C000181823

AUTOCOURSE™

THE WORLD'S LEADING GRAND PRIX ANNUAL

PUBLISHING LIMITED

 **OFFICIAL TIMEPIECE**

THE F1 FORMULA 1 LOGO IS A TRADEMARK OF FORMULA ONE
LICENSING BV, A FORMULA ONE GROUP COMPANY.

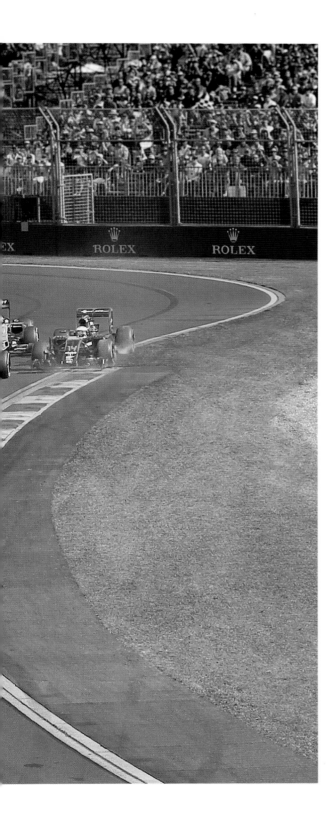

WHEN YOUR PERFORMANCE IS UNRIVALLED, YOU'VE MADE HISTORY.

This watch is a witness to timeless racing traditions. Worn by those who embody performance and precision. It doesn't just tell time. It tells history.

OYSTER PERPETUAL COSMOGRAPH DAYTONA

ROLEX

CONTENTS

AUTOCOURSE 2016–2017

is published by:
Icon Publishing Limited
Regent Lodge
4 Hanley Road
Malvern
Worcestershire
WR14 4PQ
United Kingdom

Tel: +44 (0)1684 564511

Email: info@autocourse.com
Website: www.autocourse.com

Printed in Italy by
L.E.G.O. S.p.A
Viale dell'Industria, 2
I-36100 Vicenza
Email: info@legogroup.com
www.legogroup.com

© Icon Publishing Limited 2016.
No part of this publication may be reproduced, stored in a retrieval system or transmitted, in any form or by any means, electronic, mechanical, photocopying, recording or otherwise, without prior permission in writing from Icon Publishing Limited.

ISBN: 978-1910584224

DISTRIBUTORS
Gardners Books
1 Whittle Drive, Eastbourne,
East Sussex BN23 6QH
Tel: +44 (0)1323 521555
email: sales@gardners.com

Bertram Books
1 Broadland Business Park, Norwich,
Norfolk, NR7 0WF
Tel: +44 (0)871 803 6709
email: books@bertrams.com

Chaters Wholesale Ltd
25/26 Murrell Green Business Park,
Hook, Hampshire RG27 9GR
Telephone: +44 (0)1256 765443
Fax: +44 (0)1256 769900
email: books@chaters.co.uk

NORTH AMERICA
Motorbooks
Quayside Distribution Services
400 First Avenue North, Suite 300,
Minneapolis, MN 55401, USA
Tel: (612) 344 8100
Fax: (612) 344 8691
email: customerservice@quartous.com
www.motorbooks.com

www.autocourse.com

Acknowledgements

France: ACO; Fédération Française du Sport Automobile; FIA (Jean Todt, Charlie Whiting, Matteo Bonciani, Pat Behar); **Germany:** Formula 3 Vereinigung; Mercedes-Benz (Toto Wolff, Paddy Lowe, Bradley Lord). **Great Britain:** Maurice Hamilton, Mark Hughes; McLaren (Ron Dennis, Zak Brown, Jonathan Neale, Eric Boullier, Tim Goss, Matt Bishop, Steve Cooper, Silvia Hoffer Frangipane); Red Bull Racing (Christian Horner, Rob Marshall, Paul Monaghan, Ben Wyatt, Nikki Vasiliadis, Anna Parmin); Renault Sport F1 (Nick Chester, Bob Bell, Frédéric Vasseur, Alan Permane, Andy Stobart, Clarisse Hoffmann); Force India (Bob Fernley, Andrew Green, Andy Stevenson, Will Hings); Williams F1 (Sir Frank Williams, Claire Williams, Pat Symonds, Rob Smedley, Sophie Ogg, Max Constanduros); Manor MRT F1 (Stephen Fitzpatrick, Dave Ryan, Pat Fry, Tracy Novak). **Italy:** Commissione Sportiva Automobilistica Italiana; Scuderia Ferrari (Maurizio Arrivabene, Mario Binotto, Alberto Antonini, Stefania Bocci, Roberta Vallorosi); Scuderia Toro Rosso (Franz Tost, James Key, Fabiana Valenti, Tabitha Valls Halling; Pirelli (Paul Hembery, Mario Isola, Roberto Boccafogli, Anthony Peacock). **South Africa:** Dieter Rencken. **Switzerland:** Sauber (Monisha Kaltenborn, Robert Hoepoltseder, Marleen Seilheimer). **USA:** Haas (Guenther Steiner, Rob Taylor, Mike Arning, Stuart Morrison); IndyCar Series; Indianapolis Motor Speedway.

Photographs published in AUTOCOURSE 2016–2017 have been contributed by:

Chief photographer: Peter J. Fox. Chief contributing photographers: **Lucas Gorys; Peter Nygaard of GP Photo; Jad Sherif and Jean-François Galeron of WRi2.**

Other photographs contributed by: GP2 Media Services; GP3 Media; F3 Euroseries; Formula E; IndyCar (Richard Dowdy, Joe Sibinski, Hadar Goren, Shawn Gritzmacher, Brett Kelley, Forrest Mellott, Chris Owens); Audi Communications Motorsport; Mercedes AMG; BMW Presse Club; Sahara Force India F1 Team; Mercedes AMG Petronas F1 Team; Red Bull Racing/Getty Images; McLaren Honda; Renault Sport F1; Sauber F1 Team; Scuderia Toro Rosso/Getty Images; LAT Photographic (Sam Bloxham, Andrew Ferraro, Jake Galstad, Adam Warner, Zak Mauger, David Lord); LAT Photo USA (Nigel Kinrade, Michael L. Levitt, Russell LaBounty, Brent Moist, John Harrelson, Matthew T. Thacker); BTCC; WTCC; TCR; Jakob Ebrey; Steve Mohlenkamp; WRi2 (Jerry Andre, Fritz van Eldik, Luca Bassini, Hiroshi Yamamura; Mannuel Gloria; Studio Colombo, Bryn Williams).

publisher
STEVE SMALL
steve.small@iconpublishinglimited.com

commercial director
BRYN WILLIAMS
bryn.williams@iconpublishinglimited.com

editor
TONY DODGINS

grand prix correspondent
MAURICE HAMILTON

f1 technical editor
MARK HUGHES

text editor
IAN PENBERTHY

results and statistics
DAVID HAYHOE

lap chart compiler
PETER McLAREN

chief photographer
PETER J. FOX

chief contributing photographers
JEAN-FRANÇOIS GALERON
LUKAS GORYS
PETER NYGAARD
JAD SHERIF

f1 car and circuit illustrations
ADRIAN DEAN
f1artwork@blueyonder.co.uk

Right: Mission accomplished. Nico Rosberg, world champion of 2016.
Photo: Mercedes AMG Petronas F1 Team

Title page: Red Bull Racing's Daniel Ricciardo provided the main opposition to the dominant Mercedes team.
Photo: Red Bull Racing/Getty Images

Dust jacket: Nico Rosberg, in his seventh season with the Mercedes AMG Petronas F1 Team, took the world championship crown away from his team-mate Lewis Hamilton.
Photo: Peter J. Fox

Thank you, from Nico

No driver can win the Formula 1™ World Championship alone.
Thank you to the entire MERCEDES AMG PETRONAS Formula 1™ Team.

Nico Rosberg, 2016 Formula 1™ World Champion

FOREWORD by NICO ROSBERG

Photo: Peter J. Fox

IT is very hard to put into words the feeling of having achieved my childhood dream to become world champion. I have been around racing all my life: I remember clearly sitting on the roof of my dad's car at his final DTM race, through the Motodrom in Hockenheim – and that was when I knew racing was the life I wanted, too.

There have been so many years of work to get here, and so many people who have shared in the road to this success. But most of all, I must thank my parents and my wife: it was incredible to see them straight after the race on Sunday and share the emotions with them and my friends.

The season was a tough one. We had a dominant car, thanks to the incredible job from the team, but we were left by the team to battle it out on track. That is a fantastic opportunity for a driver, but also a big challenge when your team-mate is Lewis Hamilton!

Lewis did an incredible job in 2016, driving better than ever before, and it feels like I've been racing him for a long time, with him always getting the edge. But now I've managed to turn that around: I changed some things in my approach over the winter, worked even harder and the results came.

Sure, he had some difficulties, too, but that's racing; one year it goes your way, another year it doesn't, as I know well. It was a great battle with Lewis, through all the ups and downs, over all those seasons.

Now, my thoughts are all around reaching my dream. It will be pretty cool to sit around the table at home with my parents and know there are two world champions from now on. I still can't quite believe it.

EDITOR'S INTRODUCTION
A TWIST IN THE TALE

Above: Nico Rosberg manoeuvres his Mercedes on to the grid in Abu Dhabi. Nobody knew that retirement was uppermost in his mind.
Photo: Mercedes AMG Petronas F1 Team

Top right: Jenson Button called time on his F1 career after 305 races over 17 seasons.
Photo: McLaren Honda

Top far right: A civil handshake on the Abu Dhabi podium brings to an end a near two-decade rivalry between Nico Rosberg and Lewis Hamilton.
Photo: WRi2/Jad Sherif

Above right: Joy and relief in equal measure for Vivian, Nico and Sina after the post-race celebrations.
Photo: Mercedes AMG Petronas F1 Team

Right: A star is born. Red Bull's Max Verstappen won first time out in Spain, and his amazing performances didn't stop there...
Photo: Red Bull Racing/Getty Images

MERCEDES once again dominated the F1 landscape. The world championship went down to the wire and a fabulous, nail-biting finale in Abu Dhabi, where Lewis Hamilton created controversy by winning at the slowest speed and giving team-mate and lone title rival Nico Rosberg a very difficult afternoon. The Mercedes management may not have liked it, but Lewis felt he had no option. Put through the wringer and emotionally spent, Rosberg's second place achieved for him his lifetime ambition of following in father Keke's footsteps as world champion.

"I have climbed my mountain," he said in a shock retirement announcement five days later. "I am on the peak, so this feels right. My strongest emotion right now is deep gratitude to everybody who supported me to make that dream happen." And good luck to him – an intelligent, family man who wants to move on to the next phase of his life. Although Hamilton blamed the loss of his title on an engine failure in Malaysia, ironically Mercedes' overall reliability was more impressive than ever as the team won a hat trick of constructors' titles since the 2014 advent of the hybrid era. And Lewis finished the season with 53 wins, two more than Alain Prost and now with only Michael Schumacher's 91 victories to aim at.

Red Bull Racing hit back strongly in 2016 and, as in 2014, was the only team other than Mercedes to win races. Two of them. The first, Spain, brought a fairy-tale win for 18-year-old Max Verstappen on his debut with the senior Red Bull team, after his promotion from Toro Rosso. Verstappen was a breath of fresh air for Formula One. In these pages, Red Bull chief Christian Horner talks about the dynamics of a partnership with Daniel Ricciardo that he thinks gives his team the strongest driver pairing on the grid. Ricciardo, too,

was right at the top of his game and won in Malaysia after a close fight with his new young team-mate.

While Ferrari had a tough year and dropped behind Red Bull in the pecking order, Force India had its best ever season and, on a relatively meagre budget compared to the top teams, finished a brilliant fourth in the constructors' championship. Maurice Hamilton looks at the foundations of that achievement.

McLaren Honda made progress. While it was insufficient for the team to challenge for podiums, they did manage to return to the top six. When Fernando Alonso suffered a huge accident in Australia, reserve driver Stoffel Vandoorne stepped in and scored a point on his F1 debut in Bahrain. The talented young Belgian has a race seat alongside Alonso in 2017 as Formula One bids farewell to Jenson Button after more than 300 GP starts.

The biggest story, though, was the late-season removal of Ron Dennis after 35 years at the team's helm, F1's most successful team boss falling victim to a fall-out with co-shareholder Mansour Ojjeh. In changing times for the team, the commercially astute Zak Brown arrived as executive director with an ambition to return McLaren Honda to former glory. And, off-track, the news that American global giant Liberty Media was buying a controlling stake in the F1 business set tongues wagging. Dieter Rencken examines the hopes and implications of that. Can the sport expand its footprint and attract new young fans in a changing, digital media age?

The F1 calendar had a new venue in Azerbaijan on an interesting new circuit with huge variety, which gave us a scary GP2 race, but a surprisingly incident-free first grand prix around Baku. The race and venue exceeded all expectation.

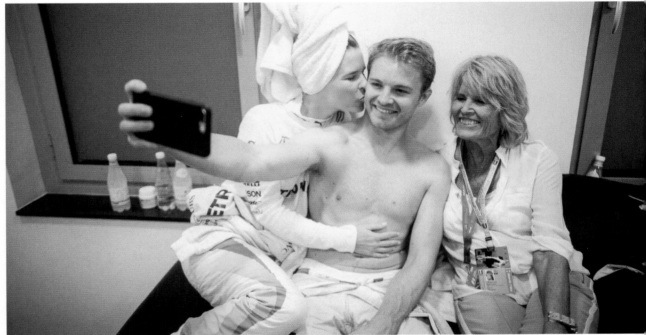

Outside Formula One, Porsche won the World Endurance Championship, with the drivers' title falling to the crew of Marc Lieb, Neel Jani and Romain Dumas, who won at Silverstone and took Le Mans right at the death after Toyota was cruelly robbed. Anthony Davidson and Sébastien Buemi went through the heartache of watching helplessly from the pits as team-mate Kazuki Nakajima suffered a loss of power on the penultimate lap, the leading Toyota hobbled by a defect in the airline between turbocharger and intercooler. It was scant consolation when Mike Conway, Stéphane Sarrazin and Kamui Kobayashi triumphed on home turf at Fuji.

Above: Blue skies and a full house for a dramatic 100th running of the Indianapolis 500.
Photo: Brett Kelley/Indycar

Right: What a difference a year makes. Alexander Rossi went from a Manor F1 reserve driver to the winner of the Indianapolis 500.

Above right: Simon Pagenaud won the Indycar title for Team Penske in their 50th year of racing.
Photos: Shawn/Gritzmacher/Indycar

Top far right: Lance Stroll totally dominated in Formula 3 and signed to race in F1 for Williams in 2017.
Photo: FIA F3 Media

Above far right: Chevrolet's Jimmie Johnson took a record-equalling seventh NASCAR title.
Photo: Michael R. Levitt/LAT South USA

Right: Friends and foes. Prema Racing team-mates Pierre Gasly and Antonio Giovinazzi fought for the GP2 title.
Photo: GP2 Media

Far right: The end of an era in sportscar racing as the big three WEC manufacturers, Porsche, Toyota and Audi, battle it out in Fuji.
Photo: Porsche

Mark Webber, Brendon Hartley and Timo Bernhard won in Nürburgring, Mexico City, Austin and Shanghai, but difficulties in the opening three races prevented them from taking the ultimate prize.

The GP2 series also went right down to an Abu Dhabi decider between Prema Racing (its debut season in F1's feeder category) team-mates Pierre Gasly and Antonio Giovinazzi. Frenchman Gasly, a Red Bull junior driver, took the crown with a dominant win in the feature event and a solid Sunday reverse-grid race.

The GP3 crown fell to Charles Leclerc, who also enjoyed four Friday FP1 practice outings with the Haas F1 team. The young Monegasque won at Barcelona, Red Bull Ring and Spa, while Thai rival Alexander Albon was victorious at Silverstone and Sepang. Britons Matt Parry and Jake Dennis also won feature races, as did Antonio Fuoco and Nyck de Vries.

In the European F3 championship, Canadian teenager Lance Stroll dominated, with 14 wins in 30 starts, securing his passage straight into the Williams F1 team alongside Valtteri Bottas for 2017. Stroll already has testing experience aboard a 2014 Williams, and his first-year F1 progress will be interesting to watch. Across the Atlantic, Frenchman Simon Pagenaud claimed the Indycar title ahead of Penske team-mates Will Power and Helio Castroneves, while former Manor F1 driver Alexander Rossi scooped the big prize with a last-gasp win in the 100th running of the Indianapolis 500.

On the NASCAR scene, Jimmie Johnson won the Sprint Cup Series for Hendrick Motorsports, while three-times champion Tony Stewart called time on his illustrious career.

Tony Dodgins
November, 2016

FIA F1 WORLD CHAMPIONSHIP 2016

TOP TEN DRIVERS

THE EDITOR'S CHOICE

Driver Portraits by Peter J. Fox

1

YOU could easily make a case for putting Nico Rosberg, Daniel Ricciardo or even Max Verstappen at No. 1 in 2016, but looking at it rationally, the only thing preventing Hamilton from taking a fourth world title had been his engine failure while leading comfortably in Malaysia. So strong was the works squad's reliability that team-mate Rosberg did not suffer a single mechanical failure.

Hamilton had his early-season problems in qualifying and was hit by Bottas in Bahrain, all adding up to a significant deficit. It was the end of May before Lewis saw the chequered flag first, in Monaco, and only then after cruel misfortune for Ricciardo. But once he did, he went on the sort of run that was widely anticipated, adding victories in Canada, Austria, Silverstone, Hungary and Germany. The only interruption was the new Baku round, where he crashed in qualifying and encountered problems in the race.

By mid-season, he had his nose ahead in the championship battle, but then came a bad patch: engine penalties at Spa, a bad start from pole at Monza, a below-par weekend in Singapore, and that engine failure at Sepang. That all gave Rosberg renewed impetus, but even then, you wouldn't have felt comfortable betting against Lewis winning the final four races, as he needed to do.

Ostensibly, it was nip and tuck between Lewis and Nico for both single-lap and race pace throughout 2016. But, strip away Hamilton's qualifying issues and consider only the 16 races leading up to Abu Dhabi, where a direct comparison is possible, and Hamilton led 11–5 with an average qualifying margin of 0.14s over Nico. It doesn't sound a lot, but only two other team-mate comparisons reveal a bigger margin (the 0.21s that Bottas and Sainz had over Massa and Kvyat respectively).

It was close, sure, but his bizarre media behaviour in Suzuka notwithstanding, Hamilton was still F1's class act. Abu Dhabi was fully understandable.

LEWIS HAMILTON

DANIEL RICCIARDO

REMOVE the works Mercedes pair, and Daniel Ricciardo was a comfortable world champion. The Australian's engaging, affable personality masks a steely competitor. And with the precociously talented Max Verstappen's arrival in the senior Red Bull team from Barcelona onwards, he needed to be!

Friendly and personable he may be, but Ricciardo doesn't like losing. After that remarkable Verstappen debut win in Spain, where Daniel was put on to a three-stop strategy that required overtaking on a circuit where it's difficult and where he had an engine deficit, he was clearly unimpressed.

Then came Monaco. He arrived in the Principality sniffing half a chance of beating the Mercs and determined to reassert himself. From the moment the cars ventured out on Thursday morning, he was imperious. He took his first pole and was in command of the season's Blue Riband race until he arrived in the pits to find no tyres. Having suffered something similar the previous year, Hamilton acknowledged Ricciardo's pain as he accepted the winner's spoils, but Daniel's face told the story. It took him three days to be in serious touch with his team again.

There then followed as near to a slump as you will get with Ricciardo: he flat-spotted his rubber and was a lacklustre seventh in Canada; the RB12 ate its tyres in Baku; and he was fifth in Austria, well beaten by his new young team-mate, who finished second, having caught him napping with an opportunistic move down the inside of Turn Eight.

Then Ricciardo hit back strongly in Hungary, Germany and Belgium, and resisted Verstappen's attack robustly through Turns 4/5/6 in a fabulous lead battle in Malaysia that gave him his first win since the three in 2014. Singapore was first rate, too.

Christian Horner thinks he has the strongest driver line-up in F1, and it's hard to disagree. The dynamic between the pair of them will be fascinating if the RB13 turns out to be a championship challenger.

NICO ROSBERG

3

Perhaps it's harsh to rank Nico only third. He beat Lewis Hamilton in the same car over a 21-race season, and that is a truly great feat.

Rosberg raced incredibly well in 2016. He won from pole in China, Baku, Belgium and Japan – all races in which Hamilton had problems, be they qualifying dramas, engine penalties or poor starts. Nico did the same with a masterful drive in Singapore, where he clearly had Hamilton's number.

Four straight wins at the start of the new season meant that Rosberg continued in the manner he'd ended 2015, but then came the first-lap collision with Hamilton in Spain, a racing incident pure and simple. Monaco, an event he was looking to win for the fourth successive year, turned out to be his weakest race, Nico losing tyre heat and struggling home seventh.

Then came the slight error at Turn One in Austria that allowed Hamilton alongside before they clashed, then a rather cack-handed overtaking attempt down the inside of the hairpin at Hockenheim that led to a penalty. It wasn't all roses, then, but they were the only smudges on an otherwise unblemished year.

It was almost as if it wasn't going to get any better, and he knew it.

"This season, I tell you, it was so damn tough. I pushed like crazy in every area after the disappointments of the last two years; they fuelled my motivation to levels I had never experienced before. And of course that had an impact on the ones I love, too – it was a whole family effort of sacrifice, putting everything behind our target. I cannot find enough words to thank my wife Vivian; she has been incredible."

The retirement decision was made 24 hours after Abu Dhabi. He reflected upon it for a day, then told those closest to him. After a quarter of a century of racing, his heart told him that it was right. A sensible move from a classy individual.

4

MAX VERSTAPPEN

WHO was the last driver to make a stronger impression upon his F1 arrival? Realistically, you can cite only two: Michael Schumacher and Ayrton Senna. Is Max in that league? Time will tell, but there were glimpses of extraordinary talent.

When Helmut Marko decided to promote Verstappen to the Red Bull senior team at the expense of Daniil Kvyat, you wondered whether the move was to appease the Verstappens, amid rumours of interest from both Mercedes and Ferrari. There were mutterings about the overly harsh treatment of Kvyat. But they lasted until roughly 4pm on Sunday in Barcelona, where Verstappen became the youngest grand prix winner in history in his first race for Christian Horner's team.

Yes, Max was fortunate: the Mercedes twins had taken care of themselves on the opening lap, and both team-mate Ricciardo and Vettel in the lead Ferrari had been switched to three-stop strategies, which proved less than optimum. But, you sensed, it was Destiny.

Some would argue that Verstappen should be ranked higher than fourth after seven podiums in 16 races heading to Abu Dhabi, the same number as Ricciardo, incidentally. Assuredly, he will be in future.

But it wasn't all roses. Next time out in Monaco, Max crashed in practice, qualifying and the race, no doubt trying to reach the bar that Ricciardo's performance established as the weekend progressed. "Long term, it will probably do him good…" smiled father Jos.

There was also the aggression and robust defence that rubbed the Establishment the wrong way, in much the same manner that Senna had done with Rosberg Sr, Piquet, Lauda, Alboreto and Prost some three decades earlier. Sometimes with full justification: the chop on Räikkönen at Spa should have brought sanction.

The peaks, though, were superb: Austria, Silverstone, Malaysia, Suzuka and that awesome wet-weather recovery in Brazil. If ever anything put you in mind of Senna… Without a doubt, Verstappen is the best thing to happen to F1 for many a long year.

FERNANDO ALONSO

HONDA made progress with its power unit over the winter of 2015/16, but not sufficiently to allow Alonso to challenge at the sharp end, where he belongs. Heading to the season finale in Abu Dhabi, Fernando was tenth in the drivers' championship, narrowly ahead of a Williams driver, where, really, he had no place to be.

In his native Spain, Alonso qualified McLaren Honda in the top ten for the first time, and he did it again at successive races in Monaco and Canada. Then he put the car seventh on the grid in Hungary and made it to Q3 again in Singapore, where he always excels, and Malaysia.

On Sunday afternoons, he was as feisty and persistent as ever, nowhere demonstrating that better than Austin. At CotA, he chased down Massa and Sainz, and scored a superb fifth position, equalling McLaren Honda's best finishing position, courtesy of his own fifth place in Monaco, where the driver accounts for a slightly higher ratio of the car/driver performance equation than elsewhere.

Alonso knows the business inside out, engages, and talks intelligently and rationally. But frustration lay just below the surface, and Fernando readily admitted that if he did not find the cars more challenging to drive when the new 2017 regulations kicked in, he would think deeply about extending his F1 career beyond the end of that year. He preferred the V10-powered Michelin/Bridgestone tyre-war days, when drivers went flat out from first to last and were physically spent by race end. He is not alone in believing that economy and conservation have no place in F1. His decision to continue beyond 2017, he said, will depend more on the enjoyment he gets from competing and driving than it will on the chance to compete for more podiums and victories. It will also be fascinating to see how he responds to the challenge of highly rated rookie team-mate Stoffel Vandoorne. He's been there with Lewis.

BOTTAS'S career seems to have lost a bit of momentum since he was being talked about as a potential Räikkönen replacement at Ferrari, but it's little to do with the level-headed Finn.

The Williams FW38 was not an easy car, often failing to achieve the same kind of stint lengths on its tyres as the Force Indias, with whom the Williams drivers fought a season-long battle, eventually coming off second best. Bottas attributed part of the struggle to mid-season updates that failed to produce the necessary improvements to keep Williams in the hunt for fourth place in the constructors' championship.

That said, Valtteri still managed to finish the season eighth in the championship, 13 points clear of Force India's Hülkenberg, and to score points in 15 of 21 race starts. The highlights were a lone podium behind Hamilton and Vettel in Canada, fourth place in Russia, and a brace of fifths in Barcelona and Malaysia.

Consider the comparative qualifying picture relative to team-mate Felipe Massa, though, and in 15 races where a comparison was valid, Valtteri was 13–2 in front, and the margin between them was joint largest on the grid, with Sainz/Kvyat, at 0.21s. Clearly, Bottas wasn't hanging around.

In 2017, he will be joined by young Canadian rookie Lance Stroll, Felipe Massa having decided to hang up his helmet after 250GP starts, and Valtteri will have to lead the Wlliams development direction. He must hope that the wider tyres and aerodynamic reset will allow Williams to take a step forward in performance.

Bottas has spent his entire F1 career with the team, and 2017 will be his fifth season as a Williams race driver. Through no fault of his own, though, his competitiveness seems to be falling, and he could do with the FW39 being a quantum leap if he wants to avoid becoming F1's forgotten man. It's a fickle business sometimes.

VALTTERI BOTTAS

7

CARLOS SAINZ

SAINZ continued to show exciting potential in 2016, despite the main focus of attention in the Red Bull camp being early-season team-mate Max Verstappen. The latter graduated to the senior Red Bull team in Sochi at the expense of Daniil Kvyat, who went the other way back to Toro Rosso.

In the four races Sainz did alongside Verstappen at the start of the season, Max qualified better on three occasions, but by such a tiny amount that the average qualifying comparison worked out in Sainz's favour, if only by a hundredth of a second!

Against Kvyat, though, that margin was up to 0.21s, the joint largest on the grid and the same advantage that Bottas enjoyed over Massa.

Sainz achieved a hat trick of top-six finishes in Barcelona, Austin, and amid the spray and aquaplaning of Brazil – a chance to show off his oft-seen wet-weather prowess.

The Toro Rosso was a good chassis, but it was compromised by the late switch to Ferrari power, which was not finalised until 1st December. And, it was a 2015-spec Ferrari engine as well…

The 11th-hour nature of the deal and the packaging compromises of the switch from Renault to Ferrari engine did Sainz no favours, and the deficit only grew as those running contemporary power units received developments. But it didn't impact on his commitment or enthusiasm, and there were places – Melbourne, Monaco, Budapest and Singapore – where the car was best of the rest behind Mercedes, Red Bull and Ferrari. That allowed him to perform.

Renault showed interest in signing Sainz, although, as Kevin Magnussen pointed out, they showed interest in everyone from the Pope south! Red Bull's Helmut Marko resisted that and continues to rate Carlos highly. Quite where he fits into the overall picture, with a lead driver pairing as strong as Ricciardo and Verstappen at the senior team, remains to be seen. What he wants is to be challenging for the world championship in a Red Bull by 2018.

SEBASTIAN VETTEL

VETTEL had the most frustrating season since his arrival on the F1 scene. After three wins for his new team in 2015, the honeymoon period at Maranello was clearly over, and a hat trick of second places in China, Canada and Baku was all he had to show for a year in which he finished fourth in the championship, some 44 points behind former Red Bull teammate Daniel Ricciardo.

'Mr Angry' from Heppenheim was a regular feature of race-day radio transmissions. His beefs were everything from slow-moving backmarkers to flaky team strategy. And, in the heat of battle in Mexico, he excelled himself, telling race director Charlie Whiting to "**** off!"

He knew he'd overstepped the mark there and was quick to apologise to Charlie, and to write a letter of apology to the FIA's Jean Todt. Those steps saved him from sanction, but the behaviour was rooted in frustration.

There were rumours of clashes with Ferrari team principal Maurizio Arrivabene who, at one stage, told an interviewer that Vettel needed to concentrate on driving the car, rather than trying to run the team. You got the feeling that those comments might actually have come from Sergio Marchionne himself.

There were lapses that were unlike Sebastian, and first-corner incidents in China, Russia, Belgium and Malaysia. The last spun Rosberg to the tail of the field, eliminated the Ferrari and earned Vettel a three-place grid penalty a week later in Suzuka.

Whereas Vettel totally shaded Kimi Räikkönen in 2015, this time the average qualifying margin between them was just 0.03s in Seb's favour going to Abu Dhabi. Kimi outqualified him there, making it 10–9 in comparable races, stripping away the evolving track conditions in Hungary and Vettel's mechanical issues in Singapore.

The continuing compatibility of the Vettel/Ferrari relationship will depend very much on what Ferrari serves him up in 2017.

SERGIO PÉREZ

PÉREZ had a good year. The top scoring driver of the battling Force India/Williams quartet, he finished seventh in the championship.

"It means a lot to be the best of the rest," he said. "It's been an incredible year for us. We started it lacking a bit of pace, but worked hard and developed the car. When we really had the turnaround was Monaco, where we made it on to the podium.

"The team has made the difference in difficult races, which is when we secured the most points. It was the whole thing: engineering made good calls at the best times, tyre strategy was good, and from the driving side, there were few mistakes. In every single race in difficult conditions, we took the maximum, I think."

For one-lap pace, Pérez and Hülkenberg were pretty evenly matched, and Sergio also raced with strong performance and consistency. Making the podium at Monaco was a personal highlight, but Baku was probably his stand-out weekend.

The VJM09 was great around F1's interesting new venue, and Pérez knew he had a car capable of the first two rows on the grid. He put pressure on himself when he crashed the car in FP3, broke the gearbox and earned himself a penalty. Without that, and with Hamilton crashing, Sergio would have started from the front row. And he beat himself up about it. But on race day, he got the job done, even passing the penalised Räikkönen in the closing stages to score his seventh F1 podium, the same number as Pedro Rodriguez! Probably his strongest drive of the year.

Pérez stays for 2017 and hopes that the rule changes might just give Force India a chance to shock the Big Three now and again. He regards Hülkenberg as one of the best and said they've pushed each other. He's also looking forward to the arrival of Esteban Ocon who, he thinks, is the best driver Force India could have taken.

NICO HÜLKENBERG

10

TEN years ago, a sports agent was asked to name two great sporting stars of the next decade. He came up with Rafael Nadal and Nico Hülkenberg.

Nadal, with two French Opens already under his belt at the age of 20, was a bit of a slam-dunk. You didn't need to be Einstein or Doris Stokes. Hülkenberg, at the time, was a Formula BMW and A1GP champion racing in the F3 Euroseries, which he won with ART.

Continuing his stellar junior career, 'the Hulk' won the GP2 title, also with ART, in his debut 2009 season, cementing a strong relationship with team boss Frédéric Vasseur, who is now in charge of the Renault F1 operation that Hülkenberg joins in 2017.

In the intervening time, while Nadal, a sportsman the tennis-playing Hülkenberg admires, has won 14 grand slam tournaments, Nico, unbelievably, is still chasing his first F1 podium.

In his first season with Williams in 2010, Hülkenberg took that fine changing-weather pole position in Brazil, but Williams was at best a mid-grid team then, while the rest of Nico's F1 career has been spent at Sauber and Force India.

Hülkenberg and Sergio Pérez proved well matched and brought Force India a fine fourth place in the constructors' championship. A fourth place at Spa was Nico's best result, and he was outscored by Pérez in a season when, more than once, he found himself the victim of first-lap aggravation.

He qualified a fine fifth in Monaco and repeated the feat in Mexico after what he reckoned had been one of the best laps of his career. In evolving wet track conditions in Austria, he lined up third. The one that got away was Baku, where, with a car that was capable of the front two rows, he spun out of Turn 16 and failed to make it out of Q2.

Thirty in 2017, Hülkenberg needed to graduate to a works team and, seeing him as a loyal servant, Force India released him to do so. Let's hope it works.

OVER AND OUT!

Faced with a fiercely competitive, determined and uncompromising team-mate in Lewis Hamilton, Nico Rosberg fought a tough campaign throughout the 2016 season and was rewarded with the ultimate prize. TONY DODGINS looks at the background to his hard-won F1 championship title...

Above: Nico and Vivian receive a dousing during the post-race championship celebrations.
Photo: Peter J. Fox

Top right: Father and son world champions, Keke and Nico, make it a family affair with their wives, Vivian and Sina.
Photo: WRi2/Jean-François Galeron

Above right: Surfing the crowd.

Right: Fighting back. Rosberg on his way to victory at the Italian GP, the middle of a run of three wins that put his title bid back on track.

Opening spread: The inevitable huge release of emotion from the 2016 world champion at the end of a marathon 21-race season.
Photos: Peter J. Fox

IT'S always a privilege to watch a man achieve a life's ambition and to share the emotion of the moment. "You got the job done," Bernie Ecclestone said as a joyful Nico Rosberg lifted the F1 boss off his feet in the Abu Dhabi pre-podium room. Moments later, when podium compere David Coulthard mentioned Nico's mother and father, the new world champion choked up.

Keke and Sina Rosberg had stayed away from the track until after the race. But, a while later, Keke gave his first interview since 1st January, 2010, when he consciously made the decision to step into the background.

Arriving from nearby Dubai, where he had watched the afternoon's drama unfold at a friend's house, Keke was in possession of a cigar and a smile. "Yes," he said, "I'm alive, but only just…"

Reflecting, he mused, "Formula 1 is a sport. It is to be enjoyed, and the pressure should always be less than the enjoyment." Prescient words in view of what followed five days later.

There was no denying Nico's unbridled joy on Sunday evening in Abu Dhabi, but no denying, either, the strain of the previous pressure-cooker seven weeks. Because it had been post-Suzuka on 9th October that Rosberg really began to feel the heat. He knew that the realisation of his ambition, his destiny if you like, was in his own hands. His team-mate could win the final four races and it still would not be enough.

From that point, there was a discernible change in Rosberg's handling of the media. Always pleasant, he was nonetheless more reluctant than ever to engage in conjecture or speculation, or in anything negative. It was as if he knew exactly how much energy he was going to need and wasn't going to waste any.

As Bernie said, he had indeed got the job done. And what a job it was. From the moment he joined Mercedes, Nico's team-mates had been Michael Schumacher and Lewis Hamilton. And you don't emerge from such pairings with a world championship unless you have earned it. Whether Hamilton had an engine failure in Malaysia or not…

At times, you almost felt sorry for Rosberg. When he outqualified Schumacher, a man with 68 pole positions, more often than not, everyone said it was because Michael was an old man. Then in 2014, when he took the inaugural pole-position trophy with 11 in 19 races against Hamilton, there was more head scratching, rather than an admission that he was just plain quick. Hamilton reversed the trend in 2015, but in 2016 there was little over a tenth between them for one-lap pace.

What Keke particularly admired about his son's approach was the 110-per cent commitment and focus that, he said, was night-and-day different from the way his own generation had gone racing.

It was evident in 2015 when, post-Belgium and the Pirelli tyre pressure increase, Nico worked diligently at the set-up changes and approach needed to ensure there were no repeats of the difficult weekend and performance fall-off Mercedes had experienced in Singapore. It set him up for a hat trick of wins to end 2015 and a four-race winning streak at the start of 2016.

When Hamilton responded and was leading the championship by mid-campaign, plenty wrote off Nico again, before he hit back hard with first-time wins at Spa, Monza and Suzuka. Okay, Hamilton suffered engine penalties at Spa, and made bad starts in Italy and Japan, but it's all part of the game.

Nico himself believes that he performed at a higher level in 2016: "I've driven my best ever races, definitely," he said. "The last couple of races weren't the real Nico, though, because the pressure slows you down. I'm just happy I came through it in the way that I did. Lewis, on the other hand, had nothing to lose. I always believed in myself and was optimistic, but there were some seriously tough moments."

His comment about Brazil and Abu Dhabi is interesting

because, although he was bested by Hamilton, those races were tremendously challenging and offered circumstances in which he could so easily have dropped the ball. Just ask Mark Webber about Korea 2010…

The spray and aquaplaning of Interlagos were precisely the sort of conditions in which all bets were off and, best car or not, it would have been so easy for Nico to finish outside the top three.

And then came Abu Dhabi, when the moment he failed to take pole, Nico was in for a seriously tough time. Surprisingly, Hamilton's tactic of backing him into the pack seemed to catch him on the hop.

"I wasn't expecting it," he said. "Maybe I was a bit naïve…"

The Mercedes team had widely anticipated it, however, and there wasn't a lot happening that surprised them. From where Lewis was, it was clearly a self-centred objective to try to retain his championship. But the objective for the team, and one employed all year long, was to finish the race as high as possible with two cars. It was a basic conflict that they hoped people would understand. With a fierce competitor like Hamilton working against the second car, it could have become very difficult for Rosberg to achieve the result he needed.

The first potential banana skin to negotiate was avoiding Hamilton backing him into the pack during the first stint on ultra-soft tyres to the extent that he was a sitting duck for an aggressive undercut by either Red Bull or Ferrari. While initially it may have been a relief to see an experienced, measured driver like Räikkönen in his mirrors on lap one, rather than a Ricciardo or Verstappen, any tiny feelings of security were short lived.

Lewis's pace in the first stint was about 0.8s off what it should have been, and the team was asking him to pick it up throughout. Once it had highlighted what Hamilton was doing, Mercedes went for the earliest pit-stop window that it could achieve with him, so that he understood that they

knew what his game was and that potentially he was going to compromise the first stint.

Hamilton even came on the radio and said that his tyres were fine and that he didn't need to stop. The team had anticipated that he might do that and stay out to increase the undercut threat. Therefore they had a back-up plan to pit Rosberg on that same lap if Hamilton hadn't responded to the pit call.

By dint of taking pole and leading, Hamilton had the right to pit first, provided he obeyed instructions, but by going slowly, he had allowed Räikkönen to stay with Rosberg, and when Kimi followed Lewis into the pits on lap seven, there was a potential undercut threat to Nico, who could only come in next time around. He responded with a rapid in-lap and very narrowly saw off the danger.

Mercedes had spent a couple of days brainstorming everything that could potentially happen, but the way Hamilton did it, one lap's difference either way on that first stop would have changed the result and the world champion. If they'd gone one lap earlier or one lap later, Rosberg would likely have found himself caught up in traffic behind Ferrari.

The next curve ball was rapidly upon Nico in the shape of Max Verstappen. The Red Bulls had started on the super-soft Pirelli tyre compound rather than the ultra-softs and were expected to run a longer opening stint. Any threat from Verstappen had appeared extinguished when he spun

to the back of the field on the opening lap after contact with Hülkenberg, but he recovered quickly and converted to a one-stop race.

Mercedes acknowledged that what Red Bull did was very good. Achieving a one-stop and taking the super-soft tyre that far was way outside the sphere of what Mercedes believed possible going into the race. But by lap 11/12, they could clearly understand Red Bull's plan, and see that the anticipated graining hadn't occurred on Verstappen's front tyres and his speed was very strong.

They told Rosberg that fundamentally the game had changed. He now had a situation where he was racing Max on pure terms. Previously, to avoid any risks, Mercedes had avoided overtaking Verstappen, but from that point onwards, especially because they could see a bit of an incline in his tyre curve, they encouraged Nico to get past. Had he not been able to do that, it was just a straight race between them with both cars having one more stop to make – a pure undercut race and a test of who was bravest going to the end of the race…

It was this that led to the most stressful moment of the race for Rosberg, as faithful race engineer Tony Ross informed him that it was critical for him to pass Verstappen within the next three laps.

"Not a nice thing to hear,"Nico said later with masterful understatement. "It's critical that you pass Max Verstappen to win the championship. Holy Moly!"

But pass Verstappen he did, with a fine move through Turns Eight and Nine, no doubt a heart-in-the-mouth moment as Verstappen defended typically robustly.

"That was definitely a great one!" Nico said. "Fair play to Max, also. He went full on aggressive of course, didn't given an inch as usual, but we didn't collide and I got by, so that felt amazingly good, an awesome feeling. Really, very relieving and so unbelievably intense. I'd never felt something like that in a car before."

That and the last ten laps were the most stressful elements of a race that Rosberg readily acknowledged as the toughest of his career: "At the end, I didn't know what Lewis was going to do and how far he was going to push it."

As Abu Dhabi entered its final laps, Hamilton indeed slowed the pace once more and Rosberg, on soft-compound Pirellis, faced the threat of a fast-closing Sebastian Vettel, the Ferrari on a fresh set of super-softs after a long middle stint. And close behind the Ferrari was still Verstappen…

With Vettel on Rosberg's gearbox and attacking in the second DRS zone, Tony Ross, calmness personified, was back on the radio: "You only need P3, Nico. You can't afford damage."

But allowing Vettel through was not in Nico's thoughts.

"I wanted to hang on to second, because if I'd dropped one place who knew what mess they might have gotten into in front of me… And I didn't want to have Verstappen right behind me either!"

Although Rosberg is not renowned as a 'physical' driver, some wondered why, with the points already in the bag and Hamilton messing him about, Nico did not make a more serious bid to relieve Lewis of the lead, knowing that any contact only favoured him.

"I was trying at times," he explained, "but Lewis was doing it really well. He pushed flat out from Turn One. In fact, from Turn 21, all the way to the end of the first sector and halfway through the second, which is where you overtake, and so I could never get close enough. Then he just backed off in the last sector, where you can't overtake."

At the end of a fine season, Nico was truly put through the wringer for 98 minutes at Yas Marina and was not found wanting. Don't let anyone tell you that he didn't earn his title or is anything other than a deserving champion.

"He knows what it means to me and to him," his proud father said. "I had three rules when I came to F1: you have to win your first race, then Monaco and then win a championship. And now he can put a cross against all three and say, 'Done that!'"

Indeed he could, and it was enough for him. Five days later, at the FIA Awards, Nico announced, "I pushed like crazy in all directions, along with everyone involved, my family. There were a lot of sacrifices, even my wife at home. Every time I was home, she understood I had to rest; I never did any nights, never had to take care of our little daughter.

"I'm cherishing the moment. The first thing I did when I saw the world championship trophy was to look, where's my dad? Amazing.

"I've achieved this childhood dream now and I'm not willing to make that sort of commitment again for another year. And I'm not interested in coming fourth or whatever. I'm a fighter and I want to win. So, not interested to do that again. I've decided to follow my heart, and my heart has told me to stop there, to call it a day and go on to other things. It's been wonderful and it just feels right."

What is it they say about making decisions when you're emotional? Let's just hope that for Nico, it is right. Bravo.

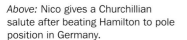

Above: Nico gives a Churchillian salute after beating Hamilton to pole position in Germany.

Left: Under pressure. Nico was under the cosh in Austria as Hamilton closed in for the kill. He was penalised for the ensuing collision, exacerbating the tensions between the two drivers.

Right: It's over! Nico and his teammates celebrate his crowning moment at Yas Marina.
Photos: Peter J. Fox

THE END OF AN ERA

As the season drew to a close, McLaren chairman and CEO Ron Dennis lost a boardroom battle when a bid to buy back control of the company with Chinese investment was rejected. Shareholders Mansour Ojjeh and the Bahraini investment fund Mumtalakat moved to have Dennis placed on gardening leave until the expiration of his contract in January, 2017. Dennis fought his suspension in the High Court, but lost. TONY DODGINS examines the story...

Photo: Peter J. Fox

Above: Boss and Boss. Ron Dennis and Mansour Ojjeh in happier times at the 2006 Brazilian Grand Prix.

Top right: A powerful trio in the mid-eighties. Alain Prost delivered two titles; Ojjeh provided the TAG engines; Dennis landed the lucrative tobacco sponsorship.

Above right: A man and his logo.

Above far right: Dennis with loyal lieutenant Martin Whitmarsh in 2003.

Right: The famous staged handshake between Dennis and Max Mosley at Spa in 2007.

Photos: WRi2/Jean-François Galeron

DENNIS has been with McLaren for the past 35 years and a central F1 figure. He has been the sport's most successful boss, his team winning a combined 17 drivers'/constructors' championships under his tenure. You could say he is right up there with Enzo Ferrari and Colin Chapman. He might even say that he outranks them.

The manner of his departure is anything but fitting, forced out of the first-class company he built by his own partners. Enzo Ferrari used to say that a company is best run by an odd number of people numbering fewer than two, and Dennis might now agree.

There is an element of Greek tragedy about the whole story, defined as a play in which the protagonist, usually a man of importance and outstanding personal qualities, succumbs to disaster through the combination of personal failing and circumstances with which he cannot deal.

A serious fall-out at McLaren boardroom level had been common knowledge for some time. At its root were personal issues between Dennis and TAG chief Mansour Ojjeh, a 25-per cent shareholder who has been involved with McLaren since Dennis persuaded him to move from Williams sponsorship in 1982 via a partnership. Ojjeh bankrolled the Porsche-built TAG turbo engine with which McLaren achieved back-to-back world drivers' championships (the first in the Dennis era) with Niki Lauda and Alain Prost (twice), in 1984, '85 and '86, and also won the constructors' title in the first two of those years.

The Ojjehs are serious heavy hitters. Mansour's father, Akram, well versed in Middle East politics and diplomacy, did business with the Saudi royal family, was involved in the arms business and is said to have negotiated a deal earning him seven per cent of all sales from French government defence manufacturing arm, Sofresa, netting him around $350m per annum by the early eighties. He was a friend of Adnan Khashoggi, once believed to be the richest man in the world, and an occasional guest on Khashoggi's $75m (in the eighties!) yacht, later bought by Donald Trump.

Mansour and wife Kathy became close friends of Ron and Lisa Dennis, the two families frequently holidaying together with their children before the Dennises split in 2008.

Dennis's marriage break-up coincided with a particularly difficult time for him professionally. After the initial success of the mid-eighties, the team had gone from strength to strength on the back of strong support from Marlboro, the poaching of Honda from Williams and the signing of Ayrton Senna, who won drivers' titles for McLaren in 1988, '90 and '91. Team-mate Alain Prost was champion in 1989 as McLaren secured four successive constructors' titles.

After the end of the Honda relationship in 1992, McLaren eventually forged an allegiance with Mercedes, which would buy a 40-per cent stakeholding, and won further drivers' and constructors' titles with Mika Häkkinen in 1998-99, after Dennis had lured design ace Adrian Newey from Williams.

But there followed an unprecedented period of domination by Ferrari in the first half of the noughties, and it was not until Lewis Hamilton won the world championship, on the last lap of the last race in 2008, that McLaren took its next title. It hasn't claimed one since.

While Dennis's drive, ambition and vision built the McLaren Technology Group into a cutting-edge company worthy of royal and prime ministerial visits, earning its founder a CBE gong in 2000, his complex personality also played a part in its more difficult moments.

Dennis had arrived in F1 in the mid-sixties as a mechanic to Jack Brabham, but in 15 years he rose to lead McLaren International with the support of Marlboro. While he could be engaging, funny, even self-deprecating, he had a compulsive attention to detail and could also be graceless, maladroit and condescending, while tending to believe that he was always right.

Famously, his "We make history, you only write about it..." went down in journalistic folklore.

His deeply considered, convoluted and sometimes unnecessarily verbose responses to questions prompted the term 'Ronspeak'. McLaren pioneered a 'Meet the Team' concept

at grands prix, where, along with his drivers, he would take questions on both the team and general F1 topics, an approach that is now widely followed by key figures throughout the paddock.

Some unkindly souls suggested that it was simply because he liked the sound of his own voice, but, for journalists, his willingness to give his time and to address matters intelligently and deeply was invaluable. There was no doubt that he cared passionately about F1 at a level more akin to custodian than competitor.

It was this trait that led him into conflict with the men who owned and ran the sport, Max Mosley and Bernie Ecclestone. Dennis disapproved strongly that while Ecclestone had first taken on his Formula One Constructors Association (FOCA) duties on behalf of the teams, on a commission basis, it had gravitated into a situation, under Max's FIA presidency, where the FIA dealt directly with Ecclestone, who took much of the burgeoning profits.

Dennis was a key figure among those who questioned the legality of developments as the FIA and FOM sought to ratify the sport's financial and governance structures with the European Commission, ahead of a potential sale or flotation, and in the face of possible interference.

Amidst it all, the BBC's *Panorama* television programme investigated the nature of the relationship between Ecclestone and Mosley and some of the deals done. They had a surprising amount of inside information and were able to put Mosley on the spot. Clearly that information had come from within, and many regarded it as a further attempt to torpedo Bernie's planned flotation. Rightly or wrongly, paddock insiders believe that the root of Dennis's strained relationship with Max and Bernie was some sort of assistance to the *Panorama* team.

Mosley always denied enmity with Dennis, but if there was any, the 'Spygate' episode presented him with an open goal. McLaren chief designer Mike Coughlan's wife went to the local copy shop to photocopy a 700-page Ferrari dossier that had come into his possession via a disaffected Ferrari employee, and the chap doing the photocopying happened to be a Ferrari fan, who phoned Maranello... You couldn't make it up!

Dennis did his best to limit the damage, saying that Coughlan was operating alone and dismissing him. But, in the middle of it all, he was counting without Fernando Alonso, who had expected number-one status when he joined McLaren, but because of the sensational first-year performance of Lewis Hamilton, wasn't getting it.

When Hamilton stitched up Alonso in Hungary and disregarded an instruction to let Fernando past to do an extra fuel-burn lap (remember those?), Alonso retaliated by blocking the pits so that Hamilton did not have time to do his final qualifying lap. All hell broke loose, and Alonso told Dennis that if he didn't sort Hamilton out and give Fernando priority, he would blow the whistle with emails implicating McLaren in a deeper understanding of Ferrari operational details. Dennis, sensing that things were out of control, phoned Mosley himself before Alonso had a chance to.

It culminated in a huge $100m fine for McLaren, whose further participation in the world championship was on a probationary basis for two years. On the announcement of the fine, Dennis was forced into a humiliating handshake with Mosley on the steps of McLaren's brand centre at Spa where, legend has it, Mosley whispered in his ear, "$5m is for the offence and $95m is for being a ****!"

Mosley had wanted to ban McLaren for two years, which risked putting them out of business, but Ecclestone talked him into the fine instead. It is also said by some in the paddock that McLaren was informed that if they wanted to keep on racing, then F1 would look a bit of a laughing stock if they went on to win either of the titles that year...

The probationary period was not over when, at the first race of 2009, Hamilton, under the team's instruction, lied to Melbourne stewards about a yellow-flag incident, in which he

Above: Dennis – back in control after ousting Martin Whitmarsh.
Photo: Wri2/Jad Sherif

Above right: Fernando Alonso was lured back to McLaren to spearhead their Honda-engined challenge, despite the Spaniard's acrimonious departure from the team at the end of 2007.
Photo: McLaren Honda

Right: After 35 years at the helm, Ron heads for the exit door.
Photo: WRi2/Jean-François Galeron

had passed Jarno Trulli, who had briefly slid off, and then erroneously been informed to let Trulli repass, which he didn't need to do, costing himself a podium.

Hamilton denied the team instruction and tried to blame Trulli, not knowing that stewards had already listened to a brief interview he'd given to a journalist, which confirmed that the instruction had in fact been given. When the stewards reconvened in Malaysia and called Hamilton and sporting director Dave Ryan again, they both lied once more, sticking to their story. Hamilton subsequently was disqualified.

The world champion, following team instruction, had now been publicly exposed as a liar, and his father was among those unhappy. At a subsequent meeting of the World Motor Sport Council in Paris, McLaren escaped with a suspended three-race ban for bringing the sport into disrepute. Martin Whitmarsh, who had recently taken over from Dennis as team principal, was praised for his open submission to the court, in which he pointed out that structural changes had been made within the McLaren organisation. Which was taken to mean an agreement that Dennis would step away from the day-to-day running of the F1 team.

This all happened just 12 months after Mosley's spanking escapade had been exposed in the *News of the World*, this revelation itself just six months after the huge 'Spygate' fine. Mosley had already been warned by Ecclestone and former Metropolitan Police Commissioner John Stevens, who ran a security company, that he was being investigated. Paddock conjecture suggested that these timelines and investigations may not have been unrelated, although now they appear to have been.

The 'Spygate' and 'Liegate' episodes seriously damaged the reputation of both Dennis and McLaren. And were manna to those in the paddock who disliked Ron's occasional pomposity and saw mirth in his sporadic malaprop-ridden butchery of the English language. More importantly, though, they were embarrassing for Mercedes, then 40-per cent stakeholders in the team. Indeed, before McLaren escaped with its suspended three-race ban for 'Liegate', chairman Dieter Zetsche had warned that a serious punishment might force Mercedes to reconsider its position as a Formula 1 engine supplier.

By then, Dennis had also upset Mercedes with the decision to launch a high-performance sportscar directly into one of the three-pointed star's market sectors. Just as McLaren launched its MP4-12C, Mercedes announced the sale back to McLaren of its 40-per cent shareholding and its decision to buy Brawn GP and run its own works team. A decision that, with hindsight and a new hybrid formula, could not have worked out better for Stuttgart, not to mention Ross Brawn!

In 2013, McLaren endured its worst season for more than three decades, finishing without a podium for the first time since 1980 and failing to find a title sponsor to replace the departing Vodafone. Some put this down to Dennis being unrealistic with the rate card against a background of tough economic times and poor team performance. It all coincided with 25-per cent stakeholder Mansour Ojjeh falling ill and needing a double lung transplant in November. As a result, he relinquished his McLaren board duties to brother Aziz.

With Jean Todt now FIA president in place of Mosley and Dennis underwhelmed by McLaren's performance, Ron saw an opportunity to return to his duties as group CEO, at the expense of Whitmarsh. Now with a 25-per cent shareholding alongside the 25 per cent of the Ojjehs, and a 50-per cent stake in the hands of the Bahraini Mumtalakat sovereign wealth fund, Dennis is believed to have persuaded Aziz Ojjeh to back him in deposing Whitmarsh and to convince the Bahrainis to do likewise. This was unlikely to have happened had Mansour still been at the helm, but it took place in January, 2014.

The way it has been described by one source close to the situation, is that when Mansour became well enough to function properly once more, the first thing he did was to hug Kathy Ojjeh; the second thing he did was to phone Whitmarsh, now a close friend, to find out how things were going at McLaren.

"I couldn't tell you," said Martin, "I'm not there anymore…"

Ojjeh, furious, confronted Dennis and the pair discussed an untenable situation. The upshot is believed to have been a set period in which Dennis needed to find the backing to buy out both Ojjeh and the Bahrainis, and to take back control of the company.

It was this that was central to the Magnussen/Button saga at the end of 2014. One of Magnussen's sponsors was Danish multi-billionaire clothing retailer Anders Pvlson, who almost made Bernie Ecclestone look like a pauper. Second only to the Maersk shipping dynasty in terms of Danish wealth, he bought Aldourie Castle on the banks of Loch Ness for £15m and, a keen sportsman, backed Danish talent such as boxer Mikkel Kessler and Magnussen. He was already involved as a McLaren backer through the Jack & Jones brand and his ASOS company, and had been identified by Dennis as a potential investor and equity partner who could facilitate Ron taking back control.

With Honda coming and Alonso signed for 2015, either Button or Magnussen had to go, and the grapevine suggested that things did not look rosy for Jenson. He and Kevin had been nip and tuck for single-lap pace throughout 2014, with Jenson perhaps racing a little better due to greater experience and tyre management. Button, too, was obviously nearing the end of his career, while Magnussen would only improve. And, at a time when the team was without a title sponsor, Button was on a hefty salary, while Magnussen brought backing. The positive delta involved in taking Kevin rather than Jenson was around £20m!

It seemed like a no-brainer, and at a McLaren board meeting where, because of the nature of the discussion, technical staff also had a contribution, the voting was 7–2 in Magnussen's favour.

Apparently, it was at this point that Button's manager, Richard Goddard, played a blinder, pointing out Dennis's game to Ojjeh and that Magnussen was central to it. Once cognisant of that, and still smarting over their personal situation and Dennis's treatment of Whitmarsh, Ojjeh and the Bahrainis overruled the board and insisted on Button, irrespective of the financial downside.

Pvlsen, it turned out, was unlikely to have been persuaded to invest, and Magnussen, having thought he was going to keep his seat, found himself as reserve driver, attending each race with a set of headphones instead of a crash helmet. It was not long before his relationship with Dennis deteriorated, too.

The catalyst seems to have been an incident in Monaco, where he accidentally forgot to settle his hotel expenses, involving personal extras amounting to about 10 euros. But apparently it was picked up by a McLaren bean-counter and became an issue. In a sorry end to the relationship at the end of the year, he received a short email from Dennis's personal assistant explaining that there would be nothing for him in the future – on his birthday.

Asked in Abu Dhabi what he thought of Dennis's removal and the arrival of Zak Brown at McLaren as executive director, Magnussen shrugged, "I think it looks quite positive what's happened there, to be honest. We'll see. Someone like Zak, who is obviously very good on the commercial side and will see things from a proper business point of view, will structure the team in a more logical way, I hope."

That is a view echoed by many, with the feeling that Dennis's controlling persona was fine for the eighties, but is less appropriate today.

Whether Dennis will receive proper recognition for his achievements remains to be seen. Clive Woodward was knighted for a single rugby world cup. We have cycling's Sir David Brailsford. We have Sir Frank Williams and Sir Patrick Head. But what of the man who gave Britain a racing and technology company to be proud of, and established an iconic Norman Foster-designed facility like the McLaren Technology Centre in Woking at a cost of more than £300m? Have those damaging episodes of the late noughties ruled out Sir Ron Dennis?

As someone put it in Abu Dhabi, "It really is a bit of a tragedy when you think about it. Two people set out to kill him. One didn't, but his former friend did. Then again, how much of a tragedy is it to be approaching your 70th birthday with half a lifetime's worth of success and £300m in the bank?"

ZAK BROWN: CHASING TITLES WITH McLAREN

ZAK BROWN, a 45-year-old American with a stellar commercial reputation, is McLaren's new executive director. In Abu Dhabi, he wore a McLaren shirt for the first time and took media questions:

Q: What is your level of authority. Are you in charge of everything to do with racing and marketing?

A: Jonathan Neale and I are, for the collective efforts of running the F1 global commercial and sports operations. Clearly I've got more of a commercial background, and Jonathan has a technical background, so I'll be focused more on external commercial business situations and Jonathan will be more involved on the technical side. Jonathan and I report to the executive committee, which is made up of Sheik Mohammad and Mansour Ojjeh.

Q: You have a race team with a chief executive [Jost Capito] and a race director [Eric Boullier] that some say clash, and a race team without an obvious technical director. Do you envisage changes?

A: I've not started yet, I don't know what I don't know and ultimately Jonathan is much closer to the whole technical side of the sport, and so we're going to be sitting down and working with the whole leadership team and those involved technically to understand what's the best way forward for McLaren to get back to the winner's circle.

Q: You were touted for a commercial role with new F1 owners Liberty Media as well as this job. Why did you choose the McLaren route?

A: McLaren has been my favourite team ever since I was growing up. McLaren Honda and the Senna/Prost era was when I first became addicted to F1 and ultimately McLaren. I've done business with McLaren for over a decade and am very close to Ron. It was a tough decision, but I'm very pleased that I'm sitting here in McLaren gear.

I know tons of the staff and it feels like home to me. I'm a racer at the end of the day, and so being in the paddock and pit lane gives me a charge. And I think the time to join McLaren is now. McLaren Honda is clearly progressing, I think there's lots of opportunity, and I just want to be part of a team that gets back to winning world championships.

Q: What's number one on the job list?

A: I don't think there's a number one. There's three legs to the stool, as I'd put it, and we need all three to be successful within the ecosystem. First is the fans. We as McLaren and F1 as a whole can improve our engagement with our consumers: the more fans we get, the more sponsors we get.

We want the fans buying our sponsors' products and services, and then the more sponsors we get, the more money we can put into our race team to go faster, and the faster we go, the more fans we are going to get because they like the teams that run at the front, so all three of those are critically important and we need to get all three right.

Clearly, a title partner is something I'm most linked to and is going to be critically important. I'm going to start taking a look at 2018 because 2017 is already here.

Q: Presumably you've been looking for a title sponsor before now, so what difference is the shirt going to make?

A: I've not been looking for a title sponsor for McLaren as part of the day job. JMI [Just Marketing International] is out there and looks after teams, so what we tend to do is find corporations and understand what their needs are, and then try to direct them where we think happens to be a good fit. We've got a lot of logos on other racing teams and are responsible for quite a few here at McLaren. I think the difference now is that I've got the shirt on and will have the business card. I'm going to put a tremendous amount of effort into that, and so hopefully that 100-per cent time versus part-time will be the difference.

Q: Given McLaren's history and the MTC facility, it's unfathomable you don't have a title sponsor. What do you put that down to? Being unrealistic with the rate card? What needs to change?

A: It's a difficult environment for all of us. Red Bull had a title sponsor. They don't now, it's themselves. Ferrari go about things a little differently, and then obviously Mercedes has been fortunate to have a title partner for some time. I think there's some serious headwinds out there, whether it's Brexit or US elections, and so it's a difficult environment. It's not an inexpensive sponsorship, but it's great value, it's global, and when you break it down it's money very well spent. But I've not been on the inside, so I don't know how many near misses McLaren has had. We've had a couple of close opportunities, but it's

Left: Zak Brown.
Photo: Wri2/Jad Sherif

Below: Men on a mission. Zak Brown,
Eric Boullier and Jonathan Neale in
the Abu Dhabi paddock.
Photo: McLaren Honda

A: I've had 22 years experience of working with corporate partners, and so I think I've got a very good understanding of what they want and how they operate, and that is different today to what it was 5, 10, 15, 20 years ago.

Measurement is critical, return on investment is critical, and then we have more competition from most other sports than we've ever had. So it's going to be hard work, understanding the market place and being flexible to a potential partner's needs.

Q: *How important are the ancillary parts of McLaren: Applied Technologies and McLaren Automotive?*

A: Very important. I don't have any direct responsibility for the groups, however. We have partners such as Glaxo Smith Kline that are involved with the F1 team and Applied Technologies, so there's a tremendous amount of synergy. That's run by Ian Rhodes.

Mike Flewitt who runs Automotive has a big passion for automobiles and motor racing, and so we are going to work very collaboratively together because some modern-day sponsorships just want a relationship with an F1 team and others want to see that relationship lead into those other businesses. That's something that gives us a broader offering than most in the pit lane.

Q: *Are you confident you can bring in new companies who aren't in F1, or should other teams be concerned you might be coming after their sponsors that you have brought in in the first place?*

A: Yes, I'm positive we will be bringing new partners.

We have for 22 years in motorsport, the last 12 in F1, and I'd like to think the well hasn't run dry on our talent in doing that. It's a competitive sport on and off the track, and everyone at times talks to each other's sponsors. It's not unusual to see sponsors move, and I don't think that will be any different moving forward.

Q: *You've been critical of F1's business model in the past. Now that you're director of a team that sits on the strategy group, what influence do you think you'll be able to bring to bear in that area?*

A: Hopefully now I'll have a louder voice and a seat at the table and be able to share my views. Business, whether it's McLaren business or F1, you can always improve, and I will push in areas where I think we can all improve. I'm super excited about it; F1 has tons of growth opportunity, and I want to personally and professionally contribute.

Q: *Obviously it's been out there that Ron didn't want to go anywhere. What's the situation between the two of you now?*

A: Ron and I are fine. I talked to him before the announcement, and post-announcement. I talked to him before I came to Abu Dhabi. I text him all the time. Ron, at the end of the day, is the one who recruited me. The last couple of years, he's left the door open. I'd been married to my existing business, so there was no opportunity, and as I saw the light at the end of the tunnel with my employment contract, I let him know and he turned up the volume in the pursuit of me. I wouldn't be standing here now if it wasn't for Ron Dennis.

hard. By no means do I have a magic wand, and nor do I think that having a title partner from 2018 will be an easy feat.

Q: *It seems that Ron is being replaced with several people, so that adds another layer of management, not always a good thing. And might you take a stake in the team?*

A: I've not been offered a stake. I don't envisage having equity in the race team, but you never know what you might get for Christmas! But you're right, Ron is our chairman and CEO; he is a significant shareholder, and so he has a significant interest in our success, and I think as these teams get larger, it requires more lieutenants to contribute and help manage the team.

Q: *You want to get McLaren back winning championships, so how long do you think that will take?*

A: I have no idea. There have been a lot of people over the years trying to make predictions like winning their first race or winning Le Mans on their debut, and from what I've seen they've gotten it wrong, so I'm going to go with the odds, keep my mouth shut and not make any predictions. But we need to get back to winning soon, and we're on a good path. Honda is producing a very good engine, we've got a great team, Eric [Boullier] and Jost [Capito] are doing a very good job, so hopefully sooner rather than later.

Q: *There's a lot of talk about sponsorship. What are you going to bring to McLaren that was lacking previously?*

MAX ATTACK...

An analysis of Red Bull's season so often centres on the design genius of Adrian Newey. But in 2016, the car was not the star. TONY DODGINS talked to Christian Horner about the driver pairing the team principal thinks is the strongest in F1...

Above: Daniel Ricciardo was a man on a mission in Monte Carlo, taking pole position from the Mercedes duo of Rosberg and Hamilton.
Photo: Peter J. Fox

Above right and far right: Joy for Max and Marko after Red Bull's triumph in Spain, but bitter disappointment for Daniel after a probable victory had slipped away in Monte Carlo.
Photos: Red Bull Racing/Getty Images

Right: Max Verstappen kept his cool and resisted the pressure from Kimi Räikkönen to take his first grand prix win in Spain.

Opening spread: Verstappen takes the applause after his fairy-tale debut win for Red Bull in Barcelona.
Photos: Peter J. Fox

DANIEL RICCIARDO had a brilliant third season with Red Bull, and when Max Verstappen was promoted to the team at the expense of Daniil Kvyat, he became the most exciting driver to hit F1 since Michael Schumacher.

Ricciardo started the season well enough, with three consecutive fourth places in Australia, Malaysia and China, which included a front-row start in Shanghai, having taken advantage of MGU-H problems for Lewis Hamilton. But the car/engine package wasn't quite there and Daniil Kvyat was struggling, notwithstanding a podium in China from sixth on the grid. But at race four in Sochi, Kvyat was outqualified significantly by Ricciardo for the fourth consecutive race and, perhaps a little desperate, braked too late for Turn Two and hit his team-mate.

Horner said that the timing was coincidental, but by Spain a fortnight later, Helmut Marko had telephoned Kvyat to break the bad news: he was on his way back to Toro Rosso, with Verstappen moving the other way.

"It was a combination of factors," Horner explained. "Daniil had been struggling with the braking characteristics of the car pretty much since day one of pre-season testing. A few things had changed. You then get into a difficult spiral and it ate into Daniil's confidence.

"We also had a very in-form Verstappen and a lot of interest swooping in on him from other teams. There was a window in his contract that if we took the opportunity, then it secured his long-term future with Red Bull Racing. And so it was almost killing two birds with one stone: it was putting our best foot forward and addressing the long-term future of

Max by putting him into what we believed was a competitive car, and it was allowing Daniil to recover his confidence in perhaps a less pressured environment.

"Also, Red Bull Racing is different to other teams, because we have four cockpits available to us and the drivers are all contracted to Red Bull Racing, so we always had that ability to move any of them around, but had never chosen to use it before."

Unbelievably, in his first race with the senior team, Verstappen stood atop the Barcelona podium as the youngest F1 winner in history, at the age of 18 years and 228 days. He beat the previous record by more than two-and-a-half years, Sebastian Vettel having been 21 years and 73 days when he won at Monza for Toro Rosso in 2008. He was also the first Dutchman ever to win a grand prix.

Fortune had favoured Verstappen. The two Mercedes had taken each other off on the opening lap and team-mate Ricciardo had been switched on to what proved to be a slower three-stop strategy, as had Vettel at Ferrari. He was left to fend off a challenge from Kimi Räikkönen in the other Maranello car, which he did brilliantly, keeping a cool head and making sure he made no mistake out of the slow final sector on to Barcelona's long main straight. Räikkönen never came close enough to challenge with the aid of DRS into Turn One, and Verstappen, mistake-free, had driven more like a seasoned veteran. Ricciardo, though, had his enthusiasm well under control…

"Barcelona was a tough one for Daniel," Horner said, "because that strategy could have gone either way. We felt we'd put Daniel on the best strategy to win the race, and

Ferrari went that route with Vettel as well. But Max did an amazing job of making the tyres last, and Daniel picking up a puncture in the last two or three laps, meant we never saw it fully play out. Strategy-wise, it could have gone either way."

Ricciardo was not convinced, questioning the wisdom of a switch to a strategy that demanded on-track overtaking while driving a car with a Renault-induced straight-line speed deficit. Caught by a TV reporter post-race, his trademark smile was missing and he was a reluctant interviewee: "I'm a little bitter right now, so it's probably best I don't say too much…"

A fortnight later, armed with a significantly upgraded Renault engine at a Monte Carlo circuit on which he fancied his chances, Ricciardo was a man on a mission.

"He was stunning all weekend," Horner said. "He'd arrived super motivated after Barcelona, wanting to re-establish himself after Max's arrival. His pole position was stunning on Saturday, completely on merit because there were no issues with Mercedes that day, and the race was a real shame because he did everything right."

Horner was referring to the fact that because of Pirelli's tyre choice of the softest three compounds in its range, with the inclusion of the ultra-soft for the first time, allied to the first stint demanding wets, there were tyres all over the place

in the tight confines of the Monaco pits. While reacting to Hamilton's strategic decisions, Red Bull got themselves in a mess, and when Daniel appeared in the pit lane, there was a crucial delay in getting the right boots ready for him. Enough of a delay to lose him a race he should have won.

His Serene Highness Prince Albert and Princess Charlene or not, Ricciardo had a face like thunder throughout the podium ceremony. As he said, it's not often that you get the chance to win the Monaco Grand Prix…

"It was very unfortunate," Horner conceded, "but Daniel quickly brushed himself down and you could see the disappointment, not just for him, but the whole team. Everybody took that quite hard."

Monte Carlo had also been a strong dose of reality for Verstappen who, trying too hard to match Ricciardo, crashed in practice, qualifying and the race. Father Jos, a hard taskmaster, wore a knowing smile. "Long term," he said, "it will probably do him good."

Spain and Monaco hinted that Red Bull could possibly even offer a challenge to Mercedes, but the next handful of races quashed that notion. Ricciardo followed up with a brace of seventh places in Canada, where he flat-spotted a tyre and gave himself a tricky afternoon, and Baku, where the car ate its rear tyres. In Austria, he was mugged by an

Above: A long time coming. Ricciardo parks in the number-one space in *parc fermé* after his victory in the Malaysian Grand Prix.
Photo: Peter J. Fox

Top right: After early-season disappointments, Daniel enjoys the winning feeling again.

Above right: Helmut Marko and Christian Horner are confident that Red Bull has the best driver pairing on the grid.

Right: Ricciardo leads Verstappen to the team's 1-2 finish in Sepang.
Photos: Red Bull Racing/Getty Images

opportunist Verstappen into the fast Turn Eight and could only get home fifth, while his young team-mate finished second to Hamilton. At Silverstone, too, he was outqualified and outraced by an outstanding Max.

In Hungary and Germany, it was the other way around, before Verstappen put the Red Bull on the front row at Spa with his best qualifying performance of the season. It was as near to a home race as possible for the Dutchman, and it prompted lengthy race-day traffic jams and a sea of orange more reminiscent of Cruyff and Neeskens and the 1974 World Cup Final!

Ricciardo was sensational in Singapore, chasing Rosberg all the way to the flag on a different strategy, having started on the front row. Then came Malaysia, where Hamilton's infamous engine blow-up meant that a battle between the Red Bull team-mates assumed far greater significance, with a race victory the prize. With staunch defence through Turns 4–6, Ricciardo took it.

"I decided to let them race, and they'd either end up in the fence or not," Horner smiled. "In fact, they showed each other a huge amount of respect and raced hard, but fair. Max said he would have squeezed much harder in Turn Six if it hadn't been Daniel, and you can see that from how he treated others! But the way that they worked together in Hockenheim, where Max conceded a place to Daniel to assist his strategy, and then Daniel did vice versa in Mexico, was great. They were working as a team."

Then, of course, came Interlagos, where, en route from 16th to the podium, Verstappen demonstrated other-worldly

feel for grip and an ability to pass where it should not have been possible.

After the prickliness of the Vettel/Webber partnership and, to a much lesser extent, Vettel and Ricciardo, it was a new dynamic for Horner and Red Bull.

"It's totally different. They're different characters to Seb and Mark. There's real respect between them, and that made a situation like Malaysia far more tenable. It's a healthy dynamic, which is what you want between two drivers. And there's also a respect for the team. On top of that, they like each other. Daniel has played pretty much an older brother type of role outside the car."

The raw statistics of their first season together make interesting reading. In Spain, where Verstappen quickly got to grips with the Red Bull and initially even looked as though he might outqualify Ricciardo, Daniel's smiling visage through the visor as he prepared for his decisive Q3 run was hardly the appearance of a haunted man. And sure enough, he produced a scintillating lap that was within a tenth of Hamilton's Mercedes and four-tenths clear of his precocious new team-mate.

Verstappen readily admitted that Ricciardo was super-quick and that he had work to do to match him for single-lap pace, but he was confident that the gap would narrow as he gained more experience of the RB12. Strip out Monaco, where Max crashed, Baku (held up by Bottas) and Austria (evolving track conditions), and by year's end, the qualifying score between them was 8–6 in Ricciardo's favour, and the average margin between them just 0.05s. In races, the score

was 10–7 in Ricciardo's favour, with 220 points scored from Barcelona onwards, versus Verstappen's 191.

"It's immensely tight," Horner agreed. "Max has got stronger and stronger as his experience has grown, and I think he has learned from Daniel and in turn has pushed Daniel. I thought initially that it was going to be an extremely strong pairing, and all that's happened during the seven months they've been together has absolutely cemented my thinking that we have the most exciting pairing in F1.

"Daniel has had a fantastic season. He's driven brilliantly well and achieved the highest standard since he arrived in F1, at a consistent level from start to finish of the year. Max's arrival has only pushed him harder."

I suggested to Horner that it was a toss-up between Hamilton and Ricciardo for 2016's No. 1 spot and he nodded: "I'd fully agree. I think it's been Daniel's best year in F1. The way he's raced, he's done some fantastic races and some of the passing moves he's made... Some of his performances on Saturday afternoon, too, have been mighty. When it's come to that last Q3 run, more often than not, he's delivered something special. He's had the additional challenge of the Verstappen factor and, I think, dealt with it fantastically well."

Finally, the $64m question: if Red Bull were to serve up a car with championship-winning potential in 2017, did Horner see his drivers' friendly, respectful relationship continuing?

"Probably not! But I think there's fundamental respect. Both are hard racers, but fair, and what they are asking from the car is very similar. From a team development point of view, that's great. Hopefully we can provide them with a competitive car next year and put a bit of pressure on Mercedes, so that they are not turning up as a foregone conclusion for pole position and the win. If so, then I believe the driver pairing we've got is really capable of taking the fight to them. We've been able to pick off the tail Mercedes now and again, certainly over the second half of this year, and hopefully we can make further progress.

"I also think that Carlos Sainz has driven a great season and is developing really well. And I'll be interested to see how Stoffel Vandoorne does. I rate him very highly. I think these are the main guys to be keeping a close eye on. But Daniel and Max – what a pairing!"

LIBERTY – EGALITE, FRATERNITE?

In late summer, 2016, US company Liberty Media announced its intention to take over control of F1's commercial rights. DIETER RENCKEN considers what that might mean for the sport and its fans...

Inset: Big players in the paddock: Liberty Media's Chase Carey and CVC's Donald Mackenzie.
Photo: Lukas Gorys

Main photo: Racing in Abu Dhabi purveys the glamorous image of Formula 1.
Photo: Peter J. Fox

Above: The speed and excitement of Formula 1 can become addictive. New sponsor Heineken clearly sees it well suited to its target audience.

Photo: Peter J. Fox

A CERTAIN irony was evident in the 7th September announcement that Liberty Media intended to acquire control of Formula 1's commercial rights in two tranches – one immediate, the other in the first quarter of 2017. The Merriam Webster dictionary defines 'liberty' as the *'quality or state of being free'* and *'free from arbitrary or despotic control'*, states many fans believe F1 had descended to under the control of CVC Capital Partners.

The cynical interpretation was that at last F1 would be 'liberated' from being treated as nothing more than a cash cow presided over by suits whose only mission appeared to be to extract top dollar in exchange for minimum – for which read 'zero' – direct investment. Thus the news was met with widespread jubilation, albeit with dollops of guarded caution among those who fear the unknown.

In simplistic terms, Liberty Media will control the sport's commercial rights via a preferential shareholding of approximately 35 per cent, with existing shareholders (including CVC's fund holders) retaining 65 per cent – although the announcement made it clear that CVC would continue in the driving seat until completion, with F1 tsar Bernie Ecclestone contractually remaining CEO for a further three years.

"After completion of the acquisition, Liberty Media will own Formula One and it will be attributed to the Liberty Media Group, which will be renamed the Formula One Group," the parties said in a statement.

"The consortium of sellers led by CVC will own approximately 65 per cent of the Formula One Group's equity and will have board representation at Formula One to support Liberty Media in continuing to develop the full potential of the sport," continued the announcement, adding that long-time media executive Chase Carey would replace long-time CVC man Peter Brabeck-Letmathe as chairman.

At the time of writing, immediately after the Mexican Grand Prix, the impressively moustached Carey had officially attended three grands prix (of five staged since the announcement), yet, worryingly, had not held a single media briefing nor met personally with all the team principals – giving rise to suggestions that Liberty was still feeling its way, despite due diligence exercises stretching back two years.

"I am thrilled to take up the role of chairman of Formula One and have the opportunity to work alongside Bernie Ecclestone, CVC and the Liberty Media team," said Carey in September. Previously, he had been vice-chairman of News Corporation and was the current incumbent of that role at 21st Century Fox.

"I greatly admire Formula One as a unique global sports entertainment franchise attracting hundreds of millions of fans each season from all around the world. I see great opportunity to help Formula One continue to develop and prosper for the benefit of the sport, fans, teams and investors alike."

For his part, Ecclestone professed to welcome working with Carey, but, intriguingly, during the American's paddock

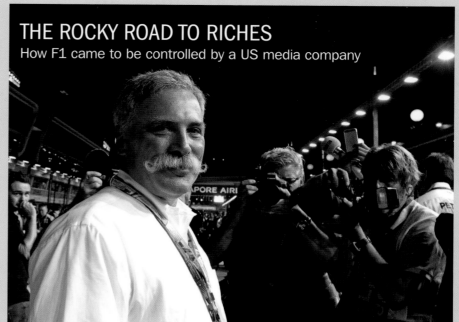

THE ROCKY ROAD TO RICHES
How F1 came to be controlled by a US media company

Photo: WRi2/Jean-François Galeron

HAVING persuaded Max Mosley's administration to sell him the FIA's commercial rights to Formula 1, Bernie Ecclestone immediately set about selling off chunks, planning to do so via a London Stock Exchange listing.

City apathy, though, scuppered the plan, so Ecclestone moved 12.5 and 37.5 per cent respectively to Morgan Grenfell and Hellman and Friedman in early 2000 – even before the EU Commission approved the FIA deal in March 2001. In turn, said equity funds, trading as Speed Investments, sold their joint 50 per cent to EM TV – better known as owner of the Muppets children's series – which promptly went bankrupt.

Munich-based Kirch Media acquired EM TV's shares, plus an additional 25 per cent, having borrowed a reported $1.6bn. The company collapsed within a year under the weight of the debt – precipitated, saliently, by lack of interest in F1's digital TV and pay-per-view offerings – and thus fell into the hands of the lending bankers, Bayern LB, JP Morgan Chase and Lehman Bros. These were soon at war with Ecclestone.

In 2005, to rid himself of the moneymen, Ecclestone arranged for CVC Capital Partners, then rights holder for MotoGP and thus *au fait* with the commercial opportunities offered by international motorsport, to acquire 66 per cent of SLEC, the holding company named after the first two letters of his then wife Slavica's first and last name. The transaction, valued at $1.6bn, gained EU approval in early 2006.

CVC hoped to emulate its other ventures by listing the company – Singapore was targeted – but the global meltdown and unwelcome publicity surrounding Ecclestone's court case (he was accused of paying a $40m bribe to a German banker to authorise the deal, and eventually paid $100m to have the charges dropped) killed those plans, but not before CVC had put in place revenue and governance structures that since have proven untenable.

With the end of its traditional ten-year investment cycle looming, CVC sought a buyer for the rights, and Liberty Media was the first to commit…

visits, they were seldom seen together. Indeed, in Mexico, a photographer was unsuccessful in snapping them together, despite lengthy sojourns outside FOM's office – signwritten 'Mr E' in celebration of Ecclestone's 86th birthday.

Various 'names' have been linked to executive positions under the new arrangement. Topping the list was Ross Brawn, the respected (now retired) former Ferrari technical director, ex-Mercedes team boss and principal of his eponymous title-winning team. Certainly, it will be fascinating to see how Ecclestone's loyal lieutenants are affected, and whom Liberty moves into the sport's various hot seats.

Liberty, ultimately owned by media mogul John Malone – also the USA's largest land owner, with real estate holdings totalling 2.1m acres – had been one of many suitors. Others were said to include sports promoter RSE Ventures, acting both in its own right and as a potential venture partner to Qatar's sovereign wealth fund, with a valuation of $12bn being optimistically bandied about by sources close to CVC.

In the end, the overall transaction value amounted to $4bn via a complicated trail that included share swaps, settlements and debt obligations, providing an enterprise value of US$8bn – 30 per cent down on CVC's original valuation. The deal is predicated upon fiscal/regulatory approval on both sides of the Atlantic, but the mere fact that an announcement was made suggests all parties are confident of obtaining the requisite clearances.

In typical CVC style, the media announcement focused on the enterprise and not transaction valuation, not surprising

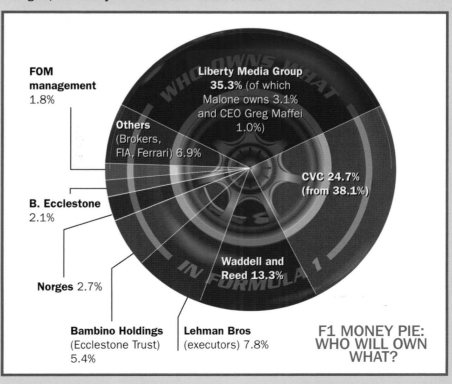

FOM management 1.8%

Others (Brokers, FIA, Ferrari) 6.9%

B. Ecclestone 2.1%

Norges 2.7%

Bambino Holdings (Ecclestone Trust) 5.4%

Lehman Bros (executors) 7.8%

Liberty Media Group **35.3%** (of which Malone owns 3.1% and CEO Greg Maffei 1.0%)

CVC 24.7% (from 38.1%)

Waddell and Reed 13.3%

F1 MONEY PIE: WHO WILL OWN WHAT?

Diagram: Adrian Dean

given that it represents a 330-per cent increase since CVC acquired two-thirds of F1's commercial rights for a largely borrowed $1.6bn in 2006, and investment funds thrive or die on perceptions of reputation. Saliently, F1 represents, by some margin, its best ever return on investment.

However, far from setting paddock minds at rest, this valuation provides cause for concern. Not only could (should?) a portion of that equity have flowed into the coffers of many a cash-strapped F1 team, but also the enterprise valuation represents a multiplier of almost 18 times F1's 2015 bottom-line earnings.

Put differently, based on F1's business model deriving its $1.8bn annual turnover from three equally-split revenue streams: pay/free-to-air TV, race hosting fees and signage/hospitality, it would take Liberty Media 17 years and eight months simply to *recover* its initial investment in F1 – an inordinately long time, given that investors generally consider return periods of half that as being only marginally attractive.

Clearly, Liberty sees massive potential in F1, despite various threats to its model. It's no secret that F1's global TV ratings plummeted 30 per cent in five years, while five of ten recent additions to F1's calendar have bombed, primarily due to astronomical hosting fees.

Even Germany, birthplace of every type of internal-combustion engine and the automobile, seems incapable of attracting sufficient fans to make an annual grand prix viable, despite fielding the most successful driver in the history of the sport (Michael Schumacher), the dominant team of the current era (Mercedes) and the present world drivers' champion (Nico Rosberg).

Finally, factor in that Force India and Sauber filed complaints with the EU Commission over inequitable governance and revenue structures – such that Ferrari is rewarded handsomely even if both red cars don't finish a race through to the end of 2020 – and that all 11 teams continue clamouring for greater shares of F1's annual revenues. Clearly, F1 faces long-term challenges of the sort that would frighten the faint-hearted.

So this arguably over-priced acquisition provides a massive fillip just when the sport needs it most, but the burning question for fans is not what F1 can do for Liberty, but what Liberty can do for F1.

The key lies in two words contained within Liberty's 'Defining Attributes', as published under the signature of president and chief executive officer Gregory B. Maffei (effectively Carey's boss) on its website.

Under 'Forward-Looking', the company states: 'We take advantage of the benefits and minimize the risks associated with the *digital transition* in the industries in which we invest.'

Liberty describes itself as an investment vehicle 'owning interests in a broad range of media, communications and entertainment businesses', including such as the Liberty Braves (Atlanta Braves baseball team), media giants Viacom and Time Warner, and concert promoters. To provide an acceptable return for investors, it needs to double F1's income at the very least.

Given F1's already mentioned primary revenue sources, it needs to grow each stream, and/or add further streams to reach that objective. Taking TV rights first, Liberty is perfectly placed to exploit opportunities presented by pay-TV, particularly as Malone controls Liberty Global, the largest cable/broadband provider outside the USA, and holds 49 and 29 per cent respectively of US TV producers/channels Starz and Discovery.

Thus fans can expect F1 gradually to migrate to subscription channels, with either no or limited free-to-air broadcasts, as is already the case in France and other territories, with Britain slated to follow suit in 2019. Liberty is also expected to increase F1's streaming services with a view to attracting Millennials via hand-held devices. Such content will likely be reformatted/packaged to cater for regional viewing preferences.

Above: Taking a watching brief thus far, Chase Carey has remained largely silent on Liberty Media's plans for Formula 1.
Photo: WRi2/Jean-François Galeron

Right: Crowds flocked to the Silverstone circuit to see Lewis Hamilton triumph, but the BRDC struggles to balance the books due to the enormous hosting fees charged by the rights holders.
Photo: Peter J. Fox

Below: Still masterminding the deals, Bernie Ecclestone remains firmly in charge.
Photo: WRi2/Jean-François Galeron

Emerging technologies, such as 4K, streaming and sim racing, plus supplemented realities are expected to change the face of broadcast content in future. In Carey, F1 clearly has an experienced executive chairman with the vision to take the sport to the next entertainment level by exploiting such 'digital' innovations.

For example, where 3D TV was once thought to be the next big thing, this technology has been supplanted by augmented/virtual-reality programs, with F1 lending itself perfectly to such developments. AR/VR is defined 'as submersive experiences in which real-world elements are supplemented by computer-generated sensory input such as sound, video, graphics or GPS data'.

Thus, imagine being in a car or a member of a pit-stop crew in real time via a compatible headset and flush credit card…

Ecclestone has long believed that expanding F1's calendar provides low-hanging fruit, for not only do hosting fee incomes increase accordingly, but other revenue streams follow suit – TV rights, 'bridge and board' signage packages, title sponsorship and hospitality income. Speculation suggests 25 races per annum under Liberty, although the jury remains out, given the challenges faced by recent additions.

That said, Liberty, as an NYSE-listed company, is obviously keen to expand its footprint in the USA, with talk of up to three US GPs: one on each coast, plus Austin, Texas. However, asterisks alongside three current grands prix – Brazil, Canada and Germany – suggest that F1 should concentrate on consolidating its 20 or so current events before eyeing expansion in territories where the sport has received a mixed reception.

But, without calendar expansion, Liberty will find it challenging to grow signage and hospitality revenues, in turn placing the full weight of expectation on media (*digital transition*). The question is whether emerging technologies and the repackaging of current formats will double revenues to meet shareholder expectations. Liberty clearly believes so.

Force India deputy team principal Robert Fernley, who triggered the EU complaint and is an outspoken critic of CVC's custodianship of what is ultimately a public sports property, is bullish about Liberty's intentions, provided that Carey and Co manage to grow the sport and, by extension, revenues that eventually flow to teams.

"In CVC, we've had a corporation there that's only been interested in extracting money," he said. "They've done what they're supposed to do as a hedge fund, which is return money to fund holders.

"Hopefully they've sold to a company that can create growth in Formula 1. When you bring in a media group, there is obviously a vested interest there in developing the sport. It pays on both sides. They bring in a lot of experience from the American sporting franchise models, and that can only be a good thing."

All well and good, but the litmus test will be whether fans are offered better overall experiences, be they sat in stands, on sofas or consuming F1 on phablets. Only then will it be possible to say that Liberty have truly liberated Formula 1 from the moneymen.

FORCING THE PACE

From lowly beginnings at the bottom of the championship table, Force India has risen steadily through the ranks of F1 teams to become 'best of the rest' outside the top three. MAURICE HAMILTON discovers the philosophy that drives the team on...

Above: Force India – speeding to fourth place in the constructors' championship in 2016.

Top right: The colour was orange. Vijay Mallya introduced his national colours on taking over the team.

Above right: The team's upward progress continued in 2011, when Adrian Sutil helped them to sixth place in the standings.
Photos: Sahara Force India F1 Team

Right: Working to a five-year programme, CEO Otmar Szafnauer has overseen steady growth at Force India.
Photo: Peter J. Fox

IN 2009, Force India finished one place from the bottom in the constructors' championship, not helped by Tonio Liuzzi and Adrian Sutil scoring zero points with 15th and a lapped 17th place in the final race in Abu Dhabi. With 13 points on the board that year, you wouldn't have put money on the little team from Silverstone rounding off the 2016 season a magnificent fourth in the table with 160 more points. Even allowing for the more generous distribution of points seven years later, it was a transformation worthy of a template for any hopeful entrant bouncing along at the bottom.

Even as the packing-up process began at the end of 2009, Force India were already looking forward to the following season, thanks to the building blocks being put in place on the foundations of what once had been Jordan Grand Prix. The restructuring had begun in October, 2007, when a consortium led by Vijay Mallya bought the business for 90m euros. The dismal picture painted by the 2009 results disguised a momentous event the previous August, when the team had scored their first points by finishing second after Giancarlo Fisichella had claimed pole at Spa. Two weeks later at Monza, Sutil had set fastest lap on his way to fourth. The demonstration of such huge potential enhanced a belief that had underpinned everything. It was a sense of conviction that Bob Fernley and Otmar Szafnauer immediately tapped into on their arrival as deputy team principal and CEO respectively.

"When James Key [technical director] left, we brought in Andy Green to supplement Mark Smith [design director]," recalled Szafnauer. "Andy came with a lot of experience, because I had worked with him at BAR and Honda, and then he went off to Jaguar and Red Bull. With his experience of bigger teams, he knew some of the systems they had that we weren't running.

"At the same time, we hired people from other teams and started putting in place the fundamental tools you need in order, first of all, to understand the car and, secondly, make it go quicker. We properly instrumented the car and brought better-quality controls so that we understood exactly what we were producing; we'd never done that before.

"Previously, the team had been using a CFD cluster in India, made by Tata. Using a computer that's on the other side of the world can make some sort of sense now, thanks to the Cloud and so on, but, back then, the connectivity failed a lot. We had to wait two or three days to get the results. That just slowed you down.

"The wind tunnel was another area that needed changing. Although improved a lot, our tunnel had started life as either a 25 or a 30 per cent model. We had made it up to 50 per cent, but the bigger you go, the better correlation you get. That led us about three years ago to Toyota and their 60 per cent tunnel, with a better rolling road and other sophistication that we didn't have."

One thing Force India did have was a compact and enthusiastic workforce, with a few key figures remaining on board from the Jordan days. Having fewer than 400 people – half the number employed by the leading teams – actually brought important benefits as well as the obvious shortfall in manpower.

"A positive is that each person does more, which means

Above: Mechanics at work on Hülkenberg's car in Sochi. A committed and loyal workforce is just one of the keys to the team's success.

Top right: Deputy team principal Bob Fernley has overseen the difficult task of keeping Force India on track over recent seasons, without the massive financial backing of the top teams.

Above right: Experienced sporting director Andy Stevenson ensures the smooth running of on-track activities.

Top far right: Joy for Sergio Pérez at Monaco, one of two podiums the Mexican delivered in 2016.

Right: In the mixed conditions, Sergio Pérez took his opportunity to grab third place at Monaco.

Photos: Sahara Force India F1 Team

they're contributing more," explained Szafnauer. "Because there is less management, they become more autonomous and make their own decisions. But you need to have the right people. For that reason, we were really careful with our choice, bearing in mind the important thing is to also make sure they all work well together.

"We did all this incrementally; our shareholders understood that this wouldn't happen overnight. We looked at the low-hanging fruit first and improved quality control. If, for example, the strakes on the front wing are out by two millimetres, they produce different results. But unless you measure that, you haven't a clue about what's happening. We also needed to start fully understanding the loads produced by different parts of the car."

Powering all of this in every sense was a liaison with McLaren and Mercedes, after Force India had ended their deal with Ferrari for the supply of engines. The association with Mercedes would be even more important with the advent of the hybrid formula at the start of 2014.

"We work on five-year programmes," said Fernley. "We moved into a five-year agreement with McLaren, the purpose of which was to identify where the weaknesses were in Force India and also for us to build on the strengths. And during that process, to take advantage where we could within the regulations of some of the McLaren facilities, such as driver simulators. That allowed us to become a solid midfield team, and it delivered, probably a little earlier than we expected.

"During a process such as that, you're looking ahead. The next five years for us was clearly being with Mercedes. So, we moved from Mercedes engine/McLaren transmission to a complete Mercedes power unit for the next five years, which is where we are today."

An outward indication of the improving standard came at Silverstone in 2015, when modifications, principally around the nose, brought a step forward in performance that ultimately led to Force India moving to fifth (from sixth) in the championship.

"Had we been able to put those bits on earlier than the British Grand Prix, we would have had an even better 2015 season, because we suffered at the beginning," said Szafnauer. "In 2016, we started with a good car. We didn't have the troubles we had in the previous winter, which were mainly resource related. We didn't have the money to do what we wanted to do. We had the development, but we couldn't produce and we had to carry some stuff over. Once you start carrying things over, like front brakes and front brake ducts, and it becomes a hybrid of the previous year and the current one, but without sufficient wind tunnel testing, it's just a mish-mash of stuff and it's no good."

The "resource related" troubles were down to money, but the problems were not as serious as paddock rumours suggested.

"We have cash-flow issues; there's no question about that," said Fernley. "But there is a difference between a cash-flow issue and a budgeting element. A cash-flow hiatus doesn't mean you don't have the money; it's just coming in at the wrong time. We've learned how to flatten that out over time and get it right. We've had rumours that we're going to close our doors every year for nine years – and we're still going! Unfortunately, when you're an independent team and you are working on a limited resource, you do hit the barriers occasionally, and the rumours will spread. It's not helpful and you've got to live with it."

Keeping the employees advised of the true situation is key during moments of media-fuelled uncertainty.

"I've always felt that reasonable people with the same information will come to the same conclusion," said Szafnauer. "So, just give them good information and be honest. A big part of what we do is getting everyone together and telling them like it is. Some people say you shouldn't be telling everybody. Okay, perhaps there is a very small number of people who could take things the wrong way and make other decisions. But I'm happy to say hardly anyone in the team is like that. Last winter, we got everyone together and

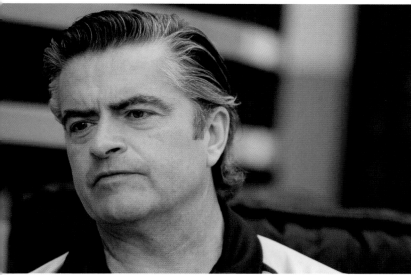

Above: Mercedes power helped Pérez to eighth on the grid at Monza.

Right: Nico Hülkenberg's last race for the team at Abu Dhabi brought him ninth place in the drivers' standings.
Photo: WRi2/Jad Sherif

Top right: Steve Curnow is developing the commercial side of the Force India operation.

Top far right: Technical director Andy Green is getting the maximum from the team's resources.

Above right: Satisfaction in Abu Dhabi for Sergio Pérez, who broke the 100-point mark in 2016, to finish seventh in the championship.
Photos: Sahara Force India F1 Team

said, 'Don't worry. This is what we're doing. Hang in there.' Some were sceptical – but not many."

"One of our main strengths has always been our staff in terms of our technical and commercial teams," said Fernley. 'We've built on that. Under Otmar, we have a very strong operational staff and, under Steve Curnow, a really efficient commercial operation. Building all of that in was part of the second-phase programme."

Fernley and his team have done what they can while operating on a budget significantly less than the rivals directly above Force India in the championship table. Each team works to the best of its ability to attract sponsorship; fair enough, that's part of the game, and Force India have been punching above their weight. But the uneven distribution of cash within the sport is something that affects Force India more than ever now that they are officially 'best of the rest'.

"The disparity shows when you look at the top three teams [Mercedes, Red Bull and Ferrari]," said Fernley. "They all receive what I call an 'off the top' payment, which is as big as our budget. So, from Day One, they receive more than we actually spend. That's the disparity; that's what's wrong with the system as it stands.

"We talk about making F1 competitive. But are we wanting to make F1 competitive as an entity? Or do we just want to make it competitive for three teams? If you redistributed the income in a proper manner – merit driven, so that you are working on reward based on success – and you also bring in some form of budget cap, then it becomes an intellectual exercise. It's immoral in my view to spend $300m – in some cases, more – to put two cars on the track for 21 races. Instead of just three teams competing at the front, you might have six or seven teams competing for that position. So, you can solve it overnight. You don't have to be clever with all the rules; just do that."

A restriction on expenditure would provide the additional benefit of placing greater emphasis on drivers, an aspect that, in any case, Force India has worked to its advantage in recent years.

"Driver choice is really important," agreed Szafnauer. "We've always tried to have the best drivers we could, and we've had some good pairings: [Paul] di Resta, Hülkenberg, Sutil. And then Sergio [Pérez] and Nico [Hülkenberg].

"With Nico leaving at the end of 2016, we had a look to see who potentially the best guy was, and I think we made the right decision with Esteban [Ocon]. We've run him twice, so we understand how fast he is – we could overlay his performances. We didn't have him in a simulator, but in two tests, and the feedback was good. He was quick. We also kept a chart and looked at his history. We knew that he had beaten [Max] Verstappen in F3 in their first year; they were very close with the number of wins."

Overseeing all of this is Mallya himself. While the Indian's business affairs have made headlines outside the sport, his commitment to the team has not wavered.

"Vijay is a very resourceful fellow and very much a part of this team," said Fernley. "He has always supported us, understood where we need to invest. He's driving that side just as much as we are. I think what you've got to remember with Force India, it is a team; it really is a racing team in its own right and not part of a wider commercial enterprise.

"I'm immensely proud of what everyone here has done. A team is only as good as the people in it. Our results in 2016 show we have super people operating the team, and we've got a good owner who supports it, but with the minimum of interference.

"Vijay celebrates ten years in F1 in 2017. That is no mean achievement these days and says everything about the man and his team."

APPRECIATIONS 2016

By MAURICE HAMILTON

Photo: SCuderia Ferrari

CHRIS AMON

CHRIS AMON, who died aged 73 on 3rd August, 2016, cut his teeth racing a Maserati 250F – often in the wet – in his native New Zealand. His throttle control was so obvious that Reg Parnell invited him to join his small F1 team in the 1963 World Championship.

At the age of 19, Amon arrived in Europe, where he formed an easy alliance with Bruce McLaren. The pair made a natural fit for Ford in the automotive giant's on-track fight with Ferrari, and they took a GT40 MkII to victory at Le Mans in 1966.

The irony was that good fortune had played its part – as it always does in the 24-hour classic – yet Amon will be remembered for the appalling luck that accompanied him everywhere else. The F1 records show that he finished second three times and managed eight third places during 96 grands prix, before his retirement part way through 1976. But the results do not give an indication of how Amon would have won more than a dozen grands prix but for an agonising catalogue of misfortune.

Enzo Ferrari was quick to spot Amon's potential, despite patchy F1 results, and he joined the Scuderia as a fourth driver in 1967. By the end of the season, he was the sole entry (Lorenzo Bandini had perished at Monaco; Ludovico Scarfiotti had fallen from favour; and Mike Parkes had been injured).

Amon bore the responsibility with such ease that he should have been champion in 1968. He retired seven times from 11 races. At Spa-Francorchamps, he had been on pole by four clear seconds; at St Jovite, he had led easily, despite having no clutch, the gearbox giving out after 73 of the 90 laps.

Bad luck applied even more in 1969, when six mechanical failures, often while leading, prompted Amon to seek reliability with the Ford-Cosworth V8, albeit one in the back of a March. It was a classic Amon move at the wrong time. A switch to Matra for 1971 meant wonderful 12-cylinder harmony, but little else. And yet, when the driver could compensate on the twisting road circuit at Clermont Ferrand in 1972, a truly dominant drive was foiled by a puncture.

Amon's poor decision making was highlighted towards the end of his career by an uncompetitive and over-complicated car built under his own name. He retired to New Zealand and returned to working the family farm while maintaining a key role as development driver for Toyota's road cars.

Photo: Autocourse Archive

ALAN HENRY

ALAN HENRY was Editor of AUTOCOURSE from 1988 to 2010. A prolific writer and towering figure in the paddocks of international motorsport for more than 40 years, he had begun his journalistic career reporting on club racing for *Autosport* and *Motoring News*, before joining the latter full time in 1971. His incisive work, combined with an encyclopaedic knowledge of the sport, ensured a swift rise to F1 reporter and then Editor. After he turned freelance in 1988, future roles would include motorsport correspondent of *The Guardian* for 20 years.

Known universally as 'AH' (a throwback to the early *Motoring News* edict that reporters should be known by their initials rather than a full by-line), Henry's dry sense of humour oiled the wheels of relationships within the prickly world of F1, a place where his honest and sometimes trenchant views would ruffle feathers – but not cause outrage, thanks to deep respect for a breadth of experience and perfectly expressed opinion.

In recent years, the onset of Parkinson's may have curtailed his activities, but did nothing to dim his wry and whimsical observations as he stayed in touch with the world he loved.

The outpouring of tributes from within and beyond F1 following his passing in March, 2016, at the age of 68, said everything about a widely-read and much-loved man.

TYLER ALEXANDER

TYLER ALEXANDER was the epitome of the term 'racer', both in looks and deed. A central member of McLaren Racing from its foundation in 1963, he had started as a mechanic and quickly became chief mechanic, later effectively running the race department. He was totally hands-on and understood how everything worked; if it didn't, he knew how to fix it.

Alexander was a key figure behind McLaren's racing in the United States in the late 1960s and early '70s, when they won CanAm championships and the Indy 500. He was also responsible for helping to hold the team together after Bruce McLaren's death in June, 1970.

In 1982, Alexander left McLaren in its latest guise and started an Indycar team with Teddy Mayer. Subsequently, he moved to the Beatrice F1 project and rejoined McLaren in 1989, where he remained until his retirement in 2008.

An intensely private man, the American did not suffer fools gladly and possessed a healthy disregard for journalists. In some respects, he was formidable, but despite the gruff exterior, it was easy to sense a tremendous passion for the sport.

Inevitably, some drivers breached the seemingly impenetrable personal defences. Apart from Bruce McLaren, of course, Tyler had a great deal of time for Johnny Rutherford, Mario Andretti, Denny Hulme and Dan Gurney, as well as having the respect of Ayrton Senna.

Tyler Alexander passed away in January, 2016, at the age of 75.

Photo: LAT Photographic

Photos: Autocourse Archive

MICHAEL MACDOWEL

MICHAEL MACDOWEL'S history as a grand prix driver may have been but a brief footnote – 17 laps of the 1957 French Grand Prix – but his motorsport career, mainly as an amateur, was actually long and very distinguished.

The Englishman earned his place on the Cooper F1 team as a result of success with sportscars in Britain, but his race with the F1 1.5 Cooper T43 at Rouen was cut short when he was asked to hand over to team leader Jack Brabham. Later that year, he finished second, ahead of a young Bruce McLaren, in the Prix de Paris at Montlhéry

After a period away from racing, Macdowel returned in 1968 to hillclimbing, taking the British championship in 1973 and 1974 with 16 wins in a fearsome 5-litre Repco-engined Brabham BT36X. He retired at the end of 1979, but stayed involved with the sport and historic racing, largely through the BRDC. Mike Dacdowel passed away in January, 2016, at the age of 83.

BERTIL ROOS

BERTIL ROOS, born in Gothenburg in October 1943, took the unusual step of pursuing his early motor racing career in North America despite speaking very little English. Reasoning this presented better opportunities than the small and isolated fishing island where he had been brought up, the Swede allowed his racing to do the talking. He won the 1973 US Super Vee title and made a name for himself further afield with impressive performances in the European F2 series and Formula Atlantic in Canada.

Roos did enough to attract the attention of Shadow, the American-backed team offering a drive in the 1974 Swedish Grand Prix at Anderstorp. He qualified 23rd and retired with transmission trouble, not having done enough to warrant further drives as Shadow switched attention to Tom Pryce. The following year, Roos founded a racing school near Pocono in Eastern Pennsylvania and built up a successful operation until selling out in 1999. He died after a long illness in March 2016.

PETER WESTBURY

PETER WESTBURY raced competitively in Formula 3 and Formula 2, but is perhaps better known for winning the British hillclimb championship. A more than competent engineer, he built up Felday Engineering in Surrey while becoming hillclimb champion, first in 1963 with a Daimler V8-powered Felday, then the following year with a Fergusson 4WD F1 car.

The Englishman used Brabhams to move into F3 and F2 – under the Felday International Racing & Sportscar Team (FIRST) banner. Apart from winning in F3 on the Chimay road course in Belgium in 1967, Westbury received credit for giving an F2 seat to Derek Bell, whose success with the BT21 attracted Ferrari's attention.

Westbury used his BT30 to race in the 1969 German Grand Prix, finishing fifth in the F2 class. A drive with BRM in the 1970 US GP came to nothing when a blown engine prevented him from qualifying.

He retired in 1973 and passed away in December, 2015, aged 77.

MARIA-TERESA DE FILIPPIS

A FEISTY pioneer, Maria-Teresa de Filippis was the first woman to race a grand prix car. She was a competitive horsewoman from a wealthy family, and was determined to prove her three brothers wrong when they said she could never succeed at motorsport.

Taken on by the Maserati sports car team, the diminutive Italian captured the imagination of the public by starting from the back of the grid (having missed practice) and finishing second in the race supporting the 1956 Naples Grand Prix.

Two years later, de Filippis moved into single-seaters, buying a Maserati 250F to run alongside the works F1 team. She finished fifth in a thin field entered for the non-championship Syracuse Grand Prix, but failed to qualify for the Monaco GP (the first round of the 1958 championship).

Having started from the back of the grid at Spa-Francorchamps, she took tenth in the Belgian Grand Prix, which would be her only finish, as she retired in Portugal and also at her home race at Monza.

A move to her friend Jean Behra's privately-run team, running a Porsche Formula 2 car for 1959, brought another failure to qualify at Monaco.

She retired from racing in August, after Behra was killed following a crash in practice in the German Grand Prix meeting Avus.

De Filippis renewed her links with racing in 1979 through active work with the Société des Anciens Pilotes. Elected vice-president in 1997, she was an integral member of this exclusive club before her death in January, 2016, at the age of 89.

Photo: Autocourse Archive

Photo: Autocourse Archive

EDDIE KEIZAN

AS a leading driver in South Africa, it was only natural that Eddie Keizan should take every opportunity to race in his home grand prix, and he did so three times between 1973 and 1975. Born in Johannesburg in 1944, he was successful racing saloons and sportscars, before moving into F5000 and winning the national title with a Surtees in 1972.

Having stepped up to the South African F1 Championship, Keizan drove the Tyrrell-Ford previously raced by Jackie Stewart, entering the world championship round with this car at Kyalami early in the 1973 season. He was unclassified, but finished 14th the following year, before switching to an ex-Fittipaldi Lotus 72 entered by Team Gunston and claiming 13th in the 1975 South African Grand Prix.

When his country's premier series switched to Formula Atlantic, Keizan moved on to saloon cars, winning the championship twice more and concentrating on his successful alloy wheel company. He passed away in May, 2016, at the age of 71.

Photo: Autocourse Archive

ANDRÉ GUELFI

BORN in Morocco and having competed in his country's only championship grand prix, André Guelfi had an eventful sporting career and a colourful life outside motor racing. Quick enough in sportscars to share a works Gordini and finish sixth (first in class) at Le Mans in 1954, he was chosen to race single-seaters for the French firm. Having moved on to rear-engine F2 Coopers, he finished a very close second in the Prix de Paris at Montlhéry in 1958. The inclusion of an F2 class for the championship grand prix at Casablanca later in the year allowed Guelfi an entry. He started from the back and finished 15th, five laps behind and fifth in class.

Guelfi continued racing for another ten years, but his name made the headlines for the wrong reasons when, having mixed in French political and business circles, he received a suspended jail sentence for his part in a corruption scandal. André Guelfi died a wealthy man in June, 2016, at the age of 97.

DR AKI HINTSA

BORN in Finland in September, 1958, Aki Hintsa qualified as a doctor and did missionary work in Africa in the 1990s.

During this time, he became intrigued by the dominance of Ethiopian distance runners, closely observing their way of life and training routines.

He brought his accumulated knowledge of medicine and mental wellbeing to Formula 1 in 1998, eventually becoming physician and chief medical officer with McLaren, a position he held for 11 years.

During that time, he developed a powerful rapport with his drivers and grew particularly close to Lewis Hamilton, helping to develop his mental as well as physical approach to the stress of competition.

Hintsa, sadly, succumbed to cancer in November, 2016.

Photos: WRi2/Jean-Francois Galeron

PAUL ROSCHE

PAUL ROSCHE, who was responsible for designing arguably the most powerful F1 engines of all time, passed away in November, 2016, at the age of 82.

Rosche joined BMW as a development engineer in the late 1950s and later would assume responsibility for the company's competition engines until it pulled out of racing in 1970. When it returned to competition three years later, BMW joined forces with March for the British manufacturer's F2 programme, leading to a string of championship titles.

Having become the technical head of BMW motorsport in 1975, Rosche began a steady campaign to convince his board to move into F1 with a turbo engine. This was agreed in 1980, the four-cylinder unit racing for the first time with Brabham in 1982. It went on to give Nelson Piquet the championship the following year.

In subsequent seasons, the 1500cc engine, in qualifying trim and on full boost, was reckoned to deliver an eye-watering 1500bhp.

When BMW withdrew from F1 at the end of 1986, Rosche's engines powered a succession of touring car championships. In the 1990s, he produced an engine for the first McLaren road car, developing the BMW V12 into a winner for McLaren at Le Mans in 1995 and a Williams-built BMW four years later. He retired at the end of 1999.

FORMULA 1 REVIEW

Team Reviews: MARK HUGHES

Car Illustrations: ADRIAN DEAN

Photo: Red Bull Racing/Getty Images

MERCEDES AMG PETRONAS F1 TEAM

6

NICO ROSBERG

44

LEWIS HAMILTON

THE steamroller continued in 2016. For the third consecutive season, Mercedes took the constructors' title *and* put its drivers 1-2 in their championship, a unique achievement in F1 history.

It did so with the W07, a more aggressive development of what had gone before than was the 2015 car. Both sides of the operation – the Paddy Lowe-run Brackley chassis squad and the Andy Cowell power unit centre at Brixworth – refused to rest on their laurels and delivered big gains on what had already been the dominant car.

On the power unit side, the initial PU106 was based very much on the upgraded engine that had been released at Monza in 2015. Improvements in the efficiency of the energy transfer to the battery had justified the use of a bigger turbine and compressor. Nineteen of the available 32 development tokens were spent during the winter, while a further two went on a fuel system upgrade for Sochi.

Phase 2 came in Canada with a reliability upgrade, which included a modification to the MGU-H that allowed the possibility of running longer in higher power modes. Phase 3 came at Spa, with a five-token combustion chamber and turbo upgrade; by now, the power unit was knocking on the door of 1,000bhp. A fourth evolution was planned, but failed to deliver the expected performance boost on the dyno, so it wasn't raced.

The chassis concept was based on two innovations: the two-piece bulkhead section (using the interpretation that had allowed Manor to adapt its 2014 car to the 2015 nose regulations) that allowed a much bigger opening for the heave damper across the front suspension. Probably of more significance was the 'W floor', which Lowe described as "the largest new concept we saw in the sport this year, in my view."

This concerned the hugely intricate arrangement of serrated vanes ahead of the sidepod. Each of these was connected to separate points of the floor's leading edge, allowing some of the flow arriving at the sidepod area to be filtered off in a controlled way to the underbody. The conventional guide vanes in this area on other cars sent the flow outboard around the sidepods. Theoretically, siphoning off some of this flow to the underbody would give a double gain: less drag from less outboard flow and more downforce from the extra energy flowing into the underbody. Aero teams usually go to a lot of trouble to ensure that flow from the outer body does not leak into the floor, to keep the underbody flow as smooth and free from turbulence as possible. The achievement of the Mercedes aero team was in incorporating the flow without introducing the turbulence.

It was an example of a more aggressive approach to the design than had been the previous year's car. "In 2015, it had been relatively straightforward to do a second lap around the original car of '14, just improving the integration aspects," said Lowe. "But that approach wouldn't have yielded much with a third iteration and therefore we had to be more innovative."

MERCEDES F1 W07 HYBRID

PARTNERS	PETRONAS • UBS • Qualcomm • Epson • Bose
TEAM PARTNERS	HUGO BOSS • IWC Schaffhausen • Monster Energy • Pure Storage • Allianz • Starwood Preferred Guest • PUMA • ebmpapst • Tumi Tata Communications • DB Schenker • Assos • Spies Hecker • Schuberth • Advanti • Endless • USI Italia • Pirelli
POWER UNIT	**Type:** Mercedes-Benz PU106C Hybrid **No. of cylinders (vee angle):** V6 (90°) **No. of valves:** 24 **Max rpm (ICE):** 15,000 **Electronics:** FIA standard ECU and FIA homologated electronic & electrical system **Fuel:** PETRONAS Primax **Lubricants:** PETRONAS Syntium **Gearbox & hydraulic oil:** PETRONAS Tutela
TRANSMISSION	**Gearbox:** Eight-speed forward, one-reverse unit with carbon-fibre main case **Gear selection:** Sequential, semi-automatic, hydraulic activation **Clutch:** Carbon plate
CHASSIS	**Structure:** Monocoque, moulded carbon-fibre and honeycomb composite structure **Front suspension:** Carbon-fibre wishbone and push-rod-activated torsion springs and rockers **Rear suspension:** Carbon-fibre wishbone and pull-rod-activated torsion springs and rockers **Brake discs and pads:** Carbone Industrie carbon/carbon discs and pads with rear brake-by-wire **Brake calipers:** Brembo **Steering:** Power-assisted rack-and-pinion **Wheels:** Advanti forged magnesium **Tyres:** Pirelli P Zero
DIMENSIONS	**Length:** 5000mm **Width:** 1800mm **Height:** 950mm **Formula weight:** 702kg, including driver and camera

Nico Rosberg winning the Spanish Grand Prix.

Photo: Peter J. Fox

TOTO WOLFF

MERCEDES AMG PETRONAS F1 TEAM: PERSONNEL

Non-Executive Chairman: Niki Lauda

Head of Mercedes-Benz Motorsport: Toto Wolff

Executive Director, Technical: Paddy Lowe

Managing Director, Mercedes AMG
High Performance Powertrains: Andy Cowell

Technology Director: Geoffrey Willis

Engineering Director: Aldo Costa

Performance Director: Mark Ellis

Head of Aerodynamics: Mike Elliott

Sporting Director: Ron Meadows

Chief Race Engineer: Andrew Shovlin

Race Engineer *(Rosberg):* Tony Ross

Race Engineer *(Hamilton):* Peter Bonnington

Chief Mechanic: Matthew Deane

Chief Engineer Trackside: Simon Cole

Head of Mercedes-Benz
Motorsport Communications: Bradley Lord

Photo: Mercedes AMG Petronas F1 Team

PADDY LOWE

There was also a steep vehicle dynamics development curve concerning the front and rear suspensions and the hydraulically controlled heave springs. This allowed further refinement in retaining chassis balance through a wide range of cornering speeds, achieving some of what had been done previously through the banned FRICS technology. Lowe lent some insight into this: "It's about getting the best from the aero platform: the best balance from high speed to low speed, and indeed even through different phases of the corner. All the teams are playing more tunes than ever they used to. Our suspension, therefore, becomes more complex year on year. Classically, a spring had a linear rate. Now we are playing with far greater and more complex ranges of non-linear compliance. That's allowing us to play games with getting the aero platform exactly where we want. It's more difficult to do than it was with FRICS, but it's the same thing really."

The W07's attitude in pitch and dive was extraordinarily finely controlled through this complex variable springing rate, and it may be one of the reasons why the team did not follow the high-rake fashion initiated by Red Bull. "If we wanted to jump to a high-rake car," said Lowe, "it would take a leap of faith and risk an investment of the wind tunnel [regulation] quota that may not deliver. The limits [on CFD capacity and wind tunnel time] mean it's especially difficult to make big departures from your existing philosophies because these cars are so highly optimised around the solutions that you have aerodynamically. If you start a new philosophy, you're always going to be starting off worse than where you were, by a significant amount."

The optimisation of the car's aero platform through its suspension sophistication made for a very benign car. Lowe continued: "If drivers from the past got into these cars, they'd be mind-blown by how well balanced they are. The degree to which we're tailoring the aero and mechanical platform almost corner by corner even gives a car where you can get to a point in the weekend where the driver is saying, 'There's nothing to tune. It's a perfectly balanced car,' whereas 20 years ago, you had to take a really very crude approximation of getting a balance at as many corners as possible while accepting the others would be rubbish."

There was one race-day failure – when a big-end bearing surrendered as Lewis Hamilton was leading the Malaysian GP. Uprated oil pumps followed, and a reversion to the previous, slightly less performant, specification of oil. Earlier in the year, Hamilton had suffered two MGU-H failures – in China and Russia – that compromised his qualifying. A turbo assembly error was found to be the culprit in both cases.

The combination of the best power unit with arguably the best chassis and balance was irresistible, winning 19 of the 21 races and setting 20 poles. However, the opposition was catching up, especially the Red Bull/Renault combination. "Our conversion rate from front-row lock-outs into a 1-2 in the race was very much lower than it was in '14 and '15," Lowe pointed out. "The reason is the reduced underlying lap time advantage. So if you get out of position, it used to be much easier to get it back. The engines are a lot closer now; by our estimation, two- to three-tenths back to Renault and Ferrari."

Unfortunately for the team, it had plenty of opportunity to measure this, as a series of poor getaways from the front row often made the races much more difficult for one or other of the drivers. An initial clutch inconsistency was improved early in the season, but subsequent poor starts were simply the result of the inherent variability of starts that the regulation regarding manual operation of the clutch was intended to induce. In other words, latterly it became more driver than car.

One weak point that remained, however, was that of braking. Partly, this was to do with optimising front duct sizing around the expectation of running at the front, where the most efficient form of brake management is for the driver to control his pace against brake temperature. That way, the aerodynamic disruption of the sort of big brake ducts seen on, for example, the Ferrari was minimised. But Lowe acknowledged that it remained a difficult area. "We haven't made the progress we'd like. Some of it is not in our hands, in that you are relying on material suppliers, and there have been no great breakthroughs there. But often you want to save your braking in order to save your tyres anyway, so the quickest race time doesn't come through a brake package that the drivers can arbitrarily take to the limit on every lap."

The Mercs of the previous two years had tended to give best to the Red Bull through low-speed corners, but in the comparison between 2016's W07 and Red Bull RB12, Lowe saw a different pattern: "We were particularly strong in the low- to medium-speed sections, and this time it was actually in some of the higher-speed corners where we could find ourselves giving up time to Red Bull. But some of that is the choices we make around set-up. According to our numbers – and Red Bull might disagree – if you normalise for power units, ours has been the quickest car at all but two of the tracks."

Above: Niki and Toto are delighted by Nico's pole lap in Spa.

Above left: Lewis sprays the bubbly after his win in Monte Carlo.

Left: The heart of the matter – the PU106C hybrid.

Right: Mission accomplished for Nico in Abu Dhabi.

Below: The championship-winning Mercedes team.

Far left: At the limit. Hamilton locks up a wheel in practice at Interlagos. He outqualified Nico by 12–9 over the 2016 season.

Photos: Mercedes AMG Petronas F1 Team

3

33

DANIEL RICCIARDO

MAX VERSTAPPEN

26

DANIIL KVYAT

RED BULL RACING

RED BULL made very significant progress after its difficult, engine-blighted 2015 season, to emerge as best of the rest behind Mercedes. The RB12 took full advantage of the gains made by Renault Sport over the winter and added a few of its own. It won twice, and only a catastrophic pit-stop error at Monaco prevented that from being three times. It tended to fall behind Ferrari at power tracks, but on balance it was a more consistently competitive car and scored the only non-Mercedes pole of the season. Also the only team other than Mercedes to win races in 2016, Red Bull finished runner-up in the constructors' championship, and its drivers, Daniel Ricciardo and Max Verstappen (recruited from race five onwards to replace Daniil Kvyat), took third and fifth in the drivers' championship.

The RB12 was the work of the same group that had produced the RB11, with Adrian Newey as chief technical officer feeding into a technical management team comprising chief engineering officer Rob Marshall, chief of aero Dan Fallows, chief car engineer Paul Monaghan and chief performance engineer Pierre Waché. As a design, it was a clear evolution of the RB11 and superficially looked almost the same. However, it had been substantially repackaged "from front to back" – as Fallows termed it – that is, with the emphasis on the front and everything else following from there. As such, the front suspension, nose and under-nose were substantially re-engineered, chasing further aerodynamic gains. The front suspension fea-

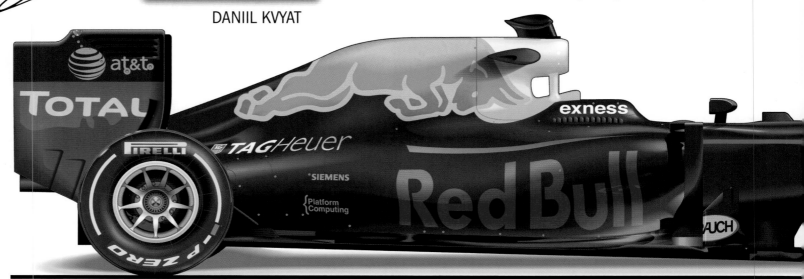

RED BULL RB12

SPONSOR	Red Bull
TEAM PARTNERS	TAG Heuer • Total • Puma • Rauch • Exness • Pepe Jeans London
INNOVATION PARTNERS	AT&T • Siemens PLM • IBM Spectrum Computing • Hexagon • DMG Mori • PWR • ANSYS • Flir • Oz Racing • Mitie • Aston Martin
TEAM SUPPLIERS	Hisense • Pirelli • Scott • Sabelt • Matrix • GoPro
POWER UNIT	Type: Red Bull Racing-TAG Heuer RB12-2016 1.6-litre turbo **No. of cylinders** *(vee angle)*: V6 (90°) **No. of valves:** 24 Bore: 80mm **Stroke:** 53mm **Max. rpm** *(ICE)*: 15,000 Fuel feed: Direct fuel injection **Electronics:** FIA standard ECU and FIA homologated electronic & electrical system **Fuel:** Total **Oil:** Total
TRANSMISSION	Eight-speed carbon-composite gearbox, longitudinally mounted with hydraulic power shift and clutch operation **Clutch:** AP Racing
CHASSIS	Carbon-fibre and aluminium honeycomb monocoque **Front suspension:** Double wishbones with push-rod-actuated torsion springs, dampers and anti-roll bar **Rear suspension:** Double wishbones with pull-rod-actuated torsion springs, dampers and anti-roll bar Dampers: Multimatic Wheel diameter: 13in, front and rear **Wheels:** OZ Racing **Tyres:** Pirelli P Zero **Brake pads, discs and calipers:** Brembo
DIMENSIONS	Not disclosed
	Formula weight: 702kg, including driver and camera

Daniel Ricciardo and Max Verstappen celebrate their 1-2 finish in Sepang.

ROB MARSHALL

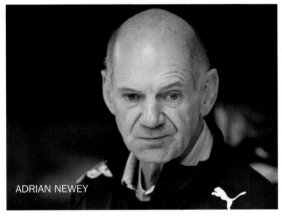
ADRIAN NEWEY

tured the Y-link blended lower wishbone (two years after it had been introduced by Mercedes). "That presented some structural entertainment," said Monaghan drily. "It was a big challenge for those guys to achieve the installation we sought with the geometry we pursued. So the chassis had to change around the wishbones, which involved a re-laying out of the carbon make-up of the chassis, to feed the loads in the required way and trying to get adequate stiffness into it."

The front suspension also featured a more vertical upper link (helped by the repositioning of the steering tie-rods), which reduced the front roll centre. The heave spring across the front of the car, which controlled the vertical stiffness, employed Belleville washers (disc-shaped springs) rather than the Merc's hydraulic operation or the Ferrari's coil.

A yet-shorter nose was scooped out further on the underside, where a new arrangement of vanes, together with a 'bat wing' – uniquely mounted on the leading edge of the floor, rather than the conventional underside of the nose – enhanced the underfloor airflow. It meant that there was no longer room for an S-duct inlet, so the feature was deleted. "The short nose, the packaging around it and trying to get the pushrods in the front suspension as close to vertical as we could, within that whole little package of regs around that part of the car, gave us some choices to make, and the S-duct was a casualty," explained

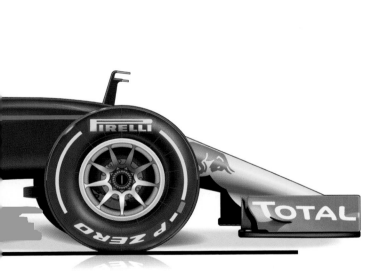

CHRISTIAN HORNER

RED BULL RACING TAG HEUER: PERSONNEL

Chairman: Dietrich Mateschitz	**Renault Sport F1, Director of Operations:** Remi Taffin
Team Principal: Christian Horner OBE	**Race Engineer** (*Ricciardo*)**:** Simon Rennie
Red Bull Motorsport Consultant: Helmut Marko	**Race Engineer** (*Kvyat/Verstappen*)**:** GianPiero Lambiase
Chief Technical Officer: Adrian Newey OBE	**No. 1 Race Mechanic** (*Ricciardo*)**:** Chris Gent
Chief Engineering Officer: Rob Marshall	**No. 1 Race Mechanic** (*Kvyat/Verstappen*)**:** Lee Stevenson
Head of Aerodynamics: Dan Fallows	**Head of Marketing:** Dominik Mitsch
Chief Engineer, Car Engineering: Paul Monaghan	**Head of Red Bull Relations & Events:** Marcus Prosser
Chief Engineer, Performance Engineering: Pierre Waché	**Head of Communications:** Ben Wyatt
Head of Electronics: Paul Everington	**Head of Partnerships:** Joanne Sinclair/Guy Richards
Race Team Manager: Jonathan Wheatley	**Press Officers:** Anna Pamin, James Ranson
Support Team Manager: Tony Burrows	

PAUL MONAGHAN

Above: By the end of the season, Daniil's fine third place in China was all but forgotten.

Top left: Helmut Marko's decision to promote Max Verstappen to the Red Bull team was immediately vindicated. The Austrian took to the Catalunya podium to celebrate.

Left: Max Verstappen drove with immense maturity, resisting the pressure from Räikkönen's Ferrari and winning the Spanish Grand Prix.

Right: Daniel Ricciardo and Max Verstappen lead the field in Sepang.

Below: The high point of the season was the team's 1-2 finish in Malaysia.

Photos: Red Bull Racing/Getty Images

Monaghan. The blown front axle continued to be used at most circuits.

At the rear, the upper wishbones were *less* inclined than before, having the effect of increasing the rear roll centre and confirming – in combination with the lower roll centre of the front suspension – the general evolution towards yet more rake, for aerodynamic reasons. So fruitful did this path prove that the car was running at rake angles in excess of those achieved during the exhaust-blown-diffuser era. "What we did at the front had knock-on consequences at the rear," Monaghan acknowledged. "For example, how to fit the rear wishbones to the gearbox, how we put the loads into it, what we did at the outboard ends."

Renault Sport's redesign of the internal-combustion and turbo parts of the power unit over the winter saved around 0.5s of lap time of itself. Onwards from Monaco (on Ricciardo's car) and Montreal (Verstappen's), it benefited from the Turbulent Jet ignition upgrade reckoned to be worth a further 0.3s. That still left it trailing Mercedes and Ferrari on outright horsepower, but brought it much closer (within an estimated 20bhp of Mercedes) than in 2015. The plenum within the engine cover had been completely redesigned over the winter to provide the engine with better breathing, and Red Bull continued to use split air-to-air intercoolers, one in each sidepod. Despite the power increase, the cooling requirement for the engine was actually reduced slightly, thanks to efficiency gains from Renault Sport.

Monaghan summarised the RB12 as "very nicely balanced from first running. It didn't have a particular understeer or oversteer tendency, and even as we evolved the car with more rake through the year, we didn't lose that balance window; it's quite narrow, as on all these cars, but that window remained accessible. Renault not only gave us more performance, but also a much more reliable power unit than before."

The only time the team ran into performance problems was during the first two stints at Baku, where the car's tyre usage was out of control, ruining the races of both drivers. "That wasn't our finest hour," admitted Monaghan. "Sometimes a team can look like an expert on tyres, the others less so; then a few races down the road, it swaps over. We changed our approach to the tyres during Friday at Baku, and it backfired on us. A stark and careful look back enabled us to understand what we'd done wrong. It was painful at the time, but as with any mistake it allows you the opportunity to learn – and I think we did." The car's performances in the rain – notably Ricciardo at Monaco, Verstappen at Silverstone and Interlagos – suggested that it may even have been quicker than the Mercedes in such conditions, when engine power counted for less and downforce more.

Although Verstappen's fairy-tale victory at Barcelona, his first race for the team, came in the aftermath of the two Mercs taking each other out on the first lap, one race later, at Monaco, Ricciardo beat the silver cars to pole and was set to trounce them in the race, too, until a communication error between the pit wall and garage resulted in his tyres not being ready as he arrived in the pit lane. That allowed Hamilton's Mercedes to steal what should have been his victory, but the tables were turned in Malaysia, where Ricciardo triumphed after Hamilton's engine blew when in the lead.

Two race wins from 20 may not sound much for a team that used to dominate, but F1 is cyclical and there's much to suggest that these were just steps along the way to a return to full competitiveness.

5

SEBASTIAN VETTEL

7

KIMI RÄIKKÖNEN

SCUDERIA FERRARI

FERRARI finished third in the constructors' championship, having contended for victory in just two races without winning either of them. It parted company with technical director James Allison – who had suffered a personal tragedy post-Melbourne – in July after a conflict of views about the disappointing performance of the SF16-T. Furthermore, strains in the relationship between senior management and Sebastian Vettel began to show. Twenty-sixteen couldn't be considered anything other than a hugely disappointing season after the promise of the previous year.

In concept, the car looked a very logical development of that which had won three 2015 grands prix. Up front, the pull-rod suspension had been ditched in favour of the pushrod system used by everyone else, allowing a bulkhead position that more comfortably facilitated a fashionably short nose. A powerfully big heave spring was fitted across the nose. At the rear, a relocation of the ERS-K to the side of the engine (rather than on the end of the gearbox) allowed the rear bodywork to be contoured in earlier, accelerating the airflow harder over the adjacent downforce-producing surfaces. A water-air intercooler – rather than air-air – was chosen for its more compact dimensions.

Former engine chief Mattia Binotto took over Allison's role as acting technical director, and he explained further the push to tighten up the rear dimensions: "It wasn't just the K unit that allowed this. We moved also the power electronics units and employed a different exhaust layout, with the same aim. We also changed the layout of the rear suspension to improve the aero efficiency." The engine itself featured the narrower block introduced at the end of the previous season.

With a shorter nose for more underbody flow, tighter rear bodywork for enhanced over-body flow and further significant power upgrades over the winter, the car was faster than its predecessor – just not by enough. Progress at Mercedes and Red Bull had been yet greater. In Melbourne for the season-opener, things looked promising as the SF16-Ts filled out the second row, seemingly losing out to Mercedes only because of the latter's continued advantage in being able to run a more aggressive qualifying-mode engine map. That disadvantage was overcome within moments of the start when the Ferraris made far faster getaways to run 1-2 by the first corner. It was difficult to see how the Scuderia could fail to control the race from there, but a red flag with 29 laps still to go gave it an awkward tyre call to make. Nervous of the medium-compound tyre that theoretically could have taken them to the end – the car was always slightly reluctant to induce heat into the rubber if the compound was on the hard side and/or conditions were cool – they fitted super-softs and accepted an extra stop. That turned out to be a disastrous decision, and

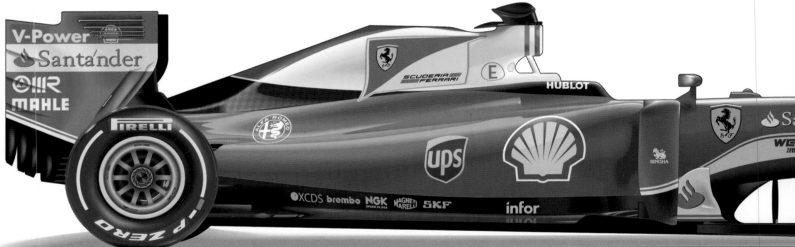

FERRARI SF16-T

MAJOR SPONSORS	Alfa Romeo • Santander • Shell • UPS • Kaspersky • Weichai • Claro • Ray-Ban • Hublot • Mahle • OMR • Singha • TNT
OFFICIAL SUPPLIERS	Pirelli • Puma • Infor • Oakley • SFK • NGK • Magneti Marelli • Brembo • XCDS • Iveco
SUPPLIERS	Bell • OZ • Honeywell • Technogym
POWER UNIT	Type: Ferrari 059/5 1.6-litre turbo **No. of cylinders** *(vee angle)*: V6 (90°) **No. of valves:** 24 **Bore:** 80mm **Stroke:** 53mm **Crank height:** 90mm **Max. rpm:** 15,000 **Power output:** Approximately 600hp (ICE) + 160hp (ERS) **Fuel injection:** Direct fuel injection, limited to 500 bar **Pressure charging:** Single turbocharger, unlimited boost pressure (typical maximum 3.5 bar abs due to fuel flow limit) **Exhaust:** Single exhaust outlet, from turbine on car centreline, with two outlet pipes connected to the wastegate **Ignition:** SKF spark plugs **ERS:** Integrated hybrid energy recovery via electrical motor generator units **Energy store:** Lithium-Ion battery (up to 4MJ per lap) **Cooling system:** Secan/Marston
TRANSMISSION	Gearbox: Ferrari eight-speed plus reverse, carbon-cased longitudinal, electronically-controlled sequential semi-automatic
CHASSIS	Carbon-fibre monocoque **Front and rear suspension:** Upper and lower wishbones, inboard springs and dampers actuated by push-rod wishbones with pull-rod-actuated inboard torsion-bar springs **Dampers:** ZF Sachs Race Engineering **Wheels:** OZ **Tyres:** Pirelli P Zero **Brakes:** Brembo calipers and ventilated carbon-fibre discs
DIMENSIONS	Height 950mm **Track width:** 1460mm (front); 1416mm (rear) **Formula weight:** 702kg, including driver and camera

Kimi Räikkönen takes a pit stop on the way to second place in Bahrain.

MAURIZIO ARRIVABENE

Photo: Scuderia Ferrari

SCUDERIA FERRARI: PERSONNEL

Chairman: Sergio Marchionne

Managing Director of Gestione Sportiva & Team Principal: Maurizio Arrivabene

Chief Technical Officer: Mattia Binotto

Chief Designer Power Unit: Lorenzo Sassi

Chief Designer: Simone Resta

Chief of Aerodynamics: Enrico Cardile

Head of Race Activities: Jock Clear

Race Team Manager: Diego Ioverno

Chief Race Engineer: Matteo Togninalli

Chief of Race Strategy: Inaki Rueda

Logistics: Sergio Bondi

Race Engineer *(Vettel)*: Riccardo Adami

Race Engineer *(Räikkönen)*: David Greenwood

Marketing Director: Lucia Pennesi

Head of Press Office: Alberto Antonini

Team Press Officer: Roberta Vallorosi

Team Press Officer: Stefania Bocchi

SERGIO MARCHIONNE

Photo; Peter J. Fox

71

as Vettel pitted, the medium-tyred Mercedes of Rosberg assumed a lead it wouldn't lose. Räikkönen, by this time, had already retired with a blown turbo.

The engine was run quite conservatively for the next two races to protect the turbo, taking the sting out of the team's challenge at a crucial time, before the Red Bull was working as well as it would subsequently. A two-token turbo modification was made in time for Russia, allowing the motor to come back on song, followed by a three-token combustion upgrade for Canada, an alteration to the MGU-K for Austria (1 token) and a further three-token upgrade for Monza, taking fuller advantage of a new brew of fuel from Shell. In addition to the 23 tokens spent during the off-season, it meant that Ferrari was the only team to use all 32 permitted engine development tokens.

"Also, a lot of the early season was spent improving the energy recovery of the MGU-H," said Binotto. "Contrary to what many would assume, despite the power units now being quite mature projects, there was still a noticeable margin of improvement. I don't want to give detailed figures, but suffice to say any increase of only 10–15 horsepower would hardly be remarked upon by a driver." It is believed that the seasonal gain of peak power was something in the order of 30bhp, putting the total at around 970bhp by the season's end, only around 10–15bhp short of Mercedes.

Of greater significance than the small power deficit was a bigger shortfall in downforce. Aerodynami- cally, the car was quite efficient, which, together with its competitive power, made it a significant factor at places such as Montreal, Spa and Monza. But raw top-end downforce was simply lacking, and once the Red Bull came on song early in the European season, the Ferrari was usually only the third quickest car – and one with a delicate gearbox. On four occasions, one of the Ferrari drivers took a five-place grid penalty for a replacement box, and the identical unit proved similarly brittle on the Haas car. Pit-wall decisions proved just as unreliable, and a potential Vettel victory at Montreal was lost through an inappropriate response to a virtual safety car period.

To test a different working method within the team, it was decided to press on with aero development late into the season, even after the others had begun concentrating full time on their 2017 cars. The fruits of this were introduced in Malaysia practice, but not actually raced until the following event at Suzuka. They followed a frank discussion between Binotto and chief designer Simone Resta about the power figures the designer was being provided by the engine department as he was calculating where to sit the drag/ downforce trade-off.

A more realistic measure had been settled upon, playing its part in the effectiveness of this upgrade. It comprised further swept-back front wing pillars to improve flow to the underbody, revisions to the turning vanes beneath the nose, a new sidepod shoulder vane, revisions to the rear brake ducts and the footplate bodywork section ahead of the rear tyres. Together, they were estimated to have found the car between 0.2 and 0.3s – and at Suzuka, the team was cheered by a significant boost in competitiveness at a very aero-demanding track. This was swiftly followed by disappointment when the car failed to sustain such form two weeks later in Austin. "It was about the specific features of the track in Austin," maintained Binotto, "which called for more combined lateral loads and traction."

The car's tyre usage was very delicately poised upon track temperatures and the hardness of the tyre compound relative to the track's demands. The softer the compound and the more stable the track temperature, the better it worked. Any sudden changes in track conditions – as happened between Saturday practice and qualifying in Barcelona, Monaco and Mexico – resulted in the team losing the set-up in a major way. It was difficult to know if this was a car trait or lack of depth in understanding the unusual tyres. Ernesto Fina was recruited from Williams quite early in the year as the team tried to bolster its tyre expertise. Quite a lot of late-season car development was devoted to reducing the heat transfer of the rear rims to the rubber.

Ferrari is too big a name and too susceptible to outside pressures for it to shrug off a winless season, especially after three wins in 2015 prompted hopes of a championship challenge. It faces the immediate future with many questions hanging over it.

Left: Kimi – in his ever-present Ray-Bans – on the Singapore grid with race engineer Dave Greenwood.

Far left: One of Sebastian Vettel's strongest performances came in Baku, where he gained second place.

Below left: Maurizio Arrivabene congratulates Ferrari Academy driver Charles Leclerc on winning the GP3 championship.

Below centre left: The massively experienced Jock Clear assumed his duties as head of race activities.

Below: Engine man Mattia Binotto was promoted to the post of chief technical officer mid-season.

Bottom: The end of a long hard season for the Scuderia's personnel, who must be hoping for better fortunes in 2017.

Photos: Scuderia Ferrari

05 | SEBASTIAN VETTEL   07 | KIMI RÄIKKÖNEN

SAHARA FORCE INDIA F1 TEAM

11

SERGIO PÉREZ

27

NICO HÜLKENBERG

WITH the Mercedes power unit and powertrain continuing to provide a rock solid base, Force India capitalised well, engaging the identically-powered Williams team in a battle for fourth in the constructors' championship, a contest that ran to the end. The prize money payments from its consistent results over three years have allowed the Silverstone-based team, with its staff of just 360, a certain independence from the financial complications surrounding owner Vijay Mallya, who was only able to attend the race in his home residence of Britain in 2016.

The Force India VJM09, with aerodynamics conceived and developed entirely in Toyota's Cologne wind tunnel, invariably qualified in the lower reaches of Q3, from where Sergio Pérez and Nico Hülkenberg could be relied upon to deliver regular points – aided by a slick race squad and Force India's now-traditional very good understanding of the tyres.

In terms of raw performance, the distinctive looking twin-nostril car was around 1.5–1.8s adrift of Mercedes and generally vied with Williams as the fourth fastest, a significant chunk off Red Bull and Ferrari, but nearly always quicker than the less powerful Toro Rosso and Haas. Overall, the VJM09 probably wasn't quite as quick as the Williams – though it had its moments, notably qualifying second quickest at both Baku and Austria – but it was a less problematic, more consistent and flexible, performer.

In its initial form in the season-opening long-haul races, essentially it was a lightly developed VJM08B, albeit with further development along the high-rake aerodynamic path. From Barcelona, it received what was in essence its pukka 2016 re-clothing, with a new front wing, sidepods, engine cover, rear wing, diffuser and McLaren-like slatted cut-outs in the aerodynamically sensitive area ahead of the rear tyre.

Although the update didn't immediately move the car up the grid, it scored some heavy points in the following few races, making the competition with Williams for a financially powerful place in the constructors' championship real. This encouraged the team to press on with development, rather than devote everything to the 2017 car, allowing a further significant upgrade to be put on for Silverstone. Development was finally switched off after the German Grand Prix.

Technical director Andy Green talked about the process of following the Red Bull-inspired path of high rake in the car's development direction. "It's a route that does seem to be quite rewarding aerodynamically. It also has its challenges mechanically. You're lifting the car up and the centre of gravity gets higher, so you have to ensure the losses arising from that are more than overcome by the aero gains. It appears to work, but it's definitely a long-term philosophy. You can't just take a quick look at it. It's an all-or-nothing commitment, not an easy concept to get working. The temptation's always there to lower the car and get the c of g down, so it goes against your natural instinct of developing a car. But we're happy with the way it's

FORCE INDIA VJM09

OFFICIAL PARTNERS	Infinitum • Telcel • NEC • Inter • Kingfisher • Hype Energy • Claro • Smirnoff • Felio Siby • NEC • Canal Latin America F1 • Quaker State
TECHNICAL PARTNERS	Koni • Pirelli • Alpinestars • Accelerate • Motegi Racing • Univa
OFFICIAL SUPPLIERS	3D Systems • Adaptavist • Apsley • Branded • Condeco • CRS • Gtechniq • ITEC • motorstore.com • The Roastery Schroth Racing • Skullcandy • Still • STL • UPS Direct • VoiP unlimited • Revolutionary Protective Solutions
POWER UNIT	**Type:** Mercedes-Benz PU106C Hybrid **No. of cylinders** *(vee angle):* V6 (90°) **No. of valves:** 24 **Max rpm** *(ICE):* 15,000 **Electronics:** FIA standard ECU and FIA homologated electronic & electrical system **Fuels and Lubricants:** Petronas
TRANSMISSION	**Gearbox:** Mercedes AMG F1 eight-speed, semi-automatic seamless-shift **Clutch:** AP Racing carbon
CHASSIS	Carbon-fibre composite monocoque with Zylon anti-intrusion panels **Front suspension:** Aluminium-alloy uprights with carbon-fibre composite wishbones, track rod and push-rod; inboard chassis-mounted torsion springs, dampers and anti-roll bar assembly **Rear suspension:** Aluminium-alloy uprights with carbon-fibre composite wishbones, track rod and pull-rod. Hydro-mechanical springs, dampers and anti-roll bar assembly. **Dampers:** Koni **Wheels:** Motegi Racing, forged to Force India specification **Tyres:** Pirelli P Zero **Brake system:** AP Racing
DIMENSIONS	**Length:** 5100mm **Width:** 1800mm **Height:** 950mm **Formula weight:** 702kg, including driver and camera

Sergio Pérez and Nico Hülkenberg were a powerful team throughout 2016.

OTMAR SZAFNAUER

VIJAY MALLYA

SAHARA FORCE INDIA F1 TEAM: PERSONNEL

Team Principal & Managing Director: Dr Vijay Mallya

Chairman & Co-owner: Subrata Roy Sahara

Shareholders: The Mol family

Deputy Team Principal: Robert Fernley

Chief Operating Officer: Otmar Szafnauer

Technical Director: Andrew Green

Sporting Director: Andy Stevenson

Production Director: Bob Halliwell

Chief Designers: Akio Haga, Ian Hall

Aerodynamics Director: Simon Phillips

Chief Engineer: Tom McCullough

Race Engineer (*Pérez*): Tim Wright

Race Engineer (*Hülkenberg*): Bradley Joyce

Race Team Operations Manager: Mark Gray

No. 1 Mechanic (*Pérez*): Andy McLaren

No. 1 Mechanic (*Hülkenberg*): Will Vickery

Commercial Director: Stephen Curnow

Head of Communications: Will Hings

ROBERT FERNLEY

Photos: Sahara Force India F1 Team

Above: Long-serving sporting director Andy Stevenson.

Above left: Technical director Andrew Green has great experience with other top teams.

Above far left: Chief engineer Tom McCullough.

Left: The crew prepares Sergio Pérez for action in Catalunya.
Photos: Sahara Force India F1 Team

Right: Nico Hülkenberg's talent shone through, despite the German suffering some terrible luck throughout his season.
Photo: WRi2/Jad Sherif

Below: The tight-knit team celebrates Checo's podium and 'the Hulk's' sixth place at Monaco.
Photo: Sahara Force India F1 Team

gone, in that every time we've brought updates to the car, the performance has materialised on the track and the driver comments reflected what we thought was going to happen. So we became increasingly confident the updates would improve the performance of the car."

Green remains delighted at the hardware provided by Mercedes. Having access to the best engine definitely played its part in the car's performance advantage over the likes of Toro Rosso and Haas. But the relationship brings with it technical and logistical challenges, as Green explained: "The timings can be very tight because obviously they want to be developing as long as possible before releasing, and we have to jump on to their schedule with a lot fewer people than the works team have. That's not easy. Technically, ours is a high-rake car and theirs is not. So the inboard pick-up points on the gearbox for the rear suspension are all optimised around a low-rake car, so we have to compromise a little. We could do our own gearbox of course, but I think it's right that we don't. It would sap a huge resource that we currently put into performance. It's a compromise, but net it's better."

Related to those difficulties, part of the Barcelona upgrade included new rear suspension designed to improve the rear end aerodynamics. But the geometry compromises referred to by Green were felt to be partly responsible for the car's subsequent difficulty with rear tyre degradation. With the new front wing also underperforming, a modified version was introduced at Silverstone – and the old rear suspension was reintroduced.

In addition to the upgrade packages of Spain and Britain, there were constant tweaks and additions to the vanes and bodywork slats as the Cologne wind tunnel programme bore fruit. Having the tunnel in a different country to the base presented logistical problems, and a rota system had to be devised. "We used to be able to run routine aero work in our own tunnel at Brackley and just use the bigger tunnel in Cologne for the higher-fidelity work and verification," explained Green. "But the regulations don't allow you to do that now – you have to nominate your tunnel for the year and use only that one. It's hard for the guys being away from home a week in every month. We had two groups of ten or twelve people – model makers, technicians and aerodynamicists – taking it in turns. It's paid us back in performance. You can look at the car in its entirety through all the different attitudes it sees throughout a lap, and it has been an enormous help in correlating our CFD – more than we anticipated."

The team capitalised fully on the significantly increased advantage offered by the Mercedes engine on Baku's super-long flat-out stretch, and Pérez was able to qualify second quickest, albeit flattered by one Mercedes having crashed out of the session. Although subsequently the Mexican was demoted for a gearbox change after crashing in practice, he made amends with a great drive to third, passing Räikkönen's penalised Ferrari on the road. This was his second such placing in three races, as he had achieved the feat in Monaco, too.

In Austria – around another heavily power-rewarding circuit – Hülkenberg used his wet-weather skills to put the car on the front row, though he faded dramatically in the dry of race day. Partly, this was due to the car's increased appetite for rubber with the 'Barcelona' rear suspension, but also 'the Hulk' – under pressure from the recent Pérez podiums – pushed too hard. "Nico could see the opportunity to score good points in Austria," said Green. "But you just can't hurry these tyres along. You have to be patient, and if you're not, you lose so much so quickly, and I think he got a little impatient, pushed too hard, too soon. Then degradation starts, he pushed even harder, and then you're in a big spiral down. He learnt the hard way and is now much more focused on what he has to do from the very first corner of the very first lap. A big lesson."

Although the team was more effective than Williams at dealing with the challenges of running the tyres at the very high minimum pressures imposed by Pirelli, allowing it to frequently beat what was usually a slightly faster car, it no longer had an advantage on most of the field in this regard. Green felt that this was just a natural outcome of gaining performance: "As you add downforce, you get more grip from the tyres, but they don't last as long – especially at these pressures. We're definitely not in the position we were two years ago, when we had advantage on tyre life. That's history now."

But the team's continued punching above its weight in the constructors' championship is also now firmly established in the history books. 'Best of the rest' behind the highly-resourced Mercedes, Red Bull and Ferrari teams is realistically the best the team could aspire to.

WILLIAMS MARTINI RACING

19

FELIPE MASSA

77

VALTTERI BOTTAS

WILLIAMS endured a difficult season, with a step-change decline in competitiveness from 2014 and '15, managing only fifth in the constructors' championship.

The FW38 – designed by Ed Wood and his group, with the aerodynamic department headed up once more by Jason Sommerville – was directly related to the previous two models and again used a customer Mercedes engine. It began the year as the fourth quickest car, but suffered a somewhat non-responsive development programme and fell behind Force India latterly.

Distinguishing the car from its predecessor was a further lengthened gearbox, which increased the gap between the engine and rear axle. Engineering director Pat Symonds explained the thinking behind this: "We wanted to tidy up the back end aerodynamically and also it allowed us to put some weight forward in the car without having to use as much ballast in the extremities, like the front wing. This was a good thing to minimise pitch inertia. People talk about polar moment of inertia, but I think pitch inertia's more important." It also helped in facilitating a generally slimmed-down sidepod arrangement.

The team was preoccupied with improving the car's tyre usage – with only partial success – and it was notable that the FW38's front wishbones ran at lower angles than those of its predecessor, inflicting a theoretical aerodynamic penalty, but better for suspension kinematics. "Most of the things we did to the car mechanically were based around dealing with the Pirelli prescriptions [on minimum pressures and maximum cambers]. A lot of our time was taken up with different suspension geometries, particularly camber gains. That is still ongoing. We've not arrived at an optimum and will have to start all over again next year [with the new wider tyres and aero regs]. The very high pressures impact all the way through the ride part of the design, and that's really dominated all our non-aero work," said Symonds.

At some circuits, the car could obtain competitive stint lengths from the tyres, but at several others it was in difficulties. In general, it lost out badly in this regard to the Force India, a defining trait that dropped Williams behind in the second half of the season. "We're not as strong as we should be on tyres," continued Symonds. "When the Pirellis do things we don't expect – like at Bahrain and Germany, where the tyres were so far away from what we expected – we didn't react well to it. You cannot pull a bloke out of another area and teach him about tyres in a year. So it's about recruitment." In September, ex-Ferrari engineer Antonio Spagnolo joined the team as 'competitor analysis and performance concept team leader'. Translation: tyre expert. Earlier in the year, the team had lost the services of the similarly specialised Ernesto Fina to Ferrari.

Although the tyre issue was an obvious disap-

WILLIAMS FW38

PARTNERS	Martini • Randstad • Rexona • Petrobras • Avanade • Financial.Org • Wihuri • Hackett • Oris • BT • DTEX • Pirelli • PPG • Alpinestars Cybex • Michael Caines • EOS Manufacturing Solutions • Spinal Injuries Association
POWER UNIT	**Type:** Mercedes-Benz PU106C Hybrid **No. of cylinders** *(vee angle):* V6 (90°) **No. of valves:** 24 **Bore:** 80mm **Stroke:** 53mm **Crank height:** 90mm (minimum allowed) **Max. rpm** *(ICE):* 15,000 **Fuel injection:** High-pressure direct injection (max 500 bar, one injector/cylinder) **Max. fuel flow rate:** 100kg/hr (above 10,500rpm) **Pressure charging:** Single-stage compressor and exhaust turbine on common shaft **Exhaust turbine max rpm:** 125,000 **Electronics:** FIA standard SECU and FIA homologated electronic & electrical system **ERS:** Mercedes AMG HPP **Fuel:** Petronas Primax **Lubricants:** Petronas Syntium **Gearbox & Hydraulic oil:** Petronas Tutela
TRANSMISSION	**Gearbox:** Williams eight-speed plus reverse seamless, sequential, semi-automatic shift **Clutch:** AP Racing carbon multi-plate
CHASSIS	Monocoque, moulded carbon-fibre and honeycomb composite structure **Front suspension:** Double wishbones and push-rod-activated springs and anti-roll bar **Rear suspension:** Double wishbones and pull-rod-activated springs and anti-roll bar **Dampers:** Williams F1 **Wheels:** APP Tech forged magnesium **Tyres:** Pirelli P Zero **Brakes:** AP six-piston front and four-piston rear calipers with carbon discs and pads **Steering:** Williams F1 power-assisted rack-and-pinion **Fuel system:** ATL Kevlar-reinforced rubber bladder
DIMENSIONS	**Length:** 5000mm **Width:** 1800mm **Height:** 950mm **Wheelbase:** more than 3000mm **Formula weight:** 702kg, including driver and camera

Felipe Massa

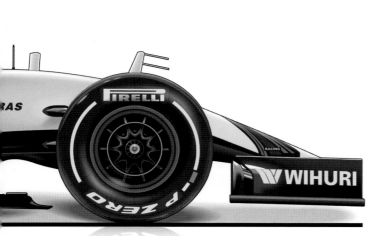

SIR FRANK WILLIAMS

Photo: Williams Martini Racing

CLAIRE WILLIAMS

Photo: WRi2/Jean-François Galeron

WILLIAMS MARTINI RACING: PERSONNEL

Team Principal: Sir Frank Williams

Deputy Team Principal: Claire Williams

Group CEO: Mike O'Driscoll

Chief Technical Officer: Pat Symonds

Chief Performance/Operations Engineer: Jakob Andreasen

Head of Vehicle Science: Max Nightingale

Head of Performance Engineering: Rob Smedley

Chief Designer: Ed Wood

Head of Aerodynamics: Jason Somerville

Senior Performance Engineer & Data Engineer *(Bottas)*: Andrew Murdoch

Senior Car Systems Engineer: Carl Gaden

Vehicle Systems Engineer: Charlie Hooper

Sporting Manager: Steve Nielsen

Car Systems Leader: Paul Leeming

Race Engineer *(Massa)*: Dave Robson

No. 1 Mechanic *(Massa)*: Ben Howard

Performance Engineer *(Massa)*: Paul Davison

Race Engineer *(Bottas)*: Jonathan Eddolls

No. 1 Mechanic *(Bottas)*: Patric Gustafsson

Chief Mechanic: Mark Pattinson

Left: Pat Symonds, Williams chief technical officer.
Photo: WRi2/Jean-François Galeron

Right: Valtteri Bottas finished eighth in the drivers' championship. He remains with the team for a fifth consecutive season in 2017.
Photo: Williams Martini Racing

Below left: Felipe Massa's F1 career ended in Abu Dhabi after 250 grand prix starts.

Below: Formula 3 Champion Lance Stroll will step into Massa's seat for the 2017 season.

Bottom: The Williams Martini Racing team assembled in Abu Dhabi.

Below right: Head of performance Rob Smedley.

Bottom right: The Williams multi-tasking steering wheel.
Photos: WRi2/Jean-François Galeron

19 FELIPE MASSA   77 VALTTERI BOTTAS

pointment to the team, Symonds did feel that it had increased its knowledge – just not by the desired amount: "We're getting a lot better at understanding our optimum balance through a corner – understanding more about the dynamics side of aerodynamics, which even though it has dynamics included in the word, it's remarkable how little attention aerodynamicists pay to the dynamic side of things. We've been trying to ensure that as the car enters a corner at a particular attitude and ride height, we get the correct migration of balance as it gets to mid-corner – at higher ride heights, yaw angles and where you're getting on the power. There was a fair bit of concentration on that type of thing. It's been a lean year for development, and we started on the '17 car early."

Aerodynamically, the development programme was based around variations of three separate families of front wing, which proved stubbornly resistant. "Yes, we put our eggs in a particular basket that hasn't been as fruitful as we'd hoped," admitted Symonds. "We are all – apart from Mercedes – trying to get more rake on the car. But you can't just keep adding rake. There's a point at which the downforce rolls off. The more successful teams have got that roll-off at a higher rear ride height and therefore the peak is higher." The FW38 was not as responsive to that development as several other cars on the grid, notably the Force India.

Part of the reason may have been the turnaround speed of new parts, which seemed slower than at other teams. In the age of rapid prototyping – and when this technology is more valuable than ever because of the regulation restrictions on wind tunnel time and CFD capacity – this seems to be an area where Williams had been rather left behind. Integral to a successful development programme is the rapid throughput of new parts, to quickly determine a fruitful direction. Quite often, when a new component would be introduced, there would only be one or two examples for more than one race. This was the case with the medium-downforce rear wing introduced in Montreal, an updated floor that came later in the season and the shorter nose introduced early-season.

One positive about the season was the spectacular manner in which the team had corrected its problem pit stops from 2015, with very often the quickest stops in the pit lane during 2016. Symonds was reluctant to give precise details of what had been changed, but said, "It was more design than anything – in the hub, the wheelnut, the wheel – but there was a bit of metallurgy in there. It wasn't a five-minute solution. It was quite empirical – we had to try a lot of things, but the results were impressive."

For 2017, Felipe Massa eases into retirement; Valtteri Bottas remains on board and is to be joined by rookie Lance Stroll. With the convergence of engine performance expected to continue, losing Williams a key advantage over several teams, how it reacts to the radically different aero regulations could well determine its trajectory for the next few years.

14

47

FERNANDO ALONSO

STOFFEL VANDOORNE

22

JENSON BUTTON

McLAREN HONDA

WHILE it was still far, far away from the performance a team of McLaren's size and standing aspires to, 2016 may have represented the beginnings of a recovery, as Honda – in the second year of its turbo hybrid programme – made significant progress. That allowed the McLaren MP4-31 to become a regular in the lower Q3 part of the grid from Spain onwards, the foundation for enough points to put the team sixth in the constructors' championship.

The primary source of Honda's improvement was an increase in size and a total redesign of the compressor and turbine, allowing it to generate higher pressures before the increased back pressure of the engine cancelled out the net gain (very much the limitation of the 2015 unit). This allowed the whole hybrid loop to capture enough energy that the motor no longer ran out of electrical deployment embarrassingly early. Deployment was now competitive with that of the other power units.

Total horsepower however, still lagged behind. Paddock estimates suggested that it was around 60bhp down on the standard-setting Mercedes at the end of the season. The siting of the split turbine and compressor was still inside the engine's vee, an intrinsic part of the 'zero-size' concept initiated the previous year with the intention of creating a greater volume of space for aerodynamic gain. But as energy transfer efficiencies were improving at a fast pace, it appeared to make the 'turbo between the vee' concept

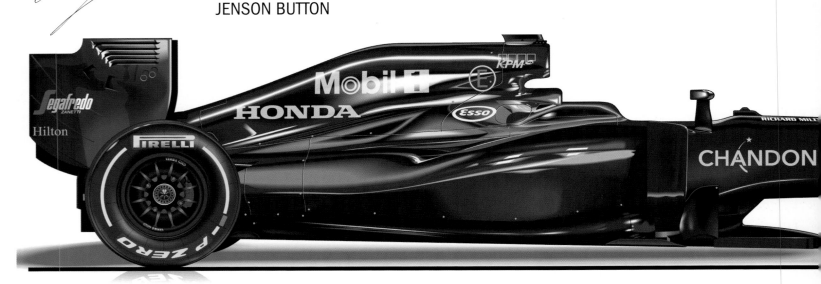

McLAREN-HONDA MP4-31

ENGINE PARTNER	Honda
TECHNOLOGY PARTNERS	Mobil 1 • SAP • Esso • NTT Communications • Pirelli • Akebono **INNOVATION PARTNER** KPMG
CORPORATE PARTNERS	Johnnie Walker • Richard Mille • Santander • Segafredo Zanetti • Hilton • CNN • Michael Kors • Norton Rose Fulbright • Sensodyne
OFFICIAL SUPPLIERS	Calsonic Kanser • Enkei • Nielsen • Volvo Trucks • Kenwood • Mazak • Sparco • Sikkens • Maxi Nutrition • Asics • TechnoGym
POWER UNIT	**Type:** Honda RA616H Hybrid **No. of cylinders** (vee angle): V6 (90°) **No. of valves:** 24 **Max. rpm** (ICE): 15,000 **Electronics:** McLaren Applied Technologies, including chassis control, engine control, data acquisition, alternator, sensors, data analysis and telemetry **Fuel:** Exxon Mobil **Oil:** Mobil 1
TRANSMISSION	**Gearbox:** McLaren eight-speed seamless-shift, carbon-composite casing **Clutch:** Carbon-carbon multi-plate
CHASSIS	Carbon-fibre composite, incorporating driver controls and fuel cell **Bodywork:** Carbon-fibre composite, including engine cover, sidepods, floor, nose, front wing and rear wing with driver-operated drag-reduction system **Front suspension:** Carbon-fibre wishbone and push-rod suspension elements operating inboard torsion-bar and damper system **Rear suspension:** Carbon-fibre wishbone and pull-rod suspension elements operating inboard torsion-bar and damper system **Wheel diameter:** 13in, front and rear **Wheels:** Enkei **Tyres:** Pirelli P Zero **Brake system:** Akebono calipers and master systems; Akebono 'brake-by-wire' rear brake controls **Steering:** McLaren power-assisted rack-and-pinion **Instruments and electronics:** McLaren Applied Technologies **Batteries:** GS Yuasa **Radio systems:** Kenwood
DIMENSIONS	**Dimensions:** not disclosed **Wheelbase:** not disclosed **Formula weight:** 702kg, including driver and camera

increasingly obsolete. The optimum sizing of the turbo is defined under these regulations by the efficiency of the power electronics and MGU-K. If the turbine can put 100kW into the MGU-H, but only 50 of that makes it to the crankshaft, the weight, volume and cooling of a bigger turbo would begin to outweigh any advantage it brought. At Mercedes, the conversion rate was around 95 per cent in 2016, justifying the use of a turbo that was significantly bigger than could be placed inside the vee of one of these engines. The 2016 Honda compressor was about as big as could be fitted inside the vee, and it was claimed by Honda to be "about the same size as Mercedes' 2014 compressor". At the time of writing, it was expected that the 2017 Honda engine would have the compressor outside the vee.

Furthermore, the Honda did not feature the Turbulent Jet ignition technology used by Mercedes, Ferrari and – from mid-season – Renault, whereby a mini combustion chamber ignited the mixture in the main combustion chamber, allowing a more energy-efficient combustion. That feature was also expected to be incorporated into Honda's 2017 motor, underlining the fact that the Japanese company had been later into the formula than the others.

In terms of the chassis, the MP4-31 was visually a refinement of the 2015 car, relatively short in wheelbase with a blown front axle, an S-duct and an extremely tightly-waisted rear end. McLaren technical director Tim Goss explained the philosophy: "It was to

Fernando Alonso on track in the McLaren MP4-31

McLAREN HONDA: PERSONNEL

Chief Executive Officer: Jost Capito

Racing Director: Eric Boullier

Operations Director: Simon Roberts

Technical Director: Tim Goss

Director of Engineering: Matt Morris

Chief Engineer: Peter Prodromou

Team Manager: Dave Redding

Above: Chief operating officer Jonathan Neale.

Above left: New chief executive officer Jost Capito took over his role late in the season.

Left: Racing director Eric Boullier continued to put on a brave face during another trying season of underachievement.

Photos: McLaren Honda

stick with the direction we were on and wring more out of it, so very much an evolution of the thinking that Peter Prodromou brought to the team aerodynamically the previous year. That and an evolution of learning what we need to do with Honda. There are three engineering directors: myself, [chief of aero] Peter Prodromou and [engineering director] Matt Morris. Peter looks after aero development and a lot of the exploitation of the car trackside. I look after design and technical development, and Matt looks after engineering operations at the factory. But there is a massive overlap between us; if one of us is away, the other will happily step in. It's been running like that for 18 months and it works well."

Probably the most significant visual difference between the MP4-31 and its predecessor was the higher engine cover. "It gave Honda a bit more to work with on the intake side," explained Goss. "It hadn't been holding us back massively the previous year, but it did allow Honda to make an improvement on the inlet to the benefit of power. From Canada, we changed the whole plenum design, again to allow the engine to breathe a bit better."

The gearbox remained a single-skinned unit, rather than the twin-case cassette type used by Mercedes. "We did look at the cassette box idea again," said Goss. "It has some advantages, but the disadvantage is the box ends up being a bit larger, and we are pushing that area of the car very hard to keep it narrow. We still think single case is better."

More substantial changes were made in the rear suspension compared to the MP4-30, as Goss explained: "The MP4-30 had an unconventional rear suspension arrangement that had its origins in MP4-29 with twin shrouds. We retained some features of that because, at the time, it was attractive aerodynamically, but as the season went on, there were some structural issues with that type of suspension. It was fine for the most part, but under braking there was some unwanted movement in the uprights that led to some instability. So for this car, we went to a more conventional shrouded rear lower wishbone. That, in turn, enabled us to tighten up the rear end further because the other suspension required more structure in the gearbox."

Both Fernando Alonso and Jenson Button valued the improvement in rear stability, with Goss claiming that Alonso in particular "likes to be able to attack the corner entry, wants to be able to brake and then when he steers, have the car instantly respond. It's easy to make a front end, but giving security at the rear at the same time is what it's all about. We've worked very hard at that, and that's one of our car's strengths – good braking and corner entry. But what we've been working on most of the season is mid to exit. This breed of engine has so much torque, there's masses of performance in just being able to get the power down. If you are down on the combined exit, you'll carry that penalty all the way down the straight. Traction you used to think of as just slow corners, but with these engines, we're now talking about Turn Three Barcelona as being a traction event."

The car was notably weak in mid- to high-speed corners and in straight-line speed, the latter partly – but not totally – a function of the power deficit. It also seemed dogged by an apparent 'dead-spot' in front wing angle, whereby the car would understeer up to a certain point of angle, but any increase beyond that would bring unacceptable levels of oversteer. That was something picked up immediately by Stoffel Vandoorne when he stood in for an injured Alonso in Bahrain, and a trait that was still present as late as Suzuka, where it proved impossible to achieve

Above: The changing of the guard. The team photo at Abu Dhabi, with Jenson Button, about to take part in his 305th grand prix, and his successor, Stoffel Vandoorne, posing on car 22.

Right: Hard at work on Alonso's car in the garage in Budapest.

Far right: The final outing in the McLaren MP4-31 for Jenson in Abu Dhabi.

Below: Even the drivers become involved in the number crunching during practice at Hockenheim.

Photos: McLaren Honda

a balance that gave the necessary direction change alacrity through the Esses, but acceptable rear stability through the faster corners. At circuits with less of a spread of corner types, it was usually possible to find a workable compromise, and at circuits without long straights or that emphasised slow corner entry, the car was respectably quick – though its best qualifying position of fifth in Austria was very much to do with Button's wet-weather skills.

Aerodynamically, Prodromou definitely followed his former Red Bull philosophies. "We were one of three genuinely high-rake cars," said Goss. "Red Bull and ourselves probably run the highest rake, with Force India somewhere close. Given the performance of the low-rake Mercedes, it's quite clear you can achieve a high performance solution in either direction. Putting more rake in the car, you generate more front end and need to get less from the front wing. You can take a route that is a lower-loss [in terms of drag] front end, and much of what we're doing is generating load out of all the devices, not just the front wing. And when you do that, you also create losses, and what you're trying not to do is have those losses impact the rear of the car where you're also trying not to generate losses."

With a complete revolution in the aero regulations due for 2017, it remains to be seen where the McLaren team pitches its car and whether it can maximise the expected gains from the Honda motor.

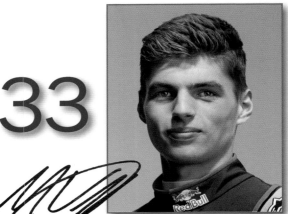

26

DANIIL KVYAT

33

MAX VERSTAPPEN

55

CARLOS SAINZ

SCUDERIA TORO ROSSO

A LATE change of engine – 2015-spec Ferrari in place of the previous Renault – rather took the sting out of STR's 2016 challenge. Not only did it disrupt and compromise the conception of the STR11, but also it left the team facing a progressively greater power deficit to the front as all the other engines were developed while theirs remained frozen. There were several glimpses of speed – it was the best of the rest after the big three at Melbourne, Monaco, Budapest and Singapore – but it was inconsistent, leaving the team in seventh place in the constructors' championship.

Once again, James Key headed the technical department of the Faenza-based team, with its wind tunnel in the UK. After some eye-catching performances in 2015, Key's target for this car was to ally the STR10's excellent high-speed aerodynamics to a better low-speed performance. In this, the team was only partly successful, and tracks with heavy longitudinal demands continued to be a weak point, particularly in traction.

But even this was connected to the late engine change imposed on the team by Red Bull senior management, which in turn was concerned with heavy politicking between Red Bull, Renault and F1's management. Key explained the challenges: "We finally got confirmation of the engine on December 1, which is normally when you'd just be finishing off

TORO ROSSO STR11

PARTNERS	Red Bull • Sapinda • Estrella Galicia • Acronis • Edifice Casio • Gi Group • Pirelli
SUPPLIERS	CD-Adapco • Riedel • App Tech • Hangar-7 • Red Bull Mobile
POWER UNIT	**Type:** Ferrari 060-2015 **No. of cylinders** (vee angle)**:** V6 (90°) **No. of valves:** 24 **Bore:** 80mm **Stroke:** 53mm **Crank height:** 90mm
	Max rpm (ICE)**:** 15,000 **Power output:** Above 600hp (ICE) + 160hp (ERS)
	Fuel injection: Direct fuel injection, limited to 500 bar **Pressure charging:** Single turbocharger, unlimited boost pressure (typical
	maximum 3.5 bar abs due to fuel flow limit) **Exhaust:** Single exhaust outlet, from turbine on car centreline **Ignition:** SKF spark plugs
	ERS: Integrated hybrid energy recovery via electrical motor generator units **Energy store:** Lithium-Ion battery (up to 4MJ per lap)
	Electronics: FIA standard ECU and FIA homologated electronic & electrical system **Cooling system:** Secan/Marston **Fuel:** Shell; **Oil:** Shell
TRANSMISSION	**Gearbox:** Scuderia Toro Rosso carbon/aluminium, eight-speed sequential, hydraulically operated **Clutch:** AP Racing
CHASSIS	Composite monocoque structure **Front suspension:** Upper and lower carbon wishbones, push-rod, torsion-bar springs, central damper and
	anti-roll bars **Rear suspension:** Upper and lower carbon wishbones, pull-rod, torsion-bar springs, central damper and anti-roll bars
	Dampers: Penske **Wheels:** APP Tech magnesium alloy **Tyres:** Pirelli P Zero **Brake discs, pads and calipers:** Brembo; Scuderia Toro Rosso
	brake-by-wire **Steering:** Scuderia Toro Rosso **Radiators:** Scuderia Toro Rosso **Fuel tank:** ATL with Scuderia Toro Rosso internals
DIMENSIONS	**Height:** 950mm **Track width:** 1460mm (front); 1416mm (rear) **Formula weight:** 702kg, including driver and camera

the details of the car. Obviously, the car was basically already configured, and we gave ourselves an added challenge by not changing the outer surfaces, so that there was no negative aerodynamic effect. But shoehorning a Ferrari in a space designed for a Renault was bloody difficult, and the team did a fantastic job.

"Under the skin, it was quite a big compromise. We couldn't get the flexibility on suspension design that we really wanted because the layout around that area of the car of the two different engines is totally different." This meant that the aero-profile rear suspension, introduced on the previous year's car, had to be altered.

"Outboard, it was the same," explained Key, "but the internals and the bellhousing, where you have the interface of gearbox to engine, that package was governed very heavily by the engine layout. What fits in that space in a certain way with one engine doesn't necessarily work with another. So we had to contort the rear suspension internals around the shape we ended up with. To do otherwise would have involved redesigning the whole gearbox and probably changing the wheelbase – which is the last thing you want to be doing late in the day." This is believed to have played a significant part in the car's weakness in longitudinal performance.

But it remained an aerodynamically sophisticated

Daniil Kvyat during the US Grand Prix at Austin.

JAMES KEY

SCUDERIA TORO ROSSO: PERSONNEL

Team Owner: Dietrich Mateschitz

Team Principal: Franz Tost

Technical Director: James Key

Head of Vehicle Performance: Jody Egginton

Team Manager: Graham Watson

Chief Race Engineer: Phil Charles

Technical Co-ordinator: Sandro Parrini

Logistics Manager: Michela Fabbri

Race Engineer *(Verstappen/Kvyat)*:
Xevi Pujolar/Pierre Hamelin

Race Engineer *(Sainz)*: Marco Matassa

Chief Mechanic: Domiziano Facchinetti

Reliability Manager: Phil Mitchell

Ferrari: Maurizio Barbieri

Sponsor Key Account and Brand Manager:
Andrea Menth

Head of Account Management – Sponsorship:
Sonja Stadlbauer

Head of Communications: Fabiana Valenti

Press Officer: Tabatha Valls Halling

Digital Manager: Diego Mandolfo

FRANZ TOST

Photos: Scuderia Toro Rosso/Getty Images

Above: Max Verstappen began the season in Melbourne as a Toro Rosso driver, but after just four races, he was promoted to the Red Bull team.

Top: Sainz waits patiently as his car is prepared for a practice run at Spielberg.

Above right: Carlos Sainz wringing the max from his car in Malaysia. Having performed impressively throughout the year, he was the subject of much interest from other teams. However, the Spaniard remains very firmly on the Red Bull driver roster.

Right: Initially, Daniil Kvyat struggled to come to terms with being dropped from Red Bull, but he ended the year with a Toro Rosso contract for 2017.

Photos: Peter J. Fox

car, as evidenced by the way it incorporated an S-duct fed by NACA ducts on the sides of the nose. The nose regulations, in place since 2015, led teams to devise combinations of a very short nose and multiple vanes beneath the nose to maximise airflow to the underbody, but at the cost of available space for an S-duct inlet. For this reason, several teams deleted or did not develop an S-duct, foregoing the benefit its high-speed jet outlet brings in reattaching the top-surface airflow that tends to become detached as it hits the nose's downward slope head-on. The NACA ducts in the side allowed the STR11 to have its intricate vanes beneath the nose *and* an S-duct outlet. Its nose was narrower than its predecessor's and it used a blown front axle at several tracks, but not the higher-speed circuits.

"We knew the world didn't stand still," said Key, giving background to the direction of the concept, "so we were aggressive in some areas on this year's car and tried to develop areas that didn't develop so well last year, so certain aspects of the front were re-evaluated. Other aspects were quite similar because we knew they were working quite well for us and we knew we could squeeze more out of them." It was notable that the car ran with ever more rake as the season progressed, almost to Red Bull levels.

There was further compromise because the 2015 Ferrari unit was slightly wider than the 2016 motor and retained the ERS-K unit on the gearbox, rather than to the side of the engine, preventing the sidepods from being brought in quite as tightly as would have been possible with the later motor. The STR11 was unable to have the extreme cut-in (in plan view)

of, say, the Red Bull or McLaren, almost certainly costing some downforce.

The way the load-carrying carbon-fibre gearbox casing was designed (with a Mercedes-like internal cage for the gearbox itself) allowed the late call on suspension pick-up points associated with the engine choice to be resolved. The car was long in the wheelbase, better allowing the packaging of the different engine, but this contributed towards a weight problem. Initially, the car could not be brought significantly under the weight limit, so there was no scope for using ballast to vary weight distribution (within the prescribed regulation limits) from track to track or to equalise driver weight. There wasn't time or space to optimise around the more space-efficient (but less heat-efficient) air-air intercooler, rather than the water-air intercooler favoured by Ferrari, thus further contributing towards the weight problem.

A complete rethink on the cooling package and a gearbox modification – introduced at Hungary – finally brought the required weight reduction. A major aerodynamic upgrade followed at Hockenheim.

At least one Toro Rosso made it into Q3 seven times in the first eight races, but only four times in the subsequent eight, giving an idea of how the development of all the other power units began to hurt. When the Hockenheim aero upgrade coincided with a drop in the car's form – Carlos Sainz and Daniil Kvyat qualifying 13th and 19th respectively – alarm bells began ringing for Key. But it turned out to be no more than the aero effect of everyone having gained more power. "In the first part of the season, Renault and Honda were bobbing about where we were on engine

power. We struggled a bit with straight-line speed, but because our aero was good, we were able to compensate for that with wing levels so we could still be competitive in the corners, but with a lower wing level than you'd normally expect to run for that kind of balance. That worked pretty well for us.

But as the season went on, and other engines developed while we had zero development from a year-old engine, it was a double whammy. That, together with some developments at other teams – McLaren, Force India – allowed them to pull some downforce off and still retain a straight-line advantage. We couldn't afford to run that low a wing level any more because suddenly any aero advantage we had was beginning to disappear because their power allowed them to run more wing. So the lack of engine development ended up having a bigger hit than we thought. From around Hockenheim onwards, you really began to see that."

Initially, however, Key was concerned that the fall-off may have been something to do with the new aero package, but unfortunately there followed a series of untypical low- or high-downforce tracks. It wasn't until Sepang, four races later, that a meaningful back-to-back comparison could be made between the two packages. "That was the next conventional track on the calendar, and it confirmed to us it was just the engine situation," Key said.

For the 2017 season, with a switch back to Renault made with plenty of notice, STR stands a realistic chance of more fully combining its aerodynamic strength with an engine that remains competitive throughout the season.

HAAS F1 TEAM

8

ROMAIN GROSJEAN

21

ESTEBAN GUTIÉRREZ

AMERICAN-owned and entered, Haas brought an entirely new type of team to F1, taking full advantage of the 2014 relaxation of the regulations concerning listed parts in defining what constitutes a bona fide constructor. So, with a team of fewer than 200 people – fewer even than Manor – it was able to field a solidly mid-grid car that scored 29 points, with a best race finish of fifth, putting it eighth in the constructors' championship. It did so with a car that employed all-Ferrari mechanical components, with aerodynamics conceived in the Ferrari wind tunnel and built by Dallara. The team's British race base – formerly Manor's F1 factory – was where the cars were prepared for each event. But the design and construction were done exclusively in Italy.

Industrialist Gene Haas had expanded his racing interests from NASCAR into F1 at the suggestion of former Jaguar Racing MD and Red Bull technical operations chief Gunther Steiner, who had had the original vision of this simplified F1 team template. To qualify as a constructor, a team cannot have another F1 team produce its survival cell, front-impact structures, roll-over structures, bodywork, wings, floor and diffuser. But there is nothing to prevent a team from contracting out the manufacture of those components to an outside supplier – in this case Dallara.

"We sent people from Banbury to Dallara to build the first car," explained Steiner. "Otherwise, Banbury is the race team only, with some administration and the rebuild people. Nothing else. The design work was all done in Dallara, and the aero all done at Ferrari. About 90 per cent of the production of new parts – the stuff we don't buy from Ferrari – is done either from Dallara or suppliers used by Dallara."

Dallara chief of aerodynamics Ben Agathangelou oversaw the aero concept of the Haas VF-16, with Rob Taylor assuming the role of chief designer. The former had worked with Steiner as aero chief at both Jaguar and Red Bull, while the latter had previously been assistant chief designer at Manor. In fact, many of the race team were ex-Manor. Engine, gearbox, suspension and running gear were all by Ferrari. Radiators are defined as bodywork and thus were shaped by Dallara. The aerodynamic work was conducted in Ferrari's Maranello wind tunnel by a team of hired Ferrari aerodynamicists, separate from those working on the Scuderia's own car – a controversial arrangement that was greeted with suspicion by rival teams, but which was fully ratified by the FIA.

The resultant car was a neat and quite sophisticated design with some notable similarities to the Ferrari, some defined by the identical mechanical components and their layout. Its nose design was quite conservative, without the extreme 'fingertip' or the tiny width of those at the cutting edge, which require very sophisticated, expensive and time-con-

HAAS VF-16

PARTNERS	Haas Automation Inc • Richard Mille • Alpinestars • Pirelli
POWER UNIT	**Type:** Ferrari 061 Hybrid **No. of cylinders** (vee angle): V6 (90°) **No. of valves:** 24 **Max. rpm** *(ICE)*: 15,000 **ERS:** Integrated hybrid energy recovery via electrical motor generator units **Electronics:** FIA standard ECU and FIA homologated electronic & electrical system (as provided by MES) **Fuel and lubricants:** Shell
TRANSMISSION	**Gearbox:** Ferrari servo-controlled hydraulic limited-slip differential with semi-automatic sequential and electronically-controlled gearbox, quick-shift (eight gears, plus reverse) **Clutch:** AP Racing carbon-carbon multi-plate
CHASSIS	Carbon-fibre and honeycomb composite structure **Suspension:** Independent, push-rod-activated torsion-bar and damper system front and rear **Dampers:** ZF Sachs **Wheels:** Oz Racing **Wheel diameter:** 13in, front and rear **Tyres:** Pirelli P Zero **Brakes:** Brembo carbon-fibre discs, pads and six-piston calipers **Cockpit instrumentation:** Ferrari
DIMENSIONS	**Height:** 950mm **Overall width:** 1800mm **Wheelbase:** not disclosed **Formula weight:** 702kg, including driver and camera

Haas F1 Team's debut in Melbourne exceeded all expectations with Romain Grosjean's sixth-place finish.

HAAS F1 TEAM: PERSONNEL

Founder and Chairman: Gene Haas

Chief Operating Officer: Joe Custer

Team Principal: Guenther Steiner

Technical Director: Rob Taylor

Team Manager: Dave O'Neill

Chief Aerodynamicist: Ben Agathangelou

Head of Logistics: Peter Crolla

Principal Race Engineer: Ayao Komatsu

Race Engineer *(Grosjean)*: Gary Cannon

Race Engineer *(Gutiérrez)*: Giuliano Salvi

Chief Mechanic: Stuart Crump

Race Mechanic *(Grosjean)*: Ian Standiforth

Race Mechanic *(Gutiérrez)*: Toby Brown

GENE HAAS

Photo: WRi2/Jean-François Galeron

Above: Guenther Steiner and Gene Haas in conversation.

Left: One for the future? Charles Leclerc was given Friday-morning track time at four races.
Photos: Haas F1 Team

Right: After failing to score a point, Esteban Gutiérrez found himself replaced by Kevin Magnussen.
Photo: Peter J. Fox

Below: On home soil. The team lines up for a photo at the Circuit of the Americas track in Austin.
Photo: Haas F1 Team

suming stress analysis to get through the regulation crash tests. Thus the theoretical airflow capacity of the underfloor was more limited. Ferrari-like guide vanes beneath the nose and chassis helped optimise that flow.

The front wing was comparatively sophisticated in its use of multiple elements and wide three-dimensional endplates with multiple vortex generators, designed to improve the aero efficiency behind the front wheels and all the way down the car. It was remarkably similar, in fact, to Ferrari's 2015 front wing... The front brake ducts initially used also appeared to be identical. It featured a blown front axle, a front suspension with fashionably conjoined lower wishbones to enhance the aero, contemporary-style sculpted sidepods and the requisite gills ahead of the rear wheel footprint to improve the efficiency of the diffuser. The rear wing was more McLaren-like than Ferrari in the design of its main plane, but with Ferrari-like endplates featuring vertical leading-edge slots to help equalise the air pressure across the wing.

"The car was pretty good in high-speed, sweeping corners," said Romain Grosjean, "but less good on stop-start tracks. I think our aero is perhaps not so good at low speed, and the braking, too."

In Australia, Grosjean scored a fairy-tale sixth place on the team's debut, aided by the way his race strategy dovetailed with a red flag. But even before that, he'd shown comparable race pace to the likes of

Force India and Williams. One race later in Bahrain, he qualified in the top ten and drove a strong race to fifth. Sixty-two per cent of the team's seasonal points score came in these first two races. These two results essentially earned the new team its respectability and a financially useful place in the constructors' championship. They would stand as the team's seasonal highlights, however, for a combination of inexperience in understanding the traits of the tyres and a necessarily small development programme caused the car to fall away from its initial competitiveness. There was a late upturn when a new four-element front wing – and corresponding changes to floor and rear brake ducts – was introduced in Suzuka, allowing Grosjean to qualify seventh both there and in Brazil. This by far was the biggest upgrade the car received, the low rate of development being the one area that revealed the team's small size. That said, Haas was one of the few teams to devote much attention to producing a special low-downforce rear wing for Monza, with a highly unconventional M-shaped profile.

Meanwhile, Grosjean and Esteban Gutiérrez suffered repeated difficulties with the car's tyre usage and its braking traits. "Everything is in how you use the tyres these days," said Steiner, "and our inexperience showed in this. How you set the car up is all in the tyres – have you overheated the rubber, not got it hot enough, how you control the temperature from the brakes, the difference between the tyre surface

and the bulk, the effects of the track temperature: all these things. Maybe in our first races, we lucked in with this, or maybe the other teams hadn't built up their understanding, either. We had vehicle dynamics people learning about this all the time, and for next year we are recruiting more, but the experienced people all have six months gardening-leave contracts and will be coming in 2017."

There was almost certainly a causal relationship between this weakness and the car's repeated braking difficulties, for it used the exact same braking system as the Ferrari, which arguably was the best braking car on the grid. Also, as the aero team attempted to develop the car, it moved away from the initial Ferrari-copy front ducts, and this may have been a contributory factor as well. The car seemed forever caught between locking fronts and unstable rear, with no window in between – especially for Grosjean who, in his forceful driving style, relies heavily upon the fronts not locking prematurely. For Brazil, he made an experimental change away from Ferrari's favoured brake supplier, Brembo, to Carbone Industrie and found an improvement in the feel it gave him through the pedal. But this was just an alleviation of the worst of the car's traits; the root underlying cause remained to be found.

Nonetheless, this was all within the context of the strongest season for a start-up Formula One team for many years.

RENAULT SPORT F1 TEAM

20
KEVIN MAGNUSSEN

30
JOLYON PALMER

THE four-times championship-winning Enstone team had been rescued from oblivion at the 11th hour, late in 2015, when Renault bought back what it had sold to Genii Capital five years before. It lost the Lotus name and the Mercedes power unit, each replaced by Renault. Otherwise, by necessity, the RS16 was essentially the 2015 Lotus E23, painted yellow and pushed along by a less powerful engine.

Bob Bell was recruited as chief technical officer, back to the team he'd left in 2010 for Mercedes. On his return, he oversaw what essentially was just a foundation season for the future. "I had mixed feelings," he admitted, "because whilst it was great to come back to a team I've great fondness for, it was sad to see the state the team had fallen into due to a lack of investment just to stay alive over the previous season-and-a-half or more. It was very heartening to see the real spirit and drive that existed among the crew of people that remained to bring it all back to life again, but there was a lot to do. The lack of investment meant it had lost a lot of people, good people, and the facilities had not been kept up to standard. From when I left, there were a couple of additional buildings and a simulator, but generally the infrastructure was the same, just more run down."

Staff numbers had fallen to 470 for a facility optimised at around 650; CFD licences had expired

months before. Development of the car had been frozen mid-2015, and for the start of the season, it was a case of re-engineering it to accept the Renault power unit and adding some of the development parts that had been designed, but not made in 2015, including the shorter nose. It was much less competitive than the 2015 car had been, illustrating just how quickly teams can fall backwards if they stand still in F1. Drivers Kevin Magnussen and Jolyon Palmer usually struggled to graduate beyond the first hurdle of Q1 in qualifying, and only eight points were scored throughout the season, leaving the team ninth in the constructors' championship.

"The team had only been with Mercedes for a year, so it wasn't as difficult as it might have been getting the car to accept the Renault power unit," said Bell. "Obviously, there's a very longstanding relationship between Enstone and Renault Sport at Viry, a lot of shared history. The relationship was already there and we understood each other very well."

Until a new gearbox could be designed and built (a very long-lead item), the box used with the Mercedes engine car was modified. "Yes, there was nothing to be particularly proud of with that one, other than the amount of man hours and effort that went into doing it in time," said Bell. "It was only in the second half of the season that we started getting the pukka 2016 gearbox coming through. For a long time, we had only

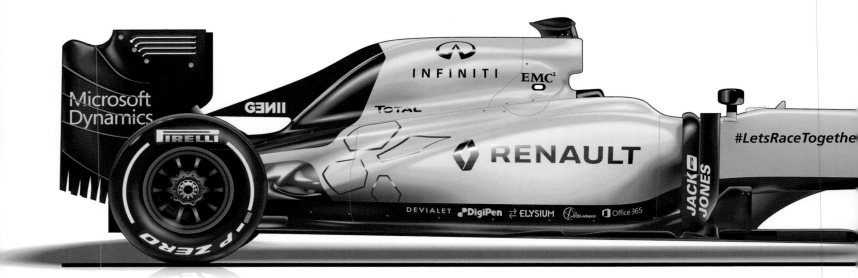

RENAULT R.S.16

OFFICIAL PARTNERS	APL • Bell & Ross • Devialet • EMC2 • Eurodatacar • Genii Business Exchange • Infiniti • Interproccian • Jack Jones • Microsoft Dynamics • Total • Pirelli
OFFICIAL SUPPLIERS	3d Systems • Alpinestars • Boeing Research & Technology • CD-adapco • Digipen • Elysium • GF Machining Solutions • Matrix OZ Racing • PerkinElmer • Siemens • Yxlon
POWER UNIT	**Type:** Renault R.S.16 Hybrid **No. of cylinders** *(vee angle):* V6 (90°) **No. of valves:** 24 **Max rpm** *(ICE):* 15,000 **Electronics:** MES-Microsoft standard electronic control unit **Fuel:** Total **Oil:** Total
TRANSMISSION	**Gearbox:** Eight-speed semi-automatic titanium with reverse gear, quick-shift system **Clutch:** AP Racing
CHASSIS	Moulded carbon fibre and aluminium honeycomb composite monocoque **Front suspension:** Upper and lower carbon-fibre wishbones, push-rod-actuated torsion-bar springs, dampers and anti-roll bar **Rear suspension:** Upper and lower carbon-fibre wishbones, pull-rod operated torsion-bar springs and transverse-mounted damper units inside gearbox casing, aluminium uprights **Wheels:** OZ magnesium **Tyres:** Pirelli P Zero **Brake pads and discs:** Carbon **Brake calipers:** AP Racing **Fuel tank:** ATL
DIMENSIONS	**Front track:** 1450mm **Rear track:** 1400mm **Overall height:** 950mm **Overall width:** 1800mm **Formula weight:** 702kg, including driver and camera

JOLYON PALMER

BOB BELL

RENAULT SPORT F1 TEAM: PERSONNEL

President: Jérome Stoll

Managing Director: Cyril Abiteboul

Racing Director: Frédéric Vasseur

F1 Technology Director: Bob Bell

Chassis Technical Director: Nick Chester

Engine Technical Director: Rémi Taffin

Trackside Operations Director: Alan Permane

Chief Designer: Martin Tolliday

Race Team Manager: Paul Seaby

Chief Mechanic: Robert Cherry

Team Head of Vehicle Performance: Chris Dyer

Race Engineer *(Magnussen)***:** Chris Richards

Engine Engineer *(Palmer)***:** Julien Simon-Chautemps

CYRIL ABITEBOUL

FRÉDÉRIC VASSEUR

Photos: Renault Sport F1 Team

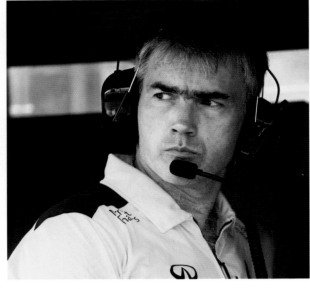

Above: Chassis technical director Nick Chester.

Above left: Head of vehicle performance Chris Dyer.

Left: Engine guru Rémi Taffin.

Right: Out of the ashes of Lotus, the team lines up for the traditional end-of-year photo in Abu Dhabi.

Below: Kevin Magnussen in action in the United States Grand Prix. The Dane could not reach an agreement to stay with the team and moves to Haas for 2017.

Below right: Trackside operations director Alan Permane oversees the cars' preparation on the grid at Suzuka.

Photos: Renault Sport F1 Team

three of those hybrid gearboxes in the system, and it's an incredible testament to the guys at Enstone that they kept them alive as long as they did." The gearbox for 2016 was a traditional Enstone unit in cast titanium.

Enstone and Viry between them opted for air-air intercoolers, rather than the more compact, but heavier water-air type. Viry had made significant progress with its power unit into the 2016 season, and there was a further step change with the introduction of Turbulent Jet ignition technology at Monaco. But even in comparison to the identical engines in the Red Bulls, there was probably a slight shortfall, as Bell explained: "There had been no budget to do a development programme with suppliers, and so we were probably behind on intercooler core technology. They worked fine, but I suspect we were a bit deficient, and others are able to operate their systems more efficiently.

"I don't think we should be anything other than blunt about it: the car was nowhere. We only started a programme before Christmas to develop this car as much as we could pre-season, and we put a few bits and pieces on it during the season, but nothing that transformed it. There wasn't time to do that. It takes a lot of time to make up for the sort of loss we saw, and there are elements of the infrastructure, because they were run down, that didn't allow us to address that as fast as we'd like. We were sadly lacking in rapid prototyping, which is crucial to feeding a very hungry wind tunnel programme. So I don't think we've

covered ourselves in glory, didn't put as much aero performance on the car as we'd have hoped. And in terms of car traits, fundamentally it lacked downforce in basic terms. But that's not the only story. From the start of year until around Hungary time, its balance and set-up window weren't as good as they could be, and we have worked at improving them aerodynamically and mechanically and made some good steps there in the second half of the season, making it much improved in terms of driveability, easier to set up, better balanced. That bodes well for the future."

In general, the car struggled to generate good front tyre temperatures and showed better at circuits with long-duration corners – Hungaroring, Sepang, Suzuka – that kept the front loaded up for longer. At those tracks, the car moved up to mid-grid, allowing Palmer to run in the top ten. Magnussen's respectable grid position in Malaysia came to nothing in the opening few moments, as he was caught up in the first-corner mayhem. From Suzuka onwards, there was a minor floor upgrade around the area ahead of the rear tyres, designed to further restrict the tyre squirt airflow from reaching the diffuser, and this coincided with a small upturn in form – perhaps the first green shoots of a recovery.

This is a long-term project – officially longer than any other team's, in fact, as it has signed a commercial agreement with F1 through to 2024 – and it will be some time before it can realistically aspire to recapture the glory years. The only way is up…

SAUBER F1 TEAM

9

MARCUS ERICSSON

12

FELIPE NASR

SAUBER began the season on a financial knife-edge, and only a mid-season buy-out ensured its survival. As a result, its 2016 car, the C35, was very little different from its 2015 contender (which, in turn, was based heavily on the 2014 car), merely modified to meet the latest side-intrusion regulation tweaks. For the same reason, the car received virtually no technical development until the money taps were turned back on under the new owners, Longbow Finance.

Mark Smith, recruited as technical director in August, 2015, left before the season was very old. Chief designer Eric Gandelin filled the role of acting TD. Head of track engineering Giampaolo Dall'Ara also left (after 15 years with the team) and was replaced by former Red Bull man Tim Malyon – who stayed just three months before returning from whence he had come. In turn, he was replaced by former Williams and Toro Rosso engineer Xevi Pujolar. Nicolas Hennel (ex-Enstone, Ferrari and Toyota) joined to fill the vacant chief-of-aero slot at around the same time. This was all a reflection of the financial uncertainty surrounding the team. The upheaval and lack of continuity obviously impacted further upon its performance. It also remained the only team without a driver-in-loop simulator, a very valuable tool in this era of restricted testing.

Ferrari provided the engine and gearbox once more, and the car largely retained its somewhat ba-sic-looking bodywork with little of the complexity seen in more modern designs. Its front wing, for example, looked particularly unsophisticated by contemporary standards. The sidepods were subtly reshaped, with more of a height reduction along their length compared to those of the C34. The mounting of the rear wing was slightly different. The 2016 Ferrari engine's narrower block and more tightly packaged gearbox should have brought Sauber some aerodynamic gain.

Marcus Ericsson and Felipe Nasr generally struggled to progress beyond the Q1 part of qualifying, the former managing it on five occasions out of 20, the latter three. The car was barely any faster than the Manor, and occasionally not even that. Operational problems and inconsistencies borne of having to manage on a super-tight budget often prevented even what small potential was in the car from being fully exploited.

Although CFD studies continued through the year, wind tunnel time was restricted on cost grounds, as was the manufacture of new parts. So it wasn't until Longbow completed its purchase of the team that the developments planned through the season could actually be made. This package first appeared on the car at Spa and was a very thorough reworking of its surfaces. It began with a shorter nose tip, increasing the airflow to the underfloor. Accompanying this was an all-new – Red Bull-like - front wing, much more sophisticated than the original, and featuring six flaps

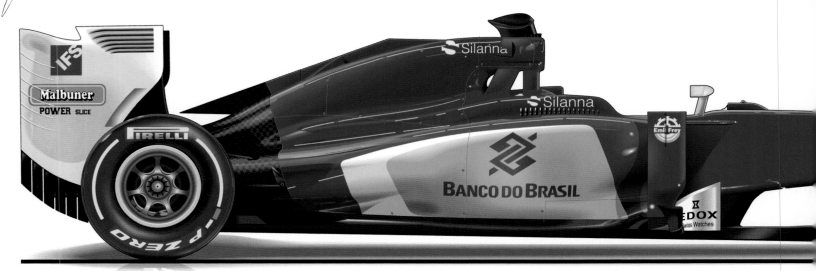

SAUBER C35

PRINCIPAL PARTNERS	Banco do Brasil • Silanna • IFS
PREMIUM PARTNERS	CNBC • Malbuner/Power Slice • Emil Frey • Edox Swiss Watches • Modo Eyewear
OFFICIAL & TECHNICAL PARTNERS	Gabrielle's Angel Foundation • Mitsubishi Electric • NetApp • OMP • Pirelli • Swiss Fibertec • Thomann Walter Meier • Wikland
PROMOTIONAL PARTNERS	Brütsch/Rüegger • Carbon Connect • Hewlett-Packard Enterprise • Interroll • Jura • MTO • nabholz • On AG • Pack Easy Powerfood • Riedel Communications • Singapore Airlines • Sport Media Group • Vebego
POWER UNIT	**Type:** Ferrari 1.6-litre turbo **No. of cylinders** (vee angle): V6 (90°) **No. of valves:** 24 **Max. rpm:** 15,000
TRANSMISSION	**Gearbox:** Ferrari eight-speed quick-shift carbon gearbox, longitudinally mounted **Clutch:** Carbon fibre
CHASSIS	Carbon-fibre monocoque **Front suspension:** Upper and lower wishbones, inboard spring and damper elements actuated by push-rods **Rear suspension:** Upper and lower wishbones, inboard spring and damper elements actuated by pull-rods **Dampers:** ZF Sachs **Wheel diameter:** 13in, front and rear **Wheels:** OZ **Tyres:** Pirelli P Zero **Brake calipers and pads:** Brembo **Discs:** Carbon Industrie **Steering wheel:** Sauber F1 Team **Instruments:** Sauber F1 Team **Fuel tank:** ATL **Electronics:** MES
DIMENSIONS	**Length:** 5150mm **Width:** 1800mm **Front track:** 1460mm **Rear track:** 1416mm **Height:** 950mm
	Formula weight: 702kg, including driver and camera

MARCUS ERICSSON

MONISHA KALTENBORN

MARCUS ERICSSON

SAUBER F1 TEAM: PERSONNEL

President of the Board of Directors: Pascal Picci

Team Principal & CEO: Monisha Kaltenborn

Operations Director: Axel Kruse

Chief Designer: Eric Gandelin

Head of Aerodynamics: Nicolas Hennel de Beaupreau

Head of Systems Engineering: Damiano Molfetta

Team Manager: Beat Zehnder

Head of Track Engineering: Xevi Pujolar

Race Engineer *(Ericsson)*: Craig Gardiner

Race Engineer *(Nasr)*: Jörn Becker

Head of Track Operations: Timothée Guerin

Chief Mechanic: Reto Camenzind

Head of Communications: Robert Höpoltseder

Head of Marketing: Kristina Fraesdorf

Photos: Sauber F1 Team

and a Mercedes-like tunnel on its underside to generate vortexes further down the side of the car. This all required a redrawing of the various turning vanes and flow conditioners beneath the nose.

The aerodynamically powerful front brake ducts were also modified, while the aerodynamically sensitive area in the footplate ahead of the rear wheels received the fashionable multiple slots that restrict outer body airflow from being sucked inwards to interfere with that of the diffuser. The sidepods received a new splitter design around their shoulders to better accelerate the airflow down the car's flanks towards the 'coke-bottle' section.

The upgrade made for a noticeable improvement in the car's competitiveness, generally pulling it clear of Manor and allowing it to compete with Renault. Ericsson managed to qualify it 16th in both Singapore and Austin, and 15th in Mexico. In the rain of Brazil, Nasr drove well on a good strategy, finishing ninth and scoring two hugely valuable points. These put Sauber ahead of Manor in the constructors' championship, thereby qualifying it for around £30 million more prize money for the future.

This further shored up the financial security provided by the new owners, and before the end of the season, it was announced that Jörg Zander would be returning to the team as technical director in 2017, having last served there ten years before as chief designer. The Swiss team's competitiveness had suffered heavily from its financial woes of the last few years, but thankfully it is still intact. Now it is to be hoped that Sauber is in the early stages of a rebuilding phase, rather than in survival mode.

Above: The team poses for a group photo at the start of what would prove to be a long, hard season.
Photo: Sauber F1 Team

Right: Despite the diabolical weather that descended upon Interlagos, Sauber and Felipe Nasr survived the conditions to net a priceless ninth-place finish.
Photo: WRi2/Jad Sherif

Left: Nasr brought a large chunk of sponsorship money from Brazil in order to keep his seat in the car.

Top right: Regardless of the long points-scoring drought, spirits remained high among the crew.
Photos: Sauber F1 Team

Above right: Marcus Ericsson celebrated his 50th grand prix start in Singapore.
Photo: WRi2/Jean-François Galeron

94

PASCAL WEHRLEIN

88

RIO HARYANTO

31

ESTEBAN OCON

MANOR RACING MRT

A SWITCH to Mercedes power for 2016 helped Manor make real progress. For the first time, it was able to race regularly with the likes of Sauber and, occasionally, Renault. Pascal Wehrlein's championship point for tenth place in Austria looked hugely valuable for the team, putting it tenth in the points table (ahead of Sauber), but the ninth place achieved by Nasr in Brazil for the Hinwil team denied Manor the chance to become a 'column 2' team, with a consequent boost in start money income.

The team was still under the ownership of Stephen Fitzpatrick, founders John Booth and Graeme Lowden having left at the end of the previous season, and it was run by former McLaren team manager Dave Ryan. Part of the Mercedes deal involved giving a seat to its junior driver, Pascal Wehrlein, and initially he was teamed with fellow rookie Rio Haryanto. When the Indonesian's backers were unable to continue payments in the season's second half, however, he was demoted to third driver and replaced by another Mercedes protégé, Esteban Ocon.

The Manor MRT05 was designed by Luca Furbatto, overseen by technical director John McQuilliam, and it was based recognisably on the car of the previous two years, but considerably refined. McQuilliam's still-born 2015 car – aborted when the team went into receivership in late 2014, with the re-emergent outfit running an adaptation of the '14 car instead – established some of the 2016 machine's general design

MANOR MRT05

PARTNERS	Rebellion • Daffy's Gin • Pirelli • Airbnb • Shazam • Rescale • Branded London • Pertamina • Kiky
POWER UNIT	**Type:** Mercedes-Benz PU106C Hybrid **No. of cylinders** *(vee angle):* V6 (90°) **No. of valves:** 24 **Bore:** 80mm **Stroke:** 53mm **Crank height:** 90mm *(minimum allowed)* **Max. rpm:** 15,000 **Fuel injection:** High-pressure direct injection (max. 500 bar, one injector/cylinder) **Pressure charging:** Single-stage compressor and exhaust turbine on a common shaft **Electronics:** FIA standard ECU and FIA homologated electronic and electrical system **ERS:** Integrated hybrid energy recovery via electrical motor generator units **Energy store:** Lithium-Ion battery **Fuel and lubricants:** Petronas
TRANSMISSION	**Gearbox:** Williams eight-speed seamless sequential semi-automatic shift, electro-hydraulically-actuated gear selection **Clutch:** Carbon-fibre plates
CHASSIS	Moulded composite with aluminium honeycomb core **Bodywork:** Moulded carbon fibre with Nomex core **Front suspension:** Manor racing full composite push-rod suspension with inboard torsion-bar and damper system **Rear suspension:** Williiams double wishbones with pull-rod-activated springs and anti-roll bar **Dampers:** Front, Penske; Rear, Williams Advanced Engineering **Wheels:** APP Tech forged magnesium **Tyres:** Pirelli P Zero **Brake system:** Carbone Industrie carbon/carbon discs and pads, AP Racing calipers, Manor Racing rear brake-by-wire **Steering:** Manor Racing power-assisted rack-and-pinion **Fuel tank:** ATL **Instruments:** Manor Racing-designed, steering wheel mounted
DIMENSIONS	**Overall length:** 5000mm **Front track:** 1799mm **Rear track:** 1799mm **Height:** 949mm **Formula weight:** 702kg, including driver and camera

Pascal Wehrlein scored the team's only point in Austria.

features. At the car's launch, McQuilliam was keen to emphasise the step forwards it represented for the team: "Even at this early stage of the game, we can easily say this is the best car we've ever launched. Certainly the most developed, the most ambitious and the most aggressive. The design team have focused almost exclusively on it since the middle of last season, and it's just a whole different ball game to any of its predecessors."

The biggest difference was the presence of a Mercedes power unit, together with a Williams gearbox. Williams also provided the rear suspension. The car featured a significantly narrower nose than its prede-

cessor, though it was considerably longer than those of all the other cars, allowing it an easier route through the crash test at the expense of some underbody airflow capacity. In this, it resembled the 2015 Ferrari SF15-T, and probably for a similar reason: the front bulkhead (in carbon composite for 2016, rather than the previous aluminium) positioning prevented it from being made any shorter.

The sidepods were more tightly sculpted than those of the MR03B and featured vortex generators on their leading edge, helping aero efficiency. The mechanical hardware defined a Mercedes-like internal layout, allowing the sidepods to close in quite

early to reveal the radiator cooling outlets towards the centreline of the car.

Bodywork around the airbox was cut away, and there were extensive developments to the rear brake ducts and rear wing endplates. By necessity, the car was visually less aerodynamically intricate than those of the top teams – as a comparison between the complexity of the respective front wings will show – but it proved well balanced with no real vices. It was conceived in the wind tunnel leased from McLaren, but developed from mid-season onwards at the Mercedes-owned Brackley tunnel. Nikolas Tombazis joined as chief of aero on the eve of the season, so had nothing to do with the car's conception, but he led its development. The car evolved steadily through the season, with tweaks to floor, endplates and diffuser, the improvement rate actually staying level with that at the front of the field.

"It was a very satisfying season," said Ryan. "Last season, the team had just been turning up and getting through the year. We'd been in survival mode. This year, we were at least competing. Though the car was done on a budget, it was a fairly big step on from what we'd had before, but really the team was in a bit of a mess. A lot of people had left, and January was very difficult. Just trying to get two cars built, getting a team of people together, testing and going to the first race was an achievement in itself. We just about had two car crews, but in testing it meant we couldn't have a night shift, so some of the things you'd normally get done just weren't possible in the time frame. Some of the rig tests you'd like to do, we just couldn't. There was a lot of compromise. We didn't get a set-up on the car until we were actually running at Barcelona. We didn't do any pit-stop practice because there was no car available. We were just 110 people then. Now we're 210."

As a result, the car's performance in qualifying for the first race made it appear that Manor would be running solidly at the back, a significant way off the pace of the penultimate team, as previously. It was a misleading picture, however, the product of nothing more than the compromised preparation. Wehrlein's characteristic flying start in Melbourne was just a portent of what was to come. At the next race, he outqualified both Saubers and a Renault, and raced strongly with them.

Among those who had left between the seasons was chief engineer Gianluca Pisanello. He was replaced at the racetrack on a consultancy basis by ex-McLaren and Ferrari engineering chief Pat Fry. "For Manor to attract people based on how they were was quite difficult," said Ryan. "Being seconds off the next slowest car on the grid, people want to know you're serious, and Stephen Fitzpatrick going out and getting us the best engine, rather than doing a cheaper deal on a year-old Ferrari or something, was a notice of intent. This car has allowed us on a good day to qualify 15th to 16th maybe. It's given us a couple of opportunities and we took them." Wehrlein got through to Q2 on five occasions, and in Austria, a track that heavily rewards horsepower and that is relatively forgiving of a lack of downforce, he even came close to making it into Q3. This pace was the basis of the crucially important championship point.

"Now we need to take the next big step and get the same sort of improvement again," continued Ryan, "and just become a solid team. But we've demonstrated that we are a serious proposition. We compete, we look more presentable, a pretty good group of guys, and we're now attracting really good people, but good guys are on six-month or one-year notice."

DAVE RYAN

JOHN McQUILLIAM

MANOR RACING MRT: PERSONNEL

Owner: Stephen Fitzpatrick

Chief Executive Officer: Thomas Mayer

Racing Director: Dave Ryan

Technical Director: John McQuilliam

Chief Designer: Luca Furbatto

Chief Aerodynamicist: Nikolas Tombazis

Engineering Consultant: Pat Fry

Chief Race Engineer: Juan Pablo Ramirez

Race Engineer (Wehrlein)**:** Josh Peckett

Performance Engineer (Wehrlein)**:** Stuart Barlow

Race Engineer (Ocon/Haryanto)**:** Juan Pablo Ramirez

Performance Engineer (Ocon/Haryanto)**:** Roberto Garcia

Chief Mechanic: Pete Vale

PR & Communications Director: Tracy Novak

Marketing Director: Simon Pavitt

STEPHEN FITZPATRICK

CHASSIS LOGBOOK 2016

COMPILED BY DAVID HAYHOE

MERCEDES F1 W07

ROUND 1 AUSTRALIAN GP

	MERCEDES	
6	Nico Rosberg	F1 W07/03
44	Lewis Hamilton	F1 W07/01
	RED BULL-TAG HEUER	
3	Daniel Ricciardo	RB12/02
26	Daniil Kvyat	RB12/01
	WILLIAMS-MERCEDES	
19	Felipe Massa	FW38/02
77	Valtteri Bottas	FW38/03
	FERRARI	
5	Sebastian Vettel	SF16-H/314
7	Kimi Räikkönen	SF16-H/317
	McLAREN-HONDA	
14	Fernando Alonso	MP4-31/01
22	Jenson Button	MP4-31/03
	FORCE INDIA-MERCEDES	
11	Sergio Pérez	VJM09/02
27	Nico Hülkenberg	VJM09/01
	TORO ROSSO-FERRARI	
33	Max Verstappen	STR11/01
55	Carlos Sainz	STR11/02
	RENAULT	
20	Kevin Magnussen	R.S.16/02
30	Jolyon Palmer	R.S.16/01
	MANOR-MERCEDES	
88	Rio Haryanto	MRT05/01
94	Pascal Wehrlein	MRT05/02
	SAUBER-FERRARI	
9	Marcus Ericsson	C35/01
12	Felipe Nasr	C35/02
	HAAS-FERRARI	
8	Romain Grosjean	VF-16/01
21	Esteban Gutiérrez	VF-16/03

ROUND 2 BAHRAIN GP

	MERCEDES	
6	Nico Rosberg	F1 W07/03
44	Lewis Hamilton	F1 W07/01
	RED BULL-TAG HEUER	
3	Daniel Ricciardo	RB12/02
26	Daniil Kvyat	RB12/01
	WILLIAMS-MERCEDES	
19	Felipe Massa	FW38/02
77	Valtteri Bottas	FW38/03
	FERRARI	
5	Sebastian Vettel	SF16-H/314
7	Kimi Räikkönen	SF16-H/317
	McLAREN-HONDA	
22	Jenson Button	MP4-31/03
47	Stoffel Vandoorne	MP4-31/02
	FORCE INDIA-MERCEDES	
11	Sergio Pérez	VJM09/02
34	Alfonso Celis	VJM09/02
27	Nico Hülkenberg	VJM09/01
	TORO ROSSO-FERRARI	
33	Max Verstappen	STR11/01
55	Carlos Sainz	STR11/02
	RENAULT	
20	Kevin Magnussen	R.S.16/02
30	Jolyon Palmer	R.S.16/01
	MANOR-MERCEDES	
88	Rio Haryanto	MRT05/01
94	Pascal Wehrlein	MRT05/02
	SAUBER-FERRARI	
9	Marcus Ericsson	C35/01
12	Felipe Nasr	C35/02
	HAAS-FERRARI	
8	Romain Grosjean	VF-16/01
21	Esteban Gutiérrez	VF-16/02

ROUND 3 CHINESE GP

	MERCEDES	
6	Nico Rosberg	F1 W07/03
44	Lewis Hamilton	F1 W07/01
	RED BULL-TAG HEUER	
3	Daniel Ricciardo	RB12/02
26	Daniil Kvyat	RB12/01
	WILLIAMS-MERCEDES	
19	Felipe Massa	FW38/02
77	Valtteri Bottas	FW38/03
	FERRARI	
5	Sebastian Vettel	SF16-H/314
7	Kimi Räikkönen	SF16-H/317
	McLAREN-HONDA	
14	Fernando Alonso	MP4-31/02
22	Jenson Button	MP4-31/03
	FORCE INDIA-MERCEDES	
11	Sergio Pérez	VJM09/02
27	Nico Hülkenberg	VJM09/01
	TORO ROSSO-FERRARI	
33	Max Verstappen	STR11/01
55	Carlos Sainz	STR11/02
	RENAULT	
20	Kevin Magnussen	R.S.16/02
30	Jolyon Palmer	R.S.16/01
	MANOR-MERCEDES	
88	Rio Haryanto	MRT05/01
94	Pascal Wehrlein	MRT05/02
	SAUBER-FERRARI	
9	Marcus Ericsson	C35/01
12	Felipe Nasr	C35/02
	HAAS-FERRARI	
8	Romain Grosjean	VF-16/01
21	Esteban Gutiérrez	VF-16/02

ROUND 4 RUSSIAN GP

	MERCEDES	
6	Nico Rosberg	F1 W07/03
44	Lewis Hamilton	F1 W07/01
	RED BULL-TAG HEUER	
3	Daniel Ricciardo	RB12/02
26	Daniil Kvyat	RB12/01
	WILLIAMS-MERCEDES	
19	Felipe Massa	FW38/02
77	Valtteri Bottas	FW38/03
	FERRARI	
5	Sebastian Vettel	SF16-H/314
7	Kimi Räikkönen	SF16-H/317
	McLAREN-HONDA	
14	Fernando Alonso	MP4-31/02
22	Jenson Button	MP4-31/03
	FORCE INDIA-MERCEDES	
11	Sergio Pérez	VJM09/02
27	Nico Hülkenberg	VJM09/01
34	Alfonso Celis	VJM09/01
	TORO ROSSO-FERRARI	
33	Max Verstappen	STR11/01
55	Carlos Sainz	STR11/02
	RENAULT	
20	Kevin Magnussen	R.S.16/02
46	Sergey Sirotkin	R.S.16/02
30	Jolyon Palmer	R.S.16/01
	MANOR-MERCEDES	
88	Rio Haryanto	MRT05/01
94	Pascal Wehrlein	MRT05/02
	SAUBER-FERRARI	
9	Marcus Ericsson	C35/01
12	Felipe Nasr	C35/03
	HAAS-FERRARI	
8	Romain Grosjean	VF-16/01
21	Esteban Gutiérrez	VF-16/02

ROUND 5 SPANISH GP

	MERCEDES	
6	Nico Rosberg	F1 W07/03
44	Lewis Hamilton	F1 W07/01
	RED BULL-TAG HEUER	
3	Daniel Ricciardo	RB12/03
33	Max Verstappen	RB12/04
	WILLIAMS-MERCEDES	
19	Felipe Massa	FW38/02
77	Valtteri Bottas	FW38/03
	FERRARI	
5	Sebastian Vettel	SF16-H/314
7	Kimi Räikkönen	SF16-H/317
	McLAREN-HONDA	
14	Fernando Alonso	MP4-31/04
22	Jenson Button	MP4-31/03
	FORCE INDIA-MERCEDES	
11	Sergio Pérez	VJM09/02
27	Nico Hülkenberg	VJM09/03
	TORO ROSSO-FERRARI	
26	Daniil Kvyat	STR11/01
55	Carlos Sainz	STR11/03
	RENAULT	
20	Kevin Magnussen	R.S.16/02
30	Jolyon Palmer	R.S.16/03
45	Esteban Ocon	R.S.16/03
	MANOR-MERCEDES	
88	Rio Haryanto	MRT05/01
94	Pascal Wehrlein	MRT05/03
	SAUBER-FERRARI	
9	Marcus Ericsson	C35/01
12	Felipe Nasr	C35/03
	HAAS-FERRARI	
8	Romain Grosjean	VF-16/01
21	Esteban Gutiérrez	VF-16/02

ROUND 6 MONACO GP

	MERCEDES	
6	Nico Rosberg	F1 W07/03
44	Lewis Hamilton	F1 W07/01
	RED BULL-TAG HEUER	
3	Daniel Ricciardo	RB12/03
33	Max Verstappen	RB12/02 (04-Fri+Sat)
	WILLIAMS-MERCEDES	
19	Felipe Massa	FW38/02
77	Valtteri Bottas	FW38/03
	FERRARI	
5	Sebastian Vettel	SF16-H/314
7	Kimi Räikkönen	SF16-H/317
	McLAREN-HONDA	
14	Fernando Alonso	MP4-31/04
22	Jenson Button	MP4-31/03
	FORCE INDIA-MERCEDES	
11	Sergio Pérez	VJM09/02
27	Nico Hülkenberg	VJM09/03
	TORO ROSSO-FERRARI	
26	Daniil Kvyat	STR11/03
55	Carlos Sainz	STR11/01
	RENAULT	
20	Kevin Magnussen	R.S.16/01
30	Jolyon Palmer	R.S.16/03
	MANOR-MERCEDES	
88	Rio Haryanto	MRT05/01
94	Pascal Wehrlein	MRT05/03
	SAUBER-FERRARI	
9	Marcus Ericsson	C35/01
12	Felipe Nasr	C35/03
	HAAS-FERRARI	
8	Romain Grosjean	VF-16/03
21	Esteban Gutiérrez	VF-16/02

TORO ROSSO STR11

Scuderia Toro Rosso

RENAULT R.S.16

Renault Sport F1

FERRARI SF16-H

Scuderia Ferrari

SAUBER C35

Sauber F1 Team

ROUND 7 CANADIAN GP

	MERCEDES	
6	Nico Rosberg	F1 W07/03
44	Lewis Hamilton	F1 W07/01
	RED BULL-TAG HEUER	
3	Daniel Ricciardo	RB12/03
33	Max Verstappen	RB12/02
	WILLIAMS-MERCEDES	
19	Felipe Massa	FW38/02
77	Valtteri Bottas	FW38/03
	FERRARI	
5	Sebastian Vettel	SF16-H/314
7	Kimi Räikkönen	SF16-H/317
	McLAREN-HONDA	
14	Fernando Alonso	MP4-31/04
22	Jenson Button	MP4-31/03
	FORCE INDIA-MERCEDES	
11	Sergio Pérez	VJM09/02
27	Nico Hülkenberg	VJM09/03
	TORO ROSSO-FERRARI	
26	Daniil Kvyat	STR11/03
55	Carlos Sainz	STR11/01
	RENAULT	
20	Kevin Magnussen	R.S.16/01 (04-Fri to Sat P3)
30	Jolyon Palmer	R.S.16/02
	MANOR-MERCEDES	
88	Rio Haryanto	MRT05/02
94	Pascal Wehrlein	MRT05/03
	SAUBER-FERRARI	
9	Marcus Ericsson	C35/01
12	Felipe Nasr	C35/03
	HAAS-FERRARI	
8	Romain Grosjean	VF-16/03
21	Esteban Gutiérrez	VF-16/02

ROUND 8 EUROPEAN GP

	MERCEDES	
6	Nico Rosberg	F1 W07/03
44	Lewis Hamilton	F1 W07/01
	RED BULL-TAG HEUER	
3	Daniel Ricciardo	RB12/03
33	Max Verstappen	RB12/02
	WILLIAMS-MERCEDES	
19	Felipe Massa	FW38/02
77	Valtteri Bottas	FW38/03
	FERRARI	
5	Sebastian Vettel	SF16-H/314
7	Kimi Räikkönen	SF16-H/317
	McLAREN-HONDA	
14	Fernando Alonso	MP4-31/04
22	Jenson Button	MP4-31/03
	FORCE INDIA-MERCEDES	
11	Sergio Pérez	VJM09/02
27	Nico Hülkenberg	VJM09/03
	TORO ROSSO-FERRARI	
26	Daniil Kvyat	STR11/03
55	Carlos Sainz	STR11/01
	RENAULT	
20	Kevin Magnussen	R.S.16/01
30	Jolyon Palmer	R.S.16/02
	MANOR-MERCEDES	
88	Rio Haryanto	MRT05/02
94	Pascal Wehrlein	MRT05/03
	SAUBER-FERRARI	
9	Marcus Ericsson	C35/01
12	Felipe Nasr	C35/03
	HAAS-FERRARI	
8	Romain Grosjean	VF-16/03
21	Esteban Gutiérrez	VF-16/02

ROUND 9 AUSTRIAN GP

	MERCEDES	
6	Nico Rosberg	F1 W07/05
44	Lewis Hamilton	F1 W07/04
	RED BULL-TAG HEUER	
3	Daniel Ricciardo	RB12/03
33	Max Verstappen	RB12/02
	WILLIAMS-MERCEDES	
19	Felipe Massa	FW38/04
77	Valtteri Bottas	FW38/03
	FERRARI	
5	Sebastian Vettel	SF16-H/314
7	Kimi Räikkönen	SF16-H/317
	McLAREN-HONDA	
14	Fernando Alonso	MP4-31/02
22	Jenson Button	MP4-31/03
	FORCE INDIA-MERCEDES	
11	Sergio Pérez	VJM09/02
34	Alfonso Celis	VJM09/02
27	Nico Hülkenberg	VJM09/03
	TORO ROSSO-FERRARI	
26	Daniil Kvyat	STR11/04 (03-Fri+Sat)
55	Carlos Sainz	STR11/01
	RENAULT	
20	Kevin Magnussen	R.S.16/01
30	Jolyon Palmer	R.S.16/02
	MANOR-MERCEDES	
88	Rio Haryanto	MRT05/01
94	Pascal Wehrlein	MRT05/03
	SAUBER-FERRARI	
9	Marcus Ericsson	C35/01
12	Felipe Nasr	C35/03
	HAAS-FERRARI	
8	Romain Grosjean	VF-16/03
21	Esteban Gutiérrez	VF-16/02

ROUND 10 BRITISH GP

	MERCEDES	
6	Nico Rosberg	F1 W07/05
44	Lewis Hamilton	F1 W07/04
	RED BULL-TAG HEUER	
3	Daniel Ricciardo	RB12/03
33	Max Verstappen	RB12/02
	WILLIAMS-MERCEDES	
19	Felipe Massa	FW38/04
77	Valtteri Bottas	FW38/03
	FERRARI	
5	Sebastian Vettel	SF16-H/314
7	Kimi Räikkönen	SF16-H/317
	McLAREN-HONDA	
14	Fernando Alonso	MP4-31/02
22	Jenson Button	MP4-31/03
	FORCE INDIA-MERCEDES	
11	Sergio Pérez	VJM09/02
27	Nico Hülkenberg	VJM09/03
	TORO ROSSO-FERRARI	
26	Daniil Kvyat	STR11/04
55	Carlos Sainz	STR11/01
	RENAULT	
20	Kevin Magnussen	R.S.16/01
45	Esteban Ocon	R.S.16/01
30	Jolyon Palmer	R.S.16/02
	MANOR-MERCEDES	
88	Rio Haryanto	MRT05/02
94	Pascal Wehrlein	MRT05/03
	SAUBER-FERRARI	
9	Marcus Ericsson	C35/02
		(01-Fri to Sat P3)
12	Felipe Nasr	C35/03
	HAAS-FERRARI	
8	Romain Grosjean	VF-16/03
21	Esteban Gutiérrez	VF-16/02
50	Charles Leclerc	VF-16/02

ROUND 11 HUNGARIAN GP

	MERCEDES	
6	Nico Rosberg	F1 W07/05
44	Lewis Hamilton	F1 W07/04
	RED BULL-TAG HEUER	
3	Daniel Ricciardo	RB12/03
33	Max Verstappen	RB12/02
	WILLIAMS-MERCEDES	
19	Felipe Massa	FW38/04
77	Valtteri Bottas	FW38/03
	FERRARI	
5	Sebastian Vettel	SF16-H/314
7	Kimi Räikkönen	SF16-H/317
	McLAREN-HONDA	
14	Fernando Alonso	MP4-31/02
22	Jenson Button	MP4-31/03
	FORCE INDIA-MERCEDES	
11	Sergio Pérez	VJM09/02
27	Nico Hülkenberg	VJM09/03
	TORO ROSSO-FERRARI	
26	Daniil Kvyat	STR11/02
55	Carlos Sainz	STR11/01
	RENAULT	
20	Kevin Magnussen	R.S.16/01
45	Esteban Ocon	R.S.16/01
30	Jolyon Palmer	R.S.16/04
	MANOR-MERCEDES	
88	Rio Haryanto	MRT05/02
94	Pascal Wehrlein	MRT05/01
	SAUBER-FERRARI	
9	Marcus Ericsson	C35/02
		(04-Fri+Sat)
12	Felipe Nasr	C35/03
	HAAS-FERRARI	
8	Romain Grosjean	VF-16/03
21	Esteban Gutiérrez	VF-16/02
50	Charles Leclerc	VF-16/02

ROUND 12 GERMAN GP

	MERCEDES	
6	Nico Rosberg	F1 W07/05
44	Lewis Hamilton	F1 W07/04
	RED BULL-TAG HEUER	
3	Daniel Ricciardo	RB12/03
33	Max Verstappen	RB12/02
	WILLIAMS-MERCEDES	
19	Felipe Massa	FW38/04
77	Valtteri Bottas	FW38/03
	FERRARI	
5	Sebastian Vettel	SF16-H/314
7	Kimi Räikkönen	SF16-H/317
	McLAREN-HONDA	
14	Fernando Alonso	MP4-31/02
22	Jenson Button	MP4-31/03
	FORCE INDIA-MERCEDES	
11	Sergio Pérez	VJM09/02
27	Nico Hülkenberg	VJM09/03
	TORO ROSSO-FERRARI	
26	Daniil Kvyat	STR11/02
55	Carlos Sainz	STR11/01
	RENAULT	
20	Kevin Magnussen	R.S.16/01
30	Jolyon Palmer	R.S.16/04
45	Esteban Ocon	R.S.16/04
	MANOR-MERCEDES	
88	Rio Haryanto	MRT05/02
94	Pascal Wehrlein	MRT05/01
	SAUBER-FERRARI	
9	Marcus Ericsson	C35/02
12	Felipe Nasr	C35/03
	HAAS-FERRARI	
8	Romain Grosjean	VF-16/03
21	Esteban Gutiérrez	VF-16/02
50	Charles Leclerc	VF-16/02

RED BULL RB12

Red Bull Racing

ROUND 13 BELGIAN GP

MERCEDES		
6	Nico Rosberg	F1 W07/05
44	Lewis Hamilton	F1 W07/04
RED BULL-TAG HEUER		
3	Daniel Ricciardo	RB12/05
33	Max Verstappen	RB12/03
WILLIAMS-MERCEDES		
19	Felipe Massa	FW38/02
77	Valtteri Bottas	FW38/03
FERRARI		
5	Sebastian Vettel	SF16-H/314
7	Kimi Räikkönen	SF16-H/317
McLAREN-HONDA		
14	Fernando Alonso	MP4-31/04
22	Jenson Button	MP4-31/03
FORCE INDIA-MERCEDES		
11	Sergio Pérez	VJM09/02
27	Nico Hülkenberg	VJM09/03
TORO ROSSO-FERRARI		
26	Daniil Kvyat	STR11/03
55	Carlos Sainz	STR11/01
RENAULT		
20	Kevin Magnussen	R.S.16/01
30	Jolyon Palmer	R.S.16/04
MANOR-MERCEDES		
31	Esteban Ocon	MRT05/02
94	Pascal Wehrlein	MRT05/03
SAUBER-FERRARI		
9	Marcus Ericsson	C35/04
12	Felipe Nasr	C35/03
HAAS-FERRARI		
8	Romain Grosjean	VF-16/03
21	Esteban Gutiérrez	VF-16/02

ROUND 15 SINGAPORE GP

MERCEDES		
6	Nico Rosberg	F1 W07/05
44	Lewis Hamilton	F1 W07/04
RED BULL-TAG HEUER		
3	Daniel Ricciardo	RB12/05
33	Max Verstappen	RB12/03
WILLIAMS-MERCEDES		
19	Felipe Massa	FW38/02
77	Valtteri Bottas	FW38/03
FERRARI		
5	Sebastian Vettel	SF16-H/314
7	Kimi Räikkönen	SF16-H/317
McLAREN-HONDA		
14	Fernando Alonso	MP4-31/04
22	Jenson Button	MP4-31/02
FORCE INDIA-MERCEDES		
11	Sergio Pérez	VJM09/02
27	Nico Hülkenberg	VJM09/03
TORO ROSSO-FERRARI		
26	Daniil Kvyat	STR11/03
55	Carlos Sainz	STR11/01
RENAULT		
20	Kevin Magnussen	R.S.16/04
30	Jolyon Palmer	R.S.16/05
MANOR-MERCEDES		
31	Esteban Ocon	MRT05/02
94	Pascal Wehrlein	MRT05/03
SAUBER-FERRARI		
9	Marcus Ericsson	C35/04
12	Felipe Nasr	C35/03
HAAS-FERRARI		
8	Romain Grosjean	VF-16/03
21	Esteban Gutiérrez	VF-16/02

McLAREN MP4-31

McLaren Honda

HAAS VF-16

Haas F1 Team

ROUND 14 ITALIAN GP

MERCEDES		
6	Nico Rosberg	F1 W07/05
44	Lewis Hamilton	F1 W07/04
RED BULL-TAG HEUER		
3	Daniel Ricciardo	RB12/05
33	Max Verstappen	RB12/03
WILLIAMS-MERCEDES		
19	Felipe Massa	FW38/02
77	Valtteri Bottas	FW38/03
FERRARI		
5	Sebastian Vettel	SF16-H/314
7	Kimi Räikkönen	SF16-H/317
McLAREN-HONDA		
14	Fernando Alonso	MP4-31/04
22	Jenson Button	MP4-31/03
FORCE INDIA-MERCEDES		
11	Sergio Pérez	VJM09/02
27	Nico Hülkenberg	VJM09/03
34	Alfonso Celis	VJM09/03
TORO ROSSO-FERRARI		
26	Daniil Kvyat	STR11/03
55	Carlos Sainz	STR11/01
RENAULT		
20	Kevin Magnussen	R.S.16/04
30	Jolyon Palmer	R.S.16/02
MANOR-MERCEDES		
31	Esteban Ocon	MRT05/02
94	Pascal Wehrlein	MRT05/03
SAUBER-FERRARI		
9	Marcus Ericsson	C35/04
12	Felipe Nasr	C35/03
HAAS-FERRARI		
8	Romain Grosjean	VF-16/03
21	Esteban Gutiérrez	VF-16/02

ROUND 16 MALAYSIAN GP

MERCEDES		
6	Nico Rosberg	F1 W07/05
44	Lewis Hamilton	F1 W07/04
RED BULL-TAG HEUER		
3	Daniel Ricciardo	RB12/05
33	Max Verstappen	RB12/03
WILLIAMS-MERCEDES		
19	Felipe Massa	FW38/02
77	Valtteri Bottas	FW38/03
FERRARI		
5	Sebastian Vettel	SF16-H/314
7	Kimi Räikkönen	SF16-H/317
McLAREN-HONDA		
14	Fernando Alonso	MP4-31/04
22	Jenson Button	MP4-31/03
FORCE INDIA-MERCEDES		
11	Sergio Pérez	VJM09/02
27	Nico Hülkenberg	VJM09/03
TORO ROSSO-FERRARI		
26	Daniil Kvyat	STR11/03
55	Carlos Sainz	STR11/01
RENAULT		
20	Kevin Magnussen	R.S.16/04
30	Jolyon Palmer	R.S.16/05
MANOR-MERCEDES		
31	Esteban Ocon	MRT05/02
94	Pascal Wehrlein	MRT05/03
SAUBER-FERRARI		
9	Marcus Ericsson	C35/04
12	Felipe Nasr	C35/03
HAAS-FERRARI		
8	Romain Grosjean	VF-16/03
21	Esteban Gutiérrez	VF-16/02

WILLIAMS FW38

Williams Martini Racing

ROUND 17 JAPANESE GP

	MERCEDES	
6	Nico Rosberg	F1 W07/05
44	Lewis Hamilton	F1 W07/04
	RED BULL-TAG HEUER	
3	Daniel Ricciardo	RB12/05
33	Max Verstappen	RB12/03
	WILLIAMS-MERCEDES	
19	Felipe Massa	FW38/02
77	Valtteri Bottas	FW38/03
	FERRARI	
5	Sebastian Vettel	SF16-H/314
7	Kimi Räikkönen	SF16-H/317
	McLAREN-HONDA	
14	Fernando Alonso	MP4-31/04
22	Jenson Button	MP4-31/03
	FORCE INDIA-MERCEDES	
11	Sergio Pérez	VJM09/02
27	Nico Hülkenberg	VJM09/03
	TORO ROSSO-FERRARI	
26	Daniil Kvyat	STR11/03
55	Carlos Sainz	STR11/01
	RENAULT	
20	Kevin Magnussen	R.S.16/04
30	Jolyon Palmer	R.S.16/05
	MANOR-MERCEDES	
31	Esteban Ocon	MRT05/02
94	Pascal Wehrlein	MRT05/03
	SAUBER-FERRARI	
9	Marcus Ericsson	C35/04
12	Felipe Nasr	C35/03
	HAAS-FERRARI	
8	Romain Grosjean	VF-16/03
21	Esteban Gutiérrez	VF-16/02

ROUND 18 UNITED STATES GP

	MERCEDES	
6	Nico Rosberg	F1 W07/05
44	Lewis Hamilton	F1 W07/04
	RED BULL-TAG HEUER	
3	Daniel Ricciardo	RB12/05
33	Max Verstappen	RB12/03
	WILLIAMS-MERCEDES	
19	Felipe Massa	FW38/02
77	Valtteri Bottas	FW38/03
	FERRARI	
5	Sebastian Vettel	SF16-H/314
7	Kimi Räikkönen	SF16-H/317
	McLAREN-HONDA	
14	Fernando Alonso	MP4-31/04
22	Jenson Button	MP4-31/03
	FORCE INDIA-MERCEDES	
11	Sergio Pérez	VJM09/02
34	Alfonso Celis	VJM09/02
27	Nico Hülkenberg	VJM09/03
	TORO ROSSO-FERRARI	
26	Daniil Kvyat	STR11/03
55	Carlos Sainz	STR11/01
	RENAULT	
20	Kevin Magnussen	R.S.16/04
30	Jolyon Palmer	R.S.16/05
	MANOR-MERCEDES	
31	Esteban Ocon	MRT05/02
94	Pascal Wehrlein	MRT05/01
42	Jordan King	MRT05/01
	SAUBER-FERRARI	
9	Marcus Ericsson	C35/04
12	Felipe Nasr	C35/03
	HAAS-FERRARI	
8	Romain Grosjean	VF-16/03
21	Esteban Gutiérrez	VF-16/02

ROUND 19 MEXICAN GP

	MERCEDES	
6	Nico Rosberg	F1 W07/05
44	Lewis Hamilton	F1 W07/04
	RED BULL-TAG HEUER	
3	Daniel Ricciardo	RB12/05
33	Max Verstappen	RB12/03
	WILLIAMS-MERCEDES	
19	Felipe Massa	FW38/02
77	Valtteri Bottas	FW38/03
	FERRARI	
5	Sebastian Vettel	SF16-H/314
7	Kimi Räikkönen	SF16-H/317
	McLAREN-HONDA	
14	Fernando Alonso	MP4-31/04
22	Jenson Button	MP4-31/03
	FORCE INDIA-MERCEDES	
11	Sergio Pérez	VJM09/02
27	Nico Hülkenberg	VJM09/03
	TORO ROSSO-FERRARI	
26	Daniil Kvyat	STR11/03
55	Carlos Sainz	STR11/01
	RENAULT	
20	Kevin Magnussen	R.S.16/04
30	Jolyon Palmer	R.S.16/02
		(05-Fri to Sat P3)
	MANOR-MERCEDES	
31	Esteban Ocon	MRT05/02
94	Pascal Wehrlein	MRT05/01
	SAUBER-FERRARI	
9	Marcus Ericsson	C35/04
12	Felipe Nasr	C35/03
	HAAS-FERRARI	
8	Romain Grosjean	VF-16/03
21	Esteban Gutiérrez	VF-16/02

ROUND 20 BRAZILIAN GP

	MERCEDES	
6	Nico Rosberg	F1 W07/05
44	Lewis Hamilton	F1 W07/04
	RED BULL-TAG HEUER	
3	Daniel Ricciardo	RB12/05
33	Max Verstappen	RB12/03
	WILLIAMS-MERCEDES	
19	Felipe Massa	FW38/02
77	Valtteri Bottas	FW38/03
	FERRARI	
5	Sebastian Vettel	SF16-H/314
7	Kimi Räikkönen	SF16-H/317
	McLAREN-HONDA	
14	Fernando Alonso	MP4-31/04
22	Jenson Button	MP4-31/03
	FORCE INDIA-MERCEDES	
11	Sergio Pérez	VJM09/02
27	Nico Hülkenberg	VJM09/03
	TORO ROSSO-FERRARI	
26	Daniil Kvyat	STR11/03
55	Carlos Sainz	STR11/01
	RENAULT	
20	Kevin Magnussen	R.S.16/04
46	Sergey Sirotkin	R.S.16/04
30	Jolyon Palmer	R.S.16/05
	MANOR-MERCEDES	
31	Esteban Ocon	MRT05/02
94	Pascal Wehrlein	MRT05/01
	SAUBER-FERRARI	
9	Marcus Ericsson	C35/02
12	Felipe Nasr	C35/03
	HAAS-FERRARI	
8	Romain Grosjean	VF-16/03
21	Esteban Gutiérrez	VF-16/02
50	Charles Leclerc	VF-16/02

ROUND 21 ABU DHABI GP

	MERCEDES	
6	Nico Rosberg	F1 W07/05
44	Lewis Hamilton	F1 W07/04
	RED BULL-TAG HEUER	
3	Daniel Ricciardo	RB12/05
33	Max Verstappen	RB12/03
	WILLIAMS-MERCEDES	
19	Felipe Massa	FW38/02
77	Valtteri Bottas	FW38/03
	FERRARI	
5	Sebastian Vettel	SF16-H/314
7	Kimi Räikkönen	SF16-H/317
	McLAREN-HONDA	
14	Fernando Alonso	MP4-31/04
22	Jenson Button	MP4-31/03
	FORCE INDIA-MERCEDES	
11	Sergio Pérez	VJM09/02
27	Nico Hülkenberg	VJM09/03
34	Alfonso Celis	VJM09/03
	TORO ROSSO-FERRARI	
26	Daniil Kvyat	STR11/03
55	Carlos Sainz	STR11/01
	RENAULT	
20	Kevin Magnussen	R.S.16/04
30	Jolyon Palmer	R.S.16/05
	MANOR-MERCEDES	
31	Esteban Ocon	MRT05/02
42	Jordan King	MRT05/02
94	Pascal Wehrlein	MRT05/01
	SAUBER-FERRARI	
9	Marcus Ericsson	C35/01
12	Felipe Nasr	C35/03
	HAAS-FERRARI	
8	Romain Grosjean	VF-16/03
21	Esteban Gutiérrez	VF-16/02

Photo: Mercedes AMG Petronas F1 Team

FIA FORMULA 1 WORLD CHAMPIONSHIP

GRANDS PRIX 2016

By TONY DODGINS and MAURICE HAMILTON

Main photo: After three successive victories to close out the 2015 season, Nico Rosberg continued his winning ways at the Melbourne opener.
Photo: Peter J. Fox

Inset: Rosberg saw off the challenges of both Hamilton and Vettel to win the 2016 curtain raiser.
Photo: Mercedes AMG Petronas F1 Team

AUSTRALIAN GRAND PRIX

MELBOURNE CIRCUIT

MELBOURNE QUALIFYING

SHORTLY before the start of the 2016 season came news that F1's qualifying format was to change. The powers that be – read Bernie Ecclestone – had decided that the Saturday show needed spicing up and he wanted a few factors that might mix up Sunday's grid. He would have preferred a qualifying race with the finishing order reversed, or the reversal of the top ten post-qualifying, but both proved unpalatable.

The compromise was a new format with a 16-minute Q1, followed by a 15-minute Q2 and a 14-minute Q3. After seven minutes of Q1, the slowest driver would be eliminated every 90 seconds until just 15 of the 22-driver entry remained.

After six minutes of Q2, the same system would operate until just eight drivers were left to go through to Q3. After five minutes of the final period, the same again until just two drivers were left for a pole shootout.

Did it work? No. It was an unmitigated disaster (*see Viewpoint*).

As expected, the new Manor line-up of DTM champion Pascal Wehrlein and Indonesia's first ever GP driver, Rio Haryanto, fell in Q1. It was no surprise, either, to see the Sauber C35s of Felipe Nasr and Marcus Ericsson fail to progress. But the other three eliminations, Red Bull's Daniil Kvyat and the new Haas-Ferraris of Romain Grosjean and Esteban Gutiérrez, which had demonstrated enough pre-season testing pace to suggest that they would be mid-grid contenders, were unexpected.

Kvyat had a compromised out-lap and failed to get enough heat into his super-soft Pirellis, and the new format meant he didn't have time for another run. Grosjean, meanwhile, had been caught in traffic and Gutiérrez had locked up. Still learning the F1 ropes and in the relatively tight confines of Melbourne's garages, Haas failed to turn the pair around quickly enough for a second run. Instead of the expected dramatic on-track suspense, we witnessed drivers 'counted out' while sitting in the pits resigned to their fate. Furthermore, for more than half of the qualifying hour – supposedly one of the most exciting elements of a grand prix weekend – we were focused on what was happening at the back rather than the front.

But Q3 was even worse. The chequered flag was waved at an empty track without a car in sight. If you had paid good money to watch qualifying, you would have been dismayed at why everyone had apparently given up. And why, with five minutes to go, Sebastian Vettel was walking down the pit lane in his jeans, waving at you...

The new countdown system had forced everyone to get in their first runs early to avoid being last when the first cut-off mark was reached, and with many running out of fresh super-softs, there were few second runs. Formula 1 sometimes displays a propensity for shooting itself in the foot, and it had done so spectacularly here.

For the record, Lewis Hamilton took pole, with 0.3s in hand over Mercedes team-mate Nico Rosberg, with Sebastian Vettel's Ferrari 0.8s away. The Mercedes drivers at least made second runs, but Vettel and Ferrari team-mate Kimi Räikkönen elected to save their fresh super-softs for the race, figuring that they had no chance of beating Mercedes to pole position. In contrast to the Mercedes twins, both had been forced into second Q2 runs to be safe.

Rosberg, behind the Ferraris after the first run, on which he'd gone wide at Turn Nine, righted that on his second attempt, making it an all-silver front row, but Hamilton was imperious.

Mercedes had clearly made further strides during the winter with an already superior power train, and its advantage was further magnified by the relatively cool 25-degree track temperature, which played more to its strengths than those of its Maranello rivals.

The fight for 'Best of the Rest' was between Toro Rosso and Williams. Red Bull's junior team now had Ferrari instead of Renault power – albeit 2015-spec units – which, early season at least, suggested they could well give the senior team a run for its money. Max Verstappen's STR11 pipped Felipe Massa's Williams FW38 to fifth, with team-mate Carlos Sainz seventh.

Daniel Ricciardo, with a TAG Heuer-badged Renault, was eighth, just a few hundredths adrift of Sainz and completing the Q3 runners under the new format, which resulted in just eight cars making it through to the final stage of qualifying.

Freedom of tyre choice at the start thus became available to those lining up ninth and tenth rather than 11th and backwards – in this case, the Force Indias of Sergio Pérez and Nico Hülkenberg – which made the opening stint potentially more interesting.

Valtteri Bottas's Williams failed to make it out of Q2, Verstappen having forced the Finn to run harder than optimum on his out-lap, meaning that the FW38's super-softs had gone away before the end of his hot lap. Subsequently a gearbox problem demoted Bottas another five slots.

The McLaren-Hondas still had a power deficit to the top teams – some said as much as 100bhp – but improved energy deployment allowed Fernando Alonso and Jenson Button to qualify 12th and 13th, ahead of Renault and Sauber. Jolyon Palmer, having his F1 debut at Renault, got off to a good start by outqualifying new team-mate Kevin Magnussen, whose F1 career had been revitalised by the non-arrival of Pastor Maldonado's Venezuelan sponsorship funds.

THE first race start of the new season was aborted when Kvyat's Red Bull suffered an electrical failure, making this the second successive Melbourne in which he'd retired before the race had even begun.

New for 2016 was the availability of three Pirelli tyre compounds at each race, instead of the previous two, the aim being to provide more strategic opportunity depending on varying chassis characteristics.

For Australia, the super-soft, soft and medium compounds were on offer, with the top eight still obliged to start on the tyres used in Q2. A one-stop race was generally reckoned to be quickest if the chosen compounds could be made to last, but tyre data was in short supply, Friday's practice sessions having been wet

Of those with free tyre choice – ninth and further back – the Force Indias of Pérez and Hülkenberg started on softs, along with Bottas, Button and both Haas cars, while everyone else opted for super-softs.

When the lights went out, Hamilton was slow away, and while Rosberg's start was better, it was Vettel's Ferrari that made a lightning getaway, the four-times champion arrowing between the Mercs on the run to Turn One. Rosberg ran a little wide, compromising Hamilton, who lightly tagged his front wing on Nico's car, allowing Räikkönen to make it a Ferrari 1-2. Verstappen and Massa also passed the pole man to make Hamilton's afternoon all the more difficult.

Behind came Sainz, Hülkenberg, Ricciardo, Alonso, Palmer, Pérez, Button, Wehrlein (up seven places!), Ericsson, Nasr, Bottas, Grosjean, Haryanto and Gutiérrez. Magnussen's Renault suffered a puncture in close-quarter combat and headed for the pits, while Hülkenberg and Ricciardo also made contact.

It took Hamilton four laps to find a way by Massa's Williams, and Rosberg, even with DRS, was unable to do anything about Räikkönen's Ferrari. The impotence of DRS in Melbourne was further illustrated by a frustrated Lewis radioing in that he couldn't do anything about Verstappen without risking using "too much energy." By which he meant rooting his tyres.

Up front, Vettel opened up a 2.5s gap to his team-mate, who still had Rosberg behind him after a dozen laps. As soon as a pit window appeared, Mercedes brought in Nico and bolted on a new set of soft tyres, getting him back out just ahead of Hülkenberg's Force India.

Ferrari responded by stopping Vettel, figuring that Räikkönen would already have been undercut by the Mercedes. They sent Seb back out on more super-softs, still 1s ahead of Nico.

Verstappen, having asked to pit, but received no response, came in of his own accord. With his tyres not quite ready, however, he suffered a delay. Hamilton now had a clear track, but had lost enough ground to Räikkönen to suggest that he would opt for a different strategy, trying to run long enough to make it through on a single stop.

Räikkönen's tyres had gone off, but Ferrari kept him out – as potentially he might have been needed to help Vettel, who was about to be the meat in a Mercedes sandwich. With Rosberg on his tail, Vettel quickly caught the old-tyred Hamilton and went by with no drama, his better tyres allowing the Ferrari to go around Lewis's outside in Turn Two.

Ferrari brought in Räikkönen on lap 16 for fresh super-softs. He was followed in by Hamilton, who had a set of the most durable mediums fitted – which meant a one-stop run.

For those attempting an undercut strategy, bringing forward the first stop was likely to mean a two-stop race, while Hamilton, Hülkenberg, Pérez and Bottas looked like making it on the one pit visit.

Once the initial stops had shaken out, Vettel's Ferrari, on super-softs, led the soft-shod Rosberg by just over 5s, with Räikkönen losing ground in third place. Hamilton, meanwhile, was passed by the undercutting strategy of Ricciardo, Verstappen and Sainz. Home hero Ricciardo had gone on to new super-softs saved from qualifying and was fourth, although some distance behind Räikkönen's Ferrari.

The added tyre variability made the situation up front interesting. The softs on Rosberg's second-place Mercedes were going to last longer than the super-softs on Vettel's lead Ferrari. But could Vettel use the initial pace advantage to eke

Above: Sebastian Vettel grabs the advantage at the start from Nico Rosberg (*left*) and Kimi Räikkönen.
Photo: Scuderia Ferrari

Left: If the cap fits… Sebastian Vettel jests with former Red Bull team-mate Daniel Ricciardo following rumours that the Australian was a target for Ferrari in 2017.
Photo: Lukas Gorys

Below left: Back in business. Kevin Magnussen returned to F1 duty as leader of the Renault team.
Photos: GP Photo/Peter Nygaard

out a pit stop's advantage? Or, pit just as Rosberg got within undercutting distance and manage to maintain track position in the final stint?

But, just then, came an almighty shunt as Gutiérrez defended against Alonso's closing McLaren-Honda on the flat-out run to Turn Three. Both men went left, Alonso's right front riding up over the Mexican Haas driver's left rear.

Alonso suffered just about every form of impact known to man, including a 46g force that would result in a couple of broken ribs being diagnosed in the days ahead. That he was able to clamber out and give the thumbs-up ("I know my mother watches on TV…") was a huge relief, and testament to the progress in safety that had been made over the previous two decades, not least with the wheel tethers, which did their job admirably.

Given the enormity of the accident, and the widespread carbon-fibre debris, it was a sensible move by the FIA to red-flag the race, meaning that everyone was free to fit new tyres for the remaining 39 laps as they awaited the restart.

When the blankets came off, Mercedes had followed what seemed to be the obvious strategy of bolting on a new set of mediums on which to run to the end. Ferrari, though, had a tendency to lose front tyre temperature early, and as temperatures fell following Melbourne's relatively late start time, Maranello was not as confident of its performance on the medium, which, added to a lack of tyre data from a wet Friday, inclined them towards super-softs, meaning they would have to pit again.

The Red Bull and Toro Rosso teams went for new softs. Further back, it was a good break for ninth-placed Grosjean on Haas's debut, the Frenchman the only driver not to have

pitted before the accident and therefore effectively getting a free stop to go on to mediums. Hamilton, meanwhile, took the opportunity to change his damaged front wing.

At the front, Mercedes had concerns that Rosberg might be vulnerable to Räikkönen at the restart if Kimi switched on the super-softs quicker than Nico's mediums, but the Finn seemed actually to lose ground at first, while Rosberg got the mediums in relatively quickly.

It became immaterial three laps later, however, when Räikkönen trailed into the pits, a healthy airbox fire the result of a turbo failure.

Initially, Vettel used his softer rubber to open up a 3s lead, but that's as far as he went, Rosberg then starting to reduce the deficit. The Mercedes looked to be in the pound seats, but what Rosberg didn't know, thanks to new radio restrictions, was that he had worryingly high front right brake caliper temperatures. The new rules said that the team could only alert him if it became 'dangerous' and, considering there was a cockpit alarm for just that eventuality, Nico was allowed to continue blissfully unaware.

"At one point, we didn't think he would make it to the end and that we would have to retire the car," team principal Toto Wolff explained, "but thankfully it stabilised." The cause was later established to be a piece of debris lodged in the brake duct.

The soft (yellow) Pirelli compound is a higher-working-range tyre, and as the track temperature fell, it was not working effectively on either Ricciardo's Red Bull or the Toro Rossos of Verstappen and Sainz.

While the Toro Rosso pit-wall team was weighing up whether to pit or soldier on, Sainz locked a front, flat-spotted

Above: Having collided with the Haas of Esteban Gutiérrez, Alonso's McLaren hits the wall and begins its terrifying path to destruction.
Photo: Lukas Gorys

Right: Alonso crawls unscathed from the wreckage.

Below right: The battered remains of the McLaren are winched away.

Far right: Fernando walked away with a couple of damaged ribs that would keep him out of the Bahrain GP.
Photos: Peter J. Fox

Top left: Nico Hülkenberg just edged Valtteri Bottas to take seventh for Force India.
Photo: Sahara Force India F1 Team

Above left: Sebastian Vettel's Ferrari on the red-marked super-soft Pirellis is stalked by Nico Rosberg on the yellow softs.
Photo: Scuderia Ferrari

Above: Romain Grosjean's Haas locks a wheel on its way to sixth place.
Photo: Peter J. Fox

Top right: A dream debut come true for Gene Haas and Romain Grosjean.
Photo: WRi2/Jean François Galeron

Above right: Sebastian Vettel takes the opportunity to give Mark Webber a dousing on the podium.

Right: The new qualifying procedure was shambolic, but Mercedes made sure they were at the head of the queue to guarantee their place on the front row of the grid.
Photos: GP Photo/Peter Nygaard

it and informed them he had to pit; he was given the go-ahead. Having switched to mediums, the promising young Spaniard pitted out in touch with Pérez's Force India.

Verstappen, meanwhile, unaware of Sainz's lock-up, saw his team-mate pitting and, as the lead Toro Rosso on the road, believed his stop should have been given priority. He promptly radioed in that he was pitting, but he arrived to find that his mediums were not ready. He was livid to rejoin behind Sainz and immediately let the team know in blue, single-syllable language!

When the Toro Rossos stopped, Hamilton finally found himself in clean air and soon began taking more than a second a lap out of third-placed Ricciardo. Then came Massa, like the Red Bull gang, also discovering that the soft was not the tyre of choice at this precise point. Grosjean, meanwhile, was taking full advantage of his earlier good fortune by keeping Hülkenberg and Bottas behind him, this pair running not far ahead of Jolyon Palmer, making an impressive F1 debut in the Renault.

Sainz relegated Pérez with a fine move into the Turn Nine chicane; Verstappen followed him through on the next lap as he charged to get back on to his team-mate's gearbox. Once he did, he was straight on the radio: "Can I pass him? He's holding me up!"

In fact, there was precious little Sainz could do about that, the pair having caught Palmer's Renault, which was defending staunchly.

When Sainz was told to move over, he developed selective amnesia, which he considered payback for Singapore in 2015, when Max had not complied with a team instruction to do likewise.

This looked like it had every chance of ending in tears… On lap 42, Sainz pulled a move on the increasingly gripless Palmer as they accelerated out of Turn Two, Verstappen also taking advantage as the Renault got off line.

With five laps to go, Sainz locked his brakes at Turn 15 and Verstappen went for it, but the pair made contact. The back of Sainz's car was tagged as Verstappen spun, but both managed to keep going and got to the line ninth and tenth respectively, right with the Hülkenberg/Bottas battle,

which was still behind a fabulous sixth place from Grosjean's debuting Haas! Temperatures were still running high at Toro Rosso a good hour afterwards…

Up front, the outcome had seemed inevitable when Vettel had been unable to drop Rosberg more conclusively on his super-softs, and so it proved. Ferrari brought him in on lap 35 for new softs, and Sebastian rejoined in fourth place, around 10s behind Hamilton, who was still inexorably hauling in Ricciardo.

Meanwhile, Rosberg's brakes were under control, but now he was experiencing a lack of grip from the left rear and backed off to eke out the remaining tyre life. He had that luxury, as Red Bull and Ricciardo eventually gave up the unequal struggle on the softs and pitted for a final run on used super-softs.

And so, despite Hamilton's slow getaway, we now had a Mercedes 1-2, with Vettel gaining on the second Mercedes. Ricciardo kept the home fans in good cheer by closing down Massa on his super-softs into Turn One and retaking fourth.

As the laps ticked down, Vettel's Ferrari got within DRS range of Hamilton, but any chance of salvaging second went out of the window when Sebastian ran wide on to the grass at Turn 15.

Thus the Mercedes steamroller began 2016 in similar fashion to 2015. That said, after a deeply unsatisfactory Saturday qualifying hour had put F1 in the headlines for all the wrong reasons, Sunday at least gave us an entertaining race with strategic interest. Rosberg might have got to the chequer first, but Ferrari had shown pace and, it could be argued, had actually thrown a potential win away by surrendering track position with a conservative strategy at the restart.

Rosberg admitted that it might have been tougher if Ferrari had taken the medium tyre for the restart, but Vettel, ever the team player, defended Maranello's call. "It's easier with hindsight," he said, "but I think it would have been difficult to come away with more than we got." Maybe so, but you did wonder what the downside was to giving it a go? It just might have been a winning start for the boys in red.

Tony Dodgins

VIEWPOINT
ANOTHER FINE MESS...

WHICHEVER way you turned during March, F1 seemed intent on driving itself into the ground. The Australian Grand Prix may have been a lively and intriguing season opener, but everything else about the weekend in Melbourne was riven with suspicion and confusion.

The new qualifying procedures turned out to be an embarrassing shambles. With the vast majority of fans, F1 insiders and anyone with a jot of common sense realising that the sport did not need an empty track at the very moment qualifying should be at its thrilling climax in the closing minutes, it was agreed immediately that the new rules should be scrapped. Good judgement prevailed.

Not so fast. Within 24 hours, there were suggestions that part of the old would merge with part of the new qualifying system – but no one was quite sure which bits would be where. This was the final straw for the Grand Prix Drivers' Association (GPDA). Never one of F1's more voluble groups, preferring to focus on matters of safety rather than upsetting their employers, the drivers stuck their heads above the parapet with an open letter.

Choosing their words carefully and avoiding criticism of anyone in particular, the drivers nevertheless expressed dismay with the state of Formula 1, noting that "some of the recent rule changes are disruptive, do not address the bigger issues our sport is facing and could jeopardise its future success ... the drivers have come to the conclusion that the decision-making process is obsolete and prevents progress being made."

A dismissive response from 85-year-old Bernie Ecclestone proved that the drivers have no political teeth, as F1's irascible chief executive swatted them off like an irritating fly. The teams were never likely to be bothered, since they help drivers maintain the high financial standards to which they have become accustomed.

Qualifying in Australia was a sad reflection of F1's chaotic state.

Maurice Hamilton

2016 FORMULA 1
ROLEX
AUSTRALIAN GRAND PRIX

ROLEX

F1 OFFICIAL TIMEPIECE

MELBOURNE 18–20 MARCH

RACE DISTANCE: 57 laps, 187.822 miles/302.271km

RACE WEATHER: Dry/sunny-overcast (track 27–38°C, air 22–25°C)

ALBERT PARK, MELBOURNE
Circuit: 3.295 miles/5.303km
58 laps
100/62 kmh/mph
Gear
— DRS zone

Turn 13 150/93
Turn 12 235/146
Turn 15 84/52
Turn 14 205/127
Turn 11 226/140
Turn 9 120/75
Turn 8 270/168
Turn 16 180/112
Turn 10 145/90
292/181
Turn 7 186/116
Turn 2 200/124
Turn 6 150/93
325/202
Turn 4 145/90
Turn 1 160/99
Turn 5 239/149
Turn 3 100/62
290/180

RACE – OFFICIAL CLASSIFICATION

Pos.	Driver	Nat.	No.	Entrant	Car/Engine	Tyres	Laps	Time/Retirement	Speed (mph/km/h)	Gap to leader	Fastest race lap	
1	**Nico Rosberg**	D	6	Mercedes AMG Petronas F1 Team	Mercedes F1 W07-Mercedes PU106C V6	P	57	1h 48m 15.565s	104.095/167.525		1m 30.557s	21
2	**Lewis Hamilton**	GB	44	Mercedes AMG Petronas F1 Team	Mercedes F1 W07-Mercedes PU106C V6	P	57	1h 48m 23.625s	103.967/167.318	8.060s	1m 30.646s	48
3	**Sebastian Vettel**	D	5	Scuderia Ferrari	Ferrari SF16-H-059/5 V6	P	57	1h 48m 25.208s	103.941/167.277	9.643s	1m 29.951s	23
4	**Daniel Ricciardo**	AUS	3	Red Bull Racing	Red Bull RB12-TAG Heuer RB12 V6	P	57	1h 48m 39.895s	103.707/166.900	24.330s	1m 28.997s	49
5	**Felipe Massa**	BR	19	Williams Martini Racing	Williams FW38-Mercedes PU106C V6	P	57	1h 49m 14.544s	103.159/166.018	58.979s	1m 32.288s	39
6	**Romain Grosjean**	F	8	Haas F1 Team	Haas VF-16-Ferrari 059/5 V6	P	57	1h 49m 27.646s	102.953/165.687	1m 12.081s	1m 32.862s	48
7	**Nico Hülkenberg**	D	27	Sahara Force India F1 Team	Force India VJM09-Mercedes PU106C V6	P	57	1h 49m 29.764s	102.920/165.633	1m 14.199s	1m 32.833s	49
8	**Valtteri Bottas**	FIN	77	Williams Martini Racing	Williams FW38-Mercedes PU106C V6	P	57	1h 49m 30.718s	102.905/165.609	1m 15.153s	1m 32.725s	51
9	**Carlos Sainz**	E	55	Scuderia Toro Rosso	Toro Rosso STR11-Ferrari 059/4 V6	P	57	1h 49m 31.245s	102.897/165.596	1m 15.680s	1m 31.671s	23
10	**Max Verstappen**	NL	33	Scuderia Toro Rosso	Toro Rosso STR11-Ferrari 059/4 V6	P	57	1h 49m 32.398s	102.879/165.567	1m 16.833s	1m 31.516s	44
11	Jolyon Palmer	GB	30	Renault Sport F1 Team	Renault R.S.16-R.E.16 V6	P	57	1h 49m 38.964s	102.776/165.402	1m 23.399s	1m 32.955s	14
12	Kevin Magnussen	DK	20	Renault Sport F1 Team	Renault R.S.16-R.E.16 V6	P	57	1h 49m 41.171s	102.741/165.346	1m 25.606s	1m 32.452s	45
13	Sergio Pérez	MEX	11	Sahara Force India F1 Team	Force India VJM09-Mercedes PU106C V6	P	57	1h 49m 47.264s	102.646/165.193	1m 31.699s	1m 32.780s	39
14	Jenson Button	GB	22	McLaren Honda	McLaren MP4-31-Honda RA616H V6	P	56			1 lap	1m 31.684s	33
15	Felipe Nasr	BR	12	Sauber F1 Team	Sauber C35-Ferrari 059/5 V6	P	56			1 lap	1m 32.711s	48
16	Pascal Wehrlein	D	94	Manor Racing MRT	Manor MRT05-Mercedes PU106C V6	P	56			1 lap	1m 32.673s	34
	Marcus Ericsson	S	9	Sauber F1 Team	Sauber C35-Ferrari 059/5 V6	P	38	rear tyre			1m 33.892s	15
	Kimi Räikkönen	FIN	7	Scuderia Ferrari	Ferrari SF16-H-059/5 V6	P	21	airbox fire			1m 30.701s	21
	Rio Haryanto	RI	88	Manor Racing MRT	Manor MRT05-Mercedes PU106C V6	P	17	transmission			1m 33.847s	15
	Esteban Gutiérrez	MEX	21	Haas F1 Team	Haas VF-16-Ferrari 059/5 V6	P	16	accident			1m 32.998s	4
	Fernando Alonso	E	14	McLaren Honda	McLaren MP4-31-Honda RA616H V6	P	16	accident			1m 32.553s	14
NS	Daniil Kvyat	RUS	26	Red Bull Racing	Red Bull RB12-TAG Heuer RB12 V6	P		power unit on the parade lap				

Race scheduled for 58 laps, but reduced by a lap due to an aborted start, Kvyat's car having failed at the end of the parade lap.

Race stopped on lap 19, due to the Alonso & Gutiérrez accident, and resumed 19m 22s later. Overall race times include the stoppage time.

Fastest race lap: Daniel Ricciardo on lap 49, 1m 28.997s, 133.291mph/214.510km/h. **Lap record:** Michael Schumacher (Ferrari F2004 V10), 1m 24.125s, 141.010mph/226.933km/h (2004).

21 · WEHRLEIN · Manor | 19 · GROSJEAN · Haas | 17 · NASR · Sauber | 15 · ERICSSON · Sauber | 13 · PALMER · Renault | 11 · ALONSO · McLaren

22 · HARYANTO · Manor
(3-place grid penalty for causing an accident in the pit lane) | 20 · GUTIÉRREZ · Haas | 18 · KVYAT · Red Bull
(did not start) | 16 · BOTTAS · Williams
(5-place grid penalty for replacing the gearbox) | 14 · MAGNUSSEN · Renault | 12 · BUTTON · McLaren

Grid order	1	2	3	4	5	6	7	8	9	10	11	12	13	14	15	16	17	18	19	20	21	22	23	24	25	26	27	28	29	30	31	32	33	34	35	36	37	38	39	40	41	42	43	44	45	46
44 HAMILTON	5	5	5	5	5	5	5	5	5	5	5	5	7	7	7	5	5	5	5	5	5	5	5	5	5	5	5	5	5	5	5	5	5	6	6	6	6	6	6	6	6	6	6	6	6	6
6 ROSBERG	7	7	7	7	7	7	7	7	7	7	7	7	44	44	44	6	6	6	6	6	6	6	6	6	6	6	6	6	6	6	6	6	6	3	3	3	3	3	3	44	44	44	44	44		
5 VETTEL	6	6	6	6	6	6	6	6	6	6	6	6	33	5	5	7	7	7	7	7	3	3	3	3	3	3	3	3	3	3	3	3	3	44	44	44	44	44	44	5	5	5	5	5		
7 RÄIKKÖNEN	33	33	33	33	33	33	33	33	33	33	33	44	6	6	6	3	3	3	33	33	33	33	33	33	33	33	33	44	44	44	5	5	5	5	5	5	19	19	19	19	3					
33 VERSTAPPEN	19	19	19	44	44	44	44	44	44	44	44	6	27	27	27	44	33	33	33	33	33	55	55	55	55	55	55	55	55	44	19	19	19	19	19	19	19	19	19	3	3	3	3	19		
19 MASSA	44	44	44	19	19	19	19	19	19	3	3	27	11	11	11	33	55	55	55	55	55	44	44	44	44	44	44	44	44	8	8	8	8	8	8	8	8	8	8	8	8	8	8	8		
55 SAINZ	55	55	55	55	55	55	55	3	3	19	27	11	33	3	3	55	44	44	44	44	44	19	19	19	19	19	19	8	27	27	27	27	27	27	27	27	27	27	27	27	27	27	27	27		
3 RICCIARDO	27	27	27	27	3	3	3	27	27	27	14	14	3	22	22	33	19	19	19	19	19	19	8	8	77	77	77	77	77	77	77	77	77	77	77	77	77	77	77	77	77	77	77	77		
11 PÉREZ	3	3	3	3	27	27	27	14	14	14	11	22	77	33	55	77	8	8	8	8	27	27	27	27	27	27	27	27	77	30	30	30	30	30	30	30	55	55	55	55	55					
27 HÜLKENBERG	14	14	14	14	14	14	14	11	11	11	22	77	3	55	19	8	77	27	27	27	77	77	77	77	77	77	77	77	55	33	55	55	55	55	55	55	55	55	33	33	33	33				
14 ALONSO	11	11	11	11	11	11	11	22	22	22	30	55	55	77	77	27	27	77	77	77	30	30	30	30	30	30	30	30	30	11	11	33	33	33	33	33	33	33	30	30	30	30	30			
22 BUTTON	22	22	22	22	22	22	22	30	30	30	77	8	19	19	8	21	30	30	30	30	22	22	22	22	22	11	11	11	55	55	33	11	11	11	11	11	11	11	11	11	11	11	11	11		
30 PALMER	30	30	30	30	30	30	94	77	19	19	8	8	21	14	11	11	11	11	11	11	20	20	20	94	94	12	12	20	20	20	20	20	20	20	20	12	12	12	12	12	12	12				
20 MAGNUSSEN	94	94	94	94	94	94	94	9	77	94	8	21	14	11	14	11	9	9	22	22	11	11	11	11	11	20	20	94	94	12	12	12	12	12	12	20	20	20	20	20	20	20	12	12		
9 ERICSSON	9	9	9	9	9	9	9	77	9	9	55	14	14	14	22	30	22	22	20	20	94	94	94	12	12	22	22	22	22	22	22	22	22	22	22	22	22	22	22	22	22	22	22			
77 BOTTAS	12	12	12	12	77	77	77	12	12	8	21	30	30	30	30	9	12	12	12	12	20	20	94	94	12	12	12	22	9	9	9	9	9	9	9	94	94	94	94	94	94	94				
12 NASR	77	77	77	77	12	12	12	8	8	55	88	9	9	9	9	12	94	94	94	94	94	20	94	94	94	12	9	9	9	9	94	94	94	94	94	94	94									
26 KVYAT	8	8	8	8	8	8	8	55	88	21	9	12	12	22	88	20	20	20	94																											
8 GROSJEAN	88	88	88	88	88	88	88	88	88	21	88	94	94	94	94	94	20																													
21 GUTIÉRREZ	21	21	21	21	21	21	21	21	55	12	12	88	88	88	88	88																														
94 WEHRLEIN	20	20	20	20	20	20	20	20	20	20	20	20	20	20	94																															
88 HARYANTO																																														

All results and data © FOM 2016

TIME SHEETS

PRACTICE 1 (FRIDAY)
Weather: Rain/overcast
Temperatures: track 18-28°C, air 16-19°C

Pos.	Driver	Laps	Time
1	Lewis Hamilton	14	1m 29.725s
2	Daniil Kvyat	14	1m 30.146s
3	Daniel Ricciardo	13	1m 30.875s
4	Nico Hülkenberg	8	1m 31.325s
5	Max Verstappen	14	1m 31.720s
6	Nico Rosberg	11	1m 31.814s
7	Fernando Alonso	11	1m 33.060s
8	Jenson Button	16	1m 33.129s
9	Sergio Pérez	6	1m 33.370s
10	Kevin Magnussen	13	1m 34.060s
11	Valtteri Bottas	6	1m 34.550s
12	Felipe Massa	6	1m 34.679s
13	Felipe Nasr	7	1m 34.796s
14	Jolyon Palmer	12	1m 35.477s
15	Marcus Ericsson	6	1m 37.956s
16	Pascal Wehrlein	6	1m 40.401s
17	Kimi Räikkönen	10	1m 40.754s
18	Esteban Gutiérrez	8	1m 41.780s
19	Rio Haryanto	7	1m 43.372s
20	Romain Grosjean	6	1m 43.443s
21	Sebastian Vettel	8	no time
22	Carlos Sainz	3	no time

PRACTICE 2 (FRIDAY)
Weather: Rain/overcast
Temperatures: track 17-21°C, air 15-18°C

Pos.	Driver	Laps	Time
1	Lewis Hamilton	7	1m 38.841s
2	Nico Hülkenberg	8	1m 39.308s
3	Kimi Räikkönen	7	1m 39.486s
4	Daniel Ricciardo	9	1m 39.535s
5	Carlos Sainz	16	1m 39.694s
6	Fernando Alonso	16	1m 39.895s
7	Jenson Button	13	1m 40.008s
8	Sebastian Vettel	7	1m 40.761s
9	Sergio Pérez	8	1m 41.256s
10	Daniil Kvyat	10	1m 42.411s
11	Esteban Gutiérrez	10	1m 42.891s
12	Pascal Wehrlein	25	1m 43.401s
13	Romain Grosjean	8	1m 43.731s
14	Rio Haryanto	22	1m 44.304s
15	Nico Rosberg	4	1m 47.356s
16	Kevin Magnussen	2	no time
17	Jolyon Palmer	5	no time
18	Felipe Massa	2	no time
19	Valtteri Bottas	2	no time
	Marcus Ericsson	-	no time
	Felipe Nasr	-	no time
	Max Verstappen	-	no time

PRACTICE 3 (SATURDAY)
Weather: Dry/overcast
Temperatures: track 29°C, air 20°C

Pos.	Driver	Laps	Time
1	Lewis Hamilton	24	1m 25.624s
2	Nico Rosberg	25	1m 25.800s
3	Sebastian Vettel	25	1m 25.852s
4	Carlos Sainz	28	1m 26.257s
5	Kimi Räikkönen	23	1m 26.435s
6	Max Verstappen	26	1m 26.701s
7	Valtteri Bottas	28	1m 26.730s
8	Daniel Ricciardo	22	1m 26.768s
9	Felipe Massa	28	1m 27.151s
10	Sergio Pérez	22	1m 27.242s
11	Fernando Alonso	20	1m 27.263s
12	Jenson Button	20	1m 27.341s
13	Daniil Kvyat	22	1m 27.430s
14	Marcus Ericsson	26	1m 27.659s
15	Kevin Magnussen	24	1m 27.871s
16	Nico Hülkenberg	22	1m 27.988s
17	Jolyon Palmer	24	1m 28.117s
18	Esteban Gutiérrez	21	1m 28.284s
19	Romain Grosjean	11	1m 28.292s
20	Felipe Nasr	26	1m 28.293s
21	Pascal Wehrlein	18	1m 29.046s
22	Rio Haryanto	23	1m 29.272s

QUALIFYING (SATURDAY)
Weather: Dry/overcast Temperatures: track 24-32°C, air 17-20°C

Pos.	Driver	First	Second	Third	Qualifying Tyre
1	Lewis Hamilton	1m 25.351s	1m 24.605s	1m 23.837s	Super-Soft (new)
2	Nico Rosberg	1m 26.934s	1m 24.796s	1m 24.197s	Super-Soft (new)
3	Sebastian Vettel	1m 26.945s	1m 25.257s	1m 24.675s	Super-Soft (new)
4	Kimi Räikkönen	1m 26.579s	1m 25.615s	1m 25.033s	Super-Soft (new)
5	Max Verstappen	1m 26.934s	1m 25.615s	1m 25.434s	Super-Soft (new)
6	Felipe Massa	1m 25.918s	1m 25.644s	1m 25.458s	Super-Soft (new)
7	Carlos Sainz	1m 27.057s	1m 25.384s	1m 25.582s	Super-Soft (new)
8	Daniel Ricciardo	1m 26.945s	1m 25.599s	1m 25.589s	Super-Soft (new)
9	Sergio Pérez	1m 26.607s	1m 25.753s	no time	
10	Nico Hülkenberg	1m 26.550s	1m 25.865s	no time	
11	Valtteri Bottas	1m 27.135s	1m 25.961s		
12	Fernando Alonso	1m 26.537s	1m 26.125s		
13	Jenson Button	1m 26.740s	1m 26.304s		
14	Jolyon Palmer	1m 27.241s	1m 27.601s		
15	Kevin Magnussen	1m 27.297s	1m 27.742s		
16	Marcus Ericsson	1m 27.435s			
17	Felipe Nasr	1m 27.958s			
18	Daniil Kvyat	1m 28.006s			
19	Romain Grosjean	1m 28.322s			
20	Esteban Gutiérrez	1m 29.606s			
21	Rio Haryanto	1m 29.627s			
22	Pascal Wehrlein	1m 29.642s			

FOR THE RECORD

1st GRAND PRIX: **Rio Haryanto, Jolyon Palmer, Pascal Wehrlein, Haas.**

1st POINTS: **Haas.**

50th POLE POSITION: **Lewis Hamilton.**

80th PODIUM POSITION: **Sebastian Vettel.**

10,000th LAP COMPLETED: **Nico Rosberg.**

DID YOU KNOW?

Rio Haryanto became the first Indonesian to enter F1.

Photo: WRi2/Jean-François Galeron

POINTS

DRIVERS

1	Nico Rosberg	25
2	Lewis Hamilton	18
3	Sebastian Vettel	15
4	Daniel Ricciardo	12
5	Felipe Massa	10
6	Romain Grosjean	8
7	Nico Hülkenberg	6
8	Valtteri Bottas	4
9	Carlos Sainz	2
10	Max Verstappen	1

CONSTRUCTORS

1	Mercedes	43
2	Ferrari	15
3	Williams	14
4	Red Bull	12
5	Haas	8
6	Force India	6
7	Toro Rosso	3

Photos: Peter J. Fox

Qualifying: head-to-head

Rosberg	0	1	Hamilton
Vettel	1	0	Räikkönen
Massa	1	0	Bottas
Ricciardo	1	0	Kvyat
Pérez	1	0	Hülkenberg
Magnussen	0	1	Palmer
Verstappen	1	0	Sainz
Ericsson	1	0	Nasr
Alonso	1	0	Button
Haryanto	1	0	Wehrlein
Grosjean	1	0	Gutiérrez

9 · PÉREZ · Force India

7 · SAINZ · Toro Rosso

5 · VERSTAPPEN · Toro Rosso

3 · VETTEL · Ferrari

1 · HAMILTON · Mercedes

10 · HÜLKENBERG · Force India

8 · RICCIARDO · Red Bull

6 · MASSA · Williams

4 · RÄIKKÖNEN · Ferrari

2 · ROSBERG · Mercedes

Lap chart

47	48	49	50	51	52	53	54	55	56	57	
6	6	6	6	6	6	6	6	6	6	6	1
44	44	44	44	44	44	44	44	44	44	44	2
5	5	5	5	5	5	5	5	5	5	5	3
3	3	3	3	3	3	3	3	3	3	3	4
19	19	19	19	19	19	19	19	19	19	19	5
8	8	8	8	8	8	8	8	8	8	8	6
27	27	27	27	27	27	27	27	27	27	27	7
77	77	77	77	77	77	77	77	77	77	77	8
55	55	55	55	55	55	55	55	55	55	55	9
33	33	33	33	33	33	33	33	33	33	33	10
30	30	30	30	30	30	30	30	30	30	30	
11	11	11	11	11	11	11	11	20	20	20	
20	20	20	20	20	20	20	11	11	11	11	
12	12	12	12	12	12	12	12	*12*	*22*	*22*	
22	22	22	22	22	22	*22*	*22*	*12*	*12*		
94	94	94	94	94	94	94	94	94	94		

6 = Pit stop   9 = Drive-thru penalty

94 = One lap or more behind

▢ Safety car deployed on laps shown

▮ Race red-flagged

RACE TYRE STRATEGIES

PIRELLI

	Driver	Race Stint 1	Race Stint 2	Race Stint 3	Race Stint 4
1	Rosberg	Super-Soft (u): 1-12	Soft (n): 13-18	Medium (n): 19-57	
2	Hamilton	Super-Soft (u): 1-16	Medium (n): 17-18	Medium (u): 19-57	
3	Vettel	Super-Soft (u): 1-13	Super-Soft (n): 14-18	Super-Soft (u): 19-35	Soft (n): 36-57
4	Ricciardo	Super-Soft (u): 1-12	Super-Soft (u): 13-18	Soft (n): 19-42	Super-Soft (u): 43-57
5	Massa	Super-Soft (u): 1-11	Soft (n): 12-18	Medium (n): 19-57	
6	Grosjean	Soft (n): 1-18	Medium (n): 19-57		
7	Hülkenberg	Soft (n): 1-16	Medium (n): 17-18	Medium (u): 19-57	
8	Bottas	Soft (n): 1-17	Medium (n): 18	Medium (u): 19-57	
9	Sainz	Super-Soft (u): 1-8	Soft (n): 9-18	Soft (n): 19-31	Medium (n): 32-57
10	Verstappen	Super-Soft (u): 1-13	Soft (n): 14-18	Soft (n): 19-32	Medium (n): 33-57
11	Palmer	Super-Soft (u): 1-12	Soft (n): 13-18	Medium (n): 19-57	
12	Magnussen	Super-Soft (u): 1	Medium (n): 2-17	Medium (u): 18-57	
13	Pérez	Soft (n): 1-16	Medium (n): 17-18	Medium (u): 19-57	
14	Button	Soft (n): 1-15	Soft (n): 16-18	Super-Soft (n): 19-30	Medium (n): 31-56
15	Nasr	Super-Soft (u): 1-10	Soft (n): 11-18	Medium (n): 19-56	
16	Wehrlein	Super-Soft (n): 1-11	Soft (n): 12-18	Soft (n): 19-32	Medium (n): 33-56
	Ericsson	Super-Soft (n): 1-11	Soft (n): 12-18	Medium (n): 19-27	Medium (n): 28-38 (dnf)
	Räikkönen	Super-Soft (u): 1-16	Super-Soft (n): 17-18	Super-Soft (u): 19-21 (dnf)	
	Haryanto	Super-Soft (u): 1-12	Soft (n): 13-17 (dnf)		
	Gutiérrez	Soft (n): 1-16 (dnf)			
	Alonso	Super-Soft (n): 1-12	Soft (n): 13-16 (dnf)		
NS	Kvyat				

The tyre regulations stipulate that at least two of three dry tyre specifications must be used during a dry race.
Pirelli P Zero logos are colour-coded on the tyre sidewalls: Red = Super-Soft; Yellow = Soft; White = Medium. (n) new (u) used

Photos: Peter J. Fox

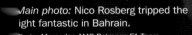

Main photo: Nico Rosberg tripped the light fantastic in Bahrain.
Photo: Mercedes AMG Petronas F1 Team

Inset: 2-0 up to Team Rosberg over Team Hamilton.
Photo: Peter J. Fox

FIA FORMULA 1 WORLD CHAMPIONSHIP · ROUND 2

BAHRAIN GRAND PRIX

SAKHIR QUALIFYING

AFTER Melbourne, everyone knew that the new qualifying system did not work. Righting such things takes time, apparently, so we were stuck with it in Bahrain as well, before reverting to the old system for China.

Although there was still the unsatisfactory scenario of cars being counted out while still in the pits in Q1/ Q2, at least the final Q3 session was more entertaining than Australia, as Ferrari thought its pace strong enough to make two runs rather than go into tyre conservation mode.

On the first of those efforts, Sebastian Vettel actually managed to split the two Mercedes W07s, but then was somewhat dismayed when Lewis Hamilton found fully half a second on his second run to snatch pole position from team-mate Nico Rosberg. The lap actually beat the quickest V10 qualifying lap of Sakhir from 2005!

At a circuit where he is always strong, Rosberg was just 0.08s adrift as Kimi Räikkönen completed the expected Stuttgart/Maranello domination of the front two rows of the grid.

With just eight cars making it into Q3 in this new – soon to be old – format, the remaining contenders were Daniel Ricciardo's Red Bull, the Williams FW38s of Valtteri Bottas and Felipe Massa, and Nico Hülkenberg's Force India.

Ricciardo got everything that could be had from the RB12, the Australian and race engineer Simon Rennie concentrating on a car set-up that paid dividends in the relatively cooler track temperatures of the 6pm qualifying start time.

For team-mate Daniil Kvyat, though, there was huge disappointment as a car that had worked well in the hotter conditions of the final free practice session, failed to translate. The young Russian was the first of those to be eliminated in Q2, meaning 15th start slot. The pressure on him was beginning to mount...

The first of those with freedom of tyre choice for Sunday was Romain Grosjean, 0.15s down on Hülkenberg, after another impressive performance by Haas.

The waters had been calmed at Toro Rosso following the 'misunderstandings' of Melbourne, but the team suspected that Sakhir might be challenging. Not only was there the long straight to address with the 2015-spec Ferrari power unit, but also traction and start-stop performance was at a premium, and the STR11 was par-ticularly adept where downforce was more important. Still, Franz Tost's cars managed tenth and eleventh, Max Verstappen shading Carlos Sainz.

At McLaren, despite two cracked ribs from his spectacular Melbourne shunt, Fernando Alonso had been passed fit to drive by his doctors, but when the FIA doctor surveyed his scans, there was disagreement. The result was reserve driver Stoffel Vandoorne hot-footing it from Japan, where he had been conducting Super Formula testing, for his F1 debut.

Without any experience of Sakhir or any simulator time, the Belgian, a dominant GP2 champion in 2015, was highly impressive, qualifying 12th, some 0.15s quicker than Jenson Button.

The Englishman, aware that everyone's eyes were on the talented rookie, was frustrated. After feeling a bit too much 'push' from the car on his first Q2 run, he asked for more front wing for his second, but tipped the balance too much towards oversteer, with the result that his tyres were past their best before the end of his hot lap.

Esteban Gutiérrez split the McLaren men with the second Haas, a couple of tenths shy of team-mate Grosjean and ahead of an impressive performance from highly-touted DTM champion Pascal Wehrlein in the Manor. The young German managed to beat both Saubers, both Renaults and Pérez's Force India, the Mexican having fallen foul of a logistical mix-up that robbed him of his second run.

Kevin Magnussen missed a weighbridge call in practice and, aware that he would have to start the race from the pit lane, made just a lone run, which was 19th fastest. Jolyon Palmer, meanwhile, was having a struggle with the second of the Regie's entries, a quarter of a second down on the Dane. It was becoming apparent that the chassis had a strong aversion to any bumps and was a handful over kerbs.

Rio Haryanto's Manor was 21st, with Felipe Nasr behind him in the second Sauber.

"I don't know what the issue is," Nasr said, "but the car feels nothing like it did when we tested in Barcelona. It's really unstable under braking, and nothing we try seems to make any difference. I think there's an aero problem somewhere." The young Brazilian was fully a second-and-a-half behind 17th-placed team-mate Marcus Ericsson.

Above: With Fernando Alonso ruled out of action, Stoffel Vandoorne was called up by McLaren Honda for his grand prix debut. He promptly out-qualified team-mate Jenson Button to take 12th on the grid.
Photo: McLaren Honda

Left: Valtteri Bottas qualified in a promising sixth place, but the race only yielded a ninth for the Finn after a first-lap contretemps with Hamilton.
Photo: Williams Martini Racing

Above right: Under scrutiny. The FIA's Jean Todt (*left*) and Charlie Whiting.
Photo: Lukas Gorys

Right: Lewis goes native in Bahrain.
Photo: Peter J. Fox

Far right: Farewell old friend. Ron Dennis, Niki Lauda and fellow journalists raise a glass in memory of former AUTOCOURSE Editor Alan Henry.
Photo: Lukas Gorys

THERE were dramas for the leading protagonists before the starting lights, bright in the twilight sky, even extinguished. Rosberg tried to pull away in second gear on the formation lap and was saved by the anti-stall, but Vettel had no such luck and did not even take the start. On the run between Turns Ten and Eleven, a telltale cloud of smoke from the back of the Ferrari signified a terminal engine problem, which, the team said later, was a different issue to the turbo failure suffered by Räikkönen in Australia. Palmer was another casualty, trailing his Renault back to the pits with a hydraulic problem.

For the second successive race, Hamilton failed to convert his pole position, this time suffering too much wheelspin. Unlike Melbourne, there was no Vettel to take advantage, but Rosberg did, leading into Turn One. If Maranello had a better starting system than Brixworth/Stuttgart, Räikkönen failed to take advantage of it, his finger slipping off the clutch paddle; the resultant rear scrabbling allowed both Williams and Ricciardo's Red Bull to blast by.

At Turn One, Bottas made a late and ill-fated attempt to get down the inside of Hamilton, thumping the Mercedes squarely in the sidepod and knocking it sideways. Lewis suffered floor and wing damage that would compromise the rest of his evening, while Bottas damaged both his front and rear wings, but continued relatively undelayed.

Behind, everyone took evasive action, and Massa was delighted to find himself running second from seventh grid slot! Ricciardo's Red Bull had endplate damage, Button outfumbled Vandoorne amid the confusion, and Hülkenberg

clobbered the back of Verstappen's Toro Rosso and needed to pit for a new front wing.

Across the line at the end of the opening lap, Rosberg doubtless could not believe his luck when his mirrors revealed a healthy advantage and a pair of Williams behind. Then came Ricciardo's Red Bull, Räikkönen's Ferrari, the Haas cars of Grosjean and Gutiérrez, with Hamilton down in eighth place. The rest of the order was Verstappen, Button, Sainz, Pérez, Vandoorne, Wehrlein, Kvyat, Ericsson, Haryanto, Nasr and Magnussen from the pits.

Next time around, Pérez had a go at Sainz going into Turn One, but misjudged it and hit the Toro Rosso, sending both to the pits, Sergio for a new nose and Carlos for a punctured right rear.

With DRS enabled, Hamilton was soon by Grosjean and chasing down the Bottas/Ricciardo/Räikkönen train that was disputing third place. Räikkönen managed to demote Ricciardo on lap six, by which time Rosberg already had almost 7.5s advantage over Massa.

Once it was obvious that Ricciardo could do nothing about the Williams straight-line speed and had fallen prey to the Ferrari, Red Bull pitted him and went on to Pirelli's soft-compound rubber rather than the medium, hinting at a three-stop race.

Williams immediately covered him with Massa, but bolted on a set of the white-walled medium, suggesting that they were trying to get Felipe through on a two-stopper. He rejoined just in front of the Red Bull.

Räikkönen, with more straight-line speed than the Red

Bulls, then managed to tow past Bottas to put the Ferrari up into second, with Hamilton also going past Valtteri on the next lap. There was now just one car between Hamilton and Rosberg, but Lewis, with damage that the team estimated was costing him a significant amount of downforce and as much as a second per lap, could do little about Räikkönen.

Williams now called in Bottas and also put him on the medium tyre, but just then came notification of a drive-through penalty for his first-lap contact with Hamilton. The second pit visit in short order dropped him to the back of the field.

Button was also an early casualty when the McLaren-Honda stopped with an ERS failure. Gutiérrez, running competitively a couple of seconds behind team-mate Grosjean and ahead of Verstappen, joined him on the sidelines with a brake issue.

Räikkönen pitted from second place after 12 laps, a quick stop on to softs getting him out fractionally ahead of Massa/Ricciardo, a situation the Australian used for an opportunistic pass of the Brazilian at Turn Four.

Such was Rosberg's lead that Mercedes was able to pit both cars on the same lap. Rosberg was sent on his way on the soft tyre for an expected three-stopper, while Hamilton was given a set of mediums in the hope that he might be able to run a two-stop race and jump Räikkönen.

He pitted out just behind Massa and Ricciardo, who was about to pass team-mate Kvyat, who had started on softs and was yet to pit. Hamilton was able to demote both the Red Bull and Williams to regain third place in short order.

Further back, after its impressive Melbourne debut, Haas was making more waves (see Viewpoint). The team conducted its first race pit stop (the Melbourne change was done under the red-flag situation) with Grosjean's lone surviving car, which was fitted with another new set of super-softs, the team having a plentiful supply after not making it to Q3. Loving the grip, the French-Swiss soon began closing in on the medium-shod Massa.

Williams was obviously struggling for pace on the harder tyre, the track temperature not dropping sufficiently to the low-20-degree levels that would have brought the rubber into its favourable working range. Hamilton was experiencing the same phenomenon. Initially, he had been closing on Räikkönen, despite running the harder compound, but now was losing ground, so Mercedes pitted him again, went back on to a three-stopper and sent him back out on super-softs.

Ferrari covered that by bringing Räikkönen straight in and doing likewise, having decided that they weren't going to be able to do anything about Rosberg and that second place was all that was on offer this day. Nico stopped a couple of laps later and also went back into the fray on super-softs.

The die was now cast and the podium positions established – Rosberg, Räikkönen, Hamilton – the third and final stops all passing off without incident.

Ricciardo was a solid fourth for Red Bull. Meanwhile, Grosjean, on his super-softs, had passed Massa into Turn One and was going quickly enough to suggest that he could make up enough time for the extra stop his strategy required and still stay ahead of the Williams.

Above: Kimi Räikkönen took advantage of Hamilton's first-lap problems to claim second for Ferrari.
Photo: Scuderia Ferrari

Top left: "I don't believe it!" Sebastian Vettel stands forlornly by his car after the Ferrari failed on the warm-up lap.
Photo: Lukas Gorys

Above left: Lewis Hamilton was lucky to survive his brush with the Williams pair with minimal damage.
Photo: GP Photo/Peter Nygaard

Left: On his impressive debut, Stoffel Vandoorne claimed tenth, and a world championship point.
Photo: McLaren Honda

Above: After surviving an early collision with Nico Hülkenberg, Max Verstappen took a fine sixth place for Toro Rosso, beating the Red Bull of Daniil Kvyat and the Williams of Felipe Massa and Valtteri Bottas.
Photo: WRi2/Beto Issa

Top right: Romain Grosjean went one better than Melbourne to claim fifth place for Haas.
Photo: WRi2/Jean-François Galeron

Above right: Not so fortunate was team-mate Esteban Gutiérrez, who was enduring a character-building start to his season.
Photo: WRi2/Jad Sherif

Right: Second place in Bahrain for Kimi Räikkönen once again.
Photo: Scuderia Ferrari

Massa, in fact, was falling back into the clutches of Verstappen's Toro Rosso, on softs. Then came Vandoorne and the delayed Bottas, with Kvyat bearing down on them, the two Saubers and the two Manors, Werhlein and Haryanto split by Magnussen. The Force Indias and Sainz followed, the Spaniard hampered by floor damage from his earlier assault by Pérez, which ultimately caused him to abandon the uphill struggle just after half-distance.

Verstappen went by Massa into Turn One, and Grosjean used his softer rubber to demote Ricciardo at Turn Four. Red Bull saw that as the signal to pit their man for a new set of softs. Grosjean would have another set of used super-softs before a final stint on the softs and ultimately got to the chequered flag just over 15s behind the Red Bull. You had to factor in that Ricciardo had lost a bit of pace to front wing damage sustained in the opening-lap skirmish, but that was negligible, and it was another strong showing by the American newcomers and deeply impressive.

In fact, you had to go back 40 years and more for a similar impression by a debutant team, strangely enough the UK-based, but American-owned Shadow team, in 1973! Back then, American George Follmer finished in the points, sixth and third in South Africa and Spain respectively after DNFs in the season openers in Argentina and Brazil. Only the first six scored points in those days, and Follmer was the only other unlapped runner in Spain as he followed 70-odd seconds behind the victorious Emerson Fittipaldi Lotus and the late Francois Cevert's Tyrrell. Enough history...

Behind Grosjean, Verstappen was making no impression with the Toro Rosso, but was comfortably clear of Massa, so the team pitted him and went on to the thus far unsuitable mediums in the hope that falling track temperature toward the end of the race might bring the tyres in and allow him to attack the Haas. It didn't happen, though, and in fact, their cars now on the same rubber, Massa began to close in again.

Toro Rosso heeded the warning and brought Verstappen back in to revert to softs with 13 laps to go. The teenager

came out in a Williams sandwich, ahead of Bottas and around 10s adrift of Massa, but irresistibly faster.

Kvyat, having started on softs and with super-softs available thereafter, was closing on Verstappen/Massa. His final stop for his last set of red-walled Pirellis brought him out behind Bottas, but he muscled by at Turn Four. Verstappen made it by Massa into Turn 11 with five laps to go, and Kvyat further demoted the Williams on the very last lap.

In a frustrating race for Williams, Bottas finished ninth; a bit further back, Stoffel Vandoorne scored a point for McLaren-Honda after an impressive GP debut.

Magnussen worked his way through from the back to within a handful of seconds of Vandoorne, a strong effort in a difficult car, with Wehrlein also impressing experienced Manor team principal Dave Ryan by splitting the Saubers as Nasr valiantly struggled on with his unbalanced chassis.

Hamilton's evening's work had been hampered by opening-lap events, the catalyst for which had been another bad start, but which then had spiralled out of his immediate control. Even so, he left Sakhir with food for thought, as Rosberg took a fifth consecutive grand prix victory. Nico had basically won as he pleased, the Ferrari threat extinguished by Vettel's installation-lap woes allied to a bad start made by Räikkönen.

The feel-good stories were Grosjean and Haas, and Verstappen's sixth for Toro Rosso. That was another stand-out performance on a track where power is needed, and let's not forget, the team was using a 2015-spec Ferrari engine.

Red Bull was left eagerly anticipating its updated Renault engine, and Williams had underperformed on the medium tyre. The qualifying debacle had not been quite so awful as in Melbourne, but as the freight crates were packed late on Sunday evening, everyone was looking forward to a return to the old system as the focus of F1's flyaway openers turned towards Shanghai. Its new system had been one of those F1 episodes conducted with the best of intentions, but which had not been properly thought through.

Tony Dodgins

VIEWPOINT
HAAS – MAKING WAVES IN F1

SCORING championship points in your first grand prix is a double-edged sword. Obvious pleasure within your team is matched by resentment beyond it. Newcomers are not supposed to be successful. They should know their place and learn to suffer in the same way that everyone else did – and, in many cases, continue to do so.

Gene Haas and his small team walking into the Melbourne paddock as newcomers and leaving it with eight points was one thing. But to go one better and finish fifth in the next race in Bahrain came close to showing a lack of respect for F1's apparent need for stress and struggle.

The small degree of luck attached to the Australian race was replaced by a Bahrain performance good enough to make previously extended hands of welcome reach for the knife rack.

Even allowing for the fact that Haas would suffer the endless woes expected of a new team at the next race in China, the potential thus far had been sufficient to trigger a mix of apprehension and displeasure among rivals – particularly midfield runners operating with three times as many people on double Haas's estimated $120m budget. It's one thing to be beaten, yet another to have been made to appear inefficient and wanting. To the growing number of discomfited critics, this was not a Haas at all; it was a Ferrari in everything but name.

But Gene Haas had read the regulations and found it was possible to create partnerships with Ferrari for the supply of the power unit and with the Italian constructor Dallara for a purpose-built chassis. Along the way, he discovered that he could call upon Ferrari to provide suspension components and brake ducts.

The likes of Force India, Toro Rosso and McLaren, ranked behind Haas in the constructors' championship after two races, felt uncomfortable, as did Williams, just a few points ahead in the table. All these teams were manufacturing many of the components – known as 'non-listed parts' – that Haas was receiving from Ferrari.

As one established technical director put it, "The term 'constructor' is gradually being eroded."

Maurice Hamilton

2

2016 FORMULA 1
GULF AIR
BAHRAIN
GRAND PRIX

SAKHIR 1–3 APRIL

ROLEX

OFFICIAL TIMEPIECE

BAHRAIN INTERNATIONAL CIRCUIT, SAKHIR
Circuit: 3.363 miles/5.412km, 57 laps
187/116 kmh/mph ⚙ Gear ━ DRS zone

RACE DISTANCE: 57 laps, 191.530 miles/308.238km
RACE WEATHER: Dry/dark (track 26–30°C, air 21–23°C)

All results and data © FOM 2016

RACE – OFFICIAL CLASSIFICATION

Pos.	Driver	Nat.	No.	Entrant	Car/Engine	Tyres	Laps	Time/Retirement	Speed (mph/km/h)	Gap to leader	Fastest race lap	
1	Nico Rosberg	D	6	Mercedes AMG Petronas F1 Team	Mercedes F1 W07-Mercedes PU106C V6	P	57	1h 33m 34.696s	122.804/197.634		1m 34.482s	41
2	Kimi Räikkönen	FIN	7	Scuderia Ferrari	Ferrari SF16-H-059/5 V6	P	57	1h 33m 44.978s	122.580/197.273	10.282s	1m 35.158s	39
3	Lewis Hamilton	GB	44	Mercedes AMG Petronas F1 Team	Mercedes F1 W07-Mercedes PU106C V6	P	57	1h 34m 04.844s	122.148/196.578	30.148s	1m 34.677s	43
4	Daniel Ricciardo	AUS	3	Red Bull Racing	Red Bull RB12-TAG Heuer RB12 V6	P	57	1h 34m 37.190s	121.452/195.458	1m 02.494s	1m 36.064s	44
5	Romain Grosjean	F	8	Haas F1 Team	Haas VF-16-Ferrari 059/5 V6	P	57	1h 34m 52.995s	121.115/194.916	1m 18.299s	1m 36.095s	42
6	Max Verstappen	NL	33	Scuderia Toro Rosso	Toro Rosso STR11-Ferrari 059/4 V6	P	57	1h 34m 55.625s	121.059/194.826	1m 20.929s	1m 35.504s	49
7	Daniil Kvyat	RUS	26	Red Bull Racing	Red Bull RB12-TAG Heuer RB12 V6	P	56			1 lap	1m 35.678s	36
8	Felipe Massa	BR	19	Williams Martini Racing	Williams FW38-Mercedes PU106C V6	P	56			1 lap	1m 37.560s	31
9	Valtteri Bottas	FIN	77	Williams Martini Racing	Williams FW38-Mercedes PU106C V6	P	56			1 lap	1m 37.077s	37
10	Stoffel Vandoorne	B	47	McLaren Honda	McLaren MP4-31-Honda RA616H V6	P	56			1 lap	1m 36.121s	44
11	Kevin Magnussen	DK	20	Renault Sport F1 Team	Renault R.S.16-R.E.16 V6	P	56			1 lap	1m 36.730s	40
12	Marcus Ericsson	S	9	Sauber F1 Team	Sauber C35-Ferrari 059/5 V6	P	56			1 lap	1m 38.003s	32
13	Pascal Wehrlein	D	94	Manor Racing MRT	Manor MRT05-Mercedes PU106C V6	P	56			1 lap	1m 35.448s	43
14	Felipe Nasr	BR	12	Sauber F1 Team	Sauber C35-Ferrari 059/5 V6	P	56			1 lap	1m 35.360s	49
15	Nico Hülkenberg	D	27	Sahara Force India F1 Team	Force India VJM09-Mercedes PU106C V6	P	56			1 lap	1m 35.188s	53
16	Sergio Pérez	MEX	11	Sahara Force India F1 Team	Force India VJM09-Mercedes PU106C V6	P	56			1 lap	1m 36.067s	39
17	Rio Haryanto	RI	88	Manor Racing MRT	Manor MRT05-Mercedes PU106C V6	P	56			1 lap	1m 36.685s	47
	Carlos Sainz	E	55	Scuderia Toro Rosso	Toro Rosso STR11-Ferrari 059/4 V6	P	29	accident damage			1m 38.408s	22
	Esteban Gutiérrez	MEX	21	Haas F1 Team	Haas VF-16-Ferrari 059/5 V6	P	9	brakes			1m 39.341s	2
	Jenson Button	GB	22	McLaren Honda	McLaren MP4-31-Honda RA616H V6	P	6	power unit			1m 39.427s	3
NS	Sebastian Vettel	D	5	Scuderia Ferrari	Ferrari SF15-H-059/5 V6	P		power unit on the parade lap			no time	
NS	Jolyon Palmer	GB	30	Renault Sport F1 Team	Renault R.S.16-R.E.16 V6	P		hydraulics on the parade lap			no time	

Fastest race lap: Nico Rosberg on lap 41, 1m 34.482s, 128.133mph/206.210km/h.

Lap record: Michael Schumacher (Ferrari F2004 V10), 1m 30.252s, 134.263mph/216.074km/h (2004, 3.366-mile/5.417km circuit).

Lap record (current configuration): Pedro de la Rosa (McLaren MP4-20-Mercedes V10), 1m 31.447s, 132.386mph/213.054km/h (2005).

21 · NASR · Sauber

19 · PALMER · Renault
(in pit lane; did not start)

17 · ERICSSON · Sauber

15 · KVYAT · Red Bull

13 · GUTIÉRREZ · Haas

11 · SAINZ · Toro Rosso

22 · MAGNUSSEN · Renault
(required to start from pit lane – failed to stop for weighing in P2)

20 · HARYANTO · Manor

18 · PÉREZ · Force India

16 · WEHRLEIN · Manor

14 · BUTTON · McLaren

12 · VANDOORNE · McLaren

Grid order	1	2	3	4	5	6	7	8	9	10	11	12	13	14	15	16	17	18	19	20	21	22	23	24	25	26	27	28	29	30	31	32	33	34	35	36	37	38	39	40	41	42	43	44	45	46
44 HAMILTON	6	6	6	6	6	6	6	6	6	6	6	6	6	6	6	6	6	6	6	6	6	6	6	6	6	6	6	6	6	6	6	6	6	6	6	6	6	6	6	44	6	6	6	6	6	6
6 ROSBERG	19	19	19	19	19	19	7	7	7	7	7	7	44	7	7	7	7	7	7	7	7	7	7	7	7	7	7	7	7	7	7	7	7	7	7	7	7	44	44	6	44	7	7	7	7	7
5 VETTEL	77	77	77	77	77	77	19	44	44	44	44	26	26	3	44	44	44	44	44	44	44	44	44	44	44	44	44	44	44	44	44	44	44	7	7	7	44	44	44	44
7 RÄIKKÖNEN	3	3	3	3	3	7	77	8	8	8	8	26	7	3	44	44	3	3	3	3	3	8	8	8	19	3	3	3	3	3	3	3	3	3	3	3	3	3	33	33	33	3
3 RICCIARDO	7	7	7	7	7	44	44	77	33	33	26	19	3	19	26	19	8	8	8	8	8	3	33	33	19	3	26	26	26	8	8	8	8	8	8	8	33	33	3	3	3	33
77 BOTTAS	8	8	8	44	44	8	8	33	26	26	19	3	19	44	19	8	19	19	19	33	33	33	33	19	19	26	19	8	8	26	33	33	33	33	33	19	19	19	19	8
19 MASSA	44	44	44	8	3	21	47	47	94	3	9	8	33	33	33	33	47	26	7	8	33	33	33	33	26	19	19	19	19	19	26	26	26	8	8	19
27 HÜLKENBERG	21	21	21	21	21	26	94	19	9	9	33	33	26	47	47	47	47	47	47	47	47	47	3	77	8	33	77	77	77	77	47	47	47	26	8	26	77	77
8 GROSJEAN	33	33	33	33	33	47	21	12	3	94	20	47	77	77	77	77	77	26	77	9	33	77	47	47	47	47	26	26	26	47	47	77	77	77	26	26
33 VERSTAPPEN	22	22	22	22	22	26	94	9	9	20	33	47	77	77	12	12	9	9	26	26	26	77	3	9	33	9	9	19	19	19	77	20	20	20	77	77	77	9	9	47	47
55 SAINZ	55	47	47	47	47	47	94	12	19	12	88	47	11	27	12	12	9	9	12	9	9	12	47	11	11	11	20	9	9	9	9	9	9	47	47	47	9	9
47 VANDOORNE	11	26	26	26	26	12	9	3	20	11	11	27	12	94	9	94	26	12	12	12	12	94	47	12	12	20	20	11	27	94	77	77	94	94	12	12	20	20
21 GUTIÉRREZ	47	94	94	94	94	9	19	20	88	33	88	77	94	9	94	20	26	94	94	94	94	20	11	94	11	11	27	27	27	11	77	94	94	12	12	20	20	12
22 BUTTON	94	12	12	12	12	20	3	88	11	47	27	12	11	27	20	20	20	20	20	20	20	11	11	47	47	94	27	20	9	94	11	11	12	12	20	20	27	27	27	12
26 KVYAT	26	9	9	9	9	88	20	77	27	27	77	94	9	20	27	88	88	88	88	88	11	11	20	88	88	88	88	27	88	88	94	94	94	77	12	11	27	27	11	94	94	94
94 WEHRLEIN	27	20	20	20	20	3	88	11	47	77	12	20	88	11	11	11	11	88	88	88	27	27	27	20	9	94	12	12	12	12	27	88	88	11	11	94	11	11	11
9 ERICSSON	9	88	88	88	88	88	27	11	27	77	12	94	88	11	11	12	27	27	27	27	27	20	20	88	94	12	88	88	88	88	88	11	11	88	88	88	88	88
11 PÉREZ	88	11	27	27	27	27	11	27	21	55	55	55	55	55	55	55	55	55	55	55	55	55	55	55	55	55
30 PALMER	12	27	11	11	11	11	55	55	55
88 HARYANTO	20	55	55	55	55	55
12 NASR						
20 MAGNUSSEN						

TIME SHEETS

FOR THE RECORD

1st GRAND PRIX: Stoffel Vandoorne

1st POINT: Stoffel Vandoorne

5,000th KM LED: Nico Rosberg

PRACTICE 1 (FRIDAY)

Weather: Dry/sunny-overcast
Temperatures: track 29–33°C, air 22–23°C

Pos.	Driver	Laps	Time
1	Nico Rosberg	24	1m 32.294s
2	Lewis Hamilton	24	1m 32.799s
3	Kimi Räikkönen	16	1m 34.128s
4	Daniel Ricciardo	27	1m 34.461s
5	Daniil Kvyat	30	1m 34.541s
6	Nico Hülkenberg	28	1m 34.601s
7	Carlos Sainz	21	1m 34.793s
8	Max Verstappen	19	1m 34.860s
9	Romain Grosjean	18	1m 35.000s
10	Felipe Massa	19	1m 35.006s
11	Sebastian Vettel	14	1m 35.073s
12	Valtteri Bottas	21	1m 35.174s
13	Esteban Gutiérrez	19	1m 35.309s
14	Jenson Button	28	1m 35.440s
15	Kevin Magnussen	27	1m 35.490s
16	Marcus Ericsson	30	1m 35.728s
17	Pascal Wehrlein	26	1m 36.371s
18	Stoffel Vandoorne	25	1m 36.392s
19	Felipe Nasr	24	1m 36.719s
20	Jolyon Palmer	28	1m 36.939s
21	Alfonso Celis	23	1m 37.287s
22	Rio Haryanto	27	1m 37.714s

QUALIFYING (SATURDAY)

Weather: Dry/dusk-dark Temperatures: track 26–28°C, air 21–23°C

Pos.	Driver	First	Second	Third	Qualifying Tyre
1	Lewis Hamilton	1m 31.391s	1m 30.039s	1m 29.493s	Super-Soft (new)
2	Nico Rosberg	1m 31.325s	1m 30.535s	1m 29.570s	Super-Soft (new)
3	Sebastian Vettel	1m 31.636s	1m 30.409s	1m 30.012s	Super-Soft (new)
4	Kimi Räikkönen	1m 31.685s	1m 30.559s	1m 30.244s	Super-Soft (new)
5	Daniel Ricciardo	1m 31.403s	1m 31.122s	1m 30.854s	Super-Soft (new)
6	Valtteri Bottas	1m 31.672s	1m 30.931s	1m 31.153s	Super-Soft (new)
7	Felipe Massa	1m 32.045s	1m 31.374s	1m 31.155s	Super-Soft (new)
8	Nico Hülkenberg	1m 31.987s	1m 31.604s	1m 31.620s	Super-Soft (new)
9	Romain Grosjean	1m 32.005s	1m 31.756s		
10	Max Verstappen	1m 31.888s	1m 31.772s		
11	Carlos Sainz	1m 31.716s	1m 31.816s		
12	Stoffel Vandoorne	1m 32.472s	1m 31.934s		
13	Esteban Gutiérrez	1m 32.118s	1m 31.945s		
14	Jenson Button	1m 31.976s	1m 31.998s		
15	Daniil Kvyat	1m 32.559s	1m 32.241s		
16	Pascal Wehrlein	1m 32.806s			
17	Marcus Ericsson	1m 32.840s			
18	Sergio Pérez	1m 32.911s			
19	Kevin Magnussen	1m 33.181s			
20	Jolyon Palmer	1m 33.438s			
21	Rio Haryanto	1m 34.190s			
22	Felipe Nasr	1m 34.388s			

PRACTICE 2 (FRIDAY)

Weather: Dry/dark
Temperatures: track 23–25°C, air 20–21°C

Pos.	Driver	Laps	Time
1	Nico Rosberg	38	1m 31.001s
2	Lewis Hamilton	32	1m 31.242s
3	Jenson Button	32	1m 32.281s
4	Max Verstappen	31	1m 32.406s
5	Kimi Räikkönen	38	1m 32.452s
6	Sebastian Vettel	26	1m 32.650s
7	Daniil Kvyat	34	1m 32.703s
8	Valtteri Bottas	39	1m 32.792s
9	Daniel Ricciardo	23	1m 32.870s
10	Felipe Massa	36	1m 32.873s
11	Stoffel Vandoorne	30	1m 32.999s
12	Esteban Gutiérrez	31	1m 33.129s
13	Carlos Sainz	36	1m 33.177s
14	Romain Grosjean	23	1m 33.384s
15	Sergio Pérez	35	1m 33.406s
16	Kevin Magnussen	34	1m 33.447s
17	Nico Hülkenberg	37	1m 33.570s
18	Jolyon Palmer	35	1m 33.640s
19	Pascal Wehrlein	21	1m 33.953s
20	Marcus Ericsson	31	1m 34.224s
21	Felipe Nasr	34	1m 34.477s
22	Rio Haryanto	33	1m 34.562s

PRACTICE 3 (SATURDAY)

Weather: Dry/sunny
Temperatures: track 35–36°C, air 25–26°C

Pos.	Driver	Laps	Time
1	Sebastian Vettel	22	1m 31.683s
2	Kimi Räikkönen	13	1m 31.723s
3	Nico Rosberg	18	1m 32.104s
4	Lewis Hamilton	14	1m 32.160s
5	Valtteri Bottas	18	1m 32.675s
6	Romain Grosjean	14	1m 33.082s
7	Daniil Kvyat	10	1m 33.113s
8	Esteban Gutiérrez	14	1m 33.337s
9	Felipe Massa	18	1m 33.363s
10	Daniel Ricciardo	20	1m 33.519s
11	Marcus Ericsson	16	1m 33.569s
12	Kevin Magnussen	9	1m 33.617s
13	Jenson Button	12	1m 33.704s
14	Stoffel Vandoorne	11	1m 33.744s
15	Max Verstappen	20	1m 33.778s
16	Carlos Sainz	20	1m 34.003s
17	Felipe Nasr	15	1m 34.013s
18	Nico Hülkenberg	16	1m 34.128s
19	Sergio Pérez	15	1m 34.281s
20	Jolyon Palmer	9	1m 34.424s
21	Rio Haryanto	15	1m 35.546s
22	Pascal Wehrlein	16	1m 35.724s

DID YOU KNOW?

This was the 19th time that a driver had won the first two races of an F1 season. On all but four of the previous occasions, the driver became champion that season.

Vandoorne was the first Belgian to score points since Thierry Boutsen in Australia, 1992. He also became the first ever F1 grand prix driver to race car No. 47.

Photo: McLaren Honda

POINTS

DRIVERS

1	Nico Rosberg	50
2	Lewis Hamilton	33
3	Daniel Ricciardo	24
4	Kimi Räikkönen	18
5	Romain Grosjean	18
6	Sebastian Vettel	15
7	Felipe Massa	14
8	Max Verstappen	9
9	Nico Hülkenberg	6
10	Daniil Kvyat	6
11	Valtteri Bottas	6
12	Carlos Sainz	2
13	Stoffel Vandoorne	1

CONSTRUCTORS

1	Mercedes	83
2	Ferrari	33
3	Red Bull	30
4	Williams	20
5	Haas	18
6	Toro Rosso	11
7	Force India	6
8	McLaren	1

Photos: Peter J. Fox

Qualifying: head-to-head

Rosberg	0	2	Hamilton
Vettel	2	0	Räikkönen
Massa	1	1	Bottas
Ricciardo	2	0	Kvyat
Pérez	1	1	Hülkenberg
Magnussen	1	1	Palmer
Verstappen	2	0	Sainz
Ericsson	2	0	Nasr
Alonso	1	0	Button
Button	0	1	Vandoorne
Haryanto	1	1	Wehrlein
Grosjean	2	0	Gutiérrez

9 · GROSJEAN · Haas

7 · MASSA · Williams

5 · RICCIARDO · Red Bull

3 · VETTEL · Ferrari
(did not start)

1 · HAMILTON · Mercedes

10 · VERSTAPPEN · Toro Rosso

8 · HÜLKENBERG · Force India

6 · BOTTAS · Williams

4 · RÄIKKÖNEN · Ferrari

2 · ROSBERG · Mercedes

(Lap chart)

47	48	49	50	51	52	53	54	55	56	57	
6	6	6	6	6	6	6	6	6	6	6	1
7	7	7	7	7	7	7	7	7	7	7	2
44	44	44	44	44	44	44	44	44	44	44	3
3	3	3	3	3	3	3	3	3	3	3	4
8	8	8	8	8	8	8	8	8	8	8	5
19	19	19	19	33	33	33	33	33	33	33	6
33	33	33	33	19	19	19	19	19	19	26	7
77	77	77	26	26	26	26	26	26	19		8
26	26	26	77	77	77	77	77	77	77		9
47	47	47	47	47	47	47	47	47	47	47	10
9	9	9	20	20	20	20	20	20	20		
20	20	20	9	9	9	9	9	9			
27	27	27	27	94	94	94	94	94	94		
94	94	94	94	11	11	11	11	11	12		
11	11	11	11	27	12	12	12	27	27		
12	12	12	12	12	27	27	27	27	11		
88	88	88	88	88	88	88	88	88	88	88	

6 = Pit stop   9 = Drive-thru penalty
94 = One lap or more behind

RACE TYRE STRATEGIES

PIRELLI

	Driver	Race Stint 1	Race Stint 2	Race Stint 3	Race Stint 4	Race Stint 5
1	Rosberg	Super-Soft (u): 1–13	Soft (n): 14–30	Super-Soft (u): 31–39	Soft (n): 40–57	
2	Räikkönen	Super-Soft (u): 1–12	Soft (n): 13–29	Super-Soft (u): 30–37	Soft (n): 38–57	
3	Hamilton	Super-Soft (u): 1–13	Medium (n): 14–28	Super-Soft (u): 29–41	Soft (n): 42–57	
4	Ricciardo	Super-Soft (u): 1–6	Soft (n): 7–24	Soft (n): 25–42	Medium (n): 43–57	
5	Grosjean	Super-Soft (n): 1–11	Super-Soft (u): 12–27	Super-Soft (u): 28–40	Soft (u): 41–57	
6	Verstappen	Super-Soft (u): 1–10	Soft (n): 11–26	Medium (n): 27–46	Super-Soft (u): 47–57	
7	Kvyat	Soft (n): 1–16	Soft (n): 17–34	Super-Soft (u): 35–44	Super-Soft (u): 45–56	
8	Massa	Super-Soft (u): 1–7	Medium (n): 8–29	Medium (n): 30–56		
9	Bottas	Super-Soft (u): 1–8	Medium (u): 9–29	Medium (u): 10–34	Soft (u): 35–56	
10	Vandoorne	Super-Soft (u): 1–9	Soft (n): 10–25	Soft (n): 26–41	Super-Soft (u): 42–56	
11	Magnussen	Soft (n): 1–12	Super-Soft (u): 13–24	Super-Soft (u): 25–38	Super-Soft (u): 39–56	
12	Ericsson	Soft (n): 1–13	Soft (n): 14–29	Medium (u): 30–56		
13	Wehrlein	Soft (n): 1–10	Soft (n): 11–29	Super-Soft (u): 30–41	Super-Soft (u): 42–56	
14	Nasr	Soft (n): 1–10	Soft (n): 11–30	Medium (u): 31–47	Super-Soft (u): 48–56	
15	Hülkenberg	Super-Soft (u): 1	Soft (n): 2–16	Medium (u): 17–35	Super-Soft (u): 36–51	Super-Soft (u): 52–56
16	Pérez	Super-Soft (n): 1–2	Super-Soft (n): 3–14	Soft (n): 15–37	Super-Soft (u): 38–56	
17	Haryanto	Soft (n): 1–2	Soft (u): 13–31	Medium (n): 32–44	Super-Soft (u): 45–56	
	Sainz	Soft (n): 1–2	Medium (n): 3–20	Soft (n): 21–29 (dnf)		
	Gutiérrez	Super-Soft (n): 1–8	Super-Soft (n): 9 (dnf)			
	Button	Super-Soft (n): 1–6 (dnf)				
NS	Vettel					
NS	Palmer					

The tyre regulations stipulate that at least two of three dry tyre specifications must be used during a dry race.
Pirelli P Zero logos are colour-coded on the tyre sidewalls: Red = Super-Soft; Yellow = Soft; White = Medium. (n) new (u) used

CHINESE GRAND PRIX

SHANGHAI CIRCUIT

MERCIFULLY, we were back to the 'old-style' qualifying system as the important hour ticked around on Saturday against a smoggy backdrop of leaden skies and a track that had pretty much dried after earlier rain. Only a patch of wet remained on the main straight, an area shaded by Shanghai International Circuit's distinctive 'wing' structure.

There was immediate Q1 drama for Lewis Hamilton, with a sudden loss of power, and for Pascal Wehrlein, who lost the Manor trying to traverse the wet patch hard on the gas with his DRS wide open. He found himself clattering the barrier on the left-hand side when the car got away from him. During the interruption, Mercedes identified an ERS-H failure, meaning that Hamilton would start from the back...

Nico Rosberg was now a shoo-in for pole, and such was the W07's margin of superiority that Nico was able to comfortably make it through to Q3 using Pirelli's soft-compound rubber rather than the super-softs, which were around a second a lap quicker, putting him in even better shape for Sunday.

Ferrari had enough pace to have done likewise, but whereas Mercedes had opted for five sets of softs for Rosberg when the tyre selections were made (pre-Christmas), Ferrari had chosen just four soft sets for Sebastian Vettel and Kimi Räikkönen. Factoring in the tyres used in practice as well meant they wouldn't have had two sets left for the race.

Thus the Ferraris topped Q2 on their super-softs, Nico Hülkenberg having interrupted the session when the left front wheel deserted his Force India. The resultant red flag was bad news for the likes of Felipe Massa and the McLaren-Honda drivers, who were on hot laps and ironically secured the Q3 passage of both Force Indias, although obviously Hülkenberg could not take part, and to add insult to injury he was the recipient of a three-place grid penalty as Force India was hit for unsafe release.

Through to the Q3 shootout, which was back to ten cars, were Rosberg, both Ferraris, the Red Bulls, Toro Rossos and Force Indias, plus Valtteri Bottas's Williams.

In the heat of FP2 on Friday afternoon, Ferrari had shown impressive pace on the super-soft, but with track temperature for Q3 down at around 23–24 degrees, it remained to be seen whether the red cars would still offer a challenge.

At first, it appeared that way, as Räikkönen shaded Rosberg after their first runs, although both drivers locked up at the Turn 14 hairpin. Sebastian Vettel had yet to reveal his hand, electing for just the one Q3 run to save his super-softs for Sunday. Daniel Ricciardo's Red Bull, meanwhile, was

about 0.3 second down after a first run on a set of used super-softs, which was promising.

On his second run, Rosberg made no mistake, a 1m 35.402s lap giving him pole by more than half a second. And, amazingly, joining him on the front row was Ricciardo's Red Bull with 1m 35.917s, six-hundredths quicker than Räikkönen's Ferrari.

It was a fine lap by the delighted Aussie, who refined the balance of the RB12 throughout the session, and gratifyingly closer to the Mercedes pace, but neither Räikkönen nor Vettel had got it properly together. Both lost time at the Turn 14 hairpin again, and Vettel, almost three-tenths down on his team-mate, was annoyed: "That was not my best lap of the weekend, and I probably asked too much of the tyres in the first sector. I thought I could do the same job with just the one run, but it didn't work out that way, which is frustrating because second was up for grabs."

In fact, the four-times champion was just 0.05s clear of Bottas's Williams. This was a fine effort by the Finn, who had been significantly quicker than team-mate Massa from the off, although Felipe had fallen foul of the Hülkenberg red flag in Q2. You did also wonder quite how much Massa's confidence had been shaken by two left rear tyre failures in Friday practice, caused by the rear brake ducts fouling the inner sidewall.

Daniil Kvyat was just a tenth shy of Bottas with the second Red Bull, but Ricciardo's front-row time, almost half a second quicker, put the young Russian somewhat in the shade. In fairness to Kvyat, though, his time was set on used super-softs and was still a decent effort.

Then there was an almost half-second gap to Sergio Pérez's Force India, a couple of hundredths in front of the Toro Rosso of Carlos Sainz, who had three-tenths in hand over team-mate Max Verstappen.

Fernando Alonso was particularly frustrated by the red flag for Hülkenberg's three-wheeled Force India, reckoning that McLaren-Honda had had a real shot at Q3 for the first time. He and team-mate Jenson Button lined up just behind Massa.

After the highs of Melbourne and Bahrain, it was back down to earth for Haas, with Romain Grosjean complaining of "no grip whatsoever." The Frenchman could not generate any tyre temperature, found the chassis correspondingly unbalanced and had plenty to say about what he considered to be unnecessarily high minimum tyre pressure recommendations from Pirelli, 23.5psi at the front and 21psi rear. It was becoming apparent that the Haas chassis was very benign in its tyre usage.

Above: Max Verstappen put his Toro Rosso into Q3.

Above left: Carlos Sainz negotiates the damp main straight.
Photos: Peter J. Fox

Top left: Fernando Alonso was back in the cockpit after missing the race in Bahrain.
Photo: McLaren Honda

Top: Marcus Ericsson makes the best of the wet in his Sauber.
Photo: Sauber F1 Team

Left: Kimi Räikkönen claimed third place on the grid, ahead of team-mate Sebastian Vettel.
Photo: Scuderia Ferrari

Above far left: Thumbs up from Ricciardo and Rosberg after securing the front row in Shanghai.

Opening spread: Three races, three wins in a perfect start to 2016. It was Nico Rosberg's sixth successive grand prix victory, matching the feats of Alberto Ascari, Sebastian Vettel and Michael Schumacher
Photos: Peter J. Fox

WITH Rosberg starting the race on the soft tyre rather than the super-soft, courtesy of Merc's superiority-afforded Q2 strategy, there was every chance that the extra grip from Ricciardo's super-softs would allow the Red Bull to lead, however temporarily, and so it proved as they headed down into the tightening Turns 1-2-3 'snail'.

Behind, Räikkönen briefly locked up and ran deep to the outside of Turn One, with Vettel on his inside. Kvyat, spotting an opportunity, rocketed his Red Bull down the inside of both, pincering Vettel and causing him to turn back out again, whereupon he made contact with his team-mate. Räikkönen was punted sideways into a light contact with the fleeing Kvyat and suffered a puncture, while Vettel lost a wing endplate and dropped to eighth.

There were repercussions for those behind trying to pick their way through the confusion: Ericsson's Sauber clobbered the nose of Grosjean's Haas, and team-mate Nasr ran into Hamilton's Mercedes, coming through from the back. The impact folded the Merc's nose under the car and sent Lewis back to the pits.

Across the line at the end of the frantic lap, Ricciardo led from Rosberg, then Kvyat, Pérez, Hülkenberg, Sainz and the delayed Vettel, who had outbraked Button's McLaren into the Turn 14 hairpin. Then came the Williamses of Massa and Bottas, Verstappen, Ericsson, Alonso, Magnussen, Wehrlein, Palmer, Gutiérrez and Haryanto. Heading for the pits, meanwhile, were Räikkönen, Hamilton, Grosjean and Nasr.

On the second lap, Ricciardo ran over a piece of debris from Hamilton's wing, which punctured his left rear and resulted in the Australian also heading for the pits, handing Rosberg a lead he would never lose. To avoid any further such occurrences, the safety car was deployed on lap four, which shuffled the pack.

Rosberg, of course, having started on the soft, didn't need to stop, which also went for those outside the top ten who had started on the more durable yellow-walled Pirelli. In track temperatures of more than 40 degrees, the super-softs used by the rest of the top ten qualifiers were quicker initially, but degraded rapidly and were reckoned to be slower than the soft tyre after around five laps. Thus all the super-soft brigade filed into the pits for softs, except Vettel, who had saved a new set of super-softs by doing just the one Q3 run and now took them to try to assist his way back through the traffic.

Mercedes, meanwhile, decided to bring in Hamilton, change his softs for super-softs, do a single lap behind the safety car and then call him back in to revert to softs, thereby getting the requirement to run the super-soft out of the way and allowing him fresh softs all the way to the end. But then, as he did his sole lap on the red-walled tyre, the team discovered a deep cut in one of the softs that had just come off, leaving him with just two sets for the 51 laps remaining, which was going to be difficult.

As everyone pitted, there was an entertaining cameo in the pit lane as Vettel took to the grass to pass Sainz and Hülkenberg before the pit entry line.

What happened here was that Hülkenberg, mindful that team-mate Pérez had pitted ahead of him, was in no great hurry to be stacked while the team turned the Mexican around, so was coming in more slowly than usual. Vettel, appreciating that you can race between the safety car line and the pit entry line, even when the safety car is out, took no prisoners in a move that was perfectly legitimate. He was attempting to ensure that he dropped no further down the order than necessary while Ferrari attended to his damaged front wing.

Once everyone was in line behind the official Mercedes, Rosberg was at the head of the queue, followed by the other soft-tyre starters: Massa, Alonso, Wehrlein and Gutiérrez. Kvyat was next, then Haryanto, Pérez, Bottas, Button, Sainz, Hülkenberg, Ericsson, Vettel, Magnussen, Ricciardo, Hamilton, Grosjean and Nasr.

We were racing again on lap eight. Kvyat despatched Gutiérrez, Wehrlein and Alonso in short order, and Vettel was making rapid progress as well, before he made contact with Bottas and lost another wing endplate. Hamilton passed Räikkönen, but once the edge went off his new tyres didn't have as much pace as he'd hoped, a function of the floor/aero damage suffered in the opening-lap skirmish.

As in Bahrain, this looked like another gilt-edged opportunity for Rosberg to make a significant points gain on his team-mate and, once again, he was in a race of his own as he edged clear, while Kvyat attacked Massa and relegated the Williams after 12 laps.

Räikkönen pitted for a set of medium-compound Pirellis a lap later, and Vettel stopped after a further four laps for a set of softs. By the time Rosberg pitted for the yellow-walled Pirellis on lap 21, he was able to get in and out without surrendering the lead.

It was an advantage that simply grew and grew, out to more than half a minute by the time Nico's middle stint was done. Behind, Vettel was closing in on Kvyat, and after his radio comments about Daniil's first corner (probably for the benefit of watching Ferrari head honcho Sergio Marchionne – see Viewpoint), one wondered if there would be a little additional spice.

Massa and Bottas were falling away in the Williamses, with Ricciardo's recovering Red Bull making inroads before both of Sir Frank's cars pitted to go on to the medium tyre and run to the end.

Vettel was now on the back of Kvyat, and although the Ferrari had more straight-line speed, the difference was not as much as might have been expected. First, Vettel's wing endplate damage meant he wasn't getting through the quick corners as well as he might have done and, second, Ferrari was having to run the engine slightly detuned due to a turbo issue, the fix for which was not anticipated until Barcelona, another month away.

In Seb's favour, though, was a new set of soft Pirellis versus the mediums that Kvyat had bolted on when both made their third stops with 20 laps to go. Although Kvyat left the pit lane still ahead, Vettel used the better warm-up and

Above: Sebastian Vettel's Ferrari sports front wing damage after his first-corner collision with team-mate Kimi Räikkönen. The German posted a fine recovery, going on to finish second to Rosberg.

Top left: Lewis Hamilton's first-lap wing damage scuppered his chances of a podium from the back of the grid. He would make the best of it with a seventh-place finish.

Photos: Peter J. Fox

Above left: Daniel Ricciardo suffered a puncture after running over debris from Lewis Hamilton's front wing. Daniil Kvyat passes his team-mate heading for the pits.

Left: Ferrari's Maurizio Arrivabene was left to rue the consequences of his drivers' first-corner collision.

Photos: Lukas Gorys

Above: Fortune favours the brave. An aggressive first-corner move helped pave the way for a third-place finish for Red Bull's Daniil Kvyat.
Photo: Red Bull Racing/Getty Images

Top right: Jenson Button's quest for championship points continued after his three-stop stategy failed to pay dividends.
Photo: McLaren Honda

Above right: Felipe Massa put in a determined drive to claim sixth place for Williams.
Photo: Williams Martini Racing

Right: This is for you. Daniil Kvyat signals his thanks to his crew.
Photo: Lukas Gorys

Top far right: Vettel and Kvyat shake hands in parc fermé. Sebastian's misplaced anger with the Russian driver would surface as they made for the podium.
Photo: WRi2/Studio Colombo

Far right: The CEO was in town and ramping up the pressure for his team to perform well.
Photo: Peter J. Fox

extra grip of his softs to get close enough for DRS and pass the Red Bull at the hairpin.

Rosberg made his final stop a lap later and resumed still in front without any drama. Ricciardo was briefly second before also stopping for a final set of mediums, which dropped him behind Vettel and his team-mate once more, plus both Williams men and Hamilton.

Lewis's Mercedes may not have been affording him the type of advantage that was typical, but that didn't stop him from surprising Bottas with a lunge up the inside of Turn Nine. Ricciardo followed him through on the next lap at the hairpin and then zapped Hamilton with a lovely high-speed pass at Turn Six, with 12 laps to go. This wasn't just anyone remember, it was Lewis Hamilton, albeit a struggling one.

Further around the same lap, Ricciardo took fourth from Massa at the hairpin. Cue delighted fist pumping from the appreciative Red Bull pit audience.

Räikkönen was now joining in as well, using his fresher soft Pirellis to good effect. When Hamilton lost time trying to attack Massa, Kimi took full advantage to DRS himself within striking distance at the hairpin and go by after a spot of tyre rubbing. He passed Massa at the same spot a lap later.

Both Toro Rossos were also top-ten contenders. Verstappen had been delayed picking a path through the first-corner shenanigans, a situation compounded by being stacked behind team-mate Sainz in the pits when both stopped under the safety car. Courtesy of a longer second stint, however, Max was able to go to the end on a set of softs rather than the mediums fitted to his team-mate's STR11. Although Max pitted out behind Carlos, he was significantly quicker.

The pair of them passed Button's McLaren-Honda and then homed in on Pérez's Force India, Sainz then having to acquiesce to a team instruction to let Verstappen through on his fresher tyres. Both managed to mug the Mexican at the hairpin, Verstappen then closing rapidly in on Bottas as the laps ticked down. Valtteri, defending valiantly, asked a little

too much of his struggling mediums at the hairpin, and the Dutchman was through.

Sainz managed to further demote Bottas to secure eighth and ninth for Franz Tosts's men, with Valtteri claiming the last point, four slots behind team-mate Massa, and ahead of Pérez and the McLaren-Hondas. Button had gone for a three-stop strategy and was closing down the two-stopping Alonso, but ran out of time.

For Rosberg, it was all too easy, and he gratefully claimed another maximum 25 points. He joined an exclusive club of drivers who have achieved six successive grand prix victories, the other members being Alberto Ascari, Michael Schumacher and Vettel.

Despite his first-corner aggravation, Sebastian was able to perform a strong exercise in damage limitation and leave Shanghai with 18 points to make up for his DNF in Bahrain.

He wasn't happy, though, berating Kvyat for his aggression on the opening lap.

Kvyat, to his credit, refused to be intimidated as Vettel firmly made his point before they joined Rosberg for the podium celebrations. The young Russian basically pointed out that he'd seen a gap and gone for it, they hadn't crashed and were both on the podium, so where was the problem? And it was hard to disagree.

The Red Bull driver could hardly be blamed, under constant pressure and comparison with team-mate Ricciardo, who was performing absolutely at the top of his game. That was emphasised once again by the Australian finishing just 7s behind, in fourth place, despite the early-race puncture that had dropped him to the tail of the field.

As everyone turned their attention to Kvyat's home race at Sochi, next on the early flyaway schedule, Rosberg no doubt could hardly believe his good fortune: after just three races of the new season, he had a 36-point advantage over team-mate Hamilton at the top of the championship table. How long could this go on?

Tony Dodgins

VIEWPOINT
A ROD FOR FERRARI'S BACK

I T may have seemed the smart, business-like thing to do, but Sergio Marchionne's macho public statements about Ferrari needing to win were doing no more than stating the obvious and creating pressure his team did not need. And that applied to the highly-paid superstar drivers just as much as to the man who polished the bodywork.

You could tell the sense of responsibility was getting to Sebastian Vettel when he launched a verbal attack against Daniil Kvyat that matched the intensity of the Russian's dive down the inside at the first corner. There was the undeniable feeling that this was an act of backside covering for the benefit of the unsmiling CEO, Seb getting his retaliation in first.

There was a double irony to this incident. Vettel was on the second row and prey to such an attack because he had messed up his single super-soft Q3 qualifying lap by braking too deep into the hairpin. And the entire scrappy first-lap affair had been triggered by his team-mate.

When Kimi Räikkönen ran wide and tried to save the moment, he turned into the corner and created one side of the pincer movement that was Seb's undoing as Kvyat came steaming down the inside with opportunism that, according to the voluble Vettel, was "suicidal".

It had been risky, yes. But no more than you would expect of a young racer who had seen a nice gap and gone for it. Kyvat would make that clear a couple of hours later when he stood his ground in the cool-down room and shrugged off Vettel's complaints after they had finished second and third. Kyvat saying "At least we're on the podium" did little to ease Vettel's frustration. This was a disappointing result at the end of a weekend that had promised much, as the Ferraris had been quickest in FP2.

And just to add a little salt to the wound, Nico Rosberg's sixth win in succession had put him on a par with Alberto Ascari, Michael Schumacher and Vettel – all of whom were Ferrari drivers past and present.

Maurice Hamilton

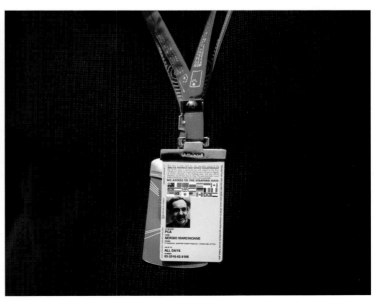

3

2016 FORMULA 1
PIRELLI
CHINESE
GRAND PRIX

SHANGHAI 15–17 APRIL

ROLEX

F1 OFFICIAL TIMEPIECE

RACE DISTANCE: 56 laps, 189.559 miles/305.066km

RACE WEATHER: Dry/sunny (track 37–45°C, air 20–22°C)

SHANGHAI INTERNATIONAL CIRCUIT
Circuit: 3.387 miles/5.451km
56 laps

187/116 kmh/mph
✹ Gear
▬ DRS zone

Turn 1 175/109
Turn 2 95/59
Turn 3 85/35
Turn 4 205/127
Turn 5 280/174
Turn 6 76/47
Turn 7 200/124
Turn 8 152/94
Turn 9 108/67
10 160/99 11 100/62
Turn 12 160/99
Turn 13 200/124
Turn 14 65/40
Turn 15 192/120
16 135/84
8 326/202

RACE – OFFICIAL CLASSIFICATION

Pos.	Driver	Nat.	No.	Entrant	Car/Engine	Tyres	Laps	Time/Retirement	Speed (mph/km/h)	Gap to leader	Fastest race lap	
1	**Nico Rosberg**	D	6	Mercedes AMG Petronas F1 Team	Mercedes F1 W07-Mercedes PU106C V6	P	56	1h 38m 53.891s	115.002/185.078		1m 40.418s	38
2	**Sebastian Vettel**	D	5	Scuderia Ferrari	Ferrari SF15-H-059/5 V6	P	56	1h 39m 31.667s	114.275/183.908	37.776s	1m 40.610s	37
3	**Daniil Kvyat**	RUS	26	Red Bull Racing	Red Bull RB12-TAG Heuer RB12 V6	P	56	1h 39m 39.827s	114.119/183.657	45.936s	1m 41.546s	38
4	**Daniel Ricciardo**	AUS	3	Red Bull Racing	Red Bull RB12-TAG Heuer RB12 V6	P	56	1h 39m 46.579s	113.990/183.449	52.688s	1m 41.015s	55
5	**Kimi Räikkönen**	FIN	7	Scuderia Ferrari	Ferrari SF16-H-059/5 V6	P	56	1h 39m 59.763s	113.740/183.046	1m 05.872s	1m 40.593s	40
6	**Felipe Massa**	BR	19	Williams Martini Racing	Williams FW38-Mercedes PU106C V6	P	56	1h 40m 09.402s	113.557/182.753	1m 15.511s	1m 41.815s	34
7	**Lewis Hamilton**	GB	44	Mercedes AMG Petronas F1 Team	Mercedes F1 W07-Mercedes PU106C V6	P	56	1h 40m 12.121s	113.506/182.670	1m 18.230s	1m 40.662s	32
8	**Max Verstappen**	NL	33	Scuderia Toro Rosso	Toro Rosso STR11-Ferrari 059/4 V6	P	56	1h 40m 13.159s	113.487/182.639	1m 19.268s	1m 40.399s	41
9	**Carlos Sainz**	E	55	Scuderia Toro Rosso	Toro Rosso STR11-Ferrari 059/4 V6	P	56	1h 40m 18.018s	113.395/182.491	1m 24.127s	1m 41.485s	35
10	**Valtteri Bottas**	FIN	77	Williams Martini Racing	Williams FW38-Mercedes PU106C V6	P	56	1h 40m 20.083s	113.356/182.428	1m 26.192s	1m 41.558s	23
11	Sergio Pérez	MEX	11	Sahara Force India F1 Team	Force India VJM09-Mercedes PU106C V6	P	56	1h 40m 28.174s	113.204/182.184	1m 34.283s	1m 41.846s	30
12	Fernando Alonso	E	14	McLaren Honda	McLaren MP4-31-Honda RA616H V6	P	56	1h 40m 31.144s	113.148/182.094	1m 37.253s	1m 42.226s	36
13	Jenson Button	GB	22	McLaren Honda	McLaren MP4-31-Honda RA616H V6	P	56	1h 40m 35.881s	113.059/181.951	1m 41.990s	1m 40.298s	46
14	Esteban Gutiérrez	MEX	21	Haas F1 Team	Haas VF-16-Ferrari 059/5 V6	P	55			1 lap	1m 40.368s	45
15	Nico Hülkenberg	D	27	Sahara Force India F1 Team	Force India VJM09-Mercedes PU106C V6	P	55			1 lap	1m 39.824s	48
16	Marcus Ericsson	S	9	Sauber F1 Team	Sauber C35-Ferrari 059/5 V6	P	55			1 lap	1m 43.269s	41
17	Kevin Magnussen	DK	20	Renault Sport F1 Team	Renault R.S.16-R.E.16 V6	P	55			1 lap	1m 42.311s	22
18	Pascal Wehrlein	D	94	Manor Racing MRT	Manor MRT05-Mercedes PU106C V6	P	55			1 lap	1m 41.489s	48
19	Romain Grosjean	F	8	Haas F1 Team	Haas VF-16-Ferrari 059/5 V6	P	55			1 lap	1m 39.923s	47
20	Felipe Nasr	BR	12	Sauber F1 Team	Sauber C35-Ferrari 059/5 V6	P	55			1 lap	1m 40.582s	42
21	Rio Haryanto	RI	88	Manor Racing MRT	Manor MRT05-Mercedes PU106C V6	P	55			1 lap	1m 42.009s	42
22	Jolyon Palmer	GB	30	Renault Sport F1 Team	Renault R.S.16-R.E.16 V6	P	55			1 lap	1m 42.232s	26

Fastest race lap: Nico Hülkenberg on lap 48, 1m 39.824s, 122.150mph/196.581km/h.

Lap record: Michael Schumacher (Ferrari F2004 V10), 1m 32.238s, 132.196mph/212.749km/h (2004).

All results and data © FOM 2016

21 · WEHRLEIN · Manor   19 · PALMER · Renault   17 · MAGNUSSEN · Renault   15 · ERICSSON · Sauber   13 · HÜLKENBERG · Force India *(3-place grid penalty for unsafe release)*   11 · ALONSO · McLaren

22 · HAMILTON · Mercedes *(5-place grid penalty for replacing the gearbox)*   20 · HARYANTO · Manor   18 · GUTIÉRREZ · Haas   16 · NASR · Sauber   14 · GROSJEAN · Haas   12 · BUTTON · McLaren

Grid order	1	2	3	4	5	6	7	8	9	10	11	12	13	14	15	16	17	18	19	20	21	22	23	24	25	26	27	28	29	30	31	32	33	34	35	36	37	38	39	40	41	42	43	44
6 ROSBERG	3	3	6	6	6	6	6	6	6	6	6	6	6	6	6	6	6	6	6	6	6	6	6	6	6	6	6	6	6	6	6	6	6	6	6	6	6	6	6	6	6	6	6	6
3 RICCIARDO	6	6	26	26	19	19	19	19	19	19	19	26	26	26	26	26	26	26	26	77	77	26	26	26	26	26	26	26	26	26	26	26	26	3	5	5	5	5	5	5	5	5	5	5
7 RÄIKKÖNEN	26	26	11	11	14	14	14	14	26	26	26	19	19	19	19	19	19	19	77	44	26	5	5	5	5	5	5	5	5	5	5	5	5	5	26	26	26	26	26	19	19	19	19	19
5 VETTEL	11	11	27	19	94	94	94	14	14	14	14	14	5	5	5	11	77	19	26	19	19	19	19	19	19	19	3	3	3	26	3	19	19	19	19	3	3	3	26	3	5	19	19	19
77 BOTTAS	27	27	55	5	21	21	21	21	94	94	94	11	5	14	14	11	5	55	44	22	44	11	11	19	22	11	77	77	77	3	3	55	7	7	7	7	7	19	77	44	44	44	19	19
26 KVYAT	55	55	5	27	26	26	26	26	21	21	11	5	11	11	11	77	77	11	55	5	22	19	19	11	11	77	11	3	3	77	55	7	55	33	33	33	33	77	44	3	3	3	44	44
11 PÉREZ	19	5	22	55	30	30	30	30	11	11	21	77	77	77	77	55	55	3	33	11	77	77	77	77	22	3	55	55	55	7	33	33	19	19	19	19	44	3	77	77	77	77	7	
55 SAINZ	5	22	77	22	88	88	88	11	77	77	5	94	22	22	55	3	3	44	22	11	9	3	3	3	3	55	7	7	33	19	19	77	77	77	77	3	33	11	7	7	11	11	55	55
33 VERSTAPPEN	22	19	19	77	11	11	88	30	5	77	94	22	94	55	22	14	44	22	33	19	9	55	9	55	55	55	7	44	44	44	77	44	44	44	44	44	44	11	11	7	11	11	11	11
19 MASSA	77	77	33	14	77	77	77	77	22	22	22	21	55	3	3	44	22	33	9	55	3	55	7	7	44	11	33	33	77	11	11	11	11	11	11	11	22	7	22	55	55	55	55	
14 ALONSO	9	33	9	33	22	22	22	22	55	55	55	55	3	44	44	22	33	5	9	14	3	7	7	44	44	44	22	33	14	14	21	14	44	22	22	22	7	22	55	22	22	22	22	
22 BUTTON	33	9	14	94	55	55	55	55	5	30	3	3	44	94	27	27	21	21	11	55	14	14	44	9	9	14	14	14	21	21	11	21	21	21	55	55	55	55	33	33	33	33	33	22
27 HÜLKENBERG	14	14	9	27	27	27	27	27	44	27	33	33	27	9	21	7	7	27	14	14	33	33	21	11	11	22	44	22	55	14	14	14	14	14	14	14	14	14	14	14	14			
8 GROSJEAN	20	20	3	21	9	9	9	9	88	3	44	7	21	21	21	9	20	9	7	44	27	27	27	9	9	22	22	44	22	14	14	27	27	27	27	27	27	27	27	27	27	27		
9 ERICSSON	94	94	94	20	5	5	5	5	3	88	7	7	7	7	33	9	9	20	8	14	8	20	20	20	20	20	20	9	9	21	21	21	21	9	9	9	9	9	9	9	9	21	9	
12 NASR	30	30	30	30	20	20	20	20	9	44	30	33	33	9	20	20	8	14	8	20	21	21	21	21	21	20	20	20	9	9	9	9	9	9	9	9	9							
20 MAGNUSSEN	21	21	21	88	3	3	3	3	20	7	33	30	9	7	94	8	14	7	7	8	94	94	94	94	94	94	94	9	8	27	27	9	9	94	94	94	94	94	94	94	94	94	94	20
21 GUTIÉRREZ	88	88	88	3	33	33	33	33	7	9	88	20	88	88	88	88	27	27	94	30	20	20	20	20	8	27	9	9	8	94	20	12	12	12	12	12	8	8	8	8				
30 PALMER	8	7	7	7	7	7	7	7	4	44	33	9	20	88	8	12	12	12	21	12	20	20	30	88	88	88	8	88	12	12	12	12	12	12	88	88	8	8	12	20	20	20	12	
88 HARYANTO	7	44	44	44	44	44	8	8	33	20	20	88	8	20	12	88	88	88	8	8	27	24	24	94	94	94	8	30	30	30	88	88	20	12	12	12	94							
94 WEHRLEIN	44	8	8	8	8	44	44	44	8	8	8	8	30	30	94	94	94	94	30	94	12	88	88	8	8	8	30	30	88	88	8	20	20	20	8	8	88	88	88	88	88			
44 HAMILTON	12	12	12	12	12	12	12	12	12	12	12	12	7	12	30	30	30	30	88	12	12	12	12	30	30	30	30	88	88	88	88	8	8	20	30	30	30	30	30	30	30	30	30	30

6 = Pit stop   9 = Drive-thru penalty   *94 One lap or more behind*

TIME SHEETS

PRACTICE 1 (FRIDAY)

Weather: Dry/sunny

Temperatures: track 34–44°C, air 21–25°C

Pos.	Driver	Laps	Time
1	Nico Rosberg	16	1m 38.037s
2	Lewis Hamilton	16	1m 38.183s
3	Sebastian Vettel	12	1m 38.665s
4	Daniel Ricciardo	13	1m 39.061s
5	Kimi Räikkönen	11	1m 39.155s
6	Daniil Kvyat	14	1m 39.625s
7	Carlos Sainz	12	1m 39.676s
8	Jenson Button	11	1m 39.974s
9	Nico Hülkenberg	13	1m 40.169s
10	Max Verstappen	13	1m 40.232s
11	Sergio Pérez	15	1m 40.347s
12	Fernando Alonso	11	1m 40.538s
13	Valtteri Bottas	10	1m 40.828s
14	Romain Grosjean	9	1m 41.358s
15	Marcus Ericsson	18	1m 41.393s
16	Rio Haryanto	20	1m 41.614s
17	Jolyon Palmer	16	1m 41.816s
18	Pascal Wehrlein	14	1m 42.908s
19	Felipe Nasr	8	1m 42.980s
20	Kevin Magnussen	6	no time
21	Esteban Gutiérrez	2	no time
22	Felipe Massa	4	no time

PRACTICE 2 (FRIDAY)

Weather: Dry/sunny-overcast

Temperatures: track 38–45°C, air 24–27°C

Pos.	Driver	Laps	Time
1	Kimi Räikkönen	35	1m 36.896s
2	Sebastian Vettel	33	1m 37.005s
3	Nico Rosberg	33	1m 37.133s
4	Lewis Hamilton	33	1m 37.329s
5	Daniel Ricciardo	31	1m 38.143s
6	Max Verstappen	28	1m 38.268s
7	Nico Hülkenberg	31	1m 38.527s
8	Carlos Sainz	32	1m 38.542s
9	Sergio Pérez	31	1m 38.569s
10	Valtteri Bottas	34	1m 38.723s
11	Fernando Alonso	31	1m 38.728s
12	Jenson Button	28	1m 38.828s
13	Daniil Kvyat	31	1m 39.178s
14	Felipe Massa	34	1m 39.214s
15	Jolyon Palmer	32	1m 39.774s
16	Romain Grosjean	22	1m 39.890s
17	Pascal Wehrlein	36	1m 39.941s
18	Marcus Ericsson	35	1m 39.979s
19	Rio Haryanto	33	1m 40.550s
20	Felipe Nasr	32	1m 41.066s
21	Esteban Gutiérrez	4	1m 42.954s
	Kevin Magnussen		no time

PRACTICE 3 (SATURDAY)

Weather: Rain/cloudy

Temperatures: track 20–24°C, air 19–20°C

Pos.	Driver	Laps	Time
1	Sebastian Vettel	3	1m 57.351s
2	Valtteri Bottas	7	1m 58.061s
3	Sergio Pérez	4	1m 58.689s
4	Carlos Sainz	9	1m 58.800s
5	Esteban Gutiérrez	7	1m 59.526s
6	Jolyon Palmer	7	1m 59.677s
7	Kevin Magnussen	9	1m 59.761s
8	Pascal Wehrlein	8	1m 59.964s
9	Max Verstappen	6	2m 00.150s
10	Nico Hülkenberg	4	2m 00.158s
11	Felipe Nasr	8	2m 00.197s
12	Kimi Räikkönen	5	2m 00.812s
13	Felipe Massa	4	2m 02.438s
14	Rio Haryanto	5	2m 02.732s
15	Jenson Button	3	no time
16	Fernando Alonso	3	no time
17	Romain Grosjean	4	no time
18	Daniil Kvyat	4	no time
19	Nico Rosberg	2	no time
20	Daniel Ricciardo	3	no time
21	Lewis Hamilton	2	no time
22	Marcus Ericsson	1	no time

QUALIFYING (SATURDAY)

Weather: Dry/cloudy Temperatures: track 23–25°C, air 22–23°C

Pos.	Driver	First	Second	Third	Qualifying Tyre
1	Nico Rosberg	1m 37.669s	1m 36.240s	1m 35.402s	Super-Soft (new)
2	Daniel Ricciardo	1m 37.672s	1m 36.815s	1m 35.917s	Super-Soft (new)
3	Kimi Räikkönen	1m 37.347s	1m 36.118s	1m 35.972s	Super-Soft (new)
4	Sebastian Vettel	1m 37.001s	1m 36.183s	1m 36.246s	Super-Soft (new)
5	Valtteri Bottas	1m 37.537s	1m 36.831s	1m 36.296s	Super-Soft (new)
6	Daniil Kvyat	1m 37.719s	1m 36.948s	1m 36.399s	Super-Soft (used)
7	Sergio Pérez	1m 38.096s	1m 37.149s	1m 36.865s	Super-Soft (new)
8	Carlos Sainz	1m 37.656s	1m 37.204s	1m 36.881s	Super-Soft (new)
9	Max Verstappen	1m 38.181s	1m 37.265s	1m 37.194s	Super-Soft (new)
10	Nico Hülkenberg	1m 38.165s	1m 37.333s	no time	
11	Felipe Massa	1m 38.016s	1m 37.347s		
12	Fernando Alonso	1m 38.451s	1m 38.826s		
13	Jenson Button	1m 37.593s	1m 39.093s		
14	Romain Grosjean	1m 38.425s	1m 39.830s		
15	Marcus Ericsson	1m 38.321s	1m 40.742s		
16	Felipe Nasr	1m 38.654s	1m 42.430s		
17	Kevin Magnussen	1m 38.673s			
18	Esteban Gutiérrez	1m 38.770s			
19	Jolyon Palmer	1m 39.528s			
20	Rio Haryanto	1m 40.264s			
21	Pascal Wehrlein	no time			
22	Lewis Hamilton	no time			

Photo: Peter J. Fox

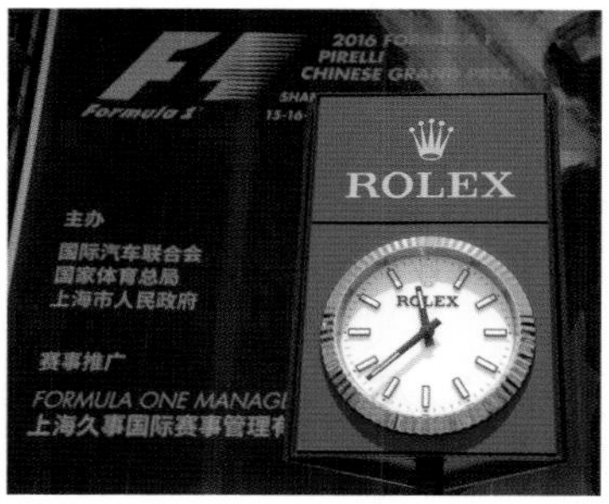

Photo: WRi2/Jad Sherif

FOR THE RECORD

400th GRAND PRIX: Mercedes engine.

100th PODIUM PLACE: Mercedes (as a constructor).

DID YOU KNOW?

Photo: Peter J. Fox

Nico Rosberg joined Alberto Ascari, Sebastian Vettel and Michael Schumacher as the only winners of six consecutive grands prix.

This was only the fifth race in F1 history where there were no retirements.

POINTS

DRIVERS

1	Nico Rosberg	75
2	Lewis Hamilton	39
3	Daniel Ricciardo	36
4	Sebastian Vettel	33
5	Kimi Räikkönen	28
6	Felipe Massa	22
7	Daniil Kvyat	21
8	Romain Grosjean	18
9	Max Verstappen	13
10	Valtteri Bottas	7
11	Nico Hülkenberg	6
12	Carlos Sainz	4
13	Stoffel Vandoorne	1

CONSTRUCTORS

1	Mercedes	113
2	Ferrari	61
3	Red Bull	57
4	Williams	29
5	Haas	18
6	Toro Rosso	17
7	Force India	6
8	McLaren	1

9 · VERSTAPPEN · Toro Rosso

7 · PÉREZ · Force India

5 · BOTTAS · Williams

3 · RÄIKKÖNEN · Ferrari

1 · ROSBERG · Mercedes

10 · MASSA · Williams

8 · SAINZ · Toro Rosso

6 · KVYAT · Red Bull

4 · VETTEL · Ferrari

2 · RICCIARDO · Red Bull

Qualifying: head-to-head

Rosberg	1	2	Hamilton
Vettel	2	1	Räikkönen
Massa	1	2	Bottas
Ricciardo	3	0	Kvyat
Pérez	2	1	Hülkenberg
Magnussen	2	1	Palmer
Verstappen	2	1	Sainz
Ericsson	3	0	Nasr
Alonso	2	0	Button
Button	0	1	Vandoorne
Haryanto	2	1	Wehrlein
Grosjean	3	0	Gutiérrez

45	46	47	48	49	50	51	52	53	54	55	56	
6	6	6	6	6	6	6	6	6	6	6	6	1
5	5	5	5	5	5	5	5	5	5	5	5	2
26	26	26	26	26	26	26	26	26	26	26	26	3
3	3	3	3	3	3	3	3	3	3	3	3	4
19	19	7	7	7	7	7	7	7	7	7	7	5
44	7	19	19	19	19	19	19	19	19	19	19	6
7	44	44	44	44	44	44	44	44	44	44	44	7
77	77	77	77	77	77	77	77	77	33	33	33	8
11	11	11	11	33	33	33	33	33	77	77	55	9
55	55	55	33	55	55	55	55	55	55	55	77	10
33	33	33	55	11	11	11	11	11	11	11	11	
14	14	14	14	14	14	14	14	14	14	14	14	
27	22	22	22	22	22	22	22	22	22	22	22	
22	27	9	9	9	21	21	21	21	21	21		
9	9	21	21	21	9	27	27	27	27	27		
21	21	27	27	27	27	9	9	9	9	9		
20	20	20	20	20	20	20	20	20	20	20		
94	94	94	94	94	94	94	94	94	94	94		
12	12	8	8	8	8	8	8	8	8	8		
8	8	12	12	12	12	12	12	12	12	12		
88	88	88	88	88	88	88	88	88	88	88		
30	30	30	30	30	30	30	30	30	30	30		

Safety car deployed on laps shown

RACE TYRE STRATEGIES

PIRELLI

	Driver	Race Stint 1	Race Stint 2	Race Stint 3	Race Stint 4	Race Stint 5	Race Stint 6
1	Rosberg	Soft (u): 1-20	Soft (n): 21-36	Medium (n): 37-56			
2	Vettel	Super-Soft (u): 1-4	Super-Soft (n): 5-17	Soft (n): 18-35	Soft (n): 36-56		
3	Kvyat	Super-Soft (u): 1-4	Soft (n): 5-19	Soft (n): 20-35	Medium (n): 36-56		
4	Ricciardo	Super-Soft (u): 1-3	Soft (n): 4-19	Soft (n): 20-37	Medium (n): 38-56		
5	Räikkönen	Super-Soft (u): 1	Soft (n): 2-14	Medium (n): 15-37	Soft (n): 38-56		
6	Massa	Soft (n): 1-19	Soft (n): 20-31	Medium (n): 32-56			
7	Hamilton	Soft (n): 1	Soft (n): 2-5	Super-Soft (n): 6	Soft (n): 7-21	Soft (u): 22-30	Medium (n): 31-56
8	Verstappen	Super-Soft (u): 1-4	Soft (n): 5-20	Medium (n): 21-39	Soft (n): 40-56		
9	Sainz	Super-Soft (u): 1-4	Soft (n): 5-19	Soft (n): 20-33	Medium (n): 34-56		
10	Bottas	Super-Soft (u): 1-4	Soft (n): 5-21	Soft (n): 22-30	Medium (n): 31-56		
11	Pérez	Super-Soft (u): 1-4	Soft (n): 5-18	Soft (n): 19-28	Medium (n): 29-56		
12	Alonso	Soft (n): 1-16	Medium (n): 17-32	Medium (n): 33-56			
13	Button	Super-Soft (u): 1-4	Medium (n): 5-27	Medium (n): 28-44	Super-Soft (u): 45-56		
14	Gutiérrez	Soft (n): 1-19	Soft (n): 20-34	Super-Soft (n): 35-43	Super-Soft (n): 44-55		
15	Hülkenberg	Super-Soft (u): 1-4	Soft (n): 5-17	Soft (n): 18-26	Medium (n): 27-46	Super-Soft (u): 47-55	
16	Ericsson	Soft (n): 1-4	Medium (n): 5-28	Medium (n): 29-55			
17	Magnussen	Super-Soft (n): 1-4	Soft (n): 5-20	Soft (n): 21-35	Medium (n): 36-55		
18	Wehrlein	Soft (n): 1-15	Soft (n): 16-27	Soft (n): 28-43	Super-Soft (n): 44-55		
19	Grosjean	Soft (n): 1	Soft (n): 2-20	Soft (n): 21-33	Super-Soft (n): 34-44	Super-Soft (u): 45-55	
20	Nasr	Soft (n): 1	Medium (n): 2-20	Medium (u): 21-40	Soft (u): 41-55		
21	Haryanto	Soft (n): 1-18	Soft (n): 19-28	Soft (u): 29-40	Medium (n): 41-55		
22	Palmer	Soft (n): 1-15	Super-Soft (n): 16-24	Soft (n): 25-38	Medium (n): 39-55		

The tyre regulations stipulate that at least two of three dry tyre specifications must be used during a dry race.

Pirelli P Zero logos are colour-coded on the tyre sidewalls: Red = Super-Soft; Yellow = Soft; White = Medium. (n) new (u) used

Commotion at the back of the field
as Gutiérrez collides with Hülkenberg,
and Haryanto bounces off Nasr.
Meanwhile, in the foreground, Kvyat
and Vettel are heading for their own
personal encounter.
Photo: Lukas Gorys

FIA FORMULA 1 WORLD CHAMPIONSHIP · ROUND 4

RUSSIAN GRAND PRIX

SOCHI CIRCUIT

LEWIS HAMILTON was not so much a man out of form as a man out of luck. Two bad starts in Melbourne and Bahrain, and some mechanical mayhem in China had resulted in a 36-point championship deficit opening up as team-mate Nico Rosberg cantered to the first three race victories of the new season.

But 36 points over 18 remaining races gave rise to simple maths: just two points per race gain over the season was all that Lewis needed to close the gap.

So, it was no big deal, right?

"It *is* a big deal," Hamilton said on Thursday in Sochi. "That's a big margin to claw back. Okay, it was 29 points in 2014, but make no mistake, it's a challenge."

By Saturday 4pm, it looked as if that challenge was becoming ever larger. After a fabulous lap in Q2, Rosberg was fully 1.3s quicker than Sebastian Vettel's Ferrari; Hamilton, half a second adrift of his team-mate, had a power unit problem. He would take no part in Q3, his sorry run of misfortune continuing.

Sochi's somewhat unique surface meant practically zero tyre degradation, multiple-lap qualifying runs and, in the absence of Pirelli's new ultrasoft tyre, what was widely expected to be a one-stop race, with the frontrunners starting on the super-softs used for qualifying and then going on to softs for the rest of the race.

To make Rosberg's life even easier, not only was Hamilton in trouble again, but also Vettel was looking at a five-place grid penalty for a gearbox change, the knock-on effect of an electrical problem that had stopped him early in second practice on Friday. This was doubly frustrating, as Ferrari had used three engine tokens for a combustion upgrade.

Vettel was nearest challenger in Q3, but he was 0.7s away from another crushingly dominant Rosberg/Mercedes display and would start the race from seventh on the grid.

Could Kimi Räikkönen step up to the plate with Vettel hampered? No. He locked up at the final turn and qualified the second Ferrari just over a tenth behind Valtteri Bottas's Williams with a time fully half a second shy of Vettel's.

With around 70 per cent of the Sochi lap run at full throttle, Williams, quick here on both previous visits, was in good shape, the cause helped by a new, shorter nose. But Felipe Massa was half a second adrift of his team-mate and perhaps a tad fortunate that it was just Räikkönen's Ferrari splitting the FW38s.

Daniel Ricciardo was a tenth shy of Massa, Red Bull more seriously hampered here by Renault's power deficit. With Ferrari having tried the 'halo' as F1 sought to protect a driver's exposed head from 2017, Ricciardo did an installation lap on Friday with Red Bull's cockpit 'canopy',

which most agreed looked a more elegant solution, although a final decision and implementation plan was still in the hands of the FIA.

Splitting the Red Bulls on the grid was Sergio Pérez's Force India, another with the benefit of Mercedes motivation. Still, this was a great effort from the Mexican, less than a tenth behind Ricciardo and a quarter of a second clear of Daniil Kvyat with the second RB12. Team-mate Nico Hülkenberg, by contrast, was languishing in 13th place, set-up changes made for Saturday having failed to translate.

Kvyat felt he could have been closer to Ricciardo, but didn't have time to do a preparation lap to get his Pirellis up to temperature and hadn't quite got the tyres in for the first sector of his flying lap.

The 2015-spec Ferrari engine was a significant handicap for Toro Rosso in Russia, but that did not stop Max Verstappen from producing a fine lap to haul his STR11 into Q3 ninth, with a lap 0.13s from Kvyat, whom he had actually outpaced in Q2.

Team-mate Carlos Sainz was unhappy to miss out on the Q3 shootout and thought he would have made it had he not encountered a slowing Kvyat, whose time was just 0.05s quicker.

McLaren-Honda threatened Q3 once more without quite making it, Jenson Button 12th, just over a tenth shy of Kvyat's Q2 time and a similar margin ahead of team-mate Fernando Alonso, the Woking men split by Hülkenberg.

Unfortunately for Haas, the Sochi performance was more China than Australia/Bahrain, with Grosjean at a loss to explain the gripless lack of performance from the car.

At Renault, Sergey Sirotkin did FP1 in place of Kevin Magnussen and was 0.78s quicker than Jolyon Palmer, who was similarly perplexed over wayward handling characteristics. This kind of thing can be damaging without explanations, but it wasn't down to Palmer, who had won the Sochi GP2 feature race with DAMS in 2014. Thankfully, attention to a new floor and some set-up tweaks allowed him to get to within a tenth of Kevin Magnussen when it mattered, although both Renaults went out in Q1.

Joining them on the sidelines were the Saubers, Felipe Nasr ahead of the Manors of Pascal Wehrlein and Rio Haryanto, and team-mate Marcus Ericsson. Having complained that his chassis was almost undrivable at the first three races of the season, Nasr had a 'new' one, but, with Ericsson last and the team cash-strapped, it was tempting to figure that they had merely swapped out of even-handedness towards those providing the folding stuff...

Internally, though, the story was that the departure of some engineering staff had meant a reshuffle, and Ericsson and his new race engineer were struggling to generate sufficient tyre temperature to get the most out of qualifying.

Left: Felilpe Nasr had a new chassis at Sauber.
Photo: Sauber F1 Team

Centre left: Daniel Ricciardo tested Red Bull's aero screen.
Photo: Red Bull Racing/Getty Images

Below centre left: Sahara Force India's Nico Hülkenberg and Sergio Pérez both celebrated taking part in their 100th grand prix.
Photo: Sahara Force India F1 Team

Below: Valtteri Bottas qualified a fine third and brought his Williams home in fourth place.
Photo: Williams Martini Racing

Far left: One race from greatness. Max Verstappen would soon be swapping chassis with electrifying effect.
Photo: Peter J. Fox

Above: Nico Rosberg takes command from the start, ahead of fast-away Räikkönen and Bottas.
Photo: Peter J. Fox

Top right: Kevin Magnussen brought some cheer (and points) to Renault with his seventh-place finish.
Photo: WRi2/Jean-François Galeron

Above right: Felipe Massa ensured a satisfactory weekend for Williams with fifth place, behind Bottas.

Right: Mayhem at Turn Two as Kvyat's Red Bull rams Sebastian Vettel's Ferrari, which in turn hits the Red Bull of Daniel Ricciardo.
Photos: WRi2/Jad Sherif

THE drag from the Sochi starting grid through the flat-out Turn One right down into the tight right at Turn Two, the field madly jockeying for position, makes for an impressive sight. When the lights changed, Rosberg converted his pole and Räikkönen, by dint of another strong Ferrari getaway, got down the inside of Bottas into Turn Two.

Team-mate Vettel also got a flier, and although Ricciardo closed the door on him through the Turn One kink, the Ferrari was down the inside of the Red Bull into Turn Two. Behind him, though, was Kvyat in the sister Red Bull. Perhaps a little over-anxious to impress in front of his home crowd and carry on the momentum of his Shanghai podium, Daniil clipped the back of Vettel's Ferrari, knocking it into team-mate Ricciardo, on Seb's outside. Ricciardo, in turn, clipped Pérez's right rear, puncturing it, as the Force India attempted to take evasive action.

Not wishing to get caught up in the action, Hamilton, Verstappen, Alonso and Grosjean all shot left across the Turn Two run-off area, barely lifting, staying left of the controversial track limits bollard, as per the rules. However well intentioned (or not!), this still afforded them all a decent gain over the likes of Button, who lifted and picked their way through Turn Two as intended.

Further back, Gutiérrez made contact with Hülkenberg, the Force India spinning into Haryanto, which ended both of their races, while Gutiérrez headed to the pits to have a new front wing fitted.

Vettel, suspecting that Kvyat's impact might have punctured his right rear, did not commit to the long, fast Turn Three as usually he would have done, which caught out the young Russian, who was tucked in right behind and looking to get a tow. The Red Bull hit the Ferrari again, harder this time, and Vettel exited stage right into the barrier. To say that he was displeased was a serious understatement, the FOM TV production guys highly active with their 'bleeper' before broadcasting Seb's radio message to the Ferrari pit wall!

With a healthy dose of carbon-fibre shards littering the exit

of the testing Turn Three, it was not long before a full safety car replaced the initial virtual safety car.

Both Red Bulls, Pérez, Gutiérrez and Ericsson were in for repairs, with Ricciardo and Kvyat interestingly sent back into the fray on Pirelli's white-walled medium tyre, which was somewhat surprising. Precious little running had been done on the compound across the weekend, and although the obvious plan was to run non-stop to the end, the medium turned out to be far too slow, potentially losing much more than the 24s needed to pit.

Kvyat would soon need to visit the pit lane again anyway, when notification came of a stop-go penalty for the first-corner contact with Vettel, but Red Bull would also later decide to bring Ricciardo in again to go back on to the softs. They had rolled the dice and it hadn't worked, meaning that Christian Horner's squad would leave Sochi without a single point. On the pit wall, meanwhile, Vettel was espied visiting his former team boss to express his displeasure, images that Kvyat could have done without and which, perhaps, speeded the unwelcome news that he would receive in the next few days (*see* Viewpoint).

Once they were all lined up behind Bernd Maylander's safety car, the order was Rosberg, Räikkönen, Bottas, Massa, Hamilton, Verstappen, Alonso, Grosjean, Magnussen, Palmer, Sainz, Nasr, Button, Wehrlein; then fresh out of the pits, Kvyat, Ericsson, Ricciardo, Pérez and Gutiérrez (who also received a stop-go for the incident with Hülkenberg).

We were racing again on lap four, and a rolling start was different from a standing one for the Ferrari/Williams performance axis, Räikkönen quickly under attack from Bottas, who repaid Kimi's first-lap opportunism into Turn One to take second. Hamilton took Massa to claim fourth, with Verstappen also having a look at the Williams, but not quite making it. By the time they flashed across the line at the end of the lap, Rosberg already had almost 3s lead, knowing that he had to make hay before Hamilton got up to second.

It was soon evident that Räikkönen potentially had greater pace than Bottas, but the Williams was quick in a straight

line, and when Kimi compromised himself with a look at Valtteri, Hamilton needed no second invitation to relieve the older Finn of third place at Turn Five.

Now it was Hamilton's turn to discover that Bottas's top-end performance made him a difficult target, and despite his desire to be past and after his team-mate, the status quo remained until Williams pitted Valtteri at the end of lap 16.

After problems with pit stops in 2015, caused by heat build-up in the wheel nuts and the difficulty of removing them, Williams had refined its equipment and set the fastest pit-stop times at all three of the season-opening races. Another mid-2s stop sent Bottas rapidly on his way again, and when Mercedes stopped Hamilton a lap later and he failed to quite hit his marks, Lewis was still fractionally behind the Williams when he returned to the track.

The pair then fought a good battle, Bottas rescuing a tank-slapper in Turn Three to hold off the Mercedes until he lost some time behind Alonso's McLaren, which had yet to stop. That allowed Ferrari to get Räikkönen in and out without losing track position to Bottas.

Up into second, Hamilton realistically was going to need assistance from another safety car to do anything about his team-mate, while behind Bottas there was a 9s gap to Massa, then Verstappen, Alonso, Grosjean and Magnussen, who headed for the pits with his Renault on lap 16. Haas responded with Grosjean, but he came out behind the Dane. Palmer, in the second Renault, was suffering with higher tyre usage and had stopped a couple of laps earlier, allowing Button to jump him with a later stop.

Rosberg arrived in the pit lane on lap 21 and rejoined on softs without losing his lead, while Hamilton had distanced himself from Räikkönen, circulating almost a second a lap quicker. The Ferrari had a 3s margin over Bottas, who now was more concerned with eking out his tyre life.

Right: Four wins on the trot, awesome. No wonder Nico looks happy.
Photo: Peter J. Fox

Below: Damage limitation. Forced to start from tenth place on the grid, Lewis Hamilton avoided the first-lap chaos and brought his Mercedes home second, behind Rosberg.
Photo: Mercedes AMG Petronas F1 Team

Far right: Kimi Räikkönen's third place was the Scuderia's 700th podium.
Photo: Lukas Gorys

Bottom right: Tunnel of Love? Parting was not such sweet sorrow for Toro Rosso's Carlos Sainz and Max Verstappen post-Sochi.
Photo: Peter J. Fox

Pérez, forced to pit on the first lap, was going well on softs, up into sixth and running ahead of Verstappen. Given Rosberg's race in 2014, when he ran all the way after pitting on the opening lap to replace flat-spotted tyres, he was worth keeping an eye on. Any such thoughts were forgotten at half-distance, however, when Force India brought him in for more rubber and he rejoined 11th, just behind Ricciardo, Magnussen, Grosjean and Sainz.

Sainz was going well in the second Toro Rosso, having spent his first stint with a piece of Kvyat's barge board stuck in his radiator. That had cost him downforce and compelled him to stop early as temperatures rose, but he received a 10s race time penalty for exceeding track linits at Turn Two while battling his way past Palmer.

As the second half of the race developed, Hamilton managed to eat into Rosberg's 12s lead as the pair encountered traffic. It was down to around 8s when Verstappen suffered an engine failure on the pit straight, which, briefly, raised Lewis's hopes of another safety car. But the Toro Rosso was efficiently removed, and Hamilton's challenge was blunted by falling water pressure. He had to accept that another grand prix was going to pass by without a victory – he hadn't won a race since Austin the previous October! – and concentrate on babying the car to the finish.

Third through fifth also seemed to be set, with Räikkönen quicker than the Williams challenge, but not Hamilton fast, while Bottas and Massa were safe enough in fourth and fifth. Felipe was wearing his tyres, however, and with a big enough gap to Alonso, Williams brought him in for another set of Pirellis with seven laps to go, just to be safe.

Rosberg stroked it home for a magnificent seventh in succession, completing his first 'grand slam' – pole, win,

fastest lap – in the process. A further seven-point gain over his team-mate took his championship lead to a very healthy 43 points at this early stage of the season.

Behind the Mercs, Räikkönen and the two Williams, an aggressive race by Alonso gave McLaren-Honda a welcome top-six finish, ahead of a strong drive to seventh by Magnussen in the difficult Renault that, nonetheless, seemed to perform better in race trim than when it was set up for qualifying.

Pérez did all he could to get his Force India up into seventh, but Grosjean, in spite of his older tyres, managed to fend off the Mexican and score the Haas team's third helping of points in four outings.

Button took the final point in the second McLaren and made the point that it might have been better had he, too, run flat out across the Turn Two run-off on the opening lap, as had some of those drivers ahead of him, including his team-mate…

With the first four flyaway races of the new season over, the paddock now turned its attention to Barcelona, a fortnight away. Rosberg was contemplating a start to the season better than he could have dared hope. "The car was just awesome today," he said. "It's always good, but it was fantastic all the way through – qualifying, race, everything. I've never felt it so connected."

In the back of his mind, though, he would have known that Hamilton was on a run of misfortune that could not continue, and that Vettel, too, was coming off a hat trick of problematic races in Sakhir/Shanghai/Sochi. But, that said, the Ferrari was not showing pace to match some of the pre-season expectations. Could this be Nico's year?

Tony Dodgins

VIEWPOINT
NO SENTIMENT AT RED BULL

DANIIL KVYAT'S career path around the time of the Russian Grand Prix would prove that a driver is only as good as his last result. Or as bad as his last collision. Having scored a first-rate podium for Red Bull in China and stood his ground, on and off the track, the Russian's home race turned out to be a nightmare with consequences.

Perhaps carried away by the excitement of Shanghai, and the resulting accolades and attention at Sochi, Kvyat's adrenalin got the better of him and he had a double collision with Sebastian Vettel (his sparring partner in China) on the first lap. Both moments of contact could be described as no more than unfortunate racing incidents, but Kvyat's problem was that the second destroyed the race of team-mate Daniel Ricciardo.

The fact that suddenly he had become unpopular within Red Bull was not the only reason that subsequently he was told he would be heading back to Toro Rosso for the rest of the season. More than anything, his timing was bad in a sense way beyond his natural reflexes in the presence of Vettel's Ferrari. Kvyat had actually set the scene for Max Verstappen's promotion at a time when the tension within the Toro Rosso garage had become noticeably edgy.

Some of this had to do with Verstappen Senior. Not a man to mess around, Jos had made sure that Helmut Marko and the Red Bull hierarchy were aware that Ferrari and Mercedes were interested in his boy. This message had also been picked up by Carlos Sainz, who, in any case, was becoming irritated by the Verstappens' constant pursuit of the best of everything in tactical and mechanical terms for their side of the garage.

The opportunity to make the switch suited Marko perfectly, and satisfied the Verstappen family's need to secure Max's long-term future. It also typified the demanding criteria for anyone in the Red Bull junior squad. Kvyat had been fast, but not consistently quick enough in such elevated company. Time to move on. Next!
Maurice Hamilton

4

2016 FORMULA 1
RUSSIAN GRAND PRIX

SOCHI 29 APRIL–1 MAY

ROLEX

OFFICIAL TIMEPIECE

RACE DISTANCE:
53 laps, 192.467miles/309.745km

RACE WEATHER:
Dry/sunny (track 34–42°C, air 16–18°C)

SOCHI OLYMPIC PARK CIRCUIT, KRASNODAR KRAI
Circuit: 3.634 miles/5.848km
53 laps

8 165/103 · 10 135/84 · 7 · 6 265/165 · 9 · 10 305/190 · 5 125/78 · 3 275/171 · 4 165/103 · 12 330/205 · 2 125/78 · 13 105/65 · 16 · 14 · 17 · 15 · Turn 1 305/190 · 18 115/71

— DRS zone

RACE – OFFICIAL CLASSIFICATION

Pos.	Driver	Nat.	No.	Entrant	Car/Engine	Tyres	Laps	Time/Retirement	Speed (mph/km/h)	Gap to leader	Fastest race lap	
1	**Nico Rosberg**	D	6	Mercedes AMG Petronas F1 Team	Mercedes F1 W07-Mercedes PU106C V6	P	53	1h 32m 41.997s	124.574/200.482		1m 39.094s	52
2	**Lewis Hamilton**	GB	44	Mercedes AMG Petronas F1 Team	Mercedes F1 W07-Mercedes PU106C V6	P	53	1h 33m 07.019s	124.016/199.584	25.022s	1m 40.266s	36
3	**Kimi Räikkönen**	FIN	7	Scuderia Ferrari	Ferrari SF16-H-059/5 V6	P	53	1h 33m 13.995s	123.861/199.335	31.998s	1m 40.101s	47
4	**Valtteri Bottas**	FIN	77	Williams Martini Racing	Williams FW38-Mercedes PU106C V6	P	53	1h 33m 32.214s	123.459/198.688	50.217s	1m 41.159s	37
5	**Felipe Massa**	BR	19	Williams Martini Racing	Williams FW38-Mercedes PU106C V6	P	53	1h 33m 56.424s	122.928/197.834	1m 14.427s	1m 39.743s	52
6	**Fernando Alonso**	E	14	McLaren Honda	McLaren MP4-31-Honda RA616H V6	P	52			1 lap	1m 40.347s	52
7	**Kevin Magnussen**	DK	20	Renault Sport F1 Team	Renault R.S.16-R.E.16 V6	P	52			1 lap	1m 41.832s	50
8	**Romain Grosjean**	F	8	Haas F1 Team	Haas VF-16-Ferrari 059/5 V6	P	52			1 lap	1m 42.026s	51
9	**Sergio Pérez**	MEX	11	Sahara Force India F1 Team	Force India VJM09-Mercedes PU106C V6	P	52			1 lap	1m 41.897s	47
10	**Jenson Button**	GB	22	McLaren Honda	McLaren MP4-31-Honda RA616H V6	P	52			1 lap	1m 41.720s	50
11	Daniel Ricciardo	AUS	3	Red Bull Racing	Red Bull RB12-TAG Heuer RB12 V6	P	52			1 lap	1m 41.179s	46
12	Carlos Sainz	E	55	Scuderia Toro Rosso	Toro Rosso STR11-Ferrari 059/4 V6	P	52	*		1 lap	1m 42.205s	41
13	Jolyon Palmer	GB	30	Renault Sport F1 Team	Renault R.S.16-R.E.16 V6	P	52			1 lap	1m 42.660s	37
14	Marcus Ericsson	S	9	Sauber F1 Team	Sauber C35-Ferrari 059/5 V6	P	52			1 lap	1m 42.050s	45
15	Daniil Kvyat	RUS	26	Red Bull Racing	Red Bull RB12-TAG Heuer RB12 V6	P	52			1 lap	1m 42.344s	44
16	Felipe Nasr	BR	12	Sauber F1 Team	Sauber C35-Ferrari 059/5 V6	P	52	**		1 lap	1m 42.253s	50
17	Esteban Gutiérrez	MEX	21	Haas F1 Team	Haas VF-16-Ferrari 059/5 V6	P	52			1 lap	1m 42.378s	52
18	Pascal Wehrlein	D	94	Manor Racing MRT	Manor MRT05-Mercedes PU106C V6	P	51			2 laps	1m 41.907s	43
	Max Verstappen	NL	33	Scuderia Toro Rosso	Toro Rosso STR11-Ferrari 059/4 V6	P	33	power unit			1m 42.029s	32
	Sebastian Vettel	D	5	Scuderia Ferrari	Ferrari SF15-H-059/5 V6	P	0	accident			no time	
	Nico Hülkenberg	D	27	Sahara Force India F1 Team	Force India VJM09-Mercedes PU106C V6	P	0	accident			no time	
	Rio Haryanto	RI	88	Manor Racing MRT	Manor MRT05-Mercedes PU106C V6	P	0	accident			no time	

* Includes 10-second penalty for forcing another driver off the track – originally finished 11th. ** Includes 5-second penalty for not respecting Race Director's instructions – position unaffected.

Fastest race lap: Nico Rosberg on lap 52, 1m 39.094s, 132.012mph/212.452km/h (new record).

Previous lap record: Valtteri Bottas (Williams FW36-Mercedes V8), 1m 40.896s, 129.654mph/208.658km/h (2014).

All results and data © FOM 2016

21 · HARYANTO · Manor

19 · NASR · Sauber

17 · MAGNUSSEN · Renault

15 · GROSJEAN · Haas

13 · HÜLKENBERG · Force India

11 · SAINZ · Toro Rosso

22 · ERICSSON · Sauber

20 · WEHRLEIN · Manor

18 · PALMER · Renault

16 · GUTIÉRREZ · Haas

14 · ALONSO · McLaren

12 · BUTTON · McLaren

Grid order	1	2	3	4	5	6	7	8	9	10	11	12	13	14	15	16	17	18	19	20	21	22	23	24	25	26	27	28	29	30	31	32	33	34	35	36	37	38	39	40	41	42
6 ROSBERG	6	6	6	6	6	6	6	6	6	6	6	6	6	6	6	6	6	6	6	6	6	6	6	6	6	6	6	6	6	6	6	6	6	6	6	6	6	6	6	6	6	6
77 BOTTAS	7	7	7	77	77	77	77	77	77	77	77	77	77	77	77	77	44	7	7	7	7	33	44	44	44	44	44	44	44	44	44	44	44	44	44	44	44	44	44	44	44	44
7 RÄIKKÖNEN	77	77	77	7	44	44	44	44	44	44	44	44	44	44	44	19	33	33	44	7	7	7	7	7	7	7	7	7	7	7	7	7	7	7	7	7	7	7	7	7	7	7
19 MASSA	19	19	19	44	44	44	7	7	7	7	7	7	7	7	7	7	77	19	33	44	7	33	77	77	77	77	77	77	77	77	77	77	77	77	77	77	77	77	77	77	77	77
3 RICCIARDO	44	44	44	19	19	19	19	19	19	19	19	19	19	19	19	19	19	33	14	14	77	77	19	19	19	19	19	19	19	19	19	19	19	19	19	19	19	19	19	19	19	19
11 PÉREZ	33	33	33	33	33	33	33	33	33	33	33	33	33	33	14	77	77	14	14	19	11	11	11	33	33	33	33	33	14	14	14	14	14	14	14	14	14	14	14	14	14	14
5 VETTEL	14	14	14	14	14	14	14	14	14	14	14	14	14	14	14	14	77	44	19	19	19	11	33	33	33	33	11	14	14	14	14	20	20	20	20	20	20	20	20	20	20	20
26 KVYAT	26	8	8	8	8	8	8	8	8	8	8	8	8	8	8	8	8	8	22	22	11	11	9	9	14	14	14	14	3	20	20	20	20	8	8	8	8	8	8	8	8	8
33 VERSTAPPEN	8	20	20	20	20	20	20	20	20	20	20	20	20	20	20	20	20	20	22	11	22	22	14	14	9	9	9	9	20	8	8	8	11	11	11	11	11	11	11	11	11	11
44 HAMILTON	20	30	30	30	30	30	30	30	30	30	30	30	30	22	22	22	11	11	9	9	9	3	3	3	3	3	3	3	55	55	11	11	55	55	55	55	55	55	55	55	55	55
55 SAINZ	30	55	55	55	55	55	55	55	55	55	22	22	22	30	11	11	9	3	3	3	20	20	20	20	20	20	55	11	11	55	55	55	22	22	22	22	22	22	22	22	22	22
22 BUTTON	55	12	12	12	12	12	12	22	22	22	11	11	11	11	9	9	3	20	20	20	8	8	8	8	8	8	9	30	22	22	22	22	30	30	30	30	30	30	30	30	30	30
27 HÜLKENBERG	12	22	22	22	22	22	22	12	11	11	94	94	94	9	3	3	3	20	8	8	30	55	55	55	55	55	55	11	30	30	30	30	9	9	9	3	3	3	3	3	3	3
14 ALONSO	14	94	94	94	94	94	12	94	12	94	55	9	9	3	3	3	30	30	30	30	55	30	30	30	30	30	30	55	3	9	9	9	3	26	26	26	26	26	26	26	26	26
8 GROSJEAN	22	26	26	26	26	9	9	11	94	12	12	3	94	55	55	55	55	55	55	55	22	22	22	22	22	22	22	22	9	12	26	3	3	26	26	26	26	26	26	26	26	26
21 GUTIÉRREZ	94	9	9	9	9	26	11	9	9	9	9	12	55	12	12	12	12	12	12	12	12	12	12	12	12	12	12	26	3	26	26	12	12	12	12	12	12	12	12	12	12	12
20 MAGNUSSEN	9	3	3	3	3	11	26	3	3	3	3	55	94	94	94	94	94	94	94	94	94	94	94	94	94	26	94	94	12	12	12	94	94	94	94	94	21	21	21	21		
30 PALMER	11	11	11	11	11	3	3	21	21	21	21	21	21	21	21	26	26	26	26	26	94	94	94	94	94	94	26	3	94	94	94	21	21	21	21	21	94	94	94	94		
12 NASR	21	21	21	21	21	21	21	26	26	26	26	26	26	26	26	26	21	21	21	21	21	21	21	21	21	21	21	21	21	21	21											
94 WEHRLEIN																																										
88 HARYANTO																																										
9 ERICSSON																																										

TIME SHEETS

PRACTICE 1 (FRIDAY)
Weather: Dry/sunny-overcast
Temperatures: track 27–31°C, air 15–16°C

Pos.	Driver	Laps	Time
1	Nico Rosberg	32	1m 38.127s
2	Lewis Hamilton	31	1m 38.849s
3	Sebastian Vettel	19	1m 39.175s
4	Kimi Räikkönen	18	1m 39.332s
5	Felipe Massa	14	1m 39.365s
6	Daniel Ricciardo	24	1m 39.650s
7	Valtteri Bottas	34	1m 39.802s
8	Daniil Kvyat	26	1m 40.218s
9	Sergio Pérez	22	1m 40.287s
10	Carlos Sainz	21	1m 40.654s
11	Jenson Button	19	1m 40.663s
12	Fernando Alonso	18	1m 40.771s
13	Sergey Sirotkin	24	1m 40.898s
14	Felipe Nasr	21	1m 41.085s
15	Max Verstappen	22	1m 41.134s
16	Esteban Gutiérrez	18	1m 41.238s
17	Romain Grosjean	20	1m 41.385s
18	Jolyon Palmer	25	1m 41.671s
19	Marcus Ericsson	22	1m 41.962s
20	Pascal Wehrlein	21	1m 42.483s
21	Rio Haryanto	8	1m 42.687s
22	Alfonso Celis	23	1m 43.432s

PRACTICE 2 (FRIDAY)
Weather: Dry/sunny-overcast
Temperatures: track 39–41°C, air 16–17°C

Pos.	Driver	Laps	Time
1	Lewis Hamilton	30	1m 37.583s
2	Sebastian Vettel	10	1m 38.235s
3	Nico Rosberg	37	1m 38.450s
4	Kimi Räikkönen	35	1m 38.793s
5	Daniel Ricciardo	34	1m 39.084s
6	Valtteri Bottas	42	1m 39.185s
7	Daniil Kvyat	32	1m 39.193s
8	Jenson Button	31	1m 39.196s
9	Felipe Massa	38	1m 39.289s
10	Fernando Alonso	30	1m 39.400s
11	Carlos Sainz	37	1m 39.465s
12	Max Verstappen	30	1m 39.501s
13	Nico Hülkenberg	31	1m 39.795s
14	Sergio Pérez	38	1m 39.867s
15	Kevin Magnussen	41	1m 40.193s
16	Romain Grosjean	24	1m 40.260s
17	Esteban Gutiérrez	26	1m 40.508s
18	Jolyon Palmer	37	1m 40.688s
19	Felipe Nasr	31	1m 40.740s
20	Rio Haryanto	38	1m 41.080s
21	Pascal Wehrlein	23	1m 41.148s
22	Marcus Ericsson	29	1m 41.652s

PRACTICE 3 (SATURDAY)
Weather: Dry/cloudy
Temperatures: track 30–32°C, air 16°C

Pos.	Driver	Laps	Time
1	Lewis Hamilton	17	1m 36.403s
2	Nico Rosberg	22	1m 36.471s
3	Sebastian Vettel	28	1m 37.007s
4	Kimi Räikkönen	14	1m 37.727s
5	Felipe Massa	16	1m 37.918s
6	Valtteri Bottas	16	1m 37.985s
7	Max Verstappen	22	1m 38.133s
8	Jenson Button	14	1m 38.260s
9	Carlos Sainz	25	1m 38.465s
10	Sergio Pérez	18	1m 38.542s
11	Daniel Ricciardo	23	1m 38.622s
12	Fernando Alonso	12	1m 38.633s
13	Daniil Kvyat	15	1m 39.047s
14	Nico Hülkenberg	16	1m 39.162s
15	Esteban Gutiérrez	18	1m 39.230s
16	Kevin Magnussen	16	1m 39.238s
17	Romain Grosjean	15	1m 39.239s
18	Jolyon Palmer	19	1m 39.589s
19	Rio Haryanto	19	1m 39.599s
20	Pascal Wehrlein	18	1m 39.663s
21	Marcus Ericsson	23	1m 39.740s
22	Felipe Nasr	19	1m 39.898s

QUALIFYING (SATURDAY)
Weather: Dry/sunny-overcast Temperatures: track 29–33°C, air 16–17°C

Pos.	Driver	First	Second	Third	Qualifying Tyre
1	Nico Rosberg	1m 36.119s	1m 35.337s	1m 35.417s	Super-Soft (new)
2	Sebastian Vettel	1m 36.555s	1m 36.623s	1m 36.123s	Super-Soft (new)
3	Valtteri Bottas	1m 37.746s	1m 37.140s	1m 36.536s	Super-Soft (new)
4	Kimi Räikkönen	1m 36.976s	1m 36.741s	1m 36.663s	Super-Soft (new)
5	Felipe Massa	1m 37.753s	1m 37.230s	1m 37.016s	Super-Soft (new)
6	Daniel Ricciardo	1m 38.091s	1m 37.569s	1m 37.125s	Super-Soft (new)
7	Sergio Pérez	1m 38.006s	1m 37.282s	1m 37.212s	Super-Soft (new)
8	Daniil Kvyat	1m 38.265s	1m 37.606s	1m 37.459s	Super-Soft (new)
9	Max Verstappen	1m 38.123s	1m 37.510s	1m 37.583s	Super-Soft (new)
10	Lewis Hamilton	1m 36.006s	1m 35.820s	no time	
11	Carlos Sainz	1m 37.784s	1m 37.652s		
12	Jenson Button	1m 38.332s	1m 37.701s		
13	Nico Hülkenberg	1m 38.562s	1m 37.771s		
14	Fernando Alonso	1m 37.971s	1m 37.807s		
15	Romain Grosjean	1m 38.383s	1m 38.055s		
16	Esteban Gutiérrez	1m 38.678s	1m 38.115s		
17	Kevin Magnussen	1m 38.914s			
18	Jolyon Palmer	1m 39.009s			
19	Felipe Nasr	1m 39.018s			
20	Pascal Wehrlein	1m 39.399s			
21	Rio Haryanto	1m 39.463s			
22	Marcus Ericsson	1m 39.519s			

Photos: Peter J. Fox

FOR THE RECORD

700th PODIUM POSITION: **Ferrari.**

100th GRAND PRIX ENTERED: **Nico Hülkenberg, Sergio Pérez.**

90th PODIUM POSITION: **Lewis Hamilton.**

40th FASTEST LAP: **Mercedes.**

DID YOU KNOW?

Nico Rosberg became the fourth driver to win four consecutive races from the start of a season (previously achieved by Ayrton Senna in 1991, Nigel Mansell in 1992, and Michael Schumacher in 1994 and 2004.

POINTS

DRIVERS

1	Nico Rosberg	100
2	Lewis Hamilton	57
3	Kimi Räikkönen	43
4	Daniel Ricciardo	36
5	Sebastian Vettel	33
6	Felipe Massa	32
7	Romain Grosjean	22
8	Daniil Kvyat	21
9	Valtteri Bottas	19
10	Max Verstappen	13
11	Fernando Alonso	8
12	Kevin Magnussen	6
13	Nico Hülkenberg	6
14	Carlos Sainz	4
15	Sergio Pérez	2
16	Jenson Button	1
17	Stoffel Vandoorne	1

CONSTRUCTORS

1	Mercedes	157
2	Ferrari	76
3	Red Bull	57
4	Williams	51
5	Haas	22
6	Toro Rosso	17
7	McLaren	10
8	Force India	8
9	Renault	6

9 · VERSTAPPEN · Toro Rosso

7 · VETTEL · Ferrari
(5-place grid penalty for replacing the gearbox)

5 · RICCIARDO · Red Bull

3 · RÄIKKÖNEN · Ferrari

1 · ROSBERG · Mercedes

10 · HAMILTON · Mercedes

8 · KVYAT · Red Bull

6 · PÉREZ · Force India

4 · MASSA · Williams

2 · BOTTAS · Williams

Qualifying: head-to-head

Rosberg	2	2	Hamilton
Vettel	3	1	Räikkönen
Massa	1	3	Bottas
Ricciardo	4	0	Kvyat
Pérez	3	1	Hülkenberg
Magnussen	3	1	Palmer
Verstappen	3	1	Sainz
Ericsson	3	1	Nasr
Alonso	2	1	Button
Button	0	1	Vandoorne
Haryanto	2	2	Wehrlein
Grosjean	4	0	Gutiérrez

43	44	45	46	47	48	49	50	51	52	53	
6	6	6	6	6	6	6	6	6	6	6	1
44	44	44	44	44	44	44	44	44	44	44	2
7	7	7	7	7	7	7	7	7	7	7	3
77	77	77	77	77	77	77	77	77	77	77	4
19	19	19	19	19	19	19	19	19	19	19	5
14	14	14	14	14	14	14	14	14	14		6
20	20	20	20	20	20	20	20	20	20		7
8	8	8	8	8	8	8	8	8	8		8
11	11	11	11	11	11	11	11	11	11		9
55	55	55	55	55	22	22	22	22	22		10
22	22	22	22	22	55	55	55	55	55		
30	30	30	30	30	30	3	3	3	3		
3	3	3	3	3	3	30	30	30	30		
9	9	9	9	9	9	9	9	9	9		
26	26	26	26	26	26	26	26	26	26		
12	12	12	12	12	12	12	12	12	12		
21	21	21	21	21	21	21	21	21	21		
94	94	94	94	94	94	94	94	94			

6 = Pit stop   9 = Drive-thru penalty

94 = One lap or more behind

RACE TYRE STRATEGIES

PIRELLI

	Driver	Race Stint 1	Race Stint 2	Race Stint 3
1	Rosberg	Super-Soft (u): 1–21	Soft (n): 22–53	
2	Hamilton	Super-Soft (u): 1–17	Soft (n): 18–53	
3	Räikkönen	Super-Soft (u): 1–20	Soft (n): 21–53	
4	Bottas	Super-Soft (u): 1–16	Soft (n): 17–53	
5	Massa	Super-Soft (u): 1–18	Soft (n): 19–46	Super-Soft (u): 47–53
6	Alonso	Super-Soft (n): 1–21	Soft (n): 22–52	
7	Magnussen	Super-Soft (n): 1–16	Soft (n): 17–52	
8	Grosjean	Super-Soft (n): 1–17	Soft (n): 18–52	
9	Pérez	Super-Soft (u): 1	Soft (u): 2–27	Soft (n): 28–52
10	Button	Super-Soft (n): 1–20	Soft (n): 21–52	
11	Ricciardo	Super-Soft (u): 1	Medium (n): 2–29	Soft (n): 30–52
12	Sainz	Super-Soft (n): 1–11	Soft (n): 12–52	
13	Palmer	Super-Soft (n): 1–14	Soft (n): 15–52	
14	Ericsson	Soft (n): 1	Super-Soft (n): 2–28	Super-Soft (n): 29–52
15	Kvyat	Super-Soft (u): 1	Medium (n): 2–52	
16	Nasr	Super-Soft (n): 1–12	Soft (n): 13–52	
17	Gutiérrez	Soft (n): 1	Medium (n): 2–9	Medium (u): 10–52
18	Wehrlein	Super-Soft (u): 1–13	Soft (n): 14–39	Super-Soft (u): 40–51
	Verstappen	Super-Soft (u): 1–22	Soft (n): 23–33 (dnf)	
	Vettel	Super-Soft (u): 0 (dnf)		
	Hülkenberg	Soft (u): 0 (dnf)		
	Haryanto	Super-Soft (u): 0 (dnf)		

The tyre regulations stipulate that at least two of three dry tyre specifications must be used during a dry race.

Pirelli P Zero logos are colour-coded on the tyre sidewalls: Red = Super-Soft; Yellow = Soft; White = Medium. (n) new (u) used

Photos: Peter J. Fox

149

SPANISH GRAND PRIX

CATALUNYA CIRCUIT

Inset, above: Max jumps for joy after vindicating Helmut Marko's decision to promote the youngster to the Red Bull team.
Photo: Red Bull Racing/Getty Images

Inset, left: Grand prix racing's youngest ever winner – at the age of 18 years and 228 days.

Main photo: A star is born. Max Verstappen lofts the winner's trophy.
Photos: Peter J. Fox

FORMULA 1 GRAN PREMIO DE ESPAÑA PIRELLI 2016

A T Catalunya, qualifying was all about recovery and saving face. After being put on the back foot by Nico Rosberg in the first four races of the season, and then making a mistake on the first of two Q3 laps, Lewis Hamilton knew he had it all to do on his last run.

Despite locking up badly going into Turn Ten the first time, Hamilton was confident he could still do it. After struggling to become comfortable with his Mercedes W07 on the first day, he had worked hard with engineer Pete Bonnington to make the small, but necessary changes. Part of the process involved checking on what Rosberg had been up to with Tony Ross on the other side of the garage.

"Nico seemed in control on Friday, but bit by bit I have been bringing the pace together," said Hamilton. "The car was not great yesterday and I had a bit of a wasted day. Today, starting from scratch, we made a few changes, more in the direction Nico had been already going and, straight away, I could feel the car beneath me. I was ready."

On that final run, Hamilton was faster than before in the first two sectors and deliberately braked a fraction early going into the downhill Turn Ten. This time, he was inch perfect, powering out to complete the lap and take pole by 0.28s. Rosberg, happy with his car, simply had to accept that his team-mate had been quicker.

Given their domination of the championship thus far, it was no surprise to see Mercedes locking out the front row. But the appearance of two Red Bulls on the second row was unexpected. Forgetting for a moment the dark blue cars being ahead of both Ferraris, the story of this qualifying session was the remarkable performance by Max Verstappen. The young Dutchman had made the switch from Toro Rosso to Red Bull and showed no nerves, but plenty of pace.

For much of qualifying, the 18-year-old was faster than the more experienced Daniel Ricciardo. Even as far as Q2, Ricciardo had been forced to make a second run, whereas Verstappen had saved a set of tyres for a second run in Q3. Instead of the pressure being on the youngster, it had switched to the Australian who, thus far in his career, had never been seriously challenged. Had that moment finally come?

Responding magnificently, Ricciardo produced a storming lap, followed by a shout of delight when informed he was P3. "Yeah, I left it late," he grinned. "To have us both on the second row is pretty awesome. I only gave myself one run in which to do it, and I knew it had to count. But I've been there before. It just adds a bit of excitement."

Ferrari did not share that sense of excitement, the Italian team being close to shock as Red Bull swept Kimi Räikkönen and Sebastian Vettel on to the third row. "Something went wrong for both drivers," said a stunned Maurizio Arrivabene. "We did not expect this. We have to check." Subsequent analysis would reveal Ferrari's difficulty in generating a working tyre temperature on a track that was too hot for optimum grip. Which outweighed any advantage that might have been derived from extensive aero upgrades.

"I couldn't get hold of the car," said Vettel, "I didn't get the feeling I had earlier in the day and couldn't nail the laps."

A lack of rear grip in the faster corners affected Williams, despite Valtteri Bottas setting seventh fastest time, albeit 0.4s off the Ferraris. At least the Finn was in Q3, unlike Felipe Massa, who had failed to get out of Q1 due to a misunderstanding over how much time was left to make a second run. The Brazilian was 18th.

In all of the hype surrounding Verstappen's sudden promotion, it was easy to overlook his former team-mate. Carlos Sainz did absolutely the right thing by allowing his performance in the Toro Rosso to do the talking – he qualified just 0.1s behind Bottas. Daniil Kvyat, massaging his psychological bruising, had to contend with being 0.4s slower as he settled back with his former team.

Major revisions to the Force India – front wing, sidepods, engine cover, rear wing and diffuser – helped Sergio Pérez into Q3 and ninth fastest, a couple of tenths quicker than Nico Hülkenberg. Splitting the Force Indias, Fernando Alonso was delighted that his home grand prix should be the moment when he and McLaren-Honda made it to Q3 for the first time. Team-mate Jenson Button was not far behind in 12th, the black cars predictably suffering most from a lack of straight-line speed.

Problems for the Haas drivers were tyre temperature related, Romain Grosjean and Esteban Gutiérrez struggling with lack of balance and grip in the slow corners. The pair were split by Kevin Magnussen's 15th fastest time. A lack of development was beginning to tell at Renault as rivals got going, Jolyon Palmer's weekend not being helped by a rear tyre failure at 190mph during free practice on the previous day. But if progress at Renault was slow, it was at a standstill at the cash-strapped Sauber team, Marcus Ericsson being the quicker of their two drivers by 0.25s; Felipe Nasr was ahead of Pascal Wehrlein and Rio Haryanto as the Manor drivers brought up the rear.

Above: Carlos Sainz's excellent performances in qualifying and the race were, perhaps, lost amid the excitement of Verstappen's win.
Photo: Peter J. Fox

Left: All smiles from the top three qualifiers. Their disposition would not be so sunny after the race.
Photo: Red Bull Racing/Getty Images

Below: No doubt Helmut Marko was happy that Red Bull supremo Dietrich Mateschitz (*right* was in attendance to watch his team emerge victorious.
Photo: Peter J. Fox

Above: Jenson Button finally broke his duck with a ninth-place finish for McLaren Honda.

Left: Ricciardo suffered a puncture on the penultimate lap, but the Australian held on to fourth, ahead of the Williams of Bottas.
Photos: Peter J. Fox

Above: Hamilton and Rosberg contrived to eliminate each other on the opening lap. Thus ended a run of ten consecutive Mercedes victories that had begun with Hamilton's win at Suzuka in 2015.

Photo: LAT Photographic/Zak Mauger

Right: Sebastian Vettel's Ferrari was switched to a three-stop strategy, which ultimately failed to bring the German a victory.

Photo: Scuderia Ferrari

Below right: Placido Domingo provides soothing words, but Kimi Räikkönen is left wondering whether that was one that got away...

Photo: GP Photo/Peter Nygaard

FINALLY, it happened. On the first lap of the Spanish Grand Prix, the Mercedes drivers crashed into each other. Given their rivalry, the surprise was that it had taken so long.

You could pinpoint any number of causes. One was motor sport's political correctness: the need to define anything and everything that a racing driver could and should be able to deal with instinctively.

When referring to a driver defending his position, Article 27 of the Sporting Regulations states: *More than one change of direction to defend a position is not permitted.* [During that single move] *a driver may use the width of the track provided no significant portion of the car attempting to pass is alongside his.* (In the case of the Spanish Grand Prix incident, this was later defined as any part of the front wing on the attacking car being alongside the rear wheel.)

This definition was introduced to prevent weaving. Apart from presupposing that all F1 drivers are hooligans, the rule legitimised a blatant move that contributed hugely to the collision between the Mercedes drivers as they fought for the lead during the opening lap at Barcelona.

Hamilton had led initially from pole. It had been a good start, but Rosberg had made a better one. Sensing this, Hamilton cut – as allowed – from left to right to block his team-mate, but Rosberg used the opportunity to slipstream the sister car on the long run to the first corner, before using the momentum to dart left and run around the outside to take the lead.

It was a bold move that did not best please the reigning world champion. Aware of the equality between the two Mercedes, and given the difficulty of overtaking on the Circuit de Barcelona-Cataluña, Hamilton knew that his chances of getting back in front were slim; added to which, Rosberg would now have the first call on pit-stop strategy.

But Hamilton perked up considerably seconds later, when a flashing light on the back of his team-mate's car indicated that Rosberg had made an error with his steering wheel settings and the power unit was suddenly back in the power-saving mode used during the parade lap. The German had forgotten to make the necessary adjustment while sitting on the grid. With the launch mode overriding everything at the start, all had seemed normal as the pair raced towards the first corner. But, when Rosberg disengaged the launch mode while going thought Turns Two and Three, the setting reverted to the lower power map. Rosberg instantly hit the overtake

button positioned on the left-hand side of the steering wheel. Meanwhile, the flashing red light at the back of the Mercedes was announcing to Lewis that Nico was in a spot of bother, and that this was likely to be his only chance to overtake.

Rosberg, of course, quickly came to the same conclusion and subconsciously thought of Article 27. As Mercedes Number 6 moved dramatically right, Mercedes Number 44 was already heading for a gap that was always going to close – thanks to the aforementioned permission to use the full width of the track.

Whether Hamilton had enough of his front wing alongside Rosberg's right rear wheel in this diminishing space will be debated forever. They were split-second decisions by both drivers, neither of whom had a sinister motive. Indeed, Rosberg was aggressive – because the rule does not actually define how bold a driver can be. A collision was inevitable.

Rosberg did not believe Hamilton would continue to go for the gap. But, once committed, Lewis had no alternative but to get on to the grass, where he lost control and speared into Nico as they arrived at Turn Four. Both drivers were eliminated before the race was barely a minute old.

With the favourites sidelined, the question was, which driver would step on to the vacant space at the top of the podium? Would he come from Red Bull or Ferrari? The eventual answer was arguably the driver you least expected.

Red Bull led Ferrari in the opening phase, Verstappen having sat it out with Vettel through Turn One to slot into what was now second place behind his team-mate. Räikkönen should have been next, but a wheel-spinning getaway by the Ferrari had allowed the fast-starting Sainz to move up one place, the Toro Rosso advancing further when Vettel ran wide at Turn Three.

With the safety car now on track, Ferrari boss Sergio Marchionne (in the paddock for a high-power meeting about F1's future with Dr Zetsche of Mercedes) had to take on board that both of his drivers were behind a trio of Red Bull cars, one of them powered by a Ferrari engine. But at least Marchionne's inner frustration had to be less than Zetsche's as the Mercedes drivers made a sheepish return on foot.

By the time Vettel had finally got past Sainz on lap seven, the Red Bull pair were already 5.5s down the road. But when Vettel began to eat into their lead, it became clear to the Red Bull pit-wall crew that Ferrari's race pace was not as bad as qualifying had suggested it might be.

Rather than risk the undercut, Red Bull brought both cars

in: Ricciardo on lap 11, Verstappen on the following lap. The medium tyres received by both drivers may have been slower than the discarded softs, but they were more durable; a conclusion that would be reached along the length of the pit lane. The only uncertainty – for the leaders at least – was whether to run with a two- or three-stop strategy, both options still being possible at this stage.

When Vettel continued to show good pace and stayed out until lap 15, Red Bull were in something of a dilemma as the Ferrari rejoined less than five seconds behind, but clearly in a good position to run longer to the second stop and therefore have fresher rubber for the final stint.

That said, Vettel would need to actually pass the Red Bulls if Ricciardo and Verstappen also remained on a two-stop tactic. The best way forward in every sense would be to run Vettel on three stops and, to cover Ferrari's options, keep Räikkönen (who had eventually got ahead of Sainz) on two. When Vettel appeared keen to run the more aggressive strategy, Ferrari decided to go down that route, bringing the German in once more on lap 29. That left Red Bull with Hobson's choice. One of the strategies would be wrong, but which one?

"Vettel was clearly three-stopping," said Red Bull's Christian Horner. "We had to take a tactical decision at that point to say, 'Do we try to cover Vettel with one of our cars?' The best car which we believed had the best chance of winning the race was the lead car [Ricciardo], and we elected to go for the three-stop with him."

Ricciardo was brought in from the lead on lap 28 and returned with a set of softs, Ferrari matching that strategy for Vettel on the next lap. That put Verstappen and Räikkönen – now a few car lengths from the Red Bull – up to the head of the race. When the Ferrari got within undercut range, Red Bull called in Verstappen on lap 33. Räikkönen pitted on the following lap, both drivers going for medium tyres. They were only 15 seconds behind their respective team-mates – both of whom would have to stop again. Could Verstappen and Räikkönen make their tyres last the remaining 32 laps? Could Verstappen hold off the seasoned Ferrari driver? This race was by no means settled.

Throwing the dice one more time, Ferrari brought Vettel back to the pits after just eight laps. Given that he had been right on Ricciardo's tail, Red Bull dared not mirror this move for fear of being caught on the undercut by fresher tyres and the potentially faster Ferrari. Daniel stayed out for another

Above: Valtteri Bottas had a lonely race to fifth place.
Photo: Williams Martini Racing

Top right: Well done mate! Hiding his undeniable disappointment, Daniel Ricciardo congratulates Verstappen on his victory.
Photo: Lukas Gorys

Above right: Following his demotion to Toro Rosso, Daniil Kvyat came back in fighting mood. The Russian claimed the fastest race lap and the final point on offer.
Photo: Peter J. Fox

Right: Verstappen carried out the task of preserving his tyres with great aplomb, which allowed him to keep the Ferraris at bay.
Photo: WRi2/Jean-François Galeron

six laps, the hope now being that he could have a tyre advantage over Vettel.

Ricciardo did catch Vettel and, at any track other than this one, he might have had a chance to overtake. As it was, they were nine seconds behind their team-mates, but, crucially, not lapping much faster than Verstappen and Räikkönen.

At this point, Vettel (on the medium tyre) turned his attention to keeping Ricciardo out of third place. On lap 58, the latter came from a long way back and dived down the inside going into the first corner. Vettel, unimpressed, was compelled to give the Red Bull room, but by running wide forced Ricciardo to concede. He would try once more, but it was clear that the Ferrari had the Red Bull's measure on the straight.

Recognising this situation, Verstappen had the presence of mind always to ensure that he used superior traction to make a clean exit from the final chicane and keep Räikkönen out of DRS range. Circumstance may have placed him in such a fortuitous position, but he was not about to throw it away. "We knew that the two-stop was going to be under a lot of pressure at the end of the race in terms of degradation," said Horner. "But Max was able to look after his tyres incredibly well and make sure that he had just enough left to fend off Kimi over the last five or six laps. Just incredible."

"When he was right with me in the last laps, it was like driving on ice," said Verstappen. "But I knew it's difficult to overtake here, and I just managed the pressure and the tyres – I made sure I did no front locking, didn't slide in the last sector and got a good exit from the chicane." It was a beautifully judged win; deceptively simple from a driver so relatively inexperienced. The youngest driver in the field had successfully fended off the oldest.

As if Ricciardo had not suffered enough disappointment, the Australian picked up a puncture on his penultimate lap, but he was far enough ahead of Bottas in the Williams to be able to pit for fresh rubber and return to claim fourth place. The fact that he had saved 12 points was irrelevant on a day when he felt he should have scored 25.

"In hindsight," said Ricciardo, "a three-stop strategy was the wrong thing to do, but maybe during the race it seemed like the right thing to the team. Winning with a three-stop would have required that I overtake two cars on track, which isn't very feasible round here. But, having been handed the lead and feeling in control, to not even make it to the podium is hard to take."

Bottas and Williams reckoned fifth was as good as could be expected; Sainz and Toro Rosso felt the same about sixth after another solid performance from the Spaniard, who had been overlooked in all of the Verstappen hype. Further back, Pérez just held off Massa, the Williams driver having stopped three times during a strong climb from 18th on the grid.

A similar feisty performance from Kvyat had been tempered somewhat when, after a late stop for soft tyres, the Russian was told to back off and not think about unlapping himself when he set fastest lap of the race and reeled in Vettel and Ricciardo. That cost him any chance of taking two championship points from Button, although he did manage tenth and to deny the Haas of Gutiérrez the final point.

Jolyon Palmer, 13th, split the Saubers after Ericsson found that three stops worked better than the two made by a frustrated Nasr. Magnussen received a five-place penalty after an improper clash of wheels with his Renault team-mate; the Manors brought up the rear, Wehrlein ahead of Haryanto.

Grosjean retired from the rear quarter of the field with no brakes after 56 laps, 11 after Alonso had disappointed his loyal supporters when the McLaren-Honda suffered a severe loss of power while running just behind his team-mate.

The list of retirements had been opened in spectacular fashion on lap one, the race stewards (with Martin Donnelly on board) ruling that the clash between the Mercedes drivers had been a racing incident. The decision was widely seen as an apt summary and, in the end, a dramatic subtext to history that was impressively made on 15th May, 2016 by F1's youngest winner.

Maurice Hamilton

VIEWPOINT
YOUNG BULLS LOCK HORNS

MUCH of the week leading up to the Spanish GP was spent discussing whether or not Daniil Kvyat had been hard done by in being demoted back to Toro Rosso in favour of Max Verstappen, orchestrated by the 'ruthless' Helmut Marko.

Sebastian Vettel had not enjoyed Kvyat's lunge down his inside on the opening lap in China, although Daniil and most of the paddock saw nothing wrong with it. Then, in Sochi, Kvyat had hit Vettel on the opening lap again – twice – and Christian Horner had apologised to the four-times champion.

All that, though, was coincidental to the timing, Red Bull said. The decision to switch the two youngsters had already been taken. Verstappen's name was already being talked about in the same sentence as Ferrari. Red Bull had him under contract, however, and wanted Max to take the next step, into the senior team. With the move done, Christian Horner was not slow to tell everyone that he believed he now had the strongest driver line-up in F1. Daniel Ricciardo, be believed, was driving better than anyone.

Here was one of those mouthwatering scenarios, where two aces had been paired together in cars with race-winning potential. When Verstappen performed so strongly throughout practice and qualifying while still getting used to the Red Bull, faster than Ricciardo for much of the time, people did start talking. But then we saw a revealing image of Ricciardo, sat in the pits, visor up, the familiar grin lighting up his face, just prior to his final Q3 run.

Ricciardo didn't look like a man under pressure who thought the game was up. And, sure enough, there followed a stupendous qualifying lap that was four-tenths quicker than young Max. For the record, the average qualifying gap between Ricciardo and Kvyat in comparable sessions across 2015 had been 0.26s.

In the race, though, Red Bull's switch to a three-stop strategy for Ricciardo, to cover Vettel's Ferrari, inadvertently handed the advantage to Verstappen who, unbelievably, scored a fairytale win on his debut for the senior team.

Being interviewed post-race, Ricciardo's 'Colgate' smile had gone. He did not want to say too much. "I'm feeling a little bitter," he said, before the team had been able to fully run through the reasoning behind their split strategy. A combustible situation had not taken long to ignite...

Tony Dodgins

5

2016 FORMULA 1
GRAN PREMIO DE ESPAÑA
PIRELLI
CATALUNYA 13–15 MAY

ROLEX

OFFICIAL TIMEPIECE

RACE DISTANCE: 66 laps, 190.826 miles/307.104km

RACE WEATHER: Dry/sunny (track 40–42°C, air 20–23°C)

CIRCUIT DE BARCELONA-CATALUNYA, BARCELONA

Circuit: 2.892 miles/4.655km
66 laps

Renault 205/127
Turn 5 120/75
Repsol 120/75
Turn 2 155/96
Turn 6 260/162
Campsa 180/112
Turn 8 175/109
Banc Sabadell 105/65
Total 120/75
315/196
Turn 7
Europcar 120/75
La Caixa 75/47
Turn 14/15 95/59
New Holland 200/124

Gear
187/116 kmh/mph
■ DRS zone

RACE – OFFICIAL CLASSIFICATION

Pos.	Driver	Nat.	No.	Entrant	Car/Engine	Tyres	Laps	Time/Retirement	Speed (mph/km/h)	Gap to leader	Fastest race lap	
1	Max Verstappen	NL	33	Red Bull Racing	Red Bull RB12-TAG Heuer RB12 V6	P	66	1h 41m 40.017s	112.618/181.241		1m 28.816s	36
2	Kimi Räikkönen	FIN	7	Scuderia Ferrari	Ferrari SF16-H-059/5 V6	P	66	1h 41m 40.633s	112.606/181.222	0.616s	1m 28.538s	38
3	Sebastian Vettel	D	5	Scuderia Ferrari	Ferrari SF15-H-059/5 V6	P	66	1h 41m 45.598s	112.515/181.075	5.581s	1m 27.974s	39
4	Daniel Ricciardo	AUS	3	Red Bull Racing	Red Bull RB12-TAG Heuer RB12 V6	P	66	1h 42m 23.967s	111.812/179.944	43.950s	1m 28.209s	46
5	Valtteri Bottas	FIN	77	Williams Martini Racing	Williams FW38-Mercedes PU106C V6	P	66	1h 42m 25.288s	111.788/179.906	45.271s	1m 29.081s	60
6	Carlos Sainz	E	55	Scuderia Toro Rosso	Toro Rosso STR11-Ferrari 059/4 V6	P	66	1h 42m 41.412s	111.496/179.435	1m 01.395s	1m 29.663s	42
7	Sergio Pérez	MEX	11	Sahara Force India F1 Team	Force India VJM09-Mercedes PU106C V6	P	66	1h 42m 59.555s	111.168/178.908	1m 19.538s	1m 29.801s	37
8	Felipe Massa	BR	19	Williams Martini Racing	Williams FW38-Mercedes PU106C V6	P	66	1h 43m 00.724s	111.147/178.874	1m 20.707s	1m 29.238s	43
9	Jenson Button	GB	22	McLaren Honda	McLaren MP4-31-Honda RA616H V6	P	65			1 lap	1m 30.260s	39
10	Daniil Kvyat	RUS	26	Scuderia Toro Rosso	Toro Rosso STR11-Ferrari 059/4 V6	P	65			1 lap	1m 26.948s	53
11	Esteban Gutiérrez	MEX	21	Haas F1 Team	Haas VF-16-Ferrari 059/5 V6	P	65			1 lap	1m 30.139s	34
12	Marcus Ericsson	S	9	Sauber F1 Team	Sauber C35-Ferrari 059/5 V6	P	65			1 lap	1m 29.715s	42
13	Jolyon Palmer	GB	30	Renault Sport F1 Team	Renault R.S.16-R.E.16 V6	P	65			1 lap	1m 29.779s	35
14	Felipe Nasr	BR	12	Sauber F1 Team	Sauber C35-Ferrari 059/5 V6	P	65			1 lap	1m 29.905s	38
15	Kevin Magnussen	DK	20	Renault Sport F1 Team	Renault R.S.16-R.E.16 V6	P	65	*		1 lap	1m 28.716s	57
16	Pascal Wehrlein	D	94	Manor Racing MRT	Manor MRT05-Mercedes PU106C V6	P	65			1 lap	1m 31.182s	37
17	Rio Haryanto	RI	88	Manor Racing MRT	Manor MRT05-Mercedes PU106C V6	P	65			1 lap	1m 29.402s	52
	Romain Grosjean	F	8	Haas F1 Team	Haas VF-16-Ferrari 059/5 V6	P	56	brakes			1m 28.974s	41
	Fernando Alonso	E	14	McLaren Honda	McLaren MP4-31-Honda RA616H V6	P	45	power unit			1m 29.750s	41
	Nico Hülkenberg	D	27	Sahara Force India F1 Team	Force India VJM09-Mercedes PU106C V6	P	20	oil leak			1m 31.810s	8
	Lewis Hamilton	GB	44	Mercedes AMG Petronas F1 Team	Mercedes F1 W07-Mercedes PU106C V6	P	0	accident			no time	
	Nico Rosberg	D	6	Mercedes AMG Petronas F1 Team	Mercedes F1 W07-Mercedes PU106C V6	P	0	accident			no time	

* includes 10-second penalty for causing an accident – originally finished 14th.

Fastest race lap: Daniil Kvyat on lap 53, 1m 26.948s, 119.761mph/192.735km/h.

Lap record: Giancarlo Fisichella (Renault R25 V10), 1m 15.641s, 136.835mph/220.213km/h (2005 – 2.875-mile/4.627km circuit).

Lap record (current configuration): Kimi Räikkönen (Ferrari F2008 V8), 1m 21.670s, 127.500mph/205.191km/h (2008).

All results and data © FOM 2016

21 · WEHRLEIN · Manor

19 · ERICSSON · Sauber

17 · PALMER · Renault

15 · MAGNUSSEN · Renault

13 · KVYAT · Toro Rosso

11 · HÜLKENBERG · Force India

22 · HARYANTO · Manor

20 · NASR · Sauber

18 · MASSA · Williams

16 · GUTIÉRREZ · Haas

14 · GROSJEAN · Haas

12 · BUTTON · McLaren

Grid order

		1	2	3	4	5	6	7	8	9	10	11	12	13	14	15	16	17	18	19	20	21	22	23	24	25	26	27	28	29	30	31	32	33	34	35	36	37	38	39	40	41	42	43	44	45	46	47	48	49	50	51	52
44	HAMILTON	3	3	3	3	3	3	3	3	3	33	5	5	5	5	3	3	3	3	3	3	3	3	3	3	3	33	33	33	33	33	7	3	3	3	3	3	3	3	33	33	33	33	33	33	33	33
6	ROSBERG	33	33	33	33	33	33	33	33	33	3	33	8	3	33	33	33	33	33	33	33	33	33	33	5	7	7	7	7	33	3	5	5	33	33	33	33	33	7	7	7	7	7	7	7	7	7
3	RICCIARDO	55	55	55	55	55	55	55	5	3	8	33	5	5	5	5	5	5	5	5	5	3	3	3	3	3	5	33	33	7	7	7	7	7	5	5	5	5	5	5	5	5	5
33	VERSTAPPEN	5	5	5	5	5	5	55	55	7	7	77	33	33	8	7	7	7	7	7	7	7	7	7	7	5	5	5	5	5	33	7	7	5	5	5	5	5	3	3	3	3	3	3	3	3	3
7	RÄIKKÖNEN	7	7	7	7	7	7	7	7	77	77	8	21	21	7	77	77	77	77	77	77	77	77	77	77	77	77	77	77	77	77	77	77	77	77	77	77	77	77	77	77	77	77	77	77	77	77
5	VETTEL	77	77	77	77	77	77	77	77	55	8	3	7	7	21	21	55	55	55	55	55	55	55	55	55	55	55	55	55	55	55	55	55	55	55	19	19	55	55	55	55	55	55	55	55
77	BOTTAS	11	11	11	11	11	11	11	22	14	14	21	77	77	77	55	11	11	11	11	11	11	11	11	11	11	11	11	14	19	19	55	55	19	11	11	11	11	11	11	11	11	11
55	SAINZ	22	22	22	22	22	22	22	14	8	21	12	55	55	55	11	22	22	22	22	22	22	22	22	22	22	22	22	22	19	14	14	11	21	21	21	21	21	21	21	21	21	21
11	PÉREZ	14	14	14	14	14	14	14	8	22	12	55	11	11	11	22	14	14	14	14	14	14	14	14	14	14	14	22	11	11	11	21	26	26	26	26	26	26	26	19	19
14	ALONSO	8	8	8	8	8	8	8	11	27	30	88	88	22	22	14	19	19	19	19	19	19	8	8	8	21	21	19	19	19	19	11	21	21	26	26	22	19	19	19	19	26	22
27	HÜLKENBERG	26	26	26	26	26	26	27	27	30	88	11	22	14	14	19	8	8	8	8	8	21	21	21	8	19	30	30	21	21	21	26	26	22	19	22	22	22	22	22	22	26
22	BUTTON	27	27	27	27	27	27	20	20	21	94	22	14	19	19	27	27	27	27	20	20	21	19	20	20	20	20	20	8	8	8	26	22	22	14	14	14	14	14	20	20	20	20	30
26	KVYAT	20	20	20	20	20	20	26	30	20	55	14	19	88	27	8	20	20	20	30	30	19	30	8	21	26	26	8	9	9	20	20	20	20	20	30	30	30	30	30	20
8	GROSJEAN	21	21	21	21	21	21	21	21	12	19	27	27	88	20	26	26	26	26	26	12	12	30	12	9	20	9	30	30	30	30	12	12	12	9	9	9	12	12	12	9	9
20	MAGNUSSEN	30	30	30	30	30	30	30	26	94	22	27	20	20	20	9	9	21	9	9	9	30	19	19	12	12	8	26	20	9	20	8	30	30	12	12	12	12	9	9	9	12	12
21	GUTIÉRREZ	12	12	12	12	12	19	19	12	88	19	20	26	26	88	30	21	9	30	30	12	9	94	94	26	26	94	94	9	20	12	30	12	12	9	9	9	9	8	8	8	8	8
30	PALMER	9	9	9	19	12	12	9	94	11	27	26	9	30	30	12	12	9	94	26	26	26	94	94	9	9	21	30	30	12	9	94	94	94	8	8	94	94	94	94	94
19	MASSA	94	94	94	19	9	9	9	19	88	19	20	9	30	30	30	12	12	94	88	9	5	9	9	20	20	94	94	94	94	94	8	8	8	94	94	94	88	88	88	88
9	ERICSSON	19	19	19	94	94	94	94	9	26	26	30	12	12	12	88	88	88	94	88	88	88	88	88	88	88	88	88	88	88	88	8	88	88	88	88	88
12	NASR	88	88	88	88	88	88	88	88	19	9	9	94	94	94	94	94	94	94	88
94	WEHRLEIN																																											
88	HARYANTO																																													

TIME SHEETS

PRACTICE 1 (FRIDAY)
Weather: Dry/sunny-overcast
Temperatures: track 23–34°C, air 16–19°C

Pos.	Driver	Laps	Time
1	Sebastian Vettel	22	1m 23.951s
2	Kimi Räikkönen	18	1m 24.089s
3	Nico Rosberg	34	1m 24.454s
4	Lewis Hamilton	33	1m 24.611s
5	Daniel Ricciardo	25	1m 25.416s
6	Max Verstappen	29	1m 25.585s
7	Valtteri Bottas	36	1m 25.672s
8	Carlos Sainz	19	1m 26.078s
9	Felipe Massa	32	1m 26.186s
10	Fernando Alonso	18	1m 26.243s
11	Kevin Magnussen	30	1m 26.576s
12	Daniil Kvyat	21	1m 26.583s
13	Nico Hülkenberg	27	1m 26.938s
14	Sergio Pérez	9	1m 27.064s
15	Felipe Nasr	27	1m 27.253s
16	Romain Grosjean	17	1m 27.258s
17	Esteban Gutiérrez	18	1m 27.283s
18	Marcus Ericsson	24	1m 27.392s
19	Jenson Button	19	1m 27.610s
20	Pascal Wehrlein	29	1m 28.084s
21	Rio Haryanto	34	1m 29.052s
22	Esteban Ocon	6	no time

PRACTICE 2 (FRIDAY)
Weather: Dry/sunny-overcast
Temperatures: track 36–43°C, air 19–21°C

Pos.	Driver	Laps	Time
1	Nico Rosberg	35	1m 23.922s
2	Kimi Räikkönen	31	1m 24.176s
3	Lewis Hamilton	27	1m 24.641s
4	Sebastian Vettel	35	1m 25.017s
5	Carlos Sainz	39	1m 25.131s
6	Daniel Ricciardo	37	1m 25.194s
7	Fernando Alonso	31	1m 25.342s
8	Max Verstappen	31	1m 25.375s
9	Sergio Pérez	32	1m 25.437s
10	Nico Hülkenberg	35	1m 25.453s
11	Valtteri Bottas	30	1m 25.708s
12	Jenson Button	20	1m 25.893s
13	Romain Grosjean	33	1m 25.899s
14	Kevin Magnussen	40	1m 26.244s
15	Daniil Kvyat	44	1m 26.375s
16	Felipe Massa	36	1m 26.491s
17	Jolyon Palmer	16	1m 26.770s
18	Pascal Wehrlein	40	1m 26.960s
19	Rio Haryanto	39	1m 27.252s
20	Felipe Nasr	40	1m 27.812s
21	Esteban Gutiérrez	9	1m 28.205s
22	Marcus Ericsson	42	1m 28.501s

PRACTICE 3 (SATURDAY)
Weather: Dry/sunny
Temperatures: track 28°C, air 18°C

Pos.	Driver	Laps	Time
1	Nico Rosberg	15	1m 23.078s
2	Lewis Hamilton	11	1m 23.204s
3	Sebastian Vettel	16	1m 23.225s
4	Max Verstappen	10	1m 23.719s
5	Daniel Ricciardo	9	1m 23.816s
6	Kimi Räikkönen	13	1m 24.110s
7	Valtteri Bottas	14	1m 24.356s
8	Sergio Pérez	15	1m 24.472s
9	Daniil Kvyat	13	1m 24.553s
10	Fernando Alonso	13	1m 24.555s
11	Nico Hülkenberg	15	1m 24.585s
12	Felipe Massa	15	1m 24.621s
13	Carlos Sainz	21	1m 24.695s
14	Romain Grosjean	13	1m 24.981s
15	Jenson Button	13	1m 25.051s
16	Kevin Magnussen	12	1m 25.100s
17	Esteban Gutiérrez	17	1m 25.130s
18	Jolyon Palmer	13	1m 25.376s
19	Felipe Nasr	22	1m 25.383s
20	Marcus Ericsson	24	1m 25.401s
21	Pascal Wehrlein	13	1m 26.097s
22	Rio Haryanto	19	1m 26.251s

QUALIFYING (SATURDAY)
Weather: Dry/sunny Temperatures: track 42–45°C, air 21–23°C

Pos.	Driver	First	Second	Third	Qualifying Tyre
1	Lewis Hamilton	1m 23.214s	1m 22.159s	1m 22.000s	Soft (new)
2	Nico Rosberg	1m 23.002s	1m 22.759s	1m 22.280s	Soft (new)
3	Daniel Ricciardo	1m 23.749s	1m 23.585s	1m 22.680s	Soft (new)
4	Max Verstappen	1m 23.578s	1m 23.178s	1m 23.087s	Soft (new)
5	Kimi Räikkönen	1m 23.796s	1m 23.504s	1m 23.113s	Soft (new)
6	Sebastian Vettel	1m 24.124s	1m 23.688s	1m 23.334s	Soft (new)
7	Valtteri Bottas	1m 24.251s	1m 24.023s	1m 23.522s	Soft (new)
8	Carlos Sainz	1m 24.496s	1m 24.077s	1m 23.643s	Soft (new)
9	Sergio Pérez	1m 24.698s	1m 24.003s	1m 23.782s	Soft (new)
10	Fernando Alonso	1m 24.578s	1m 24.192s	1m 23.981s	Soft (new)
11	Nico Hülkenberg	1m 24.463s	1m 24.203s		
12	Jenson Button	1m 24.583s	1m 24.348s		
13	Daniil Kvyat	1m 24.696s	1m 24.445s		
14	Romain Grosjean	1m 24.716s	1m 24.480s		
15	Kevin Magnussen	1m 24.669s	1m 24.625s		
16	Esteban Gutiérrez	1m 24.406s	1m 24.778s		
17	Jolyon Palmer	1m 24.903s			
18	Felipe Massa	1m 24.941s			
19	Marcus Ericsson	1m 25.202s			
20	Felipe Nasr	1m 25.579s			
21	Pascal Wehrlein	1m 25.745s			
22	Rio Haryanto	1m 25.939s			

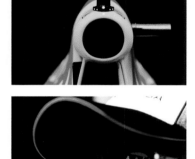

Photos: Peter J. Fox

FOR THE RECORD

1st WIN: Max Verstappen, TAG Heuer engine.

1st FASTEST LAP: Daniil Kvyat, Toro Rosso.

DID YOU KNOW?

Max Verstappen became the youngest race leader, on the podium and winner, at the age of 18 years and 228 days. It was the first time a driver had won on his first outing with a team since Alonso (Ferrari) in Bahrain, 2010, and he was the first Dutch driver to win in F1.

This was the first time since 1990 (Senna and Prost) that both cars on the front row were eliminated on the first lap.

POINTS

DRIVERS
1	Nico Rosberg	100
2	Kimi Räikkönen	61
3	Lewis Hamilton	57
4	Sebastian Vettel	48
5	Daniel Ricciardo	48
6	Max Verstappen	38
7	Felipe Massa	36
8	Valtteri Bottas	29
9	Daniil Kvyat	22
10	Romain Grosjean	22
11	Carlos Sainz	12
12	Fernando Alonso	8
13	Sergio Pérez	8
14	Kevin Magnussen	6
15	Nico Hülkenberg	6
16	Jenson Button	3
17	Stoffel Vandoorne	1

CONSTRUCTORS
1	Mercedes	157
2	Ferrari	109
3	Red Bull	94
4	Williams	65
5	Toro Rosso	26
6	Haas	22
7	Force India	14
8	McLaren	12
9	Renault	6

 9 · PÉREZ · Force India
 7 · BOTTAS · Williams
 5 · RÄIKKÖNEN · Ferrari
 3 · RICCIARDO · Red Bull
 1 · HAMILTON · Mercedes

 10 · ALONSO · McLaren
 8 · SAINZ · Toro Rosso
 6 · VETTEL · Ferrari
 4 · VERSTAPPEN · Red Bull
 2 · ROSBERG · Mercedes

Qualifying: head-to-head
Rosberg	2	3	Hamilton
Vettel	3	2	Räikkönen
Massa	1	4	Bottas
Ricciardo	4	0	Kvyat
Ricciardo	1	0	Verstappen
Pérez	4	1	Hülkenberg
Magnussen	4	1	Palmer
Verstappen	3	1	Sainz
Kvyat	0	1	Sainz
Ericsson	4	1	Nasr
Alonso	3	1	Button
Button	0	1	Vandoorne
Haryanto	2	3	Wehrlein
Grosjean	5	0	Gutiérrez

53	54	55	56	57	58	59	60	61	62	63	64	65	66	
33	33	33	33	33	33	33	33	33	33	33	33	33	33	
7	7	7	7	7	7	7	7	7	7	7	7	7	7	2
5	5	5	5	5	5	5	5	5	5	5	5	5	5	3
3	3	3	3	3	3	3	3	3	3	3	3	3		4
77	77	77	77	77	77	77	77	77	77	77	77	77	77	5
55	55	55	55	55	55	55	55	55	55	55	55	55	55	6
11	11	11	11	11	11	11	11	11	11	11	11	11	11	7
21	21	21	19	19	19	19	19	19	19	19	19	19	19	8
19	19	19	21	21	21	21	21	22	22	22	22	22	22	9
22	22	22	22	22	22	22	22	21	26	26	26	26	26	10
26	26	26	26	26	26	26	26	26	21	21	21	21		
30	30	30	30	30	30	30	30	9	9	9	9	9		
20	20	20	9	9	9	9	9	30	30	30	30	30		
9	9	12	12	12	12	12	12	12	12	12	12	12		
12	12	20		8	20	20	20	20	20	20	20	12		
8	8	8	20	94	94	94	94	94	94	94	94	94		
94	94	94	94	88	88	88	88	88	88	88	88	88		
88	88	88	88											

6 = Pit stop   9 = Drive-thru penalty

94 = One lap or more behind

■ Safety car deployed on laps shown

RACE TYRE STRATEGIES

PIRELLI

	Driver	Race Stint 1	Race Stint 2	Race Stint 3	Race Stint 4	Race Stint 5
1	Verstappen	Soft (u): 1–12	Medium (n): 13–34	Medium (n): 35–66		
2	Räikkönen	Soft (u): 1–12	Medium (n): 13–35	Medium (n): 36–66		
3	Vettel	Soft (u): 1–15	Medium (n): 16–29	Soft (u): 30–37	Medium (n): 38–66	
4	Ricciardo	Soft (u): 1–11	Medium (n): 12–28	Soft (u): 29–43	Medium (n): 44–65	Soft (u): 66
5	Bottas	Soft (u): 1–12	Medium (n): 13–39	Medium (n): 40–66		
6	Sainz	Soft (u): 1–10	Medium (n): 11–38	Medium (n): 39–66		
7	Pérez	Soft (u): 1–9	Medium (n): 10–35	Medium (n): 36–66		
8	Massa	Soft (u): 1–8	Medium (n): 9–25	Soft (u): 26–41	Medium (n): 42–66	
9	Button	Soft (u): 1–10	Medium (n): 11–36	Medium (n): 37–65		
10	Kvyat	Soft (u): 1–9	Medium (n): 10–25	Medium (n): 26–51	Soft (n): 52–65	
11	Gutiérrez	Soft (u): 1–16	Soft (u): 17–30	Medium (n): 31–65		
12	Ericsson	Soft (u): 1–9	Soft (n): 10–24	Medium (n): 25–40	Medium (n): 41–65	
13	Palmer	Soft (u): 1–11	Medium (n): 12–33	Hard (n): 34–65		
14	Magnussen	Soft (u): 1–10	Medium (n): 11–30	Hard (n): 31–55	Soft (u): 56–65	
15	Nasr	Soft (u): 1–12	Medium (n): 13–36	Medium (n): 37–65		
16	Wehrlein	Soft (u): 1–11	Medium (n): 12–33	Medium (n): 34–65		
17	Haryanto	Medium (n): 1–22	Medium (n): 23–48	Soft (u): 49–65		
	Grosjean	Soft (u): 1–15	Soft (u): 16–29	Medium (n): 30–37	Soft (u): 38–56 (dnf)	
	Alonso	Soft (u): 1–11	Medium (n): 12–39	Medium (n): 40–45 (dnf)		
	Hülkenberg	Soft (u): 1–10	Medium (n): 11–20 (dnf)			
	Rosberg	Soft (u): 0 (dnf)				
	Hamilton	Soft (u): 0 (dnf)				

The tyre regulations stipulate that at least two of three dry tyre specifications must be used during a dry race.

Pirelli P Zero logos are colour-coded on the tyre sidewalls: Yellow = Soft; White = Medium; Orange = Hard. (n) new (u) used

MONACO GRAND PRIX

MONTE CARLO CIRCUIT

Inset: Lewis thanks the heavens, after the changeable weather conditions played into his hands.

Main photo: After a slow pit stop, victory slipped from the grasp of Daniel Ricciardo, who emerged from the pit lane just too late to prevent Hamilton from taking the lead.

Photos: Peter J. Fox

MONTE CARLO QUALIFYING

RENAULT'S much awaited engine upgrade, originally scheduled for Montreal, was ready early, in time for Monaco. There had been pressure from Red Bull, who thought that they might be able to take the fight to Mercedes in Monte Carlo and even dare hope for a positive outcome.

There was one unit apiece – for Daniel Ricciardo at Red Bull and Kevin Magnussen at the works team. Max Verstappen and Jolyon Palmer would have to wait until Canada for the new power unit, complete with its combustion-improving turbulent jet ignition (as already sported by Mercedes and Ferrari). Estimates suggested that the new unit could be worth a couple of tenths around the streets of the principality and more at a power track such as Canada.

Ricciardo figured that those couple of tenths could make all the difference and was a man on a mission from first thing Thursday morning. Now he was almost able to live with the Mercs in the power-dependent sector one, which includes acceleration up the hill from Saint Devote and through Massenet. In the final sector three, through the swimming-pool section, where Ricciardo was awesome, and on to the end of the lap, the Australian had a couple of tenths in hand over everyone.

That allowed Red Bull to think bold on strategy. Pirelli's purple-walled ultra-soft tyre was on offer for the first time, along with the super-soft and soft compounds. Ricciardo alone opted for the slightly harder super-soft (yes, confusing, I know...) for his flat-out Q2 run, which of course is the tyre on which a driver qualifying in the top ten must start the race. Rain was forecast for Sunday at some stage, and the team figured that this might give them the option of running deeper into the race, hopefully allowing them to go straight on to wets when it arrived, thereby saving a pit stop.

Whatever tyre he was on, Ricciardo seemed to be in control and stopped the clock at 1m 13.622s to claim his first ever pole position.

When Nico Rosberg finished Thursday practice more than half a second shy of Ricciardo, the man who had won the previous three Monaco grands prix knew he had a battle on his hands. Yes, Mercedes had more powerful qualifying engine modes to play with, but Rosberg knew that they were unlikely to peg back that sort of deficit. He was right, too, car No. 6 managing a best of 1m 13.791s.

Over a single lap of a place like Monte Carlo, a driver can never feel totally confident of beating Lewis Hamilton, but, almost unbelievably, the reigning champion suffered more mechanical dramas. The rising temperatures and tight confines of the Monaco pits caused fuel vaporisation problems for Mercedes. Rosberg's issue was sorted in the garage, only momentarily delaying his first Q3 run, but Hamilton ground to a halt as he trundled down the pit lane, mercifully before he'd crossed the white exit line. His crew was able to pull him back and sort the problem, but not before he'd lost the time needed to do two runs.

With track temperature climbing and Lewis fuelled for a multi-lap run, his single best lap didn't come together quite as he wanted, and he could manage only 1m 13.94s, more than three-tenths from Ricciardo's pole.

The Ferraris were disappointingly off the pace in Monte Carlo. Sebastian Vettel's 1m 14.552s lap was nigh on a full second from the Red Bull pace, with Kimi Räikkönen a couple of tenths slower and pipped to fifth by a fine lap from Nico Hülkenberg in the Force India, who went a hundredth quicker than the second Ferrari. Making matters worse, Räikkönen had to suffer a five-place hit for a replacement gearbox.

Sergio Pérez is usually a star performer in Monte Carlo, but this time he had to bow to 'the Hulk' and lined up eighth, behind a fine effort from Carlos Sainz in the Toro Rosso, the young Spaniard just a hundredth behind Räikkönen's Ferrari. Daniil Kvyat couldn't get anywhere near that and was more than half a second away in ninth.

There had been bullish talk from the McLaren hierarchy pre-race – enough to make a cynic think they might have a sponsor on the hook! – and although the performance around Monaco was not quite what the team had hoped, it was good enough to get Alonso through to Q3 for the second successive race.

The reason that the low-drag Williams was such a competitive proposition at a track like Sochi also explained why it struggled at somewhere like Monaco, 11th the best that Valtteri Bottas could manage, with team-mate Felipe Massa 14th.

Esteban Gutiérrez was the first of the Haas drivers, a decent 12th, three slots ahead of team-mate Romain Grosjean. The Frenchman, however, was convinced he could have made it through to Q3 had both his Q2 flying laps not been compromised by traffic.

Kevin Magnussen put his Renault into Q2, three-tenths quicker than team-mate Jolyon Palmer – at least half of which was probably due to the upgraded engine, the pair split by Marcus Ericsson's Sauber. The Manors brought up the rear, Rio Haryanto 0.16s quicker than Pascal Wehrlein.

But what of F1's new star, Max Verstappen? It was back down to earth with a bump – literally. In third practice, he'd run wide and clipped the barrier at Massenet, and then, with the car repaired in time for qualifying, he glanced the inside barrier out of the swimming-pool section and ran across the road into the barrier. The Spanish GP and youngest-ever F1 winner was out in Q1...

Above: Charlie Whiting oversees work on the loose drain cover dislodged by Nico Rosberg.
Photo: WRi2/Studio Colombo

Top: Down to earth for Max Verstappen, who found the barriers at Massenet in both practice and the race.
Photo: WRi2/Jerry Andre

Above right: Nico Hülkenberg posted a fine fifth in qualifying for Force India and snatched sixth in the race.
Photo: Sahara Force India F1 Team

Right: Poster boy. Jackie Stewart, the race winner 50 years before.
Photo: Jad Sherif/WRi2

Below: Carlos Sainz shone once again for Toro Rosso.

Far right: Ricciardo's playground as he makes his way towards pole position.
Photos: Peter J. Fox

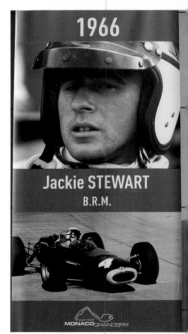

1966
Jackie STEWART
B.R.M.

SOLID grey skies on race morning confirmed the expectations of rain and, sure enough, by start time the track was wet, rain was still falling and the Monaco GP would get under way behind the safety car with everyone on the mandatory full wet Pirellis. Ricciardo still looked as confident as ever; he and the downforce-endowed Red Bull were quick in the wet, and there would be no opportunity for anyone to beat him off the line. In Monte Carlo, that can mean that a significant proportion of the job is already done.

The rain soon abated and messages began to come through from the cockpits: "It's good to go." The official Mercedes stayed out for seven laps, though, while the standing water dispersed, spray lessened and visibility improved. On a weekend when the Bianchi family announced that they were to sue the FIA over events surrounding Jules's fatal accident at Suzuka in 2014, caution was the watchword.

Once released, Ricciardo went away from the field in highly impressive fashion, more than 3s clear of Rosberg after just one racing lap, his superiority magnified by the struggle Nico was having in generating tyre temperature.

"I just couldn't get any tyre heat at all," Rosberg said, "so then I lost brake temperature, too, and there's no way you can drive quickly around Monaco when things are like that and you don't have any confidence."

Elsewhere, there were already reminders of what happens when a driver pushes a bit too hard in such conditions. Palmer, accelerating hard out of Anthony Noghes on to the front straight, suddenly had the rears spin up on a white line, which deposited him, somewhat embarrassingly, stage left into the barrier. Hard.

And even one of F1's most experienced men, Kimi Räikkönen, locked up at the hairpin, hit the barrier and tucked the nose under the Ferrari. Trying to defend his position from Massa at Portiers, he ran straight and clipped Grosjean, then trailed a shower of sparks through the tunnel before deciding that discretion was the better part of valour and parking it in the escape road at the harbour-front chicane.

Finding the right moment to switch to the intermediate Pirellis soon became the key decision, but while a drier line was emerging in sectors one and two, the final portion of the lap was still wet. Jenson Button, always an ace in changeable conditions, was one of the first to pit, while among the front-runners, Vettel rolled the dice on lap 13.

This was probably a bit early, complicated by the early stoppers dropping back out into traffic and so not providing an accurate read on the track evolution.

Ricciardo was escaping at a rate of knots, while Hamilton fretted and fumed behind the struggling Rosberg. Lewis had just decided he was going to have a go at Nico (around the outside of Massenet!) when the instruction came from Mercedes for Rosberg to let Hamilton by. Once through, he dropped his team-mate by more than 2s per lap and gave chase to Ricciardo. In the other Red Bull, Verstappen had gone on to intermediates and was going a couple of seconds a lap quicker than the leaders by lap 20, when Pérez stopped, followed by a flood of people into the pits.

Rosberg pitted and came out just ahead of the earlier-stopping Vettel. Behind him, Sainz, now running a brilliant third, and Pérez, fourth, headed for the pit lane on lap 21, when, cruelly, a stubborn front wheel nut cost the Spaniard a couple of seconds. The Mexican's Force India left the pit lane

ahead of him, and they rejoined the track just as Vettel and Hülkenberg blasted by. Pérez jumped both while the luckless Sainz dropped in behind all three. A bad break.

With the intermediates now clearly quicker, Red Bull called in Ricciardo on lap 23 of the 78 – perhaps needlessly because of his lead – and he resumed comfortably second. Now Hamilton led, and he showed no evidence of heading for the pits anytime soon. Ricciardo's pace was all too clear to Mercedes, and the only way the team could envisage beating him was to leave Hamilton out and see if he could dovetail a single stop with a switch to slicks, missing out the intermediates altogether.

This phase of the race was run quite brilliantly by Hamilton. Although the final portion of the lap still had some standing water that could be used to cool the rubber, he was managing to circulate at a similar pace to Rosberg on intermediates, without chewing up the heavier treaded Pirellis.

"I was on those tyres for a mighty long time," Hamilton smiled later. "If I'd pitted, there was no way we could have beaten Daniel, and so I was just doing everything I could to eke out that stint. It was hard to know exactly how much you could take out of the tyres, how much you could spin up the rears or how long they were going to go."

It only took Ricciardo a handful of laps on his intermediates to be right back on Hamilton's gearbox, the pair of them in a race of their own, but this being Monaco, there was no way by. In the other Red Bull, Verstappen had been making progress from the back, repeatedly diving down the inside into the harbour chicane. Ultimately, though, he ended his Monaco GP early after a second altercation with the barrier at Massenet, putting it down to experience. "Long term,

it will probably do him good…" smiled father Jos, through clenched teeth.

By lap 31, with 47 still to go, Hamilton was starting to really struggle on his full wets and pitted for the switch straight to slicks. The available tyres were the softs and super-softs, as usual, but also the ultra-softs. Although theoretically they were quicker, could he get a set of the purple-walled Pirellis to the end? Importantly, the fuel vaporisation problem that had restricted him to just the one run in Q3 meant that he had a brand-new set left, which swayed Mercedes' willingness to roll the dice and bolt on the softest rubber.

Once Hamilton stopped, Ricciardo cut loose and turned the timing screens purple. The combination of a superb in-lap from the Aussie and Hamilton skittering and opposite-locking his way around the Principality, trying desperately to get his ultra-softs into their operating window, meant that the Red Bull should have rejoined comfortably in front. But it didn't…

Team boss Christian Horner takes up the story: "We'd originally planned to fit the soft [yellow] tyres when Daniel pitted, but when we saw Lewis put on the ultra-softs, we decided to go for the super-soft instead. These would be less durable, but racier than the soft in case Hamilton started doing ballistic laps on his ultra-softs.

"Unfortunately, given the full range of tyres that had to be available – both types of wets, plus the three different compounds of slicks – all in the tight confines of the Monaco pits, the super-softs were at the back of the garage, and there was a miscommunication of what was required. Combined with Daniel's massively quick in-lap, the result was that when he arrived, we weren't ready for him."

Above: The varied conditions brought a well-earned fifth place for Fernando Alonso, and a welcome haul of points for McLaren Honda.
Photo: WRi2/Jean-François Galeron

Top left: Kimi Räikkönen blotted his copybook by hitting the barriers at the hairpin and carrying his dislodged front wing through the tunnel before ending up on the escape road.
Photo: WRi2/Studio Colombo

Above left: The race started behind the safety car, which held the field in station for seven laps before the racing started in earnest.
Photo: Peter J. Fox

Left: Nico Rosberg had a race to forget, losing out to the pursuing Nico Hülkenberg for sixth on the final lap.
Photo: Mercedes AMG Petronas F1 Team

Above: A brilliant drive by Sergio Pérez brought a podium for the Force India driver, who held off the challenge of Sebastian Vettel's Ferrari.

Top right: Pérez was very happy with his spoils.
Photos: Sahara Force India F1 Team

Above right: Commiserations from Hamilton to the unfortunate Ricciardo, who, he would happily admit, was the moral victor.
Photo: Mercedes AMG Petronas F1 Team

Right: No way past. Lewis Hamilton shuts the door firmly on Ricciardo's attempted pass.
Photo: WRi2

With sub-3s pit stops the norm in F1, Ricciardo was stationary for an agonising 12s, and by the time he exited the pit lane, Hamilton was blasting by into the lead proper.

Behind, Mercedes was able to pit Rosberg on the same lap as Hamilton, such was the distance between them, with Pérez's Force India stopping the lap before, and Vettel, Hülkenberg and Sainz all coming in at the same time as the second Mercedes.

Now it was Rosberg's turn to endure a bit of drama in the pits, a wheel-gun issue allowing Pérez to undercut him and Vettel's Ferrari to jump him in the pit lane. If that wasn't bad enough, Alonso also managed to overcut him in the McLaren-Honda by staying out a lap longer, producing a great in-lap on a clear track and getting out just ahead. The second Mercedes was now sixth.

Aboard the Red Bull, Ricciardo, seething, was able to bring in the super-softs more effectively than Hamilton managed with the ultra-softs. Monaco or not, Daniel looked determined to have a go and attempted to get down Lewis's inside into the harbour-front chicane. Hamilton was forced to brake late to repel the move, then couldn't quite get the Mercedes turned in. He missed part of the corner and compromised his exit; it looked as though the Red Bull would have a run on him down to Tabac. But Hamilton was having none of it and rudely chopped across the blue car's bows.

"What the **** was that?" Ricciardo exclaimed over the radio, but the race stewards decided that no action was necessary.

Ricciardo knew that if he was going to do something, he had to make it stick there and then, while his rubber was temporarily affording him more grip. Once Hamilton had the ultra-softs in, it would become a question of whether he could get them to the end; any realistic opportunity for the Red Bull would only come later.

But that didn't happen. Hamilton controlled the pace and

indeed managed 47 laps on his ultra-softs, which rather indicated that their moniker was something of a misnomer.

Towards the back, there was one of those moments that gives team principals apoplexy. The fact that funds were stretched to breaking point at Sauber was no secret, so it was with a mixture of disbelief and annoyance that Monisha Kaltenborn watched Marcus Ericsson slide into Felipe Nasr as he made a cack-handed attempt to pass his team-mate at Rascasse, taking both out and earning a three-place grid penalty in upcoming Montreal.

A delighted Hamilton had overcome the challenge of a slippery surface while delivering a masterclass in strategy and tyre management. But, having been victim himself of a pitting error the previous year, which had handed Rosberg a Monaco hat trick, he could feel for Ricciardo, whose brilliance all weekend he was only too willing to acknowledge.

That, though, was little consolation to the Australian. Royal presence or not, his face betrayed his feelings throughout the podium ceremony. It would be three days before he communicated at any length with his team.

Delighted to be on the podium, though, was Pérez. He and Vettel had gone for the soft tyre at their stops, knowing they would present no life issues whatsoever. They had simply got stuck in and got the Force India and Ferrari to the flag within 15s of Hamilton/Ricciardo.

Over a minute behind, Alonso had grabbed everything on offer to McLaren-Honda and more, with fifth place. Anywhere else and he'd have been swallowed up, but this was Monaco.

On the very last lap, Hülkenberg completed a dismal afternoon for Rosberg when he booted the Force India out of Rascasse and opportunistically threw it down the inside of Nico into the tight Antony Noghes final corner, pinching sixth place within sight of the flag. In a car that had just won the race, the world championship leader finished seventh...

Tony Dodgins

VIEWPOINT
BITTER PILL FOR RICCIARDO

ANYONE who had suggested that Daniel Ricciardo was a nice guy at the expense of being a hard-nosed racer, only needed to look at the podium. As Lewis Hamilton and Sergio Pérez enjoyed this precious moment, Ricciardo clearly wished he could be anywhere but up high and on display before the world.

Second place may as well have been 22nd. In fact, that would have been better, because at least he could have disappeared around the corner to Fontvieille and the quiet sanctuary of his anonymous apartment.

For a 26-year-old widely noted and loved for his happy-go-lucky demeanour, the barely concealed expression of pain said everything about the significance of losing at Monaco. Particularly on a weekend when the Australian – not a man given to boasting or self-motivating hype – had been absolutely certain from the opening lap of practice that this was going to be his weekend. A truly exquisite pole lap confirmed it. All things being equal, this race was his for the taking.

Except, of course, all things were not equal. But even allowing for things going wrong in motor racing, the breakdown in Red Bull's management communication was very hard to take. Having lost out two weeks previously in Spain was one thing; being denied at Monaco was something else. Hacked off did not begin to describe his mood.

On that basis, Nico Rosberg should have been ready to push his Mercedes into the harbour, after an afternoon struggling to coax the W07 around the damp track, and then having to move aside to let arch-rival Hamilton proceed towards the one result he did not want to see. The agony continued until the final hundred metres, when the gripless championship leader was out-accelerated by Nico Hülkenberg and pushed down to seventh place. He hadn't been that far back since Hungary the previous year.

Throwing toys out of the pram may not be Rosberg's way – and all credit to him for that – but smiles and shrugs in the late afternoon of 29th May seemed strangely out of place. Particularly when compared to the rage to win being demonstrated so quietly, yet conspicuously, on the podium.

Maurice Hamilton

6

2016 FORMULA 1
GRAND PRIX DE MONACO

MONTE-CARLO 27–29 MAY

RACE DISTANCE: 78 laps, 161.734 miles/260.286km

RACE WEATHER: Wet-drying track/cloudy
(track 19–25°C, air 17–19°C)

ROLEX

F1 OFFICIAL TIMEPIECE

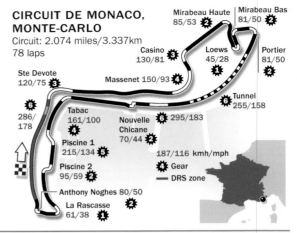

CIRCUIT DE MONACO, MONTE-CARLO
Circuit: 2.074 miles/3.337km
78 laps

Mirabeau Haute 85/53
Mirabeau Bas 81/50
Casino 130/81
Loews 45/28
Portier 81/50
Massenet 150/93
Ste Devote 120/75
Tunnel 255/158
286/178
Tabac 161/100
Nouvelle Chicane 70/44
295/183
Piscine 1 215/134
187/116 kmh/mph
Piscine 2 95/59
Gear
DRS zone
Anthony Noghes 80/50
La Rascasse 61/38

RACE – OFFICIAL CLASSIFICATION

Pos.	Driver	Nat.	No.	Entrant	Car/Engine	Tyres	Laps	Time/Retirement	Speed (mph/km/h)	Gap to leader	Fastest race lap	
1	**Lewis Hamilton**	GB	44	Mercedes AMG Petronas F1 Team	Mercedes F1 W07-Mercedes PU106C V6	P	78	1h 59m 29.133s	81.215/130.703		1m 17.939s	71
2	**Daniel Ricciardo**	AUS	3	Red Bull Racing	Red Bull RB12-TAG Heuer RB12 V6	P	78	1h 59m 36.385s	81.133/130.571	7.252s	1m 18.294s	67
3	**Sergio Pérez**	MEX	11	Sahara Force India F1 Team	Force India VJM09-Mercedes PU106C V6	P	78	1h 59m 42.958s	81.058/130.451	13.825s	1m 18.446s	64
4	**Sebastian Vettel**	D	5	Scuderia Ferrari	Ferrari SF15-H-059/5 V6	P	78	1h 59m 44.979s	81.036/130.415	15.846s	1m 18.005s	62
5	**Fernando Alonso**	E	14	McLaren Honda	McLaren MP4-31-Honda RA616H V6	P	78	2h 00m 54.209s	80.263/129.170	1m 25.076s	1m 19.170s	72
6	**Nico Hülkenberg**	D	27	Sahara Force India F1 Team	Force India VJM09-Mercedes PU106C V6	P	78	2h 01m 02.132s	80.175/129.029	1m 32.999s	1m 19.232s	74
7	**Nico Rosberg**	D	6	Mercedes AMG Petronas F1 Team	Mercedes F1 W07-Mercedes PU106C V6	P	78	2h 01m 02.423s	80.172/129.024	1m 33.290s	1m 18.763s	74
8	**Carlos Sainz**	E	55	Scuderia Toro Rosso	Toro Rosso STR11-Ferrari 059/4 V6	P	77			1 lap	1m 18.519s	70
9	**Jenson Button**	GB	22	McLaren Honda	McLaren MP4-31-Honda RA616H V6	P	77			1 lap	1m 19.670s	66
10	**Felipe Massa**	BR	19	Williams Martini Racing	Williams FW38-Mercedes PU106C V6	P	77			1 lap	1m 19.213s	69
11	Esteban Gutiérrez	MEX	21	Haas F1 Team	Haas VF-16-Ferrari 059/5 V6	P	77			1 lap	1m 19.131s	69
12	Valtteri Bottas	FIN	77	Williams Martini Racing	Williams FW38-Mercedes PU106C V6	P	77	*		1 lap	1m 19.223s	66
13	Romain Grosjean	F	8	Haas F1 Team	Haas VF-16-Ferrari 059/5 V6	P	76			2 laps	1m 20.219s	65
14	Pascal Wehrlein	D	94	Manor Racing MRT	Manor MRT05-Mercedes PU106C V6	P	76	**		2 laps	1m 20.372s	60
15	Rio Haryanto	RI	88	Manor Racing MRT	Manor MRT05-Mercedes PU106C V6	P	74			4 laps	1m 19.868s	70
	Marcus Ericsson	S	9	Sauber F1 Team	Sauber C35-Ferrari 059/5 V6	P	51	accident			1m 21.342s	51
	Felipe Nasr	BR	12	Sauber F1 Team	Sauber C35-Ferrari 059/5 V6	P	48	accident			1m 21.889s	46
	Max Verstappen	NL	33	Red Bull Racing	Red Bull RB12-TAG Heuer RB12 V6	P	34	accident			1m 26.563s	34
	Kevin Magnussen	DK	20	Renault Sport F1 Team	Renault R.S.16-R.E.16 V6	P	32	accident			1m 29.802s	27
	Daniil Kvyat	RUS	26	Scuderia Toro Rosso	Toro Rosso STR11-Ferrari 059/4 V6	P	18	accident			1m 37.895s	14
	Kimi Räikkönen	FIN	7	Scuderia Ferrari	Ferrari SF16-H-059/5 V6	P	10	accident damage			1m 47.149s	10
	Jolyon Palmer	GB	30	Renault Sport F1 Team	Renault R.S.16-R.E.16 V6	P	7	accident			1m 58.474s	2

*includes 10-second penalty for causing an accident. **includes 10-second penalty for not staying above the minimum time under the Virtual Safety Car, and 10-second penalty for ignoring blue flags.

Fastest race lap: Lewis Hamilton on lap 71, 1m 17.939s, 95.776mph/154.135km/h.
Lap record: Michael Schumacher (Ferrari F2004 V10), 1m 14.439s, 100.369mph/161.528km/h (2004).

22 · NASR · Sauber
(required to start from the pit lane – car modified in parc fermé)

20 · WEHRLEIN · Manor

18 · PALMER · Renault

16 · MAGNUSSEN · Renault

14 · MASSA · Williams

12 · GUTIÉRREZ · Haas

21 · VERSTAPPEN · Red Bull
(required to start from the pit lane – change of Survival Cell)

19 · HARYANTO · Manor

17 · ERICSSON · Sauber

15 · GROSJEAN · Haas

13 · BUTTON · McLaren

11 · RÄIKKÖNEN · Ferrari
(5-grid place penalty for replacing the gearbox)

Grid order	1 2 3 4 5 6 7 8 9 10 11 12 13 14 15 16 17 18 19 20 21 22 23 24 25 26 27 28 29 30 31 32 33 34 35 36 37 38 39 40 41 42 43 44 45 46 47 48 49 50 51 52 53 54 55 56 57 58 59 60
3 RICCIARDO	3 3 3 3 3 3 3 3 3 3 3 3 3 3 3 3 3 3 3 3 44 44 44 44 44 44 44 44 3 3 44 44 44 44 44 44 44 44 44 44 44 44 44 44 44 44 44 44 44 44 44 44 44 44 44 44 44 44 44 44
6 ROSBERG	6 6 6 6 6 6 6 6 6 6 6 6 6 6 44 44 44 44 44 44 44 3 3 3 3 3 3 3 44 44 3 3 3 3 3 3 3 3 3 3 3 3 3 3 3 3 3 3 3 3 3 3 3 3 3 3 3 3 3 3
44 HAMILTON	44 44 44 44 44 44 44 44 44 44 44 44 44 44 6 6 6 6 55 11 6 6 6 6 6 6 6 6 14 11 11 11 11 11 11 11 11 11 11 11 11 11 11 11 11 11 11 11 11 11 11 11 11 11 11 11 11 11 11 11
5 VETTEL	5 5 5 5 5 5 5 5 5 5 5 27 55 55 55 55 11 55 11 11 11 11 11 11 5 21 5 5 5 5 5 5 5 5 5 5 5 5 5 5 5 5 5 5 5 5 5 5 5 5 5 5 5 5 5 5
27 HÜLKENBERG	27 27 27 27 27 27 27 27 27 27 27 55 55 11 11 11 11 11 6 6 5 5 5 5 5 5 5 27 5 14 14 14 14 14 14 14 14 14 14 14 14 14 14 14 14 5 5 5 14 14 14 14 14 14 14 14 14 14 14 14
55 SAINZ	55 55 55 55 55 55 55 55 55 55 55 11 11 21 19 19 19 19 6 5 27 27 27 27 27 27 55 6 21 6 6 6 6 6 6 6 6 6 6 6 6 6 6 6 6 6 6 6 6 6 6 6 6 6 6 6
11 PÉREZ	11 11 11 11 11 11 11 11 11 11 11 14 77 27 5 5 5 27 55 55 55 55 55 55 14 19 6 27 27 27 27 27 27 27 27 27 27 27 27 27 27 27 27 27 27 27 27 27 27 27 27 27 27 27 27 27
26 KVYAT	14 14 14 14 14 14 14 14 14 14 14 21 19 77 21 19 27 27 27 14 14 14 21 21 21 21 55 55 55 55 55 55 55 55 55 55 55 55 55 55 55 55 55 55 55 55 55 55 55 55 55 55 55 55 55 55
14 ALONSO	77 77 77 77 77 77 77 77 77 77 77 19 5 14 14 14 14 21 21 21 21 21 14 14 27 55 33 33 22 22 22 22 22 22 22 22 22 22 22 22 22 22 22 22 22 22 22 22 22 22 22 22 22 22 22 22
77 BOTTAS	7 7 7 7 7 7 21 21 21 21 21 19 5 14 21 21 21 22 22 33 33 33 33 33 11 55 33 22 22 21 21 21 21 19 19 19 19 19 19 19 19 19 19 19 19 19 19 19 19 19 19 19 19 19 19 19
7 RÄIKKÖNEN	21 21 21 21 21 21 7 7 7 19 19 94 22 22 33 33 33 22 22 22 22 22 33 22 21 21 19 19 19 19 19 19 19 19 19 19 21 21 21 21 21 21 21 21 21 21 21 21 21 21 21 21 21 21 21 21
21 GUTIÉRREZ	22 22 22 22 22 22 22 19 19 33 94 94 94 94 22 94 94 33 19 19 19 19 19 19 19 22 19 19 77 77 77 77 77 77 77 77 77 77 77 77 77 77 77 77 77 77 77 77 77 77 77 77 77 77 77 77
22 BUTTON	19 19 19 19 19 19 19 8 8 8 94 22 22 22 27 77 77 77 77 94 94 94 94 94 94 12 88 88 88 88 94 94 94 94 94 94 94 94 94 94 94 94 94 94 94 94 94 94 94 94 94 94 94 94 94 94
19 MASSA	8 8 8 8 8 8 8 20 8 20 12 33 33 20 9 7 7 77 77 77 77 77 77 77 77 9 12 77 77 94 8 12 77 77 94 94 8 12 12 12 12 12 12 12 12 9 9 9 88 88 88 88 88 88 88 88
8 GROSJEAN	20 20 20 20 20 20 9 88 88 33 8 20 20 20 12 33 33 20 9 9 9 9 9 9 9 12 88 94 77 94 94 8 12 12 12 12 12 12 12 12 12 9 9 9 9 8 88 88 88 88 88 88 88 88
20 MAGNUSSEN	9 9 9 9 9 9 30 33 33 88 20 12 12 12 12 12 12 12 12 12 12 12 12 8 77 77 94 8 8 12 88 9 9 9 9 9 9 9 9 9 12 88 88 88
9 ERICSSON	30 30 30 30 30 30 88 94 94 94 12 33 33 33 9 9 9 9 9 88 88 88 88 88 8 8 8 8 8 12 12 9 9 88 88 88 88 88 88 88 88 88 88 88
30 PALMER	88 88 88 88 88 88 88 33 22 22 22 9 9 9 9 88 88 88 88 88 8 8 8 88 88 88 88 88 9 9 9 9 9
88 HARYANTO	94 94 94 94 94 94 94 20 20 20 88 88 88 88 8 8 8 8 20 20 20 20 20 20 20 20 20 20
94 WEHRLEIN	33 33 33 33 33 33 12 12 12 26 26 26 26 26 26 26 26 26
33 VERSTAPPEN	12 12 12 12 12 12 12 20 26 26 26 26
12 NASR	26 26 26 26 26 26 26

All results and data © FOM 2016

TIME SHEETS

PRACTICE 1 (THURSDAY)

Weather: Dry/cloudy
Temperatures: track 23-30°C, air 18-20°C

Pos.	Driver	Laps	Time
1	Lewis Hamilton	31	1m 15.537s
2	Nico Rosberg	39	1m 15.638s
3	Sebastian Vettel	26	1m 15.956s
4	Daniel Ricciardo	29	1m 16.308s
5	Max Verstappen	30	1m 16.371s
6	Daniil Kvyat	37	1m 16.426s
7	Nico Hülkenberg	34	1m 16.560s
8	Sergio Pérez	28	1m 16.697s
9	Kimi Räikkönen	24	1m 16.912s
10	Carlos Sainz	39	1m 17.130s
11	Valtteri Bottas	44	1m 17.562s
12	Romain Grosjean	33	1m 17.599s
13	Fernando Alonso	27	1m 17.838s
14	Esteban Gutiérrez	25	1m 17.909s
15	Jenson Button	26	1m 17.920s
16	Felipe Massa	29	1m 18.187s
17	Kevin Magnussen	34	1m 18.274s
18	Marcus Ericsson	33	1m 18.301s
19	Felipe Massa	10	1m 18.746s
20	Jolyon Palmer	22	1m 18.871s
21	Rio Haryanto	28	1m 20.528s
22	Pascal Wehrlein	25	1m 20.868s

QUALIFYING (SATURDAY)

Weather: Dry/sunny Temperatures: track 33-44°C, air 21-24°C

Pos.	Driver	First	Second	Third	Qualifying Tyre
1	Daniel Ricciardo	1m 14.912s	1m 14.357s	1m 13.622s	Ultra-Soft (new)
2	Nico Rosberg	1m 14.873s	1m 14.043s	1m 13.791s	Ultra-Soft (new)
3	Lewis Hamilton	1m 14.826s	1m 14.056s	1m 13.942s	Ultra-Soft (new)
4	Sebastian Vettel	1m 14.610s	1m 14.318s	1m 14.552s	Ultra-Soft (new)
5	Nico Hülkenberg	1m 15.333s	1m 14.989s	1m 14.726s	Ultra-Soft (new)
6	Kimi Räikkönen	1m 15.499s	1m 14.789s	1m 14.732s	Ultra-Soft (used)
7	Carlos Sainz	1m 15.467s	1m 14.805s	1m 14.749s	Ultra-Soft (new)
8	Sergio Pérez	1m 15.328s	1m 14.937s	1m 14.902s	Ultra-Soft (new)
9	Daniil Kvyat	1m 15.384s	1m 14.794s	1m 15.273s	Ultra-Soft (new)
10	Fernando Alonso	1m 15.504s	1m 15.107s	1m 15.363s	Ultra-Soft (new)
11	Valtteri Bottas	1m 15.521s	1m 15.273s		
12	Esteban Gutiérrez	1m 15.592s	1m 15.293s		
13	Jenson Button	1m 15.554s	1m 15.352s		
14	Felipe Massa	1m 15.710s	1m 15.385s		
15	Romain Grosjean	1m 15.465s	1m 15.571s		
16	Kevin Magnussen	1m 16.253s	1m 16.058s		
17	Marcus Ericson	1m 16.299s			
18	Jolyon Palmer	1m 16.586s			
19	Rio Haryanto	1m 17.295s			
20	Pascal Wehrlein	1m 17.452s			
21	Max Verstappen	1m 22.467s			
22	Felipe Nasr	no time			

PRACTICE 2 (THURSDAY)

Weather: Dry/sunny
Temperatures: track 34-37°C, air 18-20°C

Pos.	Driver	Laps	Time
1	Daniel Ricciardo	40	1m 14.607s
2	Lewis Hamilton	36	1m 15.213s
3	Nico Rosberg	48	1m 15.506s
4	Max Verstappen	42	1m 15.571s
5	Daniil Kvyat	53	1m 15.815s
6	Carlos Sainz	54	1m 15.981s
7	Kimi Räikkönen	38	1m 16.040s
8	Sergio Pérez	48	1m 16.120s
9	Sebastian Vettel	40	1m 16.269s
10	Jenson Button	46	1m 16.325s
11	Nico Hülkenberg	49	1m 16.487s
12	Fernando Alonso	43	1m 16.723s
13	Esteban Gutiérrez	40	1m 16.782s
14	Valtteri Bottas	47	1m 16.849s
15	Romain Grosjean	23	1m 16.874s
16	Felipe Massa	42	1m 17.286s
17	Kevin Magnussen	29	1m 17.530s
18	Marcus Ericsson	39	1m 17.562s
19	Jolyon Palmer	24	1m 17.761s
20	Felipe Nasr	49	1m 17.999s
21	Rio Haryanto	10	1m 18.647s
22	Pascal Wehrlein	46	1m 18.814s

PRACTICE 3 (SATURDAY)

Weather: Dry/sunny
Temperatures: track 33°C, air 21°C

Pos.	Driver	Laps	Time
1	Sebastian Vettel	25	1m 14.650s
2	Lewis Hamilton	24	1m 14.668s
3	Nico Rosberg	29	1m 14.772s
4	Daniel Ricciardo	22	1m 14.807s
5	Max Verstappen	17	1m 15.081s
6	Daniil Kvyat	23	1m 15.259s
7	Carlos Sainz	26	1m 15.324s
8	Sergio Pérez	21	1m 15.368s
9	Kimi Räikkönen	22	1m 15.555s
10	Nico Hülkenberg	20	1m 15.666s
11	Felipe Massa	29	1m 16.068s
12	Fernando Alonso	24	1m 16.257s
13	Jenson Button	23	1m 16.298s
14	Valtteri Bottas	21	1m 16.347s
15	Esteban Gutiérrez	23	1m 16.406s
16	Kevin Magnussen	13	1m 16.412s
17	Romain Grosjean	27	1m 16.527s
18	Felipe Nasr	23	1m 16.867s
19	Marcus Ericsson	32	1m 17.038s
20	Jolyon Palmer	17	1m 17.482s
21	Pascal Wehrlein	32	1m 17.595s
22	Rio Haryanto	34	1m 18.180s

Photo: Mercedes AMG Petronas F1 Team

FOR THE RECORD

1st POLE POSITION: Daniel Ricciardo.

100th GRAND PRIX STARTED: Nico Hülkenberg.

70th RACE WITH A FRONT ROW: Mercedes.

50th WIN: Mercedes.

DID YOU KNOW?

Ricciardo became the 11th driver to achieve his maiden pole at Monaco. The previous occasion was Jarno Trulli in 2004.

POINTS

DRIVERS

1	Nico Rosberg	106
2	Lewis Hamilton	82
3	Daniel Ricciardo	66
4	Kimi Räikkönen	61
5	Sebastian Vettel	60
6	Max Verstappen	38
7	Felipe Massa	37
8	Valtteri Bottas	29
9	Sergio Pérez	23
10	Daniil Kvyat	22
11	Romain Grosjean	22
12	Fernando Alonso	18
13	Carlos Sainz	16
14	Nico Hülkenberg	14
15	Kevin Magnussen	6
16	Jenson Button	5
17	Stoffel Vandoorne	1

CONSTRUCTORS

1	Mercedes	188
2	Ferrari	121
3	Red Bull	112
4	Williams	66
5	Force India	37
6	Toro Rosso	30
7	McLaren	24
8	Haas	22
9	Renault	6

10 · BOTTAS · Williams

8 · KVYAT · Toro Rosso

6 · SAINZ · Toro Rosso

4 · VETTEL · Ferrari

2 · ROSBERG · Mercedes

9 · ALONSO · McLaren

7 · PÉREZ · Force India

5 · HÜLKENBERG · Force India

3 · HAMILTON · Mercedes

1 · RICCIARDO · Red Bull

Qualifying: head-to-head

Rosberg	3	3	Hamilton
Vettel	4	2	Räikkönen
Massa	1	5	Bottas
Ricciardo	4	0	Kvyat
Ricciardo	2	0	Verstappen
Pérez	4	2	Hülkenberg
Magnussen	5	1	Palmer
Verstappen	3	1	Sainz
Kvyat	0	2	Sainz
Ericsson	5	1	Nasr
Alonso	4	1	Button
Button	0	1	Vandoorne
Haryanto	3	3	Wehrlein
Grosjean	5	1	Gutiérrez

RACE TYRE STRATEGIES

PIRELLI

	Driver	Race Stint 1	Race Stint 2	Race Stint 3	Race Stint 4
1	Hamilton	Wet (n): 1-31	Ultra-Soft (n): 32-78		
2	Ricciardo	Wet (n): 1-23	Inter (n): 24-32	Super-Soft (u): 33-78	
3	Pérez	Wet (n): 1-21	Inter (n): 22-30	Soft (n): 31-78	
4	Vettel	Wet (n): 1-13	Inter (n): 14-31	Soft (n): 32-78	
5	Alonso	Wet (n): 1-14	Inter (n): 15-32	Super-Soft (n): 33-78	
6	Hülkenberg	Wet (n): 1-15	Inter (n): 16-31	Soft (n): 32-78	
7	Rosberg	Wet (n): 1-20	Inter (n): 21-31	Ultra-Soft (u): 32-78	
8	Sainz	Wet (n): 1-21	Inter (n): 22-31	Super-Soft (n): 32-77	
9	Button	Wet (n): 1-8	Inter (n): 9-30	Super-Soft (n): 31-77	
10	Massa	Wet (n): 1-20	Inter (n): 21-32	Super-Soft (n): 33-77	
11	Bottas	Wet (n): 1-15	Inter (n): 16-30	Super-Soft (n): 31-49	Ultra-Soft (n): 50-77
12	Gutiérrez	Wet (n): 1-16	Inter (n): 17-32	Ultra-Soft (n): 33-77	
13	Wehrlein	Wet (n): 1-31	Ultra-Soft (n): 76		
14	Grosjean	Wet (n): 1-15	Inter (n): 16-30	Ultra-Soft (n): 31-76	
15	Haryanto	Wet (n): 1-11	Inter (n): 12-34	Ultra-Soft (n): 35-47	Ultra-Soft (u): 48-74
	Ericsson	Wet (n): 1-11	Inter (n): 12-29	Ultra-Soft (n): 30-49	Ultra-Soft (u): 50-51 (dnf)
	Nasr	Wet (n): 1-8	Inter (n): 9-32	Ultra-Soft (n): 33-48 (dnf)	
	Verstappen	Wet (n): 1-12	Inter (n): 13-31	Soft (n): 32-34 (dnf)	
	Magnussen	Wet (n): 1-7	Inter (n): 8-21	Inter (n): 22-29	Super-Soft (n): 30-32 (dnf)
	Kvyat	Wet (n): 1	Wet (u): 2	Wet (u): 3-7	Inter (n): 8-18 (dnf)
	Räikkönen	Wet (n): 1-10 (dnf)			
	Palmer	Wet (n): 1-7 (dnf)			

At least two of three dry tyre specs must be used in a dry race. If Wet or Intermediate tyres are needed, this rule is suspended. Pirelli P Zero sidewall logos are colour-coded: Red = Super-Soft; Yellow = Soft; Purple = Ultra-Soft; Blue = Wet; Green = Intermediate. (n) new (u) used

62	63	64	65	66	67	68	69	70	71	72	73	74	75	76	77	78	
44	44	44	44	44	44	44	44	44	44	44	44	44	44	44	44	44	1
3	3	3	3	3	3	3	3	3	3	3	3	3	3	3	3	3	2
11	11	11	11	11	11	11	11	11	11	11	11	11	11	11	11	11	3
5	5	5	5	5	5	5	5	5	5	5	5	5	5	5	5	5	4
14	14	14	14	14	14	14	14	14	14	14	14	14	14	14	14	14	5
6	6	6	6	6	6	6	6	6	6	6	6	6	6	6	6	27	6
27	27	27	27	27	27	27	27	27	27	27	27	27	27	27	27	6	7
55	55	55	55	55	55	55	55	55	55	55	55	55	55	55	55	55	8
22	22	22	22	22	22	22	22	22	22	22	22	22	22	22	22	22	9
19	19	19	19	19	19	19	19	19	19	19	19	19	19	19	19	19	10
21	21	21	21	21	21	21	21	21	21	21	21	21	21	21	21	17	
77	77	77	77	77	77	77	77	77	77	77	77	77	77	77	77	21	
94	94	94	94	94	94	94	94	94	94	94	94	94	94				
8	8	8	8	8	8	8	8	8	8	8	8	8	8	8	8		
88	88	88	88	88	88	88	88	88	88	88	88	88	88				

6 = Pit stop   9 = Drive-thru penalty

94 = One lap or more behind

Safety car deployed on laps shown

Photos: Peter J. Fox

CANADIAN GRAND PRIX

MONTREAL CIRCUIT

MONTREAL QUALIFYING

AFTER Red Bull's showing in Monaco, there was renewed anticipation surrounding the Canadian GP. Could Christian Horner's squad take it to Mercedes at a power track such as Montreal after its recent Renault engine upgrade? And how much difference would Ferrari's upgraded turbo make?

Throughout practice, the indication was that Mercedes still had a significant advantage, Lewis Hamilton looking totally in control at a circuit that always seems to suit his aggressive braking and reactive style. If he had a challenge, it seemed to be getting the ultra-soft Pirellis into their operating window in temperatures that had everyone reaching for fleeces and down jackets.

"I didn't really get any of my laps properly together," Hamilton said, after what had been a fairly consistent four-tenths advantage over Nico Rosberg throughout practice had shrunk to just a few hundredths as they battled for the top spot. Hamilton's pole time, in fact, was his first Q3 run, the second no improvement, as he got out of shape in Turn Eight. Rosberg's attempt to take advantage and take pole against the run of play foundered at the first corner, when he locked up.

If Ferrari's early-season races had not quite lived up to Maranello's optimism, things looked better here, as the revised engine, new Shell fuel and reworked rear bodywork allowed Sebastian Vettel to within 0.15s of pole.

"I actually thought pole was possible today," said the four-times champion, "but I think I was too greedy out of the hairpin and not greedy enough in Turn Six. I didn't leave anything out of the final chicane, though, and actually brushed Champions Wall, so I can tick that box!"

At a time when Kimi Räikkönen's continued tenure of the second Ferrari had become a subject of speculation on a race-by-race basis, he could have done with being closer to Vettel than the six-tenths that separated them, particularly as both Red Bulls managed to fill that gap.

The RB12s were much closer than they had been 12 months earlier, but the margin was still 0.35s, and they were still struggling for top-end speed on the straight versus Mercedes and Ferrari. The gap made sense later in the season, when Christian Horner let slip that the upgraded Renault, important step though it was, still lacked around 45bhp compared to the top performing power units.

Max Verstappen was the quicker of the two Red Bull drivers on the first Q3 run, but Daniel Ricciardo put the teenager in his place on the second. That left the latter to ponder again a grid sheet that had his team-mate around a quarter of a second in front, and this time with both using the same engine spec.

Montreal was good territory for a Williams-Mercedes, and Valtteri Bottas and Felipe Massa qualified seventh and eighth. The low-drag FW38 was quickest of all through the speed trap, but around half a second adrift of Red Bull over the entire lap. Massa's was a decent recovery after a big shunt into Turn One in the first session of free practice on Friday, when his car turned sharp right as he hit the brakes and the DRS closed.

Nico Hülkenberg qualified the first Force India ninth, split from team-mate Sergio Pérez by the two McLaren-Hondas – an unthinkable scenario in Montreal a year earlier!

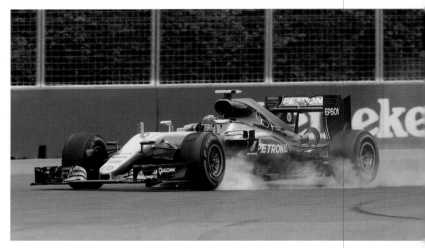

Jenson Button generally seemed to have a tenth or so in hand over Fernando Alonso throughout the practice sessions, but the Spaniard cheekily managed to go out right behind JB and use a back-straight tow from his team-mate to elevate himself into Q3 for the second successive race.

Toro Rosso had been likely Q3 candidates, but Carlos Sainz flirted too heavily with Champions Wall in Q2. Team-mate Daniil Kvyat came mightily close to the same fate before finding himself 13th, with a three-place grid demotion for his Monaco coming-together with Kevin Magnussen still to be added.

That promoted the Haas drivers, with Esteban Gutiérrez outqualifying Romain Grosjean for the first time. After such a strong start in the warmer climes of Australia and Bahrain, a constant struggle to generate tyre temperature was becoming a recurring theme for Gene Haas's men, with the relatively benign Montreal track surface and lack of real corners exaggerating it, to Grosjean's frustration in particular.

In fact, the French-Swiss only escaped Q1 by the narrowest of margins. Jolyon Palmer – in the lone Renault after Magnussen had damaged his chassis with a shunt in free practice – had appeared to be on course to demote him until Rio Haryanto put his Manor into the Turn Five wall and brought out the red flag.

Pascal Wehrlein did a strong job to outqualify both Saubers with the sister Manor. Marcus Ericsson shaded Felipe Nasr, who didn't like the feel of his brakes, before the Swede also took a three-place hit for the Rascasse assault on his team-mate a fortnight earlier in Monte Carlo.

RACE starts had been something of an Achilles heel for Lewis Hamilton throughout the 2016 season so far, and his Montreal getaway was not the best either. Vettel, by contrast, was off the line like a scalded cat, the Ferrari past both Mercedes in a trice and leading the field into Turn One.

On the outside of Hamilton, Rosberg's start was better, but the run to the first corner in Canada is a short one, and perhaps it was a bit optimistic of Nico to think his team-mate would allow him to run around his outside, as he had in Spain a month earlier. Hamilton let his car run out in the first left-hander, the pair banged wheels, and Nico was forced to bump his way across the escape road and rejoin on the exit of Turn Two.

By that time, Vettel, Hamilton, both Red Bulls, Räikkönen, Bottas, Massa, Alonso and Hülkenberg had all gone through. Nico's front-row start had translated into tenth place and a tricky afternoon.

With temperatures still lower than expected, Vettel initially seemed to bring his tyres in quicker than Hamilton and opened up an early lead, only to overdo his braking at the final chicane. He bailed out of the turn, went left past the penalty marker as required and rejoined still in front, but with Hamilton back on his gearbox.

Despite its long back straight, Montreal is not the easiest track on which to pass, and Vettel was able to keep Hamilton at bay even when DRS became active on lap three. The pair of them disappeared from the rest of the field at an impressive rate, with Verstappen, Ricciardo and Räikkönen leading the chase. The Finn looked potentially quicker than the Red Bulls, but also was unable to get by them.

Behind, Hülkenberg and Rosberg did manage to take advantage of Honda's relative lack of horsepower to demote Alonso and tag on to the back of the Williams pair.

In lower temperatures than predicted for Montreal at the time the tyre choice had been made several months in advance, it was going to be interesting to see what the tyre life of the respective compounds was like and whether anyone could make a one-stop race work. Two stops were notionally quicker, but of course they came with uncertainties surrounding traffic.

Pérez, renowned for his ability to eke out tyre life, had started 12th on the soft-compound Pirelli, which was reckoned to be good for 50 laps or more if it was quick enough, but he lost places on the opening lap because of its reduced grip compared to the softer compounds. Thus, with the Mexican in traffic early on, it was hard for the leaders to get a gauge on the true race pace of the yellow-walled tyre and to make an informed decision as to whether it had the pace, in these temperatures, to make a one-stop race properly viable.

The ultra-softs, on which the top ten qualifiers had to start the race, were reckoned to be okay for 20–25 laps, and that was the strategy conundrum occupying minds on the pit wall when the Honda in Button's McLaren let go on the back straight ten laps in. Jenson pulled off, and the race was neutralised by a virtual safety car (VSC) as the marshals set to moving the McLaren out of harm's way.

With the cars now circulating slowly to a pre-determined delta, pitting under the VSC could save time, and with Ferrari planning a two-stop race, it was deemed soon enough to bring in the red cars. It was a no-brainer if the thinking was that everyone was running a two-stop race, but arguably an error to surrender track position given that Mercedes in particular was planning to get through on a one-stop.

Ferrari might also have rolled the dice, bolted on the softs and attempted to get 59 laps out of them, but as soon as a set of the red-walled super-softs went on to Vettel's car, Mercedes and the rest knew that Ferrari was committed to a two-stop.

Above: Sebastian Vettel grabs the lead as Rosberg is pushed wide by team-mate Hamilton. The Red Bulls lead the remainder of the pack in an orderly manner.
Photo: WRi2/Jean-François Galeron

Facing page, from top:
Felipe Massa hit the wall hard in Friday free practice.
Photo: Lukas Gorys

Vettel skirted disaster in qualifying!
Photo: Peter J. Fox

Carlos Sainz, however, did a proper demolition job on his Toro Rosso!

Centre left: Nico Rosberg locks the brakes and loses his opportunity to take pole position.
Photos: Lukas Gorys

Below left: Chilly conference between Kimi Räikkönen, Jock Clear and Dave Greenwood on the grid.
Photo: Scuderia Ferrari

Opening spread: Formula 1's new promotional deal with Heineken was very much in evidence in Canada.
Photo: Peter J. Fox

The other tactic Ferrari might have adopted was to split strategy with Räikkönen, but by the time the instruction to stay out had been communicated to the Finn, he was already committed to the pit lane, where he too was given a set of super-softs.

As racing resumed, Hamilton led for the first time, from Verstappen, Ricciardo, then the reshod Vettel. The Red Bulls had struggled initially with tyre graining, Verstappen seemingly more so than his team-mate, and a radio instruction had been forthcoming for Max not to hold up Daniel. The VSC occurred before the teenager came under more pressure to act upon it, however, and with Ricciardo now struggling to get his ultra-softs back to working temperature and preoccupied with Vettel's Ferrari, Verstappen had a stay of execution.

Ricciardo resisted his former team-mate for a handful of laps before Vettel forced his way down the inside into Turn Ten. The Ferrari was past Verstappen with the help of DRS on the next lap and up into second place, Seb lapping almost a second quicker than race leader Hamilton with the benefit of his fresh super-softs.

For Mercedes, the strategy was now straightforward. They needed to get Hamilton as far as possible into the race on his ultra-soft starting tyres, so as not to ask too much of the softs (these being Pirelli's designated mandatory tyre) that he would change on to at his only stop. Provided that Vettel didn't get close enough to undercut him at the Ferrari's second stop, it would be game over.

Behind, nobody was close enough to be a threat, the only other significant mover being Rosberg in the second silver arrow. He had passed Hülkenberg before starting to close down the Williams pair.

In fact, Bottas and Massa were starting to look racier than the Red Bull pair, still struggling with graining on the ultra-softs. To protect against the undercut from the closing Finn, Red Bull pitted Verstappen after 20 laps and brought in Ricciardo a lap later.

The Dutchman rejoined in front of Räikkönen's Ferrari, in ten laps earlier under the VSC of course, while Ricciardo came out just behind the red car. The Williams pair came in a couple of laps later, the team's now customary rapid stops meaning that Bottas only narrowly failed to displace Ricciardo.

By lap 24, just over one-third distance, Vettel had his Ferrari within almost 5s of Hamilton's lead Mercedes, so Lewis was pitted, requiring him to do 46 laps on a set of softs as he rejoined just over 13s behind Vettel, who of course had another stop to make.

The pace of the Ferrari on its used super-softs versus the Mercedes on its new softs was relatively even, and with the lower ambient temperatures failing to trigger the thermal degradation so often seen with the current-generation Pirellis, Vettel and Hamilton were able to drive relatively flat out without having to concern themselves too much with minding the rubber.

Above: A welcome first podium of the season for Valtteri Bottas, after he had taken advantage of Red Bull's tyre woes.

Top left: Kimi Räikkönen might have fared better than sixth but for being put on to the same two-stop strategy as team-mate Vettel. The Finn, however, did hold off the challenge of Daniel Ricciardo.

Photos: Peter J. Fox

Above left: No way past. An obdurate Max Verstappen successfully held off the hard-charging Rosberg for fourth.

Photo: Jean-François Galeron/WRi2

Left: A win lost for Vettel? Ferrari's decision to give up track position proved costly for the German.

Photo: Peter J. Fox

VIEWPOINT
VETTEL: SEEING THE BIGGER PICTURE?

BECAUSE the Ferrari driver had appeared to be polite and politically correct, not much was made of Sebastian Vettel defending the strategy decision that possibly had cost him victory in the Canadian Grand Prix.

With hindsight, the positive talk of the team "making immense progress", and "We didn't win, but we showed we had a very good weekend," could be translated as Vettel looking after his own interests as much as those of the team. On reflection, it could also be said that Seb knew the required results might not be achieved in forthcoming races and the pressure would be even greater than it was in the aftermath of Montreal.

If that was the case, he had two options: rant and rage, or stay calm and get the team on side – his side. Vettel is no fool. He clearly chose the latter and gave the team support at a time when the accusations – not necessarily valid, but damaging nonetheless – were about to fly, as only they can when associated with the pride of Italy.

Perhaps it is no coincidence that less than a month later, Ferrari took up their option on Kimi Räikkönen for 2017. Apart from this being several weeks earlier than Ferrari's traditional pre-Monza moment for such announcements, and taking into account the Finn's age and comparative lack of consistent form, the unexpected move smacked of being Vettel's choice as much as, if not more than, that of the Ferrari management.

Was this the preference of a driver who did not wish to see Daniel Ricciardo, Carlos Sainz, Romain Grosjean or Nico Hülkenberg – names rumoured to be under consideration at Maranello – on the other side of the garage? From their time together, Vettel knew that Räikkönen, happy to be invited back at the age of 37, would not make waves in any direction affecting him.

When subsequently interviewed by Lee McKenzie for Channel 4 TV, Vettel admitted he had more personal influence at Ferrari than he had ever enjoyed at Red Bull. All of which might explain an F1 driver seeing the bigger picture and remaining noticeably calm over a victory lost through no fault of his own.

Maurice Hamilton

The fact that both were fully 'on it' was reflected by each making the odd mistake: Hamilton running too deep into the hairpin a couple of times, and Vettel again having to miss the final chicane.

"I was also more compassionate with the seagulls..." Vettel smiled. "There seemed to be a couple with a suicide pact on the apex at Turn One, and I went wide and cost myself half a second or so, but Lewis took the normal line, and happily by the time he got there they'd flown off."

Vettel took his super-softs to lap 33, giving himself nine laps less on his final set of softs when he pitted out just over 7s behind Hamilton's leading Mercedes. But, even if Seb was able to catch Lewis, what was the realistic chance of being able to pass him? You did wonder about that decision to give up track position under the VSC.

Quite possibly, Ferrari had actually based its strategy not so much on beating Mercedes (they weren't to know that Vettel would pull off a ballistic start to lead from the first lap) as on making sure they could see off Red Bull over the duration of the race.

But, in fact, Christian Horner's men were struggling. Ricciardo could not find a way past Räikkönen on his super-softs until the Ferrari made its second stop around half-distance, whereupon Daniel locked up into the final chicane and had to take the long way around, which was enough to cede fourth place to Bottas's Williams.

"It wasn't my greatest day," Ricciardo admitted. "I then locked up again into six and flat-spotted the tyre properly." It meant that a one-stop run went out of the window, and Ricciardo was in for a second set of soft-compound Pirellis after 38 laps.

Verstappen also did not have great pace on the hardest of Pirelli's three Canada compounds and bailed out of a two-stopper to fit a set of ultra-softs for the final 24 laps.

That promoted Bottas to third in the sole remaining Williams, Felipe Massa having succumbed to an overheating engine, but the recovering Rosberg was now fourth and closing in. Verstappen ran fifth, ahead of Räikkönen, with

Ricciardo once more behind the second Ferrari. Then there was a gap to Hülkenberg's Force India and an inspired Sainz, who had driven a fine recovery race after his qualifying shunt.

Just as it looked as though Rosberg would complete an exercise in damage limitation by closing down Bottas and finishing on the podium, Mercedes data revealed a slow puncture in the right rear. He was forced into an unplanned second pit visit for another set of softs.

Now comfortably the quickest car on the circuit, Nico quickly re-caught Ricciardo and Räikkönen, going by both with the assistance of DRS.

Next on the German's radar was Verstappen, which provided great closing-lap entertainment and helped Bottas in his quest for a first Williams podium of 2016.

Verstappen, remember, was on a set of ultra-softs, which afforded him a little extra grip under braking. While the Mercedes was indisputably quicker, Max had the tools with which to fight, and didn't he use them!

Coming down the back straight, the Red Bull would flick right on the approach to the final chicane, forcing Rosberg to try to go around the outside, but Verstappen was able to go deep enough into the braking area to prevent that. It was the same story at Turn One, where Max would drive a wide line out and force Nico to back off.

Approaching the last lap, Rosberg made a concerted effort into the final chicane, but Verstappen defended his fourth place as staunchly as ever and the Mercedes spun, Nico only just gathering it all up and rejoining before Räikkönen's Ferrari managed to steal fifth. Not only can Verstappen overtake, but also his racecraft is as natural as anyone's.

And so it was two in row for a delighted Hamilton as Ferrari finally showed greater competitiveness. Some figured that, as in Melbourne, Maranello had thrown away a potential win with a strategy call. But there was no accusing finger from Vettel. Not publicly anyway, and you did begin to wonder if Sebastian perhaps had one eye on the bigger overall picture (see Viewpoint).

Tony Dodgins

Above: Mercedes' one-stop strategy worked perfectly for Lewis Hamilton, who protected his Pirellis to ensure a second successive win.
Photo: Peter J. Fox

Top left: Thumbs-up from Lewis, who closed to within nine points of Rosberg's championship lead.
Photo: Lukas Gorys

Above left: Carlos Sainz recovered brilliantly from his qualifying accident to put the Toro Rosso in ninth place.
Photo: Red Bull Racing/Getty Images

Left: Good loser? Outwardly, at least, Seb appeared to take defeat with good grace.
Photo: Scuderia Ferrari

7

2016 FORMULA 1
GRAND PRIX DU CANADA

MONTRÉAL 10–12 JUNE

ROLEX

F1 **OFFICIAL TIMEPIECE**

RACE DISTANCE:

70 laps, 189.686 miles/305.270km

RACE WEATHER:

Dry/overcast (track 21–24°C, air 12–13°C)

CIRCUIT GILLES VILLENEUVE, MONTRÉAL

Turn 2 80/50
Turn 3/4 143/89
Pont de la Concorde 160/99
Turn 5 260/162
Turn 6 105/65
Virage Senna 160/99
Droit du Casino 335/208
Start/finish Chicane 145/90
301/187
Turn 8 120/75
Turn 9 160/99
Droite du Casino
Épingle 86/53

Circuit: 2.709 miles/4.361km
70 laps

187/116 kmh/mph ✿ Gear ▬ DRS zone

RACE – OFFICIAL CLASSIFICATION

Pos.	Driver	Nat.	No.	Entrant	Car/Engine	Tyres	Laps	Time/Retirement	Speed (mph/km/h)	Gap to leader	Fastest race lap	
1	**Lewis Hamilton**	GB	44	Mercedes AMG Petronas F1 Team	Mercedes F1 W07-Mercedes PU106C V6	P	70	1h 31m 05.296s	124.946/201.081		1m 15.981s	68
2	**Sebastian Vettel**	D	5	Scuderia Ferrari	Ferrari SF15-H-059/5 V6	P	70	1h 31m 10.307s	124.832/200.897	5.011s	1m 16.297s	70
3	**Valtteri Bottas**	FIN	77	Williams Martini Racing	Williams FW38-Mercedes PU106C V6	P	70	1h 31m 51.718s	123.894/199.388	46.422s	1m 16.938s	68
4	**Max Verstappen**	NL	33	Red Bull Racing	Red Bull RB12-TAG Heuer RB12 V6	P	70	1h 31m 58.316s	123.745/199.149	53.020s	1m 16.319s	49
5	**Nico Rosberg**	D	6	Mercedes AMG Petronas F1 Team	Mercedes F1 W07-Mercedes PU106C V6	P	70	1h 32m 07.389s	123.542/198.822	1m 02.093s	1m 15.599s	60
6	**Kimi Räikkönen**	FIN	7	Scuderia Ferrari	Ferrari SF16-H-059/5 V6	P	70	1h 32m 08.313s	123.522/198.789	1m 03.017s	1m 16.919s	44
7	**Daniel Ricciardo**	AUS	3	Red Bull Racing	Red Bull RB12-TAG Heuer RB12 V6	P	70	1h 32m 08.930s	123.508/198.767	1m 03.634s	1m 16.506s	51
8	**Nico Hülkenberg**	D	27	Sahara Force India F1 Team	Force India VJM09-Mercedes PU106C V6	P	69			1 lap	1m 16.604s	68
9	**Carlos Sainz**	E	55	Scuderia Toro Rosso	Toro Rosso STR11-Ferrari 059/4 V6	P	69			1 lap	1m 16.578s	54
10	**Sergio Pérez**	MEX	11	Sahara Force India F1 Team	Force India VJM09-Mercedes PU106C V6	P	69			1 lap	1m 16.559s	54
11	Fernando Alonso	E	14	McLaren Honda	McLaren MP4-31-Honda RA616H V6	P	69			1 lap	1m 17.307s	67
12	Daniil Kvyat	RUS	26	Scuderia Toro Rosso	Toro Rosso STR11-Ferrari 059/4 V6	P	69			1 lap	1m 16.942s	50
13	Esteban Gutiérrez	MEX	21	Haas F1 Team	Haas VF-16-Ferrari 059/5 V6	P	68			2 laps	1m 17.728s	48
14	Romain Grosjean	F	8	Haas F1 Team	Haas VF-16-Ferrari 059/5 V6	P	68			2 laps	1m 17.281s	50
15	Marcus Ericsson	S	9	Sauber F1 Team	Sauber C35-Ferrari 059/5 V6	P	68			2 laps	1m 18.100s	63
16	Kevin Magnussen	DK	20	Renault Sport F1 Team	Renault R.S.16-R.E.16 V6	P	68			2 laps	1m 18.224s	42
17	Pascal Wehrlein	D	94	Manor Racing MRT	Manor MRT05-Mercedes PU106C V6	P	68			2 laps	1m 18.282s	48
18	Felipe Nasr	BR	12	Sauber F1 Team	Sauber C35-Ferrari 059/5 V6	P	68			2 laps	1m 17.883s	66
19	Rio Haryanto	RI	88	Manor Racing MRT	Manor MRT05-Mercedes PU106C V6	P	68			2 laps	1m 18.658s	57
	Felipe Massa	BR	19	Williams Martini Racing	Williams FW38-Mercedes PU106C V6	P	35	water system/overheating			1m 17.424s	32
	Jolyon Palmer	GB	30	Renault Sport F1 Team	Renault R.S.16-R.E.16 V6	P	16	water leak			1m 19.879s	6
	Jenson Button	GB	22	McLaren Honda	McLaren MP4-31-Honda RA616H V6	P	9	gearbox			1m 19.456s	5

Fastest race lap: Nico Rosberg on lap 60, 1m 15.599s, 129.040mph/207.669km/h.

Lap record: Rubens Barrichello (Ferrari F2004 V10), 1m 13.622s, 132.505mph/213.246km/h (2004).

All results and data © FOM 2016

21 · ERICSSON · Sauber
(3-place grid penalty for causing an accident in round 6)

19 · HARYANTO · Manor

17 · WEHRLEIN · Manor

15 · KVYAT · Toro Rosso
(3-place grid penalty for causing an accident in round 6)

13 · GUTIÉRREZ · Haas

11 · PÉREZ · Force India

22 · MAGNUSSEN · Renault
(5-place grid penalty for replacing the gearbox – started from the pit lane)

20 · SAINZ · Toro Rosso
(5-place grid penalty for replacing the gearbox)

18 · NASR · Sauber

16 · PALMER · Renault

14 · GROSJEAN · Haas

12 · BUTTON · McLaren

Grid order	1	2	3	4	5	6	7	8	9	10	11	12	13	14	15	16	17	18	19	20	21	22	23	24	25	26	27	28	29	30	31	32	33	34	35	36	37	38	39	40	41	42	43	44	45	46	47	48	49	50	51	52	53	54
44 HAMILTON	5	5	5	5	5	5	5	5	5	44	44	44	44	44	44	44	44	44	44	44	44	44	5	5	5	5	5	5	5	5	5	5	5	5	5	44	44	44	44	44	44	44	44	44	44	44	44	44	44	44	44	44	44	44
6 ROSBERG	44	44	44	44	44	44	44	44	44	33	33	33	33	33	33	33	5	5	5	5	5	5	44	44	44	44	44	44	44	44	44	44	44	44	44	5	5	5	5	5	5	5	5	5	5	5	5	5	5	5	5	5	5	5
5 VETTEL	33	33	33	33	33	33	33	33	33	3	3	3	3	3	3	3	5	33	33	33	33	33	33	33	33	33	33	33	33	33	33	33	33	33	33	77	77	77	77	77	77	77	77	6	6	6	6	33	33	33	33			
3 RICCIARDO	3	3	3	3	3	3	3	3	3	5	5	5	5	5	5	5	3	3	77	19	33	7	7	7	7	7	7	7	7	7	3	3	77	77	77	77	77	77	77	77	77	77	6	6	6	33	33	33						
33 VERSTAPPEN	7	7	7	7	7	7	7	7	7	77	77	77	77	77	77	77	77	77	19	33	7	77	3	3	3	3	3	3	3	3	77	77	77	3	3	6	6	6	6	6	6	6	33	33	33	33	33	7	7	7				
7 RÄIKKÖNEN	77	77	77	77	77	77	77	77	77	19	19	19	19	19	19	19	6	3	3	77	77	77	77	77	77	77	77	77	6	6	6	6	6	7	7	7	7	7	7	7	7	7	3	3	3	6								
77 BOTTAS	19	19	19	19	19	19	19	19	19	6	6	6	6	6	6	6	27	7	11	11	6	6	6	6	6	6	6	6	19	19	7	7	3	3	3	3	3	3	3	3	3	3	6	6	6	3								
19 MASSA	27	27	27	27	27	27	27	27	27	27	27	27	27	27	27	27	33	11	19	6	11	11	11	11	11	11	11	19	19	19	7	7	27	27	27	27	27	27	27	27	27	27	27	27	27	27								
27 HÜLKENBERG	27	14	6	6	6	6	6	6	6	14	14	14	14	14	14	11	7	7	6	19	19	19	19	19	19	19	27	27	27	27	55	55	55	55	55	55	55	55	55	55	55	55	55	55	55	55								
14 ALONSO	6	6	14	14	14	14	14	14	14	11	11	11	11	11	11	7	11	11	11	27	27	27	27	27	27	27	55	55	55	55	8	11	11	11	11	11	11	11	11	11	14	14	14	14	14	14	14	11	11					
11 PÉREZ	22	22	22	22	22	22	22	22	11	8	8	8	8	8	7	55	55	55	55	55	55	55	55	55	55	55	11	8	8	8	8	11	8	8	26	26	26	26	26	14	14	11	26	26	26	26	14	14						
22 BUTTON	11	11	11	11	11	11	11	11	8	26	26	26	26	7	8	8	8	8	8	8	8	8	8	8	8	8	8	11	11	11	11	26	26	14	14	14	14	26	26	11	11	11	11	11	26	26								
21 GUTIÉRREZ	21	21	21	21	21	21	21	21	8	21	55	7	7	26	26	26	20	26	26	26	26	26	26	26	26	26	26	26	26	14	14	14	8	8	8	8	8	21	21	21	21	21	21	21	21	21								
8 GROSJEAN	26	8	8	8	8	21	26	55	7	30	30	30	20	20	20	14	14	14	14	14	14	14	14	14	14	14	21	21	21	21	21	21	21	21	21	21	8	8	8	8	8	8	8	8	8	8								
26 KVYAT	8	26	26	26	26	26	26	26	55	7	21	88	88	20	55	14	14	14	14	21	21	21	21	21	21	21	9	9	9	9	9	9	9	9	9	9	9	9	9	9	9	9	9	9	9									
30 PALMER	55	55	55	55	55	55	55	55	94	30	30	9	20	55	20	21	21	21	20	20	20	20	20	20	20	9	9	20	20	20	9	9	20	20	20	20	20	20	20	20	20	20	20	20										
94 WEHRLEIN	94	94	94	94	94	94	94	94	9	88	88	20	55	21	21	94	94	94	94	94	94	94	94	94	94	94	94	94	94	9	20	20	94	94	94	94	94	94	94	94	94	94	94											
12 NASR	30	30	30	9	9	9	9	9	9	9	9	21	9	9	9	9	9	9	9	9	9	9	94	94	94	88	88	88	88	88	88	12	12	12	12	12	12	12	12	12	12	12												
88 HARYANTO	9	9	9	30	30	30	30	30	88	20	20	21	94	12	12	12	12	12	12	12	12	12	12	12	12	12	12	12	12	12	88	88	88	88	88	88	88	12	88	88	88	88	88	88										
55 SAINZ	20	20	20	20	20	20	88	88	88	20	94	94	94	9	88	12	88	88	88	88	88	88	88	88	88	88	88	88	88	88	88	88	88	12																				
9 ERICSSON	88	88	88	88	88	88	20	20	20	12	12	12	12	12	88																																							
20 MAGNUSSEN	12	12	12	12	12	12	12	12	12																																														

6 = Pit stop   9 = Drive-thru penalty   94 = One lap or more behind

TIME SHEETS

PRACTICE 1 (FRIDAY)
Weather: Dry/cloudy
Temperatures: track 25–32°C, air 13–15°C

Pos.	Driver	Laps	Time
1	Lewis Hamilton	22	1m 14.755s
2	Nico Rosberg	30	1m 15.086s
3	Sebastian Vettel	22	1m 15.243s
4	Max Verstappen	29	1m 15.553s
5	Kimi Räikkönen	23	1m 15.618s
6	Valtteri Bottas	30	1m 16.301s
7	Nico Hülkenberg	24	1m 16.464s
8	Carlos Sainz	21	1m 16.543s
9	Sergio Pérez	25	1m 16.577s
10	Fernando Alonso	18	1m 16.663s
11	Daniel Ricciardo	28	1m 16.734s
12	Jenson Button	8	1m 16.788s
13	Romain Grosjean	22	1m 17.008s
14	Felipe Massa	7	1m 17.065s
15	Daniil Kvyat	24	1m 17.310s
16	Esteban Gutiérrez	24	1m 17.319s
17	Felipe Nasr	21	1m 17.855s
18	Rio Haryanto	21	1m 18.103s
19	Marcus Ericsson	8	1m 18.129s
20	Kevin Magnussen	13	1m 18.409s
21	Pascal Wehrlein	30	1m 18.453s
22	Jolyon Palmer	28	1m 18.583s

PRACTICE 2 (FRIDAY)
Weather: Dry/sunny
Temperatures: track 43–46°C, air 17–20°C

Pos.	Driver	Laps	Time
1	Lewis Hamilton	43	1m 14.212s
2	Sebastian Vettel	45	1m 14.469s
3	Nico Rosberg	46	1m 14.738s
4	Max Verstappen	29	1m 15.156s
5	Daniel Ricciardo	43	1m 15.168s
6	Valtteri Bottas	46	1m 15.213s
7	Jenson Button	35	1m 15.213s
8	Kimi Räikkönen	43	1m 15.234s
9	Nico Hülkenberg	50	1m 15.321s
10	Carlos Sainz	42	1m 15.410s
11	Fernando Alonso	40	1m 15.450s
12	Sergio Pérez	47	1m 15.493s
13	Felipe Massa	44	1m 15.513s
14	Daniil Kvyat	42	1m 15.559s
15	Romain Grosjean	35	1m 16.093s
16	Kevin Magnussen	39	1m 16.255s
17	Felipe Nasr	40	1m 16.582s
18	Esteban Gutiérrez	32	1m 16.591s
19	Marcus Ericsson	51	1m 16.902s
20	Jolyon Palmer	48	1m 17.001s
21	Pascal Wehrlein	32	1m 17.023s
22	Rio Haryanto	49	1m 17.423s

PRACTICE 3 (SATURDAY)
Weather: Dry/cloudy
Temperatures: track 19°C, air 14°C

Pos.	Driver	Laps	Time
1	Sebastian Vettel	21	1m 13.919s
2	Max Verstappen	19	1m 14.158s
3	Nico Rosberg	22	1m 14.316s
4	Kimi Räikkönen	21	1m 14.332s
5	Lewis Hamilton	19	1m 14.334s
6	Daniel Ricciardo	22	1m 14.487s
7	Carlos Sainz	21	1m 14.655s
8	Fernando Alonso	19	1m 14.801s
9	Sergio Pérez	21	1m 14.886s
10	Felipe Massa	18	1m 14.890s
11	Nico Hülkenberg	20	1m 14.918s
12	Valtteri Bottas	20	1m 14.985s
13	Jenson Button	17	1m 15.023s
14	Daniil Kvyat	20	1m 15.199s
15	Esteban Gutiérrez	16	1m 15.444s
16	Jolyon Palmer	19	1m 15.656s
17	Romain Grosjean	14	1m 15.704s
18	Marcus Ericsson	24	1m 16.078s
19	Kevin Magnussen	17	1m 16.085s
20	Felipe Nasr	24	1m 16.326s
21	Pascal Wehrlein	18	1m 16.622s
22	Rio Haryanto	15	1m 16.901s

QUALIFYING (SATURDAY)
Weather: Intermittent drizzle/overcast Temperatures: track 18–22°C, air 14–16°C

Pos.	Driver	First	Second	Third	Qualifying Tyre
1	Lewis Hamilton	1m 14.121s	1m 13.076s	1m 12.812s	Ultra-Soft (new)
2	Nico Rosberg	1m 13.714s	1m 13.094s	1m 12.874s	Ultra-Soft (new)
3	Sebastian Vettel	1m 13.925s	1m 13.857s	1m 12.990s	Ultra-Soft (new)
4	Daniel Ricciardo	1m 14.030s	1m 13.540s	1m 13.166s	Ultra-Soft (new)
5	Max Verstappen	1m 14.601s	1m 13.793s	1m 13.414s	Ultra-Soft (new)
6	Kimi Räikkönen	1m 14.477s	1m 13.849s	1m 13.579s	Ultra-Soft (new)
7	Valtteri Bottas	1m 14.389s	1m 13.791s	1m 13.670s	Ultra-Soft (new)
8	Felipe Massa	1m 14.815s	1m 13.864s	1m 13.769s	Ultra-Soft (new)
9	Nico Hülkenberg	1m 14.663s	1m 14.166s	1m 13.952s	Ultra-Soft (new)
10	Fernando Alonso	1m 15.026s	1m 14.260s	1m 14.338s	Ultra-Soft (new)
11	Sergio Pérez	1m 14.814s	1m 14.317s		
12	Jenson Button	1m 14.755s	1m 14.437s		
13	Daniil Kvyat	1m 14.829s	1m 14.457s		
14	Esteban Gutiérrez	1m 15.148s	1m 14.571s		
15	Romain Grosjean	1m 15.444s	1m 14.803s		
16	Carlos Sainz	1m 14.714s	1m 21.956s		
17	Jolyon Palmer	1m 15.459s			
18	Pascal Wehrlein	1m 15.599s			
19	Marcus Ericsson	1m 15.635s			
20	Felipe Nasr	1m 16.663s			
21	Rio Haryanto	1m 17.052s			
22	Kevin Magnussen	no time			

Photo: Peter J. Fox
Photo: WRI2/Jad Sherif

FOR THE RECORD

100th GRAND PRIX STARTED: Sergio Pérez.

14,000th LAP LED: Ferrari engine.

3,000th LAP LED: Mercedes.

2,500th LAP LED: Lewis Hamilton.

Photo: Sahara Force India F1 Team

POINTS

DRIVERS

1	Nico Rosberg	116
2	Lewis Hamilton	107
3	Sebastian Vettel	78
4	Daniel Ricciardo	72
5	Kimi Räikkönen	69
6	Max Verstappen	50
7	Valtteri Bottas	44
8	Felipe Massa	37
9	Sergio Pérez	24
10	Daniil Kvyat	22
11	Romain Grosjean	22
12	Fernando Alonso	18
13	Nico Hülkenberg	18
14	Carlos Sainz	18
15	Kevin Magnussen	6
16	Jenson Button	5
17	Stoffel Vandoorne	1

CONSTRUCTORS

1	Mercedes	223
2	Ferrari	147
3	Red Bull	130
4	Williams	81
5	Force India	42
6	Toro Rosso	32
7	McLaren	24
8	Haas	22
9	Renault	6

Qualifying: head-to-head

Rosberg	3	4	Hamilton
Vettel	5	2	Räikkönen
Massa	1	6	Bottas
Ricciardo	4	0	Kvyat
Ricciardo	3	0	Verstappen
Pérez	4	3	Hülkenberg
Magnussen	5	2	Palmer
Verstappen	3	1	Sainz
Kvyat	1	2	Sainz
Ericsson	6	1	Nasr
Alonso	5	1	Button
Button	0	1	Vandoorne
Haryanto	3	4	Wehrlein
Grosjean	5	2	Gutiérrez

9 · HÜLKENBERG · Force India

7 · BOTTAS · Williams

5 · VERSTAPPEN · Red Bull

3 · VETTEL · Ferrari

1 · HAMILTON · Mercedes

10 · ALONSO · McLaren

8 · MASSA · Williams

6 · RÄIKKÖNEN · Ferrari

4 · RICCIARDO · Red Bull

2 · ROSBERG · Mercedes

Lap chart (continuation)

56	57	58	59	60	61	62	63	64	65	66	67	68	69	70	
44	44	44	44	44	44	44	44	44	44	44	44	44	44	44	1
5	5	5	5	5	5	5	5	5	5	5	5	5	5	5	2
77	77	77	77	77	77	77	77	77	77	77	77	77	77	77	3
33	33	33	33	33	33	33	33	33	33	33	33	33	33	33	4
7	6	6	6	6	6	6	6	6	6	6	6	6	6	6	5
6	7	7	7	7	7	7	7	7	7	7	7	7	7	7	6
3	3	3	3	3	3	3	3	3	3	3	3	3	3	3	7
27	27	27	27	27	27	27	27	27	27	27	27	27	27	27	8
55	55	55	55	55	55	55	55	55	55	55	55	55	55	55	9
11	11	11	11	11	11	11	11	11	11	11	11	11	11	11	10
14	14	14	14	14	14	26	26	26	26	26	14	14	14		
26	26	26	26	26	26	14	14	14	14	14	26	26	26		
21	21	21	21	21	21	21	21	21	21	21	21	21			
9	9	9	9	9	9	9	9	9	9	9	9	9			
20	20	20	20	20	20	20	20	20	20	20	20	20			
94	94	94	94	94	94	94	94	94	94	94	94	94			
12	12	12	12	12	12	12	12	12	12	12	12	12			
88	88	88	88	88	88	88	88	88	88	88	88	88			

■ Safety car deployed on laps shown

RACE TYRE STRATEGIES

PIRELLI

	Driver	Race Stint 1	Race Stint 2	Race Stint 3	Race Stint 4
1	Hamilton	Ultra-Soft (u): 1–24	Soft (n): 25–70		
2	Vettel	Ultra-Soft (u): 1–11	Super-Soft (n): 12–37	Soft (n): 38–70	
3	Bottas	Ultra-Soft (u): 1–23	Soft (n): 24–70		
4	Verstappen	Ultra-Soft (u): 1–20	Soft (n): 21–46	Ultra-Soft (u): 47–70	
5	Rosberg	Ultra-Soft (u): 1–21	Soft (n): 22–51	Soft (u): 52–70	
6	Räikkönen	Ultra-Soft (u): 1–11	Super-Soft (n): 12–33	Soft (n): 34–70	
7	Ricciardo	Ultra-Soft (u): 1–21	Soft (n): 22–38	Soft (n): 39–70	
8	Hülkenberg	Ultra-Soft (u): 1–21	Soft (n): 22–51	Soft (n): 52–69	
9	Sainz	Ultra-Soft (u): 1–13	Soft (n): 14–48	Ultra-Soft (n): 49–69	
10	Pérez	Soft (n): 1–30	Super-Soft (u): 31–46	Soft (n): 47–69	
11	Alonso	Ultra-Soft (u): 1–17	Soft (n): 18–69		
12	Kvyat	Ultra-Soft (u): 1–17	Soft (n): 18–44	Ultra-Soft (u): 45–69	
13	Gutiérrez	Ultra-Soft (u): 1–13	Soft (n): 14–41	Ultra-Soft (u): 42–68	
14	Grosjean	Ultra-Soft (u): 1–17	Soft (n): 18–39	Ultra-Soft (u): 40–46	Ultra-Soft (u): 47–68
15	Ericsson	Ultra-Soft (u): 1–14	Soft (n): 15–39	Soft (u): 40–68	
16	Magnussen	Soft (n): 1–39	Ultra-Soft (n): 40–68		
17	Wehrlein	Ultra-Soft (u): 1–11	Soft (n): 12–38	Soft (n): 39–68	
18	Nasr	Ultra-Soft (u): 1–9	Soft (n): 10–35	Soft (n): 36–68	
19	Haryanto	Super-Soft (n): 1–15	Soft (n): 16–44	Soft (n): 45–68	
	Massa	Ultra-Soft (u): 1–22	Soft (n): 23–35 (dnf)		
	Palmer	Ultra-Soft (u): 1–16 (dnf)			
	Button	Super-Soft (n): 1–9 (dnf)			

The tyre regulations stipulate that at least two of three dry tyre specifications must be used during a dry race.
Pirelli P Zero logos are colour-coded on the tyre sidewalls: Purple = Ultra-Soft; Yellow = Soft; Red = Super-Soft. (n) new (u) used

Photos: Peter J. Fox

EUROPEAN GRAND PRIX

BAKU CITY CIRCUIT

The European Grand Prix gets under way, with Nico Rosberg taking a lead he was never to lose.
Photo: Peter J. Fox

BAKU QUALIFYING

THE return of the European Grand Prix on the impressive new 3.73-mile Baku City Circuit in Azerbaijan brought an interesting new challenge to the Formula 1 calendar. **From the exit of Turn 16, a flat-out drag through the kinks of Turns 17 to 20 and down to Turn One gave F1 its longest 'straight' of the season, at 2.1km.** Then, the run from Turn Two to Three, although it may not have looked long by comparison, was actually longer than the front straight in Budapest!

There followed a more technical section through Turns Four to Seven, before the track climbed up past the medieval castle walls and its 12th-century Maiden's Tower in a narrow, twisty section that put you in mind of Macau.

Some drivers loved it; others had reservations. Jenson Button said, "We have worked really hard at safety, but here we seem to have gone a little backwards."

A hugely quick pit-lane entry with a 'chicane' before the speed line was another concern. Daniel Ricciardo reckoned that at least half a second and perhaps even a full second could be gained with a committed entry. Nico Rosberg agreed, but reckoned that a fully committed entry risked a huge shunt.

When Bernie Ecclestone was informed that Rosberg thought the pit entry too fast, he said he'd send his guys down to check Nico's car and see if there was a brake pedal in there...

When it came to the qualifying hour, there was certainly a brake pedal in Hamilton's Mercedes because, after dominating all three free practice sessions, Lewis was suddenly locking up his super-softs everywhere after Mercedes dialled in some changes following what the team referred to as a 'messy Friday'.

After a lock-up at Turn Seven on his first Q3 run, Hamilton had just his second attempt to put a time on the board. Quickest in sector one, he then clipped the inside wall at Turn Nine, the first time anyone had done that all weekend. The track rod was broken, the right front wheel turned in on itself and out came the red flag. A cast-iron pole became tenth on the grid.

"I'm not sure why, but the car felt very different today and I just didn't get it together," admitted the chastened Mercedes driver, "but I think it will be an interesting race, and I can still come through."

Force India had good cause for frustration. The VJM09, with its Mercedes power, had been in fine shape from the off, both cars in the top five for one-lap pace in FP2 and slower only than Mercedes on the longer runs.

It genuinely looked as though the team could shoot at positions on the first two rows with both cars. But then Sergio Pérez clouted the wall at Turn 15 – a place without much time to be gained – in the dying minutes of FP3. It was something Ricciardo had done on Friday at a corner Rosberg described as one of the most difficult anywhere in F1, with a downhill entry and adverse camber falling away on the exit.

Pérez's shunt damaged the gearbox, causing a five-place grid penalty, a sin in view of the fact that he finished qualifying quicker (1m 43.515s) than everyone except Rosberg (1m 42.758s), a front-row start morphing into seventh...

Nico Hülkenberg also messed up, spinning out of Turn 16 when on a really quick lap in Q2. He pitted for a new set of super-softs, went back out, hit traffic and didn't have time for another lap. He failed to make Q3. You could imagine Force India's Bob Fernley wanting to remove parts of his drivers' anatomy, but he remained in admirably good spirits, convinced his team would get something from what was likely to be a long, difficult race. And he was right...

Red Bull struggled to switch on the tyres in Friday practice, and it didn't look promising when they found themselves taking off downforce so as not to have too much of a straight-line speed deficit on race day. That, however, did not prevent Ricciardo from hauling the car on to the front row as everyone put in one frantic lap when Q3 was resumed with just two minutes on the clock after Hamilton's *faux pas*.

The Australian's time, 1m 43.966s, was identical to Sebastian Vettel's down to the last thousandth of a second, with Sebastian breaking the timing beam just a few yards behind the Red Bull. That meant that by dint of setting the time first, Ricciardo was on the front row once Pérez's gearbox penalty was applied.

"Oh come on guys, you're joking!" was Vettel's anguished response when the Ferrari pit-wall crew informed him.

The Williams, with its low-drag, efficient chassis was expected to go well in Baku, but sixth place for Felipe Massa and a third-row slot alongside Kimi Räikkönen's Ferrari was the extent of it, a couple of tenths clear of a mighty effort from a resurgent Daniil Kvyat with the Toro Rosso at a track on which you expected the 2015-spec Ferrari engine to extract a heavier toll.

Valtteri Bottas had been the quicker Williams driver all weekend, but when it mattered in Q3, he twice became tangled up with Max Verstappen at Turn One. The first time, Williams and Bottas were convinced that Verstappen was on a warm-up lap and let a gap open up out of Turn 16, to make best use of the tow. Max was actually starting a hot lap, however, and was dismayed to find Bottas diving down his inside at Turn One, wrecking both of their laps. He was practically speechless when it happened again on the frantic one-lap second-run shootout. This time, it was simply that Valtteri was behind him in the queue with his ballistic 227mph top speed.

Verstappen, therefore, started ninth when he thought he should have been challenging his team-mate for a slot on the front row. With Hamilton tenth, Romain Grosjean's Haas was the first car with freedom of tyre choice, with the disappointed Hülkenberg lining up 12th. Further back, Button's McLaren-Honda was an unrepresentative 19th, mired in Q1 after he had gone down the escape road at Turn 15, lit up the back tyres to around 170 degrees with a spin turn and then failed to appreciate how much he'd taken out of them.

Above: The total number of fans may have been relatively modest, but the views from the small grandstands were spectacular.
Photo: Sahara Force India F1 Team

Facing page, from top:
The construction work to ready the circuit was remarkable.
Photo: Mercedes AMG Petronas F1 Team

Baku City staged an impressive event, despite the often gusty conditions.
Photo: GP Photo/Peter Nygaard

All smiles from the top three in qualifying: Ricciardo, Rosberg and Pérez.
Photo: Mercedes AMG Petronas F1 Team

Above left: The grid girls wore traditional costume.
Photo: Peter J. Fox

Left: A dog's life for Lewis in Baku.
Photo: Mercedes AMG Petronas F1 Team

Far left: Once again, Ferrari was Mercedes' main threat, with Sebastian Vettel being runner-up to Rosberg this time around.
Photo: Scuderia Ferrari

AFTER two chaotic GP2 races with multiple restarts best described as 'hairy', even before you factored in the speed differentials of varying F1 power units, the chances of the grand prix passing off without a safety car intervention seemed remote.

With numerous interruptions expected, it was perhaps surprising that after converting his pole position, Nico Rosberg disappeared at such a rate of knots instead of babying his Pirellis. For the first three laps, Daniel Ricciardo's Red Bull stayed in touch, but then the gap increased dramatically. By the end of lap four of the race's scheduled 51, it was out to 3.86s, then 7.2s next time around.

Why was Nico pushing his super-softs quite so much when any safety car would bring his pursuers right back to him?

Closer inspection revealed that, in fact, he wasn't. His opening laps actually had been remarkably consistent: 1m 50.541s, 1m 50.876s, 1m 50.251s, 1m 50.409s, 1m 50.237s. Rather, it was Ricciardo who was dropping away quite spectacularly, the comparable lap times for the second-placed RB12 being 1m 51.098s, then 1m 52.768s and 1m 53.670s.

For the first couple of laps, Ricciardo had entertained notions of challenging Rosberg, the Red Bull seemingly able to keep pace with the Mercedes while coming under no threat from Vettel's Ferrari. But then, as those lap times showed, Daniel's super-softs dropped off rapidly. At the 5pm start time, the track temperature was higher than it had been previously, still in the high forties, and, with Red Bull having removed downforce, causing additional sliding, the rears were starting to grain.

Ricciardo soon fell back into Vettel's clutches, and when the Ferrari towed past at the start of lap six, Ricciardo bailed out and headed to the pits for an early switch to softs at the end of the lap. If he was going to follow the expected single-stop strategy, that was going to require 45 laps on the softs.

The Red Bull pitted out 12th, and initially Ferrari, with Vettel and Räikkönen now running second and third, suspected this was a bold undercut strategy from Red Bull; Vettel was told to pit next time around.

Coming just a week after Montreal, where many had decried the Maranello early-stop strategy that had surrendered track position to Hamilton, the call was questioned by Vettel, who said the car felt fine and stayed out. But Räikkönen duly appeared in the pit lane after eight laps.

Kimi, though, had already fallen foul of a pit-entry revision. Its high-speed nature had spooked drivers when they considered the 200mph-plus approach at a point where they were going to be slipstreaming, and this prompted the FIA to extend the white entry line and decree that any car crossing it had to enter the pits. Räikkönen had been unsighted on the previous lap when tucked in behind Ricciardo before he headed in, and when he ducked back right, inadvertently he crossed the line, attracting a 5s penalty. Kimi rejoined 11th, some 4s and two slots behind Ricciardo.

Further back, the widely expected mayhem at the 90-degree Turn One left-hander simply had not materialised. Granted, there was a bit of bumping and boring as Gutiérrez thumped Hülkenberg's Force India, which, having started on the soft tyre, did not have quite the traction out of the turn available to those on super-softs. Then the Haas had gone right, forcing Haryanto's Manor to tag the Tecpro barrier and require a pit visit for a new front wing – a shame given that the Indonesian rookie, impressively, had been the lone driver not to appear on any incident sheet during Friday/Saturday.

Behind Rosberg, Ricciardo and the two Ferraris, Pérez had jumped Massa and Kvyat between Turns Two and Three, and the Russian was demoted again a little further around the lap by Verstappen. Sadly, after such a fine qualifying effort, the Toro Rosso was destined to last just six laps before retiring with a suspension problem that would also account for team-mate Carlos Sainz just after half-distance. Sticking dampers had caused the car to bottom out after changes to the ride height.

Valtteri Bottas completed the opening lap in ninth place, with Hamilton on his tail. The pair of them demoted Kvyat on lap three, then Lewis went by the Williams once DRS was enabled and soon set about Verstappen, who was experiencing the same tyre drop-off as Ricciardo; he headed for the pits after just five laps.

Both McLaren-Hondas were also early stoppers. Alonso had started 14th, having failed to make Q3 for the first time in four races, but he tried a bold first-corner move around the outside of Hamilton and pulled it off, only to be hung out to dry by Verstappen. That caused him to lose momentum, which allowed Grosjean to go by and limited Fernando's net gain to just two positions. Ultimately, he would fail to see the chequered flag for the second time in as many races after becoming stuck in fourth gear with ten laps to go.

With ten of the 51 laps down, Rosberg, in a race of his own, was leading by 12.5s from Vettel, who had a 10s advantage over Pérez's Force India, all three targeting a one-stop race. After running in Bottas's wheel tracks from the start, Hamilton finally managed to pull off a DRS pass of the Williams on lap 11.

Then he set his sights on Pérez, but was not actually running as quickly as the Force India. When Lewis headed for the pits on lap 15, he was 2.5s behind the Mexican. Force India responded on the next lap, bringing Pérez in,

although he still had track position over the Mercedes when he rejoined.

Clearly Lewis's recovery drive was not going to plan, and he was soon on the radio, frustrated at a lack of power. An engine mode issue was causing a problem with the delivery of the harvested ERS energy. The conversation with engineer Pete Bonnington, who, under stricter radio communication regulations, was not allowed to advise him, went like this:

Hamilton: "Derates [loss of power] everywhere. Is there no solution?"

Bonnington: "We're working on it."

Hamilton: "You guys need to pick up the pace."

Bonnington: "The problem appears to be with the engine mode that you're in."

Hamilton: "I don't know what you mean. I don't know what's wrong. This is ridiculous, guys. I don't know, I'm looking at my frickin' dash every five seconds trying to find the switch in the wrong position."

Bonnington: "Lewis, it's nothing you are doing wrong, just a setting that's incorrect."

Hamilton: "I might not finish the race. I'm going to try and change everything."

Bonnington: "We don't advise that, Lewis."

Hamilton: "Can I make suggestions and you tell me if that's okay?"

Above: With Baku's Flame Towers in the background, Sergio Pérez powers his Force India along one of the two parallel straights.
Photo: Peter J. Fox

Facing page, from top:
Team-mates Jenson Button and Fernando Alonso in relaxed mood.
Photo: McLaren Honda

A long stint on super-softs helped the one-stopping Nico Hülkenberg to finish ninth.

Bernie makes a point to Ferrari's Maurizio Arrivabene.

Left: Pascal Wehrlein locks up in the Manor behind the Renault of Kevin Magnussen.
Photos: Peter J. Fox

Above: Nico Rosberg felt "at one" with his Mercedes as he totally dominated proceedings.
Photo: Peter J. Fox

Top right: Immaculate presentation – old and new. Jenson Button's McLaren and Baku's classic architecture make an intriguing visual pairing.
Photo: McLaren Honda

Above right: Sergio Pérez took a second podium in three races for Sahara Force India.
Photo: Sahara Force India F1 Team

Right: Marshals wave their flags to celebrate the end of a race that, against expectations, produced no safety car interventions. Red Bull drivers Daniel Ricciardo and Max Verstappen struggled in Baku, finishing seventh and eighth respectively.
Photo: Red Bull Racing/Getty Images

Bonnington: "Nope, that's not allowed."

In fact, Rosberg had experienced a similar phenomenon earlier in the race, as technical director Paddy Lowe explained: "There was a configuration related to the management of the hybrid energy which was not correctly tuned during our race preparation. It caused premature derates down the straights, costing 0.3–0.4s per lap."

But crucially, as team principal Toto Wolff elaborated, there was a difference: "Nico was quite fortunate because he'd already made a switch change before the problem that led him on the right path when the problem did arise. Lewis hadn't and so didn't have the same clues."

It meant that Rosberg imperiously reeled off the 51 laps unchallenged to score his 19th GP victory and the fifth of 2016, and surely one of the most impressive of his career. When Hamilton got his full power back with about 15 laps to go, he set what was then the quickest lap of the race (1m 46.822s) on lap 42. Just for good measure, and to make a point, Rosberg went around in 1m 46.485s with three laps to go. After blips in Monaco and Montreal, he had well and truly bounced back, and his championship lead, which had been 43 points before shrinking to nine, was back out to 24.

"I was at one with the car in a way I've never felt before," Rosberg enthused.

Räikkönen's relatively early stop had allowed him to undercut team-mate Vettel, who did not pit until lap 20, but on fresher softs, Seb soon caught Kimi, who was instructed to let him by.

"Okay, but tell him to get a move on," said Räikkönen, who was concerned about opening up a 5s margin over Pérez's Force India to try to overcome his penalty.

The Force India was too quick, though, and although he had no need, Pérez went by the Ferrari into Turn One on the very last lap.

"I saw the opportunity and that it was safe enough to go for it, and it's always nice to finish ahead on the track, even though I knew he had a penalty," Pérez confirmed. "It's well deserved for the team and all my boys who fixed the car after yesterday…"

It was the second podium in three races for Pérez, who allowed that while Rosberg had been in a class of his own, without his Saturday *faux pas* he would have been pushing Vettel hard for second.

The penalised Räikkönen took fourth, some 23s clear of a glum-looking Hamilton, who salvaged fifth place at a track he had seemed to own on the opening day.

Bottas managed to make a one-stop race work and rewarded Williams with sixth, while Massa could not manage the same feat and dropped to tenth after two pit stops.

The Red Bull drivers found that their early stops for softs did not do much for their tyre issues and went on to the medium tyre when they pitted again around the 20-lap mark. The RB12s had good pace on the white-walled Pirelli, with Verstappen setting third quickest lap of the race as he closed in on his team-mate, struggling with a long brake pedal in the closing stages. Both managed to overhaul the one-stopping Hülkenberg, eking out a 31-lap stint on super-softs, in the closing laps to finish seventh and eighth.

Button just missed out on the points after a spirited drive in the McLaren-Honda, and Kevin Magnussen did a good job after a pit-lane start.

"Formula 1 needs more tracks like this," was Toto Wolff's summation, and few disagreed after a very well organised European GP. But what odds would you have got on 51 laps of Baku City Circuit without a safety car? Control and a degree of circumspection, as well as higher-than-anticipated tyre wear, had been the order of the day.

All things considered, F1 had an interesting new track and a fine event.

Tony Dodgins

VIEWPOINT
BAKU, AN INTRIGUING MIX...

THIS was old-fashioned in the best possible way. A proper street circuit, in the sense that the walls and kerbs were close at hand; it was as fast in some places as it was tight in others; no run-offs measured by the square mile; plenty of hazards to catch the unwary. And the entire track was placed near the heart of an ancient city: rushing past the new, snaking around the old. A standard FIA modern cut-out track this most certainly was not. And all the more welcome for it. Well, welcomed by most.

Jenson Button said, "It's like we have gone backwards in certain areas. We work so hard on safety, improving circuits all the time, and we come here and we have corners like T3, T7 and T14 that don't have any run-off at all. Turn Seven has three Tecpro barriers and then a concrete barrier at the edge of the circuit. There is not much you can do because there is a building in the way. It's a shame really."

This would be Button's 292nd grand prix. Thus he was fully qualified to comment; perhaps, some suggested, over-qualified at the age of 36.

Not everyone shared the 2009 world champion's concern. Both Lewis Hamilton and Daniel Ricciardo saw the track as a fresh challenge that had to be overcome. It was ironic, therefore, when both fell victim to its close confines. Ricciardo's shunt, although more extensive than Hamilton's, had less serious consequences, since it occurred in first free practice; Lewis tagged the wall at a crucial moment during qualifying.

Neither driver saw fit to change their opinion of a track that was quickly proving to be a welcome addition. This was against all odds, following predictions a few months before that the layout in the old-town section was impossibly narrow and bumpy, and that it would never be finished in time. Not only did the drivers cope, but so did the organisers, laying on a facility that could claim just one instance of insecure kerbs and another of a loose drain cover as the only black marks in an otherwise impressive debut.

Maurice Hamilton

8

2016 FORMULA 1
GRAND PRIX OF EUROPE

BAKU 17–19 JUNE

ROLEX

F1 OFFICIAL TIMEPIECE

RACE DISTANCE: 51 laps, 190.170 miles/306.049km

RACE WEATHER: Dry/sunny (track 38–46°C, air 31–33°C)

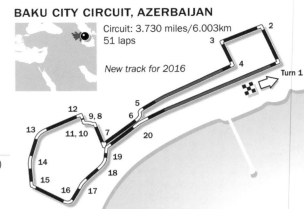

BAKU CITY CIRCUIT, AZERBAIJAN

Circuit: 3.730 miles/6.003km
51 laps

New track for 2016

All results and data © FOM 2016

RACE – OFFICIAL CLASSIFICATION

Pos.	Driver	Nat.	No.	Entrant	Car/Engine	Tyres	Laps	Time/Retirement	Speed (mph/km/h)	Gap to leader	Fastest race lap	
1	**Nico Rosberg**	D	6	Mercedes AMG Petronas F1 Team	Mercedes F1 W07-Mercedes PU106C V6	P	51	1h 32m 52.366s	122.858/197.721		1m 46.485s	48
2	**Sebastian Vettel**	D	5	Scuderia Ferrari	Ferrari SF15-H-059/5 V6	P	51	1h 33m 09.062s	122.491/197.130	16.696s	1m 47.028s	49
3	**Sergio Pérez**	MEX	11	Sahara Force India F1 Team	Force India VJM09-Mercedes PU106C V6	P	51	1h 33m 17.607s	122.304/196.829	25.241s	1m 46.990s	45
4	**Kimi Räikkönen**	FIN	7	Scuderia Ferrari	Ferrari SF16-H-059/5 V6	P	51	1h 33m 25.468s *	122.132/196.553	33.102s	1m 47.181s	41
5	**Lewis Hamilton**	GB	44	Mercedes AMG Petronas F1 Team	Mercedes F1 W07-Mercedes PU106C V6	P	51	1h 33m 48.701s	121.628/195.742	56.335s	1m 46.822s	42
6	**Valtteri Bottas**	FIN	77	Williams Martini Racing	Williams FW38-Mercedes PU106C V6	P	51	1h 33m 53.252s	121.530/195.584	1m 00.886s	1m 47.604s	50
7	**Daniel Ricciardo**	AUS	3	Red Bull Racing	Red Bull RB12-TAG Heuer RB12 V6	P	51	1h 34m 01.595s	121.351/195.295	1m 09.229s	1m 47.736s	51
8	**Max Verstappen**	NL	33	Red Bull Racing	Red Bull RB12-TAG Heuer RB12 V6	P	51	1h 34m 03.062s	121.319/195.244	1m 10.696s	1m 46.973s	50
9	**Nico Hülkenberg**	D	27	Sahara Force India F1 Team	Force India VJM09-Mercedes PU106C V6	P	51	1h 34m 10.074s	121.169/195.002	1m 17.708s	1m 48.012s	37
10	**Felipe Massa**	BR	19	Williams Martini Racing	Williams FW38-Mercedes PU106C V6	P	51	1h 34m 17.741s	121.004/194.737	1m 25.375s	1m 47.761s	35
11	Jenson Button	GB	22	McLaren Honda	McLaren MP4-31-Honda RA616H V6	P	51	1h 34m 37.183s	120.590/194.070	1m 44.817s	1m 47.622s	50
12	Felipe Nasr	BR	12	Sauber F1 Team	Sauber C35-Ferrari 059/5 V6	P	50			1 lap	1m 47.708s	48
13	Romain Grosjean	F	8	Haas F1 Team	Haas VF-16-Ferrari 059/5 V6	P	50			1 lap	1m 47.943s	48
14	Kevin Magnussen	DK	20	Renault Sport F1 Team	Renault R.S.16-R.E.16 V6	P	50			1 lap	1m 49.282s	41
15	Jolyon Palmer	GB	30	Renault Sport F1 Team	Renault R.S.16-R.E.16 V6	P	50			1 lap	1m 47.583s	48
16	Esteban Gutiérrez	MEX	21	Haas F1 Team	Haas VF-16-Ferrari 059/5 V6	P	50			1 lap	1m 47.563s	50
17	Marcus Ericsson	S	9	Sauber F1 Team	Sauber C35-Ferrari 059/5 V6	P	50			1 lap	1m 48.898s	48
18	Rio Haryanto	RI	88	Manor Racing MRT	Manor MRT05-Mercedes PU106C V6	P	49			2 laps	1m 51.365s	27
	Fernando Alonso	E	14	McLaren Honda	McLaren MP4-31-Honda RA616H V6	P	42	gearbox			1m 49.101s	27
	Pascal Wehrlein	D	94	Manor Racing MRT	Manor MRT05-Mercedes PU106C V6	P	39	brakes			1m 50.571s	33
	Carlos Sainz	E	55	Scuderia Toro Rosso	Toro Rosso STR11-Ferrari 059/4 V6	P	31	rear suspension			1m 48.804s	31
	Daniil Kvyat	RUS	26	Scuderia Toro Rosso	Toro Rosso STR11-Ferrari 059/4 V6	P	6	rear suspension			1m 53.167s	2

* Includes 5-second penalty for crossing the white line at the pit entry without entering the pit lane – position unaffected.

Fastest race lap: Nico Rosberg on lap 48, 1m 46.485s, 126.105mph/202.946km/h.

Lap record: no previous race.

22 · MAGNUSSEN · Renault
(5-place grid penalty for replacing
the gearbox – started from the pit lane)

20 · ERICSSON · Sauber

18 · SAINZ · Toro Rosso
(5-place grid penalty for replacing
the gearbox)

16 · HARYANTO · Manor

14 · GUTIÉRREZ · Haas

12 · HÜLKENBERG · Force India

21 · PALMER · Renault

19 · BUTTON · McLaren

17 · WEHRLEIN · Manor

15 · NASR · Sauber

13 · ALONSO · McLaren

11 · GROSJEAN · Haas

Grid order / lap chart

Grid order	1	2	3	4	5	6	7	8	9	10	11	12	13	14	15	16	17	18	19	20	21	22	23	24	25	26	27	28	29	30	31	32	33	34	35	36	37	38	39	40	41
6 ROSBERG	6	6	6	6	6	6	6	6	6	6	6	6	6	6	6	6	6	6	6	6	6	6	6	6	6	6	6	6	6	6	6	6	6	6	6	6	6	6	6	6	6
3 RICCIARDO	3	3	3	3	3	5	5	5	5	5	5	5	5	5	5	5	5	5	5	5	5	7	7	7	7	7	7	7	5	5	5	5	5	5	5	5	5	5	5	5	5
5 VETTEL	5	5	5	5	5	7	11	11	11	11	11	11	11	11	11	77	77	7	7	5	5	5	5	5	5	5	7	7	7	7	7	7	7	7	7	7	7	7	7	7	7
7 RÄIKKÖNEN	7	7	7	7	7	11	77	77	77	44	44	44	44	77	77	3	7	3	77	11	3	44	44	44	44	44	44	11	11	11	11	11	11	11	11	11	11	11	11	11	11
19 MASSA	11	11	11	11	11	19	7	44	44	44	77	77	77	77	44	3	7	3	77	11	3	44	44	44	44	44	44	44	44	44	44	44	44	44	44	44	44	44	44	44	44
26 KVYAT	19	19	19	19	19	3	44	7	27	27	27	27	3	3	3	7	27	27	27	44	44	19	19	19	19	19	19	77	77	77	77	77	77	77	77	77	77	77	77	77	77
11 PÉREZ	33	33	33	33	77	77	19	27	8	3	3	3	27	27	27	19	19	11	19	19	3	77	77	77	77	77	19	27	27	27	27	27	27	27	27	27	27	27	27	27	27
77 BOTTAS	26	26	77	44	44	44	8	8	94	94	7	7	7	7	19	11	11	19	27	77	77	55	55	27	27	27	3	3	3	3	3	3	3	3	3	3	3	3	3	3	3
33 VERSTAPPEN	77	77	44	77	8	8	27	94	3	7	19	19	19	19	11	44	44	44	44	3	55	14	27	55	55	3	19	19	19	19	19	19	19	19	19	19	19	19	19	19	19
44 HAMILTON	44	44	26	8	27	27	94	3	19	19	94	94	94	33	33	33	33	33	33	55	14	27	3	3	55	33	33	33	33	33	33	33	33	33	33	33	33	33	33	33	33
8 GROSJEAN	8	8	8	14	12	12	9	9	7	9	9	9	9	94	94	55	55	55	55	14	22	22	22	22	8	94	20	20	20	20	20	20	20	20	20	20	20	20	20	20	20
27 HÜLKENBERG	14	14	14	26	33	94	3	19	19	8	33	33	33	9	55	94	14	14	14	22	12	12	12	8	22	20	33	94	14	14	14	14	14	14	14	22	22	22	22	22	22
14 ALONSO	12	27	27	27	22	9	12	30	30	33	55	55	55	14	14	22	22	22	27	27	3	14	94	8	94	14	30	22	22	22	22	22	22	22	12	12	12	12			
21 GUTIÉRREZ	27	12	12	12	21	21	33	33	30	14	14	14	14	9	22	94	12	12	33	8	8	8	94	20	30	30	33	30	30	30	12	22	55	30	14	14	8	8	8	8	4
12 NASR	22	22	22	22	94	22	30	14	14	94	12	12	12	12	8	9	94	94	94	20	20	94	20	33	12	12	12	55	30	14	22	12	12	55	30	12	4				
88 HARYANTO	94	94	94	94	21	30	33	55	55	14	12	12	12	12	12	8	9	8	8	8	20	20	94	12	30	14	22	55	94	12	8	30	30	30	30	30	30	30	30	30	30
94 WEHRLEIN	21	21	21	21	9	20	14	22	22	22	30	8	8	8	9	20	20	20	30	30	30	33	21	21	21	21	8	30	9	9	21	21	21	21	21	21	21	21	21		
55 SAINZ	55	55	55	30	20	33	55	12	12	12	8	20	20	30	30	33	33	30	14	22	12	12	21	8	9	9	21	21	9	9	9	9	9	9	9	9	9	9			
22 BUTTON	30	30	30	9	30	14	22	12	20	20	20	30	30	30	30	9	8	9	12	12	12	8	8	21	94	21	94	21	94	94	94	94	94	94	94	94	88	88			
9 ERICSSON	9	9	9	20	26	55	20	8	88	88	88	88	88	21	21	21	21	21	21	21	9	9	9	88	9	9	9	94	88	88	88	88	88	88	88	88					
30 PALMER	20	20	20	55	55	88	88	21	21	21	21	21	21	21	21	9	9	88	88	88	88	88	88	9	88	88	88	88													
20 MAGNUSSEN	88	88	88	88	88	26																																			

TIME SHEETS

PRACTICE 1 (FRIDAY)
Weather: Dry/sunny
Temperatures: track 37–43°C, air 26–28°C

Pos.	Driver	Laps	Time
1	Lewis Hamilton	23	1m 46.435s
2	Nico Rosberg	32	1m 46.812s
3	Valtteri Bottas	34	1m 47.096s
4	Fernando Alonso	21	1m 47.989s
5	Sebastian Vettel	26	1m 48.627s
6	Sergio Pérez	17	1m 48.922s
7	Jenson Button	21	1m 49.019s
8	Felipe Massa	22	1m 49.125s
9	Carlos Sainz	16	1m 49.267s
10	Nico Hülkenberg	27	1m 49.301s
11	Romain Grosjean	20	1m 49.611s
12	Kimi Räikkönen	16	1m 49.635s
13	Daniel Ricciardo	17	1m 49.778s
14	Esteban Gutiérrez	25	1m 50.167s
15	Marcus Ericsson	18	1m 50.473s
16	Max Verstappen	7	1m 50.485s
17	Daniil Kvyat	19	1m 50.551s
18	Jolyon Palmer	25	1m 50.910s
19	Kevin Magnussen	27	1m 50.939s
20	Pascal Wehrlein	24	1m 51.219s
21	Felipe Nasr	11	1m 51.771s
22	Rio Haryanto	28	1m 51.925s

QUALIFYING (SATURDAY)
Weather: Dry/sunny Temperatures: track 37–48°C, air 27–29°C

Pos.	Driver	First	Second	Third	Qualifying Tyre
1	Nico Rosberg	1m 43.685s	1m 42.520s	1m 42.758s	Super-Soft (new)
2	Sergio Pérez	1m 44.462s	1m 43.939s	1m 43.515s	Super-Soft (new)
3	Daniel Ricciardo	1m 44.570s	1m 44.141s	1m 43.966s	Super-Soft (used)
4	Sebastian Vettel	1m 45.062s	1m 44.461s	1m 43.966s	Super-Soft (used)
5	Kimi Räikkönen	1m 44.936s	1m 44.533s	1m 44.269s	Super-Soft (used)
6	Felipe Massa	1m 45.494s	1m 44.696s	1m 44.483s	Super-Soft (new)
7	Daniil Kvyat	1m 44.694s	1m 44.687s	1m 44.717s	Super-Soft (used)
8	Valtteri Bottas	1m 44.706s	1m 44.477s	1m 45.246s	Super-Soft (used)
9	Max Verstappen	1m 44.939s	1m 44.387s	1m 45.570s	Super-Soft (used)
10	Lewis Hamilton	1m 44.259s	1m 43.526s	2m 01.954s	Super-Soft (new)
11	Romain Grosjean	1m 45.507s	1m 44.755s		
12	Nico Hülkenberg	1m 44.860s	1m 44.824s		
13	Carlos Sainz	1m 44.827s	1m 45.000s		
14	Fernando Alonso	1m 45.525s	1m 45.270s		
15	Esteban Gutiérrez	1m 45.300s	1m 45.349s		
16	Felipe Nasr	1m 45.549s	1m 46.048s		
17	Rio Haryanto	1m 45.665s			
18	Pascal Wehrlein	1m 45.750s			
19	Jenson Button	1m 45.804s			
20	Marcus Ericsson	1m 46.231s			
21	Kevin Magnussen	1m 46.348s			
22	Jolyon Palmer	1m 46.394s			

PRACTICE 2 (FRIDAY)
Weather: Dry/overcast
Temperatures: track 31–36°C, air 25–26°C

Pos.	Driver	Laps	Time
1	Lewis Hamilton	33	1m 44.223s
2	Nico Rosberg	26	1m 44.913s
3	Sergio Pérez	37	1m 45.336s
4	Valtteri Bottas	35	1m 45.764s
5	Nico Hülkenberg	37	1m 45.920s
6	Carlos Sainz	35	1m 46.027s
7	Max Verstappen	35	1m 46.068s
8	Sebastian Vettel	36	1m 46.219s
9	Jenson Button	32	1m 46.234s
10	Daniel Ricciardo	32	1m 46.293s
11	Fernando Alonso	27	1m 46.498s
12	Romain Grosjean	29	1m 46.681s
13	Kimi Räikkönen	32	1m 46.694s
14	Daniil Kvyat	35	1m 46.744s
15	Esteban Gutiérrez	26	1m 46.830s
16	Felipe Massa	28	1m 47.060s
17	Kevin Magnussen	38	1m 47.329s
18	Rio Haryanto	33	1m 47.487s
19	Marcus Ericsson	22	1m 47.772s
20	Jolyon Palmer	35	1m 47.794s
21	Pascal Wehrlein	36	1m 48.018s
22	Felipe Nasr	38	1m 48.081s

PRACTICE 3 (SATURDAY)
Weather: Dry/sunny
Temperatures: track 46°C, air 28°C

Pos.	Driver	Laps	Time
1	Lewis Hamilton	17	1m 44.352s
2	Nico Rosberg	22	1m 44.610s
3	Nico Hülkenberg	18	1m 45.540s
4	Daniel Ricciardo	13	1m 45.620s
5	Sebastian Vettel	20	1m 45.630s
6	Sergio Pérez	17	1m 45.735s
7	Max Verstappen	14	1m 45.901s
8	Jenson Button	17	1m 45.954s
9	Daniil Kvyat	19	1m 45.981s
10	Kimi Räikkönen	16	1m 46.024s
11	Fernando Alonso	16	1m 46.131s
12	Carlos Sainz	17	1m 46.190s
13	Romain Grosjean	21	1m 46.361s
14	Felipe Massa	20	1m 46.510s
15	Esteban Gutiérrez	21	1m 46.670s
16	Kevin Magnussen	16	1m 47.024s
17	Pascal Wehrlein	19	1m 47.100s
18	Jolyon Palmer	18	1m 47.158s
19	Marcus Ericsson	14	1m 47.328s
20	Felipe Nasr	18	1m 47.379s
21	Rio Haryanto	18	1m 47.556s
22	Valtteri Bottas	1	no time

FOR THE RECORD

60th POLE POSITION: Mercedes.

DID YOU KNOW?

Azerbaijan became the 32nd country to host a Formula 1 grand prix.

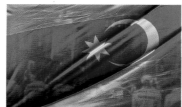

Photo: Peter J. Fox

POINTS

DRIVERS

1	Nico Rosberg	141
2	Lewis Hamilton	117
3	Sebastian Vettel	96
4	Kimi Räikkönen	81
5	Daniel Ricciardo	78
6	Max Verstappen	54
7	Valtteri Bottas	52
8	Sergio Pérez	39
9	Felipe Massa	38
10	Daniil Kvyat	22
11	Romain Grosjean	22
12	Nico Hülkenberg	20
13	Fernando Alonso	18
14	Carlos Sainz	18
15	Kevin Magnussen	6
16	Jenson Button	5
17	Stoffel Vandoorne	1

CONSTRUCTORS

1	Mercedes	258
2	Ferrari	177
3	Red Bull	140
4	Williams	90
5	Force India	59
6	Toro Rosso	32
7	McLaren	24
8	Haas	22
9	Renault	6

Photo: Scuderia Ferrari

Photo: Peter J. Fox

Qualifying: head-to-head

Rosberg	4	4	Hamilton
Vettel	6	2	Räikkönen
Massa	2	6	Bottas
Ricciardo	4	0	Kvyat
Ricciardo	4	0	Verstappen
Pérez	5	3	Hülkenberg
Magnussen	6	2	Palmer
Verstappen	3	1	Sainz
Kvyat	2	2	Sainz
Ericsson	6	2	Nasr
Alonso	6	1	Button
Button	0	1	Vandoorne
Haryanto	4	4	Wehrlein
Grosjean	6	2	Gutiérrez

10 · HAMILTON · Mercedes

8 · BOTTAS · Williams

6 · KVYAT · Toro Rosso

4 · RÄIKKÖNEN · Ferrari

2 · RICCIARDO · Red Bull

9 · VERSTAPPEN · Red Bull

7 · PÉREZ · Force India
(5-place grid penalty for replacing the gearbox)

5 · MASSA · Williams

3 · VETTEL · Ferrari

1 · ROSBERG · Mercedes

42	43	44	45	46	47	48	49	50	51	
6	6	6	6	6	6	6	6	6	6	1
5	5	5	5	5	5	5	5	5	5	2
7	7	7	7	7	7	7	7	7	11	3
11	11	11	11	11	11	11	11	11	7	4
44	44	44	44	44	44	44	44	44	44	5
77	77	77	77	77	77	77	77	77	77	6
27	27	27	27	27	27	3	3	3	3	7
3	3	3	3	3	27	33	33	33	33	8
19	19	19	33	33	33	33	27	27	27	9
33	33	33	19	19	19	19	19	19	19	10
22	22	22	22	22	22	22	22	22	22	
20	20	12	12	12	12	12	12			
12	12	20	20	8	8	8	8	8		
8	8	8	8	20	20	20	20			
30	30	30	30	30	30	30	30	30		
14	21	21	21	21	21	21	21			
21	9	9	9	9	9	9	9			
9	88	88	88	88	88	88	88			
88										

6 = Pit stop   9 = Drive-thru penalty
94 = One lap or more behind

RACE TYRE STRATEGIES

PIRELLI

	Driver	Race Stint 1	Race Stint 2	Race Stint 3
1	Rosberg	Super-Soft (u): 1–21	Soft (n): 22–51	
2	Vettel	Super-Soft (u): 1–20	Soft (n): 21–51	
3	Pérez	Super-Soft (u): 1–16	Soft (n): 17–51	
4	Räikkönen	Super-Soft (u): 1–8	Soft (n): 9–51	
5	Hamilton	Super-Soft (u): 1–15	Soft (n): 16–51	
6	Bottas	Super-Soft (u): 1–19	Soft (n): 20–51	
7	Ricciardo	Super-Soft (u): 1–6	Soft (n): 7–22	Medium (u): 23–51
8	Verstappen	Super-Soft (u): 1–5	Soft (n): 6–20	Medium (u): 21–51
9	Hülkenberg	Soft (n): 1–20	Super-Soft (n): 21–51	
10	Massa	Super-Soft (u): 1–7	Soft (n): 8–28	Soft (n): 29–51
11	Button	Super-Soft (u): 1–6	Soft (n): 7–25	Soft (n): 26–51
12	Nasr	Super-Soft (u): 1–7	Soft (n): 8–24	Soft (n): 25–50
13	Grosjean	Super-Soft (n): 1–10	Soft (n): 11–26	Medium (u): 27–50
14	Magnussen	Super-Soft (u): 1–6	Soft (n): 7–50	
15	Palmer	Super-Soft (u): 1–11	Soft (n): 12–31	Super-Soft (n): 32–50
16	Gutiérrez	Super-Soft (u): 1–8	Soft (n): 9–29	Super-Soft (u): 30–50
17	Ericsson	Soft (n): 1–16	Super-Soft (n): 17–25	Soft (u): 26–50
18	Haryanto	Super-Soft (u): 1	Soft (n): 2–49	
	Alonso	Super-Soft (n): 1–5	Soft (n): 6–24	Soft (n): 25–42 (dnf)
	Wehrlein	Soft (n): 1–29	Medium (n): 30–39 (dnf)	
	Sainz	Super-Soft (u): 1–4	Soft (n): 5–27	Super-Soft (n): 28–31 (dnf)
	Kvyat	Super-Soft (u): 1–5	Soft (n): 6 (dnf)	

The tyre regulations stipulate that at least two of three dry tyre specifications must be used during a dry race.

Pirelli P Zero logos are colour-coded on the tyre sidewalls: Red = Super-Soft; Yellow = Soft; White = Medium. (n) new (u) used

Photo: McLaren Honda

Photo: Mercedes AMG Petronas F1 Team

Inset, right: Fightback for Hamilton, after the first of a run of four successive victories.
Photo: Peter J. Fox

Inset, centre right: Christian Horner seems happy to don the lederhosen; Dr Marko looks a trifle apprehensive!
Photo: Red Bull Racing/Getty Images

Inset, far right: Nearly! Max Verstappen celebrates his second place after a one-stop strategy gave him a chance of outright victory.
Photo: Red Bull Racing/Getty Images

Main photo: Lewis Hamilton claims the lead at the start.
Photo: Peter J. Fox

FIA FORMULA 1 WORLD CHAMPIONSHIP · ROUND 9

AUSTRIAN GRAND PRIX

RED BULL RING

SPIELBERG QUALIFYING

AS the F1 fraternity gathered in the scenic Styrian mountains, the breathtaking beauty of which never fails to captivate, the intriguing gossip was all about reinstating the majestic full Österreichring, last used for F1 in 1987. Still in the planning stages, it is a mouthwatering prospect, even if a significant majority of today's F1 heroes did not seem to know of its existence, just over the brow at the new Red Bull Ring's Turn One...

For the moment, though, Austria was another battle to be fought on the relatively short nine-turn circuit that Dietrich Mateschitz had brought back to the F1 calendar in 2014.

Abuse of track limits had been an issue in 2014/15, so additional kerbing had been added at a number of corners, most notably Turns Two, Five and Eight. By Saturday evening, they were a source of controversy, after no fewer than four kerb-induced suspension failures. Max Verstappen had hit the additional yellow kerbing at Turn Five hard enough to break his Red Bull's steering and send it into the Turn Six gravel on Friday, then Nico Rosberg had suddenly turned sharp left into the barrier when the right rear suspension on his Mercedes W07 had broken in Turn Two during FP3 on Saturday morning.

It was Daniil Kvyat's turn to hit trouble in Q1, when the frequency loadings over the Turn Eight kerb broke his Toro Rosso's right rear suspension and pitched him into the barrier, eliminating him on a weekend when he'd looked confident and aggressive.

Sergio Pérez was on his second Q1 run when he felt the rear of his Force India behaving strangely. He headed for the pits, where investigation revealed another suspension failure, meaning that the Baku podium finisher would start 16th.

Both Rosberg and Lewis Hamilton's pit crews worked flat out to get car No. 6 repaired in time for qualifying, with Nico appearing to have a couple of tenths in hand over Lewis throughout practice. Unfortunately, though, the earlier impact had damaged the gearbox and Nico would suffer a five-place gird penalty. As, too, would Sebastian Vettel, whose crew discovered foreign bodies in the Ferrari's gearbox oil.

Rosberg left the pit lane 11 minutes into Q1 and made it safely through to Q2. Joining the luckless Kvyat and Pérez on the sidelines after the first session were both Renault drivers (Kevin Magnussen being a hundredth quicker than Jolyon Palmer), Manor's Rio Haryanto and both Sauber drivers, Marcus Ericsson 0.03s ahead of Felipe Nasr.

Manor got through into Q2 for the first time after a superb effort from Pascal Wehrlein, which equalled the team's best qualifying performance, a 12th place from the late Jules Bianchi on a wet track at Spa. This was in the dry, though, Wehrlein enjoying himself on a rare circuit that he already knew from DTM, and liked. Sure, it helped that he had a Mercedes engine and just nine corners to penalise the Manor's relative lack of downforce, but it was laudable to be just 2.2 per cent shy of the ultimate Q2 pace.

Carlos Sainz had a disastrous Saturday, as an electrical issue cut short FP3 on Saturday morning and then had consequences for his power unit in Q2, meaning an engine change and 15th on the grid.

Fernando Alonso was less than chuffed when he was put on used, rather than new, rubber for his first Q2 run and then found his second attempt compromised by yellow flags for team-mate Jenson Button at Turn Three. Jenson had already recorded a lap that was quick enough to progress into Q3.

Interestingly, the Ferraris of Vettel and Kimi Räikkönen, and the Red Bulls of Daniel Ricciardo and Verstappen all set their Q2 times on Pirelli's red-walled super-soft tyre, rather than the purple-walled ultra-soft. Mercedes responded, but by then rain was falling, and it was the ultra-softs on which the Mercs set their best Q2 times and hence had to use for the race start.

Given the rate at which the Mercedes drivers had chewed up the ultra-softs in high track temperatures on Saturday morning, this looked like giving Ferrari and Red Bull the potential option of running a one-stop race on Sunday, while Mercedes would have to stop twice. The forecast, though, was for the track temperature to be significantly lower on race day, clouding the picture somewhat.

At the start of Q3, the track was very wet in places, but drying in others. There was no doubt that intermediate Pirellis were needed, but the question was how quickly the surface would dry and whether slicks would come into play by the end of the session. They did, and it was one of those intriguing shootouts where everyone went faster and faster, and the last man across the line at the end had track conditions at their best.

Hamilton put in a fine lap to take pole with 1m 07.922s, more than half a second clear of team-mate Rosberg, with Nico Hülkenberg's Force India an excellent third, 'The Hulk' reminding everyone of his wet-weather Brazilian pole for Williams way back in 2010. Vettel's Ferrari was fourth; a fine lap from Button gave McLaren Honda fifth, ahead of Räikkönen's Ferrari, with Ricciardo seventh for Red Bull, Valtteri Bottas's Williams eighth, Verstappen's Red Bull ninth and Felipe Massa's Williams tenth. The Brazilian was found to have a damaged front wing, however, and the fitting of a replacement on race morning meant a pit-lane start.

The gearbox penalties for Rosberg and Vettel elevated Hülkenberg to the front row and a delighted Button to third. "I haven't been that close to the starting lights for a long time," he smiled. "They're going to seem very bright!"

Left: Nico Rosberg's FP3 accident resulted in the German receiving a grid penalty for a replacement gearbox.

Far left: Michael Schumacher's image illuminates part of the Wall of Champions in the under-track tunnel.
Photos: Lukas Gorys

Below left: Esteban Gutiérrez enjoys a quiet moment.
Photo: Peter J. Fox

Below far left: Daniil Kvyat's season took a further downward turn after a big crash in Q1. He had hit a kerb, breaking his suspension.
Photo: Lukas Gorys

Opposite page: Jenson Button shone in the variable qualifying conditions. The McLaren Honda driver ended up with fifth fastest time, and fourth on the grid after Rosberg's penalty.

Below: Over the limit. Max Verstappen takes his Red Bull over the newly-installed yellow kerbing.
Photos: Peter J. Fox

Above: The right rear Pirelli of Sebastian Vettel's Ferrari blows to shreds on lap 26.
Photo: Peter J. Fox

Right: Max Verstappen surprised Red Bull team-mate Daniel Ricciardo with a late move down the inside of Turn Eight, using all the road on exit.
Photo: Red Bull Racing/Getty Images

ALTHOUGH some lament the days when tyres were not such a dominant factor in the race performance equation, you cannot escape that such is the case in the current Pirelli era, and that track temperature and its effect on the chosen compounds (ultra-soft, super-soft and soft in Austria) are key.

As forecast, race day gave track temperatures around 20 degrees below those on which the slick compounds had been run on Friday and Saturday. Which meant that while Hamilton had trashed a set of ultra-softs in five laps on Saturday morning, he was tasked with getting his starting set to lap 23 before going on to the soft-compound tyre for the remainder of the 71 laps, thereby covering a potential one-stop race from Ferrari certainly, and possibly Red Bull, too.

For Rosberg, starting sixth after his gearbox penalty, the thinking was that he would need to be aggressive early on, make an earlier stop for softs and then complete a two-stop run with a stint on the super-softs at the end. The team simulations suggested that he would end up second to Hamilton, producing the desired Mercedes 1-2. But there were complications.

Hamilton converted his pole position without problem this time, while Hülkenberg's Force India made an awful getaway and was passed by Button's McLaren, Räikkönen's Ferrari and Ricciardo's Red Bull. Using his Mercedes grunt, however, 'The Hulk' repassed Daniel going into Turn Three, but soon began to struggle with badly graining ultra-softs. Rosberg nailed him into Turn Two and quickly got on the back of Button and Räikkönen as Jenson fought to hold off Kimi's quicker Ferrari.

The Red Bull drivers swapped positions at the end of the second lap, when Verstappen dived down the inside of Ricciardo into Turn Eight from a long way back. Daniel, about to turn in, had to sharply turn out again!

Ricciardo had been caught napping: "I was surprised. I knew the mode we were in and the fact that we were struggling a bit for pace there versus other cars, but Max was in the same mode. I looked in my mirror and he didn't seem close enough, so, yeah, good move..." And increased heart rates on the Red Bull pit wall, no doubt.

Both Räikkönen and Rosberg passed Button on lap seven, but although Hamilton was only 7s to the good, Nico's ultra-softs were struggling compared to Kimi's super-softs and the Mercedes was starting to lose ground. The team brought him in for softs after ten laps.

Meanwhile, Hamilton was doing on his ultra-softs what he'd done in Monaco on full wets: eking out stint length while still going quickly, a skill he possesses that perhaps is under-appreciated.

"It was much cooler today," he said, "but on Saturday morning, I'd killed the tyres in five laps driving a certain way. This morning, they said that for Plan A to work, I needed to get them 23 laps, and there are different driving styles you can use to nurture these tyres. I studied the lines a lot, and where to lift and coast, and it worked well. I was happy how I looked after the tyres, but it's not a surprise, I've done it in other races."

After Mercedes pitted him and he came out behind his team-mate on tyres with 13 fewer laps, with Rosberg needing to stop once more, Lewis had no reason to suspect that this was going to be other than a routine win.

Things were about to change, however, courtesy of Ferrari. Vettel had passed Ricciardo after six laps and was just 5s behind team-mate Räikkönen; both were on super-softs rather than ultra-softs, remember. When Red Bull pitted Ricciardo on lap 14 and Verstappen a lap later, the Ferraris kept going, Kimi taking the lead for a lap when Hamilton pitted, before Ferrari called him in.

Vettel, stayed out longer, however, the planned one-stop looking workable and Ferrari trying to reduce the distance he would have to run on his softs. He was not far in front of the early-stopping Rosberg when, on lap 26, his right rear Pirelli blew on the main straight. The Ferrari spun at almost 200mph and Vettel kissed the pit wall before coming to rest on the other side of the track, unscathed. Investigations revealed no obvious problem, and the incident was put down to either debris or damage sustained over kerbing, although Vettel was sceptical about the latter.

Out came the safety car for the next five laps and the field rebunched. This was a good break for Grosjean, who had yet to stop in the Haas and essentially was given a free stop, which elevated him to what effectively was seventh place.

The order behind the official Mercedes was now Rosberg, Hamilton, Verstappen, Ricciardo, Räikkönen, Bottas, Nasr (whose Sauber had started on softs and was yet to pit), Button and Grosjean. Bottas would soon fade with tyre graining worse than Williams had ever experienced.

When racing resumed, Hamilton assumed that he could cruise around behind his team-mate until Nico made his second stop and then continue on, untroubled, to victory. Which explains why he was thrown somewhat by a message from the pit wall that he would be stopping next, not Rosberg. Why had Mercedes switched strategy?

The safety car had changed the equation by closing up the gaps. Mercedes was eyeing Verstappen a little nervously, suspecting that the five laps behind the safety car would lead Red Bull to definitely take him through on a one-stopper, which was correct. Rosberg, meanwhile, would need to stop again, but he did not have a new set of softs left and therefore would have to run his final stint on super-softs. He would be quick initially, but they would fall away earlier and he might not get past Verstappen. Max's Montreal defence was fresh in the memory…

Worse, if Hamilton's 50-lap one-stopper proved tough for any reason, Verstappen was now right there and might even be a threat for the win. Converting Hamilton to a two-stop reduced the risk, but the instruction was not what Lewis was expecting, or wanted to hear.

"I didn't understand and still don't really…" he said later.

"My tyres are fine!" he said on the radio as he contemplated ignoring the pit instruction and staying out, before finally peeling into the pit lane.

You couldn't help but wonder whether seeds of doubt had been sewn by Lewis suffering considerably worse power unit reliability than any other Mercedes user (inevitably he would have to suffer a ten-place grid drop at one of the later-season races for an additional power unit) and baseless internet stories suggesting that it fitted the Mercedes agenda to have Rosberg win the championship!

Now that they were both stopping again, and with Nico in front on the road, Hamilton was given priority so that he could undercut his way past Rosberg once more, which, given the circumstances, was only fair. But Lewis's left rear proved stubborn and he had to work hard to bring his softs up to temperature on his out-lap. Nico pitted next lap and, after a good in-lap and a better stop, managed to stay in front. Any paranoia on Hamilton's part was fuelled further by Rosberg being on the red-walled super-softs.

"Why is he on different tyres to me?" Hamilton demanded, not realising that his team-mate had no softs left. The team assured Lewis that, in fact, he was on the optimum tyre.

The race was now beautifully set up. The one-stopping Verstappen led, but was unlikely to be able to fend off the fresh-tyred Mercs, now on tyres with differing performance characteristics.

As expected, Verstappen was rapidly closed down, with Rosberg, quicker than Hamilton initially on his super-softs, going by into Turn Three with ten laps remaining. Hamilton passed Verstappen at Turn Two on lap 63, and now it was a straight race between the Mercedes pair.

In terms of lap time, it was nip and tuck between the pair. Both had been forced to manage brake temperatures because the grippier resurfaced track had made that more of an issue, but with just one lap left, Rosberg suddenly

Above: After a great qualifying, Pascal Wehrlein's Manor leads Alonso, Grosjean and the two Renaults. Helped by a safety car, the Mercedes junior unlapped himself en route to tenth.
Photo: Sahara Force India F1 Team

Top right: Wehrlein scored Manor a vital point, potentially worth millions at the season's end. Sporting director Davy Ryan receives a Chandon shampoo in celebration.
Photo: Jad Sherif/WRi2

Above right: Kimi Räikkönen took a podium following Rosberg's troubles on the final lap.
Photo: Scuderia Ferrari

Right: Rosberg was reprimanded for dragging his damaged car to the line fourth, after last-lap contact with his team-mate.
Photo: Peter J. Fox

had reduced brake-by-wire effect as the system went into conservation mode.

It was a momentary distraction, but not a big issue. Nico knew that Lewis's only real opportunity would be into Turn Two and that he needed a good exit from Turn One. But he took too much inside kerb.

Hamilton was on him instantly, and Rosberg was forced to flick right early and defend the inside. Lewis tried to go the long way around into Turn Two, but Nico braked late and attempted to run him out wide. With Hamilton fractionally ahead, the pair made contact and Rosberg suffered a damaged front wing. Hamilton ran off the circuit, rejoined just ahead of Rosberg and motored away to the 25 points.

Rosberg, his front wing sparking furiously as the nose looked as though it might detach, limped home, passed en route by Verstappen and Räikkönen. In the Mercedes pit, an angry Toto Wolff smashed down his fist. The race stewards (Martin Donnelly the driver steward) found Rosberg guilty of causing a collision and awarded him a 10s penalty, effectively meaningless considering he got to the line 14s clear of Ricciardo's Red Bull.

"This is such a hard track to overtake and I didn't know if I was going to get an opportunity," beamed Hamilton. "I went for it, and that's what I live for – racing. Nico turned in early at Turn One, clipped the kerb on the apex and bounced, which you don't like to do because you can't get on the power. I saw it happen, and it's very easy to follow, do the same thing and not get the exit. But I was great on the brakes and got a really good exit. If he'd done it normally, as he'd done the lap before maybe, I wouldn't have had a chance," he added, rubbing it in.

For Rosberg, it could hardly have been worse. He'd lost

a grand prix on the last lap, through a mistake, and to his team-mate. No racing driver worth his salt is going to let someone – especially his team-mate – drive around the outside of him on the last lap, but he'd been blamed for what was probably a racing incident. To add insult to injury, he received a reprimand for dragging his damaged car to the line. Again, a bit harsh. It was the last lap, after all, and he'd been leading. What's a racing driver going to do? But then you remembered poor Justin Wilson and figured that head protection is needed sooner rather than later.

Last-lap drama was provided not just by Mercedes, but by Force India, who had been in trouble with brakes and had already retired Hülkenberg, for whom the afternoon had been something of a disaster from his front-row starting position. Braking into Turn Two, team-mate Pérez had no problem, but into T3 the pedal went to the floor and Sergio into the tyres.

This was highly significant for Manor. Wehrlein, after his great qualifying performance, ran an ultra-soft/ultra-soft/soft strategy, and after going a lap down with his two early stops, had been able to unlap himself behind the safety car. He'd driven a great race; Pérez's problem elevated him to tenth and into the points on the very last lap.

"I saw Sergio's car, but I had no idea where he had been running and I was only told about tenth place after I'd crossed the line," Pascal explained. It put Manor ahead of cash-strapped Sauber and into the all-important constructors' championship top ten.

Predictably enough, the post-race talk was all about three contacts in five races (Spain, Canada and now Austria) for the Mercedes men and the possible imposition of team orders. Yawn...

Tony Dodgins

VIEWPOINT
POLITICAL INCORRECTNESS

FINAL lap, the two drivers fighting for the lead run wheel to wheel and collide, no one gets hurt. What more could you want? This is motor racing. But it's also motor racing in the second decade of the 21st century, complete with political correctness.

Nico Rosberg, attempting to copy the use-all-of-the-track tactic exhibited by his team-mate more than once in the past, does it badly. Rather than touch wheel to wheel while attempting to persuade Lewis Hamilton that coming around the outside is not a good idea, Rosberg fouls his front wing against the sister car. The damage is bad enough to make the wing collapse. In doing so, it creates sparks and catches the attention of the race stewards.

A couple of weeks later, Mercedes boss Toto Wolff was asked what the difference was between Hamilton easing out Rosberg at the first corner of the 2015 US Grand Prix and the positions being reversed in the final lap in Austria. He couldn't – or, tactfully, wouldn't – give a straight answer. Setting aside Mercedes management's rage at a possible 1-2 being compromised, this was a clumsy racing incident, filled with passion and raw excitement in the tense closing moments of a grand prix.

The same applied to Rosberg limping home, rather than parking up and watching what had become 12 points disappear as the remaining finishers raced by. This was no Kimi Räikkönen dragging his damaged Ferrari through the tunnel in the middle of the Monaco Grand Prix. It was the final lap on a wide-open track manned by professional marshals, yellow flags at the ready.

But no. The already chastened Rosberg needed his wrist slapped, the stewards adding a reprimand to the penalty for causing the accident.

And here's the final irony. The driver steward that weekend was Martin Donnelly. If ever there was a man who would drag home a heap of wreckage if there were a championship point or hard cash waiting at the finish line, it was the tough and uncompromising Ulsterman. Rosberg could be forgiven for feeling insult had been added to self-inflicted injury.

Maurice Hamilton

9

2016 FORMULA 1
GROSSE PREIS VON ÖSTERREICH

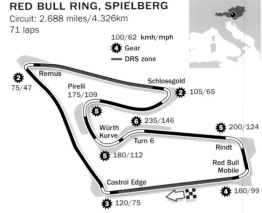

RED BULL RING, SPIELBERG
Circuit: 2.688 miles/4.326km
71 laps

SPIELBERG 1–3 JULY

RACE DISTANCE: 71 laps, 190.773 miles/307.020km

RACE WEATHER: Dry/overcast (track 26–28°C, air 15–17°C)

ROLEX
OFFICIAL TIMEPIECE

RACE – OFFICIAL CLASSIFICATION

Pos.	Driver	Nat.	No.	Entrant	Car/Engine	Tyres	Laps	Time/Retirement	Speed (mph/km/h)	Gap to leader	Fastest race lap	
1	**Lewis Hamilton**	GB	44	Mercedes AMG Petronas F1 Team	Mercedes F1 W07-Mercedes PU106C V6	P	71	1h 27m 38.107s	130.614/210.203		1m 08.411s	67
2	**Max Verstappen**	NL	33	Red Bull Racing	Red Bull RB12-TAG Heuer RB12 V6	P	71	1h 27m 43.826s	130.472/209.975	5.719s	1m 09.618s	69
3	**Kimi Räikkönen**	FIN	7	Scuderia Ferrari	Ferrari SF16-H-059/5 V6	P	71	1h 27m 44.131s	130.464/209.962	6.024s	1m 08.876s	66
4	**Nico Rosberg**	D	6	Mercedes AMG Petronas F1 Team	Mercedes F1 W07-Mercedes PU106C V6	P	71	1h 28m 04.817s*	129.954/209.141	26.710s	1m 08.491s	66
5	**Daniel Ricciardo**	AUS	3	Red Bull Racing	Red Bull RB12-TAG Heuer RB12 V6	P	71	1h 28m 09.088s	129.849/208.972	30.981s	1m 08.770s	66
6	**Jenson Button**	GB	22	McLaren Honda	McLaren MP4-31-Honda RA616H V6	P	71	1h 28m 15.813s	129.684/208.706	37.706s	1m 10.001s	70
7	**Romain Grosjean**	F	8	Haas F1 Team	Haas VF-16-Ferrari 059/5 V6	P	71	1h 28m 22.775s**	129.514/208.432	44.668s	1m 09.925s	67
8	**Carlos Sainz**	E	55	Scuderia Toro Rosso	Toro Rosso STR11-Ferrari 059/4 V6	P	71	1h 28m 25.507s	129.447/208.325	47.400s	1m 10.138s	68
9	**Valtteri Bottas**	FIN	77	Williams Martini Racing	Williams FW38-Mercedes PU106C V6	P	70			1 lap	1m 10.210s	55
10	**Pascal Wehrlein**	D	94	Manor Racing MRT	Manor MRT05-Mercedes PU106C V6	P	70			1 lap	1m 10.859s	67
11	Esteban Gutiérrez	MEX	21	Haas F1 Team	Haas VF-16-Ferrari 059/5 V6	P	70			1 lap	1m 09.694s	55
12	Jolyon Palmer	GB	30	Renault Sport F1 Team	Renault R.S.16-R.E.16 V6	P	70			1 lap	1m 10.228s	53
13	Felipe Nasr	BR	12	Sauber F1 Team	Sauber C35-Ferrari 059/5 V6	P	70			1 lap	1m 10.415s	46
14	Kevin Magnussen	DK	20	Renault Sport F1 Team	Renault R.S.16-R.E.16 V6	P	70			1 lap	1m 10.450s	56
15	Marcus Ericsson	S	9	Sauber F1 Team	Sauber C35-Ferrari 059/5 V6	P	70			1 lap	1m 10.704s	58
16	Rio Haryanto	RI	88	Manor Racing MRT	Manor MRT05-Mercedes PU106C V6	P	70			1 lap	1m 10.342s	66
17	Sergio Pérez	MEX	11	Sahara Force India F1 Team	Force India VJM09-Mercedes PU106C V6	P	69	brakes		2 laps	1m 10.120s	66
18	Fernando Alonso	E	14	McLaren Honda	McLaren MP4-31-Honda RA616H V6	P	64	power unit		7 laps	1m 11.020s	44
19	Nico Hülkenberg	D	27	Sahara Force India F1 Team	Force India VJM09-Mercedes PU106C V6	P	64	brakes		7 laps	1m 10.309s	53
20	Felipe Massa	BR	19	Williams Martini Racing	Williams FW38-Mercedes PU106C V6	P	63	brakes		8 laps	1m 09.899s	59
	Sebastian Vettel	D	5	Scuderia Ferrari	Ferrari SF15-H-059/5 V6	P	26	rear tyre			1m 11.441s	10
	Daniil Kvyat	RUS	26	Scuderia Toro Rosso	Toro Rosso STR11-Ferrari 059/4 V6	P	2	loss of power			1m 18.302s	2

* includes 10-second penalty for causing an accident – position unaffected. ** includes 5-second penalty for speeding in the pit lane – position unaffected.

Fastest race lap: Lewis Hamilton on lap 67, 1m 08.411s, 141.454mph/227.647km/h.

Lap record: Nigel Mansell (Williams FW11B-Honda V6 turbo), 1m 28.318s, 150.500mph/242.207km/h (1987 – 3.692-mile/5.942km circuit).

Lap record (current configuration): Michael Schumacher (Ferrari V10), 1m 08.337s, 141.607mph/227.894km/h (2003).

21 · NASR · Sauber
(3-place grid penalty for failing to slow for yellow flags)

19 · PALMER · Renault
(3-place grid penalty for failing to slow for yellow flags)

17 · MAGNUSSEN · Renault

15 · SAINZ · Toro Rosso

13 · GROSJEAN · Haas

11 · GUTIÉRREZ · Haas

22 · KVYAT · Toro Rosso
(required to start from the pit lane – change of Survival Cell)

20 · HARYANTO · Manor
(3-place grid penalty for failing to slow for yellow flags)

18 · ERICSSON · Sauber

16 · PÉREZ · Force India

14 · ALONSO · McLaren

12 · WEHRLEIN · Manor

6 = Pit stop   9 = Drive-thru penalty

94 = One lap or more behind

All results and data © FOM 2016

TIME SHEETS

PRACTICE 1 (FRIDAY)
Weather: Dry/sunny
Temperatures: track 31–40°C, air 19–22°C

Pos.	Driver	Laps	Time
1	Nico Rosberg	37	1m 07.373s
2	Lewis Hamilton	34	1m 07.730s
3	Sebastian Vettel	28	1m 08.022s
4	Kimi Räikkönen	31	1m 08.222s
5	Daniel Ricciardo	35	1m 08.528s
6	Carlos Sainz	34	1m 08.803s
7	Felipe Massa	39	1m 08.824s
8	Max Verstappen	21	1m 08.962s
9	Daniil Kvyat	32	1m 08.990s
10	Valtteri Bottas	40	1m 08.998s
11	Romain Grosjean	34	1m 09.078s
12	Nico Hülkenberg	43	1m 09.280s
13	Jenson Button	31	1m 09.365s
14	Fernando Alonso	30	1m 09.567s
15	Kevin Magnussen	24	1m 09.707s
16	Pascal Wehrlein	34	1m 09.775s
17	Jolyon Palmer	28	1m 09.851s
18	Marcus Ericsson	35	1m 09.929s
19	Esteban Gutiérrez	20	1m 10.110s
20	Felipe Nasr	26	1m 10.314s
21	Rio Haryanto	21	1m 10.493s
22	Alfonso Celis	37	1m 10.860s

QUALIFYING (SATURDAY)
Weather: Dry-light rain/sunny-overcast Temperatures: track 35–54°C, air 26–28°C

Pos.	Driver	First	Second	Third	Qualifying Tyre
1	Lewis Hamilton	1m 06.947s	1m 06.228s	1m 07.922s	Ultra-Soft (new)
2	Nico Rosberg	1m 06.516s	1m 06.403s	1m 08.465s	Ultra-Soft (new)
3	Nico Hülkenberg	1m 07.385s	1m 07.257s	1m 09.285s	Ultra-Soft (new)
4	Sebastian Vettel	1m 06.761s	1m 06.602s	1m 09.781s	Ultra-Soft (new)
5	Jenson Button	1m 07.653s	1m 07.572s	1m 09.900s	Ultra-Soft (new)
6	Kimi Räikkönen	1m 07.240s	1m 06.940s	1m 09.901s	Ultra-Soft (new)
7	Daniel Ricciardo	1m 07.500s	1m 06.840s	1m 09.980s	Ultra-Soft (new)
8	Valtteri Bottas	1m 07.148s	1m 06.911s	1m 10.440s	Ultra-Soft (new)
9	Max Verstappen	1m 07.131s	1m 06.866s	1m 11.153s	Ultra-Soft (new)
10	Felipe Massa	1m 07.419s	1m 07.145s	1m 11.977s	Ultra-Soft (new)
11	Esteban Gutiérrez	1m 07.660s	1m 07.578s		
12	Pascal Wehrlein	1m 07.565s	1m 07.700s		
13	Romain Grosjean	1m 07.662s	1m 07.850s		
14	Fernando Alonso	1m 07.671s	1m 08.154s		
15	Carlos Sainz	1m 07.618s	no time		
16	Sergio Pérez	1m 07.657s	no time		
17	Kevin Magnussen	1m 07.941s			
18	Jolyon Palmer	1m 07.965s			
19	Rio Haryanto	1m 08.026s			
20	Daniil Kvyat	1m 08.409s			
21	Marcus Ericsson	1m 08.418s			
22	Felipe Nasr	1m 08.446s			

PRACTICE 2 (FRIDAY)
Weather: Dry-wet/overcast
Temperatures: track 25–43°C, air 17–24°C

Pos.	Driver	Laps	Time
1	Nico Rosberg	25	1m 07.967s
2	Lewis Hamilton	19	1m 07.986s
3	Nico Hülkenberg	28	1m 08.580s
4	Sebastian Vettel	25	1m 08.589s
5	Daniel Ricciardo	30	1m 08.649s
6	Carlos Sainz	32	1m 08.713s
7	Max Verstappen	20	1m 08.761s
8	Kimi Räikkönen	23	1m 08.820s
9	Valtteri Bottas	24	1m 08.941s
10	Jenson Button	30	1m 08.994s
11	Fernando Alonso	26	1m 09.075s
12	Felipe Massa	17	1m 09.184s
13	Daniil Kvyat	26	1m 09.207s
14	Sergio Pérez	32	1m 09.226s
15	Kevin Magnussen	19	1m 09.525s
16	Jolyon Palmer	23	1m 10.020s
17	Pascal Wehrlein	20	1m 10.034s
18	Esteban Gutiérrez	16	1m 10.138s
19	Marcus Ericsson	19	1m 10.140s
20	Romain Grosjean	31	1m 10.400s
21	Felipe Nasr	22	1m 10.444s
22	Rio Haryanto	25	1m 11.328s

PRACTICE 3 (SATURDAY)
Weather: Dry/sunny
Temperatures: track 42°49°C, air 24–26°C

Pos.	Driver	Laps	Time
1	Sebastian Vettel	20	1m 07.098s
2	Kimi Räikkönen	26	1m 07.234s
3	Lewis Hamilton	20	1m 07.308s
4	Daniel Ricciardo	22	1m 07.639s
5	Max Verstappen	22	1m 07.761s
6	Valtteri Bottas	23	1m 07.814s
7	Felipe Massa	27	1m 07.831s
8	Nico Hülkenberg	23	1m 08.285s
9	Jenson Button	19	1m 08.304s
10	Fernando Alonso	17	1m 08.327s
11	Sergio Pérez	26	1m 08.442s
12	Esteban Gutiérrez	22	1m 08.475s
13	Pascal Wehrlein	29	1m 08.534s
14	Romain Grosjean	21	1m 08.550s
15	Kevin Magnussen	31	1m 08.569s
16	Daniil Kvyat	32	1m 08.786s
17	Jolyon Palmer	27	1m 08.939s
18	Carlos Sainz	11	1m 09.008s
19	Rio Haryanto	28	1m 09.116s
20	Marcus Ericsson	25	1m 09.137s
21	Felipe Nasr	20	1m 09.557s
22	Nico Rosberg	16	1m 10.959s

FOR THE RECORD

2,000th POINT: **Lewis Hamilton.**

30th FASTEST LAP: **Lewis Hamilton.**

1st POINT: **Pascal Wehrlein.**

DID YOU KNOW?

This was the 250th win for British drivers.

POINTS

DRIVERS
1	Nico Rosberg	153
2	Lewis Hamilton	142
3	Sebastian Vettel	96
4	Kimi Räikkönen	96
5	Daniel Ricciardo	88
6	Max Verstappen	72
7	Valtteri Bottas	54
8	Sergio Pérez	39
9	Felipe Massa	38
10	Romain Grosjean	28
11	Daniil Kvyat	22
12	Carlos Sainz	22
13	Nico Hülkenberg	20
14	Fernando Alonso	18
15	Jenson Button	13
16	Kevin Magnussen	6
17	Pascal Wehrlein	1
18	Stoffel Vandoorne	1

CONSTRUCTORS
1	Mercedes	295
2	Ferrari	192
3	Red Bull	168
4	Williams	92
5	Force India	59
6	Toro Rosso	36
7	McLaren	32
8	Haas	28
9	Renault	6
10	Manor	1

Photo: Peter J. Fox

Photo: Sahara Force India F1 Team

Qualifying: head-to-head
Rosberg	4	5	Hamilton
Vettel	7	2	Räikkönen
Massa	2	7	Bottas
Ricciardo	4	0	Kvyat
Ricciardo	5	0	Verstappen
Pérez	5	4	Hülkenberg
Magnussen	7	2	Palmer
Verstappen	3	1	Sainz
Kvyat	2	3	Sainz
Ericsson	7	2	Nasr
Alonso	6	2	Button
Button	0	1	Vandoorne
Haryanto	4	5	Wehrlein
Grosjean	6	3	Gutiérrez

9 · VETTEL · Ferrari
(5-place grid penalty for replacing the gearbox)

7 · BOTTAS · Williams

5 · RICCIARDO · Red Bull

3 · BUTTON · McLaren

1 · HAMILTON · Mercedes

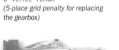

10 · MASSA · Williams
(started from the pit lane)

8 · VERSTAPPEN · Red Bull

6 · ROSBERG · Mercedes
(5-place grid penalty for replacing the gearbox)

4 · RÄIKKÖNEN · Ferrari

2 · HÜLKENBERG · Force India

56	57	58	59	60	61	62	63	64	65	66	67	68	69	70	71	
33	33	33	33	33	6	6	6	6	6	6	6	6	6	6	44	1
6	6	6	6	6	33	33	44	44	44	44	44	44	44	44	33	2
44	44	44	44	44	44	44	33	33	33	33	33	33	33	33	7	3
3	3	7	7	7	7	7	7	7	7	7	7	7	7	7	6	4
7	7	3	3	22	22	22	22	3	3	3	3	3	3	3	3	5
22	22	22	22	3	3	3	3	22	22	22	22	22	22	22	22	6
8	8	8	8	8	8	8	8	8	8	8	8	8	8	8	8	7
11	11	11	11	11	11	11	11	11	11	11	11	11	55	55		8
55	55	55	55	55	55	55	55	55	55	55	55	55	57	77		9
19	14	14	14	14	14	14	77	77	77	77	77	77	77	94		10
14	77	77	77	77	77	77	94	94	94	94	94	94	*94*	21		
77	94	94	94	94	94	94	21	21	21	21	*21*	*21*	*21*	30		
94	21	21	21	21	21	14	*14*	*30*	30	30	30	30	12			
21	19	19	19	19	19	*19*	*30*	*12*	12	12	12	12	20			
12	12	12	12	30	30	*30*	*12*	*20*	20	20	20	20	9			
30	30	30	30	12	*12*	*12*	*12*	20	9	9	9	9	88			
27	27	*27*	*27*	27	27	27	27	9	88	88	88	88				
20	20	20	20	20	20	20	20	88								
9	9	9	9	9	9	9	9	27								
88	88	88	88	88	88	88	88									

▓ Safety car deployed on laps shown

RACE TYRE STRATEGIES PIRELLI

	Driver	Race Stint 1	Race Stint 2	Race Stint 3	Race Stint 4
1	Hamilton	Ultra-Soft (u): 1-21	Soft (n): 22-54	Soft (u): 55-71	
2	Verstappen	Super-Soft (u): 1-15	Soft (n): 16-71		
3	Räikkönen	Super-Soft (u): 1-22	Soft (n): 23-71		
4	Rosberg	Ultra-Soft (u): 1-10	Soft (n): 11-55	Super-Soft (n): 56-71	
5	Ricciardo	Super-Soft (u): 1-14	Soft (n): 15-60	Ultra-Soft (n): 61-71	
6	Button	Ultra-Soft (u): 1-9	Soft (n): 10-26	Soft (u): 27-71	
7	Grosjean	Super-Soft (n): 1-26	Soft (n): 27-71		
8	Sainz	Super-Soft (n): 1-9	Soft (n): 10-28	Soft (n): 29-71	
9	Bottas	Ultra-Soft (u): 1-9	Soft (n): 10-51	Super-Soft (n): 52-70	
10	Wehrlein	Super-Soft (n): 1-13	Ultra-Soft (n): 14-23	Soft (n): 24-70	
11	Gutiérrez	Super-Soft (n): 1-21	Super-Soft (n): 22-41	Soft (u): 42-70	
12	Palmer	Super-Soft (n): 1-12	Soft (n): 13-50	Super-Soft (n): 51-70	
13	Nasr	Soft (n): 1-43	Super-Soft (n): 44-70		
14	Magnussen	Super-Soft (n): 1-12	Soft (n): 13-49	Super-Soft (u): 50-70	
15	Ericsson	Super-Soft (n): 1-12	Soft (n): 13-50	Super-Soft (u): 51-70	
16	Haryanto	Soft (n): 1-27	Super-Soft (n): 28-50	Super-Soft (u): 51-70	
17	Pérez	Ultra-Soft (n): 1-9	Super-Soft (n): 10-26	Soft (u): 27-69	
18	Alonso	Super-Soft (n): 1-9	Soft (n): 9-26	Soft (n): 27-64	
19	Hülkenberg	Ultra-Soft (u): 1-8	Super-Soft (n): 9-24	Soft (n): 25-50	Ultra-Soft (u): 51-64
20	Massa	Super-Soft (u): 1-12	Soft (u): 13-56	Super-Soft (u): 57-63	
	Vettel	Super-Soft (u): 1-26 (dnf)			
	Kvyat	Ultra-Soft (n): 1-2 (dnf)			

The tyre regulations stipulate that at least two of three dry tyre specifications must be used during a dry race.
Pirelli P Zero logos are colour-coded on the tyre sidewalls: Purple = Ultra-Soft; Yellow = Soft; Red = Super-Soft. (n) new (u) used

Red Bull Racing/Getty Images

Photo: Peter J. Fox

199

BRITISH GRAND PRIX

SILVERSTONE CIRCUIT

SILVERSTONE QUALIFYING

LEWIS HAMILTON'S fans got double value during qualifying. The home hero had claimed provisional pole early in Q3, only to have the time deleted because he ran wide. Nigel Mansell, the driver steward at Silverstone, had warned his successors that zero tolerance would be applied if they ran wide at Copse, Stowe or Club, corners where lap time could be found. Having exceeded the limits at Copse, Hamilton's time was removed from the top of the list.

"I touched a kerb, the car bounced a little and it pulled me further off the track," said Lewis. "There was nothing I could do to prevent it, and I realised a penalty might be coming."

As he sat in the pits, preparing for a final run, Hamilton was showing in tenth place. He had to do it all again and, just for good measure, Rosberg had moved to the top of the pile. The Englishman knew this lap had to count. He had been quickest in every practice session thus far, but that meant nothing when even the smallest mistake would be costly as Rosberg hovered with intent.

It may have been a moment of pressure, but this was Silverstone. Hamilton rose to the occasion magnificently, taking career pole number 55. Rosberg failed to improve on his final lap and refused to offer as an excuse his absence from the track for much of FP2 due to a water pump failure. Hamilton was simply quicker, particularly through sector two and the awesome Maggotts/Becketts complex. The gap was 0.319s over 3.194 miles (5.141km).

The discrepancy between Mercedes and Red Bull was even larger, the W07 having excelled on the high-speed sections thanks to a package of aero improvements to the nose, sidepods, diffuser and rear wing endplates. For the first time since being promoted from Toro Rosso, Max Verstappen outqualified Daniel Ricciardo, despite the Dutchman having lost his final lap due to putting all four wheels across the white line. That lap had been slower in any case, thanks to a crosswind at Copse. Ricciardo had the same problem and he failed to close the gap to his young team-mate, this increasingly intense and interesting in-house battle edging the dark blue cars even further ahead of Ferrari.

Kimi Räikkönen's signature on a new contract for 2017 must have added to his sense of wellbeing on the fast curves, as he proved to be significantly quicker than Sebastian Vettel. A scrappy weekend for the German began when he came close to losing the car at Stowe towards the end of his first Q3 lap; the same thing occurred thanks to a gust of wind at Abbey as he began his second lap. As if sixth fastest was not bad enough, he had to endure a five-place penalty thanks to his third gearbox failure of the season. Both drivers cited a lack of downforce as the major problem, despite changes to the diffuser and front and rear brake ducts.

Ferrari's disappointment was matched, if not exceeded, by Williams on their home track, Valtteri Bottas being 0.7s adrift of Vettel with a car that suffered through the fast sweeps. At least the Finn was in the top ten, which was more than could be said for Felipe Massa, languishing in 12th after being unable to prevent his rear tyres from overheating before the end of his best Q2 lap.

The battle between Williams and Force India continued apace as Nico Hülkenberg set eighth fastest time, only to have it disallowed due to a track limits infringement. Despite further aero upgrades, Silverstone-based Force India was unable to fine-tune the car's balance due to being the only team to have chosen three sets of the hard tyre for each driver, limiting the number of softs to six, compared to seven for Mercedes and eight for Ferrari. That partly accounted for Sergio Pérez being unhappy with his VJM09 in the high-speed turns and failing to better 11th.

Hülkenberg's penalty allowed Carlos Sainz into eighth; a very impressive performance given that the Toro Rosso's old-spec Ferrari was short of breath on a circuit such as this (as proved by a lowly position on the speed-trap times). Sainz's confidence in nailing the car through sector two contrasted with the slightly more tentative Daniil Kvyat and was marked by 15th on the grid for the Russian, 0.6s slower than the Spaniard, although this was partially due to Kvyat's best lap having been spoiled by a slower car.

McLaren's Fernando Alonso had been eighth before his best lap time was deleted for exceeding track limits at the final corner, the Spaniard having wrung the car's neck to make up for an estimated 70bhp shortfall from the Honda. Alonso's frustration was nothing compared to that of team-mate Jenson Button, who was eliminated in first qualifying after the rear wing endplate separated from the floor.

The Haas proved susceptible to the Silverstone crosswind, Romain Grosjean surviving a particularly lurid moment through Stowe on this way to 13th fastest time, one place ahead of Esteban Gutiérrez. The Renaults continued to struggle as a lack of development showed, Kevin Magnussen and Jolyon Palmer split by Button in 17th place. Rio Haryanto was fractionally quicker than Pascal Wehrlein, the Manors comfortably ahead of Felipe Nasr, the only Sauber on track during qualifying. This was due to Marcus Ericsson being in hospital for a check-up, following a heavy impact with the barriers after getting out of shape on the wet Astroturf at the exit of Stowe during FP3.

THE Great British Crowd was out in full force. And so was the Great British Summer. As the field gathered on the grid, the heavens opened. And as the good, the great and the not so great of F1 scuttled for cover, drivers and engineers were deep in conversation about tyre choice. A safety car start would solve that problem, since the rules dictated full wets as mandatory. But, when the dark cloud scurried east and the smiling sun returned a few minutes before the appointed hour (1pm), it seemed the decision might be premature.

In fact, it would be proved correct as the field set off behind the Mercedes AMG GT-S and created massive spray thanks to standing water on Wellington Straight and at Luffield. With the brisk wind and the passage of 22 cars, however, the racing line quickly appeared, prompting Hamilton to address race director Charlie Whiting on the radio. "Can we go now, Charlie?" was the simple request as the world champion became increasingly concerned about falling tyre pressures and temperatures. In fact, in his enthusiasm to generate heat from the brakes, Hamilton locked his fronts and came perilously close to sliding into the safety car. There had been concerns about a collision between two Mercedes on the first lap – but not like this!

As the field reached the halfway point of lap five, the lights on the official car were extinguished. Knowing they could start racing after crossing the so-called safety car line between Stowe and Club, Hamilton backed everyone up at the end of Hangar Straight – and then floored it halfway through Stowe. By the end of the lap, he was 3.7s in front. No one would get close for the rest of the afternoon.

Elsewhere, strategy options were all over the place, Räikkönen, Bottas, Sainz, Hülkenberg, Alonso, Vettel and others having followed the safety car into the pits to change to intermediates. At the end of lap six, Ricciardo led the next batch, but Wehrlein was about to change the face of the race for those who had stopped early. When the Manor slid off and became stuck in gravel on the outside of Abbey, the imposition of a virtual safety car played into the hands of the leading four (Pérez, yet to come in, having joined Hamilton, Rosberg and Verstappen). With a chance to make what was effectively a free stop, the front quartet came in, collected their intermediates and rejoined without losing track position.

Ricciardo, having been right with Verstappen, had lost almost ten seconds on his team-mate and was behind Pérez to boot. That would consign the luckless Australian to what he would later describe as a lonely and uneventful race. The only thing Ricciardo could be thankful for was not being stuck behind a Williams, as Bottas and Massa struggled to get temperature into their tyres. The Williams may have been slow, but getting past the white cars was almost impossible thanks to the high top speed of their Mercedes power units, the absence of DRS while conditions remained essentially wet and the treacherous surface immediately alongside the dry racing line.

There would be relief on lap ten, when Bottas spun out of ninth place, and Hülkenberg, Alonso, Vettel and Kyvat managed to get past while the Finn recovered. Now, Force India and McLaren were stacked up behind the other Williams of Massa, Hülkenberg surviving a massive moment when he got out of shape on the damp off-line coming out of Club. Meanwhile, Massa's tenacious driving was allowing Sainz and Räikkönen to make good their escape in sixth and seventh places.

Hamilton looked untroubled as he eased out a gap of several seconds over Rosberg. "I had more pace in hand if I needed it," he explained later. It was good that he could conserve his intermediates at this stage. He didn't want to wear them out too soon and make an unnecessary stop for a second set. Equally, he needed to prolong the moment to stop for slicks in the hope that the chosen dry tyre would last until the finish.

While Hamilton appeared to be in cruise mode, Verstappen was anything but as he put Rosberg under increasing pressure, the Red Bull working particularly well under these tricky conditions – as was the driver as he revelled in this world of fast reflexes charged by a huge natural ability. Rosberg remained totally calm in defence as the blue car climbed all over the back of the silver one. Going through Maggotts on lap 15, Rosberg touched a kerb and got slightly off line. That was all Verstappen needed. Running around the outside of Becketts – on the wet line – Max held his ground into and through Chapel to pull off the move in the most unlikely place. Hamilton was 6.3s ahead. When would he stop for slicks?

Above: Consternation abounds as the teams prepare their cars on the rain-sodden track.
Photo: Lukas Gorys

Top left: Before the storm. The Emirates grid girls appeared to be dressed for the weather.
Photo: Peter J. Fox

Above left: The heavens open, and Lewis Hamilton heads for cover while frantic preparations continue on the starting grid.
Photo: WRi2

Left: For the first five laps, Lewis Hamilton and Nico Rosberg were forced to hold station behind the safety car.

Below left: The home crowd braved the elements and were amply rewarded with a British winner.
Photos: WRi2/Bryn Williams

Opening spread: Lewis jumps for joy after his second successive British Grand Prix victory.
Photo: Peter J. Fox

Above: Max Verstappen took second place for Red Bull.
Photo: Peter J. Fox

Facing page, from top:
Sahara Force India's V.J. Mallya (*right*) made his first appearance of the year.
Photo: Sahara Force India F1 Team

Jolyon Palmer had a home race to forget after a pit-stop bungle caused him to be penalised for unsafe release.
Photo: WRi2/Bryn Williams

Disadvantaged by the safety car after Wehrlein's spin, Daniel Ricciardo had a lonely race to fourth place.
Photo: Red Bull Racing/Getty Images

Right: Nico Rosberg's gearbox problems led to an illegal radio communication from his team. His subsequent ten-second penalty demoted him to third, behind Verstappen.
Photo: WRi2/Bryn Williams

Vettel, stuck in the queue behind Massa, was the first to take the gamble at the end of lap 15. Everyone watched the timing screen with interest. When the German immediately set personal best sector times, the message was clear. But it was also clear that the track remained treacherous when the Ferrari spun at the exit of Abbey – and Vettel found himself back in the queue behind Massa who, into the bargain, had also stopped for slicks and was set to stay out for quite some time. Having jumped a couple of places by making an early stop (for wets) at Silverstone 12 months before, the reverse had happened in 2016. This was definitely not Vettel's weekend.

In truth, there may have been little to choose between the intermediate and the slick, but the leaders came in on laps 17 and 18, Hamilton rejoining 7s ahead of Verstappen, with Rosberg 4s further behind. Pérez remained a distant fourth, but Ricciardo was closing in for a rare piece of action for the Australian as he ran around the outside of the Force India at Stowe. Räikkönen was several car lengths behind, with Sainz keeping the Ferrari in sight. Hülkenberg was next, the progress of both the Toro Rosso and the Force India being interrupted by various sideways and off-track moments. Massa was ninth, with an increasingly frustrated Alonso climbing all over the back of the Williams – and, on one occasion, putting two wheels on the green concrete at 150mph on Wellington Straight. The Spaniard then announced by radio his annoyance over a late call for slicks.

The track remained tricky in parts, particularly the turn-in to Abbey, where a damp patch caused a nasty, high-speed sideways moment for the leader. Hamilton caught the slide, but finished off the corner by taking to the run-off area. Verstappen would have been in a position to take advantage – had he not done exactly the same thing. Instead of attacking, now he was defending as Rosberg closed in with a Mercedes that was handling much better in the drying conditions.

Despite his rear tyres going away, Verstappen was solid in defence, positioning his car perfectly – occasionally making a move too many for Rosberg's liking, the Mercedes driver complaining to his engineer – but showing all the mature signs demonstrated when holding off Räikkönen for that maiden win two months before in Spain. But once into DRS range and after a couple of attempts, Rosberg timed it perfectly on Hangar Straight and ran cleanly around the outside through Stowe. Hamilton was 6.7s ahead with nine laps to go.

The gap came down to 6.1s. Then, at the end of lap 46, it had jumped to 9.3s, Rosberg crossing the line with the car stuck in seventh gear. "Chassis default zero-one," he was urgently advised. The electronics did their work and he was soon under way. But the trouble was not yet over. "Avoid seventh gear," came the next command. When Rosberg asked if he should do that by going from sixth to eighth, he was instructed, "Affirmative. Go through seventh." Those words would prove costly later on. In the meantime, Rosberg was able to continue and keep Verstappen at bay, making it two Mercedes, followed by two Red Bulls and then Räikkönen half a minute behind.

Pérez (who had spun wildly through Abbey on lap 33) and Hülkenberg netted Force India 14 very important points for sixth and seventh on a day when Williams scored none. Vettel was ninth, his difficult weekend rounded off by a five-second penalty for running Massa wide when the understeering Ferrari tried to move ahead. An equally despairing Massa

then stopped for a set of softs with 14 laps to go. Alonso, having eventually got the better of Massa, lost control of the McLaren and spun, allowing Kvyat, Vettel and Button through. Then Vettel had passed Kvyat, the Toro Rosso claiming the final point.

Button finished 12th, one place ahead of Alonso, who deserved better after his relentless efforts. With Massa having dropped to 11th, Bottas was no help for Williams in 14th after a race full of uncharacteristic errors. In the closing stages, he had to fend off Nasr, who had delivered a strong race for Sauber, stopping at the right moments and making very few errors. That was some consolation for the team (although much-needed points would have been better), as Ericsson, having started from the pit lane in the rebuilt car, had been forced to retire after 11 laps with an engine misfire.

A poor race day for Haas was summed up by Grosjean stopping before the virtual safety car and then retiring from 16th place with transmission failure; Gutiérrez struggled into 16th. Renault were in an even worse state: Magnussen retired from the back of the field on lap 49 with a broken gearbox, and Palmer, having received a penalty for an unsafe three-wheeled release, also had a gearbox problem, which brought merciful release from blue-flag hell that had started as early as lap 17. After the excitement of a point for Manor in Austria, it was back to earth, literally with a bump, as Haryanto joined Wehrlein as a victim of the treacherous track at Abbey.

That was the difference between the good and the brilliant. Hamilton had survived his moment at Abbey with some style. He had been peerless and thoroughly deserved the adulation of the crowd as he joined Nigel Mansell and Jim Clark as a four-times British winner of their home grand prix.

The championship gap to Rosberg had been reduced to four points. A few hours later, it would become a single point when the stewards ruled that Nico had received an instruction and imposed a ten-second penalty. That was enough to drop the German from second to third. A brilliant day for Hamilton had suddenly become even better.

Maurice Hamilton

VIEWPOINT
THE NECESSARY SOLUTION

Right: A perfect day for Hamilton, who cruises home following his emphatic victory.
Photo: WRi2/Bryn Williams

Left: Sebastian Vettel was the latest driver to test the halo.
Photo: Scuderia Ferrari

Below left: Not a pretty sight. Vettel cruises down the pit lane prior to a track test.

Below: Max Verstappen celebrates with his third-place trophy, which was soon swapped for a larger one.
Photos: Lukas Gorys

Below right: To cap his celebrations, Hamilton surfed the adoring crowd.
Photo: Mercedes AMG Petronas F1 Team

DOMINATING Silverstone was the fallout from the Rosberg/Hamilton collision in Austria, and I've got to admit to some sympathy for Nico, booed as he was on the runner-up step of the podium.

Fair enough, Hamilton had been booed in Austria, too, but that was because a commentator had erroneously informed the spectators that Lewis had taken Nico out. If ever something had been a racing incident, that was it. No driver worth his salt is going to let someone drive around the outside of him on the last lap of a grand prix – especially his team-mate!

There was Nico, beaten up in Bahrain 2014, in Austin and Suzuka in 2015, and again on the opening lap in Montreal, but as soon as he stands his ground, albeit a bit cack-handedly, he gets a 10s penalty and two penalty points on his licence.

To add insult to injury, Rosberg was reprimanded for driving his damaged car to the end of the Austrian race to claim fourth. Realistically, was he going to park his car on the last lap of a race he'd been winning because his front wing was sparking?

My initial reaction was that when someone embarks on a career as a racing driver, they are not signing up to be an office clerk, but to something they know is risky. And that those risks might include a driver trying to finish a race on the last lap with a damaged car.

But then I remembered that, less than a year before, around 500 mourners had gathered at a church fewer than five miles from where we were standing at Silverstone, to pay tribute to Justin Wilson, killed by flying debris from Sage Karam's car in an Indycar race at Pocono.

The solution, however unpalatable to the purists, is head protection. You've just got to hope that in its final execution, it is a bit prettier than the revised Halo we saw on Sebastian Vettel's Ferrari on Friday morning. That looked like something you might snap shut in front of you on a big-dipper ride at your favourite theme park.

Tony Dodgins

10

2016 FORMULA 1
BRITISH
GRAND PRIX

SILVERSTONE 8–10 JULY

ROLEX

OFFICIAL TIMEPIECE

RACE DISTANCE: 52 laps, 190.262 miles/306.198km

RACE WEATHER: Wet track, drying/overcast-sunny
(track 22–29°C, air 17–21°C)

SILVERSTONE GRAND PRIX CIRCUIT
Circuit: 3.660 miles/5.891km, 52 laps

Club 1 130/81
Club 2 226/140
Vale 110/68
Luffield 125/78
Woodcote 280/174
Abbey 225/140
Brooklands 180/112
Stowe 180/112
Farm 285/177
Wellington Straight
Hangar straight 325/202
Village
The Loop
Copse 268/165
Chapel 252/157
Aintree
Maggotts 305/190
Gear 187/116 kmh/mph
Becketts 170/106
249/155
270/168
DRS zone

RACE – OFFICIAL CLASSIFICATION

Pos.	Driver	Nat.	No.	Entrant	Car/Engine	Tyres	Laps	Time/Retirement	Speed (mph/km/h)	Gap to leader	Fastest race lap	
1	**Lewis Hamilton**	GB	44	Mercedes AMG Petronas F1 Team	Mercedes F1 W07-Mercedes PU106C V6	P	52	1h 34m 55.831s	120.253/193.529		1m 35.771s	45
2	**Max Verstappen**	NL	33	Red Bull Racing	Red Bull RB12-TAG Heuer RB12 V6	P	52	1h 35m 04.081s	120.079/193.249	8.250s	1m 36.407s	41
3	**Nico Rosberg**	D	6	Mercedes AMG Petronas F1 Team	Mercedes F1 W07-Mercedes PU106C V6	P	52	1h 35m 12.742s*	119.897/192.956	16.911s	1m 35.548s	44
4	**Daniel Ricciardo**	AUS	3	Red Bull Racing	Red Bull RB12-TAG Heuer RB12 V6	P	52	1h 35m 22.042s	119.703/192.643	26.211s	1m 36.013s	52
5	**Kimi Räikkönen**	FIN	7	Scuderia Ferrari	Ferrari SF16-H-059/5 V6	P	52	1h 36m 05.574s	118.799/191.188	1m 09.743s	1m 36.994s	39
6	**Sergio Pérez**	MEX	11	Sahara Force India F1 Team	Force India VJM09-Mercedes PU106C V6	P	52	1h 36m 12.772s	118.651/190.950	1m 16.941s	1m 37.900s	35
7	**Nico Hülkenberg**	D	27	Sahara Force India F1 Team	Force India VJM09-Mercedes PU106C V6	P	52	1h 36m 13.543s	118.635/190.924	1m 17.712s	1m 37.618s	51
8	**Carlos Sainz**	E	55	Scuderia Toro Rosso	Toro Rosso STR11-Ferrari 059/4 V6	P	52	1h 36m 21.689s	118.468/190.655	1m 25.858s	1m 37.401s	43
9	**Sebastian Vettel**	D	5	Scuderia Ferrari	Ferrari SF15-H-059/5 V6	P	52	1h 36m 27.485s**	118.349/190.464	1m 31.654s	1m 36.933s	44
10	**Daniil Kvyat**	RUS	26	Scuderia Toro Rosso	Toro Rosso STR11-Ferrari 059/4 V6	P	52	1h 36m 28.431s	118.330/190.433	1m 32.600s	1m 37.667s	35
11	Felipe Massa	BR	19	Williams Martini Racing	Williams FW38-Mercedes PU106C V6	P	51			1 lap	1m 36.141s	40
12	Jenson Button	GB	22	McLaren Honda	McLaren MP4-31-Honda RA616H V6	P	51			1 lap	1m 37.907s	36
13	Fernando Alonso	E	14	McLaren Honda	McLaren MP4-31-Honda RA616H V6	P	51			1 lap	1m 35.669s	43
14	Valtteri Bottas	FIN	77	Williams Martini Racing	Williams FW38-Mercedes PU106C V6	P	51			1 lap	1m 37.383s	45
15	Felipe Nasr	BR	12	Sauber F1 Team	Sauber C35-Ferrari 059/5 V6	P	51			1 lap	1m 38.710s	43
16	Esteban Gutiérrez	MEX	21	Haas F1 Team	Haas VF-16-Ferrari 059/5 V6	P	51			1 lap	1m 37.713s	44
17	Kevin Magnussen	DK	20	Renault Sport F1 Team	Renault R.S.16-R.E.16 V6	P	49	gearbox		3 laps	1m 37.619s	43
	Jolyon Palmer	GB	30	Renault Sport F1 Team	Renault R.S.16-R.E.16 V6	P	37	gearbox			1m 39.755s	36
	Rio Haryanto	RI	88	Manor Racing MRT	Manor MRT05-Mercedes PU106C V6	P	24	spin			1m 41.380s	23
	Romain Grosjean	F	8	Haas F1 Team	Haas VF-16-Ferrari 059/5 V6	P	17	transmission			1m 55.507s	14
	Marcus Ericsson	S	9	Sauber F1 Team	Sauber C35-Ferrari 059/5 V6	P	11	electrics			2m 00.286s	9
	Pascal Wehrlein	D	94	Manor Racing MRT	Manor MRT05-Mercedes PU106C V6	P	6	spin			2m 48.804s	4

* includes 10-second penalty for receiving unlawful radio communication – originally finished 2nd. ** includes 5-second penalty for forcing another driver off the track – position unaffected.

Fastest race lap: Nico Rosberg on lap 44, 1m 35.548s, 137.918mph/221.957km/h.

Lap record: Nigel Mansell (Williams FW11B-Honda V6 turbo), 1m 09.832s, 153.059mph/246.324km/h (1987, 2.969-mile/4.778km circuit)

Lap record (current configuration): Fernando Alonso (Ferrari F10 V8), 1m 30.874s, 145.012mph/233.373km/h (2010)

All results and data © FOM 2016

21 · NASR · Sauber

19 · HARYANTO · Manor

17 · BUTTON · McLaren

15 · KVYAT · Toro Rosso

13 · GROSJEAN · Haas

11 · VETTEL · Ferrari
(5-place grid penalty for replacing the gearbox)

22 · ERICSSON · Sauber
(required to start from the pit lane – change of Survival Cell)

20 · WEHRLEIN · Manor

18 · PALMER · Renault

16 · MAGNUSSEN · Renault

14 · GUTIÉRREZ · Haas

12 · MASSA · Williams

Grid order	1	2	3	4	5	6	7	8	9	10	11	12	13	14	15	16	17	18	19	20	21	22	23	24	25	26	27	28	29	30	31	32	33	34	35	36	37	38	39	40	41	42
44 HAMILTON	44	44	44	44	44	44	44	44	44	44	44	44	44	44	44	44	44	33	44	44	44	44	44	44	44	44	44	44	44	44	44	44	44	44	44	44	44	44	44	44	44	44
6 ROSBERG	6	6	6	6	7	6	6	6	6	6	6	6	6	6	6	33	33	44	33	33	33	33	33	33	33	33	33	33	33	33	33	33	33	33	33	33	6	6	6	6	6	
33 VERSTAPPEN	33	33	33	33	77	3	33	33	33	33	33	33	33	33	33	6	6	6	6	6	6	6	6	6	6	6	6	6	6	6	6	6	6	6	6	6	33	33	33	33	33	
3 RICCIARDO	3	3	3	3	6	33	11	11	11	11	11	11	11	11	11	11	11	11	3	3	3	3	3	3	3	3	3	3	3	3	3	3	3	3	3	3	3	3	3	3	3	
7 RÄIKKÖNEN	7	7	7	7	55	19	12	3	3	3	3	3	3	3	3	3	3	3	11	11	11	11	11	11	11	11	11	11	11	11	11	11	11	11	11	11	11	11	11	11	11	
77 BOTTAS	77	77	77	77	33	11	9	7	7	7	7	7	7	7	7	7	55	7	7	7	7	7	55	55	7	7	7	7	7	7	7	7	7	7	7	7	7	7	7	7	7	
55 SAINZ	55	55	55	55	27	26	3	55	55	55	55	55	55	55	55	27	55	55	55	55	55	7	7	27	27	27	27	27	27	27	27	27	27	27	27	27	27	27	27	27	27	
27 HÜLKENBERG	27	27	27	27	3	22	7	19	19	19	19	19	19	19	5	19	14	27	27	27	27	27	27	55	55	55	55	55	55	55	55	55	55	55	55	55	55	55	55	55	55	
14 ALONSO	14	14	14	14	14	30	55	77	77	27	27	27	27	27	26	7	19	19	19	19	19	19	19	19	19	19	19	19	19	19	19	19	19	19	5	5	5	5	5	5	5	
11 PÉREZ	11	11	11	11	5	8	19	27	27	14	14	14	14	14	27	22	26	14	14	14	14	14	14	14	14	26	26	26	26	26	26	26	26	26	19	19	26	26	26	26		
5 VETTEL	5	5	5	5	11	12	77	14	14	5	5	5	5	14	5	14	26	26	26	26	26	5	5	5	5	26	26	26	26	26	26	26	26	26	26	26	22	22	22	22		
19 MASSA	19	19	19	19	8	9	27	5	5	26	26	26	26	26	77	19	5	5	5	5	5	22	22	22	22	22	22	22	22	22	22	22	22	22	14	19	19	19				
8 GROSJEAN	8	8	8	8	19	7	14	26	26	77	77	77	77	77	26	22	22	22	22	22	22	14	14	14	14	14	14	14	14	14	14	14	14	14	14	14	14	14				
21 GUTIÉRREZ	21	21	21	21	21	77	5	22	22	22	22	22	22	12	20	77	77	77	77	77	77	12	12	77	77	77	77	77	77	77	77	77	77	77	77	77	77	77				
26 KVYAT	26	26	26	26	20	55	26	12	12	12	12	12	12	5	12	20	12	20	20	20	20	77	77	12	12	12	12	12	12	12	12	12	12	12	12	12	12	12				
20 MAGNUSSEN	20	20	20	20	26	27	22	8	8	8	8	8	8	8	77	20	20	20	20	20	20	20	20	20	20	20	20	20	20	20	20	20	20	20	21	20	21	21				
22 BUTTON	22	22	22	22	94	14	8	30	30	30	30	30	30	30	12	21	21	21	21	21	21	21	21	21	21	21	21	21	21	21	21	21	21	21	20	21	20	20				
30 PALMER	30	30	30	30	22	5	30	20	20	20	20	20	20	8	30	30	88	88	88	88	88	30	30	30	30	30	30	30	30	30	30	30										
88 HARYANTO	88	88	88	88	30	8	20	9	9	21	21	21	21	21	21	88	88	88	30	30	30	30	30																			
94 WEHRLEIN	94	94	94	94	88	20	88	88	88	88	88	88	88	88	88	30																										
12 NASR	12	12	12	12	12	94	21	21	21	9	9																															
9 ERICSSON	9	9	9	9	9	21																																				

TIME SHEETS

FOR THE RECORD

90th RACE WITH A PODIUM: Red Bull.

70th RACE WITH A PODIUM: Mercedes.

PRACTICE 1 (FRIDAY)
Weather: Dry/overcast
Temperatures: track 18–23°C, air 16–18°C

Pos.	Driver	Laps	Time
1	Lewis Hamilton	30	1m 31.654s
2	Nico Rosberg	34	1m 31.687s
3	Nico Hülkenberg	30	1m 32.492s
4	Sebastian Vettel	20	1m 32.501s
5	Daniel Ricciardo	30	1m 32.773s
6	Kimi Räikkönen	28	1m 33.039s
7	Max Verstappen	22	1m 33.202s
8	Sergio Pérez	30	1m 33.235s
9	Carlos Sainz	19	1m 33.446s
10	Fernando Alonso	22	1m 33.527s
11	Daniil Kvyat	20	1m 33.738s
12	Jenson Button	24	1m 34.132s
13	Valtteri Bottas	38	1m 34.263s
14	Felipe Massa	34	1m 34.456s
15	Romain Grosjean	24	1m 34.547s
16	Jolyon Palmer	29	1m 34.787s
17	Felipe Nasr	21	1m 34.805s
18	Charles Leclerc	26	1m 35.869s
19	Esteban Ocon	31	1m 35.980s
20	Marcus Ericsson	19	1m 36.003s
21	Pascal Wehrlein	25	1m 36.136s
22	Rio Haryanto	29	1m 36.647s

PRACTICE 2 (FRIDAY)
Weather: Dry/sunny-overcast
Temperatures: track 33–39°C, air 20–22°C

Pos.	Driver	Laps	Time
1	Lewis Hamilton	36	1m 31.660s
2	Daniel Ricciardo	30	1m 32.051s
3	Max Verstappen	36	1m 32.286s
4	Sebastian Vettel	40	1m 32.570s
5	Kimi Räikkönen	38	1m 32.736s
6	Fernando Alonso	31	1m 33.040s
7	Valtteri Bottas	38	1m 33.493s
8	Romain Grosjean	32	1m 33.614s
9	Jenson Button	20	1m 33.763s
10	Felipe Massa	29	1m 33.801s
11	Carlos Sainz	27	1m 33.840s
12	Esteban Gutiérrez	32	1m 34.000s
13	Daniil Kvyat	35	1m 34.139s
14	Felipe Nasr	25	1m 34.154s
15	Nico Hülkenberg	35	1m 34.321s
16	Sergio Pérez	37	1m 34.356s
17	Pascal Wehrlein	40	1m 34.549s
18	Jolyon Palmer	41	1m 34.610s
19	Marcus Ericsson	36	1m 34.722s
20	Kevin Magnussen	41	1m 34.959s
21	Rio Haryanto	36	1m 35.841s
22	Nico Rosberg		no time

PRACTICE 3 (SATURDAY)
Weather: Damp-dry/overcast
Temperatures: track 20–22°C, air 17–19°C

Pos.	Driver	Laps	Time
1	Lewis Hamilton	10	1m 30.904s
2	Nico Rosberg	18	1m 30.967s
3	Daniel Ricciardo	6	1m 31.488s
4	Max Verstappen	7	1m 31.561s
5	Sebastian Vettel	10	1m 32.049s
6	Valtteri Bottas	15	1m 32.736s
7	Fernando Alonso	11	1m 32.754s
8	Nico Hülkenberg	14	1m 32.798s
9	Kimi Räikkönen	13	1m 32.833s
10	Carlos Sainz	10	1m 32.889s
11	Esteban Gutiérrez	12	1m 32.895s
12	Jenson Button	11	1m 33.042s
13	Romain Grosjean	13	1m 33.344s
14	Sergio Pérez	13	1m 33.361s
15	Felipe Massa	14	1m 33.440s
16	Daniil Kvyat	10	1m 33.538s
17	Felipe Nasr	10	1m 33.710s
18	Jolyon Palmer	13	1m 33.769s
19	Kevin Magnussen	10	1m 34.049s
20	Rio Haryanto	14	1m 34.471s
21	Marcus Ericsson	7	1m 34.551s
22	Pascal Wehrlein	11	1m 34.658s

DID YOU KNOW?

This was the 50th F1 world championship grand prix at Silverstone and the 70th in Great Britain (including GPs of Europe).

This was Kimi Räikkönen's 100th start with Ferrari.

QUALIFYING (SATURDAY)
Weather: Dry/overcast Temperatures: track 26–29°C, air 20–22°C

Pos.	Driver	First	Second	Third	Qualifying Tyre
1	Lewis Hamilton	1m 30.739s	1m 29.243s	1m 29.287s	Soft (new)
2	Nico Rosberg	1m 30.724s	1m 29.970s	1m 29.606s	Soft (new)
3	Max Verstappen	1m 31.305s	1m 30.697s	1m 30.313s	Soft (new)
4	Daniel Ricciardo	1m 31.684s	1m 31.319s	1m 30.618s	Soft (new)
5	Kimi Räikkönen	1m 31.326s	1m 31.385s	1m 30.881s	Soft (new)
6	Sebastian Vettel	1m 31.606s	1m 30.711s	1m 31.490s	Soft (new)
7	Valtteri Bottas	1m 31.913s	1m 31.478s	1m 31.557s	Soft (new)
8	Carlos Sainz	1m 32.115s	1m 31.708s	1m 31.989s	Soft (new)
9	Nico Hülkenberg	1m 32.349s	1m 31.770s	1m 32.172s	Soft (new)
10	Fernando Alonso	1m 32.281s	1m 31.740s	1m 32.343s	Soft (new)
11	Sergio Pérez	1m 32.336s	1m 31.875s		
12	Felipe Massa	1m 32.146s	1m 32.002s		
13	Romain Grosjean	1m 32.283s	1m 32.050s		
14	Esteban Gutiérrez	1m 32.237s	1m 32.241s		
15	Daniil Kvyat	1m 32.553s	1m 32.306s		
16	Kevin Magnussen	1m 32.729s	1m 37.060s		
17	Jenson Button	1m 32.788s			
18	Jolyon Palmer	1m 32.905s			
19	Rio Haryanto	1m 33.098s			
20	Pascal Wehrlein	1m 33.151s			
21	Felipe Nasr	1m 33.544s			
22	Marcus Ericsson	no time			

POINTS

DRIVERS

1	Nico Rosberg	168
2	Lewis Hamilton	167
3	Kimi Räikkönen	106
4	Daniel Ricciardo	100
5	Sebastian Vettel	98
6	Max Verstappen	90
7	Valtteri Bottas	54
8	Sergio Pérez	47
9	Felipe Massa	38
10	Romain Grosjean	28
11	Nico Hülkenberg	26
12	Carlos Sainz	26
13	Daniil Kvyat	23
14	Fernando Alonso	18
15	Jenson Button	13
16	Kevin Magnussen	6
17	Pascal Wehrlein	1
18	Stoffel Vandoorne	1

CONSTRUCTORS

1	Mercedes	335
2	Ferrari	204
3	Red Bull	198
4	Williams	92
5	Force India	73
6	Toro Rosso	41
7	McLaren	32
8	Haas	28
9	Renault	6
10	Manor	1

Photo: Peter J. Fox

Qualifying: head-to-head

Rosberg	4	6	Hamilton
Vettel	7	3	Räikkönen
Massa	2	8	Bottas
Ricciardo	4	0	Kvyat
Ricciardo	5	1	Verstappen
Pérez	5	5	Hülkenberg
Magnussen	8	2	Palmer
Verstappen	3	1	Sainz
Kvyat	2	4	Sainz
Ericsson	7	3	Nasr
Alonso	7	2	Button
Button	0	1	Vandoorne
Haryanto	5	5	Wehrlein
Grosjean	7	3	Gutiérrez

9 · ALONSO · McLaren

7 · SAINZ · Toro Rosso

5 · RÄIKKÖNEN · Ferrari

3 · VERSTAPPEN · Red Bull

1 · HAMILTON · Mercedes

10 · PÉREZ · Force India

8 · HÜLKENBERG · Force India

6 · BOTTAS · Williams

4 · RICCIARDO · Red Bull

2 · ROSBERG · Mercedes

	43	44	45	46	47	48	49	50	51	52	
	44	44	44	44	44	44	44	44	44	44	1
	6	6	6	6	6	6	6	6	6	6	2
	33	33	33	33	33	33	33	33	33	33	3
	3	3	3	3	3	3	3	3	3	3	4
	11	11	11	7	7	7	7	7	7	7	5
	7	7	7	11	11	11	11	11	11	11	6
	27	27	27	27	27	27	27	27	27	27	
	55	55	55	55	55	55	55	55	55	55	8
	5	5	5	5	5	5	5	5	5	5	9
	26	26	26	26	26	26	26	26	26	26	10
	22	22	22	22	22	22	19	19	19		
	19	19	19	19	19	19	22	22	22		
	14	14	14	14	14	14	14	14	14		
	77	77	77	77	77	77	77	77	77		
	12	12	12	12	12	12	12	12			
	21	21	21	21	21	21	21	21			
	20	20	20	20	20	20	20				

6 = Pit stop   9 = Drive-thru penalty

94 = One lap or more behind

▮ Safety car deployed on laps shown

RACE TYRE STRATEGIES

PIRELLI

	Driver	Race Stint 1	Race Stint 2	Race Stint 3	Race Stint 4
1	Hamilton	Wet (n): 1–7	Intermediate (n): 8–17	Medium (n): 18–52	
2	Rosberg	Wet (n): 1–7	Intermediate (n): 8–17	Medium (n): 18–52	
3	Verstappen	Wet (n): 1–7	Intermediate (n): 8–18	Medium (n): 19–52	
4	Ricciardo	Wet (n): 1–6	Intermediate (n): 7–17	Medium (n): 18–52	
5	Räikkönen	Wet (n): 1–5	Intermediate (n): 6–16	Medium (n): 17–52	
6	Pérez	Wet (n): 1–7	Intermediate (n): 8–17	Medium (n): 18–52	
7	Hülkenberg	Wet (n): 1–5	Intermediate (n): 6–17	Medium (u): 18–52	
8	Vettel	Wet (n): 1–5	Intermediate (n): 6–15	Medium (n): 16–52	
9	Kvyat	Wet (n): 1–6	Intermediate (n): 7–16	Medium (n): 17–52	
10	Sainz	Wet (n): 1–5	Intermediate (n): 6–17	Medium (n): 18–52	
11	Button	Wet (n): 1–6	Intermediate (n): 7–17	Medium (n): 18–51	
12	Massa	Wet (n): 1–6	Intermediate (n): 7–16	Medium (n): 17–38	Soft (n): 39–51
13	Alonso	Wet (n): 1–5	Intermediate (n): 6–17	Medium (n): 18–39	Medium (n): 40–51
14	Nasr	Wet (n): 1–7	Intermediate (n): 8–16	Medium (n): 17–51	
15	Bottas	Wet (n): 1–5	Intermediate (n): 6–16	Medium (n): 17–51	
16	Gutiérrez	Wet (n): 1–5	Intermediate (n): 6–17	Medium (n): 18–51	
17	Magnussen	Wet (n): 1–5	Intermediate (n): 6–17	Medium (n): 18–40	Soft (n): 41–49
	Palmer	Wet (n): 1–6	Intermediate (n): 7–16	Medium (n): 17–19	Medium (u): 20–37 (dnf)
	Haryanto	Wet (n): 1–6	Intermediate (n): 7–17	Medium (n): 18–24 (dnf)	
	Grosjean	Wet (n): 1–5	Intermediate (n): 6–16	Medium (n): 17 (dnf)	
	Ericsson	Wet (u): 1–7	Intermediate (n): 8–10 (dnf)		
	Wehrlein	Wet (n): 1–5	Intermediate (n): 6 (dnf)		

At least two of three dry tyre specs must be used in a dry race. If Wet or Intermediate tyres are needed, this rule is suspended. Pirelli P Zero sidewall logos are colour-coded: Blue = Wet; Green = Intermediate; White = Medium; Yellow = Soft. (n) new (u) used

Photos: Peter J. Fox

Winning streak. A fourth successive win for Lewis Hamilton put him into the lead of the drivers' championship after 11 races.
Photos: Peter J. Fox

FIA FORMULA 1 WORLD CHAMPIONSHIP · ROUND 11

HUNGARIAN GRAND PRIX

HUNGARORING CIRCUIT

HUNGARORING QUALIFYING

AFTER a Friday and Saturday morning of typically hot Budapest temperatures, the heavy clouds gathered as lunchtime approached, and with the qualifying hour ticking around, the heavens opened.

Hungaroring had been resurfaced since 2015, and Q1 would be the first experience anyone had of the new asphalt on treaded rubber. After a couple of ten-minute delays, the field ventured out on Pirelli's full wet tyres for a Q1 session that ran and ran.

Sauber had arrived in Hungary with many a relieved face, after it was announced that a Swiss-based investment group, Longbow Finance, had bought the team and committed to its future. Any Saturday celebrations had to be placed on hold, though, as Marcus Ericsson red-flagged Q1 when he dumped his C35 heavily into the barrier at Turn Eight. It was the second successive race that his car had needed to be rebuilt around a spare tub (in this case, one that Nasr had struggled with early in the season) and he would start from the pit lane.

The Hungarian circuit dries quickly, and a switch to intermediates soon looked plausible. Felipe Massa was the first to try it, but he dropped the Williams on the wet kerb at the exit of Turn Four and spun into the barrier on the opposite side of the road. Cue red flag number two.

With the track drying all the time and only five minutes on the clock, there was an almighty scramble when barrier repairs were complete.

The Mercedes were quickest, from Fernando Alonso, Sebastian Vettel, Romain Grosjean and the Toro Rossos of Carlos Sainz and Daniil Kvyat. Then, with just 1m 18s remaining, Rio Haryanto lost his Manor and brought out the final red. There would be no time to resume, so we lost the damaged Ericsson, Massa and Haryanto, plus the Renaults of the unlucky Jolyon Palmer – much happier with the feel of his car here – and Kevin Magnussen, and Pascal Wehrlein in the second Manor.

Such was the rate at which the track was drying that by the end of Q2, all times were being set on Pirelli's super-soft (available for the first time at Hungaroring, along with the soft and medium), with Valtteri Bottas the first to go on to them.

It was one of those scenarios when the track was getting quicker and quicker with each lap and whoever ran last was sitting pretty. Unfortunately for Kimi Räikkönen, Ferrari got the timing wrong and the Finn became the highest-profile casualty of Q2, 14th.

There was very nearly another one in the form of Lewis Hamilton, who was backed up by Fernando Alonso as they began their last laps – shades of 2007! Hamilton scraped into Q3 with tenth quickest Q2 time, just 0.11s ahead of Grosjean's Haas! Räikkönen apart, Sergio Pérez undoubtedly had the pace for Q3, but didn't make it, while a disgruntled Kvyat was unhappy with Toro Rosso's session management and was saying so.

"I think we did a very poor job in managing things when it really counted, especially my track position," he said. "We were slow putting the slicks on – the tyres were not ready when I came into the pits and I had to wait too long. I was then caught up in traffic and I did my last lap, the one that counted, behind Button… I always raise my hand when I do a bad job, but I think today it was a bit the other way around."

How to make friends and influence people? Kvyat, though, probably wanted the world – or Helmut Marko at least – to know. Red Bull junior driver Pierre Gasly had just won his second successive GP2 feature race and now was leading that championship…

With a properly dry track for Q3, the order reverted to type, with the two Mercs ahead of the two Red Bulls. Given Hamilton's four victories and five poles in Hungary, however, you would have fancied the three-times champion to outqualify Rosberg, whose only podium at Hungaroring had been in the GP2 sprint race in 2005. But waved yellow flags at Turn Nine, after Alonso had spun his McLaren, put paid to that.

Hamilton had been quickest after the first Q3 runs, and he found another three-tenths in the first sector before the yellows. Behind him, though, Rosberg carried on attacking, lifting marginally for the yellows (which mean slow down and be prepared to stop). Across the line, he pipped Hamilton's first run by 0.14s to take a 26th F1 pole, much to Lewis's chagrin (see Viewpoint).

Ricciardo had also improved significantly in sector one on his first run and thought he could split the Mercs, but he had to be content with a slot on the second row, some 0.27s clear of team-mate Max Verstappen.

Vettel, like Ricciardo, survived a lurid tank-slapper out of the final corner and was a further three-tenths down in the first Ferrari, ahead of an excellent effort from Carlos Sainz, who put his Toro Rosso sixth, in front of Alonso's McLaren-Honda. Jenson Button was eighth, his attempt to beat his team-mate scuppered by Fernando's spin… Then came Nico Hülkenberg's Force India, with Bottas's Williams completing the top ten.

IF the letter of the law had been strictly applied, those outside 107 per cent of the fastest Q1 time due to the variable track conditions, which included the two Red Bulls, would have started the race behind those who had achieved the time, in the order that they finished the final session of free practice. But, the FIA decreed that the conditions represented exceptional circumstances and the order stayed as it was.

There was also controversy at Mercedes. Hamilton, sore at losing pole, thought the rules needed clarification if his team-mate could get away with backing off by just 0.14s in a double-waved yellow zone, setting a sector best and taking pole. Of course, it wasn't personal interest here, you understand, it was the poor example for those young karters and junior formula drivers...

"Thanks for that...," responded Rosberg, his voice laced with sarcasm.

Hamilton stuck to his guns, though, allegedly lobbying Charlie Whiting to have the matter investigated by the stewards. This was "regrettable" said Mercedes executive director (technical) Paddy Lowe, who said that the team was perfectly capable of handling the matter without Lewis getting involved. In fact, went the rumour, the Mercedes team management was so hacked off at one of its drivers trying to get the other's time annulled (more shades of McLaren/Hungary 2007) that they seriously considered disciplinary action. But then they probably thought that they could do without a muck storm in the days leading up to Mercedes' home German GP.

It was against such a backdrop that Rosberg made a less than ballistic start from pole and found himself under attack from his team-mate on the inside, and Ricciardo's Red Bull around the outside as the field blasted into Turn One.

While there is often little between Rosberg and Hamilton in terms of single-lap pace, it is in wheel-to-wheel combat where Lewis appears to have a significant advantage. Given that he was racing Hamilton alone for the championship, Rosberg appeared to have the opportunity to move over on

the Englishman and protect the inside for Turn One. Ricciardo would have led around the outside, sure, but with a quicker car Nico could have sorted that out later, or at the stops.

What happened was that Ricciardo got around the outside, ran out a little wide and couldn't quite get the power down, chopping back on just ahead of Rosberg, while Hamilton went down the inside, got a decent T1 exit and led into T2. Rosberg got a run on Ricciardo and drew alongside the Red Bull, reasserting himself by pinching it tight and going around the outside of T2.

Across the line at the end of the opening lap, Verstappen was fourth, ahead of Vettel's Ferrari, Alonso's McLaren, Sainz's Toro Rosso and Button's McLaren. Bottas, in the only competitive Williams (Massa was in trouble with heavy steering in left-handers and light steering in right-handers, following repairs after his qualifying shunt), ran ninth, with Hülkenberg's Force India completing the top ten.

Further back, Räikkönen's Ferrari was out of position following non-representative qualifying. He had elected to start on the yellow-walled soft Pirellis, as had Kvyat (who made a poor getaway), Pérez, Palmer and the struggling Massa. Kimi managed to dispense with Gutiérrez and Pérez before catching Grosjean, who, still on the new super-softs he'd started with, was able to keep the Ferrari behind.

At the front, Hamilton opened a small margin, keeping Rosberg out of DRS range, and then began to look after his super-softs, the thinking being that a two-stop was the strategy of choice so long as tyre issues didn't force a three-stopper, which was close in terms of time, but always subject to traffic, a particular issue at Hungaroring. Pérez, always benign in his tyre usage, would actually try a one-stopper, switching to the medium tyre at his first stop, before finding the rubber uncompetitive and reverting to softs after only 13 laps.

Button lost his eighth place as early as lap four, when he suffered a hydraulics issue, one of the effects of which was his brake pedal going to the floor. New radio regulations in effect for Hungary, intended to allow teams to instruct

Above: Daniel Ricciardo and Lewis Hamilton pinch Nico Rosberg as the pack heads into the first corner.
Photo: GP Photo/Peter Nygaard

Top left: Fernando Alonso and Carlos Sainz chat happily as they leave the drivers' briefing.

Above left: Daniil Kvyat's season reached a low ebb following outspoken criticism of his team.

Left: Daniel Ricciardo puts his Pirellis to the test in taking his Red Bull to third place on the grid.
Photos: Peter J. Fox

Below left: Qualifying began with heavy rain, causing mayhem with the teams' plans. Romain Grosjean was fifth fastest in the difficult conditions of Q1.
Photo: Lukas Gorys

drivers in matters of mechanical importance that were not performance enhancing and hence did not breach the "driver must drive the car alone and unaided" edict, required the driver to pit to receive the message. When McLaren dictated a switch change to cure his problem, Button received a drive-through penalty because he did not pit soon enough.

"Really?" Button said when told. "So the brake pedal going to the floor isn't classified as a safety issue? That's quite interesting. I think someone needs to read up on what's safe and what isn't… To get penalised for stopping an incident is pathetic." Later he retired with an oil leak ten laps before the end and hardly seemed distraught.

With a dozen laps down and the first round of stops imminent, Hamilton led Rosberg by 2.5s, with Ricciardo just over 3s further back in the first of the Red Bulls. Team-mate Verstappen was as near to the back of the Australian as prudent, given the need to look after his super-softs, and with Vettel's Ferrari just 1.5s behind the second Red Bull and clearly an undercut threat.

Although tyre conservation was going on, Alonso could not run at the leaders' pace and had dropped almost ten seconds back, with Sainz close behind. Then there was a three-second gap to Bottas, who had a similar margin over Hülkenberg. Grosjean was right with the Force India, while Räikkönen, the first of those on softs, was tucked in behind, some three seconds ahead of the similarly-shod Pérez.

Before the race, Red Bull had discussed how it was going to be difficult to keep both of its cars ahead of Vettel at the first stops if they were not in free air, and Verstappen was already impatient.

"I'm driving like a grandma!" he fretted over the radio as early as lap eight.

His worst fears were realised when Ferrari pitted Vettel first, on lap 14. At the end of the previous lap, the Ferrari had been just over three seconds behind Ricciardo's third place, so Red Bull was effectively forced to respond with its lead car. Ricciardo pitted on lap 15, rejoining still just ahead of the Ferrari.

Verstappen did not get the call to pit until lap 16, and when he re-emerged, Vettel had passed the pit exit a couple of seconds earlier, and to his annoyance, Max also

found himself behind Räikkönen's Ferrari. Haas had pitted Grosjean out of Kimi's way a couple of laps earlier, and the combination of increased speed from the Finn and a less than perfect Red Bull stop, with a slight delay at the left rear, meant that Verstappen was destined to follow Räikkönen to the end of his soft-tyre stint on lap 29, by which time Ricciardo and Vettel were ten seconds further up the road.

When Hamilton stopped for his softs on lap 16, Rosberg, who would pit next time around, was a couple of seconds back, and the leader's margin over Ricciardo's Red Bull was almost eight seconds. But now, super-softs having been replaced by softs on the leading five cars, the Mercedes pace did not appear to be as strong.

Hamilton had been lapping in the mid-to-high 1m 25s on his used super-softs before pitting, but on the new softs, he was more than a second a lap slower. On lap 20, he radioed, "I'm struggling for pace."

Both Ricciardo and Vettel were going quicker and closing the gap. By lap 25, Ricciardo was just over four seconds behind Rosberg, with the Ferrari a couple of seconds further back; the Mercedes pit wall crew was starting to get jumpy.

"So, Lewis, just need to pick up the pace a little," came the instruction.

"I'm working on it," replied Hamilton, a little grumpily.

Was Hamilton genuinely in trouble on the yellow-walled Pirelli or was he deliberately backing Rosberg into Ricciardo/ Vettel before the second stops?

A cynic may well have suspected the latter when, on lap 33, Hamilton's pace dropped off by a full second.

"Okay, Lewis, so Ricciardo is about to get on the back of the train, so we really need to open this gap up," came the message from the pit wall once more.

"Well, I'm driving to the best of my ability on these tyres," responded Hamilton.

"Okay, copy that," said engineer Pete Bonnington. "But if these cars bunch up, we'll be bringing Nico in first."

Coded message: *"If you don't get a move on, we're going to prioritise Nico, and he's going to come out in front of you…"*

Hamilton: "Well why would they do that? It's not like I'm driving slow, I'm trying."

Above: A smart pit stop by Ferrari helped Sebastian Vettel to jump the Red Bull of Max Verstappen.

Left: Sauber mechanics prepare to receive Marcus Ericsson.
Photos: Peter J. Fox

Far left: Nico Hülkenberg rescued a point for Sahara Force India, claiming tenth after a difficult race.
Photo: Sahara Force India F1 Team

Above: Max Verstappen and Kimi Räikkönen locked in combat. The Finn was irked by the Red Bull driver's robust defensive moves, but the stewards found no fault with young Max's tactics.
Photo: WRi2/Jad Sherif

Facing page, from top: Ferrari's Maurizio Arrivabene was very unhappy with the stewards' decision not to penalise Verstappen.

Pleased as punch. Ricciardo was delighted to be back on the podium.
Photos: Peter J. Fox

It was dry and sunny on race day, and for the Hungaroring's celebration of hosting its 31st world championship grand prix.
Photo: Sahara Force India F1 Team

Nico Rosberg was under pressure from Daniel Ricciardo mid-race, but was never in serious concern of losing his second place.
Photo: Mercedes AMG Petronas F1 Team

Far right: Lewis Hamilton throws his trophy aloft after taking a fifth win of the season.
Photo: Mercedes AMG Petronas F1 Team

"Yeah, Lewis, just the risk is that we are putting the win in jeopardy."

On that slow lap 33 that Hamilton drove, Ricciardo had closed to within two seconds of Rosberg and Red Bull went for it, bringing Daniel straight into the pits for a new set of softs, even though that would require a fairly lengthy 37 laps on them.

And, lo and behold, after the gee-up, Hamilton found an extra second-and-a-half to two seconds in the locker, so obviously he hadn't been struggling that badly...

Mercedes knew that such pace had been available and that they didn't need to respond to Ricciardo's stop, provided Hamilton kept on it; the silver cars did not pit for another eight laps, with Hamilton in first, as was his right as lead car. Once both had been turned around and were back up to speed, Hamilton had 4.5s in hand over his team-mate, with Ricciardo a further four seconds down, but seven seconds ahead of Vettel now, after a handful of laps with his new softs at their best.

Between them was Räikkönen, who had been given a set of new super-softs at his lap-29 stop and would be back for another set of the same on lap 50, for a final 20-lap sprint to the flag.

The quickest car on the track, with his reducing fuel load and fresh red-walled Pirellis, Kimi rapidly closed the gap to Verstappen, and battle was rejoined between the pair with 15 laps to go, this time with Max in the 'defence' role. He took it right to the line in terms of acceptability, moving late at both Turn Two and Turn One, and within the braking zone, which tends to raise temperatures and blood pressures.

It certainly did for Maurizio Arrivabene on the Ferrari pit wall, and Räikkönen was moved to comment that Verstappen's driving was "not correct". The race stewards looked closely, but considered that no action was necessary.

Asked his opinion later, Hamilton pointed out, "Kimi doesn't say much, so when he does bother to speak, he's probably right!"

Up front, Hamilton was again circumspect in the early laps on his final set of softs, letting Rosberg back to within DRS range, but he never truly looked threatened. He was a little frustrated when Gutiérrez took a long while to move off line and let him through, offering the young Mexican his left middle finger as he finally went by on the front straight.

With the race just between the two of them, the Mercs had pulled out 25s over Ricciardo by the flag, Daniel reaching the line half a second clear of Vettel, whose tyres were in better shape at the end. At a track on which Red Bull thought they might be in the frame, the silver cars' pace was sobering once more.

The battling Verstappen and Räikkönen completed the top six, a further 20s in arrears, and it was only fitting that after being classified seventh in every practice session and qualifying, Alonso's McLaren-Honda should finish in that spot, too!

Countryman Sainz chased him all the way, eighth for Toro Rosso, the point-scorers being completed by Bottas for Williams and Hülkenberg for Force India.

Pérez finished 14s behind his team-mate. Half of that deficit was due to a slow second stop, when the team had abandoned its one-stop plan and, due to a miscommunication, Sergio's tyres had not been ready for him when he arrived in the pit lane.

Jolyon Palmer was just seven seconds down after a much stronger showing from Renault, but he was beating himself up at the loss of a potential point. A pit-stop race with Hülkenberg had been won on lap 39, which elevated Palmer to tenth, but ten laps later he had lost it at Turn Four, the spin costing him ten seconds.

"I'm gutted," he admitted. "I don't know what happened. Nothing seemed different. I carried a little more speed in, but we're only talking about 2kph." Still, he got to the flag 12s in front of team-mate Kevin Magnussen – a mark of the performance.

And so, as the paddock packed up and headed for Germany and the summer break, a weekend of political intra-team intrigue ended with Lewis Hamilton on top. Shades of 2007 again. You couldn't help but think back to 2007 and the McLaren shenanigans that led to 'Spygate', with Lewis centre stage there too!

Tony Dodgins

VIEWPOINT
ONE CHANCE TOO MANY?

IT continued to be a hot topic of conversation a week later in Hockenheim. Was it correct to have allowed Nico Rosberg to claim pole at the Hungaroring thanks, in part, to setting a purple sector time at the scene of waved double yellow flags?

Lewis Hamilton didn't seem to think so – and said as much. Several times. Apart from voicing his concerns at the post-qualifying press conference and picking up the theme at the winner's media briefing, the Englishman also got in touch (more than once, it was alleged) with race director Charlie Whiting to press home his view that Rosberg's time should have been disallowed.

There were extenuating circumstances: the drying track was improving all the time, meaning a purple sector was more easily attained than usual; the stricken car (Alonso's McLaren) had been on the racing line when Hamilton (and others) came through, but the track was clear – and could be seen to be free of marshals – when Rosberg arrived. Nonetheless, it was difficult to deny the damaging concept of a driver, despite having lifted off enough to satisfy the stewards, being seen to go quickly at a point were he should have been prepared to stop *if* necessary.

Even allowing for Hamilton trying – and failing – to destabilise Rosberg in public, there was a hint of hypocrisy about the complaints, as summed up by Anthony Davidson for viewers on *SkyF1*.

"Let's get this straight," said the WEC and former F1 driver. "There is not a driver out there who would not have done exactly what Rosberg did under those circumstances. That's what we're hardwired to do: take every advantage possible because, if you don't, another driver will. You make a judgement and go for it. And the same drivers will complain if another – such as Rosberg – takes a chance and gets away with it. Again, that's what racing drivers do!"

Given that drivers need to be kept in line by official dictum, a heavy-handed solution, announced a week later, was to show the red flag during a double-yellow period. The session would be disrupted unnecessarily, and some drivers would lose, but no one would gain.

Maurice Hamilton

11

2016 FORMULA 1 MAGYAR NAGYDÍJ

BUDAPEST 22–24 JULY

RACE DISTANCE: 70 laps, 190.531 miles/306.630km

RACE WEATHER: Dry/sunny (track 49–54°C, air 28–29°C)

ROLEX
OFFICIAL TIMEPIECE

HUNGARORING MOGYORÓD, BUDAPEST
Circuit: 2.722 miles/4.381km
70 laps

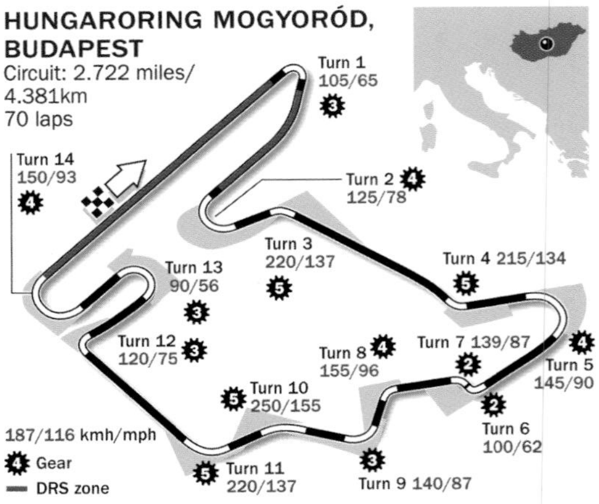

Turn 1
105/65
Turn 2
125/78
Turn 3
220/137
Turn 4 215/134
Turn 5
145/90
Turn 6
100/62
Turn 7 139/87
Turn 8
155/96
Turn 9 140/87
Turn 10
250/155
Turn 11
220/137
Turn 12
120/75
Turn 13
90/56
Turn 14
150/93
187/116 kmh/mph
Gear
DRS zone

RACE – OFFICIAL CLASSIFICATION

Pos.	Driver	Nat.	No.	Entrant	Car/Engine	Tyres	Laps	Time/Retirement	Speed (mph/km/h)	Gap to leader	Fastest race lap	
1	**Lewis Hamilton**	GB	44	Mercedes AMG Petronas F1 Team	Mercedes F1 W07-Mercedes PU106C V6	P	70	1h 40m 30.115s	113.748/183.059		1m 23.849s	69
2	**Nico Rosberg**	D	6	Mercedes AMG Petronas F1 Team	Mercedes F1 W07-Mercedes PU106C V6	P	70	1h 40m 32.092s	113.710/182.999	1.977s	1m 23.670s	60
3	**Daniel Ricciardo**	AUS	3	Red Bull Racing	Red Bull RB12-TAG Heuer RB12 V6	P	70	1h 40m 57.654s	113.230/182.226	27.539s	1m 24.608s	60
4	**Sebastian Vettel**	D	5	Scuderia Ferrari	Ferrari SF15-H-059/5 V6	P	70	1h 40m 58.328s	113.218/182.206	28.213s	1m 24.383s	59
5	**Max Verstappen**	NL	33	Red Bull Racing	Red Bull RB12-TAG Heuer RB12 V6	P	70	1h 41m 18.774s	112.837/181.593	48.659s	1m 24.687s	40
6	**Kimi Räikkönen**	FIN	7	Scuderia Ferrari	Ferrari SF16-H-059/5 V6	P	70	1h 41m 19.159s	112.830/181.582	49.044s	1m 23.086s	52
7	**Fernando Alonso**	E	14	McLaren Honda	McLaren MP4-31-Honda RA616H V6	P	69			1 lap	1m 24.958s	62
8	**Carlos Sainz**	E	55	Scuderia Toro Rosso	Toro Rosso STR11-Ferrari 059/4 V6	P	69			1 lap	1m 25.103s	67
9	**Valtteri Bottas**	FIN	77	Williams Martini Racing	Williams FW38-Mercedes PU106C V6	P	69			1 lap	1m 25.273s	59
10	**Nico Hülkenberg**	D	27	Sahara Force India F1 Team	Force India VJM09-Mercedes PU106C V6	P	69			1 lap	1m 25.392s	69
11	Sergio Pérez	MEX	11	Sahara Force India F1 Team	Force India VJM09-Mercedes PU106C V6	P	69			1 lap	1m 25.021s	65
12	Jolyon Palmer	GB	30	Renault Sport F1 Team	Renault R.S.16-R.E.16 V6	P	69			1 lap	1m 25.743s	41
13	Esteban Gutiérrez	MEX	21	Haas F1 Team	Haas VF-16-Ferrari 059/5 V6	P	69	*		1 lap	1m 25.955s	39
14	Romain Grosjean	F	8	Haas F1 Team	Haas VF-16-Ferrari 059/5 V6	P	69			1 lap	1m 25.958s	56
15	Kevin Magnussen	DK	20	Renault Sport F1 Team	Renault R.S.16-R.E.16 V6	P	69			1 lap	1m 26.230s	39
16	Daniil Kvyat	RUS	26	Scuderia Toro Rosso	Toro Rosso STR11-Ferrari 059/4 V6	P	69			1 lap	1m 24.669s	48
17	Felipe Nasr	BR	12	Sauber F1 Team	Sauber C35-Ferrari 059/5 V6	P	69			1 lap	1m 25.676s	66
18	Felipe Massa	BR	19	Williams Martini Racing	Williams FW38-Mercedes PU106C V6	P	68			2 laps	1m 25.296s	68
19	Pascal Wehrlein	D	94	Manor Racing MRT	Manor MRT05-Mercedes PU106C V6	P	68			2 laps	1m 26.524s	47
20	Marcus Ericsson	S	9	Sauber F1 Team	Sauber C35-Ferrari 059/5 V6	P	68			2 laps	1m 25.475s	47
21	Rio Haryanto	RI	88	Manor Racing MRT	Manor MRT05-Mercedes PU106C V6	P	68			2 laps	1m 27.791s	64
	Jenson Button	GB	22	McLaren Honda	McLaren MP4-31-Honda RA616H V6	P	60	*oil leak*			1m 26.744s	9

* Includes 5-second penalty for ignoring blue flags – originally finished 12th.

Fastest race lap: Kimi Räikkönen on lap 52, 1m 23.086s, 117.950mph/89.822km/h.

Lap record: Michael Schumacher (Ferrari F2004 V10), 1m 19.071s, 123.939mph/199.461km/h (2004).

All results and data © FOM 2016

21 · HARYANTO · Manor
(5-place grid penalty for replacing the gearbox)

19 · MAGNUSSEN · Renault

17 · PALMER · Renault

15 · GUTIÉRREZ · Haas

13 · PÉREZ · Force India

11 · GROSJEAN · Haas

22 · ERICSSON · Sauber
(Required to start from the pit lane – change of Survival Cell)

20 · WEHRLEIN · Manor

18 · MASSA · Williams

16 · NASR · Sauber

14 · RÄIKKÖNEN · Ferrari

12 · KVYAT · Toro Rosso

Grid order	1	2	3	4	5	6	7	8	9	10	11	12	13	14	15	16	17	18	19	20	21	22	23	24	25	26	27
6 ROSBERG	44	44	44	44	44	44	44	44	44	44	44	44	44	44	44	6	6	44	44	44	44	44	44	44	44	44	44
44 HAMILTON	6	6	6	6	6	6	6	6	6	6	6	6	6	6	6	44	44	6	6	6	6	6	6	6	6	6	6
3 RICCIARDO	3	3	3	3	3	3	3	3	3	3	3	3	3	3	3	33	3	3	3	3	3	3	3	3	3	3	3
33 VERSTAPPEN	33	33	33	33	33	33	33	33	33	33	33	33	33	33	33	55	5	5	5	5	5	5	5	5	5	5	5
5 VETTEL	5	5	5	5	5	5	5	5	5	5	5	5	5	5	55	3	7	7	7	7	7	7	7	7	7	7	7
55 SAINZ	14	14	14	14	14	14	14	14	14	14	14	14	14	14	14	5	33	33	33	33	33	33	33	33	33	33	33
14 ALONSO	55	55	55	55	55	55	55	55	55	55	55	55	55	55	77	77	11	11	11	11	11	11	11	11	11	11	11
22 BUTTON	22	22	22	22	77	77	77	77	77	77	77	77	77	77	5	7	30	30	30	30	30	30	30	30	30	30	14
27 HÜLKENBERG	77	77	77	77	27	27	27	27	27	27	27	27	27	7	7	11	20	20	20	20	20	20	20	14	14	14	55
77 BOTTAS	27	27	27	27	8	8	8	8	8	8	8	8	8	21	11	30	14	14	14	14	14	14	14	20	55	55	77
8 GROSJEAN	8	8	8	8	7	7	7	7	7	7	7	7	7	27	21	20	55	55	55	55	55	55	55	55	77	77	27
26 KVYAT	21	21	21	21	21	21	21	21	21	21	21	21	21	8	30	14	19	19	77	77	77	77	77	77	27	27	30
11 PÉREZ	11	7	7	7	11	11	11	11	11	11	11	11	11	11	20	19	77	77	19	19	19	19	19	19	21	21	21
7 RÄIKKÖNEN	7	11	11	11	12	12	12	12	12	12	30	30	30	30	19	26	26	26	26	26	26	26	26	27	8	8	8
21 GUTIÉRREZ	12	12	12	12	30	30	30	30	30	30	12	20	20	20	26	27	27	27	27	27	27	27	27	21	19	20	20
12 NASR	30	30	30	30	94	94	94	94	20	20	20	19	19	19	27	21	21	21	21	21	21	21	21	26	20	12	12
30 PALMER	94	94	94	94	20	20	20	20	94	19	19	26	26	26	88	8	8	8	8	8	8	8	8	8	12	88	88
19 MASSA	20	20	20	20	19	19	19	19	19	26	26	88	88	88	8	88	88	88	88	88	88	88	12	12	88	94	26
20 MAGNUSSEN	19	19	19	19	26	26	26	26	26	88	88	9	9	9	9	12	12	12	12	12	12	12	88	88	94	26	94
94 WEHRLEIN	26	26	26	26	88	88	88	88	88	9	9	12	12	12	12	9	94	94	94	94	94	94	94	94	26	19	19
88 HARYANTO	88	88	88	88	9	9	9	9	9	94	94	94	94	94	94	94	9	22	22	22	22	22	22	22	22	22	22
9 ERICSSON	9	9	9	9	22	22	22	22	22	22	22	22	22	22	22	22	22	9	9	9	9	9	9	9	9	9	9

Grid order	28	29	30	31	32	33	34	35	36	37	38	39	40	41	42	43	44	45	46	47	48	49	50	51	52	53	54
6 ROSBERG	44	44	44	44	44	44	44	44	44	44	44	44	44	6	6	44	44	44	44	44	44	44	44	44	44	44	44
44 HAMILTON	6	6	6	6	6	6	6	6	6	6	6	6	6	44	44	6	6	6	6	6	6	6	6	6	6	6	6
3 RICCIARDO	3	3	3	3	3	3	5	5	5	5	5	5	5	5	3	3	3	3	3	3	3	3	3	3	3	3	3
33 VERSTAPPEN	5	5	5	5	5	5	33	33	33	33	33	3	3	3	7	7	7	7	7	7	7	7	7	5	5	5	5
5 VETTEL	7	33	33	33	33	33	3	3	3	3	3	7	7	7	5	5	5	5	5	5	5	5	5	33	33	33	33
55 SAINZ	33	7	14	7	7	7	7	7	7	7	7	33	33	33	33	33	33	33	33	33	33	33	33	7	7	7	7
14 ALONSO	14	14	7	14	14	14	14	14	14	14	14	14	14	14	14	14	14	14	14	14	14	14	14	14	14	14	14
22 BUTTON	55	55	55	55	55	55	55	55	55	55	55	55	55	55	55	77	55	55	55	55	55	55	55	55	55	55	55
27 HÜLKENBERG	77	77	77	77	77	77	77	77	77	77	77	77	77	77	77	55	77	77	77	77	77	77	77	77	77	77	77
77 BOTTAS	11	11	11	11	11	11	11	11	11	11	11	11	11	26	26	26	26	26	26	30	27	27	27	27	27	27	27
8 GROSJEAN	27	27	27	27	27	27	27	27	27	27	27	27	26	30	30	30	30	30	30	27	21	21	21	21	21	21	21
26 KVYAT	30	30	30	30	30	30	30	30	30	30	30	30	30	27	27	27	27	27	27	21	11	11	11	11	11	11	11
11 PÉREZ	21	21	21	21	21	21	21	21	21	21	12	26	27	21	21	21	21	21	21	11	30	30	30	30	30	30	30
7 RÄIKKÖNEN	8	8	8	8	8	8	8	8	8	12	26	12	21	11	11	11	11	11	11	8	8	8	8	8	8	8	8
21 GUTIÉRREZ	20	20	20	20	20	20	20	20	20	26	21	21	8	8	8	8	8	8	8	20	20	20	20	20	20	20	20
12 NASR	12	12	12	12	12	12	12	12	12	8	8	8	20	20	20	20	20	20	20	26	26	26	26	26	26	26	26
30 PALMER	88	26	26	26	26	26	26	26	26	20	20	20	12	12	12	12	12	12	12	12	12	12	12	12	12	12	12
19 MASSA	26	94	94	94	94	94	94	9	9	9	9	9	9	9	9	9	9	19	19	19	19	19	19	19	19	19	19
20 MAGNUSSEN	94	19	19	19	19	9	9	19	19	19	19	19	19	19	19	19	19	9	22	22	22	22	22	22	22	22	22
94 WEHRLEIN	19	88	9	9	9	19	19	94	22	22	22	22	22	22	22	22	22	94	94	94	94	94	94	94	94	94	94
88 HARYANTO	9	9	22	22	22	22	22	22	88	88	88	88	88	94	94	94	94	94	9	9	9	9	9	9	9	9	9
9 ERICSSON	22	22	88	88	88	88	88	88	94	94	94	94	94	88	88	88	88	88	88	88	88	88	88	88	88	88	88

6 = Pit stop 9 = Drive-thru penalty

TIME SHEETS

PRACTICE 1 (FRIDAY)

Weather: Damp-dry/overcast-sunny
Temperatures: track 26-42°C, air 22-25°C

Pos.	Driver	Laps	Time
1	Lewis Hamilton	34	1m 21.347s
2	Nico Rosberg	34	1m 21.584s
3	Sebastian Vettel	22	1m 22.991s
4	Kimi Räikkönen	19	1m 23.082s
5	Daniel Ricciardo	28	1m 23.174s
6	Max Verstappen	27	1m 23.457s
7	Fernando Alonso	28	1m 23.935s
8	Jenson Button	18	1m 23.961s
9	Romain Grosjean	22	1m 24.013s
10	Sergio Pérez	29	1m 24.073s
11	Nico Hülkenberg	29	1m 24.120s
12	Felipe Massa	27	1m 24.154s
13	Valtteri Bottas	33	1m 24.370s
14	Carlos Sainz	27	1m 24.579s
15	Marcus Ericsson	19	1m 24.981s
16	Charles Leclerc	22	1m 25.181s
17	Felipe Nasr	18	1m 25.256s
18	Esteban Ocon	28	1m 25.260s
19	Daniil Kvyat	16	1m 25.324s
20	Rio Haryanto	23	1m 27.012s
21	Pascal Wehrlein	9	1m 27.249s
22	Jolyon Palmer	6	1m 28.560s

PRACTICE 2 (FRIDAY)

Weather: Dry/sunny
Temperatures: track 40-48°C, air 27-28°C

Pos.	Driver	Laps	Time
1	Nico Rosberg	45	1m 20.435s
2	Daniel Ricciardo	36	1m 21.030s
3	Sebastian Vettel	31	1m 21.348s
4	Max Verstappen	35	1m 21.770s
5	Lewis Hamilton	4	1m 21.960s
6	Kimi Räikkönen	46	1m 22.058s
7	Fernando Alonso	21	1m 22.328s
8	Jenson Button	34	1m 22.387s
9	Nico Hülkenberg	41	1m 22.449s
10	Sergio Pérez	38	1m 22.653s
11	Esteban Gutiérrez	38	1m 22.673s
12	Felipe Massa	39	1m 22.681s
13	Carlos Sainz	24	1m 22.689s
14	Valtteri Bottas	38	1m 22.773s
15	Romain Grosjean	28	1m 22.864s
16	Daniil Kvyat	43	1m 22.948s
17	Kevin Magnussen	41	1m 23.347s
18	Marcus Ericsson	36	1m 23.437s
19	Jolyon Palmer	12	1m 23.528s
20	Felipe Nasr	31	1m 23.986s
21	Pascal Wehrlein	22	1m 23.992s
22	Rio Haryanto	36	1m 24.265s

PRACTICE 3 (SATURDAY)

Weather: Dry/sunny-overcast
Temperatures: track 42-48°C, air 26-27°C

Pos.	Driver	Laps	Time
1	Nico Rosberg	25	1m 20.261s
2	Max Verstappen	10	1m 20.263s
3	Daniel Ricciardo	22	1m 20.726s
4	Lewis Hamilton	23	1m 20.769s
5	Kimi Räikkönen	18	1m 20.859s
6	Sebastian Vettel	22	1m 21.185s
7	Fernando Alonso	11	1m 21.584s
8	Valtteri Bottas	21	1m 21.649s
9	Sergio Pérez	22	1m 21.672s
10	Jolyon Palmer	19	1m 21.935s
11	Felipe Massa	28	1m 21.975s
12	Kevin Magnussen	13	1m 21.989s
13	Jenson Button	11	1m 22.009s
14	Esteban Gutiérrez	15	1m 22.142s
15	Romain Grosjean	13	1m 22.284s
16	Carlos Sainz	21	1m 22.402s
17	Nico Hülkenberg	22	1m 22.427s
18	Daniil Kvyat	18	1m 22.541s
19	Felipe Nasr	23	1m 22.816s
20	Marcus Ericsson	23	1m 23.219s
21	Pascal Wehrlein	24	1m 23.311s
22	Rio Haryanto	23	1m 23.513s

QUALIFYING (SATURDAY)

Weather: Rain-drying/overcast-sunny Temperatures: track 25-34°C, air 21-26°C

Pos.	Driver	First	Second	Third	Qualifying Tyre
1	Nico Rosberg	1m 33.302s	1m 22.806s	1m 19.965s	Super-Soft (new)
2	Lewis Hamilton	1m 34.210s	1m 24.836s	1m 20.108s	Super-Soft (new)
3	Daniel Ricciardo	1m 39.968s	1m 23.234s	1m 20.280s	Super-Soft (new)
4	Max Verstappen	1m 40.424s	1m 22.660s	1m 20.557s	Super-Soft (new)
5	Sebastian Vettel	1m 35.718s	1m 24.082s	1m 20.874s	Super-Soft (new)
6	Carlos Sainz	1m 36.115s	1m 24.734s	1m 21.131s	Super-Soft (new)
7	Fernando Alonso	1m 35.165s	1m 23.816s	1m 21.211s	Super-Soft (new)
8	Jenson Button	1m 37.983s	1m 24.456s	1m 21.597s	Super-Soft (new)
9	Nico Hülkenberg	1m 41.471s	1m 23.901s	1m 21.823s	Super-Soft (new)
10	Valtteri Bottas	1m 42.758s	1m 24.506s	1m 22.182s	Super-Soft (new)
11	Romain Grosjean	1m 35.906s	1m 24.941s		
12	Daniil Kvyat	1m 36.714s	1m 25.301s		
13	Sergio Pérez	1m 41.411s	1m 25.416s		
14	Kimi Räikkönen	1m 36.853s	1m 25.435s		
15	Esteban Gutiérrez	1m 38.959s	1m 26.189s		
16	Felipe Nasr	1m 37.772s	1m 27.063s		
17	Jolyon Palmer	1m 43.965s			
18	Felipe Massa	1m 43.999s			
19	Kevin Magnussen	1m 44.543s			
20	Marcus Ericsson	1m 46.984s			
21	Pascal Wehrlein	1m 47.343s			
22	Rio Haryanto	1m 50.189s			

Photos: Peter J. Fox

FOR THE RECORD

50th FRONT ROW: **Nico Rosberg.**

2,000th POINT: **Sebastian Vettel.**

POINTS

DRIVERS

1	Lewis Hamilton	192
2	Nico Rosberg	186
3	Daniel Ricciardo	115
4	Kimi Räikkönen	114
5	Sebastian Vettel	110
6	Max Verstappen	100
7	Valtteri Bottas	56
8	Sergio Pérez	47
9	Felipe Massa	38
10	Carlos Sainz	30
11	Romain Grosjean	28
12	Nico Hülkenberg	27
13	Fernando Alonso	24
14	Daniil Kvyat	23
15	Jenson Button	13
16	Kevin Magnussen	6
17	Pascal Wehrlein	1
18	Stoffel Vandoorne	1

CONSTRUCTORS

1	Mercedes	378
2	Ferrari	224
3	Red Bull	223
4	Williams	94
5	Force India	74
6	Toro Rosso	45
7	McLaren	38
8	Haas	28
9	Renault	6
10	Manor	1

9 · HÜLKENBERG · Force India

7 · ALONSO · McLaren

5 · VETTEL · Ferrari

3 · RICCIARDO · Red Bull

1 · ROSBERG · Mercedes

10 · BOTTAS · Williams

8 · BUTTON · McLaren

6 · SAINZ · Toro Rosso

4 · VERSTAPPEN · Red Bull

2 · HAMILTON · Mercedes

Qualifying: head-to-head

Rosberg	5	6	Hamilton
Vettel	8	3	Räikkönen
Massa	2	9	Bottas
Ricciardo	4	0	Kvyat
Ricciardo	6	1	Verstappen
Pérez	5	6	Hülkenberg
Magnussen	8	3	Palmer
Verstappen	3	1	Sainz
Kvyat	2	5	Sainz
Ericsson	7	4	Nasr
Alonso	8	2	Button
Button	0	1	Vandoorne
Haryanto	5	6	Wehrlein
Grosjean	8	3	Gutiérrez

55	56	57	58	59	60	61	62	63	64	65	66	67	68	69	70	
44	44	44	44	44	44	44	44	44	44	44	44	44	44	44	44	1
6	6	6	6	6	6	6	6	6	6	6	6	6	6	6	6	2
3	3	3	3	3	3	3	3	3	3	3	3	3	3	3	3	3
5	5	5	5	5	5	5	5	5	5	5	5	5	5	5	5	4
33	33	33	33	33	33	33	33	33	33	33	33	33	33	33	33	5
7	7	7	7	7	7	7	7	7	7	7	7	7	7	7	7	6
14	14	14	14	14	14	14	14	14	14	14	14	14	14	14		7
55	55	55	55	55	55	55	55	55	55	55	55	55	55	55		8
77	77	77	77	77	77	77	77	77	77	77	77	77	77	77		9
27	27	27	27	27	27	27	27	27	27	27	27	27	27	27		10
21	21	21	21	21	21	21	21	11	11	11	11	11	11	11		
11	11	11	11	11	11	11	11	21	21	21	21	21	21	21		
30	30	30	30	30	30	30	30	30	30	30	30	30	30	30		
8	8	8	8	8	8	8	8	8	8	8	8	8	8	8		
20	20	20	20	20	20	20	20	20	20	20	20	20	20	20		
26	26	26	26	26	26	26	26	26	26	26	26	26	26	26		
12	12	12	12	12	12	12	12	12	12	12	12	12	12	12		
19	19	19	19	19	19	19	19	19	19	19	19	19	19			
22	22	22	22	22	22	94	94	94	94	94	94	94	94			
94	94	94	94	94	94	9	9	9	9	9	9	9	9			
9	9	9	9	9	9	88	88	88	88	88						
88	88	88	88	88	88											

94 = One lap or more behind

RACE TYRE STRATEGIES

PIRELLI

	Driver	Race Stint 1	Race Stint 2	Race Stint 3	Race Stint 4
1	Hamilton	Super-Soft (u): 1-16	Soft (n): 17-41	Soft (n): 42-70	
2	Rosberg	Super-Soft (u): 1-17	Soft (n): 18-42	Soft (n): 43-70	
3	Ricciardo	Super-Soft (u): 1-15	Soft (n): 16-33	Soft (n): 34-70	
4	Vettel	Super-Soft (u): 1-14	Soft (n): 15-41	Soft (n): 42-70	
5	Verstappen	Super-Soft (u): 1-16	Soft (n): 17-38	Soft (n): 39-70	
6	Räikkönen	Soft (n): 1-29	Super-Soft (n): 30-50	Super-Soft (n): 51-70	
7	Alonso	Super-Soft (u): 1-15	Soft (n): 16-44	Soft (n): 45-69	
8	Sainz	Super-Soft (u): 1-16	Soft (n): 17-42	Soft (n): 43-69	
9	Bottas	Super-Soft (u): 1-16	Soft (n): 17-43	Soft (n): 44-69	
10	Hülkenberg	Super-Soft (u): 1-14	Soft (n): 15-39	Soft (n): 40-69	
11	Pérez	Soft (n): 1-27	Medium (n): 28-40	Soft (n): 41-69	
12	Gutiérrez	Super-Soft (n): 1-15	Soft (n): 16-37	Soft (n): 38-69	
13	Palmer	Soft (n): 1-26	Super-Soft (n): 27-39	Soft (n): 40-69	
14	Grosjean	Super-Soft (n): 1-14	Soft (n): 15-36	Soft (n): 37-69	
15	Magnussen	Super-Soft (n): 1-24	Super-Soft (n): 25-36	Soft (n): 37-69	
16	Kvyat	Soft (n): 1-24	Super-Soft (n): 25-46	Super-Soft (n): 47-69	
17	Nasr	Super-Soft (n): 1-11	Soft (n): 12-39	Soft (n): 40-69	
18	Massa	Soft (n): 1-25	Medium (n): 26-65	Super-Soft (n): 66-68	
19	Wehrlein	Super-Soft (n): 1-9	Soft (n): 10-35	Soft (n): 36-68	
20	Ericsson	Soft (n): 1-17	Soft (n): 18-45	Super-Soft (n): 46-62	Super-Soft (n): 63-68
21	Haryanto	Soft (n): 1-29	Medium (n): 30-68		
	Button	Super-Soft (n): 1-7	Soft (n): 8-28	Medium (n): 29-60 (dnf)	

The tyre regulations stipulate that at least two of three dry tyre specifications must be used during a dry race.
Pirelli P Zero logos are colour-coded on the tyre sidewalls: Red = Super-Soft; Yellow = Soft; White = Medium. (n) new (u) used

Photos: Peter J. Fox

FIA FORMULA 1 WORLD CHAMPIONSHIP · ROUND 12

GERMAN GRAND PRIX

HOCKENHEIM CIRCUIT

HOCKENHEIM QUALIFYING

THERE was a nice symmetry about Nico Rosberg claiming pole position for the German Grand Prix at Hockenheim 30 years after his father, Keke, had taken his last Formula 1 pole at the same circuit.

In truth, Rosberg was not too bothered about the historic significance of his impressive lap. More important was the fact that he had beaten his Mercedes team-mate in a straight scrap, Lewis Hamilton having made a small, but vital mistake as he tried to fight back.

Rosberg's lap seemed even sweeter because it had been completed under greater pressure than normal. Approaching the end of his first run in Q3, his engine had cut out due to a problem with the electronics. Fortunately, he was able to use 'limp-home' mode to creep back to the pits, where the problem was quickly rectified.

With Hamilton having set the fastest time so far, it meant that Rosberg had it all to do on this one lap. And just to add another degree of difficulty, he was fuelled for three laps in case of a problem on the first, the additional weight costing around 0.1s; a significant amount in battles as close as this.

Rosberg nailed it on his first lap and, as he claimed provisional pole, all eyes were on Hamilton, about half a lap behind. Through the first three corners, Lewis appeared to have the edge, but going into the hairpin at the far end of the 4.6km lap, he briefly locked his front brakes. That cost him pole by 0.107s. It may have been the blink of an eye, but it was enough to give him an unsmiling expression as his team-mate enjoyed the moment in front of his home fans.

"It was a really good feeling," said Rosberg. "It was a great lap, knowing that I had it all to do. I don't know exactly what caused the original problem. All I know is that I suddenly lost the throttle and the engine cut out. It's never happened before. I had to put all that behind me and just focus on the lap. The car was perfect. I'm sure it will be okay for the race."

"It was frustrating that it didn't work out, because I was a couple of tenths of a second up on my time," said Hamilton. "But I'm not thinking about that. It's been a very good weekend so far. I just didn't finish it off properly during qualifying. The good thing is this is a much easier track for overtaking. I'll definitely be pushing hard in the race."

As Hamilton prepared for the 67-lap race, he was aware that the Red Bulls had been closer than expected during qualifying. Daniel Ricciardo, on his usual good form all weekend, had worked on his set-up and lap time, finishing qualifying 0.363s off Rosberg's pole with a fully committed lap. Max Verstappen had never looked like challenging his team-mate, but nevertheless was clear of the Ferraris – led by Kimi Räikkönen. Sebastian Vettel never seemed truly at ease on his home track, his Ferrari appearing more nervous compared to the Finn, who seemed able to carry momentum more smoothly into and through the long corners. That translated into 0.15s and an unhappy German. "The balance didn't come together," said Vettel.

There was a similar gap to an intensely fought battle between Force India and Williams for the remaining top ten places. Nico Hülkenberg, impressively committed from the start of practice, won this particular Mercedes-power game, although he would be demoted by one place because of a mix-up with tyres and the wrong set being handed back at the end of FP3. That moved Valtteri Bottas into seventh on the grid, although there was nothing in it, as Sergio Pérez and Felipe Massa were potentially as quick as their respective team-mates.

There was more of a discrepancy between the Haas drivers. Esteban Gutiérrez looked happier than of late and pushed hard throughout practice, taking 11th, despite problems with inconsistent brakes. Romain Grosjean had similar difficulties, but much worse was a broken gearbox, which brought the penalty of another five places to add to his 15th fastest time.

Splitting the American entry, Jenson Button had the better of his team-mate, Fernando Alonso having run wide at the first corner. He claimed that he had been pushed there by Vettel, but his complaint was not upheld by the stewards. This was a decent result for Button who, on Friday, had been briefly hospitalised to deal with a tiny fragment of carbon that had got into one eye.

Carlos Sainz, in turn, split the McLaren-Hondas on paper, but the Toro Rosso would be relegated a further three places for impeding Massa on the run to Turn Two. Sainz may have felt his 2015 Ferrari engine was being outgunned on the straights, but his problems were nothing compared to those of a distraught Daniil Kvyat, after the Russian had lapped 0.559s off his team-mate and failed, for no obvious reason, to get out of Q1.

Jolyon Palmer, on the other hand, was much happier after his recent travails with the Renault, thanks to making Q2 and qualifying 16th, one place ahead of Kevin Magnussen. Following a mistake by Rio Haryanto at Turn Eight, Pascal Wehrlein was the faster of the two Manor drivers, the German almost making it into Q2, and being comfortably ahead of Felipe Nasr and Marcus Ericsson, bringing up the rear for Sauber.

HAMILTON would explain later that he had been working intently with a member of his engineering crew to perfect the two-part clutch operation as best they could. This had been prompted by some dreadful starts. The one at Hockenheim would be near perfect. Rosberg, on the other hand, having enjoyed some stonking getaways, suffered a disaster.

"I don't really understand what happened," said Nico. "It was close to perfect off the dummy grid. I did the same thing and the clutch over-engaged, so I got wheelspin." The surging engine revs accompanied the inevitable appearance of Hamilton on his right as the German helplessly and slowly gathered momentum, heading for the first corner and hoping there would not be enough time or space for others to follow his team-mate.

It was a false hope, as the Red Bulls seized their moment and sorted out second place among themselves. Initially, it appeared to be Ricciardo's, but, calm as you like – well, not so calm perhaps – Verstappen ran around the outside and, to Daniel's surprise and frustration, the daring Dutchman found plenty of grip, despite all four wheels being on the kerb, but within track limits. Fourth to second in a ballsy move.

Rosberg was determined not to cede more places as Vettel, having out-accelerated Räikkönen, looked for a way through on the run towards the hairpin while, at the same time, making sure he prevented Kimi from taking the slipstream advantage. Behind the Ferraris, the pack fanned out, led by Bottas, Hülkenberg, Button, Massa, Alonso, Magnussen and Sainz.

Palmer had already lost the advantage of his qualifying performance by damaging his front wing and heading for the pits after contact with Massa at Turn Two. Pérez was another instant loser after start-line wheelspin, as was Gutiérrez, the Haas suffering from a gripless start thanks to being the only car on the harder soft tyre amid a sea of super-softs. Nasr, on the other hand, made a great start to duck around a crowded first corner and claim 17th place as Grosjean

dealt with an attack by the Manors, before getting past his frustrated team-mate and setting after the Sauber.

When Hamilton finished the first lap 1.3s ahead of Verstappen, this demoralising performance posed more questions than it answered. Certainly, the Mercedes was quick; everyone knew that. But was Lewis opening a gap, the better a few laps later to cruise and look after his tyres? Or was he going for broke to execute a three-stop strategy? That was the question, of course: how would the super-soft fare as the track temperature remained high? The worry was thermal degradation of the rears. In theory, three stops would be faster than two, with the bonus of overtaking being comparatively easy on this track.

Rosberg might not have agreed with that last statement as he tried to stage an immediate recovery from the disastrous start. His task was made even more difficult by being up against one of the fastest and most tenacious of rivals, at the wheel of a car that was continuing to prove remarkably quick on a track that highlighted any shortfall in top-end power. Even allowing for the advances made by Renault, the Red Bull was indecently quick, helped by the RB12 running a noticeable degree of rake to permit the front end to be fully productive in terms of downforce. Clever work at Milton Keynes had found that crucial balance without upsetting the operation of the rear.

Rosberg was discovering this at first hand as he tracked Ricciardo, Nico later dismissing the view that high-speed downforce, a fundamental tenet of the Mercedes design, was compromised when running in close company. "We have an awesome car," was his clipped response. "The Red Bulls were difficult to pass because they were fast."

The use of the plural term when referring to the opposition would be made necessary by a controversial incident that we will come to shortly. For now, Rosberg was fully focused on dealing with an Australian who was very keen to make amends for losing out to his team-mate and to capitalise on having got ahead of a Mercedes at the start.

Above: The midfield pack scrambles for position on the opening lap. Kevin Magnussen's Renault heads the Toro Rossos of Sainz (*left*) and Kvyat, the latter holding off the challenge of Pérez. Gutiérrez brings up the rear.
Photo: Renault Sport Formula One Team

Top left: Sebastian Vettel delights a youngster with a selfie.
Photo: Peter J. Fox

Above left: For the third successive race meeting, Charles Leclerc was given valuable track time in the Haas.
Photo: Haas F1 Team

Left: Renault gave Esteban Ocon a second run in Friday practice.
Photo: Renault Sport Formula One Team

Below left: Nico Rosberg was top of the pile in qualifying, recording his fifth pole position of the year.
Photo: Mercedes AMG Petronas F1 Team

Opening spread: Under overcast skies, the field is already becoming strung out during the opening phase of the race.
Photo: Peter J. Fox

Above: Lewis Hamilton takes command as pole-sitter Nico Rosberg becomes boxed in behind the Red Bulls of Verstappen and Ricciardo.
Photo: Lukas Gorys

Top right: Despite a one-place grid penalty, Nico Hülkenberg drove another strong race to seventh for Force India.
Photo: Sahara Force India F1 Team

Above right: Jolyon Palmer was left to race the Saubers after an early pit stop, prompted by a collision with Felipe Massa.
Photo: Renault Sport Formula One Team

Right: Jenson Button took a heartening eighth place for McLaren Honda, just ahead of Bottas and Pérez.
Photo: McLaren Honda

On the second lap, Rosberg ducked out of Ricciardo's slipstream and dived down the inside under braking for the hairpin. Daniel used the generous circuit width to hang on to the outside line and set up a drag race to the next very fast right – which they went through side by side at 180mph in an awesome display of tenacity and trust. Having held his ground, Ricciardo was perfectly positioned to claim the line for the slow left in front of the Mercedes grandstand.

The factory employees and guests from Stuttgart enjoyed this battle – if not the result, as Rosberg had to settle for fourth for the time being – and they had the comfort of watching Hamilton extend his lead to just over two seconds. The fact that he had eased his lap time by half a second was the only outward sign of winding down the power unit in the interest of reliability. He could do this because, after six laps, Verstappen was beginning to feel his rear tyres going away to accompany the diminishing view of the leading Mercedes.

Unfortunately for Rosberg, Ricciardo was not experiencing the same difficulty; a situation predicted by long runs during practice and prompting Red Bull to consider splitting their strategy, Verstappen running one more stop than Ricciardo. With that in mind, there was no debate about bringing in Max at the end of lap 11 when they saw Mercedes preparing to do the same as Nico was switched to three stops. Both drivers took on new super-softs, but when Ricciardo came in a lap later, he received a set of softs, thanks to two stops still being an option. When Hamilton was the last of the leading quartet to come in two laps later, he also received softs, with the same strategy remaining available.

At the end of lap 15, the order was Hamilton, six seconds ahead of Verstappen, who had 1.3s in hand over his teammate, with Rosberg 2.6s behind Ricciardo. As a result of this fast game of shadow boxing at the front, the Ferraris, led by Vettel, had been dropped to the tune of five seconds.

There was a similar gap to the fight between Bottas and Hülkenberg, made interesting by Williams choosing softs, but Force India opting to continue with the super-soft – not that it would make much difference, as the higher temperature reduced the margin between the tyres as durability more or less matched the 0.9s performance difference. It caused Verstappen to announce on lap 17 that the super-soft was "not the race tyre", a fact that was becoming apparent, with three stops the answer regardless of tyre choice.

Mercedes made the first move by bringing in Rosberg for softs on lap 27, prompting Red Bull to do the same for Verstappen a lap later. That was predictable, as was an attempt by Rosberg to make the most of finding himself just behind the emerging Red Bull, but with fresh tyres that were up to temperature.

On the charge towards the hairpin, Rosberg began a bold overtaking attempt from such a long way back that Verstappen didn't see it coming. And when he did, he made a partial blocking move that would have an effect on what happened next.

Rosberg kept going straight and only turned in at the point where Verstappen had nowhere to go but off the road – an option the Dutchman took with an exaggerated sweep across the run-off in case anyone missed his opinion that Rosberg

had been unnecessarily forceful rather than at the absolute limit of his braking and successfully avoiding a lock-up. If nothing else, it showed that Rosberg was willing to grab a rare opportunity to have a go at a driver who, in a short time, had earned a reputation for being extremely difficult to pass. Whatever the motivation, the stewards did not approve of the execution and added a five-second penalty to either his next stop or race time if he did not visit the pits again.

Having got ahead of Verstappen, Rosberg used the undercut to move into second place when Ricciardo made his second stop, on lap 33. Hamilton made his pit visit a lap later and rejoined 5.7s ahead of his team-mate. While it seemed unlikely that Rosberg would close in on Hamilton, the same was not the case between the Red Bull drivers, as Ricciardo found a fresh set of super-softs to his liking and set about reducing the 2.6s gap to Verstappen (on softs that were five laps old). By lap 40, the Red Bulls were running in tandem, Verstappen dutifully allowing the faster car into third place to give chase to Rosberg. Any hope Nico had of at least holding on to second – never mind getting on terms with Hamilton – was about to be dashed by a pit-stop fumble that had a comedic value for everyone outside Mercedes.

With five seconds to be added before work could begin during this final stop, the Mercedes came to a halt. But the team manager's hand-held stopwatch failed to start. The need to ensure a safety margin resulted in 8.3 seconds of inactivity, which seemed like a lifetime to the hapless Rosberg. Such a ridiculous delay meant that the Red Bulls were home free, second and third.

VIEWPOINT
RADIO GA-GA

RESTRICTED radio messages, thankfully, were a thing of the past as the paddock assembled in Germany. You could understand the thinking behind the ban. These guys were supposed to be heroes. They were supposed to drive the car 'alone and unaided'. It didn't sound cool to have engineers telling them where to brake, when to back off, when to drive fast.

But, on the other hand, radio transmissions, some of them heated, irate, informative regarding strategy, were reckoned by many to contribute more to the 'show' and the understanding of it than they took away.

Apart from amateurish chopping and changing in the middle of the season, as with the qualifying debacle at the start of the year, you had to hope that Nico Rosberg didn't end up losing the championship by less than three points, the penalty for his Silverstone demotion from second to third when he was told not to shift through seventh gear.

Then again, there was Baku, where if Pete Bonnington had been allowed to tell Lewis Hamilton which buttons to press when he was chasing Sergio Pérez and losing power, it may have made the difference between fifth and third.

The point is that, like it or not, the hybrid-era cars are tremendously complex, and F1 is supposed to test driving skill, not mental dexterity by way of remembering what to do with a selection of modes and switches that probably would befuddle an Oxford don. Quite apart from the safety element, with Jenson Button penalised in Hungary over a brake issue.

Yes, it's not always straightforward and radio instructions are performance enhancing, but if anything, they add to the transparency of what can be a complex business. Good to have them back.

Tony Dodgins

As was Hamilton, cruising at the front. He was ten seconds to the good, and looking after his tyres and engine. When Ricciardo, who earlier had set the fastest race lap, reduced the gap to 6.3s, the Mercedes driver responded with almost insouciant ease.

There had been nothing easy-going about life at Ferrari. The mounting pressure within the team had received a public airing when Vettel questioned an instruction to make his second stop, claiming his softs were still good. When told he needed to come in to make an undercut on Verstappen, he assessed that the eight-second gap would make such a move impossible, but, less correctly perhaps, went against the pit-wall decision and remained on track. Apart from doing little for sagging morale at Maranello, it made little difference to the overall result, as Vettel led home Räikkönen by ten seconds (Kimi complaining he had been left out too long on his super-softs), the red pair a massive 33 seconds behind the winner.

Force India won the battle with Williams, Hülkenberg undercutting Bottas at the second stop and forcing the Finn to run two stops, a struggle that left Valtteri open to attack as Button claimed eighth, a happy situation for the Briton, who made better use of his fuel saving than Alonso. The Spaniard's frustration was made worse by Pérez seizing an opportunity while being lapped to push the McLaren into 11th and out of the points, a situation exacerbated when Gutiérrez snatched the place on the final lap. Despite starting from 20th, Grosjean managed to haul himself into 13th, two places and nine seconds behind his Haas team-mate.

The Toro Rosso pair finished 14th and 15th, just two seconds apart after a slow stop for Sainz, and a solid and strong recovery by the beleaguered Kvyat. Seventeenth was poor reward after a consistent drive by Wehrlein, both Manor drivers having struggled with broken front wing endplates, the pair split by Ericsson (a steady race) and Palmer (recovering from the early pit stop). There were two retirements: Nasr with an engine problem while running last; Massa with handling difficulties, possibly caused by the collision with Palmer – although some team members doubted that.

There was no doubt within Mercedes over the quality of Hamilton's totally commanding performance from the moment Rosberg's otherwise dominant weekend went the way of his slipping clutch.

"I'm really surprised to be 19 points in front," said Lewis. "There's still a long way to go in the season, and I don't want to make any assumptions, but after all the difficulties I had earlier in the year, I'm beginning to think I might have a chance of the championship – but no more than a chance. Anything can happen."

Maurice Hamilton

Above: Winner Lewis Hamilton reflects on his day's work, while the Red Bull pair of Ricciardo and Verstappen discuss their race before they all head for the podium.
Photo: Peter J. Fox

Above left: Charlie Whiting announces the FIA's decision to abandon the restrictions on radio messages between the teams and their drivers.
Photo: GP Photo/Peter Nygaard

Left: Nico Rosberg's robust move on Max Verstappen earned the German a five-second time penalty, which eventually cost him a podium place.
Photo: WRi2/Studio Colombo

12

2016 FORMULA 1
GROSSER PREIS VON DEUTSCHLAND

HOCKENHEIM 29–31 JULY

ROLEX

OFFICIAL TIMEPIECE

RACE DISTANCE: 67 laps, 190.424 miles/306.458km

RACE WEATHER: Dry/sunny-overcast (track 37–42°C, air 24–25°C)

HOCKENHEIM-RING, HOCKENHEIM
Circuit: 2.842 miles/4.574km
67 laps
187/116 kmh/mph ⚙ Gear
Einfarhrt Parabolika 100/62
Nordkurve 205/127
165/103
Sachskurve 115/71
Hochgeschwindigkeits Parabolika 300/186
Mobil 1 Kurve 200/124
325/199
Südkurve 160/99
135/84
180/112
285/177
Spitzkehre 65/40
110/68

RACE – OFFICIAL CLASSIFICATION

Pos.	Driver	Nat.	No.	Entrant	Car/Engine	Tyres	Laps	Time/Retirement	Speed (mph/km/h)	Gap to leader	Fastest race lap	
1	**Lewis Hamilton**	GB	44	Mercedes AMG Petronas F1 Team	Mercedes F1 W07-Mercedes PU106C V6	P	67	1h 30m 44.200s	125.918/202.646		1m 18.746s	52
2	**Daniel Ricciardo**	AUS	3	Red Bull Racing	Red Bull RB12-TAG Heuer RB12 V6	P	67	1h 30m 51.196s	125.757/202.386	6.996s	1m 18.442s	48
3	**Max Verstappen**	NL	33	Red Bull Racing	Red Bull RB12-TAG Heuer RB12 V6	P	67	1h 30m 57.613s	125.609/202.148	13.413s	1m 18.910s	47
4	**Nico Rosberg**	D	6	Mercedes AMG Petronas F1 Team	Mercedes F1 W07-Mercedes PU106C V6	P	67	1h 31m 00.045s	125.553/202.058	15.845s	1m 19.122s	51
5	**Sebastian Vettel**	D	5	Scuderia Ferrari	Ferrari SF15-H-059/5 V6	P	67	1h 31m 16.770s	125.170/201.441	32.570s	1m 18.710s	48
6	**Kimi Räikkönen**	FIN	7	Scuderia Ferrari	Ferrari SF16-H-059/5 V6	P	67	1h 31m 21.223s	125.068/201.277	37.023s	1m 19.572s	36
7	**Nico Hülkenberg**	D	27	Sahara Force India F1 Team	Force India VJM09-Mercedes PU106C V6	P	67	1h 31m 54.249s	124.319/200.072	1m 10.049s	1m 20.056s	46
8	**Jenson Button**	GB	22	McLaren Honda	McLaren MP4-31-Honda RA616H V6	P	66			1 lap	1m 19.781s	48
9	**Valtteri Bottas**	FIN	77	Williams Martini Racing	Williams FW38-Mercedes PU106C V6	P	66			1 lap	1m 20.442s	36
10	**Sergio Pérez**	MEX	11	Sahara Force India F1 Team	Force India VJM09-Mercedes PU106C V6	P	66			1 lap	1m 19.606s	46
11	Esteban Gutiérrez	MEX	21	Haas F1 Team	Haas VF-16-Ferrari 059/5 V6	P	66			1 lap	1m 19.883s	56
12	Fernando Alonso	E	14	McLaren Honda	McLaren MP4-31-Honda RA616H V6	P	66			1 lap	1m 20.132s	50
13	Romain Grosjean	F	8	Haas F1 Team	Haas VF-16-Ferrari 059/5 V6	P	66			1 lap	1m 20.250s	58
14	Carlos Sainz	E	55	Scuderia Toro Rosso	Toro Rosso STR11-Ferrari 059/4 V6	P	66			1 lap	1m 19.957s	54
15	Daniil Kvyat	RUS	26	Scuderia Toro Rosso	Toro Rosso STR11-Ferrari 059/4 V6	P	66			1 lap	1m 19.585s	51
16	Kevin Magnussen	DK	20	Renault Sport F1 Team	Renault R.S.16-R.E.16 V6	P	66			1 lap	1m 21.649s	42
17	Pascal Wehrlein	D	94	Manor Racing MRT	Manor MRT05-Mercedes PU106C V6	P	65			2 laps	1m 20.710s	49
18	Marcus Ericsson	S	9	Sauber F1 Team	Sauber C35-Ferrari 059/5 V6	P	65			2 laps	1m 21.212s	35
19	Jolyon Palmer	GB	30	Renault Sport F1 Team	Renault R.S.16-R.E.16 V6	P	65			2 laps	1m 21.127s	55
20	Rio Haryanto	RI	88	Manor Racing MRT	Manor MRT05-Mercedes PU106C V6	P	65			2 laps	1m 21.845s	56
	Felipe Nasr	BR	12	Sauber F1 Team	Sauber C35-Ferrari 059/5 V6	P	57	*power unit*			1m 21.420s	45
	Felipe Massa	BR	19	Williams Martini Racing	Williams FW38-Mercedes PU106C V6	P	36	*accident/handling*			1m 21.476s	31

Fastest race lap: Daniel Ricciardo on lap 48, 1m 18.442s, 130.437mph/209.918km/h.

Lap record: Riccardo Patrese (Williams FW14B V10), 1m 41.591s, 150.060mph/241.498km/h (1992, 4.235 miles/6.815km circuit).

Lap record (current configuration): Kimi Räikkönen (McLaren MP4-19B-Mercedes Benz V10), 1m 13.780s, 138.679mph/223.182km/h (2004).

21 · NASR · Sauber

19 · HARYANTO · Manor

17 · WEHRLEIN · Manor

15 · SAINZ · Toro Rosso
(3-place grid penalty for impeding another driver)

13 · ALONSO · McLaren

11 · GUTIÉRREZ · Haas

22 · ERICSSON · Sauber

20 · GROSJEAN · Haas
(5-place grid penalty for replacing the gearbox)

18 · KVYAT · Toro Rosso

16 · MAGNUSSEN · Renault

14 · PALMER · Renault

12 · BUTTON · McLaren

Grid order	1	2	3	4	5	6	7	8	9	10	11	12	13	14	15	16	17	18	19	20	21	22	23	24	25	26	27	28	29	30	31	32	33	34	35	36	37	38	39	40	41	42	43	44	45	46	47	48	49	50	51	52
6 ROSBERG	44	44	44	44	44	44	44	44	44	44	44	44	44	44	44	44	44	44	44	44	44	44	44	44	44	44	44	44	44	44	44	44	44	44	44	44	44	44	44	44	44	44	44	44	44	44	44	44	44	44	44	44
44 HAMILTON	33	33	33	33	33	33	33	33	33	33	3	3	7	7	33	33	33	33	33	33	33	33	33	33	33	33	33	3	3	3	3	3	6	6	6	6	6	6	6	6	6	3	3	3	3	3	3	3	3	3	3	3
3 RICCIARDO	3	3	3	3	3	3	3	3	3	33	5	5	33	3	3	3	3	3	3	3	3	3	3	33	5	5	7	6	6	33	33	33	33	33	33	3	3	3	33	33	5	33	33	33	33	33	33
33 VERSTAPPEN	6	6	6	6	6	6	6	6	6	5	7	33	3	6	6	6	6	6	6	6	6	6	6	5	7	7	5	33	33	3	3	3	3	33	33	33	33	6	5	7	6	6	6	6
7 RÄIKKÖNEN	5	5	5	5	5	5	5	5	5	6	77	3	6	5	5	5	5	5	5	5	5	5	5	7	6	6	7	5	7	7	7	7	7	7	7	7	7	7	33	6	5	5	5	5	5
5 VETTEL	7	7	7	7	7	7	7	7	7	7	33	6	5	7	7	7	7	7	7	7	7	7	7	6	33	33	33	7	7	7	7	7	7	7	6	6	5	7	7	7	7	7
77 BOTTAS	77	77	77	77	77	77	77	77	77	77	27	14	14	8	77	77	77	77	77	77	77	77	77	77	77	77	77	77	27	27	27	27	27	27	27	27	77	77	77	77	77	77	77	77
27 HÜLKENBERG	27	27	27	27	27	27	27	27	27	27	22	22	8	77	8	27	27	27	27	27	27	27	27	27	27	27	27	77	77	77	77	77	77	77	77	27	22	14	27	27	27	27
11 PÉREZ	22	22	22	22	22	22	22	22	22	22	14	8	77	27	27	8	22	22	22	22	22	22	22	22	22	22	22	22	22	22	22	22	22	22	22	22	14	22	14	22	22	22	22	22
19 MASSA	19	19	19	19	19	14	14	14	14	14	6	77	21	21	21	21	21	21	21	14	14	14	14	14	20	20	14	14	14	14	14	14	14	14	14	27	27	22	14	14	14	14
21 GUTIÉRREZ	14	14	14	14	14	11	11	8	19	20	8	21	22	22	14	14	14	11	11	11	11	11	20	8	8	8	8	11	11	11	11	21	21	21	21	21	21	21
22 BUTTON	20	55	55	55	55	55	55	55	8	8	20	21	27	22	11	11	11	11	21	20	8	14	14	14	11	8	8	21	21	21	21	11	55	11	11	11	55	55	55	55
14 ALONSO	55	20	20	20	20	20	20	20	55	21	21	94	9	11	14	14	14	19	20	20	20	8	8	55	11	11	20	21	21	21	8	8	8	8	8	55	11	55	55	55	20	20
30 PALMER	30	26	26	26	26	11	11	8	19	94	94	9	11	9	19	20	19	55	55	8	55	55	11	11	21	21	55	55	55	55	55	55	55	55	8	20	20	20	21	21	21	20
55 SAINZ	26	11	11	11	8	8	11	21	9	9	11	19	19	20	20	55	55	55	8	55	55	21	26	26	26	21	55	55	20	20	20	20	20	20	20	26	26	26	26	26	8	55
20 MAGNUSSEN	11	12	12	8	8	21	94	88	88	20	8	21	21	21	21	19	21	9	19	21	19	9	26	26	26	26	26	26	26	26	26	8	8
94 WEHRLEIN	12	8	8	12	12	12	94	94	11	11	19	55	55	55	9	26	26	26	26	26	94	9	26	26	26	9	94	94	94	94	94	94	94	9	9	9	9	9
26 KVYAT	21	21	21	21	21	9	9	88	19	19	20	88	26	26	94	94	94	94	94	94	21	94	94	94	94	9	19	19	9	9	9	9	9	94	94	94	94	94
88 HARYANTO	94	94	94	94	94	94	26	88	11	55	55	55	26	94	94	94	9	9	9	9	9	9	88	19	19	19	19	9	19	30	30	30	30	30	88	88	88	30	30	30
8 GROSJEAN	8	88	88	88	9	9	88	30	30	30	30	30	30	30	12	9	30	30	30	30	30	88	19	88	88	88	12	12	12	12	12	12	88	88	88	30	30	12	12	12	12
12 NASR	9	9	9	9	88	88	12	26	26	26	30	94	12	12	9	9	12	88	88	88	88	88	12	12	12	12	30	30	30	30	88	88	88	88	12	12	12	12	88	88
9 ERICSSON	88	30	30	30	30	30	30	12	12	12	12	88	88	88	88	88	88	12	12	12	12	12	12	30	30	30	30	30	88	88	88	88	88

6 = Pit stop   9 = Drive-thru penalty

All results and data © FOM 2016

TIME SHEETS

PRACTICE 1 (FRIDAY)
Weather: Dry/sunny
Temperatures: track 32-35°C, air 22-24°C

Pos.	Driver	Laps	Time
1	Nico Rosberg	32	1m 15.517s
2	Lewis Hamilton	30	1m 15.843s
3	Sebastian Vettel	29	1m 16.667s
4	Kimi Räikkönen	23	1m 16.852s
5	Max Verstappen	29	1m 16.927s
6	Daniel Ricciardo	30	1m 17.089s
7	Fernando Alonso	18	1m 17.183s
8	Jenson Button	15	1m 17.612s
9	Daniil Kvyat	25	1m 18.008s
10	Carlos Sainz	22	1m 18.044s
11	Marcus Ericsson	28	1m 18.198s
12	Valtteri Bottas	37	1m 18.210s
13	Felipe Massa	33	1m 18.322s
14	Romain Grosjean	20	1m 18.589s
15	Nico Hülkenberg	35	1m 18.591s
16	Sergio Pérez	29	1m 18.628s
17	Charles Leclerc	32	1m 18.882s
18	Kevin Magnussen	35	1m 18.933s
19	Felipe Nasr	22	1m 18.961s
20	Esteban Ocon	30	1m 18.981s
21	Rio Haryanto	34	1m 19.167s
22	Pascal Wehrlein	33	1m 19.975s

PRACTICE 2 (FRIDAY)
Weather: Dry/sunny
Temperatures: track 37-45°C, air 25-26°C

Pos.	Driver	Laps	Time
1	Nico Rosberg	43	1m 15.614s
2	Lewis Hamilton	36	1m 16.008s
3	Sebastian Vettel	39	1m 16.208s
4	Max Verstappen	40	1m 16.456s
5	Daniel Ricciardo	38	1m 16.490s
6	Kimi Räikkönen	45	1m 16.512s
7	Nico Hülkenberg	43	1m 16.781s
8	Jenson Button	16	1m 17.087s
9	Sergio Pérez	44	1m 17.148s
10	Fernando Alonso	21	1m 17.225s
11	Carlos Sainz	32	1m 17.342s
12	Daniil Kvyat	38	1m 17.367s
13	Valtteri Bottas	44	1m 17.425s
14	Romain Grosjean	13	1m 17.602s
15	Felipe Massa	40	1m 17.686s
16	Esteban Gutiérrez	42	1m 18.005s
17	Kevin Magnussen	46	1m 18.056s
18	Marcus Ericsson	28	1m 18.130s
19	Pascal Wehrlein	42	1m 18.193s
20	Jolyon Palmer	47	1m 18.313s
21	Rio Haryanto	47	1m 18.591s
22	Felipe Nasr	41	1m 19.295s

PRACTICE 3 (SATURDAY)
Weather: Dry/sunny
Temperatures: track 36-37°C, air 24-25°C

Pos.	Driver	Laps	Time
1	Nico Rosberg	16	1m 15.738s
2	Lewis Hamilton	19	1m 15.795s
3	Daniel Ricciardo	13	1m 15.837s
4	Kimi Räikkönen	16	1m 15.902s
5	Sebastian Vettel	20	1m 16.104s
6	Max Verstappen	23	1m 16.182s
7	Valtteri Bottas	28	1m 16.400s
8	Felipe Massa	26	1m 16.630s
9	Fernando Alonso	11	1m 16.916s
10	Nico Hülkenberg	16	1m 16.972s
11	Carlos Sainz	20	1m 17.028s
12	Sergio Pérez	10	1m 17.066s
13	Esteban Gutiérrez	17	1m 17.160s
14	Daniil Kvyat	19	1m 17.227s
15	Kevin Magnussen	9	1m 17.351s
16	Jolyon Palmer	23	1m 17.473s
17	Marcus Ericsson	19	1m 17.685s
18	Felipe Nasr	24	1m 18.057s
19	Jenson Button	6	1m 18.093s
20	Pascal Wehrlein	24	1m 18.270s
21	Rio Haryanto	18	1m 18.272s
22	Romain Grosjean	4	1m 25.160s

QUALIFYING (SATURDAY)
Weather: Dry/sunny-overcast Temperatures: track 37-45°C, air 24-27°C

Pos.	Driver	First	Second	Third	Qualifying Tyre
1	Nico Rosberg	1m 15.485s	1m 14.839s	1m 14.363s	Super-Soft (new)
2	Lewis Hamilton	1m 15.243s	1m 14.748s	1m 14.470s	Super-Soft (new)
3	Daniel Ricciardo	1m 15.591s	1m 15.545s	1m 14.726s	Super-Soft (new)
4	Max Verstappen	1m 15.875s	1m 15.124s	1m 14.834s	Super-Soft (new)
5	Kimi Räikkönen	1m 15.752s	1m 15.242s	1m 15.142s	Super-Soft (new)
6	Sebastian Vettel	1m 15.927s	1m 15.630s	1m 15.315s	Super-Soft (new)
7	Nico Hülkenberg	1m 16.301s	1m 15.623s	1m 15.510s	Super-Soft (new)
8	Valtteri Bottas	1m 15.952s	1m 15.490s	1m 15.530s	Super-Soft (new)
9	Sergio Pérez	1m 16.169s	1m 15.500s	1m 15.537s	Super-Soft (new)
10	Felipe Massa	1m 16.503s	1m 15.699s	1m 15.615s	Super-Soft (new)
11	Esteban Gutiérrez	1m 15.987s	1m 15.883s		
12	Jenson Button	1m 16.172s	1m 15.909s		
13	Carlos Sainz	1m 16.317s	1m 15.989s		
14	Fernando Alonso	1m 16.338s	1m 16.041s		
15	Romain Grosjean	1m 16.328s	1m 16.086s		
16	Jolyon Palmer	1m 16.636s	1m 16.665s		
17	Kevin Magnussen	1m 16.716s			
18	Pascal Wehrlein	1m 16.717s			
19	Daniil Kvyat	1m 16.876s			
20	Rio Haryanto	1m 16.977s			
21	Felipe Nasr	1m 17.123s			
22	Marcus Ericsson	1m 17.238s			

Photo: Renault Sport F1 Team

Photo: Peter J. Fox

FOR THE RECORD

100th GRAND PRIX START: Daniel Ricciardo.
50th GRAND PRIX START: Esteban Gutiérrez.
300th FRONT ROW POSITION: Mercedes engine.
10,000th LAP COMPLETED: Lewis Hamilton

POINTS

DRIVERS

1	Lewis Hamilton	217
2	Nico Rosberg	198
3	Daniel Ricciardo	133
4	Kimi Räikkönen	122
5	Sebastian Vettel	120
6	Max Verstappen	115
7	Valtteri Bottas	58
8	Sergio Pérez	48
9	Felipe Massa	38
10	Nico Hülkenberg	33
11	Carlos Sainz	30
12	Romain Grosjean	28
13	Fernando Alonso	24
14	Daniil Kvyat	23
15	Jenson Button	17
16	Kevin Magnussen	6
17	Pascal Wehrlein	1
18	Stoffel Vandoorne	1

CONSTRUCTORS

1	Mercedes	415
2	Red Bull	256
3	Ferrari	242
4	Williams	96
5	Force India	81
6	Toro Rosso	45
7	McLaren	42
8	Haas	28
9	Renault	6
10	Manor	1

9 · PÉREZ · Force India

7 · BOTTAS · Williams

5 · RÄIKKÖNEN · Ferrari

3 · RICCIARDO · Red Bull

1 · ROSBERG · Mercedes

10 · MASSA · Williams

8 · HÜLKENBERG · Force India
(1-place grid penalty for using tyres without appropriate identification)

6 · VETTEL · Ferrari

4 · VERSTAPPEN · Red Bull

2 · HAMILTON · Mercedes

Qualifying: head-to-head

Rosberg	6	6	Hamilton
Vettel	8	4	Räikkönen
Massa	2	10	Bottas
Ricciardo	4	0	Kvyat
Ricciardo	7	1	Verstappen
Pérez	5	7	Hülkenberg
Magnussen	8	4	Palmer
Verstappen	3	1	Sainz
Kvyat	2	6	Sainz
Ericsson	7	5	Nasr
Alonso	8	3	Button
Button	0	1	Vandoorne
Haryanto	5	7	Wehrlein
Grosjean	8	4	Gutiérrez

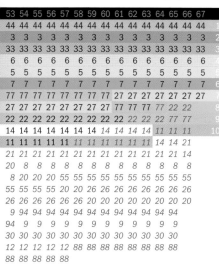

53	54	55	56	57	58	59	60	61	62	63	64	65	66	67	
44	44	44	44	44	44	44	44	44	44	44	44	44	44	44	1
3	3	3	3	3	3	3	3	3	3	3	3	3	3	3	2
33	33	33	33	33	33	33	33	33	33	33	33	33	33	33	3
6	6	6	6	6	6	6	6	6	6	6	6	6	6	6	4
5	5	5	5	5	5	5	5	5	5	5	5	5	5	5	5
7	7	7	7	7	7	7	7	7	7	7	7	7	7	7	6
77	77	77	77	77	77	77	77	27	27	27	27	27	27	27	7
27	27	27	27	27	27	27	27	77	77	77	77	22	22		8
22	22	22	22	22	22	22	22	22	22	22	22	77	77		9
14	14	14	14	14	14	14	14	14	14	14	11	11	11		10
11	11	11	11	11	11	11	11	11	11	11	14	14	21		
21	21	21	21	21	21	21	21	21	21	21	21	21	14		
20	8	8	8	8	8	8	8	8	8	8	8	8	8		
8	20	20	20	55	55	55	55	55	55	55	55	55	55		
55	55	55	55	20	20	26	26	26	26	26	26	26	26		
26	26	26	26	26	26	20	20	20	20	20	20	20	20		
9	94	94	94	94	94	94	94	94	94	94	94	94			
94	9	9	9	9	9	9	9	9	9	9	9	9			
30	30	30	30	30	30	30	30	30	30	30	30	30			
12	12	12	12	12	88	88	88	88	88	88	88	88			
88	88	88	88	88											

94 = One lap or more behind

RACE TYRE STRATEGIES

PIRELLI

	Driver	Race Stint 1	Race Stint 2	Race Stint 3	Race Stint 4
1	Hamilton	Super-Soft (u): 1-14	Soft (n): 15-34	Super-Soft (n): 35-47	Soft (u): 48-67
2	Ricciardo	Super-Soft (u): 1-12	Soft (n): 13-33	Super-Soft (u): 34-46	Super-Soft (n): 47-67
3	Verstappen	Super-Soft (u): 1-11	Super-Soft (n): 12-28	Soft (n): 29-45	Super-Soft (u): 46-67
4	Rosberg	Super-Soft (u): 1-11	Super-Soft (n): 12-27	Soft (n): 28-44	Soft (u): 45-67
5	Vettel	Super-Soft (u): 1-13	Soft (n): 14-31	Super-Soft (u): 32-46	Soft (u): 47-67
6	Räikkönen	Super-Soft (u): 1-14	Soft (n): 15-32	Super-Soft (u): 33-47	Soft (n): 48-67
7	Hülkenberg	Super-Soft (u): 1-12	Soft (n): 13-32	Super-Soft (u): 33-44	Soft (n): 45-67
8	Button	Super-Soft (u): 1-13	Soft (n): 14-31	Super-Soft (u): 32-46	Super-Soft (n): 47-66
9	Bottas	Super-Soft (u): 1-12	Soft (n): 13-33	Soft (n): 34-66	
10	Pérez	Super-Soft (u): 1-8	Soft (n): 9-27	Super-Soft (n): 28-43	Soft (n): 44-66
11	Gutiérrez	Soft (n): 1-25	Super-Soft (n): 26-47	Super-Soft (n): 48-66	
12	Alonso	Super-Soft (u): 1-14	Soft (n): 15-28	Super-Soft (n): 29-47	Super-Soft (u): 48-66
13	Grosjean	Super-Soft (u): 1-17	Soft (n): 18-43	Super-Soft (n): 44-66	
14	Sainz	Super-Soft (u): 1-9	Super-Soft (n): 10-29	Soft (n): 30-51	Super-Soft (n): 52-66
15	Kvyat	Super-Soft (u): 1-7	Soft (n): 8-28	Super-Soft (n): 29-49	Super-Soft (n): 50-66
16	Magnussen	Super-Soft (u): 1-11	Super-Soft (n): 12-32	Soft (n): 33-66	
17	Wehrlein	Super-Soft (n): 1-12	Super-Soft (u): 13-26	Soft (n): 27-46	Soft (u): 47-65
18	Ericsson	Super-Soft (n): 1-16	Super-Soft (u): 17-33	Soft (n): 34-65	
19	Palmer	Super-Soft (n): 1-2	Soft (n): 3-25	Super-Soft (u): 26-45	Super-Soft (u): 46-65
20	Haryanto	Super-Soft (u): 1-13	Soft (n): 14-32	Super-Soft (u): 33-49	Super-Soft (u): 50-65
	Nasr	Super-Soft (n): 1-7	Super-Soft (n): 8-19	Soft (n): 20-42	Soft (n): 43-57 (dnf)
	Massa	Super-Soft (u): 1-9	Soft (n): 10-26	Soft (n): 27-36 (dnf)	

The tyre regulations stipulate that at least two of three dry tyre specifications must be used during a dry race. Pirelli P Zero logos are colour-coded on the tyre sidewalls: Red = Super-Soft; Yellow = Soft. (n) new (u) used

Photo: Peter J. Fox

Photo: Mercedes AMG Petronas F1 Team

BELGIAN GRAND PRIX

SPA-FRANCORCHAMPS CIRCUIT

Three into two won't go at La Source. Max Verstappen squeezes his Red Bull on to the inside line and makes contact with Kimi Räikkönen. Sebastian Vettel bounces off his teammate's Ferrari.

Photos: Lukas Gorys

SPA-FRANCORCHAMPS QUALIFYING

RETURNING from the summer break with a 19-point deficit to triple world champion Lewis Hamilton, Nico Rosberg had an opportunity at Spa. With a maximum of five of the various power unit elements permitted, Hamilton had already used five turbochargers and five MGU-Hs (motor generator unit – heat). Thus it was inevitable that he would have to use extra components and accept a grid penalty somewhere, and Spa evidently was the place to do so. Overtaking on the stretch from Raidillon to Les Combes with the aid of DRS is not normally an issue for Mercedes engine users, and Lewis would be tasked with fighting through from the back.

A year earlier, tyre failures for Rosberg (in FP2) and Sebastian Vettel (in the closing stages of the race) had been controversial and provoked increased tyre pressures from Pirelli. Although it was suspected that a catalyst may have been an old, partly jagged section of kerbing at the top of Raidillon, allied to drivers putting the whole car over the white line to its left and rejoining the track with the right rear tyre sidewall crossing the offending section, that section of track remained unchanged for 2016.

The problems of 2015 had prompted an immediate increase in Pirelli minimum pressure stipulations, and they were higher still in Belgium this time around (22psi front, 23psi rear). The super-soft tyre was available for the first time, too, alongside the soft and medium, which gave rise to a qualifying conundrum.

In the light of the higher pressures and high temperatures, would the super-soft last the full 4.3-mile lap?

"There are quite a few places where it doesn't hold on for a lap-and-a-half, and Spa is a very long lap," Jenson Button pointed out.

Furthermore, the rate of degradation was high, and anyone starting the race on the super-soft tyre would necessarily be into the pits very early for new boots, likely dropping back out into traffic.

"I think you'll find most of the quick teams using softs, not super-softs, in Q2," Button added.

He was correct, even if none of that applied to the championship leader. By the time Hamilton had a fourth internal-combustion engine (ICE) fitted for FP1, a fifth for FP2 and a sixth for FP3, plus sundry ancillary components, he had amassed 55 places of grid penalties. Happily these days, you can only go as far as the back of the grid – no additional drive-throughs, time penalties or following race carry-overs. That being the case, it made total sense to get as many new components as possible into the pool for the rest of the year, a loophole that would be closed for 2017.

In theory, Mercedes could have installed a seventh ICE for qualifying and race, but never considered it because sending out an untried engine did not make sense. And, knowing he would start from the back, neither did it make sense for Hamilton to burn up tyres in qualifying, so a single lap was all that we saw from car No. 44.

That should have given Rosberg a straightforward run to pole, but FP3 suggested that his task was anything but simple. The Mercedes was blistering the super-soft tyre, and the best he could manage in FP3 was seventh quickest, well over half a second shy of the Ferrari/Red Bull pace, and also slower than Williams and Force India. Shades of Singapore 2015?

This time, though, the team responded in time for the qualifying hour, and Rosberg did indeed claim pole, having used the soft tyre in Q2, with a 0.15s advantage over Max Verstappen's Red Bull. The latter took super-softs to get through Q2 to save another set of the soft-compound Pirellis for the race.

Red Bull had split strategy, Ricciardo, like the Ferrari duo and Rosberg, setting his Q2 time on the yellow-walled soft tyre. Both his Q3 laps were spoiled by lost time at the first-corner La Source hairpin, however, a symptom of having to bring the super-soft tyre in very gently to get it to last the full lap, and he could only qualify fifth, behind both Ferraris.

At Maranello, four-times Spa winner Kimi Räikkönen got the better of team-mate Sebastian Vettel for the third time in four races, missing Verstappen's front-row time by just a couple of hundredths. The Finn is always quick at Spa and, but for running a bit too deep into the Bus Stop chicane, pole had actually been there for the taking.

Force India looked strong from the start, decent on both single-lap and long-run pace. Sergio Pérez put his car on row three, 0.14s clear of team-mate Nico Hülkenberg, who had a slight power unit issue, but still pipped Valtteri Bottas's Williams by 0.07s.

Both of Sir Frank's cars were troubled by a software issue that prevented the power unit from being run in qualifying spec. It made sure that they qualified behind the Force India duo that was closing in on Grove's fourth place in the constructors' championship.

Half a second shy of the first Williams was a strong effort from Button at McLaren Honda. The Japanese had a seven-token engine upgrade in the back for Belgium, and Button was delighted with a lap that allowed him to outqualify Massa's Williams, the Brazilian hampered by just the single Q3 run after needing two sets of super-softs to clear Q2. Fernando Alonso, like Hamilton, received penalties for a whole raft of engine changes and would start from the back in the second McLaren.

Fastest of those with free tyre choice was Romain Grosjean's Haas, with team-mate Gutiérrez there or thereabouts, too, but slapped with a five-place grid penalty for dangerous inattention to a fast approaching Pascal Wehrlein when tooling along in the middle of the track at Raidillon.

Benefiting from Hamilton and Alonso not going for it, both Renaults cleared Q1, ending up with Kevin Magnussen 12th and Jolyon Palmer 14th, both ahead of Carlos Sainz in the first of the Toro Rossos – outgunned with their 2015-spec Ferrari power units.

The final Q2 qualifier was Pascal Wehrlein after a fine lap in the Manor that put him ahead of new team-mate Esteban Ocon, the Mercedes-backed junior subbing for Rio Haryanto, whose Indonesian funds had run dry.

SPA is close to the Dutch border, and on Sunday morning, you could have been forgiven for thinking that you had walked into the middle of a nation en route to watch their team play the World Cup Final. Such was the extent to which Max Verstappen had caught the imagination in his native land. All around the circuit was a sea of orange, the Ferrari flag-wielding faithful for once outnumbered.

Sadly, it all went wrong for their favoured son within the first couple of hundred yards on Sunday afternoon. While Rosberg made a reasonable getaway to lead into La Source, Verstappen's Red Bull got too much wheelspin and, in a trice, both second-row Ferraris blasted past him.

If Verstappen sees a gap, he fills it. Räikkönen left half a chance on the inside of La Source and the Dutchman went for it. Unfortunately, Vettel, slightly in front of his team-mate, but on the outside, tried to pinch Kimi tight to slow his exit and did not appreciate that the Red Bull had dived inside. Kimi was left with nowhere to go and was shunted into the Red Bull, rebounding into Vettel and causing Sebastian to spin.

As Verstappen and Räikkönen blasted down to Eau Rouge, both were battle scarred: Kimi had a punctured right front and was showering sparks as the car's underbody sat down, while Verstappen had a damaged front wing and

floor that gave him big understeer and forced him into the pits. He was always going to be in early, just not that early.

He was followed in by both Ferraris, Räikkönen's underbody plank momentarily on fire such had been the friction. He rejoined lapped, with Vettel down at the back, just ahead of Verstappen.

This was very good news for Hamilton, all three being cars he would have struggled to overcome from the back of the grid, giving him a realistic shot at the podium and decent championship damage limitation. Lewis had made strong progress on the opening lap, but nothing compared to Alonso, who came by 12th at the end of it!

There was more aggravation further back. Button, fighting Pérez, was forced to lift, whereby he was collected by Wehrein, both posting retirements. Then, next lap, Sainz punctured a tyre on some of the opening-lap debris and spun on Kemmel Straight, retiring the damaged Toro Rosso and instigating a virtual safety car (VSC) while the track was cleared.

Once the VSC period was over, the drama continued when Kevin Magnussen lost his Renault at the top of Raidillon and ploughed heavily backwards into the tyres, before flicking through 180 degrees and going in again forwards for good measure.

It was a relief to see the young Dane climb out of the car

Above: A clean start from Nico Rosberg ensures that he will never be headed. Trouble brews further back as Verstappen moves out behind Räikkönen, while Lewis Hamilton begins his long journey from the back of the grid towards second place.

Photo: Red Bull Racing/Getty Images

Left: Having been given a couple of practice outings with Renault, Esteban Ocon was placed in the Manor Team by Mercedes to race alongside Pascal Wehrlein.

Photo: WRi2/Jean-François Galeron

Above: The race was red-flagged after Magnussen's crash. Leader Nico Rosberg surveys the frantic activity as the cars are lined up in the pit lane.
Photo: Lukas Gorys

Top right: Tyre marks show the path of Magnussen's Renault towards the tyre wall.

Above centre right: Magnussen's wrecked Renault is brought back to the pits.
Photos: GP Photo/Peter Nygaard

Above right: Under instructions? Ferrari's new chief technical officer Mattia Binotto takes a call.
Photo: Lukas Gorys

Right: Räikkönen is forced to limp back to the pits after his collision with Verstappen.
Photo: WRi2/Jean-François Galeron

and limp away, the safety car already deployed. Hülkenberg, Pérez, Grosjean, Palmer and Räikkönen all came straight in to switch from their super-softs, while Bottas and Gutiérrez followed suit on the next lap. The safety car was a decent break for Räikkönen, who could pass it and get back on the lead lap.

After a few laps behind the safety car, it became apparent that some heavier machinery would be needed to restore the Raidillon tyre barrier, and we had a full red-flag situation. Although the regulations would change for 2017, currently they allowed everyone to work on the cars and change rubber.

Race leader Rosberg and Pérez, therefore, could switch to mediums without having to make a pit stop, while Alonso and Hamilton, who'd started from the back on alternative-strategy mediums to run long and had gained by those ahead pitting, could take a set of the quicker soft tyre.

There were 34 laps of a probable two-stop race remaining when the race resumed under the safety car in the order Rosberg, Ricciardo, Hülkenberg, Alonso, Hamilton, Massa, Pérez, Kvyat, Palmer, Grosjean, Vettel, Bottas, Gutiérrez, Verstappen, Ocon, Nasr and Räikkönen.

At the front, Rosberg and Ricciardo eased away from Hülkenberg's Force India, Nico keeping Daniel out of DRS

range, but looking after his rubber at the same time. Alonso was powerless to stop Hamilton from blowing by on the Kemmel Straight to move up to fourth place, but the McLaren-Honda was sprightly enough through sector two to keep Williams and Pérez at bay. Grosjean struggled with a power loss that ultimately was fixed from the pit wall, but not before he had lost positions to Vettel's Ferrari, Bottas and Gutiérrez in the second Haas.

Just behind, Räikkönen was attacking Verstappen. At first, Kimi tried to run around the outside of the Red Bull into Les Combes, but Max pushed him out wide and off the track after they touched wheels, prompting an uncomplimentary radio transmission from the Finn. The Ferrari emerged ahead, but Räikkönen was informed that he needed to give the place back.

So he tried again next lap, this time on the inside. In a move highly reminiscent of the famous chop that Michael Schumacher had given Mika Häkkinen in 2000, Verstappen placed himself in the middle of the track, waited to see which way Räikkönen was going, then moved over on him. It was as iffy a bit of driving as witnessed for a long time, forcing Räikkönen to swerve and actually brake.

"That's f***ing ridiculous..." Kimi complained over the radio, understandably enough. Almost unbelievably, the

race stewards did not construe the matter to be worthy of further investigation, but even Red Bull team principal Christian Horner admitted that Verstappen had been "right on the limit."

The difference compared to 16 years before was that the closing speed was even greater, Räikkönen's tow also supplemented by DRS. Potential wheel-over-wheel contact, which you had to figure had been narrowly avoided, would have resulted in an airborne accident. A late move into Turn Two at Budapest, which Max had also done to Kimi, was one thing, but 200-plus mph at Spa, quite another.

When Schumacher had done it to Häkkinen, it so enraged Mika that he pulled that fantastic pass on the next lap when they shot either side of a bewildered Riccardo Zonta. Happily, perhaps, Max and Kimi were soon separated by varying strategy and the fact that, with the Red Bull an estimated second per lap slower due to the first-lap contact, the Ferrari was in much better shape. Of course, it is not Räikkönen's way to overreact, but clearly he was far from happy.

On the medium compound, Rosberg was looking more comfortable in front than practice had suggested he might, and when Ricciardo attempted to match him for pace, Red Bull was soon on the radio warning him of overheating tyre temperatures – one of the great frustrations of modern-day F1. Everyone was hoping that thermal degradation would not be such a pronounced feature of the new 2017 Pirellis, but nobody was holding their breath.

Against what looked like insurmountable odds after the practice sessions, Hamilton made it into the podium places when he pulled off a DRS pass of Hülkenberg down the Kemmel Straight on lap 18. His championship damage would be limited to just the ten points.

At this point, Ricciardo was just 6.5s further up the road from Lewis, both on softs of the same nine-lap vintage, but the Red Bull was actually going a tad quicker than the world champion. Lewis pitted for a new set of softs on lap 21, while Ricciardo ran a further four laps before going on to a new set of mediums. Rosberg responded on the next lap, also taking new mediums, but he was in no danger of a Red Bull undercut, having opened himself a 10s advantage. Hamilton would do just an 11-lap stint before coming in again, also to switch on to the harder tyre. It did not affect his podium finish, as he effortlessly went past Hülkenberg again, but Ricciardo's runner-up spot in a race he won in 2014, was secure.

Alonso was still pluckily holding down fifth place after a lap-23 stop for a new set of mediums, but he was under pressure from Massa and Pérez, with the recovering Vettel, Bottas and Räikkönen closing in.

Fernando was his usual canny Sunday-afternoon self. Suspecting that the Force India was quicker than Massa, he was going slowly enough to make sure that Massa was always within DRS range of the McLaren and so was not a sitting duck on the long straight for the Force India. Such a tactic would have been unthinkable with the Honda of just 12 months previously, but the power unit improvement, plus the McLaren's strong traction out of La Source, allowed Alonso to play the game.

On lap 29, though, Pérez finally displaced Massa, and a couple of laps later the Mexican was past Alonso and up into a Force India 4-5 that resulted in Vijay Mallya's Silverstone squad overhauling Williams by a couple of points in the battle for fourth place in the championship.

Vettel demoted Alonso to an eventual seventh on lap 35 and got to within 5s of Pérez by the flag, but the McLaren-Honda was able to hold off Bottas on the last lap, Valtteri a few tenths behind and a similar margin clear of Räikkönen.

Rosberg had managed to halt his team-mate's winning streak more easily than he might have done because three credible challengers had taken care of themselves at the first corner. Ferrari, in particular, had a more competitive car than for some races, but failed to take advantage, while the landscape, both on and off the track, was dominated by a certain Max Verstappen (see Viewpoint)...

Tony Dodgins

Above: Nico Hülkenberg posted a season's-best fourth place for the Force India team.
Photo: WRi2/Jean-François Galeron

Right: Sheer delight for Daniel Ricciardo and his crew, after yet another podium for the Red Bull driver.
Photo: Peter J. Fox

Top right: Nico looks suitably pleased with his victory, while no doubt Lewis was relieved to have rescued third place after his grid penalties.
Photo: WRi2/Jad Sherif

Above right: A walk in the woods for a handful of the thousands of Max Verstappen fans who had crossed the border from the Netherlands.
Photo: Red Bull Racing/Getty Images

Far right: Max Verstappen found himself the centre of unwanted attention at Spa-Francorchamps.
Photo: Peter J. Fox

VIEWPOINT
LESSONS TO LEARN

THE 'Verstappen at Spa' story was always likely to run and run from the moment Max made a late move on Räikkönen at over 200mph, and Kimi, understandably, felt compelled to complain about it.

Undeniably, Verstappen had become box office; the breath of fresh air that F1 needed. But his action on Kemmel Straight was considered by many – though not all – as too high a price to pay for the pleasure of watching such a precocious talent. Had the Red Bull and Ferrari actually made contact, the consequences of the resulting airborne accident did not bear thinking about.

Blocking is part of a driver's legitimate defence, but Verstappen's habit of waiting to see the direction of attack before moving at the last second was potentially dangerous. It may strictly have satisfied the 'one move' rule, but that was no excuse.

Max's move was reminiscent of Michael Schumacher's chop across the bow of Mika Häkkinen's McLaren in 2000. On that occasion, Häkkinen eventually got the better of the Ferrari driver by pulling off one of the greatest overtaking moves of all time, but that did not stop the Finn from having a quiet, but very serious word with Michael in *parc fermé*.

Schumacher took heed. The evidence in 2016 was that Verstappen would continue to play out the role of headstrong teenager and dismiss the views of senior drivers with a decade or more's experience. Worrying?

Verstappen may have been an 18-year-old bubbling with exuberance and confidence, and no one wanted to see the muzzling of such outrageous talent, but the feeling was that he needed to learn the importance of picking his fights rather than simply taking on everyone at every corner on every lap.

At Monza a week later, race director Charlie Whiting had a quiet word, explaining that a repeat would warrant a black-and-white-flag warning for unsportsmanlike behaviour. The unspoken hope in the event of Verstappen's continuing insouciance was that no one would be hurt during this necessary learning process.

Maurice Hamilton

13

2016 FORMULA 1
BELGIAN
GRAND PRIX

SPA-FRANCORCHAMPS 26–28 AUGUST

RACE DISTANCE: 44 laps, 191.415 miles/308.052km

RACE WEATHER: Dry/sunny (track 36–40°C, air 25–27°C)

ROLEX

OFFICIAL TIMEPIECE

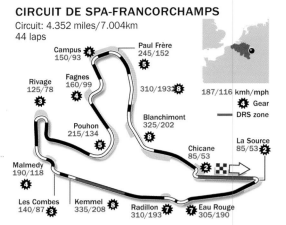

CIRCUIT DE SPA-FRANCORCHAMPS
Circuit: 4.352 miles/7.004km
44 laps

Campus 150/93
Paul Frère 245/152
Fagnes 160/99
Rivage 125/78
310/193
187/116 kmh/mph
Gear
DRS zone
Pouhon 215/134
Blanchimont 325/202
La Source 85/53
Chicane 85/53
Malmedy 190/118
Les Combes 140/87
Kemmel 335/208
Radillon 310/193
Eau Rouge 305/190

RACE – OFFICIAL CLASSIFICATION

Pos.	Driver	Nat.	No.	Entrant	Car/Engine	Tyres	Laps	Time/Retirement	Speed (mph/km/h)	Gap to leader	Fastest race lap	
1	**Nico Rosberg**	D	6	Mercedes AMG Petronas F1 Team	Mercedes F1 W07-Mercedes PU106C V6	P	44	1h 44m 51.058s	109.535/176.279		1m 51.746s	11
2	**Daniel Ricciardo**	AUS	3	Red Bull Racing	Red Bull RB12-TAG Heuer RB12 V6	P	44	1h 45m 05.171s	109.290/175.885	14.113s	1m 52.461s	11
3	**Lewis Hamilton**	GB	44	Mercedes AMG Petronas F1 Team	Mercedes F1 W07-Mercedes PU106C V6	P	44	1h 45m 18.692s	109.056/175.508	27.634s	1m 51.583s	40
4	**Nico Hülkenberg**	D	27	Sahara Force India F1 Team	Force India VJM09-Mercedes PU106C V6	P	44	1h 45m 26.965s	108.913/175.279	35.907s	1m 53.530s	41
5	**Sergio Pérez**	MEX	11	Sahara Force India F1 Team	Force India VJM09-Mercedes PU106C V6	P	44	1h 45m 31.718s	108.831/175.147	40.660s	1m 53.414s	34
6	**Sebastian Vettel**	D	5	Scuderia Ferrari	Ferrari SF15-H-059/5 V6	P	44	1h 45m 36.452s	108.751/175.017	45.394s	1m 52.728s	35
7	**Fernando Alonso**	E	14	McLaren Honda	McLaren MP4-31-Honda RA616H V6	P	44	1h 45m 50.503s	108.509/174.629	59.445s	1m 54.484s	43
8	**Valtteri Bottas**	FIN	77	Williams Martini Racing	Williams FW38-Mercedes PU106C V6	P	44	1h 45m 51.209s	108.498/174.610	1m 00.151s	1m 54.120s	31
9	**Kimi Räikkönen**	FIN	7	Scuderia Ferrari	Ferrari SF16-H-059/5 V6	P	44	1h 45m 52.167s	108.481/174.584	1m 01.109s	1m 53.498s	27
10	**Felipe Massa**	BR	19	Williams Martini Racing	Williams FW38-Mercedes PU106C V6	P	44	1h 45m 56.931s	108.400/174.453	1m 05.873s	1m 54.342s	25
11	Max Verstappen	NL	33	Red Bull Racing	Red Bull RB12-TAG Heuer RB12 V6	P	44	1h 46m 02.196s	108.310/174.308	1m 11.138s	1m 53.281s	32
12	Esteban Gutiérrez	MEX	21	Haas F1 Team	Haas VF-16-Ferrari 059/5 V6	P	44	1h 46m 04.935s	108.263/174.233	1m 13.877s	1m 54.335s	26
13	Romain Grosjean	F	8	Haas F1 Team	Haas VF-16-Ferrari 059/5 V6	P	44	1h 46m 07.532s	108.219/174.162	1m 16.474s	1m 53.803s	25
14	Daniil Kvyat	RUS	26	Scuderia Toro Rosso	Toro Rosso STR11-Ferrari 059/4 V6	P	44	1h 46m 18.155s	108.039/173.872	1m 27.097s	1m 52.081s	37
15	Jolyon Palmer	GB	30	Renault Sport F1 Team	Renault R.S.16-R.E.16 V6	P	44	1h 46m 24.223s	107.937/173.707	1m 33.165s	1m 53.251s	41
16	Esteban Ocon	F	31	Manor Racing MRT	Manor MRT05-Mercedes PU106C V6	P	43			1 lap	1m 55.734s	26
17	Felipe Nasr	BR	12	Sauber F1 Team	Sauber C35-Ferrari 059/5 V6	P	43			1 lap	1m 56.152s	31
	Kevin Magnussen	DK	20	Renault Sport F1 Team	Renault R.S.16-R.E.16 V6	P	5	*accident*			1m 56.588s	4
	Marcus Ericsson	S	9	Sauber F1 Team	Sauber C35-Ferrari 059/5 V6	P	3	*gearbox*			2m 15.255s	2
	Carlos Sainz	E	55	Scuderia Toro Rosso	Toro Rosso STR11-Ferrari 059/4 V6	P	1	*rear tyre*			no time	
	Jenson Button	GB	22	McLaren Honda	McLaren MP4-31-Honda RA616H V6	P	1	*accident*			no time	
	Pascal Wehrlein	D	94	Manor Racing MRT	Manor MRT05-Mercedes PU106C V6	P	0	*accident*			no time	

Race stopped on lap 10 after Magnussen's accident, to repair the guardrail. Resumed 16m 55s later. Overall race times include the stoppage time.

Fastest race lap: Lewis Hamilton on lap 40, 1m 51.583s, 140.411mph/225.969km/h.

Lap record: Kimi Räikkönen (McLaren MP4-19B-Mercedes Benz V8), 1m 45.108s, 148.465mph/238.931km/h (2004, 4.335-mile/6.976km circuit)

Lap record (current configuration): Sebastian Vettel (Red Bull RB5-Renault V8), 1m 47.263s, 146.066mph/235.070km/h (2009).

All results and data © FOM 2016

22 · ALONSO · McLaren
(60-place grid penalty for using additional power unit elements)

20 · ERICSSON · Sauber
(10-place grid penalty for using additional power unit element – started from the pit lane)

18 · GUTIÉRREZ · Haas
(5-place grid penalty for impeding another driver)

16 · NASR · Sauber

14 · SAINZ · Toro Rosso

12 · MAGNUSSEN · Renault

21 · HAMILTON · Mercedes
(55-place grid penalty for using additional power unit elements; 5-place penalty for replacing the gearbox)

19 · KVYAT · Toro Rosso

17 · OCON · Manor

15 · WEHRLEIN · Manor

13 · PALMER · Renault

11 · GROSJEAN · Haas

Grid order	1	2	3	4	5	6	7	8	9	10	11	12	13	14	15	16	17	18	19	20	21	22	23	24	25	26	27	28	29	30	31	32	33	34	35
6 ROSBERG	6	6	6	6	6	6	6	6	6	6	6	6	6	6	6	6	6	6	6	6	6	6	6	6	6	6	6	6	6	6	6	6	6	6	6
33 VERSTAPPEN	27	27	27	27	27	27	3	3	3	3	3	3	3	3	3	3	3	3	3	3	3	3	3	3	3	3	3	3	3	3	3	3	3	3	3
7 RÄIKKÖNEN	3	3	3	3	3	3	27	27	27	27	27	27	27	27	27	27	44	44	44	27	27	27	44	44	44	44	44	44	44	44	44	27	44	44
5 VETTEL	19	77	77	77	77	77	77	14	14	14	14	44	44	44	44	44	27	27	27	44	14	11	11	27	27	27	27	27	27	27	44	27	27
3 RICCIARDO	8	19	8	11	11	11	14	44	44	44	44	14	14	14	14	14	14	14	14	14	11	27	14	14	14	14	14	11	11	11	11	11	11
11 PÉREZ	77	8	11	8	8	8	21	19	19	19	19	19	19	19	19	19	19	19	19	5	44	14	19	19	19	11	14	14	14	14	14	5
27 HÜLKENBERG	55	11	30	30	30	30	44	11	11	11	26	11	11	11	11	11	11	11	11	19	5	7	11	11	11	19	19	19	19	5	14
77 BOTTAS	11	30	20	20	20	21	19	26	26	26	11	26	26	26	26	5	5	5	5	77	77	19	33	33	5	5	5	5	5	19	19
22 BUTTON	30	20	21	21	21	14	11	30	30	30	30	8	8	8	5	26	26	77	77	77	44	7	33	5	77	77	77	77	77	77	77
19 MASSA	20	21	14	14	14	44	26	8	8	8	8	30	5	5	8	77	77	26	26	21	7	19	5	77	7	7	7	7	7	7	7
8 GROSJEAN	21	14	31	44	44	19	30	5	5	5	5	5	30	77	77	77	8	21	21	7	8	33	77	7	7	33	21	21	21	21	21	21	21
20 MAGNUSSEN	14	31	44	31	31	31	8	77	77	77	77	77	77	30	21	21	21	8	8	7	8	21	8	26	26	21	26	26	26	33	33	33	33
30 PALMER	31	44	19	19	19	26	5	21	21	21	21	21	21	21	30	30	30	7	7	8	26	33	31	21	21	26	26	30	30	33	26	26	8
55 SAINZ	26	26	26	26	26	5	33	33	33	33	33	33	33	33	7	7	30	30	30	30	30	12	31	30	30	30	8	33	30	8	8	8	26
94 WEHRLEIN	44	9	5	5	5	33	31	31	31	31	7	7	7	7	12	12	12	12	12	12	26	30	8	8	31	8	30	30	30	30	30	30	30
12 NASR	33	5	33	33	33	12	12	12	12	12	12	12	12	12	33	31	31	31	31	31	12	26	30	31	31	31	31	31	31	31	31	31	31
31 OCON	9	33	12	12	12	7	7	7	7	7	31	31	31	31	31	33	33	31	26	12	12	12	12	12	12	12	12	12	12	12	12	12	12
21 GUTIÉRREZ	12	12	9	7	7																												
26 KVYAT	5	7	7																														
9 ERICSSON	22																																
44 HAMILTON	7																																
14 ALONSO																																	

6 = Pit stop   9 = Drive-thru penalty
94 = One lap or more behind

TIME SHEETS

PRACTICE 1 (FRIDAY)
Weather: Dry/sunny
Temperatures: track 26–33°C, air 25–28°C

Pos.	Driver	Laps	Time
1	Nico Rosberg	27	1m 48.348s
2	Lewis Hamilton	25	1m 49.078s
3	Kimi Räikkönen	24	1m 49.147s
4	Sergio Pérez	23	1m 49.274s
5	Sebastian Vettel	19	1m 49.768s
6	Daniel Ricciardo	24	1m 49.782s
7	Max Verstappen	24	1m 49.865s
8	Nico Hülkenberg	21	1m 50.088s
9	Valtteri Bottas	31	1m 50.394s
10	Esteban Gutiérrez	21	1m 50.583s
11	Romain Grosjean	18	1m 50.899s
12	Felipe Massa	28	1m 51.122s
13	Marcus Ericsson	16	1m 51.125s
14	Carlos Sainz	17	1m 51.424s
15	Felipe Nasr	19	1m 51.768s
16	Esteban Ocon	26	1m 51.787s
17	Daniil Kvyat	19	1m 52.308s
18	Jenson Button	18	1m 52.407s
19	Pascal Wehrlein	23	1m 52.837s
20	Kevin Magnussen	20	1m 53.053s
21	Jolyon Palmer	20	1m 53.089s
22	Fernando Alonso	3	no time

PRACTICE 2 (FRIDAY)
Weather: Dry/sunny
Temperatures: track 38–41°C, air 31–32°C

Pos.	Driver	Laps	Time
1	Max Verstappen	27	1m 48.085s
2	Daniel Ricciardo	27	1m 48.341s
3	Nico Hülkenberg	30	1m 48.657s
4	Sebastian Vettel	27	1m 49.023s
5	Sergio Pérez	27	1m 49.100s
6	Nico Rosberg	33	1m 49.161s
7	Kimi Räikkönen	30	1m 49.244s
8	Romain Grosjean	20	1m 49.419s
9	Jenson Button	23	1m 49.419s
10	Esteban Gutiérrez	23	1m 49.648s
11	Pascal Wehrlein	31	1m 49.716s
12	Fernando Alonso	30	1m 49.772s
13	Lewis Hamilton	33	1m 49.782s
14	Daniil Kvyat	25	1m 49.916s
15	Marcus Ericsson	27	1m 50.083s
16	Valtteri Bottas	19	1m 50.151s
17	Felipe Massa	29	1m 50.157s
18	Carlos Sainz	25	1m 50.194s
19	Kevin Magnussen	34	1m 50.375s
20	Jolyon Palmer	32	1m 50.562s
21	Esteban Ocon	25	1m 50.659s
22	Felipe Nasr	24	1m 50.719s

PRACTICE 3 (SATURDAY)
Weather: Dry/sunny
Temperatures: track 30°C, air 28°C

Pos.	Driver	Laps	Time
1	Kimi Räikkönen	11	1m 47.974s
2	Daniel Ricciardo	18	1m 48.189s
3	Sebastian Vettel	12	1m 48.297s
4	Valtteri Bottas	17	1m 48.504s
5	Lewis Hamilton	20	1m 48.635s
6	Nico Hülkenberg	12	1m 48.739s
7	Nico Rosberg	19	1m 48.742s
8	Felipe Massa	21	1m 48.783s
9	Sergio Pérez	12	1m 48.915s
10	Romain Grosjean	16	1m 49.272s
11	Fernando Alonso	9	1m 49.453s
12	Esteban Gutiérrez	16	1m 49.631s
13	Jenson Button	10	1m 49.665s
14	Kevin Magnussen	11	1m 49.716s
15	Pascal Wehrlein	15	1m 49.761s
16	Daniil Kvyat	9	1m 50.023s
17	Carlos Sainz	9	1m 50.078s
18	Jolyon Palmer	11	1m 50.241s
19	Felipe Nasr	13	1m 50.420s
20	Esteban Ocon	18	1m 50.693s
21	Marcus Ericsson	5	1m 51.319s
22	Max Verstappen	2	no time

QUALIFYING (SATURDAY)
Weather: Dry/sunny Temperatures: track 31–43°C, air 28–32°C

Pos.	Driver	First	Second	Third	Qualifying Tyre
1	Nico Rosberg	1m 48.019s	1m 46.999s	1m 46.744s	Super-Soft (new)
2	Max Verstappen	1m 48.407s	1m 47.163s	1m 46.893s	Super-Soft (new)
3	Kimi Räikkönen	1m 47.912s	1m 47.664s	1m 46.910s	Super-Soft (new)
4	Sebastian Vettel	1m 47.802s	1m 47.944s	1m 47.108s	Super-Soft (new)
5	Daniel Ricciardo	1m 48.407s	1m 48.027s	1m 47.216s	Super-Soft (new)
6	Sergio Pérez	1m 48.106s	1m 47.485s	1m 47.407s	Super-Soft (new)
7	Nico Hülkenberg	1m 48.080s	1m 47.317s	1m 47.543s	Super-Soft (new)
8	Valtteri Bottas	1m 48.655s	1m 47.918s	1m 47.612s	Super-Soft (new)
9	Jenson Button	1m 48.700s	1m 48.051s	1m 48.114s	Super-Soft (new)
10	Felipe Massa	1m 47.738s	1m 47.667s	1m 48.263s	Super-Soft (new)
11	Romain Grosjean	1m 48.751s	1m 48.316s		
12	Kevin Magnussen	1m 48.800s	1m 48.485s		
13	Esteban Gutiérrez	1m 48.748s	1m 48.598s		
14	Jolyon Palmer	1m 48.901s	1m 48.888s		
15	Carlos Sainz	1m 48.876s	1m 49.038s		
16	Pascal Wehrlein	1m 48.554s	1m 49.320s		
17	Felipe Nasr	1m 48.949s			
18	Esteban Ocon	1m 49.050s			
19	Daniil Kvyat	1m 49.058s			
20	Marcus Ericsson	1m 49.071s			
21	Lewis Hamilton	1m 50.033s			
22	Fernando Alonso	no time			

Photos: Peter J. Fox

FOR THE RECORD

1st GRAND PRIX: Esteban Ocon.

20th WIN: Nico Rosberg.

DID YOU KNOW?

Max Verstappen became the youngest driver to start on the front row. At 18 years and 333 days, he beat the record set by Ricardo Rodríguez in 1961. He was also the first Dutch driver to take a front-row start.

POINTS

DRIVERS

1	Lewis Hamilton	232
2	Nico Rosberg	223
3	Daniel Ricciardo	151
4	Sebastian Vettel	128
5	Kimi Räikkönen	124
6	Max Verstappen	115
7	Valtteri Bottas	62
8	Sergio Pérez	58
9	Nico Hülkenberg	45
10	Felipe Massa	39
11	Fernando Alonso	30
12	Carlos Sainz	30
13	Romain Grosjean	28
14	Daniil Kvyat	23
15	Jenson Button	17
16	Kevin Magnussen	6
17	Pascal Wehrlein	1
18	Stoffel Vandoorne	1

CONSTRUCTORS

1	Mercedes	455
2	Red Bull	274
3	Ferrari	252
4	Force India	103
5	Williams	101
6	McLaren	48
7	Toro Rosso	45
8	Haas	28
9	Renault	6
10	Manor	1

Qualifying: head-to-head

Rosberg	7	6	Hamilton
Vettel	8	5	Räikkönen
Massa	2	11	Bottas
Ricciardo	4	0	Kvyat
Ricciardo	7	2	Verstappen
Pérez	6	7	Hülkenberg
Magnussen	9	4	Palmer
Verstappen	3	1	Sainz
Kvyat	2	7	Sainz
Ericsson	7	6	Nasr
Alonso	8	4	Button
Button	0	1	Vandoorne
Haryanto	5	7	Wehrlein
Wehrlein	1	0	Ocon
Grosjean	9	4	Gutiérrez

10 · MASSA · Williams   8 · BOTTAS · Williams   6 · PÉREZ · Force India   4 · VETTEL · Ferrari   2 · VERSTAPPEN · Red Bull

9 · BUTTON · McLaren   7 · HÜLKENBERG · Force India   5 · RICCIARDO · Red Bull   3 · RÄIKKÖNEN · Ferrari   1 · ROSBERG · Mercedes

Lap chart

36	37	38	39	40	41	42	43	44	
6	6	6	6	6	6	6	6	6	1
3	3	3	3	3	3	3	3	3	2
44	44	44	44	44	44	44	44	44	3
27	27	27	27	27	27	27	27	27	4
11	11	11	11	11	11	11	11	11	5
5	5	5	5	5	5	5	5	5	6
14	14	14	14	14	14	14	14	14	7
19	19	19	19	19	77	77	77	77	8
77	77	77	77	77	19	7	7	7	9
7	7	7	7	7	7	19	19	19	10
33	33	33	33	33	33	33	33	33	
21	21	21	21	21	21	21	21	21	
8	8	8	8	8	8	8	8	8	
26	26	26	26	26	26	26	26	26	
30	30	30	30	30	30	30	30	30	
31	31	31	31	31	31	31	31		
12	12	12	12	12	12	12	12		

■ Safety car deployed on laps shown

▨ Race red-flagged

RACE TYRE STRATEGIES

PIRELLI

	Driver	Race Stint 1	Race Stint 2	Race Stint 3	Race Stint 4	Race Stint 5
1	Rosberg	Soft (u): 1-9	Medium (n): 10-26	Medium (n): 27-44		
2	Ricciardo	Soft (u): 1-9	Soft (u): 10-25	Medium (n): 26-44		
3	Hamilton	Medium (n): 1-9	Soft (n): 10-21	Soft (n): 22-32	Medium (u): 33-44	
4	Hülkenberg	Super-Soft (u): 1-6	Soft (u): 7-9	Soft (u): 10-23	Medium (n): 24-44	
5	Pérez	Super-Soft (u): 1-6	Soft (u): 7-9	Medium (n): 10-24	Medium (n): 25-44	
6	Vettel	Soft (u): 1	Soft (n): 2-9	Soft (u): 10-23	Medium (n): 24-44	
7	Alonso	Medium (n): 1-9	Soft (n): 10-23	Medium (n): 24-44		
8	Bottas	Super-Soft (u): 1-7	Soft (n): 8-9	Soft (n): 10-23	Medium (n): 24-44	
9	Räikkönen	Soft (u): 1	Super-Soft (u): 2-5	Soft (n): 6-9	Soft (u): 10-24	Medium (n): 25-44
10	Massa	Super-Soft (u): 1-2	Soft (n): 3-9	Soft (n): 10-22	Medium (n): 23-44	
11	Verstappen	Super-Soft (u): 1	Medium (n): 2-9	Medium (u): 10-16	Soft (u): 17-27	Soft (n): 28-44
12	Gutiérrez	Soft (n): 1-7	Soft (n): 8-9	Soft (u): 10-22	Medium (n): 23-44	
13	Grosjean	Soft (n): 1-6	Soft (n): 7-9	Soft (u): 10-23	Medium (n): 24-44	
14	Kvyat	Soft (n): 1-9	Soft (n): 10-21	Medium (n): 22-35	Super-Soft (u): 36-44	
15	Palmer	Soft (n): 1-6	Soft (n): 7-9	Soft (u): 10-22	Medium (n): 23-34	Super-Soft (n): 35-44
16	Ocon	Soft (n): 1-6	Medium (n): 7-9	Medium (n): 10-24	Medium (u): 25-43	
17	Nasr	Soft (n): 1	Medium (n): 2-9	Soft (n): 10-23	Medium (u): 24-43	
	Magnussen	Soft (n): 1-5 (dnf)				
	Ericsson	Soft (n): 1-3 (dnf)				
	Sainz	Soft (n): 1 (dnf)				
	Button	Super-Soft (u): 1 (dnf)				
	Wehrlein	Soft (n): 0 (dnf)				

The tyre regulations stipulate that at least two of three dry tyre specifications must be used during a dry race.
Pirelli P Zero logos are colour-coded on the tyre sidewalls: Red = Super-Soft; Yellow = Soft; White = Medium. (n) new (u) used

ITALIAN GRAND PRIX

MONZA CIRCUIT

MONZA QUALIFYING

GIVEN the emphasis on power and the usual Monza downforce trade-off, Mercedes were expected to dominate qualifying for the Italian Grand Prix. But no one had predicted that Lewis Hamilton would beat Nico Rosberg by almost half a second. Rosberg appeared as stunned as Hamilton was surprised.

That made it three pole positions in a row for Hamilton at Monza and his fifth for this race, putting the Englishman on a par with former champions Juan Manuel Fangio and Ayrton Senna. More important was a significant psychological advantage in the championship battle with Rosberg.

"Obviously I'm very happy," said Hamilton. "I feel incredibly honoured to have my name ranked along with Senna and Fangio; two great champions. This weekend, I've had a strong feeling, and during that pole lap, the car felt incredible, the lap was super-clean. The last corner [Parabolica] was definitely the best I've done it all weekend. It's very difficult to get the balance of the car perfect."

Hamilton's only error was to lock his brakes briefly and flat-spot the tyres he would have to use to start the race. (A further lap on another set would be spoiled by a brief moment at Parabolica.) "I had a small lock-up into Turn One," he said. "But the flat spot on the tyre is minimal and you can't really feel it. I'm not too worried about that."

Rosberg did not offer any excuses. "The car felt very good," he said. "My only problem is that Lewis did probably his best qualifying lap of the season – and that's it."

Detailed analysis would show that Hamilton had been stealing fractions all the way through the medium- to high-speed curves, from braking to higher mid-corner speed and a faster exit. It was particularly evident at Ascari, and the sum total of 0.478s blew Rosberg away in every sense.

The Mercedes in-house contest aside, the superiority of the W07 and its generous treatment of tyres meant that Hamilton and Rosberg had been able to get away with running (and therefore starting on) the soft tyre, whereas the rest had to resort to the super-soft in Q2 and consign themselves to two stops from the outset.

The home crowd at least had the consolation of seeing both Ferraris start from the second row, Sebastian Vettel having beaten Kimi Räikkönen with a storming lap and run wide at the final corner at the end of qualifying.

"I wasn't happy with my first lap," said Vettel. "I lost rhythm a bit, but I was able to get it back and went on the limit in the last corner. I'm very happy for Ferrari to lock out the second row, but not entirely happy with the gap ahead to Mercedes. But it's great to see so much support here; it's massive."

Ferrari had at least ensured an edge over Red Bull by incorporating the final three-token engine upgrade allowed for 2016 and combining the more potent power unit with an efficient low-downforce aero package.

This left Red Bull gasping, Daniel Ricciardo having urged the RB12 into an excellent fifth place, while Max Verstappen had to give best to an on-form Valtteri Bottas with what the Finn described as "one of my best qualifying laps ever". A Williams-Mercedes – albeit in the hands of Felipe Massa – was fastest through the speed trap at 357.6kph (222.2mph), but the Brazilian, in his final season in F1, had to make do with 11th fastest, after traffic on his out-lap meant that the Pirellis were not properly up to temperature.

Both Force India drivers and a Haas filled the gap between Bottas and Massa, Nico Hülkenberg having needed an extra run on the super-soft to ensure Q3, where he finished a couple of hundredths behind Sergio Pérez. Whereas the likes of Red Bull had not gone massively out of their way to produce a Monza aero special, Haas had invested much time in a low-downforce package, which, coupled with the upgraded Ferrari unit, lifted the American-entered car into Q3 for the first time. The fact that the extremely happy Esteban Gutiérrez was driving it did not go down well with Romain Grosjean, particularly when the *de facto* number one spun at Ascari because of a gearbox glitch, the subsequent box replacement adding to his woes with a penalty move from 11th to 17th on the tightly competitive grid.

Compromise at McLaren extended to trimming the rear wing even further than desirable for qualifying in the hope of being in good overtaking shape in the race, aided by having a more flexible tyre strategy based on the preferred single stop. As a result, Fernando Alonso and Jenson Button had few complaints about 13th and 15th.

The former champions were split by Pascal Wehrlein, after the young German had used Mercedes power to help him into Q2 for the third time. Gradually getting their revised act together, Manor had hoped to take advantage of Monza's high-speed demands, but their effort was diluted by a succession of difficult-to-trace electrical problems for the unfortunate Esteban Ocon, sidelined yet again before he could complete a single timed qualifying lap.

Conversely, Toro Rosso pitched up at Monza in the knowledge that undeveloped 2015 Ferrari power amounted to having one hand tied behind their back, Carlos Sainz having done well to make it through to Q2, the 0.15s difference to Daniil Kvyat crossing the divide from Q1. Felipe Nasr was marginally faster than Marcus Ericsson, in 18th and 19th respectively, and ahead of the Renaults, as high drag and a shortage of top-end power were the last things Jolyon Palmer and Kevin Magnussen needed. Magnussen tried so hard that he had a huge moment exiting Ascari. If nothing else, his mistake highlighted Palmer's clean performance, but the three-second gap to the front of the grid signalled that a large part of the race would be spent obeying blue flags – assuming the yellow cars got that far.

Above: Felipe Massa announces that he will retire as a Formula 1 driver at the end of the season.
Photo: WRi2/Jean-François Galeron

Top left: Hamilton supporters were out in force at Monza.

Above left: Carlos Sainz did well to put his underpowered Toro Rosso into Q2.
Photo: Peter J. Fox

Top: New sponsors Heineken arranged a five-a-side football match on the main straight. Fernando Alonso certainly looked the part.
Photo: GP Photo/Peter Nygaard

Left: Classic Monza light as Daniel Ricciardo looks for every ounce of speed from his Red Bull. Notice the narrowness of the track.
Photo: Red Bull Racing/Getty Images

Opposite page: On soft Pirellis, Lewis Hamilton was on scintillating form in qualifying. The Englishman comfortably took pole position.
Photo: Mercedes AMG Petronas F1 Team

Opening spread: Winner Nico Rosberg jumps for joy as the traditional Monza track invasion takes place beneath the podium.
Photo: Peter J. Fox

Above: Lewis Hamilton's poor start resulted in him being swallowed up by the pack as the field negotiated the first chicane.
Photo: GP Photo/Peter Nygaard

Top right: Heading for trouble. Jolyon Palmer and Felipe Nasr just before they collided, eliminating themselves from the race.
Photo: Renault Sport F1 Team

Above right: Sergio Pérez gained more valuable points for Force India in their battle with Williams for the constructors' honours.
Photo: Sahara Force India F1 Team

Right: The Ferraris of Vettel and Räikkönen give chase to Rosberg on the opening lap.
Photo: WRi2/Bryn Williams

THERE was every reason to justify F1 agreeing another three-year deal for the Italian Grand Prix to continue at Monza. As the cars rolled on to the grid on a glorious September afternoon, a much larger crowd than usual waited in anticipation of at least one Ferrari taking advantage of any problems for Mercedes during the 620m dash to the first chicane. And not for the first time in the season, there would indeed be difficulties at the start for a silver car.

Having warmed his soft tyres nicely on the parade lap (in anticipation of the Ferraris' super-softs providing better initial grip), Hamilton released the single clutch in the prescribed manner, only for it to over-engage, spin the wheels and send the revs into an upward spiral. The championship leader was quickly engulfed by both Ferraris, while Bottas and Ricciardo also had grabbed their opportunity by the time the leaders hit the brakes for the Rettifilio chicane.

In fact, once Vettel had ducked around Hamilton, he had felt enough momentum to take a serious look at challenging Rosberg as they pulled through the gears and accelerated hard, the Mercedes driver staying calm and maintaining the lead he had hoped for, but hadn't really expected.

Hamilton's feelings were diametrically opposed as he immediately realised his chances of winning had been heavily compromised, if not wiped out altogether. Sixth at the end of the first lap, 3.5 seconds behind Rosberg, was not where he needed to be. It mattered little that he was already edging ahead of Pérez, Massa, Alonso and Hülkenberg.

Any fears that the first three rows of the grid might have Verstappen flying over the top of them into the first chicane had been calmed by the Red Bull dropping back to 11th, thanks to the anti-stall kicking in at the start. Gutiérrez was just as frustrated, a slow getaway having dropped the Haas to the back. The Mexican only had Ocon and Button behind him. The McLaren's presence was explained by a number of incidents, triggered by Massa forcing Alonso into evasive

action, which had the knock-on effect of sending Button into the escape road. After he emerged, further overcrowding pushed him into the gravel at the Lesmos and down to last place. Massa was not yet done, however, a kerb-jumping moment at Lesmo forcing Hülkenberg wide and allowing Alonso through.

Button's only good fortune – if you could call it that – came on the second lap, when he moved up a couple of places after Nasr got out of shape through the Rettifilio chicane and collected the hapless Palmer. The Renault was forced to retire, Palmer's fury later multiplied by Nasr, having seemingly retired, too, choosing to continue to take the ten-second penalty handed down for causing the accident in the first place.

As Rosberg pulled clear of the DRS threat, it was obvious to the pursuing Vettel that only misfortune of some sort would prevent his fellow countryman from winning. That was not to say, however, that Hamilton had given up hope of at least getting into a position where he might be able to attack in the event of a problem. A fast and clean exit from the first chicane on the second lap allowed him to run around the outside of Ricciardo through Curve Grande and take fifth.

Bottas was half a second ahead, but a much more difficult proposition thanks to Mercedes power and excellent straight-line speed. If anything, the gap between the Williams and the Mercedes increased initially, along with Hamilton's feeling of helplessness as Rosberg stretched his lead to 11 seconds in ten laps. Given the super-soft strategies employed by the cars in front of Hamilton, it was clear that the Ferraris and the Williams would be stopping sooner rather than later. But Lewis could not afford to wait and, at the start of lap 11, pulled a DRS move on Bottas going into the chicane.

As the race settled down, it became clear that the Red Bull was not taking as much out of the rear super-softs as the Williams, Ricciardo moving into a threatening position on Bottas while, three places further back, Verstappen was

doing the same to Massa. The Red Bull had earlier dispensed with Hülkenberg and Alonso as Max used DRS and his now familiar confident late braking to make up for the slow start.

It was no surprise that Williams blinked first, Bottas being brought in at the end of lap 13, given the threat of the undercut by Ricciardo. There was no danger of that as the new softs on the Williams gave Bottas enough pace to prompt Red Bull to keep Ricciardo out for three more laps, the better to shuffle the pit stops towards a shorter final stint on the super-soft. The Williams plan worked against Massa, however, who was unable to come in because of the priority given to Bottas and who stayed out for an extra three laps while aiming for a one-stop. Watching all of this, Red Bull had brought in Verstappen at the end of lap 13 and sent him out to go after Pérez and be clear of Massa once the Williams had stopped.

There was never likely to be much threat to Rosberg's lead as the Ferraris were brought in (Räikkönen on lap 15; Vettel a lap later) for another set of super-softs. This allowed Hamilton to move into second.

Rosberg was 14.8s down the road. Having worked his soft tyres as much as he dared while fighting through the field, Hamilton knew he would be no match for his team-mate, who had been untroubled at the front. There was no point in observers applying Hamilton's half-second advantage seen during qualifying. It was wishful thinking on the part of anyone hoping for a decent race. The tyres simply would not let Hamilton utilise his inherent skill.

"When they told me I was 15s down, I knew I wasn't going to be able to catch Nico," said Lewis. "Maybe if the gap behind had been six seconds. But 15? No way. Even if I had closed the gap, there's no way I'd have had the tyres to pass. If we had better grip, yes, I could have done qualifying laps lap after lap. That would be great. But it hasn't been like that for a long time." Welcome to F1 in the tyre-limited era. It killed this race stone dead.

Above: It might have only been third place, but no doubt Sebastian Vettel was relieved to make his first visit to the podium since Baku.
Photo: WRi2/Bryn Williams

Above right: Keeping everybody happy. Stoffel Vandoorne, Ron Dennis and Jenson Button at the announcement of the British driver's planned sabbatical for 2017.
Photo: McLaren Honda

Right: Even on super-softs, Valtteri Bottas could not hold off the advance of Lewis Hamilton on his softs. The Finn did claim a solid sixth place for Williams, however.
Photo: WRi2/Bryn Williams

When Rosberg made his single stop just before half-distance, he rejoined on the medium, the hardest tyre available. Hamilton was given the same when he came in a lap later. He may have been behind the Ferraris once more, but the knowledge that the red cars were due to stop did not prevent the racer in Hamilton from seeing what was possible. When Vettel and Räikkönen left the way clear on lap 34, Rosberg was 11 seconds ahead. Pushing hard and consistently running close to his personal best lap set on fresh tyres, the Englishman narrowed the gap to 10.5s. But that was all she wrote. And Rosberg, carefully commanding this race, knew it.

Entertainment would have to be sought elsewhere in a field that had only four retirements, Wehrlein having joined Palmer and Nasr with a lack of oil pressure, followed by Kvyat with an overheated battery, possibly caused by floor damage sustained across a kerb on the first lap. Pérez and Verstappen had swapped places back and forth as their different two-stop strategies played out, Verstappen getting the upper hand thanks to a shorter final stint on the soft and taking seventh place on lap 48.

It was a similar story in the Bottas/Ricciardo battle, the late stop for super-softs serving the Red Bull well, as Ricciardo took fifth place on lap 47. But that straightforward description of a position change does not do justice to one of the best overtaking moves of the season. Ricciardo had come from a long, long way back and nailed Bottas with a piece of outbraking that was exquisitely timed and without wheel-locking drama.

Tyre care would play a significant part in the finishing order

at McLaren. Putting his head down after the first-lap delay and making the most of the super-soft, Button had sliced through the field, holding 12th place at the time of his first stop for softs on lap 15. He had rejoined a couple of places behind Alonso, the pair of them planning a late stop and final run on used super-softs. Even allowing for Alonso having been delayed slightly at his stop, Button not only reduced the deficit, but also ran longer in the middle stint, the better to be able to use the super-soft. Alonso couldn't manage it and had to stop early for softs. It was classic Button territory, the pity being that 12th place would be the only reward. Alonso finished 14th, relieving his frustration by making a late stop for the super-soft with the sole intention of amusing himself by setting fastest lap of the race with 12 laps to go.

Button had chased down Grosjean in the closing stages, failing by less than a second to take 11th, the same applying to the gap between Grosjean, Hülkenberg and a place in the points. It had been a disappointing day for Haas all round, Gutiérriez having recovered well, but nevertheless disappointed with 13th. He had got the better of Sainz when Toro Rosso failed to make a one-stop strategy work for the Spaniard, a similar ambitious, but failed, plan by Sauber resulting in 16th for Ericsson, half a minute ahead of the struggling Magnussen. Ocon, learning as he went, was a further lap down at the end of a difficult weekend.

That put the novice two laps behind Rosberg, who, in reality, had won this rather dull encounter within seconds of the start 78 minutes earlier. A result he would have found hard to envisage just 24 hours earlier...

Maurice Hamilton

VIEWPOINT
A GOOD SOLUTION FOR JB?

AFTER Felipe Massa announced on Thursday afternoon in Monza that he would be calling time on his F1 career at the end of the season, the world's press assembled at McLaren Honda on Saturday afternoon to see what Jenson Button was up to.

Simply, there was no room at the inn. Fernando Alonso was under contract for 2017, and already twiddling his thumbs for a year had been reigning GP2 champion and one of the sport's great young talents, Stoffel Vandoorne. It was no surprise to anybody when the team revealed that the Belgian would partner Alonso for the new season.

Jenson, however, was under contract to McLaren for the next two years. He would attend a number of races in 2017 and act as a McLaren Honda ambassador. Furthermore, the team had an option on him for 2018.

For some, however, that was an unsatisfactory conclusion, leaving Button hanging in the air somewhat.

He, though, seemed entirely happy with the situation, and you could see why. At the end of the season, he would have 305 GPs under his belt, only one shy of Michael Schumacher's total and 17 less than Rubens Barrichello, the only other two drivers in history to reach the 300 mark.

"I love what I do, it's the best job in the world, but it's been intense and it's been 17 years. Like anything, you get tired. I want to see a bit of my family, and there are things I want to do. Will I find I miss it too much? Possibly, but it's time for some 'me' time."

Button is a sponsor's dream, and it would have made no sense to push him out of the door. Neither is he past it, either mentally or physically, despite admitting to being a little tired. Before he spoke, he'd just lapped Monza nip and tuck with Alonso.

His love of triathlons means that, physically, he's more 26 than 36, but he wants to have a proper go at it and he recognises he's getting to the upper age range to do so.

And what if, in 2017, the McLaren-Honda is quick, Vandoorne performs impressively alongside Alonso and the Spaniard wants squillions to extend? Having Button under option is a good move for both Jenson and the team.

Tony Dodgins

14

2016 FORMULA 1
GRAN PREMIO
HEINEKEN
D'ITALIA

MONZA 2–4 SEPTEMBER

RACE DISTANCE: 53 laps, 190.587 miles/306.720km

RACE WEATHER: Dry/sunny (track 35–40°C, air 29–30°C)

AUTODROMO NAZIONALE DI MONZA

Circuit: 3.600 miles/5.793km, 53 laps

Lesmo 2 200/124
Lesmo 1 175/109
Curva del Serraglio 300/186
Seconda Variante 125/78
Curva Vialone 175/109
Variante Ascari 180/112
335/208
Prima Variante 70/43
Curva Biassono 305/190
Rettifilo Tribune 335/208
Curva Parabolica 250/155

187/116 kmh/mph 🔧 Gear ▬ DRS zone

RACE – OFFICIAL CLASSIFICATION

Pos.	Driver	Nat.	No.	Entrant	Car/Engine	Tyres	Laps	Time/Retirement	Speed (mph/km/h)	Gap to leader	Fastest race lap	
1	**Nico Rosberg**	D	6	Mercedes AMG Petronas F1 Team	Mercedes F1 W07-Mercedes PU106C V6	P	53	1h 17m 28.089s	147.612/237.558		1m 26.599s	26
2	**Lewis Hamilton**	GB	44	Mercedes AMG Petronas F1 Team	Mercedes F1 W07-Mercedes PU106C V6	P	53	1h 17m 43.159s	147.134/236.790	15.070s	1m 26.303s	27
3	**Sebastian Vettel**	D	5	Scuderia Ferrari	Ferrari SF15-H-059/5 V6	P	53	1h 17m 49.079s	146.948/236.490	20.990s	1m 26.310s	48
4	**Kimi Räikkönen**	FIN	7	Scuderia Ferrari	Ferrari SF16-H-059/5 V6	P	53	1h 17m 55.650s	146.741/236.157	27.561s	1m 26.016s	50
5	**Daniel Ricciardo**	AUS	3	Red Bull Racing	Red Bull RB12-TAG Heuer RB12 V6	P	53	1h 18m 18.384s	146.187/235.265	45.295s	1m 25.919s	52
6	**Valtteri Bottas**	FIN	77	Williams Martini Racing	Williams FW38-Mercedes PU106C V6	P	53	1h 18m 19.104s	146.009/234.979	51.015s	1m 26.708s	46
7	**Max Verstappen**	NL	33	Red Bull Racing	Red Bull RB12-TAG Heuer RB12 V6	P	53	1h 18m 22.325s	145.909/234.818	54.236s	1m 26.405s	50
8	**Sergio Pérez**	MEX	11	Sahara Force India F1 Team	Force India VJM09-Mercedes PU106C V6	P	53	1h 18m 33.043s	145.577/234.284	1m 04.954s	1m 26.920s	40
9	**Felipe Massa**	BR	19	Williams Martini Racing	Williams FW38-Mercedes PU106C V6	P	53	1h 18m 33.706s	145.557/234.251	1m 05.617s	1m 26.400s	50
10	**Nico Hülkenberg**	D	27	Sahara Force India F1 Team	Force India VJM09-Mercedes PU106C V6	P	53	1h 18m 46.745s	145.155/233.605	1m 18.656s	1m 26.954s	40
11	Romain Grosjean	F	8	Haas F1 Team	Haas VF-16-Ferrari 059/5 V6	P	52			1 lap	1m 27.227s	50
12	Jenson Button	GB	22	McLaren Honda	McLaren MP4-31-Honda RA616H V6	P	52			1 lap	1m 26.354s	40
13	Esteban Gutiérrez	MEX	21	Haas F1 Team	Haas VF-16-Ferrari 059/5 V6	P	52			1 lap	1m 27.106s	42
14	Fernando Alonso	E	14	McLaren Honda	McLaren MP4-31-Honda RA616H V6	P	52			1 lap	1m 25.340s	51
15	Carlos Sainz	E	55	Scuderia Toro Rosso	Toro Rosso STR11-Ferrari 059/4 V6	P	52			1 lap	1m 26.751s	41
16	Marcus Ericsson	S	9	Sauber F1 Team	Sauber C35-Ferrari 059/5 V6	P	52			1 lap	1m 28.552s	37
17	Kevin Magnussen	DK	20	Renault Sport F1 Team	Renault R.S.16-R.E.16 V6	P	52			1 lap	1m 27.618s	52
18	Esteban Ocon	F	31	Manor Racing MRT	Manor MRT05-Mercedes PU106C V6	P	51			2 laps	1m 28.534s	51
	Daniil Kvyat	RUS	26	Scuderia Toro Rosso	Toro Rosso STR11-Ferrari 059/4 V6	P	36	floor damage/battery overheating			1m 28.037s	35
	Pascal Wehrlein	D	94	Manor Racing MRT	Manor MRT05-Mercedes PU106C V6	P	26	oil pressure			1m 28.723s	18
	Jolyon Palmer	GB	30	Renault Sport F1 Team	Renault R.S.16-R.E.16 V6	P	7	accident damage			1m 31.361s	4
	Felipe Nasr	BR	12	Sauber F1 Team	Sauber C35-Ferrari 059/5 V6	P	6	accident damage			no time	

Fastest race lap: Fernando Alonso on lap 51, 1m 25.340s, 151.846mph/244.373km/h.

Lap record: Rubens Barrichello (Ferrari F2004 V10), 1m 21.046s, 159.892mph/257.320km/h (2004).

All results and data © FOM 2016

21 · MAGNUSSEN · Renault

19 · ERICSSON · Sauber

17 · GROSJEAN · Haas
(5-place grid penalty for replacing the gearbox)

15 · SAINZ · Toro Rosso

13 · WEHRLEIN · Manor

11 · MASSA · Williams

22 · OCON · Manor
(5-place grid penalty for replacing the gearbox)

20 · PALMER · Renault

18 · NASR · Sauber

16 · KVYAT · Toro Rosso

14 · BUTTON · McLaren

12 · ALONSO · McLaren

Grid order	1	2	3	4	5	6	7	8	9	10	11	12	13	14	15	16	17	18	19	20	21	22	23	24	25	26	27	28	29	30	31	32	33	34	35	36	37	38	39	40	41	42
44 HAMILTON	6	6	6	6	6	6	6	6	6	6	6	6	6	6	6	6	6	6	6	6	6	6	6	6	44	6	6	6	6	6	6	6	6	6	6	6	6	6	6	6	6	6
6 ROSBERG	5	5	5	5	5	5	5	5	5	5	5	5	5	5	5	44	44	44	44	44	44	44	44	44	6	5	5	5	5	5	5	7	44	44	44	44	44	44	44	44	44	44
5 VETTEL	7	7	7	7	7	7	7	7	7	7	7	7	7	7	44	7	5	5	5	5	5	5	5	5	5	7	7	7	7	7	7	5	7	3	3	5	5	5	5	5	5	5
7 RÄIKKÖNEN	77	77	77	77	77	77	77	77	77	77	77	44	44	44	44	7	3	7	7	7	7	7	7	7	44	44	44	44	44	44	44	3	5	5	5	3	7	7	7	7	7	7
77 BOTTAS	3	44	44	44	44	44	44	44	44	44	77	77	3	3	3	19	8	8	77	77	77	77	77	77	77	77	77	77	77	3	3	3	5	7	7	7	77	77	77	77	77	77
3 RICCIARDO	44	3	3	3	3	3	3	3	3	3	3	11	11	11	7	77	77	3	3	3	3	3	3	3	3	77	33	33	33	33	33	77	77	3	3	3	3
33 VERSTAPPEN	11	11	11	11	11	11	11	11	11	11	11	77	19	19	8	3	8	8	8	11	11	11	11	11	33	33	33	19	19	19	19	19	11	11	11	11	11	11
11 PÉREZ	19	19	19	19	19	19	19	19	19	19	19	19	8	77	11	11	11	11	11	33	33	33	33	33	11	19	19	27	27	77	77	11	33	33	33	33	33
27 HÜLKENBERG	14	14	14	14	14	14	14	14	33	33	33	33	8	8	19	19	19	27	27	77	77	11	11	33	22	19	19	19	19
21 GUTIÉRREZ	27	27	27	33	33	33	14	14	14	14	14	33	94	77	11	33	33	19	19	19	19	8	8	27	27	14	14	11	11	22	22	22	19	22	27	27	27
19 MASSA	33	33	33	33	27	27	27	27	27	27	27	14	55	55	94	19	19	55	55	27	27	27	27	8	8	14	14	11	11	11	14	22	27	27	27	27	8	8	8
14 ALONSO	94	8	8	8	8	8	8	8	8	8	8	8	22	22	9	9	27	27	55	14	14	14	14	14	8	22	22	22	14	8	8	8	8	14	14	14	14
94 WEHRLEIN	8	94	94	94	94	94	94	94	94	94	94	77	9	33	27	9	14	14	55	55	22	22	22	22	21	21	21	21	21	14	14	14	22	22	22
22 BUTTON	55	55	55	55	55	55	55	55	55	55	55	9	21	27	14	14	9	9	22	94	94	21	8	8	8	14	55	55	55	55	21	21	21
55 SAINZ	26	26	26	26	26	26	26	26	26	22	55	22	22	33	14	31	22	22	9	21	21	55	55	55	55	55	9	21	21	21	9	9	55
26 KVYAT	12	20	20	20	20	20	9	22	26	26	26	9	33	31	21	22	31	31	94	94	94	31	55	55	26	26	26	26	9	9	21	9	9	9	55	55	9
8 GROSJEAN	30	9	9	9	9	9	22	9	9	9	9	21	14	14	31	94	94	94	31	31	21	21	55	21	9	9	9	9	26	26	26	26	20	20	20	20	20
12 NASR	20	21	21	21	21	22	21	21	21	21	21	26	31	21	22	26	21	21	31	31	26	9	20	20	20	20	20	20	31	20	20	20	31	31	31	31	31
9 ERICSSON	9	22	22	22	22	21	31	20	20	20	20	20	26	31	26	26	21	26	26	26	9	9	31	31	31	31	20	31	31	31
30 PALMER	21	31	31	31	31	31	31	31	31	31	31	31	26	31	31	26	20	20	20	20	20	20	20
20 MAGNUSSEN	31	30	30	30	30	30	30	
31 OCON	22	12	12	12	12	12	

TIME SHEETS

PRACTICE 1 (FRIDAY)
Weather: Dry/sunny
Temperatures: track 29–35°C, air 26–28°C

Pos.	Driver	Laps	Time
1	Nico Rosberg	37	1m 22.959s
2	Lewis Hamilton	36	1m 23.162s
3	Kimi Räikkönen	16	1m 24.047s
4	Sebastian Vettel	17	1m 24.307s
5	Sergio Pérez	32	1m 24.650s
6	Romain Grosjean	17	1m 24.763s
7	Valtteri Bottas	37	1m 24.785s
8	Max Verstappen	25	1m 24.982s
9	Esteban Gutiérrez	19	1m 25.113s
10	Daniel Ricciardo	17	1m 25.120s
11	Jenson Button	23	1m 25.351s
12	Alfonso Celis	30	1m 25.367s
13	Fernando Alonso	14	1m 25.507s
14	Felipe Massa	18	1m 25.840s
15	Marcus Ericsson	20	1m 25.853s
16	Carlos Sainz	20	1m 25.973s
17	Daniil Kvyat	20	1m 26.074s
18	Esteban Ocon	30	1m 26.391s
19	Felipe Nasr	21	1m 26.439s
20	Pascal Wehrlein	28	1m 26.762s
21	Jolyon Palmer	35	1m 26.811s
22	Kevin Magnussen	32	1m 26.956s

PRACTICE 2 (FRIDAY)
Weather: Dry/sunny
Temperatures: track 40–43°C, air 29–31°C

Pos.	Driver	Laps	Time
1	Lewis Hamilton	40	1m 22.801s
2	Nico Rosberg	42	1m 22.994s
3	Sebastian Vettel	33	1m 23.254s
4	Kimi Räikkönen	28	1m 23.427s
5	Max Verstappen	25	1m 23.732s
6	Daniel Ricciardo	33	1m 24.003s
7	Fernando Alonso	24	1m 24.259s
8	Valtteri Bottas	41	1m 24.299s
9	Romain Grosjean	35	1m 24.516s
10	Jenson Button	28	1m 24.549s
11	Felipe Massa	20	1m 24.556s
12	Nico Hülkenberg	40	1m 24.587s
13	Sergio Pérez	42	1m 24.653s
14	Esteban Gutiérrez	33	1m 24.674s
15	Marcus Ericsson	25	1m 24.981s
16	Pascal Wehrlein	38	1m 25.083s
17	Carlos Sainz	31	1m 25.240s
18	Esteban Ocon	13	1m 25.275s
19	Kevin Magnussen	39	1m 25.555s
20	Daniil Kvyat	33	1m 25.614s
21	Felipe Nasr	31	1m 25.643s
22	Jolyon Palmer	45	1m 25.833s

PRACTICE 3 (SATURDAY)
Weather: Dry/sunny
Temperatures: track 33°C, air 27°C

Pos.	Driver	Laps	Time
1	Lewis Hamilton	14	1m 22.008s
2	Nico Rosberg	17	1m 22.401s
3	Sebastian Vettel	13	1m 22.946s
4	Kimi Räikkönen	12	1m 23.149s
5	Valtteri Bottas	20	1m 23.500s
6	Felipe Massa	19	1m 23.647s
7	Daniel Ricciardo	23	1m 23.709s
8	Max Verstappen	21	1m 23.740s
9	Sergio Pérez	20	1m 23.917s
10	Esteban Gutiérrez	15	1m 24.034s
11	Nico Hülkenberg	21	1m 24.041s
12	Jenson Button	11	1m 24.104s
13	Carlos Sainz	17	1m 24.240s
14	Romain Grosjean	4	1m 24.463s
15	Jolyon Palmer	13	1m 24.533s
16	Marcus Ericsson	20	1m 24.542s
17	Fernando Alonso	12	1m 24.658s
18	Felipe Nasr	19	1m 24.715s
19	Kevin Magnussen	12	1m 24.793s
20	Daniil Kvyat	17	1m 24.845s
21	Pascal Wehrlein	19	1m 24.893s
22	Esteban Ocon	15	1m 24.938s

QUALIFYING (SATURDAY)
Weather: Dry/sunny Temperatures: track 38–42°C, air 30–31°C

Pos.	Driver	First	Second	Third	Qualifying Tyre
1	Lewis Hamilton	1m 21.854s	1m 21.498s	1m 21.135s	Super-Soft (new)
2	Nico Rosberg	1m 22.497s	1m 21.809s	1m 21.613s	Super-Soft (new)
3	Sebastian Vettel	1m 23.077s	1m 22.275s	1m 21.972s	Super-Soft (new)
4	Kimi Räikkönen	1m 23.217s	1m 22.568s	1m 22.065s	Super-Soft (new)
5	Valtteri Bottas	1m 23.264s	1m 22.499s	1m 22.388s	Super-Soft (new)
6	Daniel Ricciardo	1m 23.158s	1m 22.638s	1m 22.389s	Super-Soft (new)
7	Max Verstappen	1m 23.229s	1m 22.857s	1m 22.411s	Super-Soft (new)
8	Sergio Pérez	1m 23.439s	1m 22.922s	1m 22.814s	Super-Soft (new)
9	Nico Hülkenberg	1m 23.259s	1m 22.951s	1m 22.836s	Super-Soft (new)
10	Esteban Gutiérrez	1m 23.386s	1m 22.856s	1m 23.184s	Super-Soft (new)
11	Felipe Massa	1m 23.489s	1m 22.967s		
12	Romain Grosjean	1m 23.421s	1m 23.092s		
13	Fernando Alonso	1m 23.783s	1m 23.273s		
14	Pascal Wehrlein	1m 23.760s	1m 23.315s		
15	Jenson Button	1m 23.666s	1m 23.399s		
16	Carlos Sainz	1m 23.661s	1m 23.496s		
17	Daniil Kvyat	1m 23.825s			
18	Felipe Nasr	1m 23.956s			
19	Marcus Ericsson	1m 24.087s			
20	Jolyon Palmer	1m 24.230s			
21	Kevin Magnussen	1m 24.436s			
22	Esteban Ocon	no time			

FOR THE RECORD

50th GRAND PRIX START: Daniil Kvyat.

50th PODIUM POSITION: Nico Rosberg.

DID YOU KNOW?

Alonso's fastest lap was the first for a Honda engine since Senna in Portugal, 1992.

POINTS

DRIVERS

1	Lewis Hamilton	250
2	Nico Rosberg	248
3	Daniel Ricciardo	161
4	Sebastian Vettel	143
5	Kimi Räikkönen	136
6	Max Verstappen	121
7	Valtteri Bottas	70
8	Sergio Pérez	62
9	Nico Hülkenberg	46
10	Felipe Massa	41
11	Fernando Alonso	30
12	Carlos Sainz	30
13	Romain Grosjean	28
14	Daniil Kvyat	23
15	Jenson Button	17
16	Kevin Magnussen	6
17	Pascal Wehrlein	1
18	Stoffel Vandoorne	1

CONSTRUCTORS

1	Mercedes	498
2	Red Bull	290
3	Ferrari	279
4	Williams	111
5	Force India	103
6	McLaren	48
7	Toro Rosso	45
8	Haas	28
9	Renault	6
10	Manor	1

Photo: Bryn Williams

9 · HÜLKENBERG · Force India

7 · VERSTAPPEN · Red Bull

5 · BOTTAS · Williams

3 · VETTEL · Ferrari

1 · HAMILTON · Mercedes

10 · GUTIÉRREZ · Haas

8 · PÉREZ · Force India

6 · RICCIARDO · Red Bull

4 · RÄIKKÖNEN · Ferrari

2 · ROSBERG · Mercedes

Qualifying: head-to-head

Rosberg	7	7	Hamilton
Vettel	9	5	Räikkönen
Massa	2	12	Bottas
Ricciardo	4	0	Kvyat
Ricciardo	8	2	Verstappen
Pérez	7	7	Hülkenberg
Magnussen	9	5	Palmer
Verstappen	3	1	Sainz
Kvyat	2	8	Sainz
Ericsson	7	7	Nasr
Alonso	9	4	Button
Button	0	1	Vandoorne
Haryanto	5	7	Wehrlein
Wehrlein	2	0	Ocon
Grosjean	9	5	Gutiérrez

(Lap chart columns 43–53)

43	44	45	46	47	48	49	50	51	52	53	
6	6	6	6	6	6	6	6	6	6	6	1
44	44	44	44	44	44	44	44	44	44	44	2
5	5	5	5	5	5	5	5	5	5	5	3
7	7	7	7	7	7	7	7	7	7	7	4
77	77	77	77	3	3	3	3	3	3	3	5
3	3	3	3	77	77	77	77	77	77	77	6
11	11	11	11	11	33	33	33	33	33	33	7
33	33	33	33	33	11	11	11	11	11	11	8
19	19	19	19	19	19	19	19	19	19	19	9
27	27	27	27	27	27	27	27	27	27	27	10
8	8	8	8	8	8	8	8	8			
14	22	22	22	22	22	22	22	22	22		
22	14	14	14	14	14	14	21	21	21		
21	21	21	21	21	21	21	14	14	14		
55	55	55	55	55	55	55	55	55	55		
9	9	9	9	9	9	9	9	9			
20	20	20	20	20	20	20	20	20			
31	31	31	31	31	31	31	31	31			

6 = Pit stop   9 = Drive-thru penalty

94 = One lap or more behind

RACE TYRE STRATEGIES

PIRELLI

	Driver	Race Stint 1	Race Stint 2	Race Stint 3	Race Stint 4
1	Rosberg	Soft (u): 1-24	Medium (n): 25-53		
2	Hamilton	Soft (u): 1-25	Medium (n): 26-53		
3	Vettel	Super-Soft (u): 1-16	Super-Soft (u): 17-33	Soft (n): 34-53	
4	Räikkönen	Super-Soft (u): 1-15	Super-Soft (u): 16-34	Soft (n): 35-53	
5	Ricciardo	Super-Soft (u): 1-16	Soft (n): 17-37	Super-Soft (u): 38-53	
6	Bottas	Super-Soft (u): 1-13	Soft (n): 14-30	Soft (n): 31-53	
7	Verstappen	Super-Soft (u): 1-13	Soft (n): 14-35	Soft (n): 36-53	
8	Pérez	Super-Soft (u): 1-15	Soft (n): 16-28	Soft (n): 29-53	
9	Massa	Soft (n): 1-16	Soft (n): 17-36	Super-Soft (n): 37-53	
10	Hülkenberg	Super-Soft (u): 1-14	Soft (n): 15-33	Soft (n): 34-53	
11	Grosjean	Soft (n): 1-28	Super-Soft (n): 29-52		
12	Button	Super-Soft (n): 1-15	Soft (n): 16-38	Super-Soft (u): 39-52	
13	Gutiérrez	Super-Soft (n): 1-16	Soft (n): 17-34	Super-Soft (n): 35-52	
14	Alonso	Super-Soft (n): 1-13	Soft (n): 14-33	Soft (n): 34-49	Super-Soft (u): 50-52
15	Sainz	Soft (n): 1-23	Super-Soft (n): 24-39	Super-Soft (n): 40-52	
16	Ericsson	Soft (n): 1-23	Medium (n): 24-52		
17	Magnussen	Super-Soft (n): 1-14	Soft (n): 15-30	Soft (n): 31-52	
18	Ocon	Medium (n): 1-32	Soft (n): 33-51		
	Kvyat	Super-Soft (n): 1-13	Soft (n): 14-33	Super-Soft (n): 34-36 (dnf)	
	Wehrlein	Soft (n): 1-16	Medium (u): 17-26 (dnf)		
	Palmer	Soft (n): 1-2	Medium (n): 3-7 (dnf)		
	Nasr	Soft (n): 1-2	Medium (n): 3-4	Soft (n): 5	Soft (u): 6 (dnf)

The tyre regulations stipulate that at least two of three dry tyre specifications must be used during a dry race.
Pirelli P Zero logos are colour-coded on the tyre sidewalls: Red = Super-Soft; Yellow = Soft; White = Medium. (n) new (u) used

Photo: Scuderia Ferrari

Photo: Peter J. Fox

ROLEX

ROLEX

FIA FORMULA 1 WORLD CHAMPIONSHIP · ROUND 15

SINGAPORE GRAND PRIX

MARINA BAY CIRCUIT

Nico Rosberg's fighting comeback
continued apace in Singapore, where
he overtook Lewis Hamilton at the top
of the drivers' championship.
Photo: WRi2/Jad Sherif

MARINA BAY QUALIFYING

THE Singapore GP, now an iconic event, dates back to 2008, but arriving at Marina Bay for the ninth time, only three drivers had won it: Sebastian Vettel four times; Lewis Hamilton and Fernando Alonso twice each. The pole-position roll of honour was dominated by the same three names, plus Felipe Massa in the inaugural 2008 race.

Nico Rosberg, though, had always gone well at the track, notwithstanding the anomalous Mercedes performance in 2015, and would have been in the frame to win it in '08 for Williams but for the 'creative' use of Nelson Piquet Jr by Renault.

This time, Rosberg produced a stupendous qualifying lap (1m 42.584s) – "one of the three best of my career" – to take pole by over half a second.

And this time, the man closest to him was not team-mate Lewis Hamilton, but Daniel Ricciardo who, while having not quite matched his Monaco pole position, did manage to put a Red Bull on the front row of the grid, albeit 0.53s adrift.

With the ultra-soft, super-soft and soft being Pirelli's tyre compounds of choice for Singapore, it was interesting that Ricciardo and team-mate Max Verstappen, who qualified fourth, comfortably cleared Q2 on the super-soft. They were the only drivers to attempt to do so, and thus would start the race on the red-walled tyre, which was reckoned to be good for an additional five laps over the ultra-soft.

That, you figured, would only afford Red Bull an advantage if they could win the start and control the pace, possibly using the second car to force Mercedes into an early stop and drop them back into traffic.

Hamilton, after his imperious Saturday at Monza a fortnight earlier, unusually was not on Rosberg's qualifying pace around Marina Bay, his on-track performance putting you more in mind of Baku. He lost much of Friday's FP2 running to a hydraulic issue, and at other times, the car appeared to be sparking more than anyone else's as the underside hit the deck, and there were lock-ups and missed apices. By contrast, Rosberg's progress was relatively serene, notwithstanding a minor straight-on moment that took the front wing off at T18 in FP1 on Friday. Lewis ended up third, 0.17s behind Ricciardo's second Q3 run and just 0.04s clear of Verstappen.

The young Dutchman was disappointed with fourth, complaining that he could not get the front tyres properly up to temperature and extract the maximum from the car. That is one of the secrets of a quick time on the long Singapore lap, with its 23 corners. The warm-up lap is key to getting the tyres in for sector one of the hot lap while trying to ensure that they are not spent by the time the tight sequence of sector three (Turns 16 through 23) is reached.

Initially, it looked as though we could be in for a three-way pole fight, with Ferrari also threatening. But, as the track rubbered in and practice progressed, it was apparent that the Maranello cars were just a little adrift. And their challenge was not helped when Sebastian Vettel encountered a problem with his car in Q1.

"The warm-up lap felt okay," he said, "but it felt strange in Turn One on my first quick lap, and then there was obviously a problem." The Ferrari was lifting its front wheels, pointing towards a broken rear anti-roll bar. Without time to address the problem, Vettel contemplated spending two hours around Marina Bay from the back...

Kimi Räikkönen, always happier when tyres from the softer end of the spectrum are on the menu, giving him a more responsive front end, qualified fifth, but was almost a full second from Rosberg's pace.

Joining Kimi on row three, after a tremendous performance in the Toro Rosso, was Carlos Sainz. The team

had been struggling for the previous three races, corresponding with an aero update introduced at Hockenheim. They weren't sure whether this was just coincidence, the drop-off in performance attributable to the relative breathlessness of its 2015-spec Ferrari engine at power tracks like Spa and Monza, or whether there was an issue with the update package. Having run inconclusive back-to-back tests at Monza, they carried on in Singapore, Sainz's car fitted with the revised package, including a different front wing, floor and sidepods, while Daniil Kvyat continued with the original specification.

As chief race engineer Phil Charles pointed out, the fact that they managed to qualify sixth and seventh in a good chassis with a lot of inherent downforce at a circuit that needs it, with Sainz 0.27s ahead and the team back into Q3, was a great fillip for everyone.

Nico Hülkenberg was a hundredth behind Kvyat and felt that there was another two- or three-tenths in the Force India, 'the Hulk' lapping just over a tenth quicker than team-mate Sergio Pérez. They were split by Fernando Alonso's McLaren-Honda.

Pérez, however, was adjudged to have committed a double-waved-yellow-flag transgression, having failed to slow sufficiently at Turns Nine and Ten for a crashed Romain Grosjean Haas, and overtaken Esteban Gutiérrez at Turn 16 when there were yellows for Jenson Button, who had pulled off after clipping the wall at Turn 14. The Mexican received a three-place grid penalty for the first offence and five more for the second, which put him 18th on the grid.

The Pérez penalty would elevate Valtteri Bottas to tenth, still with freedom of tyre choice, ahead of teammate Massa, with Button next up, in front of the Haas chassis of Esteban Gutiérrez and a troubled Grosjean, struggling with braking – again – and a loose rear end all weekend.

Marcus Ericsson did a good job to haul his Sauber into Q2, while the Q1 eliminations, Vettel apart, were team-mate Nasr, both Renaults and, unsurprisingly, both Manors, which were paying the price for a lack of downforce and traction.

Above: Daniel Ricciardo put his Red Bull on the front row of the grid.
Photo: Peter J. Fox

Left: Rolex CEO Jean-Frederic Dufour with long-time brand ambassador Sir Jackie Stewart.
Photo: WRi2/Jean-François Galeron

Centre left: Jérôme Stoll, president of Renault Sport F1, with Cyril Abiteboul, the team's managing director.
Photo: Renault Sport F1 Team

Below centre left: Now a spritely 75-year-old, former Lotus F1 driver Reine Wisell with young compatriot Marcus Ericsson.
Photo: Jean-François Galeron/WRi2

Left: McLaren's Jost Capito (*left*) and Jonathan Neale.
Photo: McLaren Honda

Far Left: Bernie Ecclestone plays wing man to Liberty Media's Chase Carey.
Photo: WRi2/Studio Colombo

Above: Kimi Räikkönen leads Fernando Alonso, the two Toro Rossos and a charging Max Verstappen in the race's early stages.

Photo: Scuderia Ferrari

Top right: Nico Rosberg narrowly avoids a marshal clearing debris from the track.

Above right: Nico Hülkenberg surveys the damage to his Force India after being pitched into the pit wall at the start of the race.

Photos: Peter J. Fox

Right: Sebastian Vettel had to settle for fifth behind his team-mate.

Photo: Scuderia Ferrari

ROMAIN GROSJEAN was out of the running before the Marina Bay race had even begun, having fallen victim to a brake-by-wire problem.

Realistically, after such a dominant qualifying performance, Rosberg's rivals were left hoping that some mechanical drama might strike car No. 6, with Mercedes starts having been an Achilles heel at times in 2016. Not this time, though. Nico got away perfectly, successfully converting his pole position, with Ricciardo's Red Bull slotting in behind as they went through Turn One.

Further back, it was Verstappen who had clutch problems, the No. 33 Red Bull suffering way too much wheelspin as Max tried to get away. As the RB12 fishtailed, Hamilton, Räikkönen and Alonso found a way by, but Hülkenberg was caught by surprise and, taking evasive action, clipped Sainz's Toro Rosso. The Force India spun into the pit wall and brought out an immediate safety car. Bottas and Button also collected each other at Turn One, and were into the pits for attention to a left rear tyre and nose respectively.

With debris littering the grid, the field was sensibly brought through the pit lane. The safety car was withdrawn at the end of the second lap, much to the consternation of a marshal still picking up carbon fibre at Turn One, who suddenly found Rosberg bearing down on him at racing speed!

Nico wanted to make hay while he still had a buffer to his team-mate, but without putting too much stress through his ultra-soft Pirellis. He was soon in command, his next hurdle being to go quickly enough to protect against any possible undercut from Ricciardo's Red Bull.

Sainz's brush with Hülkenberg had left his Toro Rosso with a flapping turning vane on the right-hand pod, and he was soon into the pits responding to a black and orange flag. That and an ERS problem spoiled a race from which both team and driver had high expectations after such a competitive qualifying session.

Mercedes now hit some brake issues as Rosberg picked up the pace to give himself a cushion as the first pit stops neared. Hamilton was warned, too. Suffering from understeer, Lewis did not appear to have the same pace as Nico and was still being pressured by Räikkönen's Ferrari.

Alonso, as he often does, had overqualified the McLaren and had a gaggle of cars behind him, but passing around Marina Bay is not the work of a moment. Verstappen was finding that out in his attempts to displace Kvyat who, no doubt, was enjoying the opportunity to deny the man who had taken his place in the senior team. Red Bull brought in Verstappen earlier than planned, at the end of lap 13, but having been trapped at Alonso's pace, he pitted out way back in the pack, behind Wehrlein's Manor.

Vettel, always strong in Singapore, had picked up places during the early laps from his lowly starting position, but found Pérez a tougher proposition, the Force India, like the Ferrari, having started on the soft-compound Pirellis (the hardest tyre on offer) with a view to a longer opening stint. Vettel would get around the Mexican by employing an undercut and switching to a set of new ultra-softs made available by his Q1 elimination.

With the brake temperatures back under control, Rosberg had been able to open a sufficient gap that Ricciardo no longer presented an undercut threat, but Red Bull still brought in Daniel first and put him on a set of super-softs. The idea was that his pace would make Rosberg stop before the gap shrank too much, and possibly give Daniel another crack at the end of the remaining stints, when they felt they might be quicker.

But Mercedes looked to have everything firmly under control. Hamilton stopped on the same lap as Ricciardo, and Rosberg was in a lap later, both fitted with the hardest-compound yellow-walled Pirellis.

Hamilton came on the radio asking why the team did not

offer up a more adventurous tyre choice, but their plan had always been to run a two-stop race with the final two stints on the soft tyre, rather than stray into potential three-stop territory, the feeling being that this was the best way of dealing with any potential threat from Räikkönen.

Thus Ferrari took the decision to keep Kimi out a little longer to reduce the length of subsequent stints, aware that they had a cushion behind due to the fact that Alonso's defence had slowed up the midfield pack, comprising Kvyat, Verstappen and Massa, with Kevin Magnussen doing his best to hang on with the Renault.

Verstappen, having recovered ground after his first stop, still could not find a way past Kvyat's Toro Rosso, a couple of attempts at Turn Seven again robustly rebuffed by the Russian. Max's attempts soon took the edge off his rubber and he was brought in for his second stop well before Kvyat, moving him in the direction of a three-stop race.

In the other Red Bull, on his softer tyres, Ricciardo started to make an impression on leader Rosberg, while Räikkönen was also closing on Hamilton, who still had brake temperature issues. The Merc's design, predicated on leading, had smaller ducts, and in races where they had to follow, the driver needed to manage the brakes. As the 61-lap race approached half-distance, Räikkönen was pressing Hamilton and looking for a way by. Lewis defended, but ultimately locked up into T7 and lost momentum, Kimi scrabbling by at T10.

Then Ferrari brought the Finn in so that Mercedes could not immediately try to undercut Hamilton back ahead, putting him on a set of softs to go to the end. Mercedes mirrored the move with Hamilton a lap later, Kimi retaining track position.

As the second stops approached for the lead pair, Ricciardo's charge ran out of steam and Rosberg upped the pace to try to create a stop margin. Both came in on lap 32 and were fitted with the soft-compound Pirelli for the final 29 laps.

Above: No way past. Daniil Kvyat proved a stubborn opponent for Max Verstappen.
Photo: WRi2/Jad Sherif

Top right: Kevin Magnussen scored a rare point for Renault.
Photo: Lukas Gorys

Above right: Ricciardo shows his delight at splitting the Mercedes.
Photo: Red Bull Racing/Getty Images

Right: A perfect race provided a third win on the bounce for Nico Rosberg.
Photo: Peter J. Fox

It looked like stalemate up front: Rosberg controlling Ricciardo, and Räikkönen ahead of Hamilton. Mercedes, though, decided to roll the dice with Lewis and convert him to a three-stop on lap 45, with 16 to go.

"We didn't really see a downside," explained Paddy Lowe. "Lewis's brake temperatures seemed under control at that stage and there was a big gap behind the leading four, so that the pit stop was effectively a free one."

Hamilton had a scrubbed set of super-softs available and would quickly close down Räikkönen again on his softs, but would the tyres have enough left to pass Kimi?

Ferrari, meanwhile, was trying to decide whether to attempt to cover Hamilton by pitting Kimi on the next lap. Vettel was flying on a set of ultra-softs he had just received as he jumped Alonso at his second stop, and Ferrari elected to pit Kimi as well.

His stop was half a second slower than Hamilton's, and that, combined with a ballistic out-lap from Lewis, ensured that the Mercedes moved back into third place.

Red Bull, seeing Vettel's pace, and with both Hamilton and Räikkönen having converted to three stops, saw no downside in doing likewise with Ricciardo. They brought in Daniel for a set of super-softs with 14 laps to go.

Mercedes now had a conundrum over what to do with race leader Rosberg. Early on his next lap, Nico received an instruction to "box". Unfortunately, though, with Ricciardo turning the timing screens purple on his super-softs, Rosberg lost time with backmarkers. Suddenly, pitting introduced a serious risk of conceding track position to the Red Bull. The strategists changed their minds and ordered Rosberg to remain out.

At the initial rate of gain, it looked as though Ricciardo might have Rosberg within range by the time the race reached its closing stages, but as the degradation increased, his gains would lessen. Ricciardo was torn between charging after the lead Merc and trying to leave enough in his tyres to mount a challenge if and when he got on to Nico's gearbox.

Rosberg was faced with the same issue: push to dishearten Ricciardo and hopefully leave enough in the tyres, or conserve his softs so that he could fight if and when Ricciardo caught him.

"Watching the gap was nail-biting and we didn't know which way it was going to go," Toto Wolff admitted. "It was a brilliant race."

In the final analysis, Rosberg judged it perfectly and took the chequered flag just under half a second clear of Ricciardo. A hat trick of victories since the summer break had put him back in the lead of the world championship.

Hamilton finished 8s behind his team-mate on one of those rare occasions when he was unable to match Nico for pace, and Räikkönen was a further 2s back in a race when he might realistically have had a podium. Vettel's fifth place from the back, just 27.6s behind Rosberg, also suggested that had he started on the front two rows, he would have had sufficient pace to have challenged for an outright win in a race he had dominated for Ferrari a year earlier.

Verstappen's switch to three stops had finally got him ahead of Kvyat, and he had homed in on Alonso, whom he passed at Turn Seven, going on to claim sixth. Behind the McLaren-Honda, Kvyat pressed Pérez hard for eighth, but year-old Ferrari power was no match for Mercedes grunt. The plucky Magnussen claimed the final point.

A year on from what had been such an uncharacteristic race in 2015, Mercedes had a double podium at what Rosberg acknowledged as a Red Bull track.

Technical director Paddy Lowe said in summary, "It could so easily have been second and fourth today, but some good strategy calls, strong pit stops, great driving and a decent slice of luck got us a hard-earned win and double podium. Lewis didn't quite have the car underneath him this weekend, but a fantastic pole and drive by Nico to win on his 200th GP weekend was well deserved." Clearly, he intended to fight for that elusive first world title.

Tony Dodgins

VIEWPOINT
A STRONGER ROSBERG

HERE was a good enough reason to consider Nico Rosberg worthy of the championship if it were to come his way in 2016. Having been 43 points to the good after five races, only to fall 19 behind Lewis Hamilton in the next phase of this roller-coaster season, Rosberg put his name back at the top of the points table in Singapore.

As the accompanying report indicates, it was the manner of his victory that impressed as much as the comeback itself. On territory normally considered to be Lewis Hamilton's patch, Rosberg produced an outstanding pole-position lap as a prelude to dealing with huge pressure during a race that lasted almost two hours in uncomfortably humid conditions.

The Singapore weekend would merely confirm the view of Ross Brawn, watching from afar, that Rosberg is a "tough little bugger". It's not an image that fits the easy stereotype summed up by a British tabloid's season preview, which referred to the German as 'Nico Lossberg'.

Brawn, with massive experience and no axe to grind, would know what he was talking about in an interview later in the season. "He's very resilient," he said. "He slips behind a bit, then he has a good talking to himself and comes back. A lot of drivers, having been punished by Lewis for a couple of years, would have gone away. In many ways, I would like him to win the world championship because he's done a fabulous job of getting beaten and coming back."

Brawn made a tellling comparison with Hamilton, a view that would be given credibility by the respective performances of the Mercedes drivers in Singapore. "Nico will put in a more consistent performance over the year, but would never quite reach the highs that Lewis could," he said. "But then Lewis dips down a bit. He's more emotional in his approach."

Proof of that last statement was not far off, thanks to Lewis's behaviour a couple of weeks later. Meanwhile, a stronger Rosberg continued to quietly impress.

Maurice Hamilton

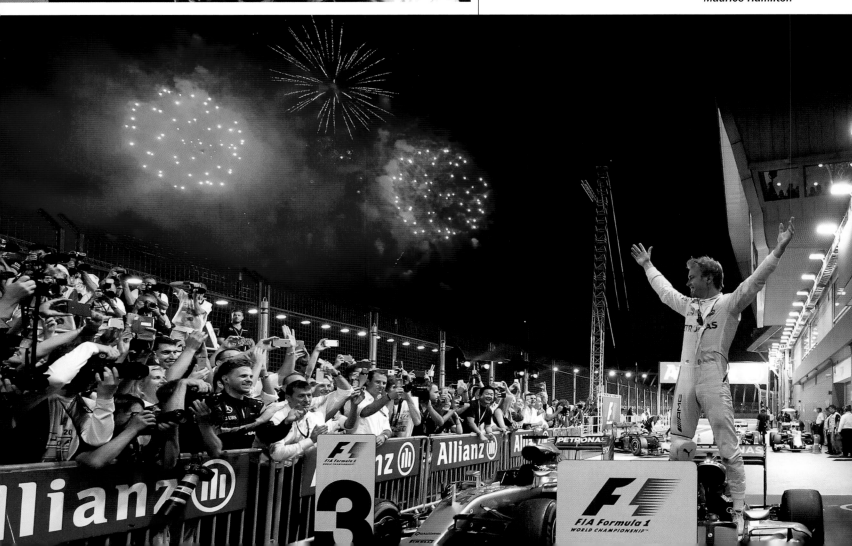

15

2016 FORMULA 1
SINGAPORE AIRLINES
SINGAPORE
GRAND PRIX

SINGAPORE 16–18 SEPTEMBER

ROLEX

OFFICIAL TIMEPIECE

RACE DISTANCE: 61 laps, 191.897 miles/308.828km

RACE WEATHER: Dry/dark (track 34–36°C, air 30–31°C)

MARINA BAY STREET CIRCUIT, SINGAPORE
Circuit: 3.147 miles/5.065km
61 laps

Stamford Road
8 94/58
Memorial 125/78
6 290/180
4 200/124
3 80/50
3 150/93
Turn 1
2
Singapore Sling 140/87
9 135/84
15 245/152
5 135/84
Raffles Boulevard
19 126/78
20
23 220/137
11
14 80/50
17 120/75
18 95/59
21 130/81
22 185/115
12 140/87
Esplanade Drive
16 85/53
Anderson Bridge 13 80/50
187/116 kmh/mph ❖ Gear ━ DRS zone

RACE – OFFICIAL CLASSIFICATION

Pos.	Driver	Nat.	No.	Entrant	Car/Engine	Tyres	Laps	Time/Retirement	Speed (mph/km/h)	Gap to leader	Fastest race lap	
1	**Nico Rosberg**	D	6	Mercedes AMG Petronas F1 Team	Mercedes F1 W07-Mercedes PU106C V6	P	61	1h 55m 48.950s	99.414/159.992		1m 50.296s	38
2	**Daniel Ricciardo**	AUS	3	Red Bull Racing	Red Bull RB12-TAG Heuer RB12 V6	P	61	1h 55m 49.438s	99.408/159.981	0.488s	1m 47.187s	49
3	**Lewis Hamilton**	GB	44	Mercedes AMG Petronas F1 Team	Mercedes F1 W07-Mercedes PU106C V6	P	61	1h 55m 56.988s	99.299/159.807	8.038s	1m 47.752s	52
4	**Kimi Räikkönen**	FIN	7	Scuderia Ferrari	Ferrari SF16-H-059/5 V6	P	61	1h 55m 59.169s	99.268/159.757	10.219s	1m 48.204s	51
5	**Sebastian Vettel**	D	5	Scuderia Ferrari	Ferrari SF15-H-059/5 V6	P	61	1h 56m 16.644s	99.020/159.357	27.694s	1m 47.345s	45
6	**Max Verstappen**	NL	33	Red Bull Racing	Red Bull RB12-TAG Heuer RB12 V6	P	61	1h 57m 00.147s	98.407/158.370	1m 11.197s	1m 49.050s	46
7	**Fernando Alonso**	E	14	McLaren Honda	McLaren MP4-31-Honda RA616H V6	P	61	1h 57m 18.148s	98.154/157.964	1m 29.198s	1m 51.249s	49
8	**Sergio Pérez**	MEX	11	Sahara Force India F1 Team	Force India VJM09-Mercedes PU106C V6	P	61	1h 57m 40.012s	97.850/157.475	1m 51.062s	1m 51.517s	34
9	**Daniil Kvyat**	RUS	26	Scuderia Toro Rosso	Toro Rosso STR11-Ferrari 059/4 V6	P	61	1h 57m 40.507s	97.844/157.464	1m 51.557s	1m 50.944s	39
10	**Kevin Magnussen**	DK	20	Renault Sport F1 Team	Renault R.S.16-R.E.16 V6	P	61	1h 57m 48.902s	97.727/157.277	1m 59.952s	1m 50.858s	44
11	Esteban Gutiérrez	MEX	21	Haas F1 Team	Haas VF-16-Ferrari 059/5 V6	P	60			1 lap	1m 51.075s	39
12	Felipe Massa	BR	19	Williams Martini Racing	Williams FW38-Mercedes PU106C V6	P	60			1 lap	1m 51.455s	53
13	Felipe Nasr	BR	12	Sauber F1 Team	Sauber C35-Ferrari 059/5 V6	P	60			1 lap	1m 51.683s	41
14	Carlos Sainz	E	55	Scuderia Toro Rosso	Toro Rosso STR11-Ferrari 059/4 V6	P	60			1 lap	1m 50.532s	56
15	Jolyon Palmer	GB	30	Renault Sport F1 Team	Renault R.S.16-R.E.16 V6	P	60			1 lap	1m 51.777s	36
16	Pascal Wehrlein	D	94	Manor Racing MRT	Manor MRT05-Mercedes PU106C V6	P	60			1 lap	1m 52.021s	40
17	Marcus Ericsson	S	9	Sauber F1 Team	Sauber C35-Ferrari 059/5 V6	P	60			1 lap	1m 50.963s	27
18	Esteban Ocon	F	31	Manor Racing MRT	Manor MRT05-Mercedes PU106C V6	P	59			2 laps	1m 51.748s	47
	Jenson Button	GB	22	McLaren Honda	McLaren MP4-31-Honda RA616H V6	P	43	*accident/brakes*			1m 51.631s	18
	Valtteri Bottas	FIN	77	Williams Martini Racing	Williams FW38-Mercedes PU106C V6	P	35	*engine*			1m 51.368s	17
	Nico Hülkenberg	D	27	Sahara Force India F1 Team	Force India VJM09-Mercedes PU106C V6	P	0	*accident*			no time	
NS	Romain Grosjean	F	8	Haas F1 Team	Haas VF-16-Ferrari 059/5 V6	P		*brakes on the reconnaissance lap*				

Fastest race lap: Daniel Ricciardo on lap 49, 1m 47.187s, 105.704mph/170.113km/h.

Lap record: Kimi Räikkönen (Ferrari F2008 V8), 1m 45.599s, 107.336mph/172.740km/h (2008, 3.148-mile/5.067km circuit).

All results and data © FOM 2016

22 · VETTEL · Ferrari
(20-place grid penalty for using additional power unit elements; 5-place penalty for changing the gearbox)

20 · GROSJEAN · Haas
(5-place grid penalty for replacing the gearbox – did not start)

18 · PALMER · Renault

16 · NASR · Sauber

14 · ERICSSON · Sauber

12 · BUTTON · McLaren

21 · OCON · Manor

19 · WEHRLEIN · Manor

17 · PÉREZ · Force India
(5-place grid penalty for ignoring yellow flags; 3-place penalty for overtaking under yellow flags)

15 · MAGNUSSEN · Renault

13 · GUTIÉRREZ · Haas

11 · MASSA · Williams

Grid order	1	2	3	4	5	6	7	8	9	10	11	12	13	14	15	16	17	18	19	20	21	22	23	24	25	26	27	28	29	30	31	32	33	34	35	36	37	38	39	40	41	42	43	44	45	46	47	48
6 ROSBERG	6	6	6	6	6	6	6	6	6	6	6	6	6	6	6	6	7	6	6	6	6	6	6	6	6	6	6	6	6	6	6	6	44	6	6	6	6	6	6	6	6	6	6	6	6	6	6	6
3 RICCIARDO	3	3	3	3	3	3	3	3	3	3	3	3	3	3	3	7	6	3	3	3	3	3	3	3	3	3	3	3	3	3	44	44	6	3	3	3	3	3	3	3	3	3	3	3	3	3	3	3
44 HAMILTON	44	44	44	44	44	44	44	44	44	44	44	44	44	7	3	3	44	44	44	44	44	44	44	44	44	44	44	44	44	3	7	3	7	7	7	7	7	7	7	7	7	7	7	44	44			
33 VERSTAPPEN	7	7	7	7	7	7	7	7	7	7	7	7	7	44	44	44	3	7	7	7	7	7	7	7	7	7	7	7	7	7	3	7	44	44	44	44	44	44	44	44	44	44	44	7	7			
7 RÄIKKÖNEN	14	14	14	14	14	14	14	14	14	14	14	26	19	20	21	11	11	11	11	11	11	11	11	14	14	14	14	14	14	26	5	5	5	5	5	33	5	5	5	33	14	14	14	14				
55 SAINZ	26	26	26	26	26	26	26	26	26	26	26	19	26	19	11	5	5	5	5	5	5	14	26	26	26	26	26	14	5	26	33	33	33	33	33	5	33	14	14	14	14							
26 KVYAT	55	55	55	55	55	55	33	33	33	33	33	33	19	14	20	21	5	21	14	14	14	14	26	33	33	19	20	20	20	20	5	5	20	20	14	14	14	14	14	14	11	11	11	33				
27 HÜLKENBERG	33	33	33	33	33	33	19	19	19	19	19	20	20	21	11	20	14	26	26	26	26	33	19	19	20	19	5	5	5	5	20	20	33	33	33	11	11	11	11	11	11	26	26	26				
14 ALONSO	19	19	19	19	19	19	20	20	20	20	20	33	21	11	5	14	26	33	33	33	33	19	11	20	33	5	21	21	21	21	33	33	14	14	14	20	19	19	19	26	33	33	33	26				
77 BOTTAS	20	20	20	20	20	20	9	21	21	11	11	11	11	5	14	33	19	20	20	20	20	55	21	11	11	33	33	11	11	11	11	19	26	20	20	26	19	20	20	20	20							
19 MASSA	9	9	9	9	9	9	21	11	11	11	11	11	11	5	12	14	33	19	20	20	20	20	55	21	11	33	33	11	11	21	19	26	20	26	26	19	20	20	20	20	55	55	55	55	21			
22 BUTTON	11	21	21	21	21	21	11	12	12	12	12	12	12	14	26	12	20	55	55	55	55	55	21	5	11	12	12	12	19	19	19	19	21	55	55	55	55	55	55	21	21	21	19					
21 GUTIÉRREZ	21	11	11	11	11	11	55	5	5	5	5	5	5	94	94	33	19	55	21	21	21	21	5	11	12	33	19	19	19	12	12	55	21	21	21	21	21	21	19	19	19	12						
9 ERICSSON	22	94	94	12	12	12	12	9	94	94	94	94	94	33	33	94	94	9	9	12	12	12	55	77	77	30	30	55	55	55	12	12	12	12	12	12	12	12	12	12	12	12	12	12				
20 MAGNUSSEN	77	31	12	94	94	5	5	94	94	94	94	9	9	9	77	77	30	30	77	55	55	30	94	94	94	22	22	22	22	30	30	30	30															
12 NASR	94	12	31	31	5	94	94	31	77	77	77	77	77	55	55	31	31	30	30	30	30	30	30	30	30	94	94	9	22	30	30	30	30	9	94	94	94	94	94	94	94	94						
11 PÉREZ	31	30	30	5	31	31	31	77	30	30	22	22	22	9	9	9	12	77	77	77	77	77	22	22	94	55	94	94	9	30	22	9	94	94	94	94	94											
30 PALMER	12	5	5	30	77	77	77	30	22	22	55	55	55	77	30	30	30	31	22	22	22	22	9	94	22	9	9	77	22	22	22	30	30	9	9	9	9	22	31	31	31	31						
94 WEHRLEIN	30	77	77	77	30	30	30	22	55	9	9	9	9	22	77	77	77	22	94	94	94	94	94	9	9	22	22	22	22	77	77	77	77	31	31	31	31	31	31	31								
8 GROSJEAN	5	22	22	22	22	22	22	55	9	55	30	30	30	30	22	22	94	31	31	31	31	31	31	31	31	31	31	31	31	31	31	31	31	31														
31 OCON																																																
5 VETTEL																																																

TIME SHEETS

PRACTICE 1 (FRIDAY)
Weather: Dry/sunny
Temperatures: track 36–37°C, air 30–32°C

Pos.	Driver	Laps	Time
1	Max Verstappen	25	1m 45.823s
2	Daniel Ricciardo	27	1m 45.872s
3	Sebastian Vettel	22	1m 46.287s
4	Lewis Hamilton	24	1m 46.426s
5	Nico Rosberg	22	1m 46.513s
6	Kimi Räikkönen	20	1m 46.890s
7	Carlos Sainz	28	1m 46.936s
8	Daniil Kvyat	29	1m 47.683s
9	Felipe Massa	27	1m 48.044s
10	Esteban Gutiérrez	23	1m 48.109s
11	Fernando Alonso	21	1m 48.202s
12	Sergio Pérez	28	1m 48.214s
13	Nico Hülkenberg	28	1m 48.359s
14	Valtteri Bottas	26	1m 48.453s
15	Felipe Nasr	16	1m 49.595s
16	Jenson Button	20	1m 49.615s
17	Jolyon Palmer	27	1m 49.794s
18	Kevin Magnussen	29	1m 50.263s
19	Pascal Wehrlein	23	1m 51.112s
20	Marcus Ericsson	16	1m 51.479s
21	Esteban Ocon	33	1m 52.379s
22	Romain Grosjean	2	no time

PRACTICE 2 (FRIDAY)
Weather: Dry/dark
Temperatures: track 32–34°C, air 29–30°C

Pos.	Driver	Laps	Time
1	Nico Rosberg	34	1m 44.152s
2	Kimi Räikkönen	34	1m 44.427s
3	Max Verstappen	29	1m 44.532s
4	Daniel Ricciardo	26	1m 44.557s
5	Sebastian Vettel	33	1m 45.161s
6	Nico Hülkenberg	35	1m 45.182s
7	Lewis Hamilton	10	1m 45.275s
8	Carlos Sainz	33	1m 45.507s
9	Fernando Alonso	30	1m 45.779s
10	Daniil Kvyat	35	1m 46.029s
11	Sergio Pérez	26	1m 46.063s
12	Jenson Button	30	1m 46.574s
13	Esteban Gutiérrez	36	1m 46.727s
14	Felipe Massa	30	1m 46.856s
15	Valtteri Bottas	30	1m 46.960s
16	Kevin Magnussen	30	1m 47.161s
17	Jolyon Palmer	34	1m 47.166s
18	Felipe Nasr	29	1m 47.531s
19	Romain Grosjean	12	1m 48.391s
20	Marcus Ericsson	32	1m 48.487s
21	Pascal Wehrlein	33	1m 48.505s
22	Esteban Ocon	29	1m 48.823s

PRACTICE 3 (SATURDAY)
Weather: Dry/dusk
Temperatures: track 36°C, air 31°C

Pos.	Driver	Laps	Time
1	Nico Rosberg	15	1m 44.352s
2	Max Verstappen	15	1m 44.411s
3	Kimi Räikkönen	15	1m 44.860s
4	Daniel Ricciardo	12	1m 44.903s
5	Sebastian Vettel	13	1m 45.104s
6	Nico Hülkenberg	13	1m 45.316s
7	Daniil Kvyat	19	1m 45.503s
8	Lewis Hamilton	9	1m 45.806s
9	Carlos Sainz	17	1m 45.879s
10	Valtteri Bottas	16	1m 45.947s
11	Sergio Pérez	15	1m 46.112s
12	Fernando Alonso	13	1m 46.164s
13	Esteban Gutiérrez	16	1m 46.316s
14	Felipe Massa	17	1m 46.529s
15	Kevin Magnussen	11	1m 47.116s
16	Jenson Button	16	1m 47.277s
17	Felipe Nasr	18	1m 47.293s
18	Romain Grosjean	20	1m 47.411s
19	Marcus Ericsson	20	1m 47.956s
20	Jolyon Palmer	13	1m 48.689s
21	Pascal Wehrlein	10	1m 49.201s
22	Esteban Ocon	14	1m 49.565s

QUALIFYING (SATURDAY)
Weather: Dry/dark Temperatures: track 32–37°C, air 29–31°C

Pos.	Driver	First	Second	Third	Qualifying Tyre
1	Nico Rosberg	1m 45.316s	1m 43.020s	1m 42.584s	Ultra-Soft (new)
2	Daniel Ricciardo	1m 44.255s	1m 43.933s	1m 43.115s	Ultra-Soft (new)
3	Lewis Hamilton	1m 45.167s	1m 43.471s	1m 43.288s	Ultra-Soft (new)
4	Max Verstappen	1m 45.036s	1m 44.112s	1m 43.328s	Ultra-Soft (new)
5	Kimi Räikkönen	1m 44.964s	1m 44.159s	1m 43.540s	Ultra-Soft (new)
6	Carlos Sainz	1m 45.499s	1m 44.493s	1m 44.197s	Ultra-Soft (new)
7	Daniil Kvyat	1m 45.291s	1m 44.475s	1m 44.469s	Ultra-Soft (new)
8	Nico Hülkenberg	1m 46.081s	1m 44.737s	1m 44.479s	Ultra-Soft (new)
9	Fernando Alonso	1m 45.373s	1m 44.653s	1m 44.553s	Ultra-Soft (new)
10	Sergio Pérez	1m 45.204s	1m 44.703s	1m 44.582s	Ultra-Soft (new)
11	Valtteri Bottas	1m 46.086s	1m 44.740s		
12	Felipe Massa	1m 46.056s	1m 44.991s		
13	Jenson Button	1m 45.262s	1m 45.144s		
14	Esteban Gutiérrez	1m 45.465s	1m 45.593s		
15	Romain Grosjean	1m 45.609s	1m 45.723s		
16	Marcus Ericsson	1m 46.427s	1m 47.827s		
17	Kevin Magnussen	1m 46.825s			
18	Felipe Nasr	1m 46.860s			
19	Jolyon Palmer	1m 46.960s			
20	Pascal Wehrlein	1m 47.667s			
21	Esteban Ocon	1m 48.296s			
22	Sebastian Vettel	1m 49.116s			

FOR THE RECORD

200th GRAND PRIX: **Nico Rosberg.**

50th GRAND PRIX: **Marcus Ericsson.**

200th GRAND PRIX: **Toro Rosso.**

50th FASTEST LAP: **Red Bull.**

150th POLE POSITION: **Mercedes engine.**

POINTS

DRIVERS

1	Nico Rosberg	273
2	Lewis Hamilton	265
3	Daniel Ricciardo	179
4	Sebastian Vettel	153
5	Kimi Räikkönen	148
6	Max Verstappen	129
7	Valtteri Bottas	70
8	Sergio Pérez	66
9	Nico Hülkenberg	46
10	Felipe Massa	41
11	Fernando Alonso	36
12	Carlos Sainz	30
13	Romain Grosjean	28
14	Daniil Kvyat	25
15	Jenson Button	17
16	Kevin Magnussen	7
17	Pascal Wehrlein	1
18	Stoffel Vandoorne	1

CONSTRUCTORS

1	Mercedes	538
2	Red Bull	316
3	Ferrari	301
4	Force India	112
5	Williams	111
6	McLaren	54
7	Toro Rosso	47
8	Haas	28
9	Renault	7
10	Manor	1

Photo: Scuderia Ferrari

Qualifying: head-to-head

Rosberg	8	7	Hamilton
Vettel	9	6	Räikkönen
Massa	2	13	Bottas
Ricciardo	4	0	Kvyat
Ricciardo	9	2	Verstappen
Pérez	7	8	Hülkenberg
Magnussen	10	5	Palmer
Verstappen	3	1	Sainz
Kvyat	2	9	Sainz
Ericsson	8	7	Nasr
Alonso	10	4	Button
Button	0	1	Vandoorne
Haryanto	5	7	Wehrlein
Wehrlein	3	0	Ocon
Grosjean	10	5	Gutiérrez

10 · BOTTAS · Williams

8 · HÜLKENBERG · Force India

6 · SAINZ · Toro Rosso

4 · VERSTAPPEN · Red Bull

2 · RICCIARDO · Red Bull

9 · ALONSO · McLaren

7 · KVYAT · Toro Rosso

5 · RÄIKKÖNEN · Ferrari

3 · HAMILTON · Mercedes

1 · ROSBERG · Mercedes

Lap chart

49	50	51	52	53	54	55	56	57	58	59	60	61	-
6	6	6	6	6	6	6	6	6	6	6	6	6	1
3	3	3	3	3	3	3	3	3	3	3	3	3	2
44	44	44	44	44	44	44	44	44	44	44	44	44	3
7	7	7	7	7	7	7	7	7	7	7	7	7	4
5	5	5	5	5	5	5	5	5	5	5	5	5	5
14	14	14	14	14	33	33	33	33	33	33	33	33	6
33	33	33	33	33	14	14	14	14	14	14	14	14	7
11	11	11	11	11	11	11	11	11	11	11	11	11	8
26	26	26	26	26	26	26	26	26	26	26	26	26	9
20	20	20	20	20	20	20	20	20	20	20	20	20	10
21	21	21	21	21	21	21	21	21	21	21	21		
19	19	19	19	19	19	19	19	19	19	19	19		
12	12	12	12	12	12	12	12	12	12	12	12		
55	55	55	55	55	55	55	55	55	55	55	55		
30	30	30	30	30	30	30	30	30	30	30	30		
94	94	94	94	94	94	94	94	94	94	94	94		
9	9	9	9	9	9	9	9	9	9	9			
31	31	31	31	31	31	31	31	31	31	31			

6 = Pit stop   9 = Drive-thru penalty

94 = One lap or more behind

⬛ Safety car deployed on laps shown

RACE TYRE STRATEGIES

PIRELLI

	Driver	Race Stint 1	Race Stint 2	Race Stint 3	Race Stint 4	Race Stint 5
1	Rosberg	Ultra-Soft (u): 1–16	Soft (n): 17–33	Soft (n): 34–61		
2	Ricciardo	Super-Soft (u): 1–15	Super-Soft (n): 16–32	Soft (n): 33–47	Super-Soft (n): 48–61	
3	Hamilton	Ultra-Soft (u): 1–15	Soft (n): 16–34	Soft (n): 35–45	Super-Soft (u): 46–61	
4	Räikkönen	Ultra-Soft (u): 1–17	Super-Soft (n): 18–33	Soft (n): 34–46	Ultra-Soft (u): 47–61	
5	Vettel	Soft (n): 1–24	Ultra-Soft (n): 25–42	Ultra-Soft (n): 43–61		
6	Verstappen	Super-Soft (u): 1–13	Super-Soft (n): 14–27	Super-Soft (n): 28–44	Soft (n): 45–61	
7	Alonso	Ultra-Soft (u): 1–14	Super-Soft (n): 15–34	Soft (n): 35–61		
8	Pérez	Ultra-Soft (u): 1	Soft (n): 2–25	Soft (n): 26–61		
9	Kvyat	Ultra-Soft (u): 1–15	Super-Soft (n): 16–37	Super-Soft (u): 38–61		
10	Magnussen	Ultra-Soft (u): 1–18	Super-Soft (n): 19–38	Super-Soft (n): 39–61		
11	Gutiérrez	Ultra-Soft (u): 1–18	Ultra-Soft (u): 19–36	Soft (u): 37–60		
12	Massa	Ultra-Soft (u): 1–16	Super-Soft (n): 17–28	Ultra-Soft (u): 29–43	Ultra-Soft (u): 44–60	
13	Nasr	Super-Soft (n): 1–17	Super-Soft (n): 18–35	Soft (n): 36–60		
14	Sainz	Ultra-Soft (u): 1–7	Super-Soft (u): 8–27	Soft (n): 28–48	Ultra-Soft (u): 49–60	
15	Palmer	Super-Soft (u): 1–11	Super-Soft (n): 12–34	Soft (n): 35–60		
16	Wehrlein	Ultra-Soft (n): 1–18	Super-Soft (n): 19–36	Ultra-Soft (n): 37–60		
17	Ericsson	Ultra-Soft (n): 1–8	Super-Soft (n): 9–25	Ultra-Soft (n): 26–36	Soft (u): 37–60	
18	Ocon	Ultra-Soft (n): 1–19	Ultra-Soft (n): 20–34	Super-Soft (n): 35–45	Super-Soft (n): 46–59	
	Button	Ultra-Soft (u): 1	Super-Soft (n): 2–15	Ultra-Soft (n): 16–27	Soft (n): 28–43 (dnf)	
	Bottas	Ultra-Soft (n): 1	Soft (n): 2–15	Super-Soft (n): 16–30	Ultra-Soft (u): 31–31	Ultra-Soft (u): 33–35 (dnf)
	Hülkenberg	0				
NS	Grosjean					

The tyre regulations stipulate that at least two of three dry tyre specifications must be used during a dry race.
Pirelli P Zero logos are colour-coded on the tyre sidewalls: Purple = Ultra-Soft; Yellow = Soft; Red = Super-Soft. (n) new (u) used

MALAYSIAN GRAND PRIX

SEPANG CIRCUIT

SEPANG QUALIFYING

ALTHOUGH the perception was that Nico Rosberg was on a roll with three back-to-back victories since the summer break – some even suggesting that with an eight-point lead over Lewis Hamilton, he was now the championship favourite – the reality was a little different.

Okay, no one could take away from Nico his fine Singapore performance, but Lewis could look at the Spa engine penalties, the poor start in Monza, and the different set-up and compromised practice in Singapore. The fact was that around Sepang, only unpredictable conditions had led to Hamilton being outqualified by a team-mate. And, this time around, he never looked close to being troubled by Rosberg.

With Sepang scheduled for a late-season date for the first time since 2000, all sessions were dry, and although car No. 6 set the quickest FP1 time, Hamilton dominated every remaining session of practice and qualifying to claim pole by 0.41s. He did it as a result of his first run, having locked up a front and aborted his second.

Rosberg, in fact, needed his second Q3 run to lock out the front row for Mercedes, having bitten off a little too much at Turn Six on his first run and ended up just fifth quickest. Until that point, Max Verstappen had looked a serious threat. Most impressive of all for long-run pace on Friday afternoon, as the teams gathered data on the soft, medium and hard Pirellis on offer in Malaysia, Max appeared to have the legs of team-mate Daniel Ricciardo. The Australian ran a different set-up on Friday, although the pair converged more on Saturday.

In the final analysis, though, Rosberg did enough. Hamilton's 1m 32.850s pole was out of reach, but Nico's 1m 33.264s shaded Verstappen by 0.16s. Ricciardo made it an all-Red Bull second row, ultimately missing his team-mate's time by just four-hundredths.

The Ferrari were close, the long-run times on Friday suggesting that the race could actually be a close-fought affair between F1's dominant three teams. For much of the weekend, Kimi Räikkönen had seemed to be the quicker Maranello driver, but in the final minutes of qualifying, it was Sebastian Vettel who took the honours with a lap just 0.12s behind Ricciardo and five-hundredths quicker than the Finn.

Force India having moved a point ahead of Williams again in the battle for fourth place in the constructors' championship post-Singapore, where Sir Frank's men had recorded only their second non-score of the season, the contest was as keenly fought as ever in Malaysia. While Marina Bay had played more to the strengths of Force India, Williams hoped to hit back again at Sepang. Initially, that had looked feasible, with Massa quickest of the four combatants in Q2. When it mattered, though, Felipe could not reproduce the time, and it was Sergio Pérez – still unconfirmed at Force India for 2017 – who took seventh on the grid, 0.17s ahead of team-mate Nico Hülkenberg.

An interloper in the contest was a certain Jenson Button in the McLaren-Honda, who produced a fine lap to go ninth, just 0.03s behind Hülkenberg and 0.15s ahead of Massa, who outqualified team-mate Bottas. The Finn missed out on Q3 and thus had freedom of tyre choice for the race.

After a character-building weekend in Singapore, the Haas team hoped they had some answers to their braking issues in Malaysia. Romain Grosjean and team-mate Esteban Gutiérrez qualified 12th and 13th, separated by just eight-thousandths, but a couple of tenths quicker than Kevin Magnussen's Renault.

The Toro Rosso drivers suspected that they might struggle more for pace in Malaysia, and those fears were realised, with Daniil Kvyat, rarely, getting the better of Carlos Sainz, albeit by just 0.01s as Franz Tost's men completed the Q2 qualifiers.

Marcus Ericsson arrived in Malaysia a little battered and bruised, having come unstuck on a cycle training ride when he hit a chicken at around 30mph and came off! He did manage to outqualify Sauber team-mate Felipe Nasr, however, the pair fractionally quicker than Jolyon Palmer, who was left to rue a mistake at the final Turn 15 that kept him mired in Q1 as pressure to impress the Renault management grew week by week.

Palmer was not the only driver to be caught out there. Parts of the Sepang layout had been reprofiled to improve drainage, most notably Turns 2, 9 and 15, with adverse camber now making the exit tricky and the ideal line less certain.

After difficult qualifying sessions in Monza and Singapore, Esteban Ocon looked more convincing at Sepang, producing a fine lap to outqualify Manor team-mate Pascal Wehrlein for the first time.

Bringing up the rear was Fernando Alonso who, with an upgraded Honda and part stockpiling (banned in 2017) giving him a 40-place grid penalty, opted to concentrate solely on race set-up. It's good that a rule that would keep a driver such as Alonso off the circuit in qualifying is in the skip...

Above: Follow my leader. The Haas mechanics march down the pit lane behind Esteban Gutiérrez.

Top: Multi-Max on screen during the post-qualifying press conference.
Photos: WRi2/Jad Sherif

Above right: Kevin Magnussen makes a hasty exit from his flaming Renault in the pit lane during Friday practice.
Photo: Lukas Gorys

Right: Daniel Ricciardo could only qualify fourth, but he would emerge victorious on race day.

Opening spread: Ricciardo's win eased some of the early-season pain, victories in Spain and Monaco having just eluded him.
Photos: Peter J. Fox

Above: Jolyon Palmer's Renault is wheeled on to the grid before the start. Tenth place brought the keen driver his first championship point.
Photo: Renault Sport F1 Team

Top right: Sebastian Vettel's race was already run after his collision with Nico Rosberg at the start.
Photo: GP Photo/Peter Nygaard

Above right: The field continues as Rosberg's Mercedes is tipped into a spin. The German was fortunate to emerge unscathed.
Photo: Lukas Gorys

Right: Rosberg's lucky day as he crosses the line in third place.
Photo: Mercedes AMG Petronas F1 Team

FIFTY per cent of the Williams challenge was blunted before the red lights even went out. Felipe Massa's car was pushed into the pit lane after the Brazilian found himself stuck in tickover mode.

What seemed like an inordinate wait for the lights to extinguish was caused by a dead engine for Carlos Sainz as the grid formed up. Fortunately, he managed to get it going via the energy recovery system before the start needed to be aborted.

Hamilton got the start right and managed to convert his pole, while behind, Vettel, battling with Verstappen, was aggressively late on the brakes down the inside. Rosberg, having realised he wasn't going to be able to challenge his team-mate, had flicked back across to the left to take the ideal line through T1. As he turned in, he was clobbered by Vettel's locked-up Ferrari.

Sebastian's left front made contact with Nico's right rear and spun the Mercedes around. Vettel was out on the spot, his wheel at 90 degrees to the direction of travel, while Rosberg rejoined at the back. Vettel, rightly, was adjudged to be at fault and given a three-place grid penalty for the following race at Suzuka.

There was more contact further back as Gutiérrez turned in on Magnussen, puncturing the Haas's rear tyre, and Kvyat's Toro Rosso thumped the back of the Renault, sending both the Dane and the Russian into the pits for repairs. The damage proved terminal for Magnussen, however, causing his rear brakes to overheat.

Cue virtual safety car (VSC) for debris removal with the pack now in the order Hamilton, Ricciardo, Pérez, Button, Räikkönen, Verstappen, Hülkenberg, Bottas, Grosjean and, into the top ten after the shananigans, Ocon's Manor. Then

came Sainz and Alonso, up to 12th from the back! Rosberg was last.

Once the VSC period had ended, Hamilton eased away from Ricciardo, while Räikkönen and Verstappen both passed Button, Max also towing past Kimi for good measure. Further illustrating his opportunistic overtaking ability, the Red Bull driver also demoted Pérez's Force India. Kimi followed him through, between T1 and T2 at the start of the fourth lap.

Alonso was soon further on the move, passing Ocon, Sainz and Grosjean. The French-Swiss was about to suffer another brake-by-wire failure as he approached the T15 hairpin...

And so we had another VSC period. The race had not gone far enough for the medium- and hard-tyre starters to make a pit stop, but with most planning a two-stop race, it was long enough to make it worthwhile taking advantage of a cheap stop and shuffling the pack. Red Bull pitted Verstappen, but left Ricciardo out.

Max dropped just the one position, his VSC stop saving him around 10s compared to a normal stop. That put the pressure on Hamilton and Mercedes, as Lewis did not have a standard stop's advantage over the young Dutchman and would be forced to increase his pace.

Pérez, Button, Hülkenberg, Alonso and the recovering Rosberg all followed Verstappen's lead and pitted, taking on either medium- or hard-compound tyres for a long stint.

As the second VSC period ended, Hamilton led from Ricciardo, Räikkönen, Verstappen and Bottas. Then came Sainz, Ocon and Ericsson, all yet to stop, followed by Pérez, Palmer, Button, Hülkenberg, Rosberg, Alonso, et al.

Rosberg soon made progress, demoting Hülkenberg, Button and Pérez, and closing the gap to Bottas once the prime-tyre starters had stopped. Verstappen was also flying

on his new tyres, lapping quicker than race leader Hamilton and gaining on Räikkönen's third-placed Ferrari.

With 20 laps down and leading by just over 5s, Hamilton headed for the pits and a change to a set of hard-compound Pirellis. Räikkönen pitted, too, and followed suit. Ricciardo stopped a lap later, which gave his young team-mate an 8s lead over Hamilton. Max ran to lap 27 before making his second stop, pitting out 16s behind Lewis, now third.

With a pit stop taking just over 23s, the choice for Mercedes and Hamilton was either to stay out and get to the end on the prime tyre, hopefully quickly enough to defend against Red Bull, or to up the pace, build the necessary pit-stop window and stop once more for fresh rubber. The fact that Hamilton had been managing his tyres between his own stop and Verstappen's prompted Mercedes to favour the second option.

Red Bull also had strategic decisions to make. Ricciardo's tyres were six laps older than his team-mate's, and Daniel was likely to need a second stop, whereas Max, his second pit visit already complete, was good to go to the end. In taking the two-stop route, though, Ricciardo would cede track position, and ultimately the better result, to his team-mate. Thus it was no surprise when he said he'd stay out.

Verstappen, meanwhile, radioed in to ask if Red Bull could move Daniel out of the way because they were on different strategies (he thought) and he needed to prevent Hamilton from opening up that 23s gap for the additional stop, which the lead Mercedes was right on the cusp of doing.

"He's beginning to cost me time now; you need to make a decision…" Max said. He was told that he was racing for position, and the team readied itself for the ensuing combat.

The key moment came on lap 40, when Verstappen got a better exit from Turn Four and tried to line up Ricciardo through the high-speed sweeping T5/T6 section of Sepang.

"I saw him coming at Turn Four," Daniel said. "I protected the inside, but I knew he'd probably get a better exit for T5. I had a bit of wheelspin as well and I thought that for sure he's going to get me, but I had just enough drive to stay on the inside for T5. That meant he had the inside for T6, but I rode it out around the outside and thankfully the marbles weren't too bad, and I held on and braked a bit later than normal for T7 on the clean line."

This was seat-of-the-pants stuff and the first of many on-circuit battles between two top drivers that we are likely to see repeated at Red Bull. Both are hard and uncompromising racers, and it was important that they did not make contact. Not just for the outcome of this race, but for the future willingness of the team to let them race in the manner that all fans want to see.

"It was close," Verstappen smiled. "For sure, if it hadn't been my team-mate, I would have squeezed a little harder in Turn Six…"

Ricciardo's defence turned out to be critical. Hamilton was on the radio asking for the blue flags to be promptly waved when, at the end of the front straight, his engine let go in the biggest possible way.

"Oh, No! No!" he shouted as flames filled his mirrors. He pulled off at Turn One, his 25 points out of the window and his angst all too apparent. There was no hiding his disappointment as we had a third VSC interruption.

Hamilton's misfortune was a good break for Ricciardo. No longer did he face having to hold off his team-mate on older tyres over the remaining 16 laps. Their lead margin, combined with the reduced-speed VSC running, meant that both Red Bull drivers could effectively execute free pit stops for fresh softs. Ricciardo's were brand new, while Verstappen's had just an install lap on them.

One can only imagine what must have gone through Rosberg's mind when he saw his team-mate's car inert at the side of the track and realised that a race in which damage limitation had been the only realistic option after Turn One, was going to afford him a handsome lead in the championship. But that did not halt his forward progress and

Above: Lewis Hamilton walks away from his smoking Mercedes.
Photo: WRi2

Above right: Someone up there doesn't like me. Divine intervention or not, Hamilton's title chase was beginning to look a tall order.
Photo: Lukas Gorys

Right: Nico's move on Räikkönen earned him a post-race time penalty.
Photo: GP Photo/Peter Nygaard

his desire to displace Räikkönen's Ferrari from third place, which he did aggressively down the inside into Turn Two, nerfing Räikkönen wide in the process.

Notification of a stewards' investigation was quickly forthcoming, and subsequently a ten-second penalty was added to Nico's race time.

"That penalty is just complete nonsense," Mercedes team principal Toto Wolff said post-race. "A couple of months ago, we decided all together that we wanted to allow racing between all the cars and that if it wasn't 100-per cent clear that someone was at fault, then we would let them race each other. And then this…"

As soon as the final VSC period began, Ferrari brought in Räikkönen for a new set of boots with which to hit back at Rosberg, but Mercedes covered that by adopting the same tactic next time around.

Pérez, Alonso and Hülkenberg, running sixth through eighth, all got a cheap late stop as well, at Button's expense.

There were now two races to resolve. Could Verstappen attack Ricciardo for the win? And could Rosberg open up the necessary ten seconds over Räikkönen to overcome his penalty and claim the final podium position?

Initially, Verstappen attacked hard, taking 2s out of Ricciardo's post-stop advantage and closing to within 1.15s with seven laps to go. That was uncomfortably close to DRS range for Ricciardo's liking, but then Max made a mistake, locking up under braking for the Turn 15 hairpin and spinning up the wheels on exit, taking the edge off his softs. He was never as close again, and a delighted Ricciardo took the chequered flag 2.4s to the good.

"I said earlier in the year that I thought we would win one, and I'm just delighted to have finally delivered on it," the beaming Aussie admitted.

Verstappen had kept him honest as Red Bull scored the 17th 1-2 finish in its relatively short history.

Every time Nico Rosberg does anything remotely aggressive, he seems to attract a penalty or reprimand – Austria sprung to mind. And so it was probably fitting, given the circumstances of Turn One at Sepang, that he managed to overcome a Ferrari to claim that final podium spot, although Kimi Räikkönen doubtless would disagree.

Initially, Rosberg had requested the use of the 'Strat 3' engine setting – basically a qualifying mode – to open up the necessary ten-second cushion, but he was only allowed

VIEWPOINT
KEEP CALM AND CARRY ON

THE moment Lewis Hamilton's engine went bang and his anguished "Oh, No! No!" was heard across the airwaves, the media – and its British representatives in particular – let out a groan. It was an expression of mild pain, partly in sympathy with the poor man's plight just as this race appeared to have been bought and convincingly paid for, but mainly because they knew what would be coming next.

If anything was guaranteed to kick-start the stupid rumours of Mercedes sabotage in favour of Nico Rosberg, it was the sight of that smoking car. The problem was that Lewis would then fan the sparks of uninformed innuendo into an inferno when microphones were shoved in his face long before his adrenalin had dropped to an unemotional level.

"I just can't believe that there's eight Mercedes cars and only my engines are the ones that have gone this way," he said. "Something just doesn't feel right. It was a brand-new engine. It's just odd. There's been like 43 engines for Mercedes, and only mine have gone."

By the time he had clarified that 'something or someone' working against him to be 'the man above', the damage had been done.

It was an unfair reflection of the dedicated workforce at Mercedes AMG High Performance Powertrains at Brixworth; a misconception that Hamilton would attempt to put right during the following days.

Nonetheless, his distress, perversely, was an indication of how reliable the power units have become. Back in the day, Lewis's hero, Ayrton Senna, would suffer engine blow-ups as regularly as Hamilton wins races. He would not be happy, but he would remain tight-lipped in front of the media and then deliver a withering volley behind closed doors at Honda's hapless project leader.

Lewis needed to bear in mind that the hybrid Mercedes had powered him to no fewer than 27 wins in 54 races, 11 of which he had finished second to Rosberg. This had been Hamilton's first engine failure since Australia in 2014. The amazing fact was that these highly-stressed units, running for five races, did not explode as readily as the offended driver.

Maurice Hamilton

to employ it for a couple of laps, the team being mindful of Hamilton's engine failure and desperate to avoid a double DNF. He didn't need it anyway, since Räikkönen had been struggling with a broken floor and resultant lack of downforce following their coming-together. Nico had the necessary gap with seven laps remaining and crossed the line 13.2s clear of Kimi.

Fifth, after a fine one-stop drive managing his Pirellis, was Valtteri Bottas, who saw off the challenge of Pérez's Force India by 2s. Alonso's McLaren-Honda finished a superb seventh from the back, 9s clear of Hülkenberg. Jenson Button finished his 300th GP with two points for ninth place, and Jolyon Palmer claimed his first Formula 1 point with a Toro Rosso-beating drive to finish tenth.

Massa's grid drama restricted him to 13th, meaning that despite Bottas's efforts, Force India made a two-point gain over Williams in the bid for fourth in the constructors' championship. The big swing, though, was between the Mercedes men, Rosberg's eight-point margin over Hamilton now out to 23 with just five races remaining. Things were starting to look difficult for Lewis…

Tony Dodgins

16

2016 FORMULA 1
PETRONAS
MALAYSIA
GRAND PRIX

ROLEX

F1 OFFICIAL TIMEPIECE

KUALA LUMPUR 30 SEPTEMBER–2 OCTOBER

RACE DISTANCE: 56 laps, 192.879 miles/310.408km

RACE WEATHER: Dry/sunny (track 49–55°C, air 32–35°C)

SEPANG INTERNATIONAL CIRCUIT, KUALA LUMPUR

Circuit: 3.444 miles/5.543km, 56 laps

187/116 kmh/mph

Gear
DRS zone

Turn 6 235/146
Turn 4 100/62
Turn 3 240/149
Turn 7 160/99
Turn 5 215/134
Hairpin 84/52
Turn 2 65/40
Turn 8 170/106
325/202
315/196
Turn 9 74/46
Turn 1 90/56
Turn 10 175/109
Turn 14 98/61
Turn 10 118/73
Turn 12 185/115
Turn 13 218/135

All results and data © FOM 2016

RACE – OFFICIAL CLASSIFICATION

Pos.	Driver	Nat.	No.	Entrant	Car/Engine	Tyres	Laps	Time/Retirement	Speed (mph/km/h)	Gap to leader	Fastest race lap	
1	Daniel Ricciardo	AUS	3	Red Bull Racing	Red Bull RB12-TAG Heuer RB12 V6	P	56	1h 37m 12.776s	119.045/191.584		1m 37.449s	44
2	Max Verstappen	NL	33	Red Bull Racing	Red Bull RB12-TAG Heuer RB12 V6	P	56	1h 37m 15.219s	191.504	2.443s	1m 37.376s	44
3	Nico Rosberg	D	6	Mercedes AMG Petronas F1 Team	Mercedes F1 W07-Mercedes PU106C V6	P	56	1h 37m 38.292s *	190.749	25.516s	1m 36.424s	44
4	Kimi Räikkönen	FIN	7	Scuderia Ferrari	Ferrari SF16-H-059/5 V6	P	56	1h 37m 41.561s	190.643	28.785s	1m 37.466s	47
5	Valtteri Bottas	FIN	77	Williams Martini Racing	Williams FW38-Mercedes PU106C V6	P	56	1h 38m 14.358s	189.582	1m 01.582s	1m 39.199s	53
6	Sergio Pérez	MEX	11	Sahara Force India F1 Team	Force India VJM09-Mercedes PU106C V6	P	56	1h 38m 16.570s	189.511	1m 03.794s	1m 39.328s	51
7	Fernando Alonso	E	14	McLaren Honda	McLaren MP4-31-Honda RA616H V6	P	56	1h 38m 17.981s	189.466	1m 05.205s	1m 38.291s	44
8	Nico Hülkenberg	D	27	Sahara Force India F1 Team	Force India VJM09-Mercedes PU106C V6	P	56	1h 38m 26.838s	189.182	1m 14.062s	1m 37.793s	43
9	Jenson Button	GB	22	McLaren Honda	McLaren MP4-31-Honda RA616H V6	P	56	1h 38m 34.592s	188.934	1m 21.816s	1m 38.740s	51
10	Jolyon Palmer	GB	30	Renault Sport F1 Team	Renault R.S.16-R.E.16 V6	P	56	1h 38m 48.242s	188.499	1m 35.466s	1m 39.350s	53
11	Carlos Sainz	E	55	Scuderia Toro Rosso	Toro Rosso STR11-Ferrari 059/4 V6	P	56	1h 38m 51.654s	188.390	1m 38.878s	1m 39.243s	44
12	Marcus Ericsson	S	9	Sauber F1 Team	Sauber C35-Ferrari 059/5 V6	P	55			1 lap	1m 39.781s	55
13	Felipe Massa	BR	19	Williams Martini Racing	Williams FW38-Mercedes PU106C V6	P	55			1 lap	1m 39.920s	53
14	Daniil Kvyat	RUS	26	Scuderia Toro Rosso	Toro Rosso STR11-Ferrari 059/4 V6	P	55			1 lap	1m 39.798s	43
15	Pascal Wehrlein	D	94	Manor Racing MRT	Manor MRT05-Mercedes PU106C V6	P	55			1 lap	1m 39.653s	55
16	Esteban Ocon	F	31	Manor Racing MRT	Manor MRT05-Mercedes PU106C V6	P	55	**		1 lap	1m 41.467s	45
	Felipe Nasr	BR	12	Sauber F1 Team	Sauber C35-Ferrari 059/5 V6	P	46	brakes			1m 40.490s	43
	Lewis Hamilton	GB	44	Mercedes AMG Petronas F1 Team	Mercedes F1 W07-Mercedes PU106C V6	P	40	engine			1m 38.595s	31
	Esteban Gutiérrez	MEX	21	Haas F1 Team	Haas VF-16-Ferrari 059/5 V6	P	39	front wheel lost			1m 41.775s	37
	Kevin Magnussen	DK	20	Renault Sport F1 Team	Renault R.S.16-R.E.16 V6	P	17	accident/brakes			1m 43.379s	3
	Romain Grosjean	F	8	Haas F1 Team	Haas VF-16-Ferrari 059/5 V6	P	7	brakes/spin			1m 42.142s	7
	Sebastian Vettel	D	5	Scuderia Ferrari	Ferrari SF15-H-059/5 V6	P	0	accident			no time	

* includes 10-second penalty for causing an accident – position unaffected. ** includes 5-second penalty for speeding in the pit lane – position unaffected.

Fastest race lap: Nico Rosberg on lap 44, 1m 36.424s, 128.592mph/206.948km/h.

Lap record: Juan Pablo Montoya (Williams FW26-BMW V10), 1m 34.223s, 131.596mph/211.782km/h (2004).

22 · ALONSO · McLaren
(45-place grid penalty for using additional power unit elements)

20 · OCON · Manor

18 · NASR · Sauber

16 · SAINZ · Toro Rosso

14 · MAGNUSSEN · Renault

12 · GROSJEAN · Haas

21 · WEHRLEIN · Manor

19 · PALMER · Renault

17 · ERICSSON · Sauber

15 · KVYAT · Toro Rosso

13 · GUTIÉRREZ · Haas

11 · BOTTAS · Williams

Grid order	1	2	3	4	5	6	7	8	9	10	11	12	13	14	15	16	17	18	19	20	21	22	23	24	25	26	27	28	29	30	31	32	33	34	35	36	37	38	39	40	41	42	43	44
44 HAMILTON	44	44	44	44	44	44	44	44	44	44	44	44	44	44	44	44	44	44	44	44	3	33	33	33	33	33	33	44	44	44	44	44	44	44	44	44	44	44	44	44	3	3	3	3
6 ROSBERG	3	3	3	3	3	3	3	3	3	3	3	3	3	3	3	3	3	3	3	3	33	44	44	44	44	44	44	3	3	3	3	3	3	3	3	3	3	3	3	3	33	33	33	3
33 VERSTAPPEN	11	11	33	33	33	33	33	33	33	7	7	7	7	7	7	7	7	7	7	7	33	44	3	3	3	3	3	33	33	33	33	33	33	33	33	33	33	33	33	33	6	6	6	6
3 RICCIARDO	7	33	11	7	7	7	7	7	7	33	33	33	33	33	33	33	33	33	33	33	7	7	7	7	7	7	7	7	7	7	7	7	7	7	7	7	7	7	6	6	6	7	7	7
5 VETTEL	33	7	7	11	11	11	11	11	77	77	77	77	77	77	77	77	77	77	6	6	6	6	6	6	6	6	6	6	6	6	6	6	6	6	6	7	77	77	77	77				
7 RÄIKKÖNEN	22	22	22	22	22	22	22	22	77	55	55	55	55	55	55	55	55	55	6	6	77	77	77	77	77	77	77	77	77	11	11	11	22	22	22	77	77	77	77	11	11	11	11	
11 PÉREZ	27	27	27	27	27	27	27	27	22	31	9	9	9	9	9	9	9	55	55	9	11	11	11	11	11	11	11	11	22	22	22	77	77	77	77	22	11	11	11	14	14	14	14	
27 HÜLKENBERG	77	77	77	77	77	77	77	77	27	9	31	11	11	11	6	6	6	9	9	11	9	22	22	22	22	22	22	22	77	77	77	11	11	11	11	11	14	14	14	22	22	27	27	
22 BUTTON	8	8	8	8	8	14	14	14	55	11	11	31	6	6	11	11	11	11	11	55	22	27	27	27	27	27	27	30	30	55	14	14	14	14	14	27	27	27	27	22	22			
19 MASSA	31	31	55	14	14	8	8	55	14	30	30	6	22	22	22	22	22	22	22	27	14	14	14	14	14	30	55	55	14	55	55	55	27	27	22	22	30	30	30	30				
77 BOTTAS	55	55	14	55	55	55	55	6	6	12	6	30	22	27	27	27	27	14	30	30	30	30	55	9	9	9	9	27	55	55	55	30	30	30	55	55	55	55						
8 GROSJEAN	14	14	31	31	31	6	6	31	31	22	22	22	27	30	30	14	14	14	14	30	12	55	55	55	55	9	14	14	27	27	27	9	9	9	9	55	55	55	9	9	9			
21 GUTIÉRREZ	9	9	9	9	9	31	31	9	9	27	27	14	14	14	30	30	30	30	30	12	55	9	9	9	9	14	27	30	12	30	30	30	30	9	9	9	12	12	12	12				
20 MAGNUSSEN	30	30	30	6	6	9	9	94	30	6	12	12	12	12	12	12	12	55	9	12	12	12	12	12	12	12	30	12	12	12	12	12	12	12	12	19	19	19	19					
26 KVYAT	94	94	94	30	30	30	94	30	94	14	14	12	26	26	26	26	26	26	26	26	26	26	26	26	31	31	26	26	26	26	26	26	26	26	26	26	26	26	26					
55 SAINZ	12	12	6	94	94	94	30	12	12	94	94	94	94	94	94	94	94	94	94	94	94	94	94	94	19	19	19	19	19	19	94	31	31	31										
9 ERICSSON	6	6	12	12	12	12	26	26	94	94	31	31	31	31	31	31	31	31	31	31	31	19	26	19	26	94	94	94	94	94	31	94	94	94										
12 NASR	26	19	19	19	19	19	26	21	21	21	21	21	21	21	19	19	19	19	19	19	26	94	21	21	21	21	21	31																
30 PALMER	19	26	26	26	26	26	21	20	20	20	20	19	19	19	21	21	21	21	21	21	21	21	31	31	31	31	31																	
31 OCON	20	20	21	21	21	21	20	19	19	19	19	20	20	20	20	20																												
94 WEHRLEIN	21	21	20	20	20	20	19																																					
14 ALONSO																																												

TIME SHEETS

PRACTICE 1 (FRIDAY)
Weather: Dry/sunny
Temperatures: track 39-50°C, air 29-32°C

Pos.	Driver	Laps	Time
1	Nico Rosberg	25	1m 35.227s
2	Lewis Hamilton	25	1m 35.721s
3	Kimi Räikkönen	16	1m 36.315s
4	Sebastian Vettel	18	1m 36.331s
5	Fernando Alonso	18	1m 36.510s
6	Daniel Ricciardo	27	1m 36.753s
7	Max Verstappen	26	1m 36.973s
8	Nico Hülkenberg	26	1m 37.513s
9	Sergio Pérez	27	1m 37.601s
10	Jenson Button	20	1m 37.613s
11	Daniil Kvyat	29	1m 37.847s
12	Valtteri Bottas	17	1m 37.861s
13	Romain Grosjean	22	1m 37.886s
14	Esteban Gutiérrez	20	1m 37.921s
15	Carlos Sainz	25	1m 38.055s
16	Felipe Nasr	18	1m 38.184s
17	Marcus Ericsson	20	1m 38.313s
18	Felipe Massa	24	1m 38.339s
19	Jolyon Palmer	23	1m 39.148s
20	Esteban Ocon	28	1m 40.036s
21	Pascal Wehrlein	26	1m 40.627s
22	Kevin Magnussen	2	no time

PRACTICE 2 (FRIDAY)
Weather: Dry/sunny
Temperatures: track 51-60°C, air 32-35°C

Pos.	Driver	Laps	Time
1	Lewis Hamilton	35	1m 34.944s
2	Nico Rosberg	36	1m 35.177s
3	Sebastian Vettel	37	1m 35.605s
4	Kimi Räikkönen	31	1m 35.842s
5	Max Verstappen	29	1m 36.037s
6	Sergio Pérez	33	1m 36.284s
7	Fernando Alonso	27	1m 36.296s
8	Daniel Ricciardo	30	1m 36.337s
9	Nico Hülkenberg	37	1m 36.390s
10	Jenson Button	22	1m 36.715s
11	Carlos Sainz	30	1m 36.836s
12	Jolyon Palmer	36	1m 36.940s
13	Valtteri Bottas	37	1m 37.016s
14	Esteban Gutiérrez	28	1m 37.048s
15	Felipe Massa	19	1m 37.110s
16	Daniil Kvyat	29	1m 37.297s
17	Marcus Ericsson	28	1m 37.449s
18	Felipe Nasr	26	1m 37.547s
19	Kevin Magnussen	19	1m 37.664s
20	Romain Grosjean	25	1m 37.789s
21	Pascal Wehrlein	34	1m 37.878s
22	Esteban Ocon	36	1m 37.990s

PRACTICE 3 (SATURDAY)
Weather: Dry/cloudy
Temperatures: track 50°C, air 32°C

Pos.	Driver	Laps	Time
1	Lewis Hamilton	16	1m 34.434s
2	Max Verstappen	14	1m 34.879s
3	Nico Rosberg	16	1m 35.053s
4	Kimi Räikkönen	15	1m 35.150s
5	Sebastian Vettel	14	1m 35.170s
6	Daniel Ricciardo	22	1m 35.461s
7	Nico Hülkenberg	16	1m 35.776s
8	Valtteri Bottas	17	1m 35.902s
9	Carlos Sainz	18	1m 36.222s
10	Felipe Massa	20	1m 36.227s
11	Sergio Pérez	15	1m 36.259s
12	Jenson Button	11	1m 36.363s
13	Esteban Gutiérrez	14	1m 36.553s
14	Jolyon Palmer	20	1m 36.604s
15	Romain Grosjean	15	1m 36.687s
16	Kevin Magnussen	19	1m 36.741s
17	Daniil Kvyat	20	1m 36.752s
18	Marcus Ericsson	19	1m 36.765s
19	Felipe Nasr	18	1m 37.106s
20	Esteban Ocon	17	1m 37.961s
21	Pascal Wehrlein	13	1m 38.089s
22	Fernando Alonso	15	1m 41.199s

QUALIFYING (SATURDAY)
Weather: Dry/cloudy Temperatures: track 38-53°C, air 30-33°C

Pos.	Driver	First	Second	Third	Qualifying Tyre
1	Lewis Hamilton	1m 34.344s	1m 33.046s	1m 32.850s	Soft (new)
2	Nico Rosberg	1m 34.460s	1m 33.609s	1m 33.264s	Soft (new)
3	Max Verstappen	1m 35.443s	1m 33.775s	1m 33.420s	Soft (new)
4	Daniel Ricciardo	1m 35.079s	1m 33.888s	1m 33.467s	Soft (new)
5	Sebastian Vettel	1m 34.557s	1m 33.972s	1m 33.584s	Soft (new)
6	Kimi Räikkönen	1m 34.556s	1m 33.903s	1m 33.632s	Soft (new)
7	Sergio Pérez	1m 35.068s	1m 34.538s	1m 34.319s	Soft (new)
8	Nico Hülkenberg	1m 34.827s	1m 34.441s	1m 34.489s	Soft (new)
9	Jenson Button	1m 35.267s	1m 34.431s	1m 34.518s	Soft (new)
10	Felipe Massa	1m 35.267s	1m 34.422s	1m 34.671s	Soft (new)
11	Valtteri Bottas	1m 35.166s	1m 34.577s		
12	Romain Grosjean	1m 35.400s	1m 35.001s		
13	Esteban Gutiérrez	1m 35.658s	1m 35.097s		
14	Kevin Magnussen	1m 35.593s	1m 35.277s		
15	Daniil Kvyat	1m 35.695s	1m 35.369s		
16	Carlos Sainz	1m 35.605s	1m 35.374s		
17	Marcus Ericsson	1m 35.816s			
18	Felipe Nasr	1m 35.949s			
19	Jolyon Palmer	1m 35.999s			
20	Esteban Ocon	1m 36.451s			
21	Pascal Wehrlein	1m 36.587s			
22	Fernando Alonso	1m 37.155s			

Photo: Peter J. Fox

FOR THE RECORD

300th GRAND PRIX START: **Jenson Button.**

100th FRONT ROW POSITION: **Lewis Hamilton.**

20th FASTEST LAP: **Nico Rosberg.**

1st POINT: **Jolyon Palmer.**

DID YOU KNOW?

This was the first time for 10 years that teams lined up in pairs for the top 8 on the grid.

This was the first time in 42 races that there was no world champion on the podium.

POINTS

DRIVERS
1	Nico Rosberg	288
2	Lewis Hamilton	265
3	Daniel Ricciardo	204
4	Kimi Räikkönen	160
5	Sebastian Vettel	153
6	Max Verstappen	147
7	Valtteri Bottas	80
8	Sergio Pérez	74
9	Nico Hülkenberg	50
10	Fernando Alonso	42
11	Felipe Massa	41
12	Carlos Sainz	30
13	Romain Grosjean	28
14	Daniil Kvyat	25
15	Jenson Button	19
16	Kevin Magnussen	7
17	Jolyon Palmer	1
18	Pascal Wehrlein	1
19	Stoffel Vandoorne	1

CONSTRUCTORS
1	Mercedes	553
2	Red Bull	359
3	Ferrari	313
4	Force India	124
5	Williams	121
6	McLaren	62
7	Toro Rosso	47
8	Haas	28
9	Renault	8
10	Manor	1

10 · MASSA · Williams
(started from the pit lane)

8 · HÜLKENBERG · Force India

6 · RÄIKKÖNEN · Ferrari

4 · RICCIARDO · Red Bull

2 · ROSBERG · Mercedes

9 · BUTTON · McLaren

7 · PÉREZ · Force India

5 · VETTEL · Ferrari

3 · VERSTAPPEN · Red Bull

1 · HAMILTON · Mercedes

Qualifying: head-to-head
Rosberg	8	8	Hamilton
Vettel	10	6	Räikkönen
Massa	3	13	Bottas
Ricciardo	4	0	Kvyat
Ricciardo	9	3	Verstappen
Pérez	8	8	Hülkenberg
Magnussen	11	5	Palmer
Verstappen	3	1	Sainz
Kvyat	3	9	Sainz
Ericsson	9	7	Nasr
Alonso	10	5	Button
Button	0	1	Vandoorne
Haryanto	5	7	Wehrlein
Wehrlein	3	1	Ocon
Grosjean	11	5	Gutiérrez

45	46	47	48	49	50	51	52	53	54	55	56	
3	3	3	3	3	3	3	3	3	3	3	3	1
33	33	33	33	33	33	33	33	33	33	33	33	2
6	6	6	6	6	6	6	6	6	6	6	6	3
7	7	7	7	7	7	7	7	7	7	7	7	4
77	77	77	77	77	77	77	77	77	77	77	77	5
11	11	11	11	11	11	11	11	11	11	11	11	6
14	14	14	14	14	14	14	14	14	14	14	14	7
27	27	27	27	27	27	27	27	27	27	27	27	8
22	22	22	22	22	22	22	22	22	22	22	22	9
30	30	30	30	30	30	30	30	30	30	30	30	10
55	55	55	55	55	55	55	55	55	55	55	55	
9	9	9	9	9	9	9	9	9	9	9	9	
12	19	19	19	19	19	19	19	19	19	19		
19	26	26	26	26	26	26	26	26	26			
26	12	94	94	94	94	94	94	94	94	94		
31	94	31	31	31	31	31	31	31	31			
94	31											

6 = Pit stop   9 = Drive-thru penalty

94 = One lap or more behind

▓ Safety car deployed on laps shown

RACE TYRE STRATEGIES

 PIRELLI

	Driver	Race Stint 1	Race Stint 2	Race Stint 3	Race Stint 4
1	Ricciardo	Soft (u): 1-21	Hard (n): 22-41	Soft (n): 42-56	
2	Verstappen	Soft (u): 1-9	Soft (u): 10-27	Hard (n): 28-41	Soft (u): 42-56
3	Rosberg	Soft (u): 1-9	Hard (n): 10-31	Soft (n): 32-41	Soft (u): 42-56
4	Räikkönen	Soft (u): 1-20	Hard (n): 21-32	Hard (u): 33-40	Soft (u): 41-56
5	Bottas	Medium (n): 1-29	Hard (n): 30-56		
6	Pérez	Soft (u): 1-9	Medium (n): 10-32	Hard (n): 33-56	
7	Alonso	Soft (n): 1-9	Hard (n): 10-27	Soft (n): 28-40	Soft (u): 41-56
8	Hülkenberg	Soft (u): 1-9	Medium (n): 10-28	Hard (n): 29-40	Soft (u): 41-56
9	Button	Soft (u): 1-9	Hard (n): 10-37	Soft (u): 38-56	
10	Palmer	Hard (n): 1-31	Soft (n): 32-56		
11	Sainz	Soft (u): 1-20	Hard (n): 21-37	Soft (u): 38-56	
12	Ericsson	Soft (u): 1-21	Soft (n): 22-37	Hard (n): 38-55	
13	Massa	Soft (u): 1	Hard (u): 2-6	Hard (u): 7-31	Medium (n): 32-55
14	Kvyat	Soft (n): 1	Hard (n): 2-29	Soft (n): 30-40	Soft (u): 41-55
15	Wehrlein	Soft (n): 1-9	Hard (n): 10-30	Hard (n): 31-41	Soft (u): 42-55
16	Ocon	Soft (n): 1-12	Hard (n): 13-31	Hard (n): 32-55	
	Nasr	Medium (n): 1-32	Hard (n): 33-46 (dnf)		
	Hamilton	Soft (u): 1-20	Hard (n): 21-40 (dnf)		
	Gutiérrez	Soft (n): 1	Soft (u): 2-22	Hard (n): 23-39 (dnf)	
	Magnussen	Medium (n): 1	Hard (n): 2-17 (dnf)		
	Grosjean	Soft (n): 1-7 (dnf)			
	Vettel	Soft (u): 0 (dnf)			

The tyre regulations stipulate that at least two of three dry tyre specifications must be used during a dry race.
Pirelli P Zero logos are colour-coded on the tyre sidewalls: Yellow = Soft; Orange = Hard; White = Medium. (n) new (u) used

Photos: Peter J. Fox

JAPANESE GRAND PRIX

SUZUKA CIRCUIT

SUZUKA QUALIFYING

NICO ROSBERG had taken the previous two Suzuka pole positions, even if team-mate Lewis Hamilton had won the races. If he could do it again, and underline that 23-point championship advantage handed to him by Hamilton's engine failure in Malaysia, it would put him in prime place from which to launch his bid for a ninth win of 2016. And if he could achieve that, it would mean he could afford to finish second to Hamilton for the remainder of the season and still claim that first world title.

It started to look good for Rosberg when he topped every session of practice and then enjoyed an almost four-tenths margin over Hamilton in Q1 and Q2. But, raising his game in Q3, Hamilton made Nico work hard for a 30th career pole, the final margin between them just thirteen-thousandths of a second as car No. 6 broke the timing beam in 1m 30.647s.

"It's been going well the whole weekend," Rosberg said. "I had a good balance in the car and was feeling good and comfortable."

Hamilton said he was happy, too, but after more of a battle.

"We kind of veered off on a tangent in terms of set-up this weekend, and it wasn't until qualifying that I went back with some big changes," he explained, "and it's not that easy to go straight into qualifying with a completely different car." Despite that, he produced a first Q3 run that overturned the deficit to Rosberg and momentarily put him on pole, until Nico snatched it back on his own final run.

A gap of just three-tenths between Rosberg and third-placed Kimi Räikkönen was less than might have been anticipated and partially down to Hamilton's Malaysian engine failure having prompted Mercedes to restrict some of its more aggressive qualifying and race engine modes. The three-pointed star also delayed the introduction of the latest-spec power unit for its customer teams.

If Maranello was delighted to claim the second-row slots ahead of Red Bull, that enthusiasm was tempered by grid penalties for both Räikkönen and team-mate Sebastian Vettel. Räikkönen had looked more convincing than Vettel throughout practice, but he was frustrated by a five-place drop for a replacement gearbox that was needed for Sunday afternoon. At a place like Suzuka, where overtaking is not the work of a moment, once again you did have to question the wisdom of such draconian penalties for mechanical mayhem beyond the control of the man in the cockpit. Wouldn't a loss of constructors' championship points, or even a fine, be a better punishment?

Vettel, meanwhile, started three places further back as a consequence of his optimistic lunge down the inside of Turn One in Malaysia, which had disrupted Rosberg's afternoon.

Red Bull's Friday-afternoon long-run pace was highly impressive, particularly from Max Verstappen, and if the single-lap pace was still slightly shy of Ferrari, the Maranello drivers' penalties ensured that Red Bull appeared to be in good shape potentially to take the race to Mercedes, especially if it rained. Verstappen qualified 0.15s behind Vettel on time, and 0.07s ahead of team-mate Ricciardo, who felt he was losing out on top speed. The Renault engines in both Red Bulls were coming to the end of their duty cycles, with new ones due to be installed in Austin.

Sergio Pérez qualified a fine seventh – which would become fifth after the Ferrari penalties – his 1m 31.961s lap matching the time of Romain Grosjean's Haas to the last thousandth of a second. The Mexican took the higher position, however, by dint of recording the time first.

Force India team-mate Nico Hülkenberg was next, 0.18s slower, with Esteban Gutiérrez completing the top ten qualifiers.

The Haas pace was a surprise, the team having put the problems of Singapore and Malaysia behind them, and extracting the most from an update package that included a new front wing.

Paying the price for the Haas advance was Williams, still embroiled in its close constructors' championship battle with Force India, but unable to put either driver into the Suzuka top ten, Valtteri Bottas missing Sergio Pérez's Q2 time by 0.08s.

With a high proportion of full-throttle running at Suzuka, the Toro Rossos were suffering with the old 2015-spec Ferrari engine as Daniil Kvyat, unusually, pipped Carlos Sainz by 0.06s for 13th.

Just 0.004s slower was Fernando Alonso, McLaren having a tough time in Hondaland. In fact, he only just scraped out of Q1 at the expense of team-mate Jenson Button, both being beaten by Jolyon Palmer's Renault.

"What was the gap to Fernando?" Jenson asked over the radio.

"Thirty milliseconds," came the response.

"Ouch!" said Button.

Alonso found a tenth to beat Palmer in Q2, while Jolyon's Renault team-mate, Kevin Magnussen, was eliminated in Q1 along with the Saubers and Manors. At the Swiss team, Marcus Ericsson got the better of Felipe Nasr by a tenth, and Esteban Ocon impressed by going a couple of tenths quicker than Pascal Wehrlein on his first visit to the challenging Suzuka.

HAMILTON'S 2016 race starts had been variable, and in Japan, before the race got under way, Lewis was concerned about a damp patch on his side of the grid after overnight rain. As the cars formed up, he tried to place his Mercedes to the left of it, but when the lights went out, rather than the excessive wheelspin he had feared, the car bogged down.

Rosberg, by contrast, got away well, but Ricciardo was forced to jink left to avoid Hamilton, who also lost out to both Ferraris, both Red Bulls and both Force Indias as he dropped to eighth place.

Vettel took advantage of Ferrari's straight-line speed superiority over Red Bull to pass Ricciardo on the run down to 130R to move up to fourth, behind Rosberg, Verstappen and Pérez. A better exit from the chicane allowed him to take third from the Mexican into Turn One at the start of the second lap – unusual without the help of DRS.

Räikkönen did need the assistance of DRS to pass Hülkenberg around the outside into T1 on lap seven, something that Hamilton also accomplished on the following lap to move up to seventh.

Rosberg was lapping in the 1m 37s range for the first seven laps, but dropped into the 1m 38s on lap eight, signalling that the first stops would not be long in coming. By this time, he had opened out a 5.3s lead over Verstappen, who now had Vettel's Ferrari within 2s of his gearbox. Then there was a 6.5s gap to Pérez, who was dictating the pace of the group behind. Ricciardo was right with the Force India, but with insufficient straight-line speed to pass, while Räikkönen was almost within DRS range and just over a second clear of Hamilton. Behind the Mercedes was a 3s gap to Hülkenberg.

Red Bull had spotted the potential undercut threat from Ferrari to each of their drivers and, with a 10s gap between them and hence no concern about losing time 'stacking' the second car in the pits, stopped both Verstappen and Ricciardo on lap ten.

Hülkenberg was in next lap. Then, on lap 12, Rosberg, Vettel, Pérez and Räikkönen all headed in, with Hamilton having to wait until lap 13.

By dint of his earlier stop, Verstappen had narrowed Rosberg's lead to just 2.6s by the end of lap 14, with Vettel 3s behind the first Red Bull. The Williams pair, Valtteri Bottas and Felipe Massa, both running a longer opening stint on harder tyres, were now fifth and sixth, ahead of Hamilton. The Mercedes driver, having been freed up when those ahead pitted, turned in a couple of ballistic laps and managed to overcut Räikkönen (trapped behind Pérez) and Sergio himself, who lost out most heavily, being passed by Räikkönen's Ferrari as they both went by Palmer.

Then Lewis demoted Ricciardo, delayed behind the Williams pair and Palmer, on the run to 130R, using the superior Mercedes straight-line speed. The Red Bull speed figures showed that Ricciardo seemed to be lacking pace, even compared to team-mate Verstappen.

"I'm not sure entirely why," Daniel said later, "but both of our engines were tired and my car was grounding out a little bit, which was probably costing me a bit of straight-line speed. I did go a slightly different route in set-up, with the rear springs, and maybe it was that."

Next, Hamilton made short work of the two Williams to elevate himself to fourth. Now he had a clear track to Vettel, the third-placed Ferrari some 13.5s up the road.

What of Haas, after qualifying both of its cars in the top ten? Romain Grosjean and Esteban Gutiérrez both managed decent getaways and came around ninth and tenth at the end of the opening lap, running just ahead of the Toro Rossos, with Kvyat heading Sainz. Grosjean had dropped around 3.5s behind Hülkenberg's Force India by the time of his first stop on lap ten.

Gutiérrez came in a lap later, but was undercut by Alonso's McLaren-Honda, which had stopped two laps earlier. Sainz made his stop two laps after the Mexican and came out

Above: With Max Verstappen ready to pounce, Nico Rosberg takes control from the start. After a poor getaway, Hamilton is mired in the pack.
Photo: Red Bull Racing/Getty Images

Top left: Jenson fans kitted out in support of their hero.
Photo: WRi2/Jean-François Galeron

Above left: Mechanics work on a Toro Rosso in the Suzuka pit.

Left: Sebastian Vettel's season was beginning to unravel.
Photos: WRi2/Jean-François Galeron

Below left: A suitably colour-coded Hülkenberg fan – with a fan.

Opening spread: Nico Rosberg forces his Pirellis into amazing shapes as he extracts the maximum from his car.
Photos: Peter J. Fox

between them, the whole train behind Button's McLaren, on a different strategy that entailed running until lap 19 before stopping for the first time. By the time Jenson pitted, Gutiérrez had lost 18.5s to team-mate Grosjean in under ten laps, which had included a spin on his out-lap. Sainz had also lost ground due to Kvyat having first pit-stop call, and then had cost himself a bit more time with an excursion into the Turn One run-off while trying to go around the outside of Alonso.

By lap 25, Hamilton had taken a couple of seconds out of third-placed Vettel's advantage, and had opened a 10s margin over Ricciardo and Räikkönen when Ferrari pitted Kimi for the second time on lap 26, from just a second behind Ricciardo.

Red Bull knew that they couldn't defend the undercut from there, so they kept the Australian out for a further seven laps, shortening his final stint. That still required the hard-compound Pirelli, however, and with almost a 20s deficit to Kimi once re-shod, it would be a tall order to catch the Ferrari again, let alone pass it.

Once rebooted, Räikkönen was the fastest man on track, and after rejoining 28.5s behind fourth-placed Hamilton, immediately started to close the gap.

At the front, Rosberg led Verstappen by 4.5s at the end of lap 26, with Vettel's Ferrari 2.2s behind the Red Bull, all three of them lapping within 0.18s. On the following lap, however, Verstappen lapped half a second slower than Vettel, which put the Ferrari within undercut range. Maranello did not react, however, keeping Vettel out a further seven laps to achieve the longer middle stint. The plan was to put him on to softs for the final stint, meaning that he needed to eke out the middle stint to make that viable. Arguably though, track position and the harder tyre would have been of more value.

Red Bull reacted to what was an unrealised undercut fear by pitting Verstappen on lap 28. When Vettel rejoined on lap 35, he was 11s behind the Red Bull with just 18 laps remaining, any chance of displacing Verstappen seemingly gone, unless Vettel had super-low degradation on his softs.

Verstappen's stop, from 5s behind Rosberg, led Mercedes to respond with the race leader next time around, handing a brief lead to Vettel for five laps. Nico's margin over Verstappen was down to 3.9s by dint of his slightly later stop, but he never appeared to be other than in complete control.

The next point of interest surrounded Hamilton and the

Ferraris. By lap 30, he had cut that initial 13.5s gap to Vettel to just 6s and was going quicker. But, 27.5s behind him on his fresh rubber, Räikkönen was still flying and lapping 1s quicker even than Lewis. Mercedes faced a conundrum: they needed to keep Hamilton out to try to get him within undercut range of Vettel, but with a stop taking around 23.5s, if they kept him out too long, losing time to Räikkönen, they risked pitting out behind the second Ferrari.

At the end of lap 31, the Vettel-Hamilton gap was 4.8s and the Hamilton-Räikkönen margin was 26.5. On lap 32, the figures were 4.2s and 24.6. Kimi was now dangerously within undercutting distance, and Mercedes had little choice but to pit Hamilton next time around. Ferrari, surely, would bring in Vettel at the same time, his lap times having dropped into the high 1m 38s range, while Räikkönen was lapping at 1m 36.1s. But no, they left Seb out for another lap, during which he encountered traffic through the Esses, despite repeatedly shouting, "Blue flags!" on the radio.

It was a great break for Mercedes. Hamilton was told to ignore bringing in his final set of hards gently and to drive a qualifying lap – track position was all. He did as instructed and had 3s in hand over Räikkönen as he rejoined. Ferrari pitted Vettel next time around, to go on to softs with 19 laps remaining, but Lewis was already sweeping around his outside into Turn One as the Ferrari left the pit lane.

Vettel, of course, was on the quicker tyre: he would need to make the 'golden' lap count. He couldn't quite do it. He was right on Hamilton's gearbox as they went into the Spoon Curve and appeared to be in the tow of the Mercedes on the run down to 130R, but he didn't have quite sufficient speed.

Hamilton was now in a podium position, and if he was to achieve the ultimate damage limitation after his awful start, he needed to catch Verstappen, who was 10s ahead with 18 laps to go, on tyres that were five laps older than Lewis's. The chase was on!

It took Hamilton just five laps to halve the deficit, and in another five, lap 45, he was within DRS range of the Red Bull and only 6.1s behind race leader Rosberg. The latter was pacing his race superbly and keeping a weather eye on developments behind.

Verstappen was not fazed by Hamilton's arrival. He made sure that he got a good exit from the chicane to protect against a DRS attack into Turn One, and used his battery deployment intelligently to aid the cause, just as he had done

Above: Hamilton makes a typically slick pit stop on his climb to third.
Photo: Peter J. Fox

Left: A slow pit stop dropped Valtteri Bottas behind team-mate Felipe Massa to take tenth at the finish.
Photo: WRi2/Hiroshi Yamamura

Right: Hülkenberg took eighth place to help his team edge a little further clear of Williams in the ongoing battle for constructors' points.
Photo: Sahara Force India F1

Above: Max Verstappen's robust defensive move forced Lewis Hamilton into making a mistake, which caused the champion to miss the chicane and lose any chance of second place behind Rosberg.
Photo: Red Bull Racing/Getty Images

Right: A third win in four races gave Nico Rosberg a substantial lead in the title race.

Below right: A rueful looking Hamilton had to be content with third.
Photos: Mercedes AMG Petronas F1 Team

Far right: Once again, Fernando Alonso endured a troubled time on Honda's home soil, though in 2016 his ire seemed to be directed at the McLaren rather than its engine.
Photo: McLaren Honda

in those final laps at Barcelona while holding Räikkönen at bay for his debut win.

On the penultimate lap, Hamilton got a strong exit from Spoon Curve, was right on the Red Bull through 130R and then jinked right to try to get down the inside into the chicane, the classic Suzuka move. Verstappen, though, knew all about it and also moved right to cover Lewis.

Once again, it was arguably a late move in the braking zone. Lewis was forced to jink left and try to go around the outside, but he ran too straight. Verstappen was now safe. Hamilton complained over the radio about Max moving in the braking area, and the stewards considered it, but no action was deemed necessary. It was nothing that hadn't happened a million times at Suzuka.

And so a delighted Rosberg crossed the line 5s clear of Hamilton and Verstappen to take win number nine of 2016, opening a 33-point advantage at the top of the championship – significant in that it allowed him to finish second in the remaining four races and still take his first world title.

A slightly disgruntled Vettel was fourth, having backed off when he realised he couldn't threaten Hamilton on his softer rubber, with Räikkönen just 7s further back.

Ricciardo finished the race 5s adrift of the second Ferrari, with Pérez's Force India getting to the flag 1.5s ahead of team-mate Hülkenberg, for whom the highlight of the race had been a lap-20 pass of Bottas into the chicane, prompting a whoop and a "See ya later!" over the radio from 'the Hulk'.

A slow pit stop for Valtteri had dropped him behind Williams team-mate Massa as Sir Frank's cars took three points for ninth and tenth, the pair dropping a little further behind Force India in that intense battle for fourth place in the constructors' championship.

Grosjean finished right with the Williams pair, but just out of the points, while under the radar, Jolyon Palmer produced one of the drives of the race, despite finishing a lap down in the difficult Renault. He had not raced at Suzuka before, yet finished 15s up the road from team-mate Kevin Magnussen – no mean feat. Whether it would be enough to keep him in the team for 2017 remained to be seen as Renault seemingly spoke to everyone from The Pope south…

Tony Dodgins

VIEWPOINT
LOSS OF FACE AT HOME

AFTER two consecutive points finishes, 16th and 18th was not merely disappointing for McLaren, it was an embarrassment on Honda's home track. Unlike 2015, however, this was not entirely the fault of the hapless engine manufacturer.

For a car that needed slow-speed corners and plenty of heavy braking to extract a few of its finer points, Suzuka was the last place McLaren needed to be from a performance point of view, never mind explaining the shortfall to the Honda hierarchy.

Alonso had been painfully vocal the year before about having a "GP2 engine" behind his shoulders, but somehow he didn't feel the need to compare the gripless McLaren with a GP2 chassis when only the Manors were consistently slower through the twisting first sector.

With Button failing to make Q2 and Alonso getting in by the skin of his teeth, the race was never going to promise much. Even another hoped-for opportunist start by Fernando would be denied when he was eased on to the run-off at the first corner. The black cars finished a lap down and played no significant part whatsoever.

"Our race today reflected the whole weekend; it was just anonymous," said Alonso. "To finish 16th and 18th is a nasty surprise. It was clear that the layout of the track didn't suit our package. We lacked downforce for the faster corners. I know our car is much more competitive than we were able to show today, and I'm disappointed about putting on such a poor show at Honda's home race."

The on-track performance did nothing to deflect media attention from gathering rumours about Ron Dennis and his future with McLaren. Having re-established himself in 2014, the team's CEO was quick to make clear that he was going nowhere. Certainly, in Japan, that could have been applied to his racing cars, which continued to have flanks devoid of blue-chip partnerships that McLaren had enjoyed in better days than this.

Maurice Hamilton

17

2016 FORMULA 1
EMIRATES
JAPANESE
GRAND PRIX

SUZUKA 7–9 OCTOBER

ROLEX

F1 OFFICIAL TIMEPIECE

RACE DISTANCE: 53 laps, 191.054 miles/307.471km

RACE WEATHER: Dry/overcast (track 25–27°C, air 21–22°C)

SUZUKA INTERNATIONAL RACING COURSE, SUZUKA-CITY

Circuit: 3.608 miles/5.807km, 53 laps

187/116 kmh/mph

☼ Gear
▬ DRS zone

Turn 14 170/106
Spoon
Turn 13 225/140
Turn 12 285/178
Degner 2 150/93
Degner 1 185/115
Turn 2 155/69
130R 315/196
Hairpin 85/53
S Curves 250/155   196/122
200/124
Casino Triangle 92/57
Turn 1 265/165
Dunlop 240/149

RACE – OFFICIAL CLASSIFICATION

Pos.	Driver	Nat.	No.	Entrant	Car/Engine	Tyres	Laps	Time/Retirement	Speed (mph/km/h)	Gap to leader	Fastest race lap	
1	**Nico Rosberg**	D	6	Mercedes AMG Petronas F1 Team	Mercedes F1 W07-Mercedes PU106C V6	P	53	1h 26m 43.333s	132.183/212.728		1m 36.049s	31
2	**Max Verstappen**	NL	33	Red Bull Racing	Red Bull RB12-TAG Heuer RB12 V6	P	53	1h 26m 48.311s	132.056/212.524	4.978s	1m 36.386s	43
3	**Lewis Hamilton**	GB	44	Mercedes AMG Petronas F1 Team	Mercedes F1 W07-Mercedes PU106C V6	P	53	1h 26m 49.109s	132.036/212.492	5.776s	1m 35.152s	36
4	**Sebastian Vettel**	D	5	Scuderia Ferrari	Ferrari SF15-H-059/5 V6	P	53	1h 27m 03.602s	131.670/211.902	20.269s	1m 35.118s	36
5	**Kimi Räikkönen**	FIN	7	Scuderia Ferrari	Ferrari SF16-H-059/5 V6	P	53	1h 27m 11.703s	131.466/211.574	28.370s	1m 35.990s	33
6	**Daniel Ricciardo**	AUS	3	Red Bull Racing	Red Bull RB12-TAG Heuer RB12 V6	P	53	1h 27m 17.274s	131.326/211.349	33.941s	1m 35.511s	36
7	**Sergio Pérez**	MEX	11	Sahara Force India F1 Team	Force India VJM09-Mercedes PU106C V6	P	53	1h 27m 40.828s	130.738/210.403	57.495s	1m 36.756s	31
8	**Nico Hülkenberg**	D	27	Sahara Force India F1 Team	Force India VJM09-Mercedes PU106C V6	P	53	1h 27m 42.510s	130.697/210.336	59.177s	1m 37.351s	39
9	**Felipe Massa**	BR	19	Williams Martini Racing	Williams FW38-Mercedes PU106C V6	P	53	1h 28m 21.096s	129.745/208.805	1m 37.763s	1m 37.785s	35
10	**Valtteri Bottas**	FIN	77	Williams Martini Racing	Williams FW38-Mercedes PU106C V6	P	53	1h 28m 21.656s	129.731/208.782	1m 38.323s	1m 37.844s	33
11	Romain Grosjean	F	8	Haas F1 Team	Haas VF-16-Ferrari 059/5 V6	P	53	1h 28m 22.587s	129.709/208.746	1m 39.254s	1m 37.020s	32
12	Jolyon Palmer	GB	30	Renault Sport F1 Team	Renault R.S.16-R.E.16 V6	P	52			1 lap	1m 37.978s	43
13	Daniil Kvyat	RUS	26	Scuderia Toro Rosso	Toro Rosso STR11-Ferrari 059/4 V6	P	52			1 lap	1m 37.597s	25
14	Kevin Magnussen	DK	20	Renault Sport F1 Team	Renault R.S.16-R.E.16 V6	P	52			1 lap	1m 38.036s	27
15	Marcus Ericsson	S	9	Sauber F1 Team	Sauber C35-Ferrari 059/5 V6	P	52			1 lap	1m 38.496s	28
16	Fernando Alonso	E	14	McLaren Honda	McLaren MP4-31-Honda RA616H V6	P	52			1 lap	1m 38.208s	29
17	Carlos Sainz	E	55	Scuderia Toro Rosso	Toro Rosso STR11-Ferrari 059/4 V6	P	52			1 lap	1m 37.723s	41
18	Jenson Button	GB	22	McLaren Honda	McLaren MP4-31-Honda RA616H V6	P	52			1 lap	1m 37.177s	39
19	Felipe Nasr	BR	12	Sauber F1 Team	Sauber C35-Ferrari 059/5 V6	P	52			1 lap	1m 38.544s	28
20	Esteban Gutiérrez	MEX	21	Haas F1 Team	Haas VF-16-Ferrari 059/5 V6	P	52			1 lap	1m 37.775s	30
21	Esteban Ocon	F	31	Manor Racing MRT	Manor MRT05-Mercedes PU106C V6	P	52			1 lap	1m 38.380s	33
22	Pascal Wehrlein	D	94	Manor Racing MRT	Manor MRT05-Mercedes PU106C V6	P	52			1 lap	1m 38.000s	39

Fastest race lap: Sebastian Vettel on lap 36, 1m 35.118, 136.566mph/219.781km/h.

Lap record: Kimi Räikkönen (McLaren MP4-20-Mercedes Benz V10), 1m 31.540s, 141.904mph/228.372km/h (2005).

21 · WEHRLEIN · Manor *(5-place grid penalty for replacing the gearbox)*

19 · NASR · Sauber

17 · MAGNUSSEN · Renault

15 · ALONSO · McLaren

13 · KVYAT · Toro Rosso

11 · BOTTAS · Williams

22 · BUTTON · McLaren *(35-place grid penalty for using additional power unit elements)*

20 · OCON · Manor

18 · ERICSSON · Sauber

16 · PALMER · Renault

14 · SAINZ · Toro Rosso

12 · MASSA · Williams

Grid order	1	2	3	4	5	6	7	8	9	10	11	12	13	14	15	16	17	18	19	20	21	22	23	24	25	26	27	28	29	30	31	32	33	34	35	36	37	38	39	40	41	42
6 ROSBERG	6	6	6	6	6	6	6	6	6	6	6	6	6	6	6	6	6	6	6	6	6	6	6	6	6	6	6	6	6	5	5	5	5	6	6	6	6	6	6	6	6	6
44 HAMILTON	33	33	33	33	33	33	33	33	33	5	5	5	44	33	33	33	33	33	33	33	33	33	33	33	33	33	33	5	5	44	44	44	6	6	33	33	33	33	33	33	33	33
33 VERSTAPPEN	11	11	5	5	5	5	5	5	5	33	11	44	33	5	5	5	5	5	5	5	5	5	5	5	5	5	5	33	44	6	6	6	44	33	44	44	44	44	44	44	44	44
3 RICCIARDO	5	5	11	11	11	11	11	11	11	11	5	11	5	77	44	44	44	44	44	44	44	44	44	44	44	33	33	33	33	33	44	5	5	5	5	5	5	5	5	5	5	5
11 PÉREZ	3	3	3	3	3	3	3	7	44	7	77	19	77	77	3	3	3	3	3	3	3	3	3	3	3	3	3	3	3	7	7	7	7	7	7	7	7	7	7	7	7	7
5 VETTEL	27	27	27	27	27	7	7	7	7	44	33	33	55	44	3	3	77	7	7	7	7	7	7	7	7	11	11	7	7	7	7	3	3	3	3	3	3	3	3	3	3	3
8 GROSJEAN	7	7	7	7	7	27	44	44	44	3	27	55	19	3	19	7	7	77	11	11	11	11	11	11	11	27	7	11	11	11	11	11	11	11	11	11	11	11	11	11	11	11
7 RÄIKKÖNEN	44	44	44	44	44	44	27	27	27	27	55	77	3	7	7	19	11	11	77	27	27	27	27	27	27	7	27	8	27	27	27	27	27	27	27	27	27	27	27	27	27	27
27 HÜLKENBERG	8	8	8	8	8	8	8	8	8	21	21	19	30	11	11	11	19	27	27	77	77	77	77	8	8	8	8	27	8	19	19	19	19	19	19	19	19	19	19	19	19	19
21 GUTIÉRREZ	21	21	21	21	21	21	21	21	21	8	77	30	11	27	27	27	27	19	19	19	19	19	8	77	55	55	19	19	77	77	77	77	77	77	77	77	77	77	77	77	77	77
77 BOTTAS	26	26	26	26	26	26	26	26	26	55	19	3	7	30	30	30	30	30	30	30	30	30	19	30	9	19	19	77	77	8	8	8	8	8	8	8	8	8	8	8	8	8
19 MASSA	55	55	55	55	55	55	55	55	55	26	30	9	27	9	9	9	9	8	8	8	8	30	30	9	14	14	77	55	55	55	55	55	55	30	30	30	30	30	30	30	30	30
26 KVYAT	77	77	77	77	77	77	77	77	77	3	20	9	20	20	8	8	9	9	9	9	9	9	9	20	55	77	22	22	22	22	22	22	22	30	55	26	26	26	26	26	26	26
55 SAINZ	19	19	19	19	19	19	19	19	19	9	27	20	8	20	20	20	20	20	20	20	20	14	19	21	21	30	30	30	30	30	30	30	30	26	26	20	20	20	20	20	20	20
14 ALONSO	14	14	14	14	14	14	14	14	30	20	12	12	12	12	12	12	12	12	12	12	55	21	22	21	21	26	26	26	20	20	20	20	20	9	9	9	9	9	9	9	9	9
30 PALMER	30	30	30	30	30	30	30	30	14	9	12	8	22	22	22	26	26	26	14	14	12	22	30	31	31	20	20	20	20	20	20	9	14	14	14	14	14	14	14	14	14	14
20 MAGNUSSEN	9	9	9	9	9	9	9	9	9	12	9	22	26	26	26	14	14	14	55	55	21	30	31	26	20	20	9	9	9	9	9	14	55	55	55	55	55	55	55	55	55	55
9 ERICSSON	20	20	20	20	20	20	20	20	12	14	14	14	14	14	22	55	55	55	26	21	19	31	26	20	9	14	14	14	14	14	12	22	22	22	22	22	22	22	22	22
12 NASR	12	12	12	12	12	12	12	12	31	22	14	14	55	55	55	55	21	21	21	22	22	26	9	14	14	31	12	12	12	12	21	12	12	12	12	12	12	12	12	12	12	12
31 OCON	31	31	31	31	31	31	31	31	94	31	21	21	21	21	21	21	31	31	31	31	12	12	14	12	12	12	12	21	21	21	12	21	21	21	21	21	21	21	21	12	12	12
94 WEHRLEIN	94	94	94	94	94	94	94	94	22	94	31	31	31	31	31	31	22	22	22	94	94	12	12	94	31	31	31	31	31	31	31	31	31	31
22 BUTTON	22	22	22	22	22	22	22	22	14	14	94	31	94	94	94	94	94	94	94	94	94	94	12	12	94	94	94	94	31	94	94	94	94	94	94	94	94	94

6 = Pit stop   9 = Drive-thru penalty

TIME SHEETS

PRACTICE 1 (FRIDAY)

Weather: Dry/overcast

Temperatures: track 30-36°C, air 22-24°C

Pos.	Driver	Laps	Time
1	Nico Rosberg	24	1m 32.431s
2	Lewis Hamilton	21	1m 32.646s
3	Sebastian Vettel	19	1m 33.525s
4	Kimi Räikkönen	17	1m 33.817s
5	Daniel Ricciardo	23	1m 34.112s
6	Max Verstappen	26	1m 34.379s
7	Nico Hülkenberg	28	1m 34.530s
8	Sergio Pérez	30	1m 34.767s
9	Fernando Alonso	10	1m 35.003s
10	Valtteri Bottas	31	1m 35.381s
11	Daniil Kvyat	23	1m 35.446s
12	Carlos Sainz	27	1m 35.672s
13	Jenson Button	24	1m 35.677s
14	Romain Grosjean	17	1m 35.688s
15	Felipe Nasr	15	1m 35.967s
16	Felipe Massa	23	1m 36.169s
17	Esteban Gutiérrez	21	1m 36.219s
18	Marcus Ericsson	19	1m 36.294s
19	Kevin Magnussen	30	1m 36.822s
20	Esteban Ocon	29	1m 37.797s
21	Pascal Wehrlein	24	1m 37.966s
22	Jolyon Palmer	13	1m 37.992s

PRACTICE 2 (FRIDAY)

Weather: Dry/overcast

Temperatures: track 31-34°C, air 24-25°C

Pos.	Driver	Laps	Time
1	Nico Rosberg	35	1m 32.250s
2	Lewis Hamilton	35	1m 32.322s
3	Kimi Räikkönen	26	1m 32.573s
4	Max Verstappen	29	1m 33.061s
5	Sebastian Vettel	34	1m 33.103s
6	Sergio Pérez	37	1m 33.570s
7	Nico Hülkenberg	35	1m 33.873s
8	Fernando Alonso	37	1m 33.985s
9	Valtteri Bottas	33	1m 34.028s
10	Carlos Sainz	33	1m 34.086s
11	Felipe Massa	33	1m 34.127s
12	Daniel Ricciardo	29	1m 34.150s
13	Romain Grosjean	33	1m 34.241s
14	Daniil Kvyat	27	1m 34.305s
15	Kevin Magnussen	36	1m 34.339s
16	Jenson Button	29	1m 34.398s
17	Esteban Gutiérrez	11	1m 34.643s
18	Jolyon Palmer	40	1m 34.760s
19	Felipe Nasr	26	1m 34.824s
20	Pascal Wehrlein	30	1m 35.292s
21	Esteban Ocon	37	1m 35.400s
22	Marcus Ericsson	26	1m 36.318s

PRACTICE 3 (SATURDAY)

Weather: Damp-dry/overcast

Temperatures: track 26-28°C, air 25-26°C

Pos.	Driver	Laps	Time
1	Nico Rosberg	14	1m 32.092s
2	Daniel Ricciardo	10	1m 32.394s
3	Sebastian Vettel	13	1m 32.731s
4	Max Verstappen	9	1m 32.784s
5	Kimi Räikkönen	12	1m 33.011s
6	Felipe Massa	13	1m 33.271s
7	Lewis Hamilton	12	1m 33.284s
8	Jolyon Palmer	13	1m 33.639s
9	Kevin Magnussen	10	1m 33.639s
10	Nico Hülkenberg	11	1m 33.646s
11	Fernando Alonso	12	1m 33.714s
12	Esteban Gutiérrez	16	1m 33.787s
13	Valtteri Bottas	9	1m 33.865s
14	Sergio Pérez	11	1m 33.921s
15	Daniil Kvyat	12	1m 34.037s
16	Romain Grosjean	13	1m 34.272s
17	Felipe Nasr	12	1m 34.388s
18	Marcus Ericsson	13	1m 34.544s
19	Jenson Button	11	1m 34.548s
20	Esteban Ocon	13	1m 35.230s
21	Pascal Wehrlein	10	1m 37.256s
22	Carlos Sainz	3	1m 56.323s

QUALIFYING (SATURDAY)

Weather: Dry/overcast Temperatures: track 26-28°C, air 23-24°C

Pos.	Driver	First	Second	Third	Qualifying Tyre
1	Nico Rosberg	1m 31.858s	1m 30.714s	1m 30.647s	Soft (new)
2	Lewis Hamilton	1m 32.218s	1m 31.129s	1m 30.660s	Soft (new)
3	Kimi Räikkönen	1m 31.674s	1m 31.406s	1m 30.949s	Soft (new)
4	Sebastian Vettel	1m 31.659s	1m 31.227s	1m 31.028s	Soft (new)
5	Max Verstappen	1m 32.487s	1m 31.489s	1m 31.178s	Soft (new)
6	Daniel Ricciardo	1m 32.538s	1m 31.719s	1m 31.240s	Soft (new)
7	Sergio Pérez	1m 32.682s	1m 32.237s	1m 31.961s	Soft (new)
8	Romain Grosjean	1m 32.458s	1m 32.176s	1m 31.961s	Soft (new)
9	Nico Hülkenberg	1m 32.448s	1m 32.200s	1m 32.142s	Soft (new)
10	Esteban Gutiérrez	1m 32.620s	1m 32.155s	1m 32.547s	Soft (new)
11	Valtteri Bottas	1m 32.383s	1m 32.315s		
12	Felipe Massa	1m 32.562s	1m 32.380s		
13	Daniil Kvyat	1m 32.645s	1m 32.623s		
14	Carlos Sainz	1m 32.789s	1m 32.685s		
15	Fernando Alonso	1m 32.819s	1m 32.689s		
16	Jolyon Palmer	1m 32.796s	1m 32.807s		
17	Jenson Button	1m 32.851s			
18	Kevin Magnussen	1m 33.023s			
19	Marcus Ericsson	1m 33.222s			
20	Felipe Nasr	1m 33.332s			
21	Esteban Ocon	1m 33.353s			
22	Pascal Wehrlein	1m 33.561s			

Photos: Peter J. Fox

FOR THE RECORD

3rd WORLD CONSTRUCTORS' TITLE: Mercedes.

100th PODIUM: Lewis Hamilton.

30th POLE POSITION: Nico Rosberg.

1,500th POINT: Nico Rosberg.

60th WIN: Mercedes.

250th RACE LED: Mercedes engine.

DID YOU KNOW?

Bottas, with 73 starts, beat Jim Clark's record of the most starts exclusively with one constructor.

This was the sixth race in F1 history where there were no retirements.

POINTS

	DRIVERS	
1	Nico Rosberg	313
2	Lewis Hamilton	280
3	Daniel Ricciardo	212
4	Kimi Räikkönen	170
5	Max Verstappen	165
6	Sebastian Vettel	165
7	Valtteri Bottas	81
8	Sergio Pérez	80
9	Nico Hülkenberg	54
10	Felipe Massa	43
11	Fernando Alonso	42
12	Carlos Sainz	30
13	Romain Grosjean	28
14	Daniil Kvyat	25
15	Jenson Button	19
16	Kevin Magnussen	7
17	Jolyon Palmer	1
18	Pascal Wehrlein	1
19	Stoffel Vandoorne	1

	CONSTRUCTORS	
1	Mercedes	593
2	Red Bull	385
3	Ferrari	335
4	Force India	134
5	Williams	124
6	McLaren	62
7	Toro Rosso	47
8	Haas	28
9	Renault	8
10	Manor	1

9 · HÜLKENBERG · Force India

7 · GROSJEAN · Haas

5 · PÉREZ · Force India

3 · VERSTAPPEN · Red Bull

1 · ROSBERG · Mercedes

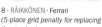

10 · GUTIÉRREZ · Haas

8 · RÄIKKÖNEN · Ferrari *(5-place grid penalty for replacing the gearbox)*

6 · VETTEL · Ferrari *(3-place grid penalty for causing an accident in round 16)*

4 · RICCIARDO · Red Bull

2 · HAMILTON · Mercedes

Qualifying: head-to-head

Rosberg	9	8	Hamilton
Vettel	10	7	Räikkönen
Massa	3	14	Bottas
Ricciardo	4	0	Kvyat
Ricciardo	9	4	Verstappen
Pérez	9	8	Hülkenberg
Magnussen	11	6	Palmer
Verstappen	3	1	Sainz
Kvyat	4	9	Sainz
Ericsson	10	7	Nasr
Alonso	11	5	Button
Button	0	1	Vandoorne
Haryanto	5	7	Wehrlein
Wehrlein	3	2	Ocon
Grosjean	12	5	Gutiérrez

43	44	45	46	47	48	49	50	51	52	53	-
6	6	6	6	6	6	6	6	6	6	6	1
33	33	33	33	33	33	33	33	33	33	33	2
44	44	44	44	44	44	44	44	44	44	44	3
5	5	5	5	5	5	5	5	5	5	5	4
7	7	7	7	7	7	7	7	7	7	7	5
3	3	3	3	3	3	3	3	3	3	3	6
11	11	11	11	11	11	11	11	11	11	11	7
27	27	27	27	27	27	27	27	27	27	27	8
19	19	19	19	19	19	19	19	19	19	19	9
77	77	77	77	77	77	77	77	77	77	77	10
8	8	8	8	8	8	8	8	8	8	8	
30	30	30	30	30	30	30	30	30	30		
26	26	26	26	26	26	26	26	26	26		
20	20	20	20	20	20	20	20	20	20		
9	9	9	9	9	9	9	9	9	9		
14	14	14	14	14	14	14	14	14	14		
55	55	55	55	55	55	55	55	55	55		
22	22	22	22	22	22	22	22	22	22		
12	12	12	12	12	12	12	12	12	12		
21	21	21	21	21	21	21	21	21	21		
31	31	31	31	31	31	31	31	31	31		
94	94	94	94	94	94	94	94	94	94		

94 = One lap or more behind

RACE TYRE STRATEGIES

PIRELLI

	Driver	Race Stint 1	Race Stint 2	Race Stint 3
1	Rosberg	Soft (u): 1-12	Hard (n): 13-29	Hard (u): 30-53
2	Verstappen	Soft (u): 1-10	Hard (n): 11-28	Hard (u): 29-53
3	Hamilton	Soft (u): 1-13	Hard (n): 14-33	Hard (u): 34-53
4	Vettel	Soft (u): 1-12	Hard (n): 13-34	Soft (n): 35-53
5	Räikkönen	Soft (u): 1-12	Hard (n): 13-26	Hard (u): 27-53
6	Ricciardo	Soft (u): 1-10	Hard (n): 11-32	Hard (n): 33-53
7	Pérez	Soft (u): 1-12	Hard (n): 13-29	Medium (n): 30-53
8	Hülkenberg	Soft (u): 1-11	Hard (n): 12-28	Medium (n): 29-53
9	Massa	Medium (n): 1-24	Hard (n): 25-53	
10	Bottas	Medium (u): 1-26	Hard (n): 27-53	
11	Grosjean	Soft (u): 1-10	Hard (n): 11-30	Hard (n): 31-53
12	Palmer	Medium (n): 1-25	Hard (n): 26-52	
13	Kvyat	Soft (n): 1-10	Soft (u): 11-23	Hard (n): 24-52
14	Magnussen	Hard (n): 1-25	Medium (n): 26-52	
15	Ericsson	Medium (n): 1-26	Hard (n): 27-52	
16	Alonso	Soft (n): 1-9	Hard (n): 10-27	Hard (n): 28-52
17	Sainz	Soft (n): 1-13	Hard (n): 14-37	Soft (u): 38-52
18	Button	Hard (n): 1-19	Soft (n): 20-36	Soft (n): 37-52
19	Nasr	Hard (n): 1-25	Medium (n): 26-52	
20	Gutiérrez	Soft (u): 1-11	Hard (n): 12-28	Hard (n): 29-52
21	Ocon	Soft (u): 1-12	Hard (n): 13-31	Hard (n): 32-52
22	Wehrlein	Soft (n): 1-13	Hard (n): 14-32	Hard (n): 33-52

The tyre regulations stipulate that at least two of three dry tyre specifications must be used during a dry race.

Pirelli P Zero logos are colour-coded on the tyre sidewalls: Yellow = Soft; Orange = Hard; White = Medium. (n) new (u) used

Photos: Peter J. Fox

CIRCUIT OF THE AMERICAS QUALIFYING

THE championship was getting down to the nitty-gritty, the tension palpable. After all the hot air about Lewis Hamilton's press-conference behaviour in Japan, Mercedes boss Toto Wolff said simply, "I think people underestimate just how much pressure these guys are under..."

Nico Rosberg's Suzuka win meant that he could drive for second place in all four remaining grands prix, but it was a notion he claimed to have put out of his mind. "I'm here to win, nothing else," he said, at a track on which he'd started from pole in the previous two seasons.

This time, though, it was three-times Austin and four-times US Grand Prix winner Lewis Hamilton who claimed his first pole at a track he loves. His final Q3 run was a great lap, and his 1m 34.999s time beat Nico by 0.22s, a margin gained exclusively in sector one.

"It's an awesome, technical track in terms of braking and positioning," Hamilton explained. "Turn One is not easy to get right, and position is everything through the following Esses. Having a good front end is important, and placing the car at a point when the tyres can be overheating. That first sector on my qually lap was my best of the weekend."

Rosberg never quite got Turn One right, running a little wide on exit on both Q3 runs. Nevertheless, he was happy with the rest of the lap and to qualify P2, with an Austin GP yet to be won from anywhere else.

The red-walled Pirelli super-soft tyre was on offer for the first time in Austin, but both Mercedes drivers managed to clear Q2 on the yellow-walled soft rubber, which was expected to provide a six-lap longer first stint, putting them in a seemingly strong position for Sunday.

But so, too, did Max Verstappen, as Red Bull locked out the second row. Team-mate Daniel Ricciardo, by contrast, had shown impressive long-run pace on the super-soft tyre in Friday afternoon's FP2 session and was happy to qualify third on the softest tyre.

"We expected it to go like this," he said. "Max was wanting to try the soft, and I was happier to go on the super-soft and was more comfortable with that tyre on the long run yesterday. The degradation was pretty good. I think we have a good chance tomorrow. The track conditions changed quite a bit today. Sure, the super-softs won't last as long in the opening stint, but they might give me a bit of an advantage at the start. And this is a place where you can overtake and change your line; it's not just a one-line circuit."

Ricciardo's intelligent Q3 lap, babying the super-softs through sector three where, for most, they were losing performance, was just 0.29s away from Rosberg's time and a quarter of a second better than his team-mate's. Max, though, had received a radio message meant for Daniel and had made a setting adjustment that had given him oversteer in sector three, so he reckoned he should have been closer.

Ferrari had appeared to make a performance step in Japan, but the gap separating Red Bull from Maranello in Austin was significant. Ricciardo's lap was 0.63s clear of Kimi Räikkönen, who again got the better of Sebastian Vettel, by more than two-tenths. With Ferrari's strategy questionable in Suzuka, and pressure from the Italian media growing daily, you had to wonder at Vettel's state of mind.

Between Suzuka and Austin, Nico Hülkenberg had been confirmed as a Renault driver for 2017, but, for the moment, his priority was protecting Force India's ten-point margin over Williams in the battle for fourth place in the constructors' championship. He did an impressive job, too – quickest man outside of F1's 'Big Three', and almost half a second clear of Valtteri Bottas's Williams.

The Finn's Q3 lap had been a good one, until the car snapped at Turn 19 and cost him some time, but having two cars in the top ten was a positive step for the Williams team, which had struggled for qualifying pace latterly. Felipe Massa had strung together a decent lap as well, just 0.15s slower than Bottas.

After what he considered one of his best ever laps, Carlos Sainz was an excellent eighth in Q2, ahead of both Williams cars, but he couldn't quite match it in Q3 and had to be content with tenth, 0.06s behind Massa. It was still an admirable effort. Behind the scenes at Toro Rosso, chief race engineer Phil Charles was absent, having moved on as he came to the end of a three-year contract with the team, seeking to spend more time in the UK for family reasons.

Sergio Pérez was struggling for pace compared to team-mate Hülkenberg, the Force India nervous in high-speed corners and losing time under braking, but P11 with freedom of tyre choice was not a bad position to be in, a fact that McLaren also put across to Fernando Alonso, who was 12th with the first McLaren, 0.06s slower than the Mexican.

Daniil Kvyat – celebrating a renewed Toro Rosso contract, which meant that he could finally relax, despite GP2 front-runner Pierre Gasly's continued presence in the team's pit – was a similar distance behind Alonso and ahead of Esteban Gutiérrez. The Mexican was the lone Haas driver to make it into Q2 at what would be a tricky home race for Gene Haas's men.

The car had been shedding body parts during Friday practice, and Haas could not run the new front wing that had helped put both cars through to Q3 in Suzuka. They generally lacked grip, and when Grosjean was held up in sector three in Q1, it brought to an end a 12-race streak of the team getting both cars through to Q2.

Jolyon Palmer was the sole Renault driver to make it out of Q1, while Marcus Ericsson produced a fine lap to also drag a Sauber into Q2.

Above: No track limits at Austin as Vettel explores the kerbs.
Photo: Scuderia Ferrari

Left: Herbie Blash, already looking forward to a happy retirement after a lifetime in Formula 1.
Photo: WRi2/Jean-François Galeron

Centre left: Nico Hülkenberg put in another storming qualifying performance to take fourth on the grid.
Photo: Sahara Force India F1 Team

Below centre left: A dream realised for Gene Haas as his team takes part in its home GP for the first time.
Photo: WRi2/Jean-François Galeron

Far left: Lewis Hamilton lifts a wheel on his way to pole.
Photo: Steve Mohlenkamp Photography

Opening spread: Lewis Hamilton turns the Austin track into his personal playground, having left Rosberg just a speck in the distance.
Photo: Peter J. Fox

Above: No mistakes this time as Lewis Hamilton makes a clean start, leading Ricciardo and Rosberg away from the pack scrabbling around Turn One.
Photo: Red Bull Racing/Getty Images

Right: The Williams of Felipe Massa was locked in battle with the Toro Rosso of Carlos Sainz over six and seventh places.
Photo: WRi2/Jean-François Galeron

A YEAR earlier, Hamilton had sealed his third world title at Circuit of the Americas, with more than a little animosity rooted in his first-corner dive down the inside, which had forced pole man Rosberg wide and let both Red Bulls through.

This time, with the points already on the board, you wondered whether Nico might adopt the same tactic.

"My start was not good enough to get down the inside, and Lewis could move across and cover that off," Rosberg explained. "Knowing that wasn't an option, I went to the outside. I thought everything was okay, but Daniel [Ricciardo] got a better drive out of Turn One, which we always knew was a possibility."

Ricciardo, of course, was on super-soft tyres, which gave him a car's length advantage off the line. Also able to brake a little later with extra grip, he grabbed second place as the field sprinted through Turn Two and the sweeps of sector one.

Further back, there was contact that eliminated Hülkenberg with broken steering.

"I was sandwiched between Vettel on my right and Bottas to the left," Nico explained. "Sebastian turned in quite aggressively, made contact and pushed me into Valtteri. I think it could have been avoided if he'd given us a bit more space. It was frustrating to have such a quick car and be out of the race in the first ten seconds..."

In what was a disastrous opening lap for Force India, Pérez was also assaulted and spun around by Daniil Kvyat at Turn 11, finishing the opening lap six places behind his starting position and with a damaged floor. The young Russian received front wing damage and a 10s penalty for his efforts.

Across the line at the end of the opening lap, Hamilton was just under a second clear of Ricciardo, from Rosberg, Räikkönen, Verstappen, Vettel, Massa, Sainz, Alonso, Gutiérrez, Button, Kvyat, the fast-starting Ericsson, Palmer, Grosjean, Magnussen, Pérez, Ocon, Nasr and Wehrlein.

Bottas was into the pits to change a punctured right front, but a damaged floor meant that he struggled for the rest of the race, battling Nasr's Sauber.

After a difficult start to the Austin weekend, Grosjean was determined to get Gene Haas a point on home turf and, making the most of the new super-softs he'd gone to the grid on, launched a move down the inside of Palmer into Turn One on lap two. Hung out to dry on exit, Palmer lost momentum and further places to team-mate Magnussen and Pérez. Then Grosjean despatched Ericsson, Kvyat and team-mate Gutiérrez by lap seven, setting his sights on Button, who had also started on super-softs.

After looking after his softs for the first few laps, Hamilton started to open a small margin over Ricciardo, the lead out to 2.35s by the end of lap seven, with Daniel's pace starting to fall away as he prepared to pit at the end of the following lap, to go from super-softs to softs. He was followed in by fourth-placed Räikkönen.

Rosberg was now second, but he crossed the line 5.3s behind his team-mate on lap nine (of 56). He pitted on the following lap – fitting a set of mediums – and rejoined still 3s behind Ricciardo. Daniel, though, had pitted out just behind Alonso after his earlier stop and had lost a bit of time getting by the McLaren, extinguishing any undercut possibility on the race leader. Hamilton was in and out without undue drama on lap 11, taking softs rather than the mediums bolted to his team-mate's car. He rejoined still 4s clear of Ricciardo as Vettel's Ferrari led for three laps, Sebastian eking out a decent 14-lap opening stint on his super-softs.

What of Verstappen? Having been jumped by Räikkönen on lap one, the young Dutchman had found himself in a Ferrari sandwich, unable to run at the car's true pace, so Red Bull, aware of the undercut threat from Vettel, pitted him the lap after his team-mate. It meant that he was unable to take advantage of the longer opening stint potential afforded by

using the soft rather than super-soft tyre in Q2, but on a new set of softs, he was quick and soon pressing Räikkönen, who really didn't like the feel of his Ferrari on the yellow-walled Pirelli tyres.

Seeing Verstappen pit, Ferrari had kept Vettel out. Max, knowing he couldn't waste time behind Räikkönen, shot down the inside of the Ferrari into T12 with the aid of DRS to take fifth on lap 13, which became fourth when Vettel pitted on the following lap and re-emerged still behind Räikkönen.

With the first stops all done, Hamilton led Ricciardo by 4.2s, with Rosberg 2s further back and Verstappen, the quickest on the track, closing in just 1.3s further back. Then came a 2.3s gap to Räikkönen, with team-mate Vettel gaining on him on his fresher softs. Massa was 8s further in arrears, a similar margin clear of Sainz, then Kvyat 4s behind. The Toro Rosso would go as far as lap 21 before pitting for mediums and attempting a one-stop strategy. Alonso was close behind, having taken a set of mediums at his lap-11 first stop.

Red Bull, seeing Verstappen lapping quicker than the first three, came on the radio and reminded him that he needed to achieve a decent stint length, to which Max responded, "I'm not here to finish fourth…"

With Ricciardo on older softs and Rosberg on mediums, Mercedes was planning to run Nico long and leave him with a short final stint on softs to attack the Red Bull driver, who made his second stop for a second set of mediums on lap 25. But with Verstappen close to Rosberg, Red Bull thought they might be able to use him to spook Mercedes into stopping Rosberg earlier than planned to protect against a possible undercut. The edge was beginning to go off Verstappen's softs, however, and he mistook a radio message telling him to push for an instruction to pit.

Without a confirmation message, Verstappen simply arrived in the pit lane on lap 26, to Red Bull's great surprise. Obviously, his tyres weren't ready, and the crew did a fine job to rescue the situation as best they could. Amid the confusion, Verstappen had to stop short of his marks, then accelerated hard into place, to the possible detriment of his transmission, had his final set of mediums fitted and, in total, lost around 12s.

He accelerated back into the fray just behind Massa's Williams, which had yet to make its final stop. Soon, though, it became obvious that there was a problem. Verstappen heard a number of unwelcome metallic-type noises as he attempted to go up through the box. The team instructed him to stay off-line and attempt to get back to the pits. But he only got as far as Turn 18, where he was forced to pull off.

This was the prompt for a lap-31 virtual safety car (VSC), which was great news for those who had not yet made their second stops. It was a good break for Mercedes, but a bad one for Red Bull. Hamilton and Rosberg effectively had cheap second stops as they headed in one behind the other, the 9s gap between them meaning that Rosberg did not lose out.

On the previous lap, Nico had been 15s ahead of Ricciardo's Red Bull with a stop to go. With a stop time of around 23s, he would have pitted out around 7–8s behind Ricciardo, on the softer rubber, with a short stint to come in which he would have had to pass the Red Bull on track.

Now, though, he was able to take on the more durable medium compound and rejoin 3s ahead of the Red Bull.

"That really sucks," a frustrated Ricciardo radioed in.

Others who had just pitted before the VSC and were left cursing were Vettel, Massa, Pérez, Grosjean, Button and the two Renault drivers.

With pressure on at Renault to secure the one remaining seat alongside the newly-confirmed Hülkenberg, Palmer had been less than impressed to concede an early place to team-mate Magnussen, courtesy of Grosjean's lunge, and had radioed in saying he was quicker than Kevin and could the team please help. Understandably in the circumstances, perhaps, they did not comply.

After just an 11-lap second stint on softs, therefore, Palmer pitted on lap 26 from just 1s behind Magnussen in an attempt to undercut him, but the Dane responded next lap and hung on.

Above: Daniel Ricciardo's Red Bull was no match for the Mercedes in Austin, but there was satisfaction in seeing the Ferraris well beaten.
Photo: Red Bull Racing/Getty Images

Top right: Romain Grosjean grabbed the final championship point for Haas.
Photo: WRi2/Jad Sherif

Above right: Nico Rosberg did enough to secure second place and keep his championship quest on track.
Photo: Lukas Gorys

Right: A pleasant surprise to see a woman on the podium as Mercedes partner services director Victoria Vowles joins in the celebrations and accepts the trophy for the winning constructor.
Photo: Mercedes AMG Petronas F1 Team

Räikkönen, too, was not helped by the VSC. After struggling on his softs for 16 laps, he had pitted for a second time on lap 24 to go back on to super-softs, on which the car felt much better. The Ferrari never seemed to work well on the medium-compound Pirelli, of which Ferrari had brought a very limited supply, and lap 30 was adjudged to be too early to go back on to the used set of softs on which it was intended that Kimi would complete the race.

He didn't get that far, however. When he pitted on lap 39, there were sparks at the right rear corner and a cross-threaded nut. Kimi did get the green light, though, and accelerated down the pit lane without the wheel properly attached. He did not get the message until past the pit exit line, and Ferrari copped a 5,000-euro fine for unsafe release. The Finn was left with nothing to do but let the car roll back down the hill into the pit lane and abandon it.

Rosberg apart, the big winners from the VSC interruption were the Spanish contingent. Beforehand, Sainz had been around 8s behind Massa, with Alonso a further 5s adrift of the Toro Rosso. Massa's Williams had just stopped for a final set of mediums before the VSC, while Sainz was able to take on a set of softs under the VSC and emerge just ahead of Felipe, with Alonso now just 4s behind the Williams.

For Hamilton, it was now a simple case of looking after the car and stroking home to the 50th grand prix victory he had been chasing since July. It was a feat that had been achieved by only two men in F1 history – Michael Schumacher and Alain Prost. The Frenchman's 51 would probably need to be passed before the end of the year if Hamilton was to claim a fourth title; Michael's total could take a while longer...

Rosberg was happy with his second place, and Ricciardo not so delighted with his third, but he was still smiling. Ferrari, after the promise of Suzuka, had not really been a factor in Austin. Vettel had suffered variable levels of rear downforce in the race, which included a scary moment in the middle of the Esses. Changing wind direction and debris affecting the wing were the only explanations he could offer as he contemplated a 43s deficit to Hamilton's winning Mercedes.

The real action was in the battle for fifth. The VSC had thrown Sainz, Massa and Alonso together for the final 25 laps. On paper, Massa's Williams had superior pace, but Sainz was on softs, while his chasers were on mediums. That allowed him to keep them at bay until the grip started to go away in the final laps.

With six laps to go, Carlos suffered a substantial lock-up into Turn 18, which distracted Massa, who momentarily left the door open. Alonso needed no second invitation to launch his McLaren down the inside. They banged wheels, but Alonso was through and Massa, furious, was on the radio complaining. Race stewards served notice of investigation, but it was adjudged to be a racing incident, despite bitter protest from Massa in the stewards' room.

This was all good news for Force India in the fourth-place constructors' championship battle. With Hülkenberg out on lap one and Pérez also suffering, it had looked as though they would take a sizeable hit. But Massa's demotion, and a great 1.8s pit stop to get Pérez out ahead of Grosjean, meant that ultimately Sergio crossed the line just one place behind the Williams driver.

Alonso wasn't finished and now attacked Sainz.

"I knew I wasn't going to keep him behind with the tyres the way they were, but I made him work for it," Carlos smiled. Alonso, though, was through with DRS into T12 on the penultimate lap, letting rip with a Texan "Yeeha" over the radio in celebration of McLaren Honda's best ever fifth-place finish. Button supplemented that with two more points for ninth, while a delighted Grosjean fittingly took the final point for Haas.

As the paddock packed up for the trip to Mexico, track action just four-and-a-half days away, Rosberg was still on target, but the gap was down to 26 points.

Tony Dodgins

VIEWPOINT
DERAILED LEWIS BACK ON TRACK

THE Lewis Hamilton in Austin should have been the one we anticipated in Japan. Putting setbacks behind him is a Hamilton trademark; it's almost as though he needs back-to-the-wall adversity to fire his adrenaline to the thrilling heights everyone knows he is capable of reaching. That's how he was expected to react at Suzuka after the bitter disappointment of that 11th-hour engine failure in Malaysia.

Instead, we witnessed a confused character who was some-one other than the carefree driver accustomed to using a sub-lime talent to expunge previous frustration. His spat with the media in Japan was guaranteed to earn a place on the pre-race official FIA press conference at CotA as journalists eagerly waited to see which Lewis Hamilton would turn up this time.

Fortunately – at least for Lewis, if not the expectant tabloid hacks – this was the Hamilton who beamed from ear to ear as he embraced everything about the country in which he happily spends much of his limited downtime. His answers were thoughtful and lengthy, the exact opposite of the embarrassing and mildly insulting display in Japan.

That demeanour continued throughout the weekend, his relaxed mood helped by the presence of the friends and family he clearly could have done with two weeks before.

In the USA, he relished a track that had brought victory three times. Rather than concern himself over "disrespect" – real or imagined – from the media, he applied his mind to the tricky first corner, a blind left-hander that had caused trouble in the past. In Q3, he nailed it as a prelude to a stunning lap, a full two-tenths faster than Rosberg. Pole – just when he needed it most.

Then there was the start to worry about. Once more, the application of thought and lengthy talks with his engineers brought a perfect getaway. Again, when he needed it most. Win number 50 was on its way.

The comeback had begun. But there was the undeniable feel-ing that it could have started a fortnight before on the other side of the world.

Maurice Hamilton

18

2016 FORMULA 1
UNITED STATES
GRAND PRIX

ROLEX

OFFICIAL TIMEPIECE

AUSTIN 21–23 OCTOBER

RACE DISTANCE: 56 laps, 191.634 miles/308.405km

RACE WEATHER: Dry/overcast (track 32–37°C, air 26–29°C)

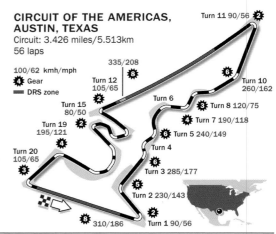

CIRCUIT OF THE AMERICAS, AUSTIN, TEXAS
Circuit: 3.426 miles/5.513km
56 laps

100/62 kmh/mph
☼ Gear
▬ DRS zone

RACE – OFFICIAL CLASSIFICATION

Pos.	Driver	Nat.	No.	Entrant	Car/Engine	Tyres	Laps	Time/Retirement	Speed (mph/km/h)	Gap to leader	Fastest race lap	
1	**Lewis Hamilton**	GB	44	Mercedes AMG Petronas F1 Team	Mercedes F1 W07-Mercedes PU106C V6	P	56	1h 38m 12.618s	117.076/188.415		1m 42.386s	45
2	**Nico Rosberg**	D	6	Mercedes AMG Petronas F1 Team	Mercedes F1 W07-Mercedes PU106C V6	P	56	1h 38m 17.138s	116.986/188.270	4.520s	1m 41.897s	34
3	**Daniel Ricciardo**	AUS	3	Red Bull Racing	Red Bull RB12-TAG Heuer RB12 V6	P	56	1h 38m 32.310s	116.685/187.787	19.692s	1m 42.555s	51
4	**Sebastian Vettel**	D	5	Scuderia Ferrari	Ferrari SF15-H-059/5 V6	P	56	1h 38m 55.752s	116.224/187.045	43.134s	1m 39.877s	55
5	**Fernando Alonso**	E	14	McLaren Honda	McLaren MP4-31-Honda RA616H V6	P	56	1h 39m 46.571s	115.238/185.458	1m 33.953s	1m 43.502s	36
6	**Carlos Sainz**	E	55	Scuderia Toro Rosso	Toro Rosso STR11-Ferrari 059/4 V6	P	56	1h 39m 48.742s	115.196/185.390	1m 36.124s	1m 42.832s	33
7	**Felipe Massa**	BR	19	Williams Martini Racing	Williams FW38-Mercedes PU106C V6	P	55			1 lap	1m 43.414s	33
8	**Sergio Pérez**	MEX	11	Sahara Force India F1 Team	Force India VJM09-Mercedes PU106C V6	P	55			1 lap	1m 43.925s	33
9	**Jenson Button**	GB	22	McLaren Honda	McLaren MP4-31-Honda RA616H V6	P	55			1 lap	1m 44.468s	37
10	**Romain Grosjean**	F	8	Haas F1 Team	Haas VF-16-Ferrari 059/5 V6	P	55			1 lap	1m 44.335s	35
11	Daniil Kvyat	RUS	26	Scuderia Toro Rosso	Toro Rosso STR11-Ferrari 059/4 V6	P	55			1 lap	1m 44.730s	48
12	Kevin Magnussen	DK	20	Renault Sport F1 Team	Renault R.S.16-R.E.16 V6	P	55	*		1 lap	1m 42.475s	45
13	Jolyon Palmer	GB	30	Renault Sport F1 Team	Renault R.S.16-R.E.16 V6	P	55			1 lap	1m 44.724s	18
14	Marcus Ericsson	S	9	Sauber F1 Team	Sauber C35-Ferrari 059/5 V6	P	55			1 lap	1m 45.140s	19
15	Felipe Nasr	BR	12	Sauber F1 Team	Sauber C35-Ferrari 059/5 V6	P	55			1 lap	1m 44.117s	55
16	Valtteri Bottas	FIN	77	Williams Martini Racing	Williams FW38-Mercedes PU106C V6	P	55			1 lap	1m 44.977s	34
17	Pascal Wehrlein	D	94	Manor Racing MRT	Manor MRT05-Mercedes PU106C V6	P	55			1 lap	1m 45.451s	36
18	Esteban Ocon	F	31	Manor Racing MRT	Manor MRT05-Mercedes PU106C V6	P	54			2 laps	1m 43.585s	46
	Kimi Räikkönen	FIN	7	Scuderia Ferrari	Ferrari SF16-H-059/5 V6	P	38	loose rear wheel			1m 41.841s	26
	Max Verstappen	NL	33	Red Bull Racing	Red Bull RB12-TAG Heuer RB12 V6	P	28	gearbox			1m 42.424s	28
	Esteban Gutiérrez	MEX	21	Haas F1 Team	Haas VF-16-Ferrari 059/5 V6	P	16	brakes			1m 45.364s	15
	Nico Hülkenberg	D	27	Sahara Force India F1 Team	Force India VJM09-Mercedes PU106C V6	P	1	accident/steering arm			no time	

All results and data © FOM 2016

* includes 5-second penalty for leaving the track and gaining an advantage – originally finished 11th.

Fastest race lap: Sebastian Vettel on lap 55, 1m 39.877s, 123.474mph/198.712km/h.

Lap record: Sebastian Vettel, 1m 39.347s, 124.133mph/199.772km (2012).

22 · OCON · Manor   20 · WEHRLEIN · Manor   18 · MAGNUSSEN · Renault   16 · ERICSSON · Sauber   14 · GUTIÉRREZ · Haas   12 · ALONSO · McLaren

21 · NASR · Sauber   19 · BUTTON · McLaren   17 · GROSJEAN · Haas   15 · PALMER · Renault   13 · KVYAT · Toro Rosso   11 · PÉREZ · Force India

Grid order	1	2	3	4	5	6	7	8	9	10	11	12	13	14	15	16	17	18	19	20	21	22	23	24	25	26	27	28	29	30	31	32	33	34	35	36	37	38	39	40	41	42	43	44
44 HAMILTON	44	44	44	44	44	44	44	44	44	44	44	5	5	5	44	44	44	44	44	44	44	44	44	44	44	44	44	44	44	44	44	44	44	44	44	44	44	44	44	44	44	44	44	44
6 ROSBERG	3	3	3	3	3	3	3	3	6	6	5	44	44	44	3	3	3	3	3	3	3	3	3	3	3	6	6	6	6	6	6	6	6	6	6	6	6	6	6	6	6	6	6	6
3 RICCIARDO	6	6	6	6	6	6	6	6	33	5	19	3	3	3	6	6	6	6	6	6	6	6	6	6	6	33	5	5	5	3	3	3	3	3	3	3	3	3	3	3	3	3	3	3
33 VERSTAPPEN	7	7	7	7	7	7	7	7	5	19	3	6	6	6	33	33	33	33	33	33	33	33	33	33	33	5	3	3	3	7	7	7	7	7	7	7	7	5	5	5	5	5	5	5
7 RÄIKKÖNEN	33	33	33	33	33	33	33	33	19	55	55	7	33	33	7	7	7	7	7	7	7	7	7	5	3	7	7	7	5	5	5	5	5	5	5	5	5	55	55	55	55	55	55	55
5 VETTEL	5	5	5	5	5	5	5	5	55	3	6	33	7	7	5	5	5	5	5	5	5	5	5	7	7	19	33	19	55	55	55	55	55	55	55	55	55	19	19	19	19	19	19	19
27 HÜLKENBERG	19	19	19	19	19	19	19	19	14	14	7	19	19	19	19	19	19	19	19	19	19	19	19	19	19	33	19	55	14	19	19	19	19	19	19	19	19	14	14	14	14	14	14	14
77 BOTTAS	55	55	55	55	55	55	55	55	7	33	36	55	55	55	55	55	55	55	55	55	55	55	55	55	55	55	55	14	19	14	14	14	14	14	14	14	14	11	11	11	11	11	11	11
19 MASSA	14	14	14	14	14	14	14	14	7	33	14	21	26	26	26	26	14	14	14	14	14	14	14	14	14	14	14	11	11	11	11	11	11	11	11	11	11	22	22	22	22	22	22	22
55 SAINZ	21	21	22	22	22	22	22	22	22	22	21	55	21	14	14	26	26	26	22	22	22	22	22	22	22	22	22	22	22	22	22	22	22	22	22	22	22	8	8	8	8	8	8	8
11 PÉREZ	22	22	21	21	21	21	8	8	8	26	9	9	9	9	22	22	22	26	11	11	11	11	11	11	11	11	11	8	8	8	8	8	8	8	8	8	8	9	9	9	9	9	9	9
14 ALONSO	26	26	26	26	8	8	21	11	11	11	9	20	14	22	22	22	11	11	11	11	8	8	8	8	8	8	9	9	9	9	9	9	9	9	9	9	26	26	26	26	26	26	26
26 KVYAT	9	9	8	8	26	11	11	21	21	20	14	20	11	11	11	8	8	8	8	8	26	12	20	20	20	20	20	9	12	26	26	26	26	26	26	26	20	20	20	20	20	20	20	30
21 GUTIÉRREZ	30	8	9	9	11	26	26	26	26	14	30	30	8	8	9	12	12	12	12	12	20	20	20	20	9	12	94	20	20	20	20	20	20	20	20	30	30	30	30	30	30	30	30	30
30 PALMER	8	20	11	11	9	9	9	9	9	94	94	22	30	30	12	12	20	20	30	30	12	12	9	12	94	26	94	30	30	30	30	30	30	30	12	12	12	12	12	12	12	12	12	12
9 ERICSSON	20	11	20	20	20	20	20	20	20	22	22	11	12	12	20	20	30	30	9	9	9	9	12	94	26	20	30	94	94	12	12	12	12	12	94	94	77	77	77	77				
8 GROSJEAN	11	30	30	30	30	30	30	30	30	11	11	8	21	31	30	9	9	9	94	94	94	94	94	26	20	30	12	12	12	94	94	94	94	94	77	77	94	94	94	94				
20 MAGNUSSEN	31	31	31	94	94	94	94	94	94	8	94	94	20	20	31	94	94	94	26	26	26	26	30	30	30	77	77	77	77	77	77	77	77	77	31	31	31	31	31	31				
22 BUTTON	12	94	94	31	31	31	12	12	12	12	12	20	31	94	94	77	77	31	31	31	31	31	77	31	31	31	31	31	31	31	31	31												
94 WEHRLEIN	94	12	12	12	12	12	31	31	31	31	31	31	94	94	77	77	31	77	77	77	77	77	31	77	77	77	31	31	31	31	31	31												
12 NASR	27	77	77	77	77	77	77	77	77	77	77	77	77	77	77	21																												
31 OCON	77																																											

TIME SHEETS

PRACTICE 1 (FRIDAY)
Weather: Dry/sunny
Temperatures: track 23–29°C, air 18–20°C

Pos.	Driver	Laps	Time
1	Lewis Hamilton	25	1m 37.428s
2	Nico Rosberg	27	1m 37.743s
3	Max Verstappen	28	1m 39.379s
4	Kimi Räikkönen	21	1m 39.407s
5	Nico Hülkenberg	27	1m 39.712s
6	Valtteri Bottas	30	1m 39.776s
7	Daniel Ricciardo	26	1m 39.963s
8	Sebastian Vettel	15	1m 39.988s
9	Daniil Kvyat	16	1m 40.131s
10	Carlos Sainz	26	1m 40.140s
11	Felipe Massa	27	1m 40.191s
12	Felipe Nasr	16	1m 40.287s
13	Fernando Alonso	26	1m 40.362s
14	Romain Grosjean	15	1m 40.826s
15	Esteban Gutiérrez	15	1m 40.970s
16	Marcus Ericsson	17	1m 41.170s
17	Alfonso Celis	27	1m 41.422s
18	Jenson Button	21	1m 41.663s
19	Kevin Magnussen	22	1m 41.942s
20	Jordan King	29	1m 42.012s
21	Jolyon Palmer	31	1m 42.332s
22	Esteban Ocon	27	1m 43.874s

PRACTICE 2 (FRIDAY)
Weather: Dry/sunny
Temperatures: track 37–38°C, air 22–23°C

Pos.	Driver	Laps	Time
1	Nico Rosberg	33	1m 37.358s
2	Daniel Ricciardo	33	1m 37.552s
3	Lewis Hamilton	32	1m 37.649s
4	Sebastian Vettel	35	1m 38.178s
5	Max Verstappen	27	1m 38.258s
6	Nico Hülkenberg	32	1m 38.508s
7	Sergio Pérez	31	1m 38.568s
8	Jenson Button	29	1m 38.713s
9	Fernando Alonso	30	1m 38.801s
10	Kimi Räikkönen	31	1m 38.865s
11	Carlos Sainz	31	1m 38.971s
12	Kevin Magnussen	23	1m 39.159s
13	Felipe Nasr	28	1m 39.189s
14	Valtteri Bottas	34	1m 39.197s
15	Daniil Kvyat	36	1m 39.202s
16	Felipe Massa	30	1m 39.281s
17	Jolyon Palmer	34	1m 39.455s
18	Romain Grosjean	24	1m 39.554s
19	Esteban Ocon	27	1m 40.086s
20	Esteban Gutiérrez	26	1m 40.114s
21	Marcus Ericsson	28	1m 40.219s
22	Pascal Wehrlein	31	1m 41.131s

PRACTICE 3 (SATURDAY)
Weather: Dry/sunny
Temperatures: track 20°C, air 17°C

Pos.	Driver	Laps	Time
1	Max Verstappen	16	1m 36.766s
2	Daniel Ricciardo	19	1m 37.032s
3	Kimi Räikkönen	15	1m 37.284s
4	Lewis Hamilton	12	1m 37.483s
5	Nico Rosberg	10	1m 37.784s
6	Sebastian Vettel	8	1m 37.894s
7	Nico Hülkenberg	17	1m 37.948s
8	Valtteri Bottas	16	1m 38.188s
9	Jenson Button	14	1m 38.212s
10	Fernando Alonso	13	1m 38.452s
11	Sergio Pérez	16	1m 38.512s
12	Jolyon Palmer	14	1m 38.528s
13	Felipe Massa	15	1m 38.607s
14	Daniil Kvyat	16	1m 38.691s
15	Carlos Sainz	6	1m 38.710s
16	Esteban Gutiérrez	13	1m 38.939s
17	Romain Grosjean	13	1m 39.097s
18	Kevin Magnussen	14	1m 39.105s
19	Marcus Ericsson	14	1m 39.239s
20	Felipe Nasr	14	1m 39.509s
21	Esteban Ocon	19	1m 39.771s
22	Pascal Wehrlein	7	1m 41.427s

QUALIFYING (SATURDAY)
Weather: Dry/sunny Temperatures: track 34–37°C, air 23–25°C

Pos.	Driver	First	Second	Third	Qualifying Tyre
1	Lewis Hamilton	1m 36.296s	1m 36.450s	1m 34.999s	Super-Soft (new)
2	Nico Rosberg	1m 36.397s	1m 36.351s	1m 35.215s	Super-Soft (new)
3	Daniel Ricciardo	1m 36.759s	1m 36.255s	1m 35.509s	Super-Soft (new)
4	Max Verstappen	1m 36.613s	1m 36.857s	1m 35.747s	Super-Soft (new)
5	Kimi Räikkönen	1m 36.985s	1m 36.584s	1m 36.131s	Super-Soft (new)
6	Sebastian Vettel	1m 37.151s	1m 36.462s	1m 36.358s	Super-Soft (new)
7	Nico Hülkenberg	1m 36.950s	1m 36.626s	1m 36.628s	Super-Soft (new)
8	Valtteri Bottas	1m 37.456s	1m 37.202s	1m 37.116s	Super-Soft (new)
9	Felipe Massa	1m 37.402s	1m 37.214s	1m 37.269s	Super-Soft (new)
10	Carlos Sainz	1m 37.744s	1m 37.175s	1m 37.326s	Super-Soft (new)
11	Sergio Pérez	1m 37.345s	1m 37.353s		
12	Fernando Alonso	1m 37.913s	1m 37.417s		
13	Daniil Kvyat	1m 37.844s	1m 37.480s		
14	Esteban Gutiérrez	1m 38.053s	1m 37.773s		
15	Jolyon Palmer	1m 38.084s	1m 37.935s		
16	Marcus Ericsson	1m 38.040s	1m 39.356s		
17	Romain Grosjean	1m 38.308s			
18	Kevin Magnussen	1m 38.317s			
19	Jenson Button	1m 38.327s			
20	Pascal Wehrlein	1m 38.548s			
21	Felipe Nasr	1m 38.583s			
22	Esteban Ocon	1m 38.806s			

Photo: Mercedes AMG Petronas F1 Team

FOR THE RECORD

50th WIN: Lewis Hamilton.

100th GRAND PRIX START: Romain Grosjean.

70th POLE POSITION: Mercedes.

DID YOU KNOW?

Hamilton now holds the record for the most circuits with a pole position – 23, which beats Alain Prost.

POINTS

DRIVERS

1	Nico Rosberg	331
2	Lewis Hamilton	305
3	Daniel Ricciardo	227
4	Sebastian Vettel	177
5	Kimi Räikkönen	170
6	Max Verstappen	165
7	Sergio Pérez	84
8	Valtteri Bottas	81
9	Nico Hülkenberg	54
10	Fernando Alonso	52
11	Felipe Massa	49
12	Carlos Sainz	38
13	Romain Grosjean	29
14	Daniil Kvyat	25
15	Jenson Button	21
16	Kevin Magnussen	7
17	Jolyon Palmer	1
18	Pascal Wehrlein	1
19	Stoffel Vandoorne	1

CONSTRUCTORS

1	Mercedes	636
2	Red Bull	400
3	Ferrari	347
4	Force India	138
5	Williams	130
6	McLaren	74
7	Toro Rosso	55
8	Haas	29
9	Renault	8
10	Manor	1

Qualifying: head-to-head

Rosberg	9	9	Hamilton
Vettel	10	8	Räikkönen
Massa	3	15	Bottas
Ricciardo	4	0	Kvyat
Ricciardo	10	4	Verstappen
Pérez	9	9	Hülkenberg
Magnussen	11	7	Palmer
Verstappen	3	1	Sainz
Kvyat	4	10	Sainz
Ericsson	11	7	Nasr
Alonso	12	5	Button
Button	0	1	Vandoorne
Haryanto	5	7	Wehrlein
Wehrlein	4	2	Ocon
Grosjean	12	6	Gutiérrez

10 · SAINZ · Toro Rosso

8 · BOTTAS · Williams

6 · VETTEL · Ferrari

4 · VERSTAPPEN · Red Bull

2 · ROSBERG · Mercedes

9 · MASSA · Williams

7 · HÜLKENBERG · Force India

5 · RÄIKKÖNEN · Ferrari

3 · RICCIARDO · Red Bull

1 · HAMILTON · Mercedes

45	46	47	48	49	50	51	52	53	54	55	56	
44	44	44	44	44	44	44	44	44	44	44	44	1
6	6	6	6	6	6	6	6	6	6	6	6	2
3	3	3	3	3	3	3	3	3	3	3	3	3
5	5	5	5	5	5	5	5	5	5	5	5	4
55	55	55	55	55	55	55	55	55	55	14	14	5
19	19	19	19	19	19	14	14	14	14	55	55	6
14	14	14	14	14	14	19	19	19	19	19		7
11	11	11	11	11	11	11	11	11	11	11		8
22	22	22	22	22	22	22	22	22	22			9
8	8	8	8	8	8	8	8	8	8			10
9	9	26	26	26	26	26	20	20	20			
26	26	9	9	9	9	20	26	26	26			
30	30	30	20	20	20	9	9	30	30	30		
20	20	20	30	30	30	30	30	9	9	9		
77	77	77	77	77	77	12	77	12	12	12		
12	12	12	12	12	12	77	12	77	77	77		
94	94	94	94	94	94	94	94	94	94	94		
31	31	31	31	31	31	31	31	31	31			

6 = Pit stop   9 = Drive-thru penalty

94 = One lap or more behind

RACE TYRE STRATEGIES

PIRELLI

	Driver	Race Stint 1	Race Stint 2	Race Stint 3	Race Stint 4
1	Hamilton	Soft (u): 1-11	Soft (n): 12-31	Medium (n): 32-56	
2	Rosberg	Soft (u): 1-10	Medium (n): 11-31	Medium (n): 32-56	
3	Ricciardo	Super-Soft (u): 1-8	Soft (n): 9-25	Medium (n): 26-56	
4	Vettel	Super-Soft (u): 1-14	Soft (n): 15-29	Medium (n): 30-53	Super-Soft (u): 54-56
5	Alonso	Soft (n): 1-11	Medium (n): 12-30	Medium (n): 31-56	
6	Sainz	Super-Soft (u): 1-11	Soft (n): 12-30	Soft (n): 31-56	
7	Massa	Super-Soft (u): 1-11	Soft (n): 12-29	Medium (n): 30-54	Super-Soft (u): 55
8	Pérez	Super-Soft (n): 1-10	Medium (n): 11-27	Medium (n): 28-55	
9	Button	Super-Soft (n): 1-10	Medium (n): 11-28	Medium (n): 29-55	
10	Grosjean	Super-Soft (u): 1-10	Soft (n): 11-27	Medium (n): 28-55	
11	Magnussen	Soft (n): 1-13	Soft (n): 14-27	Medium (n): 28-43	Super-Soft (n): 44-55
12	Kvyat	Soft (n): 1-21	Medium (n): 22-55		
13	Palmer	Soft (n): 1-15	Soft (n): 16-26	Medium (n): 27-55	
14	Ericsson	Soft (n): 1-17	Medium (n): 18-55		
15	Nasr	Medium (n): 1-29	Soft (n): 30-55		
16	Bottas	Super-Soft (u): 1	Soft (n): 2-20	Medium (n): 21-55	
17	Wehrlein	Soft (n): 1-13	Medium (n): 14-30	Medium (n): 31-55	
18	Ocon	Super-Soft (n): 1-17	Soft (n): 18-26	Soft (u): 27-44	Super-Soft (n): 45-54
	Räikkönen	Super-Soft (u): 1-8	Soft (n): 9-24	Super-Soft (u): 25-38 (dnf)	
	Verstappen	Soft (u): 1-9	Soft (n): 10-26	Medium (u): 27-28 (dnf)	
	Gutiérrez	Soft (n): 1-13	Soft (u): 14-16 (dnf)		
	Hülkenberg	Super-Soft (n): 1 (dnf)			

The tyre regulations stipulate that at least two of three dry tyre specifications must be used during a dry race.
Pirelli P Zero logos are colour-coded on the tyre sidewalls: Red = Super-Soft; Yellow = Soft; White = Medium. (n) new (u) used

Photos: Peter J. Fox

289

MEXICAN GRAND PRIX

MEXICO CITY CIRCUIT

MEXICO CITY QUALIFYING

LEWIS HAMILTON took pole position by 0.25s – quite comfortably by recent F1 standards – and then said it was his worst session of the weekend thus far. His mild frustration was a measure of how he had been gradually building up his pace during free practice and the early part of qualifying, only to fail to go faster on his final lap in Q3. It was also an indication of just how difficult it was to put in a consistently quick lap of Autodromo Hermanos Rodriguez, given the tyre and temperature combinations presented on this weekend.

In much cooler conditions than expected, the super-soft – the fastest tyre of choice – proved very difficult to switch on. If pushed too hard, the tread would overheat while the core would remain too cold. Ideally, two laps were needed to gradually build the temperature throughout the tyre. It may have been quick in terms of qualifying, but the downside was reckoned to be a comparatively short-lived run in the race. Of the front-runners, Mercedes and Ferrari were brave enough to use the soft to get through Q2 (and therefore start the race on this middle-of-the-range rubber). For Q3, of course, it was back to nursing the super-soft towards its competitive peak.

Hamilton's personal dissatisfaction had come through being unable to put together personal bests in all three sectors of each lap at any given time. But his first run in Q3 was good enough – as had seemed possible from the moment he took to the track on Friday morning. Nico Rosberg, on the other hand, had been working hard all weekend, and it was not until his final lap that he was able to work the tyres properly and leap ahead of the Red Bulls, giving Mercedes a front-row lockout for the 12th time in 2016.

"Q3 was actually not great for me," said Hamilton. "Even though I got pole, it wasn't a great lap. I lost quite a lot of time on my first Q3 lap and then more again on my second lap. I just didn't put three sectors together in either of them. If I'd put them all together, I think there was probably another three- or four-tenths in there."

"This weekend, it took a bit longer to find my rhythm," said Rosberg. "At the end of qualifying, I was quite happy with how I felt in the car and managed to pull out a good lap, but Lewis was just a bit quicker. I'm not happy to have missed out on the pole position. But, on the other hand, starting from second place here is not that bad. It will be a challenging race and we need to have an eye on Red Bull."

Rosberg was referring to Max Verstappen and Daniel Ricciardo, starting from the second row, and with the initial benefit of the grippier super-soft. The Red Bull drivers had been struggling for balance throughout, Ricciardo describing this as one of the most difficult Q3 runs of his career, after only a marginal improvement on his previous run – although his mood was probably not helped by Verstappen nicking third by seven-hundredths of a second after a very clean run, despite being unable to find the same grip level and speed enjoyed in Q2.

Ferrari were in an even worse situation. Kimi Räikkönen and Sebastian Vettel not only had been caught out by changing track temperatures – Vettel having been very happy with his soft Q2 lap, while Räikkönen had been denied a final Q3 lap thanks to a sudden loss of power – but also they suffered the additional frustration of having Nico Hülkenberg beat them to P5.

The Force India driver's lap was the standout performance of qualifying. His effort looked even better when compared to team-mate Sergio Pérez, who had disappointed himself and the large home crowd by failing to get out of Q2. When a lap on the soft was not good enough, he messed up his final chance on the super-soft by locking up and running wide at the first corner.

Williams found themselves in similar potential difficulty, the late switch to the super-soft putting both cars into Q3, where Valtteri Bottas edged Felipe Massa by less than half a second for P8. Carlos Sainz took tenth after clever work with his engineer allowed him to respond to the changing conditions and make it into Q3 for the second successive weekend. That, at least, was good news for Toro Rosso, after a sudden power loss had kept Daniil Kvyat in Q1.

Having expected to lose out a little on the long straight, McLaren then discovered they had balance issues throughout free practice, so they were happy when Fernando Alonso got the best from his tyres to take P11. The Spaniard was also content because of the race tyre choice available outside the top ten. Jenson Button did not manage his tyres so well, particularly in the first sector, and was 13th, 0.4s behind his team-mate.

Kevin Magnussen qualified 14th. He was the only Renault representative in Q2, Jolyon Palmer having been ruled out of qualifying after damaging his car on an exit kerb at the final corner of his third lap during Saturday morning practice. Palmer had dropped a wheel on the outside of the kerb, which was enough to crack the chassis and force the team to assemble another car around a spare monocoque.

There were happier times at Sauber and Manor when Marcus Ericsson and Pascal Wehrlein both made it into Q2 with impressive laps, then claimed 15th and 16th on the grid. They had been helped by the problems suffered by Kvyat and Palmer, and a disastrous Q1 for Haas, where persistent brake trouble had prompted a change of cooling duct, which had an adverse effect on the front end. A change of set-up on Saturday did not help, but worse was to come when Esteban Gutiérrez spun – right in front of Romain Grosjean as he made one last and equally desperate attempt. When subsequently Grosjean's car was found to have a damaged floor, the change to one of a different spec would mean a pit-lane start – not that it made much difference after qualifying 21st.

Felipe Nasr accounted for the half-a-second discrepancy with Ericsson by having struggled with the Sauber's handling and going nowhere. Esteban Ocon had the same trouble with his Manor, and the pair took 19th and 20th respectively.

"IT'S a long, long run down to Turn One, so the start will be important," said Hamilton. "But our long-run race pace has looked really strong and we're on the better tyre, so the signs are good. Red Bull might have a slight advantage off the line on the super-soft, but it looks like that tyre will grain quite badly. As always, our strategist has done a fantastic job there. Looking after the soft tyre, avoiding lock-ups and flat spots will give us a challenge. But the car has been great this weekend, so I hope that continues. This is a race I haven't won yet, and I'd love to tick it off the list in front of this amazing crowd, who have been really spectacular all weekend."

That crowd – 135,000 – was even more spectacular in the warmth of race day. The varying temperatures, however, gave strategists headaches that had nothing to do with too much sun – not that it was appearing that much.

The problem, as ever, was the need to second-guess tyre performance on a continually evolving track. The hardest tyre, the medium, could last all day if treated correctly. The ideal plan for those starting on the soft would be to make it last long enough for a single stop, then run the medium with confidence until the finish. Making the super-soft go far enough for a single stop was a different proposition. It was something Red Bull would have to deal with on the hoof, so to speak. Then, of course, there was the possibility of a safety car curve ball.

First, though, there was the start. Hamilton was hoping to reprise his excellent getaway seven days before at CotA. Rosberg's wish was that Lewis would suffer a repeat of Suzuka, although, more probably, his more pressing task would be to watch his mirrors for a darting Dutchman or an advancing Aussie.

There were no immediate problems as the front rows surged off the line. Hamilton was untroubled, but, as expected, Rosberg was challenged initially by Verstappen, until the Mercedes powerhouse really kicked in, an advantage enjoyed by Hülkenberg as he took a look at Verstappen. Ahead of them, the possibility of another scenario began to play out the moment Hamilton hit his brakes.

He had failed to prepare his brakes properly and the right-hand front disc was more than 200 degrees hotter than the left. It snatched and locked up, and Lewis arrived too quickly into the first corner. He took to the grass, then floored it as he ran straight towards Turn Three, bypassing Two and, in the process, maintaining his lead. Once back on the track, Hamilton lifted off enough to satisfy the race director that no advantage had been gained. This would be the cause of some contention after the race, but it would pale in significance compared to events due to unfold 70 laps later.

Meanwhile, those following Hamilton were too embroiled in their own affairs to even think about taking advantage of the leader's cross-country exploits. Having got himself alongside

Above: Dos hombres. Sergio Pérez and Esteban Gutiérrez acknowledge their home crowd.
Photo: Peter J. Fox

Left: The Red Bull drivers hit the paddock on Thursday made up for 'The Day of the Dead'. Max definitely looks scary, while Daniel looks a little sad…
Photo: Red Bull Racing/Getty Images

Opening spread: The race is run, and Lewis is about to 'abandon ship' to start his victory celebrations in front of the vast arena.
Photo: Peter J. Fox

Above: Too hot. Lewis Hamilton locks his right front and is about to cut the first corner. Meanwhile, Nico Rosberg is about to come under attack from Max Verstappen.

Photo: GP Photo/Peter Nygaard

Rosberg, Verstappen locked up and banged wheels with the Mercedes at the exit of Turn One. The force of the impact was enough to knock Rosberg sideways and on to the grass, but he retained control and position; race control considered that any off-road advantage accrued had been negated by Verstappen having caused the trouble in the first place.

Hülkenberg's flying start had put him ahead of Ricciardo. Massa and Vettel had touched with enough of an impact to make the German erroneously believe he had a puncture. The rear of the other Williams had been hit hard enough by Sainz to damage the floor. In the ensuing kaleidoscope of cars, the Toro Rosso sorted itself out through the right-hand Turn Three – where Sainz did not realise that Alonso was attacking on the outside. Eased left by cars on his right, Sainz forced Alonso on to the grass, where somehow Fernando saved the McLaren from a huge sideways moment – and he didn't lift off for a second. Making ground on the first lap is critical in this era, when passing during the race is severely limited by aerodynamic turbulence.

Further back, Gutiérrez aimed for a diminishing gap and tapped Wehrlein sideways into Ericsson. So much for their excellent qualifying: the Manor retired on the spot and the Sauber limped back to the pits for a new nose.

Wehrlein had gone in hard enough to prompt a virtual safety car (VSC), which later became a full-blown safety car, triggering the first alternate plan on the Red Bull list of possibilities. They decided to split strategies. Ricciardo, being the second of the two Red Bulls on the road, was brought in to swap the super-softs for a set of mediums, thus opening up the possibility of running non-stop, the disadvantage of rejoining in 17th place being partly negated by the bunching effect of the safety car. Renault adopted the same tactic with Palmer.

When the safety car came in at the end of the third lap,

Rosberg was more intent on watching Verstappen than thinking about getting the jump on Hamilton who, by the end of the next lap, was already out of DRS range. Nico did not have to worry for long, however. The super-softs dropped off quite quickly, and Verstappen was five seconds behind after ten laps and keeping an eye on Hülkenberg who, in turn, was only a second ahead of Räikkönen. The Ferraris were split by Massa, while the other Williams of Bottas had dropped back slightly from this trio. The status quo would remain as Räikkönen, rather than abuse his brakes at this early stage, bided his time, waiting for the super-soft-shod Force India to make an early stop. Vettel faced a similar predicament, made more difficult by the Mercedes-powered Williams being quick and untouchable on the long straight – even with the assistance of Ferrari DRS.

Eventually, Sainz would receive a five-second penalty for his part in Alonso's grasstracking experience, but by the time the Toro Rosso had finally got out of the Spaniard's way by pitting on lap 12, the McLaren driver had Ricciardo on his tail, the Red Bull quickly moving ahead and into ninth place.

At the same time, Verstappen felt his super-softs were past their best and came in for mediums, rejoining just behind Alonso, but quickly moving ahead and thinking about closing down the three-second gap to his team-mate.

The strategic thinking on the Mercedes pit wall was not so clear cut. With fresh tyres slow to reach their optimum performance, there was the danger that the undercut might not work, so much so that a rival might be faster on his used tyres, thereby bringing a so-called overcut into play. The dilemma for Mercedes was which of their two drivers to bring in first. By rights, it should have been Hamilton, because of the usual qualification of track position, but Lewis would not be best pleased if that played into Rosberg's hands thanks to an overcut.

In the end, Hamilton opened a lead of more than four seconds and that settled the matter. But it was not as straightforward as it looked for Lewis. The first-corner lock-up had flat-spotted the right front to such a degree that he actually thought he might have to change tyres because of the resulting vibration. Knowing this would seriously compromise a race he had to win, however, he had kept going and tried not to think about the eyeball-rattling vibration as he reached more than 200mph on the main straight.

Hamilton came in for mediums at the end of lap 17; Rosberg stayed out for three more laps, rejoining ahead of Ricciardo and Verstappen, the Red Bulls now in line astern. There were changes further back as Räikkönen jumped Hülkenberg thanks to the Ferrari running longer on the softs. Massa and Sainz had stopped shortly after Verstappen, but having kept going longer on his super-softs, Bottas made his later stop and quickly caught team-mate Massa, who moved aside to allow him to chase down Hülkenberg.

Apart from Nasr, Vettel was the only driver not to have stopped, the Ferrari now leading the race. With his softs in good shape, the German pressed on. Rejecting his team's call to come in after 26 laps, he stayed out until lap 32, by which time he was 3.7s ahead of Hamilton, but, more importantly, 19s and 26s ahead of Räikkönen and Hülkenberg in sixth and seventh places respectively. Having rejoined on mediums between these two, he was soon closing in on Räikkönen, who was unhappy on his mediums.

When the Finn stopped again on lap 45, Vettel – as happy with the car as he had been all weekend – was five seconds behind Ricciardo, who had given way (on team instruction) to Verstappen on fresher mediums. As the Ferrari came closer, Red Bull reacted by pulling in Ricciardo for new softs on lap 50. That dropped him behind Hülkenberg's fifth-placed Force India, but it would be the work of a moment for Ricciardo to

gain the place back and begin a charge. With Verstappen a few car lengths behind Rosberg's second-placed Mercedes, this was becoming tasty.

The first act opened when Verstappen made a lunge down the inside of the Mercedes, a move that didn't come off as he ran wide. In the process, he did his tyres no good. Vettel was closing in.

Meanwhile, the other Ferrari was pushing Hülkenberg for sixth, but Räikkönen was unable to get the power down cleanly enough out of the final corner to allow an overtake on the main straight. He seized his moment into Turn Four, the pair briefly running side by side until Hülkenberg's older tyres gave out and he spun the Force India to avoid an otherwise inevitable collision. Fortunately, Hülkenberg was far enough ahead of Bottas not to lose another place. There were five laps remaining and the race was about to become even more eventful.

Having previously tried an unsuccessful run down the inside of Rosberg at Turn Four – a move that had been foiled by the dust and marbles off line – Verstappen now came under attack from Vettel. Making the most of DRS, the Ferrari driver had a go into Turn One – where Verstappen's tyres were not up to the job and he ran wide on to the grass in a similar fashion to Hamilton 68 laps before. This time, however, the race director reported the incident to the stewards as Verstappen continued in third place.

Red Bull advised Verstappen, "You're probably going to have to surrender position." That was relayed to Vettel, but the increasingly furious German was not aware of a further Red Bull instruction for their man to hold station until the matter was resolved.

When Verstappen then checked the Ferrari's speed (Vettel claimed he was brake-tested), Sebastian became apoplectic, having realised that Verstappen was also backing

Above: The battle for third was fought out on and off the track between Max Verstappen, Sebastian Vettel and Daniel Ricciardo. The stewards would eventually promote Ricciardo to third, although he didn't get to enjoy his moment on the podium.
Photo: Lukas Gorys

Right: Another 1-2 finish for Mercedes was celebrated with the aid of suitable local attire.
Photo: WRi2/Jad Sherif

Above right: For the record. Monday morning's *Récord* got the podium right. Their witty image showed Vettel crudely expunged by Ricciardo.
Photo: WRi2/Jean-François Galeron

the Ferrari towards the rapidly advancing Ricciardo. Given Daniel's impressive late-braking capability – plus the benefit of fresher tyres – Vettel knew what was coming next. This prompted a tirade of abuse across the airwaves, aimed at the race director and employing colourful language the like of which had not been heard before – or, at least, not in public.

Perhaps because he was so distracted, Vettel left the door open approaching Turn Four and, predictably, Ricciardo pounced. Sebastian defended by changing his line in the braking zone, Ricciardo locked up, the two cars touched, but the drivers skillfully avoided a full-blown collision. Their positions were unchanged as they completed the final lap.

Räikkönen was sixth, 20s behind this controversy, with Hülkenberg seventh, pulling in extra points for Force India over Williams as Bottas and Massa came home eighth and ninth. Pérez picked up another point for Force India, but the local hero was very disappointed with tenth, having been stuck behind the Williams and unable to find a way through.

Eleventh was an excellent result for Ericsson and should have deserved a point for his effort, following a non-stop run as the result of the first-lap pit visit for a new nose. Having recovered from his first-lap excursion, Alonso also deserved better, 13th (one place behind Button, who had struggled with tyres) being the result of a wheel-nut problem during a pit stop.

Palmer did well to recover from the early stop, having outperformed his team-mate and battled with the McLarens. The Renault finished 14th, ahead of Nasr, who had run a very long first stint and had to give best to his Sauber team-mate. After such promise during practice, Sainz was disappointed with 16th, the result of the five-second penalty for the incident with Alonso and front wing damage incurred during the hectic first lap. The only consolation for Magnussen, after a race-long struggle with all three types of tyre, was nicking

17th place from Kvyat by 0.006s after the Toro Rosso driver had been penalised for exceeding track limits and dropped two places as a result. The worst weekend so far for Haas was summed up by Gutiérrez and Grosjean struggling into 19th and 20th places, ahead of final finisher Ocon, whose tough weekend had been cemented by a handling imbalance throughout the race.

Apart from the tyre vibration in the first stint, Hamilton had no such problems, having done everything he could in championship terms by leading from pole and commanding the race. Similarly, Rosberg could not complain about surviving the first-lap clash with Verstappen and withstanding mounting pressure to collect another 18 points for second.

The recipient of 15 points changed identity no fewer than three times. Verstappen made his way to the podium, only to be told in the cool-down room that the application of a five-second penalty meant the place belonged to Vettel. The Ferrari team rushed to welcome a much-needed result – only to discover not long after that third had become fifth, thanks to a ten-second penalty for their man's move in the braking zone as Ricciardo had attacked to take what had now become third place. The controversy was set to continue over this incident and the application – or not – of penalties from start to finish.

"I controlled the race from grass to finish," joked Hamilton. "It hadn't crossed my mind about the stewards penalising me. I was more concerned about the big flat spot. The vibration was rattling my brain."

"Lewis did a better job this weekend," said Rosberg. "I have to live with that. But the championship is still looking okay, but I'm not counting on anything. I'm going into the next race in Brazil with the same attitude I've had all season, which is to try and win."

Maurice Hamilton

VIEWPOINT
FRUSTRATION GETS THE BETTER OF VETTEL

THE four-times champion was not having a good time of it. Ferrari's 2016 performance, while not 2014-awful, was not what Maranello had been looking for.

The subject of a driver's key role polarises opinion. Does he need to 'lead', drive everyone forward and involve himself, like a Schumacher or Senna? Or should he simply climb in and drive the wheels off the things, like a Mansell?

Vettel's radio transmissions in 2016 suggested that all was not rosy in the Ferrari garden. Not quite 'stroppy', Seb often questioned strategy calls and, sometimes, plain disregarded them. He was also regularly upset by unco-operative backmarkers.

But Max Verstappen's late-race behaviour in Mexico made Vettel properly steamed up. This time in a car with more performance than the two Red Bulls, Vettel was furious that Verstappen had not ceded position after running off at Turn One and then backing him into the advancing Ricciardo, Daniel on better rubber. Over the radio, he told race director Charlie Whiting to "**** off!"

The right decision was made to penalise Verstappen, but perhaps it should have been applied to Hamilton, too, for lap one. And, had Vettel been aware that later he would be penalised and dropped to fifth for his defence against Ricciardo, no doubt the air would have been bluer still.

Maybe Seb had moved a little in the braking area, but he had left Ricciardo racing room. How could he be given a penalty when Verstappen had got away with far more aggressively chopping Räikkönen at 200-plus mph at Spa? Certainly there was no consistency there, something called for by Carlos Sainz post-race.

In Vettel's case, though, you sensed that it was a manifestation of frustration that had built throughout the season. Should he have been sanctioned for bringing the sport into disrepute? Maybe. But when the emotion cooled, he sought out Charlie Whiting and apologised personally, then wrote a letter to FIA President Jean Todt. Because of that, he got off, but everyone was warned that a repeat would not be tolerated. Probably good to see adult behaviour over a racing driver simply reaching boiling point.

Tony Dodgins

19

2016 FORMULA 1 GRAN PREMIO DE MÉXICO

MEXICO CITY 28–30 OCTOBER

RACE DISTANCE: 71 laps, 189.738 miles/305.354km

RACE WEATHER: Dry/sunny-overcast (track 43–50°C, air 20–23°C)

AUTODROMO HERMANOS RODRIGUEZ, MEXICO CITY
Circuit: 2.674 miles/4.304km 71 laps

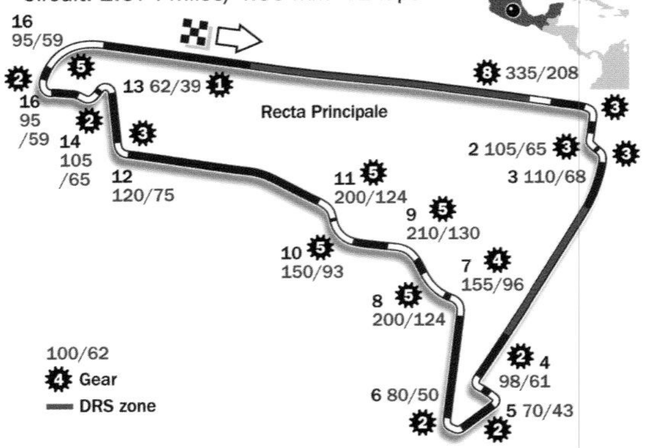
16 95/59
13 62/39
Recta Principale
335/208
16 95 /59
14 105 /65
12 120/75
2 105/65
3 110/68
11 200/124
9 210/130
10 150/93
7 155/96
8 200/124
100/62
Gear
DRS zone
4 98/61
6 80/50
5 70/43

ROLEX
OFFICIAL TIMEPIECE

RACE – OFFICIAL CLASSIFICATION

Pos.	Driver	Nat.	No.	Entrant	Car/Engine	Tyres	Laps	Time/Retirement	Speed (mph/km/h)	Gap to leader	Fastest race lap	
1	**Lewis Hamilton**	GB	44	Mercedes AMG Petronas F1 Team	Mercedes F1 W07-Mercedes PU106C V6	P	71	1h 40m 31.402s	113.250/182.258		1m 22.596s	66
2	**Nico Rosberg**	D	6	Mercedes AMG Petronas F1 Team	Mercedes F1 W07-Mercedes PU106C V6	P	71	1h 40m 39.756s	113.093/182.006	8.354s	1m 22.792s	43
3	**Daniel Ricciardo**	AUS	3	Red Bull Racing	Red Bull RB12-TAG Heuer RB12 V6	P	71	1h 40m 52.260s	112.860/181.630	20.858s	1m 21.134s	53
4	**Max Verstappen**	NL	33	Red Bull Racing	Red Bull RB12-TAG Heuer RB12 V6	P	71	1h 40m 52.725s*	112.851/181.616	21.323s	1m 22.887s	66
5	**Sebastian Vettel**	D	5	Scuderia Ferrari	Ferrari SF15-H-059/5 V6	P	71	1h 40m 58.715s**	112.739/181.436	27.313s	1m 22.497s	61
6	**Kimi Räikkönen**	FIN	7	Scuderia Ferrari	Ferrari SF16-H-059/5 V6	P	71	1h 41m 20.778s	112.330/180.778	49.376s	1m 22.512s	47
7	**Nico Hülkenberg**	D	27	Sahara Force India F1 Team	Force India VJM09-Mercedes PU106C V6	P	71	1h 41m 30.293s	112.155/180.496	58.891s	1m 23.288s	50
8	**Valtteri Bottas**	FIN	77	Williams Martini Racing	Williams FW38-Mercedes PU106C V6	P	71	1h 41m 37.014s	112.031/180.297	1m 05.612s	1m 23.540s	65
9	**Felipe Massa**	BR	19	Williams Martini Racing	Williams FW38-Mercedes PU106C V6	P	71	1h 41m 47.608s	111.837/179.984	1m 16.206s	1m 23.576s	64
10	**Sergio Pérez**	MEX	11	Sahara Force India F1 Team	Force India VJM09-Mercedes PU106C V6	P	71	1h 41m 48.200s	111.826/179.966	1m 16.798s	1m 23.607s	62
11	Marcus Ericsson	S	9	Sauber F1 Team	Sauber C35-Ferrari 059/5 V6	P	70			1 lap	1m 24.340s	65
12	Jenson Button	GB	22	McLaren Honda	McLaren MP4-31-Honda RA616H V6	P	70			1 lap	1m 23.777s	70
13	Fernando Alonso	E	14	McLaren Honda	McLaren MP4-31-Honda RA616H V6	P	70			1 lap	1m 23.668s	69
14	Jolyon Palmer	GB	30	Renault Sport F1 Team	Renault R.S.16-R.E.16 V6	P	70			1 lap	1m 24.574s	64
15	Felipe Nasr	BR	12	Sauber F1 Team	Sauber C35-Ferrari 059/5 V6	P	70			1 lap	1m 23.657s	58
16	Carlos Sainz	E	55	Scuderia Toro Rosso	Toro Rosso STR11-Ferrari 059/4 V6	P	70	***		1 lap	1m 24.467s	52
17	Kevin Magnussen	DK	20	Renault Sport F1 Team	Renault R.S.16-R.E.16 V6	P	70			1 lap	1m 23.146s	53
18	Daniil Kvyat	RUS	26	Scuderia Toro Rosso	Toro Rosso STR11-Ferrari 059/4 V6	P	70	*		1 lap	1m 23.618s	59
19	Esteban Gutiérrez	MEX	21	Haas F1 Team	Haas VF-16-Ferrari 059/5 V6	P	70			1 lap	1m 23.456s	63
20	Romain Grosjean	F	8	Haas F1 Team	Haas VF-16-Ferrari 059/5 V6	P	70			1 lap	1m 23.278s	53
21	Esteban Ocon	F	31	Manor Racing MRT	Manor MRT05-Mercedes PU106C V6	P	69			2 laps	1m 24.964s	43
	Pascal Wehrlein	D	94	Manor Racing MRT	Manor MRT05-Mercedes PU106C V6	P	0	*accident*			no time	

* includes 5-second penalty for leaving the track and gaining an advantage. ** includes 10-second penalty for illegal defending under braking *** includes 5-second penalty for forcing a car off track.

Fastest race lap: Daniel Ricciardo on lap 53, 1m 21.134, 118.665mph/190.972km/h.

Lap record: Nigel Mansell (Williams FW14 - Renault V10), 1m 16.788s, 128.790mph/207.267km (1991, 2.747-mile/4.421km circuit).

Lap record (current configuration): Nico Rosberg (Mercedes-Benz F1 W06), 1m 20.521s, 119.568mph/192.426km/h (2015).

21 · PALMER · Renault

19 · NASR · Sauber

17 · GUTIÉRREZ · Haas

15 · ERICSSON · Sauber

13 · BUTTON · McLaren

11 · ALONSO · McLaren

22 · GROSJEAN · Haas
(required to start from the pit lane – car modified in parc fermé)

20 · OCON · Manor

18 · KVYAT · Toro Rosso

16 · WEHRLEIN · Manor

14 · MAGNUSSEN · Renault

12 · PÉREZ · Force India

	Grid order	1	2	3	4	5	6	7	8	9	10	11	12	13	14	15	16	17	18	19	20	21	22	23	24	25	26	27	28	29	30	31	32	33	34	35	36	37	38	39	40	41	42	43	44	45	46	47	48	49	50	51	52	53	54	55
44	HAMILTON	44	44	44	44	44	44	44	44	44	44	44	44	44	44	44	44	44	6	6	6	5	5	5	5	5	5	5	5	5	5	5	5	44	44	44	44	44	44	44	44	44	44	44	44	44	44	44	44	44	44	44	44	44	44	44
6	ROSBERG	6	6	6	6	6	6	6	6	6	6	6	6	6	6	6	6	6	7	7	7	44	44	44	44	44	44	44	44	44	44	44	44	6	6	6	6	6	6	6	6	6	6	6	6	6	6	6	6	6	6	6	6	6	6	6
33	VERSTAPPEN	33	33	33	33	33	33	33	33	33	33	33	27	27	7	7	7	7	5	5	5	6	6	6	6	6	6	6	6	6	6	6	6	33	33	33	33	33	33	33	33	33	33	33	33	33	33	33	33	33	33	33	33	33	33	33
3	RICCIARDO	27	27	27	27	27	27	27	27	27	27	27	7	7	27	5	5	5	44	44	44	3	33	33	33	33	33	33	33	33	33	33	33	3	3	3	3	3	3	3	3	3	3	3	3	3	3	3	3	3	5	5	5	5	5	5
27	HÜLKENBERG	7	7	7	7	7	7	7	7	7	7	7	33	19	5	77	77	77	77	11	3	33	3	3	3	3	3	3	3	3	3	3	3	7	7	7	7	7	7	7	7	7	7	7	7	5	5	5	5	5	3	27	3	3	3	3
7	RÄIKKÖNEN	3	19	19	19	19	19	19	19	19	19	19	19	5	77	11	11	11	11	3	33	7	7	7	7	7	7	7	7	7	7	7	7	5	5	5	5	5	5	5	5	5	5	5	5	7	27	27	27	27	27	3	27	27	27	27
5	VETTEL	19	5	5	5	5	5	5	5	5	5	5	5	77	11	3	3	3	3	33	11	27	27	27	27	27	27	27	27	27	27	27	27	27	27	27	27	27	27	27	27	27	27	27	27	27	7	7	7	7	7	7	7	7	7	7
77	BOTTAS	5	77	77	77	77	77	77	77	77	77	77	77	11	19	33	33	33	33	77	27	19	19	77	77	77	77	77	77	77	77	77	77	77	77	77	77	77	77	77	77	77	77	77	77	77	77	77	77	77	77	77	77	77	77	77
19	MASSA	77	11	11	11	11	11	11	11	11	11	11	11	3	3	14	27	27	27	27	19	77	77	19	19	19	19	19	19	19	19	19	19	19	19	19	19	19	19	19	19	19	19	19	19	19	19	19	19	19	19	19	19	19	19	19
55	SAINZ	11	55	55	55	55	55	55	55	55	55	55	14	14	33	27	14	22	19	19	77	11	11	11	11	11	11	11	11	11	11	11	11	11	11	11	11	11	11	11	11	11	11	11	11	11	11	11	11	11	11	11	11	11	11	11
14	ALONSO	55	14	14	14	14	14	14	14	14	14	14	3	33	14	22	22	12	12	12	12	12	12	12	12	12	12	12	12	12	12	12	12	9	9	9	9	9	9	9	9	9	9	9	9	9	9	9	9	9	9	9	9	9	*9*	*9*
11	PÉREZ	14	20	20	20	20	20	20	20	20	3	3	55	22	22	12	12	19	9	9	9	9	9	9	9	9	9	9	9	9	9	9	9	12	12	12	12	12	12	12	12	12	12	12	12	12	12	12	12	*30*	*30*	*30*	*30*	*30*	*30*	*30*
22	BUTTON	20	22	22	22	22	22	22	22	3	20	20	22	12	12	19	19	9	30	30	30	30	30	30	30	30	30	30	30	30	30	30	30	30	30	30	30	30	30	30	30	30	30	30	30	30	30	30	*30*	*12*	*22*	*22*	*22*	*22*	*22*	*22*
20	MAGNUSSEN	22	21	21	21	21	21	3	3	22	22	22	20	31	31	9	9	30	55	55	55	55	55	55	55	55	55	55	55	55	55	55	55	55	55	55	55	55	55	55	55	55	55	55	55	55	55	*55*	*55*	*22*	*55*	*55*	*55*	*55*	*55*	*55*
9	ERICSSON	21	12	12	3	3	3	21	21	21	21	21	12	26	9	30	30	55	14	14	14	14	14	14	14	14	14	14	14	14	14	14	14	14	14	14	14	14	14	14	14	14	14	14	14	22	*22*	*22*	*22*	*55*	*14*	*14*	*14*	*14*	*14*	*14*
94	WEHRLEIN	12	31	31	12	12	12	12	12	12	12	12	21	9	30	31	55	14	20	20	22	22	22	22	22	22	22	22	22	22	22	22	22	22	22	22	22	22	22	22	22	22	22	22	22	*26*	*26*	*26*	*20*	*20*	*12*	*12*	*12*	*12*	*12*	*12*
21	GUTIÉRREZ	31	3	3	26	26	26	26	26	26	26	26	26	30	55	55	20	20	22	22	20	20	20	20	20	20	20	20	20	26	26	26	26	26	26	26	26	26	26	26	26	26	26	26	26	*14*	*20*	*20*	*14*	*14*	*20*	*20*	*26*	*26*	*26*	*26*
26	KVYAT	26	26	26	31	31	31	31	31	31	31	31	31	55	20	20	21	21	21	21	21	21	26	26	26	26	26	26	26	20	20	20	20	20	20	20	20	20	20	20	*20*	*20*	*20*	*20*	*20*	*20*	*21*	*14*	*21*	*26*	*26*	*26*	*20*	*20*	*20*	*20*
12	NASR	30	8	8	8	8	8	8	8	8	8	9	9	20	21	21	26	26	26	26	26	26	21	21	21	21	21	21	21	21	21	21	21	21	21	21	21	*21*	*21*	*21*	*21*	*21*	*21*	*21*	*21*	*21*	*14*	*21*	*26*	*8*	*8*	*21*	*21*	*21*	*21*	*21*
31	OCON	8	30	30	30	9	9	9	9	9	9	30	30	21	26	26	8	8	8	8	8	8	8	8	8	8	8	8	8	8	8	8	8	8	8	*8*	*8*	*8*	*8*	*8*	*8*	*8*	*8*	*8*	*8*	*8*	*8*	*8*	*8*	*31*	*21*	*31*	*31*	*8*	*8*	*8*
30	PALMER	9	9	9	9	30	30	30	30	30	30	8	8	8	8	8	31	31	31	31	31	31	31	31	31	31	31	31	31	31	31	31	31	31	31	*31*	*31*	*31*	*31*	*31*	*31*	*31*	*31*	*31*	*31*	*31*	*31*	*31*	*31*	*21*	*31*	*8*	*8*	*31*	*31*	*31*
8	GROSJEAN																																																							

6 Pit stop 9 = Drive-thru penalty *94 One lap or more behind*

All results and data © FOM 2016

TIME SHEETS

PRACTICE 1 (FRIDAY)
Weather: Dry/overcast
Temperatures: track 20-24°C, air 12-14°C

Pos.	Driver	Laps	Time
1	Lewis Hamilton	34	1m 20.914s
2	Sebastian Vettel	23	1m 20.993s
3	Kimi Räikkönen	19	1m 21.072s
4	Sergio Pérez	23	1m 21.200s
5	Nico Hülkenberg	23	1m 21.409s
6	Valtteri Bottas	34	1m 21.447s
7	Nico Rosberg	32	1m 21.673s
8	Daniel Ricciardo	27	1m 21.727s
9	Felipe Massa	31	1m 21.836s
10	Daniil Kvyat	29	1m 22.215s
11	Romain Grosjean	21	1m 22.500s
12	Carlos Sainz	32	1m 22.563s
13	Marcus Ericsson	17	1m 22.723s
14	Max Verstappen	10	1m 22.877s
15	Esteban Gutiérrez	23	1m 22.910s
16	Fernando Alonso	25	1m 23.089s
17	Felipe Nasr	12	1m 23.089s
18	Jenson Button	24	1m 23.342s
19	Kevin Magnussen	32	1m 23.556s
20	Esteban Ocon	30	1m 24.083s
21	Jolyon Palmer	35	1m 24.097s
22	Pascal Wehrlein	28	1m 24.350s

PRACTICE 2 (FRIDAY)
Weather: Dry/overcast
Temperatures: track 32-37°C, air 15-17°C

Pos.	Driver	Laps	Time
1	Sebastian Vettel	47	1m 19.790s
2	Lewis Hamilton	37	1m 19.794s
3	Nico Rosberg	46	1m 20.225s
4	Kimi Räikkönen	37	1m 20.259s
5	Daniel Ricciardo	43	1m 20.448s
6	Nico Hülkenberg	43	1m 20.574s
7	Max Verstappen	42	1m 20.619s
8	Valtteri Bottas	41	1m 20.629s
9	Carlos Sainz	46	1m 20.974s
10	Fernando Alonso	25	1m 21.003s
11	Daniil Kvyat	39	1m 21.193s
12	Jenson Button	39	1m 21.198s
13	Felipe Massa	45	1m 21.326s
14	Kevin Magnussen	39	1m 21.442s
15	Sergio Pérez	41	1m 21.579s
16	Jolyon Palmer	44	1m 21.785s
17	Pascal Wehrlein	42	1m 21.980s
18	Marcus Ericsson	42	1m 21.997s
19	Felipe Nasr	43	1m 22.037s
20	Romain Grosjean	14	1m 22.105s
21	Esteban Ocon	44	1m 22.298s
22	Esteban Gutiérrez	33	1m 22.408s

PRACTICE 3 (SATURDAY)
Weather: Dry/sunny
Temperatures: track 32°C, air 14°C

Pos.	Driver	Laps	Time
1	Max Verstappen	16	1m 19.137s
2	Lewis Hamilton	23	1m 19.231s
3	Daniel Ricciardo	17	1m 19.370s
4	Nico Rosberg	27	1m 19.618s
5	Valtteri Bottas	19	1m 19.811s
6	Sebastian Vettel	16	1m 19.937s
7	Kimi Räikkönen	16	1m 19.994s
8	Felipe Massa	22	1m 19.997s
9	Nico Hülkenberg	21	1m 20.255s
10	Carlos Sainz	22	1m 20.325s
11	Sergio Pérez	20	1m 20.472s
12	Daniil Kvyat	20	1m 20.586s
13	Fernando Alonso	18	1m 20.600s
14	Jolyon Palmer	18	1m 20.959s
15	Jenson Button	19	1m 21.152s
16	Marcus Ericsson	21	1m 21.245s
17	Esteban Gutiérrez	16	1m 21.338s
18	Kevin Magnussen	17	1m 21.345s
19	Romain Grosjean	15	1m 21.601s
20	Pascal Wehrlein	23	1m 21.758s
21	Esteban Ocon	22	1m 21.921s
22	Felipe Nasr	18	1m 22.354s

QUALIFYING (SATURDAY)
Weather: Dry/sunny Temperatures: track 24-55°C, air 13-19°C

Pos.	Driver	First	Second	Third	Qualifying Tyre
1	Lewis Hamilton	1m 19.447s	1m 19.137s	1m 18.704s	Super-Soft (new)
2	Nico Rosberg	1m 19.996s	1m 19.761s	1m 18.958s	Super-Soft (new)
3	Max Verstappen	1m 19.874s	1m 18.972s	1m 19.054s	Super-Soft (new)
4	Daniel Ricciardo	1m 19.713s	1m 19.553s	1m 19.133s	Super-Soft (new)
5	Nico Hülkenberg	1m 20.599s	1m 19.769s	1m 19.330s	Super-Soft (new)
6	Kimi Räikkönen	1m 19.554s	1m 19.936s	1m 19.376s	Super-Soft (new)
7	Sebastian Vettel	1m 19.865s	1m 19.385s	1m 19.381s	Super-Soft (new)
8	Valtteri Bottas	1m 20.338s	1m 19.958s	1m 19.551s	Super-Soft (new)
9	Felipe Massa	1m 20.423s	1m 20.151s	1m 20.032s	Super-Soft (new)
10	Carlos Sainz	1m 20.457s	1m 20.169s	1m 20.378s	Super-Soft (new)
11	Fernando Alonso	1m 20.552s	1m 20.282s		
12	Sergio Pérez	1m 20.308s	1m 20.287s		
13	Jenson Button	1m 21.333s	1m 20.673s		
14	Kevin Magnussen	1m 21.254s	1m 21.131s		
15	Marcus Ericsson	1m 21.062s	1m 21.536s		
16	Pascal Wehrlein	1m 21.363s	1m 21.785s		
17	Esteban Gutiérrez	1m 21.401s			
18	Daniil Kvyat	1m 21.454s			
19	Felipe Nasr	1m 21.692s			
20	Esteban Ocon	1m 21.881s			
21	Romain Grosjean	1m 21.916s			
22	Jolyon Palmer	no time			

Photos: Peter J. Fox

FOR THE RECORD

600th POINT: Daniel Ricciardo.

DID YOU KNOW?

Mercedes set a new record for wins in a season (17).

This was the 250th race start by Kimi Räikkönen. This includes Belgium 2001, where he retired at the first start.

POINTS

DRIVERS

1	Nico Rosberg	349
2	Lewis Hamilton	330
3	Daniel Ricciardo	242
4	Sebastian Vettel	187
5	Kimi Räikkönen	178
6	Max Verstappen	177
7	Sergio Pérez	85
8	Valtteri Bottas	85
9	Nico Hülkenberg	60
10	Fernando Alonso	52
11	Felipe Massa	51
12	Carlos Sainz	38
13	Romain Grosjean	29
14	Daniil Kvyat	25
15	Jenson Button	21
16	Kevin Magnussen	7
17	Jolyon Palmer	1
18	Pascal Wehrlein	1
19	Stoffel Vandoorne	1

CONSTRUCTORS

1	Mercedes	679
2	Red Bull	427
3	Ferrari	365
4	Force India	145
5	Williams	136
6	McLaren	74
7	Toro Rosso	55
8	Haas	29
9	Renault	8
10	Manor	1

9 · MASSA · Williams

7 · VETTEL · Ferrari

5 · HÜLKENBERG · Force India

3 · VERSTAPPEN · Red Bull

1 · HAMILTON · Mercedes

10 · SAINZ · Toro Rosso

8 · BOTTAS · Williams

6 · RÄIKKÖNEN · Ferrari

4 · RICCIARDO · Red Bull

2 · ROSBERG · Mercedes

Qualifying: head-to-head

Rosberg	9 10	Hamilton
Vettel	10 9	Räikkönen
Massa	3 16	Bottas
Ricciardo	4 0	Kvyat
Ricciardo	10 5	Verstappen
Pérez	9 10	Hülkenberg
Magnussen	12 7	Palmer
Verstappen	3 1	Sainz
Kvyat	4 11	Sainz
Ericsson	12 7	Nasr
Alonso	13 5	Button
Button	0 1	Vandoorne
Haryanto	5 7	Wehrlein
Wehrlein	5 2	Ocon
Grosjean	12 7	Gutiérrez

56	57	58	59	60	61	62	63	64	65	66	67	68	69	70	71	
44	44	44	44	44	44	44	44	44	44	44	44	44	44	44	44	1
6	6	6	6	6	6	6	6	6	6	6	6	6	6	6	6	2
33	33	33	33	33	33	33	33	33	33	33	33	33	33	33	33	3
5	5	5	5	5	5	5	5	5	5	5	5	5	5	5	5	4
3	3	3	3	3	3	3	3	3	3	3	3	3	3	3	3	5
27	27	27	27	27	27	27	27	27	27	27	7	7	7	7	7	6
7	7	7	7	7	7	7	7	7	7	7	27	27	27	27	27	7
77	77	77	77	77	77	77	77	77	77	77	77	77	77	77	77	8
19	19	19	19	19	19	19	19	19	19	19	19	19	19	19	19	9
11	11	11	11	11	11	11	11	11	11	11	11	11	11	11	11	10
9	9	9	9	9	9	9	9	9	9	9	9	9	9	9		
30	30	30	30	22	22	22	22	22	22	22	22	22	22	22		
22	22	22	22	30	30	30	30	30	30	14	14	14	14	14		
55	55	55	55	55	14	14	14	14	14	30	30	30	30	30		
14	14	14	14	14	55	55	55	55	55	55	55	55	55	55		
12	12	12	12	12	12	12	12	12	12	12	12	12	12	12		
26	26	26	26	26	26	26	26	26	26	26	26	26	26	26		
20	20	20	20	20	20	20	20	20	20	20	20	20	20	20		
21	21	21	21	21	21	21	21	21	21	21	21	21	21	21		
8	8	8	8	8	8	8	8	8	8	8	8	8	8	8		
31	31	31	31	31	31	31	31	31	31	31	31	31	31			

Safety car deployed on laps shown

RACE TYRE STRATEGIES

PIRELLI

	Driver	Race Stint 1	Race Stint 2	Race Stint 3
1	Hamilton	Soft (u): 1-17	Medium (n): 18-71	
2	Rosberg	Soft (u): 1-20	Medium (n): 21-71	
3	Vettel	Soft (u): 1-32	Medium (n): 33-71	
4	Ricciardo	Super-Soft (u): 1	Medium (n): 2-50	Soft (n): 51-71
5	Verstappen	Super-Soft (u): 1-12	Medium (n): 13-71	
6	Räikkönen	Soft (u): 1-20	Medium (n): 21-45	Medium (u): 46-71
7	Hülkenberg	Super-Soft (u): 1-14	Medium (n): 15-71	
8	Bottas	Super-Soft (u): 1-19	Medium (n): 20-71	
9	Massa	Super-Soft (u): 1-14	Medium (n): 15-71	
10	Pérez	Soft (u): 1-20	Medium (n): 21-71	
11	Ericsson	Soft (n): 1	Medium (n): 2-70	
12	Button	Soft (n): 1-17	Medium (n): 18-70	
13	Alonso	Soft (n): 1- 16	Medium (n): 17-45	Soft (n): 46-70
14	Palmer	Super-Soft (n): 1	Medium (n): 2-70	
15	Nasr	Medium (n): 1-49	Super-Soft (n): 50-70	
16	Sainz	Super-Soft (u): 1-12	Medium (n): 13-70	
17	Magnussen	Soft (n): 1-12	Medium (n): 13-51	Super-Soft (n): 52-70
18	Kvyat	Soft (n): 1-13	Soft (n): 14-47	Super-Soft (n): 48-70
19	Gutiérrez	Soft (n): 1-12	Medium (n): 13-48	Soft (n): 49-70
20	Grosjean	Soft (n): 1-11	Medium (n): 12-50	Soft (n): 51-70
21	Ocon	Soft (n): 1-15	Medium (n): 16-69	
	Wehrlein	Soft (n): 0 (dnf)		

The tyre regulations stipulate that at least two of three dry tyre specifications must be used during a dry race.
Pirelli P Zero logos are colour-coded on the tyre sidewalls: Red = Super-Soft; Yellow = Soft; White = Medium. (n) new (u) used

Photos: Peter J. Fox

BRAZILIAN GRAND PRIX

INTERLAGOS CIRCUIT

Main photo: Lewis Hamilton was never headed in the oft interrupted proceedings. Nico Rosberg managed a damage-limitation drive to second place, just resisting a brilliant effort from Max Verstappen.

Inset, left: Thumbs up from Lewis.
Photos: Peter J. Fox

INTERLAGOS QUALIFYING

WHEN the Mercedes of Lewis Hamilton and Nico Rosberg headed the queue to start Q1, it was a sign of serious intent and the need to beat the threat of rain. Neither title contender wanted a random element to interfere with their careful preparations at this stage, particularly when the weekend so far had gone reasonably well for both.

Hamilton had maintained an edge through free practice, but not enough to encourage the idea that his 60th pole position was a given. Rosberg would have a tiny advantage through the first sector, while Hamilton's split time showed magenta in sector 2 and sometimes sector 3. In the end, just a tenth of a second separated them, and it was impossible to tell where that fraction had been won and lost. Maybe there was nothing in it, but it was a sizeable psychological gap as the reigning champion continued to exude the confidence evident in the previous two races.

"I've felt very comfortable with the car all weekend so far," said Hamilton. "Every session I was in front, and this is the best I could have hoped for. Strangely, it's only my second pole here. Interlagos is a tricky track that I've struggled with in the past, but we seem to have nailed it this time."

Rosberg continued to maintain that he would take every race as it came; just like the previous 19. "The lap times were very close, which is why it's a little disappointing," said Rosberg. "My lap was good, but Lewis was quicker. But as we have seen at other races, pole isn't always everything."

While that may have been true, Rosberg knew that he was 8m closer than Hamilton to the lurking menace of Kimi Räikkönen and Max Verstappen on row two. His unspoken hope may have been to see a continuation of the no-holds-barred fight between them that had taken place at previous races, but, for now, the Finn was mildly surprised to find himself third fastest.

"I struggled the whole of qualifying in a few places in the middle sector," said the Finn. "To be honest, the last lap [his quickest] was pretty average. I think we're lacking a bit of downforce."

That may have been a problem in the middle sector, but the Ferrari made up the difference with a slight power advantage in the first and final sectors – particularly the latter with the long, uphill climb. Part of Kimi's surprise was due to Verstappen – on course during practice to be best of the rest – having failed to put together a decent final lap, largely due to poor tyre preparation and a comparative lack of grip.

Sebastian Vettel and Daniel Ricciardo, fifth and sixth, were even more disappointed. Vettel's genuine hope of claiming P3 with a car that was behaving well had been compromised when the German was too conservative through the final corner (Junção). Ricciardo had been similarly over-cautious while trying not to lock up into the two tight corners in the middle sector.

The mood at Haas was diametrically opposed to Red Bull, as Romain Grosjean had claimed an excellent seventh to give the American team their best qualifying position to date. The performance was even more of a surprise after Grosjean had struggled with inconsistent handling and power delivery, plus the familiar problem of unstable braking, albeit less than normal following a successful switch from Brembo to Carbone Industrie brakes. Haas did admit that cooler conditions on Saturday had helped tyre performance and contributed to the leap from P15 in FP1 and FP3.

Grosjean's 'scruff-of-the-neck' lap time was also a surprise for Force India and Williams, engaged in their tight battle for fourth place in the constructors' championship. Williams, having looked extremely promising on Friday, suffered the reverse of Haas when the drop in temperature brought an equivalent increase in lap time, putting Valtteri Bottas 11th, while a disappointed Felipe Massa had to accept 13th for his final grand prix appearance at home.

Esteban Gutiérrez split the Williams pair, unhappy about being dropped by Haas for 2017 and disgruntled at being left to struggle with Brembo brakes. But what really got the attention of Williams was not only Nico Hülkenberg and Sergio Pérez (separated by half a tenth) shooting into the top ten, but also the Force Indias being followed into tenth by Fernando Alonso. The Spaniard had made the most of tyre grip and the McLaren's handling in the middle sector, just where Williams had been struggling most with understeer and a lack of tyre temperature.

A sizeable gap to Daniil Kvyat and Carlos Sainz in 14th and 15th was accounted for by the Toro Rosso's deficit on this power-sensitive track. Jolyon Palmer not only outqualified Kevin Magnussen, but also made it into Q2, the Dane unhappy with the Renault's balance, while Palmer was left to rue a brake lock-up that had prevented an improvement on P16.

Jenson Button, splitting the Renaults, was very unhappy with the McLaren's inability to cope with the cooler temperatures, after being more competitive on Friday. Having failed to get out of Q1, his mood was exacerbated by his team-mate being seven places higher.

The battle between the Manor team-mates could not have been closer, five-thousandths of a second giving Pascal Wehrlein a smidgen of satisfaction after being passed over by Force India in favour of Esteban Ocon for a seat in 2017. Ocon would receive a three-place penalty for blocking Palmer, but that could not hide Sauber bringing up the rear, Marcus Ericsson being marginally quicker, despite losing track time with an engine change. Things could not have looked bleaker for Felipe Nasr at the bottom of the time sheet. This, and more, was about to change 24 hours later.

THE forecast rain may not have arrived in time for qualifying, but it more than made up for that overnight and into race day. Race Director Charlie Whiting, keen to have a standing start, delayed proceedings by ten minutes to allow a particularly heavy cloud to pass. But his fear of cars aquaplaning would be realised when Grosjean, checking the grip level on the climb towards the final curve, lost control on a stream of water and sat helplessly as the Haas went into the barrier. With seventh place on the grid now empty, it must have seemed the longest walk of the Frenchman's life as he plodded disconsolately towards the pits and through the usual scene of frantic pre-race activity. High on his perch, Whiting felt he had no option but to use the safety car for the start.

For seven laps, the field of 21 cars did its best to retain tyre and brake temperatures while following Bernd Maylander in the AMG Mercedes GT. But even in the midst of the weaving and darting, it was noticeable that Verstappen was trying different lines and searching for grip. An immediate attack on Räikkönen was certain.

Sure enough, as soon as the safety car lights were extinguished, the Red Bull was off line through Junção, the better to have a faster exit and climb up the hill. As Hamilton immediately eased away from Rosberg, the huge ball of spray headed by a red Ferrari suddenly broadened as a blue Red Bull appeared on Räikkönen's left and had no trouble taking third place into the first corner.

Diving straight into the pits, Magnussen and Renault felt a switch to intermediates (the field having been required to start on full wets) was worth a gamble. Button made the same choice a lap later. Alonso, Bottas, Kvyat, Palmer and Ericsson would follow suit at the end of lap nine, but the

benefit, such as it was, would be heavily outweighed by the serious lack of grip on that lethal run up to and over the crest leading to the main straight.

At the end of lap ten, Vettel made an unplanned stop for inters; 'unplanned' insofar as he had lost it on the uphill climb and was fortunate not to have anyone hit the gyrating Ferrari. He immediately took advantage of ending up handily placed for the pit entrance. His troubles were not over, however, the premature release of the clutch paddle causing a delay with a rear wheel and a slide down to 19th place.

Proof that the track remained utterly treacherous came on lap 12, when Ericsson spun on the uphill climb and pinballed across the track, the Sauber coming to rest at the pit-lane entrance. With debris scattered in all directions and predicting the appearance of the safety car, Red Bull called in their drivers for inters. Verstappen weaved his way past the stricken Sauber moments after it had come to a halt and the red 'pit lane closed' sign had been illuminated. It was deemed that Verstappen was committed to the move and no penalty would be given. That was not the case for Ricciardo, who would receive a five-second forfeit, to be taken at his next stop.

Part of the Red Bull plan had been to prompt Mercedes to make a similar call, but their drivers were having none of it; both Hamilton and Rosberg were of the opinion that the full wet remained the tyre to have. And so it was, thus playing into the hands of those who had not stopped, the most notable 'out-of-place' drivers being Hülkenberg and Pérez, fifth and sixth, ahead of Sainz and, from the back, Nasr. Ocon was tenth, Manor being another team to have grabbed the rare chance of points thanks to the climatic curve ball.

While the debris was cleared, Whiting was eyeing the

Above: Kimi Räikkönen's Ferrari aquaplaned into the pit wall, causing the race to be red-flagged.
Photo: WRi2/Luca Bassani

Left: Charlie Whiting joined the drivers' press conference, where there was good humour all round.
Photo: Scuderia Ferrari

Above: Sergio Pérez had hoped to score another podium for Force India, but he had to give way to Verstappen just three laps from the finish.
Photo: Sahara Force India F1 Team

Top right: Pitching gazebos was the order of the day as the teams got to work on the cars during the suspension of racing.
Photo: Red Bull Racing/Getty Images

Above right: Despite the weather on race day, the Heineken grid girls maintained a glamorous presence.
Photo: Peter J. Fox

Right: Felipe Massa, who crashed out on his farewell F1 appearance at Interlagos, is given an emotional farewell from the crowd.
Photo: WRi2/Luca Bassani

sky and the weather prediction, hoping for an easing of the streaming conditions. With several laps spent running behind the safety car, it was difficult to judge the slipperiness of the track. The race director was about to get his answer from the moment the field was released at the beginning of lap 20.

Verstappen, having rejoined in fourth place, was about to pull the same move on Räikkönen, who was obviously aware of the youngster's intentions. Considering this while applying as much power as he dared, the Finn suddenly suffered a surfeit of wheelspin and a tank-slapping moment that his desperate reactions could not cover. In an instant, the Ferrari was into the wall on the right, before spinning across the track, smacking the pit wall and coming to rest – facing the wrong way and lost in swirling spray.

Verstappen had a huge moment in trying to dodge the stricken Ferrari, while Hülkenberg hit part of its front wing. With Kimi's car virtually invisible, Ocon pulled off a remarkable last-second avoidance as others did the same to keep clear of the jinking Manor. It was as close a call as you could wish for.

Too close, in fact, and a sign of how the cold tyres were incapable of shifting huge amounts of water quickly enough. The red flag appeared immediately, the remaining runners making their way to the pits, where they would sit with engines running long enough to burn off fuel that was weighty, but no longer needed because of the comparatively slow running. But when would they run again?

It took a while to clear the mess. By the time that had been done, the rain was continuing with enough force to warrant a safety car start and, with it, the obligatory fitting of full wets. Hamilton led Rosberg and Verstappen, but Hülkenberg's wretched luck struck again when he picked up a puncture and had to depart from fourth place, rejoining 15th, between Vettel and Massa. In a continuing reverse of the expected positions, Nasr was sixth, Ocon eighth and Wehrlein ninth. This was incredibly tense for Sauber and Manor, fighting over that money-rich tenth place in the constructors' championship.

Thinking about the drivers' title and the points he needed,

Hamilton was calling for the racing to restart. They circulated for seven laps, the bedraggled crowd becoming restless, more so when the red flag was shown once more, this time for no apparent reason.

The decision had been driven by the fairly certain knowledge that the poor weather was set to continue, thus bringing further tedious safety car running as the clock ticked towards the two-hour cut-off. Far better, it was reasoned, to wait for an improvement and then get on with the racing. Unfortunately, this logic was not conveyed to either the public or the media, commentators and personalities such as Niki Lauda publicly questioning the red flag.

Fresh wet-weather tyres were fitted in readiness for another safety car restart when the rain, as forecast, began to ease. Absent from the next part of this race would be Palmer, who had hit the back of Kvyat when blinded by spray at the previous restart. The Renault had been too badly damaged to continue.

Hamilton and Verstappen, however, were more than ready when the safety car peeled off at the end of lap 31, two laps into the fresh start. As Lewis controlled the field before making a safe break along the top straight, Verstappen was all over Rosberg. Plunging into the Senna Esses, the Red Bull came out of it on an outside line into Turn Three, where Verstappen found enough grip to catapult alongside the Mercedes as Rosberg tried to adopt the normal racing line. Job done.

Now Verstappen began to think about making inroads on the lead, but Hamilton had him covered – easily, as it turned out. Others, meanwhile, were moving forward, Ricciardo getting ahead of Nasr and Sainz and into P5. Vettel joined in after overtaking three cars in as many laps and eventually getting by Ocon, who was making a better fist of the tricky conditions than his Manor team-mate, Wehrlein having lost tyre temperature in a vicious circle of performance drop-off.

On lap 37, a reminder of the continuing hazards came when Verstappen had an enormous moment as he powered on to the pit straight. Just as it looked as though the Red Bull was heading for the inside barrier, Max was calm enough to

flick the steering and apply enough power to point the car in the right direction, select a lower gear and resume as though nothing had happened. He hadn't even lost second place. Rosberg hadn't been close enough – and perhaps he didn't want to be close enough on a day when, rightly, he was thinking of the championship.

That was a thought far from the minds of Alonso and Vettel as the Ferrari closed in on the McLaren in 14th place. With no love lost between these two, it was unsurprising to watch Alonso being shoved on to the grass at the exit of Junção, a move than did not impress the Spaniard.

By now (lap 41), the rain had eased a little and Red Bull were looking for an alternative strategy to beat Mercedes. Ricciardo, in fifth place and struggling with a leaking visor, had been brought in for inters on the previous lap. Daniel took his five-second penalty and rejoined 11th, just behind Hülkenberg, who was closing on Ocon and about to take the Manor. Ricciardo followed through not long after.

Verstappen was called in at the end of lap 43, dropping from third to fifth as Pérez and Sainz took advantage. All eyes were on the Red Bull lap times, but any thoughts that conditions might be improving were dispelled by a heart-in-the-mouth moment for Rosberg as he got sideways on that treacherous stretch through the final curve. He held it, but for a fraction of a second, the championship story looked like it might be rewritten yet again as the Mercedes headed for the barrier and zero points.

In fact, Rosberg's loss was about seven seconds as Hamilton completed the 44th lap 17 seconds in front, with Pérez now five seconds behind Rosberg. Verstappen, meanwhile, was no faster than Hamilton, the inters not being the answer as the rain intensified. Then the complexion of the race changed once more when Massa, struggling on

Above: A superbly judged drive in the monsoon conditions by Felipe Nasr brought Sauber the unexpected bonus of two prized points, allowing them to leapfrog rivals Manor in the constructors' championship.
Photo: WRi2/Jean-François Galeron

Top right: The rain pitter-patters on Vettel, Hamilton and Räikkönen during the line-up for the playing of the Brazilian national anthem.

Above right: Carlos Sainz added to his burgeoning reputation with another fine drive for Toro Rosso.
Photos: Scuderia Toro Rosso/Getty Images

Right: Why all the fuss? Verstappen breezes on to the podium after his amazing drive.
Photo: Red Bull Racing/Getty Images

inters, crashed at the top of the hill. Out came the safety car yet again.

During the six laps required to clear the wreckage, Massa walked back to the pits, picking up his national flag on the way and finding the majority in the pit lane applauding his progress as the tearful Brazilian made his final appearance at home. Rarely has a driver received such a reception after crashing out.

Meanwhile, Red Bull were busy on the radio, receiving confirmation from both drivers that the inters were not the tyres to have. Ricciardo came in from tenth place on lap 52. Two laps later, Verstappen gave up fifth, to rejoin 14th. With 16 laps to go, the safety car came in, releasing the field once more and triggering an extraordinary comeback performance from Red Bull No. 33.

Verstappen would be assisted by Alonso losing it on the now infamous hill and dropping from eighth to 15th. In truth, however, Max needed no help from anyone. On successive laps, he picked off Gutiérrez (about to retire), Wehrlein and Bottas, then hauled on to his team-mate's tail and ran around the outside of Ricciardo on the downhill approach to Mergulho, a pass as unconventional as just about every move from the Dutchman on this afternoon.

Kvyat and Ocon were next, Ricciardo following through not long after. By the time he had taken Nasr on lap 62, Verstappen was seventh. How far could he get in the remaining nine laps? Was a podium possible? At this extraordinary rate of progress, *anything* seemed possible.

Up front, Hamilton headed Rosberg by six seconds. The championship leader was quite happy just to keep the car on the road and manage the ten-second gap to Pérez, who was busy keeping an eye on Sainz, just under three seconds behind, with Vettel pushing the pair of them. Hülkenberg, having taken sixth from Nasr on lap 60, was lapping almost a second faster than Vettel and closing in. But Verstappen was taking 1.5s per lap out of them both.

With six laps to go, Verstappen dived past the Force India at the Esses. Vettel was less than a second ahead, and the Red Bull was on to the Ferrari in no time. Given their

recent history (Mexico), the next move would be interesting. Ducking and weaving from Turn Four onwards on lap 66, Verstappen attacked through Mergulho and went for the inside line into Junção. Vettel, of course, refused to back off and sat it out around the outside of the left-hander, finishing on the grass for his trouble. The now predictable complaint across the airwaves received little sympathy, given that Seb had given similar treatment to his friend Fernando earlier in the afternoon. Verstappen was fifth.

Then he was fourth, thanks to a move on Sainz into Turn Four on the next lap. A podium finish became a reality two laps later with another forthright pass on Pérez. Observers were already reaching for the book of superlatives; comparisons were drawn with Michael Schumacher at Barcelona in 1996 and Ayrton Senna at Monaco in 1984.

Meanwhile... Hamilton was completing a faultless drive to a third successive win. Rosberg may have been 11 seconds down the road, but he had another 18 points in his pocket, leaving a 12-point gap between the Mercedes drivers with one race to go.

Vettel relieved Sainz of fifth place going into the Esses for the final time. Hülkenberg could only think of what might have been but for the puncture. Nonetheless, fourth and seventh places gave Force India a healthy cushion in their fight with Williams (Bottas finished 11th) for fourth in the constructors' championship.

When it came to the financial importance of position on the teams' table, no one was more overjoyed than Sauber. Nasr's steady and consistent drive on full wets from lap 28 had brought not just ninth place, but also the two points needed to open the team's account and ease Manor out of tenth (Ocon and Wehrlein finished this race 12th and 15th, the former having been in the points until demoted by Alonso on the penultimate lap).

It had been a truly dramatic race, run on a knife-edge from start to finish. The race director had called it correctly. But Lady Luck had been looking down on Autódromo José Carlos Pace on the afternoon of 13th November, 2016.

Maurice Hamilton

VIEWPOINT
CONFIRMATION OF CLASS

WHILE there had been no doubt about Max Verstappen's raw talent, it had shone, beacon-like, throughout the Brazilian GP. As Maurice Hamilton relates, the 19-year-old translated 14th place with 16 laps to go into a stunning podium finish, beaten only by the two Mercedes drivers.

The wet is so often a great barometer of the truly gifted's natural ability. Consider Jim Clark at Spa, Ayrton Senna at Monaco in 1984, his first win at Estoril in 1985, and Donington in 1993. Think of Michael Schumacher and Barcelona in 1996; Lewis Hamilton and Silverstone in 2008.

In most of the aforementioned, however, what you saw was simply a master with intuitive feeling for grip, leaving the rest trailing by an ever-growing margin. Yes, Ayrton's opening lap at Donington had included some extraordinarily opportunistic overtaking, but then it was simply a case of executing an unchallenged performance masterclass.

In Brazil, though, Verstappen had not only found grip where others could not, but had executed assured passing moves in the unlikeliest of places. Yes, he may well have been using the 'karting' line, but then haven't they all been karters these days? What was everyone else doing?

Conventional wisdom says that you don't put wheels on kerbs and white lines in the teeming rain – Marcus Ericsson well illustrated what can happen when you do – but the normal rules didn't seem to apply to Max. When a kerb did kick him sideways as he went around the outside of a victim, you sensed imminent disaster, but he simply rescued it, completed the move and carried on unperturbed.

Among it all, he passed his team-mate in the same car and the likes of four-times champion Sebastian Vettel. Lewis Hamilton, knowing he could not afford an error if he was to keep his title hopes alive, was mighty impressive all afternoon, too. You couldn't help but wonder what 2017 might serve up between these two...

Tony Dodgins

20

2016 FORMULA 1 GRANDE PRÊMIO DO BRASIL

SÃO PAULO 11–12 NOVEMBER

ROLEX
OFFICIAL TIMEPIECE

RACE DISTANCE: 71 laps, 190.083 miles/305.909km

RACE WEATHER: Heavy rain (track 19–21°C, air 18–19°C)

AUTODROMO JOSÉ CARLOS PACE, INTERLAGOS

Circuit: 2.677 miles/4.309km, 71 laps

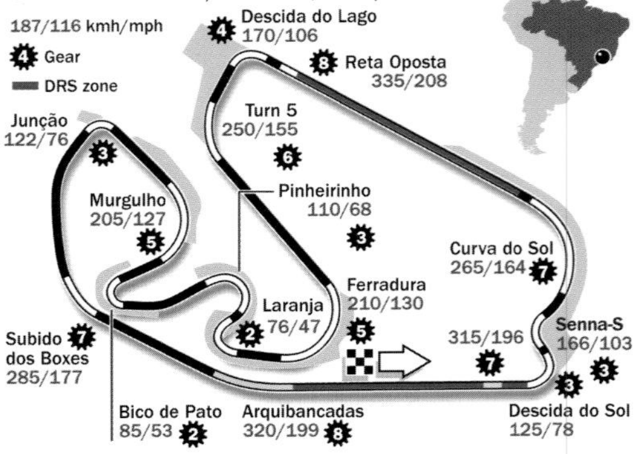

187/116 kmh/mph
4 Gear
DRS zone
Descida do Lago 170/106
Reta Oposta 335/208
Turn 5 250/155
Junção 122/76
Pinheirinho 110/68
Murgulho 205/127
Curva do Sol 265/164
Ferradura 210/130
Laranja 76/47
Subido dos Boxes 285/177
315/196
Senna-S 166/103
Bico de Pato 85/53
Arquibancadas 320/199
Descida do Sol 125/78

RACE – OFFICIAL CLASSIFICATION

Pos.	Driver	Nat.	No.	Entrant	Car/Engine	Tyres	Laps	Time/Retirement	Speed (mph/km/h)	Gap to leader	Fastest race lap	
1	**Lewis Hamilton**	GB	44	Mercedes AMG Petronas F1 Team	Mercedes F1 W07-Mercedes PU106C V6	P	71	3h 01m 01.335s	63.003/101.393		1m 25.639s	44
2	**Nico Rosberg**	D	6	Mercedes AMG Petronas F1 Team	Mercedes F1 W07-Mercedes PU106C V6	P	71	3h 01m 12.790s	62.937/101.287	11.455s	1m 26.222s	47
3	**Max Verstappen**	NL	33	Red Bull Racing	Red Bull RB12-TAG Heuer RB12 V6	P	71	3h 01m 22.816s	62.878/101.193	21.481s	1m 25.305s	67
4	**Sergio Pérez**	MEX	11	Sahara Force India F1 Team	Force India VJM09-Mercedes PU106C V6	P	71	3h 01m 26.681s	62.856/101.157	25.346s	1m 27.093s	41
5	**Sebastian Vettel**	D	5	Scuderia Ferrari	Ferrari SF15-H-059/5 V6	P	71	3h 01m 27.669s	62.850/101.148	26.334s	1m 26.195s	70
6	**Carlos Sainz**	E	55	Scuderia Toro Rosso	Toro Rosso STR11-Ferrari 059/4 V6	P	71	3h 01m 30.495s	62.834/101.122	29.160s	1m 27.153s	38
7	**Nico Hülkenberg**	D	27	Sahara Force India F1 Team	Force India VJM09-Mercedes PU106C V6	P	71	3h 01m 31.162s	62.831/101.116	29.827s	1m 26.728s	69
8	**Daniel Ricciardo**	AUS	3	Red Bull Racing	Red Bull RB12-TAG Heuer RB12 V6	P	71	3h 01m 31.821s	62.827/101.110	30.486s	1m 25.532s	42
9	**Felipe Nasr**	BR	12	Sauber F1 Team	Sauber C35-Ferrari 059/5 V6	P	71	3h 01m 43.955s	62.757/100.997	42.620s	1m 27.547s	70
10	**Fernando Alonso**	E	14	McLaren Honda	McLaren MP4-31-Honda RA616H V6	P	71	3h 01m 45.767s	62.746/100.980	44.432s	1m 27.104s	70
11	Valtteri Bottas	FIN	77	Williams Martini Racing	Williams FW38-Mercedes PU106C V6	P	71	3h 01m 46.627s	62.741/100.972	45.292s	1m 26.062s	70
12	Esteban Ocon	F	31	Manor Racing MRT	Manor MRT05-Mercedes PU106C V6	P	71	3h 01m 47.144s	62.738/100.967	45.809s	1m 27.796s	47
13	Daniil Kvyat	RUS	26	Scuderia Toro Rosso	Toro Rosso STR11-Ferrari 059/4 V6	P	71	3h 01m 52.527s	62.708/100.918	51.192s	1m 27.476s	42
14	Kevin Magnussen	DK	20	Renault Sport F1 Team	Renault R.S.16-R.E.16 V6	P	71	3h 01m 52.890s	62.705/100.914	51.555s	1m 26.524s	69
15	Pascal Wehrlein	D	94	Manor Racing MRT	Manor MRT05-Mercedes PU106C V6	P	71	3h 02m 01.833s	62.654/100.832	1m 00.498s	1m 27.919s	69
16	Jenson Button	GB	22	McLaren Honda	McLaren MP4-31-Honda RA616H V6	P	71	3h 02m 23.329s	62.531/100.634	1m 21.994s	1m 26.983s	38
	Esteban Gutiérrez	MEX	21	Haas F1 Team	Haas VF-16-Ferrari 059/5 V6	P	60	*electronics*			1m 27.805s	43
	Felipe Massa	BR	19	Williams Martini Racing	Williams FW38-Mercedes PU106C V6	P	46	*accident*			1m 26.767s	39
	Jolyon Palmer	GB	30	Renault Sport F1 Team	Renault R.S.16-R.E.16 V6	P	20	*accident/front suspension*			1m 34.334s	11
	Kimi Räikkönen	FIN	7	Scuderia Ferrari	Ferrari SF16-H-059/5 V6	P	19	*accident*			1m 28.847s	12
	Marcus Ericsson	S	9	Sauber F1 Team	Sauber C35-Ferrari 059/5 V6	P	11	*accident*			1m 31.265s	11
NS	Romain Grosjean	F	8	Haas F1 Team	Haas VF-16-Ferrari 059/5 V6	P		*accident on the reconnaissance lap*			no time	

Race stopped on lap 20, and again on lap 28, due to heavy rain and accidents. Resumed 1h 01m 17s later. Overall race times include the stoppage time.

Fastest race lap: Max Verstappen on lap 67, 1m 25.3059s, 112.994mph/181.846km/h.

Lap record: Juan Pablo Montoya (Williams FW26-BMW V10), 1m 11.473s, 134.862mph/217.038km/h (2004)

All results and data © FOM 2016

22 · OCON · Manor
(3-place grid penalty for impeding another driver)

20 · ERICSSON · Sauber

18 · MAGNUSSEN · Renault

16 · PALMER · Renault

14 · KVYAT · Toro Rosso

12 · GUTIÉRREZ · Haas

21 · NASR · Sauber

19 · WEHRLEIN · Manor

17 · BUTTON · McLaren

15 · SAINZ · Toro Rosso

13 · MASSA · Williams

11 · BOTTAS · Williams

Grid order	1	2	3	4	5	6	7	8	9	10	11	12	13	14	15	16	17	18	19	20	21	22	23	24	25	26	27	28	29	30	31	32	33	34	35	36	37	38	39	40	41	42	43	44	45	46	47	48	49	50	51	52	53	54	55
44 HAMILTON	44	44	44	44	44	44	44	44	44	44	44	44	44	44	44	44	44	44	44	44	44	44	44	44	44	44	44	44	44	44	44	44	44	44	44	44	44	44	44	44	44	44	44	44	44	44	44	44	44	44	44	44	44	44	44
6 ROSBERG	6	6	6	6	6	6	6	6	6	6	6	6	6	6	6	6	6	6	6	6	6	6	6	6	6	6	6	6	6	6	6	33	33	33	33	33	33	33	33	33	33	33	6	6	6	6	6	6	6	6	6	6	6	6	6
7 RÄIKKÖNEN	7	7	7	7	7	7	7	33	33	33	33	33	33	7	7	7	7	7	7	33	33	33	33	33	33	33	33	33	33	33	33	6	6	6	6	6	6	6	6	6	6	6	33	11	11	11	11	11	11	11	11	11	11	11	11
33 VERSTAPPEN	33	33	33	33	33	33	33	7	7	7	7	7	7	33	33	33	33	33	33	27	27	11	11	11	11	11	11	11	11	11	11	11	11	11	11	11	11	11	11	11	11	11	11	55	55	55	55	55	55	55	55	55	55	55	55
5 VETTEL	5	5	5	5	5	5	5	5	5	3	3	3	27	27	27	27	27	27	27	11	11	55	55	55	55	55	55	55	55	55	55	55	3	3	3	3	3	3	3	55	55	55	55	33	33	33	33	33	33	33	33	33	33	5	5
3 RICCIARDO	3	3	3	3	3	3	3	3	3	27	27	27	3	11	11	11	11	11	11	55	55	27	12	12	12	12	12	12	12	12	12	3	55	55	55	55	55	55	55	3	12	12	12	12	5	5	5	5	5	5	5	5	5	12	12
8 GROSJEAN	27	27	27	27	27	27	27	27	27	11	11	11	11	55	55	55	55	55	55	12	12	12	3	3	3	3	3	3	3	3	3	12	12	12	12	12	12	12	12	12	14	5	5	5	12	12	12	12	12	12	12	12	12	33	27
27 HÜLKENBERG	11	11	11	11	11	11	14	14	11	55	55	55	55	12	12	12	12	12	12	3	3	3	31	31	31	31	31	31	31	31	31	31	31	31	14	14	14	14	14	14	5	14	14	14	14	14	14	14	14	14	14	14	14	14	31
11 PÉREZ	14	14	14	14	14	14	11	11	14	12	12	12	12	3	3	3	3	3	3	31	31	31	94	94	94	94	94	94	94	94	94	14	14	14	31	31	5	5	5	5	31	31	27	27	27	27	27	27	27	27	27	27	27	27	26
14 ALONSO	77	77	77	77	77	77	19	77	55	31	31	31	31	31	31	31	31	31	31	94	94	94	14	14	14	14	14	14	14	14	14	94	94	5	5	5	31	31	31	31	27	27	31	3	3	3	3	3	3	3	3	31	31	31	77
77 BOTTAS	21	21	21	21	21	21	77	19	77	5	21	94	94	94	94	94	94	94	94	14	14	14	77	77	77	77	77	77	77	77	77	77	5	94	94	77	77	27	27	27	3	3	3	31	31	31	31	31	31	31	31	26	26	26	3
21 GUTIÉRREZ	19	19	19	19	19	19	21	26	12	21	94	21	14	14	14	14	14	14	77	77	77	77	20	20	20	20	20	20	20	20	20	5	77	77	77	27	27	77	20	20	21	21	21	21	26	26	26	26	26	26	26	77	77	77	94
19 MASSA	26	26	26	26	26	26	26	55	19	94	14	14	77	77	77	77	77	77	14	20	20	20	22	22	22	22	22	22	22	22	22	20	20	20	20	94	94	20	94	21	20	26	26	26	21	19	77	77	77	77	77	3	3	3	21
26 KVYAT	55	55	55	55	55	55	55	30	31	14	77	77	20	20	20	20	20	20	20	22	22	22	5	5	5	5	5	5	5	5	5	22	22	27	27	20	20	94	21	94	26	94	19	19	19	77	94	94	94	94	94	94	94	94	33
55 SAINZ	30	30	30	30	30	30	30	12	26	77	20	20	22	22	22	22	22	22	22	5	5	5	27	27	27	27	27	27	27	27	27	27	27	21	21	21	21	21	26	26	94	19	94	77	77	21	21	*20*	*20*	*20*	20	20	20	20	20
30 PALMER	22	22	22	22	22	22	22	9	94	20	22	22	26	26	26	26	19	19	5	19	19	19	19	19	19	19	19	19	19	19	21	21	21	26	26	26	26	26	19	19	19	77	77	94	94	94	*20*	*21*	*21*	*21*	21	21	21	21	22
22 BUTTON	20	20	20	20	20	20	12	31	21	22	26	26	19	19	19	19	5	5	19	21	21	21	21	21	21	21	21	21	21	21	26	26	26	22	19	19	19	19	77	77	77	22	22	20	20	20	*22*	*22*	*22*	*22*	22	22	22	22	14
20 MAGNUSSEN	94	94	94	94	94	94	94	94	30	26	19	19	5	5	5	5	26	21	21	26	26	26	26	26	26	26	26	26	26	26	19	19	19	19	22	22	22	22	22	22	22	20	20	22	*22*	*22*									
94 WEHRLEIN	9	9	9	9	9	9	9	21	9	19	5	5	21	21	21	21	21	26	26	30																																			
9 ERICSSON	12	12	12	12	12	12	31	22	20	30	9	30	30	30	30	30	30	30	30																																				
12 NASR	31	31	31	31	31	31	20	20	22	9	30																																												
31 OCON																																																							

6 = Pit stop 9 = Drive-thru penalty

94 = One lap or more behind

TIME SHEETS

PRACTICE 1 (FRIDAY)

Weather: Dry/sunny-overcast

Temperatures: track 36–46°C, air 26–29°C

Pos.	Driver	Laps	Time
1	Lewis Hamilton	32	1m 11.895s
2	Max Verstappen	29	1m 11.991s
3	Nico Rosberg	26	1m 12.125s
4	Daniel Ricciardo	27	1m 12.371s
5	Valtteri Bottas	36	1m 13.129s
6	Sergio Pérez	31	1m 13.289s
7	Nico Hülkenberg	33	1m 13.293s
8	Felipe Massa	33	1m 13.318s
9	Sebastian Vettel	24	1m 13.567s
10	Kimi Räikkönen	26	1m 13.569s
11	Carlos Sainz	22	1m 13.711s
12	Daniil Kvyat	15	1m 14.090s
13	Jenson Button	27	1m 14.252s
14	Fernando Alonso	26	1m 14.296s
15	Romain Grosjean	25	1m 14.507s
16	Felipe Nasr	21	1m 14.631s
17	Marcus Ericsson	23	1m 14.654s
18	Esteban Ocon	30	1m 14.827s
19	Jolyon Palmer	32	1m 14.908s
20	Pascal Wehrlein	32	1m 14.948s
21	Charles Leclerc	27	1m 15.391s
22	Sergey Sirotkin	10	1m 15.800s

PRACTICE 2 (FRIDAY)

Weather: Dry/sunny-overcast

Temperatures: track 46–54°C, air 30–32°C

Pos.	Driver	Laps	Time
1	Lewis Hamilton	41	1m 12.271s
2	Nico Rosberg	40	1m 12.301s
3	Valtteri Bottas	47	1m 12.761s
4	Felipe Massa	43	1m 12.789s
5	Daniel Ricciardo	43	1m 12.828s
6	Max Verstappen	45	1m 12.928s
7	Sebastian Vettel	45	1m 13.002s
8	Kimi Räikkönen	24	1m 13.047s
9	Nico Hülkenberg	42	1m 13.299s
10	Jenson Button	19	1m 13.440s
11	Fernando Alonso	18	1m 13.572s
12	Daniil Kvyat	46	1m 13.689s
13	Carlos Sainz	47	1m 13.801s
14	Sergio Pérez	38	1m 13.918s
15	Romain Grosjean	35	1m 14.074s
16	Kevin Magnussen	47	1m 14.109s
17	Felipe Nasr	40	1m 14.309s
18	Esteban Ocon	46	1m 14.317s
19	Jolyon Palmer	43	1m 14.436s
20	Esteban Gutiérrez	42	1m 14.558s
21	Marcus Ericsson	21	1m 14.695s
22	Pascal Wehrlein	22	1m 14.958s

PRACTICE 3 (SATURDAY)

Weather: Damp-dry/overcast

Temperatures: track 22–26°C, air 18–20°C

Pos.	Driver	Laps	Time
1	Nico Rosberg	19	1m 11.740s
2	Lewis Hamilton	21	1m 11.833s
3	Sebastian Vettel	14	1m 11.959s
4	Kimi Räikkönen	16	1m 12.027s
5	Max Verstappen	19	1m 12.077s
6	Daniel Ricciardo	21	1m 12.287s
7	Valtteri Bottas	27	1m 12.614s
8	Jolyon Palmer	19	1m 12.968s
9	Felipe Massa	26	1m 12.990s
10	Fernando Alonso	12	1m 13.002s
11	Nico Hülkenberg	14	1m 13.203s
12	Sergio Pérez	19	1m 13.231s
13	Kevin Magnussen	15	1m 13.255s
14	Carlos Sainz	20	1m 13.293s
15	Romain Grosjean	15	1m 13.344s
16	Esteban Gutiérrez	16	1m 13.596s
17	Daniil Kvyat	13	1m 13.609s
18	Jenson Button	9	1m 13.750s
19	Pascal Wehrlein	20	1m 13.972s
20	Felipe Nasr	14	1m 13.992s
21	Esteban Ocon	21	1m 14.222s
22	Marcus Ericsson	1	no time

QUALIFYING (SATURDAY)

Weather: Damp/overcast Temperatures: track 26–29°C, air 18–20°C

Pos.	Driver	First	Second	Third	Qualifying Tyre
1	Lewis Hamilton	1m 11.511s	1m 11.238s	1m 10.736s	Soft (new)
2	Nico Rosberg	1m 11.815s	1m 11.373s	1m 10.838s	Soft (new)
3	Kimi Räikkönen	1m 12.100s	1m 12.301s	1m 11.404s	Soft (new)
4	Max Verstappen	1m 11.957s	1m 11.834s	1m 11.485s	Soft (new)
5	Sebastian Vettel	1m 12.159s	1m 12.010s	1m 11.495s	Soft (new)
6	Daniel Ricciardo	1m 12.409s	1m 12.047s	1m 11.540s	Soft (new)
7	Romain Grosjean	1m 12.893s	1m 12.343s	1m 11.937s	Soft (new)
8	Nico Hülkenberg	1m 12.428s	1m 12.360s	1m 12.104s	Soft (new)
9	Sergio Pérez	1m 12.684s	1m 12.331s	1m 12.165s	Soft (new)
10	Fernando Alonso	1m 12.700s	1m 12.312s	1m 12.266s	Soft (new)
11	Valtteri Bottas	1m 12.680s	1m 12.420s		
12	Esteban Gutiérrez	1m 13.052s	1m 12.431s		
13	Felipe Massa	1m 12.432s	1m 12.521s		
14	Daniil Kvyat	1m 13.071s	1m 12.726s		
15	Carlos Sainz	1m 12.950s	1m 12.920s		
16	Jolyon Palmer	1m 13.259s	1m 13.258s		
17	Jenson Button	1m 13.276s			
18	Kevin Magnussen	1m 13.410s			
19	Pascal Wehrlein	1m 13.427s			
20	Esteban Ocon	1m 13.432s			
21	Marcus Ericsson	1m 13.623s			
22	Felipe Nasr	1m 13.681s			

Photo: Mercedes AMG Petronas F1 Team

FOR THE RECORD

800th GRAND PRIX STARTED: **McLaren.**

60th POLE POSITION: **Lewis Hamilton.**

30th 1-2 PODIUM AS TEAM-MATES: **Lewis Hamilton & Nico Rosberg.**

1st FASTEST LAP: **Max Verstappen.**

DID YOU KNOW?

Hamilton took the record for winning at the most number of circuits (24), beating Michael Schumacher.

Mercedes' 19 poles so far in 2016 was a new season record.

POINTS

DRIVERS

1	Nico Rosberg	367
2	Lewis Hamilton	355
3	Daniel Ricciardo	246
4	Sebastian Vettel	197
5	Max Verstappen	192
6	Kimi Räikkönen	178
7	Sergio Pérez	97
8	Valtteri Bottas	85
9	Nico Hülkenberg	66
10	Fernando Alonso	53
11	Felipe Massa	51
12	Carlos Sainz	46
13	Romain Grosjean	29
14	Daniil Kvyat	25
15	Jenson Button	21
16	Kevin Magnussen	7
17	Felipe Nasr	2
18	Jolyon Palmer	1
19	Pascal Wehrlein	1
20	Stoffel Vandoorne	1

CONSTRUCTORS

1	Mercedes	722
2	Red Bull	446
3	Ferrari	375
4	Force India	163
5	Williams	136
6	McLaren	75
7	Toro Rosso	63
8	Haas	29
9	Renault	8
10	Sauber	2
11	Manor	1

10 · ALONSO · McLaren

8 · HÜLKENBERG · Force India

6 · RICCIARDO · Red Bull

4 · VERSTAPPEN · Red Bull

2 · ROSBERG · Mercedes

9 · PÉREZ · Force India

7 · GROSJEAN · Haas
(did not start)

5 · VETTEL · Ferrari

3 · RÄIKKÖNEN · Ferrari

1 · HAMILTON · Mercedes

Qualifying: head-to-head

Rosberg	9	11	Hamilton
Vettel	10	10	Räikkönen
Massa	3	17	Bottas
Ricciardo	4	0	Kvyat
Ricciardo	10	6	Verstappen
Pérez	9	11	Hülkenberg
Magnussen	12	8	Palmer
Verstappen	3	1	Sainz
Kvyat	5	11	Sainz
Ericsson	13	7	Nasr
Alonso	14	5	Button
Button	0	1	Vandoorne
Haryanto	5	7	Wehrlein
Wehrlein	6	2	Ocon
Grosjean	13	7	Gutiérrez

56	57	58	59	60	61	62	63	64	65	66	67	68	69	70	71	
44	44	44	44	44	44	44	44	44	44	44	44	44	44	44	44	1
6	6	6	6	6	6	6	6	6	6	6	6	6	6	6	6	2
11	11	11	11	11	11	11	11	11	11	11	11	11	33	33	33	3
55	55	55	55	55	55	55	55	55	55	55	33	33	11	11	11	4
5	5	5	5	5	5	5	5	5	5	33	55	55	55	5	5	5
12	12	12	12	27	27	27	27	27	33	5	5	5	5	55	55	6
27	27	27	27	12	12	33	33	33	27	27	27	27	27	27	27	7
31	31	31	31	31	33	12	12	3	3	3	3	3	3	3	3	8
26	26	26	26	33	31	31	3	12	12	12	12	12	12	12	12	9
77	3	3	33	26	26	3	31	31	31	31	31	31	31	14	14	10
3	77	33	3	3	3	26	26	26	26	26	26	26	14	31	77	
94	33	77	77	14	14	14	14	14	14	14	14	14	77	77	31	
33	94	94	14	77	77	77	77	77	77	77	77	77	26	26	26	
21	21	21	94	94	94	94	94	20	20	20	20	20	20	20	20	
20	14	14	21	20	20	20	20	94	94	94	94	94	94	94	94	
22	20	20	20	22	22	22	22	22	22	22	22	22	22	22	22	
14	22	22	22	21												

Safety car deployed on laps shown

Race red-flagged

RACE TYRE STRATEGIES

PIRELLI

	Driver	Race Stint 1	Race Stint 2	Race Stint 3	Race Stint 4	Race Stint 5	Race Stint 6
1	Hamilton	Wet (n): 1–20	Wet (n): 21–28	Wet (u): 29–71			
2	Rosberg	Wet (n): 1–20	Wet (n): 21–28	Wet (u): 29–71			
3	Verstappen	Wet (n): 1–13	Intermediate (n): 14–20	Wet (n): 21–28	Wet (u): 29–43	Intermediate (n): 44–54	Wet (u): 55–71
4	Pérez	Wet (n): 1–20	Wet (n): 21–28	Wet (u): 29–71			
5	Vettel	Wet (n): 1–10	Intermediate (n): 11–20	Wet (n):21–28	Wet (u): 29–71		
6	Sainz	Wet (n): 1–20	Wet (n): 21–28	Wet (u): 29–71			
7	Hülkenberg	Wet (n): 1–20	Wet (n): 21–22	Wet (u): 23–28	Wet (u): 29–71		
8	Ricciardo	Wet (n): 1–13	Intermediate (n): 14–20	Wet (n): 21–28	Wet (u): 29–40	Intermediate (n): 41–52	Wet (u): 53–71
9	Nasr	Wet (n): 1–20	Wet (n): 21–28	Wet (u): 29–71			
10	Alonso	Wet (n): 1–9	Intermediate (n): 10–20	Wet (n): 21–28	Wet (u): 29–71		
11	Bottas	Wet (n): 1–9	Intermediate (n): 10–20	Wet (n): 21–28	Wet (u): 29–38	Intermediate (n): 39–71	
12	Ocon	Wet (n): 1–20	Wet (n): 21–28	Wet (u): 29–71			
13	Kvyat	Wet (n): 1–9	Intermediate (n): 10–17	Intermediate (n): 18–20	Wet (n): 21–28	Wet (u): 29–71	
14	Magnussen	Wet (n): 1–7	Intermediate (n): 8–20	Wet (n): 21–28	Wet (u): 29–41	Intermediate (n): 42–71	
15	Wehrlein	Wet (n): 1–20	Wet (n): 21–28	Wet (u): 29–52	Wet (u): 53–71		
16	Button	Wet (n): 1–8	Intermediate (n): 9–20	Wet (n): 21–28	Wet (u): 29–34	Intermediate (n): 35–44	Wet (u): 45–71
	Gutiérrez	Wet (n): 1–12	Intermediate (n): 13–20	Wet (n): 21–28	Wet (u): 29–47	Wet (u): 48–60 (dnf)	
	Massa	Wet (n): 1–9	Intermediate (n): 10–20	Wet (n): 21–28	Wet (u): 29–31	Intermediate (n): 32–46 (dnf)	
	Palmer	Wet (n): 1–9	Intermediate (n): 10–17	Wet (n): 18–20 (dnf)			
	Räikkönen	Wet (n): 1–19 (dnf)					
	Ericsson	Wet (n): 1–9	Intermediate (n): 10–11 (dnf)				
NS	Grosjean						

Teams may use Wet or Intermediate tyres as they see fit, but if the race is started behind the safety car due to heavy rain, Wet tyres are compulsory.
Pirelli P Zero logos are colour-coded on the tyre sidewalls: Blue = Wet; Green = Intermediate. (n) new (u) used

ABU DHABI
GRAND PRIX

YAS MARINA CIRCUIT

YAS MARINA QUALIFYING

THE signs were there from the moment Lewis Hamilton walked into the paddock. A championship contender maybe, but Hamilton appeared to be the one under the least pressure. His goal was clear: put the Mercedes on pole; win the race. He could do no more. It would be up to Nico Rosberg after that.

By comparison, there could be no disguising Rosberg's slightly tense expression. But what could he and Hamilton do once on track and away from the phalanx of cameras following their every move in the paddock?

Rosberg's first flying lap was 1m 43.949s, a time 18 drivers would fail to match in the 90 minutes of FP1. But the important riposte came from Hamilton: 1m 43.051s. Battle was joined.

Hamilton would continue to have the edge: 0.374s at the end of FP1; a scant 0.079s at the conclusion of FP2, but ahead nonetheless.

Into the continuing sunshine of Saturday afternoon, Hamilton's advantage remained. But there was a change to the script; the Mercedes may have been separated by a tenth, but they were fourth and fifth. Ahead, not one, but two Ferraris, Sebastian Vettel and Kimi Räikkönen separated by the Red Bull of Max Verstappen. And yet, despite the upturn in performance from Ferrari and the almost anticipated intrusion of Verstappen, no one really expected anything other that a shootout between the Mercedes drivers for pole as darkness fell.

Hamilton laid down another marker as early as Q1, when he became the first driver to dip into the 1m 39s, a full second faster than Rosberg. The proof, of course, would come in Q3.

First run: Hamilton 1m 39.013s; Rosberg 1m 39.359s. Nico had been faster (by 0.1s) in sector one, Lewis pulling it back in the final two. That was the key: Hamilton looking after his tyres, particularly through the first corner, and then nailing the final two-thirds of the lap. He did it again on the final run – and some: 1m 38.755s, leaving Rosberg a full three-tenths in his wake.

"I'm not taking it easy," said Rosberg in response to a suggestion that he might not have been pushing too hard. "I came here to try and win pole, but Lewis did a great job. It was not possible for me to do that time today, even though I gave it everything. But one of the reasons I'm fighting for the championship is consistency, and I plan to continue that in the race."

When he examined the practice times, there would have been an element of relief for Rosberg when he saw that the name Verstappen was back on row three and not, as expected, lurking directly behind the Mercedes pair. On course for P3, Max had locked up going into Turn 11 at the end of the back straight.

"I'm pretty disappointed with sixth," said the young Dutchman. "Qualifying up to Q3 had gone well. I had no issues; I didn't touch the car. I was a few tenths up on the last lap, but then pushed too hard."

The obvious frustration would have been magnified by team-mate Ricciardo being 'best of the rest' and slotting into P3.

"We've been chipping away all weekend and put in some good times towards the end," said Ricciardo. "We expected Mercedes to be quick in qualifying, but our long runs have been strong. We've also gone on a different strategy to Mercedes by running the super-soft [in Q2 to establish the race start tyre, Mercedes having gone for the ultra-soft]. So, let's see how that works out."

With teams having to cope with a drop in temperature between afternoon and early-evening running (qualifying and the race), it was odds-on that Ferrari would struggle to manage their narrow window of tyre performance. Räikkönen made the better job, while Vettel, by his own admission, was a little too aggressive with set-up, the red cars qualifying fourth and fifth.

The battle for fourth place in the constructors' championship may have edged further towards Force India with the result in Brazil, but the fight with Williams was by no means over. It was a good start for Force India, therefore, when Nico Hülkenberg recovered from a loss of track time (his car having been given to third driver Alfonso Celis in FP1 and then suffered technical trouble in FP3) to take seventh slot on the grid from Sergio Pérez by a scant 0.018s.

Even better news for Force India was Fernando Alonso squeezing his McLaren-Honda into ninth on the grid, ahead of the Williams pair. Fittingly, since this would be his last grand prix, Felipe Massa had made Q3, but could not match his excellent Q2 time. Valtteri Bottas, outqualified by his team-mate for only the fourth time in 2016, had been unable to make the ultra-soft work as temperatures continued to drop in the closing minutes of Q2.

Behind the white cars, there was another retiree as Jenson Button (having admitted that he was treating this as his last race, despite options being open for 2018) failed to overcome understeer on the McLaren in the cool conditions.

Qualifying ahead of his Haas team-mate was some consolation for the departing Esteban Gutiérrez, the Mexican having second-guessed the conditions more successfully that the unhappy Romain Grosjean (still struggling with brake problems). There may have been a gap of a couple of tenths to Jolyon Palmer, but that did not detract from the Englishman being the only Renault driver to make Q2, 0.4s and four places ahead of Kevin Magnussen who, apart from being called into the weighbridge at the wrong moment, said he simply had no pace.

Splitting the Renault pair, Pascal Wehrlein made it to Q2 for an impressive fifth time, outrunning Esteban Ocon (who knew the circuit well, having clinched the GP3 title there 12 months before), thanks to the Frenchman being unable to make the ultra-soft work on his Manor.

Toro Rosso probably wished their problems had been as simple as tyre performance when the wheel rim difficulties experienced in Austin returned in the shape of two left rear punctures for Daniil Kvyat in FP1. There was no alterative but to keep both cars out of the evening practice session while a cure was sought. The temporary answer (removal of aero parts) cost downforce, as painfully illustrated when neither driver could get out of Q1, Carlos Sainz's frustration being multiplied by a down-on-power engine. He took 21st place, a couple of tenths ahead of Marcus Ericsson, the slower Sauber driver, and 0.4s and three places behind Felipe Nasr.

A world away at the far end of the pit lane, the Mercedes team assessed their day and noted that Nico Rosberg had wanted pole as badly as his team-mate.

"Neither driver was playing it softly," said Niki Lauda. "Lewis did an outstanding lap. It was pure Lewis, using his talent with an aggressive attack. He did a fantastic job. But the race is another story completely. Anything can happen. We know this…"

Above: Lewis Hamilton was out on his own during practice and qualifying, ensuring he would start the race from pole position.
Photo: Mercedes AMG Petronas F1 Team

Left: Two old-timers embrace. A good-luck hug for Jenson from Fernando Alonso on the occasion of his 305th, and likely last, F1 appearance.
Photo: McLaren Honda

Far left: Who would be a team principal? Toto Wolff and Maurizio Arrivabene exchange end-of-season experiences, before rivalries are rekindled after the winter break.
Photo: Peter J. Fox

Opening spread: The 2016 World Champion leaps for joy.
Photo: Peter J. Fox

Opening spread, inset: Holding back a tear. Nico reflects on his ten-year journey to the summit of Formula 1.
Photo: Lukas Gorys

THE arrival of dusk on a warm evening somehow added to the atmosphere and feeling of anticipation as everyone gathered on the grid. From the taut expressions at the front to the more openly emotional moments further back as Massa and Button prepared for their last races, and Herbie Blash, an F1 stalwart for nearly 50 years, received fond farewells, everyone prepared for the so-called 'Duel in the Desert'.

Rosberg's ideal scenario was to jump into the lead at the first corner, but a crucially clean getaway for both Mercedes meant that Hamilton kept his advantage as the leaders aimed for the left-hander. Räikkönen did the same as he fended off a brake-locking Ricciardo, who just about saved fourth from attack by Vettel, but who would pay the price with a pair of flat spots on his super-softs (Red Bull having chosen to go against the ultra-soft form in Q2).

Verstappen did all four of his super-softs no good at all by spinning after making contact with Hülkenberg's sidepod while trying to make up for a slow getaway. His fall to 19th at least triggered anticipation of an adventurous comeback and relief for Rosberg (had he known it) that such a potential menace and game-changer had been removed from the reckoning – for the moment.

Nico was too busy watching the back of his team-mate's car, catching it in the slower turns of sector three, then watching Lewis nail it where it mattered in sector one and, particularly, the hairpin leading on to the very long main straight. The net result was a slower pace around the lap as Hamilton just managed to keep his rival out of reach. Having doubted initially that his team-mate would do such a thing, Rosberg was sensing that Lewis was hoping to allow the opposition to stay within attacking distance of the championship leader.

Räikkönen led the rest, but could not get close enough to do anything, the irony being that the comparatively slow pace was not allowing his front ultra-softs to reach the required temperature. Ricciardo couldn't do much with his vibrating fronts, and Vettel was in the same position as his team-mate. Verstappen was the one driver benefiting as he slashed his way towards the top ten without losing too much time to the leaders.

The Mercedes strategists had been on Hamilton's

case from the moment the opening lap times fell short of expectation. At this rate of going, Mercedes were laying themselves open to the undercut, as the Ferraris and Ricciardo remained within striking distance.

That's why, against the usual form, Hamilton was brought in after seven laps; Rosberg a lap later. Then came a further complication. Ferrari reacted and, with the Mercedes pit being first in line, Hamilton and Rosberg were delayed by the arrival of Räikkönen and Vettel respectively. Hamilton was running free at the front once more (after Ricciardo had stopped on lap nine), but Rosberg found himself behind Verstappen, now up to second place – and running strongly on the super-soft. In fact, his pace was so good that the thought occurred that he might be able to do a one-stop.

None of this was good news for Rosberg as Vettel stayed within reach. Despite having run the race so far as best he could, there was a chance of the championship unravelling, particularly with a loose cannon such as Verstappen now back in the mix.

At around the 18-lap mark, Rosberg got the call he did not need to hear: it was "critical" that he pass the Red Bull. Perhaps subconsciously recalling Germany and Mexico, not to mention Verstappen's audacious pass around the outside in Brazil, he steeled himself. If he messed this up, not only would his reputation be in tatters, but also possibly his championship.

Above: Sebastian Vettel makes his second pit stop, opting for the red-walled super-soft Pirellis in a late bid for the podium.
Photo: Scuderia Ferrari

Left: Over and out. Jenson and his 'Team JB' head out of the paddock into the night.

Above left: Soft-centred Mr E? Undoubtedly, in the case of the soon-to-retire Herbie Blash. Let's hope the gift was more than just chocolates!

Far left: With Force India secure in fourth place in the constructors' placings, Nico Hülkenberg and Sergio Pérez enjoyed a spirited battle over eventual seventh and eighth places.
Photos: Peter J. Fox

Above: Share the moment as AUTO-COURSE chief photographer 'Foxy' captures Nico's joy in *parc fermé*.
Photo: Peter J. Fox

Top right: Sebastian Vettel gives Rosberg his heartfelt congratulations. Lewis Hamilton's face can't hide his understandable emotions.
Photo: Lukas Gorys

Above right: Both a winner and loser. The no doubt crestfallen Lewis Hamilton joins the Mercedes post-race celebration shoot.

Right: Too close for comfort? Hamilton takes the chequered flag just ahead of Rosberg, Vettel and Verstappen.
Photos: Mercedes AMG Petronas F1 Team

However, Rosberg did pull off the move on lap 20, and he did it with a perfectly orchestrated combination of late braking into the chicane at Turns Eight and Nine and the use of carefully harvested energy to power alongside and past the Red Bull on the short back straight, sealing the deal into 11.

"The feelings I had in the battle and right after when I realised that I'd passed him, I've never had that in a race car ever in my life," Rosberg said later. "And I don't ever want to have them again."

Verstappen came in two laps later for softs, rejoining eighth, behind Pérez and Hülkenberg as they rubbed in the fact that Force India were certain to take fourth in the championship, following the retirement of Bottas with a rear suspension issue that Williams could not fix.

How were Mercedes going to fix the Hamilton issue as Rosberg set fastest laps and closed in once more on the leader? When the second stops (for softs) came and went on laps 28 and 29, Mercedes realised that there was another potential problem arising in the shape of Ferrari No. 5 at the front. As the laps ticked by and Vettel maintained a five-second lead, the threat of a short final stint on super-softs became real, as the Ferrari could catch up again in the late stages and cause havoc.

These concerns were made public when Hamilton was asked why he was going so slowly. And Hamilton's thoughts were equally evident when he showed no sign of reacting to the news that Vettel might be a threat, particularly when the Ferrari came out, as expected, on brand-new super-softs with 18 laps to go – by which stage, the Merc drivers' softs were ten laps old. Rosberg was starting to feel under siege – back and front.

The one good thing about running close to Hamilton was that Rosberg could use DRS to stay out of Verstappen's reach

once the Red Bull was a couple of car lengths behind. But the more serious threat was Vettel. Lapping over a second faster, he was given free passage by Räikkönen, picked off Ricciardo going into Turn 11 with nine laps to go and then closed in on Verstappen. With four laps remaining, Vettel passed the Red Bull at the same place. Rosberg was 1.8 seconds ahead.

By which stage, Hamilton had received a call from Paddy Lowe, the technical director's presence on the air waves indicating that this was top priority and that his words should be read as an instruction rather than advice. Once again, Hamilton studiously ignored the call to speed up and turned the screw even tighter on the hapless Rosberg. With Verstappen now in tow, the first four were covered by five seconds. Could Vettel demote Rosberg to P3 and present him to Verstappen?

Vettel would grin when recalling the scenario. "The problem when you have been passing car after car, you begin to slide, so my tyres got worse. When I was behind Nico, I was faster – but also due to the fact that Lewis was slowing down. I think... he must have had a problem!" Vettel's grin widened. "I tried everything, but they were very, very quick down the straights. I couldn't try anything really stupid like a really late dive because Lewis was so close ahead and I'd have risked hitting Lewis trying to pass Nico. Also Max was right in my mirrors, so I had to watch him, too. It was intense."

'Tell me about it' would have summed up Rosberg's thoughts as the final lap unfolded. They finished it line astern. Rosberg was 0.43s behind Hamilton and roughly the same ahead of Vettel. But the gaps didn't matter any more. The 2016 world champion emerged from his car visibly drained and emotional. It had been a long, hard journey. Right up to the final mile of this exceptionally dramatic race.

Maurice Hamilton

VIEWPOINT
DIRTY TRICKS OR HOBSON'S CHOICE?

'**Y**OU ANARCHIST!' screamed the back page of the UK's Daily Mail on the Monday morning after the Abu Dhabi GP, as it claimed that Lewis Hamilton risked having his £30m Mercedes contract ripped up as a result of the way he had driven at Yas Marina, ignoring team instruction..

In fairness, Toto Wolff, post-race, had used the word anarchy and stated that it had no place in a team or a company. But honestly, what a load of nonsense!

The constructors' championship was in the bag, and this was about the drivers' championship. A straightforward head-to-head: Lewis versus Nico. To win the championship, Lewis needed Nico to finish lower than third in the fastest car in the race. Quite obviously, he was going to drive slowly in an attempt to give Nico a hard afternoon, and anyone who thought otherwise was being naïve in the extreme.

There is nothing remotely wrong with what Hamilton did. It's not as if he'd jammed the anchors on and brake-tested Nico at the last corner, letting Seb and Max by.

If Nico had wanted to control his own pace and destiny, he needed to take pole, but he didn't manage it. From the moment Lewis claimed it, Nico was always going to be in for a tricky afternoon. It is to his credit that he came through and kept a cool head. There are others who, being messed around, would simply have forgotten to brake at Turn Eight and taken them both out. Job done. You think of Suzuka 1990... But Nico is not like that. He earned his title the hard way.

This was one race where the Mercedes team objective of achieving the highest possible finish with both cars needed to go out of the window, because it simply didn't fit the sporting contest. Yes, there might be 1,500 people at Brackley and 300,000 in Daimler, but who gives a damn? If companies can use top-class sport for PR or promotional gain, then great, but it must not obscure the real reason that people tune in on a Sunday afternoon.

What you don't want to hear is engineers telling drivers what lap time they should be doing. In the circumstances, Hamilton's responses were remarkably restrained. Had it been me, the second word would have been "off!" Yes, it would have been nice to have seen a bit more grace and magnanimity from Lewis afterwards, but you can't blame him for doing his all to defend his title.

Maybe he wasn't following the Mercedes rules of engagement, but in that race, on that evening, those rules didn't need to be there. He was certainly within the rules of motor racing, which is what should count.

Tony Dodgins

21

2016 FORMULA 1
ETIHAD AIRWAYS
ABU DHABI
GRAND PRIX

YAS MARINA 25–27 NOVEMBER

ROLEX

F1 OFFICIAL TIMEPIECE

RACE DISTANCE: 55 laps, 189.739 miles/305.355km

RACE WEATHER: Dry/sunny-dark (track 27–30°C, air 25–27°C)

YAS MARINA CIRCUIT, ABU DHABI
Circuit: 3.451 miles/5.554km
55 laps

Turn 7 65/40
Turn 8 85/53
335/208
Turn 9 98/61
300/186 4
Turns 5 & 6 100/62
Turn 21 180/112
Turn 3 270/168
Turn 10 215/134
20
Turn 2 250/155
17
19 120/75
Turn 1 170/106
Turn 18
Turn 16
Turn 15 275/171
Turn 11 102/63
Turn 14 110/68
116/187 mph/kmh
Turn 12&13 120/75
Gear
DRS zone

RACE – OFFICIAL CLASSIFICATION

All results and data © FOM 2016

Pos.	Driver	Nat.	No.	Entrant	Car/Engine	Tyres	Laps	Time/Retirement	Speed (mph/km/h)	Gap to leader	Fastest race lap	
1	**Lewis Hamilton**	GB	44	Mercedes AMG Petronas F1 Team	Mercedes F1 W07-Mercedes PU106C V6	P	55	1h 38m 04.013s	116.087/186.824		1m 45.137s	37
2	**Nico Rosberg**	D	6	Mercedes AMG Petronas F1 Team	Mercedes F1 W07-Mercedes PU106C V6	P	55	1h 38m 04.452s	116.078/186.810	0.439s	1m 45.261s	33
3	**Sebastian Vettel**	D	5	Scuderia Ferrari	Ferrari SF15-H-059/5 V6	P	55	1h 38m 04.856s	116.070/186.797	0.843s	1m 43.729s	43
4	**Max Verstappen**	NL	33	Red Bull Racing	Red Bull RB12-TAG Heuer RB12 V6	P	55	1h 38m 05.698s	116.054/186.771	1.685s	1m 45.187s	36
5	**Daniel Ricciardo**	AUS	3	Red Bull Racing	Red Bull RB12-TAG Heuer RB12 V6	P	55	1h 38m 09.328s	115.952/186.655	5.315s	1m 44.889s	29
6	**Kimi Räikkönen**	FIN	7	Scuderia Ferrari	Ferrari SF16-H-059/5 V6	P	55	1h 38m 22.829s	115.717/186.228	18.816s	1m 45.163s	35
7	**Nico Hülkenberg**	D	27	Sahara Force India F1 Team	Force India VJM09-Mercedes PU106C V6	P	55	1h 38m 54.127s	115.107/185.246	50.114s	1m 45.949s	31
8	**Sergio Pérez**	MEX	11	Sahara Force India F1 Team	Force India VJM09-Mercedes PU106C V6	P	55	1h 39m 02.789s	114.939/184.976	58.776s	1m 45.249s	30
9	**Felipe Massa**	BR	19	Williams Martini Racing	Williams FW38-Mercedes PU106C V6	P	55	1h 39m 03.449s	114.926/184.956	59.436s	1m 45.675s	33
10	**Fernando Alonso**	E	14	McLaren Honda	McLaren MP4-31-Honda RA616H V6	P	55	1h 39m 03.909s	114.917/184.941	59.896s	1m 44.495s	50
11	Romain Grosjean	F	8	Haas F1 Team	Haas VF-16-Ferrari 059/5 V6	P	55	1h 39m 20.790s	114.592/184.418	1m 16.777s	1m 44.970s	45
12	Esteban Gutiérrez	MEX	21	Haas F1 Team	Haas VF-16-Ferrari 059/5 V6	P	55	1h 39m 39.126s	114.240/183.852	1m 35.113s	1m 45.928s	45
13	Esteban Ocon	F	31	Manor Racing MRT	Manor MRT05-Mercedes PU106C V6	P	54			1 lap	1m 46.189s	46
14	Pascal Wehrlein	D	94	Manor Racing MRT	Manor MRT05-Mercedes PU106C V6	P	54			1 lap	1m 46.145s	26
15	Marcus Ericsson	S	9	Sauber F1 Team	Sauber C35-Ferrari 059/5 V6	P	54			1 lap	1m 46.216s	40
16	Felipe Nasr	BR	12	Sauber F1 Team	Sauber C35-Ferrari 059/5 V6	P	54			1 lap	1m 46.287s	44
17	Jolyon Palmer	GB	30	Renault Sport F1 Team	Renault R.S.16-R.E.16 V6	P	54			1 lap	1m 45.715s	46
	Carlos Sainz	E	55	Scuderia Toro Rosso	Toro Rosso STR11-Ferrari 059/4 V6	P	41	accident			1m 46.591s	30
	Daniil Kvyat	RUS	26	Scuderia Toro Rosso	Toro Rosso STR11-Ferrari 059/4 V6	P	14	gearbox			1m 48.752s	13
	Jenson Button	GB	22	McLaren Honda	McLaren MP4-31-Honda RA616H V6	P	12	front suspension			1m 48.753s	4
	Valtteri Bottas	FIN	77	Williams Martini Racing	Williams FW38-Mercedes PU106C V6	P	6	rear suspension			1m 47.837s	4
	Kevin Magnussen	DK	20	Renault Sport F1 Team	Renault R.S.16-R.E.16 V6	P	5	accident/front suspension			1m 48.601s	4

Fastest race lap: Sebastian Vettel on lap 43, 1m 43.729s, 119.773mph/192.756km/h.

Lap record: Sebastian Vettel (Red Bull RB5-Renault V8), 1m 40.279s, 123.894mph/199.387km/h (2009).

22 · ERICSSON · Sauber

20 · OCON · Manor

18 · MAGNUSSEN · Renault

16 · WERHLEIN · Manor

14 · GROSJEAN · Haas

12 · BUTTON · McLaren

21 · SAINZ · Toro Rosso 19 · NASR · Sauber 17 · KVYAT · Toro Rosso 15 · PALMER · Renault 13 · GUTIÉRREZ · Haas 11 · BOTTAS · Williams

Grid order	1	2	3	4	5	6	7	8	9	10	11	12	13	14	15	16	17	18	19	20	21	22	23	24	25	26	27	28	29	30	31	32	33	34	35	36	37	38	39	40	41	42	43	44
44 HAMILTON	44	44	44	44	44	44	6	6	3	44	44	44	44	44	44	44	44	44	44	44	44	44	44	44	44	44	44	44	6	5	5	5	5	5	5	5	44	44	44	44	44	44	44	44
6 ROSBERG	6	6	6	6	6	44	3	11	33	33	33	33	33	33	33	33	33	33	6	6	6	6	6	6	6	6	6	6	5	44	44	44	44	44	44	44	6	6	6	6	6	6	6	6
3 RICCIARDO	3	7	7	7	7	3	44	6	44	6	6	6	6	6	6	6	6	6	33	7	7	7	7	5	5	5	44	6	6	6	6	6	6	33	33	33	33	33	33	33
7 RÄIKKÖNEN	3	3	3	3	3	7	27	33	7	7	7	7	7	7	7	7	7	7	7	33	3	5	27	33	33	33	33	33	33	33	33	3												
5 VETTEL	5	5	5	5	5	5	5	11	6	3	3	3	3	3	3	3	3	3	3	5	5	3	27	33	3	3	3	3	3	3	3	3	7	7	5	5	5	5	5	5
33 VERSTAPPEN	11	27	27	27	27	27	27	44	7	5	5	5	5	5	5	5	5	5	27	27	27	11	11	7	7	7	7	7	7	7	7	7	5	5	7	7	7
27 HÜLKENBERG	27	11	11	11	11	11	11	19	5	22	27	27	27	27	27	27	27	27	11	11	11	33	3	11	19	19	19	14	14	14	27	27	27	27	27	27	27	27
11 PÉREZ	14	14	14	14	14	14	14	3	22	27	22	11	11	11	11	11	11	11	33	33	33	3	7	19	14	14	27	11	11	11	11	11	11	11	11	11	11
14 ALONSO	19	19	77	77	19	19	14	7	27	11	11	8	8	19	19	19	19	19	14	19	14	27	27	11	11	11	14	14	14	14	19	19	19	19
19 MASSA	77	77	19	19	77	30	33	22	8	8	19	19	8	8	8	14	14	14	14	14	14	14	14	27	11	11	19	19	19	19	14	14	14	14
77 BOTTAS	30	30	30	30	30	77	22	8	31	31	31	31	14	14	14	8	31	9	21	21	21	21	8	8	8	8	8	8	8	8	8	8	8	8
22 BUTTON	22	22	22	22	22	33	26	26	9	19	14	31	31	31	31	31	31	31	9	21	9	9	9	8	21	9	9	9	9	21	21	21	21	21	21
21 GUTIÉRREZ	26	26	26	26	33	22	30	21	19	19	9	9	9	9	9	9	21	31	8	9	9	12	12	21	19	9	9	30	30	30	94	94	94
8 GROSJEAN	12	12	12	33	26	26	21	31	14	14	14	30	30	30	30	30	21	55	55	55	55	55	21	21	12	12	30	55	55	55	30	31	31	31
30 PALMER	8	8	33	12	21	21	8	9	30	30	11	21	21	21	30	30	8	12	12	12	12	31	31	31	31	31	31	94	94	94	55	9
94 WEHRLEIN	21	33	21	21	12	8	31	14	21	21	26	26	55	55	55	55	8	12	94	94	31	31	31	30	30	30	30	55	94	9	31	31	31	12	12
26 KVYAT	31	21	8	8	8	12	9	30	26	26	26	55	55	12	12	12	12	94	31	31	30	30	55	55	55	55	94	31	31	9	9	9	30	30	30
20 MAGNUSSEN	9	31	31	31	31	9	12	55	55	55	55	12	12	94	94	94	94	30	30	94	94	94	94	94	94	94	94	12	12	12	12	12
12 NASR	33	55	55	55	55	55	55	12	12	12	94	94	94
31 OCON	55	94	94	94	94	9	94	94	94	94
55 SAINZ	94	9	9	9	9	94
9 ERICSSON	20	20	20	20	20

PRACTICE 1 (FRIDAY)
Weather: Dry/sunny
Temperatures: track 34–38°C, air 29–32°C

Pos.	Driver	Laps	Time
1	Lewis Hamilton	28	1m 42.869s
2	Nico Rosberg	31	1m 43.243s
3	Max Verstappen	26	1m 43.297s
4	Daniel Ricciardo	27	1m 43.362s
5	Sebastian Vettel	27	1m 44.005s
6	Sergio Pérez	23	1m 44.155s
7	Kimi Räikkönen	27	1m 44.556s
8	Carlos Sainz	21	1m 44.685s
9	Felipe Massa	27	1m 45.039s
10	Marcus Ericsson	20	1m 45.168s
11	Alfonso Celis	26	1m 45.476s
12	Romain Grosjean	13	1m 45.600s
13	Felipe Nasr	17	1m 45.778s
14	Esteban Gutiérrez	20	1m 45.925s
15	Valtteri Bottas	31	1m 45.940s
16	Jolyon Palmer	33	1m 46.219s
17	Kevin Magnussen	21	1m 46.372s
18	Fernando Alonso	21	1m 46.379s
19	Pascal Wehrlein	29	1m 46.458s
20	Jenson Button	10	1m 47.127s
21	Jordan King	27	1m 47.558s
22	Daniil Kvyat	4	2m 01.989s

PRACTICE 2 (FRIDAY)
Weather: Dry/twilight
Temperatures: track 27–30°C, air 25–27°C

Pos.	Driver	Laps	Time
1	Lewis Hamilton	36	1m 40.861s
2	Nico Rosberg	38	1m 40.940s
3	Sebastian Vettel	31	1m 41.130s
4	Max Verstappen	24	1m 41.389s
5	Daniel Ricciardo	33	1m 41.390s
6	Kimi Räikkönen	34	1m 41.464s
7	Valtteri Bottas	35	1m 41.959s
8	Sergio Pérez	35	1m 42.041s
9	Nico Hülkenberg	36	1m 42.264s
10	Felipe Massa	36	1m 42.268s
11	Fernando Alonso	33	1m 42.366s
12	Jenson Button	24	1m 42.823s
13	Esteban Gutiérrez	35	1m 43.012s
14	Romain Grosjean	17	1m 43.108s
15	Jolyon Palmer	33	1m 43.272s
16	Esteban Ocon	35	1m 43.600s
17	Pascal Wehrlein	33	1m 43.754s
18	Felipe Nasr	36	1m 43.903s
19	Marcus Ericsson	34	1m 44.045s
20	Kevin Magnussen	25	1m 44.117s
21	Carlos Sainz	5	1m 44.478s
22	Daniil Kvyat	4	1m 45.948s

PRACTICE 3 (SATURDAY)
Weather: Dry/sunny
Temperatures: track 34–36°C, air 29–30°C

Pos.	Driver	Laps	Time
1	Sebastian Vettel	16	1m 40.775s
2	Max Verstappen	21	1m 40.912s
3	Kimi Räikkönen	14	1m 40.999s
4	Lewis Hamilton	15	1m 41.065s
5	Nico Rosberg	19	1m 41.168s
6	Daniel Ricciardo	20	1m 41.831s
7	Sergio Pérez	19	1m 41.885s
8	Nico Hülkenberg	13	1m 42.067s
9	Valtteri Bottas	19	1m 42.076s
10	Esteban Gutiérrez	16	1m 42.354s
11	Fernando Alonso	14	1m 42.585s
12	Jolyon Palmer	18	1m 42.616s
13	Jenson Button	15	1m 42.664s
14	Felipe Massa	20	1m 42.683s
15	Romain Grosjean	17	1m 42.805s
16	Kevin Magnussen	17	1m 43.057s
17	Pascal Wehrlein	17	1m 43.145s
18	Carlos Sainz	10	1m 43.301s
19	Felipe Nasr	22	1m 43.417s
20	Esteban Ocon	15	1m 43.733s
21	Daniil Kvyat	13	1m 44.105s
22	Marcus Ericsson	20	1m 44.238s

QUALIFYING (SATURDAY)
Weather: Dry/twilight Temperatures: track 28–36°C, air 26–30°C

Pos.	Driver	First	Second	Third	Qualifying Tyre
1	Lewis Hamilton	1m 39.487s	1m 39.382s	1m 38.755s	Ultra-soft (new)
2	Nico Rosberg	1m 40.511s	1m 39.490s	1m 39.058s	Ultra-soft (new)
3	Daniel Ricciardo	1m 41.002s	1m 40.429s	1m 39.589s	Ultra-soft (new)
4	Kimi Räikkönen	1m 40.338s	1m 39.629s	1m 39.604s	Ultra-soft (new)
5	Sebastian Vettel	1m 40.341s	1m 40.034s	1m 39.661s	Ultra-soft (new)
6	Max Verstappen	1m 40.424s	1m 39.903s	1m 39.818s	Ultra-soft (new)
7	Nico Hülkenberg	1m 41.000s	1m 40.709s	1m 40.501s	Ultra-soft (new)
8	Sergio Pérez	1m 40.864s	1m 40.743s	1m 40.519s	Ultra-soft (new)
9	Fernando Alonso	1m 41.616s	1m 41.044s	1m 41.106s	Ultra-soft (new)
10	Felipe Massa	1m 41.157s	1m 40.858s	1m 41.213s	Ultra-soft (new)
11	Valtteri Bottas	1m 41.192s	1m 41.084s		
12	Jenson Button	1m 41.158s	1m 41.272s		
13	Esteban Gutiérrez	1m 41.639s	1m 41.480s		
14	Romain Grosjean	1m 41.467s	1m 41.564s		
15	Jolyon Palmer	1m 41.775s	1m 41.820s		
16	Pascal Wehrlein	1m 41.886s	1m 41.995s		
17	Daniil Kvyat	1m 42.003s			
18	Kevin Magnussen	1m 42.142s			
19	Felipe Nasr	1m 42.247s			
20	Esteban Ocon	1m 42.286s			
21	Carlos Sainz	1m 42.393s			
22	Marcus Ericsson	1m 42.637s			

Photo: Mercedes AMG Petronas F1 Team

FOR THE RECORD

1st DRIVERS' WORLD TITLE: Nico Rosberg.

250th START: Felipe Massa.

150th WIN: Mercedes (engine).

60th FRONT ROW: Rosberg.

DID YOU KNOW?

Nico Rosberg took 206 grands prix to reach his first title, a new record previously held by Nigel Mansell.

It is 34 years between Keke and Nico Rosberg's world titles, the same period as between Graham Hill's first title and Damon's.

POINTS

DRIVERS
1	Nico Rosberg	385
2	Lewis Hamilton	380
3	Daniel Ricciardo	256
4	Sebastian Vettel	212
5	Max Verstappen	204
6	Kimi Räikkönen	186
7	Sergio Pérez	101
8	Valtteri Bottas	85
9	Nico Hülkenberg	72
10	Fernando Alonso	54
11	Felipe Massa	53
12	Carlos Sainz	46
13	Romain Grosjean	29
14	Daniil Kvyat	25
15	Jenson Button	21
16	Kevin Magnussen	7
17	Felipe Nasr	2
18	Jolyon Palmer	1
19	Pascal Wehrlein	1
20	Stoffel Vandoorne	1

CONSTRUCTORS
1	Mercedes	765
2	Red Bull	468
3	Ferrari	398
4	Force India	173
5	Williams	138
6	McLaren	76
7	Toro Rosso	63
8	Haas	29
9	Renault	8
10	Sauber	2
11	Manor	1

Qualifying: head-to-head
Rosberg	9	12	Hamilton
Vettel	10	11	Räikkönen
Massa	4	17	Bottas
Ricciardo	4	0	Kvyat
Ricciardo	11	6	Verstappen
Pérez	9	12	Hülkenberg
Magnussen	12	9	Palmer
Verstappen	3	1	Sainz
Kvyat	6	11	Sainz
Ericsson	13	8	Nasr
Alonso	15	5	Button
Button	0	1	Vandoorne
Haryanto	5	7	Wehrlein
Wehrlein	7	2	Ocon
Grosjean	13	8	Gutiérrez

10 · MASSA · Williams   8 · PÉREZ · Force India   6 · VERSTAPPEN · Red Bull   4 · RÄIKKÖNEN · Ferrari   2 · ROSBERG · Mercedes

9 · ALONSO · McLaren   7 · HÜLKENBERG · Force India   5 · VETTEL · Ferrari   3 · RICCIARDO · Red Bull   1 · HAMILTON · Mercedes

Lap chart

45	46	47	48	49	50	51	52	53	54	55	
44	44	44	44	44	44	44	44	44	44	44	1
6	6	6	6	6	6	6	6	6	6	6	2
33	33	33	33	33	33	5	5	5	5	5	3
3	5	5	5	5	33	33	33	33	33	33	4
5	3	3	3	3	3	3	3	3	3	3	5
7	7	7	7	7	7	7	7	7	7	7	6
27	27	27	27	27	27	27	27	27	27	27	7
11	11	11	11	11	11	11	11	11	11	11	8
19	19	19	19	19	19	19	19	19	19	19	9
14	14	14	14	14	14	14	14	14	14	14	10
8	8	8	8	8	8	8	8	8	8	8	
21	21	21	21	21	21	21	21	21	21	21	
94	94	94	94	31	31	31	31	31	31		
31	31	31	31	94	94	94	94	94	94		
9	9	9	9	9	9	9	9	9	9		
12	12	12	12	12	12	12	12	12	12		
30	30	30	30	30	30	30	30	30	30		

6 = Pit stop   9 = Drive-thru penalty

94 = One lap or more behind

RACE TYRE STRATEGIES

PIRELLI

	Driver	Race Stint 1	Race Stint 2	Race Stint 3	Race Stint 4
1	Hamilton	Ultra-Soft (u): 1–7	Soft (n): 8–28	Soft (n): 29–55	
2	Rosberg	Ultra-Soft (u): 1–8	Soft (n): 9–29	Soft (n): 30–55	
3	Vettel	Ultra-Soft (u): 1–8	Soft (n): 9–37	Soft (n): 38–55	
4	Verstappen	Super-Soft (u): 1–21	Soft (n): 22–55		
5	Ricciardo	Super-Soft (u): 1–9	Soft (n): 10–24	Soft (n): 25–55	
6	Räikkönen	Ultra-Soft (u): 1–7	Soft (n): 8–25	Soft (n): 26–55	
7	Hülkenberg	Ultra-Soft (u): 1–8	Soft (n): 9–26	Soft (n): 27–55	
8	Pérez	Ultra-Soft (u): 1–9	Soft (n): 10–27	Soft (n): 28–55	
9	Massa	Ultra-Soft (u): 1–8	Soft (n): 9–30	Soft (n): 31–55	
10	Alonso	Ultra-Soft (u): 1–7	Soft (n): 8–38	Soft (n): 39–55	
11	Grosjean	Soft (n): 1–20	Soft (n): 21–38	Super-Soft (n): 39–55	
12	Gutiérrez	Super-Soft (n): 1–8	Soft (n): 9–28	Soft (n): 29–55	
13	Ocon	Soft (n): 1–22	Soft (n): 23–36	Super-Soft (n): 37–54	
14	Wehrlein	Ultra-Soft (u): 1–6	Soft (n): 7–24	Soft (n): 25–54	
15	Ericsson	Soft (n): 1–38	Super-Soft (n): 39–54		
16	Nasr	Super-Soft (n): 1–7	Soft (n): 8–36	Soft (n): 37–54	
17	Palmer	Ultra-Soft (u): 1–7	Soft (n): 8–21	Soft (n): 22–41	Super-Soft (n): 42–54
	Sainz	Ultra-Soft (u): 1–6	Soft (n): 7–28	Soft (n): 29–41 (dnf)	
	Kvyat	Super-Soft (n): 1–8	Soft (n): 9–14 (dnf)		
	Button	Soft (n): 1–12 (dnf)			
	Bottas	Ultra-Soft (n): 1–6 (dnf)			
	Magnussen	Soft (n): 1	Soft (n): 2–5 (dnf)		

The tyre regulations stipulate that at least two of three dry tyre specifications must be used during a dry race.

Pirelli P Zero logos are colour-coded on the tyre sidewalls: Yellow = Soft; Red = Super-Soft; Purple = Ultra-Soft. (n) new (u) used

Photo: Mercedes AMG Petronas F1 Team

STATISTICS: Compiled by DAVID HAYHOE

DRIVERS' POINTS TABLE 2016

Place	Driver	Nationality	Date of birth	Car	Australia	Bahrain	China	Russia	Spain	Monaco	Canada	Europe	Austria	Britain	Hungary	Germany	Belgium	Italy	Singapore	Malaysia	Japan	United States	Mexico	Brazil	Abu Dhabi	Points
1	**Nico ROSBERG**	D	27/6/85	Mercedes	1	1f	1p	1pf	R	7	5f	1pf	4	3f	2p	4p	1p	1	1p	3f	1p	2	2	2	2	**385**
2	**Lewis HAMILTON**	GB	7/1/85	Mercedes	2p	3p	7	2	Rp	1f	1p	5	1pf	1p	1	1	3f	2p	3	Rp	3	1p	1p	1p	1p	**380**
3	**Daniel RICCIARDO**	AUS	1/7/89	Red Bull-TAG Heuer	4f	4	4	11	4	2p	7	7	5	4	3	2f	2	5	2f	1	6	3	3f	8	5	**256**
4	**Sebastian VETTEL**	D	3/7/87	Ferrari	3	NS	2	R	3	4	2	2	9	4	5	6	3	5	R	4f	4f	5	5	5	3f	**212**
5	**Max VERSTAPPEN**	NL	30/9/97	Toro Rosso-Ferrari	10	6	8	R	–	–	–	–	–	–	–	–	–	–	–	–	–	–	–	–	–	
				Red Bull-TAG Heuer	–	–	–	–	1	R	4	8	2	3	5	3	11	7	6	2	2	R	4	3f	4	**204**
6	**Kimi RÄIKKÖNEN**	FIN	17/10/79	Ferrari	R	2	5	3	2	R	6	4	3	5	6f	6	9	4	4	4	5	R	6	R	6	**186**
7	**Sergio PÉREZ**	MEX	26/1/90	Force India-Mercedes	13	16	11	9	7	3	10	3	17*	6	11	10	5	8	8	6	7	8	10	4	8	**101**
8	**Valtteri BOTTAS**	FIN	28/8/89	Williams-Mercedes	8	9	10	4	5	12	3	6	9	14	9	9	8	6	R	5	10	16	8	11	R	**85**
9	**Nico HÜLKENBERG**	D	19/8/87	Force India-Mercedes	7	15	15f	R	R	6	8	9	19*	7	10	7	4	10	R	8	8	R	7	7	7	**72**
10	**Fernando ALONSO**	E	29/7/81	McLaren-Honda	R	–	12	6	R	5	11	R	18*	13	7	12	7	14f	7	7	16	5	13	10	10	**54**
11	**Felipe MASSA**	BR	25/4/81	Williams-Mercedes	5	8	6	5	8	10	R	10	20*	11	18	R	10	9	12	13	9	7	9	R	9	**53**
12	**Carlos SAINZ**	E	1/9/94	Toro Rosso-Ferrari	9	R	9	12	6	8	9	R	8	8	8	14	R	15	14	11	17	6	16	6	R	**46**
13	**Romain GROSJEAN**	F	17/4/86	Haas-Ferrari	6	5	19	8	R	13	14	13	7	R	14	13	13	11	NS	R	11	10	20	NS	11	**29**
14	**Daniil KVYAT**	RUS	26/4/94	Red Bull-TAG Heuer	NS	7	3	15	–	–	–	–	–	–	–	–	–	–	–	–	–	–	–	–	–	
				Toro Rosso-Ferrari	–	–	–	–	10f	R	12	R	R	10	16	15	14	R	9	14	13	11	18	13	R	**25**
15	**Jenson BUTTON**	GB	19/1/80	McLaren-Honda	14	R	13	10	9	9	R	11	6	12	R	8	R	12	R	9	18	9	12	16	R	**21**
16	**Kevin MAGNUSSEN**	DK	5/10/92	Renault	12	11	17	7	15	R	16	14	14	17*	15	16	R	17	10	R	14	12	17	14	R	**7**
17	**Felipe NASR**	BR	21/8/92	Sauber-Ferrari	15	14	20	16	14	R	18	12	13	15	17	R	17	R	13	R	19	15	15	9	16	**2**
18	**Jolyon PALMER**	GB	20/1/91	Renault	11	NS	22	13	13	R	15	12	R	12	19	15	R	15	10	12	13	14	R	17	18	**1**
19	**Pascal WEHRLEIN**	D	18/10/94	Manor-Mercedes	16	13	18	18	16	14	17	R	10	R	19	17	R	16	15	22	17	R	15	14	21	**1**
20	**Stoffel VANDOORNE**	B	26/3/92	McLaren-Honda	–	10	–	–	–	–	–	–	–	–	–	–	–	–	–	–	–	–	–	–	–	**1**
	Marcus ERICSSON	S	2/9/90	Sauber-Ferrari	R	12	16	14	12	R	15	17	15	R	20	18	R	16	17	12	15	14	11	R	15	–
	Esteban GUTIÉRREZ	MEX	5/8/91	Haas-Ferrari	R	R	14	17	11	R	13	16	11	16	13	11	12	13	11	R	20	R	19	R	12	–
	Rio HARYANTO	RI	22/1/93	Manor-Mercedes	R	17	21	R	17	15	19	18	16	R	21	20	–	–	–	–	–	–	–	–	–	–
	Esteban OCON	F	17/9/96	Renault	–	–	–	–	AP	–	–	–	AP	AP	AP	–	–	–	–	–	–	–	–	–	–	
				Manor-Mercedes	–	–	–	–	–	–	–	–	–	–	–	–	16	18	18	16	21	18	21	12	13	–

FRIDAY TESTERS

	Driver	Nationality	Date of birth	Car	Australia	Bahrain	China	Russia	Spain	Monaco	Canada	Europe	Austria	Britain	Hungary	Germany	Belgium	Italy	Singapore	Malaysia	Japan	United States	Mexico	Brazil	Abu Dhabi	
	Alfonso CELIS	MEX	18/9/96	Force India-Mercedes	–	AP	–	AP	–	–	–	AP	–	–	–	AP	–	–	AP	–	–	AP	–	–	AP	
	Jordan KING	GB	26/2/94	Force India-Mercedes	–	–	–	–	–	–	–	–	–	–	–	–	–	–	AP	–	–	AP	–	–	AP	
	Charles LECLERC	MC	16/10/97	Haas-Ferrari	–	–	–	–	–	–	–	–	AP	AP	AP	–	–	–	–	–	–	–	–	AP	–	
	Sergey SIROTKIN	RUS	27/8/95	Renault	–	–	–	–	AP	–	–	–	–	–	–	–	–	–	–	–	–	–	–	AP	–	

KEY: AP – Also practised   NS – Non-starter   R – Retired   * – Placed, but retired   f – fastest lap   p – pole position

POINTS AND PERCENTAGES

GRID POSITIONS: 2016

Pos	Driver	Starts	Best	Worst	Average
1	Nico Rosberg	21	1	6	1.81
2	Daniel Ricciardo	21	1	8	3.90
3	Lewis Hamilton	21	1	22	4.14
4	Kimi Räikkönen	21	3	14	5.33
5	Max Verstappen	21	2	21	6.05
6	Sebastian Vettel	20	3	22	6.20
7	Valtteri Bottas	21	2	16	8.29
8	Nico Hülkenberg	21	2	13	8.38
9	Sergio Pérez	21	5	18	9.76
10	Felipe Massa	21	4	20	10.43
11	Stoffel Vandoorne	1	12	12	12.00
12	Carlos Sainz	21	6	21	12.05
13	Fernando Alonso	20	7	22	12.15
14	Jenson Button	21	3	22	13.00
15	Daniil Kvyat	20	6	22	13.50
16	Esteban Gutiérrez	21	10	20	13.95
17	Romain Grosjean	19	7	22	14.11
18	Kevin Magnussen	21	12	22	17.14
19	Jolyon Palmer	20	13	21	17.15
20	Pascal Wehrlein	21	12	21	18.19
21	Marcus Ericsson	21	14	22	18.62
22	Felipe Nasr	21	15	22	18.67
23	Rio Haryanto	12	16	22	19.83
24	Esteban Ocon	9	17	22	20.44

RETIREMENTS: 2016

Number of cars to have retired

Grand Prix	Starters	At 1/4-distance	At 1/2-distance	At 3/4-distance	At full distance	Percentage of finishers
Australia	21	-	4	5	5	76.2
Bahrain	20	2	2	3	3	85.0
China	22	-	-	-	-	100.0
Russia	22	3	3	4	4	81.8
Spain	22	2	3	4	5	77.3
Monaco	22	3	5	7	7	68.2
Canada	22	2	3	3	3	86.4
Europe	22	1	1	2	4	81.8
Austria	22	1	2	2	6	72.7
Britain	22	2	4	5	6	72.7
Hungary	22	-	-	-	1	95.5
Germany	22	-	-	1	2	90.9
Belgium	22	5	5	5	5	77.3
Italy	22	2	3	4	4	81.8
Singapore	21	1	1	3	3	85.7
Malaysia	22	2	3	5	6	72.7
Japan	22	-	-	-	-	100.0
United States	22	1	3	4	4	81.8
Mexico	22	1	1	1	1	95.5
Brazil	21	1	3	4	5	76.2
Abu Dhabi	22	3	4	5	5	77.3

LAP LEADERS: 2016

Grand Prix	Hamilton	Rosberg	Vettel	Ricciardo	Verstappen	Räikkönen	Total
Australia	-	23	31	-	-	3	57
Bahrain	1	56	-	-	-	-	57
China	-	54	-	2	-	-	56
Russia	-	53	-	-	-	-	53
Spain	-	-	4	30	30	2	66
Monaco	54	-	-	24	-	-	78
Canada	47	-	23	-	-	-	70
Europe	-	51	-	-	-	-	51
Austria	22	39	4	-	5	1	71
Britain	51	-	-	-	1	-	52
Hungary	66	4	-	-	-	-	70
Germany	67	-	-	-	-	-	67
Belgium	-	44	-	-	-	-	44
Italy	1	52	-	-	-	-	53
Singapore	1	59	-	-	-	1	61
Malaysia	33	-	-	17	6	-	56
Japan	-	48	5	-	-	-	53
United States	53	-	3	-	-	-	56
Mexico	56	3	12	-	-	-	71
Brazil	71	-	-	-	-	-	71
Abu Dhabi	43	3	8	1	-	-	55
Total	**566**	**489**	**90**	**74**	**42**	**7**	**1,268**
(Per cent)	44.6	38.6	7.1	5.8	3.3	0.5	100.0

CAREER PERFORMANCES: 2016

Driver	Nationality	Races	Championships	Wins	2nd places	3rd places	4th places	5th places	6th places	7th places	8th places	9th places	10th places	Pole positions	Fastest laps	Points
Fernando Alonso	E	273	2	32	37	28	26	22	15	15	7	4	9	22	22	**1832**
Valtteri Bottas	FIN	77	–	–	2	7	5	11	4	2	7	5	3	–	1	**411**
Jenson Button	GB	305	1	15	15	20	24	27	19	12	20	14	14	8	8	**1235**
Marcus Ericsson	S	56	–	–	–	–	–	–	–	–	1	1	3	–	–	**9**
Romain Grosjean	F	102	–	–	2	8	2	1	5	8	7	3	4	–	1	**316**
Esteban Gutiérrez	MEX	59	–	–	–	–	–	–	–	1	–	–	1	–	–	**6**
Lewis Hamilton	GB	188	3	53	28	23	13	16	6	6	4	4	2	61	31	**2247**
Rio Haryanto	RI	12	–	–	–	–	–	–	–	–	–	–	–	–	–	**–**
Nico Hülkenberg	D	115	–	–	–	3	7	11	14	13	6	12	1	2	–	**362**
Daniil Kvyat	RUS	57	–	–	1	1	3	1	2	–	7	7	1	–	–	**128**
Kevin Magnussen	DK	40	–	–	1	–	–	3	1	4	4	–	4	–	–	**62**
Felipe Massa	BR	250	–	11	13	17	21	21	25	17	14	21	14	16	15	**1124**
Felipe Nasr	BR	39	–	–	–	–	–	1	1	–	1	3	1	–	–	**29**
Esteban Ocon	F	9	–	–	–	–	–	–	–	–	–	–	–	–	–	**–**
Jolyon Palmer	GB	20	–	–	–	–	–	–	–	–	–	–	1	–	–	**1**
Sergio Pérez	MEX	114	–	–	2	5	1	5	7	9	11	11	2	–	3	**367**
Kimi Räikkönen	FIN	252	1	20	32	32	21	19	17	12	11	9	10	16	43	**1360**
Daniel Ricciardo	AUS	109	–	4	5	9	9	6	5	6	4	5	9	1	8	**616**
Nico Rosberg	D	206	1	23	25	9	11	16	16	15	10	10	9	30	20	**1594.5**
Carlos Sainz	E	40	–	–	–	–	–	3	1	5	6	2	–	–	–	**64**
Stoffel Vandoorne	B	1	–	–	–	–	–	–	–	–	–	1	–	–	–	**1**
Max Verstappen	NL	40	–	1	4	2	5	1	2	2	5	3	2	–	1	**253**
Sebastian Vettel	D	178	4	42	20	24	22	15	8	3	6	2	–	46	28	**2108**
Pascal Wehrlein	D	21	–	–	–	–	–	–	–	–	–	1	–	–	–	**1**

Note: As is now common practice, drivers retiring on the formation lap are not counted as having started. Where races have been subjected to a restart, those retiring during an initial race are included as having started (Alonso and Räikkönen in Belgium, 2001 are affected).

ALL-TIME RECORDS: 2016

STARTS

Rubens Barrichello	323
Michael Schumacher	307
Jenson Button	305
Fernando Alonso	273
Riccardo Patrese	256
Kimi Räikkönen	252
Jarno Trulli	252
Felipe Massa	250
David Coulthard	246
Giancarlo Fisichella	229
Mark Webber	215
Gerhard Berger	210

FASTEST LAPS

Michael Schumacher	77
Kimi Räikkönen	43
Alain Prost	41
Lewis Hamilton	31
Nigel Mansell	30
Jim Clark	28
Sebastian Vettel	28
Mika Häkkinen	25
Niki Lauda	24
Juan Manuel Fangio	23
Nelson Piquet	23
Fernando Alonso	22

WINS

Michael Schumacher	91
Lewis Hamilton	53
Alain Prost	51
Sebastian Vettel	42
Ayrton Senna	41
Fernando Alonso	32
Nigel Mansell	31
Jackie Stewart	27
Jim Clark	25
Niki Lauda	25
Juan Manuel Fangio	24
Nelson Piquet	23
Nico Rosberg	23

POLE POSITIONS

Michael Schumacher	68
Ayrton Senna	65
Lewis Hamilton	61
Sebastian Vettel	46
Jim Clark	33
Alain Prost	33
Nigel Mansell	32
Nico Rosberg	30
Juan Manuel Fangio	29
Mika Häkkinen	26
Niki Lauda	24
Nelson Piquet	24

PODIUMS

Michael Schumacher	155
Alain Prost	106
Lewis Hamilton	104
Fernando Alonso	97
Sebastian Vettel	86
Kimi Räikkönen	84
Ayrton Senna	80
Rubens Barrichello	68
David Coulthard	62
Nelson Piquet	60
Nigel Mansell	59
Nico Rosberg	57

YOUNGEST STARTERS

Max Verstappen	17y 166d
Jaime Alguersuari	19y 125d
Mike Thackwell	19y 182d
Ricardo Rodriguez	19y 208d
Fernando Alonso	19y 218d
Esteban Tuero	19y 320d
Chris Amon	19y 324d
Daniil Kvyat	19y 324d
Esteban Ocon	19y 346d
Sebastian Vettel	19y 349d
Eddie Cheever	20y 53d
Jenson Button	20y 53d

YOUNGEST WINNERS

Max Verstappen	18y 228d
Sebastian Vettel	21y 73d
Fernando Alonso	22y 26d
Bruce McLaren	22y 104d
Lewis Hamilton	22y 154d
Kimi Räikkönen	23y 157d
Robert Kubica	23y 184d
Jacky Ickx	23y 188d
Michael Schumacher	23y 240d
Emerson Fittipaldi	23y 296d
Mike Hawthorn	24y 86d
Jody Scheckter	24y 131d

YOUNGEST CHAMPIONS

Sebastian Vettel	23y 134d
Lewis Hamilton	23y 300d
Fernando Alonso	24y 58d
Emerson Fittipaldi	25y 273d
Michael Schumacher	25y 314d
Niki Lauda	26y 197d
Jacques Villeneuve	26y 200d
Jim Clark	27y 188d
Kimi Räikkönen	28y 4d
Jochen Rindt	28y 169d
Ayrton Senna	28y 223d
James Hunt	29y 56d

YOUNGEST ON POLE

Sebastian Vettel	21y 73d
Fernando Alonso	21y 237d
Rubens Barrichello	22y 97d
Lewis Hamilton	22y 154d
Andrea de Cesaris	22y 308d
Nico Hülkenberg	23y 80d
Robert Kubica	23y 121d
Jacky Ickx	23y 216d
Kimi Räikkönen	23y 255d
David Coulthard	24y 13d
Jenson Button	24y 97d
Eugenio Castellotti	24y 238d

WORLD CHAMPIONSHIPS

Michael Schumacher	7	Jackie Stewart	3	Giuseppe Farina	1	Jochen Rindt	1
Juan Manuel Fangio	5	Fernando Alonso	2	Mike Hawthorn	1	Keke Rosberg	1
Alain Prost	4	Alberto Ascari	2	Damon Hill	1	Nico Rosberg	1
Sebastian Vettel	4	Jim Clark	2	Phil Hill	1	Jody Scheckter	1
Jack Brabham	3	Emerson Fittipaldi	2	Denny Hulme	1	John Surtees	1
Lewis Hamilton	3	Mika Häkkinen	2	James Hunt	1	Jacques Villeneuve	1
Niki Lauda	3	Graham Hill	2	Alan Jones	1		
Nelson Piquet	3	Mario Andretti	1	Nigel Mansell	1		
Ayrton Senna	3	Jenson Button	1	Kimi Räikkönen	1		

321

COOKING WITH GAS

Above: Pierre Gasly had a great weight of expectation thrust upon him. The Frenchman delivered the goods with four wins and five podiums on his way to clinching the GP2 championship.

Photo: Red Bull Content Pool

Top right: Red Bull-backed Gasly harboured hopes of racing for Toro Rosso in 2017, but the opportunity did not arise and he must wait patiently for an F1 seat.

Above right: Disappointment for Prema's Antonio Giovinazzi after losing the title battle with his team-mate.

Right: Giovinazzi, who scored five wins to Gasly's four, staged a late charge for the title, but just fell short.

Photos: GP2 Media Services

IF the 2015 GP2 Series had been a one-sided affair, thanks to the domination of Stoffel Vandoorne, the 2016 edition could not have been less so, with ten different winners and three drivers heading to the final round in contention for the title.

No fewer than six of the previous year's top ten returned for another crack at the crown – runner-up Alexander Rossi, Rio Haryanto and Richie Stanaway having joined Vandoorne in departing for pastures new – with Sergey Sirotkin the *de facto* favourite having claimed the bronze medal in 2015.

The Russian enhanced his chances by slipping into the ART cockpit vacated by Vandoorne, while fifth overall Mitch Evans, seventh-placed Raffaele Marciello and eighth man Pierre Gasly also decided on a change of scenery, joining Campos, Russian Time and series newcomer Prema Racing respectively. The Frenchman went into the season chasing a carrot familiar to the outgoing champion, the lure of an F1 seat dangling in front of him courtesy of his Red Bull backing. For a driver without a GP2 win to his name, however, it appeared a stiff task, especially since he had joined a series novice, even one as widely proven as Prema.

Alex Lynn and Nobuharu Matsushita were the other top-ten finishers to return, sticking with outgoing champion DAMS and ART for a second season respectively. The Briton, who continued to enjoy a fruitful relationship with F1 team Williams, was joined by Canadian Nicholas Latifi, who committed to a full GP2 season for the first time as DAMS attempted to wrest the teams' title back from its French rival.

Elsewhere, Racing Engineering replaced Indycar-bound Rossi with Norman Nato, pairing the mercurial Frenchman with well-funded Brit Jordan King; and Russian Time retained Artem Markelov to form an experienced line-up alongside Marciello, but the remaining combinations appeared either

unproven or uninspired. The rookie cohort was led by a pair of junior series runners-up in Luca Ghiotto, who joined Trident from GP3, and European F3's Antonio Giovinazzi at Prema, while both Jimmy Eriksson and Marvin Kirchhöfer – race winners in GP3 – offered intriguing potential at Arden and Carlin.

The grid would be slightly smaller than usual, however, with Prema taking up the entry previously held by Daiko Team Lazarus, but both Hilmer Motorsport and Status Grand Prix – the latter with no drivers signed on the very eve of its second season – falling by the wayside.

This time, the title fight would not be resolved in Sochi, for the simple fact that the former Olympic Park had dropped off the schedule, along with series stalwart Bahrain, which had held two rounds in 2015. In their place came new events on the streets of Baku, accompanying the European Grand Prix in Azerbaijan, and Sepang, which had previously featured heavily in the GP2 Asia Series. Germany also returned, having taken a finance-enforced year out, to form a midsummer double-header with Hungary.

With Bahrain off the schedule, the season opener reverted to Barcelona in May, the comparatively late start allowing for three pre-season tests to bring teams and drivers up to speed. That appeared to have served Prema well, for Gasly topped practice and took pole to add to the three with which he had closed 2015. Victory would still not come his way, however, the Frenchman struggling on the soft Pirellis and dropping to third. He bettered that with second spot in Sunday's sprint to leave the Circuit de Catalunya with the points lead, but his six-point advantage could have been even greater.

Gasly could equally have been trailing Sirotkin on Sunday evening, however, the Russian having been poised to challenge Nato for the lead of the feature when he spun and stalled. Forced to start from 21st on Sunday, he carved his

way through to 11th to serve notice of his pace, but was already playing catch-up.

If Gasly was frustrated by his lack of ultimate success in Spain, he was fit to burst in Monaco, where 15th and 13th were the result of a crash in practice, missing the weigh-bridge in qualifying and hitting Jimmy Eriksson in race one. At least he had a few points on the board, however, unlike Sirotkin, who again left with only the pole-position bonus, after crashing out of second place in the feature and posting another DNF in race two.

All that left an unlikely pair at the top of the standings, with Barcelona feature winner Nato emerging as a surprise pace-setter. The Frenchman, erratic in his rookie season, was clearly flourishing at Racing Engineering and definitely felt that he should have won the main event in Monaco as well. That he didn't was due to Markelov's uncanny pace under the virtual safety car, which had allowed him to convert a late stop for tyres into a contentious victory and second in the standings. Lynn also moved ahead of former team-mate Gasly with another solid weekend, adding fourth and fifth in Monaco to the sprint race win he had picked up in Spain.

Amazingly, given his reputation as a solid, if unspectacular, pedaller, Markelov left round three – on the brand-new street circuit encompassing the old and new parts of Baku – with the championship lead, despite only having added to his tally with fifth place in the sprint race. A chaotic Azerbaijan week-end served to close up the standings, with erstwhile leader Nato having posted two retirements – the first after surviving a lap-one clash with Gasly – and Sirotkin finally putting his season on track with a brace of podium finishes. Of greater note, however, was the emergence of both Marciello, who had been lurking on the fringes of the top five after scoring in each of the races to that point, and Giovinazzi who, after not posting a scoring finish in either Spain or Monaco, vaulted into contention with a victory double in Baku.

The Italian, who had excelled on street circuits in the latter days of his F3 career, opened his account with pole position before controlling proceedings in the feature. Starting eighth

Above: Raffaele Marciello was ultra-consistent for Russian Time. There were no wins, but the Italian made the podium six times and finished every race.

Top right: Artem Markelov's uncanny pace under the virtual safety car allowed the Russian to convert a late stop for tyres into a contentious victory in race one at Monte Carlo.

Above right: Trident's Luca Ghiotto had an impressive first GP2 season, which was topped by a win in Malaysia.

Above far right: Canadian Nicholas Lafiti scored a second place for DAMS in the first race at Barcelona, but delivered little else thereafter.

Right: Sergey Sirotkin made a rocky start to his season, but the Russian put himself into title contention with a number of classy drives in the second half of the year.

Photos: GP2 Media Services

in the sprint should not have led to a second win, especially after he had fallen back with an engine glitch, but, on a track that blended wide open stretches with confines as tight as any in Monaco, Giovinazzi benefited from some Matsushita-inspired madness at the front of the field to record the first double since Davide Valsecchi had managed the same in Bahrain four years earlier.

Perhaps more remarkable still was that the Italian was chased across the line by his team-mate, Gasly having risen from 19th on the grid following his earlier DNF. The pair ended the weekend split by a single point, Giovinazzi ahead and only eight points adrift of Markelov, while Marciello closed to within two of Gasly heading to the Red Bull Ring.

Gasly would have liked nothing more than to win at the track owned and refurbished by his paymasters, but had to cede the front row to Sirotkin and Giovinazzi, before being put on the back foot by spinning out of the lead when the heavens opened over Styria. Giovinazzi also dropped out, the result of alternator failure, and, when Sirotkin fell back during the subsequent return to slicks, Marciello completed an unexpected podium trio behind Campos duo Evans and Sean Gelael, both of whom had risen from mid-grid starts.

Marciello took over at the top of the table after adding fourth place on Sunday, while Evans's victory helped propel the Kiwi from tenth to second overall, such was the close nature of the championship battle. Gasly, meanwhile, slipped out of the top five, falling behind Oliver Rowland, who found himself sandwiched between King and Lynn on an all-British Sunday podium.

The standings had a fifth different leader in as many rounds after Silverstone, a brace of podium finishes on home soil continuing Rowland's ascent, but the bigger news concerned the end of Gasly's drought, which had stretched far beyond GP2. The Frenchman, the victim of a traffic accident on the way to the circuit on Friday, was again beaten to pole, this time by Nato and an ill-timed red flag, but he bounced back to overcome his countryman in a battle of race management in the feature.

Giovinazzi kept tabs on his team-mate by climbing from fifth to second, while, running with the unfancied MP Motorsport squad, Rowland returned to the scene of his GP2 debut to complete the top three from ninth on the grid. The Briton repeated the feat on Sunday, although again the glory went to countryman King, who converted reverse-grid pole into victory for the second meeting in succession.

The eventual title protagonists began to move clear of the pack as the series reached its halfway point at the Hungaroring, where Gasly repeated his Silverstone feature-race win, albeit after a brief scare from Marciello. The Italian was only fourth at the chequered flag, leaving Giovinazzi to keep Gasly honest at the front, limiting his gains. The rookie failed to score in the sprint race, however, having hit Matsushita and picked up a penalty, which allowed Gasly to leave Budapest with an 11-point advantage.

If anyone thought that the Frenchman, his tail up, would now fulfil his destiny and ease away from his pursuers, they were forced to think again in Germany, where a disastrous start to the weekend led not only to his exclusion from the feature, after his extinguisher had emptied itself into the cockpit, but also the loss of his points lead – to the driver who had gone to Hockenheim eighth overall!

Sergey Sirotkin's season had been in free fall through the first five rounds, his podium double in Baku surrounded by a litany of errors. However, buoyed by a return to form in Hungary – where he had finished third in the feature, before claiming a first win of the year in the sprint – he surpassed even that in Germany, winning on Saturday, despite having to retake his mandatory pit stop, and then coming through the pack to finish second on Sunday.

That was enough to put the Russian on level terms with Gasly at the head of the table, with Marciello – third and seventh at Hockenheim – 11 points adrift heading into the summer break. The four-week hiatus did not serve Sirotkin well, however, and his season reverted to type, with a brace of penalties at Spa preventing him from adding to his tally. Gasly needed no second bidding, claiming a third feature

race in four, before bolstering his renewed advantage with fourth in the sprint. Although team-mate Giovinazzi limited the damage with victory on Sunday, Gasly's lead was the biggest of the year as the series bridged the short gap to Monza.

With Sirotkin suffering another pointless weekend, the top three cemented their position at the head of the standings, Giovinazzi 'winning' on home soil after the safety car mistakenly picked up team-mate Gasly, rather than the lead group that included the Italian. Giovinazzi added third on Sunday for good measure to trim Gasly's lead from 17 to ten, even though subsequently the Frenchman chased countryman Nato home in the sprint.

Marciello also enjoyed being back in his motherland, taking second in the sprint to help put clear air between third and fourth in the points table, but it remained notable that the Russian Time driver had yet to win a race, remaining in the title hunt courtesy of some remarkable consistency. He was unable to break his duck in Malaysia, although finishes of sixth and second ensured that he went to the final round as a mathematical contender, albeit needing to secure the maximum 40 points on offer while hoping that his rivals faltered badly.

Gasly would also head for Yas Marina hoping for a mistake by his team-mate after their Sepang weekends had diverged spectacularly. Although the three title contenders would chase Luca Ghiotto across the line on Sunday, Giovinazzi's third win in four – bridging Spa, Monza and Malaysia – was achieved while pole-sitter Gasly lamented an unwanted start-line anti-stall intervention. The victory served to swap the Prema pair in the overall standings, handing Giovinazzi a seven-point cushion and the chance to emulate Nico Rosberg, Lewis Hamilton and Nico Hülkenberg as only the fourth newcomer to win the title.

Above: Williams development driver Alex Lynn took three wins for DAMS, including the season's sprint race finale at Abu Dhabi.

Top right: In his second season with Racing Engineering, Jordan King stepped up to the plate and delivered two sprint race wins.

Top far right: ART Grand Prix's Nobuharu Matsushita took a runaway win in the Monaco sprint race.

Above right: Series veteran Mitch Evans scored a feature race win in Austria for Campos Racing, but failed to make another podium appearance during the year.

Above far right: Norman Nato's stand-out performance in the safety car-punctuated Monaco feature race deserved more than second place. The Frenchman did have the consolation of winning in Barcelona and Monza, however.

Right: Oliver Rowland made a flying start to his first GP2 season, but his challenge faded against the better-funded teams later in the season.

Photos: GP2 Media Services

Gasly had spent the eight-week break between the final rounds mentally preparing himself to cope with the pressure of having to overhaul his team-mate, and it paid off immediately, as he produced what he called one of his best laps in GP2 to claim pole position and the four points that went with it. With Giovinazzi only sixth on the grid, Gasly was able to focus on leading from the front in Saturday's feature, eventually coming home seven seconds clear of the pursuit.

The Italian had made up one place early on, but could not rise higher than fifth on the road, conceding a 19-point swing for a 12-point deficit heading into a sprint race that only offered 15 for the win. When again he crossed the line fifth, the crown was officially Gasly's, even though the Frenchman had been forced to cede the final point at the close.

Gasly's eventual winning margin was eight points, although Giovinazzi enjoyed a 5-4 record as the Prema drivers took nine of the season's wins between them. With the pair having battled over the drivers' title, it was no surprise that Prema also walked off with the teams' championship, having wrapped up the silverware one round from home. Racing Engineering and Russian Time went to Abu Dhabi split by just five points, and despite Markelov rediscovering the podium, it was the Spanish outfit that eventually claimed second spot, with outgoing champion ART a close fourth.

Marciello's failure to win for a second straight year eventually prevented him from finishing third overall, on count-back, as Sirotkin overcame the 23-point deficit that had divided them heading to the finale. Marciello's racecraft, which had attracted attention from both Ferrari and Sauber in previous seasons, was evident throughout as he kept racking up the points, but he never quite had enough to reach the top step, which cost him when ranged against his rival's successes at the Hungaroring and Hockenheim.

Sirotkin was also sublime on occasion, but his season was liberally peppered with mistakes and misfortune, leaving his F1 future in limbo, despite making his free practice debut with Renault in Sochi.

The Russian was clear of the Racing Engineering pair and their personal battle for a top-five championship finish. King and Nato arrived in Abu Dhabi level on points, but a scoreless weekend for the Briton eventually handed his team-mate the advantage. Both could have expected more from their seasons, but Nato's title bid unravelled with a double DNF in Baku and Lady Luck denied him additional podiums, most notably in Belgium. King, meanwhile, emulated Marciello's consistency and matched his team-mate's two wins, before making his F1 weekend debut with Manor at the US Grand Prix.

The Briton also fell behind countryman Lynn, after the DAMS driver added a third race win in the Abu Dhabi sprint to rise from ninth to sixth in the final standings. Lynn dovetailed his campaign with the role of Williams F1 development driver and said that his sights were on securing a role in either the top flight or Formula E, rather than returning to GP2 for a third crack at the title.

After a slow start, Ghiotto emerged as a steady points scorer, picking up momentum as the year went on, before culminating in his sprint-race win at Sepang and eighth in the final table. The Italian, GP3 runner-up in 2015, will be one to watch if he returns in 2017. He ended the season by edging out Rowland after neither added to their tally at the finale.

Having vaulted to the top of the table after Silverstone, Rowland steadily faded as he failed to better fifth place at any subsequent round. He went into the finale just two points ahead of fellow Brit Lynn, but a DNF and 11th at Yas Marina left him unable to rise from ninth overall.

Markelov rounded out the top ten, after overhauling former

Russian Time team-mate Evans, courtesy of his podium in the final feature of the season. The Russian never came close to repeating his Monaco victory, while Evans likewise fell short of matching his Austrian success as his attention also turned towards Formula E.

Matsushita, having been forced to miss the Red Bull Ring thanks to his antics in Azerbaijan, also found enough in the Emirates to pass the Kiwi in the final standings. The Japanese ace was a race winner in his sophomore season, taking the other side of the Monaco double-header, but he suffered a nondescript second half that left him in championship no man's land before claiming a tactically sound second spot behind Gasly in Abu Dhabi.

Six other drivers made it to the podium in 2016, with Gelael (Austria), Kirchhöfer (Monaco) and Latifi (Barcelona) all claiming runner-up honours early in the year, and a returning Johnny Cecotto Jr doing likewise in a Yas Marina cameo. All trailed rookie Gustav Malja and veteran Arthur Pic in the overall standings, however, despite the latter pair topping out with a third place apiece, at Monza and Hockenheim respectively.

In all, 26 drivers started races during the season, all but four scoring points along the way.

For all his efforts, the new champion was not certain to land a race seat in F1 for 2017. While Giovinazzi's break-out campaign landed him a simulator role with Ferrari before the year was out, Gasly might have to look outside the top flight. The Frenchman had seemed certain that he would be a Toro Rosso driver in 2017, only to have that door slammed in his face long before the title was decided. With F3 champion Lance Stroll having bypassed GP2 en route to a Williams seat, and Gasly considering a Red Bull-funded sojourn in Japan's Super Formula, can the premier feeder series' role again be called into question?

CHARLES THE FIRST

Above: ART Grand Prix's Charles Leclerc emerged as a convincing GP3 champion. The Monegasque, with F1 testing duties for Haas already under his belt, seems destined for the top.

Top right: Nyck de Vries, Antonio Fuoco and Matt Parry share the race-one podium at Hockenheim. All three won a race during the year.

Photos: Ferrari Media

Above right: With four wins in his debut season, Alexander Albon was the main rival to team-mate Leclerc.

Photo: GP3 Media

Right: Jack Aitken, Jake Hughes and Charles Leclerc took over the Hockenheim podium after the sprint race.

Photo: Ferrari Media

Below right: Arden International's Jake Dennis ended the season on a high note with a podium in Abu Dhabi.

Photo: GP3 Media

LIKE its GP2 sibling, the 2016 GP3 Series also featured a three-way title battle heading to the final round in Abu Dhabi. Unlike GP2, however, the protagonists had emerged very early on.

Series newcomers Charles Leclerc and Alexander Albon left the opening round occupying the top two positions in the standings and, but for one month through Spa and Monza, remained there until the finale, with second-year veteran Antonio Fuoco giving vain pursuit as the top three pulled clear of the chasing pack before mid-season.

When Fuoco failed to claim pole for the Yas Marina sprint, he fell by the wayside, leaving the ART duo to squabble over the crown. The teams' title had been salted away already by the French powerhouse, which, once again, appeared to have a serious edge over the competition, not just in the calibre of driver it attracted, but also in its engineering prowess.

Given that the field had been entrusted with the new Dallara GP3/16 only at the start of the year, wrapping up the title after race one at Monza underlined ART's superiority in a season when teams were permitted to run four cars to make up for a shortfall in entries, stalwarts Carlin and Status having bowed out. Multiple GP2 champion DAMS joined the fray, but only seven teams lined up for the opening round, marking a seven-year low for the series.

As has become the norm, the campaign kicked off at the Circuit de Catalunya in Barcelona and comprised nine rounds in total, but any sense of rhythm was eliminated by lengthy hiatuses at either end of a tightly packed mid-year calendar.

That was of no concern to the drivers on that Spanish weekend, however, with both Leclerc and Albon seizing a victory apiece from third on the grid. The Monegasque had started his week by racking up enough F1 miles at Fiorano to qualify to run Friday sessions for the new Haas team, and he ended it with a four-point championship advantage over his team-mate.

Leclerc failed to score in the Barcelona sprint after a bad start, and also recorded only one scoring finish at round two in Austria, but, once again, in Saturday's feature race, he stood on the top step. Although Albon managed to rack up a brace of second places, Leclerc actually left the Red Bull Ring with a narrowly enhanced advantage, while Fuoco

moved into third overall after repeating his Sunday third place from the opening round.

After a seven-week gap between rounds, the Austrian event sparked a run of four in five weeks through July. At Silverstone, the top three in points annexed five of the six available podium spots. Leclerc did not win this time, but was second and third respectively as Albon and Fuoco took out the Saturday and Sunday races, the Thai driver closing to within two points of his team-mate overall. With Fuoco opening up a 30-point cushion over fourth place, the title battle also began to morph into its final form.

Albon won again in Hungary, taking the sprint on Sunday, and the points difference over third-placed Leclerc was briefly enough to reverse their positions at the head of the table. Normal service was resumed just a week later, however, as another podium finish for the Monegasque – on a weekend when Albon failed to make the top three in either race – resulted in him leaving Hockenheim with a restored three-point margin.

The gap grew further when the season resumed in Belgium after its summer break, Albon suffering his worst results combination of the year to net just two points, while Leclerc returned to the winner's circle and added another four points on Sunday for good measure.

Such was Albon's Spa misfortune – a mistake had cost him his qualifying lap and left him to salvage ninth from 17th on the Saturday grid – that Fuoco was able to overhaul him in the standings, and the Italian remained ahead, albeit with a reduced margin, through the Monza weekend. None of the title contenders was able to make the podium on Saturday in Italy, but Albon and Fuoco clawed back some of the extended advantage Leclerc had earned in that race when the Monegasque was taken out by the fourth ART car of Nirei Fukuzumi in the sprint.

With a 32-point gap separating him from the lead and just two rounds to go, Albon needed to make a move as the series took on Sepang for the first time. He responded in the best possible fashion by winning with fastest lap in race one. Leclerc, however, limited that damage with points for pole and third on the road as the Arden team continued its recent upturn in form to cause both title contenders a headache.

scorers on Sunday, leaving Leclerc's margin of victory at 25 points, a figure that failed to represent the intensity of his battle with Albon. Fuoco was a further 20 points adrift as the final flag fell on 2016.

The chase behind the top three was something of a shape changer, with different names seemingly in fourth and beyond after every round. By season's end, however, it had boiled down to a battle between the third ART entry of Nyck de Vries and the Arden pairing of Jake Dennis and Jack Aitken. The Dutch rookie – who had swapped a reasonable season in FR3.5 for what initially had appeared to be a step back to GP3 – had the better of the first half of the year, despite a few too many incidents with his own team-mates. Dennis and Aitken came on strong in part two, however, beginning at Spa, where Arden worked its magic on tyre management following a late switch of Pirelli compounds for the Belgian weekend.

Despite picking up three podium finishes through the first six rounds, de Vries did not win until the Monza sprint, by which time both Dennis (Monza feature) and Aitken (Spa sprint) already had P1 against their names. Dennis won for a second time in the reverse-grid race at Sepang, before de Vries made hay in the Abu Dhabi opener, but with the Arden cars finishing on the podium behind him, the trio went into the final race of the year covered by just six points. There, the reverse grid counted against de Vries, who became embroiled in a scrap with Fuoco, while Aitken and Dennis pursued podium positions. Second and fourth respectively weren't enough to reverse the British pair in the points table, but they kept McLaren protégé de Vries at bay and underlined Arden's rise to second in the team standings.

There was a similar showdown over seventh overall, with Matt Parry heading into the finale desperately trying to repel Fukuzumi and Jake Hughes. The Welshman had controlled the Hungaroring feature to take his first win at GP3 level and appeared to be on a roll, effectively carrying the Koiranen effort single-handedly as he moved into fourth overall before adding another podium in Germany. From there, however, his season bore an uncanny resemblance to 2015, bad luck at Spa and Monza derailing his effort.

Parry and Hughes also developed something of a fatal attraction, not least in Belgium, where they came together terminally in both races. However, when the DAMS driver added a second win in the Abu Dhabi sprint to a maiden success in race two at Hockenheim, it was enough to join Fukuzumi – who finished third in the final race – in demoting his rival to ninth overall.

India's Arjun Maini rounded out the top ten, despite having missed the opening two double-headers. He had posted second place behind Albon in Hungary among a solid set of results. That was enough for him to finish ahead of the only other race winner of the season, Ralph Boschung, who had missed Spa and withdrawn before the flyaways. Haas protégé Santino Ferrucci belied his baby face with some hard-nosed racing, but a third and two fourths were not enough to lift him into the top ten, while Steijn Schothorst found his feet too late in the season to better 13th overall.

For the second straight season, Oscar Tunjo failed to take in more than half the campaign, having departed before Silverstone and only reappeared for a one-off at Spa. In that time, the Colombian had still managed to rack up a podium at the opening round, but his tenuous top-14 championship position slipped at the final round as Kevin Jörg and Alex Palou overhauled him in Abu Dhabi. Matevos Isaakyan, Sandy Stuvik, Konstantin Tereschenko and Artur Janosz rounded out the top 20 in a year when 27 drivers made at least one start, although the Thai, like Palou, appeared unable to reproduce his 2015 form when it mattered.

Despite suggestions that winning the title would confirm Leclerc as Esteban Gutiérrez's replacement at Haas, the Monegasque looked certain to head for GP2 in 2017. Another immediate impact at that level, however, would likely make his stay a short one.

He also finished in front of his team-mate on Sunday, leaving Albon with a major task at Abu Dhabi.

Eighth and a DNF for Fuoco in Malaysia left the Italian clinging forlornly to his title hopes, but when he failed to go fastest in qualifying at Yas Marina, his ambitions received a fatal blow, leaving an ART head-to-head for the crown.

Although Albon took another four points off Leclerc's advantage with pole at the final round, he still trailed the Monegasque by 21 points, with a maximum 44 on the table across the two remaining races. His bid remained alive until a mistake midway through the feature sent the No. 3 machine bouncing heavily over the kerbs to sustain race-ending damage. That handed the title to Leclerc, even though he also posted a DNF.

Coming from a long way down the grid in the final race, neither contender – nor Fuoco for that matter – troubled the

FORMULA V8 3.5 REVIEW by OLLIE BARSTOW

DILLMANN DELIVERS

Above: After switching teams to AVF, Tom Dillmann brought his vast experience to bear in claiming a closely-fought championship contest with Louis Delétraz.

Above right: A champion in two single-seater categories, Dillmann added the Formula V8 3.5 title to his German F3 crown, won back in 2010.

Top right: The 19-year-old Delétraz may have been a rookie, but he took Dillmann all the way to the wire in a thrilling championship battle.

Right: Fortec's Delétraz took two wins on his way to the runner-up spot and earned himself a drive with Carlin Racing in the final GP2 meeting of 2016.

Photos: Formula V8 3.5

IT may have been a new era for one of motorsport's leading single-seater series in 2016, but the inaugural Formula V8 3.5 Championship was still one for the history books, a campaign that simmered towards a gripping climax between two worthy adversaries. Eventual champion Tom Dillmann may have been the long-time leader in the overall standings, but he was made to work very hard for his first major single-seater title against a formidable foe, Louis Delétraz.

The two drivers were at different stages in their careers. Dillmann – an old hand with credits at F3, GP3, GP2 and sportscar level – was the experience to Delétraz's youth and burgeoning talent; they would meet in the middle in a tense final-round showdown that ebbed and flowed in momentum.

Ultimately, experience won the day, Dillmann snatching the title in the very last race of the year, although the outcome was only the concluding chapter of a championship that faced more battles than merely those on track in 2016.

Indeed, while the Formula V8 3.5 Championship certainly looked and sounded familiar, it did so without the Renault backing that for more than a decade had developed the series from a fringe single-seater class into a genuine rung on the junior development ladder.

Initially, there had been fears that the series, which had honed the talents of an impressive alumni of drivers, including Daniel Ricciardo, Jules Bianchi, Robert Kubica, Kevin Magnussen and Carlos Sainz, could not survive without the finance and credibility brought by the French firm. However, thanks to the determined efforts of RPM Racing – existing promoters of the series – a deal was reached to go it alone.

Even so, the organisers had a tough time in enticing teams to follow their lead, with former title-winning outfits DAMS, Tech 1 Racing and Draco, as well as Pons, confirming that they would leave at the end of 2015. Worse was to follow within sight of the season beginning when Carlin followed suit, along with Strakka Racing, who quit despite having signed drivers.

Only four existing teams committed to the revised series – Fortec, Arden, Lotus and AVF. Fortec, champions in 2015 with Oliver Rowland, turned once more to the Formula Renault 2.0 Eurocup for its lead contender, signing runner-up Delétraz alongside Pietro Fittipaldi, son of two-times F1 World Champion Emerson.

The Charouz-run Lotus team led with ex-GP2 driver René Binder and second-year runner Roy Nissany, while Arden established itself as a pre-season favourite by re-signing two-times race winner Egor Orudzhev, to be joined by Aurélien Panis. Dillmann, meanwhile, was another returnee in 2016, heading up Adrian Valles' AVF team alongside Force India F1 development driver Alfonso Celis Jr.

New for 2016, Spirit of Race entered for the first time under the otherwise familiar SMP Racing banner and lured 2015 FR3.5 runner-up Matthieu Vaxivière, alongside youngster Matevos Isaakyan, while Teo Martin Motorsport signed Beitske Visser to join Yu Kanamaru. RP Motorsport started with Vitor Baptista and Johnny Cecotto, and Durango entered a single car for Giuseppe Cipriani.

With 18 races over nine rounds forging the path towards title glory, a somewhat meagre 15-strong grid took to the first round of the year in Motorland Aragon, the Alcaniz circuit raising the curtain on a season that generally would demonstrate quality racing to negate the somewhat stark dip in quantity.

Having ended the season as top rookie in 2015, Egor Orudzhev took pole in the first race, suggesting no loss of pace over the winter. However, a clumsy mistake early on while leading, when he ran wide at Turn Eight – before smashing his front wing against the kerb as he returned to the circuit at Turn Nine – ended his race. With a stall in race two consigning him to another non-score, the weekend would set the tone for a season in which Orudzhev would exhibit title-winning pace, if not luck.

Instead, it was Delétraz who made his mark with victory on his full-time FV8 debut in the Fortec with a well-controlled

success over Vaxivière and Dillmann, three of the more anticipated title protagonists.

There would be less fortune for the Swiss driver in race two. The youngster was tipped into a spin by Vaxivière – who retired on the spot – but showed impressive fighting spirit with a charge back to fifth. Up ahead, Arden's Panis claimed his maiden win, his better getaway over Dillmann having made the difference; Binder completed the podium.

Next, it was on to the tight, twisty Hungaroring 'dustbowl', where Dillmann appeared to be well on course for his, and also AVF's, first ever win in race one, leading from the start and establishing a sizeable gap. When a safety car period bunched up the order in the closing stages, however, an off on cold tyres at the restart opened the door for Cecotto to sweep in and claim an unlikely win. It was the first success for the new RP Motorsport team, but unfortunately for the Venezuelan – a race winner at GP2 level – it did not mark the start of his title intentions. In fact, Cecotto competed in just one more event before dwindling funds consigned him to the sidelines.

Despite his race-one disappointment, Dillmann made amends in the treacherously wet conditions of the second race, albeit not before surviving another off-track excursion and having to fend off a spirited charge by Nissany in the closing stages.

Having started from pole, Dillmann seemed once again to have scuppered his hopes after sliding on to the grass, ceding the lead to Vaxivière. When the latter waited too long to make his mandatory pit stop and was caught up behind a safety car, however, Dillmann – who had stopped before the caution – regained his advantage.

Even so, he still had to fend off a remarkable effort by Nissany, who, having spun to last just as the race started, at times was lapping two seconds faster in the closing stages to get on to Dillmann's tail by the final lap. He couldn't find

a way through, however, settling for second behind the new championship leader.

With the high-speed stretches of Spa-Francorchamps greeting the drivers for round three, it was a weekend for two of the more experienced drivers to show their less seasoned rivals the way, with Orudzhev and Vaxivière sharing the spoils. It could have been a double win for Vaxivière had he not had his pole position in race one taken away for a technical infringement. That opened the door for Orudzhev to put his faltering season on track with a hard-fought win over Dillmann.

Vaxivière made amends in the sodden conditions of race two, albeit only after long-time leader Dillmann had spun in worsening weather two laps from home. Despite the spin, Dillmann recovered to secure a sixth podium in six races, with team-mate Celis Jr completing the podium in a rare show of form for the Mexican racer.

With Paul Ricard having made a return to the schedule in 2016, Vaxivière offered hope of a home win with pole position in race one. However, a tremendous start from Orudzhev – a deft ability he would demonstrate on more than one occasion over the course of the year – allowed him to climb from third to first for a lead he'd maintain to the end as his French counterpart slipped back. Even so, he had to work hard to keep the determined Nissany behind him, the Israeli's robust attempt through the final corner leading to contact with Orudzhev, only for the Russian to hold firm and retain his lead to the chequered flag.

With the pair making up the front row for race two, this time Nissany got away well to assume an early lead, the youngster – son of former Minardi F1 test driver Chanoch Nissany – establishing a comfortable advantage in the Lotus.

However, a mistake that took him down an escape road meant that by the time he had made his pit stop, he'd return behind Delétraz. The Fortec man used his early change of

Above: Arden's Egor Orudzhev (7) steals the lead from Tom Dillmann (16) at the first corner during race one at the Circuit de Catalunya, on his way to his fifth win of the year.

Centre right, from top: Formula 2000 graduate Pietro Fittipaldi was learning the ropes with Fortec; an impressive Roy Nissany took three wins for Lotus; Dutch woman racer Beitske Visser was a consistent points scorer.

Above far right: Although a podium just eluded him, Yu Kanamaru had an encouraging sophomore season.

Top far right: Russian rookie Matevos Isaakyan, who also ran a full GP3 schedule in 2016, enjoyed a strong end to his V8 3.5 campaign, scoring a win at Jerez.

Above right: Two victories by Aurélien Panis helped Arden Morsport to take the teams' title.

Below right: In his third season in the series, Matthieu Vaxivière took two wins for SMP Racing.

Photos: Formula V8 3.5

tyres to jump ahead, clinging on until the chequered flag for his second win of the year, in front of Nissany and Orudzhev.

It was a timely win to make inroads on Dillmann's championship lead. With four of the nine rounds completed, however, the Frenchman was still comfortably out front, 22 points clear of Delétraz and 30 ahead of third-placed Panis.

It was a margin Dillmann would proceed to stretch during round five at Silverstone, despite not setting foot on the podium, as was the case for Delétraz. Marking the mid-point of the season, the British round was instead all about Nissany, the 21-year-old following his breakthrough podiums at Paul Ricard with two well-judged maiden wins.

Even so, it was a success tinged with controversy after he had collided with long-time leader Orudzhev in race one. The Russian had closed the door on his rival as they rounded Stowe, sending both into a spin. However, while Orudzhev had been forced to retire, their advantage over the pack was such that Nissany was able to rejoin in a lead he'd take to the chequered flag.

Race two was less contentious. Nissany took the lead from pole-sitter Vaxivière at Turn One and sprinted to a dominant win over Lotus team-mate Binder and Orudzhev.

Meanwhile, at the top of the standings, a pair of fourth-place results for Dillmann – compared with Delétraz's tenth- and sixth-place finishes – meant that the AVF driver headed to round six in Austria having eased his lead out to 32 points over Nissany, with Delétraz five points further back.

Delétraz looked poised to recover more ground to his rival at the Red Bull Ring with a pole position in race one. After being beaten to the first corner by SMP's Vaxivière, however, the Frenchman resisted the race-long attentions of his rival to secure a second win of the season.

Having completed the podium in race one, Dillmann would recover lost ground to Delétraz with a run to second place in race two, behind winner Panis, with his rival following up in fourth. Panis's win came at the expense of 18-year-old Isaakyan, the Russian having put in a spirited performance to lead from his maiden pole position, only to lose out to both Panis and Dillmann during the pit-stop window. Even so, third place marked his first podium of the season in the SMP Racing car.

With six rounds completed and three to go, despite having just a single win to his name after 12 races, Dillmann's eight podiums had allowed him to engineer a comfortable 32-point lead in the overall standings. It was a level of consistency that seemed to be putting him well on course towards the title with six races remaining.

Things would start to unravel for Dillmann from Monza, however, the Frenchman enduring an unusually lacklustre weekend around the high-speed Italian circuit. He was forced to pit in race one with technical issues, which left him out of the points for the first time in 2016. Then he struggled to eighth in race two. All of a sudden, his main rivals had the impetus to get back in the title fight.

This was especially true of Delétraz, whose second- and third-place finishes at Monza brought him right back into the mix, just 11 points behind his rival, while a third win of the year for Nissany put him on the cusp of a late challenge.

With the title battle invigorated, the fight would take a dramatic twist at Jerez after Dillmann and Delétraz came to blows in what threatened to become a pivotal moment for the championship. Dillmann had been leading Delétraz on the road when the latter attempted to make a pass for fourth. Instead, he collected his rival, sending him spinning into the gravel trap and out of the race.

With Delétraz going on to finish fourth, provisionally it put him one point ahead at the top of the standings. The stewards took a dim view of his actions, however, and subsequently levied a time penalty to demote him out of the points. That put Dillmann back in front.

It wasn't an advantage he'd retain for long, though, as Dillmann's stuttering form was at odds with a galvanised Delétraz. The Swiss driver's run to second place in race two, compared to his rival's eighth, allowed the youngster to ascend to the head of the standings by three points with just one round to go, and form seemingly on his side.

Mathematically, at least, seven drivers came into the Circuit de Catalunya finale with an opportunity to walk away with the title. Panis, Nissany, Orudzhev, Vaxivière and Binder were all within a shout of new leader Delétraz and Dillmann.

For many, though, the title fight was a two-horse race, with Delétraz the newly assumed favourite over a faltering

Dillmann. It was a status the Swiss driver would underline in race one, a comfortable second-place finish over Dillmann's third easing his lead out to six points with one race to go.

When Delétraz proceeded to put his Fortec on pole for the finale, with Dillmann sixth, the result seemed inevitable. But then a poor start dropped him immediately to fourth as Dillman rose to fifth. The playing field was already beginning to level.

When the pair swapped positions during their mandatory pit stops, Dillmann suddenly had the initiative to progress up the order and make the positions he needed to swing the momentum back in his favour. A series of superb laps allowed the Frenchman to pull away from Delétraz, and leapfrog Isaakyan and Nissany when they came in, putting him in the lead as his rival laboured in fourth.

With victory being enough for Dillmann to lift the title, regardless of where Delétraz finished, and though he had come into this race having scored only a single win all year, his second would prove remarkably timely. He crossed the line to take the chequered flag and with it the title.

It was a remarkable turnaround for a driver who, despite having led the standings for much of the year, had seemingly lost his momentum at the crucial moment. Though it remains to be seen whether Dillmann will follow in the wheel tracks of an impressive roll call of previous title winners by continuing his progression through the racing ranks, the result marks a welcome outcome for one of motorsport's most versatile competitors.

Despite an agonising runner-up result, 19-year-old Delétraz – son of former F1 driver Jean-Denis – nevertheless appears almost certain for greater success, his season's performance against an experienced rival belying his youth.

Behind the top two, three wins from the final five races catapulted Orudzhev up the leaderboard to third. With five victories to his name, the Russian had won more races than any other driver in 2016, but too many DNFs in the first half of the year – which dropped him 85 points behind after just six rounds – left him with too much to do to ever be a factor in the title hunt.

Similarly, Nissany made impressive gains over the course of the year in the Lotus, a third win at Monza amid seven podiums signalling an impressive rise to fourth, ahead of Panis. The Frenchman's title bid faded as the season progressed, however. But, with a total of seven wins between Panis and Orudzhev, Arden was still crowned team champion.

Vaxivière and Binder reeled off their seasons in sixth and seventh respectively, ahead of Teo Martin driver Kanamaru, Isaakyan – who had notched up an impressive maiden win at Jerez – and Fittipaldi rounding out the overall top ten.

Looking forward, despite meagre grid numbers for its inaugural season, there appears to be a bright future for FV8 3.5 as it prepares to go international for the first time, having secured a support slot on the FIA World Endurance Championship schedule. With the revised nine-round calendar now including overseas visits to Mexico City, Austin and Bahrain, it is a good opportunity for the championship to re-establish its quality and quantity for 2017.

A STROLL IN THE PARK

Above: Prema Powerteam's Lance Stroll on his way to victory at Hockenheim. The young Canadian took 14 wins from the 30 races.

Top right: Team-mate Maximillian Günther, with four wins, was runner-up to Stroll in the final standings.

Above right: With five straight wins to close out the season, Stroll was already on the fast track to Formula 1 with Williams in 2017.

Above far right: Günther kept Stroll honest for much of the season.

Right: Top rookie honours went to Sweden's Joel Erikson, who notched up a win at Spa on his way to an impressive fifth overall in the final standings.
Photos: FIA F3 Media

Below right: Sérgio Sette Câmara enjoyed Red Bull backing, but could only garner two podiums. However, the Brazilian did produce an eye-catching performance at Pau.
Photo: Red Bull

THERE were few reasons to argue against the widely-touted prediction that Lance Stroll would clinch the 2016 European Formula 3 Championship, on paper at least. With a year's experience under his belt, during which he had demonstrated encouraging pace – if a few rough edges – and a newly-acquired No. 1 status within the dominant Prema Powerteam, he came into the season with all the tools he needed to produce a convincing title charge. Predictions on paper are just that, though; Stroll still had to deliver.

Fast-forward five months. The fact that Stroll swept to the title not only comfortably, but also so dominantly as to impress the naysayers and – crucially – earn a direct path to Formula 1 with Williams, speaks volumes for the way he exceeded what had been lofty expectations.

Indeed, it had been a critical season for Stroll. Having captured the headlines for the wrong reasons during his maiden European F3 campaign, receiving more than one punishment for erratic driving, nonetheless he was a race winner by the year's end. That was enough to convince Prema that he'd earned a shot at leading the defence of the 2015 title it had won with Felix Rosenqvist.

Under substantial pressure not only to prove his maturity and lead a championship-winning team, but also to disprove the cynical perceptions of his wealthy background, as the son of billionaire businessman Lawrence Stroll, the 18-year-old achieved everything with which he was tasked. His sheer consistency during the opening half of the season set the foundation for an utterly dominant push to the title in the second half.

In truth, Stroll took time to establish some momentum, victory from the very first race of the year being his only trip to the top of the podium in the opening three triple-header rounds. Though he took until that ninth race to establish room atop the standings, thereafter he was never rivalled.

Despite Stroll's tentative start, Prema still had its bases covered in 2016 with an impressive four-man line-up, the remaining three comprising Maximillian Günther, reigning Japanese F3 champion Nick Cassidy and Formula 4 standout Ralf Aron. Between them, they ensured that a Prema driver led the standings from first lights to the final flag.

Indeed, while Stroll and Günther were winners at the Paul Ricard curtain-raiser, in race one and three respectively, a DNF for each, following a Turn One scuffle, meant that a brace of second-place finishes for Kiwi racer Cassidy was enough for him to leave France with the initial advantage over his team-mates.

From that point, Günther came to the fore in the sister car during round two at the Hungaroring with a trio of pole positions – making it five from the first six races. However, he would only go on to convert one of them into a victory in the second race of the weekend.

Even so, with two wins from the opening two rounds, Günther had established himself as a title contender, keeping Stroll on his toes. The German racer made a good early impression, following his off-season switch from Mücke to Prema. Furthermore, his early lead in the standings leaving Hungary could have been larger, had his efforts not been tempered somewhat by a DNF-inducing collision with George Russell while disputing the lead in a torrid race three. Stroll, meanwhile, favoured consistency, with one podium and three solid finishes, his more measured approach keeping him in range, if not in the headlines at this stage.

With Pau marking round three, Stroll's walk towards the head of the standings began in earnest around the iconic French street circuit. It could have been a march had he not stalled from pole in race one, which left him down in ninth. A climb to fourth in race two, however, followed by a second in race three was enough for him to leapfrog Günther – who could only manage a third and two non-scores – at the top of the standings by the end of the weekend.

Stroll left Pau with a 13-point advantage, but at no stage during the remainder of the season would the margin be so slim, the Canadian firmly asserting his authority on the championship from round four onwards at the Red Bull Ring.

Having finished second in race one around the picturesque Austrian circuit, Stroll's dominant wins in races two

and three – coupled to Günther's 3-6-3 results tally – suddenly swelled his advantage to 44 points, affirming his status as title favourite in comprehensive style.

When he pulled off an identical set of results around the streets of Nuremburg, at the Norisring, not only did he multiply his advantage over Günther, but also he headed into the second half of the season with what was already being deemed an insurmountable 86-point lead in the standings.

It was a trail of form Stroll would continue to follow during the latter half of the year, a trio of stuttering DNFs – for technical issues, rather than on-track mistakes – being negated entirely by a stunning run of results, such that by the end of the year, he had won at least one race from eight of the ten rounds.

Cruising to victory at Spa-Francorchamps, before adding another two at the Nürburgring and two more at Imola, Stroll subsequently was crowned champion for 2016 with one round to spare. It marked Prema's fourth consecutive European Formula 3 drivers' title, never mind its 2011 and 2012 titles in the preceding F3 Euroseries championship.

Stroll saw out the 2016 season in style with his first triple win at the Hockenheimring finale, ending the year having clinched 14 wins from 30 races – 13 of which came from the final 21 – and a mammoth winning margin of 187 points over Günther.

Despite the winning margin, to his credit, Günther was a worthy runner-up to his Prema team-mate. Indeed, while the 19-year-old's burgeoning title challenge had faded relatively quickly as Stroll got into his stride during the final two-thirds of the year, he remained the Canadian's most consistent rival in terms of podiums and wins.

Four wins and 13 podiums were more than enough for Günther to ensure a 1-2 for Prema at the season's end, his 'best of the rest' status strengthened by what was a more competitive season than perhaps was suggested by Stroll's dominance up top.

While grid sizes of around 20 drivers per race in 2016 paled in comparison to those of 2015, when the 'Max Verstappen effect' indirectly led to as many as 35 starters on occasion – sparking complaints about slack driving standards among ill-prepared youngsters who were promoted into a challenging series too promptly – there was arguably a 'quality over quantity' impression left by those who did race.

In fact, despite the Canadian flag flying high for much of 2016, as many as 11 drivers tasted the winner's champagne in 2016, while 16 set foot on the podium over the course of the year.

Among these was George Russell, who ensured a successful return to European F3 competition for HitechGP with a run to third place in the standings, courtesy of eye-catching wins in the blue-riband Pau and Spa-Francorchamps rounds.

Rewarded for his consistency, particularly during the latter half of the year, the former McLaren BRDC Award winner prevailed in a three-way battle for 'bronze' overall, defeating Cassidy in the third of the Prema cars and Motopark's Jimmy Erikson.

Cassidy enjoyed a strong maiden European F3 campaign, though ultimately he couldn't capitalise on some impressive results out of the box – including four second-place finishes in the opening seven races. He did claim a first win at Zandvoort, however, among three superb podium results around the Dutch venue mid-season en route to fourth overall.

Spurred on by a run of late-season form that would put him on the podium in seven of the final 13 races, Erikson comfortably ended the year as the highest placed rookie driver, in fifth. He finished just 12 points shy of third and probably would have secured the position had he not lost an almost certain win at the Norisring, where he was clumsily taken out by Ilott at one of the street circuit's famed hairpins.

Ilott, meanwhile, ended the season just behind in sixth overall, his campaign having boosted his reputation after switching from Carlin to Van Amersfoort Racing over the win-

Above: Lando Norris (31) Ricky Collard (11) and Matheus Leist run three abreast at Spa.
Photo: BRDC British F3 Championship

Top right: HitechGP's George Russell bounces off the kerbs at Imola.
Photo: FIA F3 Media

Top far right: Toby Sowery (8) won five races to edge out Thomas Randle (49) in the battle for third place in the British F3 series, behind Leist and Collard.
Photo: BRDC British F3 Championship

Above right: The experienced António Félix da Costa returned to the season closer at Macau and repeated his triumph of 2012.
Photo: LAT Photograhic

Above far right: Ben Barnicoat took a win in the wet at the Hungaroring and followed up with another triumph at Pau.
Photo: FIA F3 Media

Above centre right: Brazilian youngster Matheus Leist is presented with the British F3 Championship trophy by MSV's Jonathan Palmer.
Photo: BRDC British F3 Championship

Right: Third time lucky for Kenta Yamashita, who finally secured the elusive All-Japan Formula 3 crown.
Photo: LAT Photographic

ter. The young Briton had competed in 2015 with Red Bull backing, but a lacklustre season failed to meet the Austrian brand's famously demanding objectives, and he came into 2016 going it alone. Nonetheless, a maiden win at Paul Ricard steadied his nerves, and though ultimately it wouldn't lead to a title challenge, another victory at the Red Bull Ring suggested that the 18-year-old had regained his confidence. He will join Prema for 2017.

Two podiums – including a sure-footed win – during the second round of the season at the Hungaroring gave Prema's Ralf Aron reason to call his maiden European F3 campaign a success. Though he wouldn't set foot on the podium again en route to seventh overall, consistent results and only a single DNF all year belied his rookie status.

Making headlines with an unexpected pole-to-flag victory at the Norisring for Van Amersfoort Racing, Anthoine Hubert's season came alive during the second half of the year. Having scored just four top-ten finishes from the opening four rounds, the rookie Frenchman took a composed win over Stroll at the Norisring, which spurred a superb run of form. Two more podiums and only a single non-score from the final 18 races lifted him to eighth overall.

Other winners in 2016 included Ben Barnicoat, who displayed deft wet-weather prowess by winning at the Hungaroring, before following it up immediately with a second straight success at Pau. Leading Red Bull-backed driver Niko Kari took a victory at Imola, while Alessio Lorandi was Carlin's sole race winner at Pau, only for the Italian to quit the team and the series mid-season amid indifferent results.

If the 2016 European F3 Championship had been all about the future, then the annual jaunt to Macau for its iconic F3 Grand Prix had more than a hint of nostalgia about it. Three former winners – António Félix da Costa, Felix Rosenqvist and Daniel Juncadella – joined the ranks to raise the stakes and give up-and-comers a welcome yardstick.

On a circuit where arguably experience is more keenly felt than in any other sprint event, perhaps it is not surprising that the 'mentors' had the critical edge. Da Costa largely

dominated all weekend for Carlin, winning both the qualification race and the main final.

Even so, the Portuguese driver, who had gone on to race in DTM and Formula E since his 2012 win, was made to work hard for his success. He narrowly defeated pole-sitter George Russell in the qualifying race, before going wheel to wheel with team-mate Sérgio Sette Câmara in the final.

Câmara, whose two podiums en route to 11th in the European F3 standings hadn't seemed immediately befitting of his prized Red Bull junior status, delivered an eye-catching performance. He had looked set for a surprise win in Macau after a strong getaway, but da Costa reeled him in and passed after a safety car period. He was also passed by defending European F3 champion – and two-times Macau winner – Rosenqvist for second, but his third-place finish ensured he was the best of the relative newcomers in a hugely competitive field.

With European F3 title winner Stroll having chosen not to start in Macau, instead turning his attention to forthcoming F1 duties, Kenta Yamashita represented Japan with a run to fourth, ahead of Callum Ilott and Jake Hughes, who was racing between GP3 duties. Russell and returning 2011 winner Juncadella finished seventh and eighth.

Still one of the most prestigious stand-alone Formula 3 titles one can add to a racing CV, the 2016 edition of the Masters of F3 at Zandvoort nonetheless suffered for numbers as European championship teams ran skeleton crews, while Prema elected to skip the event altogether. In the Italian team's absence, Motopark stepped up to dominate with a 1-2-3 result, headed by its lead European F3 driver, Joel Erikson. In the final, the Swede led lights-to-flag from pole position, having headed off a challenge from team-mate Niko Kari, who stayed within a second to the finish. Sérgio Sette Câmara completed the all-Motopark podium, while Callum Ilott and HitechGP guest Alexander Albon rounded out the top five around the Dutch venue.

The once illustrious British Formula 3 Championship made a return of sorts in 2016, under a new name and with new

machinery. Known as the BRDC British Formula 3 Championship and using 2-litre, 230bhp Tatuus-Cosworth single-seaters similar to those raced in the popular Formula 4 class, British Formula 3 may have looked unfamiliar from the outset, but the return of Carlin, Double R and Fortec – among a number of new teams – gave the new-look series credence to complement its sizeable grids and competitive racing.

Across eight three-race rounds, contested by drivers from such far-flung reaches as Australia, India and South Africa, the championship generated eight different race winners over the course of the year. It would be up to Matheus Leist, however, to continue the great tradition of Brazilian drivers performing well on British soil by clinching the inaugural title for Double R Racing. A four-times race winner, Leist entered the Donington Park finale in contention for the title with Carlin's Ricky Collard – son of BTCC favourite Rob – but would emerge victorious over his home-grown rival.

Toby Sowery won five races en route to third overall for Lanan Racing, while Douglas Racing duo Thomas Randle and Enaam Ahmed completed the top five. Among other winners was highly-rated young Briton Lando Norris, who took four of the 11 guest races he started in a season when he also picked up the Formula Renault Eurocup title. Colton Herta and Force India F1 development driver Nikita Mazepin also tasted the winner's champagne during one-off appearances.

The 2016 Euroformula Open Championship produced a comfortable title winner in Campos' Leonardo Pulcini, the Italian's victory and second place from the opening round having earned him an immediate championship lead that he would protect all the way to the end of the season. Finishing off the podium in just three of the year's 16 races – and topping it on seven occasions – Pulcini was well clear of runner-up and top rookie Ferdinand Habsburg, whose comparatively scant two wins were bolstered by impressive consistency in the Drivex School car. American Colton Herta was a four-times race winner in the second half of the year and finished third overall for Carlin, ahead of Campos' Diego Menchaca and RP Motorsport's Damiano Fioravanti.

Runner-up in 2014 and 2015, Kenta Yamashita finally went one better to secure an elusive All-Japan Formula 3 Championship title in 2016, following a dramatic showdown with Jann Mardenborough. Former 'gamer to racer' GT Academy winner Mardenborough sidestepped from GP3 to Formula 3 in 2016 with backing from NISMO. He came remarkably close to taking the Japanese title at his first attempt with the B-MAX team, having gone into the Sugo triple-header finale with a six-point lead over Yamashita. However, a trio of wins from the Toyota TOM'S driver would tip the balance back in his favour, and he clinched the title over the Briton by just three points. Sho Tsuobi completed the top three, with 13 podiums from 15 races – albeit not a single win – while fourth-placed Mitsunori Takaboshi might have forged a title challenge had he started more than eight races, three of which he won.

South of the Equator, Tim Macrow notched up a third Australian Formula 3 title in the Alpine Motorsports Dallara. In a season of meagre grid numbers, he was still mightily impressive in his dominance, claiming 17 wins from 21 races to add to his 2007 and 2013 domestic F3 titles.

Matheus Iorio was crowned champion in the Brazilian Formula 3 Championship, having succeeded 2014 and 2015 title winner Pedro Piquet. With one round remaining as AUTOCOURSE went to press, Iorio was 50 points clear of Cesario F3 team-mate Guilherme Samaia, ensuring he could not be caught.

On the international stage at least, however, F3 2016 was all about Stroll. Surely even bigger opportunities await the Canadian teenager in 2017. Destined to ascend straight into F1 with esteemed Williams Martini Racing, he is following a path that bears the notable hallmarks of Max Verstappen's rise two years earlier.

Indeed, while Stroll's F1 graduation is arguably no coincidence, thanks to the trailblazing effect of the headline-grabbing Dutchman, with credentials on his side and a mature head on his shoulders, the youngster will be keenly watched in 2017…

THE WINNING COMBINATION

Above: Sébastien Buemi emerged as a deserving champion in the 2015/16 season.
Photo: Andrew Ferraro/LAT Photographic

Top right: Buemi made amends for his failure to close out the title in 2015.
Photo: Formula E

Above right: Alain Prost imparts his wisdom to son Nicolas.
Photo: Formula E

Right: Sam Bird was always a factor; he took a typically opportunist victory in Buenos Aires.
Photo: Sam Bloxham/LAT Photographic

THE electric single-seater series' sophomore campaign had a lot to live up to on track, after the inaugural season had started with a last-lap clash for the win that had sent Nick Heidfeld barrel-rolling and ended with a thrilling final-race decider. The 2015/16 season began with Sébastien Buemi revelling in a Renault e.dams package that appeared to be a step ahead of the rest and dominating the Beijing opener in late 2015. Concerns of a potential whitewash were real.

Development of the motor, gearbox and inverter had been opened up to the teams, which allowed on-the-ball Renault to steal a march. At the other end of the scale, however, the Trulli team made a complete mess of its own powertrain technology and failed to complete a timed lap in pre-season testing, before missing the Beijing and Putrajaya rounds.

The series also had a calendar in flux: the first round was delayed, Mexico City still hadn't been confirmed, while concerns over the races in Berlin, Moscow and London would escalate over the coming months.

That it came down to an explosive Battersea Park finale and a two-point winning margin for Buemi, who avenged his one-point title defeat by Nelson Piquet Jr 12 months earlier, was amazing. Formula E still has a lot of doubters, but if any of those critics had given its second season half a chance, they would have been seriously reconsidering their claim that it's not proper racing, never mind highly entertaining.

Series CEO Alejandro Agag is either the luckiest man in motorsport or he and his team are exceptionally good at

making a show. The reality of the second season of Formula E lies somewhere in between.

The series' adoption of the superpole, whereby the five fastest drivers across the four groups from qualifying fight it out in an additional session, played a major role in the mid-season troubles that dropped Buemi into Lucas di Grassi's clutches. And while the new open-warfare era of electric racing resulted in Renault having a performance advantage, it was also key to di Grassi being able to play up a 'David and Goliath' storyline in the title fight.

The irony was that while Formula E continued to promote its 'drive the future' message, the difference the drivers made was more akin to the good old days of motor racing than any conventional series seems to manage today.

While Sam Bird kept himself in the mathematical hunt until the season-ending double-header in London, it was really a two-way title fight. In the blue corner, Buemi – the super-fast Swiss, with a class-leading Renault Z.E.15 powertrain, determined to make amends for spinning away the inaugural championship crown.

After Buemi's early triumph, his car wilted in Putrajaya, but he recovered from a qualifying mistake in superpole, which had left him fifth on the grid, to make it two wins from the opening three races.

Moving into 2016, Formula E became characterised by thrilling contests that ebbed and flowed throughout. Buemi made a mistake under braking in qualifying again in Buenos Aires, but this was more serious than in Punta, for it hap-

pened in the group phase, consigning him to a back-of-the-grid start.

What transpired a few hours later was arguably the best race of the season. Bird had made the most of the fact that Buenos Aires suited his DS Virgin package more than any other track, with a superb qualifying performance to start the race from pole. While he was managing a small lead, Buemi was carving through the pack. Then, a mid-race safety car suddenly meant that a win was possible. Unfortunately, the unstoppable force met an immovable object, and Bird, dancing his tail-happy car through the twists and turns of the Puerto Madero circuit, clung to a well-deserved victory.

Second was a delight to Buemi, but his recovery drive was

the start of a succession of damage-limitation races. Another error, this time in the superpole session, put him fifth on the grid in Mexico City. In the race, with di Grassi edging into the distance, he made a meal of trying to take second from Jérôme d'Ambrosio, rear-ending him twice under braking for Turn One.

Buemi finished a frustrated third, but his luck turned on Saturday night. Di Grassi was stripped of his victory when the first of his cars failed the post-race weight check, promoting d'Ambrosio to top spot – a second win for the Belgian, after the first (Berlin 2015) had also come from a di Grassi exclusion. Buemi inherited second, and a six-point deficit to di Grassi became a 22-point advantage.

The pendulum swung away from Buemi again in Long Beach. Bird inherited pole when António Félix da Costa lost a remarkable qualifying result with Team Aguri's season-one powertrain to a tyre pressure irregularity. There was no mistake from Buemi, just unhappiness with the balance of his car – and the net result was a fourth-row start.

As di Grassi overhauled Bird to take the win, Buemi was left to rue throwing it down the inside of Robin Frijns on lap 11. He'd moved past di Grassi's team-mate, Daniel Abt, with a late dive to the inside of the hairpin, but when he tried to repeat the move on Frijns, he left it too late, locked up and rear-ended his rival, damaging his own car's nose and breaking the rear wing on the Andretti car.

Buemi was contrite afterwards, but he also had a request for e.dams that bordered on a warning. So convinced was he that something was amiss that he wanted the cars stripped down when they returned to base before the European leg of the season. The three-week gap to the Parisian round, the team's home event, afforded that opportunity for the first time since the cars had been shipped to Beijing for the opening round.

And an issue was discovered: a build-up of rust in the braking system, which was causing brake balance issues, particularly at 200kW when the cars are closer to a knife's edge. The team believed it had developed while the cars were in storage beside the harbour after the Putrajaya race, hence the issues in Punta del Este, Buenos Aires, Mexico City and Long Beach.

While that was a positive outcome, there was no immediate reprieve. The Parisian event was decidedly the coldest in Formula E's short history, and Renault e.dams was caught

Above: Three of the title contenders for the 2015/16 season shared the podium in Buenos Aires. Winner Sam Bird ultimately dropped out, leaving Sébastien Buemi and Lucas di Grassi to decide the proceedings in the London showdown.

Top right: Nicolas Prost provided able support to Buemi and was more than ready to grab wins for himself when the opportunity arose.

Photos: Andrew Ferraro/LAT Photographic

Above right: After a quiet moment to himself, the new champion wiped away the tears and composed himself before the celebrations began.

Photo: Adam Warner/LAT Photographic

Right: The crucial moment in the controversial final race as Lucas di Grassi runs into the back of the innocent Sébastien Buemi.

Photo: WRi2

out by this. Neither Buemi nor Prost had any confidence in the car, tyre warmers not being allowed, and there being a problem in getting the tyres and carbon brakes up to temperature. Buemi was eighth on the grid, and while he did well to move up to a podium place, it was a frustrating result because it meant that he travelled to Berlin in late May without having had a win in five months. That would have been an unthinkable proposition after the opening round.

The Swiss driver was able to fight back with a win from second on the grid in Germany, a vital victory that sent him to London just a point behind his chief rival. That put him in a feisty mood in Battersea, especially as he had lost one opportunity to overhaul di Grassi when the Moscow round was cancelled just weeks before its scheduled date. He dominated practice in London, before fighting wheel to wheel with di Grassi in the lower reaches of the top ten, after rain in qualifying (with both in the same group) had consigned the rivals to lowly grid slots.

A highly defensive di Grassi won that battle, much to Buemi's fury. And his anger did not subside the next day, nor in the days that followed, when di Grassi's lurid shunt into the back of him at the start of the Showdown robbed him of the opportunity to wrap up the title with a crushing victory, having absolutely dominated qualifying.

The manner in which Buemi won the title was immensely anticlimactic in the context of a stunning season. It was a farcical race for fastest lap, with Buemi suggesting that di Grassi had loitered and attempted to baulk his flying laps.

Regardless of what di Grassi supposedly had done, the Brazilian's actions at the first corner were disappointing. Had they been deliberate? Buemi, and many others, were adamant that that was the case. Di Grassi's entry speed suggested so, too; his reactive steering inputs indicated that it could have been a legitimate, if utterly unacceptable, consequence of the 'win-it-or-bin-it' mentality he had assumed in lunging down the inside of Prost, having started third.

Whatever, it was not befitting of the contender in the red corner we had seen throughout the season: di Grassi, the

ultra-consistent Brazilian without the raw pace of his rival, but with a steely determination and a Schaeffler-supported Abt Audi Sport team that had kept its French adversary on its toes.

Prior to Battersea, di Grassi had ended every race in the top three. But a mistake from the team in Mexico was almost far more costly than 25 points and a dent to his title hopes. In the immediate aftermath, he seriously considered leaving the team for the 2016/17 season.

He did not let that show in public, however. Instead, he rallied his troops and spoke before the next race in Long Beach of how he wanted Abt to continue to take risks in its pursuit of the title. His teeth had been gritted as he uttered those remarks, because, as he confessed at the end of the season, he had thought his title chances were over. One race later, though, with his title rival in disarray, di Grassi seized the opportunity in Long Beach. He passed Bird for the lead a lap after Buemi had shunted, and then survived a safety car-induced three-lap sprint at the end to take the win from Stéphane Sarrazin.

That had edged him into a one-point lead, and he made it back-to-back successes – three in a row on the road – with a fine victory in Paris. And if winning in Abt's big rival's backyard was not sweet enough, Buemi's ongoing troubles suddenly made the title a very realistic prospect.

Di Grassi could point to Berlin as the second occasion where the title was taken from him, though. And not because Buemi won. The Brazilian had a difficult qualifying session and started eighth, but in typically gritty fashion, he was running third in the closing stages – with his team-mate ahead of him. Unsurprisingly, the call came for Abt to cede the position, but to the surprise of everyone looking on, it was not heeded. Abt appeared to make a half-hearted attempt to beckon di Grassi through at the end of the penultimate lap, but it was either ignored (unlikely) or simply not seen. On the final tour, Abt kept in front for fear of letting di Grassi through and losing third to Prost in the process.

That, combined with the exclusion in Mexico, rendered the

Battersea farce somewhat obsolete. It remains a huge stain on the season, and di Grassi seriously blotted his copybook in the eyes of many, but it should not be forgotten that until that July weekend in London, he had put together the perfect season. Not many drivers can say that.

Buemi was irked by the claims (from di Grassi) that his car was comfortably the quickest. The Renault Z.E.15 powertrain had a higher peak than the Abt Schaeffler FE01, but the Abt package as a whole was the most consistent. And better to be the man accused of having the best equipment, than to be Nelson Piquet Jr, who spent his title defence languishing at the back of the field because the NextEV powertrain was too heavy and the rear structure too flexible.

Besides the title protagonists, Bird was clearly the next best in terms of overall championship performance – even though he was leapfrogged by Prost at the final weekend. His win in Buenos Aires was countered by mistakes in Long Beach and Paris, where he had been on course to finish second and third, but that is not a black mark against him, given how edgy his car was.

The DSV-01 had a single-gear, twin-motor arrangement like NextEV. It was a tricky beast and slightly heavy, but it was much better sorted than what Piquet and Oliver Turvey had to contend with. That Bird scored more than double the points of team-mate Jean-Eric Vergne, before being robbed of two top-five finishes in London, speaks volumes for the Briton's performance. Vergne had struggled after switching from Andretti to DS, and even a breakthrough podium on home soil in Paris, pole in Berlin and another podium in London could not stop him from heading for the exit door as soon as the season was over.

Prost was the season's other winner, clinching a double in London that was overlooked because of the title fight. It was enough to steal third in the points, but in truth the Frenchman had a difficult year, scoring one podium across the

opening eight races. He was the fifth different victor, which meant that Formula E's second season came surprisingly close to the inaugural campaign's tally of seven winners. It would have come even closer had da Costa's underdog heroics in the season-one Aguri package not been undone by reliability issues.

Formula E's off-track progression had a happier ending than the title fight. Trulli's departure from the series after just two rounds was immediately offset by the announcement that Jaguar would end a 12-year absence from major international motorsport with a works Formula E programme from 2016/17. And on the eve of the season finale, it was announced that Faraday Future, a Californian-based start-up technology company, would offer financial and technical support to the Jay Penske-owned Dragon Racing team, effective immediately.

There had been risk of Formula E losing momentum going into its third campaign, with no real technological changes for the 2016/17 season beyond an increase in energy harvesting from 100kW to 150kW. The Jaguar and Faraday entries were a boost – and then came even more manufacturer commitments in the off-season.

Audi had lent its name to the Abt team from the inaugural campaign, but announced between the pre-season tests at Donington Park that it would induct the Formula E entry into its official works programmes from the fourth season, but, like Faraday, it would lend more financial and technical assistance for the 2016/17 season. Within two months, Audi had announced that it would kill its World Endurance Championship project at the end of the year to focus entirely on FE, while parent company Volkswagen terminated its World Rally Championship campaign.

It was a clear changing of the guard, and also the first of three major Formula E announcements from three major manufacturers based in Germany.

Serious talk of some kind of BMW entry before the fifth season in 2018/19 emerged over the Mexico weekend. At the same time came the news that Team Aguri was pursuing a Nissan deal – most likely with Renault technology, but the Japanese manufacturer's badging.

While Aguri's eventual sale to the Techeetah entry, which Vergne had joined in a driver-cum-investor capacity after leaving DS Virgin, torpedoed the Nissan plan in the short term, BMW confirmed an engineering partnership with the Andretti team, to include serious German involvement with the ATEC-02 powertrain.

This had been expected, not least because the marque had supplied the safety car and medical vehicle from the beginning. What was not expected was the third of the German announcements: that Mercedes had secured an option for 2018/19. Formula 1's dominant team of the turbo-hybrid era wanted to take a closer look at Formula E, and had gone to the length of guaranteeing itself a spot on the grid if it wants to proceed. It is not a firm commitment, but it was an announcement that validated Formula E perhaps beyond any other – and led Agag to slap a 25 million-euro price tag on the 12th entry the series is looking to cater for.

That excitement meant that Formula E had generated a real buzz before its 2016/17 opener in Hong Kong, another coup for the series, which had also secured races in New York (Agag's dream location) and Montreal, as well as Brussels for the third season.

The calendar continues to pose a problem, though – a three-month gap between round two in Marrakech and round three in Buenos Aires is nothing short of disastrous for momentum, even if an eSports event in Las Vegas, in which all 20 drivers will compete against a handful of punters to win a share of $1 million, is scheduled for January to 'break up' the gap. There is also the not-insignificant matter of London being dropped from the calendar, after an acrimonious battle with Battersea Park locals ended with the 2016 race being the last in the area, three years before the expiry of the initial contract.

Perhaps the thorniest issue by the year's end was the New York round clashing with the World Endurance Championship's visit to the Nürburgring. With Buemi committed to his Toyota LMP1 programme, Renault e.dams was understandably concerned that missing the double-header would remove him from the title hunt. However, his lightning start to the 2016/17 season subsequently raised the very real prospect that he could win without fighting for the 58 points on offer in Brooklyn's penultimate round of the campaign.

Despite considerably improved performance from DS Virgin and NextEV – with Piquet resurgent in Hong Kong in claiming his first pole position – Buemi fought from fifth on the grid to win the opening race. And he made it two from two with a crushing Marrakech victory from seventh, having been handed a five-place grid penalty for his fire extinguisher emptying itself in qualifying and coming in under the minimum weight limit.

Formula E was undoubtedly more competitive at the front in its second season of open powertrain competition, as exhibited by Mahindra's rookie Felix Rosenqvist earning pole on merit in Marrakech, before losing out to Buemi and Bird in the race. By the year's end, however, it was a similar story to 12 months before – Buemi and Renault are the package to beat.

Above: Jaguar came to the party for year three. Adam Carroll posted a 12th-place finish on their Hong Kong debut, which the team described as "cautious".

Top: New blood, in the form of Felix Rosenqvist at Marrakech, brought fresh vigour to the driver line-up.

Top right: Under leaden skies, the field attacks the hairpin in Hong Kong.

Right: Sébastien Buemi and Renault e.dams continued to rule the roost at year's end.

Photos: Formula E

LUCKY BREAK

Main photo: Fortune smiled on the
No. 2 Porsche at Le Mans when the
leading Toyota hit trouble.
Photo: WRi2/David Lord

Inset, top: The winning Porsche
flashes by the No. 5 Toyota, which lies
abandoned against the pit wall.

Inset, above: Celebrations for Romain
Dumas, Marc Lieb and Neel Jani.
Photos: Porsche

THE stark statistics of the 2016 FIA World Endurance Championship suggest that Porsche dominated. The German manufacturer won six of the nine races, including the big one at the Le Mans 24 Hours, on the way to retaining its drivers' and manufacturers' titles. Yet the truth couldn't be further from the picture that will be painted in the record books.

The 2016 Porsche 919 Hybrid, an update of the all-new car built for the previous season, was rarely the fastest LMP1 car on the grid, at least in the second half of the season. Drivers' champions Neel Jani, Marc Lieb and Romain Dumas staggered to the title over the post-Le Mans leg of the series. And Porsche was lucky – very lucky – on the way to its 18th victory in the 24 Hours.

To say the least, it was a bizarre season. Audi, which did have the fastest car for much of the year, failed to knit together the kind of season necessary to win the championship, while Toyota had an up-and-down campaign that should have yielded its first victory at Le Mans in June, but left it struggling to compete at other times.

Jani, Lieb and Dumas succeeded team-mates Mark Webber, Timo Bernhard and Brendon Hartley as champions on the back of a big-scoring start to the season. They took maximum points at the season opener at Silverstone in April, after the winning Audi had been excluded for a technical infraction, limped home to second at Spa in May with a malfunctioning hybrid system, and then inherited a victory in the double-points Le Mans round with just five minutes to go. That gave them a 39-point advantage at the top of the championship. Remarkably, they would hang on to the lead despite failing to finish on the podium again. Three fourths, a fifth and a sixth were all they could manage.

It wasn't a satisfactory way to win the title. The eventual champions suffered a multitude of problems over the final six races, during which they swapped chassis several times. Lieb collided with a GTE Am car when leading at the Nürburgring in July, and there was another hit with a slower car, this time an LMP2; then a conservative choice of tyres in mixed conditions in Mexico City, in early September, almost certainly cost them a podium. A broken floor stymied their run in Austin,

and there were inconsistent performances at Fuji and Shanghai, in October and November respectively.

Even at the death in Bahrain in November, when the championship was more or less assured, they encountered further misfortune. Jani was side-swiped by a GTE Am Porsche, the resulting damage leaving them sixth at the flag.

They notched up just 66 points over the final six races. Their team-mates claimed 106! But such was the bad start suffered by reigning champions Webber, Bernhard and Hartley that they had just 3.5 points on the board after Le Mans. They would win four times over the remainder of the season to end up fourth in the championship, only 25.5 points behind the winners. Had they avoided any one of their misfortunes – a shunt with a backmarker for Hartley at Silverstone, two punctures at Spa, and a water pump issue at Le Mans – probably they would have retained the title.

Audi eventually claimed second position in the drivers' points with Loïc Duval, Lucas di Grassi and Oliver Jarvis at the end of what turned out to be the German manufacturer's swan-song year in the prototype ranks. They took the only two victories for the new R18 e-tron quattro – the latest and, as it turned out, last machine to carry that monicker – but should have won more.

The 2016 R18 was a complex machine. It had battery energy storage rather than the previous flywheel, and Audi warned that it might take time to hone its reliability and get on top of its radical aerodynamics. Despite those warnings, the car won on the road on debut, before André Lotterer, Marcel Fässler and Benoît Tréluyer were excluded after their car's underfloor skid block was found to be worn beyond the prescribed limits. However, poor reliability was a key reason why Audi didn't mount a challenge for the title.

Le Mans was a disaster for Audi. The Lotterer car encountered engine problems, while the sister machine was hit by a series of more minor woes, including a late change of brakes, on the way to a distant third. A wheel bearing failure hit the Duval/di Grassi/Jarvis car in Mexico, and a problem with the battery – the conventional unit, not the high-voltage energy-storage system – was among the setbacks that cost them victory in Austin in September.

Above: Audi's 'big six' have already parted from the rest as they head the field at the 6 Hours of Nürburgring.

Photo: Audi Communications Motorsport

Left: Bowing out on a high note. Lucas di Grassi, Loïc Duval and Oliver Jarvis celebrate Audi's final win on the podium in Bahrain.

Far left: The No. 1 Porsche of Timo Bernhard, Brendon Hartley and Mark Webber leads the pack around La Source at the start of the Spa race.

Photos: WEC

Above: A late-race pit stop to change brakes dashed Audi's hope for the No. 7 car of Lotterer, Fässler and Tréluyer at Le Mans.
Photo: Audi Communications Motorsport

Top right: Stunned. Toyota personnel look on in silence as their leading car hits trouble on the penultimate lap.
Photo: Adam Warner/LAT Photographic

Above right: It seemed little consolation for Toyota that the No. 6 car of Kobayashi, Conway and Sarrazin took second place.
Photo: Toyota Racing

Right: Kazuki Nakajima is consoled after his Toyota gave out with victory in sight.
Photo: Zak Mauger/LAT Photographic

Audi had the pace to win four or five of the final six races, but failed to deliver until Bahrain. It was a fitting finale for a marque that had announced the end of its programme earlier in the month. Duval and his team-mates led home the sister car to add to the more fortunate victory they had scored at Spa.

The R18 was a finicky beast that was at its best in hot conditions. There were races at which its speed waned as the temperatures cooled, nowhere more so than during the night at Le Mans.

Toyota returned to the WEC after its *annus horribilis* in 2015 with a new chassis, a new turbocharged V6 engine and a new energy storage system – like Audi, it had switched to a battery *à la* Porsche. The Japanese manufacturer intensified its focus on winning Le Mans, a race it had failed to crack in 13 factory campaigns prior to 2016, and produced an ultra-low-downforce car, which nearly delivered that elusive victory.

Both Toyotas were in the mix. The No. 6 car, shared by Kamui Kobayashi, Stéphane Sarrazin and Mike Conway, led the team's challenge for much of the way, before its performance wilted after an off from Kobayashi damaged the bodywork. After a slow start, the No. 5 car of Sebastien Buemi, Anthony Davidson and Kazuki Nakajima came into its own through the night, then got the better of the Jani/Dumas/Lieb Porsche on Sunday morning.

Toyota's long wait for victory, stretching back to 1987, appeared to be over until engine problems struck Nakajima on the penultimate lap. A broken air line between turbocharger and intercooler was the cause of the trouble. Enough power

was restored, after the Japanese driver had stopped on the start-finish straight, for the car to cross the line in second position, but the Toyota was not classified because its final lap was over the six-minute maximum.

Toyota had also lost victory at Spa, after two engine failures resulting from the forces sustained in compression at the bottom of the fast Eau Rouge corner. The TS050s were running with the high-downforce aerodynamics they had used at Silverstone, whereas Porsche and Audi were both using Le Mans-spec aero. That and Toyota's tyre choice – it correctly anticipated the warm weekend temperatures – explained why it had the edge in Belgium.

Two near misses apart, Toyota didn't look like a championship contender when the WEC regrouped after its shortened summer recess at the 'Ring at the end of July. But then the German venue was the track that required the most downforce of the circuits on the second leg of the calendar.

Toyota followed up on an average showing at the 'Ring with podiums for the Kobayashi/Sarrazin/Conway car in Mexico City and Austin, before the same trio took victory in Fuji after some creative tactics had vaulted the car ahead of the Duval/di Grassi/Jarvis Audi in the final stages. Another podium in Shanghai kept Toyota in with a sniff of the drivers' title going into the Bahrain finale, but the TS050 was at its least competitive since Nürburgring, which allowed the winning Audi crew to jump to second in the standings.

Yet again, the Anglo-Swiss Rebellion Racing squad dominated the LMP1 privateer class with its eponymous non-hybrid AER-engined chassis, even though it cut its entry from two cars to one for the flyaway races. Alexandre Imperatori,

Inset: After his final race, Mark Webber receives a farewell dousing from his fellow competitors on the podium in Bahrain.

Main photo: The No. 1 Porsche 919 Hybrid of Webber, Brendon Hartley and Timo Bernhard was often the fastest car of the year, but it suffered misfortunes to blunt their championship challenge.

Photos: Porsche

Above: The Anglo-Swiss Racing team dominated the LMP1 privateer class with Alexandre Imperatori, Dominik Kraihamer and Mathéo Tuscher.
Photo: Jakob Ebrey

Right: The LMP2 title was won by the French Signatech squad. Nicolas Lapierre, Stéphane Richelmi and Gustavo Menezes took the crown in the team's ORECA-Nissan 05.
Photo: WEC

Dominik Kraihamer and Mathéo Tuscher, who had got the better of more illustrious team-mates, including Nick Heidfeld and Nicolas Prost, in the sister car over the first half of the season, were chosen to continue the campaign. They duly ended up as champions, a long way ahead of their only rival, ByKolles, whose CLM-AER P1/01 took a solo victory at Shanghai in the hands of Pierre Kaffer, Oliver Webb and Simon Trummer.

The historic Alpine brand, part of Renault's successful 1978 Le Mans campaign, took the LMP2 title with the French Signatech squad. Nicolas Lapierre, Stéphane Richelmi and Gustavo Menezes took the crown in the team's ORECA-Nissan 05, which was dubbed an Alpine A460, on the back of a run of three consecutive wins either side of Le Mans. The Alpine trio, who never finished lower than fourth, notched up a further win in Austin and then sealed the title with fourth place with a race to go in Shanghai.

Their closest rivals were RGR Sport drivers Bruno Senna, Filipe Albuquerque and Ricardo Gonzalez. Twice they notched up class triumphs and were on the podium five more times in their Ligier-Nissan JSP2, which initially was run with assistance from the Swiss Morand squad, and then exclusively by OAK Racing post-Le Mans. It wasn't really a fair fight, however. LMP2 was again a pro-am class, and the rules stipulated that each line-up had to include a silver-rated driver. Gonzalez, 39, was a true amateur, or gentleman driver, unlike his opposite number at Signatech, 22-year-old single-seater convert Menezes.

The quickest car in P2 was the G-Drive Racing ORECA-Nissan run by the British Jota Sport squad. It notched up no fewer than six pole positions – though one was lost in the

scrutineering bay – and three victories with a revolving cast of drivers. It might have won many more and retained the title that Russian entrant G-Drive had won with OAK in 2015 but for rank misfortune, which included problems as diverse as a catastrophic gearbox failure at the 'Ring and being in the wrong place at the wrong time during the full-course-yellow virtual safety cars in Mexico.

It finally came good for G-Drive at Fuji, where Will Stevens, Alex Brundle and Roman Rusinov took a first victory of the season. This trio repeated the win at Shanghai, and then star driver René Rast returned to the line-up, having missed two races in Bahrain, to help the team take an against-the-odds hat trick after they had been relegated to the back of the grid.

Aston Martin claimed the World Endurance Cup for GT Drivers with Nicki Thiim and Marco Sørensen at the end of a season in which the manufacturers competing in the GTE Pro class shared out the victories and the important pieces of silverware. The British marque also claimed the teams' title, but Ferrari triumphed in the manufacturers' championship, while newcomer Ford took honours at Le Mans, 50 years on from the first of its four outright victories in the 1960s.

Each manufacturer claimed three wins over the course of the season, but the racing wasn't always close. The rule makers, the FIA and the Automobile Club de l'Ouest, arguably never got on top of the Balance of Performance, the means by which the different cars are equalised. New rules allowing more freedom in terms of car design were meant to make the process easier, yet the truth was that the BoP was more contentious than ever.

Constant changes through the season kept it equal in terms of what was happening in the points table, rather than

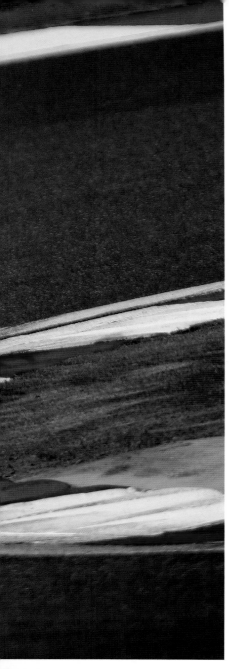

what was happening out on the racetrack. Ferrari dominated the first two races with its new turbocharged 488 GTE and also claimed victory at the Nürburgring, Sam Bird and Davide Rigon winning twice, and Gianmaria Bruni and James Calado once for the factory AF Corse team. Then the Aston Martin Vantage GTE enjoyed back-to-back victories in Mexico City and Austin, before the Ganassi Ford team took its turn and did the double in Fuji and Shanghai with Andy Priaulx and Harry Tincknell. Aston was back on top at the Bahrain finale, allowing Danes Thiim and Sørensen to duly seal the title, though the loss of a wheel post-pit stop by the sister Vantage shared by Darren Turner and Jonny Adam allowed Ferrari to grab the manufacturers' crown.

The one race that was ultra-close was Le Mans, though admittedly it was only really fought out by Ford and Ferrari. The Ferrari 488 and the Ford GT were in a class of their own around the 8.47-mile Circuit de la Sarthe.

It was a controversial race for the US manufacturer, which was represented by the two arms of the Ganassi squad competing in the WEC and the IMSA SportsCar Championship in North America, and its Italian rival. Such was the advantage enjoyed by the Ford GT and the Ferrari 488 in qualifying that they were pegged back ahead of the race, and the Aston and the Chevrolet Corvette C7.R given performance breaks, but these changes to the BoP had little bearing on the racing.

Ferrari's task was made all the harder by the retirements of the two AF Corse factory cars, but the US Risi Competizione team stepped up to the plate on its return to Le Mans after an absence of six seasons. Giancarlo Fisichella, Toni Vilander and Matteo Malucelli battled with the US-run Fords right through the race.

The eventual margin of victory was a full minute in favour of the Ford shared by Dirk Müller, Joey Hand and Sébastien Bourdais, but protests from both teams after the race reduced that to just 10s. The Ford had a total of 60s added to its time for two separate infringements, while the Ferrari was given 20s. It was an acrimonious end to a thrilling battle.

The WEC GTE Am title was won by the AF Corse Ferrari trio of Emmanuel Collard, Rui Águas and François Perrodo. Their title success was anchored by a points maximum as the first registered WEC competitor home in class at Le Mans. They notched up a further seven podiums aboard their 458 Italia, though only triumphed once, at Silverstone.

Aston Martin Racing trio Pedro Lamy, Mathias Lauda and Paul Dalla Lana were again the class act in GTE Am, but they failed to secure the title, despite winning on five occasions. A broken gearbox at Le Mans cost them dear, and then a third retirement of the season at Bahrain allowed Abu Dhabi Team Proton Porsche drivers David Heinemeier Hansson and Khaled Al Qubaisi to take the runner-up spot courtesy of a second class victory together with factory driver Pat Long.

The British Jota team finally claimed the European Le Mans Series crown after a series of near misses. The team, running under the G-Drive banner, as in the WEC, notched up a pair of victories with its Gibson-Nissan 015S shared by Harry Tincknell, Simon Dolan and ex-Formula 1 driver Giedo van der Garde in his first season of sportscar racing. They sealed the crown with victory in the Estoril finale in October, when erstwhile championship leaders Mathias Beche, Ryo Hirakawa and Pierre Thiriet, who won three times during the season in their TDS Racing ORECA, finished eighth, following a change of starter motor.

The other race winner over the course of the extended six-race season was US entrant Dragonspeed, with former Renault Formula 1 development driver Ben Hanley returning to the cockpit after a five-year absence to share with Lapierre and Henrik Hedman. The LMP3 class was won by Brundle, Christian England and Mike Guasch aboard a Ligier-Nissan JSP3 run by the Anglo-American United Autosports team, while Aston Martin Racing triumphed in GTE with a Vantage shared by Turner, Alex MacDowall and Andrew Howard.

On the other side of the sportscar divide, the reorganised Blancpain GT Series flourished in a season of monster grids and ultra-close competition that was mostly free of grumbles about the BoP. Three different manufacturers of GT3 machinery claimed the three titles up for grabs; a fourth took arguably the biggest prize on offer at the Spa 24 Hours, and another two marques made it on to the top step of the podium across the Endurance Cup and Sprint Cup legs of the series.

The Endurance Cup went down to the wire at the Nürburgring, with three crews able to overhaul points leaders Rob Bell, Côme Ledogar and Shane van Gisbergen from the

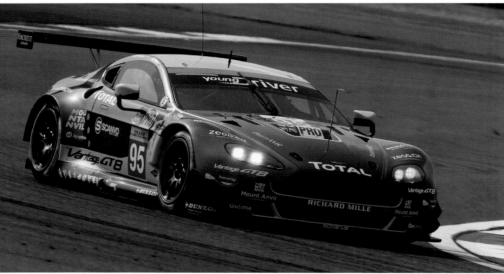

Above: Aston Martin claimed the GTE Pro class with Nicki Thiim and Marco Sørensen in the Vantage GTE.
Photo: David Lord/LAT Photographic

Above left: The G-Drive (JOTA Sport) ORECA-Nissan 05 of René Rast, Roman Rusinov and Alex Brundle was often the fastest of the P2 cars.
Photo: WEC

Top: Ford returned to Le Mans on the 50th anniversary of their historic first win, albeit in the GTE Pro class. Their experienced driver line-up of Dirk Müller, Joey Hand and Sébastien Bourdais beat off the strong challenge of the Risi Competizione Ferrari.
Photo: Jakob Ebrey/LAT Photographic

Left: The Ferrari 488 GTE of Davide Rigon and Sam Bird leads the rival Ford of Stefan Mücke and Olivier Pla in Bahrain.
Photo: Scuderia Ferrari

Garage 56 McLaren team. No one managed to do so, even though the McLaren 650S GT3, in which Duncan Tappy replaced the absent van Gisbergen, failed to trouble the scorers. That meant the Kiwi, racing in the V8 Supercars on the other side of the world that weekend, was crowned along with his regular team-mates in absentia.

The lead 650S GT3 entered by the new in-house Garage 59 set-up at McLaren GT made a flying start to the championship. They won the season opener at Monza in April, bagged some decent points at Silverstone the following month and then won again, thanks to a bit of luck, at the points-and-a-half Paul Ricard 1000km at the end of June.

That gave them a 22-point advantage after three races. They would score only a further two points over the final two races, courtesy of the eighth place in which they were running at the six-hour cut-off in the double-points Spa round at the end of July.

HTP Motorsport Mercedes trio Maximilian Buhk, Dominik Baumann and Jazeman Jaafar came closest to overhauling the McLaren drivers. Fourth place at the 'Ring in September left them just one point behind.

They had followed up on a close second at Monza with a victory aboard the new Mercedes-AMG GT3 at Silverstone in May, only for their championship challenge to go off the rails. They were out of the points at Ricard, which was followed by the bizarre episode of Mercedes' Spa assault.

The German manufacturer blocked out the top six positions in qualifying, only for an inconformity to be discovered with the new car's ignition mapping, after a thorough search lasting into the small hours of race morning. That resulted in a grid penalty and a five-minute stop-go for each of the cars that had made it through to final qualifying. Buhk and co would recover to sixth as the second Merc home.

The factory M-Sport Bentley team perhaps had the biggest gripe come the end of the season. Andy Soucek, Maxime Soulet and Wolfgang Reip, who ultimately finished a close third in the points, might have won at Spa but for a series of penalties, a poor tactical call and a mistake in the pits near the end.

More decisive in the outcome of the championship was a flash refuelling fire at the car's final pit stop at Ricard, which probably cost them the win and left them fourth at the finish. Then it all went wrong at the 'Ring, where the car sustained damage early in the race, preventing the team from removing one of the rear wheels at its first pit stop.

Fourth in the points went to Alexander Sims and Philipp Eng, who won the Spa enduro in July aboard the Rowe Motorsport BMW M6 GT3 that they shared with Maxime Martin.

The Belgian WRT Audi squad ended up only sixth in the Endurance Cup with Laurens Vanthoor, but it did add to its collection of Blancpain titles in the Sprint Cup. Belgian amateur Enzo Ide, who was partnered by Christopher Mies in four rounds and Robin Frijns in one, took the spoils after an ultra-consistent season.

Ide and Mies followed up on a podium in the Brands Hatch qualifying race with a victory in the full-points race, after which their Audi R8 LMS never finished outside the top three. Mies missed the final round at Barcelona to successfully chase the ADAC GT Masters title in Germany, and Frijns was brought in as a substitute. A third and then a second were more than enough to seal the title for Ide.

Ide's closest challengers for the title were Buhk and Baumann at HTP. They were second in the main race at the Misano opener in April, and claimed their solitary victory at the Hungaroring at the end of August. They had only an outside chance of the title going into the Barcelona decider, so opted to concentrate on maintaining their advantage at the head of the overall BGTS classification, which combined the points scored in both the sprints and the enduros.

Bell finished second overall in the BGTS after taking a pair of Sprint Cup victories with Alvaro Parente, while Vanthoor was third. Soucek and Soulet also won a sprint round on the way to fourth.

FAMILIAR FACES

Insets: Repeat champions in 2016:
Gordon Shedden (*left*), José María
López (*centre*) and Marco Wittmann.

Main: Under a sunny sky at Oulton
Park, Shedden, in the Team Dynamics
Honda Civic Type R, leads Tom Ingram
in the Speedworks Toyota Avensis.

Photos: BTCC/Jakob Ebrey/WTCC/BMW Press Club

Above: An airborne José María López took two wins around the fearsome Nürburgring Nordschleife circuit, and was the season's dominant force in his Citroën.

Centre, from top: Yvan Muller was runner-up to team-mate López, and called time on a long and successful touring car career; Tom Chilton took a victory for the Sebastien Loeb Racing-run C-Elysée in Argentina; Norbert Michelisz was part of a strong three-car Honda line-up.

Top far right: Unbridled joy on the podium for Thed Björk after scoring Volvo's maiden win in the first race at Shanghai.

Centre right: Former WTCC champion Gabriele Tarquini still had much to offer, as proved by his wins for LADA in Moscow and Losail.

Centre far right: Veteran Tom Coronel took a surprise win in Estoril with the Chevrolet Cruze.

Right: Tiago Monteiro aboard his Honda. The Portuguese driver, with two wins, was the principal challenger to the two works Citroëns' of López and Muller

Photos: Courtesy WTCC

THERE was drama and action aplenty in the touring car world over the course of 2016, although come the end of the year, it was familiar faces that emerged on top in the major championships across the globe.

In both the World and British Touring Car Championships, the title winners from 2015 would successfully defend their crowns, while the eventual victor in a hard-fought battle in Germany would be a driver with a title already to his name.

With races still to run as this edition of AUTOCOURSE closed for press, the champions in the TCR International Series and the newly-named Supercars Championship had still to be decided, with past title winners still in contention for both honours.

WORLD TOURING CAR CHAMPIONSHIP

Having taken back-to-back titles in 2014 and 2015, José María López was the man to beat going into the World Touring Car Championship season, and despite the best efforts of his rivals, the Argentine driver ended the campaign as champion for a third time.

Ahead of the season opener in France, hopes were high that 2016 could be the season when the dominant Citroën squad was beaten to the crown, the French manufacturer having downsized its factory team to two cars, and both Honda and LADA naming strong three-driver line-ups in their quest for success.

There was also the small matter of a new manufacturer, in the shape of Volvo, and a strong Independents field keen to challenge the factory outfits when the 24-race season kicked off in early April.

López topped the times in qualifying at Paul Ricard, although a change to the sporting regulations, under which the reversed-grid race each weekend was swapped from the second race to the first, meant it was Honda's Rob Huff who would take the opening victory of the campaign. Neither of the factory Citroëns was in contention at the front.

Although López converted pole into victory in race two, it was only after being forced to defend hard to keep Tiago

Monteiro's Honda at bay in the closing laps, providing the first indication that the defending champion wasn't going to have it all his own way.

Having endured a tough start to his season on home soil, López's Citroën team-mate, Yvan Muller, took pole position for round two in Slovakia. However, Monteiro would be the big winner from the weekend, moving into the championship lead with victory in race one, then maintaining his advantage with second behind López in race two.

When the series arrived in Hungary for round three, however, trouble was brewing, with an FIA investigation into the eligibility of the flat floor fitted to Honda cars. Subsequently, these were deemed to be legal. Citroën emerged on top across the weekend in Budapest, with privateer Mehdi Bennani making the right call on tyres to take victory in a wet race one, and López taking main race honours for the third straight weekend.

After Tom Coronel was a surprising winner in race one in Morocco, Honda returned to form in race two. Rob Huff led a podium lock-out, while Monteiro closed to within 14 points of López in the championship race.

That would all change on arrival at the Nürburgring, however, where stewards announced that Honda would be excluded from both the Hungarian and Moroccan weekends for running non-homologated parts; something the team would immediately appeal.

Two wins for López around the fearsome Nordschleife allowed him to extend his provisional lead over Monteiro to 69 points. The Portuguese driver had failed to score after a high-speed tyre failure in race one sent him crashing out of the lead.

Honda's appeal to the FIA would be heard before round six in Russia. The result was that the cars were reinstated for the Hungarian round, but the Moroccan exclusion was upheld, dealing a huge blow to both Monteiro and Huff in their quests for the title.

The revision to the standings put López 94 points clear. Moreover, despite suffering the lowest scoring weekend of his career in Moscow, wins for LADA pair Gabriele Tarquini

and Nicky Catsburg meant that the defending champion held an advantage of more than 100 points as the season hit the halfway stage.

Despite another poor weekend for López in Portugal, where Coronel and Monteiro had shared the victories, the Citroën driver maintained his healthy advantage in the standings, then moved further clear with victory in the main race in Argentina. Race one had gone to Tom Chilton's Sebastien Loeb Racing-run C-Elysée.

With doubts being expressed about whether the penultimate meeting of the year in Thailand would take place, the Motegi weekend suddenly became a potential championship decider. A Honda 1-2-3 in race one – headed by Norbert Michelisz – merely delayed the inevitable, as López provisionally took the title with second behind Muller in race two.

"You don't win a championship easy, you don't win a race easily," the champion reflected. "It's been a fantastic three years for me. Any driver in the world would like to achieve this. I've been lucky enough to be in the best team in the world with great team-mates, a great family, a great girlfriend, great everything.

"Everything came together these last three years, and I have only to say thank you to everybody. I wouldn't be here without Citroën today and my team-mates, so thank you to them."

Pole for López in China ensured that the manufacturers' title went to Citroën, before Thed Björk fought his way from sixth to first in a dramatic race one to give Volvo a maiden win. Then victory for López in race two confirmed him as the champion, even before the FIA announced that the Race of Thailand had indeed been cancelled.

Bennani had already wrapped up the Independents title prior to the season finale in Qatar, where he shared the wins with Tarquini. It would be a weekend that marked something of the end of an era, with LADA and Citroën both bowing out; the former to focus on domestic competition and the latter to return to the World Rally Championship.

While questions remained over LADA's drivers, Citroën's lead pairing of López and Muller also departed when the season drew to a close, with the former making a return to single-seaters in Formula E and the latter taking the decision to retire from full-time competition.

Citroën's factory withdrawal means that new champions will be crowned in 2017, with Honda and Volvo both committed to the series alongside privateer entries representing both Citroën and Chevrolet.

In the longer term, questions have been raised about the future direction of the championship, with the possibility that the series could adopt a new set of regulations, similar to those in the DTM and Super GT series, as early as 2018.

TCR INTERNATIONAL SERIES

On the back of a successful debut season, the TCR International Series would again go to the wire in year two. Returning champion Stefano Comini was hoping to successfully defend the title he had won in dramatic fashion in the final round of the inaugural campaign. As had been the case in 2015, the series would be decided through 11 rounds across Europe and Asia, including support events at the Bahrain, Singapore and Malaysian grands prix.

Having fallen short the previous season, Spaniard Pepe Oriola made the perfect start to his campaign with a double win in Bahrain, but then he was hampered by success ballast in round two at Estoril. There, Gianni Morbidelli and James Nash took a win apiece, with the former gaining a one-point lead over the Briton as a result.

The wins would continue to be spread across the field at the following two meetings, at Spa and Imola, where Aku Pellinen, Jean-Karl Vernay, Comini and Mikhail Grachev all took their first victories of the campaign. Oriola led Comini and Morbidelli going into round five in Austria.

In a somewhat chaotic weekend at the Salzburgring, Grachev and Vernay both took to the top step of the podium. Comini moved into the points lead, however, albeit with just 18 points covering the top six drivers.

That lead would change again in Germany, where Oriola's third win of the campaign helped him to move back into the top spot. However, that was only because he had more wins than Nash, as the pair were level on points.

Nash looked set to move to the top on his own after the Russian event in Sochi, but a ten-second time penalty later imposed for an incident in the first race of the weekend would cost him dear. Things seemed set to get even worse when a huge shunt in Friday testing in Thailand caused extensive damage to his SEAT León. Overnight work by his team not only allowed him to compete, but also to take a second win of the campaign, with a brace of top-two finishes putting him at the head of the championship standings.

Nash retained the lead after Vernay and Grachev shared the wins in Singapore. Then he ensured he would take a 17-point lead over Comini into the season finale in Macau with a brace of podium finishes at Sepang.

With Oriola and Vernay also in contention, drama was expected on the challenging street circuit – although not perhaps the kind of drama that unfolded as multiple incidents restricted the field to just four racing laps across the two races.

Victory in the first for Comini, and retirement for Nash after contact at Lisboa, meant half a point split the pair going into race two, with Comini at the front of the field and Nash right at the back. While the Briton was able to battle up to eighth in the limited laps available, fourth spot in a Guia Race won by WTCC regular Tiago Monteiro was enough give Comini the title for a second straight year.

Top: Nicky Catsburg, leading team-mate Hugo Valente, scored a win for LADA in Moscow.

Above: Former champion Rob Huff switched camps to Honda, but despite an opening-round victory in France, could not mount a sustained title challenge.

Photos: Courtesy WTCC

Above right: The start of race two at Estoril, with Stefano Comini (1) and James Nash (54) heading the pack.

Right: With four wins, Spanish star Pepe Oriola led the SEAT León challenge along with James Nash.

Below right: Three-times winner Jean-Karl Vernay took his WRT-run Leopard Racing Golf GTI TCR to third place in the final standings.

Far right: Stefano Comini and closest rival James Nash fought it out for the TCR championship right down to the final round, while the seemingly ageless Gianni Morbidelli was still a competitive proposition.

Photos: Courtesy TCR

BRITISH TOURING CAR CHAMPIONSHIP

An astonishing eight drivers would still be in contention for the British Touring Car Championship title when the field headed to Brands Hatch for the season finale. It was an indication of how competitive the 2016 campaign had proved to be on track.

The season had kicked off at the Kent circuit in April, when youngster Tom Ingram sprang a surprise by taking pole position and then victory in the opening race of the year. Defending champion Gordon Shedden took race-two honours for Honda, before Adam Morgan made it three different winners in race three.

It was a similar story for round two at Donington Park, where three more drivers took to the top of the podium, again racing for three different teams. Mat Jackson, Rob Collard and Matt Neal all emerged victorious, with Neal maintaining a lead he had established in the opening weekend of the campaign.

Only when the field arrived at Thruxton for round three was there a repeat winner. Morgan became the first two-times victor when he won a chaotic opening race that had to be red-flagged, following an accident caused by Neal suffering a puncture in the final chicane. It would be one of a number of tyre failures that occurred in unseasonably high temperatures. As a result, races two and three were reduced in length. They would go the way of Motorbase pair Andrew Jordan and Jackson.

Conspicuous by its absence at the front of the grid through the opening three rounds had been Team BMR with the all-new Subaru Levorg, which the team had worked around the clock to prepare for the new season. Hampered by manifold issues in the first two meetings, and then unable to compete at Thruxton because of fuel pressure concerns, the team arrived at Oulton Park with newly designed parts and was bang on the pace, Colin Turkington taking pole and then victory in race one. Sam Tordoff grabbed his first win of the year for WSR in race two, while Neal was victor in race three.

After Turkington, Collard and rookie Ash Sutton had been

Above: Sam Tordoff in the WSR BMW fell just two points short of Shedden over the thrilling season's action.

Left: Rob Collard (*left*), Sam Tordoff (*centre*) and Mat Jackson share the podium at Rockingham.

Far left: Full-on BTCC action as Colin Turkington's Team BMR Subaru and Mat Jackson's Motorbase Performance Ford Focus trade paint.

Top left: Andrew Jordan nearly loses his Ford Focus.

Above left: Team Dynamics' Matt Neal was in the championship mix until a crash at the Brands Hatch showdown ruled him out of contention.

Photos: BTCC/Jakob Ebrey

Above: Canadian Robert Wickens was fourth overall and Mercedes' highest placed DTM driver, having taken wins at Zandvoort and Moscow.
Photo: Mercedes AMG

Top right: Audi's Jamie Green looks on in admiration as BMW's Timo Glock enjoys his only win of the 2016 campaign in Austria.

Top far right: Tom Blomqvist guides his BMW M4 DTM close to the barriers at the Norisring circuit.
Photos: BMW Press Club

Above right: Gary Paffett had some strong mid-season races in the Euronics Mercedes, but had not tasted a DTM victory since 2013.
Photo: Mercedes AMG

Above far right: Close, but not touching – Bruno Spengler takes his BMW to within a whisker of the Norisring's concrete walls.
Photo: Audi Communications Motorsport

Right: BMW's Marco Wittmann drove superbly to defeat the strong challenge of Mortara's Audi and take his second DTM title in three years.
Photos: BMW Press Club

victorious at Croft, the halfway point of the campaign dawned with BMW team-mates Tordoff and Collard leading the standings, but with Neal giving chase. The three-times champion was left to fly the flag for Honda after a nightmare run for Shedden had put him down in ninth spot and more than 50 points in arrears.

The Scot returned to form when the second half of the campaign kicked off at Snetterton, however, taking his second win of the year. Turkington also enjoyed another win, and there was a third success for Jackson. It was a weekend when the issue of driving standards would be raised, however, following two huge race-stopping incidents, one of which resulted in a TV cameraman being lucky to escape injury when his gantry was felled by the rolling Chevrolet Cruze of Hunter Abbott.

Jason Plato, Neal and Jackson were the winners at Knockhill as Tordoff reclaimed the championship lead at the expense of Collard. Somehow the Yorkshireman maintained the top spot at Rockingham, having had to fight back from a disastrous qualifying session that put him towards the back of the capacity grid.

After a strong performance on race day, he joined Shedden and Aron Smith in taking victory. Tordoff was then forced to battle hard again at Silverstone, on a circuit not known to favour the BMW, to extend his lead to 11 points. Another win for Shedden, however – after earlier victories for Ingram and Jordan – meant that the Scot was now Tordoff's closest challenger for the title going into the final round.

An enthralling finale lay ahead, but it was outsider Turkington who looked like he could cause an almighty upset – pole position and two wins had put him suddenly within ten points of the lead going into the 30th and final race of the year.

Tordoff was still in the lead, but he had seen Shedden whittle down the gap to just two points. Ultimately, the superior pace of the Honda proved to be the key, Shedden chasing down and then passing his rival to become champion for the third time. It also made him the first man to successfully defend the title for nearly a decade.

"After Croft back in June, it looked like we were down and

out, but we stuck to our guns, kept plugging away and gave it absolutely everything to claw our way back," said Shedden. "It just goes to show that every single point really does count in this championship."

Tordoff ended the season as runner-up, with Jackson in third, although he missed out on the Independents title, which went to team-mate Jordan. WSR won both the manufacturers' and teams' titles, with Sutton emerging as the best of the rookie brigade.

As ever, the rumour mill was in full swing as AUTOCOURSE closed for press, although, as 12 months earlier, the only player to have revealed news was Jordan, who announced his departure from Motorbase after a single season.

GERMAN TOURING CAR CHAMPIONSHIP

Having watched F1-bound Pascal Wehrlein snatch the title from his grasp in 2015, Marco Wittmann wasted little time in reclaiming the DTM crown in 2016. The BMW driver saw off the challenge of Audi's Edoardo Mortara to secure the championship for a second time.

Wittmann's season began inauspiciously with a single points finish from the season opener at Hockenheim, where Mortara and Paul di Resta had taken a win apiece. After Audi and Mercedes had led the way in round one, BMW fought back in round two in Austria, Wittmann and Timo Glock emerging victorious from the Red Bull Ring. Wittmann's success in race one was BMW's 70th in the championship.

With points leader di Resta failing to score at the Lausitzring, Rob Wickens moved to the top of the standings with a brace of podium finishes on a weekend when Miguel Molina and Lucas Auer took the race wins. Then Mortara and Nico Müller shared the wins on a dramatic weekend at the Norisring. That meant Wittmann moved into the points lead as the field headed to Zandvoort for an event that ultimately would have a major impact on who would be crowned champion come the season's end.

Wickens beat Wittmann to take victory in race one, but the main talking point was Audi pair Mortara and Müller, who

Above: Despite taking four wins to Wittmann's three, Audi's Edoardo Mortaro ended up just four points behind the BMW champion.
Photo: Audi Communications Motorsport

Top right: Pretty in pink. Youngster Lucas Auer scored a win for Mercedes in Moscow.

Top far right: 2010 DTM champion Paul di Resta took his first win for Mercedes since returning to the series in 2014.
Photos: Mercedes AMG

Above right: Audi DTM legend Mattias Ekström scored a win in Budapest.
Photo: Audi Communications Motorsport

Above far right: New Zealander Shane van Gisbergen won out in the Australian Supercars Championship over team-mates Jamie Whincup and Craig Lowndes.
Photo: Red Bull

Right: A fixture in the DTM since 2005, Jamie Green finished third overall for Team Rosberg.
Photo: Audi Communications Motorsport

were handed drive-through penalties for going too quickly in a slow zone, introduced after Augusto Farfus had gone off into the gravel. Those penalties prevented the two drivers from scoring points, only for a post-race investigation to reveal potential discrepancies within the GPS systems used when the penalties were handed down. With no way to overturn the penalty, Mortara lost ground to Wittmann in the title race, as did Wickens when a late puncture in race two prevented him from scoring.

When racing resumed in Moscow after the summer break, Wickens took an impressive wet win in race one to assume the points lead. He lost it immediately in race two, however, as Wittmann headed a BMW 1-2-3-4.

Then the German extended his lead as he became the first driver to win three times with victory in race one at the Nürburgring. He added a third-place finish in race two, which was won by Mortara. Consequently, Wittmann went into the final two rounds 33 points clear of the Mercedes driver. It was a poor weekend for Wickens, who lost ground in third.

Anyone who thought that Wittmann was romping to the title, however, was in for a surprise in the penultimate meeting of the year in Hungary. There, Mortara headed an Audi 1–6 in race one to cut the gap to Wittmann to 14 points.

Then Wittmann and Mortara clashed at the start of race two, resulting in the latter failing to score, but Wittmann was excluded from the result for a technical infringement. That left the gap static going into the Hockenheim finale.

Wittmann finished ahead of Mortara in race one to extend his lead to 17 points, and although Mortara produced a faultless drive to win race two, fourth place was enough to give Wittmann the title by just four points.

"My success this year proves that the title in 2014 wasn't just a flash in the pan," Wittmann said. "There aren't many drivers at all who have won the DTM twice. I'm very proud to be part of this elite circle. Edoardo was a fierce rival and he would have deserved the title, too. In the end, it was close, but I think that we deserved the title."

Consolation for Audi came in the form of the teams' and manufacturers' titles, while Mercedes ended the year without a championship trophy to its name.

Big changes are afoot for 2017, with the grid set to drop from 24 to 18 cars. Each manufacturer will scale back to six cars in a year when the new Class One technical platform is introduced. In the driver market, Mortara announced a switch to Mercedes, while former champions Martin Tomczyk and Timo Scheider were among a number of drivers who confirmed that they wouldn't be returning for 2017.

SUPERCARS CHAMPIONSHIP

As AUTOCOURSE closed for press, the fight to secure the Supercars Championship title had still to be decided, with five drivers remaining in contention for top honours and two rounds left to run.

Having wrapped up the 2015 title, Mark Winterbottom was unable to defend his crown. Instead, Shane van Gisbergen emerged as the man to beat, having switched to Triple Eight over the winter.

Six wins, and only one failure to score, had given van Gisbergen a 148-point lead over team-mate Jamie Whincup going into the closing rounds, with the third Triple Eight car of Craig Lowndes holding third, albeit nearly 400 points behind. Scott McLaughlin, the only non-Holden driver remaining in the mix, and Will Davison also retained mathematical hopes of the crown.

Davison enjoyed success in the blue-riband event on the calendar, taking victory alongside Jonathon Webb at Bathurst. During the race, McLaughlin, Whincup and Garth Tander were involved in a controversial clash while dicing for the lead ten laps from home.

The cancellation of a planned event in Malaysia meant that the 2016 title was decided across 14 events, and the same will be the case in 2017, when the series introduces new Gen2 Supercar regulations. These are designed to open up the series to a wider range of body shapes and different engine configurations.

Among the early headlines was the news that Triple Eight will replace Walkinshaw Racing as the official factory Holden team, while Volvo will leave altogether after spending three seasons in the series.

THE HISTORY MAN

Inset: Seventh heaven for Jimmie Johnson after his dramatic win in the season's finale at Homestead.

Main photo: Johnson cemented his place as the greatest driver of the modern NASCAR era.

Photos: Brett Moist/LAT Photo USA

Above: Driving the No. 22 Ford for Team Penske, Joey Logano came within three points of Johnson in the final standings.
Photo: Michael R. Levitt/LAT Photo USA

Above right: Celebrating 'The Big One'. Denny Hamlin after his win in the Daytona 500.

Top far right: The 41-year-old Jimmie Johnson has plenty of miles left in the tank as he seeks a record-breaking eighth NASCAR title.
Photos: John Harrelson/LAT Photo USA

Above far right: Thinning crowds at venues such as Richmond are more commonplace as fans stay at home.
Photo: Nigel Kinrade/LAT Photo USA

Right: More empty seats under the lights at the Texas Speedway as Kyle Busch pits in his Toyota Camry.
Photo: John Harrelson/LAT Photo USA

JIMMIE JOHNSON wrote his name into American racing history by taking his seventh NASCAR Sprint Cup championship in 2016. He won the season finale at Homestead-Miami Speedway, recording the 80th victory of his career.

Thanks to NASCAR's fiendishly complex 'Chase for the Cup' rules, it's impossible to predict who will win the championship until the last of 36 races. NASCAR turned its back on a traditional season-long championship in 2004, when it instituted the 'Chase for the Cup' play-off system over the year's final ten races. Until the end of 2013, the top man in points over those ten races was the champion, but after Jimmie Johnson took his sixth title that year, NASCAR decided to add some byzantine twists to the plot.

Since that date, the 16 'Chase' qualifiers have been whittled down, with the bottom four drivers cut from the reckoning after each group of three of the ten 'Chase' races, leaving four contenders in the season finale. Any driver can advance to the next round by winning a race in each segment, and the champion is the best finisher among the final four at Homestead.

In recent years, NASCAR's TV ratings and crowds at many races have settled into a long downhill slide, and it was hoped that the unpredictable, almost random nature of the latest version of the 'Chase' would create more interest among fans, TV viewers and the media in general.

"If this is good for the sport, I'm a supporter," Johnson remarked. "I want our sport to succeed. But then again, I won six championships with a different format, so I'd much rather see it go back to that."

Yet the evidence is that the latest 'Chase' format is losing rather than gaining TV ratings. For half-a-dozen years, NASCAR's TV numbers have been in steady decline, and the trend continued in 2016. Many races were down substantially from 2015, and the year's last dozen races, including all the 'Chase' races, plunged to record low ratings.

That said, NASCAR enjoys American racing's biggest and best TV package by far, with plenty of income from handsome rights fees, and acres of TV time and space. IndyCar and IMSA are seriously hobbled on this front, with little more than race coverage and no leverage to negotiate better rights fees. NASCAR, on the other hand, is in the opening years of a pair of ten-year contracts with NBC and Fox, set to run to 2024 and worth more than $8 billion in all. So NASCAR enjoys plenty of scope to find a way to rebound before the time comes to renew its TV contracts with those companies. If the current decline continues, however, the rights fees are sure to be much smaller.

One of NASCAR's greatest drivers

Jimmie Johnson is the greatest NASCAR driver of the modern era, following in the tyre tracks of Richard Petty, Dale Earnhardt and Jeff Gordon. Johnson won his seventh NASCAR championship in 2016, thus equalling Petty and Earnhardt. He is 41 years old and reckons he has many more competitive years ahead of him, so it's likely that he will exceed Petty and Earnhardt's championship record.

Born and raised in California, Johnson has been racing at NASCAR's top level for 16 years, all with Rick Hendrick's four-car Hendrick Motorsport's Chevrolet team. He was spotted and selected by Hendrick's team leader, Jeff Gordon, who mentored Johnson through his first few years in Sprint Cup cars and remains a co-owner of Johnson's car after retiring at the end of 2015.

Johnson is an amiable, soft-spoken fellow who rarely loses his cool. He's also a complete gentleman, far removed from the traditional image of a rough-hewn Southerner. He is a clean, precise driver who is renowned for his ability to analyse a car's handling and communicate his feelings to his long-time crew chief, Chad Knaus.

"I think one of my big assets is that through all the chaos inside the car, I've always been able to communicate my feeling for the car," Johnson said. "Maybe I don't know how to fix it, but I can understand what I'm feeling and communicate it. I've been surprised that Chad has been

Above: Brad Keselowski heads the field in front of a big crowd basking in the sun at Talladega.

Left: In a close finish to the season, Kyle Busch ended up in third place in the standings, just two points behind Joey Logano.
Photos: Nigel Kinrade/LAT Photo USA

Right: Hendrick Motorsports are looking to the future with a big talent in Chase Elliott.
Photo: Brett Moist/LAT Photo USA

Below right: Matt Kenseth, champion in 2003, partnered Kyle Busch at Joe Gibbs Racing. He now has 38 wins in over 600 starts since his series debut in 2000.
Photo: Matthew T. Thacker/LAT Photo USA

Far right: Joey Logano came close to the title in 2016 and looks every inch a future NASCAR champion.
Photo: Brett Moist/LAT Photo USA

able to understand everything I've said to him over the years. That's really been the beauty of our relationship. I can be very descriptive and analytical, but it's understanding what I'm saying that is the key, and Chad is the guy who's been able to do that."

Johnson, Knaus and Hendrick's team dominated NASCAR from 2006 to 2010, winning five consecutive championships. He's been a little less effective in recent years, but has continued to win races every year, taking his sixth title in 2013. The 2016 season started well, Johnson scoring his 76th and 77th career wins in the first five races. But then followed the longest winless streak of his career as it took 24 races before he scored his 78th win at Charlotte in October, marking himself as a serious contender for the championship.

"There are times when you're on top and deserve all the accolades that you and the team receive," Johnson remarked. "And there are times when you've got to dig deep and re-create yourself and your team. The last couple of years haven't been the most productive years for myself or Hendrick Motorsport, but the commitment to getting back on top, and the work and time and effort that's going into it is pretty darn amazing.

"I'm so proud of where the company has come in the last three or four months. It wasn't a fun period of time. It was frustrating, but we had to put all that aside and make the car better. Rick [Hendrick] was tremendous. He went to a 24-hour wind tunnel test and he led by example. We were going to do everything we could. We were not going to lay down without a fight, and as soon as we found the right combination, all four of our cars had it and we were right back on top."

NASCAR's philosophy is almost diametrically opposed to Formula 1. The goal has always been to restrict technology as much as possible and to encourage close, competitive racing among as many cars as possible.

"I love Formula 1 and all the technology," Johnson grinned. "I love the concept of building the fastest vehicle, but that's not what NASCAR is. Our sanctioning body wants to put on an entertaining event, so they want to keep technology out. They intentionally want the cars to drive poorly in order to put on a better show. Everything in NASCAR is aimed at putting on a good show for the fans."

NASCAR allows its teams to use electronic data systems during testing, but data gathering and telemetry are not permitted at the track on race weekends. "By design, NASCAR tries to limit what we do," Johnson said. "But we use every tool that Formula 1 teams have to make our cars perform better within the limitations that we're allowed. Although we can't run data on the cars on race weekends, we collect data at every point in time we can otherwise. We have simulation programs, seven-poster rigs, wind tunnels, rolling-road wind tunnels and CFD models. We use everything Formula 1 does, but you can't connect the two worlds.

"In NASCAR, the driver ends up being the computer. It's my job when we come to the track to go racing to validate all of the virtual testing that we do during the week. One thing I am very proud of is the human element in NASCAR. You really have two different worlds, the virtual world of modern technology and the limited use of all that stuff at the races. I'm the one that has to flow between those two spaces, and help Chad and the team point it all in the right direction."

Johnson said he sees no signs of retirement anywhere on his horizon. "My wife and two young children prefer to stay at home, rather than travel all the time, and that makes it difficult sometimes," he said. "But I'm all in with racing. If I wasn't racing Cup cars all the time, I'd be racing something else. I can't see myself racing full-time in Cup cars when I'm 50. I guess there's an end out there that's closer than it's ever been, but I have no idea when I can identify that.

"We'll see what opportunities happen. If we were to win one or two more championships, that might sway me to consider slowing down sooner rather than later. But I plan on racing for a lot of years. I love sportscar racing and would love to do the Daytona 24 Hours again. I'd love to get back to my roots and do some off-road trucks again, because they are among the most extreme vehicles on the planet."

Jimmie Johnson is a true racer who is continuing to write his way into history. He's enjoyed a remarkable career, and it looks like he will continue to stand as NASCAR's benchmark for at least a few more years to come.

Above: Joey Logano and eventual winner Denny Hamlin lead the pack at the season opener, the Daytona 500.
Photo: Russell La Bounty/LAT South

Top right: Changing of the guard? Dale Earnhardt Jr sat out the second half of the season with concussion-like symptoms. He might not return to race in 2017.

Above right: After three NASCAR championships and 49 wins, Tony Stewart signed off with a victory at the Sonoma road course, before retiring from competition at the end of 2016.

Right: Carl Edwards executes his trademark back flip after taking victory at Richmond.
Photos: Nigel Kinrade/LAT South

NASCAR leads in cutting downforce

Over the past few years, many racing pundits have written numerous columns about cutting downforce in Formula 1 and IndyCar. We've presented arguments from many drivers and engineeers, past and present, and there's darn near unanimous agreement that downforce should be slashed. Yet F1 and IndyCar continue to make rules that increase downforce.

This is a great frustration to many observers, so it was interesting to see NASCAR tackle the job in 2016, applying a solution in a way that seems to have left everyone happy. Early in the year, NASCAR mandated much smaller spoilers and splitters, cutting downforce by as much as 30 per cent; the result was much better racing. The changes consisted of a reduction in spoiler height from 3.5 inches to 2.5 inches, a splitter reduction of two inches and a resizing of the rear deck fin to complement the spoiler change. As a result, downforce was reduced from 2,700 to about 2,000 pounds.

NASCAR will continue to remove downforce for the 2017 season by further cutting the size of spoilers and splitters, which is expected to reduce downforce by about 500 pounds to the 1,500-pound range. NASCAR's senior vice president of innovation and racing development, Gene Stefanyshyn, explained that the goal is to get down to an overall figure of 1,200 pounds.

"The objective is to put the driving back in the drivers' hands a bit more and take [more] aero dependence off the car," Stefanyshyn said. "The amount of downforce we are taking off the front and the rear is the same proportion. We're trying to keep the balance of the car identical. So it's been taken off in the same proportion to maintain the balance of the car as it was last year."

Seven-times champion Jimmie Johnson has been a big proponent of the move to low downforce. He said he couldn't be more pleased with the results. "I think taking the downforce off the cars has worked very, very well in all cases," he declared. "Ironically, there are some tracks where it doesn't show up as much as we thought it would. But I think on the tracks with abrasive surfaces, the low-downforce package has put on the best racing we've had for years and years, from each of driver, fan and statistical perspectives."

Johnson is equally happy with the way NASCAR has worked with its drivers and teams to achieve this result. "The process has been interesting and has been good for the sport," he remarked. "The drivers have a seat at the table with NASCAR in the development of specs on the car. I'm very proud of NASCAR and thankful for them taking this approach, because it's the driver who senses and feels what's going on. The engineers are very smart people, and a lot of people in the sport are very smart, but why not listen to the human element about what's going on?

"There is no quick fix in motorsports because there are many complicated elements, but it's been very good co-operation and a huge step in the right direction. I'd say the downforce changes are proof of the collaboration and working together. But honestly, it's taken some time and we're still learning how to communicate to each other properly.

"With 40 drivers, there are usually 40 different opinions. It's difficult for any sanctioning body, including NASCAR, but with the drivers' council and the seriousness that's involved, it's good to see the commitment of the drivers to doing the right thing, I think people are putting aside their own suggestions that would benefit them solely in favour of doing the right thing for the sport."

The drivers are represented by six of their number, who sit on the drivers' council. They include Johnson, Kevin Harvick, Brad Keselowski, Dale Earnhardt Jr and Joey Logano. "Each manufacturer is represented, and we have representation from the smaller teams, because the perspective of what needs to happen to the sport from the top two teams is far

different than the teams further down the field," Johnson explained.

He added that the experience of sitting on the drivers' council and working with NASCAR had been very rewarding. "It's been nice for me personally," he remarked. "As a six-time champion, I still had limited access to what's going on inside NASCAR, but now that I'm serving my first term on the drivers' council, I've learned far more about my sport than I ever knew before. It's been a very educational process for me and one that I take very seriously."

Roger Penske agreed with Johnson about the way NASCAR has worked with its teams in determining its low-downforce rules. "I think it puts the driver back in the car, and there's also a lot more strategy," Penske commented. "The tyres wear because the car is sliding around a little bit more, and there's more passing. If you have a better car at a particular time during the race, you can pass. You're not just sitting there with a bubble between you and the car in front of you.

"I think NASCAR has done a good job, and now, with the charter system, there's a competition and technical committee helping make the decisions and the timing of when any changes are going to be made, so it doesn't come overnight without any room for planning and implementation. There's a thinking process and an opportunity to judge what's happening. They're looking at it from a cost perspective, from a timing perspective and a performance perspective. Again, I think NASCAR is in great shape."

Finally, as AUTOCOURSE went to press, it appeared that Monster energy drink will replace Sprint as NASCAR's series sponsor in 2017. Sprint and its forerunner, Nextel, sponsored NASCAR's premier Cup series for 13 years. Monster is a Coca-Cola brand that enjoyed 39 per cent of the American energy market in 2015. Coca-Cola is a long-time NASCAR sponsor and has featured many top NASCAR drivers in its advertising and promotional campaigns. Monster sponsored Kurt Busch's car in 2016.

Above: Simon Pagenaud took an early-season lead and clinched the title in style with a win at Sonoma.

Top right: After a disappointing first season with Penske, Pagenaud regrouped to take the 2016 season by storm, with five wins and three second-place finishes on his way to the championship.
Photos: IndyCar/Chris Owens

Top far right: Helio Castroneves failed to take a win in 2016, but often was a factor, finishing third in the standings behind Penske team-mates Pagenaud and Power.
Photo: IndyCar/Shawn Gritzmacher

Above right: Will Power missed the opening race at Homestead, but four wins in mid-season enabled the Australian to finish the series runner-up.
Photo: IndyCar/Chris Owens

Above far right: Juan Pablo Montoya did not enjoy the best of seasons and was dropped by Penske as a full-time driver, but he opted to take up the team's offer of a ride in the 2017 Indianapolis 500.
Photo: IndyCar/Shawn Gritzmacher

Right: Will Power on his way to victory at Road America.
Photo: IndyCar/Chris Owens

Penske's 14th Indy car title

Team Penske's four cars dominated the 2016 Verizon IndyCar series, winning ten of 16 races as the team took its 14th USAC/CART/IRL/IndyCar championship amid an intra-team title battle between Simon Pagenaud and Will Power. In the end, Pagenaud was the man to beat as he led Power and Helio Castroneves to a 1-2-3 championship sweep for the team.

In his second year with Team Penske, the 32-year-old Frenchman led the championship from the second round at Phoenix in April. He won five races, finished second three times, took seven poles, and led more laps (410) and races (11) than anyone else. Pagenaud put an exclamation mark on his year by dominating the season finale at Sonoma, California, qualifying on pole and leading the race from start to finish.

"When the season started, we laid down the goals, and when I say goals, we didn't talk about results," Pagenaud said. "I think that's the key point. We don't think about results. We think about extracting 100 per cent from everybody at all the races, and that's what this team did this year.

"There were zero mistakes by the team. I made a few mistakes and we had some mechanical issues that were outside our power. That's part of racing. Sometimes you have problems, but this team has been performing at the top level all year. Now we're in a good spot, but there's still potential to improve and we've got a bright future."

What does Pagenaud expect from the next few years? "This team to me is the best team," he replied. "There's Ferrari in Formula 1, of course. But I have no desire to go anywhere else. I'm happy, and I would love to drive here at Team Penske for many years to come. I see myself racing with Team Penske trying to win as many races and championships as possible. Indy is my dream. I won't give up until I win that race."

Roger Penske said his team's advantage in 2016 came from his four drivers and their engineers working closely together and competing to get the maximum from their cars. "They all have the same cars, and it's how they want to set them up to go racing," Penske said. "I think all four of our drivers showed good speed this year. Three of them won races, and Helio was fast in many races. It's good because they're all pushing each other.

"I think we've taken advantage of all the work we've done as a whole, all the knowledge that's gone into developing and getting the best out of the suspension and mechanical part of the car. Also, the execution of our pit stops on race day has been outstanding for all four teams.

"I think our cars are quick on all types of racetracks. It's not just about shocks or any one thing. It's the way we've got the car set up. You can burn the tyres off if you're not careful. As you know, it's a very technical sport today. It's not just about having the biggest right foot. It's more about knowing when to go and how to go. I think it's understanding your roll centres and cambers and ride heights, and getting that mechanical combination operating at its best. There are so many variables."

Penske was delighted to see Pagenaud come into his own. "I think in 2016, we've executed better with Simon than in 2015, and there's no question that he's found his groove within the company," Penske observed. "I think he sees the benefit of the knowledge that surrounds him with the other three drivers, and he's stepped up his game. I think he and his engineer have done a good job.

"I think all the experience he has in sportscars and long-distance racing has helped Simon build consistency and the ability to not run off the road. He knows when it's time to go and he knows to not make mistakes. I think that's important."

Penske was equally pleased with Will Power's performances. "Will is really focused and I think he's achieved a new level overall this year," he said. "When you think about him missing the first race, then coming on strong

Penske Racing's 50th Anniversary

ROGER PENSKE began his racing team 50 years ago with just two employees, driver Mark Donohue and chief mechanic Karl Kainhofer. Donohue scored the little team's first win in July, 1966, driving a Lola T70 Can-Am car in a United States Road Racing Championship round at Kent, Washington. He went on to win two USRRC championships in 1967 and '68, three Trans-Am titles in 1968, '69 and '71, and the 1973 Can-Am championship behind the wheel of Penske's amazing turbo Porsche 917/30.

Today, Penske Racing, or Team Penske, is based in Mooresville, North Carolina, and is renowned as America's definitive racing team, with a record of more than 400 wins and 450 poles across many categories, including 16 Indy 500 victories, 14 Indy car championships and the 2012 NASCAR title.

But Penske is much more than America's most successful race team owner. He's also established himself as one of the USA's top independent businessmen. Half-a-century ago, Roger Penske retired from driving racing cars to begin his business career as a Chevrolet dealer in Philadelphia. The following year, he started Penske Racing. Since those days, Penske Corporation has grown into a global transportation industry that employs 53,000 people, leases almost a quarter of a million trucks and sells more than 400,000 cars each year.

Penske runs his business empire and race teams with the help of a fleet of seven corporate jets located in Detroit, Charlotte and Delaware. "The company has planes associated with different parts of the business," he explained. "I have one smaller plane that I use in the United States, and then we have a Gulfstream 550 that we use for the overseas and international businesses. I do somewhere between 900 and 1,000 hours in the air each year.

"It's a great place when you're in the plane, because you've got access to the internet. We've got Wi-Fi, and the phone connection is like you're sitting at your desk. You've got all the Bloomberg and other business news on the TV and internet.

"It gives you some quiet time where you get a chance to think about a lot of things that you're working on and try to develop some strategic thinking about where you're going to go. It also gives you a chance to fly with people you want to have some quiet time with, without interruption, to talk about their course or future in the business and how we can do better.

"It's about time utilisation. It think with what's happened with the use of the internet and the ability to communicate, you can make better use of your time and more utilisation of your time. Today, the guys that are processing their time better seem to get further ahead. I think with more information, in most cases, you can make a better decision."

Penske said he took particular pleasure from his team's 50th anniversary party in January, 2016. "A highlight of the year was our 50th anniversary celebration at the NASCAR Hall of Fame in Charlotte," he said. "We had almost 1,200 people there, including 42 drivers representing over 300 wins and 15 Indianapolis 500 wins. Our sponsors and our families were there, and it really showcased what's gone on over the past 50 years.

"I don't normally look back through the rearview mirror. I look forward through the windshield, but it was a great event... Racing has been a common thread through our businesses for so many years, and it was probably the highlight of my racing and business career."

Penske will celebrate his 80th birthday in February, 2017, but he remains as energetic and competitive as ever, and with Josef Newgarden's arrival, America's most successful race team should be even more dominant in the new year.

like he has over the last few months, it's been impressive. He gave Simon a good run.

"There's been some bad luck as well for all of our drivers, but [Scott] Dixon is our toughest competitor, and he's had some bad breaks too this year. Dixon is a very formidable competitor. We always have our eye on him. But it's just come together for us this year. In the end, it's all about execution, and we were able to do that this year."

Defending champion Dixon and Chip Ganassi's team had a disappointing year, as the New Zealander finished a distant sixth in IndyCar's championship. He won at Phoenix in April and Watkins Glen in September, but wasn't able to match Team Penske in most races. Team-mate Tony Kanaan finished seventh in points. He was in the hunt in many races, but was unable to score any victories.

Others to win IndyCar races in 2016 were Juan Pablo Montoya in the St Petersburg season opener; Alexander Rossi at Indianapolis; Sébastien Bourdais in Detroit; Josef Newgarden at Iowa; Ryan Hunter-Reay at Pocono; and Graham Rahal in a thriller on the high-banked Texas oval. Newgarden did a great job to finish fourth in the championship, while Rahal was fifth in points, ahead of Dixon and Kanaan.

Newgarden has demonstrated in recent seasons that he's one of the most talented American open-wheel drivers to come along in many years. He showed tremendous resilience and fortitude during 2016 as he bounced back magnificently from a big accident at the Texas Motor Speedway in June. He broke his right hand and a collarbone in Texas, but returned to action two weeks later at Elkhart Lake, before scoring a superb win on the Iowa oval only four weeks after his crash.

Newgarden drove for Ed Carpenter's very effective team over the past three years, but his performances in 2016 convinced Roger Penske to sign him for 2017. He will replace Juan Pablo Montoya, who had a tough season, finishing a distant eighth in IndyCar points. "Josef is a fantastic driver on the track and will be great with our partners off the track," Penske said. "He is hungry to win more races and win championships, and we hope to give him that opportunity as part of our team."

Left: The man most likely to? Josef Newgarden displayed both bravery and skill after bouncing back from injury in Texas to win in Iowa (*left*). For 2017, he will move to Penske and aim to be a serious championship contender.

Photo: IndyCar/Shawn Gritzmacher

Far left: 'The Captain' marked the 50th anniversary of Team Penske with a 1-2-3 Indycar triumph.

Below: Target Chip Ganassi's Scott Dixon was Penske's most feared competitor, but the reigning champion endured a somewhat luckless year, although he did score victories at Phoenix and Watkins Glen.

Photos: IndyCar/Chris Owens

Rossi's 100th Indianapolis 500

It was unfortunate that the 100th running of the Indianapolis 500 turned into a fuel-saving race, robbing the capacity crowd of a shootout among the remaining front-runners: Josef Newgarden, Tony Kanaan, Carlos Muñoz and James Hinchcliffe. Nor is there any denying that Alexander Rossi drove a steady, smart race on his way to winning the 500 on his first try.

Rossi had benefited from words of advice from team co-owners Michael Andretti and Bryan Herta. Both are very experienced, savvy racers, and it was Herta's sharp tactical thinking that put Rossi into fuel-saving mode and brought him his remarkable win at the Speedway.

Through the week of practice and qualifying leading up to the race, Rossi was fast and smooth, as he had been in all of the year's opening IndyCar races. He qualified a very respectable 11th and ran well in the race in the forward part of the midfield, amid the long snaking line of cars. Andretti team-mate Ryan Hunter-Reay was the man to beat until Townsend Bell messed up in the pits, crashing into Ryan and damaging both cars.

In the race's final segment, there was a great battle between Kanaan, Newgarden, Muñoz and Hinchcliffe. The first two led for most of the time, but Muñoz was also able to get to the front as they ran as hard as possible, knowing they had to stop for quick splashes of fuel in the closing laps. Sure enough, Kanaan stopped with seven laps to go, while

Newgarden, Muñoz and Hinchcliffe came in two laps later.

Rossi was running ninth when the final restart took place, with just over 30 laps to go, but he was able to nurse his car to the finish without stopping. He found he had half a lap's lead, and to make the finish he had to reduce his pace to a crawl. Coming out of Turn Four on the last lap, with Hunter-Reay doing all he could to tow his team-mate to the line, Rossi's car ran dry of fuel. But he was able to coast underneath the chequered flag four seconds ahead of Muñoz and Newgarden.

"I have no idea how we pulled that off," Rossi said. "We struggled a little bit on the pit stops, but Bryan came up with an unbelievable strategy. I can't believe we've done this. Ryan was unbelievable in helping me get to the finish. He was giving me a tow at the end, and it's an amazing result for Andretti Autosport. I'll cherish the fact that at one point, we were 33rd, and we rolled the dice and came through and made it happen.

"We ran out of fuel in Turn Four on the last lap," Rossi continued. "We were clutching it and coasting down the back straight. We knew it was going to be tight, but Ryan helped give me a tow to the finish over the last couple of laps. It was an amazing result."

Rossi went on to enjoy a good campaign, finishing fifth in the season-closer at Sonoma, behind Hunter-Reay and ahead of Josef Newgarden. He wound up 11th in points and was an easy Rookie of the Year winner. Rossi will continue in IndyCar with Michael Andretti's team in 2017.

Above: A full house and glorious weather greeted the 100th running of the Indianapolis 500.
Photo: IndyCar/Mike Finnegan

Top right: Alexander Rossi is stunned as the enormity of his victory begins to sink in.
Photo: IndyCar/Shawn Gritzmacher

Right: With his car virtually out of fuel, Rossi coasts over the famous line of bricks to the biggest win of his career.
Photo: Indycar/Forrest Mellott

Above: Takuma Sato endured a tough season with Foyt.

Top: Veteran Tony Kanaan raced as hard as ever for Ganassi.

Top left: Graham Rahal took a sensational win in Texas and claimed fifth in the championship standings.

Centre left: Sébastien Bourdais won in Detroit for KVSH Racing.

Left: It was a season of struggle for Marco Andretti.

Opposite page: The joy of winning for Josef Newgarden in Iowa.

Photos: IndyCar/Shawn Gritzmacher

Above: Helio Castroneves speeds through the sylvan setting during Indycar's return to Elkhart Lake.
Photo: Indycar/Chris Owens

Top right: Tommy Milner and Oliver Gavin, in the Corvette C7.R, took the IMSA Le Mans GT category.
Photo: Jake Galstad/LAT Photographic

Centre right: The WeatherTech Sports Car Championship was shaded by Eric Curran and Dane Cameron in the No. 31 Corvette Daytona prototype.
Photo: Rick Dole/LAT Photographic

Above right: Indycar, unlike Formula One, is often branded as a 'spec-racing' formula.

Above far right: Ed Jones took the Indy Lights crown and won the chance to break into Indycar in 2017.
Photos: Indycar/Chris Owens

Right: Dean Stoneman just pips Ed Jones in a photo finish at the Indianapolis Motor Speedway.
Photo: IMS/Joe Sibinski

Ed Jones wins Indy Lights

The 2016 Indy Lights championship was taken by 21-year-old Englishman Ed Jones, who won a $1 million scholarship that will enable him to compete in at least three IndyCar races in 2017, including the Indy 500. The Pro Mazda Championship was won by Aaron Telitz, 24, who received a $600,000 scholarship from Mazda and Cooper Tires to move up to Indy Lights. The US F2000 title went to 21-year-old Australian Anthony Martin, who won $363,000 to help him move up to Pro Mazda in 2017. Mazda and Cooper Tires paid $2.3 million in Road to Indy scholarships in 2016.

Action Express sweep IMSA

The Action Express team won IMSA's WeatherTech Sports Car Championship for the third year in a row, but this time around comparative newcomers Dan Cameron/Eric Curran were able to beat 2014 and '15 champions Joao Barbosa/Christian Fittipaldi to the title. Run by NASCAR veteran Gary Nelson, Action Express's pair of Corvette Daytona Prototypes usually finished in the first three, with Cameron/Curran winning two races and adding five more podiums to edge Barbosa/Fittipaldi by just three points.

The hotly-contested GT Le Mans category was won by one of the pair of factory Corvette C7.Rs driven by Tommy Milner/Oliver Gavin, beating factory or factory-backed teams from Ford, Ferrari, Porsche and BMW.

IMSA hopes its formula will enjoy a boost in 2017 with new factory-backed prototypes from Nissan, Mazda and Cadillac. In 2015, the FIA, ACO and IMSA worked together to choose four chassis constructors to build cars to compete in the FIA's LMP2 category and IMSA's new Daytona Prototype International class. The four builders selected were ORECA, Onroak Automotive (Ligier), Dallara and a joint Riley/Multimatic project.

In each of the WEC, European and Asian Le Mans series, these chassis will race in the LMP2 class, and all cars will be powered by spec Gibson V8 engines. In IMSA's WeatherTech series, the ACO/FIA configuration is eligible to compete in the new DPi category, which will take over as IMSA's premier formula. The old Daytona Prototypes will finally be parked, and current P2 cars will be allowed to race in IMSA for one more year under a grandfather clause.

LMP2 cars will compete in IMSA in the same prototype category with the new DPi cars. They will use the same four chassis, but will be powered by engines from different manufacturers and will also be required to use bodywork that's specific to each manufacturer.

Declining TV ratings and crowds

Over the past eight or nine years, NASCAR has slipped into a steady decline, losing crowds and TV ratings. The TV numbers are half what they were five years ago, and while some races continue to draw good crowds, many tracks are struggling.

It's very clear that all forms of racing in America have a lot of work to do if they wish to thrive in the long term as serious professional entities. Sportscar and Indy car racing fell off American popular culture's radar screen many years ago, amid extended struggles for control and an utter loss of brand identity or star power. Everybody's scratching their heads, trying to figure out a plan to reverse the downward spiral. What can be done?

One of the problems is that innovation, free-thinking and aesthetically pleasing elegant looks have been replaced by the plague of spec cars, cost controls and an elusive pursuit of the level playing field. Everyone has adopted NASCAR's restrictor-plate mentality, creating artificially close, competitive racing.

In IndyCar, we constantly hear the participants rave about how fiercely competitive their series is, but the TV ratings and crowds for most of IndyCar's oval races are abysmal. In the late nineties and into the turn of century, CART's races at Fontana, Michigan and Milwaukee drew huge crowds to watch beautiful, big-horsepower, high-performance race cars put on very different races than we see today.

The message about what appeals to the public and what doesn't is abundantly clear. But it's unlikely that a modern, CART-like formula can be re-created, because the spec-car plague has decimated America's Indy car building industry, while crowds, media coverage, TV ratings and the star power of the drivers have suffered a sharp decline over the past 15 years. So the delicate equation needed to produce big-time motor racing no longer exists, and IndyCar's most accomplished contemporary drivers are unknown to the general public.

One of IndyCar's most enjoyable weekends of 2016 was the return of big-time open-wheel racing to Elkhart Lake, or Road America, after a ten-year absence. The event drew the biggest crowd the circuit had seen in many years and it prompted the track to sign a long-term agreement to continue with IndyCar. Watkins Glen also rejoined IndyCar's schedule in 2016. The Glen didn't draw anything like Elkhart, but the classic road course in upstate New York also made a long-term commitment to IndyCar.

Meanwhile, IndyCar hopes to revitalise itself and attract a third manufacturer to compete against Chevrolet and Honda by freezing aero kits for 2017 and introducing a new, more attractive and effective common aero package for 2018. Given the parlous financial state of IndyCar today, this is a sensible move, but it also means that IndyCar will continue to be defined as a low-tech, spec-car formula trailing a long way behind Formula 1 and the WEC in international racing's pecking order.

NASCAR continues to enjoy star power from its top drivers, but it's going through a big transition right now, with Jeff Gordon and Tony Stewart retiring, and Dale Earnhardt Jr possibly facing the end of his career. Without doubt, Gordon, Stewart and Earnhardt are NASCAR's biggest modern stars, and it appears that their departure from the track is already having an effect on crowds and TV ratings.

Neither do the likes of Jimmie Johnson, Kyle Busch and Brad Keselowski seem to inspire the same passion from the fans, and it will be interesting to see if Kyle Larson, Chase Elliott or some of NASCAR's other up-and-comers will emerge as major personalities or superstars.

Keselowski won NASCAR's championship in 2012 with Penske Racing, which runs a pair of Fords for him and Joey Logano. For his part, Roger Penske believes NASCAR is doing well, despite recent declines in TV ratings and crowds at many of the races. "I think NASCAR is in great shape," he declared. "The average NASCAR race draws close to 100,000 people. I ran the Super Bowl in 2006 in Detroit, and we were glad when we had 75,000, so I think to have a Super Bowl every weekend in NASCAR is pretty good. All sports are suffering a little bit from the TV perspective, but you've got to add the social media aspect. There are a lot of new things out there and a lot of streaming, and I think when you look at the whole picture and combine everything, NASCAR is in great shape."

As Penske observed, many factors are at work in today's rapidly changing times, but without doubt the next few years will be critically intriguing for American motor racing. Which sanctioning body will turn the tide of decline and how will they do it?

APPRECIATIONS · by Gordon Kirby

Carl Haas

Photo: IMS/WRi2/Jean-Francois Galeron

Carl Haas

1929–2016

CARL HAAS, 86, died during the summer after a long struggle with Alzheimer's disease. One of America's most successful race team owners, Haas enjoyed wide influence in his other roles as the USA's most prolific race car salesman and chairman for many years of the SCCA's board of governors. He also promoted races at the Milwaukee Mile, sat on Road America's board of directors and ran his own Formula 1 team in 1985 and '86.

Haas owned and operated Newman/Haas Racing from 1983 to 2011 in partnership with Paul Newman, who lost his battle with cancer in 2008. Haas ran the team out of his base in Lincolnshire, Illinois, and Newman/Haas is ranked second only to Team Penske on IndyCar's all-time winners list, with a record of 107 wins, 109 pole positions and eight championships.

Haas caught the racing bug in 1951, when a friend took him to a race through the roads and streets of Elkhart Lake. The race presaged the creation a few years later of the great Road America road course, but that summer day caught young Carl's imagination and soon he was campaigning an MGTD in SCCA club races.

From Chicago's north side, he won some races aboard his MG, then traded up to a Porsche Spyder. Through the fifties and early sixties, Haas established himself as a race-winning amateur SCCA sportscar racer and began to make his name buying and selling sportscars of all types.

He met Elva boss Frank Nichols at Goodwood in 1958 and two years later started Carl Haas Auto, which sold Elva, McLaren and Lola racing cars, and Hewland gearboxes and parts. During the sixties and seventies, the business grew into the USA's largest seller of road racing cars and components to booming SCCA club and professional racing markets.

Having retired from driving, Haas formed a race team in 1967, competing in the SCCA's United States Road Racing Championship and the Can-Am series. His first driver was Masten Gregory, followed by Chuck Parsons, Peter Revson, Jackie Stewart, David Hobbs, Brian Redman, Patrick Tambay, Alan Jones, Jacky Ickx and Mario Andretti. Between 1971 and 1980, Haas's cars won 39 Can-Am and Formula 5000 races and seven championships.

During this time, famed actor/racer Paul Newman was running his own Can-Am team, buying cars from Haas. But the 'new era' Can-Am series was in trouble, and in 1982, as the series stumbled, Haas proposed to Newman that they become partners in a new CART Indy car team. He sweetened the deal by telling Newman that Mario Andretti was available to drive.

They formed a partnership towards the end of 1982, and Andretti raced the team's Lola in 1983, winning two races and finishing third in CART's Indy car championship. The following year, Andretti won six races and swept to the championship as Newman/Haas began to write its way into the history books.

Mario was the team's only driver and its

driving force for six years, until he was joined in 1989 by his son, Michael, who won Newman/Haas's second CART championship in 1991. Formula 1 World Champion Nigel Mansell drove for Newman/Haas in 1993 and '94, taking the team's third championship in his first year. Mario retired at the end of 1994, and Newman/Haas's fourth championship came in 2002, with Cristiano da Matta driving. This was followed by a remarkable string of four consecutive Champ Car championships with Sébastien Bourdais from 2004 to 2007.

John Cooper

1933–2016

JOHN COOPER, 83, died in the autumn. He was president of the Indianapolis Motor Speedway from 1979 to 1982, and president of the Daytona International Speedway from 1987 to 1990. He became USAC's first employee when the organisation was formed in 1955, and served as president of the Ontario Motor Speedway for a few years in the mid-seventies.

Cooper became president of the IMS In October, 1979, shortly after CART was formed. For a few months in 1980, he ran the Championship Racing League, a short-lived merger with CART that fell apart after only four races. He left the IMS in 1982 to serve as chairman of the Automobile Competition Committee of the United States (ACCUS). Later, he played a key role in helping to bring NASCAR to Indianapolis in 1994, and the creation of the Indy Racing League (IRL) in 1996.

Bill Smith

1928–2016

BILL SMITH passed away in 2016, aged 88. He was a director of McLaren Cars from the sixties through the seventies, in company with Bruce McLaren, Teddy Mayer and Tyler Alexander. He was also the founder of McLaren Engines in Detroit and chairman of McLaren North America.

Smith was a successful Ford dealer in Norwich, New York from 1949 to 2004. As a race car driver in the late fifties and early sixties, he won numerous SCCA Formula Junior races with Rev-Em Racing, a partnership of Peter Revson and Teddy and Timmy Mayer.

During his time with Team McLaren, the operation won five Can-Am championships, two Indianapolis 500s and two Formula One World Championships, while McLaren North America's partnership with BMW scored many IMSA wins.

Fred Opert

1939–2016

FRED OPERT passed away in 2016, aged 77. He was a leading figure in American single-seater racing in the late sixties and seventies. A racer himself, he found success as a team owner, running Brabham and Chevron Formula B and Atlantic cars for a wide range of drivers. Opert was a key man in Keke Rosberg's career, running Rosberg in Atlantic cars in 1976 and '77 in the United States, Canada and New Zealand. Occasionally, he also ran the likes of Alain Prost and Alan Jones in Atlantic cars. Over the last 30 years, the New Jersey-based Opert sold high-performance and speciality cars.

Bill Alsup

1938–2016

BILL ALSUP, 78, died in August while operating a crane at a remote site in the mountains near Silverton, Colorado. The crane rolled on a steep hill and he was killed instantly. Alsup had won both the SCCA's Super Vee championship and USAC's Mini-Indy series in 1978, before moving up to Indy cars. Running his own car, he was CART's first Rookie of the Year in 1979, and he drove in 57 Indy car races through 1984.

Alsup's best year was 1981, when he finished second to Rick Mears in CART's championship, driving a third Penske entry in most races, and his own car in the others. He finished third three times, making the podium at Michigan, Riverside and Milwaukee. He also made half-a-dozen attempts to qualify for the Indianapolis 500, but did so only once, in 1981, finishing 11th.

Born in Honolulu in July, 1938, Alsup was raised in San Francisco, but built his career in Vermont amid the burgeoning business of recreational

skiing. He started his racing career on motocross bikes and moved up through Formula Fords and Super Vees. He also raced long-distance sportscars with some success.

Tony Adamowicz

1941–2016

TONY ADAMOWICZ passed away in October, aged 75, after a battle with cancer. He raced successfully in the Can-Am, Trans-Am, Formula 5000 and IMSA, winning the 1968 Trans-Am under-2-litre championship and the SCCA's 1969 Formula 5000 championship. He also finished second in the 1971 Daytona 24 Hours, co-driving a Ferrari 512M with Ronnie Bucknum for Luigi Chinetti's North American Race Team (NART), and was third at Le Mans that year driving another NART Ferrari 512M with Sam Posey.

Later, Adamowicz drove for Nissan's factory Electramotive team, winning IMSA's GTU championship in 1981 aboard a Nissan 280ZX, and the GTO title in 1982 and '83 with a Nissan 280ZX-T. Adamowicz retired after the 1989 Daytona 24 Hours, but continued to do some historic racing for many years.

Bob Harkey

1930–2016

BOB HARKEY died in Indianapolis in January, aged 85. He raced Indy cars over the course of 17 years from 1963 to 1979. He started 85 USAC Championship races, including six Indy 500s. His best day came at Trenton in 1964, when he finished fourth. His best results at Indianapolis were a pair of eighths in 1964 and '74.

Bobby Johns

1932–2016

BOBBY JOHNS was 83 when he passed away during the summer at his home in Miami. Johns started 141 NASCAR Grand National races between 1956 and 1969, and won two major NASCAR races at Atlanta, in 1960, and Bristol, Tennessee in 1962. He finished third in NASCAR's championship in 1960, behind Rex White and Richard Petty. Johns also attempted to qualify for the Indy 500 seven times, making the field in 1965 and 1969. In 1965, he was Jim Clark's team-mate in a pair of Lotus 38-Fords, driving a steady race to finish seventh.

Bryan Clauson

Photo: Chris Owens/IMS

Bryan Clauson

1989–2016

BRYAN CLAUSON, 27, was killed in August, following a multi-car accident aboard a midget at the Belleville Nationals in Kansas. He had been leading the race when he collided with a lapped car and slammed into the barriers. Then he was hit by another car, suffering grievous head injuries.

Born in California, Clauson spent most of his life in Indiana. His father was a sprint car driver and he had grown up at racetracks across the MidWest. He was America's most successful contemporary midget and sprint car driver. A four-times USAC champion – twice in sprint cars and twice in midgets – he won 40 sprint car races and 39 midget races as well as a pair of Silver Crown races. He is tied with Gary Bettenhausen for fifth place on USAC's all-time sprint car winners list and is ranked seventh in midget wins.

In all, Clauson won 112 USAC races, including 21 in 2012, 26 in 2013, 22 in 2014 and 21 in 2015. In 2016, he was planning to start 200 races and had won 27 of the 115 he had run at the time of his death, including 18 in non-wing sprint cars, five in midgets and four in winged sprint cars. He also started the last three Indy 500s. Only a few hours after finishing 2016's 100th Indy 500, he won a sprint car race at Kokomo Speedway.

Scooter Patrick

1928–2016

VETERAN SCCA sports car driver Scooter Patrick passed away in September, aged 83. He had started his racing career in 1956, campaigning Porsches in SCCA races in California. Driving the 'PAM Special', a modified Porsche 550, he won two Pacific Coast SCCA championships. He also won a pair of SCCA national championships in 1966 and 1967, and drove a 'long tail' Porsche 908 at Le Mans. In 1967, he won the Doug Revson Trophy, a series of SCCA professional races for under-2-litre cars, driving a 906 Porsche.

The following year, Patrick was selected by Carroll Shelby to drive the new Mustang 2000 GT, and he won the SCCA's B Sports Racing championship. Patrick drove a Surtees TS8 F5000 car in 1969, and competed in the Can-Am series in 1973 and '74. He won the last Can-Am race ever run, at Road America in 1974. His last race was in a Corvette at Riverside in 1986.

MAJOR RESULTS

OTHER CHAMPIONSHIP RACING SERIES WORLDWIDE

Compiled by DAVID HAYHOE and JOÃO PAULO CUNHA - www.forix.com

FIA Formula E Championship

2015–16

SWUSP BEIJING EPRIX, Beijing Olympic Green Circuit, Beijing, China, 24 October. Round 1. 26 laps of the 2.137-mile/3.439km circuit, 55.559 miles/89.414km.
1 Sébastien Buemi, CH (Renault Z.E.15), 50m 08.835s, 66.475mph/106.981km/h; **2** Lucas di Grassi, BR (ABT Schaeffler FE01), +11.006s; **3** Nick Heidfeld, D (Mahindra M2ELECTRO), +15.681s; **4** Loïc Duval, F (Venturi VM200-FE-01), +16.009s; **5** Jérôme d'Ambrosio, B (Venturi VM200-FE-01), +16.514s; **6** Oliver Turvey, GB (NEXTEV TCR FormulaE 001), +39.466s; **7** Sam Bird, GB (Virgin DSV-01), +47.531s; **8** Nathanaël Berthon, F (Spark SRT_01E), +58.620s; **9** Stéphane Sarrazin, F (Venturi VM200-FE-01), +1m 07.814s; **10** Robin Frijns, NL (Spark SRT_01E), +1m 09.260s; **11** Daniel Abt, D (ABT Schaeffler FE01), +1m 13.351s *; **12** Jean-Éric Vergne, F (Virgin DSV-01), +1m 31.040s; **13** Bruno Senna, BR (Mahindra M2ELECTRO), +1m 50.833s; **14** Jacques Villeneuve, CDN (Venturi VM200-FE-01), -1 lap; **15** Nelson Piquet Jr, BR (NEXTEV TCR FormulaE 001), -2; Nicolas Prost, F (Renault Z.E.15), -4 (DNF-broken wing); António Félix da Costa, P (Spark SRT_01E), -13 (DNF-accident); Simona de Silvestro, CH (Spark SRT_01E), -24 (DNF-accident).
** includes 10s penalty for unsafe release.*
Fastest race lap: Buemi, 1m 39.993s, 76.933mph/123.812km/h.
Pole position: Buemi, 1m 37.297s, 79.065mph/127.243km/h.
Championship points: Drivers: 1 Buemi, 30; **2** di Grassi, 18; **3** Heidfeld, 15; **4** Duval, 12; **5** d'Ambrosio, 10; **6** Turvey, 8.
Teams: 1 Renault e.Dams, 30; **2** Dragon Racing Formula E Team, 22; **3** ABT Schaeffler Audi Sport, 18.

PUTRAJAYA EPRIX, Putrajaya Street Circuit, Persiaran Perdana, Putrajaya, Malaysia, 7 November. Round 2. 33 laps of the 1.591-mile/2.560km circuit, 52.493 miles/84.480km.
1 Lucas di Grassi, BR (ABT Schaeffler FE01), 50m 17.449s, 62.627mph/100.789km/h; **2** Sam Bird, GB (Virgin DSV-01), +13.884s; **3** Robin Frijns, NL (Spark SRT_01E), +29.776s; **4** Stéphane Sarrazin, F (Venturi VM200-FE-01), +32.628s; **5** Bruno Senna, BR (Mahindra M2ELECTRO), +34.404s; **6** António Félix da Costa, P (Spark SRT_01E), +36.925s; **7** Daniel Abt, D (ABT Schaeffler FE01), +37.283s; **8** Nelson Piquet Jr, BR (NEXTEV TCR FormulaE 001), +40.623s; **9** Nick Heidfeld, D (Mahindra M2ELECTRO), +52.904s; **10** Nicolas Prost, F (Renault Z.E.15), +53.695s; **11** Jacques Villeneuve, CDN (Venturi VM200-FE-01), +58.698s; **12** Sébastien Buemi, CH (Renault Z.E.15), +1m 07.728s; **13** Simona de Silvestro, CH (Spark SRT_01E), +1m 24.464s; **14** Jérôme d'Ambrosio, B (Venturi VM200-FE-01), -1 lap (DNF-suspension); **15** Nathanaël Berthon, F (Spark SRT_01E), -1; **16** Loïc Duval, F (Venturi VM200-FE-01), -4 (DNF-suspension); Oliver Turvey, GB (NEXTEV TCR FormulaE 001), -29 (DNF-throttle); Jean-Éric Vergne, F (Virgin DSV-01), -33 (DNF-accident).
Fastest race lap: Buemi, 1m 22.748s, 69.204mph/111.374km/h.
Pole position: Buemi, 1m 20.196s, 71.407mph/114.918km/h.
Championship points: Drivers: 1 di Grassi, 43; **2** Buemi, 35; **3** Bird, 24; **4** Heidfeld, 17; **5** Frijns, 16; **6** Sarrazin, 14.
Teams: 1 ABT Schaeffler Audi Sport, 49; **2** Renault e.Dams, 36; **3** Mahindra Racing Formula E Team, 27.

PUNTA DEL ESTE EPRIX, Punta del Este Street Circuit, Punta del Este, Uruguay, 19 December. Round 3. 33 laps of the 1.731-mile/2.785km circuit, 57.107 miles/91.905km.
1 Sébastien Buemi, CH (Renault Z.E.15), 45m 59.697s, 74.495mph/119.889km/h; **2** Lucas di Grassi, BR (ABT Schaeffler FE01), +3.534s; **3** Jérôme d'Ambrosio, B (Venturi VM200-FE-01), +6.725s; **4** Loïc Duval, F (Venturi VM200-FE-01), +6.807s; **5** Nicolas Prost, F (Renault Z.E.15), +21.057s; **6** António Félix da Costa, P (Spark SRT_01E), +22.410s; **7** Jean-Éric Vergne, F (Virgin DSV-01), +57.726s; **8** Daniel Abt, D (ABT Schaeffler FE01), +1m 00.744s; **9** Stéphane Sarrazin, F (Venturi VM200-FE-01), +1m 03.559s; **10** Robin Frijns, NL (Spark SRT_01E), +1m 03.840s; **11** Simona de Silvestro, CH (Spark SRT_01E), -1 lap; **12** Oliver Turvey, GB (NEXTEV TCR FormulaE 001), -1; **13** Oliver Rowland, GB (Mahindra M2ELECTRO), -1; **14** Nathanaël Berthon, F (Spark SRT_01E), -1; **15** Nelson Piquet Jr, BR (NEXTEV TCR FormulaE 001), -2 (DNF-spun off); Bruno Senna, BR (Mahindra M2ELECTRO), -7 (DNF-out of energy); Sam Bird, GB (Virgin DSV-01), -16 (DNF-battery); Jacques Villeneuve, CDN (Venturi VM200-FE-01), -33 (DNF-accident).
Fastest race lap: Buemi, 1m 17.413s, 80.475mph/129.513km/h.
Pole position: d'Ambrosio, 1m 15.498s, 82.516mph/132.798km/h.
Championship points: Drivers: 1 Buemi, 62; **2** di Grassi, 61; **3** d'Ambrosio, 28; **4** Bird, 24; **5** Duval, 24; **6** Heidfeld, 17.
Teams: 1 Renault e.Dams, 73; **2** ABT Schaeffler Audi Sport, 71; **3** Dragon Racing Formula E Team, 52.

BUENOS AIRES EPRIX, Puerto Madero Street Circuit, Buenos Aires, Argentina, 6 February. Round 4. 35 laps of the 1.541-mile/2.480km circuit, 53.935 miles/86.800km.
1 Sam Bird, GB (Virgin DSV-01), 45m 28.385s, 71.165mph/114.529km/h; **2** Sébastien Buemi, CH (Renault Z.E.15), +0.716s; **3** Lucas di Grassi, BR (ABT Schaeffler FE01), +7.525s; **4** Stéphane Sarrazin, F (Venturi VM200-FE-01), +9.415s; **5** Nicolas Prost, F (Renault Z.E.15), +11.316s; **6** Loïc Duval, F (Venturi VM200-FE-01), +15.660s; **7** Nick Heidfeld, D (Mahindra M2ELECTRO), +16.444s; **8** Robin Frijns, NL (Spark SRT_01E), +18.685s; **9** Oliver Turvey, GB (NEXTEV TCR FormulaE 001), +22.007s; **10** Bruno Senna, BR (Mahindra M2ELECTRO), +22.456s; **11** Jean-Éric Vergne, F (Virgin DSV-01), +24.482s; **12** Nelson Piquet Jr, BR (NEXTEV TCR FormulaE 001), +24.641s; **13** Daniel Abt, D (ABT Schaeffler FE01), +27.998s; **14** Simona de Silvestro, CH (Spark SRT_01E), +36.171s; **15** Mike Conway, GB (Venturi VM200-FE-01), +39.581s; **16** Jérôme d'Ambrosio, B (Venturi VM200-FE-01), -1 lap; António Félix da Costa, P (Spark SRT_01E), -18 (DNF-electrics); Salvador Durán, MEX (Spark SRT_01E), -21 (DNF-accident).
Fastest race lap: d'Ambrosio, 1m 10.285s, 78.930mph/127.025km/h.
Pole position: Bird, 1m 09.420s, 79.913mph/128.608km/h.
Championship points: Drivers: 1 Buemi, 80; **2** di Grassi, 76; **3** Bird, 52; **4** Duval, 32; **5** d'Ambrosio, 30; **6** Sarrazin, 28.
Teams: 1 Renault e.Dams, 101; **2** ABT Schaeffler Audi Sport, 86; **3** Dragon Racing Formula E Team, 62.

MEXICO CITY EPRIX, Autódromo Hermanos Rodríguez, Mexico City, D.F., Mexico, 12 March. Round 5. 43 laps of the 1.300-mile/2.092km circuit, 55.896 miles/89.956km.
1 Jérôme d'Ambrosio, B (Venturi VM200-FE-01), 48m 28.409s, 69.187mph/111.346km/h; **2** Sébastien Buemi, CH (Renault Z.E.15), +0.106s; **3** Nicolas Prost, F (Renault Z.E.15), +25.537s; **4** Loïc Duval, F (Venturi VM200-FE-01), +26.358s *; **5** Robin Frijns, NL (Spark SRT_01E), +28.477s; **6** Sam Bird, GB (Virgin DSV-01), +28.928s; **7** Daniel Abt, D (ABT Schaeffler FE01), +30.051s; **8** Nick Heidfeld, D (Mahindra M2ELECTRO), +36.373s; **9** Stéphane Sarrazin, F (Venturi VM200-FE-01), +37.291s; **10** Bruno Senna, BR (Mahindra M2ELECTRO), +37.603s; **11** Oliver Turvey, GB (NEXTEV TCR FormulaE 001), +38.598s; **12** Mike Conway, GB (Venturi VM200-FE-01), +38.790s; **13** Nelson Piquet Jr, BR (NEXTEV TCR FormulaE 001), +42.351s; **14** Simona de Silvestro, CH (Spark SRT_01E), +43.971s; **15** Salvador Durán, MEX (Spark SRT_01E), +1m 03.082s; **16** Jean-Éric Vergne, F (Virgin DSV-01), -1 lap; António Félix da Costa, P (Spark SRT_01E), -11 (DNF-accident).
Disqualified: Lucas di Grassi, BR (ABT Schaeffler FE01), -5.416s (car under weight).
** includes 15s penalty for missing a chicane more than three times.*
Fastest race lap: Prost, 1m 04.569s, 72.475mph/116.638km/h.
Pole position: d'Ambrosio, 1m 03.705s, 73.458mph/118.219km/h.
Championship points: Drivers: 1 Buemi, 98; **2** di Grassi, 76; **3** Bird, 60; **4** d'Ambrosio, 58; **5** Duval, 44; **6** Prost, 38.
Teams: 1 Renault e.Dams, 136; **2** Dragon Racing Formula E Team, 102; **3** ABT Schaeffler Audi Sport, 92.

LONG BEACH EPRIX, Long Beach Street Circuit, California, USA, 2 April. Round 6. 41 laps of the 1.324-mile/2.131km circuit, 54.290 miles/87.371km.
1 Lucas di Grassi, BR (ABT Schaeffler FE01), 45m 11.582s, 72.077mph/115.997km/h; **2** Stéphane Sarrazin, F (Venturi VM200-FE-01), +0.787s; **3** Daniel Abt, D (ABT Schaeffler FE01), +1.685s; **4** Nick Heidfeld, D (Mahindra M2ELECTRO), +2.343s; **5** Bruno Senna, BR (Mahindra M2ELECTRO), +4.968s; **6** Sam Bird, GB (Virgin DSV-01), +5.229s; **7** Jérôme d'Ambrosio, B (Venturi VM200-FE-01), +6.735s; **8** Loïc Duval, F (Venturi VM200-FE-01), +8.057s; **9** Simona de Silvestro, CH (Spark SRT_01E), +10.505s; **10** Mike Conway, GB (Venturi VM200-FE-01), +10.900s; **11** Nicolas Prost, F (Renault Z.E.15), +11.205s; **12** Oliver Turvey, GB (NEXTEV TCR FormulaE 001), +17.417s; **13** Jean-Éric Vergne, F (Virgin DSV-01), -1 lap; **14** Salvador Durán, MEX (Spark SRT_01E), -1; **15** Robin Frijns, NL (Spark SRT_01E), -1; **16** Sébastien Buemi, CH (Renault Z.E.15), -3; António Félix da Costa, P (Spark SRT_01E), -8 (DNF-suspension); Nelson Piquet Jr, BR (NEXTEV TCR FormulaE 001), -9 (DNF-accident).
Fastest race lap: Buemi, 57.938s, 82.276mph/132.41 km/h.
Pole position: Bird, 57.261s, 83.248mph/133.976km/h.
Championship points: Drivers: 1 di Grassi, 101; **2** Buemi, 100; **3** Bird, 71; **4** d'Ambrosio, 64; **5** Sarrazin, 48; **6** Duval, 48.
Teams: 1 Renault e.Dams, 138; **2** ABT Schaeffler Audi Sport, 132; **3** Dragon Racing Formula E Team, 112.

FIA FORMULA E CHAMPIONSHIP, Paris Street Circuit, France, 23 April. Round 7. 45 laps of the 1.193-mile/1.920km circuit, 53.686 miles/86.400km.
1 Lucas di Grassi, BR (ABT Schaeffler FE01), 52m 40.324s, 61.155mph/98.420km/h; **2** Jean-Éric Vergne, F (Virgin DSV-01), +0.853s; **3** Sébastien Buemi, CH (Renault Z.E.15), +1.616s; **4** Nicolas Prost, F (Renault Z.E.15), +2.142s; **5** Stéphane Sarrazin, F (Venturi VM200-FE-01), +3.044s; **6** Sam Bird, GB (Virgin DSV-01), +3.856s; **7** Robin Frijns, NL (Spark SRT_01E), +5.141s; **8** António Félix da Costa, P (Spark SRT_01E), +7.000s; **9** Bruno Senna, BR (Mahindra M2ELECTRO), +8.433s; **10** Daniel Abt, D (ABT Schaeffler FE01), +9.479s; **11** Jérôme d'Ambrosio, B (Venturi VM200-FE-01), +10.738s; **12** Nick Heidfeld, D (Mahindra M2ELECTRO), +12.453s; **13** Oliver Turvey, GB (NEXTEV TCR FormulaE 001), +13.721s; **14** Mike Conway, GB (Venturi VM200-FE-01), +14.833s; **15** Simona de Silvestro, CH (Spark SRT_01E), +16.049s; Nelson Piquet Jr, BR (NEXTEV TCR FormulaE 001), -6 laps (DNF-out of energy); Ma Qing Hua, CHN (Spark SRT_01E), -7 (DNF-accident); Loïc Duval, F (Venturi VM200-FE-01), -41 (DNF-gearbox).
Fastest race lap: Heidfeld, 1m 02.323s, 68.913mph/110.906km/h.
Pole position: Bird, 1m 01.616s, 69.704mph/112.178km/h.
Championship points: Drivers: 1 di Grassi, 126; **2** Buemi, 115; **3** Bird, 82; **4** d'Ambrosio, 64; **5** Sarrazin, 58; **6** Prost, 50.
Teams: 1 Renault e.Dams, 165; **2** ABT Schaeffler Audi Sport, 158; **3** Dragon Racing Formula E Team, 112.

BMW I BERLIN EPRIX, Berlin Street Circuit, Germany, 21 May. Round 8. 48 laps of the 1.197-mile/1.927km circuit, 57.474 miles/92.496km.
1 Sébastien Buemi, CH (Renault Z.E.15), 53m 46.086s, 64.135mph/103.216km/h; **2** Daniel Abt, D (ABT Schaeffler FE01), +1.767s; **3** Lucas di Grassi, BR (ABT Schaeffler FE01), +2.381s; **4** Nicolas Prost, F (Renault Z.E.15), +3.328s; **5** Jean-Éric Vergne, F (Virgin DSV-01), +4.927s; **6** Robin Frijns, NL (Spark SRT_01E), +6.501s; **7** Nick Heidfeld, D (Mahindra M2ELECTRO), +7.700s; **8** Mike Conway, GB (Venturi VM200-FE-01), +8.305s; **9** Simona de Silvestro, CH (Spark SRT_01E), +12.473s; **10** Stéphane Sarrazin, F (Venturi VM200-FE-01), +13.241s; **11** Sam Bird, GB (Virgin DSV-01), -1 lap; **12** Oliver Turvey, GB (NEXTEV TCR FormulaE 001), -1; **13** Nelson Piquet Jr, BR (NEXTEV TCR FormulaE 001), -1; **14** Ma Qing Hua, CHN (Spark SRT_01E), -1; **15** Bruno Senna, BR (Mahindra M2ELECTRO), -2; **16** Jérôme d'Ambrosio, B (Venturi VM200-FE-01), -3; René Rast, D (Spark SRT_01E), -6 (NC); Loïc Duval, F (Venturi VM200-FE-01), -9 (DNF-accident).
Fastest race lap: Senna, 59.067s, 72.977mph/117.446km/h.
Pole position: Vergne, 57.811s, 74.563mph/119.997km/h.
Championship points: Drivers: 1 di Grassi, 141; **2** Buemi, 140; **3** Bird, 82; **4** d'Ambrosio, 64; **5** Prost, 62; **6** Sarrazin, 59.
Teams: 1 Renault e.Dams, 202; **2** ABT Schaeffler Audi Sport, 191; **3** DS Virgin Racing Formula E Team, 119.

VISA LONDON EPRIX, Battersea Park Street Circuit, London, Great Britain, 2/3 July. Round 9. 2 x 33 laps of the 1.818-mile/2.925km circuit.
Race 1 (59.978 miles/96.525km).
1 Nicolas Prost, F (Renault Z.E.15), 53m 56.653s, 66.710mph/107.360km/h; **2** Bruno Senna, BR (Mahindra M2ELECTRO), +5.244s; **3** Jean-Éric Vergne, F (Virgin DSV-01), +8.195s; **4** Lucas di Grassi, BR (ABT Schaeffler FE01), +8.914s; **5** Sébastien Buemi, CH (Renault Z.E.15), +10.052s; **6** António Félix da Costa, P (Spark SRT_01E), +10.908s; **7** Sam Bird, GB (Virgin DSV-01), +10.986s; **8** Jérôme d'Ambrosio, B (Venturi VM200-FE-01), +12.106s; **9** Mike Conway, GB (Venturi VM200-FE-01), +12.456s; **10** Stéphane Sarrazin, F (Venturi VM200-FE-01), +15.918s; **11** Ma Qing Hua, CHN (Spark SRT_01E), +38.400s; **12** Nelson Piquet Jr, BR (NEXTEV TCR FormulaE 001), +52.028s; **13** Nick Heidfeld, D (Mahindra M2ELECTRO), +1m 01.264s *; **14** Simona de Silvestro, CH (Spark SRT_01E), +1m 03.079s *; **15** Oliver Turvey, GB (NEXTEV TCR FormulaE 001), -3 laps; Loïc Duval, F (Venturi VM200-FE-01), -10 (DNF-gearbox); Robin Frijns, NL (Spark SRT_01E), -14 (DNF-accident); Daniel Abt, D (ABT Schaeffler FE01), -14 (DNF-accident).
** includes 50s penalty.*
Fastest race lap: Piquet Jr, 1m 25.783s, 76.274mph/122.751km/h.
Pole position: Prost, 1m 27.192s, 75.041mph/120.767km/h.

Race 2 (59.978 miles/96.525km).
1 Nicolas Prost, F (Renault Z.E.15), 56m 32.648s, 63.643mph/102.424km/h; **2** Daniel Abt, D (ABT Schaeffler FE01), +7.633s; **3** Jérôme d'Ambrosio, B (Venturi VM200-FE-01), +22.524s; **4** Loïc Duval, F (Venturi VM200-FE-01), +23.290s; **5** Stéphane Sarrazin, F (Venturi VM200-FE-01), +24.984s; **6** Bruno Senna, BR (Mahindra M2ELECTRO), +27.174s; **7** Nick Heidfeld, D (Mahindra M2ELECTRO), +1m 07.544s *; **8** Jean-Éric Vergne, F (Virgin DSV-01), +1m 08.002s **; **9** Nelson Piquet Jr, BR (NEXTEV TCR FormulaE 001), +1m 14.270s; **10** Oliver Turvey, GB (NEXTEV TCR FormulaE 001), +1m 22.216s; **11** António Félix da Costa, P (Spark SRT_01E), +1m 58.324s ***; **12** Ma Qing Hua, CHN (Spark SRT_01E), -1 lap; **13** Mike Conway, GB (Venturi VM200-FE-01), -1; Lucas di Grassi, BR (ABT Schaeffler FE01), -15 (NC) ****; Sébastien Buemi, CH (Renault Z.E.15), -17 (NC); Robin Frijns, NL (Spark SRT_01E), -22 (DNF-accident); Simona de Silvestro, CH (Spark SRT_01E), -24 (DNF-accident); Sam Bird, GB (Virgin DSV-01), -27 (DNF-throttle).
** includes 50s penalty for exceeding energy used on second car.*
*** includes 50s penalty for exceeding energy used on second car and 1s penalty for unsafe release.*
**** includes 50s penalty for overtaking off track limits and 50s penalty for exceeding energy used on second car.*
***** includes 50s penalty for causing an accident.*
Fastest race lap: Buemi, 1m 24.150s, 77.754mph/125.133km/h.
Pole position: Buemi, 1m 22.033s, 79.761mph/128.362km/h.

Final championship points
Drivers
1 Sébastien Buemi, CH, 155; **2** Lucas di Grassi, BR, 153; **3** Nicolas Prost, F, 115; **4** Sam Bird, GB, 88; **5** Jérôme d'Ambrosio, B, 83; **6** Stéphane Sarrazin, F, 70; **7** Daniel Abt, D, 68; **8** Loïc Duval, F, 60; **9** Jean-Éric Vergne, F, 56; **10** Nick Heidfeld, D, 53; **11** Bruno Senna, BR, 52; **12** Robin Frijns, NL, 45; **13** António Félix da Costa, P, 28; **14** Oliver Turvey, GB, 11; **15** Nelson Piquet Jr, BR, 8; **16** Mike Conway, GB, 7; **17** Nathanaël Berthon, F, 4; **18** Simona de Silvestro, CH, 4.

Teams
1 Renault e.Dams, 270; **2** ABT Schaeffler Audi Sport, 221; **3** DS Virgin Racing Formula E Team, 144; **4** Dragon Racing Formula E Team, 143; **5** Mahindra Racing Formula E Team, 105; **6** Venturi Formula E Team, 77; **7** Andretti Formula E Team, 49; **8** Team Aguri, 32; **9** NEXTEV TCR Formula E Team, 19.

2016–17

HONG KONG EPRIX, Hong Kong Central Harbour Front Circuit, China, 9 October. Round 1. 45 laps of the 1.156-mile/1.860km circuit, 52.009 miles/83.700km.
1 Sébastien Buemi, CH (Renault Z.E.16), 53m 13.298s, 58.632mph/94.360km/h; **2** Lucas di Grassi, BR (Abt Schaeffler FE02), +2.477s; **3** Nick Heidfeld, D (Mahindra M3ELECTRO), +5.522s; **4** Nicolas Prost, F (Renault Z.E.16), +7.360s; **5** António Félix da Costa, P (Andretti ATEC-02), +17.987s; **6** Robin Frijns, NL (Andretti ATEC-02), +21.161s; **7** Jérôme d'Ambrosio, B (Penske 701-EV), +28.443s; **8** Oliver Tur-

vey, GB (NextEV NIO), +30.355s; 9 Maro Engel, D (Venturi VM200-FE-02), +30.898s; 10 Stéphane Sarrazin, F (Venturi VM200-FE-02), +31.734s; 11 Nelson Piquet Jr, BR (NextEV NIO), +35.256s; 12 Adam Carroll, GB (Jaguar I-type 1), +43.839s; 13 Sam Bird, GB (Virgin DSV-02), +48.058s; 14 Loïc Duval, F (Penske 701-EV), -2 laps; 15 Felix Rosenqvist, S (Mahindra M3ELECTRO), -2; Daniel Abt, D (Abt Schaeffler FE02), -11 (DNF-out of energy); Jean-Éric Vergne, F (Renault Z.E.16), -14 (DNF-out of energy); Mitch Evans, NZ (Jaguar I-type 1), -21 (DNF-mechanical); José María López, RA (Virgin DSV-02), -30 (DNF-accident); Ma Qing Hua, CHN (Renault Z.E.16), -44 (DNF-accident).
Fastest race lap: Rosenqvist, 1m 02.947s, 66.098mph/106.375km/h.
Pole position: Piquet Jr, 1m 03.099s, 65.939mph/106.118km/h.
Championship points: Drivers: 1 Buemi, 25; 2 di Grassi, 18; 3 Heidfeld, 15; 4 Prost, 12; 5 da Costa, 10; 6 Frijns, 8.
Teams: 1 Renault e.Dams, 37; 2 ABT Schaeffler Audi Sport, 18; 3 Andretti Formula E, 18.

MARRAKESH EPRIX, Circuit Moulay El Hassan, Agdal, Marrakesh, Morocco, 12 November. Round 2. 33 laps of the 1.846-mile/2.971km circuit, 60.921 miles/98.043km.
1 Sébastien Buemi, CH (Renault Z.E.16), 47m 40.840s, 76.661mph/123.374km/h; 2 Sam Bird, GB (Virgin DSV-02), +2.457s; 3 Felix Rosenqvist, S (Mahindra M3ELECTRO), +7.195s; 4 Nicolas Prost, F (Renault Z.E.16), +11.586s; 5 Lucas di Grassi, BR (ABT Schaeffler FE02), +13.771s; 6 Daniel Abt, D (ABT Schaeffler FE02), +18.233s; 7 Oliver Turvey, GB (NextEV NIO), +21.710s; 8 Jean-Éric Vergne, F (Renault Z.E.16), +28.011s; 9 Nick Heidfeld, D (Mahindra M3ELECTRO), +33.699s; 10 José María López, RA (Virgin DSV-02), +33.863s; 11 Robin Frijns, NL (Andretti ATEC-02), +37.092s; 12 Stéphane Sarrazin, F (Venturi VM200-FE-02), +40.683s; 13 Jérôme d'Ambrosio, B (Penske 701-EV), +42.034s; 14 Adam Carroll, GB (Jaguar I-Type 1), +49.026s; 15 Ma Qing Hua, CHN (Renault Z.E.16), +50.433s; 16 Nelson Piquet Jr, BR (NextEV NIO), +1m 15.452s; 17 Mitch Evans, NZ (Jaguar I-Type 1), -1 lap; 18 Loïc Duval, F (Penske 701-EV), -3; Maro Engel, D (Venturi VM200-FE-02), -7 (DNF); António Félix da Costa, P (Andretti ATEC-02), -12 (DNF).
Fastest race lap: Duval, 1m 22.600s, 80.459mph/129.486km/h.
Pole position: Rosenqvist, 1m 21.509s, 81.536mph/131.219km/h.

Provisional championship points
Drivers
1 Sébastien Buemi, CH, 50; 2 Lucas di Grassi, BR, 28; 3 Nicolas Prost, F, 24; 4 Felix Rosenqvist, S, 19; 5 Sam Bird, GB, 18; 6 Nick Heidfeld, D, 17; 7 António Félix da Costa, P, 10; 8 Oliver Turvey, GB, 10; 9 Robin Frijns, NL, 8; 10 Daniel Abt, D, 8; 11 Jérôme d'Ambrosio, B, 6; 12 Jean-Éric Vergne, F, 4; 13 Nelson Piquet Jr, BR, 3; 14 Maro Engel, D, 2; 15 Stéphane Sarrazin, F, 1; 16 José María López, RA, 1; 17 Loïc Duval, F, 1.

Teams
1 Renault e.Dams, 74; 2 ABT Schaeffler Audi Sport, 36; 3 Mahindra Racing, 36; 4 DS Virgin Racing, 19; 5 Andretti Formula E, 18; 6 NextEV NIO, 13; 7 Faraday Future Dragon Racing, 7; 8 Techeetah, 4; 9 Venturi Formula E, 3; 10 Panasonic Jaguar Racing, 0.

Results of the remaining races will be given in AUTOCOURSE 2017–2018

GP2 Series

All cars are Dallara GP2-11-Renault GP2.

GP2 SERIES, Circuit de Catalunya, Montmeló, Barcelona, Spain, 14/15 May. Round 1. 33 and 26 laps of the 2.892-mile/4.655km circuit.
Race 1 (95.374 miles/153.489 km).
1 Norman Nato, F, 58m 5.044s, 97.315mph/156.613km/h; 2 Nicholas Latifi, CDN, +1.337s; 3 Pierre Gasly, F, +4.248s; 4 Artem Markelov, RUS, +5.145s; 5 Sergio Canamasas, E, +7.294s; 6 Alex Lynn, GB, +7.596s; 7 Jordan King, GB, +8.678s; 8 Raffaele Marciello, I, +11.544s; 9 Gustav Malja, S, +13.102s; 10 Oliver Rowland, GB, +17.513s; 11 Nobuharu Matsushita, J, +18.526s; 12 Mitch Evans, NZ, +21.773s; 13 Arthur Pic, F, +23.022s; 14 Daniël de Jong, NL, +23.787s; 15 Marvin Kirchhöfer, D, +24.125s; 16 Jimmy Eriksson, S, +24.348s; 17 Sean Gelael, RI, +27.522s *; 18 Antonio Giovinazzi, I, +32.156s **; 19 Nabil Jeffri, MAL, -1 lap; Philo Paz Armand, RI, -5 (DNF-technical); Sergey Sirotkin, RUS, -10 (DNF-dpin); Luca Ghiotto, I, -33 (DNF-accident).
** includes 5s penalty.*
*** includes 20s penalty for causing an accident.*
Fastest race lap: Nato, 1m 34.050s, 110.717mph/178.181km/h.
Pole position: Gasly, 1m 27.807s, 118.588mph/190.850km/h.

Race 2 (75.126 miles/120.904km).
1 Alex Lynn, GB, 43m 50.241s, 102.931mph/165.651km/h; 2 Pierre Gasly, F, +0.377s; 3 Jordan King, GB, +1.120s; 4 Artem Markelov, RUS, +2.168s; 5 Raffaele Marciello, I, +3.382s; 6 Oliver Rowland, GB, +3.990s; 7 Nicholas Latifi, CDN, +4.584s; 8 Nobuharu Matsushita, J, +5.647s; 9 Sergio Canamasas, E, +8.115s; 10 Gustav Malja, S, +8.419s; 11 Sergey Sirotkin, RUS, +8.698s; 12 Luca Ghiotto, I, +8.828s; 13 Sean Gelael, RI, +9.178s; 14 Mitch Evans, NZ, +9.650s; 15 Marvin Kirchhöfer, D, +10.152s; 16 Norman Nato, F, +10.430s; 17 Daniël de Jong, NL, +10.726s; 18 Nabil Jeffri, MAL, +11.672s; 19 Jimmy Eriksson, S, -1 lap; Arthur Pic, F, -6 (DNF-accident); Antonio Giovinazzi, I, -6 (DNF-accident); Philo Paz Armand, RI, -13 (DNF-tecgnical).
Fastest race lap: Gasly, 1m 33.263s, 111.651mph/179.685km/h.
Pole position: Marciello.
Championship points: Drivers: 1 Gasly, 33; 2 Nato, 27; 3 Lynn, 23; 4 Latifi, 20; 5 Markelov, 20; 6 King, 16.
Teams: 1 DAMS, 43; 2 Racing Engineering, 43; 3 Prema Racing, 33.

GP2 SERIES, Monte-Carlo Street Circuit, Monaco, 27/28 May. Round 2. 40 and 30 laps of the 2.074-mile/3.337km circuit.
Race 1 (82.941 miles/133.480km).
1 Artem Markelov, RUS, 1h 01m 27.183s, 80.979mph/130.323km/h; 2 Norman Nato, F, +1.541s; 3 Oliver Rowland, GB, +3.187s; 4 Alex Lynn, GB, +8.239s; 5 Mitch Evans, NZ, +11.723s; 6 Raffaele Marciello, I, +15.025s; 7 Marvin Kirchhöfer, D, +21.153s; 8 Nobuharu Matsushita, J, +21.582s; 9 Daniël de Jong, NL, +22.343s; 10 Arthur Pic, F, +23.333s; 11 Antonio Giovinazzi, I, +25.037s *; 12 Sergio Canamasas, E, +30.192s; 13 Sean Gelael, RI, +31.295s; 14 Gustav Malja, S, +34.900s *; 15 Pierre Gasly, F, +49.748s; 16 Philo Paz Armand, RI, -1 lap; Luca Ghiotto, I, -5 (DNF-engine); Jimmy Eriksson, S, -8 (DNF-accident damage); Jordan King, GB, -13 (DNF-accident damage); Nabil Jeffri, MAL, -17 (DNF-accident); Sergey Sirotkin, RUS, -18 (DNF-accident); Nicholas Latifi, CDN, -19 (DNF-accident).
** includes 5s penalty.*
Fastest race lap: Gasly, 1m 20.469s, 92.764mph/149.289km/h.
Pole position: Sirotkin, 1m 19.186s, 94.267mph/151.708km/h.

Race 2 (62.205 miles/100.110km).
1 Nobuharu Matsushita, J, 41m 59.392s, 88.886mph/143.048km/h; 2 Marvin Kirchhöfer, D, +13.660s; 3 Raffaele Marciello, I, +15.453s; 4 Mitch Evans, NZ, +20.894s; 5 Alex Lynn, GB, +32.560s; 6 Norman Nato, F, +33.038s; 7 Oliver Rowland, GB, +33.594s; 8 Artem Markelov, RUS, +33.874s; 9 Arthur Pic, F, +36.777s; 10 Sergio Canamasas, E, +47.646s; 11 Daniël de Jong, NL, +54.291s; 12 Gustav Malja, S, +55.476s; 13 Pierre Gasly, F, +55.981s; 14 Luca Ghiotto, I, +56.501s; 15 Jimmy Eriksson, S, +58.682s; 16 Jordan King, GB, +1m 09.193s; 17 Nabil Jeffri, MAL, +1m 17.922s; 18 Antonio Giovinazzi, I, +1m 17.997s; Nicholas Latifi, CDN, -17 laps (DNF-gearbox); Sergey Sirotkin, RUS, -20 (DNF-fire extinguisher); Sean Gelael, RI, -23 (DNF-accident); Philo Paz Armand, RI, -27 (DNF-accident).
Fastest race lap: Matsushita, 1m 21.554s, 91.530mph/147.303km/h.
Pole position: Matsushita.
Championship points: Drivers: 1 Nato, 49; 2 Markelov, 48; 3 Lynn, 41; 4 Gasly, 33; 5 Marciello, 28; 6 Matsushita, 22.
Teams: 1 RUSSIAN TIME, 76; 2 Racing Engineering, 65; 3 DAMS, 61.

GP2 SERIES, Baku City Circuit, Azerbaijan, 18/19 June. Round 3. 26 and 21 laps of the 3.730-mile/6.003km circuit.
Race 1 (96.918 miles/155.974km).
1 Antonio Giovinazzi, I, 1h 03m 05.420s, 92.231mph/148.431km/h; 2 Sergey Sirotkin, RUS, +1.233s; 3 Raffaele Marciello, I, +1.343s; 4 Oliver Rowland, GB, +2.141s; 5 Mitch Evans, NZ, +2.628s; 6 Nobuharu Matsushita, J, +3.110s; 7 Sean Gelael, RI, +5.808s; 8 Daniël de Jong, NL, +6.663s; 9 Luca Ghiotto, I, +7.058s; 10 Gustav Malja, S, +7.595s; 11 Jimmy Eriksson, S, -2 laps; 12 Jordan King, GB, -2 (DNF-accident); Norman Nato, F, -8 (DNF-accident); Nabil Jeffri, MAL, -12 (DNF-tyre); Arthur Pic, F, -19 (DNF-accident); Artem Markelov, RUS, -19 (DNF-accident); Philo Paz Armand, RI, -21 (DNF-accident); Marvin Kirchhöfer, D, -26 (DNF-accident); Pierre Gasly, F, -26 (DNF-accident); Sergio Canamasas, E, -26 (DNF-accident); Alex Lynn, GB, -26 (DNF-accident); Nicholas Latifi, CDN, -26 (DNF-accident).
Fastest race lap: Matsushita, 1m 56.086s, 115.675mph/186.161km/h.
Pole position: Giovinazzi, 1m 51.752s, 120.161mph/193.381km/h.

Race 2 (78.267 miles/125.959km).
1 Antonio Giovinazzi, I, 44m 49.606s, 104.845mph/168.732km/h; 2 Pierre Gasly, F, +1.763s; 3 Sergey Sirotkin, RUS, +4.179s; 4 Jordan King, GB, +5.672s; 5 Artem Markelov, RUS, +14.809s; 6 Sergio Canamasas, E, +16.151s; 7 Nabil Jeffri, MAL, +17.693s; 8 Arthur Pic, F, +18.240s; 9 Alex Lynn, GB, +19.856s; 10 Marvin Kirchhöfer, D, +22.745s; 11 Raffaele Marciello, I, +23.645s; 12 Luca Ghiotto, I, +26.490s; 13 Nicholas Latifi, CDN, +28.862s; 14 Daniël de Jong, NL, +52.851s; 15 Oliver Rowland, GB, -1 lap; Nobuharu Matsushita, J, -8 (DNF-accident); Mitch Evans, NZ, -9 (DNF-accident); Sean Gelael, RI, -10 (DNF-accident); Gustav Malja, S, -10 (DNF-accident); Philo Paz Armand, RI, -12 (DNF-accident); Norman Nato, F, -12 (DNF-brakes); Jimmy Eriksson, S, -14 (DNF-accident).
Fastest race lap: Giovinazzi, 1m 54.792s, 116.979mph/188.260km/h.
Pole position: de Jong.
Championship points: Drivers: 1 Markelov, 54; 2 Nato, 49; 3 Giovinazzi, 46; 4 Gasly, 45; 5 Marciello, 43; 6 Lynn, 41.
Teams: 1 RUSSIAN TIME, 97; 2 Prema Racing, 91; 3 Racing Engineering, 73.

GP2 SERIES, Red Bull Ring, Spielberg, Austria, 2/3 July. Round 4. 40 and 28 laps of the 2.688-mile/4.326km circuit.
Race 1 (107.444 miles/172.914km).
1 Mitch Evans, NZ, 1h 18m 32.399s, 82.140mph/132.191km/h; 2 Sean Gelael, RI, +4.600s; 3 Raffaele Marciello, I, +10.789s; 4 Luca Ghiotto, I, +12.363s; 5 Jimmy Eriksson, S, +12.691s; 6 Oliver Rowland, GB, +15.557s; 7 Norman Nato, F, +16.559s; 8 Jordan King, GB, +22.762s; 9 Arthur Pic, F, +24.738s; 10 Nicholas Latifi, CDN, +25.629s; 11 Alex Lynn, GB, +27.000s; 12 Sergey Sirotkin, RUS, +49.708s *; 13 Gustav Malja, S, +50.258s *; 14 Daniël de Jong, NL, -1 lap; 15 Philo Paz Armand, RI, -1; 16 Rene Binder, A, -2; Antonio Giovinazzi, I, -11 (DNF-alternator); Artem Markelov, RUS, -12 (DNF-accident); Marvin Kirchhöfer, D, -14 (DNF-spin/ stall); Pierre Gasly, F, -23 (DNF-accident); Nabil Jeffri, MAL, -39 (DNF-accident damage); Sergio Canamasas, E, -40 (DNF-accident).
** includes 30s penalty for overtaking under safety car conditions.*
Fastest race lap: Evans, 1m 15.534s, 128.114mph/206.179km/h.
Pole position: Sirotkin, 1m 13.663s, 131.368mph/211.416km/h.

Race 2 (75.187 miles/121.002km).
1 Jordan King, GB, 44m 34.966s, 101.292mph/163.013km/h; 2 Oliver Rowland, GB, +6.019s; 3 Alex Lynn, GB, +7.702s; 4 Raffaele Marciello, I, +10.234s; 5 Antonio Giovinazzi, I, +10.417s; 6 Sergey Sirotkin, RUS, +11.821s; 7 Pierre Gasly, F, +12.594s; 8 Mitch Evans, NZ, +12.881s; 9 Luca Ghiotto, I, +15.878s; 10 Sergio Canamasas, E, +35.019s; 11 Artem Markelov, RUS, +57.740s; 12 Norman Nato, F, +1m 00.076s; 13 Jimmy Eriksson, S, +1m 00.107s; 14 Philo Paz Armand, RI, +1m 16.880s; 15 Rene Binder, A, +1m 17.325s; 16 Gustav Malja, S, -1 lap; 17 Nabil Jeffri, MAL, -1; 18 Arthur Pic, F, -1; 19 Marvin Kirchhöfer, D, -1; 20 Daniël de Jong, NL, -1; Nicholas Latifi, CDN, -8 (DNF-accident); Sean Gelael, RI, -25 (DNF-accident).
Fastest race lap: Nato, 1m 22.155s, 117.789mph/189.563km/h.
Pole position: King.
Championship points: Drivers: 1 Marciello, 66; 2 Evans, 56; 3 Nato, 55; 4 Markelov, 54; 5 Rowland, 54; 6 Giovinazzi, 52.
Teams: 1 RUSSIAN TIME, 120; 2 Racing Engineering, 100; 3 Prema Racing, 99.

GP2 SERIES, Silverstone Grand Prix Circuit, Towcester, Northamptonshire, Great Britain, 9/10 July. Round 5. 29 and 21 laps of the 3.660-mile/5.891km circuit.
Race 1 (106.071 miles/170.705km).
1 Pierre Gasly, F, 51m 39.383s, 123.299mph/198.431km/h; 2 Antonio Giovinazzi, I, +9.422s; 3 Oliver Rowland, GB, +16.090s *; 4 Mitch Evans, NZ, +21.667s; 5 Luca Ghiotto, I, +24.591s; 6 Nobuharu Matsushita, J, +25.165s; 7 Norman Nato, F, +25.474s; 8 Jordan King, GB, +25.651s; 9 Raffaele Marciello, I, +31.757s; 10 Artem Markelov, RUS, +33.115s; 11 Nicholas Latifi, CDN, +34.220s; 12 Marvin Kirchhöfer, D, +34.409s; 13 Sergio Canamasas, E, +37.898s; 14 Arthur Pic, F, +42.610s; 15 Jimmy Eriksson, S, +55.205s; 16 Alex Lynn, GB, +56.604s; 17 Nabil Jeffri, MAL, +57.490s; 18 Sergey Sirotkin, RUS, +1m 02.096s *; 19 Daniël de Jong, NL, +1m 23.661s; 20 Philo Paz Armand, RI, +1m 39.764s; 21 Sean Gelael, RI, -1 lap **; 22 Gustav Malja, S, -1.
** includes 5s penalty for exceeding track limits.*
*** includes 10s penalty for speeding in the pit lane.*
Fastest race lap: Evans, 1m 43.172s, 127.726mph/205.555km/h.
Pole position: Nato, 1m 38.216s, 134.171mph/215.928km/h.

Race 2 (76.787 miles/123.577km).
1 Jordan King, GB, 37m 35.325s, 122.700mph/197.468km/h; 2 Luca Ghiotto, I, +0.580s; 3 Oliver Rowland, GB, +11.664s; 4 Antonio Giovinazzi, I, +11.786s; 5 Nobuharu Matsushita, J, +17.518s; 6 Raffaele Marciello, I, +20.467s; 7 Pierre Gasly, F, +23.126s; 8 Marvin Kirchhöfer, D, +25.873s; 9 Sergio Canamasas, E, +26.721s; 10 Nicholas Latifi, CDN, +27.370s; 11 Arthur Pic, F, +28.061s; 12 Artem Markelov, RUS, +28.632s; 13 Mitch Evans, NZ, +28.844s; 14 Alex Lynn, GB, +29.598s; 15 Nabil Jeffri, MAL, +31.284s; 16 Daniël de Jong, NL, +32.249s; 17 Jimmy Eriksson, S, +35.412s; 18 Sean Gelael, RI, +40.058s; 19 Gustav Malja, S, +46.964s; 20 Philo Paz Armand, RI, +1m 30.028s; 21 Sergey Sirotkin, RUS, +1m 30.624s; 22 Norman Nato, F, -2 laps (DNF-spin).
Fastest race lap: Ghiotto, 1m 44.199s, 126.467mph/203.529km/h.
Pole position: King.
Championship points: Drivers: 1 Rowland, 79; 2 Giovinazzi, 78; 3 Gasly, 74; 4 Marciello, 72; 5 Evans, 70; 6 Nato, 65.
Teams: 1 Prema Racing, 152; 2 Racing Engineering, 129; 3 RUSSIAN TIME, 127.

GP2 SERIES, Hungaroring, Mogyoród, Budapest, Hungary, 23/24 July. Round 6. 36 and 28 laps of the 2.722-mile/4.381km circuit.
Race 1 (97.975 miles/157.676km).
1 Pierre Gasly, F, 55m 29.672s, 105.956mph/170.520km/h; 2 Antonio Giovinazzi, I, +1.365s; 3 Sergey Sirotkin, RUS, +2.835s; 4 Raffaele Marciello, I, +7.616s; 5 Arthur Pic, F, +9.908s; 6 Nobuharu Matsushita, J, +12.861s; 7 Norman Nato, F, +17.713s; 8 Jordan King, GB, +21.906s; 9 Artem Markelov, RUS, +22.101s; 10 Mitch Evans, NZ, +23.980s; 11 Oliver Rowland, GB, +29.377s; 12 Alex Lynn, GB, +34.050s; 13 Gustav Malja, S, +34.197s; 14 Marvin Kirchhöfer, D, +36.420s; 15 Daniël de Jong, NL, +38.526s; 16 Nicholas Latifi, CDN, +42.371s; 17 Luca Ghiotto, I, +51.757s *; 18 Sergio Canamasas, E, +1m 03.546s *; 19 Philo Paz Armand, RI, +1m 25.151s; 20 Nabil Jeffri, MAL, +1m 28.055s; 21 Jimmy Eriksson, S, -1 lap (DNF-engine); 22 Sean Gelael, RI, -1 *.
** includes 10s penalty for exceeding track limits.*
Fastest race lap: Rowland, 1m 29.627s, 109.342mph/175.969km/h.
Pole position: Gasly, 1m 25.612s, 114.470mph/184.221km/h.

Race 2 (76.198 miles/122.628km).
1 Sergey Sirotkin, RUS, 44m 47.059s, 102.118mph/164.344km/h; 2 Jordan King, GB, +4.953s; 3 Norman Nato, F, +7.506s; 4 Artem Markelov, RUS, +8.988s; 5 Mitch Evans, NZ, +14.146s; 6 Oliver Rowland, GB, +15.283s; 7 Pierre Gasly, F, +16.662s; 8 Raffaele Marciello, I, +20.939s; 9 Sergio Canamasas, E, +25.985s; 10 Sean Gelael, RI, +30.884s; 11 Daniël de Jong, NL, +32.518s; 12 Nicholas Latifi, CDN, +35.100s; 13 Marvin Kirchhöfer, D, +36.913s; 14 Gustav Malja, S, +39.660s; 15 Philo Paz Armand, RI, +46.412s; 16 Nabil Jeffri, MAL, +1m 00.825s; 17 Antonio Giovinazzi, I, +1m 01.928s *; Jimmy Eriksson, S, -14 laps (DNF-gearbox); Nobuharu Matsushita, J, -28 (DNF-accident); Arthur Pic, F, -28 (DNF-accident); Alex Lynn, GB, -28 (DNF-accident); Luca Ghiotto, I, -28 (DNF-accident).
** includes 10s penalty for causing an accident.*
Fastest race lap: Gasly, 1m 29.184s, 109.885mph/176.843km/h.
Pole position: King.
Championship points: Drivers: 1 Gasly, 107; 2 Giovinazzi, 96; 3 Marciello, 85; 4 Rowland, 83; 5 Nato, 81; 6 King, 80.
Teams: 1 Prema Racing, 203; 2 Racing Engineering, 161; 3 RUSSIAN TIME, 150.

GP2 SERIES, Hockenheimring Grand Prix Circuit, Heidelberg, Germany, 30/31 July. Round 7. 38 and 27 laps of the 2.842-mile/4.574km circuit.
Race 1 (108.002 miles/173.812km).
1 Sergey Sirotkin, RUS, 1h 00m 28.437s, 107.155mph/172.449km/h; 2 Luca Ghiotto, I, +13.146s; 3 Raffaele Marciello, I, +17.783s; 4 Arthur Pic, F, +25.873s; 5 Oliver Rowland, GB, +27.742s; 6 Gustav Malja, S, +28.130s; 7 Alex Lynn, GB, +32.730s *; 8 Antonio Giovinazzi, I, +36.051s; 9 Nobuharu Matsushita, J, +38.838s; 10 Marvin Kirchhöfer, D, +43.798s; 11 Nabil Jeffri, MAL, +46.523s; 12 Jimmy Eriksson, S, +48.067s; 13 Rene Binder, A, +50.706s; 14 Nicholas Latifi, CDN, +52.389s; 15 Jordan King, GB, +53.034s; 16 Philo Paz Armand, RI, +1m 15.773s; Norman Nato, F, -10 laps (DNF-spin/stall); Mitch Evans, NZ, -24 (DNF-brakes); Sean Gelael, RI, -30 (DNF-accident); Daniël de Jong, NL, -30 (DNF-accident); Artem Markelov, RUS, -32 (DNF-accident).
Disqualified: Pierre Gasly, F, +17.753s (fire extinguisher).
** includes 10s penalty for causing an accident.*
Fastest race lap: Sirotkin, 1m 25.209s, 120.078mph/193.247km/h.
Pole position: Sirotkin, 1m 22.193s, 124.484mph/200.338km/h.

Race 2 (76.738 miles/123.498km).
1 Alex Lynn, GB, 43m 20.504s, 106.232mph/170.964km/h; 2 Sergey Sirotkin, RUS, +2.922s; 3 Arthur Pic, F, +4.688s; 4 Luca Ghiotto, I, +6.206s; 5 Oliver Rowland, GB, +8.187s; 6 Pierre Gasly, F, +8.486s; 7 Raffaele Marciello, I, +9.259s; 8 Gustav Malja, S, +10.292s; 9 Artem Markelov, RUS, +14.404s *; 10 Mitch Evans, NZ, +15.162s; 11 Jordan King, GB, +16.727s; 12 Nobuharu Matsushita, J, +21.319s; 13 Jimmy Eriksson, S, +25.154s **; 14 Marvin Kirchhöfer, D, +25.292s; 15 Rene Binder, A, +25.768s; 16 Daniël de Jong, NL, +34.778s; 17 Nicholas Latifi, CDN, +41.617s ***; 18 Norman Nato, F, -1 lap; 19 Sean Gelael, RI, -3; Philo Paz Armand, RI, -5 (DNF-accident damage); Antonio Giovinazzi, I, -14 (DNF-accident); Nabil Jeffri, MAL, -21 (DNF-accident).
** includes 5s penalty for speeding in the pit lane.*
*** includes 5s penalty for forcing another driver off the track.*
**** includes 10s penalty for forcing another driver off the track.*
Fastest race lap: Markelov, 1m 25.236s, 120.040mph/193.185km/h.
Pole position: Giovinazzi.
Championship points: Drivers: 1 Sirotkin, 113; 2 Gasly, 113; 3 Marciello, 102; 4 Giovinazzi, 100; 5 Rowland, 99; 6 Nato, 81.
Teams: 1 Prema Racing, 213; 2 ART Grand Prix, 171; 3 RUSSIAN TIME, 167.

GP2 SERIES, Circuit de Spa-Francorchamps, Stavelot, Belgium, 27/28 August. Round 8.

25 and 18 laps of the 4.352-mile/7.004km circuit.
Race 1 (108.725 miles/174.976km).
1 Pierre Gasly, F, 53m 00.853s, 123.138mph/198.171km/h; **2** Jordan King, GB, +11.262s; **3** Alex Lynn, GB, +15.519s; **4** Raffaele Marciello, I, +19.163s; **5** Artem Markelov, RUS, +20.723s; **6** Antonio Giovinazzi, I, +24.616s; **7** Luca Ghiotto, I, +28.703s; **8** Gustav Malja, S, +32.404s; **9** Sergey Sirotkin, RUS, +35.778s; **10** Oliver Rowland, GB, +36.489s; **11** Nobuharu Matsushita, J, +36.620s; **12** Sergio Canamasas, E, +36.819s; **13** Nicholas Latifi, CDN, +41.909s; **14** Arthur Pic, F, +46.297s; **15** Jimmy Eriksson, S, +47.842s; **16** Mitch Evans, NZ, +51.263s; **17** Daniël de Jong, NL, +59.821s; **18** Sean Gelael, RI, +1m 10.120s; **19** Nabil Jeffri, MAL, +1m 11.915s; **20** Philo Paz Armand, RI, +1m 35.380s; Norman Nato, F, -7 laps (DNF-radiator); Marvin Kirchhöfer, D, -24 (DNF-accident damage).
Fastest race lap: Matsushita, 2m 00.976s, 129.509mph/208.424km/h.
Pole position: Giovinazzi, 1m 56.607s, 134.361mph/216.234km/h.

Race 2 (78.260 miles/125.948km).
1 Antonio Giovinazzi, I, 36m 48.422s, 127.698mph/205.510km/h; **2** Gustav Malja, S, +2.359s; **3** Luca Ghiotto, I, +3.921s; **4** Pierre Gasly, F, +4.479s; **5** Raffaele Marciello, I, +6.634s; **6** Oliver Rowland, GB, +13.133s; **7** Sergio Canamasas, E, +16.274s; **8** Norman Nato, F, +17.011s; **9** Nicholas Latifi, CDN, +18.821s; **10** Alex Lynn, GB, +19.045s *; **11** Nobuharu Matsushita, J, +20.170s; **12** Jordan King, GB, +20.458s *; **13** Mitch Evans, NZ, +20.713s; **14** Marvin Kirchhöfer, D, +24.657s; **15** Sean Gelael, RI, +34.203s; **16** Sergey Sirotkin, RUS, +35.557s **; **17** Daniël de Jong, NL, +35.989s *; **18** Nabil Jeffri, MAL, +41.645s *; **19** Philo Paz Armand, RI, +43.500s; **20** Jimmy Eriksson, S, +1m 36.962s *; **21** Artem Markelov, RUS, -1 lap (DNF-accident); **22** Arthur Pic, F, -1 *.
** includes 10s penalty for using DRS on lap 1.*
*** includes 10s penalty for causing an accident, and 10s penalty for using DRS on lap 1.*
Fastest race lap: Giovinazzi, 2m 01.329s, 129.132mph/207.818km/h.
Pole position: Malja.
Championship points: Drivers: 1 Gasly, 146; **2** Giovinazzi, 129; **3** Marciello, 120; **4** Sirotkin, 115; **5** Rowland, 104; **6** King, 98.
Teams: 1 Prema Racing, 275; **2** RUSSIAN TIME, 197; **3** Racing Engineering, 180.

GP2 SERIES, Autodromo Nazionale di Monza, Milan, Italy, 3/4 September. Round 9. 30 and 21 laps of the 3.600-mile/5.793km circuit.
Race 1 (107.796 miles/173.481km).
1 Antonio Giovinazzi, I, 52m 28.474s, 123.472mph/198.709km/h; **2** Raffaele Marciello, I, +1.457s; **3** Gustav Malja, S, +1.988s; **4** Pierre Gasly, F, +2.294s; **5** Norman Nato, F, +2.809s; **6** Luca Ghiotto, I, +2.823s; **7** Jordan King, GB, +3.896s; **8** Mitch Evans, NZ, +6.311s; **9** Oliver Rowland, GB, +7.898s; **10** Artem Markelov, RUS, +9.416s; **11** Nobuharu Matsushita, J, +10.277s; **12** Alex Lynn, GB, +11.013s; **13** Nabil Jeffri, MAL, +17.807s; **14** Sergey Sirotkin, RUS, +18.524s; **15** Nicholas Latifi, CDN, +22.201s; **16** Daniël de Jong, NL, +22.555s; **17** Marvin Kirchhöfer, D, +22.833s; **18** Jimmy Eriksson, S, +23.109s *; **19** Philo Paz Armand, RI, +23.482s; Sergio Canamasas, E, -15 (DNF-accident); Arthur Pic, F, -15 (DNF-accident).
Disqualified: Sean Gelael, RI, -1 lap.
** includes 5s penalty for forcing another driver off the track.*
Fastest race lap: Ghiotto, 1m 33.980s, 137.886mph/221.906km/h.
Pole position: Gasly, 1m 31.199s, 142.091mph/228.673km/h.

Race 2 (75.400 miles/121.344km).
1 Norman Nato, F, 33m 51.821s, 133.930mph/215.540km/h; **2** Pierre Gasly, F, +4.312s; **3** Antonio Giovinazzi, I, +8.495s; **4** Jordan King, GB, +12.775s; **5** Alex Lynn, GB, +13.576s; **6** Nobuharu Matsushita, J, +13.586s; **7** Gustav Malja, S, +21.526s *; **8** Marvin Kirchhöfer, D, +22.566s; **9** Oliver Rowland, GB, +29.225s *; **10** Artem Markelov, RUS, +32.813s **; **11** Arthur Pic, F, +34.192s; **12** Nabil Jeffri, MAL, +34.194s; **13** Sergio Canamasas, E, +36.845s; **14** Raffaele Marciello, I, +40.665s; **15** Nicholas Latifi, CDN, +41.503s **; **16** Sean Gelael, RI, +44.059s; **17** Philo Paz Armand, RI, +48.628s; **18** Jimmy Eriksson, S, -1 lap (DNF-overheating); **19** Daniël de Jong, NL, -1; Sergey Sirotkin, RUS, -15 (DNF-gearbox sensor); Mitch Evans, NZ, -21 (DNF-accident); Luca Ghiotto, I, -21 (DNF-accident).
** includes 10s penalty for causing an accident.*
*** includes 20s penalty for not slowing down for the virtual safety car.*
Fastest race lap: Markelov, 1m 33.727s, 138.258mph/222.505km/h.
Pole position: Evans.
Championship points: Drivers: 1 Gasly, 174; **2** Giovinazzi, 164; **3** Marciello, 138; **4** Sirotkin, 115; **5** King, 112; **6** Nato, 107.
Teams: 1 Prema Racing, 338; **2** Racing Engineering, 219; **3** RUSSIAN TIME, 218.

GP2 SERIES, Sepang International Circuit, Jalan Pekeliling, Kuala Lumpur, Malaysia, 1/2 October. Round 10. 29 and 22 laps of the 3.444-mile/5.543km circuit.
Race 1 (99.884 miles/160.747km).
1 Antonio Giovinazzi, I, 52m 18.049s, 114.587mph/184.410km/h; **2** Sergey Sirotkin, RUS, +5.858s; **3** Norman Nato, F, +8.015s; **4** Alex Lynn, GB, +16.214s; **5** Jordan King, GB, +18.742s; **6** Raffaele Marciello, I, +20.694s; **7** Luca Ghiotto, I, +24.964s; **8** Mitch Evans, NZ, +28.550s; **9** Gustav Malja, S, +28.741s; **10** Sergio Canamasas, E, +33.209s; **11** Pierre Gasly, F, +35.538s; **12** Oliver Rowland, GB, +35.550s; **13** Johnny Cecotto Jr, YV, +35.703s; **14** Nicholas Latifi, CDN, +41.169s; **15** Marvin Kirchhöfer, D, +41.288s; **16** Sean Gelael, RI, +42.969s; **17** Daniël de Jong, NL, +47.208s; **18** Nabil Jeffri, MAL, +1m 03.069s; **19** Philo Paz Armand, RI, +1m 06.464s; Nobuharu Matsushita, J, -7 laps (DNF-engine).
Did not start: Artem Markelov, RUS (electrics)
Fastest race lap: Matsushita, 1m 45.417s, 117.621mph/189.293km/h.
Pole position: Gasly, 1m 42.181s, 121.346mph/195.288km/h.

Race 2 (75.774 miles/121.946km).
1 Luca Ghiotto, I, 40m 22.211s, 112.618mph/181.241km/h; **2** Raffaele Marciello, I, +0.694s; **3** Pierre Gasly, F, +4.786s; **4** Antonio Giovinazzi, I, +5.402s; **5** Gustav Malja, S, +9.693s; **6** Mitch Evans, NZ, +13.333s; **7** Nobuharu Matsushita, J, +13.997s; **8** Oliver Rowland, GB, +15.893s; **9** Johnny Cecotto Jr, YV, +17.623s; **10** Nicholas Latifi, CDN, +24.245s; **11** Marvin Kirchhöfer, D, +25.837s; **12** Alex Lynn, GB, +27.198s; **13** Artem Markelov, RUS, +29.287s *; **14** Jordan King, GB, +1m 12.416s; **15** Sergio Canamasas, E, +1m 26.372s; Philo Paz Armand, RI, -4 laps (DNF-accident); Nabil Jeffri, MAL, -4 (DNF-accident); Sergey Sirotkin, RUS, -9 (DNF-gearbox); Sean Gelael, RI, -15 (DNF-spin) *; Norman Nato, F, -21 (DNF-accident); Daniël de Jong, NL, -22 (DNF-accident).
** includes 10s penalty for causing an accident.*
Fastest race lap: Canamasas, 1m 45.066s, 118.014mph/189.926km/h.
Pole position: Evans.
Championship points: Drivers: 1 Giovinazzi, 197; **2** Gasly, 190; **3** Marciello, 158; **4** Sirotkin, 135; **5** King, 122; **6** Nato, 122.
Teams: 1 Prema Racing, 387; **2** Racing Engineering, 244; **3** RUSSIAN TIME, 238.

GP2 SERIES, Yas Marina Circuit, Abu Dhabi, United Arab Emirates, 26/27 November. Round 11. 31 and 22 laps of the 3.451-mile/5.554km circuit.
Race 1 (106.913 miles/172.059km).
1 Pierre Gasly, F, 59m 14.764s, 108.344mph/174.363km/h; **2** Nobuharu Matsushita, J, +6.737s; **3** Artem Markelov, RUS, +11.309s; **4** Sergey Sirotkin, RUS, +14.111s; **5** Antonio Giovinazzi, I, +20.172s; **6** Norman Nato, F, +23.686s *; **7** Johnny Cecotto Jr, YV, +26.630s; **8** Alex Lynn, GB, +35.974s; **9** Nicholas Latifi, CDN, +39.007s; **10** Raffaele Marciello, I, +41.589s; **11** Luca Ghiotto, I, +43.486s; **12** Sergio Canamasas, E, +43.960s; **13** Jordan King, GB, +46.090s; **14** Daniël de Jong, NL, +1m 04.814s; **15** Mitch Evans, NZ, +1m 26.008s; **16** Philo Paz Armand, RI, +1m 27.892s; **17** Emil Bernstorff, GB, +1m 42.538s; Louis Delétraz, CH, -24 laps (DNF); Oliver Rowland, GB, -25 (DNF); Sean Gelael, RI, -25 (DNF); Gustav Malja, S, -26 (DNF); Nabil Jeffri, MAL, -28 (DNF).
** includes 5s penalty for speeding in the pit lane.*
Fastest race lap: Matsushita, 1m 51.175s, 111.751mph/179.846km/h.
Pole position: Gasly, 1m 47.476s, 115.597mph/186.035km/h.

Race 2 (75.853 miles/122.073km).
1 Alex Lynn, GB, 41m 36.580s, 109.479mph/176.190km/h; **2** Johnny Cecotto Jr, YV, +4.945s; **3** Sergey Sirotkin, RUS, +6.607s; **4** Nobuharu Matsushita, J, +8.078s; **5** Norman Nato, F, +13.375s; **6** Antonio Giovinazzi, I, +16.716s; **7** Artem Markelov, RUS, +17.807s; **8** Mitch Evans, NZ, +22.609s; **9** Pierre Gasly, F, +23.226s; **10** Jordan King, GB, +28.848s; **11** Oliver Rowland, GB, +30.312s; **12** Nicholas Latifi, CDN, +33.447s; **13** Raffaele Marciello, I, +37.784s; **14** Gustav Malja, S, +38.996s; **15** Emil Bernstorff, GB, +45.390s; **16** Sergio Canamasas, E, +45.936s; **17** Louis Delétraz, CH, +46.716s; **18** Philo Paz Armand, RI, +50.219s; **19** Luca Ghiotto, I, +1m 08.896s; **20** Nabil Jeffri, MAL, +1m 10.410s; **21** Sean Gelael, RI, +1m 27.122s; Daniël de Jong, NL, -22 laps (DNF-accident).
Fastest race lap: Ghiotto, 1m 52.646s, 110.291mph/177.497km/h.
Pole position: Lynn.

Final championship points
Drivers
1 Pierre Gasly, F, 219; **2** Antonio Giovinazzi, I, 211; **3** Sergey Sirotkin, RUS, 159; **4** Raffaele Marciello, I, 159; **5** Norman Nato, F, 136; **6** Alex Lynn, GB, 124; **7** Jordan King, GB, 122; **8** Luca Ghiotto, I, 111; **9** Oliver Rowland, GB, 107; **10** Artem Markelov, RUS, 97; **11** Nobuharu Matsushita, J, 92; **12** Mitch Evans, NZ, 90; **13** Gustav Malja, S, 53; **14** Arthur Pic, F, 36; **15** Sean Gelael, RI, 24; **16** Nicholas Latifi, CDN, 23; **17** Marvin Kirchhöfer, D, 21; **18** Johnny Cecotto Jr, YV, 18; **19** Sergio Canamasas, E, 17; **20** Jimmy Eriksson, S, 10; **21** Daniël de Jong, NL, 6; **22** Nabil Jeffri, MAL, 2.

Teams
1 Prema Racing, 430; **2** Racing Engineering, 258; **3** RUSSIAN TIME, 256; **4** ART Grand Prix, 251; **5** DAMS, 147; **6** Pertamina Campos Racing, 114; **7** MP Motorsport, 113; **8** Trident, 111; **9** Rapax, 107; **10** Carlin, 38; **11** Arden International, 12.

Japanese Championship Super Formula

All cars are Dallara SF14.

JAPANESE CHAMPIONSHIP SUPER FORMULA, Suzuka International Racing Course, Suzuka-shi, Mie Prefecture, Japan, 24 April. Round 1. 43 laps of the 3.608-mile/5.807km circuit, 155.157 miles/249.701km.
1 Naoki Yamamoto, J (-Honda), 1h 13m 59.415s, 125.820mph/202.487km/h; **2** Yuji Kunimoto, J (-Toyota), +11.710s; **3** Stoffel Vandoorne, B (-Honda), +13.194s; **4** Takashi Kogure, J (-Honda), +16.758s; **5** Koudai Tsukakoshi, J (-Honda), +23.270s; **6** James Rossiter, GB (-Toyota), +25.199s; **7** André Lotterer, D (-Toyota), +30.052s; **8** Bertrand Baguette, B (-Honda), +31.040s; **9** Tomoki Nojiri, J (-Honda), +37.410s; **10** João Paulo de Oliveira, BR (-Toyota), +37.971s.
Fastest race lap: Yuhi Sekiguchi, J (-Toyota), 1m 41.167s, 128.400mph/206.641km/h.
Pole position: Yamamoto, 1m 37.459s, 133.286mph/214.503km/h.

JAPANESE CHAMPIONSHIP SUPER FORMULA, Okayama International Circuit (TI Circuit Aida), Aida Gun, Okayama Prefecture, Japan, 29 May. Round 2. 8 laps of the 2.301-mile/3.703km circuit, 18.408 miles/29.624km.
1 Hiroaki Ishiura, J (-Toyota), 22m 06.947s, 49.939mph/80.370km/h; **2** Koudai Tsukakoshi, J (-Honda), +0.718s; **3** Takuya Izawa, J (-Honda), +1.749s; **4** Tomoki Nojiri, J (-Honda), +2.525s; **5** Naoki Yamamoto, J (-Honda), +3.841s; **6** Yuji Kunimoto, J (-Toyota), +5.408s; **7** Daisuke Nakajima, J (-Honda), +6.442s; **8** André Lotterer, D (-Toyota), +8.369s; **9** James Rossiter, GB (-Toyota), +9.677s; **10** Yuichi Nakayama, J (-Toyota), +10.753s.
Fastest race lap: Kamui Kobayashi, J (-Toyota), 2m 10.960s, 63.251mph/101.793km/h.
Pole position: Ishiura, 1m 13.620s, 112.515mph/181.076km/h.

JAPANESE CHAMPIONSHIP SUPER FORMULA, Fuji International Speedway, Sunto-gun, Shizuoka Prefecture, Japan, 17 July. Round 3. 55 laps of the 2.835-mile/4.563km circuit, 155.754 miles/250.661km.
1 João Paulo de Oliveira, BR (-Toyota), 1h 25m 12.917s, 109.798mph/176.702km/h; **2** Kazuki Nakajima, J (-Toyota), +2.836s; **3** Yuhi Sekiguchi, J (-Toyota), +28.542s; **4** André Lotterer, D (-Toyota), +31.889s; **5** James Rossiter, GB (-Toyota), +38.349s; **6** Hiroaki Ishiura, J (-Toyota), +43.344s; **7** Narain Karthikeyan, IND (-Toyota), +43.351s; **8** Koudai Tsukakoshi, J (-Honda), +50.014s; **9** Yuichi Nakayama, J (-Toyota), +59.488s; **10** Kamui Kobayashi, J (-Toyota), +1m 17.804s.
Fastest race lap: Nakajima, 1m 25.759s, 119.021mph/191.546km/h.
Pole position: Stoffel Vandoorne, B (-Honda), 1m 40.778s, 101.283mph/163.000km/h.

JAPANESE CHAMPIONSHIP SUPER FORMULA, Twin Ring Motegi, Motegi-machi, Haga-gun, Tochigi Prefecture, Japan, 21 August. Round 4. 52 laps of the 2.983-mile/4.801km circuit, 155.139 miles/249.672km.
1 Yuhi Sekiguchi, J (-Toyota), 1h 25m 17.584s, 109.133mph/175.633km/h; **2** André Lotterer, D (-Toyota), +6.127s; **3** Hiroaki Ishiura, J (-Toyota), +6.708s; **4** Yuji Kunimoto, J (-Toyota), +21.326s; **5** James Rossiter, GB (-Toyota), +31.996s; **6** Stoffel Vandoorne, B (-Honda), +35.761s; **7** Kazuki Nakajima, J (-Toyota), +36.334s; **8** Naoki Yamamoto, J (-Honda), +44.197s; **9** Kamui Kobayashi, J (-Toyota), +44.593s; **10** Daisuke Nakajima, J (-Honda), +1m 06.775s.
Fastest race lap: Kobayashi, 1m 36.444s, 111.364mph/179.223km/h.
Pole position: Sekiguchi, 1m 33.002s, 115.485mph/185.856km/h.

JAPANESE CHAMPIONSHIP SUPER FORMULA, Okayama International Circuit (TI Circuit Aida), Aida Gun, Okayama Prefecture, Japan, 10/11 September. Round 5. 28 and 51 laps of the 2.301-mile/3.703km circuit.
Race 5 (64.426 miles/103.684km).
1 Stoffel Vandoorne, B (-Honda), 36m 28.567s, 105.976mph/170.551km/h; **2** Yuji Kunimoto, J (-Toyota), +4.795s; **3** Narain Karthikeyan, IND (-Toyota), +9.855s; **4** Tomoki Nojiri, J (-Honda), +14.781s; **5** Koudai Tsukakoshi, J (-Honda), +17.531s; **6** Daisuke Nakajima, J (-Honda), +18.502s; **7** Hiroaki Ishiura, J (-Toyota), +19.782s; **8** João Paulo de Oliveira, BR (-Toyota), +22.013s; **9** James Rossiter, GB (-Toyota), +22.993s; **10** Naoki Yamamoto, J (-Honda), +25.032s.
Fastest race lap: Kazuki Nakajima, J (-Toyota), 1m 17.353s, 107.085mph/172.337km/h.
Pole position: Nakajima, 1m 14.038s, 111.880mph/180.053km/h.

Race 6 (117.348 miles/188.853km).
1 Yuji Kunimoto, J (-Toyota), 1h 11m 31.812s, 98.432mph/158.411km/h; **2** Kazuki Nakajima, J (-Toyota), +1.168s; **3** Hiroaki Ishiura, J (-Toyota), +1.683s; **4** André Lotterer, D (-Toyota), +5.267s; **5** João Paulo de Oliveira, BR (-Toyota), +9.490s; **6** Naoki Yamamoto, J (-Honda), +11.519s; **7** Stoffel Vandoorne, B (-Honda), +13.614s; **8** Takuya Izawa, J (-Honda), +16.056s; **9** Yuhi Sekiguchi, J (-Toyota), +19.969s; **10** James Rossiter, GB (-Toyota), +20.749s.
Fastest race lap: Ishiura, 1m 17.232s, 107.253mph/172.607km/h.
Pole position: Tomoki Nojiri, J (-Honda), 1m 14.404s, 111.330mph/179.168km/h.

JAPANESE CHAMPIONSHIP SUPER FORMULA, Sportsland-SUGO International Course, Shibata-gun, Miyagi Prefecture, Japan, 25 September. Round 6. 68 laps of the 2.302-mile/3.704km circuit, 156.517 miles/251.889km.
1 Yuhi Sekiguchi, J (-Toyota), 1h 22m 26.480s, 113.911mph/183.323km/h; **2** Daisuke Nakajima, J (-Honda), +14.278s; **3** Tomoki Nojiri, J (-Honda), +18.885s; **4** Kazuki Nakajima, J (-Toyota), +19.331s; **5** André Lotterer, D (-Toyota), +20.255s; **6** Stoffel Vandoorne, B (-Honda), +23.101s; **7** Takashi Kogure, J (-Honda), +23.990s; **8** James Rossiter, GB (-Toyota), +27.401s; **9** Bertrand Baguette, B (-Honda), +28.182s; **10** William Buller, GB (-Toyota), +38.001s.
Fastest race lap: Sekiguchi, 1m 07.736s, 122.331mph/196.872km/h.
Pole position: Sekiguchi, 1m 05.398s, 126.704mph/203.910km/h.

JAPANESE CHAMPIONSHIP SUPER FORMULA, Suzuka International Racing Course, Suzuka-shi, Mie Prefecture, Japan, 30 October. Round 7. 19 and 35 laps of the 3.608-mile/5.807km circuit.
Race 8 (68.558 miles/110.333km).
1 Yuji Kunimoto, J (-Toyota), 31m 58.809s, 128.626mph/207.003km/h; **2** André Lotterer, D (-Toyota), +1.772s; **3** Hiroaki Ishiura, J (-Toyota), +13.087s; **4** Tomoki Nojiri, J (-Honda), +22.140s; **5** Kazuki Nakajima, J (-Toyota), +24.143s; **6** Bertrand Baguette, B (-Honda), +24.951s; **7** Takashi Kogure, J (-Honda), +27.087s; **8** João Paulo de Oliveira, BR (-Toyota), +36.271s; **9** Kamui Kobayashi, J (-Toyota), +36.539s; **10** Daisuke Nakajima, J (-Honda), +36.811s.
Fastest race lap: Lotterer, 1m 40.221s, 129.612mph/208.591km/h.
Pole position: Ishiura, 1m 37.453s, 133.294mph/214.516km/h.

Race 9 (126.291 miles/203.245km).
1 Stoffel Vandoorne, B (-Honda), 1h 08m 32.427s, 110.554mph/177.920km/h; **2** André Lotterer, D (-Toyota), +0.726s; **3** Hiroaki Ishiura, J (-Toyota), +3.988s; **4** João Paulo de Oliveira, BR (-Toyota), +6.471s; **5** Bertrand Baguette, B (-Honda), +8.500s; **6** Yuji Kunimoto, J (-Toyota), +13.012s; **7** Kamui Kobayashi, J (-Toyota), +14.096s; **8** Yuhi Sekiguchi, J (-Toyota), +15.356s; **9** Takashi Kogure, J (-Honda), +18.353s; **10** Daisuke Nakajima, J (-Honda), +19.180s.
Fastest race lap: Narain Karthikeyan, IND (-Toyota), 1m 39.712s, 130.274mph/209.656km/h.
Pole position: Ishiura, 1m 37.026s, 133.880mph/215.460km/h.

Final championship points
Drivers
1 Yuji Kunimoto, J, 33; **2** André Lotterer, D, 30; **3** Yuhi Sekiguchi, J, 28.5; **4** Stoffel Vandoorne, B, 27; **5** Hiroaki Ishiura, J, 27; **6** Kazuki Nakajima, J, 22; **7** Naoki Yamamoto, J, 15.5; **8** João Paulo de Oliveira, BR, 15.5; **9** Tomoki Nojiri, J, 14.5; **10** James Rossiter, GB, 12; **11** Koudai Tsukakoshi, J, 11; **12** Daisuke Nakajima, J, 10.5; **13** Takashi Kogure, J, 8; **14** Narain Karthikeyan, IND, 5; **15** Bertrand Baguette, B, 4.5; **16** Takuya Izawa, J, 3.5; **17** Kamui Kobayashi, J, 1.

Teams
1 Project μ/cerumo-Inging, 54; **2** Vantelin Team TOM'S, 51; **3** ITOCHU ENEX Team Impul, 42; **4** DoCoMo Team Dandelion Racing, 36.5; **5** Nakajima Racing, 15; **6** Team Mugen, 14.5; **7** Real Racing, 14.5; **8** Kondo Racing, 12; **9** Drago Corse, 8; **10** Sunoco Team Lemans, 6.

GP3 Series

All cars are Dallara GP3/16 – Mecachrome GP3.

GP3 SERIES, Circuit de Catalunya, Montmeló, Barcelona, Spain, 14/15 May. Round 1. 22 and 17 laps of the 2.892-mile/4.655km circuit.
Race 1 (63.556 miles/102.284km).
1 Charles Leclerc, MC, 36m 38.694s, 104.189mph/167.677km/h; **2** Jake Hughes, GB, +6.023s; **3** Nirei Fukuzumi, J, +7.452s; **4** Antonio Fuoco, I, +19.325s; **5** Kevin Jörg, CH, +22.801s; **6** Alexander Albon, THA, +23.391s; **7** Jake Dennis, GB, +24.086s; **8** Oscar Tunjo, CO, +25.592s; **9** Nyck de Vries, NL, +26.467s; **10** Ralph Boschung, CH, +27.104s; **11** Matevos Isaakyan, RUS, +28.860s; **12** Matt Parry, GB, +30.952s; **13** Richard Gonda, SK, +33.095s; **14** Tatiana Calderón, CO, +33.871s; **15** Santino Ferrucci, USA, +34.241s; **16** Artur Janosz, PL, +36.835s; **17** Konstantin Tereschenko, RUS, +38.168s; **18** Sandy Stuvik, THA, +44.347s; **19** Alex Palou, E, +44.902s; **20** Jack Aitken, GB, +45.298s; **21** Akash Nandy, MAL, +55.655s; **22** Giuliano Alesi, F, +1m 00.294s; **23** Mahaveer Raghunathan, IND, +1m 03.391s; Steijn Schothorst, NL, -22 laps (DNF).
Fastest race lap: Leclerc, 1m 38.649s, 105.555mph/169.875km/h.
Pole position: Hughes, 1m 34.632s, 110.036mph/177.085km/h.

Race 2 (49.094 miles/79.009km).
1 Alexander Albon, THA, 28m 24.177s, 103.872mph/167.166km/h; **2** Oscar Tunjo, CO, +1.294s; **3** Antonio Fuoco, I, +7.307s; **4** Jake Dennis, GB, +8.114s; **5** Nyck de Vries, NL, +11.612s; **6** Matevos Isaakyan, RUS, +12.505s; **7** Kevin Jörg, CH, +15.012s; **8** Jake Hughes, GB, +15.670s; **9** Charles Leclerc, MC, +16.695s; **10** Ralph Boschung, CH, +18.345s; **11** Santino Ferrucci, USA, +18.757s; **12** Artur Janosz, PL, +20.796s; **13** Nirei Fukuzumi, J, +21.450s; **14** Alex Palou, E, +21.934s; **15** Sandy Stuvik, THA, +24.818s; **16** Giuliano Alesi, F, +26.107s; **17** Richard Gonda, SK, +27.024s; **18** Tatiana Calderón, CO, +27.582s; **19** Jack Aitken, GB, +29.135s; **20** Matt Parry, GB, +29.524s *; **21** Konstantin Tereschenko, RUS, +30.109s; **22** Steijn Schothorst, NL, +30.840s; **23** Akash Nandy, MAL, +33.959s; **24** Mahaveer Raghunathan, IND, +43.431s.
* includes 10s penalty.
Fastest race lap: Tunjo, 1m 38.722s, 105.477mph/169.749km/h.
Pole position: Tunjo.
Championship points: Drivers: 1 Leclerc, 27; **2** Albon, 23; **3** Hughes, 23; **4** Fuoco, 22; **5** Tunjo, 18; **6** Fukuzumi, 15.
Teams: 1 ART Grand Prix, 73; **2** DAMS, 35; **3** Trident, 22.

GP3 SERIES, Red Bull Ring, Spielberg, Austria, 2/3 July. Round 2. 24 and 17 laps of the 2.688-mile/4.326km circuit.
Race 1 (64.435 miles/103.698km).
1 Charles Leclerc, MC, 35m 01.756s, 110.500mph/177.833km/h; **2** Alexander Albon, THA, +2.292s; **3** Nyck de Vries, NL, +8.949s; **4** Ralph Boschung, CH, +11.840s; **5** Antonio Fuoco, I, +13.131s; **6** Matt Parry, GB, +15.494s; **7** Nirei Fukuzumi, J, +16.694s; **8** Jake Hughes, GB, +18.500s; **9** Jack Aitken, GB, +19.129s; **10** Sandy Stuvik, THA, +20.726s; **11** Artur Janosz, PL, +43.114s; **12** Akash Nandy, MAL, +45.524s; **13** Kevin Jörg, CH, +45.621s *; **14** Oscar Tunjo, CO, +46.119s; **15** Santino Ferrucci, USA, +46.534s *; **16** Alex Palou, E, +47.672s; **17** Tatiana Calderón, CO, +54.379s; **18** Konstantin Tereschenko, RUS, -1 lap (DNF-accident damage); **19** Richard Gonda, SK, -1 (DNF-accident); **20** Steijn Schothorst, NL, -1; Matevos Isaakyan, RUS, -20 (DNF-steering wheel); Jake Dennis, GB, -21 (DNF-throttle sensor).
Did not start: Giuliano Alesi, F (DNF-accident in practice).
* includes 10s penalty for causing an accident.
Fastest race lap: Leclerc, 1m 20.859s, 119.677mph/192.601km/h.
Pole position: Leclerc, 1m 19.041s, 122.429mph/197.031km/h.

Race 2 (45.619 miles/73.416km).
1 Ralph Boschung, CH, 33m 57.642s, 80.733mph/129.927km/h; **2** Alexander Albon, THA, +0.841s; **3** Antonio Fuoco, I, +1.784s; **4** Nyck de Vries, NL, +2.276s; **5** Jack Aitken, GB, +2.440s; **6** Jake Hughes, GB, +3.103s; **7** Matt Parry, GB, +3.486s; **8** Sandy Stuvik, THA, +4.802s; **9** Artur Janosz, PL, +5.038s; **10** Santino Ferrucci, USA, +6.017s; **11** Alex Palou, E, +6.169s; **12** Steijn Schothorst, NL, +7.080s; **13** Oscar Tunjo, CO, +7.349s; **14** Kevin Jörg, CH, +9.539s; Jake Dennis, GB, -3 laps (DNF-accident damage); Tatiana Calderón, CO, -4 (DNF-accident); Charles Leclerc, MC, -4 (DNF-accident); Akash Nandy, MAL, -7 (DNF-grass in radiators); Konstantin Tereschenko, RUS, -8 (DNF-accident); Matevos Isaakyan, RUS, -9 (DNF-electronics); Richard Gonda, SK, -12 (DNF-grass in radiators); Nirei Fukuzumi, J, -16 (DNF-water temperature).
Fastest race lap: Boschung, 1m 35.850s, 100.959mph/162.478km/h.
Pole position: Hughes.
Championship points: Drivers: 1 Leclerc, 58; **2** Albon, 53; **3** Fuoco, 42; **4** Hughes, 31; **5** de Vries, 31; **6** Boschung, 30.
Teams: 1 ART Grand Prix, 155; **2** Koiranen GP, 44; **3** Trident, 44.

GP3 SERIES, Silverstone Grand Prix Circuit, Towcester, Northamptonshire, Great Britain, 9/10 July. Round 3. 20 and 11 laps of the 3.660-mile/5.891km circuit.
Race 1 (73.127 miles/117.686km).
1 Alexander Albon, THA, 37m 53.666s, 115.915mph/186.547km/h; **2** Charles Leclerc, MC, +1.647s; **3** Antonio Fuoco, I, +12.239s; **4** Matt Parry, GB, +19.583s; **5** Nyck de Vries, NL, +25.000s *; **6** Ralph Boschung, CH, +29.094s; **7** Sandy Stuvik, THA, +33.337s; **8** Arjun Maini, IND, +34.157s; **9** Artur Janosz, PL, +35.434s **; **10** Alex Palou, E, +36.256s; **11** Nirei Fukuzumi, J, +36.476s; **12** Jake Dennis, GB, +36.696s **; **13** Jack Aitken, GB, +36.852s; **14** Steijn Schothorst, NL, +37.040s; **15** Kevin Jörg, CH, +38.077s; **16** Giuliano Alesi, F, +38.851s; **17** Tatiana Calderón, CO, +39.607s; **18** Santino Ferrucci, USA, +42.932s; **19** Akash Nandy, MAL, +43.180s; **20** Konstantin Tereschenko, RUS, +50.729s; **21** Matevos Isaakyan, RUS, +51.679s; Jake Hughes, GB, -7 laps (DNF-rear wing).
* includes 5s penalty for causing an accident.
** includes 5s penalty for exceeding track limits.
Fastest race lap: Albon, 1m 52.174s, 117.476mph/189.059km/h.
Pole position: Albon, 1m 47.348s, 122.757mph/197.559km/h.

Race 2 (40.182 miles/64.667km).
1 Antonio Fuoco, I, 27m 55.438s, 86.516mph/139.234km/h; **2** Alex Palou, E, +0.459s; **3** Charles Leclerc, MC, +0.583s; **4** Santino Ferrucci, USA, +3.695s; **5** Steijn Schothorst, NL, +5.060s; **6** Jack Aitken, GB, +5.626s; **7** Nirei Fukuzumi, J, +6.344s; **8** Nyck de Vries, NL, +6.370s *; **9** Jake Dennis, GB, +7.733s; **10** Sandy Stuvik, THA, +9.914s; **11** Kevin Jörg, CH, +10.890s; **12** Ralph Boschung, CH, +12.091s **; **13** Konstantin Tereschenko, RUS, +24.918s; **14** Alexander Albon, THA, +35.466s; **15** Artur Janosz, PL, +46.637s; **16** Matt Parry, GB, +50.407s *; **17** Jake Hughes, GB, +51.960s; **18** Matevos Isaakyan, RUS, +55.404s; **19** Arjun Maini, IND, +1m 16.796s; **20** Tatiana Calderón, CO, -1 lap (DNF-accident damage); Akash Nandy, MAL, -4 (DNF-spin); Giuliano Alesi, F, -11 (DNF-accident).
* includes 5s penalty for causing an accident.
* includes 10s penalty for causing an accident.
Fastest race lap: Albon, 2m 03.922s, 106.339mph/171.136km/h.
Pole position: Maini.
Championship points: Drivers: 1 Leclerc, 86; **2** Albon, 84; **3** Fuoco, 72; **4** de Vries, 42; **5** Boschung, 38; **6** Hughes, 31.
Teams: 1 ART Grand Prix, 227; **2** Trident, 82; **3** Koiranen GP, 64.

GP3 SERIES, Hungaroring, Mogyoród, Budapest, Hungary, 23/24 July. Round 4. 22 and 17 laps of the 2.722-mile/4.381km circuit.
Race 1 (59.864 miles/96.342km).
1 Matt Parry, GB, 35m 49.008s, 100.325mph/161.457km/h; **2** Antonio Fuoco, I, +3.283s; **3** Jake Dennis, GB, +4.208s; **4** Nirei Fukuzumi, J, +5.875s; **5** Ralph Boschung, CH, +6.444s; **6** Charles Leclerc, MC, +9.762s; **7** Alexander Albon, THA, +10.425s; **8** Arjun Maini, IND, +13.777s; **9** Jack Aitken, GB, +14.226s; **10** Kevin Jörg, CH, +14.977s; **11** Alex Palou, E, +18.728s; **12** Matevos Isaakyan, RUS, +19.943s; **13** Richard Gonda, SK, +20.320s; **14** Artur Janosz, PL, +20.914s; **15** Santino Ferrucci, USA, +22.111s; **16** Konstantin Tereschenko, RUS, +23.244s; **17** Akash Nandy, MAL, +23.790s; **18** Sandy Stuvik, THA, +25.665s; **19** Giuliano Alesi, F, +26.571s; **20** Nyck de Vries, NL, +26.885s; **21** Tatiana Calderón, CO, +27.914s; **22** Steijn Schothorst, NL, +28.312s; **23** Jake Hughes, GB, +43.965s.
Fastest race lap: de Vries, 1m 36.279s, 101.787mph/163.811km/h.
Pole position: de Vries, 1m 32.979s, 105.400mph/169.625km/h.

Race 2 (46.253 miles/74.437km).
1 Alexander Albon, THA, 30m 01.514s, 92.477mph/148.828km/h; **2** Arjun Maini, IND, +3.365s; **3** Charles Leclerc, MC, +4.363s; **4** Nirei Fukuzumi, J, +6.955s; **5** Matt Parry, GB, +8.848s; **6** Jack Aitken, GB, +10.908s *; **7** Jake Dennis, GB, +13.635s; **8** Matevos Isaakyan, RUS, +14.600s; **9** Kevin Jörg, CH, +15.820s; **10** Antonio Fuoco, I, +16.562s; **11** Santino Ferrucci, USA, +18.051s; **12** Artur Janosz, PL, +19.330s; **13** Nyck de Vries, NL, +20.150s; **14** Alex Palou, E, +22.892s; **15** Richard Gonda, SK, +23.631s; **16** Giuliano Alesi, F, +24.330s; **17** Konstantin Tereschenko, RUS, +27.348s; **18** Sandy Stuvik, THA, +28.354s; **19** Jake Hughes, GB, +28.676s; **20** Steijn Schothorst, NL, +29.312s; **21** Tatiana Calderón, CO, +30.151s; **22** Ralph Boschung, CH, +34.831s; Akash Nandy, MAL, -17 laps (DNF-accident).
* includes 5s penalty for causing an accident.
Fastest race lap: Albon, 1m 35.140s, 103.006mph/165.772km/h.
Pole position: Maini.
Championship points: Drivers: 1 Albon, 107; **2** Leclerc, 104; **3** Fuoco, 90; **4** Parry, 53; **5** Boschung, 48; **6** de Vries, 46.
Teams: 1 ART Grand Prix, 292; **2** Koiranen GP, 106; **3** Trident, 100.

GP3 SERIES, Hockenheimring Grand Prix Circuit, Heidelberg, Germany, 30/31 July. Round 5. 23 and 18 laps of the 2.842-mile/4.574km circuit.
Race 1 (65.369 miles/105.202km).
1 Antonio Fuoco, I, 38m 25.683s, 102.065mph/164.258km/h; **2** Nyck de Vries, NL, +5.988s; **3** Matt Parry, GB, +6.836s; **4** Alexander Albon, THA, +7.973s; **5** Charles Leclerc, MC, +10.519s; **6** Jack Aitken, GB, +12.291s; **7** Arjun Maini, IND, +14.828s; **8** Jake Hughes, GB, +18.246s; **9** Santino Ferrucci, USA, +20.065s; **10** Tatiana Calderón, CO, +20.206s; **11** Artur Janosz, PL, +23.964s; **12** Jake Dennis, GB, +25.332s; **13** Akash Nandy, MAL, +25.467s; **14** Kevin Jörg, CH, +37.076s; **15** Ralph Boschung, CH, +1m 01.860s; **16** Alex Palou, E, +1m 13.841s; Sandy Stuvik, THA, -9 laps (DNF-electrics); Steijn Schothorst, NL, -19 (DNF-accident); Matevos Isaakyan, RUS, -20 (DNF-accident); Nirei Fukuzumi, J, -20 (DNF-accident); Konstantin Tereschenko, RUS, -21 (DNF-accident); Giuliano Alesi, F, -23 (DNF-electrics).
Fastest race lap: Leclerc, 1m 31.703s, 111.574mph/179.562km/h.
Pole position: Albon, 1m 28.431s, 115.703mph/186.206km/h.

Race 2 (51.159 miles/82.33km).
1 Jake Hughes, GB, 29m 51.410s, 102.808mph/165.453km/h; **2** Jack Aitken, GB, +2.602s; **3** Charles Leclerc, MC, +5.884s; **4** Santino Ferrucci, USA, +6.835s; **5** Arjun Maini, IND, +7.718s; **6** Jake Dennis, GB, +8.935s; **7** Matt Parry, GB, +14.441s; **8** Nyck de Vries, NL, +16.694s; **9** Tatiana Calderón, CO, +16.940s; **10** Kevin Jörg, CH, +17.928s; **11** Nirei Fukuzumi, J, +18.562s; **12** Sandy Stuvik, THA, +27.796s; **13** Matevos Isaakyan, RUS, +28.852s; **14** Giuliano Alesi, F, +29.197s; **15** Konstantin Tereschenko, RUS, +29.641s; **16** Akash Nandy, MAL, +29.928s; **17** Steijn Schothorst, NL, +30.344s; **18** Antonio Fuoco, I, -1 lap; **19** Alex Palou, E, -2; Alexander Albon, THA, -17 (DNF-accident damage); Ralph Boschung, CH, -17 (DNF-accident); Artur Janosz, PL, -18 (DNF-accident).
Fastest race lap: Hughes, 1m 31.464s, 111.866mph/180.031km/h.
Pole position: Hughes.
Championship points: Drivers: 1 Leclerc, 126; **2** Albon, 123; **3** Fuoco, 115; **4** Parry, 70; **5** de Vries, 65; **6** Hughes, 52.
Teams: 1 ART Grand Prix, 349; **2** Trident, 125; **3** Koiranen GP, 123.

GP3 SERIES, Circuit de Spa-Francorchamps, Stavelot, Belgium, 27/28 August. Round 6. 17 and 13 laps of the 4.352-mile/7.004km circuit.
Race 1 (73.908 miles/118.944km).
1 Charles Leclerc, MC, 40m 06.695s, 110.668mph/178.103km/h; **2** Jake Dennis, GB, +2.305s; **3** Nyck de Vries, NL, +15.402s; **4** Antonio Fuoco, I, +19.427s; **5** Jack Aitken, GB, +19.837s; **6** Steijn Schothorst, NL, +21.419s; **7** Santino Ferrucci, USA, +24.337s; **8** Matevos Isaakyan, RUS, +28.856s; **9** Alexander Albon, T, +30.076s; **10** Giuliano Alesi, F, +31.045s *; **11** Kevin Jörg, CH, +39.185s; **12** Artur Janosz, PL, +42.364s; **13** Alex Palou, E, +48.122s; **14** Tatiana Calderón, CO, +51.121s; **15** Oscar Tunjo, CO, +1m 09.185s *; **16** Akash Nandy, MAL, +1m 15.690s; **17** Konstantin Tereschenko, RUS, +1m 22.750s **; Sandy Stuvik, T, -4 laps (DNF-accident damage); Niko Kari, FIN, -13 (DNF-accident damage); Nirei Fukuzumi, J, -16 (DNF-accident damage); Jake Hughes, GB, -17 (DNF-accident); Matt Parry, GB, -17 (DNF-accident); Arjun Maini, IND, -17 (DNF-accident).
* includes 10s penalty for causing an accident.
** includes 10s penalty for forcing another driver off the track.
Fastest race lap: Leclerc, 2m 09.918s, 120.595mph/194.079km/h.
Pole position: Leclerc, 2m 04.896s, 125.444mph/201.883km/h.

Race 2 (56.500 miles/90.928km).
1 Jack Aitken, GB, 31m 56.599s, 106.268mph/171.023km/h; **2** Antonio Fuoco, I, +1.769s; **3** Santino Ferrucci, USA, +5.820s; **4** Matevos Isaakyan, RUS, +7.207s; **5** Jake Dennis, GB, +7.708s; **6** Charles Leclerc, MC, +8.436s; **7** Steijn Schothorst, NL, +9.345s; **8** Nyck de Vries, NL, +9.851s; **9** Artur Janosz, PL, +11.614s; **10** Alexander Albon, T, +12.363s; **11** Alex Palou, E, +14.531s; **12** Giuliano Alesi, F, +15.919s; **13** Akash Nandy, MAL, +16.579s; **14** Niko Kari, FIN, +17.591s; **15** Nirei Fukuzumi, J, +23.275s *; **16** Arjun Maini, IND, +25.372s *; **17** Sandy Stuvik, T, -1 lap (DNF-accident damage); Kevin Jörg, CH, -5 (DNF-accident); Matt Parry, GB, -8 (DNF-accident); Jake Hughes, GB, -8 (DNF-accident); Konstantin Tereschenko, RUS, -11 (DNF-tyre); Tatiana Calderón, CO, -12 (DNF-accident).
Did not start: Oscar Tunjo, CO (accident damage).
* includes 10s penalty for causing an accident.
Fastest race lap: Aitken, 2m 09.435s, 121.045mph/194.803km/h.
Pole position: Isaakyan.
Championship points: Drivers: 1 Leclerc, 161; **2** Fuoco, 139; **3** Albon, 125; **4** de Vries, 81; **5** Parry, 70; **6** Aitken, 65.
Teams: 1 ART Grand Prix, 402; **2** Trident, 150; **3** Koiranen GP, 135.

GP3 SERIES, Autodromo Nazionale di Monza, Milan, Italy, 3/4 September. Round 7. 22 and 17 laps of the 3.600-mile/5.793km circuit.
Race 1 (78.999 miles/127.137km).
1 Jake Dennis, GB, 38m 06.844s, 124.661mph/200.623km/h; **2** Jack Aitken, GB, +1.987s; **3** Jake Hughes, GB, +2.532s; **4** Charles Leclerc, MC, +7.139s; **5** Nirei Fukuzumi, J, +7.561s; **6** Alexander Albon, T, +8.171s; **7** Nyck de Vries, NL, +8.343s; **8** Antonio Fuoco, I, +16.207s; **9** Matt Parry, GB, +16.607s; **10** Tatiana Calderón, CO, +17.003s; **11** Alex Palou, E, +19.202s; **12** Sandy Stuvik, T, +20.444s; **13** Steijn Schothorst, NL, +22.179s; **14** Arjun Maini, IND, +25.076s; **15** Akash Nandy, MAL, +27.804s; **16** Artur Janosz, PL, +30.365s; **17** Konstantin Tereschenko, RUS, +32.963s; **18** Ralph Boschung, CH, +34.813s; **19** Santino Ferrucci, USA, -1 lap; Kevin Jörg, CH, -4 (DNF-electrics); Matevos Isaakyan, RUS, -18 (DNF-accident damage).
Did not start: Giuliano Alesi, F.
* includes 10s penalty for causing an accident.
Fastest race lap: Hughes, 1m 40.706s, 128.677mph/207.085km/h.
Pole position: Leclerc, 1m 38.546s, 131.497mph/211.625km/h.

Race 2 (61.001 miles/98.172km).
1 Nyck de Vries, NL, 30m 24.854s, 120.715mph/194.273km/h; **2** Alexander Albon, T, +1.741s; **3** Antonio Fuoco, I, +6.382s; **4** Jake Dennis, GB, +7.761s; **5** Jack Aitken, GB, +8.331s; **6** Arjun Maini, IND, +11.991s; **7** Alex Palou, E, +12.264s; **8** Artur Janosz, PL, +12.504s; **9** Ralph Boschung, CH, +12.933s; **10** Jake Hughes, GB, +13.910s; **11** Santino Ferrucci, USA, +14.716s; **12** Kevin Jörg, CH, +16.886s; **13** Steijn Schothorst, NL, +17.561s; **14** Konstantin Tereschenko, RUS, +20.609s; **15** Sandy Stuvik, T, +20.958s *; **16** Tatiana Calderón, CO, +21.273s **; **17** Matt Parry, GB, +22.022s; **18** Akash Nandy, MAL, +1m 03.571s; **19** Giuliano Alesi, F, -1 lap; Matevos Isaakyan, RUS, -7 (DNF-accident damage); Nirei Fukuzumi, J, -15 (DNF-accident); Charles Leclerc, MC, -15 (DNF-accident).
* includes 5s penalty for causing an accident.
** includes 5s penalty for speeding in the pit lane.
Fastest race lap: de Vries, 1m 40.766s, 128.600mph/206.962km/h.
Pole position: Fuoco.
Championship points: Drivers: 1 Leclerc, 177; **2** Fuoco, 153; **3** Albon, 145; **4** de Vries, 104; **5** Dennis, 96; **6** Aitken, 89.
Teams: 1 ART Grand Prix, 465; **2** Arden International, 187; **3** Trident, 165.

GP3 SERIES, Sepang International Circuit, Jalan Pekeliling, Kuala Lumpur, Malaysia, 1/2 October. Round 8. 19 and 14 laps of the 3.444-mile/5.543km circuit.
Race 1 (65.441 miles/105.317km).
1 Alexander Albon, T, 35m 43.959s, 109.884mph/176.841km/h; **2** Jack Aitken, GB, +6.397s; **3** Charles Leclerc, MC, +7.166s; **4** Arjun Maini, IND, +7.746s; **5** Steijn Schothorst, NL, +18.680s; **6** Jake Dennis, GB, +19.544s; **7** Nirei Fukuzumi, J, +20.373s; **8** Antonio Fuoco, I, +21.961s; **9** Matt Parry, GB, +24.393s; **10** Sandy Stuvik, T, +25.325s; **11** Alessio Lorandi, I, +26.005s; **12** Kevin Jörg, CH, +26.949s; **13** Nyck de Vries, NL, +28.171s *; **14** Alex Palou, E, +33.273s; **15** Matevos Isaakyan, RUS, +35.555s; **16** Giuliano Alesi, F, +37.268s; **17** Konstantin Tereschenko, RUS, +48.279s; Santino Ferrucci, USA, -8 laps (DNF-electronics); Akash Nandy, MAL, -17 (DNF-mechanical); Artur Janosz, PL, -18 (DNF-accident); Jake Hughes, GB, -19 (DNF-accident); Tatiana Calderón, CO, -19 (DNF-clutch).
* includes 5s penalty for causing an accident.
Fastest race lap: Albon, 1m 51.934s, 110.773mph/178.272km/h.
Pole position: Leclerc, 1m 49.861s, 112.863mph/181.636km/h.

Race 2 (48.220 miles/77.602km).
1 Jake Dennis, GB, 26m 21.781s, 109.743mph/176.615km/h; **2** Nirei Fukuzumi, J, +3.456s; **3** Jack Aitken, GB, +5.688s; **4** Matt Parry, GB, +8.785s; **5** Charles Leclerc, MC, +9.140s; **6** Nyck de Vries, NL, +9.982s; **7** Arjun Maini, IND, +10.953s; **8** Alexander Albon, T, +18.086s; **9** Alessio Lorandi, I, +20.376s; **10** Steijn Schothorst, NL, +22.023s; **11** Kevin Jörg, CH, +22.448s; **12** Jake Hughes, GB, +23.229s; **13** Giuliano Alesi, F, +25.567s; **14** Matevos Isaakyan, RUS, +27.236s; **15** Tatiana Calderón, CO, +27.886s; **16** Artur Janosz, PL, +30.008s; **17** Konstantin Tereschenko, RUS, +30.271s; **18** Akash Nandy, MAL, +30.606s; **19** Alex Palou, E, +48.319s; **20** Sandy Stuvik, T, +1m 07.110s; Antonio Fuoco, I, -3 laps (DNF-puncture); Santino Ferrucci, USA, -10 (DNF-gearbox).
Fastest race lap: Fuoco, 1m 51.520s, 111.184mph/178.934km/h.
Pole position: Fuoco.
Championship points: Drivers: 1 Leclerc, 202; **2** Albon, 173; **3** Fuoco, 157; **4** Dennis, 121; **5** Aitken, 117; **6** de Vries, 108.
Teams: 1 ART Grand Prix, 539; **2** Arden International, 240; **3** Trident, 170.

GP3 SERIES, Yas Marina Circuit, Abu Dhabi, United Arab Emirates, 26/27 November. Round 9. 18 and 14 laps of the 3.451-mile/5.554km circuit.
Race 1 (62.048 miles/99.857km).
1 Nyck de Vries, NL, 38m 06.651s, 97.797mph/157.389km/h; **2** Jake Dennis, GB, +1.012s; **3** Jack Aitken, GB, +3.881s; **4** Kevin Jörg, CH, +9.601s; **5** Nirei Fukuzumi, J, +10.618s; **6** Steijn Schothorst, NL, +14.369s; **7** Jake Hughes, GB, +15.225s; **8** Konstantin Tereschenko, RUS, +17.292s *; **9** Santino Ferrucci, USA, +18.990s **; **10** Alex Palou, E, +20.776s; **11** Giuliano Alesi, F, +23.009s; **12** Alessio Lorandi, I, +26.262s; **13** Akash Nandy, MAL, +26.335s; **14** Arjun Maini, IND, +27.325s; **15** Sandy Stuvik, T, +32.912s; **16** Antonio Fuoco, I, +54.535s; Charles Leclerc, MC, -5 laps (DNF); Matevos Isaakyan, RUS, -6 (DNF); Alexander Albon, T, -8 (DNF); Tatiana Calderón, CO, -12 (DNF); Matt Parry, GB, -15 (DNF); Artur Janosz, PL, -16 (DNF).
* includes 5s penalty for leaving the track and gaining an advantage.
** includes 10s penalty for forcing another driver off the track.
Fastest race lap: Aitken, 2m 01.350s, 102.381mph/164.766km/h.
Pole position: Albon, 1m 55.274s, 107.777mph/173.451km/h.

Race 2 (48.244 miles/77.641km).
1 Jake Hughes, GB, 30m 21.199s, 95.504mph/153.699km/h; **2** Jack Aitken, GB, +2.825s; **3** Nirei Fukuzumi, J, +7.191s; **4** Jake Dennis, GB, +7.471s; **5** Alex Palou, E, +8.747s; **6** Konstantin Tereschenko, RUS, +8.774s; **7** Steijn Schothorst, NL, +9.158s; **8** Kevin Jörg, CH, +12.846s; **9** Charles Leclerc, MC, +14.035s; **10** Giuliano Alesi, F, +15.909s; **11** Nyck de Vries, NL, +17.639s; **12** Matt Parry, GB, +19.946s; **13** Akash Nandy, MAL, +20.467s; **14** Arjun Maini, IND, +20.925s; **15** Santino Ferrucci, USA, +21.153s; **16** Matevos Isaakyan, RUS, +23.085s; **17** Antonio Fuoco, I, +23.266s *; **18** Sandy Stuvik, T, +24.506s; **19** Artur Janosz, PL, +35.455s; **20** Alessio Lorandi, I, +1m 04.408s; Alexander Albon, T, -14 laps (DNF-accident); Tatiana Calderón, CO, -14 (DNF-accident).
* includes 5s penalty for causing an accident.

Fastest race lap: Dennis, 1m 59.847s, 103.665mph/166.832km/h.
Pole position: Tereschenko.

Final championship points
Drivers
1 Charles Leclerc, MC, 202; **2** Alexander Albon, T, 177; **3** Antonio Fuoco, I, 157; **4** Jake Dennis, GB, 149; **5** Jack Aitken, GB, 146; **6** Nyck de Vries, NL, 133; **7** Nirei Fukuzumi, J, 91; **8** Jake Hughes, GB, 90; **9** Matt Parry, GB, 82; **10** Arjun Maini, IND, 50; **11** Ralph Boschung, CH, 48; **12** Santino Ferrucci, USA, 36; **13** Steijn Schothorst, NL, 36; **14** Kevin Jörg, CH, 26; **15** Alex Palou, E, 22; **16** Oscar Tunjo, CO, 18; **17** Matevos Isaakyan, RUS, 17; **18** Sandy Stuvik, T, 9; **19** Konstantin Tereschenko, RUS, 8; **20** Artur Janosz, PL, 3; **21** Tatiana Calderón, CO, 2; **22** Giuliano Alesi, F, 1.

Teams
1 ART Grand Prix, 588; **2** Arden International, 297; **3** Trident, 170; **4** DAMS, 152; **5** Koiranen GP, 147; **6** Jenzer Motorsport, 68; **7** Campos Racing, 66.

Formula 3 European Championship

FIA FORMULA 3 EUROPEAN CHAMPIONSHIP, Circuit ASA Paul Ricard, Le Beausset, France, 2/3 April. Round 1. 25, 23 and 25 laps of the 2.387-mile/3.841km circuit.
Race 1 (59.667 miles/96.025km).
1 Lance Stroll, CDN (Dallara F316-Mercedes Benz), 34m 39.947s, 103.272mph/166.201km/h; **2** Nick Cassidy, NZ (Dallara F314-Mercedes Benz), +0.769s; **3** George Russell, GB (Dallara F315-Mercedes Benz), +6.983s; **4** Benjamin Barnicoat, GB (Dallara F316-Mercedes Benz), +8.615s; **5** Maximilian Günther, D (Dallara F315-Mercedes Benz), +9.202s; **6** Joel Eriksson, S (Dallara F315-Volkswagen), +13.040s; **7** Ralf Aron, EST (Dallara F315-Mercedes Benz), +13.453s; **8** Niko Kari, FIN (Dallara F315-Volkswagen), +16.613s; **9** Harrison Newey, GB (Dallara F316-Mercedes Benz), +19.159s; **10** Callum Ilott, GB (Dallara F312-Mercedes Benz), +19.718s.
Fastest race lap: Stroll, 1m 22.271s, 104.436mph/168.073km/h.
Pole position: Stroll, 1m 24.218s, 102.021mph/164.188km/h.

Race 2 (54.894 miles/88.343km).
1 Callum Ilott, GB (Dallara F312-Mercedes Benz), 35m 14.289s, 93.467mph/150.421km/h; **2** Nick Cassidy, NZ (Dallara F314-Mercedes Benz), +1.247s; **3** Guan Yu Zhou, CHN (Dallara F314-Volkswagen), +1.840s; **4** Mikkel Jensen, DK (Dallara F316-Mercedes Benz), +2.461s; **5** Sérgio Sette Câmara, BR (Dallara F314-Volkswagen), +4.408s; **6** Alessio Lorandi, I (Dallara F312-Volkswagen), +4.534s; **7** Ryan Tveter, USA (Dallara F316-Volkswagen), +5.094s; **8** Anthoine Hubert, F (Dallara F314-Mercedes Benz), +5.098s; **9** Joel Eriksson, S (Dallara F315-Volkswagen), +5.222s; **10** Raoul Hyman, ZA (Dallara F315-Volkswagen), +5.669s.
Fastest race lap: Cassidy, 1m 22.230s, 104.488mph/168.157km/h.
Pole position: Maximilian Günther, D (Dallara F315-Mercedes Benz), 1m 20.881s, 106.231mph/170.962km/h.

Race 3 (59.667 miles/96.025km).
1 Maximilian Günther, D (Dallara F315-Mercedes Benz), 34m 25.863s, 103.976mph/167.334km/h; **2** Nick Cassidy, NZ (Dallara F314-Mercedes Benz), +0.251s; **3** Joel Eriksson, S (Dallara F315-Volkswagen), +1.312s; **4** Mikkel Jensen, DK (Dallara F316-Mercedes Benz), +10.128s; **5** Lance Stroll, CDN (Dallara F316-Mercedes Benz), +10.827s; **6** Anthoine Hubert, F (Dallara F314-Mercedes Benz), +11.062s; **7** Ralf Aron, EST (Dallara F315-Mercedes Benz), +13.574s; **8** Guan Yu Zhou, CHN (Dallara F314-Volkswagen), +14.300s; **9** Alessio Lorandi, I (Dallara F312-Volkswagen), +17.326s; **10** Nikita Mazepin, RUS (Dallara F315-Mercedes Benz), +20.103s.
Fastest race lap: Eriksson, 1m 21.740s, 105.114mph/169.165km/h.
Pole position: Günther, 1m 20.895s, 106.212mph/170.932km/h.

FIA FORMULA 3 EUROPEAN CHAMPIONSHIP, Hungaroring, Mogyoród, Budapest, Hungary, 23/24 April. Round 2. 21, 22 and 16 laps of the 2.722-mile/4.381km circuit.
Race 1 (57.167 miles/92.001km).
1 Ralf Aron, EST (Dallara F315-Mercedes Benz), 35m 01.789s, 97.916mph/157.581km/h; **2** Niko Kari, FIN (Dallara F315-Volkswagen), +1.551s; **3** Joel Eriksson, S (Dallara F315-Volkswagen), +2.400s; **4** Lance Stroll, CDN (Dallara F316-Mercedes Benz), +11.297s; **5** Maximilian Günther, D (Dallara F315-Mercedes Benz), +11.801s; **6** Alessio Lorandi, I (Dallara F312-Volkswagen), +12.174s; **7** Sérgio Sette Câmara, BR (Dallara F314-Volkswagen), +12.612s; **8** Guan Yu Zhou, CHN (Dallara F314-Volkswagen), +13.090s; **9** Ben Barnicoat, GB (Dallara F316-Mercedes Benz), +13.632s; **10** Mikkel Jensen, DK (Dallara F312-Mercedes Benz), +14.407s.
Fastest race lap: Eriksson, 1m 34.722s, 103.460mph/166.504km/h.
Pole position: Günther, 1m 34.107s, 104.136mph/167.592km/h.

Race 2 (59.889 miles/96.382km).
1 Maximilian Günther, D (Dallara F315-Mercedes Benz), 35m 03.935s, 102.474mph/164.917km/h; **2** Ralf Aron, EST (Dallara F315-Mercedes Benz), +3.676s; **3** Guan Yu Zhou, CHN (Dallara F314-Volkswagen), +4.816s; **4** George Russell, GB (Dallara F315-Mercedes Benz), +10.451s; **5** Sérgio Sette Câmara, BR (Dallara F314-Volkswagen), +11.306s; **6** Alessio Lorandi, I (Dallara F312-Volkswagen), +15.175s; **7** Mikkel Jensen, DK (Dallara F312-Mercedes Benz), +28.495s; **8** Lance Stroll, CDN (Dallara F316-Mercedes Benz), +29.292s; **9** Callum Ilott, GB (Dallara F312-Mercedes Benz), +30.002s; **10** Ben Barnicoat, GB (Dallara F316-Mercedes Benz), +30.642s.
Fastest race lap: Günther, 1m 34.023s, 104.230mph/167.741km/h.
Pole position: Günther, 1m 33.614s, 104.685mph/168.474km/h.

Race 3 (43.556 miles/70.096km).
1 Ben Barnicoat, GB (Dallara F316-Mercedes Benz), 35m 22.885s, 73.861mph/118.869km/h; **2** Joel Eriksson, S (Dallara F315-Volkswagen), +4.998s; **3** Lance Stroll, CDN (Dallara F316-Mercedes Benz), +6.032s; **4** Guan Yu Zhou, CHN (Dallara F314-Volkswagen), +17.627s; **5** Sérgio Sette Câmara, BR (Dallara F314-Volkswagen), +18.503s; **6** Callum Ilott, GB (Dallara F312-Mercedes Benz), +19.980s; **7** Pedro Piquet, BR (Dallara F316-Mercedes Benz), +22.747s; **8** Niko Kari, FIN (Dallara F315-Volkswagen), +24.067s; **9** Nick Cassidy, NZ (Dallara F314-Mercedes Benz), +27.384s; **10** Harrison Newey, GB (Dallara F316-Mercedes Benz), +29.868s.
Fastest race lap: Stroll, 2m 00.265s, 81.486mph/131.140km/h.
Pole position: Maximilian Günther, D (Dallara F315-Mercedes Benz), 1m 33.910s, 104.355mph/167.943km/h.

FIA FORMULA 3 EUROPEAN CHAMPIONSHIP, Circuit de Pau Ville, Pau, France, 14/15 May. Round 3. 24, 25 and 25 laps of the 1.715-mile/2.760km circuit.
Race 1 (41.160 miles/66.240km).
1 Ben Barnicoat, GB (Dallara F316-Mercedes Benz), 35m 03.110s, 70.455mph/113.386km/h; **2** Nick Cassidy, NZ (Dallara F314-Mercedes Benz), +2.489s; **3** Maximilian Günther, D (Dallara F315-Mercedes Benz), +5.318s; **4** George Russell, GB (Dallara F315-Mercedes Benz), +7.034s; **5** Callum Ilott, GB (Dallara F312-Mercedes Benz), +8.156s; **6** Mikkel Jensen, DK (Dallara F312-Mercedes Benz), +16.707s; **7** Ryan Tveter, USA (Dallara F316-Volkswagen), +17.997s; **8** Sérgio Sette Câmara, BR (Dallara F314-Volkswagen), +22.166s; **9** Lance Stroll, CDN (Dallara F316-Mercedes Benz), +22.956s; **10** Alessio Lorandi, I (Dallara F315-Volkswagen), +26.906s.
Fastest race lap: Ilott, 1m 23.346s, 74.076mph/119.213km/h.
Pole position: Stroll, 1m 21.832s, 75.446mph/121.419km/h.

Race 2 (42.875 miles/69.000km).
1 George Russell, GB (Dallara F315-Mercedes Benz), 34m 18.884s, 74.967mph/120.647km/h; **2** Sérgio Sette Câmara, BR (Dallara F314-Volkswagen), +2.889s; **3** Callum Ilott, GB (Dallara F312-Mercedes Benz), +3.494s; **4** Lance Stroll, CDN (Dallara F316-Mercedes Benz), +4.471s; **5** Ben Barnicoat, GB (Dallara F316-Mercedes Benz), +5.066s; **6** Ralf Aron, EST (Dallara F315-Mercedes Benz), +6.024s; **7** Anthoine Hubert, F (Dallara F314-Mercedes Benz), +6.623s; **8** Mikkel Jensen, DK (Dallara F312-Mercedes Benz), +7.696s; **9** Joel Eriksson, S (Dallara F315-Volkswagen), +9.903s; **10** Arjun Maini, IND (Dallara F312-NBE), +10.105s.
Fastest race lap: Russell, 1m 10.911s, 87.066mph/140.119km/h.
Pole position: Russell, 1m 21.281s, 75.958mph/122.242km/h.

Race 3 (42.875 miles/69.000km).
1 Alessio Lorandi, I (Dallara F315-Volkswagen), 35m 09.190s, 73.179mph/117.770km/h; **2** Lance Stroll, CDN (Dallara F316-Mercedes Benz), +0.460s; **3** George Russell, GB (Dallara F315-Mercedes Benz), +2.385s; **4** Callum Ilott, GB (Dallara F312-Mercedes Benz), +2.806s; **5** Mikkel Jensen, DK (Dallara F312-Mercedes Benz), +6.393s; **6** Joel Eriksson, S (Dallara F315-Volkswagen), +6.920s; **7** Ryan Tveter, USA (Dallara F316-Volkswagen), +12.097s; **8** Niko Kari, FIN (Dallara F315-Volkswagen), +12.599s; **9** Arjun Maini, IND (Dallara F312-NBE), +13.179s; **10** Pedro Piquet, BR (Dallara F316-Mercedes Benz), +22.901s.
Fastest race lap: Russell, 1m 10.950s, 87.018mph/140.042km/h.
Pole position: Lorandi, 1m 21.586s, 75.674mph/121.785km/h.

FIA FORMULA 3 EUROPEAN CHAMPIONSHIP, Red Bull Ring, Spielberg, Austria, 21/22 May. Round 4. 16, 24 and 24 laps of the 2.688-mile/4.326km circuit.
Race 1 (43.009 miles/69.216km).
1 Callum Ilott, GB (Dallara F312-Mercedes Benz), 23m 54.454s, 107.937mph/173.709km/h; **2** Lance Stroll, CDN (Dallara F316-Mercedes Benz), +3.472s; **3** Maximilian Günther, D (Dallara F315-Mercedes Benz), +7.219s; **4** George Russell, GB (Dallara F315-Mercedes Benz), +14.222s; **5** Mikkel Jensen, DK (Dallara F312-Mercedes Benz), +15.679s *; **6** Nick Cassidy, NZ (Dallara F314-Mercedes Benz), +15.755s; **7** David Beckmann, D (Dallara F316-Mercedes Benz), +17.332s; **8** Harrison Newey, GB (Dallara F316-Mercedes Benz), +17.987s; **9** Ralf Aron, EST (Dallara F315-Mercedes Benz), +18.621s; **10** Ben Barnicoat, GB (Dallara F316-Mercedes Benz), +22.751s.
** includes 5s penalty for exceeding track limits.*
Fastest race lap: Ilott, 1m 23.276s, 116.203mph/187.011km/h.
Pole position: Ilott, 1m 23.969s, 115.244mph/185.468km/h.

Race 2 (64.513 miles/103.824km).
1 Lance Stroll, CDN (Dallara F316-Mercedes Benz), 35m 11.908s, 109.970mph/176.980km/h; **2** George Russell, GB (Dallara F315-Mercedes Benz), +12.424s; **3** Niko Kari, FIN (Dallara F315-Volkswagen), +12.891s; **4** Callum Ilott, GB (Dallara F312-Mercedes Benz), +14.909s *; **5** Mikkel Jensen, DK (Dallara F312-Mercedes Benz), +18.938s; **6** Maximilian Günther, D (Dallara F315-Mercedes Benz), +19.813s; **7** David Beckmann, D (Dallara F316-Mercedes Benz), +20.686s *; **8** Sérgio Sette Câmara, BR (Dallara F314-Volkswagen), +24.825s; **9** Alessio Lorandi, I (Dallara F315-Volkswagen), +28.232s; **10** Anthoine Hubert, F (Dallara F314-Mercedes Benz), +32.026s.
** includes 5s penalty for causing an accident.*
Fastest race lap: Sette Câmara, 1m 22.832s, 116.826mph/188.014km/h.
Pole position: Stroll, 1m 23.178s, 116.340mph/187.232km/h.

Race 3 (64.513 miles/103.824km).
1 Lance Stroll, CDN (Dallara F316-Mercedes Benz), 35m 15.242s, 109.797mph/176.701km/h; **2** Callum Ilott, GB (Dallara F312-Mercedes Benz), +4.867s; **3** Maximilian Günther, D (Dallara F315-Mercedes Benz), +11.067s; **4** Sérgio Sette Câmara, BR (Dallara F314-Volkswagen), +14.329s; **5** Ben Barnicoat, GB (Dallara F316-Mercedes Benz), +14.422s *; **6** Joel Eriksson, S (Dallara F315-Volkswagen), +19.040s; **7** Guan Yu Zhou, CHN (Dallara F314-Volkswagen), +19.413s; **8** Niko Kari, FIN (Dallara F315-Volkswagen), +19.872s; **9** Ralf Aron, EST (Dallara F315-Mercedes Benz), +26.071s; **10** Nick Cassidy, NZ (Dallara F314-Mercedes Benz), +27.450s.
** includes 2s penalty for overtaking under safety car conditions.*
Fastest race lap: Stroll, 1m 22.986s, 116.609mph/187.665km/h.
Pole position: Stroll, 1m 23.240s, 116.254mph/187.092km/h.

FIA FORMULA 3 EUROPEAN CHAMPIONSHIP, Norisring, Nürnberg (Nuremberg), Germany, 25/26 June. Round 5. 38, 36 and 24 laps of the 1.429-mile/2.300km circuit.
Race 1 (54.308 miles/87.400km).
1 Lance Stroll, CDN (Dallara F316-Mercedes Benz), 33m 59.186s, 95.875mph/154.296km/h; **2** Niko Kari, FIN (Dallara F315-Volkswagen), +1.064s; **3** George Russell, GB (Dallara F315-Mercedes Benz), +2.926s; **4** Ralf Aron, EST (Dallara F315-Mercedes Benz), +4.821s; **5** Ben Barnicoat, GB (Dallara F316-Mercedes Benz), +6.233s; **6** Nick Cassidy, NZ (Dallara F314-Mercedes Benz), +7.258s *; **7** Mikkel Jensen, DK (Dallara F312-Mercedes Benz), +7.401s; **8** Anthoine Hubert, F (Dallara F312-Mercedes Benz), +7.883s; **9** Pedro Piquet, BR (Dallara F316-Mercedes Benz), +8.737s; **10** David Beckmann, D (Dallara F316-Mercedes Benz), +13.285s.
** includes 5s penalty for safety car infringement.*
Fastest race lap: Callum Ilott, GB (Dallara F312-Mercedes Benz), 48.209s, 106.721mph/171.752km/h.
Pole position: Stroll, 48.148s, 106.857mph/171.969km/h.

Race 2 (51.450 miles/82.800km).
1 Anthoine Hubert, F (Dallara F312-Mercedes Benz), 34m 10.668s, 90.320mph/145.357km/h; **2** Lance Stroll, CDN (Dallara F316-Mercedes Benz), +0.532s; **3** Maximilian Günther, D (Dallara F315-Mercedes Benz), +1.461s; **4** Nick Cassidy, NZ (Dallara F314-Mercedes Benz), +2.708s; **5** Joel Eriksson, S (Dallara F315-Volkswagen), +3.040s; **6** Guan Yu Zhou, CHN (Dallara F314-Volkswagen), +4.514s; **7** Callum Ilott, GB (Dallara F312-Mercedes Benz), +4.882s; **8** Mikkel Jensen, DK (Dallara F312-Mercedes Benz), +6.324s; **9** George Russell, GB (Dallara F315-Mercedes Benz), +7.251s; **10** Ralf Aron, EST (Dallara F315-Mercedes Benz), +7.996s.
Fastest race lap: David Beckmann, D (Dallara F316-Mercedes Benz), 48.375s, 106.355mph/171.162km/h.
Pole position: Hubert, 48.163s, 106.823mph/171.916km/h.

Race 3 (34.300 miles/55.200km).
1 Lance Stroll, CDN (Dallara F316-Mercedes Benz), 34m 36.561s, 59.463mph/95.696km/h; **2** Anthoine Hubert, F (Dallara F312-Mercedes Benz), +0.787s; **3** Sérgio Sette Câmara, BR (Dallara F314-Volkswagen), +1.985s; **4** Guan Yu Zhou, CHN (Dallara F314-Volkswagen), +2.617s; **5** Maximilian Günther, D (Dallara F315-Mercedes Benz), +3.467s; **6** Nick Cassidy, NZ (Dallara F314-Mercedes Benz), +4.310s; **7** Callum Ilott, GB (Dallara F312-Mercedes Benz), +4.804s; **8** Alessio Lorandi, I (Dallara F315-Volkswagen), +5.322s; **9** Ralf Aron, EST (Dallara F315-Mercedes Benz), +7.698s; **10** Harrison Newey, GB (Dallara F316-Mercedes Benz), +9.074s.
Fastest race lap: Lorandi, 48.179s, 106.788mph/171.859km/h.
Pole position: Stroll, 48.180s, 106.786mph/171.855km/h.

FIA FORMULA 3 EUROPEAN CHAMPIONSHIP, Circuit Park Zandvoort, Netherlands, 16/17 July. Round 6. 3 x 23 laps of the 2.676-mile/4.307km circuit.
Race 1 (61.554 miles/99.061km).
1 Lance Stroll, CDN (Dallara F316-Mercedes Benz), 35m 02.366s, 105.401mph/169.627km/h; **2** Nick Cassidy, NZ (Dallara F314-Mercedes Benz), +8.026s; **3** Alessio Lorandi, I (Dallara F315-Volkswagen), +10.146s; **4** Maximilian Günther, D (Dallara F315-Mercedes Benz), +11.827s; **5** Callum Ilott, GB (Dallara F312-Mercedes Benz), +12.102s; **6** Niko Kari, FIN (Dallara F315-Volkswagen), +12.765s; **7** George Russell, GB (Dallara F315-Mercedes Benz), +13.328s; **8** Ryan Tveter, USA (Dallara F316-Volkswagen), +14.188s; **9** Anthoine Hubert, F (Dallara F312-Mercedes Benz), +15.069s; **10** David Beckmann, D (Dallara F316-Mercedes Benz), +23.100s.
Fastest race lap: Stroll, 1m 30.170s, 106.848mph/171.955km/h.
Pole position: Cassidy, 1m 28.533s, 108.823mph/175.134km/h.

Race 2 (61.554 miles/99.061km).
1 Nick Cassidy, NZ (Dallara F314-Mercedes Benz), 35m 01.732s, 105.433mph/169.678km/h; **2** Maximilian Günther, D (Dallara F315-Mercedes Benz), +1.136s; **3** Callum Ilott, GB (Dallara F312-Mercedes Benz), +4.800s; **4** Anthoine Hubert, F (Dallara F312-Mercedes Benz), +7.106s; **5** Alessio Lorandi, I (Dallara F315-Volkswagen), +16.559s; **6** Ralf Aron, EST (Dallara F315-Mercedes Benz), +20.982s; **7** David Beckmann, D (Dallara F316-Mercedes Benz), +21.352s; **8** Ben Barnicoat, GB (Dallara F316-Mercedes Benz), +22.050s; **9** George Russell, GB (Dallara F315-Mercedes Benz), +22.809s; **10** Joel Eriksson, S (Dallara F315-Volkswagen), +26.701s.
Fastest race lap: Günther, 1m 30.515s, 106.440mph/171.299km/h.
Pole position: Ilott, 1m 28.891s, 108.385mph/174.429km/h.

Race 3 (61.554 miles/99.061km).
1 Maximilian Günther, D (Dallara F315-Mercedes Benz), 35m 17.348s, 104.655mph/168.427km/h; **2** Nick Cassidy, NZ (Dallara F314-Mercedes Benz), +1.287s; **3** David Beckmann, D (Dallara F316-Mercedes Benz), +7.088s; **4** Alessio Lorandi, I (Dallara F315-Volkswagen), +11.032s; **5** George Russell, GB (Dallara F315-Mercedes Benz), +12.207s; **6** Callum Ilott, GB (Dallara F312-Mercedes Benz), +13.372s; **7** Joel Eriksson, S (Dallara F315-Volkswagen), +16.121s; **8** Ralf Aron, EST (Dallara F315-Mercedes Benz), +17.817s; **9** Ben Barnicoat, GB (Dallara F316-Mercedes Benz), +19.758s; **10** Anthoine Hubert, F (Dallara F312-Mercedes Benz), +20.602s.
Fastest race lap: Lance Stroll, CDN (Dallara F316-Mercedes Benz), 1m 31.104s, 105.752mph/170.192km/h.
Pole position: Günther, 1m 28.966s, 108.294mph/174.282km/h.

FIA FORMULA 3 EUROPEAN CHAMPIONSHIP, Circuit de Spa-Francorchamps, Stavelot, Belgium, 29/30 July. Round 7. 12, 16 and 16 laps of the 4.352-mile/7.004km circuit.
Race 1 (52.225 miles/84.048km).
1 Lance Stroll, CDN (Dallara F316-Mercedes Benz), 38m 47.746s, 80.769mph/129.985km/h; **2** Maximilian Günther, D (Dallara F315-Mercedes Benz), +0.655s; **3** Ben Barnicoat, GB (Dallara F316-Mercedes Benz), +1.701s; **4** Nick Cassidy, NZ (Dallara F314-Mercedes Benz), +2.299s; **5** George Russell, GB (Dallara F315-Mercedes Benz), +3.580s; **6** Harrison Newey, GB (Dallara F316-Mercedes Benz), +5.492s; **7** David Beckmann, D (Dallara F316-Mercedes Benz), +7.152s; **8** Ralf Aron, EST (Dallara F315-Mercedes Benz), +8.311s; **9** Ryan Tveter, USA (Dallara F316-Volkswagen), +9.103s; **10** Alessio Lorandi, I (Dallara F315-Volkswagen), +9.896s.
Fastest race lap: Stroll, 2m 33.102s, 102.333mph/164.690km/h.
Pole position: Stroll, 2m 31.409s, 103.478mph/166.531km/h.

Race 2 (69.633 miles/112.064km).
1 George Russell, GB (Dallara F315-Mercedes Benz), 35m 40.974s, 117.086mph/188.433km/h; **2** Joel Eriksson, S (Dallara F315-Volkswagen), +7.398s; **3** Mikkel Jensen, DK (Dallara F316-Mercedes Benz), +8.738s; **4** Anthoine Hubert, F (Dallara F312-Mercedes Benz), +10.587s; **5** Callum Ilott, GB (Dallara F316-Mercedes Benz), +13.708s; **6** Pedro Piquet, BR (Dallara F316-Mercedes Benz), +17.398s; **7** Maximilian Günther, D (Dallara F315-Mercedes Benz), +18.932s; **8** Guan Yu Zhou, CHN (Dallara F314-Volkswagen), +20.729s; **9** Ryan Tveter, USA (Dallara F316-Volkswagen), +22.186s; **10** Niko Kari, FIN (Dallara F315-Volkswagen), +24.485s.
Fastest race lap: Russell, 2m 12.610s, 118.147mph/190.139km/h.
Pole position: Russell, 2m 12.110s, 118.594mph/190.859km/h.

Race 3 (69.633 miles/112.064 km).
1 Joel Eriksson, S (Dallara F315-Volkswagen), 35m 32.758s, 117.537mph/189.159km/h; **2** Anthoine Hubert, F (Dallara F312-Mercedes Benz), +1.613s; **3** George Russell, GB (Dallara F315-Mercedes Benz), +3.563s; **4** Lance Stroll, CDN (Dallara F316-Mercedes Benz), +4.315s; **5**

Nick Cassidy, NZ (Dallara F314-Mercedes Benz), +5.976s; **6** Maximilian Günther, D (Dallara F315-Mercedes Benz), +9.543s; **7** Niko Kari, FIN (Dallara F315-Volkswagen), +11.124s; **8** Nikita Mazepin, RUS (Dallara F316-Mercedes Benz), +12.643s; **9** Mikkel Jensen, DK (Dallara F316-Mercedes Benz), +15.696s; **10** David Beckmann, D (Dallara F316-Mercedes Benz), +16.101s.
Fastest race lap: Russell, 2m 12.102s, 118.601mph/190.870km/h.
Pole position: Russell, 2m 12.156s, 118.553mph/190.792km/h.

FIA FORMULA 3 EUROPEAN CHAMPIONSHIP, Nürburgring, Nürburg/Eifel, Germany, 10/11 September. Round 8. 26, 24 and 26 laps of the 2.255-mile/3.629km circuit.
Race 1 (58.629 miles/94.354km).
1 Lance Stroll, CDN (Dallara F316-Mercedes Benz), 35m 40.320s, 98.613mph/158.702km/h; **2** Maximilian Günther, D (Dallara F315-Mercedes Benz), +6.648s; **3** George Russell, GB (Dallara F315-Mercedes Benz), +9.470s; **4** Nick Cassidy, NZ (Dallara F314-Mercedes Benz), +12.013s; **5** Callum Ilott, GB (Dallara F316-Mercedes Benz), +12.523s; **6** Ralf Aron, EST (Dallara F315-Mercedes Benz), +15.797s; **7** Joel Eriksson, S (Dallara F315-Volkswagen), +17.614s; **8** Niko Kari, FIN (Dallara F315-Volkswagen), +18.533s; **9** Ben Barnicoat, GB (Dallara F316-Mercedes Benz), +21.162s; **10** Anthoine Hubert, F (Dallara F312-Mercedes Benz), +21.809s.
Fastest race lap: Stroll, 1m 21.502s, 99.602mph/160.295km/h.
Pole position: Stroll, 1m 21.218s, 99.951mph/160.855km/h.

Race 2 (54.119 miles/87.096km).
1 Lance Stroll, CDN (Dallara F316-Mercedes Benz), 35m 00.191s, 92.766mph/149.293km/h; **2** Maximilian Günther, D (Dallara F315-Mercedes Benz), +3.727s; **3** Joel Eriksson, S (Dallara F315-Volkswagen), +5.855s; **4** Ralf Aron, EST (Dallara F315-Mercedes Benz), +8.600s; **5** Anthoine Hubert, F (Dallara F312-Mercedes Benz), +8.928s; **6** David Beckmann, D (Dallara F316-Mercedes Benz), +11.375s; **7** Callum Ilott, GB (Dallara F316-Mercedes Benz), +11.919s; **8** Sérgio Sette Câmara, BR (Dallara F316-Volkswagen), +14.024s; **9** Pedro Piquet, BR (Dallara F316-Mercedes Benz), +17.303s; **10** Niko Kari, FIN (Dallara F315-Volkswagen), +19.975s.
Fastest race lap: Günther, 1m 22.073s, 98.910mph/159.180km/h.
Pole position: Stroll, 1m 21.006s, 100.212mph/161.276km/h.

Race 3 (58.629 miles/94.354km).
1 Maximilian Günther, D (Dallara F315-Mercedes Benz), 35m 37.136s, 98.760mph/158.939km/h; **2** Lance Stroll, CDN (Dallara F316-Mercedes Benz), +3.025s; **3** Niko Kari, FIN (Dallara F315-Volkswagen), +3.967s; **4** Callum Ilott, GB (Dallara F316-Mercedes Benz), +8.730s; **5** Nick Cassidy, NZ (Dallara F314-Mercedes Benz), +11.353s; **6** Joel Eriksson, S (Dallara F315-Volkswagen), +17.647s; **7** George Russell, GB (Dallara F315-Mercedes Benz), +18.432s; **8** Sérgio Sette Câmara, BR (Dallara F316-Volkswagen), +22.968s; **9** Anthoine Hubert, F (Dallara F312-Mercedes Benz), +24.876s; **10** Ben Barnicoat, GB (Dallara F316-Mercedes Benz), +25.483s.
Fastest race lap: Günther, 1m 21.762s, 99.286mph/159.785km/h.
Pole position: Günther, 1m 21.154s, 100.030mph/160.982km/h.

FIA FORMULA 3 EUROPEAN CHAMPIONSHIP, Autodromo Enzo e Dino Ferrari, Imola, Italy, 1/2 October. Round 9. 21, 19 and 22 laps of the 3.050-mile/4.909km circuit.
Race 1 (64.057 miles/103.089km).
1 Niko Kari, FIN (Dallara F315-Volkswagen), 36m 05.485s, 106.490mph/171.379km/h; **2** Lance Stroll, CDN (Dallara F316-Mercedes Benz), +0.788s; **3** Joel Eriksson, S (Dallara F315-Volkswagen), +0.998s; **4** George Russell, GB (Dallara F315-Mercedes Benz), +2.701s; **5** Anthoine Hubert, F (Dallara F312-Mercedes Benz), +4.997s; **6** Guan Yu Zhou, CHN (Dallara F314-Volkswagen), +6.591s; **7** Ralf Aron, EST (Dallara F315-Mercedes Benz), +7.573s; **8** Ben Barnicoat, GB (Dallara F316-Mercedes Benz), +7.991s; **9** Harrison Newey, GB (Dallara F316-Mercedes Benz), +9.574s; **10** Nick Cassidy, NZ (Dallara F314-Mercedes Benz), +22.301s.
Fastest race lap: Stroll, 1m 36.574s, 113.706mph/182.993km/h.
Pole position: Stroll, 1m 36.001s, 114.385mph/184.085km/h.

Race 2 (57.956 miles/93.271km).
1 Lance Stroll, CDN (Dallara F316-Mercedes Benz), 35m 36.662s, 97.648mph/157.149km/h; **2** Joel Eriksson, S (Dallara F315-Volkswagen), +1.399s; **3** George Russell, GB (Dallara F315-Mercedes Benz), +2.883s; **4** Ralf Aron, EST (Dallara F315-Mercedes Benz), +3.917s; **5** Guan Yu Zhou, CHN (Dallara F314-Volkswagen), +4.897s; **6** Anthoine Hubert, F (Dallara F312-Mercedes Benz), +5.990s; **7** Nick Cassidy, NZ (Dallara F314-Mercedes Benz), +6.552s; **8** Harrison Newey, GB (Dallara F316-Mercedes Benz), +7.202s; **9** Niko Kari, FIN (Dallara F315-Volkswagen), +7.747s; **10** Mikkel Jensen, DK (Dallara F316-Mercedes Benz), +9.838s.
Fastest race lap: Stroll, 1m 36.832s, 113.403mph/182.505km/h.
Pole position: Stroll, 1m 36.192s, 114.158mph/183.720km/h.

Race 3 (67.107 miles/107.998km).
1 Lance Stroll, CDN (Dallara F316-Mercedes Benz), 35m 23.977s, 113.741mph/183.049km/h; **2** George Russell, GB (Dallara F315-Mercedes Benz), +7.559s; **3** Callum Ilott, GB (Dallara F316-Mercedes Benz), +8.702s; **4** Ralf Aron, EST (Dallara F315-Mercedes Benz), +14.007s; **5** Joel Eriksson, S (Dallara F315-Volkswagen), +15.358s; **6** Anthoine Hubert, F (Dallara F312-Mercedes Benz), +16.446s; **7** Mikkel Jensen, DK (Dallara F316-Mercedes Benz), +21.226s; **8** Nick Cassidy, NZ (Dallara F314-Mercedes Benz), +27.942s; **9** David Beckmann, D (Dallara F316-Mercedes Benz), +33.325s; **10** Guan Yu Zhou, CHN (Dallara F314-Volkswagen), +33.815s.
Fastest race lap: Stroll, 1m 35.876s, 114.534mph/184.325km/h.
Pole position: Stroll, 1m 36.448s, 113.855mph/183.232km/h.

FIA FORMULA 3 EUROPEAN CHAMPIONSHIP, Hockenheimring Grand Prix Circuit, Heidelberg, Germany, 15/16 October. Round 10. 3 x 23 laps of the 2.842-mile/4.574km circuit.
Race 1 (65.369 miles/105.202km).
1 Lance Stroll, CDN (Dallara F316-Mercedes Benz), 35m 46.986s, 109.609mph/176.399km/h; **2** Maximilian Günther, D (Dallara F315-Mercedes Benz), +6.254s; **3** Nick Cassidy, NZ (Dallara F314-Mercedes Benz), +10.679s; **4** Ralf Aron, EST (Dallara F315-Mercedes Benz), +12.638s; **5** Sérgio Sette Câmara, BR (Dallara F316-Volkswagen), +18.860s; **6** Joel Eriksson, S (Dallara F315-Volkswagen), +24.473s; **7** George Russell, GB (Dallara F315-Mercedes Benz), +26.933s; **8** Nikita Mazepin, RUS (Dallara F316-Mercedes Benz), +28.037s; **9** Alexander Sims, GB (Dallara F315-Mercedes Benz), +29.049s; **10** Anthoine Hubert, F (Dallara F312-Mercedes Benz), +31.175s *.
** includes 5s penalty for incorrect positioning on the grid.*
Fastest race lap: Stroll, 1m 32.535s, 110.571mph/177.947km/h.
Pole position: Stroll, 1m 31.639s, 111.652mph/179.687km/h.

Race 2 (65.369 miles/105.202km).
1 Lance Stroll, CDN (Dallara F316-Mercedes Benz), 35m 50.860s, 109.412mph/176.081km/h; **2** Joel Eriksson, S (Dallara F315-Volkswagen), +4.727s; **3** David Beckmann, D (Dallara F316-Mercedes Benz), +6.793s; **4** Jake Hughes, GB (Dallara F312-Volkswagen), +7.466s; **5** Ralf Aron, EST (Dallara F315-Mercedes Benz), +12.314s; **6** George Russell, GB (Dallara F315-Mercedes Benz), +14.881s; **7** Anthoine Hubert, F (Dallara F312-Mercedes Benz), +15.601s; **8** Maximilian Günther, D (Dallara F315-Mercedes Benz), +18.006s; **9** Ben Barnicoat, GB (Dallara F316-Mercedes Benz), +24.546s; **10** Nikita Mazepin, RUS (Dallara F316-Mercedes Benz), +25.423s.
Disqualified: Callum Ilott, GB (Dallara F316-Mercedes Benz), +8.702s (technical infringement).
Fastest race lap: Russell, 1m 32.892s, 110.146mph/177.263km/h.
Pole position: Stroll, 1m 31.733s, 111.538mph/179.503km/h.

Race 3 (65.369 miles/105.202km).
1 Lance Stroll, CDN (Dallara F316-Mercedes Benz), 35m 45.382s, 109.691mph/176.531km/h; **2** Joel Eriksson, S (Dallara F315-Volkswagen), +4.716s; **3** Jake Hughes, GB (Dallara F312-Volkswagen), +11.297s; **4** Nick Cassidy, NZ (Dallara F314-Mercedes Benz), +13.924s; **5** Alexander Sims, GB (Dallara F315-Mercedes Benz), +16.686s; **6** Sérgio Sette Câmara, BR (Dallara F316-Volkswagen), +24.146s; **7** Ben Barnicoat, GB (Dallara F316-Mercedes Benz), +24.777s; **8** Ralf Aron, EST (Dallara F315-Mercedes Benz), +26.447s; **9** Maximilian Günther, D (Dallara F315-Mercedes Benz), +27.329s; **10** Anthoine Hubert, F (Dallara F312-Mercedes Benz), +27.842s.
Fastest race lap: Hughes, 1m 32.489s, 110.626mph/178.036km/h.
Pole position: Eriksson, 1m 32.057s, 111.145mph/178.871km/h.

Final championship points
Drivers
1 Lance Stroll, CDN, 507; **2** Maximilian Günther, D, 322; **3** George Russell, GB, 274; **4** Nick Cassidy, NZ, 254; **5** Joel Eriksson, S, 252; **6** Callum Ilott, GB, 226; **7** Ralf Aron, EST, 176; **8** Anthoine Hubert, F, 160; **9** Ben Barnicoat, GB, 134; **10** Niko Kari, FIN, 129; **11** Sérgio Sette Câmara, BR, 117; **12** Mikkel Jensen, DK, 107; **13** Guan Yu Zhou, CHN, 101; **14** Alessio Lorandi, I, 96; **15** David Beckmann, D, 67; **16** Jake Hughes, GB, 27; **17** Ryan Tveter, USA, 26; **18** Harrison Newey, GB, 22; **19** Pedro Piquet, BR, 19; **20** Nikita Mazepin, RUS, 10; **21** Arjun Maini, IND, 3; **22** Raoul Hyman, ZA, 1.

Teams
1 Prema Powerteam, 887; **2** HitechGP, 535; **3** Motopark, 508; **4** Van Amersfoort Racing, 438; **5** kfzteile Mücke Motorsport, 321; **6** Carlin, 266; **7** ThreeBond with T-Sport, 40.

BRDC British Formula 3 Championship

All cars are Tatuus F4-016-Cosworth.

BRDC BRITISH FORMULA 3 CHAMPIONSHIP, Snetterton Circuit, Thetford, Norfolk, Great Britain, 27/28 March. 12, 9 and 10 laps of the 2.969-mile/4.778km circuit.
Round 1 (35.627 miles/57.336km).
1 Lando Norris, GB, 25m 04.753s, 85.234mph/137.171km/h; **2** Aleksanteri Huovinen, FIN, +19.095s; **3** Enaam Ahmed, GB, +28.308s; **4** Toby Sowery, GB, +33.447s; **5** Ricky Collard, GB, +34.595s *; **6** Ben Hingeley, GB, +36.388s; **7** Jan Jonck, DK, +41.945s; **8** Enzo Bortoleto, BR, +45.215s; **9** Sisa Ngebulana, ZA, +47.895s; **10** Matheus Leist, BR, +50.672s.
** includes 3s penalty.*
Fastest race lap: Norris, 2m 01.988s, 87.615mph/141.003km/h.
Pole position: Norris, 1m 44.570s, 102.209mph/164.490km/h.

Round 2 (26.720 miles/43.002km).
1 Matheus Leist, BR, 20m 01.628s, 80.051mph/128.830km/h; **2** Enaam Ahmed, GB, +1.421s; **3** Toby Sowery, GB, +2.408s; **4** Aleksanteri Huovinen, FIN, +8.112s; **5** Sisa Ngebulana, ZA, +8.581s; **6** Lando Norris, GB, +8.780s; **7** Thomas Maxwell, AUS, +10.053s; **8** Enzo Bortoleto, BR, +10.795s; **9** Tom Randle, AUS, +10.880s; **10** Jan Jonck, DK, +11.271s.
Fastest race lap: Sowery, 1m 46.934s, 99.949mph/160.853km/h.
Pole position: Bortoleto.

Round 3 (29.689 miles/47.780km).
1 Enaam Ahmed, GB, 17m 53.859s, 99.529mph/160.176km/h; **2** Toby Sowery, GB, +0.480s; **3** Lando Norris, GB, +0.821s; **4** Matheus Leist, BR, +1.553s; **5** Tom Randle, AUS, +2.004s; **6** Aleksanteri Huovinen, FIN, +2.630s; **7** Sisa Ngebulana, ZA, +4.805s; **8** Ricky Collard, GB, +19.656s; **9** Thomas Maxwell, AUS, +20.473s; **10** Ameya Vaidyanathan, IND, +20.955s.
Fastest race lap: Norris, 1m 45.768s, 101.051mph/162.627km/h.
Pole position: Sowery, 1m 46.934s, 99.949mph/160.853km/h.

BRDC BRITISH FORMULA 3 CHAMPIONSHIP, Brands Hatch Grand Prix Circuit, West Kingsdown, Dartford, Kent, Great Britain, 16/17 April. 16, 14 and 5 laps of the 2.433-mile/3.916km circuit.
Round 4 (38.931 miles/62.654km).
1 Matheus Leist, BR, 21m 57.732s, 106.358mph/171.167km/h; **2** Ricky Collard, GB, +1.748s; **3** Toby Sowery, GB, +2.591s; **4** Tom Randle, AUS, +22.169s; **5** Tarun Reddy, IND, +24.536s; **6** Faisal Al Zubair, OM, +29.647s; **7** Raoul Hyman, ZA, +29.979s; **8** Enzo Bortoleto, BR, +31.930s; **9** Thomas Maxwell, AUS, +32.288s; **10** Colton Herta, USA, +32.537s.
Fastest race lap: Leist, 1m 21.065s, 108.055mph/173.898km/h.
Pole position: Leist, 1m 20.416s, 108.927mph/175.301km/h.

Round 5 (34.065 miles/54.822km).
1 Toby Sowery, GB, 19m 10.793s, 106.564mph/171.498km/h; **2** Tarun Reddy, IND, +9.413s; **3** Enzo Bortoleto, BR, +12.985s; **4** Ricky Collard, GB, +13.169s; **5** Tom Randle, AUS, +13.328s; **6** Sisa Ngebulana, ZA, +13.981s; **7** Faisal Al Zubair, OM, +14.856s; **8** Thomas Maxwell, AUS, +15.469s; **9** Eugene Denyssen, ZA, +16.537s; **10** Quinlan Lall, USA, +17.288s.
Fastest race lap: Colton Herta, USA, 1m 20.700s, 108.544mph/174.685km/h.
Pole position: Bortoleto.

Round 6 (12.166 miles/19.579km).
1 Colton Herta, USA, 6m 54.745s, 105.601mph/169.948km/h; **2** Ricky Collard, GB, +0.573s; **3** Tom Randle, AUS, +1.328s; **4** Sisa Ngebulana, ZA, +2.213s; **5** Aleksanteri Huovinen, FIN, +3.166s; **6** Krishnaraaj Mahadik, IND, +6.726s; **7** Thomas Maxwell, AUS, +6.827s; **8** Quinlan Lall, USA, +8.015s; **9** Akhil Rabindra, IND, +9.946s; **10** Faisal Al Zubair, OM, +10.106s.
Fastest race lap: Collard, 1m 21.401s, 107.609mph/173.180km/h.
Pole position: Herta, 1m 20.700s, 108.544mph/174.685km/h.

BRDC BRITISH FORMULA 3 CHAMPIONSHIP, Rockingham Motor Speedway, Corby, Northamptonshire, Great Britain, 30 April/1 May. 14, 13 and 15 laps of the 1.940-mile/3.122km circuit.
Round 7 (27.160 miles/43.710km).
1 Lando Norris, GB, 17m 22.876s, 93.756mph/150.885km/h; **2** Ricky Collard, GB, +1.633s; **3** Matheus Leist, BR, +2.772s; **4** Tom Randle, AUS, +4.621s; **5** Aleksanteri Huovinen, FIN, +8.404s; **6** Enaam Ahmed, GB, +11.550s; **7** Ameya Vaidyanathan, IND, +12.677s; **8** Tarun Reddy, IND, +13.942s; **9** Thomas Maxwell, AUS, +21.417s; **10** Quinlan Lall, USA, +22.138s.
Fastest race lap: Leist, 1m 13.760s, 94.685mph/152.381km/h.
Pole position: Norris, 1m 12.577s, 96.228mph/154.865km/h.

Round 8 (25.220 miles/40.588km).
1 Tom Randle, AUS, 16m 09.259s, 93.671mph/150.749km/h; **2** Ameya Vaidyanathan, IND, +1.232s; **3** Lando Norris, GB, +1.694s; **4** Matheus Leist, BR, +8.121s; **5** Aleksanteri Huovinen, FIN, +9.301s; **6** Tarun Reddy, IND, +10.912s; **7** Ricky Collard, GB, +11.159s; **8** Toby Sowery, GB, +11.622s; **9** Thomas Maxwell, AUS, +15.015s; **10** Jan Jonck, DK, +17.240s.
Fastest race lap: Norris, 1m 13.574s, 94.924mph/152.766km/h.
Pole position: Reddy.

Round 9 (29.100 miles/46.832km).
1 Ricky Collard, GB, 20m 12.229s, 86.419mph/139.078km/h; **2** Matheus Leist, BR, +1.228s; **3** Lando Norris, GB, +2.182s; **4** Tom Randle, AUS, +12.551s; **5** Enaam Ahmed, GB, +16.829s; **6** Toby Sowery, GB, +17.293s; **7** Aleksanteri Huovinen, FIN, +17.628s; **8** Tarun Reddy, IND, +18.784s; **9** Thomas Maxwell, AUS, +20.409s; **10** Quinlan Lall, USA, +21.014s.
Fastest race lap: Collard, 1m 13.974s, 94.411mph/151.940km/h.
Pole position: Norris, 1m 13.574s, 94.924mph/152.766km/h.

BRDC BRITISH FORMULA 3 CHAMPIONSHIP, Oulton Park Circuit, Tarporley, Cheshire, Great Britain, 28/30 May. 6, 14 and 18 laps of the 2.692-mile/4.332km circuit.
Round 10 (16.152 miles/25.994km).
1 Ricky Collard, GB, 9m 17.780s, 104.247mph/167.770km/h; **2** Tom Randle, AUS, +0.905s; **3** Colton Herta, USA, +1.574s; **4** Matheus Leist, BR, +2.641s; **5** Jan Jonck, DK, +3.910s; **6** Enzo Bortoleto, BR, +4.509s; **7** Toby Sowery, GB, +5.237s; **8** Enaam Ahmed, GB, +5.761s; **9** Thomas Maxwell, AUS, +10.409s; **10** Quinlan Lall, USA, +11.117s.
Disqualified: Sisa Ngebulana, ZA (originally finished 9th).
Fastest race lap: Collard, 1m 31.533s, 105.876mph/170.391km/h.
Pole position: Collard, 1m 30.360s, 107.250mph/172.603km/h.

Round 11 (37.688 miles/60.653km).
1 Toby Sowery, GB, 21m 32.480s, 104.974mph/168.939km/h; **2** Enaam Ahmed, GB, +0.171s*; **3** Enzo Bortoleto, BR, +0.464s; **4** Matheus Leist, BR, +0.832s; **5** Jan Jonck, DK, +1.319s; **6** Colton Herta, USA, +1.924s; **7** Tom Randle, AUS, +2.628s; **8** Ricky Collard, GB, +4.520s; **9** Quinlan Lall, USA, +5.246s; **10** Thomas Maxwell, AUS, +9.663s.
** includes 6s penalty for unsafe driving.*
Fastest race lap: Collard, 1m 30.535s, 107.043mph/172.270km/h.
Pole position: Ahmed.

Round 12 (48.456 miles/77.982km).
1 Ricky Collard, GB, 27m 35.956s, 105.341mph/169.531km/h; **2** Tom Randle, AUS, +1.854s; **3** Colton Herta, USA, +2.802s; **4** Enaam Ahmed, GB, +12.852s; **5** Matheus Leist, BR, +13.259s; **6** Enzo Bortoleto, BR, +16.409s; **7** Toby Sowery, GB, +16.862s; **8** Jan Jonck, DK, +17.381s; **9** Quinlan Lall, USA, +18.218s; **10** Sisa Ngebulana, ZA, +25.640s.
Fastest race lap: Herta, 1m 31.306s, 106.139mph/170.815km/h.
Pole position: Collard, 1m 30.535s, 107.043mph/172.270km/h.

BRDC BRITISH FORMULA 3 CHAMPIONSHIP, Silverstone Grand Prix Circuit, Towcester, Northamptonshire, Great Britain, 11/12 June. 6, 8 and 10 laps of the 3.660-mile/5.891km circuit.
Round 13 (21.962 miles/35.345km).
1 Matheus Leist, BR, 11m 47.594s, 111.737mph/179.823km/h; **2** Tom Randle, AUS, +4.396s; **3** Tarun Reddy, IND, +8.374s; **4** Ricky Collard, GB, +9.037s; **5** Enaam Ahmed, GB, +9.405s; **6** Sisa Ngebulana, ZA, +11.316s; **7** Toby Sowery, GB, +11.740s; **8** Jan Jonck, DK, +12.106s; **9** Thomas Maxwell, AUS, +15.850s; **10** Eugene Denyssen, ZA, +18.692s.
Fastest race lap: Leist, 1m 57.126s, 112.506mph/181.061km/h.
Pole position: Randle, 1m 56.808s, 112.812mph/181.554km/h.

Round 14 (29.283 miles/47.127km).
1 Toby Sowery, GB, 21m 08.219s, 83.124mph/133.775km/h; **2** Lando Norris, GB, +1.002s; **3** Matheus Leist, BR, +1.692s; **4** Tom Randle, AUS, +2.979s; **5** Enaam Ahmed, GB, +3.522s; **6** Ben Hingeley, GB, +4.373s; **7** Tarun Reddy, IND, +5.186s; **8** Enzo Bortoleto, BR, +6.814s; **9** Jeremy Wahome, EAK, +7.499s; **10** Aleksanteri Huovinen, FIN, +8.120s.
Disqualified: Sisa Ngebulana, ZA (originally finished 4th).
Fastest race lap: Sowery, 2m 10.890s, 100.675mph/162.021km/h.
Pole position: Jonck.

Round 15 (36.604 miles/58.908km).
Race cancelled due to heavy rain and thunderstorm.
Pole position: Matheus Leist, BR, 1m 57.126s, 112.506mph/181.061km/h.

BRDC BRITISH FORMULA 3 CHAMPIONSHIP, Circuit de Spa-Francorchamps, Stavelot, Belgium, 8/9 July. 5, 9 and 9 laps of the 4.352-mile/7.004km circuit.
Round 16 (21.760 miles/35.020km).
1 Lando Norris, GB, 13m 52.048s, 94.150mph/151.520km/h; **2** Matheus Leist, BR, +1.384s; **3** Ricky Collard, GB, +1.858s; **4** Enaam Ahmed, GB, +2.131s; **5** Toby Sowery, GB, +3.213s; **6** Tarun Reddy, IND, +7.909s; **7** Ben Hingeley, GB, +10.659s; **8** Faisal Al Zubair, OM, +13.153s; **9** Tom Randle, AUS, +15.395s; **10** Enzo Bortoleto, BR, +16.044s.

Fastest race lap: Sowery, 2m 18.809s, 112.870mph/181.648km/h.
Pole position: Norris, 2m 16.820s, 114.511mph/184.288km/h.

Round 17 (39.169 miles/63.036km).
1 Tom Randle, AUS, 20m 50.659s, 112.746mph/181.448km/h; **2** Toby Sowery, GB, +0.469s; **3** Tarun Reddy, IND, +3.696s; **4** Enaam Ahmed, GB, +3.882s; **5** Matheus Leist, BR, +4.096s; **6** Ricky Collard, GB, +4.551s; **7** Sisa Ngebulana, ZA, +8.424s; **8** Ben Hingeley, GB, +9.430s; **9** Faisal Al Zubair, OM, +10.568s; **10** Enzo Bortoleto, BR, +10.685s.
Fastest race lap: Will Palmer, GB, 2m 17.088s, 114.287mph/183.928km/h.
Pole position: Zubair.

Round 18 (39.169 miles/63.036km).
1 Lando Norris, GB, 20m 56.613s, 112.212mph/180.588km/h; **2** Matheus Leist, BR, +0.508s; **3** Will Palmer, GB, +3.065s; **4** Toby Sowery, GB, +8.561s; **5** Tom Randle, AUS, +8.881s; **6** Ricky Collard, GB, +10.187s; **7** Thomas Maxwell, AUS, +10.694s; **8** Eugene Denyssen, ZA, +11.076s; **9** Tarun Reddy, IND, +11.806s; **10** Ben Hingeley, GB, +15.200s.
Fastest race lap: Leist, 2m 18.665s, 112.988mph/181.836km/h.
Pole position: Palmer, 2m 17.088s, 114.287mph/183.928km/h.

BRDC BRITISH FORMULA 3 CHAMPIONSHIP, Snetterton Circuit, Thetford, Norfolk, Great Britain, 6/7 August. 15, 16 and 16 laps of the 2.969-mile/4.778km circuit.
Round 19 (44.533 miles/71.670km).
1 Ricky Collard, GB, 30m 26.838s, 87.758mph/141.233km/h; **2** Matheus Leist, BR, +3.179s; **3** Toby Sowery, GB, +7.469s; **4** Ben Hingeley, GB, +12.708s; **5** Harrison Scott, GB, +13.025s; **6** Tom Randle, AUS, +13.566s; **7** Tarun Reddy, IND, +22.456s; **8** Nikita Mazepin, RUS, +23.047s; **9** Aleksanteri Huovinen, FIN, +23.432s; **10** Eugene Denyssen, ZA, +25.807s.
Fastest race lap: Collard, 1m 43.884s, 102.884mph/165.576km/h.
Pole position: Collard, 1m 43.156s, 103.610mph/166.744km/h.

Round 20 (47.502 miles/76.448km).
1 Nikita Mazepin, RUS, 28m 06.426s, 101.402mph/163.192km/h; **2** Tarun Reddy, IND, +1.976s; **3** Harrison Scott, GB, +2.293s; **4** Tom Randle, AUS, +3.247s; **5** Toby Sowery, GB, +4.010s; **6** Matheus Leist, BR, +6.638s; **7** Ricky Collard, GB, +9.258s; **8** Aleksanteri Huovinen, FIN, +14.117s; **9** Enzo Bortoleto, BR, +18.286s; **10** Eugene Denyssen, ZA, +24.819s.
Fastest race lap: Ben Hingeley, GB, 1m 44.230s, 102.542mph/165.026km/h.
Pole position: Mazepin.

Round 21 (47.502 miles/76.448km).
1 Ricky Collard, GB, 28m 13.037s, 101.007mph/162.555km/h; **2** Matheus Leist, BR, +1.533s; **3** Ben Hingeley, GB, +13.022s; **4** Enaam Ahmed, GB, +13.282s; **5** Harrison Scott, GB, +13.817s; **6** Tom Randle, AUS, +14.811s; **7** Toby Sowery, GB, +15.467s; **8** Nikita Mazepin, RUS, +16.050s; **9** Tarun Reddy, IND, +17.003s; **10** Quinlan Lall, USA, +17.781s.
Fastest race lap: Leist, 1m 44.624s, 102.156mph/164.405km/h.
Pole position: Collard, 1m 43.884s, 102.884mph/165.576km/h.

BRDC BRITISH FORMULA 3 CHAMPIONSHIP, Donington Park National Circuit, Castle Donington, Great Britain, 10/11 September. 8, 13 and 13 laps of the 2.487-mile/4.003km circuit.
Round 22 (19.898 miles/32.023km).
1 Matheus Leist, BR, 13m 31.610s, 88.261mph/142.043km/h; **2** Harrison Scott, GB, +0.519s; **3** Ben Hingeley, GB, +1.279s; **4** Toby Sowery, GB, +1.596s; **5** Thomas Maxwell, AUS, +3.239s; **6** Enaam Ahmed, GB, +4.209s; **7** Aleksanteri Huovinen, FIN, +6.363s; **8** Eugene Denyssen, ZA, +6.658s; **9** Omar Ismail, GB, +7.301s; **10** Akhil Rabindra, IND, +8.443s.
Fastest race lap: Leist, 1m 27.225s, 102.657mph/165.210km/h.
Pole position: Hingeley, 1m 43.539s, 86.482mph/139.179km/h.

Round 23 (32.335 miles/52.038km).
1 Toby Sowery, GB, 20m 47.328s, 93.324mph/150.190km/h; **2** Eugene Denyssen, ZA, +7.624s; **3** Thomas Maxwell, AUS, +8.203s; **4** Harrison Scott, GB, +8.337s; **5** Matheus Leist, BR, +8.640s; **6** Enaam Ahmed, GB, +9.898s; **7** Tarun Reddy, IND, +10.632s; **8** Tom Randle, AUS, +10.756s; **9** Omar Ismail, GB, +11.806s; **10** Ricky Collard, GB, +12.091s.
Fastest race lap: Sowery, 1m 25.250s, 105.035mph/169.038km/h.
Pole position: Denyssen.

Round 24 (32.335 miles/52.038km).
1 Toby Sowery, GB, 18m 41.224s, 103.820mph/167.082km/h; **2** Enaam Ahmed, GB, +4.479s; **3** Tom Randle, AUS, +4.751s; **4** Harrison Scott, GB, +5.165s; **5** Matheus Leist, BR, +6.134s; **6** Ricky Collard, GB, +6.436s; **7** Tarun Reddy, IND, +15.115s; **8** James Pull, GB, +16.532s; **9** Thomas Maxwell, AUS, +16.899s; **10** Jeremy Wahome, EAK, +24.030s.
Fastest race lap: Sowery, 1m 25.580s, 104.630mph/168.386km/h.
Pole position: Sowery, 1m 25.250s, 105.035mph/169.038km/h.

Final championship points
Drivers
1 Matheus Leist, BR, 493; **2** Ricky Collard, GB, 466; **3** Toby Sowery, GB, 457; **4** Tom Randle, AUS, 424; **5** Enaam Ahmed, GB, 349; **6** Tarun Reddy, IND, 284; **7** Thomas Maxwell, AUS, 265; **8** Lando Norris, GB, 247; **9** Aleksanteri Huovinen, FIN, 245; **10** Ben Hingeley, GB, 232; **11** Enzo Bortoleto, BR, 220; **12** Faisal Al Zubair, OM, 196; **13** Eugene Denyssen, ZA, 194; **14** Sisa Ngebulana, ZA, 176; **15** Quinlan Lall, USA, 149; **16** Jan Jonck, DK, 142; **17** Harrison Scott, GB, 130; **18** Akhil Rabindra, IND, 124; **19** Colton Herta, USA, 109; **20** Krishnaraaj Mahadik, IND, 104; **21** Jeremy Wahome, EAK, 98; **22** Ameya Vaidyanathan, IND, 95; **23** Nikita Mazepin, RUS, 51; **24** Omar Ismail, GB, 47; **25** Will Palmer, GB, 39; **26** James Pull, GB, 33; **27** Raoul Hyman, ZA, 15; **28** Paul Sieljes, NL, 10.

All-Japan Formula 3 Championship

ALL-JAPAN FORMULA 3 CHAMPIONSHIP, Suzuka International Racing Course, Suzuka-shi, Mie Prefecture, Japan, 23/24 April. 12 and 17 laps of the 3.608-mile/5.807km circuit.
Round 1 (43.300 miles/69.684km).
1 Kenta Yamashita, J (Dallara F312-Toyota), 24m 09.954s, 107.506mph/173.014km/h; **2** Jann Mardenborough, GB (Dallara F314-Volkswagen), +1.324s; **3** Sho Tsuboi, J (Dallara F314-Toyota), +4.867s; **4** Katsumasa Chiyo, J (Dallara F315-Volkswagen), +6.807s; **5** Daiki Sasaki, J (Dallara F312-Volkswagen), +7.002s; **6** Keishi Ishikawa, J (Dallara F316-Toda), +8.709s; **7** Hiroki Ohtsu, J (Dallara F312-Mugen Honda), +12.300s; **8** Tadasuke Makino, J (Dallara F314-Toda), +13.090s; **9** Sena Sakaguchi, J (Dallara F312-Mugen Honda), +15.666s; **10** Ai Miura, J (Dallara F312-Toyota), +23.961s.
Fastest race lap: Sasaki, 1m 53.109s, 114.844mph/184.823km/h.
Pole position: Yamashita, 1m 51.681s, 116.312mph/187.18 km/h.

Round 2 (61.341 miles/98.719km).
1 Kenta Yamashita, J (Dallara F312-Toyota), 32m 12.516s, 114.270mph/183.899km/h; **2** Sho Tsuboi, J (Dallara F314-Toyota), +1.184s; **3** Jann Mardenborough, GB (Dallara F314-Volkswagen), +8.301s; **4** Daiki Sasaki, J (Dallara F312-Volkswagen), +16.062s; **5** Keishi Ishikawa, J (Dallara F316-Toda), +16.713s; **6** Tadasuke Makino, J (Dallara F314-Toda), +25.886s; **7** Sena Sakaguchi, J (Dallara F312-Mugen Honda), +26.945s; **8** Katsumasa Chiyo, J (Dallara F315-Volkswagen), +27.264s; **9** Hiroki Ohtsu, J (Dallara F312-Mugen Honda), +29.268s; **10** Ai Miura, J (Dallara F312-Toyota), +41.490s.
Fastest race lap: Yamashita, 1m 53.207s, 114.745mph/184.663km/h.
Pole position: Yamashita, 1m 51.575s, 116.423mph/187.365km/h.

ALL-JAPAN FORMULA 3 CHAMPIONSHIP, Fuji International Speedway, Sunto-gun, Shizuoka Prefecture, Japan, 14/15 May. 15 and 21 laps of the 2.835-mile/4.563km circuit.
Round 3 (42.530 miles/68.445km).
1 Daiki Sasaki, J (Dallara F312-Volkswagen), 23m 57.282s, 106.525mph/171.436km/h; **2** Jann Mardenborough, GB (Dallara F314-Volkswagen), +0.612s; **3** Sho Tsuboi, J (Dallara F314-Toyota), +2.547s; **4** Katsumasa Chiyo, J (Dallara F315-Volkswagen), +5.454s; **5** Kenta Yamashita, J (Dallara F312-Toyota), +6.416s; **6** Tadasuke Makino, J (Dallara F314-Toda), +9.727s; **7** Keishi Ishikawa, J (Dallara F316-Toda), +10.701s; **8** Sena Sakaguchi, J (Dallara F312-Mugen Honda), +16.380s; **9** Hiroki Ohtsu, J (Dallara F312-Mugen Honda), +17.211s; **10** Ai Miura, J (Dallara F312-Toyota), +20.742s.
Fastest race lap: Sasaki, 1m 35.113s, 107.316mph/172.708km/h.
Pole position: Mardenborough, 1m 34.608s, 107.889mph/173.630km/h.

Round 4 (59.542 miles/95.823km).
1 Daiki Sasaki, J (Dallara F312-Volkswagen), 33m 25.035s, 106.906mph/172.048km/h; **2** Kenta Yamashita, J (Dallara F312-Toyota), +2.644s; **3** Sho Tsuboi, J (Dallara F314-Toyota), +7.981s; **4** Jann Mardenborough, GB (Dallara F314-Volkswagen), +14.054s; **5** Keishi Ishikawa, J (Dallara F316-Toda), +15.839s; **6** Tadasuke Makino, J (Dallara F314-Toda), +16.417s; **7** Sena Sakaguchi, J (Dallara F312-Mugen Honda), +22.662s; **8** Ai Miura, J (Dallara F312-Toyota), +24.164s; **9** Hiroki Ohtsu, J (Dallara F312-Mugen Honda), +44.043s; **10** Tairoku Yamaguchi, J (Dallara F316-Toyota), +44.586s.
Fastest race lap: Sasaki, 1m 34.933s, 107.519mph/173.036km/h.
Pole position: Sasaki, 1m 33.885s, 108.720mph/174.967km/h.

ALL-JAPAN FORMULA 3 CHAMPIONSHIP, Okayama International Circuit (TI Circuit Aida), Aida Gun, Okayama Prefecture, Japan, 28/29 May. 18 and 25 laps of the 2.301-mile/3.703km circuit.
Round 5 (41.417 miles/66.654km).
1 Kenta Yamashita, J (Dallara F312-Toyota), 25m 04.942s, 99.074mph/159.444km/h; **2** Sho Tsuboi, J (Dallara F314-Toyota), +5.598s; **3** Katsumasa Chiyo, J (Dallara F315-Volkswagen), +6.194s; **4** Mitsunori Takaboshi, J (Dallara F312-Volkswagen), +6.831s; **5** Hiroki Ohtsu, J (Dallara F312-Mugen Honda), +26.587s; **6** Sena Sakaguchi, J (Dallara F312-Mugen Honda), +27.826s; **7** Tairoku Yamaguchi, J (Dallara F316-Toyota), +35.186s; **8** Jann Mardenborough, GB (Dallara F314-Volkswagen), +35.798s; **9** Ai Miura, J (Dallara F312-Toyota), +51.319s; **10** Yoshiaki Katayama, J (Dallara F306-Toyota), +1m 10.651s.
Fastest race lap: Yamashita, 1m 22.604s, 100.278mph/161.382km/h.
Pole position: Mardenborough, 1m 21.171s, 102.048mph/164.231km/h.

Round 6 (57.523 miles/92.57km).
1 Jann Mardenborough, GB (Dallara F314-Volkswagen), 43m 24.904s, 79.498mph/127.939km/h; **2** Tadasuke Makino, J (Dallara F314-Toda), +25.803s; **3** Sho Tsuboi, J (Dallara F314-Toyota), +30.032s; **4** Sena Sakaguchi, J (Dallara F312-Mugen Honda), +32.988s; **5** Keishi Ishikawa, J (Dallara F316-Toda), +33.954s; **6** Kenta Yamashita, J (Dallara F312-Toyota), +59.887s; **7** Hiroki Ohtsu, J (Dallara F312-Mugen Honda), +1m 00.773s; **8** Mitsunori Takaboshi, J (Dallara F312-Volkswagen), +1m 22.259s; **9** Katsumasa Chiyo, J (Dallara F315-Volkswagen), +1m 43.630s; **10** Yoshiaki Katayama, J (Dallara F306-Toyota), -1 lap.
Fastest race lap: Mardenborough, 1m 42.917s, 80.486mph/129.530km/h.
Pole position: Mardenborough, 1m 20.990s, 102.277mph/164.598km/h.

ALL-JAPAN FORMULA 3 CHAMPIONSHIP, Suzuka International Racing Course, Suzuka-shi, Mie Prefecture, Japan, 11/12 June. 12 and 17 laps of the 3.608-mile/5.807km circuit.
Round 7 (43.300 miles/69.684km).
1 Mitsunori Takaboshi, J (Dallara F312-Volkswagen), 23m 08.378s, 112.274mph/180.687km/h; **2** Sho Tsuboi, J (Dallara F314-Toyota), +2.162s; **3** Katsumasa Chiyo, J (Dallara F315-Volkswagen), +5.002s; **4** Tadasuke Makino, J (Dallara F314-Toda), +7.025s; **5** Keishi Ishikawa, J (Dallara F316-Toda), +10.639s; **6** Hiroki Ohtsu, J (Dallara F312-Mugen Honda), +13.767s; **7** Sena Sakaguchi, J (Dallara F312-Mugen Honda), +15.195s; **8** Ai Miura, J (Dallara F312-Toyota), +21.350s; **9** Tairoku Yamaguchi, J (Dallara F316-Toyota), +33.315s; **10** Jann Mardenborough, GB (Dallara F314-Volkswagen), +38.875s *.
** includes 40s penalty (originally finished 1st).*
Fastest race lap: Mardenborough, 1m 54.526s, 113.423mph/182.537km/h.
Pole position: Kenta Yamashita, J (Dallara F312-Toyota), 1m 52.521s, 115.444mph/185.789km/h.

Round 8 (61.341 miles/98.719km).
1 Mitsunori Takaboshi, J (Dallara F312-Volkswagen), 32m 48.882s, 112.159mph/180.503km/h; **2** Kenta Yamashita, J (Dallara F312-Toyota), +0.993s; **3** Jann Mardenborough, GB (Dallara F314-Volkswagen), +1.412s; **4** Katsumasa Chiyo, J (Dallara F315-Volkswagen), +3.288s; **5** Keishi Ishikawa, J (Dallara F316-Toda), +17.735s; **6** Tadasuke Makino, J (Dallara F314-Toda), +22.888s; **7** Sena Sakaguchi, J (Dallara F312-Mugen Honda), +23.618s; **8** Hiroki Ohtsu, J (Dallara F312-Mugen Honda), +24.767s; **9** Ai Miura, J (Dallara F312-Toyota), +30.759s; **10** Tairoku Yamaguchi, J (Dallara F316-Toyota), +54.175s.
Fastest race lap: Mardenborough, 1m 54.908s, 113.046mph/181.930km/h.
Pole position: Yamashita, 1m 52.314s, 115.657mph/186.132km/h.

ALL-JAPAN FORMULA 3 CHAMPIONSHIP, Fuji International Speedway, Sunto-gun, Shizuoka Prefecture, Japan, 16/17 July. 15 and 21 laps of the 2.835-mile/4.563km circuit.
Round 9 (42.530 miles/68.445km).
1 Jann Mardenborough, GB (Dallara F314-Volkswagen), 30m 03.942s, 84.874mph/136.591km/h; **2** Sho Tsuboi, J (Dallara F314-Toyota), +4.092s; **3** Tadasuke Makino, J (Dallara F314-Toda), +5.438s; **4** Katsumasa Chiyo, J (Dallara F315-Volkswagen), +5.469s; **5** Sena Sakaguchi, J (Dallara F312-Mugen Honda), +10.850s; **6** Kenta Yamashita, J (Dallara F312-Toyota), +10.953s; **7** Keishi Ishikawa, J (Dallara F316-Toda), +11.128s; **8** Hiroki Ohtsu, J (Dallara F312-Mugen Honda), +11.444s; **9** Hong Li Ye, CHN (Dallara F315-Volkswagen), +12.841s; **10** Takamitsu Matsui, J (Dallara F306-Toyota), +18.215s.
Fastest race lap: Chiyo, 1m 37.458s, 104.734mph/168.553km/h.
Pole position: Mardenborough, 1m 51.268s, 91.735mph/147.633km/h.

Round 10 (59.542 miles/95.823km).
1 Katsumasa Chiyo, J (Dallara F315-Volkswagen), 37m 05.246s, 96.326mph/155.022km/h; **2** Jann Mardenborough, GB (Dallara F314-Volkswagen), +1.492s; **3** Sho Tsuboi, J (Dallara F314-Toyota), +1.653s; **4** Kenta Yamashita, J (Dallara F312-Toyota), +1.905s; **5** Tadasuke Makino, J (Dallara F314-Toda), +2.734s; **6** Hiroki Ohtsu, J (Dallara F312-Mugen Honda), +4.504s; **7** Hong Li Ye, CHN (Dallara F315-Volkswagen), +6.281s; **8** Sena Sakaguchi, J (Dallara F312-Mugen Honda), +6.844s; **9** Keishi Ishikawa, J (Dallara F316-Toda), +7.764s; **10** Tairoku Yamaguchi, J (Dallara F316-Toyota), +8.267s.
Fastest race lap: Chiyo, 1m 35.320s, 107.083mph/172.333km/h.
Pole position: Mardenborough, 1m 49.962s, 92.824mph/149.386km/h.

ALL-JAPAN FORMULA 3 CHAMPIONSHIP, Twin Ring Motegi, Motegi-machi, Haga-gun, Tochigi Prefecture, Japan, 20/21 August. 14 and 20 laps of the 2.983-mile/4.801km circuit.
Round 11 (41.768 miles/67.219km).
1 Jann Mardenborough, GB (Dallara F314-Volkswagen), 31m 28.195s, 79.634mph/128.159km/h; **2** Tadasuke Makino, J (Dallara F314-Toda), +4.765s; **3** Sho Tsuboi, J (Dallara F314-Toyota), +6.522s; **4** Keishi Ishikawa, J (Dallara F316-Toda), +10.018s; **5** Kenta Yamashita, J (Dallara F312-Toyota), +11.255s; **6** Sena Sakaguchi, J (Dallara F312-Mugen Honda), +13.024s; **7** Mitsunori Takaboshi, J (Dallara F315-Volkswagen), +13.399s; **8** Hong Li Ye, CHN (Dallara F315-Volkswagen), +15.678s; **9** Tairoku Yamaguchi, J (Dallara F316-Toyota), +44.483s; **10** Ai Miura, J (Dallara F312-Toyota), +46.922s.
Fastest race lap: Mardenborough, 2m 00.092s, 89.435mph/143.931km/h.
Pole position: Makino, 2m 01.545s, 88.365mph/142.210km/h.

Round 12 (59.669 miles/96.028km).
1 Jann Mardenborough, GB (Dallara F314-Volkswagen), 35m 44.454s, 100.169mph/161.206km/h; **2** Kenta Yamashita, J (Dallara F312-Toyota), +8.121s; **3** Sho Tsuboi, J (Dallara F314-Toyota), +19.508s; **4** Hong Li Ye, CHN (Dallara F315-Volkswagen), +21.147s; **5** Tadasuke Makino, J (Dallara F314-Toda), +22.836s; **6** Sena Sakaguchi, J (Dallara F312-Mugen Honda), +27.264s; **7** Keishi Ishikawa, J (Dallara F316-Toda), +27.731s; **8** Mitsunori Takaboshi, J (Dallara F315-Volkswagen), +32.083s; **9** Tairoku Yamaguchi, J (Dallara F316-Toyota), +37.416s; **10** Ai Miura, J (Dallara F312-Toyota), +42.326s.
Fastest race lap: Mardenborough, 1m 46.578s, 100.775mph/162.181km/h.
Pole position: Mardenborough, 2m 00.794s, 88.915mph/143.095km/h.

ALL-JAPAN FORMULA 3 CHAMPIONSHIP, Okayama International Circuit (TI Circuit Aida), Aida Gun, Okayama Prefecture, Japan, 10/11 September. 18 and 25 laps of the 2.301-mile/3.703km circuit.
Round 13 (41.417 miles/66.654km).
1 Kenta Yamashita, J (Dallara F312-Toyota), 25m 33.933s, 97.202mph/156.431km/h; **2** Mitsunori Takaboshi, J (Dallara F315-Volkswagen), +0.552s; **3** Sho Tsuboi, J (Dallara F314-Toyota), +8.801s; **4** Jann Mardenborough, GB (Dallara F314-Volkswagen), +9.558s; **5** Tadasuke Makino, J (Dallara F314-Toda), +11.623s; **6** Sena Sakaguchi, J (Dallara F312-Mugen Honda), +15.843s; **7** Hong Li Ye, CHN (Dallara F315-Volkswagen), +16.380s; **8** Hiroki Ohtsu, J (Dallara F312-Mugen Honda), +26.877s; **9** Keishi Ishikawa, J (Dallara F316-Toda), +27.280s; **10** Ai Miura, J (Dallara F312-Toyota), +29.231s.
Fastest race lap: Yamashita, 1m 24.195s, 98.383mph/158.332km/h.
Pole position: Yamashita, 1m 21.981s, 101.040mph/162.608km/h.

Round 14 (57.523 miles/92.575km).
1 Mitsunori Takaboshi, J (Dallara F315-Volkswagen), 35m 31.953s, 97.134mph/156.321km/h; **2** Sena Sakaguchi, J (Dallara F312-Mugen Honda), +15.852s; **3** Tadasuke Makino, J (Dallara F314-Toda), +16.624s; **4** Sho Tsuboi, J (Dallara F314-Toyota), +17.028s; **5** Kenta Yamashita, J (Dallara F312-Toyota), +17.275s; **6** Hong Li Ye, CHN (Dallara F315-Volkswagen), +21.302s; **7** Keishi Ishikawa, J (Dallara F316-Toda), +21.801s; **8** Jann Mardenborough, GB (Dallara F314-Volkswagen), +22.673s; **9** Ai Miura, J (Dallara F312-Toyota), +35.301s; **10** Yoshiaki Katayama, J (Dallara F306-Toyota), +1m 08.423s.
Fastest race lap: Takaboshi, 1m 24.252s, 98.317mph/158.225km/h.
Pole position: Takaboshi, 1m 22.097s, 100.897mph/162.379km/h.

ALL-JAPAN FORMULA 3 CHAMPIONSHIP, Sportsland-SUGO International Course, Shibata-gun, Miyagi Prefecture, Japan, 24/25 September. 25, 18 and 18 laps of the 2.302-mile/3.704km circuit.
Round 15 (57.543 miles/92.606km).
1 Kenta Yamashita, J (Dallara F312-Toyota), 34m 29.508s, 100.098mph/161.093km/h; **2** Jann Mardenborough, GB (Dallara F314-Volkswagen), +1.594s; **3** Sho Tsuboi, J (Dallara F314-Toyota), +5.667s; **4** Tadasuke Makino, J (Dallara F314-Toda), +5.765s; **5** Keishi Ishikawa, J (Dallara F316-Toda), +7.127s; **6** Hiroki Ohtsu, J (Dallara F312-Mugen Honda), +8.723s; **7** Sena Sakaguchi, J (Dallara F312-Mugen Honda), +9.487s; **8** Hong Li Ye, CHN (Dallara F315-Volkswagen), +10.239s; **9** Yoshiaki Katayama, J (Dallara F306-Toyota), +32.727s; **10** Dragon, J (Dallara F306-Toyota), +33.986s.
Fastest race lap: Yamashita, 1m 14.242s, 111.610mph/179.620km/h.
Pole position: Yamashita, 1m 13.253s, 113.117mph/182.045km/h.

Round 16 (41.431 miles/66.677km).
1 Kenta Yamashita, J (Dallara F312-Toyota), 22m 34.066s, 110.151mph/177.270km/h; **2** Jann Mardenborough, GB (Dallara F314-Volkswagen), +1.019s; **3** Sho Tsuboi, J (Dallara F314-Toyota), +2.281s; **4** Keishi Ishikawa, J (Dallara F316-Toda), +11.470s; **5** Sena Sakaguchi, J (Dallara F312-Mugen Honda), +16.182s; **6** Hong Li Ye,

CHN (Dallara F315-Volkswagen), +17.432s; **7** Katsumasa Chiyo, J (Dallara F315-Volkswagen), +19.975s; **8** Hiroki Ohtsu, J (Dallara F312-Mugen Honda), +21.900s; **9** Tadasuke Makino, J (Dallara F314-Toda), +23.236s; **10** Ai Miura, J (Dallara F312-Toyota), +45.065s.
Fastest race lap: Tsuboi, 1m 14.374s, 111.412mph/179.301km/h.
Pole position: Yamashita, 1m 13.417s, 112.865mph/181.638km/h.

Round 17 (41.431 miles/66.677km).
1 Kenta Yamashita, J (Dallara F312-Toyota), 26m 34.338s, 93.551mph/150.555km/h; **2** Jann Mardenborough, GB (Dallara F314-Volkswagen), +2.943s; **3** Sho Tsuboi, J (Dallara F314-Toyota), +3.249s; **4** Keishi Ishikawa, J (Dallara F316-Toda), +11.555s; **5** Sena Sakaguchi, J (Dallara F312-Mugen Honda), +15.185s; **6** Hiroki Ohtsu, J (Dallara F312-Mugen Honda), +17.501s; **7** Tadasuke Makino, J (Dallara F314-Toda), +18.374s; **8** Katsumasa Chiyo, J (Dallara F315-Volkswagen), +18.873s; **9** Hong Li Ye, CHN (Dallara F315-Volkswagen), +19.048s; **10** Ai Miura, J (Dallara F312-Toyota), +25.892s.
Fastest race lap: Mardenborough, 1m 14.771s, 110.821mph/178.349km/h.
Pole position: Yamashita.

Final championship points
Drivers
1 Kenta Yamashita, J, 113; **2** Jann Mardenborough, GB, 110; **3** Sho Tsuboi, J, 87; **4** Mitsunori Takaboshi, J, 42; **5** Tadasuke Makino, J, 41; **6** Katsumasa Chiyo, J, 34; **7** Daiki Sasaki, J, 29; **8** Keishi Ishikawa, J, 22; **9** Sena Sakaguchi, J, 20; **10** Hiroki Ohtsu, J, 6.

Drivers (National Class)
1 Yoshiaki Katayama, J, 139; **2** Dragon, J, 113; **3** Kizuku Hirota, J, 82; **4** Alex Yang, CHN, 56; **5** Zene Okazaki, J, 29; **6** Takamitsu Matsui, J, 24; **7** Masayuki Ueda, J, 15; **8** Katsuaki Kubota, J, 2.

Teams
1 B-MAX Racing Team with NDDP, 145; **2** TOM'S, 128; **3** Toda Racing, 50; **4** HFDP Racing, 24.

Major Non-Championship Formula 3

ZANDVOORT MASTERS OF FORMULA 3, Circuit Park Zandvoort, Netherlands, 21/20 August. 25 and 12 laps of the 2.676-mile/4.307km circuit.
Qualification race (32.115 miles/51.684km).
1 Joel Eriksson, S (Dallara F315-Volkswagen), 18m 33.323s, 103.845mph/167.123km/h; **2** Callum Ilott, GB (Dallara F316-Mercedes Benz), +1.461s; **3** Niko Kari, FIN (Dallara F315-Volkswagen), +2.251s; **4** Alexander Albon, T (Dallara F315-Mercedes Benz), +5.793s; **5** Sérgio Sette Câmara, BR (Dallara F316-Volkswagen), +7.670s; **6** Pedro Piquet, BR (Dallara F316-Mercedes Benz), +9.792s; **7** Anthoine Hubert, F (Dallara F312-Mercedes Benz), +10.753s; **8** Alessio Lorandi, I (Dallara F312-Volkswagen), +12.022s; **9** David Beckmann, D (Dallara F316-Mercedes Benz), +12.831s; **10** Guan Yu Zhou, CHN (Dallara F314-Volkswagen), +13.223s.
Fastest race lap: Eriksson, 1m 31.826s, 104.921mph/168.854km/h.
Pole position: Ilott, 1m 29.820s, 107.264mph/172.625km/h.

Race (66.906 miles/107.675km).
1 Joel Eriksson, S (Dallara F315-Volkswagen), 38m 53.053s, 103.239mph/166.147km/h; **2** Niko Kari, FIN (Dallara F315-Volkswagen), +0.838s; **3** Sérgio Sette Câmara, BR (Dallara F316-Volkswagen), +5.816s; **4** Callum Ilott, GB (Dallara F316-Mercedes Benz), +6.625s; **5** Alexander Albon, T (Dallara F315-Mercedes Benz), +7.256s; **6** Pedro Piquet, BR (Dallara F316-Mercedes Benz), +9.135s; **7** Anthoine Hubert, F (Dallara F312-Mercedes Benz), +9.523s; **8** Alessio Lorandi, I (Dallara F312-Volkswagen), +17.195s; **9** Sam MacLeod, GB (Dallara F312-Mercedes Benz), +18.375s; **10** David Beckmann, D (Dallara F316-Mercedes Benz), +19.428s.
Fastest race lap: Guan Yu Zhou, CHN (Dallara F314-Volkswagen), 1m 31.709s, 105.054mph/169.069km/h.
Pole position: Eriksson.

63RD FORMULA 3 MACAU GRAND PRIX, Circuito da Guia, Macau, 20/19 November. 15 and 10 laps of the 3.803-mile/6.120km circuit.
Race 1 (38.028 miles/61.200km).
1 António Félix da Costa, P (Dallara F312-Volkswagen), 27m 07.011s, 84.142mph/135.413km/h; **2** Callum Ilott, GB (Dallara F316-Mercedes Benz), +0.850s; **3** Sérgio Sette Câmara, BR (Dallara F315-Volkswagen), +5.030s; **4** Kenta Yamashita, J (Dallara F314-Threebond), +5.797s; **5** George Russell, GB (Dallara F315-Mercedes Benz), +7.351s; **6** Felix Rosenqvist, S (Dallara F316-Mercedes Benz), +7.889s; **7** Daniel Juncadella, E (Dallara F316-Mercedes Benz), +10.136s; **8** Daniel Ticktum, GB (Dallara F313-Mercedes Benz), +17.416s; **9** Alexander Sims, GB (Dallara F313-Mercedes Benz), +17.859s; **10** Jake Hughes, GB (Dallara F312-Volkswagen), +20.564s.
Fastest race lap: Ilott, 2m 11.445s, 104.150mph/167.613km/h.
Pole position: Russell, 2m 10.100s, 105.227mph/169.346km/h.

Race 2 (57.042 miles/91.800km).
1 António Félix da Costa, P (Dallara F312-Volkswagen), 37m 57.447s, 90.167mph/145.109km/h; **2** Felix Rosenqvist, S (Dallara F316-Mercedes Benz), +1.603s; **3** Sérgio Sette Câmara, BR (Dallara F315-Volkswagen), +3.194s; **4** Kenta Yamashita, J (Dallara F314-Threebond), +3.862s; **5** Callum Ilott, GB (Dallara F316-Mercedes Benz), +4.348s; **6** Jake Hughes, GB (Dallara F312-Volkswagen), +6.191s; **7** George Russell, GB (Dallara F315-Mercedes Benz), +7.027s; **8** Daniel Juncadella, E (Dallara F316-Mercedes Benz), +7.840s; **9** Pedro Piquet, BR (Dallara F316-Mercedes Benz), +9.361s; **10** Alexander Sims, GB (Dallara F313-Mercedes Benz), +11.294s.
Fastest race lap: Rosenqvist, 2m 11.080s, 104.440mph/168.080km/h.
Pole position: da Costa.

Formula V8 3.5

All cars are Dallara FR35-12-Zytek.

FORMULA V8 3.5, MotorLand Aragón, Alcañiz, Aragon, Spain, 16/17 April. Round 1. 24 and 23 laps of the 3.321-mile/5.344km circuit.
Race 1 (79.695 miles/128.256km).
1 Louis Delétraz, CH, 41m 53.608s, 114.138mph/183.688km/h; **2** Matthieu Vaxivière, F, +11.842s; **3** Tom Dillmann, F, +13.026s; **4** Rene Binder, A, +15.661s; **5** Aurélien Panis, F, +16.251s; **6** Alfonso Celis, MEX, +22.333s; **7** Roy Nissany, IL, +34.627s; **8** Vitor Baptista, BR, +49.552s; **9** Johnny Cecotto Jr, YV, +52.185s; **10** Beitske Visser, NL, +1m 00.395s *.
** includes 10s penalty.*
Fastest race lap: Delétraz, 1m 43.626s, 115.358mph/185.652km/h.
Pole position: Egor Orudzhev, RUS, 1m 40.328s, 119.151mph/191.755km/h.

Race 2 (76.374 miles/122.912km).
1 Aurélien Panis, F, 40m 03.536s, 114.392mph/184.096km/h; **2** Tom Dillmann, F, +2.024s; **3** Rene Binder, A, +12.309s; **4** Yu Kanamaru, J, +14.007s; **5** Louis Delétraz, CH, +18.868s; **6** Johnny Cecotto Jr, YV, +27.120s; **7** Roy Nissany, IL, +29.261s; **8** Alfonso Celis, MEX, +33.788s; **9** Pietro Fittipaldi, BR, +33.908s; **10** Matevos Isaakyan, RUS, +37.855s.
Fastest race lap: Delétraz, 1m 42.011s, 117.185mph/188.591km/h.
Pole position: Dillmann, 1m 40.461s, 118.993mph/191.501km/h.

FORMULA V8 3.5, Hungaroring, Mogyoród, Budapest, Hungary, 23/24 April. Round 2. 27 and 19 laps of the 2.722-mile/4.381km circuit.
Race 1 (73.500 miles/118.287km).
1 Johnny Cecotto Jr, YV, 42m 58.954s, 102.599mph/165.118km/h; **2** Tom Dillmann, F, +2.290s; **3** Louis Delétraz, CH, +3.075s; **4** Aurélien Panis, F, +14.082s; **5** Matthieu Vaxivière, F, +14.443s; **6** Roy Nissany, IL, +16.162s; **7** Beitske Visser, NL, +16.855s; **8** Pietro Fittipaldi, BR, +17.291s; **9** Yu Kanamaru, J, +17.957s; **10** Vitor Baptista, BR, +20.429s.
Fastest race lap: Dillmann, 1m 29.706s, 109.245mph/175.814km/h.
Pole position: Dillmann, 1m 26.729s, 112.995mph/181.849km/h.

Race 2 (51.722 miles/83.239km).
1 Tom Dillmann, F, 43m 10.395s, 71.881mph/115.681km/h; **2** Roy Nissany, IL, +0.898s; **3** Aurélien Panis, F, +11.854s; **4** Louis Delétraz, CH, +24.631s; **5** Matthieu Vaxivière, F, +27.164s; **6** Johnny Cecotto Jr, YV, +38.590s; **7** Rene Binder, A, +39.380s; **8** Pietro Fittipaldi, BR, +55.150s; **9** Egor Orudzhev, RUS, +1m 13.425s; **10** Yu Kanamaru, J, +1m 39.983s.
Fastest race lap: Nissany, 1m 57.701s, 83.261mph/133.997km/h.
Pole position: Dillmann.

FORMULA V8 3.5, Circuit de Spa-Francorchamps, Stavelot, Belgium, 21/22 May. Round 3. 21 and 13 laps of the 4.352-mile/7.004km circuit.
Race 1 (91.394 miles/147.084km).
1 Egor Orudzhev, RUS, 43m 37.476s, 125.700mph/202.295km/h; **2** Tom Dillmann, F, +0.229s; **3** Louis Delétraz, CH, +0.820s; **4** Yu Kanamaru, J, +2.029s; **5** Rene Binder, A, +2.683s; **6** Vitor Baptista, BR, +6.363s; **7** Beitske Visser, NL, +17.168s; **8** Aurélien Panis, F, +22.634s; **9** Giuseppe Cipriani, I, +1m 18.576s; **10** Alfonso Celis, MEX, +1m 36.080s.
Fastest race lap: Orudzhev, 2m 02.713s, 127.675mph/205.474km/h.
Pole position: Panis, 1m 58.369s, 132.361mph/213.015km/h.

Race 2 (56.577 miles/91.052km).
1 Matthieu Vaxivière, F, 43m 24.368s, 78.206mph/125.860km/h; **2** Tom Dillmann, F, +6.268s; **3** Alfonso Celis, MEX, +10.277s; **4** Vitor Baptista, BR, +17.636s; **5** Aurélien Panis, F, +20.715s; **6** Rene Binder, A, +36.885s; **7** Yu Kanamaru, J, +42.023s; **8** Giuseppe Cipriani, I, +58.157s; Beitske Visser, NL, -3 laps (DNF); Pietro Fittipaldi, BR, -6 (DNF).
Fastest race lap: Dillmann, 2m 33.683s, 101.946mph/164.067km/h.
Pole position: Dillmann, 1m 59.745s, 130.840mph/210.567km/h.

FORMULA V8 3.5, Circuit ASA Paul Ricard, Le Beausset, France, 25/26 June. Round 4. 22 and 23 laps of the 3.630-mile/5.842km circuit.
Race 1 (79.861 miles/128.524km).
1 Egor Orudzhev, RUS, 41m 42.225s, 114.897mph/184.909km/h; **2** Roy Nissany, IL, +0.541s; **3** Rene Binder, A, +5.647s; **4** Tom Dillmann, F, +6.572s; **5** Matthieu Vaxivière, F, +18.289s; **6** Louis Delétraz, CH, +18.398s; **7** Yu Kanamaru, J, +19.218s; **8** Aurélien Panis, F, +19.642s; **9** Beitske Visser, NL, +21.571s; **10** Matevos Isaakyan, RUS, +23.606s.
Fastest race lap: Orudzhev, 1m 52.801s, 115.851mph/186.445km/h.
Pole position: Vaxivière, 1m 49.087s, 119.795mph/192.792km/h.

Race 2 (83.491 miles/134.366km).
1 Louis Delétraz, CH, 43m 44.351s, 114.530mph/184.318km/h; **2** Roy Nissany, IL, +2.878s; **3** Egor Orudzhev, RUS, +9.722s; **4** Aurélien Panis, F, +13.381s; **5** Rene Binder, A, +14.317s; **6** Tom Dillmann, F, +22.114s; **7** Pietro Fittipaldi, BR, +23.489s; **8** Alfonso Celis, MEX, +24.984s; **9** Artur Janosz, PL, +32.318s; **10** Beitske Visser, NL, +37.204s.
Fastest race lap: Delétraz, 1m 51.350s, 117.361mph/188.874km/h.
Pole position: Nissany, 1m 47.933s, 121.076mph/194.854km/h.

FORMULA V8 3.5, Silverstone Grand Prix Circuit, Towcester, Northamptonshire, Great Britain, 23/24 July. Round 5. 23 and 24 laps of the 3.660-mile/5.891km circuit.
Race 1 (84.191 miles/135.493km).
1 Roy Nissany, IL, 40m 20.221s, 125.232mph/201.541km/h; **2** Matthieu Vaxivière, F, +6.248s; **3** Rene Binder, A, +7.653s; **4** Tom Dillmann, F, +8.445s; **5** Aurélien Panis, F, +11.908s; **6** Pietro Fittipaldi, BR, +12.839s; **7** Yu Kanamaru, J, +14.365s; **8** Vitor Baptista, BR, +18.958s; **9** Beitske Visser, NL, +22.488s; **10** Louis Delétraz, CH, +27.764s.
Fastest race lap: Nissany, 1m 43.960s, 126.758mph/203.997km/h.
Pole position: Vaxivière, 1m 40.586s, 131.010mph/210.840km/h.

Race 2 (87.852 miles/141.384km).
1 Roy Nissany, IL, 42m 19.344s, 124.546mph/200.438km/h; **2** Rene Binder, A, +17.091s; **3** Egor Orudzhev, RUS, +20.092s; **4** Tom Dillmann, F, +25.205s; **5** Aurélien Panis, F, +24.424s *; **6** Louis Delétraz, CH, +25.967s; **7** Matthieu Vaxivière, F, +26.622s; **8** Vitor Baptista, BR, +30.239s; **9** Yu Kanamaru, J, +34.412s; **10** Beitske Visser, NL, +50.856s.
** includes drop of 1 place.*
Fastest race lap: Nissany, 1m 43.816s, 126.934mph/204.280km/h.
Pole position: Vaxivière, 1m 40.836s, 130.685mph/210.317km/h.

FORMULA V8 3.5, Red Bull Ring, Spielberg, Austria, 10/11 September. Round 6. 31 and 30 laps of the 2.683-mile/4.318km circuit.
Race 1 (83.176 miles/133.858km).
1 Matthieu Vaxivière, F, 42m 26.793s, 117.572mph/189.213km/h; **2** Louis Delétraz, CH, +0.977s; **3** Tom Dillmann, F, +4.527s; **4** Alfonso Celis, MEX, +8.836s; **5** Aurélien Panis, F, +10.268s; **6** Roy Nissany, IL, +10.504s; **7** Yu Kanamaru, J, +11.060s; **8** Beitske Visser, NL, +13.800s; **9** Marco Bonanomi, I, +15.874s; **10** Vitor Baptista, BR, +16.412s.
Fastest race lap: Vaxivière, 1m 17.415s, 124.770mph/200.798km/h.
Pole position: Delétraz, 1m 15.914s, 127.237mph/204.768km/h.

Race 2 (80.492 miles/129.540km).
1 Aurélien Panis, F, 41m 26.486s, 116.539mph/187.551km/h; **2** Tom Dillmann, F, +0.676s; **3** Matevos Isaakyan, RUS, +4.051s; **4** Louis Delétraz, CH, +5.771s; **5** Egor Orudzhev, RUS, +6.137s; **6** Matthieu Vaxivière, F, +8.820s; **7** Alfonso Celis, MEX, +12.055s; **8** Vitor Baptista, BR, +14.185s; **9** Beitske Visser, NL, +19.894s; **10** Marco Bonanomi, I, +21.118s.
Fastest race lap: Roy Nissany, IL, 1m 17.038s, 125.380mph/201.780km/h.
Pole position: Isaakyan, 1m 15.674s, 127.640mph/205.417km/h.

FORMULA V8 3.5, Autodromo Nazionale di Monza, Milan, Italy, 1/2 October. Round 7. 26 and 22 laps of the 3.600-mile/5.793km circuit.
Race 1 (93.590 miles/150.618km).
1 Roy Nissany, IL, 42m 03.914s, 133.492mph/214.834km/h; **2** Louis Delétraz, CH, +12.422s; **3** Matthieu Vaxivière, F, +19.343s; **4** Aurélien Panis, F, +26.918s; **5** Rene Binder, A, +27.481s; **6** Yu Kanamaru, J, +32.082s; **7** Egor Orudzhev, RUS, +42.083s; **8** Vitor Baptista, BR, +48.757s; **9** Alfonso Celis, MEX, +51.242s; **10** William Buller, GB, +53.848s.
Fastest race lap: Nissany, 1m 36.331s, 134.521mph/216.491km/h.
Pole position: Nissany, 1m 33.646s, 138.378mph/222.698km/h.

Race 2 (79.191 miles/127.446km).
1 Egor Orudzhev, RUS, 41m 44.066s, 113.850mph/183.224km/h; **2** Rene Binder, A, +0.965s; **3** Louis Delétraz, CH, +4.106s; **4** Pietro Fittipaldi, BR, +6.725s; **5** Yu Kanamaru, J, +8.221s; **6** Roy Nissany, IL, +8.856s; **7** William Buller, GB, +9.265s; **8** Tom Dillmann, F, +9.898s; **9** Beitske Visser, NL, +15.013s; **10** Alfonso Celis, MEX, +24.692s.

Fastest race lap: Nissany, 1m 36.256s, 134.626mph/216.659km/h.
Pole position: Nissany, 1m 34.798s, 136.696mph/219.991km/h.

FORMULA V8 3.5, Circuito Permanente de Jerez, Jerez de la Frontera, Spain, 29/30 October. Round 8. 2 x 27 laps of the 2.751-mile/4.428km circuit.
Race 1 (74.289 miles/119.556km).
1 Matevos Isaakyan, RUS, 43m 04.008s, 103.497mph/166.563km/h; **2** Egor Orudzhev, RUS, +0.513s; **3** Matthieu Vaxivière, F, +5.100s; **4** Aurélien Panis, F, +8.252s; **5** Rene Binder, A, +9.167s; **6** Yu Kanamaru, J, +11.470s; **7** Beitske Visser, NL, +11.516s; **8** Roy Nissany, IL, +12.167s; **9** Pietro Fittipaldi, BR, +13.827s; **10** Vitor Baptista, BR, +15.744s.
Disqualified: Jack Aitken, GB (originally finished 10th).
Fastest race lap: Vaxivière, 1m 32.205s, 107.425mph/172.884km/h.
Pole position: Jack Aitken, GB, 1m 26.978s, 113.881mph/183.273km/h.

Race 2 (74.289 miles/119.556km).
1 Egor Orudzhev, RUS, 42m 07.482s, 105.812mph/170.288km/h; **2** Louis Delétraz, CH, +2.019s; **3** Matthieu Vaxivière, F, +17.876s; **4** Jack Aitken, GB, +20.306s; **5** Beitske Visser, NL, +21.136s; **6** Matevos Isaakyan, RUS, +22.558s; **7** Rene Binder, A, +31.442s; **8** Tom Dillmann, F, +38.753s; **9** Alfonso Celis, MEX, +42.548s; **10** Yu Kanamaru, J, +43.183s.
Fastest race lap: Delétraz, 1m 31.847s, 107.844mph/173.558km/h.
Pole position: Delétraz, 1m 26.943s, 113.926mph/183.347km/h.

FORMULA V8 3.5, Circuit de Catalunya, Montmeló, Barcelona, Spain, 5/6 November. Round 9. 2 x 25 laps of the 2.892-mile/4.655km circuit.
Race 1 (72.312 miles/116.375km).
1 Egor Orudzhev, RUS, 39m 40.100s, 109.375mph/176.022km/h; **2** Louis Delétraz, CH, +9.891s; **3** Tom Dillmann, F, +12.240s; **4** Aurélien Panis, F, +13.422s; **5** Matevos Isaakyan, RUS, +22.646s; **6** Vitor Baptista, BR, +26.592s; **7** Pietro Fittipaldi, BR, +31.454s; **8** Yu Kanamaru, J, +32.139s; **9** Roy Nissany, IL, +35.321s; **10** Beitske Visser, NL, +37.188s.
Fastest race lap: Delétraz, 1m 34.359s, 110.354mph/177.598km/h.
Pole position: Dillmann, 1m 44.909s, 99.256mph/159.738km/h.

Race 2 (72.312 miles/116.375km).
1 Tom Dillmann, F, 39m 47.303s, 109.045mph/175.490km/h; **2** Roy Nissany, IL, +1.405s; **3** Pietro Fittipaldi, BR, +10.434s; **4** Louis Delétraz, CH, +12.489s; **5** Matevos Isaakyan, RUS, +12.998s; **6** Rene Binder, A, +14.055s; **7** Egor Orudzhev, RUS, +16.262s; **8** Beitske Visser, NL, +39.609s; **9** Jack Aitken, GB, +41.250s; **10** Yu Kanamaru, J, +41.923s.
Fastest race lap: Orudzhev, 1m 33.239s, 111.680mph/179.731km/h.
Pole position: Delétraz, 1m 31.953s, 113.241mph/182.245km/h.

Final championship points
Drivers
1 Tom Dillmann, F, 237; **2** Louis Delétraz, CH, 230; **3** Egor Orudzhev, RUS, 197; **4** Roy Nissany, IL, 189; **5** Aurélien Panis, F, 183; **6** Matthieu Vaxivière, F, 175; **7** Rene Binder, A, 161; **8** Yu Kanamaru, J, 85; **9** Matevos Isaakyan, RUS, 70; **10** Pietro Fittipaldi, BR, 59; **11** Alfonso Celis, MEX, 55; **12** Vitor Baptista, BR, 51; **13** Beitske Visser, NL, 48; **14** Johnny Cecotto Jr, YV, 43; **15** Jack Aitken, GB, 14; **16** William Buller, GB, 7; **17** Giuseppe Cipriani, I, 6; **18** Marco Bonanomi, I, 3; **19** Artur Janosz, PL, 2.

Teams
1 Arden Motorsport, 380; **2** Lotus, 350; **3** AVF, 292; **4** Fortec Motorsports, 289; **5** SMP Racing, 245; **6** Teo Martin Motorsport, 133; **7** Rp Motorsport, 120; **8** Durango Racing Team, 6.

FIA World Endurance Championship

6 HOURS OF SILVERSTONE, Silverstone Grand Prix Circuit, Towcester, Northamptonshire, Great Britain, 17 April. Round 1. 194 laps of the 3.667-mile/5.901km circuit, 711.342 miles/1144.794km.
1 Romain Dumas/Neel Jani/Marc Lieb, F/CH/D (Porsche 919 Hybrid '16), 6h 01m 53.028s, 117.939mph/189.805km/h; **2** Stéphane Sarrazin/Mike Conway/Kamui Kobayashi, F/GB/J (Toyota TS050 HYBRID), -1 lap; **3** Mathéo Tuscher/Dominik Kraihamer/Alexandre Imperatori, CH/A/CH (Rebellion R-One-AER), -11; **4** Nicolas Prost/Nelson Piquet Jr/Nick Heidfeld, F/BR/D (Rebellion R-One-AER), -13; **5** Ricardo González/Filipe Albuquerque/Bruno Senna, MEX/P/BR (Ligier JS P2-Nissan), -15; **6** Ryan Dalziel/Luis Derani/Chris Cumming, GB/BR/CDN (Ligier JS P2-Nissan), -15; **7** Roman Rusinov/Nathanaël Berthon/René Rast, RUS/F/D (ORECA 05-Nissan), -15; **8** Gustavo Menezes/Nicolas Lapierre/Stéphane Richelmi, USA/F/MC (Alpine A460-Nissan), -16; **9** Nick Leventis/Danny Watts/Jonny Kane, GB/GB/GB (Gibson 015S-Nissan), -17; **10** Matt Rao/Richard Bradley/Roberto Merhi, GB/GB/E (ORECA 05-Nissan), -17.

Disqualified: Marcel Fässler/André Lotterer/Benoît Tréluyer, CH/D/F (Audi R18 E-Tron Quattro '16) for a technical infringement (originally finished 2nd).
Fastest race lap: Jani, 1m 40.303s, 131.602mph/211.794km/h.
Pole position: Marcel Fässler/André Lotterer/Benoît Tréluyer, CH/D/F (Audi R18 E-Tron Quattro '16), 1m 53.204s, 116.605mph/187.657km/h.

6 HOURS OF SPA-FRANCORCHAMPS, Circuit de Spa-Francorchamps, Stavelot, Belgium, 7 May. Round 2. 160 laps of the 4.352-mile/7.004km circuit, 696.323 miles/1120.624km.
1 Lucas di Grassi/Loïc Duval/Oliver Jarvis, BR/F/GB (Audi R18 E-Tron Quattro '16), 6h 00m 32.112s, 115.881mph/186.493km/h; **2** Romain Dumas/Neel Jani/Marc Lieb, F/CH/D (Porsche 919 Hybrid '16), -2 laps; **3** Mathéo Tuscher/Dominik Kraihamer/Alexandre Imperatori, CH/A/CH (Rebellion R-One-AER), -4; **4** Nicolas Prost/Nelson Piquet Jr/Nick Heidfeld, F/BR/D (Rebellion R-One-AER), -5; **5** Marcel Fässler/André Lotterer/Benoît Tréluyer, CH/D/F (Audi R18 E-Tron Quattro '16), -5; **6** Simon Trummer/Oliver Webb/James Rossiter, CH/GB/GB (CLM P1/01-AER), -9; **7** Gustavo Menezes/Nicolas Lapierre/Stéphane Richelmi, USA/F/MC (Alpine A460-Nissan), -9; **8** Ryan Dalziel/Luis Derani/Chris Cumming, GB/BR/CDN (Ligier JS P2-Nissan), -9; **9** Matt Rao/Richard Bradley/Roberto Merhi, GB/GB/E (ORECA 05-Nissan), -9; **10** Ricardo González/Filipe Albuquerque/Bruno Senna, MEX/P/BR (Ligier JS P2-Nissan), -9 *.
** includes 23s penalty.*
Fastest race lap: Brendon Hartley, NZ (Porsche 919 Hybrid '16), 1m 58.431s, 132.290mph/212.900km/h.
Pole position: Timo Bernhard/Mark Webber/Brendon Hartley, D/AUS/NZ (Porsche 919 Hybrid '16), 1m 55.793s, 135.304mph/217.750km/h.

24 HEURES DU MANS, Circuit International Du Mans, Les Raineries, Le Mans, France, 18 June. Round 3. 384 laps of the 8.469-mile/13.629km circuit, 3251.969 miles/5233.536km.
1 Romain Dumas/Neel Jani/Marc Lieb, F/CH/D (Porsche 919 Hybrid), 24h 00m 38.449s, 135.438mph/217.967km/h; **2** Stéphane Sarrazin/Mike Conway/Kamui Kobayashi, F/GB/J (Toyota TS050 HYBRID), -3 laps; **3** Lucas di Grassi/Loïc Duval/Oliver Jarvis, BR/F/GB (Audi R18 E-Tron Quattro '16), -12; **4** Marcel Fässler/André Lotterer/Benoît Tréluyer, CH/D/F (Audi R18 E-Tron Quattro '16), -17; **5** Gustavo Menezes/Nicolas Lapierre/Stéphane Richelmi, USA/F/MC (Alpine A460-Nissan), -27; **6** Roman Rusinov/Will Stevens/René Rast, RUS/GB/D (ORECA 05-Nissan), -27; **7** Vitaly Petrov/Victor Shaytar/Kirill Ladygin, RUS/RUS/RUS (BR Engineering BR01-Nissan), -31; **8** Nick Leventis/Danny Watts/Jonny Kane, GB/GB/GB (Gibson 015S-Nissan), -33; **9** Pu Jun Jin/Tristan Gommendy/Nick de Bruijn, CHN/F/NL (ORECA 05-Nissan), -36; **10** Memo Rojas/Julien Canal/Nathanaël Berthon, MEX/F/F (Ligier JS P2-Nissan), -36; **11** Nicolas Minassian/Maurizio Mediani/Mikhail Aleshin, F/I/RUS (BR Engineering BR01-Nissan), -37; **12** Fabien Barthez/Paul-Loup Chatin/Timothé Buret, F/F/F (Ligier JS P2-Nissan), -37; **13** Timo Bernhard/Mark Webber/Brendon Hartley, D/AUS/NZ (Porsche 919 Hybrid), -38; **14** John Pew/Oswaldo Negri Jr/Laurens Vanthoor, USA/BR/B (Ligier JS P2-HPD), -39; **15** Ricardo González/Bruno Senna/Filipe Albuquerque, MEX/BR/P (Ligier JS P2-Nissan), -40; **16** Scott Sharp/Ed Brown/Johannes van Overbeek, USA/USA/USA (Ligier JS P2-Nissan), -43; **17** Michael Munemann/Chris Hoy/Andréa Pizzitola, GB/GB/F (Ligier JS P2-Nissan), -43; **18** Joey Hand/Dirk Müller/Sébastien Bourdais, USA/D/F (Ford GT), -44 *; **19** Giancarlo Fisichella/Toni Vilander/Matteo Malucelli, I/FIN/I (Ferrari 488 GTE), -44 **; **20** Ryan Briscoe/Richard Westbrook/Scott Dixon, AUS/GB/NZ (Ford GT), -44; **21** Olivier Pla/Stefan Mücke/Billy Johnson, F/D/USA (Ford GT), -45; **22** Tracy Krohn/Nic Jönsson/João Barbosa, USA/S/P (Ligier JS P2-Nissan), -46; **23** Nicki Thiim/Marco Sørensen/Darren Turner, DK/DK/GB (Aston Martin Vantage V8), -46; **24** Richie Stanaway/Fernando Rees/Jonathan Adam, NZ/BR/GB (Aston Martin Vantage V8), -47; **25** Jan Magnussen/Antonio García/Ricky Taylor, DK/E/USA (Chevrolet Corvette C7.R), -48; **26** Bill Sweedler/Townsend Bell/Jeff Segal, USA/USA/USA (Ferrari F458 Italia), -53; **27** François Perrodo/Emmanuel Collard/Rui Águas, F/F/P (Ferrari F458 Italia), -53; **28** Khaled Al Qubaisi/David Heinemeier-Hansson/Patrick Long, UAE/DK/USA (Porsche 911 RSR), -54; **29** Nicolas Prost/Nick Heidfeld/Nelson Piquet Jr, F/D/BR (Rebellion R-One-AER), -54; **30** Weng Sun Mok/Keita Sawa/Rob Bell, MAL/J/GB (Ferrari F458 Italia), -55; **31** Richard Lietz/Michael Christensen/Philipp Eng, A/DK/A (Porsche 911 RSR '16), -55; **32** Vincent Capillaire/Erik Maris/Jonathan Coleman, F/F/GB (Ligier JS P2-Judd), -56; **33** Mike Wainwright/Adam Carroll/Ben Barker, GB/GB/GB (Porsche 911 RSR), -56; **34** Ben Keating/Jeroen Bleekemolen/Marc Goossens, USA/NL/B (ORECA 03R-Nissan), -61; **35** Johnny Laursen/Mikkel Mac/Christina Nielsen, DK/DK/DK (Ferrari F458 Italia), -65; **36** Andrew Howard/Liam Griffin/Gary Hirsch, GB/GB/CH (Aston Martin Vantage V8), -66; **37** Yutaka Yamagishi/Pierre Ragues/Jean-Philippe Belloc, J/F/F (Chevrolet Corvette C7.R), -68; **38** Frédéric Sausset/Christophe Tinseau/Jean-Bernard Bouvet, F/F/F (Morgan LMP2-Nissan), -69; **39** Johnny O'Connell/Oliver Bryant/Mark Patterson, USA/GB/USA (Chevrolet Corvette C7.R), -78; **40** Marino Franchitti/Andy Priaulx/Harry Tincknell, GB/GB/GB (Ford GT), -78; **41** Christian Ried/Wolf Henzler/Joël Camathias, D/D/CH (Porsche 911 RSR), -84; **42** Ryan Dalziel/Luis Derani/Chris Cumming, GB/BR/CDN (Ligier JS P2-Nissan), -87; **43** Niki Leutwiler/Shinji Nakano/James Winslow, CH/J/GB (ORECA 03R-Judd), -87 ***; **44** Duncan Cameron/Matt Griffin/Aaron Scott, GB/IRL/GB (Ferrari F458 Italia), -95; Anthony Davidson/Sébastien Buemi/Kazuki Nakajima, GB/CH/J (Toyota TS050 HYBRID), -11.625s (final lap too slow); Inès Taittinger/Remy Striebig/Leo Roussel, F/F/F (Morgan LMP2-Nissan), -92 (DNF-fire); Tor Graves/Matt Rao/Roberto Merhi, GB/GB/E (ORECA 05-Nissan), -101 (DNF-accident); Paul Dalla Lana/Pedro Lamy/Mathias Lauda, CDN/P/A (Aston Martin Vantage V8), -103 (DNF-gearbox); Pierre Thiriet/Mathias Beche/Ryo Hirakawa, F/CH/J (ORECA 05-Nissan), -143 (DNF-accident damage); David Cheng/Ho-Pin Tung/Nelson Panciatici, USA/CHN/F (Alpine A460-Nissan), -150 (DNF-accident); Simon Dolan/Jake Dennis/Giedo van der Garde, GB/GB/NL (Gibson 015S-Nissan), -162 (DNF-accident damage); Oliver Gavin/Tommy Milner/Jordan Taylor, GB/USA/USA (Chevrolet Corvette C7.R), -165 (DNF-accident); Simon Trummer/Oliver Webb/Pierre Kaffer, CH/GB/D (CLM P1/01-AER), -178 (DNF-fire); Mathéo Tuscher/Alexandre Imperatori/Dominik Kraihamer, CH/CH/A (Rebellion R-One-AER), -184 (DNF-fuel system); Gianmaria Bruni/James Calado/Alessandro Pier Guidi, I/GB/I (Ferrari 488 GTE), -205 (DNF-electrics); Davide Rigon/Sam Bird/Andrea Bertolini, I/GB/I (Ferrari 488 GTE), -241 (DNF-wheel); Frédéric Makowiecki/Earl Bamber/Jörg Bergmeister, F/NZ/D (Porsche 911 RSR '16), -244 (DNF-engine); Patrick Pilet/Kévin Estre/Nick Tandy, F/F/GB (Porsche 911 RSR '16), -249 (DNF-suspension); Tsugio Matsuda/Matt Howson/Richard Bradley, J/GB/GB (ORECA 05-Nissan), -268 (DNF-electronics); Cooper MacNeil/Leh Keen/Marc Miller, USA/USA/USA (Porsche 911 RSR), -334 (DNF-accident).
** includes 70s penalty.*
*** includes 20s penalty.*
**** includes 8-lap and 2-minute penalty.*
Fastest race lap: Kobayashi, 3m 21.445s, 151.343mph/243.562km/h.
Pole position: Dumas/Jani/Lieb, 3m 19.733s, 152.640mph/245.650km/h.

6 HOURS OF NURBURGRING, Nürburgring, Nürburg/Eifel, Germany, 24 July. Round 4. 194 laps of the 3.199-mile/5.148km circuit, 620.571 miles/998.712km.
1 Timo Bernhard/Mark Webber/Brendon Hartley, D/AUS/NZ (Porsche 919 Hybrid), 6h 01m 16.183s, 103.064mph/165.866km/h; **2** Lucas di Grassi/Loïc Duval/Oliver Jarvis, BR/F/GB (Audi R18 E-Tron Quattro '16), +53.787s; **3** Marcel Fässler/André Lotterer, CH/D (Audi R18 E-Tron Quattro '16), +54.483s; **4** Romain Dumas/Neel Jani/Marc Lieb, F/CH/D (Porsche 919 Hybrid), +1m 37.324s; **5** Anthony Davidson/Sébastien Buemi/Kazuki Nakajima, GB/CH/J (Toyota TS050 HYBRID), -1 lap; **6** Stéphane Sarrazin/Mike Conway/Kamui Kobayashi, F/GB/J (Toyota TS050 HYBRID), -4; **7** Mathéo Tuscher/Dominik Kraihamer/Alexandre Imperatori, CH/A/CH (Rebellion R-One-AER), -16; **8** Gustavo Menezes/Nicolas Lapierre/Stéphane Richelmi, USA/F/MC (Alpine A460-Nissan), -16; **9** Ricardo González/Bruno Senna/Filipe Albuquerque, MEX/BR/P (Ligier JS P2-Nissan), -16; **10** Ryan Dalziel/Luis Derani/Chris Cumming, GB/BR/CDN (Ligier JS P2-Nissan), -18.
Fastest race lap: Fässler, 1m 40.325s, 114.784mph/184.727km/h.
Pole position: Fässler/Lotterer, 1m 39.444s, 115.801mph/186.364km/h.

6 HOURS OF MEXICO, Autódromo Hermanos Rodríguez, Mexico City, D.F., Mexico, 3 September. Round 5. 230 laps of the 2.674-mile/4.304km circuit, 615.108 miles/989.920km.
1 Timo Bernhard/Mark Webber/Brendon Hartley, D/AUS/NZ (Porsche 919 Hybrid), 6h 00m 43.702s, 102.310mph/164.653km/h; **2** Marcel Fässler/André Lotterer, CH/D (Audi R18 E-Tron Quattro '16), +1m 01.442s; **3** Stéphane Sarrazin/Mike Conway/Kamui Kobayashi, F/GB/J (Toyota TS050 HYBRID), +1m 09.709s; **4** Romain Dumas/Neel Jani/Marc Lieb, F/CH/D (Porsche 919 Hybrid), +1m 30.004s; **5** Mathéo Tuscher/Dominik Kraihamer/Alexandre Imperatori, CH/A/CH (Rebellion R-One-AER), -12 laps; **6** Ricardo González/Bruno Senna/Filipe Albuquerque, MEX/BR/P (Ligier JS P2-Nissan), -20; **7** Gustavo Menezes/Nicolas Lapierre/Stéphane Richelmi, USA/F/MC (Alpine A460-Nissan), -20; **8** Ryan Dalziel/Luis Derani/Chris Cumming, GB/BR/CDN (Ligier JS P2-Nissan), -23; **9** Nick Leventis/Lewis Williamson/Jonny Kane, GB/GB/GB (Gibson 015S-Nissan), -23; **10** Roberto González/Bruno Junqueira/Luis Diaz, MEX/BR/MEX (Gibson 015S-Nissan), -23.
Fastest race lap: Hartley, 1m 25.880s, 112.107mph/180.419km/h.
Pole position: Lucas di Grassi/Loïc Duval/Oliver Jarvis, BR/F/GB (Audi R18 E-Tron Quattro '16), 1m 25.069s, 113.176mph/182.139km/h.

6 HOURS OF CIRCUIT OF THE AMERICAS, Circuit of the Americas, Austin, Texas, USA, 17 September. Round 6. 186 laps of the 3.426-mile/5.513km circuit, 637.165 miles/1025.418km.
1 Timo Bernhard/Mark Webber/Brendon Hartley, D/AUS/NZ (Porsche 919 Hybrid), 6h 01m 30.181s, 105.752mph/170.192km/h; **2** Lucas di Grassi/Loïc Duval/Oliver Jarvis, BR/F/GB (Audi R18 E-Tron Quattro '16), +23.641s; **3** Stéphane Sarrazin/Mike Conway/Kamui Kobayashi, F/GB/J (Toyota TS050 HYBRID), +26.096s; **4** Romain Dumas/Neel Jani/Marc Lieb, F/CH/D (Porsche 919 Hybrid), -1 lap; **5** Anthony Davidson/Sébastien Buemi/Kazuki Nakajima, GB/CH/J (Toyota TS050 HYBRID), -2; **6** Marcel Fässler/André Lotterer/Benoît Tréluyer, CH/D/F (Audi R18 E-Tron Quattro '16), -6; **7** Mathéo Tuscher/Dominik Kraihamer/Alexandre Imperatori, CH/A/CH (Rebellion R-One-AER), -12; **8** Gustavo Menezes/Nicolas Lapierre/Stéphane Richelmi, USA/F/MC (Alpine A460-Nissan), -14; **9** Ricardo González/Bruno Senna/Filipe Albuquerque, MEX/BR/P (Ligier JS P2-Nissan), -15; **10** Roman Rusinov/René Rast/Alex Brundle, RUS/D/GB (ORECA 05-Nissan), -15.
Fastest race lap: Duval, 1m 47.052s, 115.198mph/185.394km/h.
Pole position: Fässler/Lotterer/Tréluyer, 1m 45.750s, 116.616mph/187.676km/h.

6 HOURS OF FUJI, Fuji International Speedway, Sunto-gun, Shizuoka Prefecture, Japan, 16 October. Round 7. 244 laps of the 2.835-mile/4.563km circuit, 691.817 miles/1113.372km.
1 Stéphane Sarrazin/Mike Conway/Kamui Kobayashi, F/GB/J (Toyota TS050 HYBRID), 6h 00m 37.284s, 115.104mph/185.242km/h; **2** Lucas di Grassi/Loïc Duval/Oliver Jarvis, BR/F/GB (Audi R18 E-Tron Quattro '16), +1.439s; **3** Timo Bernhard/Mark Webber/Brendon Hartley, D/AUS/NZ (Porsche 919 Hybrid), +17.339s; **4** Anthony Davidson/Sébastien Buemi/Kazuki Nakajima, GB/CH/J (Toyota TS050 HYBRID), +53.779s; **5** Romain Dumas/Neel Jani/Marc Lieb, F/CH/D (Porsche 919 Hybrid), -1 lap; **6** Mathéo Tuscher/Dominik Kraihamer/Alexandre Imperatori, CH/A/CH (Rebellion R-One-AER), -15; **7** Roman Rusinov/Alex Brundle/Will Stevens, RUS/GB/GB (ORECA 05-Nissan), -21; **8** Ricardo González/Bruno Senna/Filipe Albuquerque, MEX/BR/P (Ligier JS P2-Nissan), -21; **9** Gustavo Menezes/Nicolas Lapierre/Stéphane Richelmi, USA/F/MC (Alpine A460-Nissan), -21; **10** Antonio Giovinazzi/Giedo van der Garde/Sean Gelael, I/NL/RI (Ligier JS P2-Nissan), -21.
Fastest race lap: Duval, 1m 24.645s, 120.587mph/194.066km/h.
Pole position: di Grassi/Duval/Jarvis, 1m 23.570s, 122.138mph/196.563km/h.

6 HOURS OF SHANGHAI, Shanghai International Circuit, Shanghai, China, 6 November. Round 8. 195 laps of the 3.387-mile/5.451km circuit, 660.483 miles/1062.945km.
1 Timo Bernhard/Mark Webber/Brendon Hartley, D/AUS/NZ (Porsche 919 Hybrid), 6h 00m 27.901s, 109.938mph/176.928km/h; **2** Stéphane Sarrazin/Mike Conway/Kamui Kobayashi, F/GB/J (Toyota TS050 HYBRID), +59.785s; **3** Anthony Davidson/Sébastien Buemi/Kazuki Nakajima, GB/CH/J (Toyota TS050 HYBRID), +1m 06.038s; **4** Romain Dumas/Neel Jani/Marc Lieb, F/CH/D (Porsche 919 Hybrid), +1m 40.855s; **5** Lucas di Grassi/Loïc Duval/Oliver Jarvis, BR/F/GB (Audi R18 E-Tron Quattro '16), -3 laps; **6** Marcel Fässler/André Lotterer/Benoît Tréluyer, CH/D/F (Audi R18 E-Tron Quattro '16), -14; **7** Simon Trummer/Oliver Webb/Pierre Kaffer, CH/GB/D (CLM P1/01-AER), -14; **8** Roman Rusinov/Alex Brundle/Will Stevens, RUS/GB/GB (ORECA 05-Nissan), -15; **9** Antonio Giovinazzi/Tom Blomqvist/Sean Gelael, I/GB/RI (Ligier JS P2-Nissan), -16; **10** Ricardo González/Bruno Senna/Filipe Albuquerque, MEX/BR/P (Ligier JS P2-Nissan), -16.
Fastest race lap: Hartley, 1m 45.935s, 115.103mph/185.241km/h.
Pole position: Bernhard/Webber/Hartley, 1m 44.462s, 116.727mph/187.853km/h.

6 HOURS OF BAHRAIN, Bahrain International Circuit, Sakhir, Bahrain, 19 November. Round 9. 201 laps of the 3.363-mile/5.412km circuit, 675.935 miles/1087.812km.
1 Lucas di Grassi/Loïc Duval/Oliver Jarvis, BR/F/GB (Audi R18 E-Tron Quattro '16), 6h 00m 12.387s, 112.591mph/181.198km/h; **2** Marcel Fässler/André Lotterer/Benoît Tréluyer, CH/D/F (Audi R18 E-Tron Quattro '16), +16.419s; **3** Timo Bernhard/Mark Webber/Brendon Hartley, D/AUS/NZ (Porsche 919 Hybrid), +1m 17.001s; **4** Anthony Davidson/Sébastien Buemi/Kazuki Nakajima, GB/CH/J (Toyota TS050 HYBRID), -1 lap; **5** Stéphane Sarrazin/Mike Conway/Kamui Kobayashi, F/GB/J (Toyota TS050 HYBRID), -1; **6** Romain Dumas/Neel Jani/Marc Lieb, F/CH/D (Porsche 919 Hybrid), -3; **7** Mathéo Tuscher/Dominik Kraihamer/Alexandre Imperatori, CH/A/CH (Rebellion R-One-AER), -10; **8** Simon Trummer/Oliver Webb/Pierre Kaffer, CH/GB/D (CLM P1/01-AER), -14; **9** Roman Rusinov/René Rast/Alex Brundle, RUS/D/GB (ORECA 05-Nissan), -17; **10** Ricardo González/Filipe Albuquerque/Bruno Senna, MEX/P/BR (Ligier JS P2-Nissan), -17.
Fastest race lap: di Grassi, 1m 41.511s, 119.260mph/191.931km/h.
Pole position: di Grassi/Duval/Jarvis, 1m 39.207s, 122.030mph/196.389km/h.

Final championship points
Drivers
1 Romain Dumas, F, 160; 1 Marc Lieb, D, 160; 1 Neel Jani, CH, 160; **2** Loïc Duval, F, 147.5; **2** Lucas di Grassi, BR, 147.5; **2** Oliver Jarvis, GB, 147.5; **3** Stéphane Sarrazin, F, 145; **3** Kamui Kobayashi, J, 145; **3** Mike Conway, GB, 145; **4** Brendon Hartley, NZ, 134.5; **4** Timo Bernhard, D, 134.5; **4** Mark Webber, AUS, 134.5; **5** André Lotterer, D, 104; **5** Marcel Fässler, CH, 104; **6** Benoît Tréluyer, F, 70; **7** Alexandre Imperatori, CH, 66.5; **7** Dominik Kraihamer, A, 66.5; **7** Mathéo Tuscher, CH, 66.5; **8** Anthony Davidson, GB, 60; **8** Sébastien Buemi, CH, 60; **8** Kazuki Nakajima, J, 60; **9** Gustavo Menezes, USA, 47; **9** Nicolas Lapierre, F, 47; **9** Stéphane Richelmi, MC, 47; **10** Roman Rusinov, RUS, 36;

Drivers (LMP2)
1 Gustavo Menezes, USA, 199; 1 Nicolas Lapierre, F, 199; 1 Stéphane Richelmi, MC, 199; **2** Bruno Senna, BR, 166; **2** Filipe Albuquerque, P, 166; **2** Ricardo González, MEX, 166; **3** Roman Rusinov, RUS, 162;

Drivers (GT)
1 Marco Sørensen, DK, 156; 1 Nicki Thiim, DK, 156; **2** Davide Rigon, I, 134; **2** Sam Bird, GB, 134; **3** Gianmaria Bruni, I, 128; **3** James Calado, GB, 128;

Drivers (LMGTE Am)
1 Emmanuel Collard, F, 188; 1 François Perrodo, F, 188; 1 Rui Águas, P, 188; **2** David Heinemeier Hansson, DK, 151; **2** Khaled Al Qubaisi, UAE, 151; **3** Mathias Lauda, A, 149; **3** Paul Dalla Lana, CDN, 149; **3** Pedro Lamy, P, 149;

Manufacturers
1 Porsche, 324; **2** Audi, 266; **3** Toyota, 229.

Manufacturers (GT)
1 Ferrari, 294; **2** Aston Martin, 287; **3** Ford, 241.5; **4** Porsche, 123.

Teams (LMP1)
1 Rebellion Racing (car 13), 193; **2** ByKOLLES Racing Team (4), 109; **3** Rebellion Racing (12), 104.

Teams (LMP2)
1 Signatech Alpine (car 36), 199; **2** RGR Sport by Morand (43), 169; **3** G-Drive Racing (26), 164;

Teams (LMGTE Pro)
1 Aston Martin Racing (car 95), 156; **2** Ford Chip Ganassi Team UK (67), 141; **3** AF Corse (71), 134;

Teams (LMGTE Am)
1 AF Corse (car 83), 188; **2** Abu Dhabi-Proton Racing (88), 151; **3** Aston Martin Racing (98), 149;

European Le Mans Series

4 HOURS OF SILVERSTONE, Silverstone Grand Prix Circuit, Towcester, Northamptonshire, Great Britain, 16 April. Round 1. 118 laps of the 3.667-mile/5.901km circuit, 432.672 miles/696.318km.
1 Simon Dolan/Harry Tincknell/Giedo van der Garde, GB/GB/NL (Gibson 015S-Nissan), 4h 01m 45.391s, 107.382mph/172.814km/h; **2** Stefano Coletti/Julián Leal/Andreas Wirth, MC/CO/D (BR Engineering BR01-Nissan), +1m 35.052s; **3** Vincent Capillaire/Olivier Lombard/Jonathan Coleman, F/F/GB (Ligier JS P2-Judd), -1 lap; **4** Tracy Krohn/Nic Jönsson/Björn Wirdheim, USA/S/S (Ligier JS P2-Nissan), -1; **5** Sean Gelael/Mitch Evans/Antonio Giovinazzi, RI/NZ/I (BR Engineering BR01-Nissan), -1; **6** Niki Leutwiler/James Winslow/Franck Mailleux, CH/GB/F (ORECA 03R-Nissan), -2; **7** Patrice Lafargue/Paul Lafargue/Dimitri Enjalbert, F/F/F (Ligier JS P2-Judd), -2; **8** Memo Rojas/Julien Canal/Kuba Giermaziak, MEX/F/PL (Ligier JS P2-Nissan), -3; **9** Fabien Barthez/Timothé Buret/Paul-Loup Chatin, F/F/F (Ligier JS P2-Nissan), -4; **10** Michael Munemann/Chris Hoy/Parth Ghorpade, GB/GB/IND (Ligier JS P2-Nissan), -4.
Fastest race lap: Chatin, 1m 50.426s, 119.538mph/192.378km/h.
Pole position: Pierre Thiriet/Mathias Beche/Ryo Hirakawa, F/CH/J (ORECA 05-Nissan), 2m 06.471s, 104.373mph/167.972km/h.

4 HOURS OF IMOLA, Autodromo Enzo e Dino Ferrari, Imola, Italy, 15 May. Round 2. 121 laps of the 3.050-mile/4.909km circuit, 369.088 miles/593.989km.
1 Pierre Thiriet/Mathias Beche/Ryo Hirakawa, F/CH/J (ORECA 05-Nissan), 4h 01m 13.223s, 91.805mph/147.745km/h; **2** Simon Dolan/Harry Tincknell/Giedo van der Garde, GB/GB/NL (Gibson 015S-Nissan), +19.257s; **3** Henrik Hedman/Nicolas Lapierre/Benjamin Hanley, S/F/GB (ORECA 05-Nissan), +30.810s; **4** Stefano Coletti/Julián Leal/Andreas Wirth, MC/CO/D (BR Engineering BR01-Nissan), +33.991s; **5** Pu Jun Jin/Nick de Bruijn/Tristan Gommendy, CHN/NL/F (ORECA 05-Nissan), +45.472s; **6** Björn Wirdheim/Nic Jönsson/Olivier Pla, S/S/F (Ligier JS P2-Nissan), -1 lap; **7** Fabien Barthez/Timothé Buret/Paul-Loup Chatin, F/F/F (Ligier JS P2-Nissan), -1; **8** Memo Rojas/Julien Canal/Kuba Giermaziak, MEX/F/PL (Ligier JS P2-Nissan), -3; **9** Niki Leutwiler/James Winslow/Shinji Nakano, CH/GB/J (ORECA 03R-Nissan), -3; **10** Sean Doyle/Patrick McClughan/Gary Findlay, IRL/GB/GB (ORECA 03R-Nissan), -3.
Fastest race lap: Lapierre, 1m 34.799s, 115.835mph/186.419km/h.
Pole position: Hedman/Lapierre/Hanley, 1m 33.780s, 117.094mph/188.445km/h.

4 HOURS OF RED BULL RING, Red Bull Ring, Spielberg, Austria, 17 July. Round 3. 160 laps of the 2.688-mile/4.326km circuit, 430.088 miles/692.160km.
1 Pierre Thiriet/Mathias Beche/Ryo Hirakawa, F/CH/J (ORECA 05-Nissan), 4h 00m 04.366s, 107.489mph/172.987km/h; **2** Pu Jun Jin/Nick de Bruijn/Tristan Gommendy, CHN/NL/F (ORECA 05-Nissan), +51.622s; **3** Simon Dolan/Harry

Tincknell/Giedo van der Garde, GB/GB/NL (Gibson 015S-Nissan), +59.108s; **4** Stefano Coletti/Julián Leal/Andreas Wirth, MC/CO/D (BR Engineering BR01-Nissan), -1 lap; **5** Michael Munemann/Andréa Pizzitola/Jonathan Hirschi, GB/F/CH (Ligier JS P2-Nissan), -1; **6** Memo Rojas/Julien Canal/Nathanaël Berthon, MEX/F/F (Ligier JS P2-Nissan), -1; **7** Fabien Barthez/Timothé Buret/Paul-Loup Chatin, F/F/F (Ligier JS P2-Nissan), -1; **8** Guglielmo Belotti/Sean Doyle/Karun Chandhok, I/IRL/IND (ORECA 03R-Nissan), -4; **9** Alex Brundle/Michael Guasch/Christian England, GB/USA/GB (Ligier JS P3-Nissan), -9; **10** David Hallyday/Dino Lunardi/David Droux, F/F/CH (Ligier JS P3-Nissan), -9 *.
** includes 4s penalty.*
Fastest race lap: van der Garde, 1m 22.392s, 117.450mph/189.018km/h.
Pole position: Barthez/Buret/Chatin, 1m 20.700s, 119.913mph/192.981km/h.

4 HOURS OF PAUL RICARD, Circuit ASA Paul Ricard, Le Beausset, France, 28 August. Round 4. 124 laps of the 3.598-mile/5.791km circuit, 446.197 miles/718.084km.
1 Pierre Thiriet/Mathias Beche/Mike Conway, F/CH/GB (ORECA 05-Nissan), 4h 00m 58.207s, 111.100mph/178.798km/h; **2** Stefano Coletti/Julián Leal/Andreas Wirth, MC/CO/D (BR Engineering BR01-Nissan), -1 lap; **3** Henrik Hedman/Nicolas Lapierre/Benjamin Hanley, S/F/GB (ORECA 05-Nissan), -1; **4** Nick de Bruijn/Tristan Gommendy, NL/F (ORECA 05-Nissan), -1; **5** Simon Dolan/Harry Tincknell/Giedo van der Garde, GB/GB/NL (Gibson 015S-Nissan), -1; **6** Memo Rojas/Julien Canal/Nathanaël Berthon, MEX/F/F (Ligier JS P2-Nissan), -1; **7** Andrea Roda/Jonathan Hirschi/Andréa Pizzitola, I/CH/F (Ligier JS P2-Nissan), -3; **8** Tracy Krohn/Nic Jönsson/Olivier Pla, USA/S/F (Ligier JS P2-Nissan), -3; **9** Sean Doyle/Jonathan Coleman/Kevin Ceccon, IRL/GB/I (ORECA 03R-Nissan), -3 *; **10** Patrice Lafargue/Paul Lafargue/Dimitri Enjalbert, F/F/F (Ligier JS P2-Judd), -3.
** includes 30s penalty.*
Fastest race lap: Conway, 1m 49.548s, 118.250mph/190.305km/h.
Pole position: Thiriet/Beche/Conway, 1m 47.033s, 121.029mph/194.777km/h.

4 HOURS OF SPA-FRANCORCHAMPS, Circuit de Spa-Francorchamps, Stavelot, Belgium, 25 September. Round 5. 96 laps of the 4.352-mile/7.004km circuit, 417.794 miles/672.374km.
1 Henrik Hedman/Nicolas Lapierre/Benjamin Hanley, S/F/GB (ORECA 05-Nissan), 4h 01m 13.639s, 103.917mph/167.238km/h; **2** Laurens Vanthoor/Will Stevens/Dries Vanthoor, B/GB/B (Ligier JS P2-Judd), +2m 20.556s; **3** Pierre Thiriet/Mathias Beche/Ryo Hirakawa, F/CH/J (ORECA 05-Nissan), +3m 00.523s; **4** Memo Rojas/Julien Canal/Nathanaël Berthon, MEX/F/F (Ligier JS P2-Nissan), +3m 46.865s; **5** Simon Dolan/Harry Tincknell/Giedo van der Garde, GB/GB/NL (Gibson 015S-Nissan), +5m 21.062s; **6** Stefano Coletti/Andreas Wirth/Vitaly Petrov, MC/D/RUS (BR Engineering BR01-Nissan), -1 lap; **7** Fabien Barthez/Timothé Buret/Paul-Loup Chatin, F/F/F (Ligier JS P2-Nissan), -1; **8** Patrice Lafargue/Paul Lafargue/Dimitri Enjalbert, F/F/F (Ligier JS P2-Judd), -1; **9** Michael Munemann/Jonathan Hirschi/Andréa Pizzitola, GB/CH/F (Ligier JS P2-Nissan), -2; **10** Eric Trouillet/Paul Petit/Enzo Guibbert, F/F/F (Ligier JS P3-Nissan), -4 *.
** includes 30s penalty.*
Fastest race lap: Beche, 2m 08.796s, 121.644mph/195.767km/h.
Pole position: Hedman/Lapierre/Hanley, 2m 06.603s, 123.751mph/199.158km/h.

4 HOURS OF ESTORIL, Autódromo Fernanda Pires da Silva, Estoril, Portugal, 23 October. Round 6. 145 laps of the 2.599-mile/4.182km circuit, 376.793 miles/606.390km.
1 Simon Dolan/Harry Tincknell/Giedo van der Garde, GB/GB/NL (Gibson 015S-Nissan), 4h 01m 32.368s, 93.597mph/150.631km/h; **2** Henrik Hedman/Nicolas Lapierre/Benjamin Hanley, S/F/GB (ORECA 05-Nissan), +51.157s; **3** Stefano Coletti/Andreas Wirth/Vitaly Petrov, MC/D/RUS (BR Engineering BR01-Nissan), +1m 20.903s; **4** Nic Jönsson/Olivier Pla, S/F (Ligier JS P2-Nissan), +1m 28.961s; **5** Tristan Gommendy/Frédéric Vervisch/Michael Lyons, F/B/GB (ORECA 05-Nissan), -2 laps *; **6** Patrice Lafargue/Paul Lafargue/Dimitri Enjalbert, F/F/F (Ligier JS P2-Judd), -4; **7** Thomas Laurent/Yann Ehrlacher/Alexandre Cougnaud, F/F/F (Ligier JS P3-Nissan), -5; **8** Fabien Barthez/Timothé Buret/Paul-Loup Chatin, F/F/F (Ligier JS P2-Nissan), -6; **9** Mark Patterson/Matthew Bell/Wayne Boyd, USA/GB/GB (Ligier JS P3-Nissan), -7; **10** Eric Trouillet/Paul Petit/Enzo Guibbert, F/F/F (Ligier JS P3-Nissan), -7.
** includes 45s penalty.*
Fastest race lap: Lapierre, 1m 32.898s, 100.700mph/162.061km/h.
Pole position: Hedman/Lapierre/Hanley, 1m 44.146s, 89.824mph/144.558km/h.

Final championship points
Drivers (LMP2)
1 Simon Dolan, GB, 103; 1 Giedo van der Garde, NL, 103; 1 Harry Tincknell, GB, 103; **2** Pierre Thiriet, F, 96; **2** Mathias Beche, CH, 96; **3** Andreas Wirth, D, 83; **3** Stefano Coletti, MC, 83; **4** Nicolas Lapierre, F, 76; **4** Henrik Hedman, S, 76; **4** Benjamin Hanley, GB, 76; **5** Ryo Hirakawa, J, 70; **6** Julián Leal, CO, 60; **7** Tristan Gommendy, F, 50; **8** Nick de Bruijn, NL, 40; **9** Nic Jönsson, S, 39; **10** Julien Canal, F, 36; **10** Memo Rojas, MEX, 36.

Drivers (LMP3)
1 Alex Brundle, GB, 109.5; 1 Michael Guasch, USA, 109.5; 1 Christian England, GB, 109.5; **2** Paul Petit, F, 93; **2** Eric Trouillet, F, 93; **3** Enzo Guibbert, F, 81; **4** David Hallyday, F, 62; **4** Dino Lunardi, F, 62; **5** Wayne Boyd, GB, 59; **5** Matthew Bell, GB, 59; **5** Mark Patterson, USA, 59; **6** David Droux, CH, 50; **7** Terrence Woodward, GB, 48; **7** Ross Kaiser, GB, 48; **7** James Swift, GB, 48; **8** Yann Ehrlacher, F, 36; **8** Alexandre Cougnaud, F, 36; **8** Thomas Laurent, F, 36; **9** Simon Gachet, F, 30.5; **9** Eric Debard, F, 30.5; **9** Valentin Moineault, F, 30.5; **10** Matthieu Lahaye, F, 26; **10** Jean-Baptiste Lahaye, F, 26; **10** François Heriau, F, 26.

Drivers (LMGTE)
1 Alex MacDowall, GB, 98; 1 Darren Turner, GB, 98; 1 Andrew Howard, GB, 98; **2** Robert Smith, AUS, 93; **2** Rory Butcher, GB, 93; **2** Andrea Bertolini, I, 93; **3** Alexander Talkanitsa, BY, 79; **3** Alexander Talkanitsa Jr, BY, 79; **4** Mike Hedlund, USA, 66; **4** Wolf Henzler, D, 66; **5** Alessandro Pier Guidi, I, 64; **6** Duncan Cameron, GB, 64; **6** Matt Griffin, IRL, 64; **6** Aaron Scott, GB, 64; **7** Christian Ried, D, 60; **7** Gianluca Roda, I, 60; **8** Rui Águas, P, 50; **8** Piergiuseppe Perazzini, I, 50; **8** Marco Cioci, I, 50; **9** Johnny Laursen, DK, 40; **9** Mikkel Mac, DK, 40; **10** Marco Seefried, D, 40.

Teams (LMP2)
1 G-Drive Racing (car 38), 103; **2** Thiriet by TDS Racing (46), 96; **3** SMP Racing (32), 83; **4** DragonSpeed (21), 76; **5** Eurasia Motorsport (33), 50; **6** Krohn Racing (40), 39.

Teams (LMP3)
1 United Autosports (car 2), 109.5; **2** Graff (9), 93; **3** Duqueine Engineering (19), 62; **4** United Autosports (3), 59; **5** 360 Racing (6), 48; **6** M.Racing - Ymr (18), 36.

Teams (LMGTE)
1 Aston Martin Racing (car 99), 98; **2** JMW Motorsport (66), 93; **3** AT Racing (56), 79; **4** Proton Competition (77), 66; **5** AF Corse (55), 64; **6** Proton Competition (88), 60.

IMSA WeatherTech Sportscar Championship

54TH ROLEX 24 AT DAYTONA, Daytona International Speedway, Daytona Beach, Florida, USA, 30 January. 736 laps of the 3.560-mile/5.729km circuit, 2620.160 miles/4216.739km.
1 Scott Sharp/Ed Brown/Johannes van Overbeek/Luis Derani, USA/USA/USA/BR (Ligier JS P2-HPD), 24h 00m 34.607s, 109.130mph/175.627km/h; **2** Ricky Taylor/Jordan Taylor/Max Angelelli/Rubens Barrichello, USA/USA/I/BR (Corvette DP-Chevrolet), +26.166s; **3** Ryan Dalziel/Marc Goossens/Ryan Hunter-Reay, GB/B/USA (Corvette DP-Chevrolet), +1m 27.276s; **4** Christian Fittipaldi/João Barbosa/Filipe Albuquerque/Scott Pruett, BR/P/P/USA (Corvette DP-Chevrolet), -5 laps; **5** Lance Stroll/Alexander Wurz/Brendon Hartley/Andy Priaulx, CDN/A/NZ/GB (Riley DP-Ford), -11; **6** Dane Cameron/Eric Curran/Simon Pagenaud/Jonathan Adam, USA/USA/F/GB (Corvette DP-Chevrolet), -12; **7** Oliver Gavin/Tommy Milner/Marcel Fässler, GB/USA/CH (Chevrolet Corvette C7.R), -14; **8** Antonio García/Jan Magnussen/Mike Rockenfeller, E/DK/D (Chevrolet Corvette C7.R), -14; **9** Earl Bamber/Frédéric Makowiecki/Michael Christensen, NZ/F/DK (Porsche 911 RSR), -14; **10** Alessandro Pier Guidi/Alexandre Prémat/Daniel Serra/Memo Rojas, I/F/BR/MEX (Ferrari 488 GTE), -15.
Fastest race lap: Derani, 1m 39.192s, 129.204mph/207.934km/h.
Pole position: Maurizio Mediani/Nicolas Minassian/Mikhail Aleshin/Kirill Ladygin, I/F/RUS/RUS (BR Engineering BR01-Nissan), 2m 05.793s, 101.882mph/163.963km/h.

64TH ANNUAL MOBIL 1 TWELVE HOURS OF SEBRING FUELED BY FRESH FROM FLORIDA, Sebring International Raceway, Florida, USA, 19 March. 238 laps of the 3.740-mile/6.019km circuit, 890.120 miles/1432.509km.
1 Scott Sharp/Ed Brown/Johannes van Overbeek/Luis Derani, USA/USA/USA/BR (Ligier JS P2-HPD), 12h 00m 59.881s, 74.074mph/119.211km/h; **2** Dane Cameron/Eric Curran/Scott Pruett, USA/USA/USA (Corvette DP-Chevrolet), +2.926s; **3** Christian Fittipaldi/João Barbosa/Filipe Albuquerque/Scott Pruett, BR/P/P/USA (Corvette DP-Chevrolet), +3.940s; **4** Henrik Hedman/Nicolas Lapierre/Nicolas Minassian, S/F/F (ORECA 05-Nissan), +4.339s; **5** Ryan Dalziel/Marc Goossens/Ryan Hunter-Reay, GB/B/USA (Corvette DP-Chevrolet), +18.078s; **6** Jonathan Bomarito/Tristan Nunez/Spencer Pigot, USA/USA/USA (Lola B12/80 Coupe-Mazda), +29.735s; **7** John Pew/Oswaldo Negri Jr/Olivier Pla, USA/BR/F (Ligier JS P2-HPD), -1 lap (DNF-not running); **8** Joel Miller/Tom Long/Ben Devlin/Keiko Ihara, USA/USA/GB/J (Lola B12/80 Coupe-Mazda), -1; **9** Jon Bennett/Colin Braun/Mark Wilkins, USA/USA/CDN (ORECA FLM09-Chevrolet), -2; **10** Tom Kimber-Smith/Jose Gutierrez/Robert Alon, GB/MEX/USA (ORECA FLM09-Chevrolet), -2.
Fastest race lap: Pla, 1m 52.397s, 119.790mph/192.783km/h.
Pole position: Pew/Negri Jr/Pla, 1m 51.217s, 121.061mph/194.828km/h.

BUBBA BURGER SPORTS CAR GRAND PRIX AT LONG BEACH, Long Beach Street Circuit, California, USA, 16 April. 75 laps of the 1.968-mile/3.167km circuit, 147.600 miles/237.539km.
1 Ricky Taylor/Jordan Taylor, USA/USA (Corvette DP-Chevrolet), 1h 40m 58.937s, 87.699mph/141.137km/h; **2** João Barbosa/Christian Fittipaldi, P/BR (Corvette DP-Chevrolet), +2.958s; **3** Dane Cameron/Eric Curran, USA/USA (Corvette DP-Chevrolet), +4.159s; **4** Tom Long/Joel Miller, USA/USA (Lola B12/80 Coupe-Mazda), +7.618s; **5** Tristan Nunez/Jonathan Bomarito, USA/USA (Lola B12/80 Coupe-Mazda), +10.606s; **6** Marc Goossens/Ryan Hunter-Reay, B/USA (Corvette DP-Chevrolet), +31.943s; **7** John Pew/Oswaldo Negri Jr, USA/BR (Ligier JS P2-HPD), +33.061s; **8** Mikhail Goikhberg/Stephen Simpson, CDN/ZA (ORECA FLM09-Chevrolet), -1 lap; **9** Renger van der Zande/Alex Popow, NL/YV (ORECA FLM09-Chevrolet), -1; **10** James French/Kyle Marcelli, USA/CDN (ORECA FLM09-Chevrolet), -2 (DNF-not running).
Fastest race lap: Cameron/Curran, 1m 15.279s, 94.114mph/151.462km/h.
Pole position: Barbosa/Fittipaldi, 1m 14.962s, 94.512mph/152.102km/h.

CONTINENTAL TIRE MONTEREY GRAND PRIX POWERED BY MAZDA, Mazda Raceway Laguna Seca, Monterey, California, USA, 1 May. 80 and 82 laps of the 2.238-mile/3.602km circuit.
Race 4 (179.040 miles/288.137km).
1 John Pew/Oswaldo Negri Jr, USA/BR (Ligier JS P2-HPD), 2h 00m 11.145s, 89.382mph/143.846km/h; **2** Marc Goossens/Ryan Dalziel, B/GB (Corvette DP-Chevrolet), +30.099s; **3** Dane Cameron/Eric Curran, USA/USA (Corvette DP-Chevrolet), +30.954s; **4** Tristan Nunez/Jonathan Bomarito, USA/USA (Lola B12/80 Coupe-Mazda), +1m 03.035s; **5** Katherine Legge/Sean Rayhall, GB/USA (DeltaWing DWC13-Elan), +1m 08.594s; **6** Ryan Briscoe/Richard Westbrook, AUS/GB (Ford GT '16), -1 lap; **7** Alessandro Pier Guidi/Daniel Serra, I/BR (Ferrari 488 GTE), -1; **8** Ricky Taylor/Jordan Taylor, USA/USA (Corvette DP-Chevrolet), -2; **9** Earl Bamber/Frédéric Makowiecki, NZ/F (Porsche 911 RSR), -2; **10** Antonio García/Jan Magnussen, E/DK (Chevrolet Corvette C7.R), -2.
Fastest race lap: Tom Long, USA (Lola B12/80 Coupe-Mazda), 1m 19.206s, 101.720mph/163.702km/h.
Pole position: Nunez/Bomarito, 1m 18.143s, 103.103mph/165.929km/h.

Race 5 (183.516 miles/295.340km).
1 Robert Alon/Tom Kimber-Smith, USA/GB (ORECA FLM09-Chevrolet), 2h 00m 31.047s, 91.364mph/147.036km/h; **2** Renger van der Zande/Alex Popow, NL/YV (ORECA FLM09-Chevrolet), +1.736s; **3** Jon Bennett/Colin Braun, USA/USA (ORECA FLM09-Chevrolet), +15.483s; **4** James French/Kyle Marcelli, USA/CDN (ORECA FLM09-Chevrolet), +21.661s; **5** Mikhail Goikhberg/Stephen Simpson, CDN/ZA (ORECA FLM09-Chevrolet), +24.067s; **6** Matt McMurry/Johnny Mowlem, USA/GB (ORECA FLM09-Chevrolet), -1 lap; **7** Mark Kvamme/Ashley Freiberg, USA/USA (ORECA FLM09-Chevrolet), -2; **8** Mario Farnbacher/Alex Riberas, D/E (Porsche 991 GT3 R), -3; **9** Christina Nielsen/Alessandro Balzan, DK/I (Ferrari 458 Italia GT3), -3; **10** James Davison/Brandon Davis, AUS/USA (Aston Martin V12 Vantage), -3.
Fastest race lap: Braun, 1m 20.380s, 100.234mph/161.311km/h.
Pole position: Alon/Kimber-Smith, 1m 21.146s, 99.288mph/159.788km/h.

CHEVROLET SPORTS CAR CLASSIC PRESENTED BY THE METRO DETROIT CHEVY DEALERS, The Raceway at Belle Isle, Detroit, Michigan, USA, 4 June. 57 laps of the 2.350-mile/3.782km circuit, 133.950 miles/215.572km.
1 Ricky Taylor/Jordan Taylor, USA/USA (Corvette DP-Chevrolet), 1h 40m 11.998s, 80.210mph/129.085km/h; **2** João Barbosa/Christian Fittipaldi, P/BR (Corvette DP-Chevrolet), +1.740s; **3** Renger van der Zande/Alex Popow, NL/YV (ORECA FLM09-Chevrolet), +33.643s; **4** Jon Bennett/Colin Braun, USA/USA (ORECA FLM09-Chevrolet), +37.117s; **5** Robert Alon/Tom Kimber-Smith, USA/GB (ORECA FLM09-Chevrolet), +48.082s; **6** James French/Kyle Marcelli, USA/CDN (ORECA FLM09-Chevrolet), +51.278s; **7** Tristan Nunez/Jonathan Bomarito, USA/USA (Lola B12/80 Coupe-Mazda), +1m 00.977s; **8** Johnny Mowlem/Tomy Drissi, GB/USA (ORECA FLM09-Chevrolet), +1m 01.468s; **9** Tom Long/Joel Miller, USA/USA (Lola B12/80 Coupe-Mazda), -1 lap; **10** Ben Keating/Jeroen Bleekemolen, USA/NL (Dodge Viper GT3-R), -1.
Fastest race lap: Dane Cameron, USA (Corvette DP-Chevrolet), 1m 23.138s, 101.759mph/163.764km/h.
Pole position: Barbosa/Fittipaldi, 1m 23.815s, 100.937mph/162.442km/h.

SAHLEN'S SIX HOURS OF THE GLEN, Watkins Glen International, New York, USA, 3 July. 197 laps of the 3.400-mile/5.472km circuit, 669.800 miles/1077.939km.
1 João Barbosa/Christian Fittipaldi/Filipe Albuquerque, P/BR/P (Corvette DP-Chevrolet), 6h 00m 21.671s, 111.521mph/179.476km/h; **2** Dane Cameron/Eric Curran/Filipe Albuquerque, USA/USA/P (Corvette DP-Chevrolet), +0.709s; **3** John Pew/Oswaldo Negri Jr/Olivier Pla, USA/BR/F (Ligier JS P2-HPD), +1.048s; **4** Ricky Taylor/Jordan Taylor/Max Angelelli, USA/USA/I (Corvette DP-Chevrolet), +7.302s; **5** Tom Long/Joel Miller/Ben Devlin, USA/USA/GB (Lola B12/80 Coupe-Mazda), -1 lap; **6** Marc Goossens/Ryan Dalziel, B/GB (Corvette DP-Chevrolet), -1; **7** Renger van der Zande/Alex Popow, NL/YV (ORECA FLM09-Chevrolet), -2; **8** James French/Kyle Marcelli/Kenton Koch, USA/CDN/USA (ORECA FLM09-Chevrolet), -2; **9** Mark Kvamme/Richard Bradley/Remo Ruscitti, USA/GB/CDN (ORECA FLM09-Chevrolet), -2; **10** Mikhail Goikhberg/Stephen Simpson, CDN/ZA (ORECA FLM09-Chevrolet), -3.
Fastest race lap: Pla, 1m 34.515s, 129.503mph/208.415km/h.
Pole position: Scott Sharp/Luis Derani/Johannes van Overbeek, USA/BR/USA (Ligier JS P2-HPD), 1m 35.207s, 128.562mph/206.900km/h.

MOBIL 1 SPORTSCAR GRAND PRIX PRESENTED BY HAWK PERFORMANCE, Mosport International Raceway, Bowmanville, Ontario, Canada, 10 July. 125 laps of the 2.459-mile/3.957km circuit, 307.375 miles/494.672km.
1 Dane Cameron/Eric Curran, USA/USA (Corvette DP-Chevrolet), 2h 41m 22.601s, 114.282mph/183.920km/h; **2** João Barbosa/Christian Fittipaldi, P/BR (Corvette DP-Chevrolet), +10.112s; **3** Ricky Taylor/Jordan Taylor, USA/USA (Corvette DP-Chevrolet), +18.124s; **4** Marc Goossens/Ryan Dalziel, B/GB (Corvette DP-Chevrolet), +32.183s; **5** Tom Long/Joel Miller, USA/USA (Lola B12/80 Coupe-Mazda), +42.575s; **6** Jon Bennett/Colin Braun, USA/USA (ORECA FLM09-Chevrolet), -2 laps; **7** Renger van der Zande/Alex Popow, NL/YV (ORECA FLM09-Chevrolet), -2; **8** Robert Alon/Tom Kimber-Smith, USA/GB (ORECA FLM09-Chevrolet), -2; **9** James French/Kyle Marcelli, USA/CDN (ORECA FLM09-Chevrolet), -2; **10** Mikhail Goikhberg/Stephen Simpson, CDN/ZA (ORECA FLM09-Chevrolet), -3.
Fastest race lap: Cameron, 1m 10.404s, 125.737mph/202.354km/h.
Pole position: Tristan Nunez/Jonathan Bomarito, USA/USA (Lola B12/80 Coupe-Mazda), 1m 10.126s, 126.236mph/203.157km/h.

NORTHEAST GRAND PRIX, Lime Rock Park, Lakeville, Connecticut, USA, 23 July. 169 laps of the 1.474-mile/2.372km circuit, 249.106 miles/400.897km.
1 Renger van der Zande/Alex Popow, NL/YV (ORECA FLM09-Chevrolet), 2h 40m 43.254s, 92.996mph/149.662km/h; **2** Robert Alon/Tom Kimber-Smith, USA/GB (ORECA FLM09-Chevrolet), +0.815s; **3** James French/Kyle Marcelli, USA/CDN (ORECA FLM09-Chevrolet), -1 lap; **4** Matt McMurry/Johnny Mowlem, USA/GB (ORECA FLM09-Chevrolet), -1; **5** Oliver Gavin/Tommy Milner, GB/USA (Chevrolet Corvette C7.R), -2; **6** Antonio García/Jan Magnussen, E/DK (Chevrolet Corvette C7.R), -2; **7** Ryan Briscoe/Richard Westbrook, AUS/GB (Ford GT '16), -2; **8** Giancarlo Fisichella/Toni Vilander, I/FIN (Ferrari 488 GTE), -2; **9** Joey Hand/Dirk Müller, USA/D (Ford GT '16), -2; **10** Mark Kvamme/Remo Ruscitti, USA/CDN (ORECA FLM09-Chevrolet), -4.
Fastest race lap: van der Zande, 49.250s, 107.744mph/173.397km/h.
Pole position: Alon/Kimber-Smith, 48.840s, 108.649mph/174.853km/h.

CONTINENTAL TIRE ROAD RACE SHOWCASE AT ROAD AMERICA, Road America, Elkhart Lake, Wisconsin, USA, 7 August. 73 laps of the 4.048-mile/6.515km circuit, 295.504 miles/475.568km.
1 Dane Cameron/Eric Curran, USA/USA (Corvette DP-Chevrolet), 2h 40m 56.808s, 110.162mph/177.289km/h; **2** João Barbosa/Christian Fittipaldi, P/BR (Corvette DP-Chevrolet), +0.626s; **3** Ricky Taylor/Jordan Taylor, USA/USA (Corvette DP-Chevrolet), +1.460s; **4** John Pew/Oswaldo Negri Jr, USA/BR (Ligier JS P2-HPD), +18.283s; **5** Tristan Nunez/Jonathan Bomarito, USA/USA (Lola B12/80 Coupe-Mazda), +22.114s; **6** Marc Goossens/Ryan Dalziel, B/GB (Corvette DP-Chevrolet), +34.499s; **7** Robert Alon/Tom Kimber-Smith, USA/GB (ORECA FLM09-Chevrolet), -1 lap; **8** Jon Bennett/Colin Braun, USA/USA (ORECA FLM09-Chevrolet), -1; **9** James French/Kyle Marcelli, USA/CDN (ORECA FLM09-Chevrolet), -1; **10** Jose Gutierrez/Gustavo Yacamán, MEX/CO (ORECA FLM09-Chevrolet), -1.
Fastest race lap: Nunez, 1m 55.458s, 126.217mph/203.127km/h.
Pole position: Nunez/Bomarito, 1m 54.507s, 127.266mph/204.814km/h.

MICHELIN GT CHALLENGE AT VIR, Virginia International Raceway, Alton, Virginia, USA, 28 August. 90 laps of the 3.270-mile/5.263km circuit, 294.300 miles/473.630km.
1 Antonio García/Jan Magnussen, E/DK (Chevrolet Corvette C7.R), 2h 40m 13.166s, 110.211mph/177.368km/h; **2** Joey Hand/Dirk Müller, USA/D (Ford GT '16), +0.802s; **3** Earl Bamber/Frédéric Makowiecki, NZ/F (Porsche 911 RSR), +1.448s; **4** Ryan Briscoe/Richard Westbrook, AUS/GB (Ford GT '16), +6.004s; **5** Bill Auberlen/Dirk Werner, USA/D (BMW M6 GTLM), +6.243s; **6** Patrick Pilet/Nick Tandy, F/GB (Porsche 911 RSR), +7.168s; **7** Giancarlo Fisichella/Toni Vilander, I/FIN (Ferrari 488 GTE), +25.016s; **8** John Michael Edwards/Lucas Luhr, USA/D (BMW M6 GTLM), -1 lap; **9** Bryan Sellers/Madison Snow, USA/USA (Audi R8 LMS ultra), -2; **10** Lawson Aschenbach/Matt Bell, USA/USA (Audi R8 LMS), -2.
Fastest race lap: Oliver Gavin, GB (Chevrolet Corvette C7.R), 1m 42.603s, 114.733mph/184.646km/h.
Pole position: García/Magnussen, 1m 41.557s, 115.915mph/186.547km/h.

LONE STAR LE MANS, Circuit of the Americas, Austin, Texas, USA, 17 September. 75 laps of the

3.400-mile/5.472km circuit, 255.000 miles/410.383km.
1 Ricky Taylor/Jordan Taylor, USA/USA (Corvette DP-Chevrolet), 2h 41m 55.076s, 94.492mph/152.071km/h; **2** Dane Cameron/Eric Curran, USA/USA (Corvette DP-Chevrolet), +1.421s; **3** João Barbosa/Christian Fittipaldi, P/BR (Corvette DP-Chevrolet), +47.256s; **4** Tom Long/Joel Miller, USA/USA (Lola B12/80 Coupe-Mazda), +1m 46.420s; **5** Renger van der Zande/Alex Popow, NL/YV (ORECA FLM09-Chevrolet), -1 lap; **6** Robert Alon/Tom Kimber-Smith, USA/GB (ORECA FLM09-Chevrolet), -1; **7** James French/Nick Boulle, USA/USA (ORECA FLM09-Chevrolet), -1; **8** Katherine Legge/Sean Rayhall, GB/USA (DeltaWing DWC13-Elan), -1; **9** Matt McMurry/Bruno Junqueira, USA/BR (ORECA FLM09-Chevrolet), -1; **10** Earl Bamber/Frédéric Makowiecki, NZ/F (Porsche 911 RSR), -1.
Fastest race lap: Taylor, 1m 59.721s, 102.238mph/164.536km/h.
Pole position: Taylor/Taylor, 1m 58.712s, 103.107mph/165.934km/h.

PETIT LE MANS POWERED BY MAZDA, Road Atlanta Motorsports Center, Braselton, Georgia, USA, 1 October. 412 laps of the 2.540-mile/4.088km circuit, 1046.480 miles/1684.146km.
1 John Pew/Oswaldo Negri Jr/Olivier Pla, USA/BR/F (Ligier JS P2-HPD), 10h 00m 30.023s, 104.561mph/168.274km/h; **2** Scott Sharp/Luis Derani/Johannes van Overbeek, USA/BR/USA (Ligier JS P2-HPD), +3.524s; **3** Ricky Taylor/Jordan Taylor/Max Angelelli, USA/USA/I (Corvette DP-Chevrolet), +11.745s; **4** Eric Curran/Dane Cameron/Simon Pagenaud, USA/USA/F (Corvette DP-Chevrolet), +14.258s; **5** João Barbosa/Christian Fittipaldi/Filipe Albuquerque, P/BR/P (Corvette DP-Chevrolet), -2 laps; **6** Robert Alon/Jose Gutierrez/Tom Kimber-Smith, USA/MEX/GB (ORECA FLM09-Chevrolet), -8; **7** James French/Kyle Marcelli/Kenton Koch, USA/CDN/USA (ORECA FLM09-Chevrolet), -9; **8** Tom Long/Joel Miller/Spencer Pigot, USA/USA/USA (Lola B12/80 Coupe-Mazda), -11; **9** Giancarlo Fisichella/Toni Vilander/James Calado, I/FIN/GB (Ferrari 488 GTE), -14; **10** Joey Hand/Dirk Müller/Sébastien Bourdais, USA/D/F (Ford GT '16), -14.
Fastest race lap: Pla, 1m 13.478s, 124.445mph/200.275km/h.
Pole position: Pew/Negri Jr/Pla, 1m 13.061s, 125.156mph/201.419km/h.

Final championship points
Drivers (Prototype)
1 Dane Cameron, USA, 314; 1 Eric Curran, USA, 314; **2** João Barbosa, P, 311; **2** Christian Fittipaldi, BR, 311; **3** Jordan Taylor, USA, 309; **3** Ricky Taylor, USA, 309; **4** Oswaldo Negri Jr, BR, 282; **5** Marc Goossens, B, 273; **6** Tom Long, USA, 258; **6** Joel Miller, USA, 258; **7** Tristan Nunez, USA, 257; **7** Jonathan Bomarito, USA, 257; **8** John Pew, USA, 255; **9** Ryan Dalziel, GB, 247; **10** Katherine Legge, GB, 247.

Drivers (Prototype Challenge)
1 Alex Popow, YV, 355; 1 Renger van der Zande, NL, 355; **2** Tom Kimber-Smith, GB, 355; **2** Robert Alon, USA, 355; **3** Mikhail Goikhberg, CDN, 317; **3** Stephen Simpson, ZA, 317; **4** James French, USA, 305; **5** Kyle Marcelli, CDN, 274; **6** Johnny Mowlem, GB, 246; **7** Jon Bennett, USA, 245; **7** Colin Braun, USA, 245; **8** Jose Gutierrez, MEX, 210; **9** Mark Kvamme, USA, 186; **10** Matt McMurry, USA, 138.

Drivers (GT Le Mans)
1 Oliver Gavin, GB, 345; 1 Tommy Milner, USA, 345; **2** Richard Westbrook, GB, 328; **2** Ryan Briscoe, AUS, 328; **3** Jan Magnussen, DK, 319; **3** Antonio García, E, 319; **4** Earl Bamber, NZ, 313; **4** Frédéric Makowiecki, F, 313; **5** Toni Vilander, FIN, 305; **5** Giancarlo Fisichella, I, 305; **6** Dirk Müller, D, 301; **6** Joey Hand, USA, 301.

Drivers (GT Daytona)
1 Christina Nielsen, DK, 332; 1 Alessandro Balzan, I, 332; **2** Jeroen Bleekemolen, NL, 303; **2** Ben Keating, USA, 303; **3** Bryan Sellers, USA, 293; **3** Madison Snow, USA, 293; **4** Andrew Davis, USA, 290; **4** Robin Liddell, GB, 290; **5** Mario Farnbacher, D, 285; **5** Alex Riberas, E, 285; **6** Bret Curtis, USA, 279; **6** Jens Klingmann, D, 279.

Manufacturers (Prototype)
1 Chevrolet, 338; **2** Honda, 324; **3** Mazda, 304.

Manufacturers (GT Le Mans)
1 Chevrolet, 359; **2** Ford, 341; **3** Porsche, 330.

Manufacturers (GT Daytona)
1 Audi, 334; **2** Ferrari, 328; **3** Porsche, 322.

Teams (Prototype)
1 Action Express Racing (car 31), 314; **2** Action Express Racing (5), 311; **3** Wayne Taylor Racing (10), 309.

Teams (Prototype Challenge)
1 Starworks Motorsport (car 8), 355; **2** PR1/Mathiasen Motorsports (52), 355; **3** Performance Tech Motorsports (38), 330.

Teams (GT Le Mans)
1 Corvette Racing (car 4), 345; **2** Ford Chip Ganassi Racing (67), 328; **3** Corvette Racing (3), 319.

Teams (GT Daytona)
1 Scuderia Corsa (car 63), 332; **2** Riley Motorsports (33), 303; **3** Paul Miller Racing (48), 293.

Autobacs Super GT Series (Japan)

AUTOBACS SUPER GT SERIES, Okayama International Circuit (TI Circuit Aida), Aida Gun, Okayama Prefecture, Japan, 10 April. Round 1. 82 laps of the 2.301-mile/3.703km circuit, 188.677 miles/303.646km.
1 Tsugio Matsuda/Ronnie Quintarelli, J/I (Nissan GT-R), 1h 56m 22.730s, 97.273mph/156.547km/h; **2** James Rossiter/Ryo Hirakawa, GB/J (Lexus RC F), +15.334s; **3** Satoshi Motoyama/Katsumasa Chiyo, J/J (Nissan GT-R), +15.756s; **4** Kazuya Oshima/Andrea Caldarelli, J/I (Lexus RC F), +54.581s; **5** Hironobu Yasuda/João Paulo de Oliveira, J/BR (Nissan GT-R), +54.825s; **6** Yuji Tachikawa/Hiroaki Ishiura, J/J (Lexus RC F), +1m 03.303s; **7** Heikki Kovalainen/Kohei Hirate, FIN/J (Lexus RC F), +1m 06.980s; **8** Daisuke Ito/Nick Cassidy, J/NZ (Lexus RC F), +1m 08.346s; **9** Yuhi Sekiguchi/Yuji Kunimoto, J/J (Lexus RC F), -1 lap; **10** Naoki Yamamoto/Takuya Izawa, J/J (Honda NSX Concept-GT), -1.
Fastest race lap: Rossiter, 1m 20.887s, 102.406mph/164.807km/h.
Pole position: Rossiter/Hirakawa, 1m 18.126s, 106.025mph/170.632km/h.

AUTOBACS SUPER GT SERIES, Fuji International Speedway, Sunto-gun, Shizuoka Prefecture, Japan, 4 May. Round 2. 110 laps of the 2.835-mile/4.563km circuit, 311.885 miles/501.930km.
1 Tsugio Matsuda/Ronnie Quintarelli, J/I (Nissan GT-R), 2h 58m 58.430s, 104.557mph/168.269km/h; **2** Heikki Kovalainen/Kohei Hirate, FIN/J (Lexus RC F), +2.666s; **3** James Rossiter/Ryo Hirakawa, GB/J (Lexus RC F), +14.346s; **4** Daisuke Ito/Nick Cassidy, J/NZ (Lexus RC F), +15.025s; **5** Kazuya Oshima/Andrea Caldarelli, J/I (Lexus RC F), +20.158s; **6** Kosuke Matsuura/Tomoki Nojiri, J/J (Honda NSX Concept-GT), +1m 00.064s; **7** Satoshi Motoyama/Katsumasa Chiyo, J/J (Nissan GT-R), -1 lap; **8** Yuhi Sekiguchi/Yuji Kunimoto, J/J (Lexus RC F), -1; **9** Daiki Sasaki/Masataka Yanagida, J/J (Nissan GT-R), -1; **10** Daisuke Nakajima/Bertrand Baguette, J/B (Honda NSX Concept-GT), -1.
Fastest race lap: Sasaki, 1m 30.470s, 112.823mph/181.571km/h.
Pole position: Hironobu Yasuda/João Paulo de Oliveira, J/BR (Nissan GT-R), 1m 27.453s, 116.715mph/187.835km/h.

Round 3 at Autopolis was cancelled due to earthquakes. As a replacement, an additional race was held over the weekend of Motegi in November.

AUTOBACS SUPER GT SERIES, Sportsland-SUGO International Course, Shibata-gun, Miyagi Prefecture, Japan, 24 July. Round 4. 74 laps of the 2.302-mile/3.704km circuit, 170.327 miles/274.115km.
1 Daiki Sasaki/Masataka Yanagida, J/J (Nissan GT-R), 1h 42m 08.887s, 100.047mph/161.010km/h; **2** Heikki Kovalainen/Kohei Hirate, FIN/J (Lexus RC F), +0.358s; **3** Yuji Tachikawa/Hiroaki Ishiura, J/J (Lexus RC F), +0.518s; **4** Kazuya Oshima/Andrea Caldarelli, J/I (Lexus RC F), +1.048s; **5** Yuhi Sekiguchi/Yuji Kunimoto, J/J (Lexus RC F), +2.152s; **6** Koudai Tsukakoshi/Takashi Kogure, J/J (Honda NSX Concept-GT), +7.001s; **7** Hideki Mutoh/Oliver Turvey, J/GB (Honda NSX Concept-GT), +26.109s; **8** James Rossiter/Ryo Hirakawa, GB/J (Lexus RC F), +28.735s; **9** Tsugio Matsuda/Ronnie Quintarelli, J/I (Nissan GT-R), +29.387s; **10** Naoki Yamamoto/Takuya Izawa, J/J (Honda NSX Concept-GT), +30.204s.
Fastest race lap: Kogure, 1m 12.818s, 113.793mph/183.132km/h.
Pole position: Oshima/Caldarelli, 1m 10.516s, 117.507mph/189.110km/h.

AUTOBACS SUPER GT SERIES, Fuji International Speedway, Sunto-gun, Shizuoka Prefecture, Japan, 7 August. Round 5. 66 laps of the 2.835-mile/4.563km circuit, 187.131 miles/301.158km.
1 Hironobu Yasuda/João Paulo de Oliveira, J/BR (Nissan GT-R), 1h 51m 53.223s, 100.349mph/161.497km/h; **2** Koudai Tsukakoshi/Takashi Kogure, J/J (Honda NSX Concept-GT), +25.424s; **3** Naoki Yamamoto/Takuya Izawa, J/J (Honda NSX Concept-GT), +28.650s; **4** Tsugio Matsuda/Ronnie Quintarelli, J/I (Nissan GT-R), +28.940s; **5** Daisuke Ito/Nick Cassidy, J/NZ (Lexus RC F), +30.831s; **6** Kosuke Matsuura/Tomoki Nojiri, J/J (Honda NSX Concept-GT), +36.730s; **7** Yuji Tachikawa/Hiroaki Ishiura, J/J (Lexus RC F), +45.837s; **8** Heikki Kovalainen/Kohei Hirate, FIN/J (Lexus RC F), +49.017s; **9** Kazuya Oshima/Andrea Caldarelli, J/I (Lexus RC F), +55.310s; **10** Yuhi Sekiguchi/Yuji Kunimoto, J/J (Lexus RC F), +1m 33.221s.
Fastest race lap: Oliveira, 1m 30.687s, 112.553mph/181.137km/h.
Pole position: Yasuda/Oliveira, 1m 28.458s, 115.389mph/185.701km/h.

AUTOBACS SUPER GT SERIES, Suzuka International Racing Course, Suzuka-shi, Mie Prefecture, Japan, 28 August. Round 6. 173 laps of the 3.608-mile/5.807km circuit, 624.236 miles/1004.611km.
1 Yuji Tachikawa/Hiroaki Ishiura, J/J (Lexus RC F), 5h 45m 34.230s, 108.383mph/174.426km/h; **2** Daisuke Ito/Nick Cassidy, J/NZ (Lexus RC F), +1.242s; **3** Satoshi Motoyama/Mitsunori Takaboshi, J/J (Nissan GT-R), +1m 15.104s; **4** Kazuya Oshima/Andrea Caldarelli, J/I (Lexus RC F), +1m 31.514s; **5** Yuhi Sekiguchi/Yuji Kunimoto, J/J (Lexus RC F), +1m 48.254s; **6** Tsugio Matsuda/Ronnie Quintarelli, J/I (Nissan GT-R), -1 lap; **7** Naoki Yamamoto/Takuya Izawa, J/J (Honda NSX Concept-GT), -1; **8** Heikki Kovalainen/Kohei Hirate, FIN/J (Lexus RC F), -1; **9** Kosuke Matsuura/Tomoki Nojiri, J/J (Honda NSX Concept-GT), -2; **10** Koudai Tsukakoshi/Takashi Kogure, J/J (Honda NSX Concept-GT), -2.
Fastest race lap: Daiki Sasaki, J (Nissan GT-R), 1m 50.924s, 117.106mph/188.464km/h.
Pole position: Hideki Mutoh/Oliver Turvey, J/GB (Honda NSX Concept-GT), 1m 47.456s, 120.885mph/194.546km/h.

AUTOBACS SUPER GT SERIES, Buriram International Circuit, Buriram, Thailand, 9 October. Round 7. 66 laps of the 2.830-mile/4.554km circuit, 186.762 miles/300.564km.
1 Yuhi Sekiguchi/Yuji Kunimoto, J/J (Lexus RC F), 1h 37m 58.745s, 114.368mph/184.058km/h; **2** Hideki Mutoh/Tadasuke Makino, J/J (Honda NSX Concept-GT), +2.917s; **3** Kazuya Oshima/Andrea Caldarelli, J/I (Lexus RC F), +17.583s; **4** Hironobu Yasuda/João Paulo de Oliveira, J/BR (Nissan GT-R), +24.166s; **5** Daisuke Nakajima/Bertrand Baguette, J/B (Honda NSX Concept-GT), +26.506s; **6** Koudai Tsukakoshi/Takashi Kogure, J/J (Honda NSX Concept-GT), +26.703s; **7** Heikki Kovalainen/Kohei Hirate, FIN/J (Lexus RC F), +35.763s; **8** Kosuke Matsuura/Tomoki Nojiri, J/J (Honda NSX Concept-GT), +42.193s; **9** James Rossiter/Ryo Hirakawa, GB/J (Lexus RC F), +45.064s; **10** Naoki Yamamoto/Takuya Izawa, J/J (Honda NSX Concept-GT), +45.182s.
Fastest race lap: Yamamoto, 1m 25.833s, 118.684mph/191.003km/h.
Pole position: Sekiguchi/Kunimoto, 1m 24.307s, 120.832mph/194.460km/h.

AUTOBACS SUPER GT SERIES, Twin Ring Motegi, Motegi-machi, Haga-gun, Tochigi Prefecture, Japan, 12/13 November. Rounds 3 and 8. 2 x 53 laps of the 2.983-mile/4.801km circuit. Round 3 (158.122 miles/254.473km).
1 Daiki Sasaki/Masataka Yanagida, J/J (Nissan GT-R), 1h 40m 10.155s, 94.713mph/152.425km/h; **2** Heikki Kovalainen/Kohei Hirate, FIN/J (Lexus RC F), +0.239s; **3** Daisuke Ito/Nick Cassidy, J/NZ (Lexus RC F), +6.003s; **4** Kazuya Oshima/Andrea Caldarelli, J/I (Lexus RC F), +6.327s; **5** Yuhi Sekiguchi/Yuji Kunimoto, J/J (Lexus RC F), +10.156s; **6** Yuji Tachikawa/Hiroaki Ishiura, J/J (Lexus RC F), +25.940s; **7** Hironobu Yasuda/João Paulo de Oliveira, J/BR (Nissan GT-R), +34.239s; **8** Satoshi Motoyama/Katsumasa Chiyo, J/J (Nissan GT-R), +34.548s; **9** Tsugio Matsuda/Ronnie Quintarelli, J/I (Nissan GT-R), +43.835s; **10** Naoki Yamamoto/Takuya Izawa, J/J (Honda NSX Concept-GT), +57.450s.
Fastest race lap: Hirate, 1m 39.954s, 107.453mph/172.929km/h.
Pole position: Kovalainen/Hirate, 1m 45.885s, 101.434mph/163.242km/h.

Round 8 (158.122 miles/254.473km).
1 Heikki Kovalainen/Kohei Hirate, FIN/J (Lexus RC F), 1h 31m 57.828s, 103.163mph/166.026km/h; **2** Kazuya Oshima/Andrea Caldarelli, J/I (Lexus RC F), +0.472s; **3** Yuhi Sekiguchi/Yuji Kunimoto, J/J (Lexus RC F), +7.471s; **4** Daisuke Ito/Nick Cassidy, J/NZ (Lexus RC F), +14.666s; **5** James Rossiter/Ryo Hirakawa, GB/J (Lexus RC F), +16.160s; **6** Satoshi Motoyama/Katsumasa Chiyo, J/J (Nissan GT-R), +19.132s; **7** Tsugio Matsuda/Ronnie Quintarelli, J/I (Nissan GT-R), +20.461s; **8** Hironobu Yasuda/João Paulo de Oliveira, J/BR (Nissan GT-R), +25.829s; **9** Yuji Tachikawa/Hiroaki Ishiura, J/J (Lexus RC F), +29.152s; **10** Daiki Sasaki/Masataka Yanagida, J/J (Nissan GT-R), +36.738s.
Fastest race lap: Hirate, 1m 39.971s, 107.434mph/172.899km/h.
Pole position: Kovalainen/Hirate, 1m 36.491s, 111.309mph/179.135km/h.

Final championship points
Drivers (GT500)
1 Heikki Kovalainen, FIN, 82; 1 Kohei Hirate, J, 82; **2** Andrea Caldarelli, I, 69; **2** Kazuya Oshima, J, 69; **3** Tsugio Matsuda, J, 62; **3** Ronnie Quintarelli, I, 62; **4** Yuji Kunimoto, J, 58; **4** Yuhi Sekiguchi, J, 58; **5** Daisuke Ito, J, 54; **5** Nick Cassidy, NZ, 54; **6** Hiroaki Ishiura, J, 52; **6** Yuji Tachikawa, J, 52; **7** Masataka Yanagida, J, 43; **7** Daiki Sasaki, J, 43; **8** João Paulo de Oliveira, BR, 43; **8** Hironobu Yasuda, J, 43; **9** James Rossiter, GB, 38; **9** Ryo Hirakawa, J, 38; **10** Satoshi Motoyama, J, 36.

Drivers (GT300)
1 Takamitsu Matsui, J, 78; 1 Takeshi Tsuchiya, J, 78; **2** Kouki Saga, J, 60; **2** Yuichi Nakayama, J, 60; **3** Richard Lyons, GB, 57; **3** Tomonobu Fujii, J, 57.

Other Sportscar races

64TH ANNUAL MOBIL 1 TWELVE HOURS OF SEBRING FUELED BY FRESH FROM FLORIDA, Sebring International Raceway, Florida, USA, 19 March. 238 laps of the 3.740-mile/6.019km circuit, 890.120 miles/1432.509km.
1 Scott Sharp/Ed Brown/Johannes van Overbeek/Luis Derani, USA/USA/USA/BR (Ligier JS P2-HPD), 12h 00m 59.881s, 74.074mph/119.211km/h; **2** Dane Cameron/Eric Curran/Scott Pruett, USA/USA/USA (Corvette DP-Chevrolet), +2.926s; **3** Christian Fittipaldi/João Barbosa/Filipe Albuquerque/Scott Pruett, BR/P/P/USA (Corvette DP-Chevrolet), +3.940s; **4** Henrik Hedman/Nicolas Lapierre/Nicolas Minassian, S/F/F (ORECA 05-Nissan), +4.339s; **5** Ryan Dalziel/Marc Goossens/Ryan Hunter-Reay, GB/B/USA (Corvette DP-Chevrolet), +18.078s; **6** Jonathan Bomarito/Tristan Nunez/Spencer Pigot, USA/USA/USA (Lola B12/80 Coupe-Mazda), +29.735s; **7** John Pew/Oswaldo Negri Jr/Olivier Pla, USA/BR/F (Ligier JS P2-HPD), -1 lap (DNF-not running); **8** Joel Miller/Tom Long/Ben Devlin/Keiko Ihara, USA/USA/GB/J (Lola B12/80 Coupe-Mazda), -1; **9** Jon Bennett/Colin Braun/Mark Wilkins, USA/USA/CDN (ORECA FLM09-Chevrolet), -2; **10** Tom Kimber-Smith/Jose Gutierrez/Robert Alon, GB/MEX/USA (ORECA FLM09-Chevrolet), -2.
Fastest race lap: Pla, 1m 52.397s, 119.790mph/192.783km/h.
Pole position: Pew/Negri Jr/Pla, 1m 51.217s, 121.061mph/194.828km/h.

ADAC-ZüRICH-24H-RENNEN, Nürburgring, Nürburg/Eifel, Germany, 28 May. 134 laps of the 15.769-mile/25.378km circuit, 2113.067 miles/3400.652km.
1 Bernd Schneider/Maro Engel/Adam Christodoulou/Manuel Metzger, D/D/GB/D (Mercedes AMG GT3), 24h 07m 46.500s, 87.572mph/140.933km/h; **2** Christian Vietoris/Marco Seefried/Christian Hohenadel/Renger van der Zande, D/D/D/NL (Mercedes AMG GT3), +5.697s; **3** Uwe Alzen/Lance David Arnold/Maximilian Götz/Jan Seyffarth, D/D/D/D (Mercedes AMG GT3), -1 lap; **4** Hubert Haupt/Yelmer Buurman/Maro Engel/Dirk Müller, D/NL/D/D (Mercedes AMG GT3), -1; **5** Alexander Sims/Philipp Eng/Maxime Martin/Dirk Werner, GB/A/B/D (BMW M6 GT3), -1; **6** Kenneth Heyer/Sebastian Asch/Luca Ludwig/Daniel Keilwitz, D/D/D/D (Mercedes AMG GT3), -3; **7** Christopher Brück/Christian Menzel/Guy Smith/Fabian Hamprecht, D/D/GB/D (Bentley Continental GT3), -3; **8** Stuart Leonard/Robin Frijns/Edward Sandström/Frédéric Vervisch, GB/NL/S/B (Audi R8 LMS), -4; **9** Peter Dumbreck/Wolf Henzler/Martin Ragginger/Alexandre Imperatori, GB/D/A/CH (Porsche 991 GT3 R), -4; **10** Marc Busch/Dennis Busch/Christian Mamerow/René Rast, D/D/D/D (Audi R8 LMS), -4.
Fastest race lap: Schneider/Engel/Christodoulou/Metzger, 8m 19.002s, 113.765mph/183.087km/h.
Pole position: Haupt/Buurman/Engel/Müller, 8m 14.515s, 114.797mph/184.748km/h.

For the 24 Heures Du Mans, see under FIA World Endurance Championship.

SPA 24 HOURS, Circuit de Spa-Francorchamps, Stavelot, Belgium, 30 July. 531 laps of the 4.352-mile/7.004km circuit, 2310.957 miles/3719.124km.
1 Maxime Martin/Philipp Eng/Alexander Sims, B/A/GB (BMW M6 GT3), 24h 02m 18.980s, 96.135mph/154.715km/h; **2** Tristan Vautier/Renger van der Zande/Felix Rosenqvist, F/NL/S (Mercedes AMG GT3), +1m 55.408s; **3** Laurens Vanthoor/René Rast/Nico Müller, B/D/CH (Audi R8 LMS), +2m 00.586s; **4** Andy Soucek/Wolfgang Reip/Maxime Soulet, E/B/B (Bentley Continental GT3), -1 lap; **5** Thomas Jäger/Maximilian Götz/Gary Paffett, D/D/GB (Mercedes AMG GT3), -1; **6** Dominik Baumann/Jazeman Jaafar/Maximilian Buhk, A/MAL/D (Mercedes AMG GT3), -2; **7** Grégory Guilvert/Mike Parisy/Christopher Haase, F/F/D (Audi R8 LMS), -4; **8** Adrien De Leener/Bertrand Baguette/Pierre Kaffer, B/B/D (Audi R8 LMS), -4; **9** Marlon Stöckinger/Filip Salaquarda/Edoardo Mortara, PH/CZ/I (Audi R8 LMS), -4; **10** Maxime Jousse/Thierry Cornac/Raymond Narac/Patrick Pilet, F/F/F/F (Porsche 911 GT3 R), -4.
Fastest race lap: Vanthoor, 2m 18.793s, 112.884mph/181.669km/h.
Pole position: Vanthoor/Rast/Müller, 2m 18.505s, 113.119mph/182.047km/h.

International V8 Supercars Championship

Cars are: Holden Commodore VF; Ford Falcon FG; Mercedes E63 AMG); Nissan Altima L33; Volvo S60.

2015

The following races were run after AUTOCOURSE 2015–2016 went to press.

COATES HIRE SYDNEY 500, Sydney Olympic Park Street Race, New South Wales, Australia, 5/6 December. Round 14. 37, 37 and 74 laps of the 2.125-mile/3.420km circuit.
Race 1 (78.628 miles/126.540km).
1 Jamie Whincup, AUS (Holden), 56m 13.3631s, 83.910mph/135.041km/h; **2** Shane van Gisbergen, NZ (Holden), +1.0856s; **3** Jason Bright, AUS (Holden), +14.0368s; **4** James Courtney, AUS (Holden), +15.3603s; **5** Mark Winterbottom, AUS (Ford), +22.5070s; **6** Tim Slade, AUS (Holden), +22.9746s; **7** Rick Kelly, AUS (Nissan), +23.6382s; **8** Scott McLaughlin, NZ (Volvo), +24.7737s; **9** David Reynolds, AUS (Ford), +25.4748s; **10** Fabian Coulthard, NZ (Holden), +28.1885s.
Fastest race lap: van Gisbergen, 1m 29.4299s, 85.545mph/137.672km/h.

Pole position: Winterbottom, 1m 27.7596s, 87.173mph/140.292km/h.

Race 2 (78.628 miles/126.540km).
1 Jamie Whincup, AUS (Holden), 58m 11.3197s, 81.075mph/130.479km/h; **2** David Reynolds, AUS (Ford), +1.8208s; **3** Mark Winterbottom, AUS (Ford), +5.4817s; **4** James Courtney, AUS (Holden), +7.1248s; **5** Scott McLaughlin, NZ (Volvo), +8.0469s; **6** Shane van Gisbergen, NZ (Holden), +10.3743s; **7** Craig Lowndes, AUS (Holden), +10.7670s; **8** Rick Kelly, AUS (Nissan), +11.2252s; **9** Scott Pye, AUS (Ford), +14.6492s; **10** Lee Holdsworth, AUS (Holden), +15.1038s.
Fastest race lap: van Gisbergen, 1m 28.8799s, 86.074mph/138.524km/h.
Pole position: Whincup, 1m 27.6420s, 87.290mph/140.480km/h.

Race 3 (157.257 miles/253.080km).
1 Shane van Gisbergen, NZ (Holden), 1h 59m 24.7481s, 79.015mph/127.162km/h; **2** Jamie Whincup, AUS (Holden), +0.4058s; **3** Rick Kelly, AUS (Nissan), +2.7401s; **4** Mark Winterbottom, AUS (Ford), +3.6779s; **5** David Reynolds, AUS (Ford), +4.4087s; **6** Craig Lowndes, AUS (Holden), +5.4626s; **7** Lee Holdsworth, AUS (Holden), +6.7619s; **8** Michael Caruso, AUS (Nissan), +7.4152s; **9** Scott Pye, AUS (Ford), +8.0493s; **10** Fabian Coulthard, NZ (Holden), +8.6930s.
Fastest race lap: Whincup, 1m 28.8504s, 86.103mph/138.570km/h.
Pole position: James Courtney, AUS (Holden), 1m 28.0667s, 86.869mph/139.803km/h.

Final championship points
Drivers
1 Mark Winterbottom, AUS, 3246; **2** Craig Lowndes, AUS, 3008; **3** David Reynolds, AUS, 2910; **4** Shane van Gisbergen, NZ, 2712; **5** Jamie Whincup, AUS, 2647; **6** Garth Tander, AUS, 2584; **7** Fabian Coulthard, NZ, 2542; **8** Scott McLaughlin, NZ, 2205; **9** Rick Kelly, AUS, 2154; **10** James Courtney, AUS, 2110; **11** Chaz Mostert, AUS, 2017; **12** Michael Caruso, AUS, 1898; **13** Tim Slade, AUS, 1764; **14** Lee Holdsworth, AUS, 1699; **15** Will Davison, AUS, 1672; **16** Jason Bright, AUS, 1671; **17** Todd Kelly, AUS, 1664; **18** James Moffat, AUS, 1643; **19** Scott Pye, AUS, 1589; **20** Dale Wood, AUS, 1325.

Teams
1 Red Bull Racing Australia, 5690; **2** Pepsi Max Crew, 5554; **3** Holden Racing Team, 5191; **4** Brad Jones Racing, 4288; **5** Jack Daniels-Nissan Motorsport, 3818.

2016

CLIPSAL 500, Adelaide Steet Circuit, South Australia, Australia, 5/6 March. Round 1. 39, 39 and 48 laps of the 2.001-mile/3.220km circuit.
Race 1 (78.032 miles/125.580km).
1 Jamie Whincup, AUS (Holden), 56m 43.1447s, 82.545mph/132.844km/h; **2** James Courtney, AUS (Holden), +3.9266s; **3** Shane van Gisbergen, NZ (Holden), +7.5750s; **4** Scott McLaughlin, NZ (Volvo), +8.4653s; **5** Garth Tander, AUS (Holden), +11.0611s; **6** Todd Kelly, AUS (Nissan), +14.5524s; **7** Craig Lowndes, AUS (Holden), +18.1015s; **8** Mark Winterbottom, AUS (Ford), +18.8276s; **9** Rick Kelly, AUS (Nissan), +19.3622s; **10** Fabian Coulthard, NZ (Ford), +21.0549s.
Fastest race lap: Whincup, 1m 21.5714s, 88.302mph/142.108km/h.
Pole position: Scott Pye, AUS (Ford), 1m 20.0168s, 90.017mph/144.869km/h.

Race 2 (78.032 miles/125.580km).
1 James Courtney, AUS (Holden), 59m 37.1268s, 78.530mph/126.382km/h; **2** Jamie Whincup, AUS (Holden), +0.6310s; **3** Chaz Mostert, AUS (Ford), +2.5254s; **4** Scott McLaughlin, NZ (Volvo), +3.1846s; **5** Shane van Gisbergen, NZ (Holden), +6.2934s; **6** Michael Caruso, AUS (Nissan), +12.7098s; **7** Scott Pye, AUS (Ford), +16.4450s; **8** Jason Bright, AUS (Holden), +17.1323s; **9** Will Davison, AUS (Holden), +18.7421s; **10** Craig Lowndes, AUS (Holden), +20.5421s.
Fastest race lap: van Gisbergen, 1m 22.2343s, 87.590mph/140.963km/h.
Pole position: Mostert, 1m 20.3724s, 89.619mph/144.228km/h.

Race 3 (96.039 miles/154.560km).
1 Nick Percat, AUS (Holden), 1h 49m 03.6598s, 52.836mph/85.031km/h; **2** Michael Caruso, AUS (Nissan), +7.1095s; **3** Garth Tander, AUS (Holden), +8.7639s; **4** Cameron Waters, AUS (Ford), +11.2829s; **5** David Reynolds, AUS (Holden), +12.9074s; **6** Todd Kelly, AUS (Nissan), +13.5218s; **7** Rick Kelly, AUS (Nissan), +13.9870s; **8** Jason Bright, AUS (Holden), +15.1646s; **9** Mark Winterbottom, AUS (Ford), +16.4074s; **10** Shane van Gisbergen, NZ (Holden), +17.0926s.
Fastest race lap: van Gisbergen, 1m 23.4595s, 86.304mph/138.893km/h.
Pole position: Fabian Coulthard, NZ (Ford), 1m 21.3006s, 88.596mph/142.581km/h.

TYREPOWER TASMANIA SUPERSPRINT, Symmons Plains Raceway, Launceston, Tasmania, Australia, 2/3 April. Round 2. 50 and 84 laps of the 1.491-mile/2.400km circuit.
Race 1 (74.565 miles/120.000km).
1 Shane van Gisbergen, NZ (Holden), 44m 25.1871s, 100.718mph/162.089km/h; **2** Jamie Whincup, AUS (Holden), +0.9388s; **3** Will Davison, AUS (Holden), +1.1345s; **4** Rick Kelly, AUS (Nissan), +7.5154s; **5** Craig Lowndes, AUS (Holden), +10.1212s; **6** Jason Bright, AUS (Holden), +13.0117s; **7** Cameron Waters, AUS (Ford), +15.3148s; **8** Tim Slade, AUS (Holden), +17.2873s; **9** Mark Winterbottom, AUS (Ford), +17.6234s; **10** Chaz Mostert, AUS (Ford), +18.1670s.
Fastest race lap: Davison, 51.7471s, 103.747mph/166.965km/h.
Pole position: Winterbottom, 51.1530s, 104.952mph/168.905km/h.

Race 2 (125.268 miles/201.600km).
1 Will Davison, AUS (Holden), 1h 20m 51.7031s, 92.950mph/149.588km/h; **2** Craig Lowndes, AUS (Holden), +2.5702s; **3** Mark Winterbottom, AUS (Ford), +3.9809s; **4** Scott McLaughlin, NZ (Volvo), +6.3942s; **5** Chaz Mostert, AUS (Ford), +8.5446s; **6** Garth Tander, AUS (Holden), +9.6302s; **7** James Courtney, AUS (Holden), +15.7248s; **8** Fabian Coulthard, NZ (Ford), +19.3809s; **9** Lee Holdsworth, AUS (Holden), +20.8972s; **10** Jason Bright, AUS (Holden), +25.3161s.
Fastest race lap: Coulthard, 51.9251s, 103.392mph/166.393km/h.
Pole position: Davison, 51.0177s, 105.231mph/169.352km/h.

WD-40 PHILLIP ISLAND SUPERSPRINT, Phillip Island Grand Prix Circuit, Cowes, Victoria, Australia, 16/17 April. Round 3. 27 and 45 laps of the 2.762-mile/4.445km circuit.
Race 1 (74.574 miles/120.015km).
1 Scott McLaughlin, NZ (Volvo), 42m 39.8093s, 104.877mph/168.783km/h; **2** Jamie Whincup, AUS (Holden), +1.2420s; **3** Fabian Coulthard, NZ (Ford), +10.9012s; **4** Shane van Gisbergen, NZ (Holden), +16.8142s; **5** Mark Winterbottom, AUS (Ford), +17.1988s; **6** Craig Lowndes, AUS (Holden), +19.9153s; **7** James Moffat, AUS (Volvo), +23.4090s; **8** Tim Slade, AUS (Holden), +23.5464s; **9** Garth Tander, AUS (Holden), +29.8960s; **10** Jason Bright, AUS (Holden), +30.3079s.
Fastest race lap: McLaughlin, 1m 32.1163s, 107.941mph/173.715km/h.
Pole position: McLaughlin, 1m 30.4880s, 109.883mph/176.841km/h.

Race 2 (124.290 miles/200.025km).
1 Scott McLaughlin, NZ (Volvo), 1h 17m 33.4257s, 96.153 mph/154.744km/h; **2** Mark Winterbottom, AUS(Ford), +1.0055s; **3** Scott Pye, AUS (Ford), +2.8871s; **4** Jamie Whincup, AUS (Holden), +3.2976s; **5** Craig Lowndes, AUS (Holden), +3.8049s; **6** Michael Caruso, AUS (Nissan), +6.3987s; **7** James Courtney, AUS (Holden), +7.0172s; **8** Chaz Mostert, AUS (Ford), +7.9024s; **9** Will Davison, AUS (Holden), +9.6799s; **10** Shane van Gisbergen, NZ (Holden), +10.7458s.
Fastest race lap: McLaughlin, 1m 32.3759s, 107.638mph/173.226km/h.
Pole position: McLaughlin, 1m 30.7018s, 109.624mph/176.424km/h.

PERTH SUPERSPRINT, Barbagallo Raceway Wanneroo, Perth, Western Australia, Australia, 7/8 May. Round 4. 50 and 83 laps of the 1.504-mile/2.420km circuit.
Race 1 (75.186 miles/121.000km).
1 Craig Lowndes, AUS (Holden), 51m 03.2882s, 88.359mph/142.200km/h; **2** Shane van Gisbergen, NZ (Holden), +5.8635s; **3** Jamie Whincup, AUS (Holden), +6.5746s; **4** Will Davison, AUS (Holden), +7.4392s; **5** Garth Tander, AUS (Holden), +9.9291s; **6** James Courtney, AUS (Holden), +15.0999s; **7** Todd Kelly, AUS (Nissan), +15.7231s; **8** Chris Pither, NZ (Ford), +17.2098s; **9** Rick Kelly, AUS (Nissan), +18.0263s; **10** Tim Slade, AUS (Holden), +19.8672s.
Fastest race lap: James Moffat, AUS (Volvo), 56.5913s, 95.657mph/153.945km/h.
Pole position: Cameron Waters, AUS (Ford), 59.6256s, 90.789mph/146.111km/h.

Race 2 (124.809 miles/200.860km).
1 Mark Winterbottom, AUS (Ford), 1h 22m 22.8550s, 90.901mph/146.291km/h; **2** Scott McLaughlin, NZ (Volvo), +0.3067s; **3** Craig Lowndes, AUS (Holden), +0.7789s; **4** Shane van Gisbergen, NZ (Holden), +1.3782s; **5** Rick Kelly, AUS (Nissan), +1.7169s; **6** Chaz Mostert, AUS (Ford), +5.1626s; **7** Garth Tander, AUS (Holden), +5.4301s; **8** James Courtney, AUS (Holden), +6.4573s; **9** Michael Caruso, AUS (Nissan), +7.1298s; **10** Will Davison, AUS (Holden), +9.7537s.
Fastest race lap: Mostert, 56.6037s, 95.636mph/153.912km/h.
Pole position: Mostert, 55.0538s, 98.329mph/158.245km/h.

WOODSTOCK WINTON SUPERSPRINT, Winton Motor Raceway, Benalla, Victoria, Australia, 21/22 May. Round 5. 40 and 67 laps of the 1.864-mile/3.000km circuit.
Race 1 (74.565 miles/120.000km).
1 Tim Slade, AUS (Holden), 54m 40.4946s, 81.826mph/131.687 m/h; **2** Scott McLaughlin, NZ (Volvo), +4.3606s; **3** Mark Winterbottom, AUS (Ford), +4.5835s; **4** Rick Kelly, AUS (Nissan), +5.1772s; **5** Jamie Whincup, AUS (Holden), +5.4525s; **6** Will Davison, AUS (Holden), +6.2263s; **7** Chaz Mostert, AUS (Ford), +6.5241s; **8** Michael Caruso, AUS (Nissan), +10.5782s; **9** Shane van Gisbergen, NZ (Holden), +10.7344s; **10** Lee Holdsworth, AUS (Holden), +11.0443s.
Fastest race lap: Fabian Coulthard, NZ (Ford), 1m 19.7092s, 84.191mph/135.492km/h.
Pole position: Slade, 1m 19.0660s, 84.876mph/136.594km/h.

Race 2 (124.896 miles/201.000km).
1 Tim Slade, AUS (Holden), 1h 33m 49.3933s, 79.870mph/128.539km/h; **2** Mark Winterbottom, AUS (Ford), +6.6803s; **3** Fabian Coulthard, NZ (Ford), +7.3574s; **4** Shane van Gisbergen, NZ (Holden), +14.0846s; **5** Cameron Waters, AUS (Ford), +18.1457s; **6** David Reynolds, AUS (Holden), +20.1356s; **7** Scott Pye, AUS (Ford), +21.4509s; **8** Craig Lowndes, AUS (Holden), +23.7776s; **9** Jamie Whincup, AUS (Holden), +25.8858s; **10** Michael Caruso, AUS (Nissan), +30.2359s.
Fastest race lap: Reynolds, 1m 19.8523s, 84.040mph/135.249km/h.
Pole position: Chaz Mostert, AUS (Ford), 1m 18.7603s, 85.205mph/137.124km/h.

SKYCITY TRIPLE CROWN DARWIN, Hidden Valley Raceway, Darwin, Northern Territory, Australia, 18/19 June. Round 6. 42 and 70 laps of the 1.783-mile/2.870km circuit.
Race 1 (74.900 miles/120.540km).
1 Michael Caruso, AUS (Nissan), 50m 12.3730s, 89.510mph/144.053km/h; **2** Jamie Whincup, AUS (Holden), +1.7795s; **3** Chaz Mostert, AUS (Ford), +5.0879s; **4** Will Davison, AUS (Holden), +6.0353s; **5** Scott Pye, AUS (Ford), +7.1937s; **6** Fabian Coulthard, NZ (Ford), +9.6089s; **7** Todd Kelly, AUS (Nissan), +12.5336s; **8** Lee Holdsworth, AUS (Holden), +13.1064s; **9** Mark Winterbottom, AUS (Ford), +14.5127s; **10** Scott McLaughlin, NZ (Volvo), +15.4055s.
Fastest race lap: Caruso, 1m 07.0001s, 95.820mph/154.208km/h.
Pole position: Shane van Gisbergen, NZ (Holden), 1m 06.0923s, 97.136mph/156.326km/h.

Race 2 (124.833 miles/200.900km).
1 Shane van Gisbergen, NZ (Holden), 1h 32m 52.6896s, 80.643mph/129.782km/h; **2** Tim Slade, AUS (Holden), +1.5655s; **3** Craig Lowndes, AUS (Holden), +1.9608s; **4** Will Davison, AUS (Holden), +2.5982s; **5** James Courtney, AUS (Holden), +6.2058s; **6** Michael Caruso, AUS (Nissan), +7.4821s; **7** Scott McLaughlin, NZ (Volvo), +8.2234s; **8** Jamie Whincup, AUS (Holden), +8.8271s; **9** David Reynolds, AUS (Holden), +9.2415s; **10** James Moffat, AUS (Volvo), +9.9414s.
Fastest race lap: Jason Bright, AUS (Holden), 1m 07.3169s, 95.369mph/153.483km/h.
Pole position: van Gisbergen, 1m 06.6797s, 96.281mph/154.949km/h.

CASTROL EDGE TOWNSVILLE 400, Townsville Street Circuit, Queensland, Australia, 9/10 July. Round 7. 2 x 70 laps of the 1.777-mile/2.860km circuit.
Race 1 (124.399 miles/200.200km).
1 Jamie Whincup, AUS (Holden), 1h 31m 34.8721s, 81.500mph/131.162km/h; **2** Shane van Gisbergen, NZ (Holden), +3.5772s; **3** Mark Winterbottom, AUS (Ford), +5.1043s; **4** Chaz Mostert, AUS (Ford), +6.6957s; **5** Will Davison, AUS (Holden), +7.8709s; **6** James Courtney, AUS (Holden), +7.8845s; **7** Garth Tander, AUS (Holden), +8.4527s; **8** Fabian Coulthard, NZ (Ford), +8.7106s; **9** Michael Caruso, AUS (Nissan), +9.2471s; **10** Todd Kelly, AUS (Nissan), +9.5132s.
Fastest race lap: Whincup, 1m 13.3474s, 87.223mph/140.373km/h.
Pole position: Whincup, 1m 12.1443s, 88.678mph/142.713km/h.

Race 2 (124.399 miles/200.200km).
1 Shane van Gisbergen, NZ (Holden), 1h 35m 25.6070s, 78.216mph/125.876km/h; **2** James Courtney, AUS (Holden), +1.2583s; **3** Mark Winterbottom, AUS (Ford), +1.2912s; **4** Jamie Whincup, AUS (Holden), +2.5076s; **5** Scott McLaughlin, NZ (Volvo), +3.8390s; **6** Cameron Waters, AUS (Ford), +4.8648s; **7** Scott Pye, AUS (Ford), +5.7577s; **8** Michael Caruso, AUS (Nissan), +6.1444s; **9** Jason Bright, AUS (Holden), +6.7541s; **10** Craig Lowndes, AUS (Holden), +7.9279s.
Fastest race lap: van Gisbergen, 1m 13.3018s, 87.278mph/140.460km/h.
Pole position: Winterbottom, 1m 12.4077s, 88.355mph/142.194km/h.

COATES HIRE IPSWICH SUPERSPRINT, Queensland Raceway, Ipswich, Queensland, Australia, 23/24 July. Round 8. 38 and 65 laps of the 1.939-mile/3.120km circuit.
Race 1 (73.670 miles/118.560km).
1 Shane van Gisbergen, NZ (Holden), 45m 59.3567s, 96.113mph/154.679km/h; **2** Jamie Whincup, AUS (Holden), +0.8218s; **3** Craig Lowndes, AUS (Holden), +1.0891s; **4** Mark Winterbottom, AUS (Ford), +1.3332s; **5** Chaz Mostert, AUS (Ford), +1.8348s; **6** Tim Slade, AUS (Holden), +7.2672s; **7** Will Davison, AUS (Holden), +25.3741s; **8** Rick Kelly, AUS (Nissan), +26.5054s; **9** James Moffat, AUS (Volvo), +27.2664s; **10** Fabian Coulthard, NZ (Ford), +27.4977s.
Fastest race lap: Mostert, 1m 10.5470s, 98.930mph/159.213km/h.
Pole position: Chris Pither, NZ (Ford), 1m 10.0378s, 99.649mph/160.370km/h.

Race 2 (126.014 miles/202.800km).
1 Craig Lowndes, AUS (Holden), 1h 19m 07.4961s, 95.555mph/153.782km/h; **2** Jamie Whincup, AUS (Holden), +2.6015s; **3** Chaz Mostert, AUS (Ford), +4.9417s; **4** Michael Caruso, AUS (Nissan), +5.8420s; **5** Mark Winterbottom, AUS (Ford), +7.8479s; **6** Scott McLaughlin, NZ (Volvo), +9.6116s; **7** Tim Slade, AUS (Holden), +10.0683s; **8** Chris Pither, NZ (Ford), +22.2238s; **9** Todd Kelly, AUS (Nissan), +24.3472s; **10** Fabian Coulthard, NZ (Ford), +26.9276s.
Fastest race lap: James Courtney, AUS (Holden), 1m 10.4685s, 99.040mph/159.39 km/h.
Pole position: Whincup, 1m 09.4113s, 100.549mph/161.818km/h.

SYDNEY MOTORSPORT PARK SUPERSPRINT, Sydney Motorsport Park, Eastern Creek, New South Wales, Australia, 27/28 August. Round 9. 31 and 51 laps of the 2.442-mile/3.930km circuit.
Race 1 (75.702 miles/121.830km).
1 Shane van Gisbergen, NZ (Holden), 48m 51.0408s, 92.979mph/149.635km/h; **2** Jamie Whincup, AUS (Holden), +0.2460s; **3** James Courtney, AUS (Holden), +3.1382s; **4** Chaz Mostert, AUS (Ford), +3.8169s; **5** Scott McLaughlin, NZ (Volvo), +13.4811s; **6** Craig Lowndes, AUS (Holden), +14.0953s; **7** Tim Slade, AUS (Holden), +14.9800s; **8** Garth Tander, AUS (Holden), +15.1070s; **9** Rick Kelly, AUS (Nissan), +23.1119s; **10** Fabian Coulthard, NZ (Ford), +23.3512s.
Fastest race lap: Michael Caruso, AUS (Nissan), 1m 31.2409s, 96.351mph/155.062km/h.
Pole position: Mostert, 1m 28.8272s, 98.969mph/159.275km/h.

Race 2 (124.541 miles/200.430km).
1 Jamie Whincup, AUS (Holden), 1h 20m 45.1664s, 92.535mph/148.921km/h; **2** Craig Lowndes, AUS (Holden), +2.6586s; **3** Chaz Mostert, AUS (Ford), +8.1308s; **4** Fabian Coulthard, NZ (Ford), +15.4497s; **5** Shane van Gisbergen, NZ (Holden), +21.6294s; **6** Scott McLaughlin, NZ (Volvo), +23.8455s; **7** Garth Tander, AUS (Holden), +25.6939s; **8** James Courtney, AUS (Holden), +26.1077s; **9** Todd Kelly, AUS (Nissan), +45.1169s; **10** Michael Caruso, AUS (Nissan), +45.2961s.
Fastest race lap: Lowndes, 1m 30.9796s, 96.627mph/155.507km/h.
Pole position: Mostert, 1m 29.4413s, 98.289mph/158.181km/h.

WILSON SECURITY SANDOWN 500, Sandown International Motor Raceway, Melbourne, Victoria, Australia, 18 September. Round 10. 143 laps of the 1.926-mile/3.100km circuit, 275.454 miles/443.300km.
1 Garth Tander/Warren Luff, AUS/AUS (Holden), 3h 30m 56.7695s, 78.348mph/126.089km/h; **2** Shane van Gisbergen/Alexandre Prémat, NZ/F (Holden), +0.3485s; **3** Will Davison/Jonathon Webb, AUS/AUS (Holden), +14.7574s; **4** Scott McLaughlin/David Wall, NZ/AUS (Volvo), +15.9156s; **5** Chaz Mostert/Steve Owen, AUS/AUS (Ford), +16.3113s; **6** Fabian Coulthard/Luke Youlden, NZ/AUS (Ford), +22.6739s; **7** Todd Kelly/Matt Campbell, AUS/AUS (Nissan), +25.8458s; **8** Craig Lowndes/Steven Richards, AUS/NZ (Holden), +33.3303s; **9** Nick Percat/Cameron McConville, AUS/AUS (Holden), +36.1446s; **10** Rick Kelly/Russell Ingall, AUS/AUS (Nissan), +37.5299s.
Fastest race lap: Percat/McConville, 1m 09.7140s, 99.470mph/160.082km/h.
Pole position: Jamie Whincup/Paul Dumbrell, AUS/AUS (Holden).

SUPERCHEAP AUTO BATHURST 1000, Mount Panorama, Bathurst, New South Wales, Australia, 9 October. Round 11. 161 laps of the 3.861-mile/6.213km circuit, 621.553 miles/1000.293km.
1 Will Davison/Jonathon Webb, AUS/AUS (Holden), 6h 19m 25.3237s, 98.289mph/158.181km/h; **2** Shane van Gisbergen/Alexandre Prémat, NZ/F (Holden), +0.1434s; **3** Nick Percat/Cameron McConville, AUS/AUS (Holden), +2.8554s; **4** Cameron Waters/Jack Le Brocq, AUS/AUS (Ford), +3.2351s; **5** Scott Pye/Tony D'Alberto, AUS/AUS (Ford), +3.8215s; **6** Fabian Coulthard/Luke Youlden, NZ/AUS (Ford), +4.0336s; **7** Tim Slade/Ashley Walsh, AUS/AUS (Holden), +4.1968s; **8** Michael Caruso/Dean Fiore, AUS/AUS (Nissan), +6.0884s; **9** Dale Wood/David Russell, AUS/AUS (Nissan), +8.3833s; **10** Tim Blanchard/Macauley Jones, AUS/AUS (Holden), +8.8587s.
Fastest race lap: David Reynolds/Craig Baird, AUS/NZ (Holden), 2m 06.2769s, 110.060mph/177.125km/h.
Pole position: Jamie Whincup/Paul Dumbrell, AUS/AUS (Holden), 2m 05.4263s, 110.806mph/178.326km/h.

CASTROL GOLD COAST 600, Surfer's Paradise Street Circuit, Queensland, Australia, 22/23 October. Round 12. 2 x 102 laps of the 1.854-mile/2.984km circuit.
Race 1 (189.126 miles/304.368km).
1 Shane van Gisbergen/Alexandre Prémat, NZ/F (Holden), 2h 21m 45.5490s, 80.047mph/128.824km/h; **2** Scott McLaughlin/David Wall, NZ/AUS (Volvo), +0.6107s; **3** Jamie Whincup/Paul Dumbrell, AUS/AUS (Holden), +1.1408s; **4** Mark Winterbottom/Dean Canto, AUS/AUS (Ford),

+5.6598s; **5** James Moffat/James Golding, AUS/AUS (Volvo), +7.3729s; **6** Craig Lowndes/Steven Richards, AUS/NZ (Holden), +7.5249s; **7** Dale Wood/David Russell, AUS/AUS (Nissan), +8.6342s; **8** Todd Kelly/Matt Campbell, AUS/AUS (Nissan), +9.6827s; **9** Chaz Mostert/Steve Owen, AUS/AUS (Ford), +10.8286s; **10** Chris Pither/Richie Stanaway, NZ/NZ (Ford), +12.0549s.
Fastest race lap: van Gisbergen/Prémat, 1m 11.4567s, 93.413mph/150.334km/h.
Pole position: van Gisbergen/Prémat, 1m 10.6544s, 94.474mph/152.041km/h.

Race 2 (189.126 miles/304.368km).
1 Jamie Whincup/Paul Dumbrell, AUS/AUS (Holden), 2h 09m 10.5096s, 87.846mph/141.374km/h; **2** Shane van Gisbergen/Alexandre Prémat, NZ/F (Holden), +9.0794s; **3** Scott McLaughlin/David Wall, NZ/AUS (Volvo), +14.1244s; **4** Craig Lowndes/Steven Richards, AUS/NZ (Holden), +14.6334s; **5** Mark Winterbottom/Dean Canto, AUS/AUS (Ford), +20.1092s; **6** Chaz Mostert/Steve Owen, AUS/AUS (Ford), +23.4891s; **7** Lee Holdsworth/Karl Reindler, AUS/AUS (Holden), +24.3335s; **8** Tim Slade/Ashley Walsh, AUS/AUS (Holden), +25.4178s; **9** Michael Caruso/Dean Fiore, AUS/AUS (Nissan), +29.6574s; **10** James Courtney/Jack Perkins, AUS/AUS (Holden), +40.6360s.
Fastest race lap: van Gisbergen/Prémat, 1m 11.3587s, 93.541mph/150.540km/h.
Pole position: Whincup/Dumbrell, 1m 10.8872s, 94.163mph/151.542km/h.

ITM AUCKLAND SUPERSPRINT, Pukekohe Park Raceway, Auckland, New Zealand, 5/6 November. Round 13. 4 x 35 laps of the 1.808-mile/2.910km circuit.
Race 1 (63.287 miles/101.850km).
1 Jamie Whincup, AUS (Holden), 45m 37.7579s, 83.218mph/133.927km/h; **2** Shane van Gisbergen, NZ (Holden), +6.5047s; **3** Scott McLaughlin, NZ (Volvo), +8.0252s; **4** Mark Winterbottom, AUS (Ford), +10.1999s; **5** Garth Tander, AUS (Holden), +10.9381s; **6** James Courtney, AUS (Holden), +13.6761s; **7** Rick Kelly, AUS (Nissan), +17.3744s; **8** Michael Caruso, AUS (Nissan), +21.1881s; **9** Scott Pye, AUS (Ford), +22.0267s; **10** Will Davison, AUS (Holden), +22.6654s.
Fastest race lap: Whincup, 1m 03.5126s, 102.491mph/164.943km/h.
Pole position: van Gisbergen, 1m 02.5122s, 104.131mph/167.583km/h.

Race 2 (63.287 miles/101.850km).
1 Shane van Gisbergen, NZ (Holden), 37m 36.1250s, 100.983mph/162.517km/h; **2** Jamie Whincup, AUS (Holden), +2.1810s; **3** Chaz Mostert, AUS (Ford), +9.2872s; **4** Fabian Coulthard, NZ (Ford), +12.3475s; **5** Mark Winterbottom, AUS (Ford), +13.8627s; **6** Will Davison, AUS (Holden), +18.1188s; **7** Scott McLaughlin, NZ (Volvo), +19.8719s; **8** David Reynolds, AUS (Holden), +25.6250s; **9** Michael Caruso, AUS (Nissan), +26.6475s; **10** Garth Tander, AUS (Holden), +27.8165s.
Fastest race lap: van Gisbergen, 1m 03.7365s, 102.131mph/164.364km/h.
Pole position: van Gisbergen, 1m 02.2186s, 104.622mph/168.374km/h.

Race 3 (63.287 miles/101.850km).
1 Mark Winterbottom, AUS (Ford), 38m 06.2689s, 99.652mph/160.374km/h; **2** Scott Pye, AUS (Ford), +10.1496s; **3** Shane van Gisbergen, NZ (Holden), +12.9927s; **4** Craig Lowndes, AUS (Holden), +13.8946s; **5** Fabian Coulthard, NZ (Ford), +15.4129s; **6** Chaz Mostert, AUS (Ford), +16.3033s; **7** Scott McLaughlin, NZ (Volvo), +18.0338s; **8** Will Davison, AUS (Holden), +20.5726s; **9** Rick Kelly, AUS (Nissan), +20.8591s; **10** Garth Tander, AUS (Holden), +21.7133s.
Fastest race lap: Jamie Whincup, AUS (Holden), 1m 04.0351s, 101.654mph/163.597km/h.
Pole position: van Gisbergen, 1m 02.9107s, 103.471mph/166.521km/h.

Race 4 (63.287 miles/101.850km).
1 Jamie Whincup, AUS (Holden), 37m 37.1619s, 100.937mph/162.442km/h; **2** Shane van Gisbergen, NZ (Holden), +8.7366s; **3** Scott McLaughlin, NZ (Volvo), +19.4780s; **4** Chaz Mostert, AUS (Ford), +19.8987s; **5** Mark Winterbottom, AUS (Ford), +20.6497s; **6** Craig Lowndes, AUS (Holden), +21.1349s; **7** Garth Tander, AUS (Holden), +21.9262s; **8** Fabian Coulthard, NZ (Ford), +23.5691s; **9** Scott Pye, AUS (Ford), +24.4027s; **10** James Moffat, AUS (Volvo), +25.3593s.
Fastest race lap: Whincup, 1m 03.9394s, 101.807mph/163.842km/h.
Pole position: Whincup, 1m 02.6857s, 103.843mph/167.119km/h.

Provisional championship points
Drivers
1 Shane van Gisbergen, NZ, 3089; **2** Jamie Whincup, AUS, 2898; **3** Craig Lowndes, AUS, 2596; **4** Scott McLaughlin, NZ, 2575; **5** Will Davison, AUS, 2403; **6** Mark Winterbottom, AUS, 2384; **7** Chaz Mostert, AUS, 2235; **8** Michael Caruso, AUS, 2110; **9** Tim Slade, AUS, 2083; **10** Garth Tander, AUS, 1976; **11** Fabian Coulthard, NZ, 1964; **12** James Courtney, AUS, 1949; **13** Rick Kelly, AUS, 1733; **14** Todd Kelly, AUS, 1691; **15** Scott Pye, AUS, 1678; **16** Jason Bright, AUS, 1408; **17** Cameron Waters, AUS, 1381; **18** David Reynolds, AUS, 1357; **19** Chris Pither, NZ, 1318; **20** Nick Percat, AUS, 1313.

Teams
1 Red Bull Racing Australia, 5997; **2** Holden Racing Team, 3945; **3** Wilson Security Racing GRM, 3908; **4** Prodrive Racing Australia, 3815; **5** DJR Team Penske, 3612.

Results of the Sydney races will be given in AUTOCOURSE 2017–2018

Other Australian V8 races

COATES HIRE V8 SUPERCARS CHALLENGE, Albert Park Circuit, Melbourne, Victoria, Australia, 18/20 March. 11, 12, 12 and 12 laps of the 3.295-mile/5.303km circuit.
Race 1 (36.246 miles/58.333km).
1 Shane van Gisbergen, NZ (Holden), 26m 24.0911s, 82.373mph/132.567km/h; **2** Jamie Whincup, AUS (Holden), +0.5208s; **3** Chaz Mostert, AUS (Ford), +2.6165s; **4** Fabian Coulthard, NZ (Ford), +3.6343s; **5** Scott Pye, AUS (Ford), +4.5422s; **6** Garth Tander, AUS (Holden), +5.0588s; **7** Craig Lowndes, AUS (Holden), +6.3712s; **8** James Courtney, AUS (Holden), +7.4274s; **9** Scott McLaughlin, NZ (Volvo), +8.4415s; **10** Cameron Waters, AUS (Ford), +9.0468s.
Fastest race lap: Coulthard, 1m 58.3178s, 100.259mph/161.351km/h.
Pole position: Whincup, 1m 56.5634s, 101.768mph/163.780km/h.

Race 2 (39.542 miles/63.636km).
1 Shane van Gisbergen, NZ (Holden), 23m 48.6448s, 99.639mph/160.354km/h; **2** Craig Lowndes, AUS (Holden), +3.7758s; **3** Jamie Whincup, AUS (Holden), +4.4747s; **4** Fabian Coulthard, NZ (Ford), +8.2075s; **5** Chaz Mostert, AUS (Ford), +8.6498s; **6** Garth Tander, AUS (Holden), +11.3949s; **7** James Courtney, AUS (Holden), +11.6172s; **8** Scott McLaughlin, NZ (Volvo), +13.0456s; **9** Tim Slade, AUS (Holden), +17.0594s; **10** Michael Caruso, AUS (Nissan), +17.2164s.
Fastest race lap: van Gisbergen, 1m 57.7184s, 100.769mph/162.173km/h.
Pole position: van Gisbergen.

Race 3 (39.542 miles/63.636km).
1 Jamie Whincup, AUS (Holden), 23m 47.6194s, 99.711mph/160.469km/h; **2** Shane van Gisbergen, NZ (Holden), +6.6025s; **3** Craig Lowndes, AUS (Holden), +6.8834s; **4** Garth Tander, AUS (Holden), +7.4864s; **5** Fabian Coulthard, NZ (Ford), +10.1469s; **6** Chaz Mostert, AUS (Ford), +10.7016s; **7** James Courtney, AUS (Holden), +11.2252s; **8** Michael Caruso, AUS (Nissan), +11.4986s; **9** Tim Slade, AUS (Holden), +15.7079s; **10** Rick Kelly, AUS (Nissan), +17.5100s.
Fastest race lap: Lowndes, 1m 57.4613s, 100.990mph/162.528km/h.
Pole position: van Gisbergen.

Race 4 (39.542 miles/63.636km).
1 Shane van Gisbergen, NZ (Holden), 23m 53.8276s, 99.279mph/159.774km/h; **2** Fabian Coulthard, NZ (Ford), +1.2666s; **3** Craig Lowndes, AUS (Holden), +2.7884s; **4** James Courtney, AUS (Holden), +4.0098s; **5** Michael Caruso, AUS (Nissan), +4.5394s; **6** Garth Tander, AUS (Holden), +6.4085s; **7** Scott Pye, AUS (Ford), +7.2935s; **8** Rick Kelly, AUS (Nissan), +7.6883s; **9** Chaz Mostert, AUS (Ford), +10.0461s; **10** Tim Slade, AUS (Holden), +10.3879s.
Fastest race lap: van Gisbergen, 1m 58.4726s, 100.128mph/161.141km/h.
Pole position: Whincup.

Final championship points
Drivers
1 Shane van Gisbergen, NZ, 294; **2** Craig Lowndes, AUS, 245; **3** Fabian Coulthard, NZ, 244; **4** Garth Tander, AUS, 213; **5** Chaz Mostert, AUS, 212; **6** Jamie Whincup, AUS, 208; **7** James Courtney, AUS, 201; **8** Michael Caruso, AUS, 175; **9** Scott Pye, AUS, 164; **10** Tim Slade, AUS, 157.

FIA World Touring Car Championship

FIA WORLD TOURING CAR CHAMPIONSHIP, Circuit ASA Paul Ricard, Le Beausset, France, 3 April. 16 and 17 laps of the 2.387-mile/3.841km circuit.
Round 1 (38.187 miles/61.456km).
1 Rob Huff, GB (Honda Civic WTCC), 24m 26.764s, 93.725mph/150.836km/h; **2** Mehdi Bennani, MA (Citroën C-Elysée WTCC), +2.184s; **3** Norbert Michelisz, H (Honda Civic WTCC), +6.737s; **4** Tiago Monteiro, P (Honda Civic WTCC), +7.911s; **5** Hugo Valente, F (Lada Vesta WTCC), +12.554s; **6** José María López, RA (Citroën C-Elysée WTCC), +12.955s; **7** Thed Björk, S (Volvo S60 WTCC), +22.162s; **8** Nicky Catsburg, NL (Lada Vesta WTCC), +23.708s; **9** Tom Coronel, NL (Chevrolet RML Cruze TC1), +24.892s; **10** Grégoire Demoustier, F (Citroën C-Elysée WTCC), +25.738s.
Fastest race lap: Huff, 1m 30.455s, 94.987mph/152.867km/h.
Pole position: Valente.

Round 2 (40.574 miles/65.297 km).
1 José María López, RA (Citroën -Elysée WTCC), 25m 53.030s, 94.051mph/151.361km/h; **2** Tiago Monteiro, P (Honda Civic WTCC), +0.284s; **3** Norbert Michelisz, H (Honda Civic WTCC), +3.111s; **4** Yvan Muller, F (Citroën C-Elysée WTCC), +8.652s; **5** Nicky Catsburg, NL (Lada Vesta WTCC), +9.814s; **6** Rob Huff, GB (Honda Civic WTCC), +19.934s; **7** Hugo Valente, F (Lada Vesta WTCC), +21.792s; **8** Mehdi Bennani, MA (Citroën C-Elysée WTCC), +22.130s; **9** Tom Chilton, GB (Citroën C-Elysée WTCC), +22.389s; **10** Fredrik Ekblom, S (Volvo S60 WTCC), +27.554s.
Fastest race lap: Muller, 1m 30.762s, 94.665mph/152.350km/h.
Pole position: López, 1m 28.950s, 96.594mph/155.453km/h.

FIA WORLD TOURING CAR CHAMPIONSHIP, Automotodróm Slovakia Ring, Orechová Potôn, Slovakia, 17 April. 11 and 12 laps of the 3.680-mile/5.922km circuit.
Round 3 (40.403 miles/65.023km).
1 Tiago Monteiro, P (Honda Civic WTCC), 23m 30.309s, 103.321mph/166.280km/h; **2** Mehdi Bennani, MA (Citroën C-Elysée WTCC), +2.526s; **3** Rob Huff, GB (Honda Civic WTCC), +3.119s; **4** Gabriele Tarquini, I (Lada Vesta WTCC), +9.247s; **5** José María López, RA (Citroën C-Elysée WTCC), +9.453s; **6** Norbert Michelisz, H (Honda Civic WTCC), +10.085s; **7** Yvan Muller, F (Citroën C-Elysée WTCC), +10.659s; **8** Tom Chilton, GB (Citroën C-Elysée WTCC), +11.606s; **9** Fredrik Ekblom, S (Volvo S60 WTCC), +12.567s; **10** Nicky Catsburg, NL (Lada Vesta WTCC), +14.766s.
Disqualified: Thed Björk, S (Volvo S60 WTCC), originally finished 8th.
Fastest race lap: Huff, 2m 07.105s, 104.221mph/167.729km/h.
Pole position: Valente.

Round 4 (44.083 miles/70.945km).
1 José María López, RA (Citroën C-Elysée WTCC), 25m 44.212s, 102.941mph/165.667km/h; **2** Tiago Monteiro, P (Honda Civic WTCC), +0.700s; **3** Nicky Catsburg, NL (Lada Vesta WTCC), +3.260s; **4** Norbert Michelisz, H (Honda Civic WTCC), +4.620s; **5** Yvan Muller, F (Citroën C-Elysée WTCC), +4.737s; **6** Mehdi Bennani, MA (Citroën C-Elysée WTCC), +5.262s; **7** Tom Chilton, GB (Citroën C-Elysée WTCC), +5.950s; **8** Fredrik Ekblom, S (Volvo S60 WTCC), +7.551s; **9** Tom Coronel, NL (Chevrolet RML Cruze TC1), +18.969s; **10** John Filippi, F (Chevrolet RML Cruze TC1), +19.345s.
Disqualified: Thed Björk, S (Volvo S60 WTCC), originally finished 4th.
Fastest race lap: López, 2m 06.669s, 104.580mph/168.306 km/h.
Pole position: Muller, 2m 03.910s, 106.909mph/172.053km/h.

FIA WORLD TOURING CAR CHAMPIONSHIP, Hungaroring, Mogyoród, Budapest, Hungary, 24 April. 14 and 17 laps of the 2.722-mile/4.381km circuit.
Round 5 (38.111 miles/61.334km).
1 Mehdi Bennani, MA (Citroën C-Elysée WTCC), 30m 49.813s, 74.169mph/119.364km/h; **2** Tom Chilton, GB (Citroën C-Elysée WTCC), +3.313s; **3** Nicky Catsburg, NL (Lada Vesta WTCC), +6.367s; **4** Fredrik Ekblom, S (Volvo S60 WTCC), +13.918s; **5** Gabriele Tarquini, I (Lada Vesta WTCC), +14.566s; **6** Hugo Valente, F (Lada Vesta WTCC), +29.575s; **7** Grégoire Demoustier, F (Citroën C-Elysée WTCC), +34.530s; **8** John Filippi, F (Chevrolet RML Cruze TC1), +47.418s; **9** René Münnich, D (Chevrolet RML Cruze TC1), +1m 48.021s; **10** Rob Huff, GB (Honda Civic WTCC), +1m 58.809s.
Disqualified: Ferenc Ficza, H (originally finished 10th).
Fastest race lap: José María López, RA (Citroën C-Elysée WTCC), 2m 09.820s, 75.489mph/121.488km/h.
Pole position: Bennani.

Round 6 (46.278 miles/74.477km).
1 José María López, RA (Citroën C-Elysée WTCC), 38m 37.180s, 71.897mph/115.708km/h; **2** Yvan Muller, F (Citroën C-Elysée WTCC), +2.821s; **3** Tiago Monteiro, P (Honda Civic WTCC), +14.981s; **4** Thed Björk, S (Volvo S60 WTCC), +18.026s; **5** Tom Chilton, GB (Citroën C-Elysée WTCC), +19.834s; **6** Rob Huff, GB (Honda Civic WTCC), +24.535s; **7** Tom Coronel, NL (Chevrolet RML Cruze TC1), +26.979s; **8** Mehdi Bennani, MA (Citroën C-Elysée WTCC), +27.898s; **9** Hugo Valente, F (Lada Vesta WTCC), +36.557s; **10** Norbert Michelisz, H (Honda Civic WTCC), +36.867s.
Fastest race lap: López, 2m 10.774s, 74.938mph/120.601km/h.
Pole position: López, 1m 46.109s, 92.358mph/148.635km/h.

FIA WORLD TOURING CAR CHAMPIONSHIP, Circuit Moulay El Hassan, Agdal, Marrakech, Morocco, 8 May. 21 and 22 laps of the 1.846-mile/2.971km circuit.
Round 7 (38.768 miles/62.391km).
1 Tom Coronel, NL (Chevrolet RML Cruze TC1), 29m 30.458s, 78.829mph/126.864km/h; **2** José María López, RA (Citroën C-Elysée WTCC), +0.319s; **3** Yvan Muller, F (Citroën C-Elysée WTCC), +2.185s; **4** Gabriele Tarquini, I (Lada Vesta WTCC), +9.517s; **5** Tom Chilton, GB (Citroën C-Elysée WTCC), +11.403s; **6** Mehdi Bennani, MA (Citroën C-Elysée WTCC), +12.294s; **7** Fredrik Ekblom, S (Volvo S60 WTCC), +16.540s; **8** Grégoire Demoustier, F (Citroën C-Elysée WTCC), +31.551s; **9** Thed Björk, S (Volvo S60 WTCC), +52.376s *.
** includes 30s penalty.*
Disqualified: Tiago Monteiro, P (Honda Civic WTCC); Norbert Michelisz, H (Honda Civic WTCC); Rob Huff, GB (Honda Civic WTCC).
Fastest race lap: Hugo Valente, F (Lada Vesta WTCC), 1m 23.087s, 79.987mph/128.727km/h.
Pole position: Thompson.

Round 8 (40.614 miles/65.362km).
1 José María López, RA (Citroën C-Elysée WTCC), 34m 34.047s, 70.495mph/113.451km/h; **2** Yvan Muller, F (Citroën C-Elysée WTCC), +7.206s; **3** Gabriele Tarquini, I (Lada Vesta WTCC), +7.807s; **4** Hugo Valente, F (Lada Vesta WTCC), +29.793s; **5** Mehdi Bennani, MA (Citroën C-Elysée WTCC), +33.433s; **6** James Thompson, GB (Chevrolet RML Cruze TC1), +34.512s; **7** Nicky Catsburg, NL (Lada Vesta WTCC), +43.985s; **8** Tom Coronel, NL (Chevrolet RML Cruze TC1), +1m 02.113s; **9** John Filippi, F (Chevrolet RML Cruze TC1), +1m 05.006s; **10** Thed Björk, S (Volvo S60 WTCC), -1 lap.
Disqualified: Rob Huff, GB (Honda Civic WTCC); Norbert Michelisz, H (Honda Civic WTCC); Tiago Monteiro, P (Honda Civic WTCC); Tom Chilton, GB (Citroën C-Elysée WTCC).
Fastest race lap: Tarquini, 1m 32.550s, 71.809mph/115.565km/h.
Pole position: Rob Huff, GB (Honda Civic WTCC), 1m 21.743s, 81.302mph/130.844km/h.

FIA WORLD TOURING CAR CHAMPIONSHIP, Nürburgring, Nürburg/Eifel, Germany, 28 May. 2 x 3 laps of the 15.769-mile/25.378km circuit.
Round 9 (47.307 miles/76.134km).
1 José María López, RA (Citroën C-Elysée WTCC), 26m 36.640s, 106.665mph/171.661km/h; **2** Tom Chilton, GB (Citroën C-Elysée WTCC), +0.526s; **3** Norbert Michelisz, H (Honda Civic WTCC), +6.653s; **4** Rob Huff, GB (Honda Civic WTCC), +7.971s; **5** Mehdi Bennani, MA (Citroën C-Elysée WTCC), +10.126s; **6** Hugo Valente, F (Lada Vesta WTCC), +12.568s; **7** Gabriele Tarquini, I (Lada Vesta WTCC), +12.890s; **8** Fredrik Ekblom, S (Volvo S60 WTCC), +12.983s; **9** Nicky Catsburg, NL (Lada Vesta WTCC), +20.389s; **10** Sabine Schmitz, D (Chevrolet RML Cruze TC1), +29.462s.
Fastest race lap: Chilton, 8m 47.586s, 107.601mph/173.167km/h.
Pole position: Monteiro.

Round 10 (47.307 miles/76.134km).
1 José María López, RA (Citroën C-Elysée WTCC), 26m 29.665s, 107.133mph/172.415km/h; **2** Norbert Michelisz, H (Honda Civic WTCC), +0.435s; **3** Tom Chilton, GB (Citroën C-Elysée WTCC), +0.915s; **4** Rob Huff, GB (Honda Civic WTCC), +1.908s; **5** Mehdi Bennani, MA (Citroën C-Elysée WTCC), +2.431s; **6** Nicky Catsburg, NL (Lada Vesta WTCC), +4.905s; **7** Fredrik Ekblom, S (Volvo S60 WTCC), +6.072s; **8** Thed Björk, S (Volvo S60 WTCC), +8.008s; **9** Gabriele Tarquini, I (Lada Vesta WTCC), +8.675s; **10** Hugo Valente, F (Lada Vesta WTCC), +13.860s.
Fastest race lap: López, 8m 48.359s, 107.443mph/172.914km/h.
Pole position: López, 8m 35.541s, 110.115mph/177.213km/h.

FIA WORLD TOURING CAR CHAMPIONSHIP, Moscow Raceway, Volokolamsk Oblast, Russia, 12 June. 15 and 17 laps of the 2.443-mile/3.931km circuit.
Round 11 (36.548 miles/58.818km).
1 Gabriele Tarquini, I (Lada Vesta WTCC), 29m 39.384s, 74.125mph/119.293km/h; **2** Nicky Catsburg, NL (Lada Vesta WTCC), +4.782s; **3** Yvan Muller, F (Citroën C-Elysée WTCC), +16.062s; **4** Hugo Valente, F (Lada Vesta WTCC), +23.683s; **5** José María López, RA (Citroën C-Elysée WTCC), +28.092s; **6** Tiago Monteiro, P (Honda Civic WTCC), +28.803s; **7** Rob Huff, GB (Honda Civic WTCC), +29.266s; **8** James Thompson, GB (Chevrolet RML Cruze TC1), +30.164s; **9** Mehdi Bennani, MA (Citroën C-Elysée WTCC), +35.037s; **10** Norbert Michelisz, H (Honda Civic WTCC), +43.985s.
Fastest race lap: Catsburg, 1m 57.084s, 75.103mph/120.867km/h.
Pole position: Monteiro.

Round 12 (41.433 miles/66.680km).
1 Nicky Catsburg, NL (Lada Vesta WTCC), 33m 00.149s, 75.491mph/121.491km/h; **2** Gabriele Tarquini, I (Lada Vesta WTCC), +1.011s; **3** Norbert Michelisz, H (Honda Civic WTCC), +13.681s; **4** Rob Huff, GB (Honda Civic WTCC), +20.120s; **5** Tiago Monteiro, P (Honda Civic WTCC), +25.497s; **6** James Thompson, GB (Chevrolet RML Cruze TC1), +29.838s; **7** Hugo Valente, F (Lada Vesta WTCC), +30.611s; **8** José María López, RA (Citroën C-Elysée WTCC), +36.168s; **9** Ferenc Ficza, H (Honda Civic WTCC), +37.289s; **10** Mehdi Bennani, MA (Citroën C-Elysée WTCC), +42.772s.
Fastest race lap: Ficza, 1m 53.843s, 77.241mph/124.308km/h.
Pole position: Catsburg, 1m 57.722s, 74.696mph/120.212km/h.

FIA WORLD TOURING CAR CHAMPIONSHIP, Circuito Internacional de Vila Real, Portugal, 26 June. 13 and 14 laps of the 2.973-mile/4.785km circuit.
Round 13 (38.634 miles/62.175km).
1 Tom Coronel, NL (Chevrolet RML Cruze TC1), 26m 11.089s, 88.567mph/142.536km/h; **2** Tom

Chilton, GB (Citroën C-Elysée WTCC), +0.597s; **3** Nicky Catsburg, NL (Lada Vesta WTCC), +2.626s; **4** Mehdi Bennani, MA (Citroën C-Elysée WTCC), +3.145s; **5** José María López, RA (Citroën C-Elysée WTCC), +3.626s; **6** Rob Huff, GB (Honda Civic WTCC), +4.332s; **7** Thed Björk, S (Volvo S60 WTCC), +5.155s; **8** Norbert Michelisz, H (Honda Civic WTCC), +5.452s; **9** Yvan Muller, F (Citroën C-Elysée WTCC), +7.411s; **10** Tiago Monteiro, P (Honda Civic WTCC), +8.054s.
Fastest race lap: López, 2m 00.432s, 88.877mph/143.035km/h.
Pole position: Coronel.

Round 14 (41.607 miles/66.960km).
1 Tiago Monteiro, P (Honda Civic WTCC), 27m 53.321s, 89.553mph/144.122km/h; **2** Yvan Muller, F (Citroën C-Elysée WTCC), +0.821s; **3** Norbert Michelisz, H (Honda Civic WTCC), +2.181s; **4** Rob Huff, GB (Honda Civic WTCC), +3.402s; **5** José María López, RA (Citroën C-Elysée WTCC), +16.164s; **6** Thed Björk, S (Volvo S60 WTCC), +17.374s; **7** Nicky Catsburg, NL (Lada Vesta WTCC), +17.904s; **8** Mehdi Bennani, MA (Citroën C-Elysée WTCC), +21.614s; **9** Hugo Valente, F (Lada Vesta WTCC), +23.054s; **10** Tom Chilton, GB (Citroën C-Elysée WTCC), +23.364s.
Fastest race lap: Huff, 1m 58.385s, 90.414mph/145.508km/h.
Pole position: Monteiro, 1m 56.633s, 91.772mph/147.694km/h.

FIA WORLD TOURING CAR CHAMPIONSHIP, Autódromo Termas de Río Hondo, Santiago del Estero, Argentina, 7 August. 13 and 14 laps of the 2.986-mile/4.806km circuit.
Round 15 (38.714 miles/62.304km).
1 Tom Chilton, GB (Citroën C-Elysée WTCC), 23m 08.487s, 100.653mph/161.985km/h; **2** Rob Huff, GB (Honda Civic WTCC), +0.792s; **3** Yvan Muller, F (Citroën C-Elysée WTCC), +1.384s; **4** Tiago Monteiro, P (Honda Civic WTCC), +2.471s; **5** José María López, RA (Citroën C-Elysée WTCC), +7.646s; **6** Norbert Michelisz, H (Honda Civic WTCC), +9.897s; **7** Tom Coronel, NL (Chevrolet RML Cruze TC1), +11.528s; **8** Mehdi Bennani, MA (Citroën C-Elysée WTCC), +13.150s; **9** James Thompson, GB (Chevrolet RML Cruze TC1), +15.333s; **10** John Filippi, F (Chevrolet RML Cruze TC1), +17.352s.
Fastest race lap: López, 1m 45.994s, 101.427mph/163.231km/h.
Pole position: Filippi.

Round 16 (41.700 miles/67.110km).
1 José María López, RA (Citroën C-Elysée WTCC), 24m 52.898s, 100.814mph/162.245km/h; **2** Tom Coronel, NL (Chevrolet RML Cruze TC1), +2.032s; **3** Rob Huff, GB (Honda Civic WTCC), +2.583s; **4** Tiago Monteiro, P (Honda Civic WTCC), +3.956s; **5** Yvan Muller, F (Citroën C-Elysée WTCC), +4.305s; **6** Esteban Guerrieri, RA (Chevrolet RML Cruze TC1), +8.740s; **7** Mehdi Bennani, MA (Citroën C-Elysée WTCC), +9.126s; **8** Norbert Michelisz, H (Honda Civic WTCC), +11.649s; **9** Tom Chilton, GB (Citroën C-Elysée WTCC), +12.659s; **10** John Filippi, F (Chevrolet RML Cruze TC1), +14.693s.
Fastest race lap: López, 1m 45.899s, 101.518mph/163.378km/h.
Pole position: López, 1m 43.044s, 104.331mph/167.904km/h.

FIA WORLD TOURING CAR CHAMPIONSHIP, Twin Ring Motegi, Motegi-machi, Haga-gun, Tochigi Prefecture, Japan, 4 September. 13 and 14 laps of the 2.983-mile/4.801km circuit.
Round 17 (38.782 miles/62.413km).
1 Norbert Michelisz, H (Honda Civic WTCC), 26m 07.443s, 89.071mph/143.346km/h; **2** Rob Huff, GB (Honda Civic WTCC), +1.358s; **3** Tiago Monteiro, P (Honda Civic WTCC), +2.173s; **4** José María López, RA (Citroën C-Elysée WTCC), +3.609s; **5** Yvan Muller, F (Citroën C-Elysée WTCC), +4.805s; **6** Thed Björk, S (Volvo S60 WTCC), +8.049s; **7** Nicky Catsburg, NL (Lada Vesta WTCC), +8.738s; **8** Tom Chilton, GB (Citroën C-Elysée WTCC), +9.385s; **9** Néstor Girolami, RA (Volvo S60 WTCC), +10.135s; **10** Gabriele Tarquini, I (Lada Vesta WTCC), +10.456s.
Fastest race lap: Björk, 1m 58.156s, 90.892mph/146.277km/h.
Pole position: Michelisz.

Round 18 (41.765 miles/67.214km).
1 Yvan Muller, F (Citroën C-Elysée WTCC), 28m 03.653s, 89.301mph/143.717km/h; **2** José María López, RA (Citroën C-Elysée WTCC), +1.045s; **3** Tiago Monteiro, P (Honda Civic WTCC), +2.561s; **4** Mehdi Bennani, MA (Citroën C-Elysée WTCC), +3.280s; **5** Néstor Girolami, RA (Volvo S60 WTCC), +5.204s; **6** Tom Chilton, GB (Citroën C-Elysée WTCC), +7.638s; **7** Thed Björk, S (Volvo S60 WTCC), +9.159s; **8** Norbert Michelisz, H (Honda Civic WTCC), +12.094s; **9** Rob Huff, GB (Honda Civic WTCC), +15.769s; **10** Gabriele Tarquini, I (Lada Vesta WTCC), +16.746s.
Fastest race lap: López, 1m 58.061s, 90.965mph/146.395km/h.
Pole position: López, 1m 55.602s, 92.900mph/149.509km/h.

FIA WORLD TOURING CAR CHAMPIONSHIP, Shanghai International Circuit, Shanghai, China, 25 September. 16 and 15 laps of the 2.860-mile/4.603km circuit.
Round 19 (45.763 miles/73.648km).
1 Thed Björk, S (Volvo S60 WTCC), 31m 58.340s, 85.879mph/138.209km/h; **2** Norbert Michelisz, H (Honda Civic WTCC), +0.361s; **3** Yvan Muller, F (Citroën C-Elysée WTCC), +0.528s; **4** José María López, RA (Citroën C-Elysée WTCC), +2.215s; **5** Nicky Catsburg, NL (Lada Vesta WTCC), +2.315s; **6** Hugo Valente, F (Lada Vesta WTCC), +6.290s; **7** Tom Coronel, NL (Chevrolet RML Cruze TC1), +6.911s; **8** Fredrik Ekblom, S (Volvo S60 WTCC), +12.151s; **9** Rob Huff, GB (Honda Civic WTCC), +13.494s; **10** Tiago Monteiro, P (Honda Civic WTCC), +16.586s.
Fastest race lap: Björk, 1m 52.578s, 91.462mph/147.193km/h.
Pole position: Filippi.

Round 20 (42.903 miles/69.045km).
1 José María López, RA (Citroën C-Elysée WTCC), 28m 18.258s, 90.945mph/146.362km/h; **2** Yvan Muller, F (Citroën C-Elysée WTCC), +11.037s; **3** Mehdi Bennani, MA (Citroën C-Elysée WTCC), +12.742s; **4** Nicky Catsburg, NL (Lada Vesta WTCC), +13.205s; **5** Gabriele Tarquini, I (Lada Vesta WTCC), +15.715s; **6** Fredrik Ekblom, S (Volvo S60 WTCC), +18.176s; **7** Thed Björk, S (Volvo S60 WTCC), +18.516s; **8** Tiago Monteiro, P (Honda Civic WTCC), +23.878s; **9** Tom Chilton, GB (Citroën C-Elysée WTCC), +24.700s; **10** Tom Coronel, NL (Chevrolet RML Cruze TC1), +26.509s.
Fastest race lap: López, 1m 52.224s, 91.750mph/147.658km/h.
Pole position: López, 1m 49.339s, 94.171mph/151.554km/h.

FIA WORLD TOURING CAR CHAMPIONSHIP, Losail International Circuit, Doha, Qatar, 25 November. 14 and 15 laps of the 3.343-mile/5.380km circuit.
Round 21 (46.802 miles/75.320km).
1 Gabriele Tarquini, I (Lada Vesta WTCC), 46m 16.258s, 60.688mph/97.668km/h; **2** Tom Chilton, GB (Citroën C-Elysée WTCC), +5.321s; **3** Rob Huff, GB (Honda Civic WTCC), +5.930s; **4** Yvan Muller, F (Citroën C-Elysée WTCC), +7.608s; **5** Norbert Michelisz, H (Honda Civic WTCC), +9.070s; **6** Thed Björk, S (Volvo S60 WTCC), +9.675s; **7** Robert Dahlgren, S (Volvo S60 WTCC), +10.255s; **8** Nicky Catsburg, NL (Lada Vesta WTCC), +10.871s; **9** José María López, RA (Citroën C-Elysée WTCC), +11.591s; **10** James Thompson, GB (Chevrolet RML Cruze TC1), +15.375s.
Fastest race lap: Tarquini, 2m 01.760s, 98.839mph/159.067km/h.
Pole position: Chilton.

Round 22 (50.145 miles/80.700km).
1 Mehdi Bennani, MA (Citroën C-Elysée WTCC), 32m 38.479s, 92.173mph/148.339km/h; **2** Thed Björk, S (Volvo S60 WTCC), +1.176s; **3** José María López, RA (Citroën C-Elysée WTCC), +4.815s; **4** Norbert Michelisz, H (Honda Civic WTCC), +10.575s; **5** Tiago Monteiro, P (Honda Civic WTCC), +11.827s; **6** Yvan Muller, F (Citroën C-Elysée WTCC), +12.390s; **7** Gabriele Tarquini, I (Lada Vesta WTCC), +14.994s; **8** Rob Huff, GB (Honda Civic WTCC), +17.037s; **9** Tom Coronel, NL (Chevrolet RML Cruze TC1), +18.379s; **10** James Thompson, GB (Chevrolet RML Cruze TC1), +20.819s.
Fastest race lap: Nicky Catsburg, NL (Lada Vesta WTCC), 2m 02.550s, 98.202mph/158.041km/h.
Pole position: Bennani, 2m 00.456s, 99.909mph/160.789km/h.

Final championship points
Drivers
1 José María López, RA, 381; **2** Yvan Muller, F, 257; **3** Tiago Monteiro, P, 214; **4** Norbert Michelisz, H, 212; **5** Mehdi Bennani, MA, 206; **6** Rob Huff, GB, 200; **7** Nicky Catsburg, NL, 175; **8** Tom Chilton, GB, 163; **9** Gabriele Tarquini, I, 147; **10** Thed Björk, S, 117; **11** Tom Coronel, NL, 111; **12** Hugo Valente, F, 78; **13** Fredrik Ekblom, S, 47; **14** James Thompson, GB, 26; **15** Néstor Girolami, RA, 12; **16** Grégoire Demoustier, F, 11; **17** John Filippi, F, 9; **18** Esteban Guerrieri, RA, 9; **19** Robert Dahlgren, S, 6; **20** René Münnich, D, 2; **21** Ferenc Ficza, H, 2; **22** Sabine Schmitz, D, 1.

Manufacturers
1 Citroën, 957; **2** Honda, 675; **3** Lada, 536; **4** Volvo, 321.

TCR International Series

TCR INTERNATIONAL SERIES, Bahrain International Circuit, Sakhir, Bahrain, 2/3 April. 2 x 10 laps of the 3.363-mile/5.412km circuit.
Round 1 (33.476 miles/53.874km).
1 Pepe Oriola, E (SEAT León TCR), 22m 25.883s, 89.946mph/144.754km/h; **2** Gianni Morbidelli, I (Honda Civic TCR), +2.372s; **3** James Nash, GB (SEAT León TCR), +3.219s; **4** Sergei Afanasiev, RUS (SEAT León TCR), +4.995s; **5** Aku Pellinen, FIN (Honda Civic TCR), +9.902s; **6** Dušan Borkovic, SRB (SEAT León TCR), +9.919s; **7** Stefano Comini, CH (Volkswagen Golf Gti TCR), +20.087s; **8** Mat'o Homola, SK (SEAT León TCR), +23.319s; **9** Davit Kajaia, GE (Volkswagen Golf Gti TCR), +23.364s; **10** Mikhail Grachev, RUS (Volkswagen Golf Gti TCR), +24.555s.
Fastest race lap: Morbidelli, 2m 12.602s, 91.298mph/146.929km/h.
Pole position: Afanasiev, 2m 12.541s, 91.340mph/146.997km/h.

Round 2 (33.476 miles/53.874km).
1 Pepe Oriola, E (SEAT León TCR), 22m 36.458s, 89.245mph/143.626km/h; **2** James Nash, GB (SEAT León TCR), +1.572s; **3** Dušan Borkovic, SRB (SEAT León TCR), +6.463s; **4** Davit Kajaia, GE (Volkswagen Golf Gti TCR), +10.265s; **5** Sergei Afanasiev, RUS (SEAT León TCR), +15.063s; **6** Jordi Oriola, E (Opel Astra OPC), +23.461s; **7** Gianni Morbidelli, I (Honda Civic TCR), +23.617s; **8** Luigi Ferrara, I (Subaru STi TCR), +24.851s; **9** Salman Al-Khalifa, BRN (SEAT Leon Cup Racer), +31.718s; **10** Aku Pellinen, FIN (Honda Civic TCR), +34.372s *.
** includes 30s penalty for jump start.*
Fastest race lap: Oriola, 2m 13.511s, 90.676mph/145.929km/h.
Pole position: Kajaia.

TCR INTERNATIONAL SERIES, Autódromo Fernanda Pires da Silva, Estoril, Portugal, 24 April. 2 x 15 laps of the 2.599-mile/4.182km circuit.
Round 3 (38.979 miles/62.730km).
1 Gianni Morbidelli, I (Honda Civic TCR), 27m 53.287s, 83.860mph/134.960km/h; **2** Jean-Karl Vernay, F (Volkswagen Golf Gti TCR), +1.026s; **3** Stefano Comini, CH (Volkswagen Golf Gti TCR), +4.113s; **4** Mat'o Homola, SK (SEAT León TCR), +5.463s; **5** Sergei Afanasiev, RUS (SEAT León TCR), +5.841s; **6** James Nash, GB (SEAT León TCR), +7.513s; **7** Aku Pellinen, FIN (Honda Civic TCR), +14.651s; **8** Pepe Oriola, E (SEAT León TCR), +20.515s; **9** Loris Hezemans, B (SEAT León TCR), +20.716s; **10** Francisco Mora, P (SEAT Leon Cup Racer), +21.078s.
Fastest race lap: Homola, 1m 49.276s, 85.607mph/137.772km/h.
Pole position: Homola, 1m 48.518s, 86.205mph/138.734km/h.

Round 4 (38.979 miles/62.730km).
1 James Nash, GB (SEAT León TCR), 27m 46.901s, 84.181mph/135.477km/h; **2** Stefano Comini, CH (Volkswagen Golf Gti TCR), +2.252s; **3** Gianni Morbidelli, I (Honda Civic TCR), +7.241s; **4** Sergei Afanasiev, RUS (SEAT León TCR), +9.592s; **5** Jean-Karl Vernay, F (Volkswagen Golf Gti TCR), +11.622s; **6** Aku Pellinen, FIN (Honda Civic TCR), +16.759s; **7** Davit Kajaia, GE (Volkswagen Golf Gti TCR), +19.190s; **8** Mat'o Homola, SK (SEAT León TCR), +20.927s; **9** Francisco Mora, P (SEAT Leon Cup Racer), +21.259s; **10** Pepe Oriola, E (SEAT León TCR), +32.535s.
Fastest race lap: Morbidelli, 1m 49.095s, 85.749mph/138.000km/h.
Pole position: Hezemans.

TCR INTERNATIONAL SERIES, Circuit de Spa-Francorchamps, Stavelot, Belgium, 6/7 May. 2 x 9 laps of the 4.352-mile/7.004km circuit.
Round 5 (39.168 miles/63.035km).
1 Aku Pellinen, FIN (Honda Civic TCR), 23m 19.800s, 100.732mph/162.113km/h; **2** Pepe Oriola, E (SEAT León TCR), +0.376s; **3** Dušan Borkovic, SRB (SEAT León TCR), +1.294s; **4** Mat'o Homola, SK (SEAT León TCR), +5.476s; **5** Gianni Morbidelli, I (Honda Civic TCR), +6.724s; **6** Kevin Gleason, USA (Honda Civic TCR), +7.208s; **7** Davit Kajaia, GE (Volkswagen Golf Gti TCR), +9.669s; **8** James Nash, GB (SEAT León TCR), +16.593s; **9** Sergei Afanasiev, RUS (SEAT León TCR), +17.076s; **10** Antti Buri, FIN (Volkswagen Golf Gti TCR), +17.734s.
Fastest race lap: Jean-Karl Vernay, F (Volkswagen Golf Gti TCR), 2m 33.702s, 101.932mph/164.044km/h.
Pole position: Borkovic, 2m 33.065s, 102.357mph/164.727km/h.

Round 6 (39.168 miles/63.035km).
1 Jean-Karl Vernay, F (Volkswagen Golf Gti TCR), 23m 15.816s, 101.020mph/162.576km/h; **2** Stefano Comini, CH (Volkswagen Golf Gti TCR), +2.262s; **3** Antti Buri, FIN (Volkswagen Golf Gti TCR), +4.584s; **4** Mat'o Homola, SK (SEAT León TCR), +6.791s; **5** Aku Pellinen, FIN (Honda Civic TCR), +7.728s; **6** James Nash, GB (SEAT León TCR), +11.555s; **7** Pepe Oriola, E (SEAT León TCR), +12.326s; **8** Kevin Gleason, USA (Honda Civic TCR), +13.032s; **9** Sergei Afanasiev, RUS (SEAT León TCR), +13.356s; **10** Pierre-Yves Corthals, B (SEAT Leon Cup Racer), +18.534s.
Fastest race lap: Vernay, 2m 33.945s, 101.771mph/163.786km/h.
Pole position: Buri.

TCR INTERNATIONAL SERIES, Autodromo Enzo e Dino Ferrari, Imola, Italy, 22 May. 14 and 13 laps of the 3.050-mile/4.909km circuit.
Round 7 (42.704 miles/68.726km).
1 Stefano Comini, CH (Volkswagen Golf Gti TCR), 28m 11.944s, 90.863mph/146.230km/h; **2** Pepe Oriola, E (SEAT León TCR), +2.235s; **3** Davit Kajaia, GE (Volkswagen Golf Gti TCR), +3.328s; **4** Sergei Afanasiev, RUS (SEAT León TCR), +10.570s; **5** Mat'o Homola, SK (SEAT León TCR), +15.423s; **6** Jordi Gené, E (Volkswagen Golf Gti TCR), +17.268s; **7** Attila Tassi, H (SEAT León TCR), +18.700s; **8** Mikhail Grachev, RUS (Honda Civic TCR), +21.347s; **9** Carlotta Fedeli, I (SEAT Leon Cup Racer), +29.519s; **10** Alessandra Neri, I (SEAT Leon Cup Racer), +48.726s.
Fastest race lap: Oriola, 1m 54.575s, 95.842mph/154.243km/h.
Pole position: Gianni Morbidelli, I (Honda Civic TCR), 1m 53.228s, 96.982mph/156.078km/h.

Round 8 (39.654 miles/63.817km).
1 Mikhail Grachev, RUS (Honda Civic TCR), 25m 07.401s, 94.702mph/152.408km/h; **2** Mat'o Homola, SK (SEAT León TCR), +1.795s; **3** Stefano Comini, CH (Volkswagen Golf Gti TCR), +2.438s; **4** Jean-Karl Vernay, F (Volkswagen Golf Gti TCR), +2.946s; **5** Pepe Oriola, E (SEAT León TCR), +3.807s; **6** Jordi Gené, E (Volkswagen Golf Gti TCR), +8.698s; **7** Attila Tassi, H (SEAT León TCR), +11.521s; **8** Davit Kajaia, GE (Volkswagen Golf Gti TCR), +11.789s; **9** Jordi Oriola, E (Honda Civic TCR), +12.807s; **10** Alain Menu, CH (Honda Civic TCR), +13.380s.
Fastest race lap: Oriola, 1m 54.582s, 95.836mph/154.233km/h.
Pole position: Tassi.

TCR INTERNATIONAL SERIES, Salzburgring, Salzburg, Austria, 5 June. 2 x 17 laps of the 2.635-mile/4.240km circuit.
Round 9 (44.788 miles/72.080km).
1 Mikhail Grachev, RUS (Honda Civic TCR), 27m 40.614s, 97.095mph/156.260km/h; **2** James Nash, GB (SEAT León TCR), +1.420s; **3** Mat'o Homola, SK (SEAT León TCR), +1.627s; **4** Gianni Morbidelli, I (Honda Civic TCR), +2.304s; **5** Jean-Karl Vernay, F (Volkswagen Golf Gti TCR), +8.244s; **6** Attila Tassi, H (SEAT León TCR), +10.746s; **7** Davit Kajaia, GE (Volkswagen Golf Gti TCR), +11.305s; **8** Stefano Comini, CH (Volkswagen Golf Gti TCR), +12.387s; **9** Florian Janits, A (Volkswagen Golf Gti TCR), +12.864s; **10** Michela Cerruti, I (Alfa Romeo Giulietta TCR), +28.268s.
Fastest race lap: Nash, 1m 26.787s, 109.286mph/175.878km/h.
Pole position: Vernay, 1m 39.079s, 95.727mph/154.058km/h.

Round 10 (44.788 miles/72.080km).
1 Jean-Karl Vernay, F (Volkswagen Golf Gti TCR), 30m 51.124s, 87.102mph/140.178km/h; **2** Sergei Afanasiev, RUS (SEAT León TCR), +0.955s; **3** Stefano Comini, CH (Volkswagen Golf Gti TCR), +2.065s; **4** James Nash, GB (SEAT León TCR), +5.698s; **5** Mat'o Homola, SK (SEAT León TCR), +7.889s; **6** Gianni Morbidelli, I (Honda Civic TCR), +8.297s; **7** Jordi Oriola, E (Honda Civic TCR), +9.392s; **8** Attila Tassi, H (SEAT León TCR), +16.390s; **9** Mikhail Grachev, RUS (Honda Civic TCR), +16.846s; **10** Florian Janits, A (Volkswagen Golf Gti TCR), +31.036s.
Fastest race lap: Vernay, 1m 36.507s, 98.278mph/158.164km/h.
Pole position: Tassi.

TCR INTERNATIONAL SERIES, Motorsport Arena Oschersleben, Germany, 19 June. 19 and 17 laps of the 2.297-mile/3.696km circuit.
Round 11 (43.635 miles/70.224km).
1 Mat'o Homola, SK (SEAT León TCR), 34m 31.336s, 75.838 mph/122.049 km/h; **2** Dušan Borkovic, SRB (SEAT León TCR), +1.438s; **3** James Nash, GB (SEAT León TCR), +2.383s; **4** Sergei Afanasiev, RUS (SEAT León TCR), +3.080s; **5** Antti Buri, FIN (SEAT Leon Cup Racer), +3.741s; **6** Jean-Karl Vernay, F (Volkswagen Golf Gti TCR), +5.031s; **7** Gianni Morbidelli, I (Honda Civic TCR), +5.533s; **8** Davit Kajaia, GE (Volkswagen Golf Gti TCR), +11.085s; **9** Niklas Mackschin, D (Volkswagen Golf Gti TCR), +11.562s; **10** Pepe Oriola, E (SEAT León TCR), +26.593s.
Fastest race lap: Homola, 1m 36.468s, 85.704mph/137.927km/h.
Pole position: Borkovic, 1m 34.872s, 87.146mph/140.247km/h.

Round 12 (39.042 miles/62.832km).
1 Pepe Oriola, E (SEAT León TCR), 27m 32.124s, 85.073mph/136.911km/h; **2** Dušan Borkovic, SRB (SEAT León TCR), +2.164s; **3** James Nash, GB (SEAT León TCR), +5.928s; **4** Sergei Afanasiev, RUS (SEAT León TCR), +7.881s; **5** Mat'o Homola, SK (SEAT León TCR), +12.375s; **6** Stefano Comini, CH (Volkswagen Golf Gti TCR), +15.413s; **7** Attila Tassi, H (SEAT León TCR), +17.703s; **8** Niklas Mackschin, D (Volkswagen Golf Gti TCR), +17.954s; **9** Michela Cerruti, I (Alfa Romeo Giulietta TCR), +21.470s; **10** Gianni Morbidelli, I (Honda Civic TCR), +23.274s.
Fastest race lap: Borkovic, 1m 35.577s, 86.503mph/139.213km/h.
Pole position: Kajaia.

TCR INTERNATIONAL SERIES, Sochi Autodrom, Sochi, Russia, 3 July. 2 x 11 laps of the 3.634-mile/5.848km circuit.
Round 13 (39.972 miles/64.328km).
1 Stefano Comini, CH (Volkswagen Golf Gti TCR), 26m 08.805s, 91.724mph/147.616km/h; **2** Pepe Oriola, E (SEAT León TCR), +1.915s; **3** Gianni Morbidelli, I (Honda Civic TCR), +8.078s; **4** Mikhail Grachev, RUS (Honda Civic TCR), +16.704s; **5** Jean-Karl Vernay, F (Volkswagen Golf Gti TCR), +17.718s; **6** Petr Fulín, CZ (Alfa Romeo Giulietta TCR), +20.396s; **7** Davit Kajaia, GE (Volkswagen Golf Gti TCR), +21.173s; **8** James Nash, GB (SEAT León TCR), +22.867s *; **9** Mat'o Homola, SK (SEAT León TCR), +23.080s; **10** Attila Tassi, H (SEAT León TCR), +23.995s.
* includes 10s penalty for causing an accident.
Fastest race lap: Comini, 2m 21.315s, 92.570mph/148.977km/h.
Pole position: Comini, 2m 21.130s, 92.691mph/149.173km/h.

Round 14 (39.972 miles/64.328km).
1 Mikhail Grachev, RUS (Honda Civic TCR), 26m 14.025s, 91.420mph/147.126km/h; **2** Jean-Karl Vernay, F (Volkswagen Golf Gti TCR), +1.254s; **3** Attila Tassi, H (SEAT León TCR), +5.954s; **4** James Nash, GB (SEAT León TCR), +6.589s; **5** Stefano Comini, CH (Volkswagen Golf Gti TCR), +7.962s; **6** Dušan Borkovic, SRB (SEAT León TCR), +8.253s; **7** Sergei Afanasiev, RUS (SEAT León TCR), +13.977s; **8** Petr Fulín, CZ (Alfa Romeo Giulietta TCR), +16.128s; **9** Mat'o Ho-

mola, SK (SEAT León TCR), +20.603s *; **10** Vladimir Sheshenin, RUS (Volkswagen Golf Gti TCR), +24.691s.
** includes 5s penalty for incorrect grid position.*
Fastest race lap: Comini, 2m 21.213s, 92.637mph/149.085km/h.
Pole position: Tassi.

TCR INTERNATIONAL SERIES, Buriram International Circuit, Buriram, Thailand, 28 August. 14 and 16 laps of the 2.830-mile/4.554km circuit.
Round 15 (39.616 miles/63.756km).
1 Pepe Oriola, E (SEAT León TCR), 24m 32.596s, 96.848mph/155.861km/h; **2** James Nash, GB (SEAT León TCR), +1.280s; **3** Gianni Morbidelli, I (Honda Civic TCR), +2.410s; **4** Stefano Comini, CH (Volkswagen Golf Gti TCR), +6.633s; **5** Jean-Karl Vernay, F (Volkswagen Golf Gti TCR), +7.467s; **6** Kusiri Kantadhee, T (Honda Civic TCR), +11.551s; **7** Dušan Borkovic, SRB (SEAT León TCR), +14.115s; **8** Attila Tassi, H (SEAT León TCR), +20.302s; **9** Sergei Afanasiev, RUS (SEAT León TCR), +22.446s; **10** Davit Kajaia, GE (Volkswagen Golf Gti TCR), +23.892s.
Fastest race lap: Morbidelli, 1m 44.528s, 97.457mph/156.842km/h.
Pole position: Oriola, 1m 43.634s, 98.297mph/158.195km/h.

Round 16 (45.276 miles/72.864km).
1 James Nash, GB (SEAT León TCR), 30m 31.095s, 89.013mph/143.253km/h; **2** Mikhail Grachev, RUS (Honda Civic TCR), +7.272s; **3** Dušan Borkovic, SRB (SEAT León TCR), +11.332s; **4** Stefano Comini, CH (Volkswagen Golf Gti TCR), +12.122s; **5** Davit Kajaia, GE (Volkswagen Golf Gti TCR), +15.181s; **6** Attila Tassi, H (SEAT León TCR), +18.516s; **7** Sergei Afanasiev, RUS (SEAT León TCR), +18.753s; **8** Jean-Karl Vernay, F (Volkswagen Golf Gti TCR), +19.870s; **9** Kusiri Kantadhee, T (Honda Civic TCR), +20.208s; **10** Mat'o Homola, SK (SEAT León TCR), +20.538s.
Fastest race lap: Nash, 1m 44.251s, 97.716mph/157.258km/h.
Pole position: Grachev.

TCR INTERNATIONAL SERIES, Marina Bay Street Circuit, Singapore, 17/18 September. 10 and 9 laps of the 3.147-mile/5.065km circuit.
Round 17 (31.387 miles/50.513km).
1 Jean-Karl Vernay, F (Volkswagen Golf Gti TCR), 24m 33.044s, 76.914mph/123.781km/h; **2** Stefano Comini, CH (Volkswagen Golf Gti TCR), +3.132s; **3** Pepe Oriola, E (SEAT León TCR), +7.101s; **4** Mat'o Homola, SK (SEAT León TCR), +9.688s; **5** James Nash, GB (SEAT León TCR), +11.570s; **6** Sergei Afanasiev, RUS (SEAT León TCR), +12.589s; **7** Dušan Borkovic, SRB (SEAT León TCR), +13.489s; **8** Kevin Gleason, USA (Honda Civic TCR), +15.735s; **9** Attila Tassi, H (SEAT León TCR), +17.835s; **10** Gianni Morbidelli, I (Honda Civic TCR), +18.264s.
Fastest race lap: Vernay, 2m 25.954s, 77.627mph/124.929km/h.
Pole position: Vernay, 2m 24.511s, 78.402mph/126.177km/h.

Round 18 (28.240 miles/45.448km).
1 Mikhail Grachev, RUS (Honda Civic TCR), 25m 55.217s, 65.564mph/105.516km/h; **2** Dušan Borkovic, SRB (SEAT León TCR), +0.456s; **3** James Nash, GB (SEAT León TCR), +0.751s; **4** Stefano Comini, CH (Volkswagen Golf Gti TCR), +0.903s; **5** Mat'o Homola, SK (SEAT León TCR), +1.423s; **6** Jean-Karl Vernay, F (Volkswagen Golf Gti TCR), +1.681s; **7** Gianni Morbidelli, I (Honda Civic TCR), +2.423s; **8** Davit Kajaia, GE (Volkswagen Golf Gti TCR), +3.070s; **9** Petr Fulín, CZ (Alfa Romeo Giulietta TCR), +3.567s; **10** Kevin Gleason, USA (Honda Civic TCR), +3.924s.
Fastest race lap: Grachev, 2m 27.637s, 76.742mph/123.505km/h.
Pole position: Grachev.

TCR INTERNATIONAL SERIES, Sepang International Circuit, Jalan Pekeliling, Kuala Lumpur, Malaysia, 30 September/1 October. 11 and 10 laps of the 3.444-mile/5.543km circuit.
Round 19 (37.887 miles/60.973km).
1 Roberto Colciago, I (Honda Civic TCR), 26m 46.089s, 84.922mph/136.669km/h; **2** Stefano Comini, CH (Volkswagen Golf Gti TCR), +0.176s; **3** James Nash, GB (SEAT León TCR), +4.341s; **4** Pepe Oriola, E (SEAT León TCR), +5.111s; **5** Jean-Karl Vernay, F (Volkswagen Golf Gti TCR), +6.392s; **6** Dušan Borkovic, SRB (SEAT León TCR), +7.445s; **7** Attila Tassi, H (SEAT León TCR), +8.085s; **8** Kevin Gleason, USA (Honda Civic TCR), +8.558s; **9** Sergei Afanasiev, RUS (SEAT León TCR), +10.570s; **10** Mat'o Homola, SK (SEAT León TCR), +10.972s.
Fastest race lap: Comini, 2m 17.268s, 90.329mph/145.371km/h.
Pole position: Colciago, 2m 15.021s, 91.832mph/147.790km/h.

Round 20 (34.443 miles/55.430km).
1 Kevin Gleason, USA (Honda Civic TCR), 24m 37.307s, 83.932mph/135.075km/h; **2** James Nash, GB (SEAT León TCR), +1.735s; **3** Gianni Morbidelli, I (Honda Civic TCR), +2.421s; **4** Dušan Borkovic, SRB (SEAT León TCR), +7.961s; **5** Jean-Karl Vernay, F (Volkswagen Golf Gti TCR), +9.853s; **6** Loris Hezemans, NL (SEAT Leon Cup Racer), +10.241s; **7** Sergei Afanasiev, RUS (SEAT León TCR), +10.850s; **8** Andy Yan, HK (Volkswagen Golf Gti TCR), +10.860s; **9** Attila Tassi, H (SEAT León TCR), +11.125s; **10** Davit Kajaia, GE (Volkswagen Golf Gti TCR), +11.800s.
Fastest race lap: Stefano Comini, CH (Volkswagen Golf Gti TCR), 2m 17.196s, 90.376mph/145.447km/h.
Pole position: Sritrai.

TCR INTERNATIONAL SERIES, Circuito da Guia, Macau, 20 November. 5 and 7 laps of the 3.803-mile/6.120km circuit.
Round 21 (19.014 miles/30.600km).
1 Stefano Comini, CH (Volkswagen Golf Gti TCR), 37m 08.856s, 30.710mph/49.424km/h; **2** Jean-Karl Vernay, F (Volkswagen Golf Gti TCR), +1.040s; **3** Tiago Monteiro, P (Honda Civic TCR), +1.467s; **4** Dušan Borkovic, SRB (SEAT León TCR), +1.844s; **5** Pepe Oriola, E (SEAT León TCR), +2.192s; **6** Tin Sritrai, T (Honda Civic TCR), +3.253s; **7** Andrea Belicchi, I (Alfa Romeo Giulietta TCR), +3.933s; **8** Rafaël Galiana, F (SEAT León TCR), +14.443s; **9** Mikhail Grachev, RUS (Honda Civic TCR), +15.238s; **10** Josh Files, GB (Honda Civic TCR), +17.230s.
Fastest race lap: Davit Kajaia, GE (Volkswagen Golf Gti TCR), 2m 59.237s, 76.379mph/122.921km/h.
Pole position: Vernay, 3m 00.602s, 75.802mph/121.992km/h.

Round 22 (26.620 miles/42.840km).
1 Tiago Monteiro, P (Honda Civic TCR), 45m 38.635s, 34.992mph/56.314km/h; **2** Jean-Karl Vernay, F (Volkswagen Golf Gti TCR), +0.926s; **3** Pepe Oriola, E (SEAT León TCR), +1.441s; **4** Stefano Comini, CH (Volkswagen Golf Gti TCR), +2.594s; **5** Dušan Borkovic, SRB (SEAT León TCR), +3.077s; **6** Josh Files, GB (Honda Civic TCR), +3.499s; **7** Mikhail Grachev, RUS (Honda Civic TCR), +9.742s; **8** James Nash, GB (SEAT León TCR), +9.965s; **9** Andrea Belicchi, I (Alfa Romeo Giulietta TCR), +10.473s; **10** Andy Yan, HK (Volkswagen Golf Gti TCR), +11.179s.
Fastest race lap: Oriola, 2m 35.494s, 88.042mph/141.690km/h.
Pole position: Comini.

Final championship points
Drivers
1 Stefano Comini, CH, 267.5; **2** James Nash, GB, 264; **3** Jean-Karl Vernay, F, 246; **4** Pepe Oriola, E, 241.5; **5** Mat'o Homola, SK, 175; **6** Gianni Morbidelli, I, 174; **7** Dušan Borkovic, SRB, 173; **8** Mikhail Grachev, RUS, 145; **9** Sergei Afanasiev, RUS, 141; **10** Davit Kajaia, GE, 80; **11** Attila Tassi, H, 68; **12** Aku Pellinen, FIN, 63; **13** Kevin Gleason, USA, 46; **14** Roberto Colciago, I, 30; **15** Antti Buri, FIN, 30; **16** Tiago Monteiro, P, 23; **17** Jordi Oriola, E, 17; **18** Jordi Gené, E, 16; **19** Petr Fulín, CZ, 15; **20** Kusiri Kantadhee, T, 10.

Teams
1 Team Craft-Bamboo LUKOIL, 594.5; **2** Leopard Racing, 521.5; **3** West Coast Racing, 466; **4** B3 Racing Team Hungary, 416; **5** Liqui Moly Team Engstler, 129.5; **6** Target Competition, 66.5; **7** Mulsanne Racing, 27; **8** LMS Racing, 14; **9** Eakie BBR Kaiten, 10; **10** Baporo Motorsport, 8.

German Touring Car Championship (DTM)

GERMAN TOURING CAR CHAMPIONSHIP (DTM), Hockenheimring Grand Prix Circuit, Heidelberg, Germany, 7/8 May. Round 1. 25 and 37 laps of the 2.842-mile/4.574km circuit.
Race 1 (71.054 miles/114.350km).
1 Edoardo Mortara, I (Audi RS **5** DTM), 42m 11.606s, 101.040mph/162.608km/h; **2** Robert Wickens, CDN (Mercedes C 63 DTM), +1.657s; **3** Nico Müller, CH (Audi RS **5** DTM), +4.454s; **4** Paul Di Resta, GB (Mercedes C 63 DTM), +8.818s; **5** Christian Vietoris, D (Mercedes C 63 DTM), +10.192s; **6** Bruno Spengler, CDN (BMW M4 DTM), +20.097s; **7** António Félix da Costa, P (BMW M4 DTM), +35.882s *; **8** Maxime Martin, B (BMW M4 DTM), +41.360s; **9** Mattias Ekström, S (Audi RS **5** DTM), +46.455s; **10** Miguel Molina, E (Audi RS **5** DTM), +47.198s.
** includes 5s penalty.*
Fastest race lap: Wickens, 1m 35.465s, 107.178mph/172.486km/h.
Pole position: Müller, 1m 33.876s, 108.992mph/175.406km/h.

Race 2 (105.160 miles/169.238km).
1 Paul Di Resta, GB (Mercedes C 63 DTM), 1h 01m 42.654s, 102.244mph/164.546km/h; **2** Augusto Farfus, BR (BMW M4 DTM), +13.905s; **3** Maxime Martin, B (BMW M4 DTM), +14.493s; **4** Gary Paffett, GB (Mercedes C 63 DTM), +15.055s; **5** Robert Wickens, CDN (Mercedes C 63 DTM), +19.377s; **6** Tom Blomqvist, GB (BMW M4 DTM), +21.690s; **7** Nico Müller, CH (Audi RS **5** DTM), +22.220s; **8** Marco Wittmann, D (BMW M4 DTM), +23.790s; **9** Martin Tomczyk, D (BMW M4 DTM), +24.454s; **10** Mike Rockenfeller, D (Audi RS **5** DTM), +31.303s.
Disqualified: Timo Glock (originally finished 2nd).
Fastest race lap: Di Resta, 1m 35.335s, 107.324mph/172.721km/h.
Pole position: Di Resta, 1m 34.060s, 108.779mph/175.063km/h.

GERMAN TOURING CAR CHAMPIONSHIP (DTM), Red Bull Ring, Spielberg, Austria, 21/22 May. Round 2. 30 and 42 laps of the 2.688-mile/4.326km circuit.
Race 1 (80.642 miles/129.780km).
1 Marco Wittmann, D (BMW M4 DTM), 42m 10.795s, 114.711mph/184.609km/h; **2** Tom Blomqvist, GB (BMW M4 DTM), +0.726s; **3** Edoardo Mortara, I (Audi RS **5** DTM), +1.251s; **4** Timo Glock, D (BMW M4 DTM), +5.566s; **5** Martin Tomczyk, D (BMW M4 DTM), +6.222s; **6** Maxime Martin, B (BMW M4 DTM), +10.712s; **7** Paul Di Resta, GB (Mercedes C 63 DTM), +12.182s; **8** Adrien Tambay, F (Audi RS **5** DTM), +12.736s; **9** Augusto Farfus, BR (BMW M4 DTM), +15.146s; **10** Nico Müller, CH (Audi RS **5** DTM), +15.750s.
Fastest race lap: Mattias Ekström, S (Audi RS **5** DTM), 1m 23.442s, 115.973mph/186.640km/h.
Pole position: Wittmann, 1m 22.795s, 116.879mph/188.098km/h.

Race 2 (112.898 miles/181.692km).
1 Timo Glock, D (BMW M4 DTM), 1h 01m 30.006s, 110.144mph/177.260km/h; **2** Mattias Ekström, S (Audi RS **5** DTM), +2.215s; **3** Jamie Green, GB (Audi RS **5** DTM), +6.014s; **4** Augusto Farfus, BR (BMW M4 DTM), +10.399s; **5** Maxime Martin, B (BMW M4 DTM), +11.012s; **6** Tom Blomqvist, GB (BMW M4 DTM), +11.643s; **7** Marco Wittmann, D (BMW M4 DTM), +12.242s; **8** Mike Rockenfeller, D (Audi RS **5** DTM), +14.301s; **9** Bruno Spengler, CDN (BMW M4 DTM), +16.607s; **10** Timo Scheider, D (Audi RS **5** DTM), +20.127s.
Fastest race lap: Robert Wickens, CDN (Mercedes C 63 DTM), 1m 23.446s, 115.967mph/186.631km/h.
Pole position: Green, 1m 22.680s, 117.041mph/188.360km/h.

GERMAN TOURING CAR CHAMPIONSHIP (DTM), EuroSpeedway Lausitz, Klettwitz, Dresden, Germany, 4/5 June. Round 3. 32 and 46 laps of the 2.161-mile/3.478km circuit.
Race 1 (69.156 miles/111.296km).
1 Miguel Molina, E (Audi RS **5** DTM), 42m 04.244s, 98.628mph/158.727km/h; **2** Jamie Green, GB (Audi RS **5** DTM), +2.034s; **3** Robert Wickens, CDN (Mercedes C 63 DTM), +4.175s; **4** Marco Wittmann, D (BMW M4 DTM), +8.724s; **5** Christian Vietoris, D (Mercedes C 63 DTM), +9.759s; **6** Mattias Ekström, S (Audi RS **5** DTM), +10.398s; **7** Lucas Auer, A (Mercedes C 63 DTM), +10.794s; **8** Edoardo Mortara, I (Audi RS **5** DTM), +14.437s; **9** Maxime Martin, B (BMW M4 DTM), +17.808s; **10** Nico Müller, CH (Audi RS **5** DTM), +18.414s.
Fastest race lap: Molina, 1m 18.149s, 99.554mph/160.217km/h.
Pole position: Molina, 1m 16.619s, 101.542mph/163.416km/h.

Race 2 (99.412 miles/159.988km).
1 Lucas Auer, A (Mercedes C 63 DTM), 1h 02m 11.261s, 95.919mph/154.360km/h; **2** Mattias Ekström, S (Audi RS **5** DTM), +3.763s; **3** Robert Wickens, CDN (Mercedes C 63 DTM), +6.386s; **4** Jamie Green, GB (Audi RS **5** DTM), +6.770s; **5** Gary Paffett, GB (Mercedes C 63 DTM), +12.292s; **6** Marco Wittmann, D (BMW M4 DTM), +16.839s; **7** Christian Vietoris, D (Mercedes C 63 DTM), +17.355s; **8** Nico Müller, CH (Audi RS **5** DTM), +18.099s; **9** Bruno Spengler, CDN (BMW M4 DTM), +21.872s; **10** Timo Glock, D (BMW M4 DTM), +24.865s.
Fastest race lap: Green, 1m 17.840s, 99.949mph/160.853km/h.
Pole position: Auer, 1m 16.861s, 101.223mph/162.902km/h.

GERMAN TOURING CAR CHAMPIONSHIP (DTM), Norisring, Nürnberg (Nuremberg), Germany, 25/26 June. Round 4. 49 and 72 laps of the 1.429-mile/2.300km circuit.
Race 1 (70.029 miles/112.700km).
1 Edoardo Mortara, I (Audi RS **5** DTM), 41m 09.983s, 102.067mph/164.260km/h; **2** Jamie Green, GB (Audi RS **5** DTM), +0.531s; **3** Paul Di Resta, GB (Mercedes C 63 DTM), +0.903s; **4** Marco Wittmann, D (BMW M4 DTM), +4.135s; **5** Bruno Spengler, CDN (BMW M4 DTM), +6.731s; **6** Maxime Martin, B (BMW M4 DTM), +9.951s; **7** Adrien Tambay, F (Audi RS **5** DTM), +10.875s; **8** Maximilian Götz, D (Mercedes C 63 DTM), +13.501s; **9** António Félix da Costa, P (BMW M4 DTM), +15.337s; **10** Christian Vietoris, D (Mercedes C 63 DTM), +15.477s.
Fastest race lap: Mortara, 48.746s, 105.546mph/169.860km/h.
Pole position: Vietoris, 48.144s, 106.866mph/171.984km/h.

Race 2 (102.899 miles/165.600km).
1 Nico Müller, CH (Audi RS **5** DTM), 1h 01m 03.139s, 101.125mph/162.746km/h; **2** Tom Blomqvist, GB (BMW M4 DTM), +0.670s; **3** Maxime Martin, B (BMW M4 DTM), +1.543s; **4** Paul Di Resta, GB (Mercedes C 63 DTM), +4.701s; **5** Lucas Auer, A (Mercedes C 63 DTM), +4.950s; **6** Marco Wittmann, D (BMW M4 DTM), +5.197s; **7** Bruno Spengler, CDN (BMW M4 DTM), +5.907s; **8** Edoardo Mortara, I (Audi RS **5** DTM), +6.228s; **9** Timo Glock, D (BMW M4 DTM), +6.981s; **10** Martin Tomczyk, D (BMW M4 DTM), +7.224s.
Fastest race lap: Blomqvist, 48.328s, 106.459mph/171.329km/h.
Pole position: Blomqvist, 47.820s, 107.590mph/173.149km/h.

GERMAN TOURING CAR CHAMPIONSHIP (DTM), Circuit Park Zandvoort, Netherlands, 16/17 July. Round 5. 25 and 39 laps of the 2.676-mile/4.307km circuit.
Race 1 (66.906 miles/107.675km).
1 Robert Wickens, CDN (Mercedes C 63 DTM), 41m 55.441s, 95.753mph/154.100km/h; **2** Marco Wittmann, D (BMW M4 DTM), +7.217s; **3** Christian Vietoris, D (Mercedes C 63 DTM), +8.987s; **4** Gary Paffett, GB (Mercedes C 63 DTM), +10.657s; **5** Jamie Green, GB (Audi RS **5** DTM), +12.626s; **6** António Félix da Costa, P (BMW M4 DTM), +18.178s; **7** Mattias Ekström, S (Audi RS **5** DTM), +18.877s; **8** Daniel Juncadella, E (Mercedes C 63 DTM), +19.166s; **9** Esteban Ocon, F (Mercedes C 63 DTM), +19.838s; **10** Maxime Martin, B (BMW M4 DTM), +23.592s.
Fastest race lap: Wickens, 1m 32.841s, 103.774mph/167.008km/h.
Pole position: Wickens, 1m 30.727s, 106.192mph/170.900km/h.

Race 2 (104.374 miles/167.973km).
1 Jamie Green, GB (Audi RS **5** DTM), 1h 01m 54.997s, 101.143mph/162.773km/h; **2** Gary Paffett, GB (Mercedes C 63 DTM), +9.731s; **3** Edoardo Mortara, I (Audi RS **5** DTM), +14.153s; **4** Marco Wittmann, D (BMW M4 DTM), +18.833s; **5** Nico Müller, CH (Audi RS **5** DTM), +19.629s; **6** Timo Glock, D (BMW M4 DTM), +21.455s; **7** Mattias Ekström, S (Audi RS **5** DTM), +24.135s; **8** Paul Di Resta, GB (Mercedes C 63 DTM), +28.983s; **9** Lucas Auer, A (Mercedes C 63 DTM), +29.430s; **10** Tom Blomqvist, GB (BMW M4 DTM), +29.875s.
Fastest race lap: Daniel Juncadella, E (Mercedes C 63 DTM), 1m 33.087s, 103.500mph/166.567km/h.
Pole position: Green, 1m 30.696s, 106.228mph/170.958km/h.

GERMAN TOURING CAR CHAMPIONSHIP (DTM), Moscow Raceway, Volokolamsk Oblast, Russia, 20/21 August. Round 6. 22 and 40 laps of the 2.443-mile/3.931km circuit.
Race 1 (53.737 miles/86.482km).
1 Robert Wickens, CDN (Mercedes C 63 DTM), 42m 29.196s, 75.889mph/122.131km/h; **2** Paul Di Resta, GB (Mercedes C 63 DTM), +10.955s; **3** Gary Paffett, GB (Mercedes C 63 DTM), +12.293s; **4** Maximilian Götz, D (Mercedes C 63 DTM), +25.270s; **5** Mattias Ekström, S (Audi RS **5** DTM), +25.874s; **6** Maxime Martin, B (BMW M4 DTM), +27.243s; **7** Jamie Green, GB (Audi RS **5** DTM), +27.752s; **8** Edoardo Mortara, I (Audi RS **5** DTM), +30.108s; **9** Timo Scheider, D (Audi RS **5** DTM), +31.671s; **10** Felix Rosenqvist, S (Mercedes C 63 DTM), +32.848s.
Fastest race lap: Daniel Juncadella, E (Mercedes C 63 DTM), 1m 48.220s, 81.255mph/130.767km/h.
Pole position: Paffett, 1m 41.443s, 86.683mph/139.503km/h.

Race 2 (97.704 miles/157.240km).
1 Marco Wittmann, D (BMW M4 DTM), 1h 02m 03.216s, 94.471mph/152.036km/h; **2** Tom Blomqvist, GB (BMW M4 DTM), +4.123s; **3** Bruno Spengler, CDN (BMW M4 DTM), +18.119s; **4** Augusto Farfus, BR (BMW M4 DTM), +24.650s; **5** Robert Wickens, CDN (Mercedes C 63 DTM), +38.818s; **6** Edoardo Mortara, I (Audi RS **5** DTM), +38.885s; **7** Nico Müller, CH (Audi RS **5** DTM), +39.158s; **8** Adrien Tambay, F (Audi RS **5** DTM), +41.193s; **9** Mattias Ekström, S (Audi RS **5** DTM), +41.223s; **10** Lucas Auer, A (Mercedes C 63 DTM), +42.138s.
Fastest race lap: Müller, 1m 30.269s, 97.413mph/156.771km/h.
Pole position: Wittmann, 1m 28.776s, 99.052mph/159.408km/h.

GERMAN TOURING CAR CHAMPIONSHIP (DTM), Nürburgring, Nürburg/Eifel, Germany, 10/11 September. Round 7. 30 and 43 laps of the 2.255-mile/3.629km circuit.
Race 1 (67.649 miles/108.870km).
1 Marco Wittmann, D (BMW M4 DTM), 42m 47.780s, 94.843mph/152.635km/h; **2** Tom Blomqvist, GB (BMW M4 DTM), +7.136s; **3** Jamie Green, GB (Audi RS **5** DTM), +9.031s; **4** Edoardo Mortara, I (Audi RS **5** DTM), +9.783s; **5** Timo Glock, D (BMW M4 DTM), +11.768s; **6** Paul Di Resta, GB (Mercedes C 63 DTM), +15.256s; **7** Lucas Auer, A (Mercedes C 63 DTM), +16.086s; **8** Maxime Martin, B (BMW M4 DTM), +23.232s; **9** Robert Wickens, CDN (Mercedes C 63 DTM), +32.197s; **10** Maximilian Götz, D (Mercedes C 63 DTM), +34.656s.
Fastest race lap: Green, 1m 24.468s, 96.106mph/154.667km/h.
Pole position: Wittmann, 1m 23.028s, 97.772mph/157.349km/h.

Race 2 (96.963 miles/156.047km).
1 Edoardo Mortara, I (Audi RS **5** DTM), 1h 01m 31.597s, 94.557mph/152.175km/h; **2** Lucas Auer, A (Mercedes C 63 DTM), +3.726s; **3** Marco Wittmann, D (BMW M4 DTM), +7.526s; **4** Mattias Ekström, S (Audi RS **5** DTM), +7.849s; **5** Nico Müller, CH (Audi RS **5** DTM), +9.182s; **6** Bruno Spengler, CDN (BMW M4 DTM), +11.812s; **7** Gary Paffett, GB (Mercedes C 63 DTM), +18.973s; **8** Tom Blomqvist, GB (BMW M4 DTM), +20.895s; **9** Daniel Juncadella, E (Mercedes C 63 DTM), +21.826s; **10** Maxime Martin, B (BMW M4 DTM), +27.220s.
Fastest race lap: Müller, 1m 24.103s, 96.523mph/155.338km/h.
Pole position: Auer, 1m 22.728s, 98.127mph/157.920km/h.

GERMAN TOURING CAR CHAMPIONSHIP (DTM), Hungaroring, Mogyoród, Budapest,

Hungary, 24/25 September. Round 8. 26 and 36 laps of the 2.722-mile/4.381km circuit.
Race 1 (70.778 miles/113.906km).
1 Edoardo Mortara, I (Audi RS **5** DTM), 42m 20.736s, 100.286mph/161.395km/h; **2** Jamie Green, GB (Audi RS **5** DTM), +1.090s; **3** Miguel Molina, E (Audi RS **5** DTM), +9.240s; **4** Mike Rockenfeller, D (Audi RS **5** DTM), +10.602s; **5** Nico Müller, CH (Audi RS **5** DTM), +11.535s; **6** Adrien Tambay, F (Audi RS **5** DTM), +21.045s; **7** Marco Wittmann, D (BMW M4 DTM), +23.177s; **8** Felix Rosenqvist, S (Mercedes C 63 DTM), +24.729s; **9** Timo Scheider, D (Audi RS **5** DTM), +25.754s; **10** Robert Wickens, CDN (Mercedes C 63 DTM), +26.916s.
Fastest race lap: Mortara, 1m 36.959s, 101.074mph/162.663km/h.
Pole position: Mortara, 1m 35.282s, 102.853mph/165.525km/h.

Race 2 (98.000 miles/157.716km).
1 Mattias Ekström, S (Audi RS **5** DTM), 59m 09.402s, 99.397mph/159.964km/h; **2** Adrien Tambay, F (Audi RS **5** DTM), +4.350s; **3** António Félix da Costa, P (BMW M4 DTM), +24.209s; **4** Tom Blomqvist, GB (BMW M4 DTM), +26.067s; **5** Timo Glock, D (BMW M4 DTM), +26.813s; **6** Timo Scheider, D (Audi RS **5** DTM), +31.792s; **7** Maxime Martin, B (BMW M4 DTM), +38.310s; **8** Mike Rockenfeller, D (Audi RS **5** DTM), +38.675s; **9** Martin Tomczyk, D (BMW M4 DTM), +39.966s; **10** Robert Wickens, CDN (Mercedes C 63 DTM), +40.327s.
Disqualified: Daniel Juncadella, E (Mercedes C 63 DTM), originally finished 3rd; Marco Wittmann, D (BMW M4 DTM), originally finished 4th.
Fastest race lap: Ekström, 1m 36.538s, 101.515mph/163.372km/h.
Pole position: Edoardo Mortara, I (Audi RS **5** DTM), 1m 34.984s, 103.175mph/166.045km/h.

GERMAN TOURING CAR CHAMPIONSHIP (DTM), Hockenheimring Grand Prix Circuit, Heidelberg, Germany, 15/16 October. Round 9. 27 and 39 laps of the 2.842-mile/4.574km circuit.
Race 1 (76.738 miles/123.498km).
1 Miguel Molina, E (Audi RS **5** DTM), 43m 02.346s, 106.979mph/172.166km/h; **2** Marco Wittmann, D (BMW M4 DTM), +1.661s; **3** Edoardo Mortara, I (Audi RS **5** DTM), +2.805s; **4** António Félix da Costa, P (BMW M4 DTM), +4.870s; **5** Mike Rockenfeller, D (Audi RS **5** DTM), +6.064s; **6** René Rast, D (Audi RS **5** DTM), +7.992s; **7** Timo Glock, D (BMW M4 DTM), +11.858s; **8** Jamie Green, GB (Audi RS **5** DTM), +15.970s; **9** Tom Blomqvist, GB (BMW M4 DTM), +17.188s; **10** Paul Di Resta, GB (Mercedes C 63 DTM), +19.048s.
Fastest race lap: da Costa, 1m 34.500s, 108.272mph/174.248km/h.
Pole position: da Costa, 1m 32.344s, 110.800mph/178.316km/h.

Race 2 (110.844 miles/178.386km).
1 Edoardo Mortara, I (Audi RS **5** DTM), 1h 02m 52.131s, 105.786mph/170.246km/h; **2** Christian Vietoris, D (Mercedes C 63 DTM), +3.040s; **3** Paul Di Resta, GB (Mercedes C 63 DTM), +4.294s; **4** Marco Wittmann, D (BMW M4 DTM), +5.030s; **5** Timo Glock, D (BMW M4 DTM), +6.103s; **6** Maxime Martin, B (BMW M4 DTM), +8.947s; **7** Tom Blomqvist, GB (BMW M4 DTM), +13.857s; **8** Jamie Green, GB (Audi RS **5** DTM), +15.054s; **9** Robert Wickens, CDN (Mercedes C 63 DTM), +16.012s; **10** Martin Tomczyk, D (BMW M4 DTM), +21.313s.
Fastest race lap: Glock, 1m 34.659s, 108.091mph/173.955km/h.
Pole position: António Félix da Costa, P (BMW M4 DTM), 1m 32.525s, 110.584mph/177.967km/h.

Final championship points
Drivers
1 Marco Wittmann, D, 206; **2** Edoardo Mortara, I, 202; **3** Jamie Green, GB, 145; **4** Robert Wickens, CDN, 124; **5** Paul Di Resta, GB, 116; **6** Tom Blomqvist, GB, 113; **7** Mattias Ekström, S, 107; **8** Maxime Martin, B, 90; **9** Nico Müller, CH, 88; **10** Timo Glock, D, 84; **11** Gary Paffett, GB, 73; **12** Lucas Auer, A, 68; **13** Miguel Molina, E, 66; **14** Christian Vietoris, D, 60; **15** Bruno Spengler, CDN, 51; **16** Augusto Farfus, BR, 44; **17** António Félix da Costa, P, 43; **18** Adrien Tambay, F, 40; **19** Mike Rockenfeller, D, 31; **20** Maximilian Götz, D, 17; **21** Martin Tomczyk, D, 16; **22** Timo Scheider, D, 13; **23** René Rast, D, 8; **24** Daniel Juncadella, E, 6; **25** Felix Rosenqvist, S, 5; **26** Esteban Ocon, F, 2.

Manufacturers
1 Audi, 700; **2** BMW, 647; **3** Mercedes, 471.

Teams
1 Audi Sport Team Abt Sportsline, 319; **2** BMW Team RMG, 290; **3** BMW Team RBM, 203; **4** Audi Sport Team Rosberg, 185; **5** Audi Sport Team Abt, 154; **6** Mercedes-AMG, 133; **7** SILBERPFEIL Energy/UBFS invest Mercedes-AMG, 130; **8** BWT Mercedes-AMG, 128; **9** BMW Team MTEK, 95; **10** EURONICS/FREE MEN'S WORLD Mercedes-AMG, 80; **11** BMW Team Schnitzer, 59; **12** Audi Sport Team Phoenix, 42.

British Touring Car Championship

BRITISH TOURING CAR CHAMPIONSHIP, Brands Hatch Indy Circuit, West Kingsdown, Dartford, Kent, Great Britain, 3 April. 27, 26 and 27 laps of the 1.208-mile/1.944km circuit.
Round 1 (32.613 miles/52.486km).
1 Tom Ingram, GB (Toyota Avensis), 23m 44.664s, 82.410mph/132.627km/h; **2** Gordon Shedden, GB (Honda Civic Type-R), +2.284s; **3** Matt Neal, GB (Honda Civic Type-R), +3.925s; **4** Ashley Sutton, GB (MG 6 GT), +6.070s; **5** Josh Cook, GB (MG 6 GT), +6.423s; **6** Rob Collard, GB (BMW 125i M Sport), +7.908s; **7** Árón Smith, IRL (Volkswagen Passat CC), +10.314s; **8** Mat Jackson, GB (Ford Focus ST), +11.720s; **9** Adam Morgan, GB (Mercedes A-Class), +13.495s; **10** Jack Goff, GB (BMW 125i M Sport), +13.615s.
Fastest race lap: Goff, 48.720s, 89.253mph/143.639km/h.
Pole position: Ingram, 47.990s, 90.611mph/145.824km/h.

Round 2 (31.405 miles/50.542km).
1 Gordon Shedden, GB (Honda Civic Type-R), 22m 27.048s, 83.931mph/135.074km/h; **2** Matt Neal, GB (Honda Civic Type-R), +0.848s; **3** Árón Smith, IRL (Volkswagen Passat CC), +3.132s; **4** Andrew Jordan, GB (Ford Focus ST), +4.165s; **5** Mat Jackson, GB (Ford Focus ST), +7.176s; **6** Ashley Sutton, GB (MG 6 GT), +8.647s; **7** Jack Goff, GB (BMW 125i M Sport), +9.682s; **8** Adam Morgan, GB (Mercedes A-Class), +10.076s; **9** Sam Tordoff, GB (BMW 125i M Sport), +10.395s; **10** Jeff Smith, GB (Honda Civic Type-R), +10.588s.
Fastest race lap: Jordan, 49.053s, 88.647mph/142.664km/h.
Pole position: Ingram.

Round 3 (32.613 miles/52.486km).
1 Adam Morgan, GB (Mercede A-Class), 23m 49.834s, 82.112mph/132.147km/h; **2** Sam Tordoff, GB (BMW 125i M Sport), +0.136s; **3** Jack Goff, GB (BMW 125i M Sport), +0.449s; **4** Andrew Jordan, GB (Ford Focus ST), +3.832s; **5** Matt Neal, GB (Honda Civic Type-R), +3.869s; **6** Rob Collard, GB (BMW 125i M Sport), +4.192s; **7** Jeff Smith, GB (Honda Civic Type-R), +4.195s; **8** Árón Smith, IRL (Volkswagen Passat CC), +5.702s; **9** Aiden Moffat, GB (Mercedes A-Class), +6.391s; **10** Ashley Sutton, GB (MG 6 GT), +10.862s.
Fastest race lap: Morgan, 48.816s, 89.078mph/143.357km/h.
Pole position: Tordoff.

BRITISH TOURING CAR CHAMPIONSHIP, Donington Park National Circuit, Castle Donington, Great Britain, 17 April. 15, 19 and 16 laps of the 1.979-mile/3.185km circuit.
Round 4 (29.647 miles/47.712km).
1 Mat Jackson, GB (Ford Focus ST), 18m 16.822s, 97.431mph/156.800km/h; **2** Josh Cook, GB (MG 6 GT), +1.860s; **3** Tom Ingram, GB (Toyota Avensis), +2.077s; **4** Jack Goff, GB (BMW 125i M Sport), +8.794s; **5** Ash Sutton, GB (MG 6 GT), +9.149s; **6** Rob Collard, GB (BMW 125i M Sport), +10.324s; **7** Jeff Smith, GB (Honda Civic Type-R), +14.807s; **8** Árón Smith, IRL (Volkswagen Passat CC), +16.423s; **9** Sam Tordoff, GB (BMW 125i M Sport), +17.990s; **10** Colin Turkington, GB (Subaru Levorg GT), +19.589s.
Fastest race lap: Jackson, 1m 10.466s, 101.104mph/162.711km/h.
Pole position: Sutton, 1m 11.729s, 99.323mph/159.846km/h.

Round 5 (37.563 miles/60.452km).
1 Rob Collard, GB (BMW 125i M Sport), 25m 07.394s, 89.798mph/144.517km/h; **2** Mat Jackson, GB (Ford Focus ST), +1.670s; **3** Árón Smith, IRL (Volkswagen Passat CC), +3.307s; **4** Gordon Shedden, GB (Honda Civic Type-R), +3.429s; **5** Jack Goff, GB (BMW 125i M Sport), +4.939s; **6** Matt Neal, GB (Honda Civic Type-R), +5.547s; **7** Josh Cook, GB (MG 6 GT), +9.967s; **8** Sam Tordoff, GB (BMW 125i M Sport), +10.311s; **9** Aiden Moffat, GB (Mercedes A-Class), +11.124s; **10** Rob Austin, GB (Toyota Avensis), +11.378s.
Fastest race lap: Tordoff, 1m 10.650s, 100.840mph/162.287km/h.
Pole position: Jackson.

Round 6 (31.626 miles/50.897km).
1 Matt Neal, GB (Honda Civic Type-R), 19m 08.350s, 99.263mph/159.748km/h; **2** Gordon Shedden, GB (Honda Civic Type-R), +0.222s; **3** Sam Tordoff, GB (BMW 125i M Sport), +2.690s; **4** Rob Collard, GB (BMW 125i M Sport), +2.908s; **5** Ash Sutton, GB (MG 6 GT), +4.142s; **6** Jack Goff, GB (BMW 125i M Sport), +9.245s; **7** Aiden Moffat, GB (Mercedes A-Class), +9.379s; **8** Rob Austin, GB (Toyota Avensis), +13.028s; **9** Josh Cook, GB (MG 6 GT), +17.535s; **10** Andrew Jordan, GB (Ford Focus ST), +18.146s.
Fastest race lap: Goff, 1m 10.545s, 100.990mph/162.529km/h.
Pole position: Tordoff.

BRITISH TOURING CAR CHAMPIONSHIP, Thruxton Circuit, Andover, Hampshire, Great Britain, 8 May. 11, 12 and 12 laps of the 2.356-mile/3.792km circuit.
Round 7 (25.916 miles/41.708km).
1 Adam Morgan, GB (Mercedes A-Class), 14m 41.826s, 105.800mph/170.269km/h; **2** Tom Ingram, GB (Toyota Avensis), +3.310s; **3** Andrew Jordan, GB (Ford Focus ST), +3.820s; **4** Jeff Smith, GB (Honda Civic Type-R), +5.115s; **5** Martin Depper, GB (Honda Civic Type-R), +5.824s; **6** Rob Collard, GB (BMW 125i M Sport), +6.464s; **7** Sam Tordoff, GB (BMW 125i M Sport), +6.932s; **8** Jack Goff, GB (BMW 125i M Sport), +8.179s; **9** Daniel Welch, GB (Proton Persona), +8.672s; **10** Jake Hill, GB (Toyota Avensis), +8.809s.
Fastest race lap: Morgan, 1m 18.420s, 108.156mph/174.060km/h.
Pole position: Ingram, 1m 16.161s, 111.364mph/179.223km/h.

Round 8 (28.272 miles/45.499km).
1 Andrew Jordan, GB (Ford Focus ST), 15m 59.415s, 106.084mph/170.726km/h; **2** Rob Collard, GB (BMW 125i M Sport), +0.401s; **3** Adam Morgan, GB (Mercedes A-Class), +1.791s; **4** Gordon Shedden, GB (Honda Civic Type-R), +1.978s; **5** Jack Goff, GB (BMW 125i M Sport), +2.786s; **6** Sam Tordoff, GB (BMW 125i M Sport), +3.017s; **7** Daniel Lloyd, GB (Honda Civic Type-R), +3.483s; **8** Mat Jackson, GB (Ford Focus ST), +6.201s; **9** Daniel Welch, GB (Proton Persona), +7.034s; **10** Rob Austin, GB (Toyota Avensis), +7.260s.
Fastest race lap: Tordoff, 1m 17.713s, 109.140mph/175.643km/h.
Pole position: Morgan.

Round 9 (28.272 miles/45.499km).
1 Mat Jackson, GB (Ford Focus ST), 15m 54.641s, 106.615mph/171.580km/h; **2** Matt Neal, GB (Honda Civic Type-R), +0.256s; **3** Adam Morgan, GB (Mercedes A-Class), +4.568s; **4** Josh Cook, GB (MG 6 GT), +4.766s; **5** Ash Sutton, GB (MG 6 GT), +5.006s; **6** Rob Collard, GB (BMW 125i M Sport), +5.460s; **7** Rob Austin, GB (Toyota Avensis), +6.082s; **8** Sam Tordoff, GB (BMW 125i M Sport), +6.291s; **9** Daniel Lloyd, GB (Honda Civic Type-R), +10.533s; **10** Michael Epps, GB (Toyota Avensis), +11.333s.
Fastest race lap: Aiden Moffat, GB (Mercedes A-Class), 1m 17.660s, 109.214mph/175.763km/h.
Pole position: Welch.

BRITISH TOURING CAR CHAMPIONSHIP, Oulton Park Circuit, Tarporley, Cheshire, Great Britain, 5 June. 15, 16 and 15 laps of the 2.226-mile/3.582km circuit.
Round 10 (33.390 miles/53.736km).
1 Colin Turkington, GB (Subaru Levorg GT), 21m 56.702s, 91.291mph/146.919km/h; **2** Sam Tordoff, GB (BMW 125i M Sport), +2.424s; **3** Jason Plato, GB (Subaru Levorg GT), +9.954s; **4** Gordon Shedden, GB (Honda Civic Type-R), +14.457s; **5** Tom Ingram, GB (Toyota Avensis), +16.249s; **6** Daniel Lloyd, GB (Honda Civic Type-R), +16.388s; **7** Josh Cook, GB (MG 6 GT), +19.119s; **8** Árón Smith, IRL (Volkswagen Passat CC), +19.312s; **9** Matt Neal, GB (Honda Civic Type-R), +20.395s; **10** Andrew Jordan, GB (Ford Focus ST), +20.819s.
Fastest race lap: Plato, 1m 26.673s, 92.457mph/148.796km/h.
Pole position: Turkington, 1m 26.264s, 92.896mph/149.501km/h.

Round 11 (35.616 miles/57.318km).
1 Sam Tordoff, GB (BMW 125i M Sport), 24m 15.404s, 88.097mph/141.779km/h; **2** Colin Turkington, GB (Subaru Levorg GT), +1.638s; **3** Jason Plato, GB (Subaru Levorg GT), +2.309s; **4** Gordon Shedden, GB (Honda Civic Type-R), +5.544s; **5** Tom Ingram, GB (Toyota Avensis), +6.217s; **6** Josh Cook, GB (MG 6 GT), +12.302s; **7** Matt Neal, GB (Honda Civic Type-R), +12.552s; **8** Andrew Jordan, GB (Ford Focus ST), +13.207s; **9** Jack Goff, GB (BMW 125i M Sport), +13.848s; **10** Mat Jackson, GB (Ford Focus ST), +13.989s.
Fastest race lap: Rob Collard, GB (BMW 125i M Sport), 1m 27.251s, 91.845mph/147.810km/h.
Pole position: Turkington.

Round 12 (33.390 miles/53.736km).
1 Matt Neal, GB (Honda Civic Type-R), 22m 18.716s, 89.790mph/144.503km/h; **2** Sam Tordoff, GB (BMW 125i M Sport), +9.481s; **3** Jason Plato, GB (Subaru Levorg GT), +11.662s; **4** Tom Ingram, GB (Toyota Avensis), +11.760s; **5** Josh Cook, GB (MG 6 GT), +11.827s; **6** Rob Collard, GB (BMW 125i M Sport), +12.015s; **7** Colin Turkington, GB (Subaru Levorg GT), +12.056s; **8** Andrew Jordan, GB (Ford Focus ST), +12.299s; **9** Jake Hill, GB (Toyota Avensis), +12.494s; **10** Adam Morgan, GB (Mercedes A-Class), +12.936s.
Fastest race lap: Collard, 1m 27.376s, 91.713 mph/147.599km/h. **Pole position:** Neal.

BRITISH TOURING CAR CHAMPIONSHIP, Croft Racing Circuit, Croft-on-Tees, North Yorkshire, Great Britain, 19 June. 18, 16 and 18 laps of the 2.125-mile/3.420km circuit.
Round 13 (38.250 miles/61.557km).
1 Colin Turkington, GB (Subaru Levorg GT), 29m 56.374s, 76.654mph/123.363km/h; **2** Jason Plato, GB (Subaru Levorg GT), +1.353s; **3** Ash Sutton, GB (MG 6 GT), +2.305s; **4** Jack Goff, GB (BMW 125i M Sport), +2.689s; **5** Andrew Jordan, GB (Ford Focus ST), +6.429s; **6** Jake Hill, GB (Toyota Avensis), +7.136s; **7** Rob Collard, GB (BMW 125i M Sport), +7.306s; **8** Mat Jackson, GB (Ford Focus ST), +8.025s; **9** Tom Ingram, GB (Toyota Avensis), +8.279s; **10** Árón Smith, IRL (Volkswagen Passat CC), +9.191s.
Fastest race lap: Turkington, 1m 25.266s, 89.719mph/144.389km/h.
Pole position: Turkington, 1m 23.608s, 91.498mph/147.252km/h.

Round 14 (34.000 miles/54.718 km).
1 Rob Collard, GB (BMW 125i M Sport), 23m 59.017s, 85.058mph/136.887km/h; **2** Jason Plato, GB (Subaru Levorg GT), +2.341s; **3** Colin Turkington, GB (Subaru Levorg GT), +5.152s; **4** Jack Goff, GB (BMW 125i M Sport), +7.038s; **5** Ash Sutton, GB (MG 6 GT), +12.363s; **6** Mat Jackson, GB (Ford Focus ST), +15.335s; **7** Tom Ingram, GB (Toyota Avensis), +15.815s; **8** Sam Tordoff, GB (BMW 125i M Sport), +16.062s; **9** Andrew Jordan, GB (Ford Focus ST), +17.782s; **10** Matt Neal, GB (Honda Civic Type-R), +18.117s.
Fastest race lap: Goff, 1m 25.464s, 89.511mph/144.054km/h.
Pole position: Turkington.

Round 15 (38.250 miles/61.557km).
1 Ash Sutton, GB (MG 6 GT), 32m 50.206s, 69.891mph/112.478km/h; **2** Sam Tordoff, GB (BMW 125i M Sport), +1.337s; **3** Tom Ingram, GB (Toyota Avensis), +2.284s; **4** Rob Collard, GB (BMW 125i M Sport), +2.860s; **5** Andrew Jordan, GB (Ford Focus ST), +3.759s; **6** Josh Cook, GB (MG 6 GT), +4.324s; **7** Colin Turkington, GB (Subaru Levorg GT), +4.683s; **8** Árón Smith, IRL (Volkswagen Passat CC), +4.947s; **9** Jack Goff, GB (BMW 125i M Sport), +5.942s; **10** Jason Plato, GB (Subaru Levorg GT), +6.290s.
Fastest race lap: Sutton, 1m 33.231s, 82.054mph/132.053km/h.
Pole position: Tordoff.

BRITISH TOURING CAR CHAMPIONSHIP, Snetterton Circuit, Thetford, Norfolk, Great Britain, 31 July. 12, 10 and 10 laps of the 2.969-mile/4.778km circuit.
Round 16 (35.627 miles/57.336km).
1 Colin Turkington, GB (Subaru Levorg GT), 23m 46.178s, 89.930mph/144.728km/h; **2** Gordon Shedden, GB (Honda Civic Type-R), +2.771s; **3** Mat Jackson, GB (Ford Focus ST), +4.042s; **4** Adam Morgan, GB (Mercedes A-Class), +5.400s; **5** Jason Plato, GB (Subaru Levorg GT), +6.880s; **6** Tom Ingram, GB (Toyota Avensis), +8.994s; **7** Sam Tordoff, GB (BMW 125i M Sport), +9.607s; **8** Matt Neal, GB (Honda Civic Type-R), +10.172s; **9** Warren Scott, GB (Subaru Levorg GT), +11.160s; **10** James Cole, GB (Subaru Levorg GT), +12.647s.
Fastest race lap: Hunter Abbott, GB (Chevrolet Cruze), 1m 57.186s, 91.205mph/146.781km/h.
Pole position: Shedden, 1m 55.627s, 92.435mph/148.760km/h.

Round 17 (29.689 miles/47.780km).
1 Mat Jackson, GB (Ford Focus ST), 19m 48.286s, 89.945mph/144.752km/h; **2** Colin Turkington, GB (Subaru Levorg GT), +1.190s; **3** Matt Neal, GB (Honda Civic Type-R), +1.950s; **4** Rob Collard, GB (BMW 125i M Sport), +2.140s; **5** Adam Morgan, GB (Mercedes A-Class), +7.255s; **6** Jason Plato, GB (Subaru Levorg GT), +7.687s; **7** Tom Ingram, GB (Toyota Avensis), +8.421s; **8** Sam Tordoff, GB (BMW 125i M Sport), +9.935s; **9** Rob Austin, GB (Toyota Avensis), +11.649s; **10** Gordon Shedden, GB (Honda Civic Type-R), +11.989s.
Fastest race lap: Collard, 1m 56.362s, 91.851mph/147.820km/h.
Pole position: Turkington.

Round 18 (29.689 miles/47.78km).
1 Gordon Shedden, GB (Honda Civic Type-R), 19m 56.310s, 89.341mph/143.781km/h; **2** Rob Collard, GB (BMW 125i M Sport), +0.525s; **3** Rob Austin, GB (Toyota Avensis), +3.738s; **4** Jason Plato, GB (Subaru Levorg GT), +4.306s; **5** Andrew Jordan, GB (Ford Focus ST), +4.406s; **6** Colin Turkington, GB (Subaru Levorg GT), +5.278s; **7** Adam Morgan, GB (Mercedes A-Class), +6.288s; **8** Aiden Moffat, GB (Mercedes A-Class), +6.434s; **9** Josh Cook, GB (MG 6 GT), +6.621s; **10** Matt Neal, GB (Honda Civic Type-R), +7.219s.
Fastest race lap: Shedden, 1m 57.560s, 90.915mph/146.314km/h.
Pole position: Tordoff.

BRITISH TOURING CAR CHAMPIONSHIP, Knockhill Racing Circuit, Dunfermline, Fife, Scotland, Great Britain, 14 August. 3 x 27 laps of the 1.271-mile/2.046km circuit.
Round 19 (34.325 miles/55.241km).
1 Jason Plato, GB (Subaru Levorg GT), 25m 30.213s, 80.753mph/129.960km/h; **2** Jack Goff, GB (BMW 125i M Sport), +0.503s; **3** Colin Turkington, GB (Subaru Levorg GT), +1.003s; **4** Tom Ingram, GB (Toyota Avensis), +2.375s; **5** Sam Tordoff, GB (BMW 125i M Sport), +2.781s; **6** Andrew Jordan, GB (Ford Focus ST), +4.034s; **7** Dave Newsham, GB (Chevrolet Cruze), +5.265s; **8** Matt Neal, GB (Honda Civic Type-R), +7.605s; **9** Gordon Shedden, GB (Honda Civic Type-R), +8.143s; **10** Rob Austin, GB (Toyota Avensis), +8.357s.
Fastest race lap: Turkington, 51.982s, 88.043mph/141.692km/h.
Pole position: Plato, 51.521s, 88.831mph/142.960km/h.

Round 20 (34.325 miles/55.241km).
1 Matt Neal, GB (Honda Civic Type-R), 25m 42.020s, 80.135mph/128.965km/h; **2** Sam Tordoff, GB (BMW 125i M Sport), +1.249s; **3** Jason Plato, GB (Subaru Levorg GT), +2.340s; **4** Colin Turkington, GB (Subaru Levorg GT), +2.830s; **5** Rob Collard, GB (BMW 125i M Sport), +2.836s; **6** Mat Jackson, GB (Ford Focus ST), +3.640s; **7** Jack Goff, GB (BMW 125i M Sport), +4.175s; **8** Andrew Jordan, GB (Ford Focus ST), +4.756s; **9** Gordon Shedden, GB (Honda Civic Type-R), +5.554s; **10** Aiden Moffat, GB (Mercedes A-Class), +6.706s.
Fastest race lap: Adam Morgan, GB (Mercedes A-Class), 52.045s, 87.936mph/141.520km/h.
Pole position: Plato.

Round 21 (34.325 miles/55.241km).
1 Mat Jackson, GB (Ford Focus ST), 25m 19.259s, 81.335mph/130.897km/h; **2** Sam Tordoff, GB (BMW 125i M Sport), +0.236s; **3** Jason Plato, GB (Subaru Levorg GT), +0.804s; **4** Gordon Shedden, GB (Honda Civic Type-R), +1.297s; **5** Matt Neal, GB (Honda Civic Type-R), +2.256s; **6** Adam Morgan, GB (Mercedes A-Class), +4.328s; **7** Rob Austin, GB (Toyota Avensis), +4.933s *; **8** Aiden Moffat, GB (Mercedes A-Class), +8.875s; **9** Andrew Jordan, GB (Ford Focus ST), +9.316s; **10** Jack Goff, GB (BMW 125i M Sport), +10.196s.
** includes 1s penalty.*
Fastest race lap: Shedden, 52.339s, 87.443mph/140.725km/h.
Pole position: Jackson.

BRITISH TOURING CAR CHAMPIONSHIP, Rockingham Motor Speedway, Corby, Northamptonshire, Great Britain, 28 August. 18, 16 and 19 laps of the 1.940-mile/3.122km circuit.
Round 22 (34.920 miles/56.198km).
1 Gordon Shedden, GB (Honda Civic Type-R), 26m 36.324s, 78.750mph/126.737km/h; **2** Mat Jackson, GB (Ford Focus ST), +2.561s; **3** Jason Plato, GB (Subaru Levorg GT), +2.869s; **4** Colin Turkington, GB (Subaru Levorg GT), +3.165s; **5** Josh Cook, GB (MG 6 GT), +8.741s; **6** Ash Sutton, GB (MG 6 GT), +12.144s; **7** Andrew Jordan, GB (Ford Focus ST), +14.072s; **8** Matt Neal, GB (Honda Civic Type-R), +18.244s; **9** Dave Newsham, GB (Chevrolet Cruze), +23.899s; **10** Sam Tordoff, GB (BMW 125i M Sport), +24.168s.
Fastest race lap: Shedden, 1m 23.375s, 83.766mph/134.808km/h.
Pole position: Shedden, 1m 36.338s, 72.494mph/116.669km/h.

Round 23 (31.040 miles/49.954km).
1 Sam Tordoff, GB (BMW 125i M Sport), 22m 44.838s, 81.873mph/131.762km/h; **2** Andrew Jordan, GB (Ford Focus ST), +2.886s; **3** Rob Collard, GB (BMW 125i M Sport), +3.085s; **4** Mat Jackson, GB (Ford Focus ST), +6.863s; **5** Ash Sutton, GB (MG 6 GT), +15.027s; **6** Matt Neal, GB (Honda Civic Type-R), +18.661s; **7** Árón Smith, IRL (Volkswagen Passat CC), +21.341s; **8** Adam Morgan, GB (Mercedes A-Class), +22.624s; **9** Aiden Moffat, GB (Mercedes A-Class), +25.489s; **10** Gordon Shedden, GB (Honda Civic Type-R), +28.536s.
Fastest race lap: Collard, 1m 24.042s, 83.101mph/133.738km/h.
Pole position: Shedden.

Round 24 (36.860 miles/59.320km).
1 Árón Smith, IRL (Volkswagen Passat CC), 29m 49.905s, 74.135mph/119.309km/h; **2** Gordon Shedden, GB (Honda Civic Type-R), +0.400s; **3** Colin Turkington, GB (Subaru Levorg GT), +0.572s; **4** Matt Neal, GB (Honda Civic Type-R), +3.491s; **5** Mat Jackson, GB (Ford Focus ST), +4.519s; **6** Rob Collard, GB (BMW 125i M Sport), +4.936s; **7** Adam Morgan, GB (Mercedes A-Class), +5.686s; **8** Jake Hill, GB (Toyota Avensis), +6.227s; **9** Aiden Moffat, GB (Mercedes A-Class), +10.578s; **10** Jason Plato, GB (Subaru Levorg GT), +10.899s.
Fastest race lap: Smith, 1m 23.729s, 83.411mph/134.238km/h.
Pole position: Smith.

BRITISH TOURING CAR CHAMPIONSHIP, Silverstone National Circuit, Towcester, Northamptonshire, Great Britain, 18 September. 22, 25 and 22 laps of the 1.640-mile/2.640km circuit.
Round 25 (36.089 miles/58.079km).
1 Tom Ingram, GB (Toyota Avensis), 21m 49.891s, 99.183mph/159.620km/h; **2** Andrew Jordan, GB (Ford Focus ST), +3.478s; **3** Rob Austin, GB (Toyota Avensis), +7.464s; **4** Adam Morgan, GB (Mercedes A-Class), +10.121s; **5** Jake Hill, GB (Toyota Avensis), +16.570s; **6** Árón Smith, IRL (Volkswagen Passat CC), +18.131s; **7** Rob Collard, GB (BMW 125i M Sport), +18.307s; **8** Colin Turkington, GB (Subaru Levorg GT), +18.431s; **9** Aiden Moffat, GB (Mercedes A-Class), +18.554s; **10** Jason Plato, GB (Subaru Levorg GT), +18.785s.
Disqualified: Ash Sutton, GB (MG 6 GT) originally finished 1st; Josh Cook, GB (MG 6 GT), originally finished 2nd.
Fastest race lap: Morgan, 58.923s, 100.223mph/161.293km/h.
Pole position: Ash Sutton, GB (MG 6 GT), 58.321s, 101.257mph/162.958km/h.

Round 26 (41.010 miles/65.999km).
1 Andrew Jordan, GB (Ford Focus ST), 26m 44.945s, 91.988mph/148.040km/h; **2** Adam Morgan, GB (Mercedes A-Class), +0.884s; **3** Tom Ingram, GB (Toyota Avensis), +2.456s; **4** Colin Turkington, GB (Subaru Levorg GT), +2.662s; **5** Jason Plato, GB (Subaru Levorg GT), +3.001s; **6** Mat Jackson, GB (Ford Focus ST), +3.253s; **7** Rob Collard, GB (BMW 125i M Sport), +3.471s; **8** Gordon Shedden, GB (Honda Civic Type-R), +4.409s; **9** Aiden Moffat, GB (Mercedes A-Class), +5.043s; **10** Hunter Abbott, GB (Chevrolet Cruze), +5.993s.
Fastest race lap: James Cole, GB (Subaru Levorg GT), 59.296s, 99.592mph/160.278km/h.
Pole position: Ingram.

Round 27 (36.089 miles/58.079km).
1 Gordon Shedden, GB (Honda Civic Type-R), 21m 54.766s, 98.815mph/159.028km/h; **2** Mat Jackson, GB (Ford Focus ST), +0.668s; **3** Rob Collard, GB (BMW 125i M Sport), +1.087s; **4** Colin Turkington, GB (Subaru Levorg GT), +2.009s; **5** Matt Neal, GB (Honda Civic Type-R), +2.426s; **6** Sam Tordoff, GB (BMW 125i M Sport), +2.586s; **7** Josh Cook, GB (MG 6 GT), +5.399s; **8** Andrew Jordan, GB (Ford Focus ST), +7.119s; **9** Aiden Moffat, GB (Mercedes A-Class), +7.914s; **10** Ash Sutton, GB (MG 6 GT), +9.275s.
Fastest race lap: Sutton, 59.016s, 100.065mph/161.039km/h.
Pole position: Shedden.

BRITISH TOURING CAR CHAMPIONSHIP, Brands Hatch Grand Prix Circuit, West Kingsdown, Dartford, Kent, Great Britain, 2 October. 16, 17 and 18 laps of the 2.433-mile/3.916km circuit.
Round 28 (38.931 miles/62.654km).
1 Colin Turkington, GB (Subaru Levorg GT), 25m 56.267s, 90.056mph/144.932km/h; **2** Rob Austin, GB (Toyota Avensis), +4.570s; **3** Josh Cook, GB (MG 6 GT), +5.314s; **4** Jason Plato, GB (Subaru Levorg GT), +5.903s; **5** Gordon Shedden, GB (Honda Civic Type-R), +10.750s; **6** Adam Morgan, GB (Mercedes A-Class), +11.130s; **7** Matt Neal, GB (Honda Civic Type-R), +11.620s; **8** Aiden Moffat, GB (Mercedes A-Class), +17.894s; **9** Ash Sutton, GB (MG 6 GT), +18.077s; **10** Sam Tordoff, GB (BMW 125i M Sport), +19.564s.
Fastest race lap: Turkington, 1m 31.372s, 95.866mph/154.282km/h.
Pole position: Turkington, 1m 31.838s, 95.380mph/153.499km/h.

Round 29 (41.364 miles/66.570km).
1 Colin Turkington, GB (Subaru Levorg GT), 28m 52.932s, 85.930mph/138.291km/h; **2** Jason Plato, GB (Subaru Levorg GT), +1.128s; **3** Gordon Shedden, GB (Honda Civic Type-R), +1.535s; **4** Josh Cook, GB (MG 6 GT), +1.827s; **5** Sam Tordoff, GB (BMW 125i M Sport), +2.431s; **6** Aiden Moffat, GB (Mercedes A-Class), +2.931s; **7** Mat Jackson, GB (Ford Focus ST), +3.046s; **8** Adam Morgan, GB (Mercedes A-Class), +3.336s; **9** Tom Ingram, GB (Toyota Avensis), +3.626s; **10** Rob Collard, GB (BMW 125i M Sport), +3.963s.
Fastest race lap: Matt Neal, GB (Honda Civic Type-R), 1m 31.570s, 95.659mph/153.948km/h.
Pole position: Turkington.

Round 30 (43.798 miles/70.485km).
1 Mat Jackson, GB (Ford Focus ST), 30m 42.447s, 85.577mph/137.723km/h; **2** Aiden Moffat, GB (Mercedes A-Class), +1.016s; **3** Gordon Shedden, GB (Honda Civic Type-R), +1.454s; **4** Adam Morgan, GB (Mercedes A-Class), +1.660s; **5** Sam Tordoff, GB (BMW 125i M Sport), +2.600s; **6** Tom Ingram, GB (Toyota Avensis), +2.734s; **7** Josh Cook, GB (MG 6 GT), +3.046s; **8** Jake Hill, GB (Toyota Avensis), +4.093s; **9** Rob Collard, GB (BMW 125i M Sport), +4.188s; **10** Jason Plato, GB (Subaru Levorg GT), +5.937s.
Fastest race lap: Jack Goff, GB (BMW 125i M Sport), 1m 31.742s, 95.479mph/153.660km/h.
Pole position: Jackson.

Final championship points
Drivers
1 Gordon Shedden, GB, 308; **2** Sam Tordoff, GB, 306; **3** Mat Jackson, GB, 292; **4** Colin Turkington, GB, 289; **5** Rob Collard, GB, 278; **6** Matt Neal, GB, 275; **7** Jason Plato, GB, 256; **8** Andrew Jordan, GB, 255; **9** Adam Morgan, GB, 241; **10** Tom Ingram, GB, 219; **11** Jack Goff, GB, 193; **12** Josh Cook, GB, 175; **13** Ash Sutton, GB, 162; **14** Aiden Moffat, GB, 138; **15** Árón Smith, IRL, 132; **16** Rob Austin, GB, 129; **17** Jake Hill, GB, 83; **18** Jeff Smith, GB, 55; **19** Hunter Abbott, GB, 38; **20** Daniel Lloyd, GB, 36; **21** Martin Depper, GB, 28; **22** Dave Newsham, GB, 28; **23** Daniel Welch, GB, 23; **24** Michael Epps, GB, 23; **25** James Cole, GB, 15; **26** Ollie Jackson, GB, 14; **27** Warren Scott, GB, 7; **28** Alex Martin, GB, 3; **29** Matt Simpson, GB, 1.

Manufacturers
1 BMW, 790; **2** Honda, 737; **3** Subaru, 722; **4** MG, 571.

Drivers (Independents)
1 Andrew Jordan, GB, 415; **2** Mat Jackson, GB, 412; **3** Adam Morgan, GB, 361; **4** Tom Ingram, GB, 338; **5** Aiden Moffat, GB, 278; **6** Rob Austin, GB, 272; **7** Árón Smith, IRL, 243; **8** Jake Hill, GB, 218; **9** Jeff Smith, GB, 187; **10** Michael Epps, GB, 155.

Drivers (Jack Sears Trophy)
1 Ash Sutton, GB, 442; **2** Michael Epps, GB, 424; **3** Matt Simpson, GB, 345; **4** Mark Howard, GB, 269; **5** Kelvin Fletcher, GB, 212; **6** Chris Smiley, GB, 183; **7** Daniel Lloyd, GB, 124.

Teams
1 Team JCT600 with GardX, 574; **2** Halfords Yuasa Racing, 557; **3** Motorbase Performance, 538; **4** Silverline Subaru BMR Racing, 531; **5** MG Racing RCIB Insurance, 332; **6** WIX Racing, 234; **7** Speedworks Motorsport, 202; **8** Team IHG Rewards Club, 192; **9** Laser Tools Racing, 137; **10** Handy Motorsport, 136.

Verizon Indycar Series

All cars are Dallara DW12.

FIRESTONE GRAND PRIX OF ST. PETERSBURG, St. Petersburg Street Circuit, Florida, USA, 13 March. Round 1. 110 laps of the 1.800-mile/2.897km circuit, 198.000 miles/318.650km.
1 Juan Pablo Montoya, CO (-Chevrolet), 2h 13m 28.4650s, 89.006mph/143.241km/h; **2** Simon Pagenaud, F (-Chevrolet), +2.3306s; **3** Ryan Hunter-Reay, USA (-Honda), +8.8764s; **4** Hélio Castroneves, BR (-Chevrolet), +9.3237s; **5** Mikhail Aleshin, RUS (-Honda), +9.7167s; **6** Takuma Sato, J (-Honda), +26.0373s; **7** Scott Dixon, NZ (-Chevrolet), +40.7056s; **8** Carlos Muñoz, CO (-Honda), +55.9459s; **9** Tony Kanaan, BR (-Chevrolet), +59.1204s; **10** Charlie Kimball, USA (-Chevrolet), -1 lap (DNF-accident); **11** Jack Hawksworth, GB (-Honda), -1; **12** Alexander Rossi, USA (-Honda), -1; **13** Conor Daly, USA (-Honda), -1; **14** Spencer Pigot, USA (-Honda), -1; **15** Marco Andretti, USA (-Honda), -1; **16** Graham Rahal, USA (-Honda), -1; **17** Max Chilton, GB (-Chevrolet), -1; **18** Oriol Servià, E (-Chevrolet), -1; **19** James Hinchcliffe, CDN (-Honda), -1; **20** Luca Filippi, I (-Honda), -2; **21** Sébastien Bourdais, F (-Chevrolet), -23 (DNF-accident); **22** Josef Newgarden, USA (-Chevrolet), -63 (DNF-electrics); Will Power, AUS (-Chevrolet), -110 (DNF-physical).
Most laps led: Pagenaud, 48.
Fastest race lap: Newgarden, 1m 02.2307s, 104.129mph/167.579km/h.
Pole position: Power, 1m 00.2450s, 107.561mph/173.102km/h.
Championship points: Drivers: 1 Montoya, 51; **2** Pagenaud, 43; **3** Hunter-Reay, 36; **4** Castroneves, 32; **5** Aleshin, 30; **6** Sato, 28.

DESERT DIAMOND WEST VALLEY PHOENIX GRAND PRIX, Phoenix International Raceway, Arizona, USA, 2 April. Round 2. 250 laps of the 1.022-mile/1.645km circuit, 255.500 miles/411.187km.
1 Scott Dixon, NZ (-Chevrolet), 1h 49m 38.3855s, 139.822mph/225.021km/h; **2** Simon Pagenaud, F (-Chevrolet), +0.6825s; **3** Will Power, AUS (-Chevrolet), +1.7264s; **4** Tony Kanaan, BR (-Chevrolet), +1.9589s; **5** Graham Rahal, USA (-Honda), +2.5272s; **6** Josef Newgarden, USA (-Chevrolet), +2.7457s; **7** Max Chilton, GB (-Chevrolet), +2.9914s; **8** Sébastien Bourdais, F (-Chevrolet), +3.9491s; **9** Juan Pablo Montoya, CO (-Chevrolet), +4.4548s; **10** Ryan Hunter-Reay, USA (-Honda), +5.2143s; **11** Hélio Castroneves, BR (-Chevrolet), +8.0324s; **12** Charlie Kimball, USA (-Chevrolet), +9.3366s; **13** Marco Andretti, USA (-Honda), +10.0918s; **14** Alexander Rossi, USA (-Honda), +13.0555s; **15** Takuma Sato, J (-Honda), -1 lap; **16** Conor Daly, USA (-Honda), -1; **17** Mikhail Aleshin, RUS (-Honda), -2; **18** James Hinchcliffe, CDN (-Honda), -2; **19** Jack Hawksworth, GB (-Honda), -4; **20** Luca Filippi, I (-Honda), -7; **21** Ed Carpenter, USA (-Chevrolet), -55 (DNF-accident); **22** Carlos Muñoz, CO (-Honda), -134 (DNF-accident).
Most laps led: Dixon, 155.
Fastest race lap: Kanaan, 19.7379s, 186.403mph/299.986km/h.
Pole position: Castroneves, 38.2604s, 192.324mph/309.516km/h (over **2** laps).
Championship points: Drivers: 1 Pagenaud, 83; **2** Dixon, 79; **3** Montoya, 74; **4** Hunter-Reay, 56; **5** Kanaan, 54; **6** Castroneves, 53.

42ND TOYOTA GRAND PRIX OF LONG BEACH, Long Beach Street Circuit, California, USA, 17 April. Round 3. 80 laps of the 1.968-mile/3.167km circuit, 157.440 miles/253.375km.
1 Simon Pagenaud, F (-Chevrolet), 1h 33m 54.4835s, 100.592mph/161.887km/h; **2** Scott Dixon, NZ (-Chevrolet), +0.3032s; **3** Hélio Castroneves, BR (-Chevrolet), +10.8376s; **4** Juan Pablo Montoya, CO (-Chevrolet), +12.2162s; **5** Takuma Sato, J (-Honda), +12.2918s; **6** Tony Kanaan, BR (-Chevrolet), +17.6267s; **7** Will Power, AUS (-Chevrolet), +18.7449s; **8** James Hinchcliffe, CDN (-Honda), +19.0362s; **9** Sébastien Bourdais, F (-Chevrolet), +22.9147s; **10** Josef Newgarden, USA (-Chevrolet), +23.6654s; **11** Charlie Kimball, USA (-Chevrolet), +24.2179s; **12** Carlos Muñoz, CO (-Honda), +40.1250s; **13** Conor Daly, USA (-Honda), +47.1809s; **14** Max Chilton, GB (-Chevrolet), +53.9106s; **15** Graham Rahal, USA (-Honda), +56.9082s; **16** Mikhail Aleshin, RUS (-Honda), +1m 01.2966s; **17** Luca Filippi, I (-Honda), +1m 08.0543s; **18** Ryan Hunter-Reay, USA (-Honda), +1m 30.3302s; **19** Marco Andretti, USA (-Honda), -1 lap; **20** Alexander Rossi, USA (-Honda), -1; **21** Jack Hawksworth, GB (-Honda), -3.
Most laps led: Castroneves, 47.
Fastest race lap: Kimball, 1m 07.6661s, 104.702mph/168.502km/h.
Pole position: Castroneves, 1m 07.1246s, 105.547mph/169.861km/h.
Championship points: Drivers: 1 Pagenaud, 134; **2** Dixon, 120; **3** Montoya, 106; **4** Castroneves, 92; **5** Kanaan, 82; **6** Sato, 73.

HONDA INDY GRAND PRIX OF ALABAMA, Barber Motorsports Park, Birmingham, Alabama, USA, 24 April. Round 4. 90 laps of the 2.300-mile/3.701km circuit, 207.000 miles/333.134km.
1 Simon Pagenaud, F (-Chevrolet), 1h 48m 42.3334s, 114.254mph/183.873km/h; **2** Graham Rahal, USA (-Honda), +13.7476s; **3** Josef Newgarden, USA (-Chevrolet), +15.8039s; **4** Will Power, AUS (-Chevrolet), +16.7315s; **5** Juan Pablo Montoya, CO (-Chevrolet), +21.1160s; **6** James Hinchcliffe, CDN (-Honda), +23.6222s; **7** Hélio Castroneves, BR (-Chevrolet), +25.5391s; **8** Tony Kanaan, BR (-Chevrolet), +27.9007s; **9** Charlie Kimball, USA (-Chevrolet), +31.8726s; **10** Scott Dixon, NZ (-Chevrolet), +39.0603s; **11** Ryan Hunter-Reay, USA (-Honda), +40.7485s; **12** Marco Andretti, USA (-Honda), +53.3648s; **13** Takuma Sato, J (-Honda), +55.2122s; **14** Carlos Muñoz, CO (-Honda), +1m 03.5214s; **15** Alexander Rossi, USA (-Honda), +1m 04.8661s; **16** Sébastien Bourdais, F (-Chevrolet), -1 lap; **17** Mikhail Aleshin, RUS (-Honda), -1; **18** Luca Filippi, I (-Honda), -1; **19** Jack Hawksworth, GB (-Honda), -1; **20** Conor Daly, USA (-Honda), -1; **21** Max Chilton, GB (-Chevrolet), -1.
Most laps led: Pagenaud, 84.
Fastest race lap: Dixon, 1m 08.4533s, 120.958mph/194.664km/h.
Pole position: Pagenaud, 1m 06.7262s, 124.089mph/199.702km/h.
Championship points: Drivers: 1 Pagenaud, 188; **2** Dixon, 140; **3** Montoya, 136; **4** Castroneves, 118; **5** Kanaan, 106; **6** Rahal, 100.

ANGIE'S LIST GRAND PRIX OF INDIANAPOLIS, Indianapolis Motor Speedway, Speedway, Indiana, USA, 14 May. Round 5. 82 laps of the 2.439-mile/3.925km circuit, 199.998 miles/321.866km.
1 Simon Pagenaud, F (-Chevrolet), 1h 50m 18.5823s, 108.784mph/175.070km/h; **2** Hélio Castroneves, BR (-Chevrolet), +4.4748s; **3** James Hinchcliffe, CDN (-Honda), +5.0807s; **4** Graham Rahal, USA (-Honda), +7.0715s; **5** Charlie Kimball, USA (-Chevrolet), +7.4234s; **6** Conor Daly, USA (-Honda), +12.1838s; **7** Scott Dixon, NZ (-Chevrolet), +12.9226s; **8** Juan Pablo Montoya, CO (-Chevrolet), +13.6912s; **9** Ryan Hunter-Reay, USA (-Honda), +15.1933s; **10** Alexander Rossi, USA (-Honda), +16.3134s; **11** Spencer Pigot, USA (-Honda), +20.5172s; **12** Carlos Muñoz, CO (-Honda), +29.6369s; **13** Mikhail Aleshin, RUS (-Honda), +43.3094s; **14** Max Chilton, GB (-Chevrolet), +43.3785s; **15** Marco Andretti, USA (-Honda), +44.6339s; **16** Matthew Brabham, USA (-Chevrolet), +45.5107s; **17** Gabby Chaves, CO (-Honda), +47.0326s; **18** Takuma Sato, J (-Honda), +56.3389s; **19** Will Power, AUS (-Chevrolet), +57.4410s; **20** Jack Hawksworth, GB (-Honda), +1m 03.7229s; **21** Josef Newgarden, USA (-Chevrolet), +1m 08.6234s; **22** J.R. Hildebrand, USA (-Chevrolet), -1 lap; **23** Alex Tagliani, CDN (-Honda), -1; **24** Sébastien Bourdais, F (-Chevrolet), -62 (DNF-mechanical); **25** Tony Kanaan, BR (-Chevrolet), -82 (DNF-accident).
Most laps led: Pagenaud, 57.
Fastest race lap: Rossi, 1m 09.5535s, 126.240mph/203.163km/h.
Pole position: Pagenaud, 1m 08.6868s, 127.832mph/205.726km/h.
Championship points: Drivers: 1 Pagenaud, 242; **2** Dixon, 166; **3** Montoya, 160; **4** Castroneves, 159; **5** Rahal, 133; **6** Kanaan, 111.

100TH RUNNING OF THE INDIANAPOLIS 500 PRESENTED BY PENNGRADE MOTOR OIL, Indianapolis Motor Speedway, Speedway, Indiana, USA, 29 May. Round 6. 200 laps of the 2.500-mile/4.023km circuit, 500.000 miles/804.672km.
1 Alexander Rossi, USA (-Honda), 3h 00m 02.0872s, 166.634mph/268.172km/h; **2** Carlos Muñoz, CO (-Honda), +4.4975s; **3** Josef Newgarden, USA (-Chevrolet), +4.9304s; **4** Tony Kanaan, BR (-Chevrolet), +10.4963s; **5** Charlie Kimball, USA (-Chevrolet), +10.5218s; **6** J.R. Hildebrand, USA (-Chevrolet), +11.3459s; **7** James Hinchcliffe, CDN (-Honda), +12.7744s; **8** Scott Dixon, NZ (-Chevrolet), +15.1607s; **9** Sébastien Bourdais, F (-Chevrolet), +21.0613s; **10** Will Power, AUS (-Chevrolet), +21.5171s; **11** Hélio Castroneves, BR (-Chevrolet), +22.1015s; **12** Oriol Servià, E (-Honda), +23.8140s; **13** Marco Andretti, USA (-Honda), +24.9700s; **14** Graham Rahal, USA (-Honda), +28.2494s; **15** Max Chilton, GB (-Chevrolet), +28.7589s; **16** Jack Hawksworth, GB (-Honda), +32.1748s; **17** Alex Tagliani, CDN (-Honda), +32.1993s; **18** Pippa Mann, GB (-Honda), -1 lap; **19** Simon Pagenaud, F (-Chevrolet), -1; **20** Gabby Chaves, CO (-Honda), -1; **21** Townsend Bell, USA (-Honda), -1; **22** Matthew Brabham, USA (-Chevrolet), -1; **23** Bryan Clauson, USA (-Honda), -2; **24** Ryan Hunter-Reay, USA (-Honda), -2; **25** Spencer Pigot, USA (-Honda), -5; **26** Takuma Sato, J (-Honda), -37 (DNF-accident); **27** Mikhail Aleshin, RUS (-Honda), -74 (DNF-accident); **28** Stefan Wilson, GB (-Chevrolet), -81 (DNF-electrics); **29** Conor Daly, USA (-Honda), -85 (DNF-accident); **30** Buddy Lazier, USA (-Chevrolet), -100 (DNF-wheel lost); **31** Ed Carpenter, USA (-Chevrolet), -102 (DNF-engine); **32** Sage Karam, USA (-Chevrolet), -107 (DNF-accident); **33** Juan Pablo Montoya, CO (-Chevrolet), -137 (DNF-accident).
Most laps led: Hunter-Reay, 52.
Fastest race lap: Rossi, 39.9488s, 225.288mph/362.566km/h.
Pole position: Hinchcliffe, 2m 36.0063s, 230.760mph/371.372km/h (over 4 laps).
Championship points: Drivers: 1 Pagenaud, 292; **2** Dixon, 235; **3** Castroneves, 224; **4** Newgarden, 211; **5** Hinchcliffe, 205; **6** Rossi, 203.

CHEVROLET DUAL IN DETROIT RACE 1, The Raceway at Belle Isle, Detroit, Michigan, USA, 4/5 June. Round 7. 2 x 70 laps of the 2.350-mile/3.782km circuit.
Race 1 (164.500 miles/264.737km).
1 Sébastien Bourdais, F (-Chevrolet), 1h 40m 51.6838s, 97.857mph/157.486km/h; **2** Conor Daly, USA (-Honda), +2.0401s; **3** Juan Pablo Montoya, CO (-Chevrolet), +5.7067s; **4** Graham Rahal, USA (-Honda), +7.4793s; **5** Hélio Castroneves, BR (-Chevrolet), +40.0139s; **6** Carlos Muñoz, CO (-Honda), +40.7592s; **7** Ryan Hunter-Reay, USA (-Honda), +42.2990s; **8** Charlie

Kimball, USA (-Chevrolet), +44.4699s; **9** Tony Kanaan, BR (-Chevrolet), +45.5832s; **10** Alexander Rossi, USA (-Honda), +48.2961s; **11** Takuma Sato, J (-Honda), +51.1067s; **12** Gabby Chaves, CO (-Honda), +51.3256s; **13** Simon Pagenaud, F (-Chevrolet), +52.5313s; **14** Josef Newgarden, USA (-Chevrolet), +1m 06.2350s; **15** Mikhail Aleshin, RUS (-Honda), +1m 14.1421s; **16** Marco Andretti, USA (-Honda), -1 lap; **17** Spencer Pigot, USA (-Chevrolet), -1; **18** James Hinchcliffe, CDN (-Honda), -5; **19** Scott Dixon, NZ (-Chevrolet), -14 (DNF-electrics); **20** Will Power, AUS (-Chevrolet), -26 (DNF-mechanical); **21** Max Chilton, GB (-Chevrolet), -62 (DNF-accident); **22** Jack Hawksworth, GB (-Honda), -70 (DNF-mechanical).
Most laps led: Pagenaud, 35.
Fastest race lap: Dixon, 1m 14.6675s, 113.302 mph/182.342 km/h.
Pole position: Pagenaud, 1m 14.9166s, 112.926 mph/181.736 km/h.

Race 2 (164.500 miles/264.737km).
1 Will Power, AUS (-Chevrolet), 1h 42m 22.2672s, 96.414mph/155.163km/h; **2** Simon Pagenaud, F (-Chevrolet), +0.9203s; **3** Ryan Hunter-Reay, USA (-Honda), +1.4711s; **4** Josef Newgarden, USA (-Chevrolet), +2.4602s; **5** Scott Dixon, NZ (-Chevrolet), +3.1575s; **6** Conor Daly, USA (-Honda), +7.1263s; **7** Tony Kanaan, BR (-Chevrolet), +11.3012s; **8** Sébastien Bourdais, F (-Chevrolet), +12.9361s; **9** Marco Andretti, USA (-Honda), +26.4201s; **10** Takuma Sato, J (-Honda), +27.7105s; **11** Graham Rahal, USA (-Honda), +28.0410s; **12** Alexander Rossi, USA (-Honda), +28.5507s; **13** Gabby Chaves, CO (-Honda), +29.2530s; **14** Hélio Castroneves, BR (-Chevrolet), +29.6631s; **15** Carlos Muñoz, CO (-Honda), +30.4879s; **16** Charlie Kimball, USA (-Chevrolet), +30.6922s; **17** Mikhail Aleshin, RUS (-Honda), +1m 10.5229s; **18** Spencer Pigot, USA (-Chevrolet), -3 laps; **19** Jack Hawksworth, GB (-Honda), -22 (DNF-mechanical); **20** Juan Pablo Montoya, CO (-Chevrolet), -37 (DNF-accident); **21** James Hinchcliffe, CDN (-Honda), -70 (DNF-accident); **22** Max Chilton, GB (-Chevrolet), -70 (DNF-accident).
Most laps led: Pagenaud, 40.
Fastest race lap: Newgarden, 1m 14.5568s, 113.471mph/182.613km/h.
Pole position: Pagenaud, 1m 14.0379s, 114.266mph/183.893km/h.
Championship points: Drivers: 1 Pagenaud, 357; **2** Dixon, 277; **3** Castroneves, 271; **4** Newgarden, 259; **5** Rossi, 242; **6** Muñoz, 242.

KOHLER GRAND PRIX, Road America, Elkhart Lake, Wisconsin, USA, 26 June. Round 8. 50 laps of the 4.014-mile/6.460km circuit, 200.700 miles/322.995km.
1 Will Power, AUS (-Chevrolet), 1h 39m 10.3044s, 121.426mph/195.416km/h; **2** Tony Kanaan, BR (-Chevrolet), +0.7429s; **3** Graham Rahal, USA (-Honda), +5.9608s; **4** Ryan Hunter-Reay, USA (-Honda), +9.3597s; **5** Hélio Castroneves, BR (-Chevrolet), +10.5340s; **6** Charlie Kimball, USA (-Chevrolet), +10.9966s; **7** Juan Pablo Montoya, CO (-Chevrolet), +12.6191s; **8** Josef Newgarden, USA (-Chevrolet), +13.8835s; **9** Spencer Pigot, USA (-Chevrolet), +15.7290s; **10** Carlos Muñoz, CO (-Honda), +17.1132s; **11** Jack Hawksworth, GB (-Honda), +18.7152s; **12** Marco Andretti, USA (-Honda), +19.9030s; **13** Simon Pagenaud, F (-Chevrolet), +21.1530s; **14** James Hinchcliffe, CDN (-Honda), +22.1333s; **15** Alexander Rossi, USA (-Honda), +22.5908s; **16** Mikhail Aleshin, RUS (-Honda), +23.5531s; **17** Takuma Sato, J (-Honda), +35.3665s; **18** Sébastien Bourdais, F (-Chevrolet), -1 lap; **19** Gabby Chaves, CO (-Honda), -1; **20** Max Chilton, GB (-Chevrolet), -2; **21** Conor Daly, USA (-Honda), -11 (DNF-accident); **22** Scott Dixon, NZ (-Chevrolet), -44 (DNF-engine).
Most laps led: Power, 46.
Fastest race lap: Chilton, 1m 44.1196s, 138.787mph/223.355km/h.
Pole position: Power, 1m 42.2105s, 141.379mph/227.527km/h.
Championship points: Drivers: 1 Pagenaud, 375; **2** Castroneves, 301; **3** Power, 294; **4** Dixon, 285; **5** Newgarden, 283; **6** Kanaan, 280.

IOWA CORN 300, Iowa Speedway, Newton, Iowa, USA, 10 July. Round 9. 300 laps of the 0.894-mile/1.439km circuit, 268.200 miles/431.626km.
1 Josef Newgarden, USA (-Chevrolet), 1h 52m 16.3613s, 143.330mph/230.667km/h; **2** Will Power, AUS (-Chevrolet), +4.2828s; **3** Scott Dixon, NZ (-Chevrolet), +5.5085s; **4** Simon Pagenaud, F (-Chevrolet), +6.1827s; **5** Mikhail Aleshin, RUS (-Honda), +7.0386s; **6** Alexander Rossi, USA (-Honda), -1 lap; **7** Tony Kanaan, BR (-Chevrolet), -1; **8** Sébastien Bourdais, F (-Chevrolet), -1; **9** James Hinchcliffe, CDN (-Honda), -1; **10** Charlie Kimball, USA (-Chevrolet), -1; **11** Takuma Sato, J (-Honda), -2; **12** Carlos Muñoz, CO (-Honda), -2; **13** Hélio Castroneves, BR (-Chevrolet), -2; **14** Marco Andretti, USA (-Honda), -2; **15** Jack Hawksworth, GB (-Honda), -2; **16** Graham Rahal, USA (-Honda), -3; **17** Gabby Chaves, CO (-Honda), -7; **18** Ed Carpenter, USA (-Chevrolet), -16; **19** Max Chilton, GB (-Chevrolet), -26; **20** Juan Pablo Montoya, CO (-Chevrolet), -121 (DNF-engine); **21** Conor Daly, USA (-Honda), -159 (DNF-handling); **22** Ryan Hunter-Reay, USA (-Honda), -195 (DNF-engine).
Most laps led: Newgarden, 282.
Fastest race lap: Newgarden, 17.9317s, 179.481mph/288.847km/h.
Pole position: Pagenaud, 34.6334s, 185.855mph/299.105km/h (over 2 laps).

Championship points: Drivers: 1 Pagenaud, 409; **2** Newgarden, 336; **3** Power, 334; **4** Dixon, 321; **5** Castroneves, 318; **6** Kanaan, 306.

HONDA INDY TORONTO, Toronto Street Circuit, Ontario, Canada, 17 July. Round 10. 85 laps of the 1.786-mile/2.874km circuit, 151.810 miles/244.315km.
1 Will Power, AUS (-Chevrolet), 1h 42m 38.6925s, 88.739mph/142.812km/h; **2** Hélio Castroneves, BR (-Chevrolet), +1.5275s; **3** James Hinchcliffe, CDN (-Honda), +2.5303s; **4** Tony Kanaan, BR (-Chevrolet), +3.7758s; **5** Takuma Sato, J (-Honda), +4.0568s; **6** Mikhail Aleshin, RUS (-Honda), +5.1145s; **7** Sébastien Bourdais, F (-Chevrolet), +5.6393s; **8** Scott Dixon, NZ (-Chevrolet), +6.1020s; **9** Simon Pagenaud, F (-Chevrolet), +6.6355s; **10** Marco Andretti, USA (-Honda), +6.9746s; **11** Charlie Kimball, USA (-Chevrolet), +7.4782s; **12** Ryan Hunter-Reay, USA (-Honda), +8.0690s; **13** Graham Rahal, USA (-Honda), +8.5989s; **14** Luca Filippi, I (-Honda), +8.9217s; **15** Conor Daly, USA (-Honda), +9.4068s; **16** Alexander Rossi, USA (-Honda), +9.6896s; **17** Carlos Muñoz, CO (-Honda), +10.0568s; **18** Max Chilton, GB (-Chevrolet), +10.6502s; **19** Spencer Pigot, USA (-Chevrolet), +11.4494s; **20** Juan Pablo Montoya, CO (-Chevrolet), -1 lap; **21** Jack Hawksworth, GB (-Honda), -5 (DNF-accident); **22** Josef Newgarden, USA (-Chevrolet), -28 (DNF-accident).
Most laps led: Dixon, 56.
Fastest race lap: Castroneves, 1m 00.8127s, 105.728mph/170.153km/h.
Pole position: Dixon, 59.9073s, 107.326mph/172.724km/h.
Championship points: Drivers: 1 Pagenaud, 432; **2** Power, 385; **3** Castroneves, 358; **4** Dixon, 349; **5** Newgarden, 344; **6** Kanaan, 339.

THE HONDA INDY 200 AT MID-OHIO, Mid-Ohio Sports Car Course, Lexington, Ohio, USA, 31 July. Round 11. 90 laps of the 2.258-mile/3.634km circuit, 203.220 miles/327.051km.
1 Simon Pagenaud, F (-Chevrolet), 1h 49m 59.6875s, 110.853mph/178.400km/h; **2** Will Power, AUS (-Chevrolet), +4.1620s; **3** Carlos Muñoz, CO (-Honda), +6.5662s; **4** Graham Rahal, USA (-Honda), +7.0196s; **5** James Hinchcliffe, CDN (-Honda), +11.1260s; **6** Conor Daly, USA (-Honda), +11.8526s; **7** Spencer Pigot, USA (-Chevrolet), +12.8831s; **8** Charlie Kimball, USA (-Chevrolet), +15.0016s; **9** Takuma Sato, J (-Honda), +18.0128s; **10** Josef Newgarden, USA (-Chevrolet), +18.5404s; **11** Juan Pablo Montoya, CO (-Chevrolet), +20.6074s; **12** Tony Kanaan, BR (-Chevrolet), +23.9632s; **13** Marco Andretti, USA (-Honda), +24.7606s; **14** Alexander Rossi, USA (-Honda), +25.5191s; **15** Hélio Castroneves, BR (-Chevrolet), +26.6191s; **16** Max Chilton, GB (-Chevrolet), +26.8199s; **17** Mikhail Aleshin, RUS (-Honda), +42.7274s; **18** Ryan Hunter-Reay, USA (-Honda), +53.5383s; **19** R.C. Enerson, USA (-Honda), -1 lap; **20** Sébastien Bourdais, F (-Chevrolet), -4 (DNF-spin); **21** Jack Hawksworth, GB (-Honda), -30 (DNF-accident); **22** Scott Dixon, NZ (-Chevrolet), -63 (DNF-mechanical).
Most laps led: Aleshin, 33.
Fastest race lap: Power, 1m 05.2600s, 124.560mph/200.460km/h.
Pole position: Pagenaud, 1m 03.8700s, 127.271mph/204.823km/h.
Championship points: Drivers: 1 Pagenaud, 484; **2** Power, 426; **3** Castroneves, 373; **4** Newgarden, 364; **5** Dixon, 357; **6** Kanaan, 357.

ABC SUPPLY 500, Pocono Raceway, Long Pond, Pennsylvania, USA, 22 August. Round 12. 200 laps of the 2.500-mile/4.023km circuit, 500.000 miles/804.672km.
1 Will Power, AUS (-Chevrolet), 2h 46m 28.9856s, 180.198mph/290.001km/h; **2** Mikhail Aleshin, RUS (-Honda), +1.1459s; **3** Ryan Hunter-Reay, USA (-Honda), +5.9076s; **4** Josef Newgarden, USA (-Chevrolet), +7.0750s; **5** Sébastien Bourdais, F (-Chevrolet), +7.5285s; **6** Scott Dixon, NZ (-Chevrolet), +7.8896s; **7** Carlos Muñoz, CO (-Honda), +11.5938s; **8** Juan Pablo Montoya, CO (-Chevrolet), +13.4345s; **9** Tony Kanaan, BR (-Chevrolet), +13.7988s; **10** James Hinchcliffe, CDN (-Honda), +14.2235s; **11** Graham Rahal, USA (-Honda), +14.3471s; **12** Marco Andretti, USA (-Honda), +16.3334s; **13** Max Chilton, GB (-Chevrolet), +17.1907s; **14** Jack Hawksworth, GB (-Honda), +18.5585s; **15** Charlie Kimball, USA (-Chevrolet), -1 lap; **16** Conor Daly, USA (-Honda), -2; **17** Pippa Mann, GB (-Honda), -3; **18** Simon Pagenaud, F (-Chevrolet), -43 (DNF-accident); **19** Hélio Castroneves, BR (-Chevrolet), -137 (DNF-accident); **20** Alexander Rossi, USA (-Honda), -137 (DNF-accident *); **21** Ed Carpenter, USA (-Chevrolet), -143 (DNF-engine); **22** Takuma Sato, J (-Honda), -199 (DNF-accident).
Most laps led: Aleshin, 87.
** includes 20s penalty for causing an accident.*
Fastest race lap: Power, 41.1901s, 218.499mph/351.640km/h.
Pole position: Aleshin, 1m 21.6530s, 220.445mph/354.772km/h (over 2 laps).
Championship points: Drivers: 1 Pagenaud, 497; **2** Power, 477; **3** Newgarden, 397; **4** Dixon, 386; **5** Castroneves, 384; **6** Kanaan, 380.

FIRESTONE 600, Texas Motor Speedway, Fort Worth, Texas, USA, 27 August. Round 13. 248 laps of the 1.455-mile/2.342-km circuit, 360.840 miles/580.716km.
Race scheduled for 11 June, but postponed until the following day due to rain. The race had to be abandoned after 71 laps due to the accident of Josef Newgarden and Conor Daly. The race could not be continued because of storms and was resumed on 27 August.
1 Graham Rahal, USA (-Honda), 2h 29m 24.8886s, 144.901mph/233.196km/h; **2** James Hinchcliffe, CDN (-Honda), +0.0080s; **3** Tony Kanaan, BR (-Chevrolet), +0.0903s; **4** Simon Pagenaud, F (-Chevrolet), +0.4773s; **5** Hélio Castroneves, BR (-Chevrolet), +9.3424s; **6** Charlie Kimball, USA (-Chevrolet), -1 lap; **7** Carlos Muñoz, CO (-Honda), -1; **8** Will Power, AUS (-Chevrolet), -1; **9** Juan Pablo Montoya, CO (-Chevrolet), -2; **10** Sébastien Bourdais, F (-Chevrolet), -2; **11** Alexander Rossi, USA (-Honda), -2; **12** Marco Andretti, USA (-Honda), -3; **13** Ryan Hunter-Reay, USA (-Honda), -3; **14** Gabby Chaves, CO (-Honda), -3; **15** Max Chilton, GB (-Chevrolet), -5; **16** Mikhail Aleshin, RUS (-Honda), -17 (DNF-accident); **17** Jack Hawksworth, GB (-Honda), -21 (DNF-accident); **18** Ed Carpenter, USA (-Chevrolet), -25 (DNF-accident); **19** Scott Dixon, NZ (-Chevrolet), -37 (DNF-accident); **20** Takuma Sato, J (-Honda), -88 (DNF-handling); **21** Conor Daly, USA (-Honda), -206 (DNF-accident); **22** Josef Newgarden, USA (-Chevrolet), -207 (DNF-accident).
Most laps led: Hinchcliffe, 188.
Fastest race lap: Dixon, 24.3797s, 214.851mph/345.769km/h.
Pole position: Muñoz, 48.2460s, 217.137mph/349.448km/h (over **2** laps).
Championship points: Drivers: 1 Pagenaud, 529; **2** Power, 501; **3** Kanaan, 416; **4** Castroneves, 415; **5** Newgarden, 406; **6** Dixon, 397.

INDYCAR GRAND PRIX AT THE GLEN PRESENTED BY HITACHI, Watkins Glen International, New York, USA, 4 September. Round 14. 60 laps of the 3.370-mile/5.423km circuit, 202.200 miles/325.409km.
1 Scott Dixon, NZ (-Chevrolet), 1h 41m 39.8592s, 119.334mph/192.049km/h; **2** Josef Newgarden, USA (-Chevrolet), +16.5308s; **3** Hélio Castroneves, BR (-Chevrolet), +21.4417s; **4** Conor Daly, USA (-Honda), +24.3349s; **5** Sébastien Bourdais, F (-Chevrolet), +25.3815s; **6** Charlie Kimball, USA (-Chevrolet), +29.4268s; **7** Simon Pagenaud, F (-Chevrolet), +31.1118s; **8** Alexander Rossi, USA (-Honda), +32.0710s; **9** R.C. Enerson, USA (-Honda), +32.3965s; **10** Max Chilton, GB (-Chevrolet), +32.9478s; **11** Carlos Muñoz, CO (-Honda), +34.7869s; **12** Marco Andretti, USA (-Honda), +35.3813s; **13** Juan Pablo Montoya, CO (-Chevrolet), +37.7024s; **14** Ryan Hunter-Reay, USA (-Honda), +42.4644s; **15** Spencer Pigot, USA (-Chevrolet), +45.3829s; **16** Jack Hawksworth, GB (-Honda), +45.7584s; **17** Takuma Sato, J (-Honda), +1m 07.4937s; **18** James Hinchcliffe, CDN (-Honda), -1 lap; **19** Tony Kanaan, BR (-Chevrolet), -1; **20** Will Power, AUS (-Chevrolet), -22 (DNF-accident); **21** Graham Rahal, USA (-Honda), -41 (DNF-accident); **22** Mikhail Aleshin, RUS (-Honda), -46 (DNF-accident).
Most laps led: Dixon, 50.
Fastest race lap: Kanaan, 1m 23.9436s, 144.526mph/232.591km/h.
Pole position: Dixon, 1m 22.5259s, 147.008mph/236.587km/h.
Championship points: Drivers: 1 Pagenaud, 555; **2** Power, 512; **3** Dixon, 451; **4** Castroneves, 451; **5** Newgarden, 446; **6** Kanaan, 427.

GOPRO GRAND PRIX OF SONOMA, Infineon Raceway, Sears Point, Sonoma, California, USA, 18 September. Round 15. 85 laps of the 2.385-mile/3.838km circuit, 202.725 miles/326.254km.
1 Simon Pagenaud, F (-Chevrolet), 2h 00m 12.9424s, 101.181mph/162.834km/h; **2** Graham Rahal, USA (-Honda), +3.2523s; **3** Juan Pablo Montoya, CO (-Chevrolet), +18.0157s; **4** Ryan Hunter-Reay, USA (-Honda), +29.7224s; **5** Alexander Rossi, USA (-Honda), +30.6649s; **6** Josef Newgarden, USA (-Chevrolet), +32.2754s; **7** Hélio Castroneves, BR (-Chevrolet), +32.8490s; **8** Marco Andretti, USA (-Honda), +34.3002s; **9** Charlie Kimball, USA (-Chevrolet), +34.9353s; **10** Sébastien Bourdais, F (-Chevrolet), +43.8965s; **11** Mikhail Aleshin, RUS (-Honda), +49.3242s; **12** James Hinchcliffe, CDN (-Honda), +51.1304s; **13** Tony Kanaan, BR (-Chevrolet), +52.1792s; **14** Takuma Sato, J (-Honda), +52.6331s; **15** Carlos Muñoz, CO (-Honda), +56.6756s; **16** Max Chilton, GB (-Chevrolet), +1m 09.2581s; **17** Scott Dixon, NZ (-Chevrolet), +1m 21.1112s; **18** Jack Hawksworth, GB (-Honda), -1 lap; **19** R.C. Enerson, USA (-Honda), -1; **20** Will Power, AUS (-Chevrolet), -8; **21** Conor Daly, USA (-Honda), -49 (DNF-overheating); **22** Spencer Pigot, USA (-Chevrolet), -50 (DNF-gearbox).
Most laps led: Pagenaud, 76.
Fastest race lap: Kanaan, 1m 19.2623s, 108.324mph/174.330km/h.
Pole position: Pagenaud, 1m 16.2565s, 112.594mph/181.202km/h.

Final championship points
Drivers
1 Simon Pagenaud, F, 659; **2** Will Power, AUS, 532; **3** Hélio Castroneves, BR, 504; **4** Josef Newgarden, USA, 502; **5** Graham Rahal, USA, 484; **6** Scott Dixon, NZ, 477; **7** Tony Kanaan, BR, 461; **8** Juan Pablo Montoya, CO, 433; **9** Charlie Kimball, USA, 433; **10** Carlos Muñoz, CO, 432; **11** Alexander Rossi, USA, 430; **12** Ryan Hunter-Reay, USA, 428; **13** James Hinchcliffe, CDN, 416; **14** Sébastien Bourdais, F, 404; **15** Mikhail Aleshin, RUS, 347; **16** Marco Andretti, USA, 339; **17** Takuma Sato, J, 320; **18** Conor Daly, USA, 313; **19** Max Chilton, GB, 267; **20** Jack Hawksworth, GB, 229; **21** Spencer Pigot, USA, 165; **22** Gabby Chaves, CO, 121; **23** J.R. Hildebrand, USA, 84; **24** Oriol Servià, E, 72; **25** Ed Carpenter, USA, 67; **26** Luca Filippi, I, 61; **27** Townsend Bell, USA, 55; **28** R.C. Enerson, USA, 55; **29** Pippa Mann, GB, 46; **30** Matthew Brabham, USA, 37; **31** Alex Tagliani, CDN, 35; **32** Sage Karam, USA, 22; **33** Bryan Clauson, USA, 21; **34** Stefan Wilson, GB, 14; **35** Buddy Lazier, USA, 12.

Rookies
1 Alexander Rossi, 430; **2** Conor Daly, 313; **3** Max Chilton, 267.

Engine manufacturers
1 Chevrolet, 1814; **2** Honda, 1710.

NASCAR Sprint Cup Series

THE 58TH ANNUAL DAYTONA 500, Daytona International Speedway, Daytona Beach, Florida, USA, 21 February. Round 1. 200 laps of the 2.500-mile/4.023km circuit, 500.000 miles/804.672km.
1 Denny Hamlin, USA (Toyota Camry), 3h 10m 25s, 157.549mph/253.551km/h; **2** Martin Truex Jr, USA (Toyota Camry), +0.010s; **3** Kyle Busch, USA (Toyota Camry), +0.102s; **4** Kevin Harvick, USA (Chevrolet SS), +0.147s; **5** Carl Edwards, USA (Toyota Camry), +0.199s; **6** Joey Logano, USA (Ford Fusion), +0.235s; **7** Kyle Larson, USA (Chevrolet SS), +0.352s; **8** Regan Smith, USA (Chevrolet SS), +0.358s; **9** Austin Dillon, USA (Chevrolet SS), +0.469s; **10** Kurt Busch, USA (Chevrolet SS), +0.551s.
Pole position: Chase Elliott, USA (Chevrolet SS), 45.845s, 196.314mph/315.936km/h.
Drivers' championship points: 1 Hamlin, 45; **2** Truex Jr, 40; **3** Busch (Kyle), 39; **4** Harvick, 37; **5** Edwards, 36; **6** Logano, 35.

57TH ANNUAL FOLDS OF HONOR QUIKTRIP 500, Atlanta Motor Speedway, Hampton, Georgia, USA, 28 February. Round 2. 330 laps of the 1.540-mile/2.478km circuit, 508.200 miles/817.869km.
1 Jimmie Johnson, USA (Chevrolet SS), 3h 15m 38s, 155.863mph/250.837km/h; **2** Dale Earnhardt Jr, USA (Chevrolet SS), +0.557s; **3** Kyle Busch, USA (Toyota Camry), +0.569s; **4** Kurt Busch, USA (Chevrolet SS), +0.974s; **5** Carl Edwards, USA (Toyota Camry), +1.408s; **6** Kevin Harvick, USA (Chevrolet SS), +1.420s; **7** Martin Truex Jr, USA (Toyota Camry), +1.629s; **8** Chase Elliott, USA (Chevrolet SS), +1.803s; **9** Brad Keselowski, USA (Ford Fusion), +1.845s; **10** Ricky Stenhouse Jr, USA (Ford Fusion), +4.976s.
Pole position: Busch, 28.938s, 191.582mph/308.321km/h.
Drivers' championship points: 1 Busch (Kyle), 78; **2** Harvick, 74; **3** Edwards, 73; **4** Johnson, 70; **4** Hamlin, 70; **6** Busch (Kurt), 69.

19TH ANNUAL KOBALT 400, Las Vegas Motor Speedway, Nevada, USA, 6 March. Round 3. 267 laps of the 1.500-mile/2.414km circuit, 400.500 miles/644.542km.
1 Brad Keselowski, USA (Ford Fusion), 2h 53m 55s, 138.170mph/222.362km/h; **2** Joey Logano, USA (Ford Fusion), +0.675s; **3** Jimmie Johnson, USA (Chevrolet SS), 267 laps; **4** Kyle Busch, USA (Toyota Camry), +0.830s; **5** Austin Dillon, USA (Chevrolet SS), +1.282s; **6** Ryan Blaney, USA (Ford Fusion), +1.911s; **7** Kevin Harvick, USA (Chevrolet SS), +2.399s; **8** Dale Earnhardt Jr, USA (Chevrolet SS), +5.622s; **9** Kurt Busch, USA (Chevrolet SS), +6.064s; **10** Kasey Kahne, USA (Chevrolet SS), +8.928s.
Pole position: Busch, 27.505s, 196.328mph/315.959km/h.
Drivers' championship points: 1 Busch (Kyle), 116; **2** Johnson, 110; **3** Harvick, 109; **4** Logano, 104; **5** Busch (Kurt), 102; **6** Keselowski, 98.

12TH ANNUAL GOOD SAM 500, Phoenix International Raceway, Arizona, USA, 13 March. Round 4. 313 laps of the 1.000-mile/1.609km circuit, 313.000 miles/503.725km.
1 Kevin Harvick, USA (Chevrolet SS), 2h 45m 53s, 113.212mph/182.197km/h; **2** Carl Edwards, USA (Toyota Camry), +0.010s; **3** Denny Hamlin, USA (Toyota Camry), +0.370s; **4** Kyle Busch, USA (Toyota Camry), +0.478s; **5** Dale Earnhardt Jr, USA (Chevrolet SS), +0.647s; **6** Kurt Busch, USA (Chevrolet SS), +0.705s; **7** Matt Kenseth, USA (Toyota Camry), +1.065s; **8** Chase Elliott, USA (Chevrolet SS), +1.272s; **9** Austin Dillon, USA (Chevrolet SS), +1.429s; **10** Ryan Blaney, USA (Ford Fusion), +1.535s.
Pole position: Busch, 26.014s, 138.387mph/222.712km/h.
Drivers' championship points: 1 Harvick, 154; **2** Busch (Kyle), 154; **3** Johnson, 140; **4** Busch (Kurt), 137; **5** Edwards, 136; **6** Hamlin, 131.

20TH ANNUAL AUTO CLUB 400, California Speedway, Fontana, California, USA, 20 March. Round 5. 205 laps of the 2.000-mile/3.219km circuit, 410.000 miles/659.831km.
1 Jimmie Johnson, USA (Chevrolet SS), 2h 59m 17s, 137.213mph/220.823km/h; **2** Kevin Harvick, USA (Chevrolet SS), +0.772s; **3** Denny Hamlin, USA (Toyota Camry), +1.030s; **4** Joey Logano, USA (Ford Fusion), +1.292s; **5** Ricky Stenhouse Jr, USA (Ford Fusion), +2.509s; **6** Chase Elliott, USA (Chevrolet SS), +2.512s; **7** Carl Edwards,

USA (Toyota Camry), +2.607s; **8** A.J. Allmendinger, USA (Chevrolet SS), +2.650s; **9** Brad Keselowski, USA (Ford Fusion), +2.769s; **10** Jamie McMurray, USA (Chevrolet SS), +3.159s.
Pole position: Austin Dillon, USA (Chevrolet SS), 38.200s, 188.482mph/303.332km/h.
Drivers' championship points: 1 Harvick, 195; **2** Johnson, 184; **3** Edwards, 171; **4** Hamlin, 170; **5** Busch (Kyle), 170; **6** Logano, 165.

67TH ANNUAL STP 500, Martinsville Speedway, Virginia, USA, 3 April. Round 6. 500 laps of the 0.526-mile/0.847km circuit, 263.000 miles/423.257km.
1 Kyle Busch, USA (Toyota Camry), 3h 17m 02s, 80.088mph/128.889km/h; **2** A.J. Allmendinger, USA (Chevrolet SS), +0.663s; **3** Kyle Larson, USA (Chevrolet SS), +1.408s; **4** Austin Dillon, USA (Chevrolet SS), +2.306s; **5** Brad Keselowski, USA (Ford Fusion), +2.720s; **6** Carl Edwards, USA (Toyota Camry), +3.129s; **7** Brian Vickers, USA (Chevrolet SS), +3.346s; **8** Paul Menard, USA (Chevrolet SS), +3.520s; **9** Jimmie Johnson, USA (Chevrolet SS), +3.861s; **10** Ryan Newman, USA (Chevrolet SS), +4.654s.
Pole position: Joey Logano, USA (Ford Fusion), 19.513s, 97.043mph/156.176km/h.
Drivers' championship points: 1 Harvick, 220; **2** Johnson, 216; **3** Busch (Kyle), 215; **4** Edwards, 206; **5** Logano, 196; **6** Keselowski, 178.

20TH ANNUAL DUCK COMMANDER 500, Texas Motor Speedway, Fort Worth, Texas, USA, 9 April. Round 7. 334 laps of the 1.500-mile/2.414km circuit, 501.000 miles/806.281km.
1 Kyle Busch, USA (Toyota Camry), 3h 37m 16s, 138.355mph/222.661km/h; **2** Dale Earnhardt Jr, USA (Chevrolet SS), +3.904s; **3** Joey Logano, USA (Ford Fusion), +4.841s; **4** Jimmie Johnson, USA (Chevrolet SS), +6.661s; **5** Chase Elliott, USA (Chevrolet SS), +6.888s; **6** Martin Truex Jr, USA (Toyota Camry), +7.297s; **7** Carl Edwards, USA (Toyota Camry), +8.927s; **8** Kasey Kahne, USA (Chevrolet SS), +11.860s; **9** Kurt Busch, USA (Chevrolet SS), +12.521s; **10** Kevin Harvick, USA (Chevrolet SS), +13.843s.
Pole position: Edwards, 27.748s, 194.609mph/313.192km/h.
Drivers' championship points: 1 Busch (Kyle), 259; **2** Johnson, 253; **3** Harvick, 252; **4** Edwards, 241; **5** Logano, 234; **6** Earnhardt Jr, 211.

56TH ANNUAL FOOD CITY 500, Bristol Motor Speedway, Tennessee, USA, 17 April. Round 8. 500 laps of the 0.533-mile/0.858km circuit, 266.500 miles/428.890km.
1 Carl Edwards, USA (Toyota Camry), 3h 15m 52s, 81.637mph/131.382km/h; **2** Dale Earnhardt Jr, USA (Chevrolet SS), +0.766s; **3** Kurt Busch, USA (Chevrolet SS), +0.880s; **4** Chase Elliott, USA (Chevrolet SS), +1.137s; **5** Trevor Bayne, USA (Ford Fusion), +1.898s; **6** Matt DiBenedetto, USA (Toyota Camry), +2.071s; **7** Kevin Harvick, USA (Chevrolet SS), +2.424s; **8** Clint Bowyer, USA (Chevrolet SS), +2.689s; **9** Ryan Newman, USA (Chevrolet SS), +2.815s; **10** Joey Logano, USA (Ford Fusion), +2.944s.
Pole position: Edwards, 14.991s, 127.997mph/205.991km/h.
Drivers' championship points: 1 Harvick, 287; **2** Edwards, 286; **3** Johnson, 271; **4** Logano, 266; **5** Busch (Kyle), 262; **6** Earnhardt Jr, 250.

62ND ANNUAL TOYOTA OWNERS 400, Richmond International Raceway, Virginia, USA, 24 April. Round 9. 400 laps of the 0.750-mile/1.20-km circuit, 300.000 miles/482.803km.
1 Carl Edwards, USA (Toyota Camry), 3h 05m 26s, 97.070mph/156.219km/h; **2** Kyle Busch, USA (Toyota Camry), +0.675s; **3** Jimmie Johnson, USA (Chevrolet SS), +2.689s; **4** Kasey Kahne, USA (Chevrolet SS), +3.735s; **5** Kevin Harvick, USA (Chevrolet SS), +4.903s; **6** Denny Hamlin, USA (Toyota Camry), +5.329s; **7** Matt Kenseth, USA (Toyota Camry), +5.929s; **8** Joey Logano, USA (Ford Fusion), +7.738s; **9** Martin Truex Jr, USA (Toyota Camry), +8.409s; **10** Kurt Busch, USA (Chevrolet SS), +8.799s.
Pole position: Harvick.
Drivers' championship points: 1 Edwards, 331; **2** Harvick, 324; **3** Johnson, 310; **4** Busch (Kyle), 302; **5** Logano, 299; **6** Busch (Kurt), 279.

47TH ANNUAL GEICO 500, Talladega Superspeedway, Alabama, USA, 1 May. Round 10. 188 laps of the 2.660-mile/4.281km circuit, 500.080 miles/804.801km.
1 Brad Keselowski, USA (Ford Fusion), 3h 34m 15s, 140.046mph/225.382km/h; **2** Kyle Busch, USA (Toyota Camry), +0.111s; **3** Austin Dillon, USA (Chevrolet SS), +0.125s; **4** Jamie McMurray, USA (Chevrolet SS), +0.223s; **5** Chase Elliott, USA (Chevrolet SS), +0.196s; **6** Tony Stewart, USA (Chevrolet SS), +0.317s; **7** Clint Bowyer, USA (Chevrolet SS), +0.347s; **8** Kurt Busch, USA (Chevrolet SS), +0.308s; **9** Ryan Blaney, USA (Ford Fusion), +0.388s; **10** Trevor Bayne, USA (Ford Fusion), +0.550s.
Pole position: Elliott, 49.704s, 192.661mph/310.057km/h.
Drivers' championship points: 1 Harvick, 351; **2** Busch (Kyle), 342; **3** Edwards, 337; **4** Johnson, 329; **5** Logano, 316; **6** Busch (Kurt), 312.

6TH ANNUAL GO BOWLING 400, Kansas Speedway, Kansas City, Kansas, USA, 7 May. Round 11. 267 laps of the 1.500-mile/2.414km circuit, 400.500 miles/644.542km.
1 Kyle Busch, USA (Toyota Camry), 2h 49m 20s, 141.909mph/228.381km/h; **2** Kevin Harvick, USA (Chevrolet SS), +1.112s; **3** Kurt Busch, USA (Chevrolet SS), +2.723s; **4** Matt Kenseth, USA (Toyota Camry), +4.139s; **5** Ryan Blaney, USA (Ford Fusion), +6.178s; **6** Austin Dillon, USA (Chevrolet SS), +7.150s; **7** Ryan Newman, USA (Chevrolet SS), +7.884s; **8** A.J. Allmendinger, USA (Chevrolet SS), +8.594s; **9** Chase Elliott, USA (Chevrolet SS), +9.124s; **10** Brad Keselowski, USA (Ford Fusion), +9.791s.
Pole position: Martin Truex Jr, USA (Toyota Camry), 28.284s, 190.921mph/307.257km/h.
Drivers' championship points: 1 Harvick, 390; **2** Busch (Kyle), 386; **3** Edwards, 367; **4** Johnson, 353; **5** Busch (Kurt), 350; **6** Keselowski, 332.

47TH ANNUAL AAA 400 DRIVE FOR AUTISM, Dover International Speedway, Delaware, USA, 15 May. Round 12. 400 laps of the 1.000-mile/1.609km circuit, 400.000 miles/643.738km.
1 Matt Kenseth, USA (Toyota Camry), 3h 39m 29s, 109.348mph/175.978km/h; **2** Kyle Larson, USA (Chevrolet SS), +0.187s; **3** Chase Elliott, USA (Chevrolet SS), +0.633s; **4** Kasey Kahne, USA (Chevrolet SS), +2.670s; **5** Kurt Busch, USA (Chevrolet SS), +3.308s; **6** Brad Keselowski, USA (Ford Fusion), +4.238s; **7** Denny Hamlin, USA (Toyota Camry), +4.260s; **8** Ryan Blaney, USA (Ford Fusion), +6.500s; **9** Martin Truex Jr, USA (Toyota Camry), +6.706s; **10** Trevor Bayne, USA (Ford Fusion), +8.380s.
Pole position: Harvick.
Drivers' championship points: 1 Harvick, 418; **2** Busch (Kyle), 397; **3** Busch (Kurt), 386; **4** Edwards, 381; **5** Johnson, 370; **6** Keselowski, 368.

57TH ANNUAL COCA-COLA 600, Lowe's Motor Speedway, Concord, Charlotte, North Carolina, USA, 29 May. Round 13. 400 laps of the 1.500-mile/2.414km circuit, 600.000 miles/965.606km.
1 Martin Truex Jr, USA (Toyota Camry), 3h 44m 05s, 160.655mph/258.548km/h; **2** Kevin Harvick, USA (Chevrolet SS), +2.572s; **3** Jimmie Johnson, USA (Chevrolet SS), +4.591s; **4** Denny Hamlin, USA (Toyota Camry), +6.406s; **5** Brad Keselowski, USA (Ford Fusion), +7.221s; **6** Kurt Busch, USA (Chevrolet SS), +7.221s; **7** Matt Kenseth, USA (Toyota Camry), +10.526s; **8** Chase Elliott, USA (Chevrolet SS), +11.493s; **9** Joey Logano, USA (Ford Fusion), +14.087s; **10** Ryan Newman, USA (Chevrolet SS), +16.084s.
Pole position: Truex Jr, 28.077s, 192.328mph/309.522km/h.
Drivers' championship points: 1 Harvick, 457; **2** Busch (Kurt), 421; **3** Johnson, 409; **4** Busch (Kyle), 405; **5** Edwards, 404; **6** Keselowski, 404.

35TH ANNUAL AXALTA WE PAINT WINNERS 400, Pocono Raceway, Long Pond, Pennsylvania, USA, 6 June. Round 14. 160 laps of the 2.500-mile/4.023km circuit, 400.000 miles/643.738km.
1 Kurt Busch, USA (Chevrolet SS), 3h 11m 15s, 125.490mph/201.957km/h; **2** Dale Earnhardt Jr, USA (Chevrolet SS), +1.126s; **3** Brad Keselowski, USA (Ford Fusion), +1.402s; **4** Chase Elliott, USA (Chevrolet SS), +2.727s; **5** Joey Logano, USA (Ford Fusion), +4.614s; **6** Kasey Kahne, USA (Chevrolet SS), +5.593s; **7** Matt Kenseth, USA (Toyota Camry), +6.304s; **8** Carl Edwards, USA (Toyota Camry), +6.441s; **9** Kevin Harvick, USA (Chevrolet SS), +6.981s; **10** Ryan Blaney, USA (Ford Fusion), +19.276s.
Pole position: Keselowski, 49.525s, 181.726mph/292.460km/h.
Drivers' championship points: 1 Harvick, 490; **2** Busch (Kurt), 465; **3** Keselowski, 442; **4** Edwards, 437; **5** Busch (Kyle), 416; **6** Johnson, 415.

48TH ANNUAL FIREKEEPERS CASINO 400, Michigan International Speedway, Brooklyn, Michigan, USA, 12 June. Round 15. 200 laps of the 2.000-mile/3.219km circuit, 400.000 miles/643.738km.
1 Joey Logano, USA (Ford Fusion), 2h 58m 47s, 134.241mph/216.039km/h; **2** Chase Elliott, USA (Chevrolet SS), +0.889s; **3** Kyle Larson, USA (Chevrolet SS), +3.069s; **4** Brad Keselowski, USA (Ford Fusion), +3.901s; **5** Kevin Harvick, USA (Chevrolet SS), +4.775s; **6** Carl Edwards, USA (Toyota Camry), +5.298s; **7** Tony Stewart, USA (Chevrolet SS), +6.144s; **8** Austin Dillon, USA (Chevrolet SS), +6.966s; **9** Jamie McMurray, USA (Chevrolet SS), +7.537s; **10** Kurt Busch, USA (Chevrolet SS), +7.729s.
Pole position: Logano, 36.080s, 199.557mph/321.155km/h.
Drivers' championship points: 1 Harvick, 526; **2** Busch (Kurt), 496; **3** Keselowski, 480; **4** Edwards, 472; **5** Logano, 455; **6** Elliott, 453.

28TH ANNUAL TOYOTA/SAVE MART 350, Infineon Raceway, Sears Point, Sonoma, California, USA, 26 June. Round 16. 110 laps of the 1.990-mile/3.203km circuit, 218.900 miles/352.285km.
1 Tony Stewart, USA (Chevrolet SS), 2h 42m 13s, 80.966mph/130.302km/h; **2** Denny Hamlin, USA (Toyota Camry), +0.625s; **3** Joey Logano, USA (Ford Fusion), +0.981s; **4** Carl Edwards, USA (Toyota Camry), +1.865s; **5** Martin Truex Jr, USA (Toyota Camry), +2.980s; **6** Kevin Harvick, USA (Chevrolet SS), +3.350s; **7** Kyle Busch, USA (Toyota Camry), +4.065s; **8** Ryan Newman, USA (Chevrolet SS), +4.984s; **9** Kasey Kahne, USA (Chevrolet SS), +5.724s; **10** Kurt Busch, USA (Chevrolet SS), +6.772s.
Pole position: Edwards, 1m 14.799s, 95.777mph/154.138km/h.
Drivers' championship points: 1 Harvick, 562; **2** Busch (Kurt), 527; **3** Edwards, 510; **4** Keselowski, 506; **5** Logano, 493; **6** Elliott, 473.

58TH ANNUAL COKE ZERO 400 POWERED BY COCA-COLA, Daytona International Speedway, Daytona Beach, Florida, USA, 2 July. Round 17. 161 laps of the 2.500-mile/4.023km circuit, 402.500 miles/647.761km.
1 Brad Keselowski, USA (Ford Fusion), 2h 40m 38s, 150.342mph/241.953km/h; **2** Kyle Busch, USA (Toyota Camry), +0.159s; **3** Trevor Bayne, USA (Ford Fusion), +0.266s; **4** Joey Logano, USA (Ford Fusion), +0.298s; **5** Ricky Stenhouse Jr, USA (Ford Fusion), +0.432s; **6** Kyle Larson, USA (Chevrolet SS), +0.439s; **7** Austin Dillon, USA (Chevrolet SS), +0.503s; **8** Greg Biffle, USA (Ford Fusion), +0.576s; **9** Clint Bowyer, USA (Chevrolet SS), +0.597s; **10** Michael McDowell, USA (Chevrolet SS), +0.602s.
Pole position: Biffle, 46.643s, 192.955mph/310.531km/h.
Drivers' championship points: 1 Harvick, 565; **2** Keselowski, 551; **3** Busch (Kurt), 545; **4** Logano, 531; **5** Edwards, 527; **6** Busch (Kyle), 492.

6TH ANNUAL QUAKER STATE 400 PRESENTED BY ADVANCE AUTO PARTS, Kentucky Speedway, Fort Mitchell, Kentucky, USA, 9 July. Round 18. 267 laps of the 1.500-mile/2.414km circuit, 400.500 miles/644.542km.
1 Brad Keselowski, USA (Ford Fusion), 3h 06m 53s, 128.583mph/206.934km/h; **2** Carl Edwards, USA (Toyota Camry), +0.175s; **3** Ryan Newman, USA (Chevrolet SS), +2.318s; **4** Kurt Busch, USA (Chevrolet SS), +8.035s; **5** Tony Stewart, USA (Chevrolet SS), +14.859s; **6** Greg Biffle, USA (Ford Fusion), +15.046s; **7** Jamie McMurray, USA (Chevrolet SS), +16.767s; **8** Matt Kenseth, USA (Toyota Camry), +17.419s; **9** Kevin Harvick, USA (Chevrolet SS), +17.721s; **10** Martin Truex Jr, USA (Toyota Camry), +18.106s.
Pole position: Harvick.
Drivers' championship points: 1 Harvick, 599; **2** Keselowski, 595; **3** Busch (Kurt), 583; **4** Edwards, 566; **5** Logano, 533; **6** Busch (Kyle), 521.

24TH ANNUAL NEW HAMPSHIRE 301, New Hampshire International Speedway, Loudon, New Hampshire, USA, 17 July. Round 19. 301 laps of the 1.058-mile/1.703km circuit, 318.458 miles/512.508km.
1 Matt Kenseth, USA (Toyota Camry), 2h 57m 53s, 107.416mph/172.869km/h; **2** Tony Stewart, USA (Chevrolet SS), +1.982s; **3** Joey Logano, USA (Ford Fusion), +3.671s; **4** Kevin Harvick, USA (Chevrolet SS), +3.690s; **5** Greg Biffle, USA (Ford Fusion), +4.265s; **6** Jamie McMurray, USA (Chevrolet SS), +5.483s; **7** Ryan Newman, USA (Chevrolet SS), +5.989s; **8** Kyle Busch, USA (Toyota Camry), +6.138s; **9** Denny Hamlin, USA (Toyota Camry), +6.566s; **10** Ricky Stenhouse Jr, USA (Ford Fusion), +7.144s.
Pole position: Jimmie Johnson, USA (Chevrolet SS), 28.430s, 133.971mph/215.606km/h.
Drivers' championship points: 1 Harvick, 636; **2** Keselowski, 622; **3** Busch (Kurt), 602; **4** Edwards, 587; **5** Logano, 571; **6** Busch (Kyle), 556.

23RD ANNUAL CROWN ROYAL PRESENTS THE COMBAT WOUNDED COALITION 400 AT THE BRICKYARD, Indianapolis Motor Speedway, Speedway, Indiana, USA, 24 July. Round 20. 170 laps of the 2.500-mile/4.023km circuit, 425.000 miles/683.971km.
1 Kyle Busch, USA (Toyota Camry), 3h 17m 46s, 128.940mph/207.509km/h; **2** Matt Kenseth, USA (Toyota Camry), +2.126s; **3** Jimmie Johnson, USA (Chevrolet SS), 170 laps; **4** Denny Hamlin, USA (Toyota Camry), 170; **5** Kyle Larson, USA (Chevrolet SS), 170; **6** Kevin Harvick, USA (Chevrolet SS), 170; **7** Joey Logano, USA (Ford Fusion), 170; **8** Martin Truex Jr, USA (Toyota Camry), 170; **9** Austin Dillon, USA (Chevrolet SS), 170; **10** Paul Menard, USA (Chevrolet SS), 170.
Pole position: Busch, 48.745s, 184.634mph/297.140km/h.
Drivers' championship points: 1 Harvick, 671; **2** Keselowski, 647; **3** Busch (Kurt), 627; **4** Logano, 606; **5** Busch (Kyle), 601; **6** Edwards, 593.

43RD ANNUAL PENNSYLVANIA 400, Pocono Raceway, Long Pond, Pennsylvania, USA, 1 August. Round 21. 138 laps of the 2.500-mile/4.023km circuit, 345.000 miles/555.224km.
1 Chris Buescher, USA (Ford Fusion), 2h 42m 15s, 127.581mph/205.322km/h; **2** Brad Keselowski, USA (Ford Fusion), +0.432s; **3** Regan Smith, USA (Chevrolet SS), +0.468s; **4** Kevin Harvick, USA (Chevrolet SS), +0.912s; **5** Tony Stewart, USA (Chevrolet SS), +3.054s; **6** Kyle Larson, USA (Chevrolet SS), +3.503s; **7** Denny Hamlin, USA (Toyota Camry), +4.027s; **8** Carl Edwards, USA (Toyota Camry), +4.549s; **9** Kyle Busch, USA (Toyota Camry), +5.167s; **10** Kurt Busch, USA (Chevrolet SS), +5.657s.
Pole position: Martin Truex Jr, USA (Toyota Camry), 50.211s, 179.244mph/288.465km/h.
Drivers' championship points: 1 Harvick, 709; **2** Keselowski, 687; **3** Busch (Kurt), 658; **4** Busch (Kyle), 634; **5** Edwards, 626; **6** Logano, 612.

31ST ANNUAL CHEEZ-IT 355 AT THE GLEN, Watkin**s Glen International, New York, USA, 7 August. Round 22. 90 laps of the 2.450-mile/3.943km circuit, 220.500 miles/354.860km.**
1 Denny Hamlin, USA (Toyota Camry), 2h 27m 48s, 89.513mph/144.057km/h; **2** Joey Logano, USA (Ford Fusion), +2.065s; **3** Brad Keselowski, USA (Ford Fusion), +2.327s; **4** A.J. Allmendinger, USA (Chevrolet SS), +4.656s; **5** Tony Stewart, USA (Chevrolet SS), +4.879s; **6** Kyle Busch, USA (Toyota Camry), +5.145s; **7** Martin Truex Jr, USA (Toyota Camry), +6.388s; **8** Jamie McMurray, USA (Chevrolet SS), +6.272s; **9** Trevor Bayne, USA (Ford Fusion), +6.607s; **10** Matt Kenseth, USA (Toyota Camry), +7.449s.
Pole position: Carl Edwards, USA (Toyota Camry), 1m 09.689s, 126.562mph/203.682km/h.
Drivers' championship points: 1 Keselowski, 727; **2** Harvick, 718; **3** Busch (Kurt), 689; **4** Busch (Kyle), 670; **5** Edwards, 653; **6** Logano, 652.

56TH ANNUAL BASS PRO SHOPS NRA NIGHT RACE, Bristol Motor Speedway, Tennessee, USA, 20 August. Round 23. 500 laps of the 0.533-mile/0.858km circuit, 266.500 miles/428.890km.
1 Kevin Harvick, USA (Chevrolet SS), 3h 25m 05s, 77.968mph/125.478km/h; **2** Ricky Stenhouse Jr, USA (Ford Fusion), +1.933s; **3** Denny Hamlin, USA (Toyota Camry), +2.088s; **4** Austin Dillon, USA (Chevrolet SS), +4.989s; **5** Chris Buescher, USA (Ford Fusion), +5.088s; **6** Carl Edwards, USA (Toyota Camry), +6.312s; **7** Jimmie Johnson, USA (Chevrolet SS), +6.446s; **8** Jamie McMurray, USA (Chevrolet SS), +7.455s; **9** A.J. Allmendinger, USA (Chevrolet SS), +7.549s; **10** Joey Logano, USA (Ford Fusion), +9.877s.
Pole position: Edwards, 14.602s, 131.407mph/211.479km/h.
Drivers' championship points: 1 Harvick, 762; **2** Keselowski, 735; **3** Busch (Kurt), 692; **4** Edwards, 689; **5** Logano, 684; **6** Busch (Kyle), 674.

4**7TH ANNUAL PURE MICHIGAN 400, Michigan International Speedway, Brooklyn, Michigan, USA, 28 August. Round 24. 200 laps of the 2.000-mile/3.219km circuit, 400.000 miles/643.738km.**
1 Kyle Larson, USA (Chevrolet SS), 2h 27m 29s, 162.730mph/261.889km/h; **2** Chase Elliott, USA (Chevrolet SS), +1.478s; **3** Brad Keselowski, USA (Ford Fusion), +2.064s; **4** Ryan Blaney, USA (Ford Fusion), +4.108s; **5** Kevin Harvick, USA (Chevrolet SS), +4.559s; **6** Jimmie Johnson, USA (Chevrolet SS), +4.773s; **7** Carl Edwards, USA (Toyota Camry), +6.371s; **8** Jamie McMurray, USA (Chevrolet SS), +6.722s; **9** Denny Hamlin, USA (Toyota Camry), +7.748s; **10** Joey Logano, USA (Ford Fusion), +7.791s.
Pole position: Logano, 35.697s, 201.698mph/324.601km/h.
Drivers' championship points: 1 Harvick, 799; **2** Keselowski, 764; **3** Edwards, 724; **4** Busch (Kurt), 721; **5** Logano, 716; **6** Busch (Kyle), 696.

67TH ANNUAL BOJANGLES' SOUTHERN 500, Darlington Raceway, South Carolina, USA, 4 September. Round 25. 367 laps of the 1.366-mile/2.198km circuit, 501.322 miles/806.800km.
1 Martin Truex Jr, USA (Toyota Camry), 3h 57m 54s, 126.437mph/203.480km/h; **2** Kevin Harvick, USA (Chevrolet SS), +0.606s; **3** Kyle Larson, USA (Chevrolet SS), +1.667s; **4** Denny Hamlin, USA (Toyota Camry), +2.555s; **5** Joey Logano, USA (Ford Fusion), +3.269s; **6** Matt Kenseth, USA (Toyota Camry), +5.397s; **7** Kasey Kahne, USA (Chevrolet SS), +5.865s; **8** Ryan Newman, USA (Chevrolet SS), +6.033s; **9** Brad Keselowski, USA (Ford Fusion), +6.510s; **10** Chase Elliott, USA (Chevrolet SS), +7.186s.
Pole position: Harvick.
Drivers' championship points: 1 Harvick, 840; **2** Keselowski, 797; **3** Logano, 752; **4** Edwards, 746; **5** Hamlin, 729; **6** Busch (Kurt), 728.

59TH ANNUAL FEDERATED AUTO PARTS 400, Richmond International Raceway, Virginia, USA, 10 September. Round 26. 407 laps of the 0.750-mile/1.207km circuit, 305.250 miles/491.252km.
1 Denny Hamlin, USA (Toyota Camry), 3h 33m 31s, 85.778mph/138.046km/h; **2** Kyle Larson, USA (Chevrolet SS), +0.609s; **3** Martin Truex Jr, USA (Toyota Camry), +0.695s; **4** Brad Keselowski, USA (Ford Fusion), +0.903s; **5** Kevin Harvick, USA (Chevrolet SS), +1.434s; **6** Kasey Kahne, USA (Chevrolet SS), +1.485s; **7** Jamie McMurray, USA (Chevrolet SS), +1.574s; **8** Kurt Busch, USA (Chevrolet SS), +1.614s; **9** Kyle Busch, USA (Toyota Camry), +1.729s; **10** Joey Logano, USA (Ford Fusion), +1.843s.
Pole position: Hamlin, 22.069s, 122.344mph/196.893km/h.
Drivers' championship points: 1 Busch (Kyle), 2012; **2** Keselowski, 2012; **3** Hamlin, 2009; **4** Harvick, 2006; **5** Edwards, 2006; **6** Truex Jr, 2006.

16TH ANNUAL TEENAGE MUTANT NINJA TURTLES 400, Chicagoland Speedway, Chicago, Illinois, USA, 18 September. Round 27. 270 laps of the 1.500-mile/2.414km circuit, 405.000 miles/651.784km.
1 Martin Truex Jr, USA (Toyota Camry), 2h 47m 24s, 145.161mph/233.614km/h; **2** Joey Logano, USA (Ford Fusion), +0.776s; **3** Chase Elliott, USA (Chevrolet SS), +1.121s; **4** Ryan Blaney, USA (Ford Fusion), +1.126s; **5** Brad Keselowski, USA (Ford Fusion), +1.327s; **6** Denny Hamlin, USA (Toyota Camry), +1.427s; **7** Kasey Kahne, USA (Chevrolet SS), +1.931s; **8** Kyle Busch, USA (Toyota Camry), +2.243s; **9** Matt Kenseth, USA (Toyota Camry), +2.276s; **10** Alex Bowman, USA (Chevrolet SS), +2.393s.
Pole position: Busch.

Drivers' championship points: 1 Truex Jr, 2050; **2** Keselowski, 2049; **3** Busch (Kyle), 2046; **4** Hamlin, 2045; **5** Logano, 2043; **6** Elliott, 2039.

20TH ANNUAL BAD BOY OFF ROAD 300, New Hampshire International Speedway, Loudon, New Hampshire, USA, 25 September. Round 28. 300 laps of the 1.058-mile/1.703km circuit, 317.400 miles/510.806km.
1 Kevin Harvick, USA (Chevrolet SS), 2h 54m 15s, 109.291mph/175.887km/h; **2** Matt Kenseth, USA (Toyota Camry), +0.442s; **3** Kyle Busch, USA (Toyota Camry), +1.731s; **4** Brad Keselowski, USA (Ford Fusion), +2.159s; **5** Kurt Busch, USA (Chevrolet SS), +2.600s; **6** Carl Edwards, USA (Toyota Camry), +3.057s; **7** Martin Truex Jr, USA (Toyota Camry), +3.270s; **8** Jimmie Johnson, USA (Chevrolet SS), +3.835s; **9** Kasey Kahne, USA (Chevrolet SS), +4.628s; **10** Kyle Larson, USA (Chevrolet SS), +5.194s.
Pole position: Edwards, 28.119s, 135.453mph/217.990km/h.
Drivers' championship points: 1 Keselowski, 2087; **2** Truex Jr, 2086; **3** Busch (Kyle), 2085; **4** Kenseth, 2078; **5** Logano, 2073; **6** Harvick, 2071.

47TH ANNUAL CITIZEN SOLDIER 400, Dover International Speedway, Delaware, USA, 2 October. Round 29. 400 laps of the 1.000-mile/1.609km circuit, 400.000 miles/643.738km.
1 Martin Truex Jr, USA (Toyota Camry), 3h 03m 15s, 130.969mph/210.774km/h; **2** Kyle Busch, USA (Toyota Camry), +7.527s; **3** Chase Elliott, USA (Chevrolet SS), +12.381s; **4** Brad Keselowski, USA (Ford Fusion), +12.741s; **5** Matt Kenseth, USA (Toyota Camry), +17.501s; **6** Joey Logano, USA (Ford Fusion), +24.116s; **7** Jimmie Johnson, USA (Chevrolet SS), -1 lap; **8** Austin Dillon, USA (Chevrolet SS), -1; **9** Denny Hamlin, USA (Toyota Camry), -1; **10** Jeff Gordon, USA (Chevrolet SS), -1.
Pole position: Keselowski.
Drivers' championship points: 1 Truex Jr, 3000; **2** Harvick, 3000; **3** Busch (Kyle), 3000; **4** Kenseth, 3000; **5** Logano, 3000; **6** Elliott, 3000.

57TH ANNUAL BANK OF AMERICA 500, Lowe's Motor Speedway, Concord, Charlotte, North Carolina, USA, 9 October. Round 30. 334 laps of the 1.500-mile/2.414km circuit, 501.000 miles/806.281km.
1 Jimmie Johnson, USA (Chevrolet SS), 3h 42m 47s, 134.929mph/217.148km/h; **2** Matt Kenseth, USA (Toyota Camry), +1.474s; **3** Kasey Kahne, USA (Chevrolet SS), +2.949s; **4** Ryan Newman, USA (Chevrolet SS), +3.788s; **5** Kyle Larson, USA (Chevrolet SS), +4.380s; **6** Kyle Busch, USA (Toyota Camry), +4.918s; **7** Brad Keselowski, USA (Ford Fusion), +7.228s; **8** Kurt Busch, USA (Chevrolet SS), +8.492s; **9** Tony Stewart, USA (Chevrolet SS), +9.790s; **10** Jamie McMurray, USA (Chevrolet SS), +9.981s.
Pole position: Kevin Harvick, USA (Chevrolet SS), 27.547s, 196.029mph/315.477km/h.
Drivers' championship points: 1 Johnson, 3045; **2** Kenseth, 3040; **3** Busch (Kyle), 3036; **4** Keselowski, 3034; **5** Busch (Kurt), 3033; **6** Edwards, 3029.

16TH ANNUAL HOLLYWOOD CASINO 400, Kansas Speedway, Kansas City, Kansas, USA, 16 October. Round 31. 267 laps of the 1.500-mile/2.414km circuit, 400.500 miles/644.542km.
1 Kevin Harvick, USA (Chevrolet SS), 3h 00m 28s, 133.155mph/214.292km/h; **2** Carl Edwards, USA (Toyota Camry), +1.183s; **3** Joey Logano, USA (Ford Fusion), +4.544s; **4** Jimmie Johnson, USA (Chevrolet SS), +5.135s; **5** Kyle Busch, USA (Toyota Camry), +6.943s; **6** Austin Dillon, USA (Chevrolet SS), +7.322s; **7** Alex Bowman, USA (Chevrolet SS), +9.724s; **8** A.J. Allmendinger, USA (Chevrolet SS), +10.753s; **9** Matt Kenseth, USA (Toyota Camry), +10.874s; **10** Kasey Kahne, USA (Chevrolet SS), +11.369s.
Pole position: Kenseth, 28.112s, 192.089mph/309.137km/h.
Drivers' championship points: 1 Johnson, 3082; **2** Kenseth, 3074; **3** Busch (Kyle), 3072; **4** Edwards, 3069; **5** Busch (Kurt), 3062; **6** Truex Jr, 3058.

48TH ANNUAL HELLMANN'S 500, Talladega Superspeedway, Alabama, USA, 23 October. Round 32. 192 laps of the 2.660-mile/4.281km circuit, 510.720 miles/821.924km.
1 Joey Logano, USA (Ford Fusion), 3h 11m 38s, 159.905 mph/257.343 km/h; **2** Brian Scott, USA (Ford Fusion), +0.124s; **3** Denny Hamlin, USA (Toyota Camry), +0.258s; **4** Kurt Busch, USA (Chevrolet SS), +0.264s; **5** Ricky Stenhouse Jr, USA (Ford Fusion), +0.423s; **6** Kyle Larson, USA (Chevrolet SS), +0.427s; **7** Kevin Harvick, USA (Chevrolet SS), +0.467s; **8** Aric Almirola, USA (Ford Fusion), +0.495s; **9** Austin Dillon, USA (Chevrolet SS), +0.524s; **10** A.J. Allmendinger, USA (Chevrolet SS), +0.529s.
Pole position: Martin Truex Jr, USA (Toyota Camry), 49.508s, 193.423mph/311.285km/h.
Drivers' championship points: 1 Logano, 4000; **2** Johnson, 4000; **3** Harvick, 4000; **4** Kenseth, 4000; **5** Edwards, 4000; **6** Hamlin, 4000.

68TH ANNUAL GOODY'S FAST RELIEF 500, Martinsville Speedway, Virginia, USA, 30 October. Round 33. 500 laps of the 0.526-mile/0.847km circuit, 263.000 miles/423.257km.
1 Jimmie Johnson, USA (Chevrolet SS), 3h 20m 55s, 78.540mph/126.398km/h; **2** Brad Keselowski, USA (Ford Fusion), +1.291s; **3** Denny Hamlin, USA (Toyota Camry), +5.722s; **4** Matt Kenseth, USA (Toyota Camry), +6.705s; **5** Kyle Busch, USA (Toyota Camry), +7.914s; **6** Jeff Gordon, USA (Chevrolet SS), +8.796s; **7** Martin Truex Jr, USA (Toyota Camry), +9.269s; **8** Jamie McMurray, USA (Chevrolet SS), +10.995s; **9** Joey Logano, USA (Ford Fusion), +14.666s; **10** A.J. Allmendinger, USA (Chevrolet SS), +16.324s.
Pole position: Truex Jr, 19.282s, 98.206mph/158.047km/h.
Drivers' championship points: 1 Johnson, 4044; **2** Hamlin, 4039; **3** Kenseth, 4039; **4** Busch (Kyle), 4037; **5** Logano, 4033; **6** Harvick, 4021.

12TH ANNUAL AAA TEXAS 500, Texas Motor Speedway, Fort Worth, Texas, USA, 6 November. Round 34. 293 laps of the 1.500-mile/2.414km circuit, 439.500 miles/707.307km.
1 Carl Edwards, USA (Toyota Camry), 3h 16m 00s, 134.541mph/216.522km/h; **2** Joey Logano, USA (Ford Fusion), +0.620s; **3** Martin Truex Jr, USA (Toyota Camry), +2.624s; **4** Chase Elliott, USA (Chevrolet SS), +3.262s; **5** Kyle Busch, USA (Toyota Camry), +3.934s; **6** Kevin Harvick, USA (Chevrolet SS), +4.553s; **7** Matt Kenseth, USA (Toyota Camry), +5.465s; **8** Kasey Kahne, USA (Chevrolet SS), +6.143s; **9** Denny Hamlin, USA (Toyota Camry), +7.365s; **10** Ryan Newman, USA (Chevrolet SS), +8.172s.
Pole position: Austin Dillon, USA (Chevrolet SS), 28.081s, 192.301mph/309.478km/h.
Drivers' championship points: 1 Busch (Kyle), 4074; **2** Johnson, 4074; **3** Logano, 4074; **4** Kenseth, 4073; **5** Hamlin, 4072; **6** Harvick, 4056.

29TH ANNUAL CAN-AM 500, Phoenix International Raceway, Arizona, USA, 13 November. Round 35. 324 laps of the 1.000-mile/1.609km circuit, 324.000 miles/521.427km.
1 Joey Logano, USA (Ford Fusion), 3h 08m 59s, 102.866mph/165.547km/h; **2** Kyle Busch, USA (Toyota Camry), +0.587s; **3** Kyle Larson, USA (Chevrolet SS), +0.756s; **4** Kevin Harvick, USA (Chevrolet SS), +1.052s; **5** Kurt Busch, USA (Chevrolet SS), +1.261s; **6** Alex Bowman, USA (Chevrolet SS), +1.420s; **7** Denny Hamlin, USA (Toyota Camry), +1.488s; **8** Ryan Blaney, USA (Ford Fusion), +2.275s; **9** Chase Elliott, USA (Chevrolet SS), +2.637s; **10** Paul Menard, USA (Chevrolet SS), +2.714s.
Pole position: Bowman, 25.619s, 140.521mph/226.146km/h.
Drivers' championship points: 1 Logano, 5000; **2** Johnson, 5000; **3** Edwards, 5000; **4** Busch (Kyle), 5000; **5** Kenseth, 2296; **6** Hamlin, 2288.

18TH ANNUAL FORD ECOBOOST 400, Homestead-Miami Speedway, Florida, USA, 20 November. Round 36. 268 laps of the 1.500-mile/2.414km circuit, 402.000 miles/646.956km.
1 Jimmie Johnson, USA (Chevrolet SS), 3h 07m 10s, 128.869mph/207.395km/h; **2** Kyle Larson, USA (Chevrolet SS), +0.466s; **3** Kevin Harvick, USA (Chevrolet SS), +0.498s; **4** Joey Logano, USA (Ford Fusion), +1.221s; **5** Jamie McMurray, USA (Chevrolet SS), +1.333s; **6** Kyle Busch, USA (Toyota Camry), +1.551s; **7** Matt Kenseth, USA (Toyota Camry), +2.073s; **8** A.J. Allmendinger, USA (Chevrolet SS), +2.651s; **9** Denny Hamlin, USA (Toyota Camry), +2.970s; **10** Michael McDowell, USA (Chevrolet SS), +2.995s.
Pole position: Harvick, 30.399s, 177.637mph/285.880km/h.

Final championship points
Drivers
1 Jimmie Johnson, USA, 5040; **2** Joey Logano, USA, 5037; **3** Kyle Busch, USA, 5035; **4** Carl Edwards, USA, 5007; **5** Matt Kenseth, USA, 2330; **6** Denny Hamlin, USA, 2320; **7** Kurt Busch, USA, 2296; **8** Kevin Harvick, USA, 2289; **9** Kyle Larson, USA, 2288; **10** Chase Elliott, USA, 2285; **11** Martin Truex Jr, USA, 2271; **12** Brad Keselowski, USA, 2267; **13** Jamie McMurray, USA, 2231; **14** Austin Dillon, USA, 2223; **15** Tony Stewart, USA, 2211; **16** Chris Buescher, USA, 2169; **17** Kasey Kahne, USA, 898; **18** Ryan Newman, USA, 895; **19** A.J. Allmendinger, USA, 830; **20** Ryan Blaney, USA, 812; **21** Ricky Stenhouse Jr, USA, 772; **22** Trevor Bayne, USA, 762; **23** Greg Biffle, USA, 691; **24** Danica Patrick, USA, 689; **25** Paul Menard, USA, 678; **26** Aric Almirola, USA, 638; **27** Clint Bowyer, USA, 628; **28** Casey Mears, USA, 556; **29** Landon Cassill, USA, 530; **30** Michael McDowell, USA, 500;

Manufacturers
1 Toyota, 1477; **2** Chevrolet, 1452; **3** Ford, 1388.

Sunoco Rookie of the Year: Chase Elliott, USA.

Other NASCAR races

SPRINT UNLIMITED, Daytona International Speedway, Daytona Beach, Florida, USA, 13 February. 79 laps of the 2.500-mile/4.023km circuit, 197.500 miles/ 317.845km.
1 Denny Hamlin, USA (Toyota Camry), 1h 32m 16s, 128.432mph/ 206.691km/h; **2** Joey Logano, USA (Ford Fusion), 79 laps; **3** Paul Menard, USA (Chevrolet SS), 79; **4** Kyle Larson, USA (Chevrolet SS), 79; **5** Casey Mears, USA (Chevrolet SS), 79; **6** Ricky Stenhouse Jr, USA (Ford Fusion), 79; **7** Kurt Busch, USA (Chevrolet SS), 79; **8** Austin Dillon, USA (Chevrolet SS), 79; **9** Brad Keselowski, USA (Ford Fusion), 79; **10** Greg Biffle, USA (Ford Fusion), 79.
Pole position: Jimmie Johnson, USA (Chevrolet SS).

NASCAR SPRINT ALL-STAR RACE, Lowe's Motor Speedway, Concord, Charlotte, North Carolina, USA, 21 May. 113 laps of the 1.500-mile/2.414km circuit, 169.500 miles/272.784km
1 Joey Logano, USA (Ford Fusion), 1h 43m 40s, 98.103mph/ 157.881km/h; **2** Brad Keselowski, USA (Ford Fusion), 1h 43m 41.142s; **3** Dale Earnhardt Jr, USA (Chevrolet SS), 113 laps; **4** Carl Edwards, USA (Toyota Camry), 113; **5** Kurt Busch, USA (Chevrolet SS), 113; **6** Chase Elliott, USA (Chevrolet SS), 113; **7** Trevor Bayne, USA (Ford Fusion), 113; **8** Greg Biffle, USA (Ford Fusion), 113; **9** Denny Hamlin, USA (Toyota Camry), 113; **10** Kyle Busch, USA (Toyota Camry), 113.
Pole position: Kevin Harvick, USA (Chevrolet SS).

Firestone Indy Lights

All cars are Dallara IL15-Mazda.

INDY LIGHTS GRAND PRIX OF ST. PETERSBURG PRESENTED BY LUCAS SCHOOL OF RACING, St. Petersburg Street Circuit, Florida, USA, 12/13 March. Round 1. 30 and 45 laps of the 1.800-mile/2.897km circuit.
Race 1 (54.000 miles/86.905km).
1 Félix Serrallés, USA, 34m 14.4964s, 94.622mph/152.279km/h; **2** Scott Hargrove, CDN, +5.5336s; **3** Kyle Kaiser, USA, +6.1320s; **4** Santiago Urrutia, U, +7.8009s; **5** R.C. Enerson, USA, +8.4345s; **6** André Negrão, BR, +12.1840s; **7** Felix Rosenqvist, S, +12.8449s; **8** Dean Stoneman, GB, +13.5796s; **9** Juan Piedrahita, CO, +15.7225s; **10** Ed Jones, UAE, +36.1840s.
Fastest race lap: Zach Veach, USA, 1m 07.6582s, 95.776mph/154.136km/h.
Pole position: Kaiser, 1m 05.8728s, 98.371mph/158.313km/h.

Race 2 (81.000 miles/130.357km).
1 Felix Rosenqvist, S, 51m 45.8621s, 93.887mph/151.096km/h; **2** Kyle Kaiser, USA, +4.3675s; **3** Zach Veach, USA, +7.4736s; **4** Félix Serrallés, USA, +11.0357s; **5** André Negrão, BR, +13.4341s; **6** Dean Stoneman, GB, +14.2443s; **7** Ed Jones, UAE, +19.2592s; **8** Juan Piedrahita, CO, +19.8197s; **9** Scott Anderson, USA, +1m 07.6326s; **10** Dalton Kellett, CDN, +1m 08.9158s.
Fastest race lap: Rosenqvist, 1m 06.9544s, 96.782mph/155.756km/h.
Pole position: Rosenqvist, 1m 06.0851s, 98.055mph/157.805km/h.

INDY LIGHTS GRAND PRIX OF PHOENIX, Phoenix International Raceway, Arizona, USA, 2 April. Round 2. 90 laps of the 1.022-mile/1.645km circuit, 91.980 miles/148.027km.
1 Kyle Kaiser, USA, 36m 57.9123s, 149.297mph/240.270km/h; **2** Ed Jones, UAE, +1.0088s; **3** R.C. Enerson, USA, +1.2089s; **4** Santiago Urrutia, U, +1.6121s; **5** Dean Stoneman, GB, +2.5229s; **6** André Negrão, BR, +3.2298s; **7** Félix Serrallés, USA, +4.5529s; **8** Zach Veach, USA, +5.3458s; **9** Neil Alberico, USA, +6.4200s; **10** Dalton Kellett, CDN, +6.9455s.
Fastest race lap: Kaiser, 22.5541s, 163.128mph/262.529km/h.
Pole position: Kaiser, 43.8334s, 167.872mph/270.164km/h (over **2** laps).

LEGACY INDY LIGHTS 100, Barber Motorsports Park, Birmingham, Alabama, USA, 23/24 April. Round 3. 35 and 30 laps of the 2.300-mile/3.701km circuit.
Race 1 (80.500 miles/129.552km).
1 Ed Jones, UAE, 47m 58.6238s, 100.673mph/162.018km/h; **2** Félix Serrallés, USA, +1.5881s; **3** Zach Veach, USA, +2.6705s; **4** Shelby Blackstock, USA, +3.3133s; **5** Zachary Claman DeMelo, CDN, +5.3350s; **6** R.C. Enerson, USA, +6.5415s; **7** Juan Piedrahita, CO, +14.9831s; **8** André Negrão, BR, +15.7903s; **9** Dalton Kellett, CDN, +17.7290s; **10** Scott Anderson, USA, +17.7891s.
Fastest race lap: Santiago Urrutia, U, 1m 15.3545s, 109.881mph/176.836km/h.
Pole position: Jones, 1m 12.6738s, 113.934mph/183.359km/h.

Race 2 (69.000 miles/111.045km).
1 Santiago Urrutia, U, 38m 16.2572s, 108.176mph/174.092km/h; **2** Ed Jones, UAE, +4.2437s; **3** Dean Stoneman, GB, +5.2194s; **4** R.C. Enerson, USA, +6.0994s; **5** Shelby Blackstock, USA, +8.1662s; **6** Kyle Kaiser, USA, +8.6812s; **7** Zachary Claman DeMelo, CDN, +9.3748s; **8** Felix Rosenqvist, S, +13.5499s; **9** Dalton Kellett, CDN, +18.9099s; **10** Zach Veach, USA, +20.6633s.
Fastest race lap: Urrutia, 1m 15.9253s, 109.055mph/175.506km/h.
Pole position: Jones, 1m 12.9396s, 113.519mph/182.690km/h.

MAZDA INDY LIGHTS GP OF INDIANAPOLIS, Indianapolis Motor Speedway, Speedway, Indiana, USA, 13/14 May. Round 4. 30 and 35 laps of the 2.439-mile/3.925km circuit.
Race 1 (73.170 miles/117.756km).
1 Ed Jones, UAE, 41m 15.4848s, 106.408mph/171.247km/h; **2** Santiago Urrutia, U, +0.9501s; **3** Dean Stoneman, GB, +1.8290s; **4** Felix Rosenqvist, S, +2.6537s; **5** Zach Veach, USA, +4.4604s; **6** Kyle Kaiser, USA, +4.8941s; **7** Félix Serrallés, USA, +6.2507s; **8** R.C. Enerson, USA, +7.3795s; **9** André Negrão, BR, +11.7029s; **10** Shelby Blackstock, USA, +44.6846s.
Fastest race lap: Zachary Claman DeMelo, CDN, 1m 16.3696s, 114.972mph/185.030km/h.
Pole position: Jones, 1m 14.6743s, 117.583mph/189.231km/h.

Race 2 (85.365 miles/137.382km).
1 Dean Stoneman, GB, 46m 45.5881s, 109.536mph/176.282km/h; **2** Santiago Urrutia, U, +0.8659s; **3** Kyle Kaiser, USA, +1.7083s; **4** Ed Jones, UAE, +3.0719s; **5** Félix Serrallés, USA, +3.5488s; **6** Felix Rosenqvist, S, +4.5985s; **7** Shelby Blackstock, USA, +30.5273s; **8** Scott Anderson, USA, +33.4589s; **9** Scott Hargrove, CDN, +1m 16.3693s; **10** Zach Veach, USA, -1 lap.
Fastest race lap: Rosenqvist, 1m 15.7230s, 115.954mph/186.610km/h.
Pole position: Jones, 1m 15.0014s, 117.070mph/188.406km/h.

FREEDOM 100, Indianapolis Motor Speedway, Speedway, Indiana, USA, 27 May. Round 5. 40 laps of the 2.500-mile/4.023km circuit, 100.000 miles/160.934km.
1 Dean Stoneman, GB, 41m 08.6299s, 145.830mph/234.690km/h; **2** Ed Jones, UAE, +0.0024s; **3** Dalton Kellett, CDN, +1.1024s; **4** Shelby Blackstock, USA, +1.2109s; **5** Scott Hargrove, CDN, +1.5703s; **6** Félix Serrallés, USA, +1.5862s; **7** Neil Alberico, USA, +1.9533s; **8** Juan Piedrahita, CO, +2.2687s; **9** Felix Rosenqvist, S, +3.2538s; **10** Zach Veach, USA, +3.2686s.
Fastest race lap: Alberico, 45.4526s, 198.008mph/318.664km/h.
Pole position: Jones.

MAZDA INDY LIGHTS GP OF ROAD AMERICA, Road America, Elkhart Lake, Wisconsin, USA, 25/26 June. Round 6. 2 x 20 laps of the 4.014-mile/6.460km circuit.
Race 1 (80.280 miles/129.198km).
1 Zach Veach, USA, 41m 40.3748s, 115.586mph/186.017km/h; **2** Dean Stoneman, GB, +7.9841s; **3** Félix Serrallés, USA, +8.8199s; **4** Ed Jones, UAE, +12.2401s; **5** Zachary Claman DeMelo, CDN, +13.6079s; **6** Kyle Kaiser, USA, +14.1648s; **7** Garett Grist, CDN, +16.1469s; **8** James French, USA, +17.0672s; **9** Santiago Urrutia, U, +18.3453s; **10** André Negrão, BR, +19.5340s.
Fastest race lap: DeMelo, 1m 54.6326s, 126.058mph/202.871km/h.
Pole position: Veach, 1m 52.9410s, 127.946mph/205.910km/h.

Race 2 (80.280 miles/129.198km).
1 Santiago Urrutia, U, 49m 07.6614s, 98.047mph/157.791km/h; **2** André Negrão, BR, +8.1504s; **3** Zach Veach, USA, +13.1818s; **4** Zachary Claman DeMelo, CDN, +25.1035s; **5** Shelby Blackstock, USA, +27.6994s; **6** Kyle Kaiser, USA, +31.0848s; **7** Juan Piedrahita, CO, +37.1282s; **8** James French, USA, +46.2237s; **9** Dean Stoneman, GB, +1m 01.4885s; **10** Garett Grist, CDN, +1m 16.0240s.
Fastest race lap: Stoneman, 1m 59.1410s, 121.288mph/195.194km/h.
Pole position: Ed Jones, UAE, 1m 52.9746s, 127.908mph/205.849km/h.

INDY LIGHTS, Iowa Speedway, Newton, Iowa, USA, 10 July. Round 7. 100 laps of the 0.894-mile/1.439km circuit, 89.400 miles/143.875km.
1 Félix Serrallés, USA, 34m 44.5047s, 154.396mph/248.477km/h; **2** Zach Veach, USA, +0.6681s; **3** Ed Jones, UAE, +6.9920s; **4** Dean Stoneman, GB, +9.7051s; **5** Santiago Urrutia, U, +10.4118s; **6** Kyle Kaiser, USA, -1 lap; **7** Juan Piedrahita, CO, -1; **8** Zachary Claman DeMelo, CDN, -1; **9** Dalton Kellett, CDN, -1; **10** Heamin Choi, ROK, -2.
Fastest race lap: Veach, 20.2232s, 159.144mph/256.117km/h.
Pole position: Jones.

COOPER TIRES INDY LIGHTS GP OF TORONTO, Toronto Street Circuit, Ontario, Canada, 16/17 July. Round 8. 35 and 45 laps of the 1.786-mile/2.874km circuit.
Race 1 (62.510 miles/100.600km).
1 Felix Rosenqvist, S, 45m 23.5496s, 82.626mph/132.974km/h; **2** Félix Serrallés, USA, +7.3433s; **3** Kyle Kaiser, USA, +11.9393s; **4** Santiago Urrutia, U, +15.8913s; **5** Dean Stoneman, GB, +19.2259s; **6** Ed Jones, UAE, +24.4726s; **7** Garett Grist, CDN, +26.1752s; **8** Dalton Kellett, CDN, +40.2590s; **9** Zach Veach, USA, -1 lap (DNF-accident); **10** Shelby Blackstock, USA, -1.
Fastest race lap: Rosenqvist, 1m 06.0052s, 97.411mph/156.767km/h.
Pole position: Rosenqvist, 1m 06.0106s, 97.403mph/156.754km/h.

Race 2 (80.370 miles/129.343km).
1 Felix Rosenqvist, S, 50m 26.4304s, 95.602mph/153.856km/h; **2** André Negrão, BR, +7.2614s; **3** Kyle Kaiser, USA, +9.4310s; **4** Santiago Urrutia, U, +10.0098s; **5** Ed Jones, UAE, +30.1368s; **6** Zach Veach, USA, +33.7780s; **7** Garett Grist, CDN, +51.2215s; **8** Neil Alberico, USA, +56.5379s; **9** Shelby Blackstock, USA, -1 lap; **10** Félix Serrallés, USA, -1.
Fastest race lap: Serrallés, 1m 06.3066s, 96.968mph/156.054km/h.
Pole position: Rosenqvist, 1m 06.0052s, 97.411mph/156.767km/h.

COOPER TIRES INDY LIGHTS GP OF MID-OHIO, Mid-Ohio Sports Car Course, Lexington, Ohio, USA, 30/31 July. Round 9. 30 and 38 laps of the 2.258-mile/3.634km circuit.
Race 1 (67.740 miles/109.017km).
1 Santiago Urrutia, U, 36m37.7836s, 110.959mph/ 178.571km/h; 2 André Negrão, BR, +6.4947s; 3 Dean Stoneman, GB, +10.6592s; 4 Félix Serrallés, USA, +11.0222s; 5 Zach Veach, USA, +17.2890s; 6 Ed Jones, UAE, +26.8029s; 7 Zachary Claman DeMelo, CDN, +31.4995s; 8 Shelby Blackstock, USA, +31.8321s; 9 Kyle Kaiser, USA, +34.9169s; 10 Garett Grist, CDN, +35.7667s.
Fastest race lap: Urrutia, 1m 11.9975s, 112.904mph/181.701km/h.
Pole position: Urrutia, 1m10.9428s, 114.582mph/ 184.403km/h.

Race 2 (85.804 miles/138.088km).
1 Santiago Urrutia, U, 53m 44.7955s, 95.787mph/ 154.155km/h; 2 Dean Stoneman, GB, +1.5270s; 3 André Negrão, BR, +1.8158s; 4 Zach Veach, USA, +3.4408s; 5 Shelby Blackstock, USA, +4.6633s; 6 Kyle Kaiser, USA, +7.0184s; 7 Zachary Claman DeMelo, CDN, +9.9542s; 8 Neil Alberico, USA, +11.4517s; 9 Dalton Kellett, CDN, +46.6342s; 10 Félix Serrallés, USA, -4 laps (DNF-accident).
Fastest race lap: Serrallés, 1m 12.6939s, 111.822mph/179.961km/h.
Pole position: Urrutia, 1m11.1604s, 114.232mph/ 183.839km/h.

MAZDA INDY LIGHTS GRAND PRIX OF WATKINS GLEN PRESENTED BY COOPER TIRES, Watkins Glen International, New York, USA, 3 September. Round 10. 25 laps of the 3.370-mile/5.423km circuit, 84.250 miles/ 135.587km.
1 Zach Veach, USA, 40m 01.9326s, 126.273mph/ 203.217km/h; 2 Ed Jones, UAE, +3.6268s; 3 André Negrão, BR, +4.1322s; 4 Kyle Kaiser, USA, +6.0913s; 5 Neil Alberico, USA, +12.6164s; 6 Shelby Blackstock, USA, +14.7333s; 7 Félix Serrallés, USA, +40.4377s; 8 Garett Grist, CDN, +41.1031s; 9 Zachary Claman DeMelo, CDN, +1m 09.5228s; 10 Dean Stoneman, GB, +1m 29.6110s.
Fastest race lap: Stoneman, 1m 33.6921s, 129.488mph/208.391km/h.
Pole position: Santiago Urrutia, U, 1m 32.2997s, 131.441mph/211.534km/h.

MAZDA INDY LIGHTS GRAND PRIX OF MONTEREY PRESENTED BY COOPER TIRES, Mazda Raceway Laguna Seca, Monterey, California, USA, 10/11 September. Round 11. 30 and 38 laps of the 2.238-mile/3.602km circuit.
Race 1 (67.140 miles/108.051km).
1 Kyle Kaiser, USA, 39m 44.0768s, 101.383mph/ 163.160km/h; 2 Ed Jones, UAE, +7.9169s; 3 Zach Veach, USA, +9.0832s; 4 Sean Rayhall, USA, +12.8022s; 5 Santiago Urrutia, U, +17.6840s; 6 Neil Alberico, USA, +24.9271s; 7 Dalton Kellett, CDN, +38.9544s; 8 Félix Serrallés, USA, +40.1397s; 9 André Negrão, BR, +40.8827s; 10 Shelby Blackstock, USA, +41.2400s.
Fastest race lap: Kaiser, 1m 17.5598s, 103.879mph/167.176km/h.
Pole position: Kaiser, 1m15.2733s, 107.034mph/ 172.254km/h.

Race 2 (85.044 miles/136.865km).
1 Zach Veach, USA, 51m 15.6018s, 99.544mph/ 160.201km/h; 2 Santiago Urrutia, U, +2.8798s; 3 Kyle Kaiser, USA, +3.5402s; 4 Ed Jones, UAE, +19.6642s; 5 Félix Serrallés, USA,

+20.6958s; 6 André Negrão, BR, +21.6949s; 7 Zachary Claman DeMelo, CDN, +23.4277s; 8 Sean Rayhall, USA, +26.2047s; 9 Dean Stoneman, GB, +27.5982s; 10 Neil Alberico, USA, +28.5777s.
Fastest race lap: Veach, 1m 17.6563s, 103.749mph/166.969km/h.
Pole position: Jones, 1m15.4259s, 106.817mph/ 171.906km/h.

Final championship points
Drivers
1 Ed Jones, UAE, 363; 2 Santiago Urrutia, U, 361; 3 Kyle Kaiser, USA, 334; 4 Zach Veach, USA, 332; 5 Dean Stoneman, GB, 316; 6 Félix Serrallés, USA, 311; 7 André Negrão, BR, 268; 8 Shelby Blackstock, USA, 227; 9 Zachary Claman DeMelo, CDN, 199; 10 Dalton Kellett, CDN, 193; 11 Neil Alberico, USA, 193; 12 Felix Rosenqvist, S, 185; 13 Juan Piedrahita, CO, 135; 14 R.C. Enerson, USA, 111; 15 Garett Grist, CDN, 102; 16 Scott Hargrove, CDN, 93; 17 Scott Anderson, USA, 61; 18 Heamin Choi, ROK, 40; 19 Sean Rayhall, USA, 32; 20 James French, USA, 26; 21 Davey Hamilton Jr, USA, 14.

Teams
1 Carlin, 413; 2 Schmidt Peterson Motorsports with Curb-Agajanian, 384; 3 Belardi Auto Racing, 322; 4 Andretti Autosport, 281; 5 Juncos Racing, 275; 6 Team Pelfrey, 135.

Atlantic Championship

All cars are Swift 014.a-Toyota.

ATLANTIC CHAMPIONSHIP, Road Atlanta Motorsports Center, Braselton, Georgia, USA, 9/10 April. Round 1. 30 and 27 laps of the 2.540-mile/4.088km circuit.
Race 1 (76.200 miles/122.632km).
1 Ryan Norman, USA, 30 laps; 2 Lee Alexander, USA, 30; 3 Bruce Hamilton, USA, 30; 4 GianPaolo Ciancimino, USA, 30; 5 Lewis Cooper Jr, USA, 30; 6 Chris Ash, USA, -1; 7 Rich Zober, USA, -8; Kirk Kindsfater, USA, -20 (DNF); Keith Grant, USA, -25 (DNF); Bob Corliss, USA, -30 (DNF).
Fastest race lap: Norman, 1m 18.632s, 116.289mph/187.148km/h.
Pole position: Norman, 1m18.198s, 116.934mph/ 188.187km/h.

Race 2 (68.580 miles/110.369km).
1 Keith Grant, USA, 27 laps; 2 Bob Corliss, USA, 27; 3 Bruce Hamilton, USA, 27; 4 Kirk Kindsfater, USA, 27; 5 Rich Zober, USA, -5; 6 Ryan Norman, USA, -5; 7 GianPaolo Ciancimino, USA, -14; Chris Ash, USA, -26 (DNF); Lewis Cooper Jr, USA, -27 (DNF); Lee Alexander, USA, -27 (DNF).
Fastest race lap: Norman, 1m 18.281s, 116.810mph/187.987km/h.
Pole position: Grant, 1m 18.238s, 116.874mph/ 188.091km/h.

ATLANTIC CHAMPIONSHIP, Watkins Glen International, New York, USA, 14/15 May. Round 2. 17 and 20 laps of the 3.400-mile/5.472km circuit.
Race 3 (57.800 miles/93.020km).
1 Ryan Norman, USA, 17 laps; 2 Dudley Fleck, USA, 17; 3 Keith Grant, USA, 17; 4 Bruce Hamilton, USA, 17; 5 Lee Alexander, USA, 17; 6 Bob Corliss, USA, 17; 7 Rich Zober, USA, 17; 8 Chris Ash, USA, -1; 9 Mark Sherwood, USA, -1; 10 Connor Burke, USA, -1.
Fastest race lap: Norman, 1m 50.961s, 110.309mph/177.525km/h.
Pole position: Grant, 1m 44.796s, 116.798mph/ 187.969km/h.

Race 4 (68.000 miles/109.435km).
1 Ryan Norman, USA, 20 laps; 2 Keith Grant, USA, 20; 3 Bruce Hamilton, USA, 20; 4 Lee Alexander, USA, 20; 5 Rich Zober, USA, 20; 6 Kirk Kindsfater, USA, 20; 7 Mark Sherwood, USA, 20; 8 Bob Corliss, USA, 20; 9 Lewis Cooper Jr, USA, -1; 10 Chris Ash, USA, -1.
Fastest race lap: Norman, 1m 43.256s, 118.540mph/190.772km/h.
Pole position: Grant, 1m 45.396s, 116.133mph/ 186.899km/h.

ATLANTIC CHAMPIONSHIP, Virginia International Raceway, Alton, Virginia, USA, 4/5 June. Round 3. 2 x 22 laps of the 3.270-mile/ 5.263km circuit.
Race 5 (71.940 miles/115.776km).
1 Ryan Norman, USA, 22 laps; 2 Keith Grant, USA, 22; 3 Chris Ash, USA, 22; 4 Rich Zober, USA, 22; 5 John Burke, USA, 22; 6 Bob Corliss, USA, -1; 7 Lewis Cooper Jr, USA, -5; 8 Bruce Hamilton, USA, -11; David Grant, USA, -20 (DNF).
Did not start: Connor Burke, USA.
Fastest race lap: Norman, 1m 44.349s, 112.814mph/181.556km/h.
Pole position: Norman, 1m43.506s, 113.733mph/ 183.035km/h.

Race 6 (71.940 miles/115.776km).
1 Ryan Norman, USA, 22 laps; 2 Keith Grant, USA, 22; 3 David Grant, USA, 22; 4 Bob Corliss, USA, 22; 5 Chris Ash, USA, 22; 6 Lewis Cooper Jr, USA, -1; 7 Bruce Hamilton, USA, -6; 8 Rich Zober, USA, -10; Connor Burke, USA, -15 (DNF).
Fastest race lap: Norman, 1m 43.847s, 113.359mph/182.434km/h.
Pole position: Norman, 1m43.243s, 114.022mph/ 183.501km/h.

ATLANTIC CHAMPIONSHIP, Mid-Ohio Sports Car Course, Lexington, Ohio, USA, 2/3 July. Round 4. 2 x 29 laps of the 2.258-mile/3.634km circuit.
Race 7 (65.482 miles/105.383km).
1 David Grant, USA, 29 laps; 2 Keith Grant, USA, 29; 3 Ryan Norman, USA, 29; 4 Rich Zober, USA, -1; 5 Lewis Cooper Jr, USA, -1; 6 Chris Ash, USA, -1; 7 Bob Corliss, USA, -2; 8 Bruce Hamilton, USA, -2.
Did not start: Kirk Kindsfater, USA.
Fastest race lap: Grant, 1m 18.448s, 103.620mph/166.761km/h.
Pole position: Grant, 1m 17.135s, 105.384mph/ 169.599km/h.

Race 8 (65.482 miles/105.383km).
1 Ryan Norman, USA, 29 laps; 2 Keith Grant, USA, 29; 3 David Grant, USA, 29; 4 Rich Zober, USA, 29; 5 Lewis Cooper Jr, USA, -1; 6 Chris Ash, USA, -1; 7 Bob Corliss, USA, -1; Bruce Hamilton, USA, -29 (DNF).
Fastest race lap: Grant, 1m 17.283s, 105.182mph/169.274km/h.
Pole position: Grant, 1m 16.858s, 105.764mph/ 170.210km/h.

ATLANTIC CHAMPIONSHIP, Pittsburgh International Race Complex, Pennsylvania, USA, 6/7 August. Round 5. 2 x 24 laps of the 1.600-mile/ 2.575km circuit.
Race 9 (38.400 miles/61.799km).
1 David Grant, USA, 24 laps; 2 Keith Grant, USA, 24; 3 Lee Alexander, USA, 24; 4 Chris Ash, USA, 24; 5 Kirk Kindsfater, USA, 24; 6 John Burke, USA, 24; 7 Bob Corliss, USA, -1; 8 Theodoras Zorbas, USA, -1; 9 Ryan Norman, USA, -9; Connor Burke, USA, -19 (DNF).
Fastest race lap: Norman, 1m 33.056s, 61.898mph/99.616km/h.

Pole position: Norman, 1m 32.218s, 62.461mph/ 100.521km/h.

Race 10 (38.400 miles/61.799km).
1 David Grant, USA, 24 laps; 2 Keith Grant, USA, 24; 3 Connor Burke, USA, 24; 4 Bob Corliss, USA, 24; 5 Ryan Norman, USA, 24; 6 Chris Ash, USA, 24; 7 Bruce Hamilton, USA, 24; 8 Kirk Kindsfater, USA, 24; 9 Theodoras Zorbas, USA, -2.
Did not start: Lee Alexander, USA.
Fastest race lap: Grant, 1m32.395s, 62.341mph/ 100.328km/h.
Pole position: Norman, 1m31.231s, 63.136mph/ 101.608km/h.

ATLANTIC CHAMPIONSHIP, New Jersey Motorsports Park - Thunderbolt, Millville, New Jersey, USA, 27/28 August. Round 6. 2 x 31 laps of the 2.200-mile/3.541km circuit.
Race 11 (68.200 miles/109.757km).
1 Ryan Norman, USA, 31 laps; 2 David Grant, USA, 31; 3 Keith Grant, USA, 31; 4 Connor Burke, USA, 31; 5 Bob Corliss, USA, 31; 6 Bruce Hamilton, USA, 31; 7 John Burke, USA, 31; 8 Lee Alexander, USA, -1; 9 Lee Brahin, USA, -1; 10 Rich Zober, USA, -1.
Fastest race lap: Norman, 1m 12.484s, 109.265mph/175.846km/h.
Pole position: Norman, 1m11.113s, 111.372mph/ 179.236km/h.

Race 12 (68.200 miles/109.757km).
1 David Grant, USA, 31 laps; 2 Ryan Norman, USA, 31; 3 Bruce Hamilton, USA, 31; 4 Connor Burke, USA, 31; 5 Keith Grant, USA, 31; 6 Chris Ash, USA, 31; 7 Lee Alexander, USA, 31; 8 John Burke, USA, -1; 9 Rich Zober, USA, -1; Lee Brahin, USA, -18 (DNF).
Fastest race lap: Grant, 1m 12.880s, 108.672mph/174.890km/h.
Pole position: Norman, 1m11.600s, 110.615mph/ 178.017km/h.

ATLANTIC CHAMPIONSHIP, Virginia International Raceway, Alton, Virginia, USA, 1/2 October. Round 7. 12 and 7 laps of the 3.270-mile/ 5.263km circuit.
Race 13 (39.240 miles/63.151km).
1 Ryan Norman, USA, 12 laps; 2 Keith Grant, USA, 12; 3 David Grant, USA, 12; 4 Bob Corliss, USA, 12; 5 Rich Zober, USA, 12; 6 Dudley Fleck, USA, 12; 7 Bruce Hamilton, USA, 12; 8 Lewis Cooper Jr, USA, 12.
Fastest race lap: Grant, 1m 42.915s, 114.386mph/184.086km/h.
Pole position: Grant, 1m 44.092s, 113.092mph/ 182.004km/h.

Race 14 (22.890 miles/36.838km).
1 David Grant, USA, 7 laps; 2 Ryan Norman, USA, 7; 3 Keith Grant, USA, 7; 4 Chris Ash, USA, 7; 5 Dudley Fleck, USA, 7; 6 Lewis Cooper Jr, USA, 7; 7 Bruce Hamilton, USA, 7; 8 Bob Corliss, USA, 7.
Fastest race lap: Grant, 1m 44.337s, 112.827mph/181.577km/h.
Pole position: Grant, 1m 43.845s, 113.361mph/ 182.437km/h.

Final championship points
Drivers
1 Ryan Norman, USA, 562; 2 Keith Grant, USA, 470; 3 Bob Corliss, USA, 449; 4 Bruce Hamilton, USA, 438; 5 Chris Ash, USA, 320; 6 David Grant, USA, 318; 7 Rich Zober, USA, 318; 8 Lee Alexander, USA, 216; 9 John Burke, USA, 206; 10 Lewis Cooper Jr, USA, 188; 11 Connor Burke, USA, 179; 12 Kirk Kindsfater, USA, 129; 13 Mark Sherwood, USA, 79; 14 GianPaolo Ciancimino, USA, 68; 15 Dudley Fleck, USA, 67; 16 Theodoras Zorbas, USA, 58; 17 Lee Brahin, USA, 32.